Understanding Children's Development

Sixth Edition

Understanding Children's Development

Sixth Edition

Peter K. Smith / Helen Cowie / Mark Blades

WILEY

Registered office

10074656 3 0

John Wiley & Sons Ltd, The Atrium, Southern Gate, Chichester, West Sussex, PO19 8SQ, United Kingdom

For details of our global editorial offices, for customer services and for information about how to apply for permission to reuse the copyright material in this book please see our website at www.wiley.com.

Library of Congress Cataloging-in-Publication Data

Smith, Peter K.
    Understanding children's development / Peter K. Smith, Helen Cowie, Mark Blades.—Sixth edition.
        pages cm
    Includes bibliographical references and index.
    ISBN 978-1-118-77298-0 (pbk.)
        1. Child psychology. 2. Child development. I. Cowie, Helen. II. Blades, Mark. III. Title.
    BF721.S57325   2015
    155.4—dc23

                                                                                    2015005897

ISBN: 9781118772980 (pbk)
ISBN: 9781119025030 (ebk)
ISBN: 9781119025078 (ebk)

A catalogue record for this book is available from the British Library.

Set in 11 / 12.5pt Dante MT by SPi Global

Printed in Italy by Printer Trento

BRIEF CONTENTS

Preface to Sixth Edition   *xxi*

Acknowledgements   *xxv*

PART I   THEORIES AND METHODS   1

CHAPTER 1   **Studying Development**   3

CHAPTER 2   **Biological and Cultural Theories of Development**   31

PART II   PRENATAL DEVELOPMENT AND BIRTH   77

CHAPTER 3   **Prenatal Development and Birth**   79

PART III   THE SOCIAL WORLD OF THE CHILD   105

CHAPTER 4   **Parents and Families**   107

CHAPTER 5   **Siblings and the Peer Group**   161

CHAPTER 6   **Developing Emotional Intelligence and Social Awareness**   199

CHAPTER 7   **Play**   233

CHAPTER 8   **Children and Media**   265

CHAPTER 9   **Helping Others and Moral Development**   297

CHAPTER 10   **Social Dominance, Aggression and Bullying**   339

PART IV   CHILDREN'S DEVELOPING MINDS   377

CHAPTER 11   **Perception**   379

CHAPTER 12   **Language**   405

CHAPTER 13   **Cognition: Piaget's Theory**   443

CHAPTER 14   **Cognition: The Information Processing Approach**   471

CHAPTER 15   **Children's Understanding of Mind**   513

CHAPTER 16 **Learning in a Social Context** 545
CHAPTER 17 **Intelligence and Attainment** 579
CHAPTER 18 **Deprivation and Enrichment: Risk and Resilience** 605

PART V ADOLESCENCE 643

CHAPTER 19 **Adolescence** 645

References (Visit the website to download the references - **www.wiley.com/college/smith**)
Index *693*

CONTENTS

Preface to Sixth Edition   *xxi*

Acknowledgements   *xxv*

PART I   THEORIES AND METHODS   1

CHAPTER 1   Studying Development   3

Development Observed 5

What is 'Development'? 6

    Baltes's Conceptualization of Life-Span Development 8

    Bronfenbrenner's Ecological Model of Human Development 10

Obtaining Information about Behaviour and Development 12

    What Degree of Control? 12

    Recording Data 15

    Reliability and Validity 16

    Participant Characteristics 17

    Children/Young People as Active Participants in Research 17

Working with the Data: Quantitative and Qualitative Methods 19

    Objectivity and Bias 19

    Ethical Issues 20

What Implications Does Psychological Knowledge have for Society? 21

    The Rights of Children 22

    The Well-being of Children 25

The Scientific Status of Psychology 27

Chapter Summary 29

Discussion Points 29

Further Reading 30

CHAPTER 2   Biological and Cultural Theories of Development   31

Genetics and the Groundplan for Development 32

    Twin Studies 33

    Adoption Studies 34

    Genes, and Shared and Non-Shared Environment 35

    Identifying Genes and the Human Genome Project 36

    Chromosomal Abnormalities 38

    Down Syndrome 38

The Brain and Developmental Neuroscience 39

How Behaviour Develops: Nature and Nurture 41

    Instinct, Maturation and Learning 42

    Rigidity and Flexibility 42

    Imprinting and the Concept of Sensitive Periods 44

Individual and Social Learning Processes 45
Social Learning, Tradition and Culture 47
Communication Systems in Monkeys and Apes 47
Teaching 48
Thinking in Primates 49
The Evolution of High Intelligence 50
The Evolution of 'Mindreading' and of Metarepresentational
Thought 51
Apes, Humans and Culture 54
Evolution and Human Behaviour 54
Evolutionary Theory 55
Evolutionary Theory and Human Behaviour 58
Box 2.1: Parent–offspring weaning conflicts among the Bofi
farmers and foragers of Central Africa 59
Evolutionary Psychology and Evolutionary
Developmental Psychology 62
Criticisms of the Evolutionary Approach 63
Belsky and Pluess' Three Models of Human Plasticity 63
Culture and Development 65
Cultural-Ecological Models 66
Box 2.2: Development through participation in
sociocultural activity 69
Social Constructionist Approaches 71
Deconstructing Developmental Psychology 73
Chapter Summary 75
Discussion Points 75
Further Reading 76

PART II   PRENATAL DEVELOPMENT AND BIRTH   77

CHAPTER 3   Prenatal Development and Birth   79

From Conception to Birth 80
Germinal Stage 80
Embryonic Stage 81
Fetal Stage 81
Sex Hormones and Male–Female Differentiation 81
Fetal Learning 82
Prenatal Risks 82
Box 3.1: Newborn and fetal response to the human
voice 83
Pregnancy Sickness 85
The Nature of Birth 85
Interaction Immediately after Birth 88
Breastfeeding 89

Premature and Low Birthweight Babies 90
Box 3.2: Cognitive status, language attainment and prereading skills of 6-year-old very preterm children and their peers: the Bavarian Longitudinal Study 92
Early Social Behaviour and Social Interactions 95
Behaviours that Operate Primarily in Social Situations 95
Behaviours to which Social Responses are Given 96
An Ability to Learn 96
An Enjoyment of Contingent Responding by Others 96
Early Behavioural Routines 98
Imitation 98
The Respective Roles of Infant and Caregiver 98
Very Early Bonding: The Work of Klaus and Kennell 100
Temperament 100
The Millennium Cohort Study (MCS): Patterns of Infant Care in the UK at 9 Months 103
Chapter Summary 104
Discussion Points 104
Further Reading 104

PART III   THE SOCIAL WORLD OF THE CHILD   105

CHAPTER 4   Parents and Families   107

The Development of Attachment Relationships 108
Who are Attachments Made With? 109
The Security of Attachment 110
Implications of Infant Attachment Security 111
Is the Strange Situation Valid Cross-Culturally? 112
Why do Infants Develop Certain Attachment Types? 112
Box 4.1: Infant–mother attachment among the Dogon of Mali 113
Disorganized Attachment and Unresolved Attachment Representations 116
Attachment beyond Infancy and Internal Working Models 117
The Adult Attachment Interview 119
Are Attachment Types Stable over Time? 120
Are Attachment Types Stable over Generations? 122
Attachment Theory as a Paradigm 124
Bowlby's 'Maternal Deprivation' Hypothesis 124
Box 4.2: The effect of early institutional rearing on the behaviour problems and affectional relationships of 4-year-old children 127

Care Outside the Family 130
    Fostering 130
    Childminding and Day Care 130
    The NICHD Longitudinal Study 132
    Day Care: An Overview 134
Fathers 134
    Historical Changes in Father Involvement 135
    Fathering and Child Outcomes 136
    Non-resident or Absent Fathers 137
Grandparents 138
    Grandparents as Surrogate Parents 139
    Grandparents and Divorced Families 139
Types of Family 140
    Lesbian and Gay Parents 141
Styles of Parenting 141
    Conflict between Parents 143
Divorce 144
Step-Parenting 146
Physical Punishment and the 'Smacking' Debate 147
Child Maltreatment, Neglect and Abuse 149
    Assessment and Extent of Child Maltreatment 150
    The Effects of Child Maltreatment 153
    Causes of Child Maltreatment 153
Models of Parenting 154
The Millennium Cohort Study (MCS): Patterns
of Childcare in the UK at 3 and 5 Years 156
Chapter Summary 158
Discussion Points 158
Further Reading 159

CHAPTER 5   **Siblings and the Peer Group**   161

Early Peer Relationships 162
Siblings 163
    Siblings in the Home Environment 164
    Sibling Influences: Play, Teaching 165
    Sibling Influences: Conflict and Social Comparison 165
    Sibling Influences: Theory of Mind 167
    Twins and Multiplets 167
    Only Children 168
    Family Size, Birth Order, Intelligence and
    Creative Lives 169
Peer Relationships in Preschool and School 170
    Measuring Peer Relationships: Sociometry 172
    The Concept of Sociometric Status 173
        Box 5.1: Dimensions and types of social status: a cross-age
        perspective 174

A Social Information Processing Model 176
Rejected Children 177
Subtypes of Rejected Children 177
Popular and Controversial Children 178
Perceived Popularity 178
Neglected Children, Loneliness and Social
Withdrawal 179
Friendship 181
What Characterizes Friendship? 181
Origins of Friendship 182
Conceptions of Friendship 183
Quality of Friendship 183
Box 5.2: Monthly instability in early adolescent friendship
networks and depressive symptoms 185
The Importance of Peer Relations and Friendship 188
A Long-term Study of Correlates of Childhood
Friendship and Sociometric Status 190
Enemies 190
Social Skills Training 191
Immigration, Acculturation and Friendships
in Multicultural Settings 192
Family and Peer Relationships 193
Group Socialization Theory and the Role of the Peer Group:
How Important are Families? 194
Chapter Summary 196
Discussion Points 196
Further Reading 197

CHAPTER 6   **Developing Emotional Intelligence
and Social Awareness**   199
How Children Begin to Understand Self and Others 200
The Infant's Recognition of Self 201
How Children Categorize Others 202
Emotional Development 203
Producing Emotions 203
Recognizing Emotions in Others 204
Understanding Others' Emotions, Desires and Beliefs 206
Developing Emotional Intelligence 208
Emotional Regulation 208
Emotional Intelligence 210
Box 6.1: Trait emotional intelligence and children's peer
relations at school 212
Self-Concept and Self-Esteem 215
Box 6.2: Circle Time for social and emotional learning in
primary schools 216
Early Sex Differences and the Development of Gender Identity 218
Sex Differences among Children in Western Societies 219

Awareness of Gender Identity and Sex Differences 219
Cross-cultural Studies 221
Theories of Sex-Role Identification 221
Biological Factors 222
Social Learning Theory 223
Social Constructionist Approaches 224
Cognitive-developmental Theory and Gender Schemas 225
Social Cognitive Theory 226
Children's Awareness of and Attitudes to Different Ethnic and National Groups 228
Ethnic Awareness and Preference 228
Emphasizing Diversity 230
Chapter Summary 230
Discussion Points 231
Further Reading 231

CHAPTER 7   Play   233

Characteristics of Playful Behaviour 234
Exploration and Play 236
The Development of Play 237
Play Types and Sequences 237
Physical Activity Play 239
Rough-and-tumble Play 239
Play with Objects 240
Fantasy and Sociodramatic Play 241
Box 7.1: Universal, developmental and variable aspects of young children's play: a cross-cultural comparison of pretending at home 244
Imaginary Companions 246
Language Play 246
War Toys and War Play 247
Video and Computer Games 248
Games with Rules 249
Factors Affecting Play 249
Play in Different Cultures and the 'Play Ethos' 250
Play Theorists 250
The Benefits of Play: The Evidence 253
The Forms of Play 253
Correlational Studies 255
Box 7.2: Boys' and girls' uses of objects for exploration, play and tools in early childhood 256
Experimental Studies 258
Play Therapy 260
Models of Benefits of Play 262
The Benefits of Play: An Overview 263
Chapter Summary 263
Discussion Points 264
Further Reading 264

CHAPTER 8   Children and Media   265

Children's Use of Media 266
Children and Television 268
    Learning from Television 270
    Sesame Street 271
    Television in Relation to Other Activities 271
    Influence of Television: Stereotypes 273
    Influence of Television: Aggression and Violence 275
    A Longitudinal, Correlational Study on Adolescents 276
    A Two-site Longitudinal Study 276
Computer Games 279
Advertising to Children 282
    Unhealthy Food Products 282
        Box 8.1: Food choice and overconsumption: effect of a
        premium sports celebrity endorser 283
    Children's Understanding of Advertisements 285
    Product Placement and Advergames 286
    Effects of Advertising on Children 288
        Box 8.2: Exploring the relationship between children's
        knowledge of text message abbreviations and school literacy
        outcomes 289
Media Interventions 291
    Restrictive Interventions 291
    Co-viewing 293
    Media Literacy 293
Chapter Summary 294
Discussion Points 294
Further Reading 295

CHAPTER 9   Helping Others and Moral Development   297

The Development of Prosocial Behaviour 298
    Experimental Studies 300
    Observational Studies 301
Factors Influencing Prosocial Behaviour 302
    Parenting 302
    Siblings 305
    School and the Peer Group 306
    Peer Support Systems in Schools 308
    Sex Differences in Prosocial Behaviour 308
        Box 9.1: The effects of primary division, student-mediated
        conflict resolution programs on playground aggression 310
    Cross-cultural Differences in Prosocial Behaviour 313
The Development of Moral Reasoning 315
    Piaget's Theory 315
    Kohlberg's Theory 318
    Early Criticisms of Kohlberg's Theory 321

Later Revisions of Kohlberg's Theory 322
The Social-Cognitive Domain Approach
to Moral Development 324
  Box 9.2: Does moral and social-conventional reasoning predict
  British young people's judgements about the rights of asylum
  seeker youth? 325
The Age of Moral Responsibility in the Context of Youth Crime 329
Can We Teach Moral Values? 331
Emotional Literacy 332
The PATHS Intervention 333
Results of the PATHS intervention 334
Chapter Summary 336
Discussion Points 337
Further Reading 337

CHAPTER 10   Social Dominance, Aggression and Bullying   339

Dominance in Children 340
Social Dominance in Younger Children 340
Social Dominance in Older Children 341
Aggression in Children 342
Types and Typologies of Aggressive Behaviour 343
Developmental Changes in Aggression 345
Is Aggression Maladaptive? 346
  Box 10.1: Strategies of control, aggression and morality in
  preschoolers: an evolutionary perspective 347
Origins of Aggression: Genetic Factors and Temperament 350
Callous-unemotional Traits 351
Origins of Aggression: Parenting 352
Origins of Aggression: Peer Group Factors 353
Origins of Aggression: Neighbourhood Factors 354
Disruptive Behaviour and Oppositional Defiant Disorder 355
Delinquency 356
Interventions 357
Bullying in School 358
Finding Out about Bullying 359
Types of Bullying 362
Cyberbullying 364
Incidence and Structural Features of Bullying 365
Causes of Bullying 366
Consequences of being Victimized 367
Interventions against Bullying 368
Large-scale School-based Intervention Programmes 371
  Box 10.2: Bully/victim problems among schoolchildren: basic
  facts and effects of a school-based intervention programme 372
Chapter Summary 375
Discussion Points 375
Further Reading 376

PART IV   CHILDREN'S DEVELOPING MINDS   377

CHAPTER 11   Perception   379

Methods for Studying Infants' Perception 381
   Preference Technique 381
   Habituation 381
      Box 11.1: Is face processing species-specific during the first year
      of life? 382
   Conditioning 384
   Summary of Methods 385
Visual Perception 386
   Investigating Infants' Visual Perception 386
   Pattern Perception 387
   Face Perception 388
   Perceptual Constancies 392
   Object Separation 393
   Depth Perception 395
      Box 11.2: Effects of prior experience on 4.5-month-old infants'
      object segregation 396
Auditory Perception 398
   Effects of the Environment on Perceptual Development 400
Intermodal Perception 401
Chapter Summary 403
Discussion Points 403
Further Reading 403

CHAPTER 12   Language   405

Main Areas of Language Development 406
Sequences in Language Development 407
   Shared Rhythms 407
   Babbling and Echolalia 408
   First Words and Sentences 411
      Box 12.1: Facilitating children's syntax development 413
   Gleitman's Syntactic Bootstrapping Hypothesis 416
   Barrett's Multi-Route Model 417
   From 3 to 5 Years 417
The Transition to Literacy 418
   Prereading and Prewriting Skills 418
      Box 12.2: Categorizing sounds and learning to read: a causal
      connection 420
   Taking Account of One's Own and Others' Perspective
   Through Narrative Experiences 423
Learning to Read 424
Dyslexia 425
   Explanations of Dyslexia 426

Helping Children with Dyslexia to Cope 428
Theories of Language Development 428
The Innate Basis of Language: Chomsky's Views 429
Pinker and the Evidence from Pidgin and Creoles 432
Language and Cognition: A Piagetian Perspective 433
Cognitive-Functional Linguistics 434
Adult–Child Speech 437
A Continuing Debate 439
Chapter Summary 441
Discussion Points 441
Further Reading 442

CHAPTER 13 Cognition: Piaget's Theory 443

Underlying Assumptions: Structure and Organization 446
The Stages of Cognitive Development 448
The Sensorimotor Stage 448
Reinterpretations of Piaget: The Sensorimotor Stage 451
The Preoperational Stage 453
The Preconceptual Period 453
The Intuitive Period 455
Box 13.1: Piaget's mountains revisited: changes in the egocentric landscape 456
Reinterpretations of Piaget: The Preoperational Stage 460
Box 13.2: Conservation accidents 462
The Concrete Operational Stage 464
Reinterpretations of Piaget: The Concrete Operational Stage 465
The Formal Operational Stage 465
Reinterpretations of Piaget: The Formal Operational Stage 466
Piaget's Theory: An Overview 468
Educational Implications 468
Chapter Summary 469
Discussion Points 470
Further Reading 470

CHAPTER 14 Cognition: The Information Processing Approach 471

Information Processing Limitations 474
Stage-Like Performance in Information Processing 476
Problem-solving Strategies 478
Box 14.1: The strategies of scientific reasoning 479
Attention 487
Memory Development 488
Encoding Strategies 488
Retrieval Strategies 490
How do memory strategies develop? 491
Metacognition 492

Knowledge and Memory Development 493

Constructive Memory and Knowledge 494

Summary of the Information Processing Approach 496

Children's Eyewitness Research 497

Children's Suggestibility 498

    Box 14.2: The effects of stereotypes and suggestions on preschoolers' reports 499

    Why are Children Misled? 503

Interviewing Procedures 506

    The Cognitive Interview 506

    Achieving Best Evidence 507

Stress and Recall 507

Summary of Eyewitness Research 509

Chapter Summary 510

Discussion Points 510

Further Reading 511

CHAPTER 15   Children's Understanding of Mind   513

The False-Belief Task 515

    Box 15.1: Beliefs about beliefs: representations and constraining function of wrong beliefs in young children's understanding of deception 516

Children's Knowledge of Mind Before About 4 Years of Age 522

    Distinguishing Mental States in Language 522

    Understanding the Relationship between Seeing and Knowing 522

    Understanding the Appearance–Reality Distinction 523

    Predicting Behaviour 524

When is Theory of Mind Achieved? 524

Theory of Mind After 4 Years of Age 526

Theories About the Development of Understanding the Mind 529

Do Children with Autism or ASD Lack an Understanding of Others' Minds? 533

    Box 15.2: Domain specificity in conceptual development: neuropsychological evidence from autism 537

How Far Can a Deficit in Understanding Mental Representations Contribute to an Explanation of ASD? 540

Chapter Summary 542

Discussion Points 542

Further Reading 543

CHAPTER 16   Learning in a Social Context   545

The Challenge of Vygotsky 546

Individual Mental Functioning: Its Sociocultural Origins 547

    Cole's Work with the Kpelle 549

    The Zone of Proximal Development (ZPD) 551

    Hedegaard's Teaching Experiment 552

Language and Thought 554
The Impact of Bruner 555
    Scaffolding in Practice 556
        Box 16.1: Capturing and modelling the process of conceptual change 557
    Guided Participation in Sociocultural Activity 562
    Collective Argumentation 564
    The Community of Inquiry 568
Implications for Education 569
        Box 16.2: Mathematics in the streets and in schools 570
    The Role of Peers as Tutors 574
Is Synthesis Possible? 575
Chapter Summary 577
Discussion Points 577
Further Reading 578

CHAPTER 17 Intelligence and Attainment 579

The Development of Intelligence Tests 580
    The First Tests 580
    Revisions of the Binet–Simon Scale 582
    Other Intelligence Scales 583
Reliability and Validity 586
    Reliability 586
    Validity 587
The Early Uses of Intelligence Tests 587
Concepts of Intelligence 589
    Sternberg's Theory of Intelligence 590
        Box 17.1: People's conceptions of intelligence 590
Savants 593
        Box 17.2: Calendar calculating by 'idiot savants'. How do they do it? 594
Intelligence in a Social-Cultural Context 596
The Use of Intelligence Tests 599
    Children with Learning Difficulties 599
    Gifted Children 599
Attainment Tests 601
Chapter Summary 603
Discussion Points 603
Further Reading 604

CHAPTER 18 Deprivation and Enrichment: Risk and Resilience 605

Deprivation 606
Extreme Deprivation and Neglect 607
    Feral Children 607
    The Koluchova Twins 608
    Genie 610

The Effects of Institutional Rearing on Children's Development 612
Early Studies 612
Romanian Adoptees: The English and
Romanian Adoptees (ERA) Study 613
Socially Disadvantaged Children 616
Social Disadvantage in the UK 616
The Impact of Racial Prejudice and Discrimination 617
Street Children 619
The Social Reintegration of Children Associated
with Armed Forces 620
Box 18.1: Participation as principle and tool in
social integration: young mothers formerly associated
with armed groups in Sierra Leone, Liberia and
Northern Uganda 620
Explanatory Models 624
The 'Deficit' and 'Difference' Models 624
Risk and Protective Factors 625
Resilience in the face of adversity: the Kauai study 626
Interventions: The Role of Families 628
Nurture Groups 630
Compensatory Education Programmes in the USA 631
USA Compensatory Programmes Evaluated 631
Box 18.2: What makes a difference: Early Head Start
evaluation findings in a developmental context 633
Compensatory Education Programmes in the UK 635
Sure Start 635
A Continuing Debate 638
Chapter Summary 640
Discussion Points 641
Further Reading 641

PART V ADOLESCENCE

643

CHAPTER 19 Adolescence

645

The Biological and Physical Changes of Puberty 646
Variations in Physical Maturation Rates 649
The Secular Trend in Age of Puberty 650
Theories Concerning Pubertal Timing 652
Psychological Effects of Puberty 653
Effects of Physical Changes 653
Box 19.1: The associations among perceived pubertal
timing, parental relations and self-perception in Turkish
adolescents 654
Effects of Hormones 657
Brain Development at Puberty 657
Effects of Cognitive Changes 659
Effects of Early and Late Maturation 660

Relations With Peers 663
The social brain 663
Romantic Development 665
Sexting 667
Adolescent Sexuality 667
Lesbian and Gay Adolescents 668
Adolescence as a Period of Turmoil, or 'Storm and Stress' 669
Identity Development and the 'Identity Crisis' 670
Conflicts with Parents 673
Adolescent Bedtimes 675
Mood Disruption 676
Risk-Taking Behaviours 678
Box 19.2: Cultural bases of risk behaviour: Danish adolescents 679
Adolescence in Different Cultures 681
Margaret Mead and Samoa 682
Broad and Narrow Socialization 683
Historical Changes in Adolescent Behaviour 684
Sexual Attitudes and Behaviour 684
Leisure Pursuits 685
Mobile Phones and the Internet 686
Adolescent Mental Health 688
Chapter Summary 690
Discussion Points 691
Further Reading 691

References (Visit the website to download the references - **www.wiley.com/college/smith**)
Index 693

PREFACE TO SIXTH EDITION

This textbook now has a history of over 25 years! It has already been through four editions, published by Blackwell. The first (1988) and second (1991) editions were by Peter Smith and Helen Cowie, with Mark Blades joining as third author for the third (1998) and fourth (2003). The fifth (2011) edition was published by Wiley-Blackwell.

We have enjoyed regularly bringing this book up to date and renewing it, and the three of us are pleased to be bringing out a sixth edition.

OPINIONS ON CHILD DEVELOPMENT

We are bombarded by opinions on child development. Everyone has a view of how children should be brought up, and explanations for why people have turned out the way they have. Even if you have not studied psychology before, you no doubt already have views on how children develop. You may agree or disagree with the following statements, but you will probably have heard them or opinions very much like them.

1. 'Animal behaviour is instinctive; human behaviour is learned. That's the difference.'
2. 'She gave me a lovely smile. I'm sure she recognized me even though she's only 2 months old.'
3. 'I wouldn't leave my child at a nursery. If you have a baby you should look after it yourself.'
4. 'A good smack never did a child any harm. That's how they learn what is right and what is wrong.'
5. 'If things go wrong in the early years of a child's life there's not much you can do about it.'
6. 'Parents shouldn't try to teach their children to read. That's best left to the school.'
7. 'They don't do any work at Paul's school. They just play all day.'
8. 'You can't understand how a child's mind works. They just think differently from us, and that's all there is to it.'
9. 'Bullying is part of growing up—just stand up for yourself!'
10. 'Children see far too much violence on television and the media.'
11. 'IQ tests don't tell us anything about real intelligence. They're a means of social control.'
12. 'Just wait until they are teenagers. That's when the trouble starts.'
13. 'Adolescents spend so much time social networking, it is having harmful effects.'
14. 'Teenagers don't get enough sleep!'
15. 'Psychologists can't teach us much. What they say is just common sense.'
16. 'Children from poor backgrounds are doomed to fail.'

In this book we don't aim to provide absolute answers to the many questions that arise in the course of rearing children and understanding their development. But we do aim to provide up-to-date and balanced accounts of research in this area. We hope to present controversies and to outline the various ways in which child psychologists' research findings enhance our understanding of the developmental process, from gestation and birth, up to and including adolescence.

CHILD DEVELOPMENT MATTERS

There is plenty of evidence that childhood experiences matter. At the time of going to press, Richard Layard and colleagues (Layard et al., 2014) have published some analyses from the British Cohort Study or BCS. The BCS study is detailed in Table 1.1, and it assessed over 17,000 children born in April 1970, following them up regularly into adulthood. Layard and colleagues looked at three main measures in childhood: intellectual performance, good conduct and emotional health. These were assessed at 5, 10 and 16 years, together with family background factors such as family income and parental education. They related these to outcomes as an adult at 26 and 34 years: income, educational achievement, social and personal adjustment, and an overall measure of life satisfaction—'How dissatisfied or satisfied are you about the way your life has turned out so far?'.

Not surprisingly, intellectual performance in childhood was a good predictor of adult educational achievement, and also of adult income. However, it was a poor predictor of adult life satisfaction. The best childhood predictor of adult life satisfaction was emotional health, followed by good conduct. These predictive effects became stronger through ages 5, 10 and 16. While noting limitations to the analyses, the authors do suggest there may be strong policy implications, especially as such research is extended and refined. So far, it points to how childhood emotional well-being is particularly important for how satisfied we are with our adult lives.

USING THIS BOOK

This book is divided into five sections: Theories and Methods; Prenatal Development and Birth; The Social World of the Child; Children's Developing Minds; and Adolescence, comprising 19 chapters in total.

Each chapter starts with a summary paragraph indicating the content to come. At various points through the text we have inserted 'stop and think' suggestions. These might help you as the reader to think actively about some of the issues being discussed, which are often open to debate.

We have tried to emphasize the variety, strengths and weaknesses of different kinds of psychological investigation, and to bring this out vividly each chapter (after the first) includes two 'boxes'. Each box consists of a detailed description of one particular study, discussing its aims, design, results, analysis, and strengths and limitations. Study of these boxes should be useful not only in terms of the content of the studies themselves, but also in helping you to get a feel for how psychological research is carried out.

More advanced students may wish to pursue the references to original work given throughout the text, while beginners should read the book without being distracted by them. The references are provided for use by teachers, for those who wish to follow up areas or studies in detail, and because acknowledgement should be made to those psychologists who have put forward certain theories or carried out particular studies.

Each chapter offers suggestions for further reading, giving indications of level and content. There are also ideas for discussion points, which might be taken up as essay titles or topics for debate in class.

CHANGES IN THE SIXTH EDITION

We hope that this new edition will continue to keep abreast of the exciting new developments in our discipline, while retaining coverage of the core components of knowledge from previous research.

This sixth edition maintains the same chapter structure as the fifth edition (which had had some substantive changes from earlier editions). Besides general updating, some of the more major revisions are indicated below.

Part I (Theories and Methods) has two chapters.

Chapter 1 on *Studying Development* again covers core principles and methods; we have particularly reworked sections on children as researchers, ethical considerations in research, and on children's rights. We cover participatory research methods which offer an innovative way of accessing the inner worlds of children and young people in ways that traditional approaches often fail to do. Researchers in this field typically have a strong desire to enable their participants' voices to be heard, particularly in the context of marginalized young people, such as young carers, children in care and young offenders.

Chapter 2, *Biological and Cultural Theories of Development*, runs through a range of theoretical approaches, from genetics and evolution through to social constructionist viewpoints. We have introduced a new section on Belsky and Pluess' three models of human plasticity.

Part II (Prenatal Development and Birth) has one chapter.

Chapter 3 on *Prenatal Development and Birth* has been updated and includes new material on breastfeeding and cognitive development.

Part III (The Social World of the Child) has seven chapters.

Chapter 4 on *Parents and Families* includes a new section on fostering, more findings from the NICHD longitudinal study, more on non-resident or absent fathers, material on parenting styles in China, on effects of domestic violence on children, and substantial reworking of the sections on physical punishment, and on child maltreatment.

Chapter 5 on *Siblings and the Peer Group* includes an update on adjustment of only children, and a new section on immigration, acculturation and friendships in multicultural settings.

Chapter 6 on *Developing Emotional Intelligence and Social Awareness* has expanded material on the development and fostering of emotional intelligence in children; it includes a new box on the impact of a widely used classroom method, Circle Time, on students' emotional health and well-being.

Chapter 7, on *Play*, includes more discussion of the benefits of object or constructive play, and more on recent debate on the developmental significance of play.

Chapter 8, on *Children and the Media*, has been completely updated to take into account the rapid changes in the media environment. There is additional information about the use of computer games for positive and educational purposes, more material on media literacy, and a new box about the use of celebrities in advertising aimed at children.

Chapter 9, on *Helping Others and Moral Development*, has a new box describing a study that measures young people's moral and conventional reasoning when discussing the religious and secular self-determination and nurturance rights of young asylum seekers in the UK.

Chapter 10 on *Social Dominance, Aggression and Bullying* includes a new section on disruptive behaviour and oppositional defiant disorder, and a substantial reworking of the sections on bullying, including more on homophobic bullying and cyberbullying, and on interventions.

Part IV (Children's Developing Minds) has eight chapters.

Chapter 11 on *Perception* has been updated with additional examples of studies and more references to research with newborn children.

Chapter 12 on *Language* includes new material on dyslexia.

Chapter 13 on *Cognition: Piaget's Theory* discusses the relevance and importance of Piaget's work for contemporary developmental psychology.

Chapter 14 on *Cognition: the Information Processing Approach* includes more examples of empirical studies, and has revised sections on eyewitness interviewing procedures and the effects of stress on child eyewitnesses.

Chapter 15 on *Children's Understanding of Mind* includes references to the large number of new publications in this area and extends the discussion of theory of mind to research considering very young children and also research with older children.

Chapter 16 on *Learning in a Social Context* includes more examination of the cultural practices that underpin everyday informal learning as children 'pitch in' with family and community activities. A key feature of this kind of learning is that it is embedded in the child's sense of *belonging* with all the personal and emotional commitment that is involved.

Chapter 17 on *Intelligence and Attainment* has been updated with more information about contemporary intelligence scales.

Chapter 18 on *Deprivation and Enrichment: Risk and Resilience* includes recent work on developing intercultural competence through education. There are two new boxes. One describes an innovative study of the social reintegration into their home communities of young mothers abducted by armed groups in Sierra Leone, Liberia and Northern Uganda. A second describes a large-scale evaluation of the impact of Early Head Start intervention on preschool children from deprived backgrounds.

Part V (Adolescence) has just the final chapter.

Chapter 19 on *Adolescence* has been extensively revised again, reflecting the growth of work on the social brain and insights from neuroscience; evolutionary perspectives on risk taking; more on peer relationships and romantic development; new sections on sexting and on adolescent bedtimes; and updating and expansion of the section on use of mobile phones and the internet.

As the book has extensive website support, appendices on ethical principles in research and on careers, together with much other useful material, can be found at www.wiley.com/college/smith.

ACKNOWLEDGEMENTS

For the sixth edition, we wish to thank Martyn Barrett, Carmel Cefai, Paul Cooper, Carmen Huser, Dawn Jennifer, Alice Jones, Renata Milijevic-Ridicki, Lorraine Radford, Ian Rivers, Edurne Scott Loinaz, Harriet Tenenbaum and Angela Veale for providing useful materials or helpful comments on drafts of various sections. John Bock, Sara E. Johnson and Tony Pellegrini kindly provided photographs that have been used in this edition.

PART I

THEORIES AND METHODS

Chapter 1   Studying Development

Chapter 2   Biological and Cultural Theories of Development

CHAPTER
1

Studying Development

CHAPTER OUTLINE

- Development Observed
- What is 'Development'?
- Obtaining Information about Behaviour and Development
- Working with the Data: Quantitative and Qualitative Methods
- What Implications does Psychological Knowledge have for Society?
- The Scientific Status of Psychology

The study of how behaviour develops forms part of the science of psychology. But what do we mean by terms such as 'science', 'psychology' and 'development'? This chapter aims to supply the answer, but although it comes first in the book, it may not necessarily be best to read it thoroughly at the outset. Especially if you have not studied psychology before, it might be useful to read it through quickly at this stage and return to it later, even after finishing the rest of the book, for a more thorough understanding. The issues raised in this chapter are important, but understanding them fully will be easier if you already know something of psychological theories and methods of investigation.

In an important sense, we are all psychologists. We are all interested in understanding behaviour, both our own and that of our parents, children, family and friends. We try to understand why we feel the way we do about other people, why we find certain tasks easy or difficult, or how certain situations affect us; we try to understand and predict how other people behave, or how their present behaviour and situation may affect their future development. Will a child settle well with a childminder, or do well at school? Will watching violent films on television be harmful? Will a child be bullied at school? Can we teach children to cooperate? What level of moral reasoning can we expect a child to understand?

Nicholas Humphrey (1984) described us as 'nature's psychologists', or *homo psychologicus*. By this he means that, as intelligent social beings, we use our knowledge of our own thoughts and feelings—'introspection'—as a guide for understanding how others are likely to think, feel and therefore behave. Indeed, Humphrey went further and argued that we are conscious, that is, we have self-awareness, precisely because this is so useful to us in this process of understanding others and thus having a successful social existence. He argued that consciousness is a biological adaptation to enable us to perform this introspective psychology. Whether this is right or not (and you might like to think about this again after you have read Chapter 2), we do know that the process of understanding others' thoughts, feelings and behaviour is something that develops through childhood and probably throughout our lives (see Chapter 15). According to one of the greatest child psychologists, Jean Piaget, a crucial phase of this process occurs in middle childhood, though more recent research has revealed how much has developed before this.

If we are already nature's psychologists, then why do we need an organized study of the science of psychology? A professional psychologist would probably answer that it is to try and arrive at greater insight, and greater agreement on contentious issues. Sometimes, common-sense beliefs are divided. For example, attitudes to physical punishment of young children as a form of discipline are sharply divided and polarized in many countries (see Chapter 4). Sometimes, common beliefs are wrong. In the course of researching the lives of children of mixed parentage, Tizard and Phoenix (1993, p. 1) reported to a group of journalists that many of the young people in their sample saw advantages in their family situation through the meeting of two distinctive cultures. The journalists responded with incredulity, since the findings ran contrary to the popular belief that these children inevitably suffered from identity problems, low self-esteem and problem behaviour!

By systematically gathering knowledge and by carrying out controlled experiments, we can develop a greater understanding and awareness of ourselves than would otherwise be possible. There is still much progress to be made in psychology and in the psychological study of development. We are still struggling to fully understand areas such as the role of play in development, the causes of delinquency and the nature of stages in cognitive development. Most psychologists would argue, however, that the discipline of child development has made much progress, and even in the most difficult areas knowledge has now become more systematic, with theories being put forward. We now know more, for example, about the importance of social attachments in infancy (Chapter 4), the process by which a child learns its native language (Chapter 12) and how our understanding of others' minds develops (Chapter 15) than previous generations ever did or could have done without organized study.

So, how can we go about this?

DEVELOPMENT OBSERVED

The biologist Charles Darwin, famous for his theory of evolution, made one of the earliest contributions to child psychology in his article 'A biographical sketch of an infant' (1877), which was based on observations of his own son's development. By the early 20th century, however, most of our understanding of psychological development could still not have been described as 'scientific' knowledge; much was still at the level of anecdote and opinion. Nevertheless, knowledge was soon being organized through both observation and experiment, and during the 1920s and 1930s the study of child development got seriously under way in the USA with the founding of Institutes of Child Study or Child Welfare in university centres such as Iowa and Minnesota. Careful observations were made of development in young children and of normal and abnormal behaviour and adjustment. In the 1920s, Jean Piaget started out on his long career as a child psychologist, blending observation and experiment in his studies of children's thinking (see Chapter 13).

Observation of behaviour in natural settings fell out of favour with psychologists in the 1940s and 1950s (though it continued in the study of animal behaviour by zoologists; see Chapter 2). Perhaps as a reaction against the absence of experimental rigour in philosophy and early psychology, and the reliance on introspection (that is, trying to understand behaviour by thinking about one's own mental processes), many psychologists moved to doing experiments under laboratory conditions. As we will discuss later, such experiments do have advantages but they also have drawbacks. Much of the laboratory work carried out in child development in the 1950s and 1960s was described by Urie Bronfenbrenner (1979) as 'the science of the behavior of children in strange situations with strange adults'.

We hope that in the course of reading this text you will begin the process of integrating perspectives—for example, by reflecting on the links made by psychologists between the concept of the child's 'internal working model of relationships' (Chapter 4) and discoveries about 'theory of mind' (Chapter 15). We hope too that you find the opportunity to recognize the complementary virtues of various different methods of investigation and gain a sense that the child's developmental processes and the social context in which they exist are closely intertwined, each having an influence on the other.

WHAT IS 'DEVELOPMENT'?

The term 'development' refers to the process by which an organism (human or animal) grows and changes through its life-span. In humans, the most dramatic developmental changes occur in prenatal development, infancy and childhood, as the newborn develops into a young adult capable of becoming a parent himself or herself. From its origins, much of developmental psychology has thus been concerned with child psychology, and with the changes from conception and infancy through to adolescence. These are the primary areas covered in this book.

Generally, developmental processes have been related to age. A typical 3-year-old has, for example, a particular mastery of spoken language (see Chapter 12), and a 4-year-old has typically progressed further. A developmental psychologist may then wish to find out, and theorize about, the processes involved in this progression. What experiences, rewards, interactions and feedback have helped the child develop in this way? Two important but different research strategies have commonly been used in this endeavour: 'cross-sectional' and 'longitudinal' designs. Each method has advantages and disadvantages.

Cross-sectional design: In a cross-sectional design, an investigator might look at several age groups simultaneously. For example, she might record language ability in 3-year-olds and 4-year-olds, at the same point in time. The cross-sectional design is quick to do, and is appropriate if the main interest is in describing what abilities or behaviours are typical at certain ages. Because of the convenience of the method, the majority of developmental studies have been cross-sectional. However, they do not give insight into the causal processes involved in developmental change.

Longitudinal design: In a longitudinal design, the investigator follows certain individuals over a given time period, measuring change. For example, our investigator might have recorded the language ability for a sample of 3-year-olds and a year later visited the same children to get a sample of what they can do as 4-year-olds. Longitudinal designs are generally preferable if the focus of interest is the process of change, and the relationship between earlier and later behaviour. In our example, it is longitudinal data that give us the most ready access to information on what kinds of experience foster language development, and whether individual differences at 3 years of age predict anything about individual differences a year later, at age 4.

Although longitudinal studies are more powerful in this way, they have a number of drawbacks. One is simply the possibility of subject attrition—some participants may move away, lose contact, or refuse or be unable to participate by the next time of testing. This could influence the generality of conclusions, especially if the reason for participant loss is related to the dependent variables of the study.

Another problem with longitudinal designs is that they are time-consuming! In our example, a wait of one year may not be too off-putting. But if you wanted to see whether friendships in childhood related to happiness as an adult (see Chapter 5), you might find yourself having to wait 20 years! Some longitudinal studies have now in fact proceeded for this length of time and longer, for example in relating infant attachment security to later attachment type as an adult (see Chapter 4).

A few major studies that originated in the USA in the 1930s, as well as some nationwide surveys starting in Britain since the 1940s, have provided or are providing longitudinal data from birth and continuing over a time-span of 20, 30, 40 or even 50 years. Table 1.1 shows two examples from the USA, five examples from the UK (four are national cohort studies,

Table 1.1   Some major longitudinal studies in the USA, UK and New Zealand.

Study	Acronym	Birth date of sample	Initial sample size	Follow-up surveys	Website
Some longitudinal programmes in the USA					
Early Childhood Longitudinal Program	ECLS-B	2001	14,000	Five follow-ups to 2007–2008, ages 6–7	http://nces.ed.gov/ecls/
NICHD Study of Early Child Care and Youth Development	SECCYD	1991	1,364	Three follow-ups to 2005–2007, age 15	https://www.nichd.nih.gov/research/supported/pages/seccyd.aspx
Some longitudinal programmes in the UK					
National Survey of Health and Development	NSHD	March 1946	13,687	20 follow-ups, to 2008–2009, ages 60–64	www.nshd.mrc.ac.uk
National Child Development Study	NCDS	March 1958	17,634	Nine follow-ups, to 2012, age 55	www.cls.ioe.ac.uk
British Cohort Study	BCS70	April 1970	17,287	Seven follow-ups to 2012, age 42	www.cls.ioe.ac.uk
Avon Longitudinal Study of Parents and Children	ALSPAC	April 1991–December 1992	14,138	Many follow-ups to 2013, age 21, more planned up to 2019	http://bristol.ac.uk/alspac
Millennium Cohort Study	MCS	September 2000–August 2001	18,819	Four follow-ups to 2012, age 11	www.cls.ioe.ac.uk
A longitudinal study in New Zealand					
Dunedin Multidisciplinary Health and Development Study	DMHDS	April 1972–March 1973	1,037	Ages 3, 5, 7, 9, 11, 13, 15, 18, 21, 26, 32, and 38 years; next follow-up at 44–45 years	http://dunedinstudy.otago.ac.nz

while ALSPAC is based on families in the Avon area around Bristol) and a longitudinal study based in the Otago region of New Zealand. Such long-term studies give us some of our most powerful evidence on the nature of development.

However, when a study goes on for so long, another problem may arise. When the study was initially designed decades ago, it may not have asked the sort of questions that we now find most interesting. Any long-term longitudinal study will be dated in its conception. It will also be dated in its conclusions, which will refer to developmental outcomes for people born decades ago. Such conclusions may not always be applicable to today's children. For example, the effects of parental divorce on a child's later adjustment may be different now, when divorce is more frequent and socially acceptable, than 50 years ago when the social stigma attached to divorce in Western societies was greater (see Chapter 4).

Stop and Think

Longitudinal studies can be powerful, but what are their practical and theoretical limitations?

Baltes's Conceptualization of Life-Span Development

Paul Baltes, a German psychologist, was influential in emphasizing the life-span nature of development and the importance of historical influences (see Baltes et al., 1980). Baltes pointed out that age-related trends, the traditional staple of developmental psychology, constitute only one of three important influences on development throughout the life-span (Figure 1.1). Each of these influences is determined by an interaction of biological and environmental factors (see Chapter 2), though one or the other may predominate in particular cases.

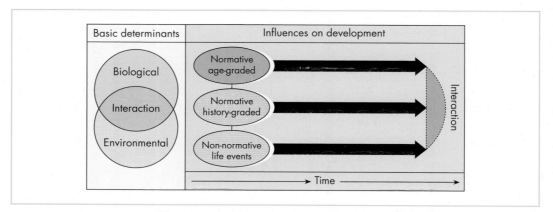

Figure 1.1   Three major influence systems on life-span development: normative age-graded, normative history-graded and non-normative life events. These influence systems interact and differ in their combinational profile for different individuals and for different behaviours.

Source: Adapted from Baltes, P.B., Reese, H.W., & Lipsitt, L.P. (1980). Life-span developmental psychology. *Annual Review of Psychology, 31,* 65–110, by permission of Annual Reviews.

Normative age-graded influences have a fairly strong relationship with chronological age. The advent of puberty at adolescence (see Chapter 19) would be an example of a normative age-graded influence with a strong biological component, while entering school at 5 years (in Britain) would be a normative age-graded influence with little biological determination.

Normative history-graded influences are those associated with historical time for most members of a given generation (or 'cohort'; see below). A famine or natural disaster, such as the earthquake in Haiti in 2010 or the earthquake and tsunami in eastern Japan in 2011, would be examples. The advent of television in the 1950s and the internet and mobile phone use in the 1980s and 1990s (see Chapter 8, for example Table 8.1), or historical changes in family size (for example, the 'one child' policy in China since the early 1980s) are other examples brought about by human agency.

Non-normative life events are those that do not occur in any normative age-graded or history-graded manner for most individuals. The effects of brain damage in an accident would be an example with strong biological determinants; the effects of job loss or moving house are examples with less strong biological determinants. All are significant events that can occur in the life-span of an individual at many age points and at many historical times.

Many developmental studies examine normative age-graded influences, for example the effects of puberty or changes in cognitive development with age, as in Piaget's theory (see Chapter 13). Some examine the effects of a particular kind of non-normative life event when it happens, such as the effects of divorce or of a traumatic event such as the sinking of a cruise ship; this might be done irrespective of age or with age as another factor.

Rather fewer studies have examined the effects of normative history-graded influences, such as exposure to warfare, or how the advent of television or the internet changed children's behaviour. However, the consideration of history-graded influences leads to further designs for studying development apart from the cross-sectional and longitudinal ones already mentioned. One of these is cohort design.

Cohort design: Here, different cohorts (i.e. samples of children born in different years) are compared at the same ages. This design will inform us of the impact of historical change. For example, if we compare the leisure activities of 8-year-old children born in a Western society in 1930, 1970 and 2010, we will see changes influenced by (among other factors) the advent of television in the 1950s and the widespread use of the internet and mobile phones in the last 20 years.

The characteristics of the three designs mentioned so far are as follows:

Cross-sectional design
Different participants | Different ages | Same historical time

Longitudinal design
Same participants | Different ages | Different historical times

Cohort design
Different participants | Same ages | Different historical times

Yet another design is a combination called cohort-sequential design.

Cohort-sequential design: This combines aspects of all the above three designs to create a very powerful analytical tool for studying developmental processes. As an example of this, we might look at the effects of compensatory preschool programmes (see Chapter 18) on children born in 1980, 1985 and 1990, following each cohort longitudinally through from

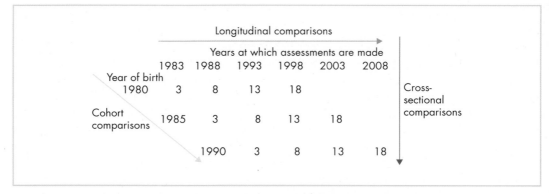

Figure 1.2 A hypothetical study design, combining cross-sectional, longitudinal and cohort comparisons, to examine the effects of compensatory preschool programmes at different ages and different historical periods. It starts in 1983 and continues until 2008. The ages of each sample of children from each cohort and at each year of study are shown in years.

age 3 years to, say, age 18 years. As well as several sets of cross-sectional and longitudinal data, this hypothetical design (Figure 1.2) would let us see whether historical change over the last two decades (for example, in educational policy or the relative position of minority groups in society) had an impact on long-term effects of the programmes. Obviously, this would be very time-consuming and, so far, cohort-sequential designs have been rather rarely used; one example is given in Box 10.2.

Bronfenbrenner's Ecological Model of Human Development

The American psychologist Urie Bronfenbrenner proposed another influential conceptualization of development (Bronfenbrenner, 1979). He emphasized the importance of studying 'development-in-context', or the ecology of development. 'Ecology' refers here to the environmental settings that the person or organism is experiencing or is linked to directly or indirectly. Bronfenbrenner conceived of this ecological environment as a set of four nested systems (Figure 1.3) and as an interaction amongst the processes of person, context and time.

Microsystem: This inner level refers to what an individual experiences in a given setting, and is the most familiar to psychologists. For a young child, one microsystem may comprise the home environment with parents and siblings. Another microsystem may be the school environment, with teachers and peers. Most psychological research is carried out at the level of one microsystem, for example looking at mother's talk and child's speech in the home (Chapter 12), or peer popularity and aggression at school (Chapter 10).

Mesosystem: This next level refers to links amongst settings in which the individual directly participates. For example, the quality of the child's home environment might affect his or her school performance or confidence with peers.

Exosystem: This third level refers to links to settings in which the individual does not participate directly, but that do affect the individual. For example, the mother's or father's work environment may affect their behaviour at home, and hence the quality of parental care. The child does not directly experience the parent's work environment, but he or she experiences the effects indirectly.

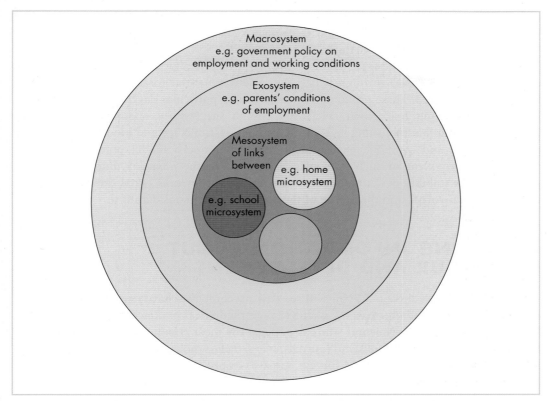

Figure 1.3 The nested circles of macro-, exo-, meso- and microsystems proposed by Bronfenbrenner (1979), with examples relevant to a school-age child.
Source: Adapted from Bronfenbrenner (1979)

Macrosystem: This fourth level refers to the general pattern of ideology and organization of social institutions in the society or subculture the individual is in. Thus, the effects of parental stress at work, or unemployment, will be affected by such factors as working hours in that society, rates of pay, holiday and leave entitlement, occupational status, or the degree of social stigma attached to unemployment.

Bronfenbrenner's model illustrates how a decision or change in the macrosystem (e.g. change in employment conditions) may affect the exosystem (parent's work experience), and hence a child's mesosystem and microsystem. This is not controversial in itself. However, recognizing these links does suggest the importance of trying to conceptualize and design psychological investigations extending beyond just the microsystem level.

Bronfenbrenner proposed that we view human development as the process of understanding and restructuring our ecological environment at successively greater levels of complexity. The child first comes to understand its primary caregivers, then its home and nursery or school environment, then wider aspects of society. Changes in the ecological environment (or 'ecological transitions') are especially important in development. Examples might be having a new sibling; entering school; getting a job; being promoted; getting married; taking a holiday. (Note the similarity to Baltes's ideas of life events.) At such times, the person is faced with a challenge and has to adapt, and thus development takes place. Indeed, Bronfenbrenner feels that seeing how a person copes with change is essential to understanding that person: 'If you want to understand something, try to change it'.

Bronfenbrenner and Ceci (1994) later proposed empirically testable basic mechanisms called *proximal processes* through which the genetic potential for effective psychological functioning is realized. These proximal processes lead to particular developmental outcomes, including controlling one's own behaviour, coping successfully under stress, acquiring knowledge and skill, establishing mutually satisfying relationships and modifying one's own physical, social and symbolic environment. Bronfenbrenner's model predicts systematic variation in the extent of such outcomes as a result of the interplay amongst proximal processes, their stability over time, the contexts in which they take place, the characteristics of the persons involved and the nature of the outcome under consideration.

OBTAINING INFORMATION ABOUT BEHAVIOUR AND DEVELOPMENT

As you read through this book, you will see that psychologists have used a wide variety of means to obtain useful information, whatever their theoretical or conceptual orientation has been. Some form of experimental study is perhaps the most common form of investigation reported in psychological books and journals. Nevertheless, non-experimental methods, such as naturalistic observation or field surveys, are also respectable procedures provided there is a clear aim to the research. The crucial variable here is the degree of control the investigator has over what is happening. We shall discuss this in some detail, together with two other aspects of obtaining data—the way behaviour is recorded and the selection of participants. These aspects are also highlighted in the boxes within all the subsequent chapters.

What Degree of Control?

A great deal can be learned from recording behaviour in natural situations or settings. Suppose we were interested in what kinds of help are shown by preschool children to others in distress (see Chapter 9). Perhaps the most suitable approach here is for the investigator simply to observe children in natural settings such as the home, or ask parents or adults to keep diary records of events. Or we might try to save time simply by interviewing parents or giving a questionnaire. The investigator interferes as little as possible, only to the extent of making sure he or she gets reliable data. This kind of approach is most suitable when we do not yet have much systematic knowledge about the phenomenon in question, and need to gather this descriptive data. As an example, Dunn and Kendrick (1982) gathered observational records of interactions between siblings in the first few years of life (see Chapter 5). Even though some experimental work had been done on sibling relationships, this study produced a richness of detail and uncovered a wide variety of phenomena that fully justified such a naturalistic approach.

From this kind of study, we can learn what kinds of behaviour occur, and how frequently. But do we advance our understanding of the processes involved? To some extent, the answer is yes. For instance, we can carry out correlational analyses of various kinds.

Correlational analyses: Here we examine whether a behaviour occurs systematically or more frequently together with some other particular behaviour or in some particular situation.

A large set of correlations is called a *matrix*. For an example, see Box Table 6.1.2, which presents an intercorrelation matrix of trait emotional intelligence (EI) scores and peer nomination scores in 10-year-old children. As another example, we may find that how children categorize sounds at preschool is correlated with reading and spelling scores four years later (see Box 12.2).

Such findings certainly suggest explanations as to the processes involved. For example, emotional intelligence might help a child develop better peer relationships or a child's practice in rhyming and alliteration may have a causal relationship with learning to read and spell. However, can we be confident that these explanations are better than some other, different explanations? Not really.

Firstly, the relation between cause and effect might be reversed: for example, children who have better peer relationships may have more opportunity to develop emotional intelligence.

Secondly, some third factor may account for the correlation. As discussed in Box 12.2, general intelligence, or memory for words, might help in earlier sound categorization skills, and in later reading and spelling achievement.

This weakness of correlational evidence is a most important concept to grasp. If you find it difficult, think of this example. Suppose you correlated, from day to day through the year, the number of people wearing shorts and the number of people eating ice creams. You would probably get a positive association or correlation. This does not mean that wearing shorts causes people to eat ice creams, or vice versa; we know that in this case the daily variation in temperature, a third variable, is the likely cause of both.

To some extent, the weakness of correlational methods can be alleviated by using regression analyses, or by using cross-lagged correlations. In *regression analyses*, quite a wide range of correlates are considered as possibly influencing a certain variable; the statistical procedure of regression then tells us which correlates are most predictive of the outcome variable, once the other correlates are taken into account (see, for example, looking at effects of father involvement on child outcomes separately from mother involvement, p. 137). In *cross-lagged correlations*, measurements are taken at two or more time points in a longitudinal study. Besides correlations between two variables at one time point, the cross-lagged correlations (those from time 1 to time 2, etc.), when compared, can give stronger suggestions as to which variable is influencing which other one (see pp. 186, 277).

The other way in which psychologists have tried to proceed further is to use some form of experiment. In an experiment, we focus on one or a small number of variables of interest that we think are important, then we try to exclude other variables from our possible explanations.

Quasi-experiments: These are the weakest form of experiments (see Cook & Campbell, 1979, for extended discussion). Here the variable that the investigator thinks is important is changed naturally, and the investigator watches what happens. For example, in 1955 Himmelweit, Oppenheim and Vince (1958) carried out a before-and-after study of the effects on children's behaviour of introducing a new television transmitter in Norwich. The investigators felt that the introduction of the opportunity to watch TV was an important normative history-graded variable and they took the opportunity to measure its effects.

Unfortunately, quasi-experiments are not much more powerful than correlational studies at excluding alternative explanations. Usually, we know too little about (i.e. have too little control over) the characteristics of our participants and the circumstances of the variable that is changing. For example, in the situation just described, which parents first acquired television sets when they were available? They would almost certainly be different in various ways from those who did not acquire television sets (and indeed, the study identified some such differences). Also, children might differentially view programmes of certain types, depending on personality and interest. How can we tell whether changes in behaviour are due to watching the programmes, or whether the programme watching is just a by-product of differences in behaviour due to other factors?

True or controlled experiments: These provide the most powerful way to answer cause-and-effect questions. We can distinguish field experiments and laboratory experiments, but both share two important features. The first is that there are two or more well-specified 'conditions' that participants can experience. The second is that participants are assigned to conditions in a systematic fashion. In these ways, the experimenter seeks to ascribe an outcome definitely to differences between certain conditions. Strongest of all is the *randomly controlled treatment design* (RCT), in which participants are assigned totally randomly to the different conditions. Alternative explanations in terms of other uncontrolled differences between conditions, or between the participants in different conditions, can then be excluded.

Let us take further the idea that television viewing may affect children's social behaviour. Suppose we invite children in small groups to a laboratory, where we randomly assign them to one of three conditions. In one condition, they see several violent cartoon programmes; in another, they see several non-violent cartoons; in the third (called a *control* condition), they do not watch television at all but do something else, like drawing. Afterwards they go to a playroom and are filmed by the experimenter, who records their social behaviour.

Suppose the experimenter finds a significant difference. Children who watched the violent cartoons are more aggressive to each other in the playroom than those who watched non-violent cartoons or did drawing. This difference in aggressiveness can confidently be ascribed to watching the violent cartoons. It cannot be explained by systematic differences in the participants (we assigned them randomly) and it cannot be explained by unknown variations in the children's experiences (we chose the cartoons, and made the children sit through all of them).

Sometimes the investigator compares the effects of two or more conditions he or she is interested in (for example, violent and non-violent cartoon films). Sometimes it is appropriate to include a *control group*, which is a condition including all the same experiences except that which the investigator is particularly interested in. The children who experienced drawing, above, were a control group for the general experience of coming to the laboratory and meeting the experimenters. Any differences between the control group and the two experimental groups showed the effects of watching cartoons. Any difference between the two experimental groups further showed the effects of whether the cartoons were violent or non-violent.

In all experiments we can identify *independent variables* and *dependent variables*. Independent variables are those controlled or manipulated by the experimenter—in our example, the experience of watching cartoons, and whether the cartoons were violent or not. The dependent variables are those we choose to examine for possible effects—in our example, social behaviour in the playroom.

The laboratory experiment allows tight control of assignment of participants and of the independent variables—but is it rather artificial? What do the participants feel about coming to the laboratory? Would they normally choose to watch such cartoons? Can we expect a reasonable range of normal behaviour in this environment? Perhaps not. To some extent, we can try to overcome these objections in a *field experiment*. For example, we might try showing different kinds of television cartoons to different groups of children at a school or at a summer camp. The children would normally be at the school or camp, and watching some television might be part of their expected programme.

In general, in a field experiment the investigator attempts to combine the rigorous control of true experimental design with the advantages of a naturalistic setting (see Box 9.1 for an example). This can, at its best, be a very powerful method. However, it is difficult to maintain both experimental control and naturalness, and the field experiment may either slip into becoming a quasi-experiment or into becoming more constrained and unnatural, like many laboratory experiments.

Thus, in all investigations the naturalness of the setting needs to be balanced against the degree of knowledge and control we have over the setting. Where the balance is best struck depends very much on the kind of behaviour or skill we are interested in. We do want to be reasonably sure that the conclusions we draw from our study apply to the 'real world'. This concern has been labelled as the need for 'ecological validity'. Bronfenbrenner (1979) defined ecological validity as 'the extent to which the environment experienced by the participants in a scientific investigation has the properties it is supposed or assumed to have by the investigator'. In other words, is it reasonably representative as regards the conclusions we wish to draw from the study? If we felt that the results of a laboratory experiment on cartoon watching were not representative of the effects of real-life television watching, then we would say this experiment lacked ecological validity.

Stop and Think

When is it important to use tightly controlled experimental designs, despite a possible lack of ecological validity?

Recording Data

Whatever design of investigation we are using, we also have to decide how to record the data. A variety of methods is available. Sometimes several types of data may be gathered in one study.

Observational methods: Here the investigator watches the participant(s) and makes systematic records of whether certain behaviours occur (e.g. Box 2.1, where observations were made of mother and infant activities in Bofi farmers and foragers). Usually the investigator defines certain *behaviour categories* in advance, and then scores when they occur. Some method of *time sampling* is often employed to assist in quantifying the scoring (see Martin & Bateson, 2007, for extended discussion).

Very often such studies are described as *non-participant observation*; this means that the observer watches the behaviour from 'outside' and does not interact much or at all with those observed. An alternative is *participant observation*, or *ethnographic study*, where the observer is also one of the actors in the situation. For example, in a study of a Chicago gang of adolescent delinquents, Whyte (1943) acted as a gang member in order to get insight into what was really going on. Patrick (1973) described a similar study of a gang in Glasgow, from the insider perspective. This kind of study is more difficult in terms of recording data, but will give unique insights as well. Another approach is where the investigator asks the participant(s) to keep his or her own records or observations of their own behaviour; perhaps a daily record of occurrences, sometimes called a *diary method*. Sandstrom and Cillessen (2003) used a diary method with 10–13-year-old children, to get records of negative interactions with peers such as victimization and exclusion.

Interviews and questionnaires: In an interview, the investigator asks participants about a topic and explores their thoughts, feelings or attitudes with them (e.g. Box 2.2). Often some degree of structure is imposed on the kinds of questions asked in the interview (e.g. Boxes 5.2, 16.1). A still more structured approach is to give participants a questionnaire in which they fill in replies to preset questions (e.g. Box 19.2). A questionnaire is often given individually, but can be given in groups. A questionnaire sent to large numbers of participants is called a survey (e.g. Box 10.2).

Focus groups: These provide a less structured interview approach, in which several participants (usually around six is seen as a good number) discuss some topic—for example, what is good or not so good about school. The debate amongst peers can often bring out interesting facets that individual interviews might not, although peer pressures need to be borne in mind.

Tests: Here a participant, either individually or in a group, is asked certain questions and is often asked to carry out certain actions (for example, solve certain puzzles). The test differs from the interview in that it is designed to measure a particular ability or trait, and it is scored in a strictly defined way that can be compared with normative values obtained earlier in the process of test design (see Chapter 17 for the case of intelligence tests).

Experimental techniques: There are many more specialized experimental procedures, which may be used for specific purposes. For example, ultrasound scanning may be used to study the fetus *in utero* (see Box 3.1); conditioning and habituation may be used to study infant perception (see Chapter 11); genotypes can be identified from DNA extracted from buccal (cheek) swabs (see Chapter 2); and a variety of neuroimaging techniques may be used by developmental cognitive neuroscientists to study changes in the brain (see Chapter 2).

Reliability and Validity

Whatever measuring instrument or method we use, we need to be sure of its *reliability*. Basically, a reliable method is one that would give the same answer if you, or another investigator, were to repeat the measurement in the same conditions. For example, if we recorded aggressive behaviour in children but did not define our behaviour categories or method of time sampling, this would be unreliable; someone else might have a different idea of what is aggressive, and get different results even if watching the same behaviour. Methods need to be carefully specified, and tried out, if they are to be reliable.

Reliability is often confused with *validity*: both are very important in any investigation. We have just seen that reliability refers to the recording of data. Validity, in contrast, refers to whether the data we obtain are actually meaningful.

There are a number of threats to validity. One problem might be that our measurement instrument, although reliable in the sense of well defined, might be poorly conceived in terms of what it is measuring. For example, our definition of aggression might include unintentional as well as intentional hurt (cf. Chapter 10), rendering it less meaningful.

A common issue is that of *ecological validity*, discussed above. Our measurements in a laboratory experiment might be very reliable (well specified and repeatable) but this does not guarantee that they are valid in the sense of meaningful in the 'real world'. Also, in experiments there can be *experimenter effects*. The experimenter may unwittingly inhibit some behaviours, or help some participants more than others, or score some participants more leniently. One type of experimenter effect is known as the 'Clever Hans' effect. Clever Hans was a horse that apparently could count. If his trainer asked, 'What is three and four?' Hans would tap with his front foot seven times. However, the German psychologist Oskar Pfungst (1911) discovered that Hans actually relied on subtle non-verbal (and unintentional) cues from his trainer, who inclined his head slightly forward after Hans had tapped the correct number of times. Hans was clever, but not in the way originally thought. The demonstration was a reliable one, but the conclusions drawn initially were not valid.

Problems of validity actually arise in all kinds of investigation. If we are making records in a natural setting, the presence of an observer might change the behaviour being observed. If you stand in a playground recording children's aggressive behaviour, will less aggression occur than usual because you are there? This is a problem of *observer effects*.

Participant Characteristics

One aspect of validity concerns the representativeness of the participants investigated. A key factor is the size of the sample. A data set obtained from one person is called a *case study*. Normally a case study tells us little about the general population but if we can obtain very extensive records (for example, the records Piaget obtained of his own children described in Chapter 13) or if the person is especially interesting (for example, the case studies of extreme deprivation described in Chapter 18) then this method may be very valuable. A case study may often serve as a source of ideas or hypotheses for later study (e.g. the case studies of the Koluchova twins and of Genie, pp. 608–612).

Many psychological investigations are done on small samples of some 10–50 individuals, who can be brought to a laboratory or observed in a single setting. Again, valuable findings may be obtained, but if the sample is small (e.g. Box 6.2) then it is difficult to generalize to a much wider population.

Sometimes a survey or other investigation is carried out on a large sample of hundreds or thousands of participants. In certain circumstances, such a sample may be regarded as normative, or representative, of some section of the population. For example, it may correspond to characteristics of the wider population such as age, gender, ethnicity or socioeconomic status. The NSHD longitudinal study in Britain included all the children born in one week of March 1946, and this could reasonably be taken as representative of children born in Britain in the later 1940s. Other major longitudinal studies have adopted a similar sampling procedure (see Table 1.1).

Children/Young People as Active Participants in Research

Some studies have gone beyond observing or interviewing children or young people, and have moved to involving them as researchers themselves. It can be argued that children have the right to be consulted, informed, and also involved, in order for their voice to be truly heard (e.g. Alderson, 2008; Harcourt & Einarsdottir, 2011). Treseder (1997) provided a model which identified five different levels of participation in research:

Assigned but informed: Adults decide on the project and young people volunteer. Adults respect the young people's views and provide appropriate information to ensure that the young participants understand the project.

Consulted and informed: The project is designed and run by adults, but young people are consulted. They have a full understanding of the process and their opinions are taken seriously.

Adult-initiated shared decisions with young people: Adults have the initial idea but young people are involved in every step of the planning and implementation. Not only are their views considered, but young people are also involved in taking the decisions.

Young people-initiated and directed: Young people have the initial idea and decide how the project is to be carried out. Adults are available but do not take charge.

Young people-initiated shared decisions with adults: Young people have the ideas, set up projects and come to adults for advice, discussion and support. The adults do not direct but offer their expertise for young people to consider.

A key concept is a belief in the competency of children to construct their own meanings. The challenge for the researcher is to design tools to facilitate the expression of that voice. To meet this challenge, the multi-method Mosaic Approach (Clark, 2011) adopts playful methods, for example, running group conferences, giving children cameras to record their everyday lived experience and encouraging children to create maps of their environment through photos and drawings. Other participatory researchers have designed methods that are appropriate for older children and adolescents. Kernaghan and Elwood (2013) established a young participants' Research Advisory Group (RAG) to monitor their research into cyber-bullying. The RAG offered illuminating insights into issues of communication, recruitment and interpretation. Researchers have also developed methods that show sensitivity to the particular emotional needs of participants. Veale (2005) used participatory methods (social mapping, story games, drawings and drama) in rural Rwanda post genocide to explore the impact of violence on social relations as it impacted on children without intruding insensitively on their personal stories; ownership and control of the material generated rested with the young people.

Participatory methods like these offer an innovative way of accessing the inner worlds of children and young people in ways that traditional approaches often fail to do. Cowie, Huser and Myers (2014) indicate that participatory research is characterized by a concern for the rights of children and young people. Researchers in this field typically have a strong desire to enable their participants' voices to be heard, particularly in the context of marginalized young people, such as young carers, children in care and young offenders. This concern is often balanced by huge enthusiasm on the part of the participants who typically express their deep desire to share their experiences and to represent others in a similar situation as if they were young ambassadors. The quality of the research may actually be enhanced by using alternative forms of communication like play, activities, songs, drawing and stories so that children, who are practised in these types of activities, may experience the research process more meaningfully than if they were participating using a traditional format.

However, these participatory methods have yet to be fully accepted. Data can appear to be unsystematic or even chaotic. There is an urgent need to develop sophisticated qualitative methods of analysis, as the Mosaic Approach has demonstrated, in order to gain credibility with mainstream academia.

 Stop and Think

How feasible is it to use child participatory methods in the research process, beyond just providing data?

WORKING WITH THE DATA: QUANTITATIVE AND QUALITATIVE METHODS

Once we have our data, what do we do with it? There has been much debate here about the advantages and disadvantages of quantitative and qualitative methods. Sometimes, disciplinary and professional biases have led to unproductive disputes about these approaches, rather than productive selection of methods that best suit the aims of the study. However, most psychologists now recognize the value of both kinds of approach, depending of course on the topic of study and the current state of knowledge (Coolican, 2009).

Quantitative methods: Here, the emphasis is on predetermined categories, and the researcher has often already decided what he or she is interested in—they are not 'exploring the area' but 'looking for the answer to certain questions'. Often, quantitative researchers use experiments or data from non-participant observation. Usually statistical tests are carried out to look at correlations, or at differences between subgroups in the sample, and to see whether the results are sufficiently stable or characteristic that it is likely they would be true of larger samples. The means of carrying out simple statistical tests (such as correlation, *t* test and chi-square) are described in texts such as Robson (1999), together with the meaning of probability or *p* values. Examples of the results of such tests are given in many of the boxes in this book.

Qualitative methods: Here, the emphasis is on the meaning of the behaviour or experience for the person concerned. The data recording methods usually used are unstructured or semi-structured interviews, focus groups or participant observation. Often, qualitative researchers obtain transcripts of interviews, and then use specialized methods such as grounded theory and discourse analysis to extract dimensions of meaning and experience from these. While clearly not suitable for very young children, such methods can be used with older children. An example is a study of girls' bullying by Owens et al. (2000). Qualitative methods can also be illuminating in studies of how parents think about child rearing (Phoenix et al., 1991).

It is possible to combine both approaches (a 'mixed methods' approach, see p. 59 as an example), or to move from initial, exploratory qualitative study to more focused quantitative study as an investigation progresses.

Objectivity and Bias

Scientific investigation is supposed to be objective, not biased by the personal beliefs or values of the individual investigator or the wider society. In practice, this is not entirely the case. The kinds of problems chosen for study, and the way they are tackled, are inevitably affected by personal or societal ideas of what is important. Some qualitative researchers believe that this is quite intrinsic to research, as the investigator is part of society too; the best the researcher can do is to describe their own orientation and background so that others are aware of it. Quantitative researchers tend to believe that by defining units of measurement closely, and training observers or interviewers, a degree of objectivity can be obtained.

Some areas of psychology may be especially susceptible to decreased objectivity, when personal beliefs are closely involved. Stephen Gould (1996) argued this in the instance of the study of intelligence testing and the view held by some psychologists that there were innate racial differences in intelligence. The kinds of study carried out in the earlier 20th century, and the way those studies were interpreted, clearly reflected bias (for example, racial prejudice) in some investigators. At times this involved misconceived inferences from results or observer bias in scoring or testing. At extremes, it bordered on fraudulence (see the next section). Gould, in turn, has been accused of misrepresenting aspects of his case (Rushton, 1997). Even though objectivity is far from perfect, it is possible to recognize and expose biases, at least after the event. Much more sophisticated studies of the issues involved in race and intelligence have now been carried out, bearing these past errors in mind (see Chapter 17, and Nisbett, 2009).

Ethical Issues

Whenever an investigation is made with human or animal participants, investigators should have due respect for their rights and welfare. Investigations with animals kept for experimental purposes are usually controlled by strict guidelines, for example by the Home Office in the UK.

General principles: For human investigations, general principles are as follows.

- *Informed consent*: participants should know what will be involved in a study they are invited to participate in, and be able to give or withhold consent without any pressure or duress. Occasionally, temporary deception concerning the purpose of the study may be thought necessary; this would need to be very carefully justified.
- *Confidentiality* of information obtained: participants should know that they will not be personally identifiable (by name or other means) in any reports or publications. Any exception would have to be agreed to by the person involved.
- *Lack of harm* to participants themselves or to others: some investigations may involve some disturbance of privacy, or inconvenience to participants. Even when legally permissible, any negative outcomes should be balanced carefully against the likely benefits from carrying out the investigations; they must be very carefully justified, and should never be a feature of student experiments or investigations.

Many psychological societies have issued ethical guidelines for the planning of investigations. For example, the ethical principles approved by the British Psychological Society (BPS, 2009) are available at www.bps.org.uk. However, the guidelines contain very little on research with children and young people.

Ethics of research with children: Special ethical issues arise around research on children. Firstly, infants and younger children cannot give fully informed consent, and consent by parents or carers (or those 'in lieu' of parents, such as teachers in school) must be obtained. However, consent from children themselves should also be obtained so far as possible. It is essential that the information be provided in a form that is easily understood by the child with proper regard for their age and level of capability. To this end, researchers working with children have adopted a number of strategies, including leaflets, packs and posters written in child-friendly language and often illustrated with pictures, drawings and cartoons.

Regarding confidentiality, children need to be reassured that adults, such as parents and teachers, will not listen to any tape recording that is made and that none of their responses will be traced back to them personally. This kind of reassurance could be crucial where researchers are investigating such sensitive topics as the mental or physical health of parents (for example, in research into young carers) or the child's own experiences of abuse, whether from peers or family members.

Confidentiality is a key ethical issue in research and children should be offered the same degree of anonymity as adult participants. However, complete confidentiality can never be totally guaranteed to a child participant if, for example, a child discloses that he or she is at risk of harm through, for example, bullying or abuse. Any such limitations of confidentiality should be carefully explained to the child prior to data collection at the point at which informed consent is sought.

Certainly, researchers should guarantee that the location where the research took place should not be identified, anonymity should be ensured through use of pseudonyms and any identifying features should be changed or omitted. As we saw in the earlier section on children as active participants in research, there are a number of methods that can be adopted by researchers to safeguard the rights of the child and to facilitate active involvement in the research process.

Reporting of results: Another ethical issue relates to the accurate reporting of results. It is clearly the duty of investigators to report their results in as accurate and unbiased a way as possible, but there have been occasions when this principle is known to have been violated. The British psychologist Sir Cyril Burt reported data on twins, which he claimed to have gathered for many years, in order to prove that intelligence was largely inherited. His results were published in numerous articles as his sample of twins accumulated. However, a strong case has been made that in the latter part of his life Burt did not gather more data, but invented it (Hearnshaw, 1979). Thus a great deal of his twin data set is believed by most psychologists to be fraudulent, and the conclusions drawn from it unwarranted. This deception attracted much attention, partly because of the social implications of the theory of hereditary intelligence, and partly because fraud on this scale is believed to be rare. Drawing attention to any such misdemeanours hopefully serves to make future occurrences less probable.

WHAT IMPLICATIONS DOES PSYCHOLOGICAL KNOWLEDGE HAVE FOR SOCIETY?

Bronfenbrenner and Ceci (1994) argued that many people have a potential for development that goes far beyond the capacities that they currently display, and proposed that this untapped potential might be realized through appropriate public policies and programmes of intervention. They argued that social changes in both developed and developing countries have 'undermined conditions necessary for healthy psychological development' (op cit., p. 583).

Bronfenbrenner was concerned about what he called the 'growing chaos' in America's children, youth and families, which he saw as being caused by disruptive trends in society over the previous four decades. In fact, alarmist writings about the state of youth and families are not new. Pearson (1983) showed how worries about the unruliness of adolescents, and the increase in rates of delinquency and adolescent crime and violence, appear to resurface in each generation. Looking at newspapers, books and journals over a period of some 150 years, he found that each generation was bemoaning rising crime and harking back to a golden age of a generation ago! We can go a long way back with such thoughts—Sommerville (1982) cited a tablet from Mesopotomia that stated, 'Our Earth is degenerate in these latter days ... Children no longer obey their parents'; this was dated to 2800 BC!

However, whether new or not, there are clearly important social problems that developmental and child psychologists have a responsibility to address. As a society, we have knowledge of ways in which we can foster competence in the young and of interventions that can act as buffers against dysfunction in the family. Bronfenbrenner was one of the founders of Project Head Start, an intervention that had positive and long-lasting effects on disadvantaged children (see Chapter 18). He was convinced that the belief systems of parents, peers, teachers and mentors can change as a function of education, intervention programmes and the mass media; the internet is also a growing source of influence. We need to ensure that new knowledge, and new technologies, are used effectively for human betterment.

The Rights of Children

Are we agreed on what human betterment is, and what is best for children? The United Nations' *Convention on the Rights of the Child* (UNCRC; United Nations, 1989) advocates rights on behalf of all children, and places emphasis on non-discrimination, acting in the best interests of the child and listening to the views of the child. The Convention built on earlier legislation by specifying children's rights not only to protection and provision, but also to participation—so giving some political rights to children. In the context of participation, it addressed such contentious issues as child labour and children's rights to freedom of thought and speech. Its recommendations are binding on those countries that ratified it (including the UK, which signed it in 1991; the USA is one country that did not sign).

Lopatka (1992), the chairman of the United Nations working group that drafted the Convention, argued that the rights of the child are universal, yet he also asserted the need to take into account the cultural values of the child's community. However, a criticism of the Convention concerns difficulties in implementing it in societies where families are very poor, civil liberties are severely constrained or a country is at war. The tension between a child's universal developmental needs and the realities of his or her social situation may be nearly impossible to resolve. We look at an example of extreme violation of children's rights in Box 18.1; this describes a project about the reintegration back into their communities of young mothers who had, as children, been abducted and raped by soldiers during armed conflict in Sierra Leone, Liberia and Northern Uganda (Veale et al., 2013).

European Forum on the Rights of the Child: The European Commission adopted 'an EU Agenda for the Rights of the Child' in 2011. This aimed to ensure the effectiveness of children's rights and to step up efforts in protecting and promoting the rights of the child. The Eighth European Forum on the Rights of the Child, held in 2013, emphasized the need for integrated, multidisciplinary approaches to children's rights issues. Four issues of particular concern were parental child abduction (where one parent illegally takes a child away from the other parent, usually to another country); children on the move (this includes child trafficking for sexual or labour exploitation), bullying and cyberbullying (considered in Chapter 10), and female genital mutilation (considered next).

Female genital mutilation: An example of the contravention of children's rights is the practice of female genital mutilation (FGM), or cutting (FGM/C). FGM involves the partial or whole removal of the outer sexual organs. It happens in a number of countries throughout the world, but especially in Africa. It is carried out on girls for traditional or religious reasons, although the practice is related to the social control of girl's and women's sexuality. FGM is a very painful procedure, carried out in childhood, usually with the consent of the parents but without the consent of the girls themselves. The World Health Organization estimates that up to 140 million girls and women have been subjected to FGM.

Besides the pain involved, FGM can have severe health consequences. In a study in The Gambia, where prevalence of FGM/C was 78% in 2006, Kaplan et al. (2011) examined 871 cases. In 34.3% of these there were health complications due to FGM, primarily haemorrhage (excessive bleeding), anaemia, infections and abnormal scarring. A review by Berg and Underland (2013) showed that FGM/C has a later negative impact on birth, being associated with prolonged labour, obstetric lacerations, instrumental delivery, obstetric haemorrhage and difficult delivery.

There have been extensive efforts by the World Health Organization, NGOs, health professionals and others to protect children from the immediate and long-term physical and psychological damage of FGM/C. The United Nations has declared 6 February each year as the International Day Against Female Genital Mutilation. In some countries this campaigning has had some success; for example, in Senegal, where the NGO Tostan is working alongside local women to achieve large-scale abandonment of FGM. The success of this project is claimed to come through respect for the culture and through a process of consultation, cooperation and education, rather than from prohibition (see www.tostan.org/female-genital-cutting). However, progress is slow and it seems likely that legal sanctions will need to be invoked in order to end this abhorrent practice.

In the European Union, FGM is criminalized in all member states. However, with the exception of France (with 29 court cases up to January 2012), prosecutions have been rare. In the UK, the practice is illegal but at the time of writing no successful prosecutions had taken place. Nevertheless, young women themselves are organizing campaigns to heighten awareness of the huge psychological and health risks involved and the UK government has pledged that strong action will now be taken against parents and medical practitioners who inflict FGM on girls.

A global agenda for children's rights in the digital age: The rapidly changing ICT environment means that children and young people are encountering an increasing number of risks as well as opportunities in their use of mobile phones and the internet. Children have rights as well as responsibilities in this domain, and these are active areas of social concern and research (Livingstone & Smith, 2014; see also Chapters 10 and 19). Livingstone and Bulger (2013) suggest a research agenda to develop this area. They claim that there is currently insufficient knowledge of how to promote beneficial online opportunities for children, of what makes children vulnerable to risk and how to protect them, and inadequate assessment of those initiatives that have been undertaken.

The Children Act: The England and Wales Children Act (Department for Children, Schools and Families, 2004) states that the child's welfare must be paramount and that adults must ascertain what the wishes and feelings of the child are. All local authority agencies should work together in the best interests of protecting the child. This means, amongst other things, that teachers are legally obliged to share their knowledge of abuse or significant harm to the child with other agencies, most frequently social services. Additionally, children and young people should be consulted on matters that affect them. To this end, the Children's Commissioner for England regularly consults with children to find out their views and, for example, provides a helpful website on which young people can have their say and access information about important aspects of childhood, at www.childrenscommissioner. gov.uk.

The Children Act shifts the emphasis from parents' rights over their children to their responsibilities towards the young people in their care. For example, when parents divorce, the local authorities have a duty to protect and promote the welfare of the children involved, and the courts must now pay due attention to the wishes of the child. A process of conciliation is now more common, in line with its intention to benefit children in this situation. In practice, courts have the right to judge the child's competence to make autonomous decisions, and may as a result disregard children's wishes in the wider context of 'the best interests of the child'. It is difficult to achieve the balance between what the child thinks he or she wants at the time and what in the view of adults may be best for the child in the longer term. And who is right—the adult or the child?

The Children's Rights Alliance for England: The Children's Rights Alliance for England (CRAE) is a pressure group for protecting the rights of children by lobbying government, supporting test cases and providing free legal information and advice. CRAE also mobilizes children and young people to take positive action to promote and protect children's human rights, and publishes an annual report on its findings. CRAE has raised concern about a general climate in the UK of intolerance and negative public attitude towards young people, especially adolescents, who are so often portrayed in the media as 'yobs' or 'thugs', and would like to see greater opportunities for young people themselves to promote more positive images of youth.

Following an inquiry by Lord Justice Leveson (2012), a review of the Editors' Code of Practice required that the press must avoid making pejorative references to certain personal characteristics, such as race and disability. However, the review did not mention 'age'. CRAE (2013) called for age to become a protected ground of discrimination in the code. CRAE has also challenged the UK government on harmful age and disability discrimination against children, for example, through the government's decision to exclude schools and children's homes from the age element of the public sector's duty to promote equality of opportunity for all children and young people. This decision means that some children may be prevented from enjoying full protection of their rights as set out in the UN Convention on the Rights of the Child. Some other countries, such as Australia, Finland and Sweden, have already prohibited age discrimination. Furthermore, CRAE argues that more could be done by public authorities in the UK, including schools, health services, police and social services, to promote the equal worth of children and young people and to give them more opportunities to participate in decision making about issues that concern them.

The CRAE (2013) report indicates that the UK has been condemned by two United Nations treaty bodies, the Committee against Torture and the Committee on the Elimination of Discrimination against Women, for consistently failing to address certain violations of children's rights, including 'the unlawful use of restraint against children in detention, the low age of criminal responsibility and the persisting legality of corporal punishment' (p. 4). Other examples of violation include the increased use of tasers against children (323 times in 2011 compared with 71 in 2008) (Office for National Statistics, 2013a). Similarly, Lord Carlile (Carlile of Berwick, 2006), in a report commissioned by the Howard League for Penal Reform, expressed grave concern about the extent of mental health difficulties being experienced by young offenders in the UK. He found that their access to treatment and protection, during and after detention, was less than that offered to children in society at large, a state of affairs that contravenes their rights according to the Children Act 2004, and the UN Convention on the Rights of the Child. Although this legislation aims to uphold children's right to be consulted in matters that affect them, rarely are young offenders given a voice on their own mental health issues, and their suggestions for supportive provision.

Stop and Think

In what additional areas of children's rights might research on children's development be important?

The Well-being of Children

Several cross-national surveys and reports have been published regarding aspects of children's development. One source is the Programme for International Student Assessment (PISA), organized through the Organization for Economic Cooperation and Development (OECD), which began in 2000. This is conducted every three years and assesses reading; mathematics and science literacy; study and learning practices; family resources and structure; and the organization of schools and school environments. Another is the Health Behavior in School-age Children (HBSC) survey, undertaken by the World Health Organization; this includes measures of material well-being, children's relationships and behaviours, and subjective well-being.

UNICEF also produces regular Report Cards on children's well-being. For example, UNICEF Report Card 11, issued in 2013, reported on children's well-being in 29 rich countries (European countries plus Canada and the USA). Well-being was assessed along five dimensions: material well-being; health and safety; education; behaviour and risks; and housing and environment (UNICEF, 2013). Despite some variations, the picture was generally one of improvement—for example, infant mortality rates fell in all 29 countries. As the data were mostly gathered a few years previously, they may not show effects of the economic recession starting around 2008 but the analysis did not find a strong relationship between per capita gross domestic product (GDP) and overall child well-being.

The UNICEF data are based on *objective* indicators, such as infant mortality rates, proportion of young people in higher education, etc. Using this and some other sources, Martorano et al. (2014) ranked the 29 countries on each dimension. They also derived a composite index based on the five dimensions cited above. These rankings are shown in Table 1.2.

It is also possible to assess children's *subjective* well-being, based on what children and young people report themselves. The HBSC surveys provide these sorts of data. Using this (from the HBSC 2009–2010 data set, reported in detail by Currie et al., 2012), Bradshaw et al. (2013) derived measures of subjective well-being in four domains: life satisfaction; peer and family relationships; subjective education; and subjective health. Their composite measure of overall subjective well-being correlated 0.67 with the overall objective measure. The ranks for overall subjective well-being are also shown for each of the 29 countries, in Table 1.2. It needs to be borne in mind (for both objective and subjective data sets) that the data were obtained some years previously (in around 2008–2010) and the

Table 1.2 Ranks of 29 rich countries on composite objective and subjective measures of child well-being.

Country	Objective well-being	Subjective well-being
Netherlands	1	1
Norway	2	10
Iceland	3	2
Finland	4	11
Sweden	5	7
Germany	6	5
Luxembourg	7	16
Switzerland	8	8
Belgium	9	15
Ireland	10	12
Denmark	11	9
Slovenia	12	3
France	13	22
Czech Republic	14	24
Portugal	15	14
United Kingdom	16	20
Canada	17	25
Austria	18	4
Spain	19	6
Hungary	20	13
Poland	21	27
Italy	22	28
Estonia	23	17
Slovakia	24	21
Greece	25	18
USA	26	29
Lithuania	27	26
Latvia	28	19
Romania	29	23

Source: Adapted from Bradshaw, J., Hoelscher, P. & Richardson, D. (2007) An index of child well-being in the European Union. *Social Indicators Research*, 80, 133–177.

quality does vary, although the composite measures should be more reliable than individual components.

The Netherlands does best on both indicators of child well-being, and the Scandinavian countries generally do well; some eastern European countries do poorly, as does the USA. Comparing the HBSC data from 2009–2010 to earlier data from 2001–2002, subjective well-being showed some changes. Some countries improved their scores (notably the UK, which had very low scores in the earlier data set); in others there was some decline, for example in Greece.

THE SCIENTIFIC STATUS OF PSYCHOLOGY

This chapter began by briefly considering the nature of psychology as a scientific discipline. We shall conclude by discussing briefly what is meant by the term 'science', and whether this is what psychologists practise. The nature of scientific inquiry has been written about by philosophers of science; we shall summarize the views of two: Popper and Kuhn.

For a long time it was generally held that science proceeded by gathering factual data, by observation and experiment, and by deriving general laws from these facts. This has been called the 'traditional' or 'inductivist' view. However, throughout the 20th century, scientists and philosophers of science have put more emphasis on the role of hypotheses or theories in science. A hypothesis, or theory, is a proposition that some relationship holds amongst certain phenomena. For example, some psychological hypotheses discussed in this book include: that the fetus can learn characteristics of the mother's voice (p. 83); that the first hours after birth are critically important for mother–infant bonding (p. 100); that viewing violent television programmes makes children behave more aggressively (pp. 275–278); that children are attracted to a level of moral reasoning just above their current level (p. 321); that children cannot understand another's point of view until about 8 years of age (p. 455); that preschool 'Sure Start' programmes can benefit a child educationally throughout the school years (pp. 635–648).

The 'traditional' view would be that hypotheses such as these are derived from facts we have gathered, and that if we get enough factual support then the theory will have been 'proved' correct. However, this view is not now generally held. Instead, most scientists and philosophers believe that the role of theory is a primary one, and that theories cannot be proved, only disproved. A most articulate proponent of this viewpoint was Sir Karl Popper (1902–1994), who argued that our ideas about the world, or 'common-sense beliefs', serve as the starting point for organizing knowledge from which scientific investigation proceeds. Thus, theory serves a primary role and, indeed, structures what and how we observe or categorize 'facts' or observations about the world. Psychologists are in a good position to appreciate this argument, as part of their discipline (and part of this book, e.g. Chapters 11, 13 and 14) is concerned with how children construct hypotheses about perceptual data and how they gain greater knowledge about the world through forming hypotheses to test against experience. Indeed, we started this chapter by considering how people are 'nature's psychologists' in this sense (see also Chapter 15).

Popper considered that science and knowledge progress by advancing hypotheses, making deductions from them, and continuing to do so until some deductions are proved wrong, or 'falsified'. The hypothesis is then changed to cope with this. A hypothesis can thus never be finally proved correct, as there is always the possibility that some further observation or experiment might discredit it. A hypothesis can, however, be falsified and it is through this process that science progresses.

You can think about this by examining the hypotheses we have just listed above. Have any been falsified? (Some have.) Did the falsifying lead to better hypotheses? (Sometimes.) Could any be 'proved' beyond question?

Popper's notion of falsification has been a powerful one, and he used it to distinguish 'science' from 'non-science'. If propositions, hypotheses or theories cannot actually be falsified, then, according to Popper, this is not science. It may be interesting and enlightening, like a novel, but it is not science. Not all philosophers of science agree with Popper's approach.

At least, not many believe that scientists spend most of their time trying to disprove their theories. A different view was put by Thomas Kuhn (1922–1996), who saw a mature branch of any science as having an accepted 'paradigm'. A paradigm is a basic set of assumptions, or way of trying to solve problems. Atomic theory provided a paradigm in the natural sciences, for example.

In psychology, 'psychoanalysis', 'behaviourism' and 'sociobiology' (see Chapter 2) could be taken as paradigms in this sense. So too could 'attachment theory' (see Chapter 4) and the 'information processing' approach (viewing the brain as a computer; see Chapter 14). An influential paradigm informing much child development research is the 'cognitive-developmental' approach; this links behaviour to the kind of cognitive development or thinking ability expected at the age or level of development the individual is at. Piaget's theory of cognitive development (see Chapter 13) is an obvious example, but the approach is much wider than this.

Kuhn described how a branch of science might develop; it starts in a 'preparadigmatic stage', where it would be characterized by rather random fact gathering and many schools of thought that quarrel about fundamental issues. With maturity, one paradigm is accepted and directs the way observations and experiments are made. Kuhn called this phase 'normal science'. Scientists work within the paradigm, extending and defending it. The paradigm is not rejected unless many difficulties or falsifications accumulate and, in addition, a superior paradigm appears. A period of 'revolutionary science' with competing paradigms then emerges, with one eventually proving superior, when 'normal science' resumes.

Kuhn characterized a science as having a fruitful paradigm that can unify the efforts and direction of study of many scientists. Falsification has a relatively minor role to play, he argued, since all theories have some anomalies (phenomena that cannot yet be well explained). Only the appearance of another paradigm can really upset things.

Kuhn's ideas have been criticized, and modified, but his idea of a paradigm, while rather vague in practice, has had considerable impact. Psychologists in particular often seem to be claiming that a particular approach or theory is setting up a 'new paradigm'! Kuhn himself seems to have thought that psychology and other social sciences may well still be at a pre-paradigmatic stage. It is indeed true that no single paradigm as yet unites the whole of child psychology. Still, certain paradigms (e.g. the cognitive-developmental approach) do seem to be fruitful and capable of bringing together several areas. Perhaps, after working through this book, the reader may decide for himself or herself what kind of scientific status the study of psychological development has, what it has achieved, and what it may reasonably hope to achieve in the foreseeable future.

CHAPTER SUMMARY

- Development refers to the process of growth and change in the child, or organism.
- Two main approaches to studying development are cross-sectional design and longitudinal design. Cohort studies can take account of historical changes in developmental processes.
- Both Baltes and Bronfenbrenner contributed important models of human development.
- There are many methods of obtaining data relevant to developmental processes, varying in the degree of control of the situation, from free observations through to quasi-experiments and controlled experimental design.
- Data can be recorded using observational methods, interviews, questionnaires, focus groups and tests.
- A relatively new procedure is to use young people as researchers.
- Reliability, validity and participant characteristics are important aspects of any research study.
- Both quantitative and qualitative methods can be useful, separately or in combination, depending on the aims of the study.
- Ethical implications of research should always be considered.
- Child development research has bearings on issues such as the rights of children and children's well-being, with policy implications.
- Child development can be considered as an important area of social science, which gathers factual data and uses them to test theories and hypotheses, thus helping us to advance beyond common-sense knowledge and opinions.

DISCUSSION POINTS

1. Has our knowledge of psychological development advanced beyond 'common sense'?
2. What is meant by 'development' and how can we study it?
3. What are the advantages and disadvantages of carrying out experiments in psychology?
4. What impact has psychological knowledge had on society?
5. In what ways can psychology be considered to be, or not to be, a science?
6. Are children themselves capable of investigating childhood?

FURTHER READING

- Breakwell, G.M., Smith, J.A. & Wright, D.B. (Eds.) (2012). *Research methods in psychology* (4th ed.). London: Sage, and Howitt, D. & Cramer, D. (2010). *Introduction to research methods in psychology* (3rd ed.). Harlow: Pearson, provide good overviews of a range of research methodologies. Other useful sources are Coolican, H. (2014). *Research methods and statistics in psychology* (6th ed.). London: Hodder Arnold, and Gray, D.E. (2014). *Doing research in the real world* (3rd ed.). London: Sage.
- Martin, P. & Bateson, P. (2007). *Measuring behaviour: An introductory guide* (3rd ed.). Cambridge: Cambridge University Press, is especially useful on observational methods.
- For an introduction to qualitative methods, see Smith, J. (2008). *Qualitative psychology: A practical guide to research methods* (2nd ed.). London: Sage. For particular methods, see, for example, Kvale, S. & Brinkmann, S. (2008). *Interviews* (2nd ed.). London: Sage, and Yin, R.K. (2009). *Case study research* (4th ed.). London: Sage. Also recommended is Christensen, P. & James, A. (Eds.) (2008). *Research with children: Perspectives and practices* (2nd ed.). New York: Routledge.
- There are many good statistics texts available for psychology and the social/behavioural sciences. These include Howitt, D. & Cramer, D. (2005) *Introduction to statistics for psychology* (3rd ed.). Hemel Hempstead: Prentice-Hall, and Howell, D.C. (2009). *Statistical methods for psychology* (7th ed.). Belmont, CA: Wadsworth.
- The journal *Childhood* is a good source for issues around children's rights and young people as researchers. See also Montgomery, H.K., Burr, R. & Woodhead, M. (Eds.) (2003). Changing childhoods: Local and global. *Childhood*, Vol 4, Chichester: John Wiley.
- An accessible general overview to ideas in the philosophy of science is in Chalmers, A.F. (1999). *What is this thing called science?* (3rd ed.). Milton Keynes: Open University Press.

CHAPTER
2

Biological and Cultural Theories of Development

CHAPTER OUTLINE

- Genetics and the Groundplan for Development
- The Brain and Developmental Neuroscience
- How Behaviour Develops: Nature and Nurture
- Evolution and Human Behaviour
- Culture and Development
- Social Constructionist Approaches

In this chapter, we look at the way behaviour develops. We start with our genetic inheritance and how the genetic blueprint interacts with our environment to channel growth and development along a particular pathway. We examine these issues in two ways—ontogenetically and phylogenetically. Ontogenesis refers to the development of behaviour in the individual. Most of the book is concerned with this! Phylogenesis refers to the evolution of behaviour; we briefly examine issues of instinct, maturation and learning in birds and mammals, including our closest non-human relatives, the monkeys and apes. This evolutionary perspective continues with an overview of socio-biology and behavioural ecology, which provide the most successful approach to explaining why animals behave as they do, and which some researchers have tried to apply to human behaviour through the disciplines of evolutionary psychology and evolutionary developmental psychology. But in addition to our biological heritage, the environments we have created for ourselves have enormous impact. Cross-cultural psychologists have written about the ways in which different cultural experiences shape development. Most psychologists see approaches that integrate biological and cultural factors as being the most relevant. Social constructionist approaches emphasize the extent to which we construct ourselves and our environments, and deemphasize biological factors.

GENETICS AND THE GROUNDPLAN FOR DEVELOPMENT

Our bodies are made up of cells—brain cells, blood cells, muscle cells, bone cells and so on. But we all started life as just one cell, the 'zygote', formed by the union of mother's egg and father's sperm, which develops through various stages (described in the next chapter). Let's look at the code for this development, the instructions that enable this development to take place.

If we look at cells under powerful microscopes, we find that each cell has a nucleus containing thread-like structures called chromosomes (Figure 2.1). These chromosomes are typically arranged in pairs: four pairs in fruit flies, 24 pairs in chimpanzees and 23 pairs for humans. Each chromosome, in turn, consists of a chain of genes; the genes are strung along the chromosomes like beads on a necklace. The genes, in turn, are composed of DNA (deoxyribonucleic acid), which is made up of strands of complex molecules twisted around each other in a double spiral configuration. It is the genes that provide instructions for the production of materials in the body for growth and development.

The whole gene sequence of an organism is called the 'genome'. The instructions coming from the genome lead to an organism having basic body organs—having wings, or not; having legs, or not; and also what kind of wings, legs, etc. As humans, we owe our basic body plan—that we have two eyes, a nose, a mouth, two arms, two legs, etc.—to the human genome. But individuals vary in other ways; the genetic constitution of a particular individual is called his or her 'genotype'. Genotypes vary, as the genes at particular points can have different 'alleles'—alternative forms that have different effects. Such aspects as the colour of our hair or of our eyes, and whether our hair is curly, depend on which particular genetic alleles we have.

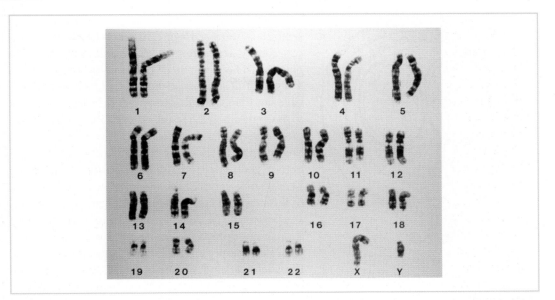

Figure 2.1 Human chromosome complement arranged into a standard karyotype, numbered as shown. The sex chromosomes, labelled X and Y, are at the lower right.
Source: Department of Clinical Cytogenetics, Addenbrookes Hospital/Science Photo Library.

In sexual reproduction, the egg cells (ova) of the mother and the sperm cells of the father contain only a half-set of chromosomes—one from each pair, following some reassortment of genes among each pair. After mating and fertilization, the zygote (fertilized egg) now has a new set of chromosome pairs, with one set of each pair from the mother and one set from the father. The offspring thus receives a mixture of the genes of each parent, approximately half from each, reassembled into new combinations. Thus we inherit aspects such as hair colour from our parents, although not always in obvious ways. Besides physical development, the genotype also influences behavioural development—a topic known as behavioural genetics (Plomin et al., 2013). There is no doubt that features of the genotype can affect behavioural development in the human species. Some genes affect one particular characteristic strongly, others affect several more weakly or in interactive combination. For most of the behavioural traits that psychologists are interested in, there are likely to be multiple genes involved, each having a small effect. Effects are typically probabilistic rather than deterministic.

Behaviour geneticists study these influences. Two traditional methods of estimating genetic and environmental influences on a trait are twin studies and adoption studies.

Twin Studies

Although mothers usually conceive only one infant at a time, about one in every 80 pregnancies involves twins. Twins can be monozygotic or dizygotic.

Monozygotic: Identical twins, who come from a single fertilized egg cell that has split into two early in development. Usually, the twins share the placenta and surrounding membrane, but have their own umbilical cord to the mother's blood supply and their own amniotic sac (Figure 2.2). They are genetically identical (they will have the same genetic alleles) and hence are the same sex.

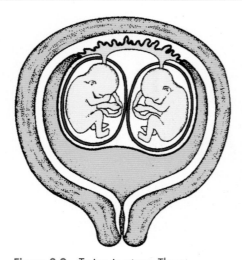

Figure 2.2   Twins *in utero*. These identical twins have a single placenta but individual amniotic sacs.

Source: Arey, L. B. (1965). *Developmental anatomy: A textbook and laboratory manual of embryology* (7th ed.). Philadelphia, London: W.B. Saunders Company.

Dizygotic: Fraternal twins, who come from two separately fertilized egg cells, each of which develops totally separately in the womb with its own placenta. They may be of the same or different sex. They are full siblings (although it is technically possible, and has been documented, for fraternal twins to be half-siblings; Segal, 2000). Full siblings are often described as having 50% of genes in common; this actually refers to the alleles that distinguish one human genotype from another, which are known as 'segregating genes'. Siblings have in common 50% of the variation between their parents in these alleles.

Twins can be considered as being reared in very similar environments—normally by the same parents, at the same time and in the same circumstances. But identical and fraternal twins differ in genetic similarity (100% versus 50% of segregating genes). Thus, it can be argued, if identical twins grow up to be more similar in certain respects than fraternal twins, this should be due to heredity or genetic factors (which differ) rather than environmental factors (which they have in common).

In fact, identical twins do often show greater similarity to one another than do fraternal twins (Figure 2.3). The extent to which this occurs is taken by behaviour geneticists as an indication of the heritability of the trait in question (the heritability is in fact twice the difference between the MZ and DZ correlations). So, for example, Figure 2.3 suggests higher heritability for verbal reasoning than for memory.

There are, of course, some questionable assumptions here; in particular, it is possible that identical twins are treated in more similar ways by parents than are fraternal twins, so that their environment is more similar as well as their genetic inheritance. Behaviour geneticists have attempted to avoid this confusion by obtaining data on identical twins reared apart (rather few in number, however) and by using other methods such as comparing adopted and non-adopted siblings (Plomin et al., 2013).

Adoption Studies

Children tend to resemble their parents to some extent, for example in appearance or temperament—'He takes after his dad'. Of course, this similarity could be due to genetic and/or environmental influences, as usually the parents are providing their children with both genes and a rearing environment. 'Family studies', which look at similarities and dissimilarities between relatives according to degrees of relatedness (e.g. are cousins less alike than siblings?), suffer from this confound of genetic with environmental factors.

Studies of adopted children can avoid this confound. Especially when adopted early, these children have the rearing environment provided by their adoptive parents, but a genetic inheritance from their natural, biological parents. So whom do they resemble most, as they grow up? If environment is more important, it should be the adoptive parents; if genetic factors, the

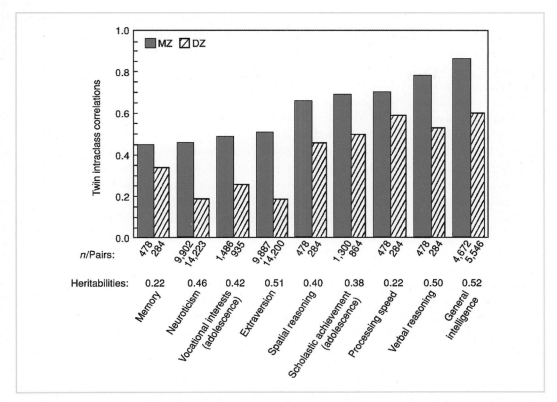

Figure 2.3   MZ and DZ twin intraclass correlations for personality (neuroticism and extraversion), interests in adolescence, scholastic achievement in adolescence, specific cognitive abilities in adolescence (memory, spatial reasoning, processing speed, verbal reasoning), and general intelligence.

Source: From Plomin, R., Owen, M. J. & McGuffin, P. (1994). The genetic basis of complex human behaviours. *Science, 264*, 1733–1739. Reprinted with permission from AAAS and Professor Robert Plomin.

biological parents. There are assumptions in this method too, as adoption is typically non-random; adoptive parents are usually screened and they may tend to choose, or have assigned to them, infants who resemble them physically or temperamentally, or with whom they feel compatible. Generally, twin studies have been used more than adoption studies in recent behaviour genetic work, but the conclusions from the two methods are broadly similar (Gregory et al., 2011).

Genes, and Shared and Non-Shared Environment

Using twin and adoption studies, behaviour geneticists usually partition influences on development into three kinds: heritability, shared environment and non-shared environment.

Heritability refers to variation explained by genetic differences.

Shared environment refers to aspects of the family environment that make brothers and sisters similar irrespective of genetics; for example, family economic circumstances or general parental rearing style.

Non-shared environment refers to environmental variation in which siblings differ. For example, siblings differ in birth order, and perhaps in the schools they go to and the friends they make. Also, parents may treat individual children differently.

Besides the main effects of these three factors, there can be what is called *genotype–environment interaction*. To some extent, children help create their own rearing environment. A child's temperament, for example (which appears to be strongly genetically influenced), influences the ways parents behave towards that child and the expectations they have of them. Also, what are called 'sibling differentiation processes' may operate. Siblings who are close in age may consciously choose to differentiate themselves in forming their own identity. Feinberg and Hetherington (2000) studied 720 sibling pairs in adolescence and found that, generally, siblings closer in age were *less* similar on measures of adjustment than those more distant in age. These kinds of phenomena complicate conclusions from behaviour genetic studies.

Two main findings from much behavioural genetic research in the 1980s and 1990s were that, first, heritability was an important factor in many aspects of development (such as personality, intelligence, antisocial behaviour) and second, that most environmental influence was of the non-shared kind. It was argued that shared environment contributed very little to understanding individual differences. For example, children adopted into the same family showed very little similarity as they grew up (Plomin & Daniels, 1987). Harris (1995, 1998; see Chapter 5) took the importance of the non-shared environment as a starting point for her 'group socialization' theory of development.

As more evidence and critical analysis have accumulated, this rather strong conclusion has been moderated, and shared environment is recognized as an important factor in some cases. As an example, Taylor et al. (2000b) used a twin study to examine heritability of delinquency in adolescence. For both boys and girls, they estimated that genetic factors accounted for about 18% of the variance, non-shared environment for 56% and shared environment for 26%. All three sources were important; the high percentage for non-shared environment here is plausibly related to the importance of peer groups and delinquent gangs in adolescence, which could vary a lot between siblings from the same family (see also Chapter 18 for discussion of street children and gangs in Brazil, and Chapter 19).

Although most studies suggest an important role for heritability, this is not always the case. Discussing several twin and family studies of attachment type (see Chapter 4), van IJzendoorn et al. (2000) found that concordance for major mother–infant attachment type was similar for same-sex siblings and monozygotic twins. They concluded that there was 'a relatively small role for a genetic component in attachment security' (p. 1096) and larger roles for both shared environment (e.g. general maternal sensitivity to infants) and non-shared environment (e.g. effects of birth order and maternal experience at child rearing).

Identifying Genes and the Human Genome Project

The Human Genome Project started in 1990 and was completed in 2003. Coordinated in the US, it was an international endeavour, with the aim of mapping the sequence of DNA base pairs in all the human chromosomes. This amounts to identifying all the genes we have, and how they are laid out along our chromosomes. There are some 3 billion building blocks for the DNA, and some 20–30,000 genes, so this has been an ambitious task! Following draft completion in April 2003, a fuller completion, with more detail for each chromosome, was announced in May 2006. The entire collection of human chromosome DNA sequences is now freely available to the worldwide research community, as are the genomes of a number of other species. Recent techniques enable us to identify genes and some of their effects more directly than in twin and adoption studies. Genes can be linked to phenotypic outcomes by linkage (cotransmission of genes and traits, often within large family pedigrees) or by association (correlating presence of a gene with a trait, often in unrelated individuals). We all possess two alleles of each gene (since we get a set from each parent). A number of specific genetic alleles have now been linked to specific behavioural outcomes, in the sense that individuals with different alleles of a certain gene may react differently in varying environmental situations.

Belsky and Pluess (2009; Table 3) list 36 such studies which show differential susceptibility (this and related terms are described more fully later, see p. 63). The genes in question are generally concerned with the production and regulation of neurotransmitters such as serotonin and dopamine. For example, a gene on the X chromosome called MAOA can have a low-activity allele, which some studies have linked to a risk of greater antisocial behaviour under stressful circumstances such as child maltreatment (see Chapter 10).

Some genes relate primarily to serotonin, a neurotransmitter substance important in mediating mood and in feelings of happiness or depression. One gene, called 5-HTTLPR, can have short or long alleles, and variations in this have been found to impact on outcomes such as depression, anxiety and attention deficit hyperactivity disorder (ADHD). The findings can be complex. A meta-analysis of 30 studies by van IJzendoorn and Bakermans-Kranenburg (2012) found that in most studies, those homozygous for the long allele (l/l) were less suscep-tible to the effects of negative environments than those with short/long (s/l) or short-short (s/s) alleles. However, this did depend on ethnicity, a suggestion supported by a study by Davies and Cicchetti (2014) (described in more detail in Chapter 10).

Other genes relate primarily to dopamine, a neurotransmitter substance important in mediating the reward system. Here, a gene called DRD4 has various forms, and attention has been paid particularly to one variant called the 7-repeat allele. This has been linked to out-comes such as disorganized attachment (see Chapter 4), sensation seeking, and externalizing behaviour. A study by Belsky and Pluess (2013) looking at social functioning in childhood as a result of early childcare experiences, as mediated by variations in both DRD4 and 5-HTTLPR, is described in Chapter 4.

There are also links from particular genes to aspects of cognitive development. For example, Diamond et al. (2004) looked at two tasks that depend upon the dorsolateral pre-frontal cortex, a part of the front area of the brain particularly involved in planning, memory and inhibition. In both tasks, children (mostly 8–10 years old) responded to stimuli on a computer screen. One task was called the 'dots-mixed' task and involved pressing the same or other side of the screen in response to a dot stimulus, depending on whether the dot was grey or striped. This task involves inhibition (but few memory demands) and is known to be influenced by the amount of dopamine in this brain area. The second task was called 'self-ordered pointing'; this involved touching each of an array of stimuli in any order, but only once. This task involves memory demands (but not much need to inhibit responses) and is not influenced by the amount of dopamine. The researchers looked at two alleles of a gene called COMT, on chromosome 22, which gives instructions for producing an enzyme to break down dopamine. The two alleles are called Met and Val, and the Met allele is slower in producing dopamine breakdown. Children could be Met-Met, Val-Met or Val-Val; the children homozy-gous for the Met allele did much better on the 'dots-mixed' task, but no better on the 'self-ordered pointing' task. (They also did no better on two other tasks, recall memory and mental rotation, that involved other brain areas.) This link from a genetic allele to a cognitive task is plausibly linked to the production and action of dopamine.

Research relating specific genes to behaviour is expanding rapidly, and will inform us about the pathways by which genes affect behaviour, gene–environment interactions, and environmental risks associated with certain genes or genotypes.

Stop and Think

Does the Human Genome Project have implications for psychologists studying child development?

Chromosomal Abnormalities

Another source of evidence for genetic effects on behaviour comes from changes at the level of chromosomes. Of the 23 pairs of chromosomes in humans, 22 pairs (the 'autosomes') are basically matched pairs similar in structure. The 23rd pair, the 'sex chromosomes', is different. One type, called the X chromosome, is considerably longer and more complex than the alternative, the Y chromosome (see Figure 2.1). If you receive two X chromosomes, you will normally develop as a female; if you receive one X and one Y chromosome, you will normally develop as a male. This, of course, has very definite implications for development, and is discussed further in Chapter 6.

Occasionally some mistake is made in genetic transmission, often a change or 'mutation' at the gene level. Sometimes the mistake can take place at a whole chromosome level. The best known example relates to the 21st chromosome pair; occasionally this pair may fail to separate in forming the egg or sperm, and the offspring may end up having three chromosomes—a trio instead of a pair at this location. This trisomy 21 condition is usually referred to as Down (or Down's) syndrome.

Down Syndrome

Down syndrome (DS) occurs in approximately one in 800 live births. The chromosomal abnormality usually originates in damage to the ovum prior to conception. A woman's ova are present from birth so they are increasingly vulnerable to damage over time; hence, older mothers are more likely than younger mothers to have a baby with DS. Mothers aged 20–24 have a 1 in 9,000 chance of having a baby with DS, whereas in mothers aged 45 or over the chances rise to 1 in 30. Paternal age is also associated with increased likelihood of having a baby with DS.

A photograph of a person with DS is shown in Figure 2.4. There are specific physical characteristics in DS, including a flat appearance to the face, with a low bridge to the nose, high cheekbones and upward and outward slanting eyes, with a conspicuous upper eyelid fold. In addition, muscles may be floppy, contributing to poor motor coordination. Most children with DS reach developmental milestones later than is usual. So far as behavioural and cognitive development is concerned, people with DS vary greatly. Most have mild to moderate retardation, but children with DS are capable of developing skills throughout their lives and have a wide range of abilities. There is likely to be particular difficulty taking in visual, auditory and other sensory information at speed, and slow reaction times; particularly poor memory for heard speech, leading to poor speech comprehension; poor speech pronunciation; and poor number ability. The child with DS is likely to have better visual skills than hearing and speech skills, so they may find it easier to sign or even to read than to acquire intelligible speech. Their level of spontaneous activity is low, and they need extra encouragement to explore, experiment and learn. Some people with DS show a deterioration of mental abilities and sometimes difficult behaviour as they get older but on the positive side, some do continue intellectual development beyond adolescence (Rauh et al., 1991). Also, children with DS are often sociable and show few negative behaviours; a study of 8–16-year-olds found they were generally positive about their peer relationships

Figure 2.4   A child with Down syndrome.
Source: Image copyright R. Gino Santa Maria. Used under licence from Shutterstock.com.

(Begley, 1999). Programmes designed to develop play and communication at an early age are helpful and many children with DS go to school and enjoy the same sorts of activities as other children; a few go on to study at college, and some are able to live independent lives in the community.

THE BRAIN AND DEVELOPMENTAL NEUROSCIENCE

We know that the human brain consists of different areas (Figure 2.5). Neurophysiologists have long known, through studies of brain injuries, electroencephalograph (EEG) recordings and electrical stimulation of brain areas, that certain regions of the brain are broadly associated with certain faculties. For example, the temporal lobes are involved in memory functions, frontal lobes and prefrontal cortex are associated with 'higher' mental faculties such as planning and inhibition of immediate emotional responses.

This century has seen a remarkable growth in techniques to study brain activity, and progress in linking brain areas and brain activity to particular abilities and behaviours. Much of this relates to cognitive activities such as perception, memory, learning and language, and has come to be called *cognitive neuroscience*—but some findings are also relevant to social behaviour.

A number of specialist techniques are now available to neuroscientists (Johnson, 2005). *Neuroimaging techniques* provide measures of brain processes, and include the following processes:

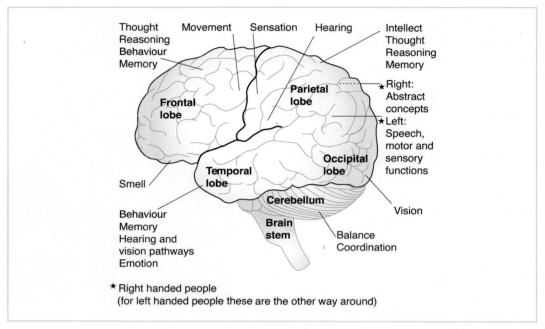

Figure 2.5 Functional areas of the human brain.
Source: Peter Gardiner/Science Photo Library.

- *High-density event-related potentials (HD-ERPs):* electrodes placed on the scalp pick up electrical activity in the brain, for example in response to a stimulus presentation.
- *Positron emission tomography (PET):* this detects changes in blood flow in regions of the brain.
- *Functional magnetic resonance imaging (fMRI):* blood oxygen levels in quite specific areas of the brain are assessed, as a measure of brain activity.
- *Near infra-red spectroscopy (NIRS):* this also measures oxygen in the blood, by means of the scattering of light beams.
- *Transcranial magnetic stimulation (TMS):* studies the effects of a temporary disruption of brain activity.

Combined with knowledge of how the brain develops through infancy, childhood and adolescence, this becomes *developmental cognitive neuroscience*, which is now a substantial area of study (Blakemore & Frith, 2005; Johnson, 2005). In infancy, there is a rapid growth in nerve fibres, the connections between the nerve cells that make up the brain. This is called *synaptogenesis*. The stems or axons between nerve cells, which conduct electrical signals, also become more efficient due to an increase in their insulating coating of myelin. Frequently used connections between nerve cells are strengthened and disused ones are eliminated, a process called *synaptic pruning*. This provides the substrate for learning and behavioural development to occur.

To study this, developmental neuroscientists have also used what are called *marker tasks*. Here, if a brain area is known to be associated with a certain kind of task performance, it can be studied at different ages and in different contexts, in order to understand better how brain developments affect the task concerned. Theories about such development can also be made explicit by *computational modelling*.

Johnson (2005) described three approaches to understanding how brain development interacts with behavioural development: maturation; skill learning; and interactive specialization.

The *maturational* view sees developments in the brain (especially the cerebral cortex) as having a direct facilitative influence on behaviour. Thus, what develops is the brain, and the behaviour follows. This might be an especially useful viewpoint in the neonatal period (see Chapter 3) and for perception abilities in infancy (see Chapter 11), when cortical development is rapid and substantial.

A contrasting viewpoint is *skill learning*; this supposes that the relevant brain region for a specific task is available (it is already developed), and that it is active practice or training in a task that improves competence levels. Thus what develops is the psychological skill, not the physiological substrate. This might be a useful viewpoint for many skills learned in middle childhood (for example, learning to ride a bicycle, learning algebraic formulas), which might also be learned in a similar way at any age.

A more complex viewpoint is *interactive specialization*. Here, it is supposed that different brain regions may start with poorly defined functions, and how these develop depends on both interactions with the environment and changes in connectivity within different brain regions themselves. This may be more realistic as a general viewpoint, and would be consistent with the idea of sensitive periods in development (see p. 44).

Much of the work in developmental cognitive neuroscience focuses on the infancy period. However, there are also important changes in adolescence, especially affecting the prefrontal cortex, which are thought to play an important role in many features of the adolescent period; this is discussed further in Chapter 19. New developments are likely to include greater linkage between behaviour genetic studies and developmental neuroscience, in order to understand how individual differences in brain structure and development are linked to genetic differences (Diamond & Anso, 2008).

HOW BEHAVIOUR DEVELOPS: NATURE AND NURTURE

The genes determine the first stages in cell growth and differentiation in the body, and in the brain and nervous system. Thus, they are often thought of as providing a blueprint for growth and also for behaviour. The actual course of growth and of behavioural development, however, depends upon, and is influenced by, the external environment. Not only does the environment provide the 'building materials' such as food and water, but the particular environmental experiences of the organism also interact with the genetic instructions to determine in detail which exact course of development is followed.

Figure 2.6 depicts in very simple form the interaction of information from the genotype and information from the environment in determining behaviour. Both genotype and environment are obviously essential for any behaviour. Thus, we cannot say that a particular behaviour is genetic and another behaviour environmental; nor can we sensibly say that a behaviour comprises some percentage of each. The diagram in Figure 2.6 is a simple one. Although our genotype is given at birth, the expression of genes, or their functional consequences, can be influenced by the environment—a process called *epigenesis*. In other words,

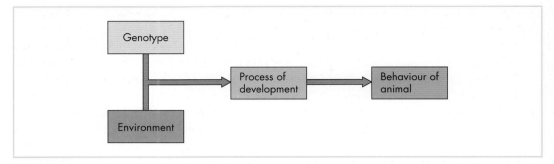

Figure 2.6   Simple model of how both information from the genotype and information from the environment combine and interact to determine the course of behaviour development.

the environment can affect our behaviour not only through processes of learning (see below) but also by influencing the way genes are functioning in our development. Another version of this diagram is given later when we look at social cultural theory (see Figure 2.17).

Although we cannot say that a behaviour is mostly genetic or environmental, we can say that the difference in behaviour between two individuals is mostly genetic or environmental. In humans, for example, differences in eye colour can usually be ascribed to genetic differences (although both genotype and environment are necessary for the development of eye colour), whereas differences in spoken language can usually be ascribed to environmental differences (although both genotype and environment are necessary for the development of language). Genes and environment interact in complex ways (Rutter, 2012), and three models of interaction are described later (p. 63).

Instinct, Maturation and Learning

Many writers have used the terms 'instinct', 'maturation' and 'learning' in discussing the development of behaviour. There are problems with the definition of these terms, and some psychologists prefer not to use the term 'instinct' at all. However, in order to understand discussion on these matters, we need to know what writers who use such terms intend. Representative definitions are given below.

Instinct: Instinctive behaviour is observed in all normal healthy members of a species. Thus, it is little influenced by the environment. The genetic instructions provide detailed information for the development of instinctive behaviour, and only quite general environmental input (such as is necessary for healthy growth) is needed for its expression.

Maturation: Maturation refers to the emergence of instinctive behaviour patterns at a particular point in development. The genetic instructions facilitate the expression of certain behaviour patterns when a certain growth point is reached or a certain time period has elapsed.

Learning: Learning refers to the influence of specific environmental information on behaviour. Within a wide range of variation, the way an animal behaves depends on what it learns from the environment. Thus, individuals of a species may differ considerably in their learned behaviour patterns.

Rigidity and Flexibility

It can be rather simplistic to say that a behaviour is either 'instinctive' or 'learned'. Many psychologists now prefer to talk in terms of the 'rigidity' or 'flexibility' of behaviour, or of how 'modifiable' or 'canalized' behavioural development is. Rigid behaviour is less susceptible to environmental modification; flexible behaviour is more so. A helpful way of conceptualizing this issue is shown in Figure 2.7. This type of figure, produced by Waddington (1957), is called an 'epigenetic landscape'. The ball represents the organism, while the landscape represents the possibilities for development constrained by the genotype. The movement of the ball down the slope represents development. The direction of travel (development) is influenced by the shape of the landscape, as it is easier for the ball to roll down the troughs, or canals. However, environmental influences can also influence the direction of travel, pushing the ball in certain directions.

At certain times, there are choice or decision points in development, and environmental influences may easily affect the direction of development at such points (for example, the point marked A in Figure 2.7). At other times, environmental influence, unless extreme, will have little effect (the point marked B, for instance).

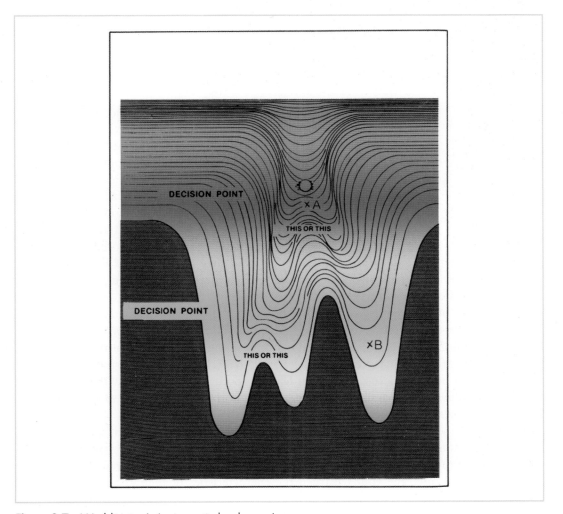

Figure 2.7   Waddington's 'epigenetic landscape'.

Source: Fishbein, H.D. (1976) *Evolution, Development, and Children's Learning*. Pacific Palisades, CA: Goodyear Publishing Company.

Waddington, and others since, talked of the 'canalization' of behaviour. This is another way of referring to the rigidity as opposed to flexibility of behaviour. We talk of canalized behaviour when the troughs or canals in the epigenetic landscape are deep and environmental variations have little effect. If the canals are shallow, the environment produces much greater variation.

Imprinting and the Concept of Sensitive Periods

The concept of imprinting stems from work by the Austrian ethologist Konrad Lorenz (see Lorenz, 1981). He noted that the young in some species, such as ducks, hens and deer (called precocial species), learn to follow their mother around very soon after birth. But how do they learn whom to follow? Lorenz discovered that while the following mechanism is highly canalized ('instinctive'), there is some flexibility in learning what (or whom) is to be followed. Generally, the young bird or mammal learns the characteristics of a conspicuous moving object nearby during a period soon after birth or hatching; it then follows this object around. This process of learning which object to follow was described as imprinting. Usually, imprinting occurs to the mother, since she is the main figure the offspring encounters during the critical, or sensitive, period after birth. But imprinting to other objects can occur.

Figure 2.8   Young ducklings 'imprinted' on Konrad Lorenz follow him wherever he goes (Atkinson, Atkinson and Hilgard, 1981).
Source: Nina Leen/The LIFE Picture Collection/Getty Images.

Lorenz imprinted some ducklings on himself, so that they then followed him everywhere (Figure 2.8). This is easy to do with sheep as well (as in the nursery song, where 'everywhere that Mary went, the lamb was sure to go').

Lorenz also introduced the term 'critical period' to describe the restricted period of time in which he believed imprinting took place. In ducklings, this period is about 9–17 hours after hatching (Figure 2.9). Lorenz also believed that imprinting was irreversible after this period. Subsequent research has suggested that the learning that takes place in imprinting is not quite as rigid as this, but that nevertheless such learning occurs most readily within a restricted period. Researchers now usually refer to this as a 'sensitive period'. Another example might be the development of kin recognition in littermates.

Imprinting in which the young learn the characteristics of the parent is known as 'filial imprinting'. It is important in precocial species in order to ensure that the young follow the correct animal (unless an experimenter such as Lorenz intervenes!). Lorenz also believed that, at the same time, the young learned the characteristics of their species, so that they would ultimately choose a member of their own species to mate with. This is called 'sexual imprinting' (Irwin & Price, 1999). Bateson (1982) showed that early experience is important

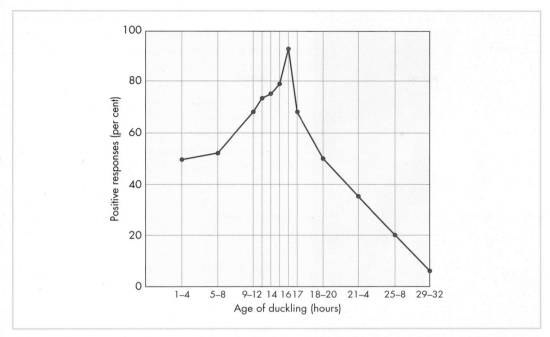

Figure 2.9   Results of an experiment showing that ducklings follow a model more readily that is seen 9–17 hours after hatching than at other times.

for mating preference in Japanese quail; they prefer as mating partners other quail that differ in appearance slightly, but not a lot, from those they were reared with. If quail are reared normally with siblings, then as adults they prefer to mate with cousins, rather than with siblings or unrelated birds. However, such choices can be altered if they are reared with non-sibling quail of different appearance. This species imprinting seems normally to involve learning the appearance of kin, and then later selecting as a mate an individual who would be related, but not too closely, thus achieving a balance between the costs of inbreeding and outbreeding.

Individual and Social Learning Processes

Imprinting is often presented as a special form of learning, highly constrained in what is learned and when it is learned. Many forms of learning are more flexible, especially in mammals, though the idea that there are some constraints on learning (some degree of canalization in development; see Figure 2.7) seems to apply widely (Hinde & Stevenson-Hinde, 1973).

The behaviourist tradition, exemplified by the work of Watson and of Skinner (e.g. Skinner, 1938), studied individual learning processes, such as classical conditioning and operant conditioning, in terms of stimulus and response associations. The degree to which the individual is rewarded or 'reinforced' in its behaviour is indeed one important aspect in understanding actual behaviour—although the processes can be complex; for example, rats will learn not to eat food that produces nausea, even if the nausea occurs an hour later

Figure 2.10   A chimpanzee pokes a twig into a termite nest.

Source: Mary Beth Angelo/Science Photo Library.

(Garcia et al., 1966). However, the behaviourists ignored higher cognitive processes, and the kinds of learning that can occur without obviously being evident in behaviour at the time. A lot of learning occurs through observation, as well as through individual exploration and 'trial and error'.

A particularly interesting kind of learning is *social learning*; here, the presence of another animal of the same species (a conspecific) assists in the learning process. There are several ways in which social learning can take place.

Local enhancement: It could be that the presence of a conspecific simply draws the attention of an animal to something, such as a food source. For example, a monkey sees another monkey washing and eating potatoes, and that draws its attention to the potatoes, which it then starts to manipulate and perhaps eat, through individual learning. This kind of process is also referred to as social facilitation.

Obviously, the role of the other animal is very limited here. Two other processes give other animals a more direct function, via observation of what they are doing.

Emulation: Here, the animal sees another one trying to achieve some goal and then also tries to achieve that goal. Perhaps it sees another monkey wash a potato in the sea before eating it, but itself washes the potato in a pool of water nearby instead of going into the sea.

Imitation: Here, the animal imitates the actual actions of the conspecific. It observes the actions (e.g. going into sea water and washing a potato) and then carries out very similar actions itself.

An interesting example of social learning is that of tool making and the use of tools in chimpanzees. Chimpanzees enjoy eating termites; however, these are found in hard, inaccessible nests. Chimpanzees have learned how to prepare sticks of the right size and length (by stripping off the side bits) to insert into holes in the nest and draw the termites out (Figure 2.10). Young chimpanzees appear to learn such skills by watching their mothers closely as they do them (van Lawick-Goodall, 1968). Lonsdorf (2005) found that young female chimpanzees acquire termite-fishing skills a year earlier than young males, probably because they stay closer to their mothers and watch and imitate their technique, whereas males may rely more on trial-and-error learning.

 Stop and Think

What different ways of learning are there? How many of these depend on other people (social learning)?

Social Learning, Tradition and Culture

Social learning is seen as a precondition of *culture*. There are many definitions of culture, and many arguments about its existence or not in non-human species (see Kendal, 2008). One definition (Laland & Janik, 2006) is: 'group-typical behavioural patterns, shared by community members that rely upon socially learned and transmitted information'. This more or less equates culture with social learning, such that local mating sites in shoals of fish or food-eating patterns in groups of rats, passed on by social learning in that group, could be seen as culture. A counter argument is that these examples are *animal traditions*, not true culture. A stronger requirement of culture would be that it: (i) has a repertoire: it is not just restricted to one or two aspects, such as how to eat nuts; and (ii) is cumulative, so that further beneficial modifications are acquired and passed on to others, resulting in gradually increased complexity and efficiency (see also p. 66). Some definitions also require that culture is transmitted symbolically, which comes close to requiring the existence of language. Animals communicate, sometimes in sophisticated ways, but generally not in a way that would facilitate cultural transmission in this sense.

Communication Systems in Monkeys and Apes

In communication, a signal is sent from one individual to another, which may influence the latter's behaviour. Signals used by monkeys and apes seem especially complex (see Seyfarth & Cheney, 1984). For example, vervet monkeys (a ground-living, social species) have three kinds of alarm call, with corresponding responses. 'Leopard alarms' cause other monkeys to run to trees; 'eagle alarms' cause them to look up in the air or run into bushes; and 'snake alarms' cause the monkeys to rise on their hind legs and look into the grass around them. These conclusions, based first on observation, have been confirmed by controlled experiments involving playback of tape-recorded calls. Vervet monkeys also 'grunt' at other monkeys, and the same methods have shown that grunts that sound the same to a human observer differ in spectrographic analysis according to whether the grunt is directed to a dominant animal, a subordinate animal or a monkey from another group.

The most dramatic studies of animal communication have been made with captive apes, usually chimpanzees. A husband and wife team, Gardner and Gardner (1969), taught American Sign Language (ASL) to Washoe, a young female chimpanzee who lived with them. Washoe acquired a large number of signs, and could convey messages such as 'please tickle' and 'give drink' (Figure 2.11). The Gardners claimed that Washoe could use several signs strung together meaningfully, that she used signs in new situations (e.g. 'water bird' when she first saw a swan), and that altogether Washoe had language competence not dissimilar to that of a 2-year-old human child. Similar methods have been used successfully with other chimpanzees, with a female gorilla called Koko (Patterson, 1978), and with an orang-utan, Princess (Shapiro, 1982).

Figure 2.11 Washoe, a young female chimpanzee taught to use sign language, for example, 'hat' for woollen cap.

Other methods have also been used. Premack (1971) taught a female chimpanzee, Sarah, to communicate using plastic shapes, and Savage-Rumbaugh and Rumbaugh (1978) used a computer keyboard to similar effect, teaching Lana (another female chimpanzee) to communicate with the experimenter in verb-object phrases.

Criticisms have been made of these studies, for example that only rote learning is taking place or that the experimenter, as with 'Clever Hans' (see p. 17), is giving unintentional cues to the animal as to the right response. Terrace et al. (1979), working with a chimpanzee called Nim, strongly criticized some of the Gardners' more ambitious claims and the selective way in which they reported their data. The Gardners defended their position, pointing out that their claims and methods of data reporting are no worse, and often better, than the methods used by those studying child language (Drumm et al., 1986; van Cantfort & Rimpau, 1982).

Human language is much more flexible than any non-human communication system, but it too has a biological underpinning. Liebermann (2007) discusses the genetic, anatomical and neural bases underlying human speech, and Steven Pinker's book *The language instinct* (1994) strongly expresses this biological viewpoint. We discuss this perspective, and human language development generally, in Chapter 12.

Teaching

We use language for teaching, which is a very special kind of learning process. Again, there are debates about the definition of teaching, and about the extent to which it is seen in non-human species.

Definitions of teaching usually incorporate three criteria: first, there is some cost to the teacher (for example, they do the task less efficiently or in a simpler form than they normally do); second, the pupil learns faster than they would do by themselves; and third, there is some feedback between teacher and pupil (for example, the teacher adapts to the pupil's progress or state of knowledge).

Surprisingly, one of the first clear demonstrations of teaching in a non-human species appears to be in ants! Franks and Richardson (2006) showed that an ant may guide another to a food source and, while doing so, goes slower than it would normally do. The other ant follows and gives 'feedback' by tapping on the leading ant's body if she is going too slowly. This is an intriguing example, but it illustrates very canalized ('instinctive') behaviours rather than the more flexible efforts to teach a pupil that characterize human behaviour.

Another example is the meerkat, a member of the mongoose family (Thornton & McAuliffe, 2006). Meerkats are known to be able to deal with scorpions, on which they prey and which can be very dangerous—a scorpion sting is potentially lethal. Adults are skilled at this, but youngsters have to learn. Adult meerkats bring scorpions to young ones to kill; the adult may kill it first, making it very easy for the young meerkat to deal with. Otherwise, they may disable the sting, or they may leave it intact, depending on the age of the meerkat pup.

A possible example of teaching in chimpanzees came from more anecdotal observations by Boesch (1991). He watched infants observing their mother cracking nuts, which chimpanzees do by putting a nut on an 'anvil' (some suitable strong flat surface) and striking it hard with a 'hammer' (usually a stone). Sometimes a mother chimpanzee would provide an infant with a suitable nut to crack, or a suitable hammer, which certainly helps the infant learn but does not fulfil the third aspect of teaching (feedback). However, on two occasions, Boesch observed a chimpanzee mother taking account of her infant's failure to crack a nut by assisting further, repositioning the nut or hammer and/or demonstrating a correct blow.

Thinking in Primates

In the more advanced mammals, especially monkeys and apes, it seems as though we are encountering the beginnings of mental activity ('thinking') as we are familiar with it. This involves a kind of internal, symbolic representation of the world in the brain; thinking consists of the internal manipulation of these symbols. Some examples of behaviour seen in monkeys certainly suggest this kind of thinking. In species such as macaques and baboons, individuals will sometimes form cliques against a rival (for example, Packer's observations on p. 58), or will give different vocalizations to animals of different social status or relatedness (Seyfarth & Cheney, 1984). It appears as though monkeys are thinking in quite complex ways about their social relationships. This goes along with a relatively large cerebral cortex in these species. With this sort of brain, behaviour becomes much more flexible, and learning during development much more important. This is especially true of the great apes—the chimpanzee, the gorilla and the orang-utan. Studies have been made of these, both in the wild and in laboratories. Let's look at some examples of advanced abilities in the great apes.

Tool use and making: Tool use has been observed in a number of species, but tool making—deliberately altering a natural object to a specific end—was long thought to be uniquely characteristic of humans. However, it has been observed in chimpanzees in natural conditions (see Figure 2.10) and in other great apes in experimental situations. Related to this is an ability to use objects in insightful ways, for example stacking boxes on top of each other to access an out-of-reach clump of bananas, or using poles as ladders to get over fences.

Learned symbolic communication: All three species of great ape have been trained to communicate using non-verbal signals (see p. 47); this is at least a rudimentary kind of learned language. These instances are based on laboratory studies, but there is an example of learned communication in natural surroundings too. Nishida (1980) has described a 'leaf-clipping display' amongst wild chimpanzees in Tanzania. A chimpanzee picks several stiff leaves and repeatedly pulls them from side to side between its teeth; this makes a distinctive and conspicuous ripping sound. It is used as possessive behaviour or courtship display by a male to a female, or a female in oestrus to a male. This display has not been seen to be used in this way in other chimpanzee populations, and may be a social custom of this particular group.

Traditions and/or culture: There are traditions in tool use and tool making, in different chimpanzee communities. For example, to get ants out of nests, some use short sticks held by one hand, others use longer sticks held by two hands. Also, in symbolic communication, some communities use the 'leaf-clipping display' (above) and others do not. There is certainly a case to be made for cultural traditions in chimpanzees (McGrew, 2004).

Self-recognition: Chimpanzees and orang-utans can recognize themselves in a mirror (just as human infants can from around 18 months; see Chapter 6). This has been shown by so-called 'mirror image stimulation' (MIS) studies (Gallup, 1982). An animal is first accustomed to a mirror. Then, while anaesthetized, it is marked conspicuously (for example, with red dye) on an ear, nose or eyebrow in a way that it cannot see directly. Its reaction on seeing its mirror reflection is noted. Monkeys will reach for the mirror image as if it was another animal. However, after a few days of prior mirror exposure, a chimpanzee or orang-utan will reach for its own body part, strongly suggesting that it recognizes itself in the image. For a while it was thought that gorillas could not do this, but some have now succeeded, albeit less easily or consistently than the other great apes (Allen & Schwartz, 2008).

Pretence: There are some observations of chimpanzees using objects in 'pretend' ways (for a discussion of pretend play in children, see Chapter 7). A classic example is of a chimpanzee called Viki, home-reared by two psychologists. Viki was observed at times to be acting as if she had an imaginary pulltoy.

> Very slowly and deliberately she was marching around the toilet, trailing the fingertips of one hand on the floor. Now and then she paused, glanced back at the hand, and then resumed her progress . . . she interrupted the sport one day to make a series of tugging motions . . . She moved her hands over and around the plumbing knob in a very mysterious fashion; then placing both fists one above the other in line with the knob, she strained backwards as in tug of war. Eventually there was a little jerk and off she went again, trailing what to my mind could only be an imaginary pulltoy.
>
> *(Hayes, 1952)*

The Evolution of High Intelligence

Why has such high intelligence evolved in the primates, and especially the great apes? There is a cost to high intelligence—large brains use up more energy for maintenance, and a longer developmental period entails greater risks. So there must be benefits to counterbalance these.

An older view was that high intelligence helps animals cope with the physical environment. Parker and Gibson (1979) suggested that high intelligence evolved as a means of better obtaining food. For example, tool use, tool making and imitative learning are all involved in food gathering in chimpanzees.

An alternative argument is that high intelligence has been selected for because of its advantages in social interaction (Byrne & Whiten, 1988). Primates are clever in social contexts—recognizing and deceiving others, forming alliances and achieving dominant status. Being socially clever could have considerable advantages for an animal's reproductive success. Byrne and Whiten (1988) called this 'Machiavellian intelligence', or tactical deception. Deception is involved when an individual sends a signal to another individual, who then acts appropriately towards the signal according to its obvious meaning, which is, however, untrue. Deception is well known in many animal species, but is particularly complex in primates. As an example, consider an observation made on chimpanzees by Plooij (in Byrne & Whiten, 1987).

> An adult male (A) was about to eat some bananas that only he knew about, when a second male (T) came into view at the edge of the feeding area. The first quickly walked several metres away from the food, sat down and looked around as though nothing had happened (Figure 2.12a).

Here, A is deceiving T by giving signals that 'there is nothing of interest around here' (untrue!). If A looked at the bananas, then T (being more dominant) would take them instead. However, the observation continues.

> The newcomer (T) left the feeding area (Figure 2.12b) but as soon as he was out of sight he hid behind a tree and peered at the male who remained (A). As soon as A approached the food and took it, T returned, displaced the other and ate the bananas.

This is actually counter-deception by the second chimpanzee, who seems to have realized that the first was hiding something!

Deception itself is not necessarily a sign of high intelligence; it depends on what level the deception is at. Mitchell (1986) has described levels of deception.

Level-one deception describes situations where an animal is programmed to give a deceptive signal, irrespective of circumstances (for example, an insect that is palatable but that mimics in appearance a brightly coloured and inedible wasp).

(a)   (b)

Figure 2.12 Tactical deception in chimpanzees.
Source: Byrne, R. & Whiten, A. 1987: The thinking primate's guide to deception, *New Scientist, 1589*(116): 54–6.
3 Dec 1987. Reproduced by permission of David Bygott.

Level-two deception is when an animal's signal is still programmed or 'instinctive', but is given only in response to certain stimuli. For example, some birds will 'pretend' to be injured when certain predators approach their nest. By feigning a broken wing, for instance, they may distract the predator and lure it away from the eggs or chicks. The display is fairly stereotyped, but only elicited if a predator appears.

Level-three deception is when the animal's signal can be modified by learning. An example might be a dog which, by limping (even though it is not injured), gets more petting and attention; this differs from the bird's feigned injury in that it has been learned in ontogeny as a successful strategy. However, it may be no more than stimulus–response learning of the type 'lifting my paw in a certain way results in my being petted'. Many cases of tactical deception (Whiten & Byrne, 1988) are likely to be of this kind.

Level-four deception indicates an understanding of deceptive intent and a flexibility of response, such that the animal deliberately corrects or changes its signals so as to encourage the receiver to act in certain ways. It is as if the animal doing the deceiving knows, and calculates, the effects on the recipient. The chimpanzee examples described above would come at this level.

The Evolution of 'Mindreading' and of Metarepresentational Thought

At these higher levels of intelligence and intentional action, it would seem as though an animal has some idea of what is going on in another animal's mind—it is, as it were, 'mindreading'. A more common term is 'theory of mind', implying that an individual can hypothesize about what is going on in another's mind. (It might be thinking 'that animal is hungry' or 'that animal is hiding food', for example.) Level-four tactical deception is a good indicator of this. Somewhat similar skills can be seen developing in children (see Chapter 15). More generally, mindreading skills, and also the other aspects of high intelligence mentioned previously, can be taken as examples of 'second-order representation' or 'metarepresentation'. A first-order representation is symbolizing something in your mind—for example, an object, such as a table or a banana, or a state, such as being hungry. In a second-order representation or metarepresentation, one or more first-order representations are themselves represented.

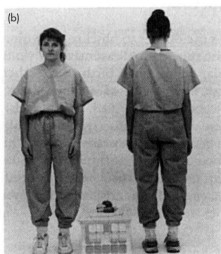

Figure 2.13   (a) The stimulus configuration for bucket probe trials. (b) The stimulus configuration for back-versus-front probe trials.

Source: Povinelli, D. J. & Eddy, T. J. (1996). III Understanding who can see you: Preliminary investigations. *Monographs of the Society for Research in Child Development, 61*(3), 23–66. Photographs preprinted with permission from Professor Povinelli.

For example, in tool making, the first-order representation of the actual action is manipulated relative to the representation of the desired object; this process involves second-order representation. In pretence, the representation of the actual object coexists with the representation of it as having pretend characteristics (Leslie, 1987). In self-recognition, the representation of the mirror image is related to the representation of one's own self, or body. In symbolic communication, symbols (non-verbal or verbal) stand for or represent other objects or actions. And in level-four deception, the intentionality of deceit implies that the sender can represent both the true and the falsely signalled state of affairs (somewhat analogous to pretence).

Some researchers have argued that these abilities all represent a second-order representational capacity, which is found in the great apes and which is also an important aspect of children's development (Suddendorf & Whiten, 2001). Other researchers have pointed out the distinctive differences that remain between the great apes and the human species. Povinelli and Eddy (1996) reported a series of studies on chimpanzees, in which they examined what young chimpanzees know about seeing. They trained chimpanzees to gesture for food, and then gave them a choice of two people to beg from; one of the people could see the chimpanzee and the other could not. Could the chimpanzee 'mindread', or at least understand that one person could see their gesture while another was unable to do so?

Figure 2.13 shows one condition in which they succeeded. If one person was facing the chimpanzee and the other had their back to the chimpanzee, the chimpanzee would beg from the person facing them. Not surprising, perhaps. But what was surprising was the failure of the chimpanzees in the other conditions. Here, both persons would face the chimpanzee, but one would be blindfolded or have a bucket over his/her head. The chimpanzees begged to the blindfolded person or the person with the bucket over their head, as much as to the other person. In another study, the chimpanzees could not discriminate between two persons with their backs to them, even when one person had his/her head turned round, looking over their shoulder at the chimpanzee.

This suggests a lack of mindreading abilities in chimpanzees and pushes us to a more behaviourist interpretation of the anecdotal and naturalistic evidence cited earlier. There are caveats to the work by Povinelli and Eddy. Are the experiments ecologically valid, for example (Smith, 1996)? A chimpanzee persistently begging from someone who is not looking at them might seem stupid, but in the wild it could make sense—another chimpanzee is likely to respond to the grunts or at least see the outstretched hand. Who is being stupid—a chimpanzee begging from a person with a bucket over their head, or the person with the bucket over their head who fails to respond to the begging grunts of the chimpanzee? This general issue about ecological validity has occurred also with work on children (see p. 259). Despite this caveat, other experimental work using non-verbal false belief tasks have found that apes typically fail them, whereas children typically pass them by around 4 years of age (Call & Tomasello, 1999).

Suddendorf and Whiten (2001), however, have reaffirmed the mental achievements of the great apes, compared to other species. There seems little doubt that chimpanzees are at least very clever behaviourists—very adept at learning links between stimulus situations and behaviour, and more so than monkeys. But maybe they lack the kind of motivation to understand others' mental states that humans, even human infants, seem to have.

An example of this is pointing at objects to communicate interest, or a desire to get the object. Infants do this from an early age, but apes do not; apes may approach an object and stretch out an arm to reach it, but they do not point with a finger. An experiment to demonstrate this child–ape difference was reported by van der Goot, Tomasello and Liszkowski (2014). They arranged experimental set-ups in which 1-year-old infants, and separately chimpanzees or bonobos, were shown desirable objects (toys, or bananas for the apes) and then presented with a situation where a similar object was out of reach but with the experimenter nearby. About half of the infants pointed at the object, but none of the apes did so—they approached as near as they could and stretched out for it. In contrast, many of the infants pointed at the object, even when the situation changed so that they could have crawled up to the object to obtain it—clearly showing the communicative intent of the pointing.

As Tomasello (1996) pointed out:

> In their natural habitats, chimpanzees do not spontaneously point for others to distal entities in their environments, either with or without finger extension. They also do not hold objects up to show them to others, or try to bring others to locations so that they can observe things there, or actively offer objects to other individuals by holding them out to them. Chimpanzees and other apes also do not engage in the intentional teaching of offspring. (p. 165)

This latter point ignores the Boesch (1991) report (see p. 38), but it is true that chimpanzee teaching is not seen in any normative or systematic fashion.

What would happen if chimpanzee infants were raised in a human environment where they *did* receive intentional teaching? There are a number of studies of such 'human-raised' or 'enculturated' apes—indeed, Washoe was an early example. Some studies have focused on indices of mindreading and intentionality, such as imitating and pointing. Tomasello (1999) concluded that enculturated apes do show more human-like skills of social cognition; they are more likely to show deferred imitation of a human action, for example. But there remain differences, and so far it looks as though even human-raised apes lack the motivation for sharing experiences with other intentional beings, which human infants seem to develop in a canalized way.

Stop and Think

In what ways do human children show capabilities and potentials that can lead to greater representational learning than is found in other primates?

Apes, Humans and Culture

Tomasello (1999) argued that the crucial difference between apes and humans is that humans understand other individuals as intentional agents like the self. This facilitates joint attention to what others are doing (and intending to do), and imitative learning. This imitative learning is not just at a motor level, but also at a representational level, constituting what Tomasello calls cultural learning. This is evident in the way in which children learn words and language, as well as the way they learn about object use and social conventions, and acquire a theory of mind. All these abilities allow for the accumulation of cultural skills—language, tool use, social conventions—over time, and for a true process of cultural evolution to take place in which learned accomplishments are retained and built upon by future generations.

Empirical evidence to support this viewpoint comes from comparative work by Herrmann et al. (2007). They directly compared the abilities of 2-year-old children with those of chimpanzees and orang-utans on a battery of cognitive tests. The abilities of the young children and the apes were fairly comparable on physical cognitive skills, but the children were markedly better at social cognitive skills. Much more than the apes, they would follow an adult's gaze, use pointing, and observe and imitate what adults did, making use of the social context of learning.

Csibra and Gergely (2006) have argued that humans, including human infants, are specifically adapted to transfer knowledge to, and receive knowledge from, conspecifics by teaching; an adaptation they call *pedagogy*. They cite particular characteristics of human infants that demonstrate this: interest in human faces; following an adult's gaze; and imitating novel actions. (These and other adaptations are considered further in Chapter 3.) These infant adaptations facilitate the ability of adults to transmit cultural information to them (ways of using objects, ways of using words, ways of interacting with other people). Pedagogy (unlike the earlier examples of animal learning) conveys generalizable knowledge that is valid beyond the actual situation. Of course, pedagogy also depends on a teacher who will provide cultural information and take account of the learner's less advanced state. The ideas of Vygotsky and Bruner in Chapter 16 develop this social context of learning further.

EVOLUTION AND HUMAN BEHAVIOUR

Although as humans we are very different from non-human species, we share the basic principles of genetic transmission and the interaction of genes with environment in determining behaviour. We have an evolutionary history, being primates (the taxonomic group that includes monkeys and the great apes). Our closest animal relatives are the great apes—the chimpanzee, gorilla and orang-utan. We know that early humans, or 'hominids', had become different from the early apes by 5 million years ago. In East Africa, scientists such as Richard Leakey and Donald Johanson have unearthed fossil remains of hominids that are 3–4 million years old

(Johanson & Edey, 1981; Lewin, 2004). These very early hominids, called *australopithecines*, were smaller than us (about 4 feet tall) and had smaller brains, but already walked erect and had moved from the ape habitat of forest to the hominid habitat of open grassland.

Over the next few million years, fossil remains document the increasing body size and especially brain size of the hominids and their increasing technological and cultural sophistication, as evidenced by stone tool manufacture. *Homo habilis*, and later *Homo erectus*, show these trends, and later, shelter construction, use of fire and cave art. These latter are evidenced by the *Neanderthals*, who probably evolved from *Homo erectus* and occupied Europe and parts of Asia for some hundreds of thousands of years. They were eventually superseded by our own species, *Homo sapiens*.

It is generally thought that modern humans originated in Africa some 100,000 years ago and moved out from there. In Europe they would have met the Neanderthals. Although considered a distinct species or subspecies, recent work has succeeded in reconstructing the Neanderthal genome from well-preserved skeletal remains (Pääbo, 2014). It appears that some interbreeding did take place, as many modern humans have some 2–4% of Neanderthal genes (but modern African people have 0% as they did not encounter the Neanderthals). Research on the distinctive aspects of the Neanderthal genome and their functional significance can be expected to shed further light on what makes us distinctively human.

Changes over the past 50,000 years have been largely cultural, not biological, as *Homo sapiens* learned to domesticate animals, cultivate plants, build cities, pursue the systematic advance of knowledge and develop modern technology (Renfrew, 2007). So, does our primate and hominid ancestry tell us anything useful about ourselves now? This has been a very controversial issue.

Some scientists studying animal behaviour have made strong links to human behaviour. Ethologists such as Irenaus Eibl-Eibesfeldt (1971, 1989) developed a field called human ethology, which took ideas such as those of Lorenz and other animal ethologists and applied them to humans. An example of this is an experimental study by Sternglanz et al. (1977) on how the 'cute' facial and bodily appearance of infants elicits caring and parental behaviour. When shown the stimuli in Figure 2.14(a), young adults rated the one shown at (b) as being most attractive. It has quite large eyes and a moderately large forehead. Dolls and 'cute' animals in film cartoons have similar facial proportions (c).

More recently, a deeper understanding of evolutionary theory has led to the development of fields such as human sociobiology, evolutionary psychology and evolutionary developmental psychology. The last of these is particularly relevant for us. First, a brief summary of evolutionary theory, stemming from the work of Charles Darwin in the 19th century, will be useful.

Evolutionary Theory

Darwin's evolutionary theory was concerned with the ways in which the characteristics of an animal were selected, over generations, to be especially suited to or 'adapted' for the kind of environment in which it lived. The giraffe's long neck was adapted for feeding on the kinds of leaves and buds found high up on trees and bushes, for example. Although Darwin was writing before modern genetic theory was developed around 1900, the idea of the gene provides a crucial link in modern evolutionary theory. As we saw earlier, the genes code information about development, and they are passed on from parent to offspring.

Giraffes, for example, have genes for long neck growth. In the past, as giraffes were evolving, those individuals that had genes for especially long necks fed better, and thus had more

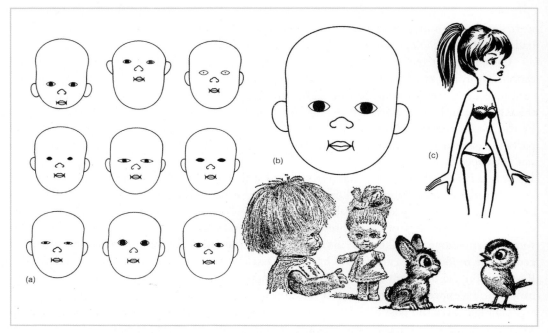

Figure 2.14 (a) Facial stimuli used by Sternglanz et al. (1997). (b) The stimulus noted as most effective. (c) Dolls and cartoon animals with similar facial proportions.

Source: (a, b) Sternglanz, S. H., Gray, J. L. & Murukami, M. (1977). Adult preference for infantile facial features: An ethological approach. *Animal Behaviour, 25,* 108–115. (c) Eibl-Eibesfeldt, I. (1971). *Love and hate: The natural history of behaviour patterns.* London: Methuen. Reproduced by permission of Transaction Aldine.

offspring, who themselves were more likely than average to have genes for long necks. Thus, genes for long necks, and actual long necks, came to typify the modern giraffe species.

Behaviour can be selected for during evolution, just as body characteristics can. For example, birdsong and communication signals are characteristic of a species and seem to have adaptive value. In considering social behaviour, however, a long-standing controversy has existed about whether we should think of the behaviour as being adaptive for the individual animal, or for the social group it is in, or even for the entire species.

Darwin's approach implied that behaviour should be adaptive for the individual, as the genes that are selected are only passed from parent to offspring. However, it was difficult to explain examples of cooperation and altruism on this basis. A consideration of Figure 2.15 may help to explain this. Consider a behaviour by animal A that affects animal B. The behaviour might have a benefit or a cost to A, and a benefit or cost to B. We measure benefits and costs in terms of how the behaviour increases the chances of surviving and rearing offspring. Animal A's behaviour could be mutualistic, selfish, altruistic or spiteful, according to this framework. Now, if we argue that behaviour is selected for individual benefits, then we should only expect behaviour in the top two cells in Figure 2.15. We would not expect altruistic behaviour, and yet this does occur; for example, *communal suckling* (lionesses in a pride will suckle other cubs as well as their own) or communal defence (elephants will defend other calves in their group as well as their own).

For a long time, the predominant response to this was to argue that behaviour was selected for the good of the whole social group, or species. The difficulty with this approach,

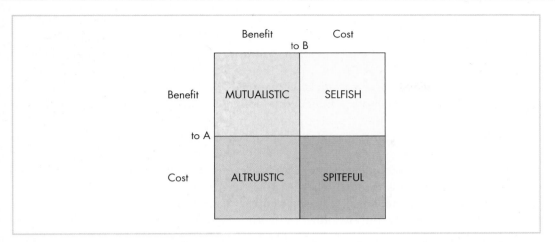

Figure 2.15   Cost and benefit to two animals, A and B, of a social interaction between A and B.

appealing as it may seem, is that it predicts only behaviour in the left-hand cells of Figure 2.15. No selfish behaviour is expected. Yet selfish behaviour is also common; for example, in many species, communal suckling or communal defence does *not* occur and in most species, individuals will show aggression to others over territory and mating rights.

Sociobiological theory provides a solution. It predicts the mixture of mutualistic, altruistic and selfish behaviour that we actually observe in animal societies. The key idea, put forward by Hamilton (1964), is that of 'kin selection'. This is the hypothesis that an animal will behave altruistically towards its kin, especially those closely related. This was always taken for granted for an individual's offspring, as it was only through offspring that genes were directly passed on. Hamilton's insight was that an animal would share a greater than average proportion of genes with relatives, too, especially close relatives such as siblings and cousins. Helping relatives is another way in which particular genes get passed on to the next generation—admittedly only an indirect way, compared with having offspring oneself.

Kin selection theory then predicts that helpful or altruistic behaviour may be directed towards relatives, provided that it is not too harmful to the animal giving the help, and provided that the other animal is closely enough related to make it worthwhile. Close relatives will be helped more. Much evidence supports this theory. Examples include communal suckling in lions, or communal defence in elephants, where the females in the group are usually sisters or cousins.

Another prediction of kin selection theory is that males will only assist females and offspring if it is likely that they are the genetic father (or a close relative). The likelihood that a male is the genetic father is referred to as *paternity certainty*. Paternity certainty will be higher in monogamous species, and it is indeed in such species that males help most in rearing the young (e.g. many nesting birds, a few mammals such as hunting dogs and marmosets). For implications of this for human behaviour, see pp. 89 and 153.

In an interesting extension of kin selection theory, Trivers (1974) postulated that we should expect to see *parent–offspring conflict*. This is because the genetic interests of parent and offspring are not identical. The mother is related to all her offspring equally, and would be selected (other things being equal) to provide each with the same amount of parental investment or help. However, an individual offspring would be selected to favour itself over its siblings, with whom it shares only half its genes; thus, according to Trivers, it should seek more than its fair share of parental investment. This should lead to conflict with the mother, over the amount and duration of parental investment, and also to conflict with siblings, or sibling rivalry. Since Trivers wrote his article, there have been many observations of parent–offspring and sibling conflict in animals. In mammals, suckling is a very important form of parental investment by the mother. In many species, the infant seems to try to continue suckling for longer than the mother wishes; the mother may reject the attempts of older infants to suckle, quite forcefully. Siblings may also compete with each other for access to the mother in feeding situations.

There is more to sociobiology than just kin selection, however. Another way of explaining altruistic behaviour is through what is called 'reciprocal altruism' (Trivers, 1971). The hypothesis is that one individual will help another, at some smaller cost to itself, if it can expect similar help back from the other animal in the future. This is the old adage, 'If you scratch my back, I'll scratch yours'. There is some evidence of reciprocal altruism, the most convincing being in monkeys and apes, where it is clear that individuals do recognize each other and could thus stop helping individuals who failed to reciprocate ('cheats'). In a study of baboons, Packer (1977) found that pairs of unrelated males would help each other in challenging a dominant male. Individuals that gave such help to a particular male often received help back from the same male. As the males were unrelated, kin selection could not explain this.

Evolutionary Theory and Human Behaviour

Evolutionary theory provides the prevailing theoretical paradigm for explaining why non-human species behave in the way they do, in terms of the evolutionary costs and benefits of behaviours. Sociobiologists such as E. O. Wilson (1978) wondered whether human behaviour, like animal behaviour, works to maximize the survival and reproductive success of individuals. For example, do the predictions of kin selection apply to humans? It does seem to be the case that people are most generous or altruistic to close kin, even when it is not socially sanctioned. In agricultural and tribal societies (i.e. people not yet living in large cities), kinship is a very important organizing framework, affecting expectations about whom you will marry as well as expectations for help and alliance in warfare.

Almost all human societies are either monogamous or polygynous (though a few tribes are or have been polyandrous, notably in Sri Lanka and Tibet). Sociobiology can explain this; monogamous societies tend to be those where fathers can help directly in child rearing, whereas in polygynous societies men compete for status, for example by acquiring wealth or cattle, and do little to help their wives directly. What seem to be characteristic sex differences in men and women, for example in abilities, in aggression and in attitudes to sexual behaviour, have also been given an evolutionary explanation (Buss & Schmitt, 1993; Symons, 1979; Wilson, 1978). Some of these ideas have applications in studying children. Young children experience a greater risk of abuse or maltreatment with stepparents compared to natural parents, and this has had an explanation based on kin selection theory (Daly & Wilson, 1996; see Chapter 4). An attempt to test Trivers' theory of parent–offspring conflict in humans is described in Box 2.1.

The idea of sexual imprinting (p. 44) has also been applied to humans. The so-called Westermarck effect predicts that children who are cosocialized (reared together) will not be sexually attracted to each other as adults (Silverman & Bevc, 2005). (Conversely, siblings

Box 2.1 Parent–offspring weaning conflicts among the Bofi farmers and foragers of Central Africa

This study by Fouts et al. (2005) examines weaning, and conflict associated with weaning, in two neighbouring but different African communities. Bofi is a language spoken in the Congo Basin rainforest in the Central African Republic. The Bofi foragers live by hunting (mainly net hunting of small animals) and gathering nuts, fruit, honey and other forest foods. (They are relatives of the Aka community, mentioned on p. 135). The Bofi farmers mainly practise slash-and-burn agriculture, growing manioc and other crops. The two groups (the foragers and the farmers) are culturally and ethnically distinct, but share the same language and trade together on a daily basis. Bofi foragers are relatively egalitarian and cooperative, but respect personal autonomy and do not usually sanction each other's behaviour. Bofi farmers are more hierarchical and there are greater disparities in wealth; there are strong clan loyalties and stricter expectations about individual behaviour (for example, whom one should marry).

The two groups have different 'parental ethnotheories'; that is, different culturally accepted ideas about how to bring up children. For example, in the foraging community, children are held by adults a lot more (they can be carried on hunting and gathering trips), and caregivers respond more quickly to fussing and crying. Child obedience is much more stressed in the farming community and, by 4 or 5 years, children may be required to help look after younger siblings. In regard to weaning, Bofi foragers follow a child-led policy. Weaning takes place between 36 and 53 months, with the fourth year of life thought of as the normal time for this. On the other hand, Bofi farmers wean their children between 18 and 27 months, with 2 years seen as the normally

appropriate time (Box Figure 2.1.1). Unlike the foragers, the farmer mothers use direct discouragement of weaning: overt prohibition, bandaging the nipples, or putting nail polish on the nipples.

In this study, the researchers examined parent–offspring conflict and what would predict levels of conflict. They were influenced by Trivers' (1974) theory of parent–offspring conflict, but were also very aware of cultural factors, believing that 'biological and cultural perspectives are complementary and that the two perspectives can accommodate each other' (p. 48).

A combination of quantitative and qualitative methodology was used. The quantitative data were obtained by focal child observations: each target child was observed over repeated short periods, for a total of nine hours over two or three days. Twenty-two forager children (aged 18.5–58 months) and 21 farmer children (aged 18.5–55 months) were observed, in order to record nursing status (time spent breastfeeding, divided at the median into 'high' or 'low'; or fully weaned), any fussing or crying behaviour, and mother and child activities (including whether the child was held by a caregiver). In addition, interviews were held with both parents to clarify cultural practices and parental ethnotheories, and to assess mother's current pregnancy status.

Box Table 2.1.1 shows the percentage of time a child was observed fussing or crying, as well as the percentage of time mothers spent working, and the percentage of time the child was held by a caregiver (usually the mother, especially while the child is still nursing, but for weaned infants often a father, grandmother or aunt). For the forager children, the sample is

Box Figure 2.1.1   Bofi forager woman nursing her 2-year-old child (a) and Bofi farmer woman nursing her 1-year-old child (b).

Source: Philip Hoffman (a) and Hillary Fouts (b).

Box Table 2.1.1   Variations in child fussing and crying, maternal work, and total holding (percentages of time during daylight hours), in Bofi foragers and farmers.

	Child fussing or crying	Maternal work	Total holding
Forager: high-level nursing, N = 9	4.0	14.8	54.6
Forager: low-level nursing, N = 5	6.6	48.4	46.4
Forager: fully weaned, N = 8	4.9	52.2	29.2
Farmer: low-level nursing without overt maternal resistance, N = 5	5.4	54.7	23.8
Farmer: low-level nursing with overt maternal resistance, N = 3	9.7	32.8	21.9
Farmer: fully weaned, N = 13	2.05	71.2	3.4

Source: Adapted from Table 5 in Fouts et al. (2005). (The original table mistakenly labels farmer children as forager children.)

split into those receiving high-level nursing, those receiving low-level nursing and those fully weaned (the latter ranging from 37 to 58 months). None of the farmer children were receiving high-level nursing; the sample is split into those receiving low-level nursing, three infants whose mothers overtly prohibited them from nursing, and those who were fully weaned (the latter ranging from 29 to 55 months).

The table shows that low-level nursing, where the mother is starting to wean the infant, is related to higher levels of fussing and crying. The researchers carried out a linear regression analysis on the whole sample, to see which factors statistically predicted fussing and crying. The two independently significant predictors were low levels of nursing and maternal pregnancy (eight mothers were pregnant, including the three farmer mothers who overtly prohibited nursing). Neither infant age, cultural group, nursing/weaned nor maternal work were significant predictors.

The researchers took the findings as showing some support for Trivers' theory of parent–offspring conflict. Not only was there more fussing and crying when the mother was in the process of weaning, but this was also exacerbated when the mother was pregnant, so that the infant's interests were in conflict with those of his or her future sibling. However, the nature and degree of distress are clearly influenced by cultural context, as are maternal strategies. In other words, 'the maximization of reproductive fitness in a particular ecology certainly influences observed differences and shapes caregiving' (p. 39).

The authors mention 'the forager children's lower distress levels' (p. 39), but the forager children showed *higher* distress levels overall (average 4.3 versus 3.9), although the difference in distress between the two groups was not significant on the regression analysis. However, the highest levels of distress did come from those farmer infants where the mother was using overt prohibition—a tactic not used in foragers. On the other hand, once weaned, the farmer infants showed the lowest distress; this may be connected to the greater training for obedience, and the growing requirement for them to help care for younger siblings.

It is noticeable from the table that high-level nursing does hold back the time forager mothers can spend working and that, for farmer mothers, full weaning releases them for more work activity. Also striking is how forager infants are held a lot more than farmer infants, irrespective of their weaning status.

This article is followed by nine commentaries, and the author's reply. The small sample size (especially for the subgroups in the table) is clearly a drawback, although this is difficult to circumvent in such research. The commentators also raised issues such as how the interviews were carried out (for example, in which language), and about the role of other kin such as fathers. In general, however, this was seen as a careful attempt to integrate biological and cultural perspectives in studying an important aspect of child rearing. Although not explicitly pursued as such in the article, the study can be seen as an example of the developmental niche approach of Super and Harkness (1997), whereby the physical setting and ecology (for example, here, the nature of the mother's work requirements), ethnotheories (here, the timetable of normal weaning and expectations of sibling caregiving) and culturally regulated customs (here, what strategies are used to achieve weaning) interact to produce distinct culturally adaptive patterns.

Based on material in Fouts, H.N., Hewlett, B.S. & Lamb, M.E. (2005). *Current Anthropology*, 46(1), 29–50.

reared apart may feel sexual attraction if they meet as adults.) The postulated function of the Westermarck effect is to reduce inbreeding, and it normally operates for siblings or close relatives, but studies of Israeli kibbutzim have shown that children reared together communally in these settlements hardly ever marry each other, even though they are unrelated (Shepher, 1983).

Evolutionary Psychology and Evolutionary Developmental Psychology

The field of evolutionary psychology argues that our present-day psychology—the way we think, feel emotions and act—can be explained by our evolutionary history. Specifically, these theorists argue that our hominid ancestors evolved for some millions of years in a nomadic hunter-gatherer environment and social organization, and that we have evolved psychological mechanisms that reflect these; as an example, males are better at complex spatial orientation tasks (which might have been useful in tracking and hunting animals), whereas females are better at remembering locations of objects (which might have been useful in remembering where to find and gather plant foods) (Eals & Silverman, 1994). Evolutionary psychologists generally argue that these adaptations are strongly genetically influenced in their development, and represent modularized capacities in the human brain.

The discipline of evolutionary developmental psychology applies many of these ideas from evolutionary psychology to the study of human development, and especially child development. In doing so, it tends to be less dogmatic about the strength of genetic influence and of modular organization of the brain, and to assume that there is a complex interaction of genetic and environmental factors in development (Bjorklund & Pellegrini, 2000; Geary & Bjorklund, 2000).

These theorists have argued that many features of childhood prepare the way for adulthood. An example is sex differences in play (see Chapter 7). Boys engage in more vigorous rough-and-tumble play than girls, and this is seen as a preparation for adult hunting and fighting skills, and/or dominance assertion. Girls are described as engaging in more play parenting (e.g. doll play). The sex difference in physical aggression (boys doing more; see Chapter 10) is also seen as having adaptive value, as males invest less in offspring and more in mating competition. Early experiences have also been hypothesized to facilitate early, or late, pubertal development (see Chapter 19). However, see also Chapter 6, in which the large overlap in boys' and girls' behaviour is discussed.

Some aspects of development are seen as adaptive at that time, rather than a preparation for later. An example is the tendency for young children to overestimate their competence in a wide range of tasks, which may facilitate their persistence at the task and increase what they learn.

Generally, evolutionary theorists see behaviour as adaptive. However, the reference point for this adaptation is taken as our ancestral environment—what is sometimes called the 'environment of evolutionary adaptedness'. This concept can be a bit nebulous, but it is generally taken as being a kind of hunter-gatherer existence. Certainly, settled agricultural and urban life is seen as different from this. As a consequence, some of our developmental adaptations are *not* well adapted to contemporary living.

One example of this is that children love sweets. This is bad for their teeth, and not especially healthy. However, in hunter-gatherer environments, taking in energy-rich food such as honey when occasionally available would be adaptive. As another example, formal schooling is a new cultural invention; it may be that ADHD, to which much attention has been given in recent years, represents a pattern of high motor activity and attention switching that might have been quite adaptive in the environment of evolutionary adaptiveness, but which is not when formal schooling becomes a universal requirement.

Evolutionary developmental psychology has had considerable application in understanding the typical changes occurring in adolescence; this is considered further in Chapter 19.

 Stop and Think

What examples are there where our evolutionary history helps us understand contemporary child development?

Criticisms of the Evolutionary Approach

Some scientists believe that even to attempt evolutionary explanations is misplaced, because of the dangers of, for example, making sex differences seem natural and inevitable. These scientists believe that the flexibility of human learning is so great that nothing useful is learned from evolutionary theorizing (e.g. Rose et al., 1984). Evolutionary explanations are criticized as 'just so' stories, made up but not really testable. At times the debate has become more personal than scientific.

A problem for evolutionary thinking is that human behaviour seems to be an order of magnitude more flexible even than that of other advanced mammals. There are enormous cultural variations in the behaviour of people in different societies, for example in the language spoken, technology used, moral or religious beliefs held and methods of child rearing used. These are learned variations. A Chinese baby brought up in China learns Chinese and Chinese manners; brought up in the USA, it learns American English and American manners. In addition to this flexibility of learning, humans can cumulatively pass on and build up knowledge and beliefs through cultural traditions (e.g. the development of the idea of democracy; the development of electronic and computer technology).

It may, however, be justified to think of some human behaviour development as reasonably canalized (see p. 43). Thus, the development of human language, from babbling to one-word utterances to syntax, may be fairly strongly canalized (see Chapter 12), whereas the actual language learned is weakly canalized, if at all. Probably some sex differences are somewhat canalized, such that they will develop unless positive steps are taken to prevent them, whereas other sex differences may not be canalized at all and could easily be changed.

Some variations in development can be argued to be adaptive responses to environmental situations. An example is whether delayed puberty can be explained in terms of environmental or psychosocial stressors (see Chapter 19).

Belsky and Pluess' Three Models of Human Plasticity

Besides the undoubted general flexibility or plasticity of human behaviour, individuals may vary in how susceptible or reactive they are to certain environmental situations. This might be due to genetic factors, physiology, or temperament, for example. Three models have been proposed to describe such varied sensitivity: diathesis-stress, differential susceptibility, and vantage sensitivity.

Diathesis-stress: The most frequent examples of this have been studies that show how some individuals are more susceptible to adverse environmental conditions (such as poor-quality parenting or stressful life events). An example of this is shown in Figure 10.1, illustrating an interaction between variants in the MAOA neurotransmitter and the likelihood of developing antisocial behaviour as a result of childhood maltreatment. Belsky and Pluess (2009) labelled this as a *diathesis-stress* model or dual-risk model. Diathesis is a medical term referring to susceptibility to a particular disease; here, it can be taken as meaning risk or disposition. The term *dual-risk* refers to a negative outcome only when two risks are combined (e.g. low MAOA activity and severe childhood maltreatment, in Figure 10.2). The most characteristic form of diathesis-stress is shown in Figure 2.16(a). Here, some individuals are relatively insensitive to variations in the environmental stress, while others are noticeably affected by it in a negative way. A range of studies, primarily over the last decade, have found evidence for this model in relation to diathesis (risk) factors such as difficult temperament,

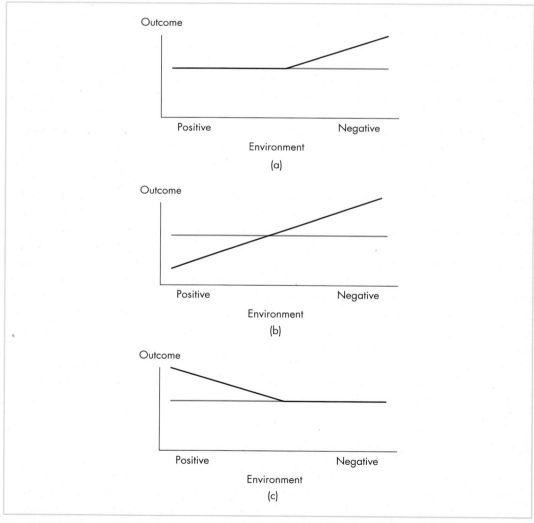

Figure 2.16 Three models of human plasticity: (a) diathesis-stress, (b) differential susceptibility, (c) vantage sensitivity.

cardiovascular reactivity, and genetic alleles of the serotonin or dopamine neurotransmitter systems, in relation to a range of parental, family or life circumstance stressors.

Differential susceptibility: While not discounting the importance of the diathesis-stress model, Belsky and Pluess (2009) argued for some reinterpretation of many of these studies, on both theoretical and empirical grounds. Theoretically, they suggested that on evolutionary grounds, one might expect individuals to vary in plasticity—in how strongly they reacted to either environmental stresses or environmental opportunities. A financial analogy might be helpful in understanding this. Suppose you have money to invest: a balanced portfolio might include some 'safe' investments and some 'risky' ones. The 'risky' ones might pay off handsomely, or might plummet, depending on the subsequent financial environment. Correspondingly, it might be beneficial for parents to have some offspring who are 'safe' investments—fairly stable whatever the environment—and some who are 'risky', reacting strongly to environmental circumstances.

Clearly this implies that the 'risky' offspring will sometimes do well and sometimes do badly. Differential susceptibility describes this situation, as shown in Figure 2.16(b). In a favourable environment they do well and in an unfavourable environment badly, compared to the less reactive offspring. For the empirical part of their argument, Belsky and Pluess (2009) reexamined and in some cases reanalysed a large number of studies that had argued for diathesis-stress effects, in this light. This included the early study by Caspi et al. (2002), shown in Figure 10.2. Looking at this figure, one can see an indication of differential susceptibility, in terms of the reactive, low MAOA group doing slightly better when there was no childhood maltreatment. Subsequent studies replicating this link between genotype for low or high activity MAOA and antisocial behaviour have, according to Belsky and Pluess, confirmed that a differential susceptibility interpretation is a plausible one.

Vantage sensitivity: A third model was explicitly proposed by Pluess and Belsky (2013), which they label *vantage sensitivity*. Vantage can be defined as a position that provides an advantage, and vantage sensitivity describes phenomena where the more reactive person benefits from a positive environment (but is not disadvantaged by a negative environment). It is thus a converse to diathesis-stress—what the authors call a 'bright side' to developmental plasticity, as compared to the 'dark side' emphasized by many earlier studies. This model is illustrated in Figure 2.16(c), and Pluess and Belsky identified some studies as likely candidates for vantage sensitivity. For example, a study in the Netherlands by Kegel et al. (2011) found that children carrying the DRD4 7-repeat gene especially benefited from positive feedback when used in computer games to improve early literacy (but showed no benefit when this positive feedback feature was absent).

Clearly distinguishing these three models will not always be easy. Roisman et al. (2012) suggested two measures ('proportion of the interaction' and 'proportion affected') to help in this. Besides the example shown in Figure 10.2, other examples will be discussed later in relation to early childcare effects (Chapter 4), and to maternal unresponsiveness and children's disruptive problems (Chapter 10).

CULTURE AND DEVELOPMENT

Anthropologists have long been impressed by the varieties of child-rearing customs, and the variations in human behaviour, between cultures. In the early decades of the 20th century, anthropologists such as Margaret Mead and Ruth Benedict emphasized how these different 'patterns of culture' would mould a child: 'from the moment of his birth the customs into which he is born shape his experience and behaviour' (Benedict, 1934, p. 2). Mead (who also trained as a child psychologist) did admit some influence of an infant's temperament on development, but generally the view of these authors (and most anthropologists) was that biology had little to say about development within a culture. A particular example in relation to adolescent development is discussed in Chapter 19. The 'culture and personality' school of anthropology followed the work of Benedict, Mead and others in particular societies, by trying to draw more generalized explanations about cultural variability. Barry et al. (1959) related the subsistence nature of a society to its childhood socialization practices (see also p. 221). For example, agricultural and peasant societies seemed to put particular value on obedience and conformity in children. The 'Six Cultures Study' (Whiting & Edwards, 1988; and see p. 221) made very detailed observations in six different societies, with the premise that parents' daily routines would mediate between the organization of a society and its subsistence practices, and the child's socialization environment. Parental practices such as sleeping arrangements, warmth from and control by mothers, extent and nature of fathers' involvement with infants, extent of caregiving by older siblings and chores given to young children were all seen as both influenced by the nature of the society and, in turn, directing the child's development. As an example, children assigned to take care of younger siblings (as in Kenya) learned more nurturant behaviour, whereas those who spent more time with peers (as in their USA sample) learned more competitive and attention-seeking behaviours.

Cultural-Ecological Models

Several anthropologists have developed more sophisticated models linking culture and ecology to development, building on the earlier decades of work in anthropology and incorporating advances in psychology and other disciplines.

Michael Cole has been influential in promoting the argument that changes in psychological perspectives on cognition have led to a more contextualized approach to the study of development, and a shift of emphasis in the study of socialization away from specific child-rearing practices to the wider context in which children learn about culturally appropriate behaviour (Cole, 1996). Cole is well known for investigating the cultural-historical claims of Vygotsky about cross-cultural differences in mental make-up (Cole et al., 1971; Cole & Scribner, 1974). On the basis of his research in this field, in particular his research on Vygotsky's concept of the zone of proximal development, or ZPD (see Chapter 16), Cole challenged traditional individualistic views in psychology about mental development, arguing instead that cognitive functioning is linked to its *sociocultural* context, and that children learn through a form of apprenticeship with adults. Cole (2005, pp. 2–3) describes culture as:

> . . . the entire pool of artifacts accumulated by the social group in the course of its historical experience. In the aggregate, the accumulated artifacts of a group, culture, is then seen as the species-specific medium of human development. It is 'history in the present'. The capacity to develop within that medium and to arrange for its reproduction in succeeding generations is *the* distinctive characteristic of our species.

The norms of one culture can differ extensively from those of another and so radically affect the ways in which children learn. For example, one culture may place high value on individual achievement, whereas another may stress the achievements of the group. In one culture it is desirable to be competitive; in another, competitiveness may meet with disapproval. Such interaction with adults and more competent peers is, from this standpoint, the foundation on which all children's learning occurs. From this perspective, members of a particular society collectively invent the properties of the social world that they inhabit. Meanings are constructed through the interactions that people have with one another. So children learn the symbolic systems, such as language, religion and mathematics, through their membership of a particular culture and historical period, and through interaction with more knowledgeable members of that culture. The key to understanding how cognitive development takes place lies in the 'activity settings' in which learners operate; for example, children's experience in an instructional context such as a school setting results in a particular kind of discourse. A diagram illustrating Cole's view of this (a variant of Figure 2.6) is shown in Figure 2.17.

This perspective has led psychologists to consider more deeply the relationship between culture and learning, and it challenged the widespread view at the time that non-literate peoples in less developed countries were less intelligent than Western people, or that some cultures did not push young people far enough (as, for example, schooling does) so that their cognitive structures operated at a lower level. Cole's view is that children can be viewed as novice participants in their culture and that their induction into the culture is achieved through shared joint activity. As they come to understand objects and relationships, they recreate their culture within themselves. In particular, Cole and Scribner's research undermined the view that a psychologist could administer cognitive tests that had been developed in one culture in order to measure the abilities of people in another culture. Within Western societies, this principle has frequently been applied to 'culturally disadvantaged children' (see Chapter 18) to explain their relative underachievement in comparison with more privileged groups.

Barbara Rogoff (Rogoff et al., 1995; Rogoff, 2003) has taken forward the idea that children's cognitive development takes place as they participate in culturally and historically shaped events. So individual development is inseparable from interpersonal and community

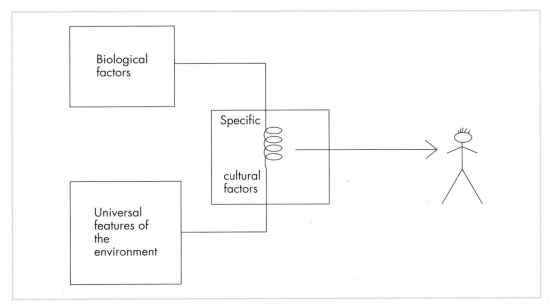

Figure 2.17 Cole's cultural context model of development.

Source: Adapted from Cole, M. (2005) *Culture in Development.* In M. Lamb & M. Bornstein(Eds.) *Developmental Science: An Advanced Textbook.* Hillsdale, NJ: Lawrence Erlbaum Associates. By permission of Taylor & Francis.

processes, and individuals' changing roles are mutually defined with those of other people and with dynamic cultural processes. The process is two-way: 'When individuals participate in shared endeavors, not only does individual development occur, but the process transforms (develops) the practices of the community' (Rogoff et al., 1995, pp. 45–46). To illustrate this sociocultural model, Rogoff and her colleagues investigated historical changes in the practice of Girl Scout cookie sales in the USA, to demonstrate how generations of Girl Scouts and cookie companies have contributed to the ongoing, developing community processes involved in that practice (see Box 2.2). Rogoff (2003) argued that human development can only be understood if we take cultural factors as a central part of the process. Individuals develop in communities, and in order to understand their social, cognitive and emotional development, we must explore the social practices and knowledge of those communities.

Looking generally at social and cognitive aspects of child development in different cultures, Super and Harkness (1997) proposed the concept of a *developmental niche*. The developmental niche 'conceptualizes both the child and the environment as active and interactive systems' (Harkness, 2002). The child is seen as bringing its own temperament, as well as species-specific potentials, to the developmental niche provided by its culture. The niche itself is divided into three major components or subsystems.

1. *The physical and social settings of the child's daily life* (for example, what sort of living space or house is the child in, does he/she have his her own bedroom, etc.)
2. *Culturally regulated customs of childcare and rearing* (for example, scheduling of activities such as children's clubs or TV programmes)
3. *The psychology of the caretakers, especially their belief systems or 'ethnotheories'* (for example, do parents believe that a regular and restful sleep schedule is vital for healthy development; see Box 2.1 for ethnotheories concerning weaning).

These three subsystems are seen as homeostatically coordinated; parents tend to feel comfortable if their own developmental theories and belief systems accord with cultural customs; cultural customs conform to physical and social settings; and all are generally functionally embedded in the larger ecology.

These anthropological perspectives on child development do strongly emphasize the importance of culture. Examples of cultural differences are taken up in several places in this book, for example relating to attachment security (p. 112) sex roles (p. 221), and adolescence (p. 681). Nevertheless researchers such as Rogoff, Cole, and Super and Harkness do not ignore or disparage genetic or biological factors as having a role to play, both through individual child temperament and through universal features of our genetic endowment.

 Stop and Think

Most developmental studies are carried out in Western societies. Is it important to consider evidence from other cultures?

Box 2.2 Development through participation in sociocultural activity

This study by Rogoff et al. (1995) illustrated how the community practice of Girl Scout cookie sales developed through the contributions of individuals and groups, and how transformations in the practice related to historical changes in other institutions, such as family structure and maternal employment.

In 1990, the time of the study, Girl Scouts of America, a voluntary organization dedicated to girls' moral education, development at home, academic and outdoor skills and career preparation, had an annual fundraising event centred on the sale of cookies. The average Scout troop raised $420; nationwide revenues were $400 million. Cookie sales were considered to be an educational tool to teach the girls social responsibility, goal setting and business principles.

This highly organized, nationwide annual event had evolved from much simpler, informal sales of home-baked cakes for local fundraising in the early years of the Girl Scout movement in the 1930s. Many Scouts had mothers or older sisters who had in their time participated in a similar event. Older customers were often eager to buy since it reminded them of their own experience as Girl Scouts years before. (If members of the community were not invited to buy, they were often offended at being left out.) By the 1990s, large baking companies were licensed by Girl Scouts of America to supply the cookies and deliver orders to a deadline. The administration of the cookie sales had expanded on a regional basis and had developed over time from a simple system of tear-off order stubs to an elaborate system of colour-coded order forms and sales training information. The administrative forms supplied to the participating Scouts were not adapted to be easy for children to use, but were retail forms similar to those used by adult salespeople. The layout of the 1990s official form designed by the Girl Scout organization required the girls to calculate amounts of money, present colour-coded information to customers that identified seven different types of cookie, and administer a system for tracking colour-coded deliveries as they arrived at the regional centre for collection by individual Scouts. Understandably, new aspects of the activity that had not been deemed to be necessary in the 1930s had evolved. There was now an elaborate training course for Scouts and the organization was required to send out letters of advice and informed consent to the parents.

The researchers used observational methods and interviews with a small sample consisting of one troop of Girl Scouts, and also researched the history of the movement since its origins by consulting the organization's archives. Their aim was to investigate the processes of guided participation through which the Girl Scouts gained mastery of a complex set of skills. They were also interested to find out how an analysis of individual development requires the researcher to refer to other planes of analysis, such as the group and the wider community. The children involved in the activity of cookie sales were learning to solve complex problems that had been defined and organized by their community; at the same time, the changes in the children's roles and understanding extended to their efforts in similar activities in the future, and so contributed to transformation of the activities in which they participated. For example, the girls in the study began to use and extend cultural tools for calculating and keeping track of customer orders. These cultural tools tied their efforts in to practices in other institutions of their culture, including the number system used in the community and the calculation box used on the order form provided by their organization. Their means of handling the problems of sales and delivery involved using tools borrowed from others, for example using elastic bands to bundle together orders or Post-its to identify customer addresses. In making calculations, the girls would use tools borrowed from teachers or parents; for example, for larger orders, considering that a box of cookies might cost one quarter of $10 rather than multiplying each unit price of $2.50.

Rogoff and her colleagues observed that the girls' roles changed as they became salespersons. There were commonalities among the girls, for example transformations in confidence and a growing identity as cookie sellers. There were also differences that often related to the extent and degree of help that the girls received from others, including parents, troop leaders, customers and siblings. The family circumstances of the girls differed, and these differences had an impact on the adoption of the main responsibility for the role of seller. One girl struggled with the primary responsibility herself; others worked in pairs; still others allowed their families to organize the sales for them. Rogoff called this a process of *guided participation*. Each girl had to coordinate her individual efforts with guidance from other participants; at the group level, she was guided through materials and practices developed over decades by previous Scouts, leaders and customers. There were also links with other systems, such as family structure. Let's look at two case studies to illustrate.

Darlene's parents were divorced, her mother worked long hours and Darlene spent much of her time after school alone by herself. Darlene treated sales as primarily her own responsibility and asked many anxious questions about potential problems at the weekly training meetings. As a result, initially she found it very difficult to work up confidence to approach potential customers, to organize orders and manage deliveries to the deadline. The researchers observed, however, that members of the community played a guiding role in inducting her into the practice of selling cookies. One customer, recognizing Darlene's shyness, invited Darlene to practise her sales skills on her roommates. This encouraged Darlene to practise her sales manner on her mother and stepfather. Another customer helped her to fill out the complex form. With practice, Darlene became a skilled salesperson. She learned to communicate knowledge of her product, used the order form effectively and adjusted her sales pitch to each customer. However, she found it very difficult to coordinate money collection and product delivery, ended up by collecting too much money and had to spend time on her own recalculating all her orders in order to track the errors.

By contrast, Carla depended heavily on the leadership of family members. Both her sister and her mother, each of whom had been a Girl Scout, called their friends in advance to let them know that Carla was on her way to sell cookies. Family members also helped her to carry out calculations so that the day's orders tallied correctly, and even did some of the door-to-door selling for her. Carla's mother administered all the names of customers, matched them to the colour-coded boxes as they arrived from the company and then telephoned customers to tell them that their order was ready for delivery.

Not surprisingly, Carla was the first Girl Scout to submit all her money, correctly tallied.

In each case, the girls, new to cookie selling, changed in the process of participating with others to become more expert than they had been before in making sales, planning orders, calculating income and organizing deliveries. They did not simply acquire these skills. Rather, they went through a process of personal transformation. Their experience of shared endeavours varied from person to person, as the two case studies show, but each girl participated in, and contributed to, intellectual and economic institutions and traditions of their society with associated cultural values, such as efficiency and honesty. In turn, these individual efforts, along with the thousands of similar individual efforts throughout the USA, would influence the historically changing institution of the Girl Scout movement.

By looking at development from the sociocultural perspective, the researchers challenged the idea of a boundary between internal knowledge (such as knowledge of arithmetic) and external phenomena (for example, the availability of order forms listing price information). Rather, the individual develops through participation in an activity and changes in ways that contribute both to the ongoing event (in this case the sale of cookies) and to the person's preparation for involvement in other similar events in the future. This study was based on a prior hypothesis about how individuals learn through guided participation. The researchers used methods similar to those adopted by anthropologists. They were already involved as 'cookie chairs' in their local Girl Scout troop, which gave them easy access to data and gave them a naturalistic role in this particular activity. The study relied on participant observation, interviews and examination of archival records and used these qualitative methods to confirm the prediction. Although the sample was small, involving only selected girls from the troop, it provides an example of real-life research grounded in authentic cultural practices.

Based on material in Rogoff, B., Baker-Sennett, J., Lacasa, P. & Goldsmith, D. (1995). In J.J. Goodnow, P.J. Miller and F. Kessel (Eds.), *Cultural practices as contexts for development. New directions for child development, 67*, Spring, pp. 45–65. San Francisco, CA: Jossey-Bass Publishers.

SOCIAL CONSTRUCTIONIST APPROACHES

Some theorists have chosen to explore childhood itself as a social construction, in effect discounting significant biological or genetic influences. Such an approach is often linked to sociological frames of discourse. Social constructionism focuses on culture and context in understanding what happens in society and in constructing knowledge based on those understandings. Burr (2003, pp. 2–5) argued that the following principles lie at the heart of social constructionism.

- A critical stance towards what we take for granted about the world.
- The belief that all ways of understanding are culturally and historically relative.

- Our knowledge of the world is not derived from its 'objective' nature; rather, we construct our knowledge of it through our daily interactions.
- Understanding is negotiated through these interactions, so there are many possible constructions of the world.

Some social constructionists have argued that, whereas developmental psychologists distinguish between children and adults and have often focused on the child's relatively lesser ability in a range of domains, in fact there is nothing 'natural' about childhood; childhood is a social construct that has more to do with how people define it. People's attitudes towards childhood are influenced by the dominant belief systems of the society in which they are located, and so will vary across time and culture. We can only begin to understand our views of childhood if we take account of our own position in a particular social, political and cultural context. For example, in some societies it is taken as given that adults have rights over children, whereas in contemporary Western society, political debate focuses more on the tensions between the rights of children to protection and their rights to participation and self-determination. Traditionally, research conducted with children and young people has been dominated by approaches that view children as objects of research rather than as active participants, with the focus on outcomes rather than processes and on child variables rather than children as individuals (Hill, 2005). The social constructionist approach tends towards a view of children as competent social actors, a move that requires a commitment to respecting their rights to participation. Such a view affects the status ascribed to children, which in turn influences the strategies that researchers employ to provide children with the opportunity to take an active role in the research process (see also p. 17). It further impacts upon the ethical and methodological approach that researchers take with regard to establishing contact with and recruiting prospective participants (Thomas & O'Kane, 2000).

James and Prout (1997) are two sociologists who have argued for a social constructionist paradigm in thinking about children's development. They stated the following key features of the paradigm.

1. Childhood is understood as a social construction. As such it provides an interpretive frame for contextualising the early years of human life. Childhood, as distinct from biological immaturity, is neither a natural nor a universal feature of human groups but appears as a specific structural and cultural component of many societies.
2. Childhood is a variable of social analysis. It can never be entirely divorced from other variables such as class, gender and ethnicity. Comparative and cross-cultural analysis reveals a variety of childhoods rather than a single or universal phenomenon.
3. Children's social relationships and cultures are worthy of study in their own right, independent of the perspective and concern of adults.
4. Children are and must be seen as active in the construction and determination of their own social lives, the lives of those around them and of the societies in which they live. Children are not just passive subjects of social structures and processes.
5. Ethnography is a particularly useful methodology for the study of childhood. It allows children a more direct voice and participation in the production of sociological data than is possible through experimental or survey styles of research.

6. Childhood is a phenomenon in relation to which the double hermeneutic of the social sciences is acutely present. That is to say, to proclaim a new paradigm of childhood sociology is also to engage in and respond to the process of reconstructing childhood.

(James & Prout, 1997, pp. 8–9)

Most developmental psychologists would have little problem with features (3) and (4) above, which simply reflect all recent thinking on the topic. Features (1) especially, and (2), emphasize the core social constructionist belief that childhood is specific to particular social or cultural conditions and does not have natural or universal features, a viewpoint at odds with the interactionist views of most developmental psychologists or, for example, Figure 2.16. Feature (5) emphasizes one particular methodological approach. Feature (6) refers to the possibility of reconstructing (and first, deconstructing) childhood.

Deconstructing Developmental Psychology

Influenced by social constructionism and also feminist theory, some psychologists and sociologists (e.g. Burman, 2007; Kitzinger, 2007; Singer, 1992) have challenged the ideas that underpin mainstream developmental psychology. Burman claimed to 'deconstruct' developmental psychology by scrutinizing the moral and political themes that are dominant in current frameworks in order to look beyond them and explore where they fit into the social practices in which psychology functions. In this sense, she addressed the 'discourses' (that is, the socially organized frameworks of meaning) that define the domains of concern to the developmental psychologist, arguing that these discourses do not represent reality—they actually create it. As an example, developmental psychologists have extensively documented behavioural and social differences between boys and girls ('boys engage in rough and tumble play'; 'girls are cooperative'). From a feminist standpoint, such stereotypical observations simply provide *social* expectations of gender. A critical outcome for children who do not conform to these social norms of behaviour can be that they are labelled as 'deviant' or 'dysfunctional'. For example, a boy might be diagnosed as having a gender identity disorder if he demonstrated 'symptoms', such as avoiding rough and tumble play, preferring the friendship of girls and dressing up in girls' clothes. From the social constructionist perspective, it would be necessary to question the actual definition of what it means to be a 'boy' or a 'girl', and to be aware of the concept of gender diversity. A critical question would be, 'What are the processes through which gender boundaries are defined by the culture in which the child is growing up?'.

Similarly, Ringrose and Renold (2011) argued that discourses around bullying tend to reinforce the institutionalized structures of normative femininity and masculinity, giving participants no way of breaking out of the stereotypes. From this perspective, the categories of 'bully' and 'victim' pathologize young people and reinforce the power relation of gender norms. In their words (Ringrose & Renold, 2011, p. 192), '. . . these discourses . . . have become so normalized and "common sense" for considering issues of aggression, bullying and violence among young people that they are unquestioningly adopted'. Two critical questions that these authors raise are: 'What kinds of images of feminine and masculine aggression do girls and boys bring with them into the school context?' and 'How are different kinds of femininity and masculinity acted out in different contexts, inside school and beyond the school gate?'.

The kinds of questions posed by those writers who challenge traditional perspectives include: 'How does developmental psychology come to be the arbiter of what is "normal"?', 'Why is developmental psychology about the child?', 'Would it be different if developmental psychologists focused on the contexts in which people grow?'. In particular, they challenge assumptions about parenting. A key theme in this perspective concerns the ideological assumptions inherent in selecting child and mother as a focus for research, since this could more accurately be perceived as reflecting 'the widespread and routine subjection of women to the developmental psychological gaze' (Burman, 1994, p. 4). Such a focus, Burman (1994, 2007) argued, results in 'individualistic' interpretations of socially constructed phenomena, often leading to the blaming of women for failing to mother their children adequately.

This perspective, in contrast to traditional models of developmental psychology, has focused less on the individual than on the interpersonal, cultural, historical and political contexts in which constructions of childhood are situated. In other words, these writers have problematized the very nature of the research carried out by mainstream developmental psychologists, by asserting that, since each person is positioned within a discourse of history, politics, gender and culture, it is impossible to take a detached, objective stance.

As an example, Singer (1992) pointed out that Bowlby's (1953) research on maternal deprivation (see Chapter 4) was highly influential, for example in the UK, at a time when men were returning from World War II to reclaim the jobs that had effectively been carried out by women. The nurseries that had proliferated in the early 1940s to enable women to work for the war effort largely closed down and mothers were advised that it was in their child's interest for them to stay at home to provide the nurture that was essential for their children's healthy emotional growth. At a stroke, women were consigned to the home during the early years of their children's development. If the mother failed to provide loving care and support, then she was responsible for any later behavioural or emotional difficulties that might arise. As Burman (1994, p. 80) wrote, 'Maternal presence therefore functions as the essential feature in the maintenance of the social-political order'.

Most developmental psychologists see some virtue in taking account of the social context, but many would not go as far as to redefine their discipline. Nor would they accept such radical undermining of their capacity to carry out objective studies of, for example, the relationships between children and their parents. Nevertheless, the questions posed in this section about the concept of childhood are challenging and open up critical debates about children's rights, issues around child protection, and the role of culture and politics in shaping the concerns of developmental psychology.

CHAPTER SUMMARY

- The Human Genome Project has advanced our understanding of genetics. Behaviour genetic techniques such as twin and adoption studies show how the human genome provides a groundplan for development.
- Chromosomal abnormalities such as Down syndrome have significant developmental consequences.
- The genes (nature) and the environment (nurture) interact in complicated ways to channel an individual's development. Some developmental pathways are easier than others.
- Recent developments in developmental cognitive neuroscience can help us understand more about how changes in regions of the brain are related to behavioural development.
- There are many forms of learning, including imprinting and sensitive periods, individual learning (such as trial and error) and social learning (local enhancement, emulation, imitation).
- Teaching, and the transmission of culture, are not totally unique to humans; nevertheless, these, and higher forms of mindreading ability, are characteristic of the development of human infants in a social context, for which humans seem particularly well adapted.
- Evolutionary theory provides some important insights into child development; the field of evolutionary developmental psychology exemplifies this approach.
- In addition to a common evolutionary heritage, there are significant cultural differences in the nature of child development, to which anthropologists as well as cultural psychologists have contributed.
- Social constructionist approaches emphasize a sociological approach to development. In its strong version, this is antagonistic to viewpoints from behaviour genetics and evolutionary theory. However, it does provide an important counterpoint to uncritical acceptance of the 'status quo' in matters of child development.

DISCUSSION POINTS

1. How relevant is behaviour genetics for understanding human behaviour?
2. What is meant by 'canalization' and is it a useful metaphor?
3. Can chimpanzees engage in mindreading?
4. What is meant by evolutionary developmental psychology?
5. Are ideas of social constructionism and social cultural theory antithetical to those of behaviour genetics and evolutionary psychology?

FURTHER READING

- For a readable account of behaviour genetics with special relevance to human behaviour, see Plomin, R., DeFries, J.C., Knopik, V.S. & Neiderhiser, J.M. (2013). *Behavioural genetics* (6th ed.). London: Worth. Twin studies are described by Wright, L. (1999). *Twins: Genes, environment and the mystery of identity*. London: Wiley, and by Segal, N. (2000). *Entwined lives: Twins and what they tell us about human behavior*. New York: Plume. A site for the human genome is at www.ensembl.org/Homo_sapiens/index.html

- For methods in developmental neuroscience, see Johnson, M.H. & de Haan, M. (2010). *Developmental cognitive neuroscience* (3rd ed.). Chichester: Wiley-Blackwell, and Blakemore, S-J. & Frith, U. (2005). *The learning brain*. Oxford: Blackwell. A more advanced collection is Romer, D. & Walker, E.F. (2007). *Adolescent psychopathology and the developing brain*. Oxford: Oxford University Press. A collection considering implications for education is Mareschal, D., Butterworth, B. & Tolmie, A. (2013). *Educational neuroscience*. Chichester: Wiley-Blackwell.

- Tomasello, M. (1999). *The cultural origins of human cognition*. Cambridge, MA: Harvard University Press, and (2009). *Why we cooperate*. Cambridge, MA: MIT Press, cover many comparative aspects of ape and human cognition. Bjorklund, D.F. & Pellegrini, A.D. (2002). *The origins of human nature: Evolutionary developmental psychology*. Washington, DC: APA Books, describes this area of theorizing. Ellis, B.J. & Bjorklund, D.F. (Eds.) (2005). *Origins of the social mind: Evolutionary psychology and child development*. New York: Guilford Press, provides an interesting collection; and Bjorklund, D.F. (2007). *Why youth is not wasted on the young: Immaturity in human development*. Oxford: Blackwell, is an accessible overview of childhood from this perspective. Konner, M. (2010). *The evolution of childhood: Relationships, emotion, mind*. Cambridge, MA: Harvard University Press, is a weighty and authoritative source.

- For cultural views of childhood, see Rogoff, B. (2003). *The cultural nature of human development*. Oxford: Oxford University Press, and Nabuzoka, D. & Empson, J.E. (Eds.) (2010). *Culture and psychological development*. London: Palgrave Macmillan. For an anthropological perspective, see Lancy, D.F. (2008). *The anthropology of childhood*. Cambridge: Cambridge University Press, or Montgomery, H. (2009). *An introduction to childhood: Anthropological perspectives on children's lives*. Oxford: Wiley-Blackwell. Smith, P.B., Bond, M.H. & Kagitçibasi, C. (2006). *Understanding social behaviour across cultures*. London: Sage, gives a general overview of cross-cultural psychology with some material on childhood.

- For sociological/social constructionist perspectives, see James, A. & Prout, A. (1997). *Constructing and reconstructing childhood*. Basingstoke: Falmer. A challenge to the fundamental assumptions of developmental psychologists can be found in Burman, E. (2007). *Deconstructing developmental psychology*. London: Routledge.

PART II

PRENATAL DEVELOPMENT AND BIRTH

Chapter 3   Prenatal Development and Birth

CHAPTER
3

Prenatal Development and Birth

CHAPTER OUTLINE

- From Conception to Birth
- The Nature of Birth
- Early Social Behaviour and Social Interactions
- Temperament
- The Millennium Cohort Study (MCS): Patterns of Infant Care in the UK at 9 Months

In this chapter, we examine the process from conception to birth, a period when genetic determination of development is at its strongest. We look at risk factors in development—prenatal, perinatal and psychosocial. We describe the birth process, and consider the particular situation of babies born prematurely.

The newborn baby has a lot to find out about the social world, and we discuss some of the ways in which the baby, and his or her caregivers, contribute to this during the first months of life, including infant temperament.

FROM CONCEPTION TO BIRTH

This period of about 9 months (a full-term birth is at about 38 weeks from conception) constitutes the beginning of human development—itself divided into three stages. Aspects of this are illustrated in Figure 3.1.

Germinal Stage

The baby is conceived when a sperm cell from the father unites with an egg cell or ovum from the mother. The fertilized egg is called a *zygote*. The zygote starts dividing, and dividing again,

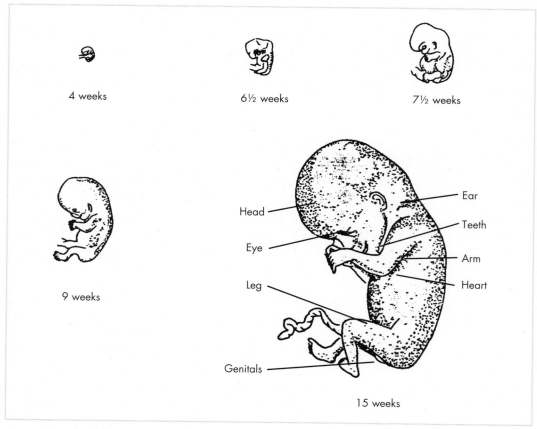

Figure 3.1   Stages of prenatal growth.

with cells rapidly differentiating. After about a week, it starts to implant onto the wall of the mother's uterus. This is complete after 2 weeks, at which point it is called an *embryo*.

Embryonic Stage

This lasts from about the third to the eighth week after conception. By the end of this time, although only an inch long, the embryo has the basic plan of a human body, with head, arms, legs, hands and feet. It connects to the *placenta*, by means of the umbilical cord. The placenta is a special area on the wall of the uterus. Here, the blood supply from the mother meets that of the embryo and they intermingle through thousands of tiny blood vessels. By this means, the mother supplies oxygen and nutrients to the growing embryo. By the eighth week, the embryo is also safely cushioned in a kind of water-bed—the amniotic sac—which surrounds it and keeps it at a constant temperature.

Fetal Stage

By now, the major structures of the body have differentiated, and bone cells develop, marking the stage of the fetus. Relatively small features develop—fingernails, eyelids, eyebrows—and cartilage in the bones is starting to harden. By the third month, the fetus is starting to move, and its heartbeat can be heard; the movements become obvious to the mother by the fourth and fifth months. By the seventh month the fetus is able to breathe, cry, swallow, digest and excrete, and has a realistic chance of surviving premature birth. The last 2 months of normal conception see a considerable increase in size and weight, with birth usually at 9 months.

The process of prenatal growth is 'canalized'—that is to say, it is strongly predetermined (see p. 44). There are clear genetic instructions for the zygote to differentiate into the embryo, and for the embryo to develop into the fetus, in ways broadly similar for every human being at this period. Prenatal development is an example where nature (i.e. genetic instructions) is very important. But nurture (i.e. the child's environment) is important too.

Sex Hormones and Male–Female Differentiation

We saw in Chapter 2 how females have two X chromosomes, while males have one X and one Y chromosome. These determine the development of the sexual organs and the production of sex hormones. These hormones, which are already differentiating at the fetal stage, although levels of sex hormones remain relatively low until puberty (see Chapter 19).

Nevertheless, it is possible that early levels of sex hormones such as testosterone, even at the fetal stage, can affect psychological characteristics later, for example in middle childhood. Baron-Cohen and colleagues (Auyeung et al., 2006; Chapman et al., 2006) have proposed an E-S model of sex differences (see also Chapter 6), in which females typically score higher on empathizing abilities (E) and males typically score higher on systematizing abilities (S). Systematizing implies analysing or constructing systems. (In fact, Baron-Cohen argues that an extreme version of this is related to autism spectrum disorders, where there can be an obsessional emphasis on ordering.) In a longitudinal study, levels of fetal testosterone were measured in around 200 fetuses, by analysing small amounts of amniotic fluid extracted during amniocentesis for medical reasons, between 14 and 22 weeks of gestational age. Later, at 6–9 years of age, assessments were made of E and S type abilities. E was measured by parental report of empathy (e.g. 'my child likes to look after other people') and by the child's performance on the 'eyes' test, where feelings or emotions are ascribed to pictures of someone's eyes (Chapman et al., 2006). S was measured by parental report of systematizing

Table 3.1 Correlations between fetal testosterone levels, and empathy, social cognition ('eyes test') and systematizing in middle childhood.

	Empathy	Eyes test	Systematizing
Fetal testosterone	−.28**	−.43**	.38**
Sex (female)	.30**	.16	−.33**

**p < .01.
Source: Adapted from Auyeung et al. (2006) and Chapman et al. (2006).

(e.g. 'my child likes to create lists of things') (Auyeung et al., 2006). Fetal testosterone levels correlated significantly with S and negatively with E, as predicted (Table 3.1). The correlations were also in the expected direction for boys and girls separately, with some indication that fetal testosterone had an influence irrespective of simply being a boy or a girl, and possibly through organizational influences on neural development.

Fetal Learning

Just as the fetus can be affected by environmental stimuli in the uterus, it is also capable of learning from the environment. This is especially so during the last 3 months in the womb. During this period, the fetus responds to sounds (auditory stimuli), which are filtered through the amniotic fluid. Sounds can reliably affect fetal heart rate and motor responses from as early as 20 weeks of gestational age; in fact, congenital deafness can be diagnosed during the prenatal period (see Shahidullah & Hepper, 1993b). A number of experiments have shown that the fetus actively processes this auditory input, and distinguishes between music, language and other sounds (Karmiloff-Smith, 1995). Box 3.1 describes a study showing how the neonate's discrimination of the mother's voice is linked to auditory experience *in utero*. Tastes and smells are also being learned. One study found that if the mother eats garlic during pregnancy, then her newborn will show less aversion to garlic (Schaal et al., 2000)!

Hepper (2008) states that 'the fetus is continually active in and reactive to its environment' (p. 475), and that this is probably important for its development both before and after birth. Familiarity with the mother's voice and smell may facilitate attachment, and in general fetal activity may be an important contributor to physical and neural development up to birth. Based on neurological evidence, and also on studies with non-human primates, Coe and Lubach (2008) argue that fetal activity has stimulation and priming effects that are essential for optimal development. The mother's diet and behaviour may impact on the fetus, but 'the baby is an active participant in the success and progress of this gestational duet' (p. 39).

Prenatal Risks

Although strongly canalized, things can go wrong in early development. Sometimes, the abnormalities are genetic, as with Down syndrome, a condition arising from a chromosomal abnormality that we discussed earlier (p. 38). Sometimes, they are environmentally caused. One class of environmental hazards are called *teratogens*. *Teratogen* is an ancient Greek work meaning 'creating a monster', a reference to the marked abnormalities that can sometimes

Box 3.1 Newborn and fetal response to the human voice

Research in the 1980s had shown that newborn infants could distinguish between the voice of their own mother and that of an unfamiliar female. DeCasper and Fifer (1980) established this for infants only 1–3 days old and Querleu et al. (1984) found a similar result for infants only 2 hours after birth, largely ruling out the possibility of rapid learning of the mother's voice postnatally. Studies had also found that the fetus could respond to auditory stimuli, with head and body movements. For example, Shahidullah and Hepper (1993a) demonstrated this using an ultrasound scanner, which produces a visual picture of the fetus, in this case showing the head, upper body and arms (see Box Figure 3.1.1). A headphone for the auditory signals was placed on the mother's abdomen. As early as 20 weeks of gestational age, the fetus would show a slow, diffuse bodily response to auditory stimuli presented in this way and by 25 weeks, an immediate startle-type response was seen.

Thus, it seemed likely that learning of the mother's voice occurred *in utero*; however, the fetus would not hear the mother's voice in the same way as the newborn infant, since the sound would be transmitted internally, through the body, as well as externally. Interestingly, a study by Fifer and Moon (1989) found that 2-day-old newborns preferred the sound of their mother's voice filtered to sound as it would have done in the womb, to the mother's natural voice!

The aim of this series of three studies was to examine further the origins of learning the mother's voice in the fetus. Two of the three studies were carried out with fetuses in the mother's womb and using the ultrasound equipment described earlier. In each of the two studies, 10 fetuses of 36 weeks gestational age participated. All of the fetuses were subsequently born

at 39–40 weeks, without complications and with healthy Apgar scores (over 8, at 1 and 5 minutes; see Table 3.2).

In one study, two conditions were compared: the mother speaking normally and a tape recording of the mother's voice played through the speaker on the mother's abdomen. This was the independent variable: each fetus experienced both conditions, with order being counterbalanced. The dependent variable was the mean number of movements elicited in the fetus (recorded on video). This averaged 5.2 for the mother speaking normally and 6.7 for

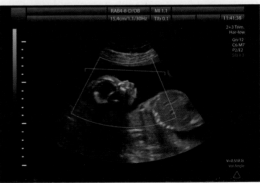

Box Figure 3.1.1 An ultrasound scanner on the mother (*top*) produces an image of the fetus.

Source: (*Top*) Image copyright Robyn MacKenzie. Used under licence from Shutterstock.com. (*Bottom*) Image copyright Valentina Razumova. Used under licence from Shutterstock.com.

the tape of the mother's voice, the difference being just significant at $p < .05$ on a matched pairs t test. The fetuses responded more to the tape of the mother's voice, which the researchers argued would be a more novel stimulus, lacking some components of the mother's voice that would come internally through the body to the fetus when the mother spoke normally. The researchers reported no obvious differences in mother's heart rate or general physical activity between the two conditions, which if present would confound the results.

In the second study of 10 fetuses, two tapes were presented to each: one of the mother's voice speaking normally and one of a strange female (in fact, another fetus's mother) speaking normally. Again, order was counterbalanced. The mean number of movements elicited in the fetus was 7.2 for the mother's voice and 6.0 for the strange female's voice. This difference did not approach statistical significance on a matched pairs t test. The researchers concluded that the fetus could not distinguish the mother's voice from a strange female's voice when both were heard externally.

In a third study, the same researchers worked with 35 newborn infants aged 2–4 days. They compared the movement responses of the newborns to tape recordings of the mother's voice and that of a strange female. For half the infants, the voices were normal; for the other half, the voices were in 'motherese', an older term used to describe simplified speech mothers often use to children, with exaggerated intonation. An analysis of variance found a significant interaction ($p < .01$); basically, the mother's normal voice elicited fewer movements than did the mother's motherese voice, or either version of the strange female's voice.

In looking at these studies, it seems as though the fetus and newborn infant are going through stages in familiarizing themselves with the auditory stimulus they are most often encountering, the mother's voice. First, the fetus is familiar with the mother's voice as experienced *in utero*; all other voices, even a tape of the mother's voice, appear different. A few hours and days after birth, newborns still prefer the mother's voice as they heard it in the womb (Fifer & Moon, 1989), but they can now distinguish the mother's normal voice from that of other females. However, the mother's 'motherese' voice still seems as strange as an adult female's voice, and recognition of this will come later.

These experiments are ingenious, and carried out in difficult circumstances. Careful precautions were followed in having standard testing conditions and presentation of stimuli. It would be reassuring to have the experiments with the fetuses replicated, since the sample sizes were small and a crucial finding in the first study only just reached statistical significance. Also, no direct statistical comparison was made for fetal response to the mother's actual speech and a tape of a strange female, even though the mean movement scores were closer than for the comparison with the tape of the mother's voice. Finally, it would be important that the videotapes of fetal movements were scored blind to condition, to avoid experimenter effects (see Chapter 1).

As Karmiloff-Smith (1995) put it, 'Prior to any *ex utero* experience, newborns show that they have already extracted information about some of the invariant, abstract features of mother's voice during their period in the womb'. Research such as this forms part of a variety of studies indicating that human development is strongly canalized in the early stages, and that the newborn infant is far from being the 'blank slate' postulated by some earlier theorists.

Based on material in Hepper, P.G., Scott, D. & Shahidullah, S. (1993). Newborn and fetal response to maternal voice. *Journal of Reproductive and Infant Psychology, 11,* 147–153.

occur in prenatal development. This is especially so in the embryonic period—this is when the basic ground plan of the body is being formed, with differentiation of major organs including arms and legs. Drugs and other harmful substances can reach the embryo through the mother's bloodstream and if they do so in the embryonic period, some can cause gross body or limb abnormalities. For example, the drug thalidomide, prescribed to prevent recurrent miscarriages in the 1950s, led to babies being born with severe limb deformities, but only when the drug was taken during the first 2 months of pregnancy. Thalidomide is no longer prescribed in these cases. But other drugs such as cocaine, heavy consumption of alcohol during pregnancy and heavy cigarette smoking are among risk factors for healthy prenatal development.

These are *prenatal risk factors*—ones implicated before birth (we look later at perinatal risk factors, at the time of birth). Other prenatal risk factors include poor maternal nutrition, infectious diseases such as rubella (German measles), exposure to radiation and possibly maternal stress. A risk factor means that later problems are not inevitable but they are more likely, especially if other risk factors or adverse circumstances are present.

Pregnancy Sickness

Many mothers experience pregnancy sickness in the early stages of pregnancy; they may feel nausea at the sight and smell of foods they previously enjoyed, vomit easily, and especially feel 'morning sickness' on rising in the morning. Profet (1992) has argued that pregnancy sickness has been selected for in evolution, as an adaptive mechanism to protect the embryo against teratogens, especially toxic chemicals from foods. She argues that certain foods, including certain plant foods, contain toxins that would not harm the mother but could harm the embryo, notably during the period when major organs are being formed. Her argument is supported by the fact that pregnancy sickness appears to coincide with the period of maximum vulnerability to teratogens, with a peak at around 6–8 weeks; that it is found cross-culturally; and that women who experience nausea and vomiting have lower rates of spontaneous abortion than those women who do not.

 Stop and Think

How important is it to consider fetal development in order to get a full understanding of the infancy period?

THE NATURE OF BIRTH

A full-term pregnancy lasts about 9 months, and then the infant is born. Nine months may seem like a long time to be pregnant but in fact, from the point of view of our position compared with other primates, including the great apes, 9 months is short. We can compare humans with other primates on the basis of general growth, gestation period and brain size at birth.

- *Growth*: complete at age 11 for chimpanzees and gorillas, at age 20 for humans.
- *Average gestation period*: 228 days in chimpanzees, 256 days in gorillas, 267 days in humans.
- *Brain size at birth as a percentage of adult size*: 41% for chimpanzees, 25% for humans.

On the basis of general growth rates, we might expect the gestation period in humans to be about twice that in the great apes, or about 18 months, but it is not—it is quite similar. As a consequence, human neonates are, in a comparative sense, quite immature, with only one-quarter of brain size achieved at birth compared with about one-half in primates generally. The human infant's brain size only reaches one-half adult size by 1 year (and three-quarters of adult size by 3 years).

The 'additional' 9 months after birth results in a very helpless infant, and this condition is sometimes referred to as *exterogestation* or *secondary altriciality* (Montagu, 1961; Trevathan, 1987). There are two main explanations for this: the 'obstetric dilemma' (OD) or 'energetics of gestation and growth' (EGG).

OD hypothesis: This locates the reason for secondary altriciality in terms of limitations in growth of the female pelvis and width of the birth canal, following the evolution of bipedalism. A significant development in hominid evolution was bipedalism—being able habitually and easily to walk around on two legs, with an erect posture; the apes can only do this rather awkwardly and for shorter periods, often going on all fours or brachiating (climbing in trees). This shift to bipedalism seems to have gone along with a change in climate and an opportunity for early hominids to gather, scavenge and hunt for food on more open, savannah grasslands (Lovejoy, 1981). Bipedalism also freed up the hands; instead of walking on hands and knuckles, humans could use their hands for carrying, and also for making tools—something incipient in chimpanzees (see Chapter 2) but a hallmark of human evolution.

With bipedalism, the pelvic bones and hip joints had to be refashioned; this in turn meant a restriction on the pelvic opening through which the infant is born—a greater restriction than in the brachiating great apes. Leutenegger (1981) proposed that there were therefore two competing trends occurring in our evolutionary history: increased efficiency of bipedal locomotion but also increasing brain size (taking advantage of the manual opportunities of bipedalism and the social opportunities of group living on the savannah). Each was vital, but increased brain size means larger heads, whereas the constraints on size from the birth canal were becoming more restrictive.

EGG hypothesis: Dunsworth et al. (2012) argued that the evidence for decreased loco-motor efficiency with increasing pelvic size in human females was not well substantiated. Instead, they suggested that, as appears to be the case in mammals generally, mothers give birth once the energetic demands of the growing fetus exceed what the mother can reasonably cope with. Metabolic demands on the mother increase during pregnancy, rising to twice the basal (resting) metabolic rate, which is thought to be a maximum sustainable limit over a long period. Thus, 'extending gestation by even one month would likely require metabolic investment beyond the mother's capacity' (p. 15215).

Whatever the reason for secondary altriciality in humans, it might seem a disadvantage; human infants do need a lot of care and attention for the first year, if they are to survive. But it has been argued that this actually reinforced the trend to increasing sociality and cooperative group living in early hominids. Basically, mothers needed help with their infants (Lovejoy, 1981; Trevathan, 1987). This help is often needed in parturition (the actual birth process), as well as subsequently. The help can come from the mother's own mother, the father of the infant, other relatives or friends. In traditional societies, some older women would be experienced in assisting at births; in modern societies, some nurses are trained as midwives for this purpose.

Figure 3.2 shows the usual position in which the infant is born—head first, and with the head facing away from the mother's face. Because of the size of the infant, especially the head, the birth process is not easy; most women find it quite painful. As birth approaches, the mother feels contractions of the uterus (the largest muscle in the human female, it can exert a force of up to 60 pounds during labour). Irregular contractions can occur before, but with the onset of true labour these become regular; there may be difficulties in sleeping, and persistent backache. After some hours, these contractions become more

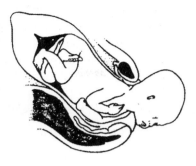

Figure 3.2 Typical birth position.

forceful and occur around every 5 minutes. By this time the mother has usually sought out assistance or (in modern societies) gone into hospital. She may be lying on a bed, although the more usual position in traditional societies is to be in a semi-reclining or squatting position.

Contractions become stronger and closer together. The cervix (through which the infant must pass) has softened and dilated. Experiences of pain may actually lessen here, but effort increases and the woman is straining and pushing (hence the term 'labour'). The fetal membranes rupture now, if they have not already done so. The infant's head starts to emerge, often accompanied by a cry from the mother. The midwife, or perhaps the mother herself, helps rotate the head to get the shoulders in the best position to come out. The infant is born, attached still by the umbilical cord. The cord is still pulsating, and for a few minutes the infant is 'cushioned' by the maternal blood supply as its lungs start to fill and it takes its first breaths and cries. The cord is cut, and within 30 minutes the placenta is also expelled.

This moment of birth is something totally new for the infant, and its cry is a sign of health as it adapts to its new, extrauterine environment. It is often a climactic experience for the mother, and one of joy for the father and other relatives. Here is a transcript of a birth conversation, recorded by Trevathan in Texas, USA, with a bilingual Hispanic mother.

Midwife:	Push, Karen. The baby's coming out now. Push hard. Good. Coming down. Grab the baby! Grab the whole thing! There you go.
Mother:	Oh, my love. Oh, my baby. Oh, I love you.
Father:	It's a boy?
Midwife:	Is it really? [Laughs] I told you, huh!
Mother:	It's a boy?
Father:	It's a boy.
Midwife:	One minute Apgar? Let's see . . . a little floppy . . . pink feet . . . [suctioning with bulb aspirator].
Mother:	What's that?
Midwife:	If he gets that down into his lungs he'll end up with pneumonia.
Mother:	[Baby crying.] It's alright poor baby, oh, it's alright. Oh my baby, yes, yes. I waited for you so long, now you're here. Oh, my baby, oh, it's OK, it's OK, I love you. It's OK. [To father.] You wanna see it? He's the most beautiful thing [laughs]. Never, never, ever seen a baby so beautiful. Oh God, oh baby,

	I love you. [Baby cries.] No, no, no. Oh you do very good, you do very good, good, yes, yes, yes. It's alright. You cry some more? Oh, why you cry? Why you cry, oh yes. Shshshshshshsh. No, nooooooo.
Midwife:	Give her [mother] some orange juice.
Mother:	[To midwife in normal pitch voice.] Can I sit up so I can breastfeed the baby? [Baby cries, mother continues to talk, but hard to hear.] Oh, my baby, don't cry, I'm sorry, I love you. Yes, it's alright.
Midwife:	What are you spitting up, fellow?
Father:	He's big, huh?
Mother:	He's the strongest little thing.
Midwife:	Got a good grip, huh?

In the above, the midwife refers to the 'one minute Apgar'. The Apgar score (Apgar, 1953) is a simple and quick way of evaluating an infant's well-being immediately after birth (often, at 1 minute and 5 minutes). The scoring is shown in Table 3.2. A total score of 7–10 is healthy, 4–6 somewhat depressed, and below 4 cause for serious concern, especially at 5 minutes. In modern societies, women are often given medication during labour, to relieve pain. This can result in lower Apgar scores and a less immediately responsive infant; hence, many women now prefer a more natural labour where possible.

Delivery of the baby is not always straightforward. Some 3–4% are 'breech' deliveries; here, the baby is not in the usual, head-first position for coming out, and instead the buttocks, knees or feet may come first with the head last. This prolongs the delivery process, since the buttocks, knees or feet do not dilate the cervix so well as the head. The baby may attempt to breathe before its head is delivered. Even in modern societies, mortality is 10–20% in breech deliveries. This again suggests that help at birth has a long evolutionary history (Trevathan, 1987).

Interaction Immediately after Birth

Behaviour after birth is strongly influenced by cultural practices and expectations and if the infant is taken away soon after birth in a hospital delivery, mother–infant interaction is obviously curtailed! This is discussed further on p. 100. Normally, however, the mother will stimulate the infant in a variety of ways: touching, stroking and rubbing its body, making eye

Table 3.2   The Apgar scoring technique for each of five indicators.

Score	0	1	2
Colour	Blue, pale	Body pink, extremities blue	Completely pink
Heart rate	Absent	Slow, <100	Over 100
Reflex irritability	No response	Grimace	Cry
Muscle tone	Flaccid	Some flexion of extremities	Active motion
Respiratory effort	Absent	Slow, irregular	Good, crying

Source: Apgar, V. (1953). A proposal for a new method of evaluation of the newborn infant, *Anesthesiology and Analgesia, 32,* 260–267.

contact while facing it, bringing it up to her chest, and talking to it. Usually within the first hour she will breastfeed the infant. Characteristically, mothers will comment on the appearance of the baby, and often on how it resembles the father—perhaps to reassure the father of his paternity (Daly & Wilson, 1982; and p. 57).

Breastfeeding

In traditional societies, breastfeeding was essential for the infant's survival. Breastfeeding is normally done by the mother, but in some societies and in some historical periods (early modern Europe is an example), wet-nursing (breastfeeding of someone else's infant by a mother who is already breastfeeding) has been quite common. In modern societies, mothers can dispense with breastfeeding and use bottle feeding if they wish. An advantage of this is that fathers can participate equally! However, human milk is particularly well suited to the needs of human infants.

The primary constituents of milk are fat, protein and carbohydrate. Ben Shaul (1962) surveyed the milk composition of a range of mammals, and found that it depends on lifestyle. Mammals that live in cold, wet environments, such as dolphins, produce large amounts of fat in their milk to help maintain body warmth. Those mammals that leave their infants in a nest or den site for a long time (such as lions, rabbits, many rodents and carnivores) have relatively large amounts of protein and fat in the milk to sustain the infants between feeding periods. Mammals that carry their young with them (marsupials like kangaroos, species with precocial young such as deer and antelope, and most primates) have milk lower in fat and protein and higher in carbohydrates. Primates have milk especially high in carbohydrates, including lactose, which is a key nutrient for brain growth.

Human milk follows the primate pattern closely. The milk composition is typical for a species where feeding would be on demand (as it would be in traditional societies where mothers carried their infants with them) and where brain growth continues rapidly after birth.

Actually, the very first milk produced by the mother after birth is not typical. It is called the colostrum, and is yellowish or bluish and different from the 'true milk' that appears within about 3 days. The colostrum appears to be useful in providing the infant with a high concentration of a variety of antibodies, providing early immunological protection; it also contains vitamin K, which is essential for blood clotting (and this may prevent blood loss at the site of the umbilical cord). Given these advantages, it is surprising that quite a number of societies, including traditional societies, practise 'colostrum denial'; the infant is nursed by another mother or fed a substitute such as sweetened water, for the first 3 days. There appear to be no advantages and some disadvantages to this practice, and the reason why these beliefs are held in some societies is not clear (Barkow, 1989).

Breastfeeding and cognitive development: A number of studies have suggested modest but consistent benefits in IQ for infants who are breast fed compared to those who are bottle fed. However, these have been correlational studies, and although many controlled for socioeconomic status, it is possible other factors might have accounted for the differences. However, Kramer and colleagues (2008) reported on a large-scale study in Belarus, using a randomized experimental design. This was with nearly 7,000 children of mothers who intended to do some breastfeeding. Half of the sample experienced PROBIT, a Promotion of Breastfeeding Intervention Trial, designed to support duration and exclusivity of breastfeeding over the first year. When the infants had reached 6.5 years they were given subsets of the Wechsler IQ scales (see Chapter 17) and were also evaluated by teachers on academic achievement. On both means of assessment, the experimental group did better than the control group.

Besides the comparison of experimental and control groups, the team also looked at variations in breastfeeding within each group; the trends supported the same conclusions. Altogether, the effects on global IQ scores averaged 3.3 points with exclusive breastfeeding for 3–6 months, and 5.6 points with exclusive breastfeeding of 6 months or more. Suggested possible mechanisms for this effect include actual beneficial constituents of human milk; physiological changes associated with breastfeeding; or enhanced verbal interaction with the mother associated with breastfeeding.

Premature and Low Birthweight Babies

A baby born around 38–42 weeks after conception is considered *full-term*. Babies born much earlier than this are considered *premature*, or *preterm*. Being born 1 or 2 weeks early is not a major risk, but the more preterm the infant is, the lower its chances of survival. Modern medical practices of intensive neonatal care have meant, however, that even infants born as early as 23 weeks gestational age may be able to survive. An infant born before 32 weeks of gestational age is considered as a *very preterm infant* (VPI). Premature birth can be a risk for the neonate. They are at greater risk of physical injury and neurological impairment during the birth process, and this can affect their psychological development. Another risk factor is low birthweight—often associated with prematurity but full-term infants can have low birthweight too. A normal birthweight is around 3,000–4,000 g. An infant weighing less than 2,500 g at birth is generally considered as *low birthweight*. Those weighing below 1,500 g are usually classed as *very low birthweight* (VLBW), and below 1,000 g as *extremely low birthweight* (ELBW).

These sorts of risk factors—prematurity and low birthweight—are called *perinatal risk factors*, as they refer to difficulties around the time of birth. Other perinatal risk factors are respiratory difficulties and difficult (e.g. breech) deliveries. By contrast, *psychosocial risk factors* relate to the care of the infant after birth; these will be indexed by the quality of hospital care (when needed), parental care and the amount of stimulation in the environment.

Generally, research has found that perinatal factors are outweighed by psychosocial factors, in the long term. In other words, if an infant is at risk because of prematurity or low birthweight, the prognosis will be good if there is high-quality care of the infant and a stimulating environment for them to grow up in. A research programme by Emmy Werner and colleagues on the island of Kauai in Hawaii is a classic statement of this relatively optimistic conclusion. Werner and Smith (1982) followed all 698 children born during 1 year in Kauai, from birth to adulthood. They documented both perinatal risk factors and psychosocial risk factors, and looked at later outcomes such as educational achievement, mental health and criminality. One finding that emerged was that boys were more susceptible to risk factors, generally, than girls were. Another finding was that temperament (see p. 100) was important in predicting later outcomes. Most pertinent to our discussion here, however, was the finding that although perinatal risk factors were important, they could be largely overridden by beneficial psychosocial factors. The latter included, for example, a happy and intact family, availability of substitute caregivers, absence of prolonged separation from parents early in life, spacing between siblings and absence of poverty in the home (Werner, 1993).

Another long-term study was reported by Swamy et al. (2008) from Norway. They analysed records for over 1 million people born in the period 1967–1988, using the Medical Birth

Registry database. About 5% of the sample was preterm (taken here as before 37 weeks gestational age). Those born preterm had higher mortality rates through childhood, achieved less well academically and were less likely to have children themselves. However, these effects were most marked and significant for those classed as extremely preterm (before 27 weeks gestational age); their mortality rates were some 5–10 times higher than for those born at term (although still low in absolute terms, i.e. most of them survived). Effects at adulthood could be quite large, as well; of those who were extremely premature, only 14% of men and 25% of women had had children, compared to 50% of men and 68% of women who had been term babies. Historical factors must be borne in mind in extrapolating these results to the present day, as the people in the Norwegian study were born some 30 or more years ago. Practice and care of premature infants have improved over that period. Other studies of infants over recent decades have shown that low to moderate perinatal risk factors can often be overcome. Neonatal care practices at the time of birth are important here. If neurological impairment is avoided, then stimulation programmes in the hospital and to help mothers after the infant is discharged from hospital are helpful for a favourable outcome (Rosenblith, 1992).

Nevertheless, the picture remains less optimistic when perinatal risk factors are severe, as is the case for very preterm infants and very low birthweight infants (VPIs and VLBWs). One longitudinal study in Germany (Laucht et al., 1997) found that prenatal, perinatal and psychosocial risk factors all contributed to negative outcomes by 4.5 years of age. Biological (prenatal and perinatal) risk factors did become relatively less important with age, but were especially associated with poorer motor outcomes. Box 3.2 details another large-scale longitudinal study from Germany, showing that VPIs (who are also usually VLBW) have what may be a specific cognitive impairment in simultaneous information processing at 6 years, which impacts on other cognitive, language and reading skills. A study in Canada (Tessier et al., 1997) reported that both premature and low birthweight children showed greater levels of internalized social problems (shyness, isolation, depression) at 11 years. Another study in the USA (Taylor et al., 2000a) found that ELBW children (below 750 g at birth in this study) performed less well than VLBW, who in turn performed less well than full-term children, on a range of cognitive, academic and behavioural measures at 11 years—some of these differences remaining significant even after IQ was controlled for.

Some investigators have examined whether genetic factors may play a part in the developmental difficulties often experienced by very premature infants. One report (Koeppen-Schomerus et al., 2000) used the Twins Early Development Study to throw light on this. This is a study of all twins born in England and Wales in 1944. Of a sample of 2,223 twin pairs for which good information was available, the researchers found 5% to be very preterm (25–31 weeks gestation; mean birthweight 1,370 g), 9% to be preterm (32–33 weeks gestation; mean birthweight 1,860 g), and 86% to be at or near full term (34+ weeks gestation; mean birthweight 2,590 g). They assessed cognitive and language development at 24 months of age, and found the expected gradient of scores according to perinatal risk (degree of prematurity). For the very preterm group, the comparison of monozygotic and dizygotic twins (see pp. 33–34) found no genetic influence, and a very large influence of shared environmental factors—presumably reflecting the environmental experiences associated with prematurity. For the other two groups, there was some genetic contribution and a reduced (although still large) effect of shared environment. This finding suggests that for the very preterm group, the perinatal risk factors are sufficiently severe that any contribution of genetic factors (which might be manifested in temperament, for example) are overwhelmed.

Box 3.2 Cognitive status, language attainment and prereading skills of 6-year-old very preterm children and their peers: the Bavarian Longitudinal Study

The Bavarian Longitudinal Study followed children born between 1 February 1985 and 31 March 1986 in southern Bavaria, in south Germany. It focused on 7,505 infants (out of 70,600 total births) who required admission to hospital within the first 10 days of birth; these infants ranged from very ill preterm infants to those just requiring brief inpatient observation. A control group of 916 healthy infants receiving normal postnatal care was also included.

The aim of the study reported here was to examine whether prematurity had any implications for cognitive and language development just before the children had started school, at 6 years 3 months of age. Of the 7,505 infants followed up, 560 were VPIs—very preterm infants with a gestation age of less than 32 weeks (see Box Figure 3.2.1). Of these 560, 158 died during the initial hospitalization, and another seven died before they reached 6 years 3 months of age. Consent to participate was refused for four, and the investigators did not continue study with infants of 42 non-German speaking families. Of the remaining 349 VPIs, 85 could not be traced, leaving 264 who provided data for the study. These VPIs had a mean gestation period of 29.5 weeks, and a mean birthweight of 1,288 g.

These 264 VPIs were compared with a control group drawn from the 916 healthy infants. Of these 916 babies, 718 had continued with assessments, and 689 of these were full term (gestational age greater than 36 weeks). From these, a sample of 264 was

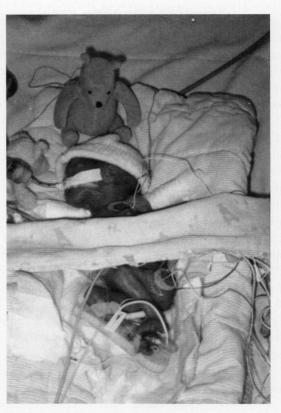

Box Figure 3.2.1   A premature baby (gestational age 28 weeks) in intensive care.

Source: Photograph courtesy of Professor Dieter Wolke, with permission.

drawn, matched with the VPIs for sex, family socioeconomic status, parental marital status and mother's age. The control group infants had a mean gestation period of 39.6 weeks, and a mean birthweight of 3,407 g.

These groups provided the independent variable of the study. The dependent variables were the assessments made at 6 years 3 months. These were:

- *Cognitive status*: a German version of the Kaufman Assessment Battery for Children (K-ABC), which is a test of intellectual functioning (especially simultaneous and sequential information processing) and of knowledge
- *Language development*: subtests of grammatical understanding and production; an articulation test; and quality of speech and grammatical correctness as rated by the research team
- *Prereading skills*: a measure of phonological awareness based on rhyming and sound-to-word matching tasks (see p. 420), and naming of letters and numbers.

In comparing these outcome measures, the obvious step was to compare the VPIs with the control group children. However, the researchers took two other steps in reporting results. First, they noted that 33 of the 264 VPIs had severe medical impairments and disabilities, including severe cerebral palsy and congenital abnormalities; they therefore reported findings when these 33 children were excluded from the VPI sample. In addition, data were available from a normative sample of 311 infants born in Bavaria, drawn from the total 70,600 born in the period and representative of this total sample on a range of characteristics.

Box Table 3.2.1 shows the main findings. Both the normative sample and the control group have near-average scores on cognitive status, and a relatively small proportion (around 7–11%) score in the lowest 10th centile for language and prereading skills (since the 10th centile refers to the lowest 10% in the distribution, this is as expected). By contrast, the VPI group scores less well on all of the assessments. These differences are all appreciable, and statistically significant. Excluding the 33 VPIs with

very severe disabilities reduces these differences, but only to a modest extent.

Further analyses were carried out in order to deepen the understanding of these results. First, the researchers checked on the 85 children who had dropped out of the VPI sample by 6 years. The medical and biological background data from the birth period showed that (in almost all respects) these children did not differ significantly from the remaining 264; thus, differential dropout was not likely to contribute much to the findings.

Next, they examined effects of socioeconomic status (SES), comparing children from families of upper, middle and lower SES. SES did have an expected, and significant, effect on cognitive status, with differences of 6–11 points on the K-ABC scales. These were less than the differences associated with being very preterm, however; no overlap of scores between the very preterm infants and controls was found.

Finally, the researchers examined whether differences in intellectual ability could account for the other deficits. They took the two information processing scores from the K-ABC as a measure of intellectual ability, and then used this as a *covariate*; that is, they looked to see if the other differences—in language and prereading skills—would still be found if the differences in intellectual ability were partialled out. In other words, at a given level of intellectual ability, would VPIs and control infants differ on these other measures? By and large, the answer was in the negative; these differences seemed mostly attributable to the differences in intellectual development.

This study found that the very preterm children scored, on average, about one standard deviation below the norm on cognitive tests, and with an especial impairment in simultaneous information processing. This was a more severe finding than the .5 standard deviation

Box Table 3.2.1   Measures of cognitive status, language development and prereading skills in full-term and preterm infants, when 6 years 3 months of age.

MEASURE	Normative sample N=311	Control group N=264	Very preterm infants without severe impairment N=231	Very preterm infants (total sample) N=264
K-ABC: Simultaneous information processing	103.0	103.2	87.0	83.7
K-ABC: Sequential information processing	96.1	96.0	89.0	86.9
K-ABC: Knowledge achievement scale	100.5	100.9	87.2	84.6
Grammatical understanding and production	51.1	51.3	47.8	47.0
Articulation test below 10th centile	8.7	4.8	23.5	26.2
Poor quality of speech and grammatical correctness	7–8%	About 7%	22–23%	25–26%
Poor phonological awareness	9–11%	9%	25–30%	30–34%
Poor naming of letters and numbers	9–10%	8–11%	28–31%	32–35%

reported by many previous studies. However, this study had the advantages of being very representative of all children born in the study area, of having good control of dropouts, and of having a control group closely matched to the VPI sample. The authors stress the importance of further follow-up of these children, and of further research to identify the process that tends to associate early prematurity with cognitive deficits.

Based on material in Wolke, D., & Meyer, R. (1999). *Developmental Medicine and Child Neurology, 41,* 94–109.

In considering the outcomes of these and other studies, Wolke (1998) argued that larger preterm infants (above 1,500 g) are at only slightly greater risk for long-term psychological deficits. A good psychosocial environment—stimulation and sensitive care—can compensate, in large measure or in most cases, for this degree of perinatal risk. However, it seems that so far, the outlook is less optimistic for VLBW infants (below 1,500 g) born very prematurely. There is much less evidence that a good psychosocial environment after birth can compensate for this more severe degree of perinatal risk. Intensive intervention programmes have had disappointing results. It may be that these children are more likely to suffer some central nervous system damage (as yet not well understood) that affects their later development adversely, even in a very facilitating environment. It is possible that in the future we will find ways to help such children more effectively, but at present these findings present a practical challenge to public health services, and an ethical challenge to our views of very intensive neonatal care to keep alive very preterm infants who are at the limits of survival.

EARLY SOCIAL BEHAVIOUR AND SOCIAL INTERACTIONS

The human infant is fairly helpless (or altricial) at birth. He or she depends on parents, or caregivers, for food, warmth, shelter and protection. For these reasons alone, it is important for human infants, as for any other young mammal, that an attachment develops between the infant and the mother (or father, or other caregiver; we will use the term 'caregiver' generically). In addition, human infants acquire something from this relationship that is largely absent in other mammals: the beginnings of symbolic communication and cultural meaning. We saw in Chapter 1 how Csibra and Gergely (2006) have argued the importance of this 'natural pedagogy' for social learning and social cognition. The particular relevance of early caregiver—infant interaction for language development is considered in Chapter 12.

Although fairly helpless, the human infant does have some reflexive (instinctive or highly canalized) abilities that assist the development of social interactions with caregivers. These are:

1. Behaviours that operate primarily in social situations.
2. Behaviours to which social responses are given.
3. An ability to learn, including discriminating social stimuli and attempting to imitate certain observed behaviours.
4. An enjoyment of contingent responding by others.

Let us consider these in turn.

Behaviours that Operate Primarily in Social Situations

The types of auditory and visual stimulation that adults provide are especially attractive to infants at or soon after birth (see also Chapter 11). For example, infants orientate to (i.e. turn their head towards) patterned sounds rather than monotones, and especially to patterned sounds within the frequency range of human speech. They are interested in visual stimuli that move around and that have a lot of contour information. The human face provides moving stimulation with much contour information, often at just the right distance for the infant to fixate easily. Infant reflexes, such as grasping, and rooting and sucking at the breast, are also used primarily with caregivers. None of these reflexive behaviours is directed only to adults, but all are well designed to operate with adults and to give the infant an initial orientation to social situations.

Behaviours to which Social Responses are Given

Newborn babies will both smile and cry. In both cases, this behaviour has no social meaning to the baby at first. She smiles apparently randomly from time to time, and cries if hungry or uncomfortable. However, caregivers respond to these signals as if they were social. They tend to smile and talk back if the infant smiles, and to pick up an infant and talk to her if she is crying (one study found that picking up an infant reduced crying on 88% of occasions, which is very rewarding for the adult). Gradually, the infant will learn the social consequences of smiling and crying, because of the social meaning and social responses that caregivers give to them. It is similar with babbling, which begins around 2 months of age.

An Ability to Learn

The development of perceptual abilities in infancy is discussed in detail in Chapter 11. We saw earlier (and in Box 3.1) how some aspects of the mother's voice are learned even before birth; infants learn to discriminate the sound of the mother's voice from that of a stranger within a few days of birth (p. 84) and learn to prefer pictures of faces to similar but scrambled up pictures by 2 months of age (p. 389; see Figure 11.6). Throughout the first months of life, infants are discriminating social stimuli and learning the consequences of social actions. By around 6 months of age they quite clearly discriminate between familiar and unfamiliar adults, for example in orienting and in ease of being comforted.

Even a few hours after birth, neonates are also able to perceive temporal relationships between events—that one stimulus event is regularly followed by another. For example, if pressing the infant on the forehead on the left or right side is followed by a drop of water on that side, the infant learns to look to that side after the press on the forehead (Blass et al., 1994). This early capacity to perceive regularities and to anticipate B from A rapidly includes social events, and forms one aspect of the enjoyment of contingent responses.

An Enjoyment of Contingent Responding by Others

From quite early on, it seems as though infants like to get 'contingent' stimulation—that is, stimulation that appropriately follows quickly on some action of their own; as it were, a 'reply' to their own action.

An early experiment that demonstrated this was carried out by Watson and Ramey (1972). They used the 'contingency mobile' shown in Figure 3.3, with 40 8-week-old infants. The mobile was attached to the infant's cot and hung about 18 inches above the infant's head. There were three conditions.

1. *The 'contingency' condition*: a pressure-sensing pillow was put in the cot. Small changes in pressure on the pillow activated an electric motor and caused the display to rotate. When the infant was lying with her head on the pillow, she could cause the display to rotate by making small head movements.

2. *The 'non-contingency' condition*: the pressure-sensing pillow was disconnected from the motor. The display rotated once every 3 or 4 seconds, independent of the infant's actions.

3. *The 'stable' condition*: the pressure-sensing pillow was disconnected from the motor. The display did not rotate at all.

The infants with the contingency mobile significantly increased the number of pillow activations they made per session. For the non-contingency mobile and the stable condition, the changes were not significant. This showed that, as early as 8 weeks, infants can learn a simple response to produce contingent stimulation. However, the investigators obtained another interesting

Figure 3.3 Apparatus used as a 'contingency mobile'
Source: Adapted from Watson & Ramey (1972).

result. It turned out that almost all the mothers in the 'contingency' condition reported that their infants smiled and cooed at the mobile, after a few sessions. As one mother said', You have to see it, when he's with his mobile, you can't distract him, he loves it'. Almost none of the mothers in the other two conditions reported this kind of strong positive emotional response.

Usually, it is caregivers (and not 'contingency' mobiles!) that provide contingent responding in a rapid and appropriate fashion, when they react to the infant's smiling, crying, cooing or babbling, or a bit later on when they engage in games such as peekaboo. A number of studies suggest that infants not only enjoy contingent responsiveness, but also come to expect it from familiar caregivers and to be upset when such expectations are violated. One paradigm used to demonstrate this is called the 'still face' (Tronick et al., 1978). A mother is asked to interact with her infant normally for, say, 3 minutes, then adopt a 'still face' pose, then return to normal interaction. Infants tend to fuss or look away during the still face episode. It could be argued that the still face is artificial and just less interesting for the infant, independent of contingency. Another paradigm, called double video (DV) live-replay, gets around this difficulty. This was first used by Murray and Trevarthen (1985). They set up a video link between mothers and their 6–12-week-old infants. First they recorded a section of live mother–infant interaction on video. Then they replayed a previously recorded section to the infant, instead of the live video picture; now, the mother was still giving social and communicative signals to the infant, but not contingently to the infant's responses. Murray and Trevarthen found that the infants (previously happy and attentive) now tended to frown and look away.

A possible criticism of this work is that, over time, the infants were getting more fussy in the experimental conditions. It would be better to have a live-replay-live condition to control for this possibility. This was done by Nadel et al. (1999), with 9-week old infants; they also avoided a break between the episodes, providing a seamless video transition. They replicated the findings of Murray and Trevarthen, and also found that the infants 'recovered' their normal levels of attention and positive behaviour once contingency was restored.

Early Behavioural Routines

Enjoyment of contingent responsiveness can develop into turn taking and proper interactions such as conversations or games. A common example is peekaboo. This is initially structured solely by the adult, who takes advantage of the infant's pleasure at the surprise generated by the sudden appearance and disappearance of the adult's face or a teddy bear; it becomes a more genuine turn-taking sequence as the infant comes to expect the next repetition of the game and thus take a more active part itself in the exchange (see Bruner & Sherwood, 1976).

Even at a few months old, infants can not only enjoy songs and rhythmic games, but develop expectations of the interaction. Fantasia et al. (2014) studied infants aged 3 months, playing early social games with their mothers, such as Row the boat or Hickory dickory dock. Besides the normal play condition, they asked mothers to sometimes do the game without the sounds (only the gestures), and sometimes to do it without the gestures (only the sounds). In both these latter conditions, where the game structure was violated, the infants gazed away more, showed less positive affect and more negative affect, and often appeared puzzled. Thus even at this early age, infants appear to have developed clear expectancies about the structures of social exchanges.

Imitation

An important aspect of infant learning is imitation. Research by Kaye and Marcus (1978, 1981) showed that clear imitation of social stimuli occurs between 6 months and 12 months of age. These investigators tried presenting infants with certain actions each time they got their attention. For example, they might open and close their mouth five times, like a goldfish, or clap their hands in front of the infant, four times. Each action sequence was contingent on the infant reestablishing eye contact with the experimenter. Besides often establishing eye contact, the infants also tried to imitate the actions themselves, often trying to copy one feature at a time; the imitations improved over trials, and as the infants got older. In fact, there is evidence of imitation at earlier ages. Meltzoff and Moore (1977) studied 12–21-day-old babies and found that they showed some imitation of actions such as tongue protrusion, mouth opening and lip pursing, as performed by an adult. There have since been many studies of imitation by infants (Nadel & Butterworth, 1999). An issue in very early imitation is the extent to which the imitative action by the infant involves an active partnership on their part, or is rather just a 'matching', an automatic and involuntary response by the infant that matches or mirrors the adult action (Papousek & Papousek, 1989).

The Respective Roles of Infant and Caregiver

The various abilities of infants, discussed above, assist them in getting into social interaction sequences with adult caregivers. However, the adult has a vital role to play in this, by responding in appropriate ways and at appropriate times. Kaye (1982) calls this 'scaffolding' (see also Chapter 16), and likens the infant to an apprentice who is learning the craft of social interaction and communication from an expert. At the beginning, the adult has to do most of the work to keep things going: picking the infant up, putting their face at the right distance, responding whenever the infant makes a signal, perhaps having the 'illusion' that the infant is replying when she smiles or grimaces. Things get less one-sided as the infant develops her own social repertoire and begins to learn to take turns in social interaction. Even so, gearing one's behaviour at an appropriate pace and level to the child remains important through infancy and beyond.

Other researchers give a greater role to the infant. Rather than seeing the infant as mainly being paced by the caregiver, Fogel prefers to talk about *co-regulation*, which he defines as 'a social process by which individuals dynamically alter their actions with respect to the ongoing and anticipated actions of their partners' (Fogel, 1993, p. 12). He thus sees these early social interactions as a more negotiated and dynamic process than the 'scaffolding' metaphor would imply.

Trevarthen has consistently argued that infants have much to contribute, from very early on. He has made detailed frame-by-frame analysis of video recordings of mothers and babies, and believes that infants have an innate capacity for intersubjectivity. He refers to *primary intersubjectivity* as being an active and immediate response by an infant to an adult's communicative intentions, and *secondary intersubjectivity* as integrating a person-person-object awareness, with joint attention to and action on objects (Trevarthen & Aitken, 2001; Trevarthen & Hubley, 1978 and cf. p. 53).

Trevarthen describes secondary intersubjectivity as emerging at around 9 months, and primary intersubjectivity much earlier. For example:

> In the gentle, intimate, affectionate, and rhythmically regulated playful exchanges of proto-conversation, 2-month-old infants look at the eyes and mouth of the person addressing them while listening to the voice. In measured and predictable cycles of response to regular time patterns in the adult's behaviour, the infant moves its face, hands and vocal system to modified patterns of adult vocal expression . . . the communicatively active hands of young infants may make expressive movements in rhythmic coordination with a person's speech . . .
> *(Trevarthen & Aitken, 2001, p. 6)*

In fact, these researchers believe that in appropriate conditions—if a newborn is alert, rested, free of stress and with a sensitive caregiver—then primary intersubjectivity is discernible from birth.

> The interactions are calm, enjoyable, and dependent upon sustained mutual attention and rhythmic synchrony of short 'utterances' which include, beside vocalizations, touching and showing the face and hands, all these expressions being performed with regulated reciprocity and turn-taking. Newborn and adult spontaneously display a mutually satisfying intersubjectivity . . .
> *(Trevarthen & Aitken, 2001, p. 6)*

Not everyone accepts these conclusions, which do depend on the way in which one interprets very detailed video records. Research with very young infants is not easy to do! Often they are asleep, and often the requirements of a research project may make it more difficult for them to be 'alert, rested, free of stress and with a sensitive caregiver' for long periods.

In many areas of infancy research, debate continues about how early various abilities and behaviours can be found, with confidence and robustness.

 Stop and Think

From an evolutionary perspective, are infants well adapted to benefit from adult caregivers?

Very Early Bonding: The Work of Klaus and Kennell

Although infants learn about their particular parents or caregivers through the first year, it has been claimed that the mother very quickly forms a bond with the infant, in the first hours or days after birth. In its strongest form, it is claimed that the first 6–12 hours after birth are a sensitive period for the mother to form a strong emotional bond with her infant through physical contact. If she is absent, the bond is less strong, and later maltreatment or abuse more likely. This 'early bonding' hypothesis was proposed by Klaus and Kennell (1976), on the basis of a study of 28 mothers in an American maternity hospital. Fourteen had the traditional treatment—5 minutes' contact at delivery, then separation for some 6–12 hours followed by half-hour feeding sessions every 4 hours. The other 14 had extra contact—an hour of cuddling after birth, and then an extra 5 hours each day. One month later, and also 1 year later, there appeared to be some differences favouring the extra contact group. For example, the mothers were more likely to soothe the baby if it cried. This suggests that the extra contact in the first day or so makes a difference.

Subsequently a number of similar studies were carried out by other investigators, some with larger samples. Some observed small effects, some none at all. Reviews of this evidence (Goldberg, 1983; Myers, 1984) suggest that while early contact is pleasurable for the mother and may have some short-term effects, the long-term effects are very small or non-existent. The positive results of the early study were flawed by methodological drawbacks, a small sample, and focusing attention on a small number of significant results out of a very large number of measurements. Thus, the existence of this sensitive period is now thought to be very questionable; many other influences are important in the mother's relationship to the infant, and over a longer time period.

Over the last decades there have been changes in hospital practice, allowing mothers more ready and continuous access to newborns, which is probably beneficial. But parents who miss the first few hours or so of contact (some mothers, most fathers and all adoptive parents) need not feel that they have lost out on a period crucial for later relationships with the baby.

TEMPERAMENT

So far, we have considered infants in rather general terms. But infants vary considerably in their behavioural characteristics. Some will cry a lot, others will be equable; some will be active, others less so; and so on. In a longitudinal study in New York, Thomas and Chess (1977) interviewed mothers about this at regular 3-month intervals, and found considerable consistency in what they call characteristics of infant temperament. Based largely on questionnaires, they identified nine main dimensions of temperament, shown in Table 3.3.

Table 3.3 Temperament dimensions from the work of Thomas and Chess.

Activity level—the amount of physical activity during sleep, feeding, play, dressing, etc.

Regularity—of bodily functioning in sleep, hunger, bowel movements, etc.

Adaptability to change in routine—the ease or difficulty with which initial response can be modified in socially desirable ways.

Response to new situations—initial reaction to new stimuli, to food, people, places, toys or procedures.

Level of sensory threshold—the amount of external stimulation, such as sounds or changes in food or people, necessary to produce a response in the child.

Intensity of response—the energy content of responses regardless of their quality.

Positive or negative mood—amount of pleasant or unpleasant behaviour throughout day.

Distractibility—the effectiveness of external stimuli (sounds, toys, people, etc.) in interfering with ongoing behaviour.

Persistence and attention span—duration of maintaining specific activities with or without external obstacles.

Source: Thomas, A., & Chess, S. (1977). *Temperament and development:* New York, Brunner/Mazel.

On the basis of these dimensions, the researchers distinguished *difficult* babies (negative, irregular and unadaptable) and *easy* babies (positive, regular and adaptable). Subsequent work has tended to group infants according to three major aspects (Rothbart, 2007; Sanson et al., 2011).

1. *Reactive emotionality or negative affectivity*: irritability, negative mood, inflexibility and high-intensity negative reactions
2. *Self-regulation or effortful control*: persistence, non-distractibility and emotional control
3. *Approach/withdrawal or extraversion/surgency*: tendency to approach, or withdraw from and be wary of, novel situations and people.

Temperamental characteristics seem evident in very young babies, and probably have some biological basis. There is evidence from behaviour genetic studies (Chapter 2) of considerable heritability in temperament (Sanson et al., 2011). In addition, some signs can be detected during fetal growth. DiPietro et al. (1996) monitored fetal heart rate and movement in 31 fetuses from gestational age 20 weeks to 36 weeks, and gathered maternal reports at 3 and 6 months. In general, more active fetuses were described later by mothers as more difficult, unpredictable, unadaptable and active infants. By 36 weeks gestation, fetal behaviour was found to be quite strongly predictive of infant temperament.

Thomas and Chess tended to see temperamental characteristics as inherent in the child; an alternative view is that since temperament is usually based on mother (or caregiver) ratings, it is a dyadic characteristic that much more reflects the mother's own psychological state and how she understands her child's behaviour (St James-Roberts & Wolke, 1984). Bornstein et al. (1991) devized an *Infant Temperament Measure* (ITM) that looks at 10 infant behaviours (such as: smiles and laughs to a stranger; fusses/cries) and combines mothers' global ratings and both mothers' and observers' ratings during a 30-minute session.

This multi-method assessment is intentionally designed to assess different perspectives on the infant's temperament.

Temperament may be an important aspect to consider in child development and parenting outcomes. A number of studies have looked at how the approach/withdrawal dimension in infancy may be predictive of shyness and social isolation in the preschool years. Kagan (1997) argues that 4-month-old infants who are easily aroused and distressed by unfamiliar stimuli are more likely to be fearful and subdued in early childhood, while those with a high arousal threshold are more likely to become bold and sociable.

Most investigators consider that a transactional model of development is useful in this context. The infant may bring some temperamental characteristics with them, but how caregiver(s) respond is an important part of a developing process. Temperamentally difficult babies are more of a challenge for parents to cope with, and seem to be more at risk for later behaviour problems. This was shown directly in a study by Stright et al. (2008). In a large US sample from the NICHD (see Table 1.1), they assessed temperament at 6 months, and also parenting quality (providing emotional support and encouraging autonomy) from 6 months through to 6 years. They also looked at outcome in first grade at school, from teacher-rated academic and social competence. For 'difficult' infants, the outcome was greatly affected by parenting quality; difficult infants with poor parenting did worse than average, but difficult infants with high-quality parenting did better than average (see also p. 133).

The best outcome is if parents are able to respond over time in a way suited to the baby or toddler—providing extra motor opportunities for active babies, for example, or especially encouraging approach in shy babies (cf. Figure 4.2). The cultural environment is also important. For example, Chen et al. (1998) found that behavioural inhibition is a temperamental trait that is more accepted in Chinese infants than in North American infants.

Temperament shows some continuity over time and can be assessed in middle childhood. Rothbart (2007) and colleagues devised a *Children's Behaviour Questionnaire*, which, using parent reports for children aged 3–7 years, yielded three main dimensions as indicated on the previous page. In a longitudinal study, Kagan et al. (2007) assessed temperament at 4 months (from observational data) and followed up at intervals, the latest assessment being at around 15 years. Children who were 'high reactive' rather than 'low reactive' at 4 months (that is, motorically vigorous and crying a lot) were more likely to be subdued in unfamiliar situations at age 15, to be anxious and more religious.

Caspi (2000) reported long-term correlates of temperament, based on the Dunedin study (see Table 1.1). At age 3, about 40% of the sample could be categorized as temperamentally easy or well adjusted; about 10% as undercontrolled (impulsive and negativistic); and about 8% as inhibited (slow to warm up, fearful). Some relations to aggression in childhood are mentioned in Chapter 10. Caspi followed the sample up to ages 18 and 21, and there continued to be significant differences in these three main groups of persons (as assigned by temperament at age 3) on measures such as mental health, employment and quality of relationships in adult life. Although the actual size of effects is generally small, this is impressive evidence for some degree of continuity in temperamentally based characteristics.

THE MILLENNIUM COHORT STUDY (MCS): PATTERNS OF INFANT CARE IN THE UK AT 9 MONTHS

This longitudinal study is following the development of more than 18,000 infants born in the UK in 2000–2001 (see Table 1.1). Dex and Joshi (2005) reported a range of findings from the first major assessments, when the infants were 9 months old, which gives a good indication of patterns of infant care in the UK at the time. The mean age of mothers at birth was 29 years. About 58% of mothers said that the pregnancy was planned; this was much lower, 16%, for mothers under 20 years.

Almost all mothers had their babies in hospital; only 2% had home deliveries. The father was present for 85% of births, and the mother's mother (or mother-in-law) for 16%; few had no social support apart from medical staff. About 7% of the infants were preterm births (here defined as 28–36 weeks of gestational age). Some 30% of mothers had induction to speed timing of delivery, and around 21% had a caesarean section.

At 9 months, about 86% of infants were with both parents, and about 14% in one-parent (usually lone mother) families. Ethnically, lone mothers were most frequent in Black Caribbean families, and least frequent in South Asian (Indian, Pakistani, Bangladeshi) families. Also, about half of teenage mothers were lone parents. Some 58% of infants had at least one sibling, family size being largest in Bangladeshi families. Around 6% had at least one grandparent living in the family, this being highest in South Asian families.

Some interesting findings came from studies of breastfeeding. Altogether, about 70% of mothers initiated breastfeeding with their infants. But there were marked regional variations in this, with the highest rates in London (83%) and the lowest in Northern Ireland (51%). Rates of breastfeeding fell off considerably over the first 6 months; in the sample as a whole, the 70% who breastfed at birth fell to 48% at 1 month, 33% at 4 months and 22% at 6 months.

The MCS is the latest in a set of British cohort studies (see Table 1.1), and the researchers were able to compare breastfeeding rates in the different studies. As we saw, nearly half the Millennium Cohort mothers breastfed their babies at 1 month, in 2000–2001. This is much higher than in 1970, where the BCS70 survey had a rate of about 22%. It is also higher than the 44% found in 1958 from the NCDS survey. However, it is less than the 62% found by the first survey, NSHD, in 1946. Clearly, rates of breastfeeding have followed a U-shaped curve, declining from high levels in the post-WWII period, as bottle feeding became cheaper and apparently more convenient and fashionable; this decline reversing again as the nutritional and health advantages of breastfeeding came to be advocated by health workers and paediatricians.

Some further findings from the MCS are discussed in Chapter 4.

CHAPTER SUMMARY

- From conception, the embryo and fetus develop following canalized pathways, which, however, can be affected by prenatal risk factors such as teratogens.
- Fetal learning occurs and fetal activity may well be important for development after birth.
- Bipedalism in hominids led to infants being born relatively early in terms of brain development.
- Medical advances have enabled premature babies to survive at increasingly earlier ages. However, very preterm infants are at risk in aspects of later development.
- Newborn infants are well adapted to take advantage of adult caregivers (usually primarily the mother) and develop early interactions with them. The adult caregiver 'scaffolds' these interactions, but the role gradually shifts to a more equal one.
- Temperament is an important source of variation among infants, which contributes to the nature and quality of their interactions and later development.

DISCUSSION POINTS

1. To what extent is the birth process affected by cultural practices?
2. What practical and moral issues are posed by modern means of intensive neonatal care?
3. How do infants become social?
4. What is the relative contribution of infant and caregiver to social interaction in the first year?
5. Is research on temperament likely to be strongly affected by how we measure temperament?

FURTHER READING

- The development of the fetus, and of the young infant, are covered in greater detail in Rosenblith, J.F. (1992). *In the beginning: Development from conception to age two*. London: Sage. The birth process and comparisons of humans with other species are discussed in Trevathan, W.R. (1987). *Human birth: An evolutionary perspective*. New York: Aldine de Gruyter.
- For early infancy, a comprehensive collection is Bremner, J.G. & Wachs, T.D. (Eds.) (2010). *Wiley-Blackwell handbook of infant development* (2nd ed.). Oxford: Wiley-Blackwell. Nadel, J. & Butterworth, G. (Eds.) (1999). *Imitation in infancy*. Cambridge: Cambridge University Press, provides a good source for the large literature on this topic.
- Dex, S. & Joshi, H. (Eds.) (2005). *Children of the 21st century: From birth to nine months*. Bristol: Policy Press, gives initial findings from the Millennium Cohort Study in the UK.

PART III

THE SOCIAL WORLD OF THE CHILD

Chapter 4   Parents and Families

Chapter 5   Siblings and the Peer Group

Chapter 6   Developing Emotional Intelligence and Social Awareness

Chapter 7   Play

Chapter 8   Children and Media

Chapter 9   Helping Others and Moral Development

Chapter 10   Social Dominance, Aggression and Bullying

CHAPTER
4

Parents and Families

CHAPTER OUTLINE

- The Development of Attachment Relationships
- Bowlby's 'Maternal Deprivation' Hypothesis
- Care Outside the Family
- Fathers
- Grandparents
- Types of Family
- Styles of Parenting
- Divorce
- Step-Parenting
- Physical Punishment and the 'Smacking' Debate
- Child Maltreatment, Neglect and Abuse
- Models of Parenting
- The Millennium Cohort Study (MCS): Patterns of Childcare in the UK at 3 and 5 Years

In this chapter we look first at the development of attachment relationships between infants and parents. The importance of such attachments for later development is considered, with its implications for policy issues such as institutional rearing, day care and childminding for young children. Although many attachment theorists tend to focus on the mother when discussing the child's early social relationships, the child has important relationships with other family members such as the father and grandparents (we discuss siblings in Chapter 5). We look at the effects of growing up in different types of family, research on parenting styles and the effects of parental divorce. We also examine the debate on physical punishment, and issues around child maltreatment and abuse. Finally, we examine some of the factors affecting successful and less successful parenting.

THE DEVELOPMENT OF ATTACHMENT RELATIONSHIPS

Suppose you are watching a 1- or 2-year-old infant with his mother in a park. This is what you might observe. The mother sits down on a bench and the infant runs off. Every now and then he will stop to look around, point to objects or events, and examine things on the ground such as leaves, stones and bits of paper, or crawl or jump over grass verges. The infant periodically stops and looks back at the mother, and now and then may return close to her or make physical contact, staying close for a while before venturing off again. Usually the infant does not go further than about 200 feet from the mother, who may, however, have to retrieve him if the distance gets too great or if she wants to move off herself.

The infant seems to be exploring the environment, using the mother as a secure base to which to return periodically for reassurance. This is one of the hallmarks of an 'attachment relationship'. The development of attachment was described in detail by John Bowlby (1969). The observations of children in parks were made in London by Anderson (1972), a student of Bowlby's.

Bowlby described four phases in the development of attachment, subsequently extended to a fifth.

1. The infant orientates and signals without discriminating between different people. We have already described this as characteristic of the infant in the first few months of life (excepting unusual laboratory situations).
2. The infant preferentially orientates to and signals at one or more discriminated persons. This marks the beginning of attachment. The infant is more likely to smile at the mother or important caregivers, for example, or to be comforted by them if distressed. Exactly when this occurs depends on the measures used, but it is commonly observed at around 5–7 months of age.
3. The infant maintains proximity preferentially to a discriminated person by means of locomotion and signals. For example, the infant crawls after the person, or returns periodically for contact, or cries or protests if the person leaves ('separation protest'). This is often taken as the definition of attachment to a caregiver. From 7–9 months usually

brings the onset of attachment, in this sense. An important related criterion is that the infant becomes wary or even fearful of unfamiliar persons ('fear of strangers').

4. The formation of a goal-corrected partnership occurs between child and caregiver. Until now the mother has served as a resource for the child, being available when needed. The goal-corrected partnership refers to the idea that the child also begins to accommodate to the mother's needs, for example being prepared to wait alone if requested until mother returns. Bowlby saw this as characterizing the child from 3 years of age, though there is evidence that 2-year-olds can partly accommodate to verbal requests by the mother to await her return (Weinraub & Lewis, 1977).

5. Lessening of attachment as measured by the child maintaining proximity. Characteristic of the school-age child and older is the idea of a relationship based more on abstract considerations such as affection, trust and approval, exemplified by an internal working model of the relationship (p. 118).

Bowlby saw attachment as a canalized developmental process. As we saw in Chapter 3, both the largely instinctive repertoire of the newborn and certain forms of learning are important in early social interactions. Some aspects of cognitive sensorimotor development (Chapters 11, 13) are also essential for attachment; until the infant has some idea of cause–effect relations, and of the continued existence of objects or persons when they are out of sight, he or she cannot consistently protest at separation and attempt to maintain proximity. Sensori-motor development is also a canalized process, and an ethological and a cognitive-learning approach to attachment development need not be in opposition.

Many of the characteristic behaviours in attachment were described by Mary Ainsworth (1967, 1973). She observed babies both in the Ganda people of Uganda and in Baltimore in the USA. She described babies smiling and vocalizing preferentially to the mother, and being comforted; crying when the mother left, following her and greeting her by smiling, lifting arms, hugging or scrambling over her and burying the face in her lap; using the mother as a secure base for exploration, and as a haven of safety if frightened.

Who are Attachments Made With?

Some earlier articles and textbooks defined the attachment relationship as being to the mother (e.g. Sylva & Lunt, 1981). But studies suggest that early attachments are usually multiple and, although the strongest attachment is often to the mother, this need not always be so.

In a study in Scotland, mothers were interviewed and asked to whom their babies showed separation protest (Schaffer & Emerson, 1964). The proportion of babies having more than one attachment figure increased from 29% when separation protest first appeared to 87% at 18 months. Furthermore, for about one-third of the babies, the strongest attachment seemed to be to someone other than the mother, such as father, grandparent or an older sibling. Generally, attachments were formed to responsive persons who interacted and played a lot with the infant; simple caregiving such as nappy changing was not in itself such an important factor.

Studies in other cultures bear out these conclusions. In the Israeli kibbutzim, for example, young children spend the majority of their waking hours in small communal nurseries, in the charge of a nurse or *metapelet*. A study of 1- and 2-year-olds reared in this way found that the infants were strongly attached to both the mother and the *metapelet*; either could serve as a base for exploration and provide reassurance when the infant felt insecure (Fox, 1977). In many agricultural societies, mothers work in the fields, and often leave young infants in the village, in the care of grandparents or older siblings, returning periodically to breastfeed. In a survey of data on 186 non-industrial societies, it was found that the mother was rated as the 'almost exclusive' caretaker in infancy in only five of them. Other persons had important caregiving roles in 40% of societies during the infancy period, and in 80% of societies during early childhood (Weisner & Gallimore, 1977).

The Security of Attachment

Ainsworth and her colleagues developed the *Strange Situation* (SS) as a method for assessing how well the infant uses the caregiver as a secure base for exploration and is comforted by the caregiver after a mildly stressful experience (Ainsworth et al., 1978). It has been used extensively with 12–24-month-old infants in many countries as a measure of attachment security.

The Strange Situation involves seven short episodes, which take place in a comfortably equipped room, usually at a research centre where the episodes can be filmed. Besides caregiver or mother (M) and infant (I), there is a stranger (S) whom the infant has not seen before. The episodes are: (1) M and I in room, I explores for 3 minutes; (2) S enters, sits for 1 minute, talks to M for 1 minute and gets down on the floor to play with I, 1 minute; (3) M leaves, S plays with I then withdraws if possible, up to 3 minutes; (4) M returns, S leaves unobtrusively, M settles I and then sits down for 3 minutes; (5) M leaves, I is alone for up to 3 minutes; (6) S comes in, attempts to settle I then withdraws if possible, up to 3 minutes; (7) M returns, S leaves unobtrusively, M settles I and sits down (session ends, after about 20 minutes).

In a well-functioning attachment relationship, it is postulated that the infant will use the mother as a base to explore (episodes 1, 2 and end of episode 4) but be stressed by the mother's absence (episodes 3, 5 and 6; these episodes are curtailed if the infant is very upset or the mother wants to return sooner). Special attention is given to the infant's behaviour in the reunion episodes (4 and 7), to see if he or she is effectively comforted by the mother. On the basis of such measures, Ainsworth and others distinguished a number of different attachment types. The primary ones are type A (Avoidant), type B (Secure) and type C (Ambivalent); later, type D (Disorganized) was added.

Type A   babies are characterized by conspicuous avoidance of proximity to or interaction with the mother in the reunion episodes. Either the baby ignores the mother on her return, greeting her casually if at all, or he mingles his welcome with avoidance responses such as turning away, moving past or averting gaze. During separation, the baby is not distressed, or distress seems due to being left alone rather than to mother's absence.

Type B   babies are characterized by actively seeking and maintaining proximity, contact or interaction with the mother, especially in the reunion episodes. They may or may not be distressed during the separation episodes, but any distress is related to mother's absence.

Type C   babies are characterized by conspicuous contact- and interaction-resisting behaviour in the reunion episodes. Rather than ignoring the mother, this is combined with some seeking of proximity and contact, thus giving the impression of being ambivalent or resistant.

Type D   babies show very disorganized or disoriented behaviour in the SS; there is no one clear pattern, but inconsistent and often bizarre responses to separation/reunion. Main and her colleagues (1985) believed this type to be a useful extension of the original Ainsworth classification.

There are subtypes of these main types, but most studies do not refer to them. In older studies, type D babies, who are often difficult to classify as they do not show a clear pattern, were 'forced' into the three-way scheme; and some contemporary analyses carry out analyses of both three-way and four-way classifications.

There has also been some criticism of the assumption that variations in attachment are best described typologically, rather than dimensionally. Fraley and Spieker (2003), using SS data on 15-month olds from the NICHD study (see Table 1.1), argued that a two-dimensional approach, with one dimension being Proximity-Seeking versus Avoidance and a second dimension being the extent of Angry-Resistant behaviour, was consistent with extant research, better described findings and, potentially, could yield stronger effect sizes.

The SS remains the main method of assessing attachment security in infants, but other methods have been used (Prior & Glaser, 2006). The Attachment Q-set method (AQS) uses descriptive items written on cards, which are used by caregivers to describe their relationship with an infant (or child), or by an observer who has watched them over some period of time.

Implications of Infant Attachment Security

An important test of the utility of attachment types is that they should predict to other aspects of development. There is now considerable evidence for this (Booth-LaForce & Kerns, 2008). Often, type B babies (secure) are contrasted with types A and C (insecure), and secure attachment tends to be seen as developmentally more normative, or advantageous.

For example, Oppenheim et al. (1988) found that secure attachment to mother at 12 months predicted curiosity and problem solving at age 2, social confidence at nursery school at age 3, and empathy and independence at age 5; Lewis et al. (1984) found that it predicted a lack of behaviour problems (in boys) at age 6.

Kochanska (2001) followed infants longitudinally from 9 to 33 months and observed their emotions in standard laboratory episodes designed to elicit fear, anger or joy. Over time, type A (avoidant) infants became more fearful, type C (resistant) infants became less joyful and type D (disorganized) became more angry, whereas type B (secure) infants showed less fear, anger or distress.

A study by McCartney et al. (2004) used 1,364 children from the NICHD Study of Early Child Care (see Table 1.1). The SS was given at 15 months, and Q-set ratings (based on home observations) by mothers at 24 months. The Q-set ratings significantly predicted internalizing and externalizing behaviour problems at 3 years, regardless of whether these were rated by mother or (for children in 10+ hours/week of non-maternal care) caregivers. However, the SS did not predict behaviour problems in this study.

There are at least two critical points to consider about the normative assumption that 'B is best'. The first is a practical point, that attachment security is a dyadic measure, and thus not really a characteristic of an infant but of a relationship. Infant–mother attachment type is not necessarily the same as infant–father attachment type, and in fact a meta-analysis (Van IJzendoorn & De Wolff, 1997) found a very modest association between the two.

The second point is a more theoretical one, coming from evolutionary developmental psychology. Given that 'insecure' attachment is quite common, is it correct to see it as maladaptive? Or are different attachment types adaptive for different situations or prevailing environments? Such arguments have been advanced by Belsky et al. (1991; see also Chapter 19 in relation to timing of puberty) and Chisholm (1996). The basic idea is that, whereas secure attachment and trusting models of relationships are adaptive for supportive environments with adequate resources and reliable caregivers, insecure attachment and a less trusting model of relationships may be more useful when resources are scarce or unpredictable, caregivers are inconsistent or abusive, and more opportunistic strategies may be advantageous (Simpson, 1999).

Is the Strange Situation Valid Cross-Culturally?

Van IJzendoorn and Kroonenberg (1988) provided a cross-cultural comparison of SS studies in a variety of different countries. In American studies, some 70% of babies were classified as securely attached to their mothers (type B), some 20% as type A and some 10% as type C. However, some German investigators found that some 40–50% of infants were type A (Grossman et al., 1981), while a Japanese study found 35% type C (Miyake et al., 1985). Such percentages raise questions about the nature and adaptiveness of 'insecure attachment', but also about comparability of procedures across cultures.

Takahashi (1990) argued that the SS must be interpreted carefully when used across cultures. He found that Japanese infants were excessively distressed by the infant alone episode (episode 5) because normally in Japanese culture they are never left alone at 12 months. Hence, fewer Japanese infants scored as B. Also, there was no chance for them to show avoidance (and score as A), since mothers characteristically went straight and without hesitation to pick up the baby. This may explain why so many Japanese babies were type C at 12 months (yet they are not at 24 months, and neither are adverse consequences apparent). This distortion might be avoided by virtually omitting episode 5 for such babies. Rothbaum et al. (2000) take a more radical stance in comparing the assessment of attachment security in the US and Japan. They argue that these two cultures put different cultural values on constructs such as independence, autonomy, social competence and sensitivity, such that some fundamental tenets of attachment theory are called into question as cross-cultural universals.

Cole (1998) suggested that the SS may be a valid indicator, but we need to redefine the meaning of the categories of avoidant, secure and ambivalent according to the local culture; although the SS is a standardized test, it is really a different situation in different cultural circumstances. However, for successful use of the SS in a non-Western culture (the Dogon people of Mali), see Box 4.1.

Why do Infants Develop Certain Attachment Types?

Are infants born predisposed to develop a certain kind of attachment, just as they may be predisposed to have a certain kind of temperament? Probably not. As mentioned in Chapter 2, Van IJzendoorn et al. (2000) argued that genetics has only a modest influence on attachment type. This is shown by twin studies; for example, O'Connor and Croft (2001) assessed twin pairs in the SS, and found concordance of 70% in monozygotic twins and 64% in dizygotic twins—not significantly different. Their model suggested estimates of only 14% of variance in attachment type due to genetics, 32% to shared environment and 53% to non-shared environment. A study of 485 same-sex twin pairs from the ECLS-B study (see Table 1.1) by Roisman and Fraley (2008) found that both shared and non-shared environment contributed appreciably to attachment security (here measured by a Q-sort technique), whereas the genetic contribution was small to negligible. A study of attachments formed by babies to foster mothers (Dozier et al., 2001) found as good a concordance between these mothers' state of mind regarding attachment (from the Adult Attachment Interview, see below) and infant attachment type from the SS, as for biological mother–infant pairs. All these studies find little genetic influence on attachment security.

Box 4.1 Infant–mother attachment among the Dogon of Mali

Although Ainsworth's pioneering work on attachment had been carried out amongst the Ganda people of Uganda, rather few subsequent studies in attachment have used non-urban populations. This study is an exception. It took place amongst the Dogon people of eastern Mali, a primarily agrarian people living by subsistence farming of millet and other crops, as well as cash economy in the towns (Box Figure 4.1.1). The study was carried out in two villages (population around 400) and one town (population 9,000), with the researchers attempting to get a complete coverage of infants born between mid-July and mid-September 1989. Not all infants could take part, due to relocation or refusal, and the researchers excluded two infants who had birth defects and eight suffering from severe malnutrition. In addition, after recruitment, two infants died before or during the 2-month testing period. Finally, 42 mother–infant pairs took part and provided good-quality data. The infants were 10–12 months old at the time of testing.

The Dogon are a polygamous society, and mothers typically live in a compound with an open courtyard, often shared with cowives.

Box Figure 4.1.1 Dogon mother spinning cotton, with child on her lap.

Box Figure 4.1.2 Dogon mother breastfeeding her child.

Source: Reproduced by permission of Lelia Pisani, supplied by ORISS archives, Lari, Italy.

There was some degree of shared care of infants, but about half were cared for primarily or exclusively by the mother and about one-third primarily by the maternal grandmother, with the mother, however, being responsible for breastfeeding (Box Figure 4.1.2). Breastfeeding is a normative response by the mother to signs of distress in Dogon infants. Three related features of infant care in the Dogon—frequent breastfeeding on demand, quick response to infant distress and constant proximity to the mother or caregiver—are seen as adaptive when there is high infant mortality (as in some other traditional African cultures).

The researchers had several objectives. They wished to see if the Strange Situation could be used successfully in Dogon culture; what distribution of attachment types was obtained; whether infant security correlated with maternal sensitivity (a test of the Maternal Sensitivity Hypothesis); whether infant attachment type related to patterns of attachment-related communications in mother–infant interaction (a test of what the authors call the Communication Hypothesis); and if frightened or frightening behaviour by the mother predicted disorganized infant attachment.

Three situations were used to obtain relevant data, with behaviour being recorded on videotape in each case. One, which was rather unusual, was the weigh-in, part of a regular well-infant examination in which the mother handed over the infant to be weighed on a scale—a mildly stressful separation for the infant, especially in Dogon culture. The other two were more standard: the Strange Situation, carried out in an area of a courtyard separated by hanging mats; and two 15-minute observations in the infant's home when the mother was cooking and bathing/caring for the infant.

The following data were obtained.

- Infant attachment classification (from the Strange Situation).

- A rating of infant security on a nine-point scale (from the Strange Situation).
- Mother and infant communication related to attachment, coded by five-point Communications Violations Rating scales (from the weigh-in).
- Maternal sensitivity, rated in terms of promptness, appropriateness and completeness of response to infant signals (from the home observations).
- Frightened or frightening behaviours by the mother, such as aggressive approach, disorientation, trance state, rough handling as if baby is an object, on a five-point scale (from the home observations and the weigh-in).

The Strange Situation was found to be feasible, following quite standard procedures. The distribution of attachment types was 67% B, 0% A, 8% C and 25% D (or on a forced three-way classification, 87% B, 0% A, 13% C). This is unusual in having no avoidant (A) classifications; D is high but not significantly greater than Western norms.

The Maternal Sensitivity Hypothesis only received weak support. The correlation between infant security and maternal sensitivity was $r = .28$, with $p < .10$; the difference in means between attachment classifications was not statistically significant (B = 5.26, C = 5.00, D = 4.20).

The Communications Hypothesis did get support. Infant security correlated .54 with Communications Violations ($p < .001$), and the attachment classifications differed significantly (B = 2.66, C = 3.50, D = 3.89; $p < .01$).

Finally, frightened or frightening behaviour by the mother correlated $r = .40$ ($p < .01$) with infant security, and was particularly high in children with disorganized attachment (B = 1.23, C = 1.33, D = 2.35; $p < .01$).

Besides demonstrating the general applicability of the Strange Situation procedure in a non-Western culture, the findings provide support for the Communications Hypothesis. The case here would have been stronger if the different kinds of communication patterns for each attachment classification had been described in more detail. For example, the authors earlier predicted that ambivalently attached (C) infants would be 'inconsistent and often unable to convey their intent, or to terminate their own or another's arousal', whereas disorganized (D) infants would 'manifest contextually irrational behaviours and dysfluent communication' (p. 1451). As it is, the main finding shows that insecure infants show more communications violations, but do not describe the detailed typology. Indeed, since some of the Communications Violation rating scales were of 'avoidance, resistance, and disorganization' (p. 1456), there is a possible danger of conceptual overlap between this scale and the attachment classifications.

Although support for the Maternal Sensitivity Hypothesis was weak, the correlation of r = .28 is in line with the average of r = .24 found in the meta-analysis by De Wolff and Van IJzendoorn (1997) on mainly Western samples. The researchers used a multiple regression analysis to examine the contributions of both maternal sensitivity and mother's frightened/frightening behaviour to attachment security. They found that the contribution of maternal sensitivity remained modest, whereas the contribution of mother's frightened/frightening behaviour was substantial and significant; ratings of maternal sensitivity do not normally take account of mother's frightened/frightening behaviour, and the researchers suggest that this might explain the modest effects found for maternal sensitivity to date.

The absence of avoidant (A) type infants is interesting. The researchers argue that, given the close contact mothers maintain with Dogon infants, and the normal use of breastfeeding as a comforting activity, it would be very difficult for a Dogon infant to develop an avoidant strategy (this may have some similarity with the low proportion of A type in Japanese infants, see p. 112). If avoidant attachment is rare or absent when infants are nursed on demand (which probably characterized much of human evolution, see p. 89), this might suggest that A type attachment was and is rare, except in Western samples in which infants tend to be fed on schedule, and often by bottle rather than breast, so that the attachment and feeding systems are effectively separated.

Most Dogon infants showed secure attachment, but one-quarter scored as disorganized (though mostly with secure as the forced three-way classification). The researchers comment that the frightened or frightening behaviours were mild to moderate, and did not constitute physical abuse. But why should mothers show these sorts of behaviour at all? An intriguing possibility is that it is related to the high level of infant mortality prevalent in the Dogon. About one-third of infants die before 5 years of age, and most mothers will have experienced an early bereavement. Unresolved loss experienced by a mother is hypothesized to be connected to disorganized attachment; perhaps frightened behaviours are more rational or expected, when the risks for infants are so much higher.

This study took great efforts to be sensitive to the cultural venue, when using procedures and instruments derived mainly from Western samples. A Malian researcher assisted in developing the maternal sensitivity coding, and Dogon women acted as strangers in the Strange Situation. The weigh-in and home observations were natural settings. The authors comment, however, that future work might make more effort to tap the perceptions of mothering and attachment held by the Dogon people themselves, in addition to the constructs coming from Western psychology.

Based on material in True, M.M., Pisani, L. & Oumar, F. (2001). Infant–mother attachment among the Dogon of Mali. *Child Development*, *72*, 1451–1466. Photos reproduced by permission of Lelia Pisani, supplied by ORISS archives, Lari, Italy.

So, what are the environmental influences that lead to different attachment types? An early candidate was the Maternal Sensitivity Hypothesis. This had been suggested by Ainsworth's original research (Ainsworth et al., 1978) that had established the nature of attachment types. This, and a number of later studies, reported that the quality and sensitivity of mother–infant face-to-face interaction from as early as a few months and through the first year or so predicted secure or insecure attachment (see also Box 4.1). A meta-analysis of relevant studies by De Wolff and Van IJzendoorn (1997) found an average effect size of .24 (an effect size is a measure of the influence of one variable on another in terms of standard deviations; an effect size of 1 would mean a shift of one standard deviation, obviously substantial; an effect size of .24 is seen as moderate). For fathers—who often get left out in such research—a similar meta-analysis of a much smaller number of studies (Van IJzendoorn & De Wolff, 1997) found a mean effect size of .13, less than for mothers. The importance of maternal sensitivity has been confirmed in predicting later attachment security (see later section on the Adult Attachment Interview).

As these effects sizes are moderate to small, other environmental influences must be at work. Meins et al. (2001) suggested that mothers' *mind-mindedness* is an important construct. This is defined as the mother treating her infant as an individual with a mind, rather than just a creature with needs to be satisfied. The emphasis is on responding to an infant's inferred state of mind, rather than simply their behaviour. In a longitudinal study of 71 mother–infant pairs, they found that maternal sensitivity (responding to infant cues) and some aspects of mind-mindedness, especially *appropriate mind-related comments* by the mother, measured at 6 months, both independently predicted security of attachment at 12 months. True et al. (2001) found evidence that a mother's frightened or frightening behaviour may also contribute independently to attachment security (see Box 4.1).

Another factor may be maternal depression. Kemppinen et al. (2006) assessed maternal sensitivity in Finnish mothers when their child was 2 months and 24 months. Maternal sensitivity ratings were quite strongly correlated between the two assessment points. Mothers with low maternal sensitivity scores together with high maternal control predicted low child cooperation, and many of these mothers (80%) reported prenatal depressive symptoms. In an Australian sample, McMahon et al. (2006) found that mothers who were depressed tended to have insecurely attached infants, with this association being moderated by maternal state of mind regarding attachment. We must also remember that a lot of the variance in attachment type appears to be related to non-shared environment, and this cannot be explained by generalized maternal sensitivity or depression. Perhaps mothers are more sensitive and behave differently to some infants than others, depending on birth order, gender and infant characteristics, suggesting the need for a family systems perspective on these issues (Van IJzendoorn et al., 2000).

Disorganized Attachment and Unresolved Attachment Representations

The disorganized pattern of infant attachment from the Strange Situation, D, came to be recognized later than the other main attachment types, and has distinctive correlates. Disorganized infants may show stereotypical behaviours such as freezing or hair pulling; contradictory behaviour such as avoiding the mother despite being very distressed on separation; and misdirected behaviour such as seeking proximity to the stranger instead of the parent. These are seen as signs of unresolved stress and anxiety. It seems that for these infants, the parent is a source of fright rather than of safety (see Table 4.4) (see Baer & Martinez, 2006; Green & Goldwyn, 2002).

Van IJzendoorn et al. (1999) reviewed a number of studies on disorganized attachment. Disorganized attachment is higher in infants with severe neurological abnormalities (cerebral palsy, autism, Down syndrome)—around 35%, compared with around 15% in normal samples. It is also especially high for mothers with alcohol or drug abuse problems (43%), or who have maltreated or abused their infants (48%). A study in Greece of infants reared in residential group care from birth found that 66% showed disorganized attachment (Vorria et al., 2003). However, D is not higher in infants with physical disabilities. Also, it is not strongly related to maternal sensitivity as such, but there is evidence relating it to maternal unresolved loss or trauma.

Whereas the Maternal Sensitivity Hypothesis suggested that maternal (in)sensitivity predicts secure (B) or insecure (A,C) attachment, a different hypothesis has been proposed to explain disorganized attachment (see Table 4.4). This is that it results from frightened or frightening behaviour by the mother (or caregiver) to the infant, resulting from the mother's own unresolved mental state related to attachment issues (for example, abuse by her own parent; violent death of a parent; sudden loss of a child).

A study by Hughes et al. (2001) in London compared unresolved scores on the Adult Attachment Interview (see below) for 53 mothers who had infants born next after a stillbirth, with 53 controls. Fifty-eight per cent of the mothers who had previously had stillborn infants scored as unresolved, compared to 8% of controls; furthermore, 36% had disorganized (D) infants, compared to 13% of controls. A statistical path analysis (looking at relationships among all the variables) showed that the stillbirth experience predicted unresolved maternal state of mind, and that this latter variable then predicted infant disorganization.

The hypothesized behavioural aspects of maternal unresolved state of mind were supported by the study in Mali reported in Box 4.1. A study in Germany by Jacobsen et al. (2000) provided further support. They examined 33 children and their mothers at 6 years of age. Disorganized attachment (assessed from a reunion episode) was significantly related to high levels of maternal expressed emotion, defined as speech to the child that was highly critical of them or overinvolved with them.

In their review, Van IJzendoorn et al. (1999) also found that infant disorganized attachment predicted for later aggressive behaviour and child psychopathology. Carlson (1998) found significant prediction from attachment disorganization at 24 and 42 months, to child behaviour problems in preschool, elementary school and high school. Given the prior links to parental maltreatment and abuse, it may be that the disorganized attachment pattern will be found to be the most relevant aspect of attachment in understanding severely maladaptive or antisocial behaviours in later life.

Van IJzendoorn et al. (1999) argued for mainly environmental causation of D, as for security of attachment generally. But as we saw in Chapter 2, there is some evidence for genetic factors in disorganized infant attachment, specifically linked to the DRD4 gene (Belsky & Pluess, 2009).

Attachment beyond Infancy and Internal Working Models

The SS measures security of attachment in terms of behaviours; especially, how the infant behaves at reunion after a separation. It is typically used in the 12–24 months age range. For 3–6-year-olds, variants of the SS, such as reunion episodes after separation, have been used with some success (Main & Cassidy, 1988; McCartney et al., 2004).

But attachment has become a life-span construct, with corresponding attempts to measure it at different developmental stages. We have seen how as the infant becomes older, in Bowlby's fourth and fifth stages, attachment relationships become less dependent on physical proximity and overt behaviour, and more dependent on abstract qualities of the relationship such as affection, trust, approval, internalized in the child and also of course in the adult. The child is then thought of as having an *internal working model* of his or her relationship with the mother, and other attachment figures (Bowlby, 1988; Main, Kaplan & Cassidy, 1985; Bretherton & Munholland, 2008). Internal working models are cognitive structures embodying the memories of day-to-day interactions with the attachment figure. They may be 'schemas' or 'event scripts', which guide the child's actions with the attachment figure, based on their previous interactions and the expectations and affective experiences associated with them.

Dyads of differing attachment type would be expected to have differing working models of the relationship. Secure attachment would be based on models of trust and affection, and a securely attached child would communicate openly and directly about attachment-related circumstances (such as how they felt if left alone for a while). By contrast, a boy with a type A avoidant relationship with his mother may have an internal working model of her that leads him not to expect secure comforting from her when he is distressed. She may in fact reject his approaches. His action rules then become focused on avoiding her, thus inhibiting approaches to her that could be ineffective and lead to further distress. This in turn can be problematic, as there is less open communication between mother and son, and their respective internal working models of each other are not being accurately updated. Type C infants with an ambivalent relationship might not know what to expect from their mother, and they in turn would be inconsistent in their communication with her and often unable to convey their intent.

Attachment quality in older children is assessed by tapping in to their internal working models (Brumariu & Kerns, 2011). One approach is by narrative tasks, often using doll play; children use a doll family and some props, and complete a set of standardized attachment-related story beginnings. Another method is the *Separation Anxiety Test*, or SAT, in which children or adolescents respond to photographs showing separation experiences; an example is shown in Figure 4.1. The child is asked how the child in the picture would feel and act, and then how he/she would feel and act if in that situation (Main et al., 1985). Wright et al. (1995) found the SAT to have good rater reliability and consistency for 8–12-year-olds. They found large differences in responses between children having clinical treatment for behaviour

Figure 4.1   Boy by Land Rover; a picture from the Separation Anxiety Test.

Source: Main, Kaplan & Cassidy (1985). Reproduced with permission.

Table 4.1   Two protocols from the Separation Anxiety Test.

From control sample:

Child:	Mum is going shopping and the boy is staying at home alone.
Interviewer:	How would you feel?
Child:	A bit scared and try to have some fun.
Interviewer:	Why?
Child:	Because someone can break in and kidnap me.
Interviewer:	What would you do?
Child:	Try and have fun and think mum and dad are in the house and no-one can kidnap me.

From clinical sample:

Child:	Mum is going shopping and the boy is staying at home alone.
Interviewer:	How would he feel?
Child:	Bad.
Interviewer:	Why?
Child:	'Cause he's often seen the video Home Alone and get burglars.
Interviewer:	What would he do?
Child:	So he sets booby traps and ends up hitting mum in the face with iron bars and blow-torches. So he sits and watches TV but he gets burnt by the fire and goes to hospital, his mum visits him and he's dead.

---

disturbance and a normal control group (Table 4.1). Securely attached children generally acknowledge the anxiety due to the separation, but come up with a coherent account and feasible coping responses; insecurely attached children generally either deny the anxiety or give inappropriate, incoherent or bizarre coping responses.

Avezier et al. (2002) assessed attachment in 66 Israeli kibbutz children at 2 years (SS) and followed up to 11–12 years (SAT). At the latter age they also measured IQ, self-esteem and sleeping arrangements after age 6 (whether communal or family). They were interested in what predicted two outcome measures: school achievement and teacher-rated emotional security, using regression analyses (p. 13). Not surprisingly, they found that good academic self-esteem and high IQ predicted both their outcome measures. But, in addition, school achievement was independently predicted by a secure SS and a coherent SAT, while emotional maturity was independently predicted by sleeping arrangement (not collective after age 6), and a secure SS.

The Adult Attachment Interview

Internal working models of relationships can normally be updated, or modified, as new interactions develop. It may be that for younger children, such change must be based on actual physical encounters. However, Main et al. (1985) suggest that in adolescents or adults who have achieved formal operational thinking (Chapter 13), it is possible to alter internal working models without having such direct interaction. To measure attachment in older adolescents and adults, they developed the *Adult Attachment Interview*, a semi-structured interview that probes memories of one's own early childhood experiences. The transcripts are coded, not on the basis of the experiences themselves so much as on how the person reflects on and evaluates them, and how coherent the total account is.

Main et al. (1985) reported that the Adult Attachment Interview (AAI) yielded four main patterns.

1. *Autonomous*: persons who can recall their own earlier attachment-related experiences objectively and openly, even if these were not favourable
2. *Dismissive*: persons who dismiss attachment relationships as of little concern, value or influence
3. *Enmeshed*: persons who seem preoccupied with dependency on their own parents and still actively struggle to please them
4. *Unresolved*: persons who have experienced a trauma, or the early death of an attachment figure, and have not come to terms with this or worked through the mourning process.

Van IJzendoorn (1995) summarized work using the AAI, which he argued has satisfactory coding reliability. Van IJzendoorn and Bakermans-Kranenburg (1996) looked at the distribution of AAI codings across different groups of people, from 33 separate studies, as summarized in Table 4.2. Mothers, fathers and older adolescents do not differ significantly in their distribution across the three main categories. People from lower socioeconomic groups are slightly more likely to score as Dismissive. However, the large difference is in persons having clinical treatment, the great majority of whom do not score as Autonomous on the AAI.

Are Attachment Types Stable over Time?

Does security of attachment change through life, or does infant–parent attachment set the pattern not only for later attachment in childhood but even for one's own future parenting? As attachment has become a life-span construct, these questions have generated considerable research and debate. Several studies have found some continuity of attachment classification over the first few years, but also some discontinuities that can partly be explained by taking account of life events that affect the family system. Vaughn et al. (1979) examined Strange Situation security at 12 and 18 months in a sample of US infants from families living in stressful situations. There was significant continuity, but also a lawful pattern of change. Infants who changed from secure to insecure usually had mothers who reported negative

Table 4.2   Normative data on AAI codings (percentages).

33 studies	Dismissive	Autonomous	Enmeshed
Mothers	24	58	18
Fathers	22	62	16
Adolescents	27	56	17
Lower socioeconomic status	33	48	18
Clinical patients	41	13	46

changes—loss of partner, worse financial circumstances. Conversely, infants who changed from insecure to secure usually had mothers who reported positive changes.

Bar-Heim et al. (2000) assessed infants at 14 and 24 months using the Strange Situation, and at 58 months using a reunion measure (behavioural measure) and the SAT (representational measure). There was significant continuity from 14 to 24 months (64% of children remained in the same A, B or C category), but not from either 14 or 24 months to 58 months. At 58 months, there was some significant agreement between the behavioural and representational measures of attachment. Again, some of the discontinuity with age could be explained by life events affecting the families; for infants who changed category between infancy and childhood, mothers reported fewer positive and more negative life events over the past year.

Several studies have now spanned a period of some 20 years to examine whether Strange Situation classification in infancy predicts AAI classification as young adults. The outcome is varied, but some of these studies do find significant continuity of the three main attachment types; that is, from Secure to Autonomous, Avoidant to Dismissive, and Resistant to Enmeshed. Also, several studies found relationships between discontinuities in attachment classification, and negative life events such as experience of parental divorce. A meta-analysis of longitudinal attachment studies by Fraley (2002) showed that attachment security-insecurity shows moderate stability from 1 year to 1.5, 4, 6 and 19 years, with an average stability coefficient of around .40.

A large sample longitudinal study was reported by Booth-LaForce and Roisman (2014). This was based on the SECCYD study in the USA (see Table 1.1), which provided early SS type data, with a follow-up of 857 participants given the AAI at about 18 years. The findings found 'low levels of stability' (p. 63) with an averaged stability coefficient of r = .12 —significant, but a small effect size. However, this study was able to explain some of the discontinuity in terms of parent factors and life events, as shown in Table 4.3, with maternal sensitivity throughout the period being a particularly important factor.

Table 4.3 Factors distinguishing different trajectories of attachment from early childhood to 18 years.

	Maternal factors	Paternal factors	Life events
Stable insecure compared to stable secure	Lower levels and greater decline in maternal sensitivity	Lower likelihood of living with father	Larger increase in negative life events
Stable insecure compared to insecure → secure	Lower level of maternal sensitivity		
Secure → insecure compared to stable secure	Lower level of maternal sensitivity	Lower likelihood of living with father; higher levels of paternal depression	

Source: Booth-LaForce, C. & Roisman, G.I. (2014). The Adult Attachment Interview: Psychometrics, stability and change from infancy, and developmental origins. *Monographs of the Society for Research in Child Development*, 79(3), 1–185.

Are Attachment Types Stable over Generations?

Besides some degree of continuity over time for an individual's attachment typing, there is also evidence for the transmission of attachment type across generations; specifically, from the parent's AAI coding and their infant's SS coding. Main et al. (1985) reported some evidence for such a link, and indeed the AAI coding system is premised on it; it was argued that Autonomous adults would have Secure infants; Dismissing adults would have Avoidant infants; Enmeshed adults would have Ambivalent infants; and Unresolved adults would have Disorganized infants; see Table 4.4.

Van IJzendoorn (1995) looked at a large number of available studies in the decade since Main's work; the results for parent–infant concordance are shown in Table 4.5. There is considerable linkage between adult AAI and infant SS coding; Van IJzendoorn argued that this 'intergenerational transmission' of attachment may be via parental responsiveness and sensitivity; we discussed above how this is only a partial explanation, and other aspects of maternal behaviour and of family systems may also be involved.

There appears to be considerable evidence for some degree of continuity of attachment security through life, and on to the next generation but also considerable evidence that this can be affected by parental factors and life events. An adult's attachment security might also be influenced by counselling or clinical treatment, or simply by reflection.

Some insight into this comes from a study reported by Fonagy et al. (1994). They carried out a longitudinal study with 100 mothers and 100 fathers, in London, who were given the AAI and other measures shortly before their child was born. The SS was used subsequently to measure security of attachment, to mother at 12 months and to father at 18 months. As other studies have found (see Table 4.5), the parent's AAI scores predicted the infant's SS scores. The researchers also obtained estimates of the amount of deprivation and disrupted parenting that the parents had themselves experienced. They looked to see if this, too, influenced infant attachment. Interestingly, it did, but it interacted strongly with the way in which the parents had dealt with their own representations of their experiences of being parented.

Table 4.4   Hypothesized relationships between maternal stage of mind (AAI), maternal behaviour and child attachment type.

Maternal behaviour with infant	Mother's state of mind	Infant Strange Situation type
Mother is sensitive to child's cues	Mother is open to and freely accesses attachment-related experiences: Autonomous on AAI	Secure
Mother is unresponsive to child's cues	Mother cuts off or minimizes past attachment memories and feelings: Dismissive on AAI	Avoidant
Mother is inconsistent; sometimes responsive, sometimes not	Mother is angry about or enmeshed in past attachment experiences: Enmeshed on AAI	Ambivalent
Mother exhibits frightened or frightening behaviour to child	Mother has unresolved state of mind about past attachment-related trauma or loss: Unresolved on AAI	Disorganized

Table 4.5 Concordance between infant Strange Situation coding and parental AAI coding.

Three-way:

18 studies	Dismissing	Autonomous	Enmeshed
Avoidant	116	46	27
Secure	53	304	46
Ambivalent	10	19	40

Four-way:

9 studies	Dismissing	Autonomous	Enmeshed	Unresolved
Avoidant	62	29	14	11
Secure	24	210	14	39
Ambivalent	3	9	10	6
Disorganized	19	26	10	62

Coding the AAI, the researchers developed a *reflective self-function* scale to assess the ability parents had to reflect on conscious and unconscious psychological states, and conflicting beliefs and desires. Of 17 mothers with deprived parenting and low reflective self-function scores, 16 had insecurely attached infants, as might be expected. By contrast, of 10 mothers who had experienced deprived parenting but had high reflective self-function scores, all had securely attached infants. The researchers argued that reflective self-function may be a way to change internal working models, and demonstrate resilience to adversity and a way of breaking the intergenerational transmission of insecure attachment.

Adults who experienced difficult childhoods but have overcome early adversity and insecure attachment by a process of reflection, counselling or clinical help are called *earned secures*. They could be contrasted with *continuous secures*, who had a positive upbringing. Phelps et al. (1998) made home observations of mothers and their 27-month-old children. They found that earned secures, like continuous secures, showed positive parenting; under conditions of stress, both these groups showed more positive parenting than insecure mothers.

Another fascinating perspective on the issue of intergenerational transmission comes from the Holocaust study (Sagi-Schwartz et al., 2003). The Holocaust refers to the experiences of Jews and other persecuted minorities in the concentration camps of World War II (1939–1945). Besides mistreatment and torture, many people were killed in the camps, leaving children as orphans in traumatic circumstances. Did such experiences impact on attachment, and was this transmitted intergenerationally to children? The study encompasses three generations: those, now grandparents, who came through the Holocaust typically as children who had lost their parents; their children, now parents; and their grandchildren. These generations are compared with comparable three-generation families who had not suffered from the Holocaust.

The effects of the Holocaust were evident in the grandparent generation. The Holocaust grandparents showed distinctive patterns on the AAI, scoring high on Unresolved, as would be predicted, and high on unusual beliefs—another predicted effect of trauma and unresolved attachment issues. They displayed avoidance of the Holocaust topic; a common finding was that the experiences had been so horrific that they were unable to talk about them even with their own children. However, intergenerational transmission of attachment type was quite low for this group. The Holocaust parents ('children of the Holocaust') showed rather small differences from controls, scoring just slightly higher on Unresolved on the AAI. This normalization process continued to the next generation ('grandchildren of the Holocaust'), for whom no significant differences in attachment security were found, from controls.

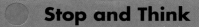

Stop and Think

How useful has the development of attachment theory been, from its origins in infancy into a life-span approach?

Attachment Theory as a Paradigm

Attachment theory is an important and vigorous approach to early social development (see Ainsworth & Bowlby, 1991, or Bretherton, 1992, for accounts of its origins) that constitutes something of a paradigm in the sense of Kuhn (see Chapter 1). It has developed rapidly. There are some internal challenges; for example, Crittenden (2000) believes that the three-fold or four-fold AAI classification homologous to the SS classification is too simple, and has proposed a more complex circumplex model. Other criticisms have been made from outside the field. Some feminist psychologists have objected to implications they see coming from attachment theory, for example, that women's identity is expected to be tied to child rearing; they see a high price being paid for maternal sensitivity, in other areas such as careers and self-esteem (Singer, 1992; Woollett & Phoenix, 1991). Some of these criticisms may be misplaced, however, being reactions to Bowlby's earlier maternal deprivation hypothesis (see below).

BOWLBY'S 'MATERNAL DEPRIVATION' HYPOTHESIS

The 'maternal deprivation' hypothesis is that children should not be 'deprived' of contact with the mother during a critical period when the primary attachment relationship is being formed. It was proposed by Bowlby (1953, 1969) in an early stage of his development of attachment theory, and while most attachment theorists later dissociated themselves from it, Bowlby did not. The hypothesis carried strong practical policy implications. Many aspects of it have been strongly criticized, however (Rutter, 1981; Clarke & Clarke, 1998).

Bowlby first put forward his views publicly in a 1951 report to the World Health Organization, published in 1953 as *Child Care and the Growth of Love*. The report was inspired by the needs of refugee or homeless children, separated from or without parents in the aftermath of the Second World War. At that time, institutional care focused on the physical needs of the child, good food and a clean environment—but little on the child's emotional needs, which were poorly recognized. On the basis of his emerging views on attachment, Bowlby proposed that 'mother love in infancy and childhood is as important for mental health as are vitamins and proteins for physical health'. This viewpoint provided an important corrective to the prevailing current of opinion. Bowlby went further, however. In a now notorious passage, he stated:

> What is believed to be essential for mental health is that the infant and young child should experience a warm, intimate and continuous relationship with his mother (or permanent mother-substitute—one person who steadily 'mothers' him) in which both find satisfaction and enjoyment.
>
> *(Bowlby, 1953, p. 11)*

This statement was backed up elsewhere in Bowlby's writings by assertions that mothers should not be separated from their young children, for example by work (even part-time) or hospitalization, and that if such separations do occur, there is a poor prognosis for social and cognitive development. The period from about 6 months to 3 years was regarded as especially crucial. Even if not universally believed, this statement had a profound effect on a generation of mothers.

Bowlby held this belief for reasons that now seem much less convincing than in the 1960s. The maternal deprivation hypothesis, at least in its strong form, has become largely discredited.

1. Bowlby's idea of a critical period for attachment formation came from ethological work on imprinting and the following response. However, the 'imprinting' characteristic of precocial birds and some mammals is not characteristic of primates (see Chapter 2). The 9-month 'fear of strangers' was supposed to prevent subsequent attachment bonds being formed, but more recent evidence suggests that 1- and 2-year-olds can form new social relationships with adults and characteristically form several strong attachment relationships. The crux of the issue here is whether infants only get attached to one person (which Bowlby called 'monotropism') or whether shared care by several attachment figures is normal and satisfactory. In fact, as we saw earlier (p. 109), moderate shared care of young children seems to be very common, harmless and even perhaps beneficial.

2. Observations of young children separated from parents and placed in an institution while the mother had a second baby and was to be in hospital for about a week showed that the children went through a characteristic sequence: first protesting but able to be comforted; secondly despair, and being inconsolable; thirdly, denial and detachment, with the child superficially unconcerned at the separation, but denying any affection or response to the mother on eventual reunion. These stages were vividly shown in a series of films made by J. and J. Robertson (1967–1973), entitled *Young Children in Brief Separation*.

   However, separation from the mother could be compensated for by the presence of another attachment figure. The Robertsons' work found just this. They found that institutional care led to the phases of protest, despair and denial, but that short-term foster care in a family, especially if the foster mother got to know the child beforehand, very greatly alleviated the child's distress. Similarly, if a young child is in hospital, regular visits or stays by mother, father and/or other attachment figures can prevent obvious distress.

3. Bowlby quoted much research evidence that suggested that children in long-term institutional care, in orphanages and foundling homes, were severely retarded in social, language and cognitive development, presumably as a result of the effects of maternal separation.

   However, the research on the effects of institutional rearing has been reevaluated (see also Chapter 18). No one denies the terrible effects of the prewar orphanages, which were poorly equipped and staffed by people with little understanding of the psychological needs of the child. However, any effects of separation from the mother were confounded with the generally unstimulating environment provided. It is not surprising that children become linguistically and cognitively retarded if they are hardly spoken to and given few toys and little sensory stimulation. It is not surprising that they are socially immature if they receive little social contact and few socially contingent responses. Such was often the case, but these are not necessary concomitants of institutional care. More recent research has found that improved institutional care has fewer dramatically harmful effects (see Box 4.2).

4. The adverse effects of long-term maternal separation were apparently further confirmed by research carried out with rhesus monkeys in the USA. Harry and Margaret Harlow (Harlow, 1958; Harlow & Harlow, 1969) reported a series of studies in which young rhesus monkeys were separated from their mothers and raised in isolation. Either they were placed in total isolation, in steel cages with diffused light and filtered sound, or they were placed in partial isolation, in wire cages where they could see and hear, but could not contact, other monkeys. Either way, when such an isolation-reared monkey was released and placed with other monkeys, it showed complete social maladjustment, usually being terrified of other monkeys, crouching, rocking and biting itself, and occasionally being hyperaggressive even to a play invitation. If isolated for only the first 3 months, a young monkey could recover, but isolation for 6 or 12 months seemed to produce irreversible effects. At adolescence, these animals were unable to mate satisfactorily, and if a female did have a baby, she abused it rather than cared for it.

   This research apparently gave experimental backing for the long-term and irreversible effects of maternal deprivation, in another primate species. Yet these studies also confounded maternal deprivation with general social and sensory deprivation. Moreover, later research in this programme showed how severe deficits can be ameliorated (Novak, 1979; Suomi & Harlow, 1972). The breakthrough came when the isolation-reared monkeys, instead of being released directly into a peer group, were first placed individually with a younger monkey. For example, 6-month isolates were paired with 3-month-old 'therapist' monkeys. The younger monkey approaches and clings to the older one, rather than attacking it, and seems to help it catch up on the sort of physical contact experiences it has missed. Even 12-month isolates can be helped by this method. This research showed that deprivation effects may not be irreversible, if the right corrective treatment is used. It also suggests that peers can be as effective as mothers in reducing the effects of social isolation.

5. Bowlby cited evidence, from retrospective studies, that linked delinquency or behaviour problems in adolescence to some form of separation experience in childhood, such as hospitalization or a 'broken home' brought about by parental separation or divorce. Bowlby's interpretation was that the separation experience caused the later behaviour problems.

   However, this evidence is open to various interpretations. No clear causal link can be inferred. For example, suppose a correlational link has been found between delinquency and a 'broken home' in early childhood. Parental separation may mean that there was increased discord at the time, or later, or perhaps less supervision of the child given by a single parent. These might be the real causes of the delinquency, not the separation itself. Rutter (1981) argued that it is the discord often present in separating or divorcing families that led to later behaviour problems. It is not separation as such, since the death of a parent, while obviously affecting the child, does not usually lead to the negative outcomes that were ascribed to maternal deprivation.

In the long term, Bowlby's work in the 1960s had some beneficial effects. Together with other research, it led to a marked improvement in the standard of institutional care (see Box 4.2)

Box 4.2 The effect of early institutional rearing on the behaviour problems and affectional relationships of 4-year-old children

The objective of this study was to see whether institutional rearing in early life resulted in behaviour problems and disturbances in affectional relationships. The research was carried out in London, and focused on 26 children aged 4 years who had been admitted to a residential nursery before 4 months of age and were still there. (In 17 cases the mother or putative father still spoke of reclaiming the child; the remaining nine had not been adopted, for various other reasons.) There were two comparison groups. One consisted of 39 children who had also been admitted to a residential nursery before 4 months, but had either been adopted (24 children) or restored to their mothers (15 children) before 4 years of age. The other group comprised 30 children from local working-class homes who had not experienced any residential care. All the children were assessed at age 4.

The residential nurseries contained around 15–25 children, in small mixed-age groups. They were well provided with books and toys. Owing to rota systems and high staff turnover, the average number of staff who had worked with each child for at least a week over the previous 2 years was 26 (range 4–45).

Each child was interviewed individually, usually with a familiar nurse or the mother present. An intelligence test was given, ratings made of the child's observed behaviour, and questionnaires given to the parent or nurse about the child's behaviour problems and attachments. Most comparisons of the three groups employed chi-squared tests of significance. On the ratings of the child's behaviour, the main differences were between the adopted

/restored children and the other two groups. The adopted/restored children were more friendly to the interviewer and more cooperative and talkative during testing.

The institutional children had the highest score for behaviour problems, but only marginally. Their scores were significantly higher for 'poor concentration', 'problems with peers', 'temper tantrums' and 'clinging'. However, the home-reared children scored significantly higher for 'poor appetite or food fads', 'overactivity' and 'disobedience'. In the answers to the attachment questionnaire, the nurses reported that many of the institutional children (18 of the 26) did 'not care deeply about anyone'. While sometimes clinging and following, their attachments seemed shallow. Some of them, and some of the adopted/restored children (who otherwise had good attachments to natural or adoptive parents), were also described as being 'overfriendly' to strangers.

The independent variable in this study is the early rearing experience; the dependent variables are measures of behaviour problems and social behaviour. The encouraging findings of the study are that the children who had experienced institutional rearing did not have very marked or severe behaviour problems (and a related study found quite good linguistic and cognitive development in this group; see Chapter 18). Also, the adopted children generally did well and formed good relations with foster parents. However, most of the children still in institutional care had failed to form any strong attachments; this is not surprising, as staff turnover was high and staff tended to discourage strong specific relationships from developing.

A real-life study such as this cannot be as neatly designed as a laboratory experiment. The children in the three groups differed in some respects (including sex and racial background), so rearing experience is confounded by these other factors. Ideally, also, the investigator would not know the background of each child interviewed, but this was not possible. Finally, the interview material relies on nurses' or mothers' reports, which may be less objective than actual observations of the child's behaviour.

A follow-up of the same children at 8 years of age was subsequently reported (Tizard & Hodges, 1978). Only eight of the 26 children now remained in institutions. The late adopted children generally had good relations with their adoptive parents. The children all had reasonably good scores on IQ tests, and the early adopted children especially had high IQ and reading test scores. However, the long-term effects of the institutional-rearing experience did show up in teachers' ratings. Compared with the home-reared controls, the children who had experienced some institutional rearing were rated as more attention seeking, restless, disobedient and not getting on well with other children. Teachers' ratings, however, could be biased by negative stereotyping (i.e. if the teachers had negative beliefs about the effects of having been brought up in an institution, irrespective of the child's actual behaviour).

A further follow-up of the same children was made when they were 16 years of age (Hodges & Tizard, 1989). The sample available was now only about two-thirds of the original one, and a new comparison group of home-reared children was used, matched for sex, social class and family position. The findings were fairly clear. IQ scores were similar to those at 8 years, and the small variations were with family placement (adoptive/restored) rather than whether the child had or had not experienced early institutional care. However, both parents and teachers rated the ex-institutional children higher on emotional and behavioural problems than the home-reared children. Ex-institutional children had more problems with social relationships, both inside the family (mainly for children restored to natural parents) and outside the family, with peers (for both adopted and restored children). The adopted children tended to score higher on symptoms of anxiety, while those who had been restored to natural families tended to score higher on antisocial behaviour and school problems. These findings were supported by interviews with the young people themselves, suggesting they were not just due to stereotyped judgements by adults.

The careful follow-up of these children is an excellent example of the power of a longitudinal study, even with a relatively small sample size. The findings do indicate that experiencing extreme multiple caretaking in the first few years of life can be a noticeable risk factor for developing satisfactory social relationships, even by adolescence.

Based on material in Tizard, B. & Rees, J. (1975). *Journal of Child Psychology and Psychiatry, 16,* 61–73.

and in many areas the phasing out of institutional care in favour of fostering arrangements. It also led to much easier access of parents to a child in hospital care. A greater awareness of the child's emotional needs was stimulated. However, there were some effects that many people now see as detrimental, particularly a feeling of guilt amongst mothers who, often out of necessity, went out to work while their children were young, and placed their children in some form of alternative care (see next section). It is widely held that Bowlby was wrong to put such a strong emphasis on mothers, and on 'monotropism'.

However, it does seem that extreme shared care, with tens of adults involved, can lead to some problems. Perhaps in such situations children cannot form *any* strong attachment relationship. We have two different sources of evidence for this.

One source is institutional rearing. Children reared in homes can experience many short-term caregivers, and find it difficult to form a strong relationship. Studies by Tizard and colleagues in London (see Box 4.2) document this, and the kind of clinginess, attention seeking and hyperactivity that may be a consequence. A possible critique of this conclusion is that the adverse effects might be due to genetic factors, or prior adverse experiences, since the children tend to come from very troubled families with multiple psychosocial adversities. Another study by Roy, Rutter and Pickles (2000, 2004) compared outcomes at around 6 years for 19 children who had been in institutional care, with 19 children who had been in continuous foster care but who came from similar troubled birth families. Both groups had worse outcomes at school than classmates, but some of the boys from the institutional care group scored significantly worse on inattention, hyperactivity and emotional disturbance. The likely hypothesis here is that this difference was due to the high levels of multiple caregiving they experienced.

A different source of evidence comes from the Israeli kibbutzim. These communities have had a strong egalitarian philosophy, which led to children being raised communally, sleeping in large dormitories away from their parents, and being educated by nurses or *metaplot* (singular: *metapelet*); children would see their parents for an hour or two each day, but were otherwise raised in a group environment. A comprehensive review of the effects of this system was made by Aviezer et al. (1994). They concluded that collective sleeping arrangements were a problematic aspect of the kibbutz system; in fact, many kibbutzim have now reverted to children sleeping with their parents. Collective sleeping arrangements were associated with a greater incidence of insecure (ambivalent) attachment, as assessed by the Strange Situation; the authors concluded that in this respect the traditional kibbutzim deviated too far from what is natural for human infants and their parents. The study by Avezier et al. (2002) described earlier (p. 119) found that collective sleeping arrangements after age 6 predicted less emotional security at age 11. Scharf (2001) reported that adolescents who had experienced prolonged communal sleeping arrangements in kibbutzim had less autonomous attachment representations on the AAI. Despite possibly negative effects of communal rearing on attachment, however, it can foster group-oriented skills and close peer relationships (Avezier et al., 1994).

An overall assessment is that it is a normal process for 1- and 2-year-olds to form strong attachments to a few persons, characterized by proximity seeking and separation protest. Bonds can be formed later, as studies of late adoption show, and many of the apparent adverse effects of 'maternal deprivation' are now seen as due to other factors, perhaps not specific to the first 2 or 3 years of life. But in certain more limited senses than Bowlby first proposed, it may be that this early period is more crucial for social adjustment than are later years, and the issue has resurfaced more recently in renewed debates about full-time early non-maternal care (see below).

CARE OUTSIDE THE FAMILY

Fostering

Foster care involves long-term parental care by non-family members. As the previous section has evidenced, foster care can be beneficial as an alternative to institutional care, though obviously the circumstances and context of both are important.

In fact, anthropological studies have shown that in many traditional societies, kinship-based fostering is common. Often in middle childhood, children may go to spend considerable time with relatives—aunts/uncles or cousins. Leinaweaver (2014) documents how this can bring notable benefits—such as expanding the family from the perspective of the child, and giving him/her new opportunities for education or apprenticeship—if the relatives live in a town with better schooling, for example, or are skilled in a certain trade. However, she notes that such practices are not always beneficial—for example, if a foster child is treated differently from birth children, or if poorer relatives place a child with wealthier relatives who use them as 'child labour'. The child's own wishes are an important factor in this.

Childminding and Day Care

In many Western societies, one view, held quite widely in the mid-20th century, has been that mothers of young children should stay at home to look after them until they are old enough to go to nursery or infant school—that is, 3–5 years of age. Nevertheless, it has always been the case that many mothers of young children have gone out to work, either through preference or through financial necessity. Some parents manage to share care in their own home with grandparents, older siblings, friends or neighbours. The alternatives are to place the child with a childminder or in a day care centre (such as a crèche or day nursery).

A study of 5,107 infants in Australia (part of a longitudinal study of Australian children; Harrison & Ungerer, 2005) found that 36% of infants aged up to 1 year were being cared for regularly by someone other than the parents they lived with. Of these, the most frequent arrangements relied on grandparents (37%), followed by day care centres/nurseries/crèches (22%), other informal care (12%), a mixture of grandparent and informal care (8%) and family day care (8%), with smaller numbers in other mixed arrangements (for some comparable UK figures, see p. 138).

Childminding, often called family day care or home-based day care, can provide a convenient form of day care with high adult to child ratios, and can be provided by professional minders. A review of childminding in England (Kinnaird & Jones, 2007) found that there were some 58,000 active registered childminders (paid to look after one or more children under 8 for more than 2 hours a day) looking after some quarter of a million children (around four children per childminder). More than half of these children were preschoolers, and 18% were under 2 years. However, about one-third of childminders had no relevant qualification for the job.

There has been considerable controversy over both childminding and centre-based day care. Some research in the 1950s and 1960s (including the writings of Bowlby reviewed above) led to cautions about these alternative forms of day care. Some earlier studies in the UK of (non-relative) childminding were very critical of the effects; Mayall and Petrie (1983) found that the children often appeared insecure in the minder's home, and scored below expectations on tests of language or cognitive ability. American research also found that much family childcare was unregulated and poorly paid, and had high staff turnover (Golbeck & Harlan, 1997).

More nuanced findings emerged from a study in London by Melhuish and colleagues (1990a, 1990b). They compared the progress of children who (starting before 9 months of age) had experienced three main types of non-maternal care: with relatives, childminding or nursery care. Melhuish et al. improved on some earlier work by controlling for measures of social class (such as mothers' education) that discriminated between the three groups. They found that the adult–child ratio was best for care by a relative, next for childminders and lowest for nursery care. At 18 months, communication to children, and also some aspects of the children's language development, were highest for children cared for by relatives and lowest in the nursery group. By 3 years of age, the children in nurseries continued to receive less language stimulation; their naming vocabulary was the least developed, though they did not differ on other language measures. There were no significant differences in cognitive development, however, and the nursery children did show more prosocial behaviour such as sharing, cooperation and empathy with others. In this research, childminding came out rather intermediate in outcomes, but doubtless much depends on the quality of the childminding experience. Although childminders should be registered, and checks on quality made, it is known that much illegal childminding can occur (Jackson & Jackson, 1979).

Nursery or centre-based day care is normally registered, but large variations in quality can still occur in terms of staff–child ratios, staff turnover and whether there is a stimulating, well-provided environment. In the 1970s and 1980s, a large body of research (much of it carried out in the USA) suggested that day care does not have adverse effects provided that it is of high quality. In such circumstances, it was concluded that day care had no overall effects on intellectual development and did not disrupt the child's attachment relationship with the mother (Belsky & Steinberg, 1978; Clarke-Stewart, 1982), although it did increase the degree to which the child interacts, both positively and negatively, with peers.

The controversy over day care was reopened in the late 1980s. Combining data from five studies, Belsky (1988, p. 401) concluded that 'a rather robust association emerges between extensive non-maternal care experience initiated in the first year of life and insecure infant–mother attachment assessed in the Strange Situation'; when day care of more than 20 hours per week began before the child was 1 year of age, the risk of insecure attachment to the mother was 43%, compared to 26% for infants with less or no day care. Not everyone agreed with Belsky's conclusion. Clarke-Stewart (1989) queried whether the SS is a valid procedure for infants of working mothers (who experience many more routine separations); whether insecure attachment to mothers can be generalized to general emotional security; and whether the differences may be due to other factors (e.g. differences between mothers who choose to work and those who do not).

Subsequent research has generally used a broader range of measures and has attempted to control for other factors by using large samples. The findings are not always consistent, and some have not supported Belsky's (1988) hypothesis. For example, a study of 1,100 Bermudan children by Scarr and Thompson (1994) compared infants placed in non-maternal care either before or after 1 year of age, and for more or less than 20 hours per week, and made assessments when the children were 2 years and 4 years old. The researchers found no differences in socioemotional or cognitive measures.

Specifically looking at outcomes for aggression, Borge et al. (2004) actually found that children in home care showed more mother-rated physical aggression at 2 and 3 years than children in day care. This was a large sample of 3,431 Canadian children, and the researchers divided the sample into low risk and high risk based on a family functioning scale. As can be

Table 4.6   Mother-rated physical aggression of children in home care and day care, in low-risk and high-risk families.

	Home care	Day care
Low risk	4.1%	4.1%
High risk	11.5%	7.9%

Source: Data from Borge, A.I.H., Rutter, M.; Cote, S. & Tremblay, R.E. (2004). Early childcare and physical aggression: Differentiating social selection and social causation. *Journal of Child Psychology and Psychiatry*, 45, 367–376.

seen in Table 4.6, ratings of physical aggression were unaffected by care arrangements for low-risk families, which made up 84% of the sample; these children were mostly not especially aggressive. But for high-risk families, children in day care were significantly *less* physically aggressive, suggesting that, here, day care was a protective factor. This is nevertheless a surprising finding, as the more usual concern has been that early day care makes children *more* aggressive.

In a study of 935 preschool children in Norway, the type and quantity of childcare experience up to 4.5 years had no significant relationship to teacher-rated social competence, behaviour problems or externalizing behaviours (Solheim, Wichstrom, Belsky & Berg-Nielsen, 2013). The only significant finding was that more time spent in childcare (as opposed to family-based care) predicted greater child–caregiver conflict; however, the effect size for this was small. Quality of care was not assessed in this study, but the researchers argued that this was generally high in the Norwegian context.

The NICHD Longitudinal Study

The National Institute of Child Health and Development (NICHD) Longitudinal Study of Early Child Care and Youth Development (SECCYD; see Table 1.1) has provided important evidence on day care effects, from a large sample at 10 sites in the USA. Altogether, 1,364 children with various childcare experiences have been followed up.

An early report on attachment outcomes by 2 years (NICHD Early Child Care Research Network, 1997) did not find any main effects of day care amount or quality on attachment security, but there was more insecure attachment for boys with long or poor-quality day care who also experienced low maternal sensitivity/responsiveness. A report on peer interaction (NICHD Early Child Care Research Network, 2001) found that children with more hours in day care were rated by caregivers as more negative in peer play, but this was not supported by observational data.

Subsequent reports followed up the children at 4.5, 7, 9, 11 and 12 years (Belsky et al., 2007b; NICHD Early Child Care Research Network, 2006). The consensus from these reports appears to give different sets of longer term outcomes, for cognitive/language development and social development.

Cognitive/language development: High-quality day care is related to better language and cognition scores, and to higher academic achievement in the primary school years. These effects decrease over time, with just a small positive effect on vocabulary scores by 11 years (5th grade in the USA).

Social development: Quantity of day care, but not quality, is related to higher levels of aggression and disobedience. This appears to be more so for non-relative day care than for relative day care (e.g. by grandparents). The effects decrease over time but, for centre-based day care only, do remain significant even by 12 years (6th grade).

Two other important and consistent findings qualified the above (NICHD Early Child Care Research Network, 2006). First, both the positive (cognitive, language) and negative (behaviour problems) outcomes of day care were highest for centre-based day care rather than other forms, such as home-based care and care by relatives; in fact, further analyses of these data suggest that there are no adverse effects of paternal or grandparental care (Linting & Van IJzendoorn, 2009). Second, the effect sizes are generally outweighed by measures of parenting quality (e.g. Belsky et al., 2007b).

Three further factors mentioned in recent research are temperament interactions, group effects and genetic moderation.

Temperament interactions: Pluess and Belsky (2009), further analysing NICHD data on teacher-rated behaviour problems and social competence at 4.5 years, found that, although there was no overall effect of childcare quality, there was an interaction effect: children with difficult temperament showed more behaviour problems when in low-quality childcare, but less when in high-quality childcare.

Group effects: Dmitrieva et al. (2007) used data from another US longitudinal study, the ECLS (see Table 1.1). What they found evidence for was a kind of contagion or diffusion effect: if there were more children with extensive exposure to childcare (especially centre-based care) in a classroom, then there was more teacher-rated externalizing behaviour, even when individual factors (family background, individual experiences of childcare) were accounted for. On the positive side, there were indications of a similar diffusion effect for academic achievement.

This finding has been used to argue that, although the effects of day care may be fairly small in terms of individual effect size, this does not mean that the effects are unimportant. Many children may be affected, and even if the average effect on a child is small, for some it may be considerable. Furthermore, there is the possibility of contagion or diffusion. As Belsky (2009, p. 236) argued, 'it could prove very misguided to dismiss small effects of personal childcare history on individual functioning, whether they be of the adverse or beneficial variety'.

Genetic moderation: Belsky and Pluess (2013) used data from a subset of the NICHD sample, comprising 508 Caucasian children where consent was given for DNA testing at age 15. Interest was on the DRD4 and 5-HTTLPR alleles, related to dopamine and serotonin transmission respectively (see Chapter 2). Measures included childcare quality, child temperament, parenting quality from 6 to 54 months, and several child outcomes at preschool, kindergarten and annually up to 6th grade. The DRD4 7-repeat allele was found to interact with parenting quality to predict some child outcomes, but not beyond 1st grade. Specifically, teacher-reported externalizing problems at 54 months were predicted by poor childcare quality (as found in the main NICHD study), but this was only significant for children carrying the 7-repeat allele. Although a small crossover interaction was present (see Figure 2.16(b)), the statistical analyses suggested a diathesis-stress model fitted best (see Figure 2.16(a)). However, for teacher-reported social skills in kindergarten, a significant crossover interaction was found, supporting a differential susceptibility model (see Figure 2.16(b)). Overall, better childcare quality predicted better social skills in kindergarten, but children with the 7-repeat allele did noticeably worse when they had experienced poor-quality childcare, and noticeably better when they had experienced better-quality childcare. This is similar to the temperament finding reported by Pluess and Belsky (2009), above, but further analyses suggested that the DRD4 effect was largely independent of the temperament effect.

Stop and Think

Does the evidence support concerns expressed about early, intensive day care?

Day Care: An Overview

Issues of day care are clearly complex and influenced by many variables. Interaction effects are important. The findings from Borge et al. (2004) in Canada and Solheim et al. (2013) in Norway, noted earlier, might appear inconsistent with the NICHD findings from the USA, as regards effects of childcare experiences on aggression, but if the Canadian and Norwegian facilities were generally of high quality, then this is in fact more consistent with the Pluess and Belsky (2009) analyses. Similarly, Harrison and Ungerer (2005) point out that the NICHD findings might not apply to the Australian situation.

Research in this area moves fast and may be overtaken by historical changes. In the UK, the 1989 Children Act helped bring about an expansion of interest in nursery care, and quality of care may have improved in the period since the Melhuish et al. (1990a, 1990b) study. Similarly, the NICHD study findings in the USA are based on children born in 1991.

A broad perspective is also useful. Besides looking at effects on children, we need to bear in mind that help with childcare can be liberating for mothers. A mother who stays at home to look after young children full time can feel frustrated or isolated, particularly if she has little support from her husband or relatives. Research on the causes of depression in women has identified a number of contributory factors, one of which is being at home full time with two or more children under 5 if other stresses are present (Brown & Harris, 1978).

Interestingly, in Sweden, each parent has non-transferable rights to about 2 months of highly compensated parental leave (at least 80% of pay); in addition, they have about 9 more highly paid months, which they can share as they wish. Almost all fathers take paid parental leave, and 22% of all highly paid parental leave days taken are taken by fathers. Thus, the concern about day care starting in the first year need not worry the Swedes (Haas et al., 2009).

FATHERS

How important is the other parent—the father? And has the role of the father changed in recent years, as is often suggested? Research in a number of societies has shown that fathers can fulfil a parenting role just as much as mothers, for example in single-parent father families, but that typically, fathers do not have such a large part in child-rearing and domestic tasks as do mothers, especially when children are young (Lewis & Lamb, 2007).

Father involvement can be measured along a number of dimensions. Lewis and Lamb (2007) mention three in particular:

1. *Engagement*: direct interaction between father and child
2. *Accessibility*: potential availability for interaction
3. *Responsibility*: providing resources and care for child's needs.

although it is recognized that other activities (such as working to earn money to support the household) can be important aspects of fathering that do not imply direct involvement.

So far, the highest degree of father involvement in any human society seems to be amongst the Aka, a hunter-gatherer people in the Central African Republic. Fathers were found to be present with an infant or child for 88% of the time, and to be holding an infant for 22% of the time. This high degree of physical intimacy by fathers seems to be encouraged by the overlapping subsistence activities of men and women. Men do not just leave women in the campsite to look after children while they go hunting; women often assist in hunting, and men often carry infants back after the hunt. Nevertheless, even in this society mothers still engage in more childcare than fathers (Hewlett, 1987).

Another society where paternal care and involvement are encouraged is Sweden. Here, equality between the sexes has been encouraged since the 1960s, including legislation about work opportunities and parental leave, and a continuous series of advertising campaigns to encourage fathers to take childcare responsibilities seriously (Klinth, 2008). While this has had some impact, it is still true that, in dual-earner families, Swedish mothers do more housework and provide more childcare than fathers do, although over time the gender gap in unpaid work has lessened (see Haas & Hwang, 2008, for a review).

Historical Changes in Father Involvement

> I think more's expected of fathers now than 30 years ago. 30 years ago the man's responsibility was to go out to work and come home . . . but I think gradually it's become that way where from a man having maybe 10% of the responsibility, his responsibility has gone up, he's going up like 50%.
>
> *(White British father, cited in Hauari & Hollingworth, 2009, p. 43)*

In Western societies, there is evidence that fathering involvement has shown some increase since the mid-20th century (Dette-Hagenmeyer, Erzinger & Reichle, 2014). Lewis (1986) carried out an interview study of 100 fathers of 1-year-old children in Nottingham, UK, and was able to compare his data, obtained in 1980, with similar data obtained by Newson and Newson (1963) in 1960. One change over that period was that the majority of fathers began attending all stages of the birth of their child; in the 1950s, fathers were discouraged from attending hospital deliveries. There were also significant increases in the number of fathers helping in the period after birth, and getting up for the baby at night.

However, mothers predominantly did the childcare, feeding and nappy changing. At least two factors seemed to contribute to this. First, the father will more often be in longer hours of employment. Lewis (1986) did find that fathers contributed more when the mother was also working. Secondly, it is easy for fathers to feel marginalized in baby care; mothers are seen as the 'experts' at this. Indeed, it is only mothers who can breastfeed! In addition, mothers may contribute to keeping their own areas of expertise, as the following interview demonstrates.

Interviewer:	How about changing him? Do you often change his nappies?
Father (to wife):	Don't think I've done that, have I?
Wife:	In the first week when I weren't well.
Interviewer:	Is there any reason why you haven't?
Wife:	Only 'cause I've always been there. They don't bother me in the slightest, you know.
Father:	Nappies don't bother me, you know. If Jan [wife] turned round to me and said, 'Could you do it for me, then?'. . . Like I say, she's a very competent mother.

(Lewis, 1986, p. 100)

Since the 1980s, the evidence is that there may have been some further increase in fathers' involvement, but that it is patchy and slow (Flouri, 2005; Lewis & Lamb, 2007). Many factors complicate these trends, for example, changes in employment rates for men and women. In the USA, Cabrera et al. (2000) suggested that a dramatic increase in mothers working over the previous 40 years had led to an appreciable increase in the time fathers spend with their children. Also relevant are changes in population composition; for example, many Western European countries have experienced considerable immigration from other cultures in the last 30 years. In a detailed study of 29 British families from White British, Pakistani and Black African and Caribbean backgrounds, Hauari and Hollingworth (2009) noted suggestions of ethnic differences; for example, some Pakistani fathers held quite traditional views.

> I mean all fathers, me too, I don't want to work for my house, my wife is there for cooking, for looking after my kids. That's all.
>
> *(Pakistani father, cited in Hauari & Hollingworth, 2009, p. 36)*

However, these views were subject to challenge.

> He's from back home [Pakistan], he's been here what, 13, 14 years, he doesn't believe men should do the cooking or cleaning or anything. I teach my boy to vacuum and clean up as well, which he [husband] doesn't like.
>
> *(Pakistani mother, cited in Hauari & Hollingworth, 2009, p. 37)*

Differences in the mother's and father's behaviour with children may lessen after infancy, especially when mothers are also working outside the home. While mothers continue to spend more time in caregiving tasks, and remain closer to children, fathers do spend more time in play and recreational activities (Lamb, 2010; Lewis & Lamb, 2007).

Fathering and Child Outcomes

In normally functioning and intact families, there is considerable evidence that more father involvement is correlated with positive child outcomes. It is of course difficult to disentangle cause and effect (father involvement may help child adjustment, or poorly behaved children may lessen father involvement, or both may reflect other factors such as poverty). However, longitudinal studies, for example using the NCDS or the BCS70 (see Table 1.1), do suggest some positive effects of father involvement, even when many other factors are accounted for by using regression analyses. Flouri (2005) reported a number of studies carrying out such analyses on samples in the UK. The findings were complex and varied, but some are as follows.

- Father involvement and mother involvement covaried, so that in some families both parents were more involved, in others less so, but it is still possible to separate out some father effects that were found independently of mother effects.
- Some positive effects of father involvement were found for their children's mental health as adults, but only significantly for daughters.
- Father involvement generally had positive effects on their children's academic development, including, for example, educational attainment by age 20.
- Father involvement was inversely related to their child's aggression with peers, and also to delinquency in adolescence in the case of sons.

Of course, these positive findings do suppose that the father involvement is of a positive kind. The Dunedin Longitudinal Study in New Zealand (Jaffee et al., 2003; and see Table 1.1) found that when fathers engaged in a lot of antisocial behaviour, then father involvement actually predicted greater conduct problems in their children (whereas the usual trend, as in Flouri's studies, was for greater father involvement to predict less antisocial behaviour).

Non-resident or Absent Fathers

Dunn (2004a) reviewed the evidence regarding non-resident fathers and how they impact on their children. She concluded that positive adjustment outcomes were related to four factors: the economic support provided by the non-resident father; the quality of the father–child relationship (specifically involvement, closeness and authoritative parenting style); and, to some extent, the frequency of father–child contact and the quality of the father–mother relationship.

In a longitudinal study of single teenage mothers in a deprived area (Borkowski et al., 2007), it was found that the support of families was crucial for the healthy development of the children. Often this came from the maternal grandmother. However, where the teenage (absent) father maintained some form of contact with his child, that factor resulted in significantly greater emotional health in the children. The absent father's involvement in adolescence was also a protective factor against psychological distress at that point in the young person's development.

Lanz et al. (1999) found that teenagers in non-intact families found it harder to talk to their parents about their fears and anxieties. There is consistent evidence too that father involvement is inversely related to adolescents' aggression with peers. In other words, young people in families where the father is absent are more likely to be involved in fighting and arguing with their peers.

There does seem to be a link between father absence and teenage pregnancy (see also Chapter 19). Early father-absent girls have the highest rates of early sexual activity and teenage pregnancy, followed by late father-absent girls, followed by father-present girls (Ellis et al., 2003).

It is important to consider the social contexts within which father absence takes place and the constructions that mothers and their children place on the absence. The death of a father is clearly a traumatic event in a child's life but it will be experienced differently from the absence of a father, perhaps through separation/divorce. Some of the outcomes will be similar (grief and loss) and others will be different (feelings of abandonment). Whatever the circumstances, it is important for fathers to be involved with their children and to maintain that contact in whatever form they can. The presence of a father is a protective factor against emotional distress in boys and girls; it also seems to be a protective factor against early teenage pregnancy. Families take many and diverse forms. The nuclear family is one form but by no means the only one. The important thing is for a child to feel loved and secure in the family where they are being nurtured.

GRANDPARENTS

About 70% of middle-aged and older people become grandparents. Since the average age of becoming a grandparent, in Western societies, is about 50 years for women and a couple of years older for men, they are likely to remain grandparents for some 25 years or more; about a third of their life-span. Grandparenthood is thus an important part of the life cycle for most people (Broad, 2007; Dench & Ogg, 2002; Glaser et al., 2010).

Grandparents can have considerable influence on their grandchildren's behaviour and development. Tinsley and Parke (1984) described both indirect and direct influences.

Indirect influence has an effect without there necessarily being any direct interaction. For example, the parent–child interaction will be influenced by the way the parent has been brought up and the experiences of child rearing that the parent has had modelled by his or her parent, i.e. the grandparent (see discussion of intergenerational transmission of attachment, p. 122). Grandparents can also provide emotional and financial support for parents, which will be especially valuable at times of emotional or financial stress. Some research on bringing up children with disabilities suggests that family functioning is helped by the grandparent's support of the parents, more than directly to the (grand)children (Trute, 2003).

Direct influence depends on direct interactions between grandparent and grandchild. These are typically reasonably frequent. In the UK, Dench and Ogg (2002) found that (according to grandparent reports), 30% saw their grandchild(ren) several times a week, and 68% at least once a month. Many grandparents live fairly close to their grandchildren and proximity is important for frequency of face-to-face contact but, increasingly, grandparents are keeping in contact with grandchildren through email and the internet (Quadrello et al., 2005). While only a small proportion of grandparents live in the same house as grandchildren in Western societies, in the Pacific Rim countries of China, Japan and Korea, family ties including grandparental bonds tend to be especially close. In these countries, many grandparents still live in three-generation households, and family ties are perceived as very close (Hwang & St James-Roberts, 1998).

Usually, grandparents have quite satisfying contacts with grandchildren, though, as with any relationship, there can be conflicts. In modern Western societies, the grandparental role is generally seen as being one of support, but not of authority or discipline. Lavers and Sonuga-Barke (1997) found that parents' satisfaction is high in these circumstances, but can be less so if grandparents are seen as underinvolved (not willing to help out or support grandchildren) or overinvolved (interfering in matters, such as discipline, which parents regard as their responsibility).

Direct influences can take many forms. Grandparents can pass on information and values directly to grandchildren. They are particularly well placed to pass on the family history and knowledge of times past. A grandparent can act as a companion and be an important part of the child's social network. Many grandparents enjoy conversations with grandchildren, asking them to run errands and giving them small gifts. The process is not always one-way. Jessel et al. (2004) observed families of Bangladeshi origin in the East End of London, and found examples of synergistic learning interactions between grandparents and grandchildren. The grandparent would help the grandchild learn about their Bengali language and heritage, while the grandchild would be helping the grandparent to learn how to use computers and word processing.

Grandparents as Surrogate Parents

Sometimes grandparents step into the role of parents. This is usually in a part-time capacity, when grandparents act as babysitters or childminders for working parents. In fact, this may be the most common form of non-parental care in many societies, although it is often ignored in statistics. In the UK, Dench and Ogg (2002) found that 53% of grandparents reported helping with daytime childcare at least monthly, and 22% weekly or more. A pan-European survey found that 58% of grandmothers and 50% of grandfathers had provided regular or occasional childcare in the past year for their grandchildren aged 15 or under (Hank & Buber, 2009).

In China, a survey by Falbo (1991) found that grandparental preschool care was associated with somewhat better school performance than parental care. There are possible confounds in this finding (such as socioeconomic status), but frequency of grandparental contact, plus grandparental educational attainment, did predict language and mathematics scores in 1st and 5th grade children. Similarly, Korean grandmothers from a sample of 1,326 extended families were accredited with increasing their grandchildren's resilience by providing sources of attachment, affection and knowledge, as well as having indirect effects through their support of parents (Hwang & St James-Roberts, 1998).

More rarely, a grandparent acts as a full-time surrogate parent. This can be either in a grandparent-maintained household or in a household where the grandparent is coresident (for example, in a single-parent family or with a teenage pregnancy). It is most often the maternal grandmother who fills these roles. However, grandfathers can be important too. Radin et al. (1991) studied families of teen mothers, where the young mother lived with her parents and the father was absent. Here, grandfather involvement was found to have a direct positive influence on young grandchildren of teen mothers, especially for grandsons.

In the case of full custodial care by grandparents (grandparent-maintained households), a rather consistent picture is that many such grandparents report high levels of stress and poor health. It is difficult to disentangle cause and effect here, as often the grandparents are acting as surrogate parents because of ongoing psychological and financial difficulties in the family. Support for grandparents in such situations appears an important priority (Broad, 2007; Carlini-Marlatt, 2005).

Grandparents and Divorced Families

Grandparents can act directly as a source of emotional support, acting as a 'buffer' in cases where a grandchild is in conflict with parents or where the parents are in conflict with each other. For example, Johnson (1983) analysed the responses of 58 US grandmothers to the divorce of one of their children. These grandmothers generally maintained their level of contact with the grandchildren, and the younger ones especially (below 65 years of age) often increased their level of contact. One grandmother described how she filled a gap in the custody arrangements.

I pick them up on Friday after work. We go to the Pizza Hut for dinner—then home to watch TV. I keep lots of goodies around for them. They fight, I shush them. Then they zonk out. The next morning, I fix breakfast—they watch TV. Then I take them to their dad's and dump them. It's kinda nice.

(Johnson, 1983, pp. 553–554)

In these more difficult family situations, grandparents can often provide some stability, support and nurturance to the grandchild(ren) and family, as well as financial assistance or childcare (Dench & Ogg, 2002; Ferguson et al., 2004). Lussier et al. (2002), using data from the ALSPAC longitudinal study in the UK (see Table 1.1), found that closeness to maternal (but not paternal) grandparents was significantly associated with grandchild adjustment when parents had separated, even when other family variables were controlled for. Attar-Schwartz et al. (2009) studied a sample of more than 1,500 secondary school students, and found that greater grandparental involvement was associated with fewer emotional problems and more prosocial behaviour generally, but that this was especially so for those adolescents from one-parent and step-families.

However, it is not always easy for grandparents to see grandchildren after parental divorce. Some paternal grandparents, especially, may be prevented from seeing grandchildren after an acrimonious divorce and when the children stay with the mother. The issue of rights of access of grandparents to their grandchildren has been of recent concern in many countries, and grandparents' rights groups have sprung up to represent their interests. A study in Canada of such grandparents deprived of access to grandchildren found a strong grief reaction, with nearly half reporting related health problems and emotional difficulties (Kruk, 1995). In a similar UK sample, Drew and Smith (1999) found that many grandparents were experiencing chronic grief, mental health problems, symptoms of posttraumatic stress (mostly intrusive thoughts) and lowered life satisfaction.

Since the loss of my grandson it has been a dreadful time mentally and physically, my health has suffered, I don't sleep well, and some days the pain is unbearable. Birthdays and Christmas time are devastating. I just long to give him a big hug and tell him how much I love him. What really worries me, is does my grandson think I've abandoned him and that I don't love him anymore, he is such a special little boy.

(Drew & Smith, 1999, p. 114)

TYPES OF FAMILY

The stereotypical family is of a heterosexual married couple with their biological children (usually two of them!). But in reality there is much variation in types of families. In Britain, for example, Clarke (1992) found that 80% of children under 16 were with both natural parents and 9% were with one natural parent and one step-parent; 10% were in lone-parent families (usually, but not always, the mother) and about 1% in other arrangements. These figures applied to one moment of time, and it was estimated that through their entire childhood, only about half of British children (53%) stayed with both married natural parents. More recent UK statistics show that lone-parent families have remained at around 10% from 1991 through to 2013 (Office for National Statistics, 2013b). In the USA, Cabrera et al. (2000) noted an increase in the number of single-parent families (usually mother-headed families) from 6% in 1960 to 24% by 2000; as in the UK, some 50% of children will experience their parents divorcing (Lansford, 2009).

This could be seen as a worrying trend, in that supportive father involvement with children is generally related to positive outcomes, as we saw above. However, mother-headed families cover a wide range—including families still suffering from the stress of separation and divorce (see below); families where fathers retain active involvement through joint custody or frequent visits; and families where fathers are effectively absent. The Dunedin Longitudinal Study (see Table 1.1) found that, of young men aged 26, 19% had become fathers, but that those who had experienced a stressful rearing environment and had a history of conduct problems were more likely to become fathers at an early age, and to spend less time living with their child (Jaffee et al., 2001). The authors concluded that these absent fathers might have difficulty providing positive parenting without effective support to help them deal with poor social-psychological adjustment.

Lesbian and Gay Parents

A small number of children are brought up by gay or lesbian parents. What are the effects of this on children? Patterson (1992) reviewed a number of relevant studies. She concluded that gender identity, gender role behaviour and sexual preferences of children of gay and lesbian parents fall within the normal range of variation; peer relationships were found to be satisfactory. This is supported by more recent research.

Golombok et al. (1997) compared children aged around 6 years in the UK in 30 lesbian mother families, 42 single heterosexual mother families and 41 two-parent heterosexual families. They found little difference between lesbian and heterosexual single-mother families. In the fatherless families (whether lesbian or heterosexual), there was actually greater mother interaction and attachment security, although children had lower self-esteem. In a follow-up of these families at adolescence, MacCallum and Golombok (2004) found both more interaction and more conflict in fatherless families, but no negative effects on social and emotional development and no major differences for children in lesbian families. Rivers et al. (2008) found that children raised by female same-sex couples did not differ from others in victimization at school, psychosocial functioning or social support.

In the Netherlands, Bos et al. (2004) found few differences between lesbian and heterosexual couples except, perhaps not surprisingly, that lesbian mothers 'appear less attuned to traditional child-rearing goals' than heterosexual mothers. In the US, Chan et al. (1998) reported findings from 80 families with children aged around 7 years, conceived by donor insemination: 55 were lesbian and 25 heterosexual families, 50 were couples and 30 were single-parent families. They found that child adjustment was unrelated to number of parents or sexual orientation (but was related to parental stress and conflict, irrespective of family type).

To date, this research does not suggest that children of gay or lesbian parents develop differently in any significant sense (see also p. 225). Other aspects of parenting (such as parenting style and conflict between parents) appear to be more important.

STYLES OF PARENTING

Independent of the body of research on attachment security, studies have been made of how parents may vary in their styles of child rearing. Some parents believe in strong discipline, others do not, for example. An American psychologist, Diana Baumrind, tried to conceptualize three global styles of child rearing in the USA (Baumrind, 1967, 1980).

1. *Authoritarian*: parents who have strict ideas about discipline and behaviour that are not open to discussion
2. *Authoritative*: parents who have ideas about behaviour and discipline that they are willing to explain and discuss with children and, at times, are willing to adapt
3. *Permissive*: parents who have relaxed ideas about behaviour and discipline.

Maccoby and Martin (1983) felt that it would be best to separate out two dimensions of parenting style: how demanding or undemanding parents are about their children's behaviour, on the one hand, and how responsive or unresponsive they are to their children on the other. They therefore produced the four-fold classification shown in Table 4.7. This approach to parenting styles, typically measured by questionnaires given to parents, has been widely used and does predict aspects of children's development, such as academic achievement; for a review, see Spera (2005). Let's look at a few examples.

Dekovic and Janssens (1992) had a sample of 112 children aged 6–11 years. They ascertained their sociometric status in school (see Chapter 5), and their prosocial behaviour from ratings by teachers and classmates (see Chapter 9). They estimated parenting style from observations at home in the evenings when both parents were present (time-consuming but probably more valid than self-report questionnaires). They found that authoritative parents tended to have popular, prosocial children; authoritarian parents tended to have sociometrically rejected children.

Steinberg et al. (1992) carried out a larger, longitudinal study, of 6,400 adolescents aged 14–18. For this size sample, they obviously had to rely on questionnaire measures of parenting style. They also asked the adolescents to report on parental involvement in their schooling, and obtained their school grades for achievement. They found that authoritative parenting was related to better school performance. Interestingly, there was a mediating effect of parental involvement, usually thought of as helpful in this context. The parent's involvement in the adolescent's school work was especially helpful when it came from authoritative parents, but not so much when it came from authoritarian parents—maybe the latter can be too critical and not so supportive as authoritative parents. *Laissez-faire* or undemanding parents were not involved very much with school.

Steinberg et al. (1992) characterized authoritative parenting in their study as having three components: parental acceptance and warmth; behavioural supervision and strictness; and psychological autonomy granting or democracy. However, this highlights a difficulty with the Maccoby and Martin scheme (see Table 4.7), which includes the last two components but does not explicitly include warmth—nor, indeed, other possibly important dimensions such as parental punitiveness. Baumrind's original global approach does include more components (Baumrind identified authoritative parents as being warm and accepting of their children, in contrast to authoritarian parents), but confounds them so that one does not know which component is responsible for the differences found. These difficulties were

Table 4.7   Styles of parenting from Maccoby and Martin (1983).

	Responsive	Unresponsive
Demanding	Authoritative	Authoritarian
Undemanding	Permissive	Uninvolved

discussed in a review by Darling and Steinberg (1993), who also pointed out the cultural specificity of this work.

Cultural differences may be important (Stewart & Bond, 2002). In the USA, where much of the research has been done, these parenting-style schemes appear to have greater predictiveness for European-American families than they do for African-American families. A study in Spain by Martinez and Garcia (2007) found that, in Spanish 13–16-year-olds, indulgent (permissive) parenting (followed by authoritative parenting) was correlated with higher academic and family self-esteem than authoritarian or neglectful parenting. Martinez and Garcia characterize Spain as a horizontal-collectivist culture (horizontal in terms of egalitarian rather than hierarchical relations, collectivist in terms of influence of others on oneself); they contrast Spain in this way with a vertical-collectivist culture (such as China) or a vertical-individualistic culture (such as the USA).

Parenting styles in China have had some scrutiny, especially following the publication of Amy Chua's (2011) book on being a 'tiger mother'—a semi-popular book in which she drew on research and her own experience to extol a (perhaps extreme) version of Chinese parenting which put great pressure on her children to achieve academically, with severe criticism or shaming of any failure. It is in fact the case, as evidenced by international surveys of academic achievement such as the Program for International Student Assessment (PISA) (2013), that Chinese children do well academically—better than children in the USA or UK in mathematics, for example. Pomerantz et al. (2014) suggest that this may be due to a holistic style of parenting in China, which combines strong involvement in learning-related activities with a rather authoritarian, controlling style that puts more emphasis on correcting mistakes than on praising success. Whereas a Western mother might say, 'Eight of ten right—you did well!', a Chinese mother might say, 'Why did you make two mistakes?'. Pomerantz et al. suggest that Chinese children feel pressured to do well in school to please their parents, and this does enhance academic achievement, but may have a cost in terms of emotional well-being and happiness. In an empirical comparison of Chinese, European-American and African-American mothers, Ng, Pomerantz and Deng (2014) found that Chinese mothers were more controlling than American mothers with their early adolescent children (especially European-American mothers; African-American mothers were intermediate on controlling). For Chinese mothers, controlling was associated with a feeling that their own worth was contingent on their child's performance, whereas American mothers saw their child's performance in a more individualistic and autonomous light. Pomerantz et al. (2014) thus see costs and benefits to both styles of parenting.

Stop and Think

Do parenting styles provide a radically different approach to parenting from attachment theory, or are they complementary?

Conflict between Parents

There is considerable research evidence that conflict between parents and intimate partner violence (IPV) can in itself be distressing for children, whether it precedes marital separation and divorce or not. A study by Gottman and Katz (1989) in Illinois, USA, of 56 families with a 4–5-year-old child used both laboratory observations and home interviews. The researchers found that more maritally distressed couples had more stressed children who showed more negative peer interactions and more illness. A follow-up of the same families was made when the children were 8 years old (Katz & Gottman, 1993). Teacher ratings of the children's internalizing and externalizing behaviour problems were made. Earlier marital mutual hostility predicted later externalizing (antisocial) behaviour in the children, and earlier husband angry-withdrawn behaviour predicted later internalizing (self-blame) behaviour in children.

In a meta-analytic review, Evans, Davies and DiLillo (2008) examined 60 studies of domestic violence and its effects on children. Exposure to domestic violence predicted both internalizing symptoms and externalizing symptoms for some children, especially boys. Such links are likely to contribute to the effects found in studies of separation and divorce (see below), though other factors are certainly important. However, there is considerable variation in child outcomes. Some light on such variation was shed by research by Manning, Davies and Cicchetti (2014). A sample of 201 2-year-old children, and their mothers, participated in three waves of data collection over a 2-year period. While IPV did predict children's later externalizing behaviours, this was only significant when maternal sensitivity was low. High maternal sensitivity acted as a protective factor for the effects of IPV on the child. An explanation for this was proposed in terms of whether children responded in an angry reactive way to IPV—this was more likely in the context of insensitive maternal behaviour.

Because of its effects on children, IPV is sometimes included as a form of child maltreatment (see later in this chapter).

DIVORCE

Divorce has become more common in modern Western societies, and this often affects young children. In England and Wales, nearly half (48%) of couples divorcing in 2012 had at least one child aged under 16; of these, 21% were under 5 years old and 64% were under 11 (Office for National Statistics, 2014a). It can be distressing for children when the apparently secure base of the family is broken in this way. There is likely to be conflict between spouses, uncertainty for the future, effects on family income, possible relocation and possible loss of contact with one parent and related kin (Richards, 1995).

Wallerstein (1985) described three phases in the divorce process. First is an acute phase, typically lasting about 2 years, in which the emotional and physical separation takes place. Second is a transitional phase, in which each parent experiences marked ups and downs while they establish separate lives. Third is a postdivorce phase, in which each parent has established a new lifestyle, either as a single parent or remarried.

What are the consequences of this for the child's development? The effects of divorce have been found to vary considerably with the child's age when the separation occurs (Hetherington & Stanley-Hagan, 1999). Preschool children, although upset, are least able to understand what is going on. By middle childhood the changes are better understood, but there may be persistent wishes for or fantasies of the parents reuniting. For early adolescents, the reaction may more often be one of shame or anger, perhaps siding with one parent or the other. The impact on children varies over time, as well; clearly, longitudinal studies are vital to get any real understanding of the impact of divorce on children. Several such studies have been made.

One influential study commenced with 144 middle-class White families in Virginia, USA (Hetherington et al., 1982). Half the children were from divorced, mother-custody families, and half from non-divorced families; their average age at separation was 4 years. After 1 year, most children from divorced families (and many parents) experienced emotional distress and behaviour problems associated with the disruptions in family functioning. This was much improved after 2 years; the main exception was that some boys had poor relations with their custodial mothers and showed more antisocial and non-compliant behaviour than boys from non-divorced families.

A follow-up was made after 6 years—when the children had an average age of 10 years—of 124 of the original 144 families. By now, 42 out of 60 divorced mothers had remarried (and two of these had redivorced); also, 11 of 64 originally non-divorced families had divorced. A general finding was that children of divorced parents experienced more independence and power in decision making at an earlier age, and their activities were less closely monitored by parents. They 'grew up faster'. Mother–daughter relationships were generally not much different from those in non-divorced families. However, mother–son relations continued to be rather tense for divorced mothers who had not remarried; even despite warmth in the relationship, sons were often non-compliant and mothers ineffective in their attempts at control.

Another study, starting in 1971, was of 131 children from 60 divorcing families in northern California (Wallerstein, 1987). The children were aged between 2.5 and 18 years at the time of decisive parental separation. Initially, virtually all the children were very distressed at the separation. Things were not much better after 18 months; some of the younger girls had recovered somewhat but some of the younger boys showed significantly more disturbance. A follow-up after 5 years showed a more complex picture. What was most important now was the overall quality of life within the postdivorce or remarried family. About one-third of the children, however, still showed moderate to severe depression.

At a follow-up after 10 years, some 90% of the original sample could still be located. Interviews with children now 16–18 years old, who had perhaps experienced the separation at the most vulnerable time, showed that many still felt sad and wistful about what had happened, while often accepting its inevitability. As one girl said:

> I don't know if divorce is ever a good thing, but if it is going to happen, it is going to happen. If one person wants out, he wants out. It can't be changed. I get depressed when I think about it. I get sad and angry when I think about what happened to me.
>
> *(Wallerstein, 1987, p. 205)*

All the children had been in the legal and physical custody of their mothers; about 40% had moved in with their fathers for a while during adolescence but most had returned; visits to father varied greatly but were not usually more than weekly, due in part to geographical separation. However, the quality of the father–child relationship was an important determinant of adjustment.

Although traditionally custody is given to one parent, usually the mother, joint custody is being increasingly advocated where possible (i.e. where both parents live fairly close and maintain a reasonable relationship). Luepnitz (1986) compared children who were in sole custody with the mother, sole custody with the father, or joint custody, 2 years or more after final separation. In fact, measures of child adjustment were found to be independent of custody type. Joint custody has the advantages of the child being able to develop two independent relationships, and of reducing financial and parenting pressures on a single parent.

Luepnitz reported that 'the vast majority of children in joint custody were pleased and comfortable with the arrangement'. Single custody can, however, protect wives from possible abuse, and give more flexibility to relocation and remarriage.

Interestingly, Luepnitz found that only 11% of her sample of children showed signs of maladjustment. This is less than one-third the level reported in Wallerstein's study, and may be due to sample differences. Wallerstein recruited subjects by promising counselling, and thus may have recruited particularly distressed families, whereas Luepnitz may have recruited rather non-distressed families who were willing to discuss custody arrangements and their outcome. Whatever the extent of maladjustment, however, all the major studies agree that experiencing good relationships with both parents and an absence of continuing conflict are generally conducive to the most positive outcome for the children involved. Hetherington (1989; see also Hetherington & Stanley-Hagan, 1999) describes 'winners, losers, and survivors' of parental divorce. Depending on circumstances, some children may continue to be damaged and insecure through to adulthood; others recover and 'survive'; yet others may develop particularly caring and competent ways of behaving as a result of coping with the experience.

Some of the ill effects of divorce are probably attributable to conflicts that predate the actual separation of the parents (cf. p. 143). A longitudinal analysis was made by Cherlin et al. (1991) of 7–11-year-olds in Britain, using the NCDS of children born in 1958 (see Table 1.1), and of 7–11-year-olds and 11–16-year-olds in the USA, using the National Survey of Children, which began in 1976. These analyses looked at children's school achievement and behaviour problems before, as well as after, divorce. Generally, the apparent effects of divorce (compared with children in non-divorcing families) were considerably reduced when the predivorce situation was taken into account. As the authors put it, 'at least as much attention needs to be paid to the processes that occur in troubled, intact families as to the trauma that children suffer after their parents separate'.

This conclusion tends to be supported by results from the ALSPAC study in the UK (see Table 1.1). O'Connor et al. (1999) used retrospective data from up to 13,000 mothers in this sample, and found a link between parental divorce and depression in adulthood (also found in the NCDS). However, this link was mediated by a number of factors, including the quality of parent–child and parent marital relationships (in that person's childhood), as well as by concurrent stress and social support.

Reviewing the evidence of effects of parental divorce on children, Lansford (2009) concludes that there is a range of short-term effects, and that a minority of children do show some long-term effects (although a majority do not). The age of the child at the time of divorce is an important factor but a complex one; younger children are more at risk of negative behavioural outcomes, but adolescents are more at risk for academic and social outcomes (especially when parents remarry; see below). Many factors mediate the effects, including prior and ongoing parental conflict, parenting practices, parental well-being and financial circumstances. Public policies and support for families (for example, conciliation services) are also important.

STEP-PARENTING

Divorced parents often remarry. In England and Wales in 2011, 11% of couple families with dependent children were stepfamilies (defined as couple families where there is at least one stepchild in the family; Office for National Statistics, 2014b).

The parents have chosen a new partner, but their children usually have the choice thrust upon them. How do they adapt to this? Remarriage does generally increase the life satisfaction of the adults, but forming strong relationships in the reconstituted family is often a gradual and difficult process. Step-parents are almost inevitably seen as intruders by stepchildren, and often try to tread an uneasy path between assisting their spouse in discipline problems (which may lead to their rejection by stepchildren) and disengagement.

According to the study of divorced families by Hetherington et al. (1982), remarriage and the presence of a stepfather seemed to improve matters for sons, who perhaps responded well to a male figure to identify with; however, the stepfamily situation often made matters worse for daughters, with the stepfather–stepdaughter relationship being a particularly difficult one.

The difficulties facing some stepfamilies were also documented by a study in London by Ferri (1984); however, many such families had successfully met the challenge. As with divorced families, the problems of stepfamilies may be exaggerated, in the sense that other associated factors may often be responsible for difficulties. This was suggested by a longitudinal study of 907 children in Christchurch, New Zealand, by Nicholson et al. (1999). Following the progress of these children up to age 18, they found that entering a stepfamily between ages 6 to 16 meant a higher risk of drug abuse, juvenile crime and poor school achievement. But these differences largely disappeared when account was taken of the families' socioeconomic status, parent characteristics, any family history of conflict and pre-existing child problems.

In reviewing research on children in stepfamilies, Dunn (2002) points out that there are many different types of stepfamily situation. Comparison of children in stepfamilies with those in intact families does show that they typically experience a greater level of adjustment problems. However, the effect size is not large; for example, 13–17% of stepfamily children have problems compared to 10% in intact families (Pryor & Rodgers, 2001). Complex stepfamilies (with both parents bringing children from previous relationships) are more challenging than simple stepfamilies with no new step-siblings. Also, just as with the research on the effects of divorce on children, the challenges of living in a stepfamily are mediated by many factors such as the background and mental health of the parents, the quality of parent–child relationships and relationships amongst siblings and step-siblings.

 Stop and Think

Does parental divorce necessarily have adverse effects on children?

PHYSICAL PUNISHMENT AND THE 'SMACKING' DEBATE

The earlier discussion of parenting styles brought up the issue of parents setting limits on children's behaviour. But how should parents do this and what methods of discipline should they use if children go beyond the limits set? Verbal reasoning/discussion, imposing additional chores/tasks, time out, grounding and withdrawal of privileges are common and widely accepted approaches (May-Chahal & Cawson, 2005). But more controversial has been the use of physical punishment with children. Is it acceptable for a parent to physically punish a child, for example by smacking and hitting? Is this a form of bullying or abuse, or is it sometimes a necessary form of parental control? Opinions are divided.

Surveys in many countries show that corporal punishment is extensively used (see www.endcorporalpunishment.org for a summary). In the UK, a national survey by the National Society for Prevention of Cruelty to Children (NSPCC) (Radford et al., 2011), carried out in 2009, found that 39.4% of parents of under-11-year-olds reported using physical punishment over the last year, and 45.9% of young people themselves aged 11–17 years reported this. Similarly high figures are found in the USA; for example, nearly two-thirds of parents of 1- and 2-year-olds use physical punishment (Gershoff, 2008). In New Zealand, retrospective data from 26-year-old adults in the Dunedin study (Millichamp et al., 2006; see Table 1.1) suggested that 20% had received no physical punishment, 29% reported smacking with the open hand (as most severe), 45% reported being hit with an object (as most severe) and 6% reported extreme physical punishment (involving injury or bruises).

Nevertheless, many countries have legally abolished the use of corporal punishment; 24 such countries were listed by Gershoff (2008), and this had reached 35 countries by 2014 (Österman, Björkqvist & Wahlbeck, 2014). In the UK and the USA it is still widely accepted, although pressure groups are attempting to change the law, for example the Children Are Unbeatable Alliance in the UK (www.childrenareunbeatable.org.uk) and the Center for Effective Discipline in the USA (www.StopHitting.org). Advocates of banning corporal punishment argue that it infringes the rights of the child, a position supported by the UN Convention on the Rights of the Child (see also p. 22). It is also argued that physical punishment is ineffective, provides an inappropriate role model of parenting, is humiliating for the child and will increase later aggressive behaviour by the child (Gershoff, 2013).

What does the research evidence show? Many studies have found correlations between parental punitiveness and childhood misbehaviour and aggression (Gershoff, 2013). However, it may depend on the context of the punishment. Moderation by other factors was shown by Deater-Deckard, Ivy and Petrill (2006) in a study of 3–9-year-olds in the USA. They confirmed an often found association between harsh maternal physical discipline and child externalizing problems. They looked at this in both biological and adoptive families to see if genetic effects were important. In fact, the correlations were very similar. This points to an environmental influence rather than a genetic one (although it does not distinguish parent to child or child to parent effects). However, their other main finding was an interaction with maternal warmth (assessed both by self-ratings and by observation). The association of harsh discipline with child externalizing behaviour was quite high and significant if mother's warmth was below average but much less so, and sometimes non-significant, if mother's warmth was above average.

A review by Larzelere (2000) concluded that smacking could be an effective, unharmful form of discipline, provided that: (1) it was not too severe; (2) it was kept under control and not done in moments of anger; (3) it was limited to the 2–6-year age range; and (4) it was used in conjunction with reasoning. Critics have pointed out that these limitations are stringent and often infringed. If smacking often slides into inappropriate and severe chastisement, this could be seen as becoming abusive behaviour (which has clear negative outcomes, as Larzelere acknowledged; see next section). However, smacking does need to be compared with other disciplinary tactics. Larzelere and Kuhn (2005) reported a meta-analysis of 26 studies, where they differentiated between four types of physical punishment:

1. *Conditional*: spanking under limited conditions
2. *Customary*: spanking (smacking) used as one of a range of disciplinary methods

3. *Overly severe*: use of excessive force, hitting with an object, slapping the face
4. *Predominant*: the primary disciplinary method.

The authors compared these spanking methods with other disciplinary techniques. *Conditional* came out well (better in 10 out of 13 comparisons) and *Customary* came out as equal to other techniques. Both *Overly severe* and *Predominant* use of physical punishment led to worse child outcomes. Larzelere thus argued that limited and conditional smacking is an effective discipline technique, a position also taken by Baumrind (Baumrind et al., 2002).

The Dunedin-based study (Millichamp et al., 2006) also gave some support to this view; at 26 years, there was no difference between the no punishment and smacking groups in terms of signs of emotional distress when discussing their experiences (both 1%). It was slightly higher for the hit with object group (2%) but very much higher for the extreme physical punishment group (22%), who clearly suffered physical abuse (see below). These findings are not always cited by opponents of physical punishment (e.g. Gershoff, 2013).

Another issue relates to direction of effect: for example, does an aggressive child bring about a punitive response from parents? A meta-analysis by Ferguson (2013) focused on longitudinal studies of spanking (smacking) and of corporal punishment (CP; also including hitting, pushing, slapping, etc.), since these are most able to indicate cause and effect. He identified 45 data sets, and found that spanking and CP did have negative predictive correlations to externalizing and internalizing behaviours, and to cognitive performance (suggesting parent to child effect). However, these findings were qualified in two important ways. First, spanking and CP fared no worse than negative verbal discipline or arbitrary discipline—although positive discipline did lead to better outcomes for externalizing behaviours. Second, the effect sizes were small—correlations around the .10 level, which means accounting for only about 1% of the variance. Ferguson concluded that 'spanking and CP do appear to be significantly associated with small increases in negative outcomes, although these correlations may not be as substantial as sometimes implied in public discussions or scholarly comments on the topic' (op. cit., p. 202).

A powerful argument from the anti-smacking lobby is that it is safer to make all smacking illegal (as many countries have successfully done) than condone behaviour for which the boundary of acceptability may be dangerously vague and difficult for parents to follow. Sweden was the first country that made smacking illegal, in 1979. According to Durrant (1999), this was successful in both changing attitudes towards physical punishment and reducing its use. The Swedish example has also been challenged, as general assaults against children in Sweden increased, though whether this has any causal connection to the smacking ban is disputable (Durrant & Janson, 2005; Larzelere, 2004). The second country to have a complete ban on corporal punishment was Finland, in 1983. An analysis by Österman et al. (2014) found that most forms of physical punishment decreased after this law was introduced.

CHILD MALTREATMENT, NEGLECT AND ABUSE

Usually, parents love and care for their children. No parent is perfect, but most provide 'good enough' parenting. Some conflict between parents and their offspring is inevitable (and indeed is predicted from evolutionary theory; see p. 57), but generally this is kept within reasonable bounds. However, some children suffer maltreatment: neglect, or physical, emotional or sexual abuse from parents or other adult caregivers.

The World Health Organization (2002, p. 59) defines child *maltreatment* as:

> All forms of physical and/or emotional ill treatment, sexual abuse, neglect or negligent treatment or commercial or other exploitation, resulting in actual or potential harm to the child's health, survival, development or dignity in the context of a relationship of responsibility, trust or power.

This is clearly quite an inclusive definition, covering neglect as well as active abuse. Also as worded, it could include smacking (see above); as we have seen, there is dispute about whether mild smacking has detrimental effects, but there is consensus that severe and prolonged physical chastisement is detrimental to child welfare and would constitute physical abuse.

The WHO (2002, p. 60) also gives the following definitions:

- *Neglect*: the failure of a parent to provide for the development of the child—where the parent is in a position to do so—in one or more of the following areas: health, education, emotional development, nutrition, shelter, and safe living conditions.
- *Physical abuse*: those acts of commission by a caregiver that cause actual physical harm or have the potential for harm.
- *Emotional abuse*: acts that have an adverse effect on the emotional health and development of a child. Such acts include restricting a child's movement, denigration, ridicule, threats and intimidation, discrimination, rejection and other non-physical forms of hostile treatment.
- *Sexual abuse*: those acts where a caregiver uses a child for sexual gratification.

Assessment and Extent of Child Maltreatment

The extent of child neglect and abuse is difficult to determine, as naturally parents are secretive about it, and children are often too young or too frightened to seek help. Some large-scale studies have used retrospective interviewing of young adults, asking about specific experiences, but embedded in other more general questions about childhood.

Questioning of young children has to be done carefully to maximize the accuracy and usefulness of children's testimony (Fundudis, 1989). In the case of sexual abuse, observation of unstructured play with anatomically correct dolls may be useful. Unlike conventional dolls, these dolls have sexual organs and characteristics. Some studies suggest that most children, while noticing the characteristics of the dolls, do not show sexually explicit play with them; when it is observed, such explicit play (for example, sucking a doll's penis) may well arise from the child's preoccupations based on previous exposure to explicit sexual information or activity (Glaser & Collins, 1989). However, the use of these dolls remains controversial (Westcott et al., 1989).

It can also be very difficult and distressing for victims of child abuse to speak out. At times they may not be believed, and interviews by police and judges can seem very intimidating (see Chapter 14). In the USA and the UK, it is possible to allow children to give evidence by means of a closed circuit television 'video link' so that they need not directly face their abuser (Davies, 1988). Psychologists are closely involved in this work, and in attempts to help victims of abuse recover from their experiences (British Psychological Society, 1990).

Childhood neglect is generally the most frequent type of maltreatment recorded, but has not had as much research attention as active abuse. Stoltenborgh, Bakermans-Kranenburg and Van IJzendoorn (2013) found 16 relevant studies of neglect on which to carry out a meta-analysis—all 16 included emotional neglect and 13 also covered physical neglect.

Eleven of the studies were from the USA. The overall prevalence rates were 18.4% for emotional neglect and 16.3% for physical neglect but with considerable variation between different studies.

In the UK, a national survey by the NSPCC carried out in 2009 (Radford et al., 2011, 2013) gathered data from 2,160 parents of children aged 1 month to 10 years, and from 2,275 young people themselves aged 11–17 years. Rates for four types of maltreatment are shown in Table 4.8, for the past year (excluding neglect) and for lifetime so far. The higher rates for the 11–17-year-olds than the under-11s, even for the past year, while they might be real, more likely reflect difficulties in getting valid information—perhaps parents/caregivers are less willing to admit maltreatment, or do not interpret it as such as readily as their children do. In this study, rates of neglect are comparable with other studies. This survey found that children or young people who experienced maltreatment by a parent or guardian were also more likely to experience it from others outside the family—that is, they were *polyvictims*. These others were most likely relatives, neighbours or family friends for the under-11s, but more often strangers for the 11–17s. However, an encouraging finding was that, compared to a similar survey carried out in the UK in 1998, some measures of maltreatment had shown a decline.

In the USA, Hussey et al. (2010), as part of a national longitudinal study of adolescent health, carried out structured interviews with a nationally representative sample of more than 10,000 young adults (aged 18–26), which included retrospective questions about maltreatment experiences with parents or adult caregivers before 6th grade (11 years). The four questions were about:

1. *Supervision neglect*: left home alone when an adult should have been with you
2. *Physical assault*: slapped, hit or kicked
3. *Physical neglect*: basic needs not taken care of, such as keeping clean, providing food or clothing
4. *Contact sexual abuse*: touched in a sexual way, forced to touch him/her in a sexual way, or to have sexual relations.

Table 4.8   Rates of types of maltreatment by a parent or caregiver over the past year, or over lifetime so far, in the UK (past year data not available for neglect).

Type/Age of child		Under-11s	11–17s
Neglect	Lifetime	5.0	13.3
Physical violence	Past year	0.7	2.4
	Lifetime	1.3	6.9
Emotional abuse	Past year	1.8	3.0
	Lifetime	3.6	6.8
Sexual abuse	Past year	0	0
	Lifetime	0.1	0.1
All forms of maltreatment	Past year	2.5	6.0
	Lifetime	8.9	21.9

Source: Adapted from Radford, L., Corral, S., Bradley, C., Fisher, H., Bassett, C., Howat, N. & Collishaw, S. (2011). *Child abuse and neglect in the UK today*. London: NSPCC. Adapted by permission of NSPCC.

The percentages they obtained are shown in Table 4.9. Supervision neglect was relatively frequent, reported by 41.5%, followed by physical assault at 28.4%; less frequent was physical neglect at 11.8%, and least frequent was contact sexual abuse at 4.5%. These are high figures, although for half or more it was only reported as happening once or twice. Females were more at risk for sexual abuse, but males more at risk for the other three categories. Low family income was a general risk factor, and lesser parental education a risk factor especially for physical neglect.

A meta-analysis of studies of sexual abuse of children (up to age 18) by Barth et al. (2013) located 55 studies from 24 countries, during the period 2002–2009. Prevalence rates for males and females for four types of sexual abuse are shown in Table 4.10. These figures are much higher than those in Tables 4.8 or 4.9, as most sexual abuse is from people other than parents (for example, figures from the NSPCC survey for *all* perpetrators of sexual abuse are about 17% for 11–17-year-olds). Non-contact abuse, the most common, included inappropriate sexual solicitation and indecent exposure. Contact abuse included unwanted touching/fondling and kissing. Forced intercourse includes any kind, including attempted. Mixed refers to when the report only included one overall prevalence rate. Rates are about twice as high for females but appreciable for males as well. Again, there was great variation among studies, with, for example, high rates reported from individual studies in Ethiopia and Nigeria.

Table 4.9   Retrospective reports of experiences of child maltreatment by parents/caregivers in the USA.

Type of maltreatment	Supervision neglect	Physical assault	Physical neglect	Contact sexual abuse
Once or twice	22.4	14.2	6.8	2.9
Three times or more	19.1	14.2	5.0	1.6

Source: Adapted from Hussey, J.M., Chang, J.J. & Kotch, J.B. (2010). Child maltreatment in the United States: Prevalence, risk factors and adolescent health consequences. *Pediatrics, 118*, 933–942.

Table 4.10   Rates of four types of child sexual abuse, from all perpetrators, by gender.

Type/Gender of child	Male	Female
Non-contact	17	31
Mixed	8	15
Contact	6	13
Forced intercourse	3	9

Source: Barth, J., Bermetz, L., Heim, E., Trelle, S. & Tonia, T. (2013). The current prevalence of child sexual abuse worldwide: A systematic review and meta-analysis. *International Journal of Public Health, 58*, 469–483.

The Effects of Child Maltreatment

For the great majority of children who survive such experiences, the effects of child abuse can be wide-ranging and long-lasting. In the UK, the NSPCC survey (Radford et al., 2011) found that all forms of abuse in childhood were generally associated with poorer mental health and increased likelihood of delinquent behaviour. For example, 11–17-year-olds who reported severe maltreatment by a parent/guardian were 6.4 times more likely to have current suicidal thoughts. In the USA, the survey by Hussey et al. (2010) found that each of their four types of maltreatment was associated with a range of adolescent mental health factors, assessed in interviews 7 years earlier at ages 11–19; these included depression, obesity, drug use and involvement in violence.

Other factors can moderate the effects of abuse—for example, the kinds of coping strategies used by the individual, the nature of support they have and the way in which they are able to appraise and understand what has happened to them. Collishaw et al. (2007a) carried out a follow-up of a study in the Isle of Wight (referred to in more detail in Chapter 19). They had available detailed interview data from 571 adolescents when they were 14–15 years old, and they succeeded in interviewing 378 of them as adults, aged 44–45 years. The adults were asked for retrospective reports of physical and sexual abuse, up to age 16; of these, 44 were identified as reporting serious abuse. The adolescent data revealed that these individuals had had a higher rate of psychiatric disorder in adolescence, and rates of adult psychopathology (for example, depression, or suicidal thoughts or attempts) were also high. Nevertheless, 14 of the 44 were judged as not seriously affected and were labelled as resilient. For these resilient individuals, the abuse had often been less serious or sustained, but other protective factors appeared to be personality (not neurotic) and having some good relationships (one caring parent, and/or peer relationships, and/or a stable partner relationship).

Relationship quality emerges as an important factor in much research in this area. McCarthy and Taylor (1999) found that adult love relationship difficulties were six times more common in those with childhood abuse experiences; avoidant/ambivalent attachment style acted as a significant mediator between abusive childhood experiences and adult relationship difficulties.

Causes of Child Maltreatment

The peak of physical abuse is in early childhood, with boys being more at risk than girls; the peak for sexual abuse appears to be later in middle childhood, with girls primarily at risk. In cases of physical abuse, mothers and fathers are about equally likely to be involved (though there are obvious questions about who is willing to admit abuse—a mother may 'shelter' an abusing father or cohabitee). In cases of sexual abuse, some 95% involve males as the perpetrators. Another risk factor, for young children, is abuse by step-parents. Studies in Canada, the UK and elsewhere indicate that the risk of abuse, including fatal abuse, is much greater for children with stepfathers (Daly & Wilson, 1996).

What leads a parent to abuse a child? For the step-parent data, Daly and Wilson take an evolutionary perspective, arguing that it is not in the stepfather's genetic interest to divert parental investment to children not related to him (see p. 57); in terms of proximal mechanisms, some stepfathers may just not develop strong attachments to their new stepchildren. More generally, abusing parents have been found very often to have insecure attachment relationships with their children. In one study, 70% of maltreated infants were found to have insecure attachments to their caregivers, compared with only 26% of infants with no record of maltreatment (Browne, 1989).

Crittenden (1988) examined the representations of relationships in abusing parents, using the idea of internal working models discussed on p. 188. She interviewed 124 mothers in Virginia, USA, many of whom had abused or maltreated their children, and gave them the SAT. She reported that adequate mothers generally had warm and secure relationships with both their children and their partner. By contrast, abusing mothers appeared to conceptualize relationships in terms of power struggles. They tended to be controlling and hostile, with anxiously attached children, and to have angry and unstable adult relationships. Another group, of neglecting mothers, appeared to conceive of relationships as emotionally empty. They were unresponsive to their anxiously attached children, and were involved in stable but affectless relationships with partners. Crittenden argued that 'the problem for those offering treatment to abused and abusing individuals is to find ways both to change their experience and also to change their conceptualization of it. Without a change in the representational model, the new experience will be encoded in terms of the old model and will be rendered useless' (Crittenden, 1988, p. 197).

Collishaw et al. (2007b) used data from the ALSPAC longitudinal study (see Table 1.1) to examine intergenerational continuity in abuse, and mediating factors. They obtained data from 5,619 families on mothers' retrospective memories of childhood abuse, and their children's adjustment at ages 4 and 7 years. The children of mothers who had experienced severe abuse had poorer adjustment scores at age 4, with these tending to persist or even get worse by age 7. The researchers identified several factors that fully mediated or explained this linkage. These included the children experiencing physical assaults and frightening parental behaviours, separations from parents and step-parenting, and other stressful events such as moving house, changing school and losing touch with friends.

Although there is some intergenerational continuity in abusive parenting, in fact only a minority of formerly abused adults go on to abuse their children. Ward and Davies (2011) reviewed the effectiveness of treatment for abused children and abusive parents. For young children, play therapy (see Chapter 7) can be helpful in diagnosis and perhaps for treatment. Other prevention aspects include nurse visits to parents and parent education (WHO, 2014).

MODELS OF PARENTING

We have looked at aspects of parenting where there are difficulties—where parents separate or divorce, or where there is actual abuse of children. But what about the more normal range of parenting? There is still a lot of variation in how different parents carry out the task. Belsky (1984) advocated a model of parental functioning that distinguishes three main influences on the quality of parental functioning. In order of suggested importance, these are:

1. *Personal psychological resources of the parent*: this will include parental mental health, the quality of internal representations of relationships and their development history
2. *Contextual sources of support*: including the social network of support from partner, relatives and friends, and job conditions and financial circumstances
3. *Characteristics of the child*: in particular, easy or difficult temperament (see p. 101).

Belsky's actual process model of factors influencing parenting is illustrated in Figure 4.2. The model is also useful for understanding how variations in family functioning, satisfactory as well as unsatisfactory, may come about, and in thinking of ways to help parents with difficult

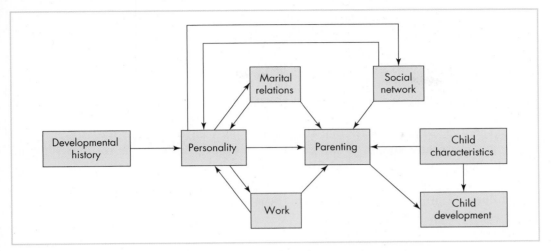

Figure 4.2 Belsky's process model of the determinants of parenting.
Source: Belsky, J. (1984). The determinants of parenting: a process model. *Child Development, 55,* 83–96.

or disruptive children. There has been considerable interest in the area of parenting skills and in ways of helping parents change, improve their coping and child management skills or develop a more secure relationship with their child. These approaches have mainly focused on the first area of Belsky's model, that of the personal psychological resources of the parent.

Van IJzendoorn et al. (1995) reviewed 16 studies that involved working with parents to improve parental sensitivity and attachment security. Interventions were varied but covered increased support from home visitors, use of videos, parent education and individual (mother) and joint (mother–child) psychotherapy. Generally, short-term, preventive interventions seemed more effective than long-term, therapy-based interventions. There were appreciable improvements in many studies in maternal sensitivity to the child, but only small improvements in attachment security.

This review suggested that it is easier to produce changes at the behavioural level than at the representational level. This need not be surprising; changes at the representational level may be deeper and need more sustained effort to bring about. Subsequently, Bakermans-Kranenburg et al. (2003) traced 70 intervention studies with 88 effect size results on parental sensitivity or attachment. They confirmed the earlier conclusions that the most effective interventions used a moderate number of sessions and a clear-cut behavioural focus. Interventions effective in enhancing maternal sensitivity were also more effective in enhancing attachment security (supporting a causal role for sensitivity in secure attachment). The mean effect size was greater for enhancing maternal sensitivity (d = .33) than for enhancing attachment security (d = .20).

Some examples of successful interventions that had limited sessions and a clear focus are:

- Promoting use of baby carriers/slings to encourage physical contact and sensitivity (Anisfeld et al., 1990).
- Providing adolescent mothers with a videotape to promote mealtime communications with infants (Black & Teti, 1997).
- Three 2-hour visits by a professional, to focus on mother's sensitive responsiveness to 'irritable' infants (van den Boom, 1994).

These studies used theoretical models based on attachment theory, or on social skills and behavioural approaches. Belsky's model also draws attention to the wider social context: the employment status of parents, housing conditions and social support.

The extent to which parents make a difference to children's development has, however, been disputed. Scarr (1992) argued that, by and large, parents need only provide a basically warm, supportive and nurturant environment for their children to develop their innate potential. She supported her argument by reference to studies in behaviour genetics (see Chapter 2), which indicate that the shared family environment—the aspects of the family environment common to all siblings—contributes rather little to understanding individual differences in many areas. To some extent, children help create their own rearing environment. A child's temperament, for example, which appears to be strongly genetically influenced, influences the ways parents behave towards that child and the expectations they have of them.

Of course, no one denies that extremes of environment can adversely affect development; studies of children reared in profoundly non-stimulating environments, and studies of environmental enrichment, show that children can be held back if they do not receive a basic minimum of language and intellectual stimulation, and love and affection (see Chapter 18). Scarr accepted this, and said that children require an average expectable environment for normal development but that beyond this, individual variation in development is mainly due to inherited individual potential, finding expression in a reasonably good environment that is partly created by the person for themselves.

Scarr's views give greater prominence to genetic factors than some psychologists think is justified, and they appear to downplay the importance of parenting beyond the basic minimum or good enough parenting. They also imply that many parent–child similarities are due to genetic rather than environmental factors. These issues are controversial (Baumrind, 1993). The importance of parents (after the preschool years) is also downplayed by Harris (1995) in her group socialization theory; this is discussed further in Chapter 5.

THE MILLENNIUM COHORT STUDY (MCS): PATTERNS OF CHILDCARE IN THE UK AT 3 AND 5 YEARS

This longitudinal study (see Table 1.1) assessed over 18,000 infants at 9 months (see Chapter 3, p. 103) and further assessments were made of more than 15,000 children and their families, at age 3 years (in 2003–2004) and age 5 years (in 2006). Hansen et al. (2010) reported a range of findings from these second and third assessment waves.

Non-maternal childcare provision had been assessed at 9 months, and was assessed again at 3 and 5 years. At 9 months, 60% of the infants were receiving some non-maternal care: 49% informal, usually grandparents (30%) or partner (25%), and 20% formal, usually day nursery (12%) or childminder (10%). At 3 years, the balance had shifted to less informal care (now 27%) and more formal care (now 76%), with 31% attending a nursery school or class and 25% a playgroup. (By 5 years they had started school.)

At age 5, 60.3% of children were with both married parents and 15.1% were with cohabiting parents. Another 19.2% were with a lone parent (almost always the mother), 5.2% were with a natural parent and a step-parent, while just .2% were with neither natural

Table 4.11 **Relationships between family status and children's emotional well-being (based on SDQ scores) at 5 years.**

Family status	Externalizing difficulties	Internalizing difficulties
Married	13.5	15.9
Cohabiting	21.4	18.2
Lone parent	28.0	22.8
Stepfamily	29.6	20.5

Source: Kiernan, K. & Mensah, F. (2010). Partnership trajectories, parent and child well-being. In K. Hansen, M. Joshi and S. Dex (Eds.), *Children of the 21st century: The first five years*. Bristol: Policy Press. © 2010. Reproduced by permission of The Policy Press.

parent. As at 9 months, lone mothers were most frequent in Black Caribbean families and least frequent in South Asian (Indian, Pakistani, Bangladeshi) families; cohabiting was highest in White families.

Family composition was found to relate to child outcomes, as measured by the Strengths and Difficulties Questionnaire (SDQ). Table 4.11 shows the percentages of children judged as experiencing either externalizing or internalizing difficulties, by four main family types. The differences are highly significant, although much can be explained by taking account of other factors. The researchers used regression analyses to account for child gender, ethnicity, poverty, maternal depression, maternal education and several other measures. When this was done, the differences in externalizing behaviour were considerably reduced but still significant; the differences in internalizing behaviours were non-significant after taking all these factors into account.

Clearly, children not growing up in married parent families are more at risk but, as the researchers say (Kiernan & Mensah, 2010, p. 94), 'this is not to say that a parent's partnership situation . . . affects children directly, but rather it reflects parental situations and inputs, which in turn affect outcomes for these families'. The quality of the parental relationship had some relationship to parenting and to child outcomes but, again, relatively little when other factors were accounted for.

Many factors affect parenting and how it impacts on children, and the causes of the differences found in Table 4.11 are open to a number of interpretations. It is worth noting that there is no behaviour genetic evidence available in the MCS reports, so they do not address the controversy noted above about the real extent of parental influence. However, these reports do provide a wealth of evidence on the recent situation of families of young children in the UK.

CHAPTER SUMMARY

- Family relationships are important. While the relationship with the mother has been studied most, other adult family members such as fathers and grandparents can have significant and usually helpful influences on development. The quality of relationships matters more than the composition of the family.
- An important and long-standing approach to parenting comes from attachment theory. This has developed from an infancy-based approach to a life-span approach. Another perspective is from parenting styles.
- Bowlby's earlier views on 'maternal deprivation' have been largely discredited, but children do need close relationships and there remains some controversy over intensive day care for young children, especially in the first year.
- The use of physical punishment as a disciplinary strategy is another area with contrasting views.
- Parental divorce has effects on children's development, especially in the short term, and a number of factors influence the long-term outcomes.
- While most parenting is loving and at least 'good enough', some parents/carers do neglect or abuse their children. The consequences of this can be severe and long-lasting, though again mediated by many factors.
- Belsky's (1984) model of parental functioning provides a useful conceptualization of the factors involved in parenting.

DISCUSSION POINTS

1. What is meant by 'secure' and 'insecure' attachment? Are these culturally biased terms?
2. What did Bowlby mean by 'maternal deprivation'? How useful or valid has this concept proved to be?
3. Do mothers, fathers and grandparents have different influences on a child's behaviour?
4. What impact does parental divorce have on children?
5. What are the problems in diagnosing, and treating, child abuse?

FURTHER READING

- Holmes, J. (2014). *John Bowlby and attachment theory* (2nd ed.). London: Routledge, provides a readable biography and assessment of Bowlby's work; his last book was published as Bowlby, J. (1988). *A secure base: Clinical applications of attachment theory*. London: Tavistock/Routledge.
- For a good overview of attachment theory, see Goldberg, S. (2000). *Attachment and development*. London: Psychology Press; for measurement procedures and interventions, see Prior, V. & Glaser, D. (2006). *Understanding attachment and attachment disorders*. London: Jessica Kingsley. A detailed and thorough source is Cassidy, J. & Shaver, P.R. (Eds.) (2008). *Handbook of attachment: Theory, research, and clinical applications* (2nd ed.). New York: Guilford Press.
- On fatherhood, Lamb, M.E. (Ed.) (2010). *The role of the father in child development* (5th ed.). Chichester: Wiley is a useful source. Golombok, S. (2000). *Parenting: What really counts?* London: Routledge, is a readable overview of many relevant topics. Pryor, J. & Rodgers, B. (2001) *Children in changing families: Life after parental separation*. Oxford: Blackwell, is a useful overview of issues around divorce, step-parenting and family transitions. For the impact of different family forms, see Parke, R.D. (2013). *Future families: Diverse forms, rich possibilities*. New York: Wiley.
- For child maltreatment and abuse, see Howe, D. (2005). *Child abuse and neglect: Attachment, development and intervention*. London: Palgrave Macmillan; for a more general approach, Finkelhor, D. (2007). *Childhood victimization: Violence, crime, and abuse in the lives of young people*. Oxford: Oxford University Press; and, for example, websites such as the US Administration for Children and Families: www.acf.hhs.gov
- An encyclopaedic reference for parenting issues is the series of volumes edited by Bornstein, M. (2002). *Handbook of parenting* (2nd ed.). Mahwah, NJ: Erlbaum.

CHAPTER
5

Siblings and the Peer Group

CHAPTER OUTLINE

- Early Peer Relationships
- Siblings
- Peer Relationships in Preschool and School
- Friendship
- The Importance of Peer Relations and Friendship
- Family and Peer Relationships
- Group Socialization Theory and the Role of the Peer Group: How Important are Families?

I n this chapter we look at children's relationships with other children—with siblings and with peers. Eighty per cent of us have siblings. Sibling relationships can be intense, and provide opportunities for early social and cognitive learning. Usually, siblings only differ in age by a few years. A 'peer' is someone who is about the same age as yourself; for children, this is usually someone in the same year, class or age grade. Peer relationships are very important throughout the school years. Here, we consider the concept of 'sociometric status', work on peer rejection and sociometric and perceived popularity. We also examine the concept of friendship: what is a friend? How do we measure friendship? We conclude by examining the controversy over the relative influence of parents and peers on children's development.

EARLY PEER RELATIONSHIPS

From an early age, peers seem to be especially interesting to children. In one study of 12–18-month-old infants, two mother–infant pairs who had not previously met shared a playroom together. The investigators observed whom the infants touched and whom they looked at. The results are shown in Figure 5.1. The infants touched their mothers a lot (thus remaining in proximity to them, as we would expect from attachment theory; see Chapter 4). However, they looked most at the peer, who was clearly interesting to them (and interested in them!) (Lewis et al., 1975).

The interactions between under-2s have been examined using video film. Video is very useful, since at this age range peer interactions are short, subtle and easy to miss. They often consist of just looking at another child and perhaps smiling, or showing a toy, or making a

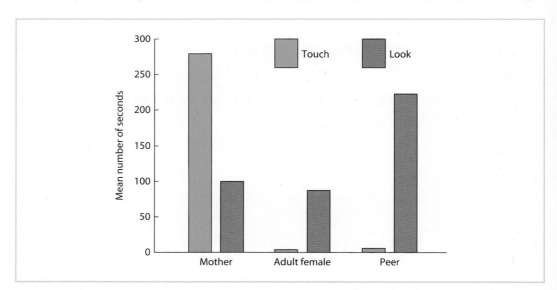

Figure 5.1   Amount of time during a 15-minute period in which children aged 12–18 months touched and looked at mother, an unfamiliar adult female and an unfamiliar peer.
Source: From Lewis et al. (1975). Reproduced with permission from John Wiley & Sons.

noise. In toddler groups an infant might make such overtures to another child once every minute or so, and each may last only a matter of seconds (Mueller & Brenner, 1977). This rather low level of peer interaction is because infants are not yet very accomplished at the skills of social interaction, such as knowing what are appropriate behaviours in certain situations, knowing what behaviour to expect back and waiting to take one's turn. As we saw in Chapter 3, adults can 'scaffold' social interactions with infants, but it takes young children some 2–3 years to become really competent at interacting socially with age-mates.

Early peer experience in toddler groups or day nurseries can assist these peer skills (p. 134), as can being 'securely attached' to the mother or caregiver (p. 111). Under-2s also have some abilities that help develop peer interaction. One of these is imitation, which we also discussed in Chapter 3. A study in France by Nadel-Brulfert and Baudonniere (1982) observed 2-year-olds in a laboratory playroom equipped with pairs of identical objects. It was found that when one child picked up or played with an object, the other child was very likely to pick up the corresponding identical object; these imitations had a definite social function, helping to initiate or maintain communication and play between the children.

Another study of French children showed evidence of a different range of abilities at 11 months and at 23 months (Tremblay-Leveau & Nadel, 1996). Here, pairs of toddlers from the same day care centre were observed with a familiar experimenter and some toys (that is, a 'triadic' situation). Both dyadic and triadic interactions were observed, with some degree of turn taking even by the younger, 11-month-old children. The particularly interesting feature of the results from this study was the differing reactions of infants when they were 'included' within an ongoing interaction with the adult, or 'excluded'. When temporarily out of the interaction, the other child made many more attempts to interact with the peer, perhaps by 'showing off' or interposing their body between the adult and peer, or by naming the toy being played with, or another toy, and smiling. At 11 months, they were five times more likely to attempt interactions with the peer when excluded; they were eight times more likely to do so at 23 months. The researchers concluded that this shows an early awareness of one's social position and an active attempt to overcome loneliness when excluded, and also of attention to others and, perhaps, some awareness of their mental states. If so, this would be a precursor of the kind of theory of mind abilities that we consider further in Chapter 15.

It was probably important in this study that the toddlers knew each other. However, the situation in which young children will know each other best of all is when they are raised in the same family: typically, siblings aged a year or so apart.

SIBLINGS

With the exception of twins or further multiplets, siblings will differ in age by at least a year and typically 2–3 years. They are not exactly 'peers', and there is a power imbalance depending on the age gap, but they are usually close enough in age, and similar enough in interests and developmental stages, to be important social partners for each other in the home and family environment. Characteristically, older siblings can show great tolerance for younger ones, and can act as an important model for more competent behaviour. They can also show hostility and ambivalence, and this has been observed in many different societies (Eibl-Eibesfeldt, 1989).

A study by Stewart (1983) in the USA showed that older siblings can act as attachment figures in the Strange Situation (see p. 109). Stewart used an extended version of the procedure with 54 family groups. At one point, the older sibling (who was aged from 30 to 58 months) was left alone with the infant (who was aged from 10 to 20 months). Every infant responded to the mother's departure with some degree of distress. Within 10 seconds of the mother's departure, 28 of the older siblings had responded by showing some form of caregiving behaviour, for example approaching and hugging the infant, offering verbal reassurance of the mother's return or carrying the infant to the centre of the room to distract him or her with toys. These actions were quite effective. The other 26 older siblings, however, ignored or moved away from the infant and did not show caregiving responses. This pattern of pronounced variation in the quality of sibling relationships is, in fact, a recurrent one in studies of siblings.

Siblings in the Home Environment

What is found in actual sibling relationships in the home? Extensive research of this kind has been carried out by Judy Dunn and her colleagues (Dunn, 1984; Dunn, 2004b; Dunn & Kendrick, 1982; Dunn et al., 1991). They carried out observations in the homes of 40 first-born children living with both parents in Cambridge, England. At first visit, a new sibling was due in a month or so and the first child was in most cases nearing their second birthday. Subsequent visits were made after the birth of the sibling, when the second child was about 1 month old, and again at 8 months and at 14 months. Besides interviewing the parents, the natural behaviour between the siblings and with their parents was observed.

Naturally enough, many first-borns showed some signs of jealousy when the new sibling arrived. Previously, they had been the centre of attention from mother, father or grandparents; now, the new brother or sister got the most attention. Parents do of course make some efforts to involve the first-born in this, for example in feeding sessions, but inevitably rates of interaction with first-borns do decline overall (at times, fathers can play a more important role with the older child while the mother is undertaking primary caregiving responsibilities with the new baby). At this point, much of the jealousy and ambivalence of the first-born is directed towards parents.

> *Mother:*   He keeps having tantrums and misery. Anything sets him off. He's just terrible.
>
> *(Dunn & Kendrick, 1982, p. 31)*

Not many first-borns show much overt hostility to the infant but some do, and some behaviour can be ambivalent. In the following example, it is difficult to know if the behaviour is friendly, hostile or (more probably) a mixture of both.

> *Mother:*   He wants to play with her but he's so rough. Lies on top of her. Then she cries. He wants to roll all over her. I have to keep her away from him 'cause I can't let her be bashed about yet.
>
> *(p. 36)*

Other children may express hostility in conversation, as the following extract shows.

> *Child:*   Baby, baby (caressing her). Monster. Monster.
> *Mother:*   She's not a monster.
> *Child:*   Monster.
>
> *(p. 68)*

However, such hostility really is ambivalent. The great majority of the first-borns do show much interest and affection towards their new sibling.

Mother: He asks where she is first thing in the morning. He's happy when he can see her.

(p. 34)

They may also show empathy and prosocial behaviour (see also Chapter 9).

Mother: When she cries he's very concerned. Gets her dummy [pacifier], then comes and tells me.

(p. 32)

There was considerable variation in the typical response when the infant was upset. Fourteen of the 40 first-borns were themselves upset, like the boy just mentioned. Ten were neutral. Five were sometimes gleeful, while 10 children actually increased their younger sibling's upset. Overall, Dunn and Kendrick (1982) felt that the sibling relationship is one in which considerable emotions may be aroused—both of love and of envy. (Evolutionary developmental psychologists would not be surprised at finding sibling rivalry; see p. 58.) However, the title of Dunn and Kendrick's (1982) book, *Siblings: Love, envy, and understanding*, brings out another important feature, that of the enhanced understanding that this close and emotionally powerful relationship may generate. This may be an optimal situation in which to learn how to understand and hence influence others.

Sibling Influences: Play, Teaching

Dunn (2004b) argues that an older brother or sister may contribute a lot to a child's pretend play experiences (see also Chapter 7). Based on her observations, she compared how mothers, and older siblings, might engage in pretend play with the younger sibling. She comments that mothers almost always focused on object-based pretence, using objects as props (on 97% of occasions, in fact). Mothers would make relevant comments and suggestions, as 'interested spectators'. In contrast, the older siblings would take part in complementary role-playing with their younger brother or sister. They would closely mesh their play, using talk and non-verbal actions. Some 27% of their bouts did not involve objects at all.

A number of studies have used semi-naturalistic paradigms to look at sibling teaching; usually the older sibling is taught some task, such as constructing a toy or how to play a game, and then is asked to teach the younger sibling (Howe et al., 2006). When the older sibling is of school age, he or she is more likely to use detailed verbal instructions, and to scaffold the process (see Chapter 16), whereas when the older sibling was still a preschooler, he or she more often used demonstration.

Sibling Influences: Conflict and Social Comparison

From early on (under 2 years of age), siblings seem to be learning how to frustrate, tease, placate, comfort or get their own way with their brother or sister. This is true not only of the older siblings but also of the younger ones as they grow up. Consider the following observation of Callum, aged 14 months, with his older sister Laura, aged 3 years (Dunn & Kendrick, 1982, p. 116).

> Callum repeatedly reaches for and manipulates the magnetic letters Laura is playing with. Laura repeatedly says NO gently. Callum continues trying to reach the letters. Finally, Laura picks up the tray containing the letters and carries it to a high table that Callum cannot reach. Callum is furious and starts to cry. He turns and goes straight to the sofa where Laura's comfort objects, a rag doll and a pacifier, are lying. He takes the doll and holds it tight, looking at Laura. Laura for the first time is very upset, starts crying, and runs to take the doll.

The obvious interpretation here is that Callum has figured out how to annoy Laura so as to get his own back on her. Indeed, rivalry and conflict are an integral part of the sibling experience. Often these are over toys and other possessions, as in the example above. There seems to be some consistency in the levels of aggression from older siblings (some consistently do more, others less), whereas generally younger siblings seem to respond to the level of aggression received from the older sibling (Perlman et al., 2007).

Conflict can be unpleasant in the short term and, if it is a repeated pattern of pervasive behaviour, may be detrimental. Dunn et al. (1991) found that in early adolescence, someone who had grown up with an unfriendly or hostile sibling was more likely to be anxious, depressed or aggressive. Cicirelli (1989) found that attachment to siblings related to well-being in later life.

Nevertheless, some level of conflict is normative, and conflicts can provide various learning experiences. Siblings will be learning about what behaviours are acceptable in the family, and moral rules about property rights and turn taking. They may also be getting practice in understanding other's feelings, and conflict resolution skills. Ross et al. (2006) found that siblings in the 3.5–12 years age range were able to reach or negotiate some sort of compromise in conflicts about half of the time, and to reach an agreeable win–loss outcome about one-fifth of the time.

The way mothers talk to one sibling about the other sibling, or discuss feelings within the family, can be important. This was illustrated by an observational study of 40 pairs of siblings in home settings in Japan (Kojima, 2000). The younger siblings were aged around 2–3 years and the older siblings around 5–6 years. Each sibling showed a fair balance of positive and negative behaviours to each other. When siblings argued, mothers might try distraction— mainly to the younger sibling, perhaps offering some different toy. Also, they would often explain the actions or emotional states of one sibling to the other. Mothers' use of such explanations to the older sibling correlated quite highly ($r = .50$) with the older sibling's positive behaviour to the younger one. Similarly, in a follow-up of the Cambridge sample at middle childhood, Dunn et al. (1991) found that mothers' talk about siblings' feelings related to later understanding and emotional quality of relationships.

Siblings may also engage in a social comparison process; for example, one sibling doing well (such as in school achievement) and getting praise from parents might lead the other sibling to have lower academic self-esteem—or it might spur them to greater efforts or to redirect their energies into a different area, such as sports. A related possibility is a 'sibling barricade' effect, in which parental treatment results in opposite effects for the siblings—for example, negative treatment of one sibling affects him/her negatively but the other sibling positively, through a social comparison process. Feinberg et al. (2000) found some evidence for these effects in an adolescent US sample. Updegraff et al. (2000) found that in adolescence, brother–sister pairs engaged in social comparison processes; for example, in older sister– younger brother pairs, sex-typed choices of friends were particularly exaggerated. However, sisters (both first- and second-born) learned control tactics from their brothers, which they applied in their friendships.

Sibling Influences: Theory of Mind

The experiences of siblings, both in joint pretend play and in conflicts and conflict resolution, may be important in helping young children learn to understand the thoughts and emotions of others and more generally develop 'theory of mind' capabilities (see Chapter 15). For example, Howe et al. (1998) found that at 5–6 years, siblings who did a lot of pretend play were more likely to use internal state terms, especially in high-level negotiations about play. A number of studies have indeed suggested that having siblings, and especially an older sibling, accelerates theory of mind development in preschoolers.

Perner et al. (1994) reported two experiments using false belief tasks with English children aged 3–5 years. Children with two siblings did better than those with one sibling, who in turn did better than those with no siblings. This was quite a substantial effect: the authors reported that 'the benefit children get from interacting with two siblings rather than none is worth about as much as one year of experience' (p. 1230). Subsequently, Ruffman et al. (1998) reported findings from four experiments with false belief tasks in England and Japan. They located the benefit as being due to older siblings. In all four experiments, the number of older siblings (none, one or two) contributed linearly to false belief understanding, whereas the number of younger siblings had no effect.

A longitudinal study in Australia by McAlister and Peterson (2013) followed 157 children aged 3–5 years over 12 months. They too found that having a sibling was advantageous for theory of mind, especially having more siblings, although in this study it did not matter very much if siblings were older or younger. This difference (and associated progress in executive functioning) was maintained over the 1-year period.

Of course, it might not only be older siblings that have this effect. Lewis et al. (1996) gave similar false belief tasks to 3–5-year-old children in Cyprus and Crete, where children lived with more extended families. They found significant effects not only for number of siblings, but also more generally for the number of older children seen the day before. They argued for an 'apprenticeship' model, with children acquiring theory of mind from adults, older siblings and other older children in their extended family or neighborhood.

Twins and Multiplets

There is normally an age gap of at least a year between siblings, but the exception is for twins and higher multiplets. As we saw in Chapter 2, twins can be identical or fraternal, and the study of these two types of twins has told us a lot about genetic and environmental influences on development. Twins occur in about 1 in 80 births and identical twins make up about one-third of this number (Segal, 2000), although there is some variation by ethnic background and some increase amongst people using assisted reproductive techniques (such as *in vitro* fertilization [IVF] and embryo transfer) in cases of infertility.

Twins are often thought of as having a 'special relationship' or 'friendship extraordinaire' (Segal, 2000). Of course, all is not harmony, even between twins, and they can fight and quarrel but generally speaking, they have close, cooperative and harmonious relationships with each other. This is especially so for identical twins. Segal observed both identical and fraternal twins completing a puzzle together; identical twins showed more cooperation and were more likely to complete the puzzle successfully.

One downside to the closeness of twins is that they may fall behind on conventional measures of language development (Chapter 12); again, this is more marked in identical twins. Although mothers may talk as much to twins as to singletons, each twin may get shorter utterances and less joint attention because the mother often has to share attention between the twins. Twins often develop their own speech patterns ('autonomous language' or 'twin speech'), which can be difficult for others to understand.

Only Children

Given the arguments that siblings' experiences can bring a number of benefits in early development, how do only children fare? The work on theory of mind, cited above, showed that only children are relatively delayed in passing false belief tasks: '. . . having no siblings is particularly disadvantageous in the acquisition of false belief understanding' (Lewis et al., 1996, p. 2937).

It is worth bearing in mind that children can get the kind of experiences we have discussed (such as pretend play and resolving conflicts) with adults and peers, as well as with siblings. But is there something special about having a sibling, or at least a close peer of similar age, to interact with? This was suggested by one study in Norway. Hollos and Cowan (1973) compared 7-year-old children growing up in three different contexts: isolated farm communities, villages and towns. At the time, children did not start school in Norway until 7 years, and the farm children lived in remote areas and saw few other children, compared to those in villages and towns. The farm children performed worse than the other two groups on social cognitive skills (role-taking abilities, understanding others' emotions). By contrast, they did just as well on non-social tasks, such as Piagetian conservation tests.

Kitzmann et al. (2002) compared the social competence of only children and first- and second-borns in two-child families, at 6–12 years, as assessed by peers from school. They did not find any significant differences in self-concept or loneliness, or in self-rated number and quality of friendships. However, in terms of social preference (getting 'liked most' and not 'liked least' nominations from classmates, see p. 173), second-borns were the most liked, and only children the least liked. Only children were also nominated most often as aggressive, victimized and withdrawn. Some of the findings are shown in Table 5.1. Kitzmann et al. (2002) concluded that 'having a sibling may be especially helpful for learning to manage conflict' (p. 299). In fact,

Table 5.1   Mean scores on social competence measures for only children, and for first- and second-borns in two-child families.

	Only children	First-born children	Second-born children
Not statistically significant:			
Number of mutual friends	4.60	5.32	5.43
Global self-esteem	2.84	2.82	2.97
Loneliness	2.21	1.73	1.86
Statistically significant:			
Social preference	−.33	.14	.45
Aggressive/disruptive	.17	−.18	−.36
Victimized	.39	−.09	−.39
Passive withdrawal	.46	−.18	−.28

Source: Adapted from Kitzmann, K.M., Cohen, R. & Lockwood, R.L. (2002). Are only children missing out? Comparison of the peer-related social competence of only children and siblings. *Journal of Social and Personal Relationships, 19,* 299–316.

having an older sibling again seems to be most advantageous, although not all the differences between first- and second-borns shown in Table 5.1 were significant.

Prosocial behaviour (Chapter 9) may also play a role in this. Caputi, Lecce, Pagnin and Banerjee (2012), in a longitudinal study of Italian children from 5 through to 6 and 7 years, found that early theory of mind abilities predicted later peer acceptance and lower peer rejection, in part through greater prosocial behaviour. (However, although a third of their sample were only children, this aspect was not analysed in their study.)

Differences between only children and those with siblings may be dependent on cultural context. In China, the one-child policy has been normative in urban areas since the 1980s. A study by Chen et al. (1994) of 8- and 10-year-olds in primary schools in Shanghai recruited 498 only children and 67 sibling children. They found no significant differences between these two groups, on sociometric assessments by peers, teacher ratings of school competence or academic achievement. The authors attributed this to the fact that only children are in the majority in contemporary China; clearly, if most children are only children, then it will be more difficult to get a general finding that only children are 'liked least'! Also, most children in China go to public day nurseries from an early age and therefore get a lot of peer experience, which may substitute for lack of siblings in the only children.

Despite any possible drawbacks in social-cognitive skills with peers, on many measures only children do just as well as others, and they may do well on achievement and intelligence. Falbo and Polit (1986) carried out a meta-analysis of 20 relevant studies; they found that only children tended to have more positive relations with parents, and parents spent more time with them and conversed with them more. The mean effect size here (difference in terms of standard deviations) was just .08 for only children compared to two-child families, but it rose to a more substantial .20 for only children compared to families with five or more children. This appears to be an effect of family size, rather than of being an only child *per se*. In a more recent review, Falbo (2012) argued that in general, only children do well academically (possibly a family size effect), and that findings concerning personality and social behaviour are inconsistent. Like Chen et al. (1994), she argued the importance of context. Whereas in China only children are the norm, in the USA (for example) there are fewer only-children families, and they are often single-parent families or those in disadvantaged circumstances— issues not often controlled for in the available research.

Family Size, Birth Order, Intelligence and Creative Lives

In contrast to the effects favouring children with older siblings in theory of mind tasks, different findings appear for tests of general intellectual ability. Large sample national surveys in industrialized countries find consistent trends favouring older born children and children from smaller families, on tests of intelligence and academic achievement (Cicirelli, 1978). Wider spacing between siblings is also beneficial in this respect (Powell & Steelman, 1993).

Zajonc and Markus (1975; Zajonc, 1983) hypothesized that these findings can be explained by the confluence model, in which a child's intellectual development is influenced by 'some function of the absolute intellectual level of its [the family's] members'. Children in smaller families get more adult stimulation and a higher-level intellectual environment. An alternative explanation is the resource dilution hypothesis, in which children in larger families have fewer intellectual, social and economic resources generally (Downey, 2001). While the family size effect appears fairly robust, the effects of birth order on intellectual development are still being debated (see Rodgers, 2001; Zajonc, 2001).

Birth order and family size are obviously closely related, but it is important to consider gender, sibling age gaps and developmental status (that is, preschool, school-age and so on). In addition, any effects may depend upon socioeconomic and cultural factors. For example, the resource dilution hypothesis would suggest greater impact of family size on poorer families; better-off families can afford good food, toys and good-quality substitute or extra care, even with a larger family.

Perhaps because of these complications and confounding factors, there are many conflicting results on birth order in the literature (Furman & Lanthier, 2002). Most reviews do not find substantial effects of birth order *per se* on personality or achievement. There is some evidence that first-borns get more parental attention when young and may be more pressured for achievement as they get older, and that first-borns are more parent oriented. But some studies find that the youngest child may be the most favoured.

A provocative theory about effects of birth order was advanced by Frank J. Sulloway (1996) in his book *Born to rebel*. Using a mixture of evolutionary theory and historical analysis, Sulloway argued that siblings had a characteristic 'niche' in the family, according to birth order. First-borns would tend to be conservative, wishing to keep the 'status quo' (which would typically have them as the oldest sibling, having the most resources). Later-born siblings would then tend to be more rebellious and creative, more willing to overthrow the 'status quo'. In terms of 'big five' personality types, first-borns would be higher on Conscientiousness, Neuroticism (Emotional Instability) and Extraversion; later-borns would be higher on Openness to Experience and Agreeableness.

Sulloway claimed evidence for this from looking at the birth order characteristics of those involved in scientific revolutions. For example, adherents of Darwin's theory (especially early on) were more often later-borns. However, Sulloway's book and methods have been heavily criticized; the main accusations are of selective use of evidence and unsystematic use of caveats (for example, invoking social class, sibship size, age gap, gender or parental conflict, at different points, to explain anomalous findings). The debate became acrimonious and litigious (see Townsend, 2000, and commentaries; also www.sulloway.org/chronology.html).

Stop and Think

What sort of influences on development do birth order, having siblings and family size have? How easy is it to disentangle their relative influence?

PEER RELATIONSHIPS IN PRESCHOOL AND SCHOOL

By 2 or 3 years of age, a child is usually thought ready for nursery school. Certainly the period from 2 to 4 years sees a great increase in the skills children have interacting with same-age peers. As we will see in Chapter 7, sociodramatic play and rough-and-tumble play with one or more partners become frequent in this age range. Parallel with this, the child is beginning to develop concrete operational thought and beginning to be able to take the perspective of others in simple ways (Chapters 13 and 15).

The increase in social behaviour in preschool children was documented by Mildred Parten at the Institute of Child Development in Minnesota in the late 1920s. She observed 2–4-year-olds and described how they might be 'unoccupied' or an 'onlooker' on others' activities; or (if engaged in an activity), 'solitary', in 'parallel' activity with others or in 'associative' or 'cooperative' activity with others. Parallel activity is when children play near each other with the same materials but do not interact much—playing independently at the same sandpit, for example. Associative activity is when children interact together in an activity, doing similar things, perhaps each adding building blocks to the same tower. Cooperative activity is when children interact together in complementary ways; for example, one child gets blocks out of a box and hands them to another child, who builds the tower. Parten (1932) found that the first four categories declined with age, whereas associative and cooperative activity—the only ones involving much interaction with peers—increased with age.

Subsequent researchers have frequently used Parten's categories, though often simplified to 'solitary' (including unoccupied and onlooker), 'parallel' and 'group' (comprising associative and cooperative). Studies in the UK and the USA have found that, very approximately, preschool children in free play divide their time equally amongst these three categories, with the balance shifting more towards 'group' activity as they get older (Smith, 1978). Most group activity involves just two or three children playing together, though the size of groups does tend to increase in older preschoolers. These trends continue in the early school years. According to a study of more than 400 Israeli children, group activity rises to about 57% of the time in outdoor free play, while parallel activity falls to about 6%; the number of groups comprising more than five children increased from about 12% to 16% between 5 and 6 years of age (Hertz-Lazarowitz et al., 1981). The size of children's groups continues to increase through the middle school years, especially in boys, as team games such as football become more popular (Eifermann, 1970).

By the middle school years, sex segregation of children's groups is becoming very marked. In fact, children tend to choose same-sex partners even in nursery school, but by no means exclusively; typically, some two-thirds of partner choices may be same-sex, though this is influenced by such factors as the class size, toys available and the role of teachers in encouraging (or not) cross-sex play. However, by the time children are getting into team games, from about 6 or 7 years onward, sex segregation in the playground is very much greater (Maccoby, 1998).

In a study of 10–11-year-old children in American playgrounds, Lever (1978) found that there were distinct differences between boys' and girls' activities and friendships. Boys more often played in larger, mixed-age groups, while girls were more often in smaller groups or same-age pairs. Boys tended to play competitive team games that were more complex in their rules and role structure, and seemed to emphasize 'political' skills of cooperation, competition and leadership in their social relations. Girls seemed to put more emphasis on intimacy and exclusiveness in their friendships (Maccoby, 1998).

The nature of children's groups changes again as adolescence is reached. Large, same-sex 'cliques' or 'gangs' become common in early adolescence, changing as sexual relationships become more important in later adolescence. A study of Australian adolescents aged 13–21 years (Dunphy, 1963) presents a picture of this process. Natural observations were supplemented by questionnaires, diaries and interviews in this study. At the younger end of this age range, many teenagers went around in cliques comprising some 3–9 individuals of the same sex.

They would interact little outside their own clique. A few years later, however, adolescents would be participating in larger groups or 'crowds', made up of several interacting cliques. These would still be same-sex groups, but the more mature or higher-status members of the crowd would start to initiate contact with members of the opposite sex. Gradually, other members of the crowd would follow their lead. This would lead to a stage where (heterosexual) crowds were made up of male and female cliques in loose association. Finally, young people associated most in (heterosexual) couples, going on dates, and loosely associated with other couples, prior to engagement and marriage. This research related to heterosexual relationships; there is more on adolescent relationships, including homosexual relationships, in Chapter 19.

Measuring Peer Relationships: Sociometry

How can we find out about the structure of children's peer relationships? This has been done in three main ways: by direct observation of behaviour; by asking another person, such as a teacher or parent; or by asking the child (see Pepler & Craig, 1998, for a review).

If you watch a class of children, you can record which children are interacting together. If you do this at regular intervals, it is possible to build up a picture of the social structure in the class. For example, in a study of two classes in a nursery school, Clark et al. (1969) observed a child for 10 seconds to see whom he was playing with, then they observed another child, and so on through the class; this was continued over a 5-week period. From these data, the authors constructed a 'sociogram' for each class, as shown in Figure 5.2. Each symbol represents a child; the number of lines joining two children represents the percentage of observations on which they were seen playing together. The concentric circles show the number of play partners a child has: if there are many, that child's symbol is towards the middle; if none, it is at the periphery. This enables us to see at a glance that in class A, for example, there is one very popular girl who links two large subgroups; one boy and one girl have no clear partners. In class B, there are several subgroups and, unlike class A, there is almost complete segregation by sex; two boys have no clear partners. This is a very neat way of illustrating social structure, provided the class is not very large.

Observation gives a valid measure of who associates with whom. An alternative procedure is to ask a teacher, for example, 'Who are John's best friends in the class?' or to ask John himself, 'Who are your best friends?'. These nomination methods also give

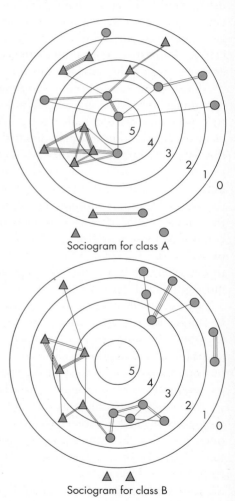

Sociogram for class A

Sociogram for class B

Figure 5.2   Sociograms of association networks in two classes of preschool children; circles represent girls, triangles represent boys.

Source: Clark, A.H., Wyon, S.M. & Richards, M.P.M. (1969). Free-play in nursery school children. *Journal of Child Psychology and Psychiatry, 10*, 205–216.

data that can be plotted on a sociogram. If John chooses Richard as a 'best friend' but Richard does not choose John, this can be indicated by an arrow from John to Richard; if the choice is reciprocated, the arrow would point both ways on the sociogram.

A common nomination method is to ask each child to name their three best friends. Other methods are to ask children to rate each child for liking (for example, asking them to sort names into three piles of 'like', 'neutral' and 'don't like') or to ask them which they prefer of all possible pairs of children. For younger children who cannot read well, photographs of classmates can be used.

For older children—approaching or in adolescence—Robert Cairns developed a method for examining the more complex cliques or groups that characterize this period. Besides asking for friendship nominations, Cairns and his colleagues got information on social groups and networks by asking questions like, 'Are there people who hang around together a lot at school? Who are they?'. By combining information from different informants, it is possible to develop a 'social-cognitive map' of the peer group structure in adolescents. Besides looking at the position of an individual in the group (as in traditional sociometry, such as in Figure 5.2), it is then also possible to look at the centrality of a group or clique in the wider peer group network of the school (Cairns et al., 1995). Gest et al. (2003) found that social-cognitive maps obtained from children aged 10–13 years showed significant agreement with classroom observations made by researchers of actual classroom interaction frequencies.

The Concept of Sociometric Status

The earliest sociometric approaches focused on liking and popularity. For example, in the sociogram in Figure 5.2, the main dimension of difference is between the 'stars' or highly liked children in the centre and the isolated children at the periphery. However, since the 1980s, investigators have also asked children to say whom they do not like. This procedure was initiated in a seminal study by Coie, Dodge and Coppotelli (1982), described in Box 5.1; see especially Box Figure 5.1.1. Researchers who have obtained both positive and negative nominations have not constructed sociograms (which would then look very complicated), but have rather categorized children into 'sociometric status types', as 'popular', 'controversial', 'rejected', 'neglected' or 'average', according to whether they are high or low on positive and negative nominations. This gives a more complicated, two-dimensional picture of variations in social status (Box Figure 5.1.1).

Sociometric status typologies attracted researchers into a large number of studies during the 1980s and 1990s. Newcomb et al. (1993) reviewed many such studies, some 10 years after the initial work of Coie and colleagues. They concluded that rejected peer status was associated with high levels of aggression and withdrawal, and low levels of sociability and cognitive abilities, whereas neglected peer status was associated with less sociability and less aggression. Controversial children compensated for high aggression with better cognitive and social abilities.

Hymel et al. (2011) review different types of sociometric assessment developed over this period. Metaanalyses show that there is some stability of sociometric status over time (Jiang & Cillessen, 2005). Stability is higher in older children, and for shorter time intervals; it is also higher for continuous measures of status (assessed on a scale) than for categorical measures (assigning children to a definite category, as in Box Figure 5.1.1). Hymel et al. also discuss the ethical issues involved. This is an issue, since questions about 'not liking' someone might bring about increased negative behaviour to unliked peers; however, so far there is little evidence for such effects (Mayeux, Underwood & Risser, 2007).

Box 5.1 Dimensions and types of social status: a cross-age perspective

Two studies were carried out in this investigation of the types of social status in children's groups and the kinds of behaviours that correlated with them.

In the first study, approximately 100 children at each of three age levels (8, 11 and 14 years) were interviewed at two schools in North Carolina, USA. Each child was seen individually, and asked to name the three classmates whom he or she liked most, and the three classmates whom he or she liked least. Then, he or she was asked to name the three children who best fitted each of 24 behavioural descriptions, such as 'disrupts the group' or 'attractive physically'. The interview was repeated 12 weeks later to check that the data were reliable.

The scores used were the total nominations each child received for each of the 26 questions (liked most, liked least and 24 behavioural descriptions). The correlations between the liked most and liked least scores, and some of the behavioural descriptions, are shown in Box Table 5.1.1. (The results were similar when each age group was treated separately.) The interesting thing about these results is that different behavioural descriptions correlate significantly with the 'liked most' and 'liked least' ratings. The two measures are not simply opposites of each other. 'Liked most' children tend to be supportive, cooperative leaders and attractive physically; 'liked least' children tend to be disruptive, aggressive and snobbish.

If 'liked most' is not just the opposite of 'liked least', the researchers argued that it made sense to think of these as independent measures (in fact, the correlation between them was .21, which is quite a small value). In that case, there are four possible status outcomes

Box Table 5.1.1 Correlations between nominations for 'most liked' and 'least liked' and behavioural descriptions for 311 children aged 8–14.

	Liked most	Liked least
Supports peers	.63*	−.24*
Leads peers	.51*	−.08*
Cooperates with peers	.51*	−.31*
Attractive physically	.57*	−.25*
Remains calm	.43*	−.28*
Defends self in arguments	.37*	.03*
Acts shy	−.12*	−.05*
Gets rejected by peers	−.28*	.30*
Acts snobbish	−.04*	.66*
Starts fights	−.02*	.70*
Gets into trouble with teacher	−.03*	.71*
Disrupts the group	−.07*	.78*

*$p < .001$.

shown in Box Figure 5.1.1 and mentioned in the text above (see p. 173), with a fifth if 'average' children are included.

In the second study, the differences between these five status groups were examined more closely. More children of the same ages were interviewed at the same schools over the next 2 years. They were asked to nominate the three peers whom they liked most and liked least, and who best fitted the descriptions 'cooperates', 'disrupts', 'shy', 'fights', 'seeks help' and 'leader'. Out of a total of 848 children, 486 were selected who clearly fitted one of the five social status groups. It was then possible to calculate the average 'behavioural profile' for children of

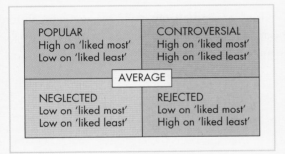

Box Figure 5.1.1 Five types of sociometric status.

each social status in terms of the six behavioural descriptions obtained from peers. Box Table 5.1.2 shows the results. Children who lead in a cooperative way are 'popular'. Children who lead but fight and are disruptive are 'controversial', liked by some but disliked by others. Disruptive children who lack any cooperative or leadership skills are 'rejected'. Children who lack cooperative or leadership skills and are not aggressive either are 'neglected'. The pattern of results was similar across the three ages, for both sexes and for different ethnic groups.

The strengths of this study are the large pool of participants and the attempt to make important distinctions in types of sociometric status. The authors speculate, for example, that 'controversial' children, high on both leadership and aggression, may become leaders of delinquent peer groups in adolescence. A weakness is that no direct observational measures were taken; we do not know that 'rejected' children really fight a lot, for example, only that other children (who do not like them) say they do. Some subsequent work (see p. 177) has linked the status groups to more direct behavioural measures.

Box Table 5.1.2   Behavioural profiles associated with five types of sociometric status in 486 children.

	Leads peers	Cooperates	Acts shy	Seeks help	Fights	Disrupts group
Popular	HIGH	HIGH		Low	Low	Low
Controversial	HIGH		Low	High	HIGH	HIGH
Rejected	Low	LOW		HIGH	HIGH	HIGH
Neglected	Low	Low		Low	Low	Low
Average						

Note: Use of upper case denotes a stronger difference than lower case; a blank cell implies the score was near the average for all the children.

Based on material in Coie, J.D., Dodge, K.A. & Coppotelli, H. (1982). Dimensions and types of social status: A cross-age perspective. *Developmental Psychology*, 18, 557–570.

A Social Information Processing Model

The sort of findings summarized by Newcomb et al. (1993) can be taken to suggest that children of different sociometric status types vary in some social-cognitive skills, in important ways. This is a widely held view, and was developed by Dodge et al. (1986) who suggested that the social skills of peer interaction can be envisaged as an exchange model of social information processing, or SIP (Figure 5.3). Suppose child A is interacting with child B. According to this model, she has to: (1) encode the incoming information to perceive what child B is doing; (2) interpret this information; (3) search for appropriate responses; (4) evaluate these responses and select the best; and (5) enact that response. For example, suppose child B is running forward with arms raised, shouting and smiling. Child A needs to perceive all these actions, interpret their meaning (is this friendly or aggressive?), search for appropriate responses (run away? ignore? play fight?), select what seems best and then do it effectively. Child B, of course, will be engaged in a similar process with respect to child A.

Crick and Dodge (1994) summarized evidence relating to this SIP model, together with some reformulation of its details. Subsequently, Lemerise and Arsenio (2000) suggested that the Crick and Dodge model is primarily cognitive, and presented a revised model in which emotion processes are integrated.

Models of this kind are certainly helpful in conceptualizing some reasons why children may be successful, or less successful, in peer relations. However, other factors are involved too. We will look at some evidence for the main status types.

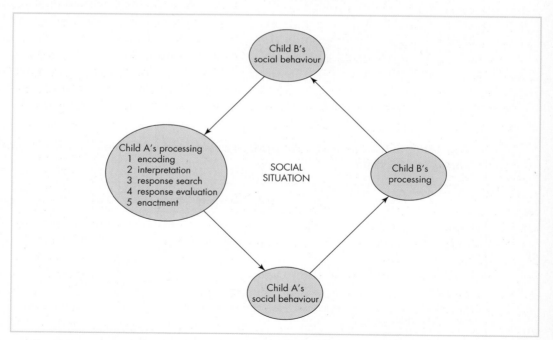

Figure 5.3   A model of social skills and social exchange in peer interaction.

Source: Adapted from Dodge, K. A., Petit, G. S., McClasky, C. L. & Brown, M. M. 1986: Social competence in children. *Monographs of the Society for Research in Child Development, 51*: 2, 1–85 by permission of John Wiley & Sons Inc.

Rejected Children

The greatest interest and concern of researchers, in the first decades of work on sociometric status, focused on rejected children. In an early study of 8- and 11-year-olds over a 4-year period, Coie and Dodge (1983) looked at the stability of sociometric status categories on a year-to-year basis, and found that this was highest for 'rejected' children; 30% of those rejected at the start of the investigation were still rejected 4 years later; another 30% were 'neglected'. By contrast, those merely 'neglected' at the start of the study tended to become 'average'.

Other studies found that 'rejected' children differ in their behaviour in what seem to be maladaptive ways. Ladd (1983) observed 8- and 9-year-olds in playground breaks. Rejected children, compared with average or popular children, spent less time in cooperative play and social conversation, and more time in arguing and fighting; they tended to play in smaller groups, and with younger or less popular companions. In another study, Dodge et al. (1983) looked at how 5-year-olds attempted to get into ongoing play between two other peers. They suggested that whereas popular children first waited and watched, then gradually got themselves incorporated by making group-orientated statements, and neglected children tended to stay at the waiting and watching stage, rejected children tended to escalate to disruptive actions such as interrupting the play.

Subtypes of Rejected Children

Following the early work in the 1980s, several studies have investigated subtypes of rejected children, and different reasons for peer rejection. In particular, there appears to be a major distinction between some children who are rejected because they are aggressive and others who are rejected because they are submissive—a distinction between externalizing and internalizing problems in behaviour (Asher et al., 1990).

A study in the Netherlands by Cillessen et al. (1992) provided evidence on this. From a sample of 784 boys, aged 5–7 years, they gathered peer nominations, teacher and peer ratings, observations of behaviour, and a measure of skills in problem solving. They found 98 rejected children. They used a statistical procedure called cluster analysis on the full range of measures, to see what natural groupings of children with similar characteristics their sample fell into. They found that the largest cluster (48% of their sample) was of rejected-aggressive children. Besides being aggressive, these boys tended to be dishonest, impulsive and non-cooperative. A smaller cluster (13%) was of the rejected-submissive children; these were shy children, not particularly aggressive (or cooperative). The remaining 39% of their rejected children formed two further clusters that were not so well defined and seemed more average in their characteristics. The researchers examined the stability of rejected status 1 year later; this was highest for the rejected-aggressive groups, with 58% of these children still being rejected; it was only true for 34% of the other children. These two subgroups may also differ in academic achievement. In a study of 11–13-year-olds, Wentzel and Asher (1995) found that rejected-aggressive children had problematic academic profiles, whereas rejected-submissive children did not have such problems.

Many researchers think that rejected-aggressive children are lacking in components of social skills. For example, on the SIP model discussed above (see Figure 5.3), they might misinterpret others' behaviour (at stage 2) or too readily select aggressive responses (at stage 4); there is some evidence for both of these. However, not all aggressive behaviour may be due to lack of social skills. Some aggressive children may be quite skilled at manipulating others. And some rejected children may simply be reacting to exclusion by the popular cliques and would not necessarily be rejected or lacking in social skills in other situations outside the classroom. Sandstrom and Coie (1999) looked at factors involved in children escaping from 'rejected' status over a 2-year period. Important factors for this were the child's own perception of their social status, participation in extracurricular activities, internal locus of control and high parental monitoring. Interestingly, aggressive behaviour was *positively* related to status improvement amongst initially rejected boys, an indication that aggressive behaviour is not always maladaptive. This is an issue considered further in Chapter 10.

Popular and Controversial Children

The Newcomb et al. (1993) meta-analysis (p. 173) suggested that popular children have good interpersonal skills, are not high in aggression and are not withdrawn. Other factors also affect popularity. Popularity may be influenced by the composition of the peer group a child is in. It may be difficult for a child to be popular if he or she differs in salient respects (such as ethnicity, interests, intelligence) from most others in the class. Around puberty, early physical maturation is also a variable affecting popularity and status (Chapter 19).

Another factor is physical attractiveness. Children, like adults, differ in how their physical attraction is rated by persons who know them. In one study (Vaughn & Langlois, 1983), ratings of physical attractiveness were obtained for 59 preschool children. The correlation with sociometric preference using a paired-comparison method was .42 ($p < .01$); the correlation was higher for girls (.66, $p < .01$) than for boys (.22, n.s.). Several other studies have found that ratings of physical attractiveness correlate with sociometric status (e.g. Box Table 5.1.1).

The relationship between popularity and aggression is complex; it varies with age and social context. In preschool and early school years, aggressive children tend to be disliked and unpopular, as we saw in the summary of 'rejected' sociometric status. Such studies usually make it clear that it is unprovoked aggression that causes such children to be actively disliked—they may push another child or disrupt a game, with little or no reason or provocation. By adolescence, the picture is much more mixed, with several studies finding that aggressive boys, especially, may appear tough, competent and popular (Pellegrini & Bartini, 2001; Rodkin et al., 2000; and see Chapter 10).

Even before adolescence, some children are quite aggressive but not clearly disliked. These are the 'controversial' children in Box Figure 5.1.1. Such children can be both highly socially skilful and highly aggressive. Peers may describe them as good leaders, but also as starting fights—a pattern of behaviour that appeals to some peers but not to others. In other words, some children may use aggressive behaviour as a means of acquiring status in the peer group (see Chapter 10).

Perceived Popularity

Following the earlier focus on rejected children, more recent work in the sociometric status tradition has focused more on popularity, and the distinction between sociometric popularity and perceived popularity (Hymel et al., 2011). Sociometric popularity is a measure of how much pupils are actually liked, and not disliked, by classmates. Another way of looking at peer popularity has been developed, called 'perceived popularity'. Perceived popularity is a measure of social visibility. It is obtained by asking classmates not who they actually like, but rather who they think is popular with classmates (for example, 'Who are the most [or least] popular students?').

This distinction was first studied empirically by Parkhurst and Hopmeyer (1998). They found that there was an overlap between the two measures of popularity, but a more limited one than one might expect. Of 700 students in grades 7–8 (ages 13–14 years), only 31% of the 'perceived popular' students were sociometrically 'popular'; another 19% were 'controversial' and 40% were average or unclassified.

Sociometrically popular children are usually also nominated as cooperative and prosocial. However, perceived popularity picks up other aspects, as the relatively high proportion of controversial children in the Parkhurst and Hopmeyer study indicates. Perceived popularity also picks up aspects of social dominance, or leadership, and sometimes aggression. Children who are seen as popular may be dominant, and sometimes aggressive or antisocial, in high-status cliques and network centrality (Cillessen & Mayeux, 2004; Rodkin et al., 2000). Correlations of perceived popularity with measures of social dominance (see Chapter 10) are quite high (Lease, Kennedy and Axelrod, 2002; Parkhurst & Hopmeyer, 1998).

Consistent with this, Cillessen and Borch (2006) found that the overlap between sociometric and perceived popularity declines with age. They obtained quite a high overlap in primary or elementary school, but a much less substantial one in secondary or high school. Interestingly, there was also a strong gender difference here; whereas the relationship between the two constructs remained positive (although smaller in magnitude) for boys, Cillessen and Borch found that it turned negative for girls. Whereas for older boys, being liked and being seen as popular stay fairly compatible, this seems to be more difficult for older girls.

Some light on this comes from a study by Closson (2009), who obtained descriptions from 8th-grade adolescents on what it meant to be popular. Being 'cool' was the most common response, and 'attractive' for girls. However, more boys mentioned 'athletic' and 'funny', whereas more girls mentioned 'mean', 'snobby' and 'rude'. It may be that the characteristics of perceived popularity in some older girls, especially, are more related to relational aggression (Chapter 10) and are less likeable, hence there is less overlap in the constructs compared to boys. Of course, the best outcomes may be associated with being high on both sociometric popularity and perceived popularity. Lease et al. (2002) found that these children seem to be prosocial and socially skilled, but not overly aggressive.

Neglected Children, Loneliness and Social Withdrawal

Neglected children have not been studied so much as rejected children, although as they receive few 'liked most' nominations, they may be lonely and lack friends (see below). However, in their US sample of 11–13-year-olds, Wentzel and Asher (1995) found that neglected children were quite well liked by teachers, being prosocial and compliant, and did fairly well academically.

Do neglected (or rejected) status children feel lonely? Asher and Wheeler (1985) developed a Loneliness and Social Dissatisfaction questionnaire, which is a 24-item self-report scale for children. It includes 16 items such as 'It's hard for me to make friends at school' and 'I have nobody to talk to in class', as well as eight 'filler' items about hobbies and interests. This and subsequent work found that neglected children did *not* score particularly highly; in fact, it was rejected children, especially the rejected-submissive subgroup, who scored highest on self-reported loneliness (Asher et al., 1990).

Neglected children do seem to be low on sociability (Newcomb et al., 1993). A related construct is *social withdrawal*, defined by Rubin et al. (2002) as the consistent display of all forms of solitary behaviour when encountering familiar and/or unfamiliar peers. Rubin et al.

argue that this may develop from the temperamental attribute of behavioural inhibition in childhood (which shows moderate stability), augmented by ambivalent (type C; see p. 110) attachment type, which results in emotional dysregulation in unfamiliar or threatening circumstances. Overprotective or oversolicitous parenting can also contribute to children (especially boys) showing social withdrawal if they have not developed good interpersonal coping skills. The sociometric status of socially withdrawn children is not well investigated, but they may be sociometrically rejected as much as neglected.

In a sample of English children aged 4–9 years, Qualter and Munn (2002) distinguished peer rejection (which they referred to as social loneliness, but was actually a measure of peer rejection) and emotional loneliness (based on self-reported feelings). Out of 640 children in their sample, 374 were neither rejected nor lonely; 60 were rejected but not lonely; 145 were lonely but not rejected; and 61 were both rejected and lonely. Qualter and Munn found that peer rejection was related to externalizing problems, while being lonely was related to internalizing and low self-esteem.

Chen et al. (2004) looked at correlations between peer-assessed behaviours and self-reported loneliness in 9–12-year-old children in Brazil, Canada, China and Italy. Some of their findings are shown in Table 5.2. They found some similarities in all four countries; for example, in all the samples, self-perceived loneliness correlated negatively to peer-assessed sociability, peer preference and having mutual friends. But they also found some differences; in China, but not in the other countries, loneliness was associated with peer-assessed aggression but not associated with peer-assessed shyness-sensitivity.

Stop and Think

Has the concept of sociometric status types proved useful? Does it have limitations in understanding peer relations?

Table 5.2 Correlations between loneliness and other social adjustment variables, in 9–12-year-old children from four countries.

	Brazil	Canada	Italy	China
Loneliness:				
and sociability	−.21**	−.26**	−.24**	−.27**
and peer preference	−.14**	−.32**	−.24**	−.31**
and mutual friends	−.14**	−.24**	−.14**	−.25**
and aggression	.00	.07	.11*	.14**
and shyness	.14**	.24**	.16**	−.01

*$p < .05$,
**$p < .001$.
Source: Adapted from Chen, X.et al. (2004) Loneliness and social adaptation in Brazilian, Canadian, Chinese and Italian children: a multi-national comparative study, *Journal of Child Psychology and Psychiatry, 45*, 1373–1384 by permission of John Wiley & Sons Ltd.

FRIENDSHIP

Usually we take friendship to mean a close relationship between two particular people, as indicated by their association together or their psychological attachment and trust. Friendship is related to social participation and to sociometric status, but it is not the same thing. While a solitary child obviously does not have friends, a child who interacts a lot with others may or may not have friends. A rejected child might be generally disliked but still have a good, close friendship with a peer.

What Characterizes Friendship?

What actually characterizes friendship? It may seem an obvious question, but it deserves looking at in some detail. Only if we know what friendship involves can we start seriously examining what a lack of friendships is likely to lead to.

A considerable body of research was summarized by Newcomb and Bagwell (1995), and by Hartup (1996). Newcomb and Bagwell concluded that relations between friends, compared with non-friends, exhibit four particular features: reciprocity and intimacy; more intense social activity; more frequent conflict resolution; and more effective task performance. Let's look at a few studies that illustrate these characteristics.

Howes et al. (1994) observed pairs of 4-year-olds, who were videotaped in a room at a childcare centre. Of 24 dyads, six had been long-term friends for about 3 years; 12 had been short-term friends for about 6 months; and six had never been friends (based on observation and nomination). The levels of communication and play between the dyads were recorded over 20-minute sessions.

Two main findings emerged from the analysis. First, friends (whether long- or short-term) engaged in more complex levels of pretend play than did non-friends (for Howes' work on levels of pretend play, see Chapter 7). Secondly, there were differences in the amount of high-level cooperative pretend play, and in the communications that served to extend such play; here, friends did more than non-friends but, in addition, long-term friends did more than short-term friends. These differences were substantial, as shown in Table 5.3, and statistically significant despite the small sample.

This finding illustrates two of the main characteristics of friendship: there is more intense social activity between friends, and this goes along with more intimacy and reciprocity, as in the cooperative forms of pretend play in this study. A third characteristic was

Table 5.3 Differences in behaviour in dyads of differing friendship status.

	Long-term friends	Short-term friends	Never friends
Parallel play	3.2	4.1	11.5
Simple social play	24.7	24.2	13.0
Complex pretend	11.5	12.8	4.3
Cooperative pretend	2.0	.7	0

Source: Adapted from Howes, C., Droege, K. & Matheson, C. C. (1994) Play and communicative processes within long- and short-term friendship dyads, *Journal of Social and Personal Relationships, 11*: 401–10.

more frequent conflict resolution; an Italian study by Fonzi et al. (1997) illustrates this. Friendship pairs of 8-year-old children were compared with pairs of non-friends in two structured tasks designed to simulate real-life situations of potential conflict—games in which equipment had to be shared or turns had to be taken. Friends were more effective about this: they made more proposals than non-friends, spent more time negotiating sharing arrangements and were more able to make compromises. Those friendship pairs that had been stable through the school year showed more sensitivity in negotiations. More generally, as Newcomb and Bagwell (1995) found over many studies, friends may well have conflicts but they differ from non-friends in that they are better able to resolve these conflicts. A conflict with a friend is more likely to be made up than a conflict with a non-friend.

A study of older children by Azmitia and Montgomery (1993) demonstrates more effective task performance in friends. This was carried out with 11-year-olds in schools in California. Same-sex pairs of pupils were given scientific reasoning tasks (these were tasks of formal operational thinking, which will be discussed in Chapter 13). There were 18 pairs of friends (who had each nominated the other as a friend, so they were mutual friends), and 18 pairs of acquaintances (who had not nominated the other as a friend but who did not dislike them either). The problem-solving efforts were recorded on videotape and audiotape.

The researchers found that friends achieved higher problem-solving accuracy, especially in the harder problems, than did the non-friends. This seemed to be related to greater transaction between them in evaluating possible solutions. Friends appeared more willing to elaborate and critique each other's reasoning; even if they disagreed, they could handle this constructively to take things further. Besides the more effective task performance, friends appeared better able to handle disagreements or conflict of view.

However, Kutnick and Kingston (2005) found that, in primary school children, this effect interacted with gender. They gave science reasoning tasks to children aged 5, 7 and 9 years in English schools. Pairs were either friends or just acquaintances. Girl friendship pairings performed at the highest level, better than acquaintances, but for boy pairings, this pattern was reversed. In this study, boy pairs who were friends seemed to get distracted into non-task activities and conversation. Friendship was still a relevant variable, but whether it assists task performance may depend on age and the context in which the task is set.

Origins of Friendship

The work of John Gottman and colleagues has examined the processes of developing and maintaining friendships in young children. Gottman (1983) observed pairs of children (aged 3 up to 9 years) playing in their homes. In one study, the pairs were previously unacquainted, and Gottman observed them over three sessions. Often, children would establish a simple common-ground activity, such as colouring with crayons, which they could do side by side (a kind of 'parallel play'); they might 'escalate' this by 'information exchange' or 'self-disclosure', perhaps commenting on the other's activity or saying something about what they liked or wished to do. If successful, the pair would move on to introducing a joint activity. Often, such joint activity would involve pretend activity.

For example, Gottman (1983, pp. 56–57) describes interactions between D (in his own house) and J (visiting), both young 4-year-olds. After some information exchange,

J says, 'Pretend like those little roll cookies too, OK?' and D replies, 'And make, um, make a, um, pancake, too'. Later, D tries to introduce role-play, and there is some negotiation.

D: I'm the mummy.
J: Who am I?
D: Um, the baby.
J: Daddy.
D: Sister.
J: I wanna be the daddy.
D: You're the sister.
J: Daddy.
D: You're the big sister!
J: Don't play house. I don't want to play house.

Despite D offering progressively higher status roles (but not equal to 'mummy'!), this negotiation ended in failure and what Gottman calls a 'deescalation'. For a while, they returned to pretend meal preparation.

Gottman describes the social skill of friendship formation as managing levels of closeness ('amity') and conflict, by escalating and when necessary deescalating levels of play. Colouring side by side has low risks and low benefits (in friendship terms). Simple pretend (for example, pretending blocks are cookies) is a step up, and role-play is a step further. Thus, in Gottman's model, pretend play has a central role in the development of friendship.

Conceptions of Friendship

How do children themselves conceive of friendship? In one research programme (Bigelow & La Gaipa, 1980), children aged 6–14 years were asked to write an essay in class about their expectations of best friends. Essays were obtained from 480 Scottish children and also from 480 Canadian children, and analysed for their content. Results were similar in Scotland and Canada. At the earlier ages, children mentioned sharing common activities, receiving help and living nearby; later, admiring and being accepted by the partner; later still, such aspects as loyalty and commitment, genuineness and potential for intimacy. These last were found to be especially important in adolescence. Bigelow and La Gaipa suggested a three-stage model for friendship expectations (Table 5.4).

In similar research, Selman and Jaquette (1977) interviewed 225 persons aged from 4 to 32 years on their understanding and awareness of friendship relations. They documented five stages of understanding, also outlined in Table 5.4, linked to stages in perspective-taking abilities (Chapter 13). Although different in detail, there are considerable correspondences between the two schemes. There clearly seems to be a shift towards more psychologically complex and mutually reciprocal ideas of friendship during the middle school years, with intimacy and commitment becoming especially important later in adolescence (Berndt, 1982). Older children are obviously aware of characteristics of friendship such as reciprocity and intimacy.

Quality of Friendship

In his review, Hartup (1996) suggested that it is not only having a friend that may be important; it is also important to consider who your friends are—whether they are of high or low status in the peer group, for example—and what the quality of the friendship is.

Table 5.4 Two analyses of stages of understanding friendship.

Bigelow & La Gaipa (1980)	*Reward–cost stage* Common activities, living nearby, similar expectations	Around 7–8 years
	Normative stage Shared values, rules and sanctions	Around 9–10 years
	Empathic stage Understanding, self-disclosure, shared interests	Around 11–12 years
Selman & Jaquette (1997)	*Momentary physical playmate* Playing together, being in proximity	Around 3–7 years
	One-way assistance A friend helps you, but no notion of reciprocation	Around 4–9 years
	Fairweather cooperation Reciprocity focused on specific incidents rather than the friendship itself; conflicts may sever the relationship	Around 6–12 years
	Intimate; mutual sharing Awareness of intimacy and mutuality in a relationship that continues despite minor setbacks	Around 9–15 years
	Autonomous interdependence Awareness that relationships grow and change; reliance on friends but acceptance of their need for other relationships	Around 12–adult

Source: Adapted from Bigelow & La Gaipa (1980) and Selman & Jaquette (1977).

Bukowski et al., (1994) used some of the suggested characteristics of friendship to develop a Friendship Qualities Scale. This is an instrument in which children can rate friends and peers on several subscales, as indicated in Table 5.5. Bukowski et al. used this scale with 10–12-year-olds and found that the subscales of Companionship, Help, Security and Closeness were related; that is, someone rated high on one of these tended to be rated highly on the others. Reciprocated friends rated higher on these subscales than non-reciprocated friends and in a longitudinal sample, friends who had remained friends after 6 months scored higher than those who had not stayed friends.

The remaining Conflict subscale related negatively to the others. Reciprocated friends scored lower on Conflict than non-reciprocated friends; however, stable friends did not differ on Conflict from non-stable friends. Note that the Conflict items here refer mainly to frequency of conflict. Items to do with resolving conflicts successfully appear in the Security subscale (see Table 5.5), again illustrating how conflict resolution is an important aspect of friendship and one that predicts the stability of friendship more than does simple frequency of conflict.

Table 5.5 **Sample items from the Friendship Qualities Scale.**

Companionship	My friend and I spend all our free time together.
Help	My friend helps me when I am having trouble with something.
Security	If I have a problem at school, I can talk to my friend about it.
	If my friend and I have a fight or argument, we can say 'I'm sorry' and everything will be all right.
Closeness	If my friend had to move away, I would miss him.
Conflict	My friend and I disagree about many things.

Source: Adapted from Bukowski, W.M., Hoza, B. & Boivin, M. (1994). Measuring friendship quality during pre- and early adolescence: The development and psychometric properties of the Friendship Qualities Scale. *Journal of Social and Personal Relationships, 11*, 471–484.

One study suggesting the importance of friendship quality was reported by Ladd et al. (1996). They studied 82 children aged 5 years, all of whom had a reciprocated and stable 'best friend' in their classroom. The quality of this friendship was associated with the children's development and adjustment in school; for example, perceived conflict in friendships was (for boys) associated with more loneliness and less liking of school.

The Bukowski et al., (1994) study indicated that stability of friendships is one correlate of friendship quality: better-quality friendships last longer. This stability or instability of friendships might be a useful indicator to relate to other outcomes. Chan and Poulin (2009) examined this construct in relation to depression, and their study is described in Box 5.2. They did indeed find links to depression, but the direction of effect seemed to be more from depression to friendship instability than vice versa.

Box 5.2 Monthly instability in early adolescent friendship networks and depressive symptoms

The aim of this study was to examine the relation between perceived friendship network instability and depressive symptoms among young adolescents. Friendship stability is often taken as a positive aspect of good-quality friendships. Depressed feelings are not uncommon in adolescence (see Chapter 19) and the authors surmised that friendship instability might be related to this.

To study this, they decided to use repeated telephone interviews with participants, over a 5-month period (February to June). The interview sample consisted of 109 young people, falling to 102 who provided satisfactory data (51 boys, 51 girls; mostly aged 12 years). They lived in the greater Montreal region, Canada. Once a month, a researcher would telephone each participant for an interview lasting about 15 minutes. The main questions were about current friends, and three best friends, both in school and in other out-of-school contexts. Each participant was also asked about depressive symptoms—sadness, loss of interest at school, irritability, feeling like crying, loneliness, appetite loss, sleep problems or worry—over the past week. A depression inventory was also given in class.

The researchers constructed a monthly friendship stability index, and then a global index, based on the number of friends renominated (up to four times) over the five interviews. A proportion score was then calculated from 0 to 1 (0 would mean the young person did not nominate any of the same persons from one month to another; 1 would mean that exactly the same friends were nominated each time). This index was calculated overall, and separately for best friends. It could also be calculated separately for school friends, out-of-school friends and multiple context friends (both in and out of school).

The overall stability index was found to be .66. Perhaps not surprisingly, it was greater for best friends, at .86. For most of these young people, the same best friends were nominated each month. For secondary friends (those never nominated as best friends), the index fell to .55, indicating some consistency but also a fair degree of change. The index did not vary greatly by context, but was highest for multiple context friends at .72, compared to school only at .63 and non-school only at .62. Possibly, multiple context friends are more likely to be best friends, although this was not ascertained in the published study.

The researchers were mainly interested in the links between friendship stability and depression. The two depression measures (interview and questionnaire) correlated at .54; the correlations between the friendship stability measures and the depression measures were all consistently negative. They ranged from −.16 to −.30 for the interview measure, and from −.21 to −.35 for the questionnaire measure (most of

Box Table 5.2.1 Correlations over 1-month intervals, between monthly friendship stability index and monthly depression scores, for 102 children aged around 12 years; cross-lagged correlations are in the top half, stability correlations in the bottom half.

	Earlier friendship stability to later depression	Earlier depression to later friendship stability
March–April	−.06	−.20*
April–May	.07	−.13
May–June	−.04	−.21*

	Earlier to later friendship stability	Earlier to later depression stability
March–April	.57**	.71**
April–May	.48**	.81**
May–June	.54**	.75**

*p < .05.
** < .01.

the correlations being statistically significant). A regression analysis showed that gender was not important in this relationship; the pattern applied to both boys and girls.

The strength of the longitudinal design is that it is possible to see if depression predicts later friendship instability or if friendship instability predicts later depression. These are called cross-lagged correlations (see also p. 13). The researchers used cross-lagged structural equation modelling (SEM) to examine this. They report the cross-lagged correlations for the intervals from March to April, April to May and May to June. (It is not clear why the first February to March interval is not included.) The pattern of correlations is shown in Box Table 5.2.1, with the cross-lagged correlations in the top half. Perhaps surprisingly, the correlations between earlier friendship stability to depression scores 1 month later are small, non-significant and inconsistent (one actually being positive in direction). In contrast, the correlations between earlier depression to friendship stability 1 month later are consistently negative; although not very large in magnitude, two of the three are significant statistically.

Further analyses suggested that the relationship between depression and friendship stability was strongest for best friends (compared to secondary friends) and for school friendships (rather than non-school or multiple context friendships).

A strength of this study is the longitudinal design, with repeated measurements at relatively short time intervals—what the researchers call a 'microscopic analysis'. The sample size is reasonably large and could detect some relatively small effects. A modest but consistent relationship between friendship instability and depression was indeed found. However, the main finding was perhaps unexpected, as the cross-lagged correlations suggest that earlier depression predicted later friendship instability, rather than vice versa. Perhaps children feeling depressed withdraw somewhat from interactions or are less attractive as friendship partners, so that their friendships (perceived or perhaps actually) become less stable. The researchers speculate that depressive symptoms are more stable than friendship stability—which indeed they found, as can be seen in the lower set of correlations in Box Table 5.2.1. Another possibility is that effects of friendship instability on depression might still be found but would be more long term than the 5-month period examined here. Also, the authors point out that friendship instability need not always be maladaptive; changing friends can be positive if a previous friendship becomes less satisfying or even abusive (as in some girls' bullying, see Chapter 10), and a new friendship proves more rewarding.

The main limitation of the study is the reliance on self-report measures. Both friendship stability and depression were based on participants' own judgements. This is a problem of 'shared-method variance'; some participants might, for example, tend to give positive or self-enhancing answers (to both friendship and depression questions), leading to some relationships that are more due to this personality-type factor than to any genuine friendship-depression relationships. Multiple informant data (such as data from peers, parents or teachers) could overcome this limitation.

Based on material in Chan, A. & Poulin, F. (2009). *Social Development, 18*, 1–23.

THE IMPORTANCE OF PEER RELATIONS AND FRIENDSHIP

We have seen that there are immediate benefits to being sociometrically accepted and to having friends; you can avoid feelings of loneliness, engage in more intense and reciprocal social activities and, with the help of friends, solve tasks more effectively. So, is having friends an important developmental milestone? Hartup (1996) suggested that both aspects—sociometric status and/or having close, trustworthy friends—could be important. However, as he also pointed out, these are difficult questions to answer and they are not easy to test experimentally. However, several sources of evidence support the general idea that sociometric status and friendship have a wider importance, both at the time and for later development (Hartup, 1996).

An interesting small-scale study at the preschool age range was carried out by Field (1984) in a US kindergarten. This class of 28 children had been together from the age of 6–12 months and half the children were now due to leave the kindergarten. Field noted in the 2-week period prior to their leaving that these children showed increased rates of fussiness, negative affect, aggressive behaviour, physical contact and fantasy play—possibly signs of anticipation and attempted coping with the separation from peers and their familiar environment. Also, this could be due to anxiety about attending a new school. However, in observing the children who stayed behind, Field found these children showed similarly increased agitated behaviour after the other children had left. This could have been, on a small scale, a 'grief' response to the friends they had lost.

This suggests that friendships are affectively important to a child, even at 3 or 4 years of age. Do they have other consequences? In a study of preadolescents, Mannarino (1980) identified those who had 'chums'—close, stable best friendships—and compared them with those who did not, on measures of altruism and self-concept. Preadolescents with chums had higher levels of altruism and higher levels of self-concept than those who lacked chums. This is further support for the importance of friendship although, being a correlational study, it does not prove that having a chum in itself caused the greater altruism or self-concept (rather than, for example, the other way round).

Are peer relationships in childhood important for later development? In one US study, data were gathered on a large number of 8-year-olds in school, including IQ scores, school grades, attendance records, teachers' ratings and peer ratings. Eleven years later, when the subjects were nearly adult, the researchers checked mental health registers to see who had needed any psychiatric help during this period. Those who had were 2.5 times more likely to have had negative peer ratings at 8 years; indeed, the peer ratings were the best of all the earlier measures at predicting appearance in the mental health registers (Cowen et al., 1973).

Parker and Asher (1987), and more recently, Deater-Deckard (2001), have reviewed links from childhood peer relationships to psychopathology in childhood and adolescence. Parker and Asher looked at three measures of peer relationships: peer acceptance/rejection; aggressiveness to peers; and shyness or withdrawal from peers. They examined the relationship of these to three main kinds of later outcome: dropping out of school early; being involved in juvenile and adult crime; and adult psychopathology (mental health ratings or needing psychiatric help of any kind).

Parker and Asher found that different studies were very consistent in linking low peer acceptance (or high peer rejection) with dropping out of school, and suggestive but not so consistent in linking it with juvenile/adult crime. Conversely, the studies were very consistent in linking aggressiveness at school with juvenile/adult crime, and suggestive but not so consistent in linking it with dropping out of school. The data on effects of shyness/withdrawal, and on predictors of adult psychopathology, were less consistent; while some studies found significant effects, others did not, and thus any links or effects remain unproven at present.

Most of the studies were 'follow-back' designs; that is, retrospective data on peer relations were sought for people who were currently dropping out of school, getting in trouble with the law or seeking psychiatric help. A smaller number were 'follow-up' designs—taking a large sample of schoolchildren, obtaining data on peer relations and seeing what happens later. Whichever design is used, the data are correlational in nature. We cannot be certain that low peer acceptance, for example, is a causal predictor of later problems. However, longitudinal 'follow-up' designs, while more costly to organize, are likely to provide more valid data for establishing predictive links.

Two somewhat different causal models, discussed by Parker and Asher (1987) in the context of low peer acceptance, are shown in Figure 5.4. In (a), the low peer acceptance has a direct causal role; in (b), it is an outcome of more enduring traits, such as aggressiveness or shyness, rather than a cause in itself. (In both models, the original reasons for the deviant behaviour are not spelt out; you might consider whether some of the factors discussed in Chapter 4 would be relevant in making the models more complete.) These models could of course apply to other peer relationship or friendship difficulties, as well as peer acceptance.

Woodward and Fergusson (2000), in a longitudinal study of children from 9 to 18 years in Christchurch, New Zealand, argued that both these causal models have some validity. Peer relationship problems at age 9 did predict educational underachievement and unemployment at age 18. Further analyses suggested that personal characteristics (such as low IQ) and adverse family and socioeconomic circumstances explained some of this association (effectively, model (b) above). However, the childhood peer relationship problems did appear to lead directly to later relationship difficulties with peers and teachers and earlier school leaving (effectively, model (a) above).

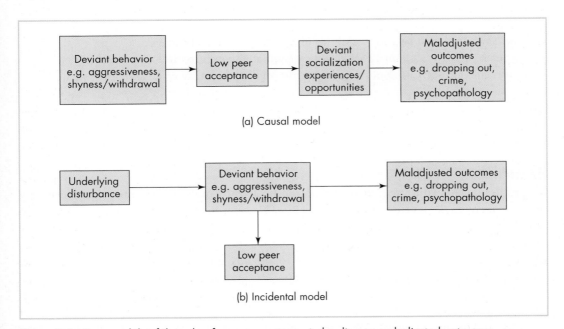

Figure 5.4 Two models of the role of peer acceptance in leading to maladjusted outcomes.

Source: Parker, J.G. & Asher, S.R. (1987). Peer relations and later personal adjustment: are low-accepted children at risk? *Psychological Bulletin, 102*, 357–389.

Deater-Deckard (2001) argued that peer rejection is strongly implicated in the development of psychopathology, particularly when considered in conjunction with aggression and delinquency, but that there are important moderating factors such as age, gender, ethnicity, peer group behavioural norms and quality of close friendships. We will look at many of these in more detail when considering aggression and bullying, in Chapter 10.

A Long-term Study of Correlates of Childhood Friendship and Sociometric Status

A study that looked at the separate contributions of sociometric status (specifically, peer rejection) and friendship to later adjustment was reported by Bagwell, Newcomb and Bukowski (1998). This was a longitudinal, follow-up study in the mid-west USA, of students in school (at 10 years) to when they were young adults (at 23 years). At school, 334 students were asked to name three best friends and three classmates they liked least, of the same sex, twice (once month apart). The researchers then formed two subgroups.

- *Friended subgroup* (N=58): these children had a stable, reciprocated best friend at both times.
- *Chumless subgroup* (N=55): these children had no reciprocated friendship choice at either time.

In addition, they scored *Peer rejection* from the liked most/least ratings.

At the follow-up, 30 young adults from each subgroup (15 male, 15 female) were given questionnaires to assess life status, self-esteem, psychopathological symptoms and quality of adult friendships. The main findings were:

- *Peer rejection* predicted poorer life status (job aspiration and performance, extent of social activities).
- *Friendship* predicted relations with family members and self-esteem.
- *Both lack of friendship and peer rejection* predicted psychopathological symptoms.
- *Neither lack of friendship nor peer rejection* predicted quality of adult friendships.

This study suggests that both presence/absence of a close friend in preadolescence, and the experience of peer rejection, may be important for later well-being, but with each being stronger predictors of different aspects of later life.

Enemies

While there has been a great deal of research on friends in childhood, there has been very little on enemies. As Hartup and Abecassis (2002) point out, mutual antipathies ('Whom do you dislike more than anyone else?') are rare among very young children, but become more common by middle childhood. They argued that we should analyse the correlates and consequences of having enemies, as we have done for friends, and that it is an additional factor to consider, separate from sociometric status or peer rejection.

Card (2010), in a meta-analysis of 16 research studies on child and adolescent antipathetic relationships, found that the average prevalence rate was 35%; around one-third of children and young people have at least one antipathetic relationship at any given time.

Boys were slightly more likely than girls to have this kind of relationship, but there were no significant differences by age or by ethnic group. Card found that antipathetic relationships were associated with externalizing problems, such as aggression and disruptive behaviour, as well as with internalizing behaviours, such as depression and social withdrawal. Having enemies was associated with victimization and rejection by peers and having fewer friends. Another interesting finding was that a substantial number of 'enemies' were former friends whose relationship had been undermined by some violation, such as breaking trust or telling an intimate secret. This kind of phenomenon has been illustrated by recent studies of cyber-bullying (see Chapter 10) where intimate secrets or photographs are posted online by young people about their previous romantic/sexual partners.

Aldridge et al. (2011) used a narrative method to elicit children's perceptions of jealousy in relationships. They found interesting age differences: 5–6-year-olds tended to focus on the basic emotion of anger, whereas 7–8-year-olds spoke of a variety of emotions, including jealousy, unhappiness, anger, sadness and annoyance. These findings suggest that the child's conception of jealousy begins with a negative feeling and increasingly develops in complexity as the child understands additional relevant information. The older children in this study were much more able to identify a rival and to take the perspective of others.

Social Skills Training

Many psychologists believe that social skills training may be useful for those children who lack friends; this training is usually directed to changing behaviours that are the correlates of peer rejection (such as high aggression or high withdrawal).

Attempts have been made to help improve social skills in neglected children and rejected children. In one study (Furman et al., 1979), 4- and 5-year-olds who seldom played with other children were identified by observation. Some were given special play sessions with a younger partner to see if this might give them more confidence in social interaction. This did seem to help, and more so than play sessions with a same-age peer or no intervention at all. However, this study only used levels of social interaction as the measure of adjustment, so it does not directly address the issue of friendship and rejection.

Other researchers, working with middle-school children, have used more direct means of encouraging social skills—modelling techniques, for example. A child might watch a film showing an initially withdrawn child engaged in a series of increasingly complex peer interactions. Watching such films has been shown to increase social interaction subsequently (O'Connor, 1972). A more instructional approach was used by Oden and Asher (1977). They coached 8- and 9-year-old children identified as socially isolated (neglected or rejected) on skills such as how to participate in groups, cooperate and communicate with peers; they did this in special play sessions with the target child and one other peer. These children improved in sociometric status more than those who had special play sessions without the coaching. This effect was present a year later at a follow-up assessment, and was also replicated by an independent study (Ladd, 1981). However, another study with 9-year-olds found that academic skill training was even more effective than social skill training (Coie & Krehbiel, 1984). The hypothesis that rejected children are lacking in social skills, while promising, may not be the whole story. Malik and Furman (1993) provide an overview of clinical interventions to help children's social skills in peer relationships, while Ladd, Buhs and Troop (2002) give a wider overview of interventions in school settings.

Stop and Think

Given its basis in social information processing theory, for which kinds of children will social skills training be most helpful?

Immigration, Acculturation and Friendships in Multicultural Settings

Across the industrialized countries, recent decades have seen a rapid increase in immigration all over Europe. Immigrants face a number of challenges, including adjusting to a new culture and often a new language, and not uncommonly experiencing some prejudice from the native population. Berry, Phinney, Sam and Vedder (2006) describe this as *acculturative stress*. As a stressful life event, immigrant families and their children may be more subject to depression, loneliness or lower self-esteem. However, findings are very mixed (Strohmeier & Schmitt-Rodermund, 2008). Sam et al. (2008) discuss what has been called the *immigrant paradox phenomenon*, namely that first-generation immigrants may show better adaptation than native peers, despite often having lower socioeconomic status. A factor here may be that those who choose or manage to migrate to a different country may be particularly enterprising or adaptable.

For immigrant children, an important aspect of acculturation will be friendships they make in their school and neighbourhood. Reviewing this topic, Titzmann (2014) found that making friends with non-immigrant peers was predicted by good language proficiency in the language of the host country. It is also predicted by attitudes on both sides—immigrant children may vary in terms of their willingness to engage with those outside their family culture, and native children may vary in prejudicial attitudes to immigrants.

In schools, a factor will be the proportions of different ethnic groups. For example, in a study in German secondary schools, Titzmann (2014) describes how most children reported having intraethnic friends (i.e. friends from the same ethnic group as themselves), but that this tendency decreased with length of stay in the new country. However, this increase in interethnic friendships was strongest when there was a smaller proportion of own-ethnic children in the school. If the concentration of own-ethnic pupils was as high as 30% or more, the tendency to form more interethnic friendships over time was greatly reduced.

Generalizations in this area have proven difficult, as there are so many factors involved, including which specific immigrant cultures are involved, and whether one is thinking of first- or second-generation immigrants—or indeed later generations, as in many countries where there has been a long process of acculturation, and where it makes no sense to describe many ethnic minority families as 'immigrant'. For example, in the UK, many non-white families are very well established as Black British or Asian British (although there are also many first-generation immigrant children, from a large variety of countries).

In many London secondary schools the percentage of ethnic minority children is now comparable to the percentage of White British students (Office for National Statistics, 2012). A study by Bagci et al. (2014) in nine secondary schools in Greater London focused on 11-year-old White European and South Asian British students. They completed measures of same-/cross-ethnic friendship numbers, and quality of three best cross-ethnic friends. Both numbers and quality of cross-ethnic friendships had positive associations with psychological well-being and resilience, for children of both ethnic groups. In addition, some aspects of friendships buffered the negative effects of any perceived ethnic discrimination.

Graham, Munniiksma and Juvonen (2014) studied 396 6th-grade students, mean age 11.5 years, in 66 multiethnic classrooms in the USA. They examined same-/cross-ethnic friendships between Latino and African-American children. Cross-ethnic friendships predicted less individual vulnerability—a composite of feelings about school safety, peer victimization and loneliness.

Studies like these suggest that although children show ethnic awareness and some degree of ethnic preference by the time they are in primary school (Chapter 6), interethnic friendships are now not uncommon and may have some advantages for the children concerned. The extent of this is probably strongly affected by cultural and historical factors.

FAMILY AND PEER RELATIONSHIPS

Although the family and the world of peer relationships—basically, home and school—are often considered separately, they do of course interact. We saw in Chapter 4 how parent–child attachment characteristics can predict aspects of peer relationships; perhaps the internal model of relationships that children form with parents transfers in some ways to peer group relationships. Also important may be other aspects of parenting, such as parenting style.

Cohn et al. (1991) reviewed evidence on the links between attachment quality, parenting and peer relations; they concluded that if parents are high in warmth, authoritative and interested but not overcontrolling, children tend to be socially confident with peers and socially accepted. As an example, Ladd and Golter (1988) examined preschoolers' interactions in kindergarten. They found that parents who used indirect monitoring at home (periodic observations of what their children were doing) had children who were more accepted by peers; parents who used more direct control at home (staying around, being intrusive) had children who were more rejected by peers. Reich and Vandell (2011) provide a review of these kinds of interplay between parents and peers.

A study by Patterson et al. (1991) related both home background factors and life events to sociometric status in peers, in a sample of 949 children aged 7–9 years. They assessed eight home background factors and seven major life events. They found that rejected status was associated with four home background factors: biological mother not at home; biological father not at home; lack of educational stimulation; and low income. The presence of these four home factors increased risk of peer rejection cumulatively—if one factor was present, risk increased by 10%, but if all four were present, by 30%. In addition, four recent life events were associated with peer rejection: illness in the family; death of a family member; the child transferring schools; or the separation/divorce of parents. The presence of these four life events also increased risk of peer rejection cumulatively, from 11% to 40%. Put together, home background factors plus recent life events proved a very powerful predictor of whether a child would be rejected by peers. If no home background variables or life events were present, the risk of peer rejection was less than 10% but if three or more home background variables and two or more life events were present, the risk of peer rejection rose to 75%.

GROUP SOCIALIZATION THEORY AND THE ROLE OF THE PEER GROUP: HOW IMPORTANT ARE FAMILIES?

As we saw in Chapter 4, many developmental psychologists have assumed that parents have a formative and even decisive influence on the development of children. Important theoretical views have buttressed this assumption, including the psychoanalytic tradition of Freud, carried forward into more modern views of attachment theory by Bowlby, as well as the learning theory views of Watson and Skinner. The last three decades have seen very many studies of parenting styles and parenting influences on children's development, which have largely looked at the nature of such effects rather than querying whether such effects exist.

Judith Harris provided a vigorous challenge to this view. Her 'group socialization' theory of development was expounded in 1995 and taken further in her 1998 book, *The nurture assumption*. There are undoubtedly similarities between parents and children, but Harris suggests two main reasons for this, which do not involve children learning from parents. These are, first, genetic effects and second, community effects mediated by the peer groups children are in.

Parents and children share genes in common. From behaviour genetic work using data from adoption and twin studies (e.g. Plomin et al., 2013; and see Chapter 2), behaviour geneticists have argued that a substantial proportion of differences in individual children's development can be ascribed to genetic factors. Perhaps more surprising and challenging, however, were their conclusions about the nature of the remaining environmental influences. Particularly relevant were findings on many measures and in many studies, that children of the same family grow up to be quite different from each other; also, adopted children show increasingly little similarity to their adoptive parents as they grow up. The conclusion drawn by behaviour geneticists was that the influence of environmental factors can mostly be ascribed to non-shared environment, and rather little to shared environment. Shared environment refers to the common experiences that children (siblings) get by being brought up in the same family. The shared environment of a household, with particular parents, has not made siblings substantially more alike than if they were not in the same household with the same parents.

If such shared environment effects are indeed small, then two conclusions seem to follow.

1. Parents do not have such a strong direct environmental effect on children's development as is often supposed. Indeed, Scarr (1992) proposed that it is good enough for parents to provide an average expectable environment, and then their children develop according to their own genetic potential. It is only if parents fail to do this that there are strong direct parenting effects.
2. We need to establish what the important aspects of the non-shared environment are. It could be parents behaving differently to different children (because of birth order, temperament, etc.), or it could be the peer group.

Harris argued that the major environmental factor in growing up is the child's peer group. She believes that, at least after infancy, the peer group provides the major important reference group for children. They adapt to peer group norms and compare themselves to their peers (for similar views in relation to sex differences, see Maccoby, 2000). Harris invoked ideas from social psychology and evolutionary psychology to suggest the importance of group processes, especially within the peer group, such as group affiliation, hostility to strangers, improving one's status in the group and forming close dyadic relationships from within the group. In the peer group, children can learn to behave in quite different ways from the home.

The situation of immigrant children provided what Harris saw as a compelling argument for her views. She took as an exemplar a family coming to a country such as the USA from a quite different country—say, Poland. The parents speak Polish and, although they learn English, they speak the language with a strong accent; they also keep many Polish traditions. Their children, however, once they enter school, very rapidly learn American English and an American way of life; the strong influence of the peer group produces assimilation in a generation or, at most, two. 'Code switching', or the context dependency of learning, is an important part of Harris's argument. Here, code can refer to a language, or values, or ways of behaving. Even if children learn one code for the home context, they learn another code for the peer context.

Thus, Harris argued that what children learn from parents specifically (rather than peers, and others generally) is transient to the infancy period and/or limited to the home context. But what about all the evidence showing some similarities between parent and child in temperament, personality and intelligence? Some similarities can be expected (to biological parents) from genetic factors. In addition, Harris argued, correlations found between parents and children may reflect effects of children on parents (rather than vice versa), or similarities of peer groups for children within a particular subcultural group.

For example, punitive parents tend to have aggressive children (Chapter 10); this is conventionally taken to be a parent-to-child effect, but it could be a child-to-parent effect if temperamentally difficult children are both naturally aggressive and evoke more punitive behaviour from exasperated parents.

At a cultural and subcultural level, there will also be some correspondence between peer group values and parental values. Depending on ethnicity and social class, there are likely to be some shared values and assumptions held widely in a community. These will be shared in the peer group of children, and also in the older generation 'peer group' of parents. Thus, some similarity of parents and children will simply reflect this general community similarity of values. Harris argued that this similarity comes via the peers rather than directly via the parents.

Harris's theory occasioned considerable controversy and some hostility from those committed to the view that the behaviour of parents can have strong positive or negative effects on their children's development. The issues were debated further by Vandell (2000) and Harris (2000a); see also Reich and Vandell (2011). Rutter (1999) suggested that the challenge of Harris's theory was to be welcomed, but that it was premature to accept all her conclusions. Like Scarr (1992), he believes that even if parents have rather little effect within the normal range of parenting, there is good evidence for specific effects at the extremes (for example, in cases of child abuse). He suggested that Harris also neglects the more complex effects of parents on children's development, via their choice of neighbourhoods, schools and peer groups for their children.

CHAPTER SUMMARY

- Peer interactions start in the first year but are initially short and infrequent.
- Siblings can provide an early opportunity for social interactions with non-adults. Many processes go on in sibling interactions, and they can foster early theory of mind development.
- Research on only children, family size and birth order produces a complex pattern of results.
- Peer interactions develop rapidly in the preschool years, from 2 to 4 or 5 years.
- Sociometry is a way of measuring peer relations and friendships, and sociometric status refers to being liked or disliked in the peer group, yielding five sociometric status types. Rejected children have problematic peer relationships.
- A social information processing model has been widely used in understanding peer interactions and interaction difficulties. Some interventions are based on social skills training.
- Conceptions of friendship change through childhood. Quality of friendship is an important aspect, in addition to number of friends. In modern multicultural societies, cross-ethnic friendships may bring some benefits.
- There is some debate about the relative roles of parents and peers in development, once children start attending school.

DISCUSSION POINTS

1. How special are sibling relationships compared with peer relationships?
2. Are friendships important for children? How can we find out?
3. Why are some children popular and others not?
4. How useful is a social skills model in understanding peer relationships?
5. Are families or peers more important in development?

FURTHER READING

- For sibling relationships, see Dunn, J. (1984). *Sisters and brothers*. Glasgow: Fontana/Open Books; and more generally, Dunn, J. (1993). *Young children's close relationships: Beyond attachment*. London: Sage, and Howe, N., Ross, H.S. & Recchia, H. (2011). Sibling relationships in early and middle childhood. In P.K. Smith & C.H. Hart (Eds.), *Wiley-Blackwell handbook of childhood social development* (2nd ed.). Oxford: Wiley-Blackwell.
- Good overviews of peer relations in childhood are Schneider, B. (2015). *Friends and enemies* (2nd ed.). London: Psychology Press, focusing on the psychological literature; Pellegrini, A.D., Blatchford, P. & Barnes, E. (2014). *The child at school* (2nd ed.). London: Psychology Press, having a wider coverage of peer relations, friendship, play and aggression in the school setting; Kupersmidt, J.B. & Dodge, K.A. (Eds.) (2004). *Children's peer relations*. Washington, DC: American Psychological Association, a collection focusing mainly on the sociometric tradition; and Hay, D.F., Payne, A. & Chadwick, A. (2004). Peer relations in childhood. *Journal of Child Psychology and Psychiatry*, 45, 84–108, which outlines a developmental model of peer relations.
- A classic collection on children's friendships is Bukowski, W.M., Newcomb, A.F. & Hartup, W.W. (Eds.) (1996). *The company they keep: Friendship in childhood and adolescence*. Cambridge: Cambridge University Press. Dunn, J. (2004). *Children's friendships: The beginnings of intimacy*. Oxford: Blackwell, is a readable account of peer relations and friendship development. Cillessen, A.H.N., Schwartz, D. & Mayeux, L. (Eds.) (2011). *Popularity in the peer system*. New York: Guilford, is a useful source. For challenges facing immigrant children, see Masten, A.S., Liebkind, K., & Hernandez, D.J. (Eds.) (2012). *Realizing the potential of immigrant youth*. New York: Cambridge University Press.

CHAPTER
6

Developing Emotional Intelligence and Social Awareness

CHAPTER OUTLINE

- How Children Begin to Understand Self and Others
- Emotional Development
- Understanding Others' Emotions, Desires and Beliefs
- Developing Emotional Intelligence
- Early Sex Differences and the Development of Gender Identity
- Theories of Sex-Role Identification
- Children's Awareness of and Attitudes to Different Ethnic and National Groups

So far, we have looked at the child developing in the context of the family, the peer group and the school. In this chapter we shall look at how the child develops an understanding of him- or herself and of others. There are various influences on the ways in which children develop an understanding of themselves. The child's sense of self is closely related to the ways in which they express and manage their emotions. We will start by considering children's developing sense of self; their understanding of their own emotions; and how they learn to categorize others and understand *their* emotional expressions. (This further relates to the developing awareness of others' mental states, beliefs and desires—what has been called a 'theory of mind' or skills in 'mindreading', discussed in Chapter 15.) The emotions play a key role in the ways that adults and children work, interact and learn together, and have a strong influence on the quality of children's interpersonal relationships. In this context, we examine Harris's theory about how children come to understand other people's emotions, desires and beliefs. We also look at the development of the skills of emotion regulation, which influence the ways in which children relate to both peers and adults in their social worlds. We consider recent work on the development of emotional intelligence and consider some controversies in this relatively new field. We also explore some of the intervention programmes that aim to increase children's prosocial behaviour, reduce aggression and enhance their capacity to relate well to one another. We explore sex differences and the development of gender identity, and compare a number of theoretical explanations for the development of gender identity. We end by exploring research studies of how children develop ethnic awareness and their attitudes to others of different ethnicity, and nationality.

HOW CHILDREN BEGIN TO UNDERSTAND SELF AND OTHERS

'Self-awareness is arguably the most fundamental issue in psychology, from both a developmental and an evolutionary perspective' (Rochat, 2003, p. 717). Rochat (2010) argues that almost from birth babies have a complex sense of their own bodies as differentiated from others. He calls this the *social mirror* of others. The emergent self-awareness of the baby refers to the capacity to become the object of one's own attention and it has both private (awareness of self) and public (awareness of self as perceived by others) aspects.

From a very early age, babies begin to show some awareness of their separateness from the parents by appearing to search for them when they are out of sight. Babies are fascinated by the game of 'Peekaboo' where the parent seems to disappear and then reappear. This is an early landmark of 'person permanence' and implies an internal representation of a social being, corresponding to that person's continuity in time and space. Closely related to the concept of person permanence is that of 'object permanence', applied to non-social objects, and discussed in Chapter 13. Both are achieved during the sensorimotor period (up to about 18 months of age), with major progress in the degree of permanence achieved (measured by the success of the infant's search strategies) towards the end of the first year.

The Infant's Recognition of Self

While person permanence experiments show that an infant can recognize particular others and expect them to continue existing, they do not tell us specifically about the infant's own sense of self. Lewis and Brooks-Gunn (1979) found evidence that infants as young as 9–12 months were capable of some differentiation between pictorial representation of themselves and others; for example, they would smile more and look longer at pictures of themselves than at pictures of other same-age babies. By 15–18 months, children are using verbal labels such as 'baby', or their own name, to distinguish pictures of themselves and others.

One ingenious technique to assess self-recognition has been the 'mirror test', also used with primates (see p. 49). In a study of this kind, Lewis and Brooks-Gunn (1979) used 16 infants at each of six age groups: 9, 12, 15, 18, 21 and 24 months. Each infant was first placed by the mother in front of a fairly large mirror, and their behaviour observed for about 90 seconds. Then the infant's nose was wiped with rouge discreetly, on the pretence of wiping the infant's face (only one of the 96 infants immediately felt for his nose after this). The infant was subsequently placed in front of the mirror again and observed for another 90 seconds. How would the infant react?

At all ages, most of the infants smiled at their image in the mirror (Table 6.1) and many pointed to the mirror or reached out to touch it. However, in the first, 'no rouge' condition, very few touched their own nose, and not many touched their own body at all. When the rouge had been applied, the effect depended markedly on the infant's age. The 9- and 12-month-old infants never touched their own nose, despite being able to see their unusually red nose in the mirror; a minority of 15- and 18-month-olds, and most 21- and 24-month-olds did reach for their own noses. This suggests that after about 18 months, an infant has a pretty good idea that the reflection in the mirror is a representation of him- or herself.

What can we infer about the baby's emergent sense of self? Fernyhough (2008, p. 123) describes how his daughter, Athena, at 4.5 months, was fascinated by mirrors. When she saw her parents in the mirror and they waved at her, she would wave back and then turn, as if to check the real parents with those reflected in the mirror. When placed directly in front of the mirror, she looked at the image of herself, reached forward to the 'stranger' and looked up and down as noting the similarities of the movements. But when her mother put rouge on Athena's nose, she did not pay any attention to the red blob on the nose of the reflected image. However, at around 14 months, she named the baby in the mirror as 'Athena'. At that point, when the mother put the rouge on Athena's nose, she looked at the reflection, did a

Table 6.1 Percentages of infants smiling and touching own nose on viewing their reflection in a mirror.

Infants' behaviour	Age (months)	9	12	15	18	21	24
Smiling	No rouge	86	94	88	56	63	60
	Rouge	99	74	88	75	82	60
Touching own nose	No rouge	0	0	0	6	7	7
	Rouge	0	0	19	25	70	73

Source: Lewis, M. & Brooks-Gunn, J. (1979) *Social Cognition and the Acquisition of Self*. New York: Plenum Press. With kind permission from Springer Science and Business Media.

double take, gazed with more purpose and then touched her *own* nose, laughing in surprise. The test had become a game. She touched the reflection, then her own nose. In Fernyhough's words (pp. 124–150), Athena was doing something amazing—'seeing herself as others see her and somehow identifying with the image'.

By 2 years, the image in the mirror is associated with different behaviours since the toddler will now demonstrate self-consciousness, for example by seeming to be embarrassed. This shows that the child is now seeing himself through the eyes of others. Povinelli (2001), through careful studies of preschoolers as they watched themselves in video-recordings, found that it is not until around 3 years that children fully grasp the temporal dimension of the self; that is, that the self refers to 'the now' as well as to what they experienced 'then' in the past. This evolving sense of self-awareness is a dynamic process that continues into adulthood. As Rochat (2003, p. 723) argues, 'As adults, we are constantly oscillating in our levels of awareness: from dreaming or losing awareness about ourselves during sleep, to being highly self-conscious in public circumstances or in a state of confusion and dissociation as we immerse ourselves in movies or novels'.

How Children Categorize Others

We have seen how infants achieve person permanence through the sensorimotor period, often ahead of object permanence. As concepts of particular persons become more stable, persons can begin to be categorized along social dimensions. Lewis and Brooks-Gunn (1979) argued that the three earliest social dimensions learned are familiarity, age and gender. They argue that these are concurrently developed in relation to oneself and to other persons.

The importance of familiarity is apparent from the research that shows that infants behave differently to familiar and to strange adults by around 7–9 months of age (when attachment relationships have usually formed), if not earlier (see Chapter 4; and Sroufe, 1977). A bit later, infants respond differently to familiar and unfamiliar peers. Jacobson (1980) found that wariness of an unfamiliar peer (compared with a familiar peer) developed between 10 and 12 months. Greater previous experience with the familiar peer predicted an earlier onset of wariness of the unfamiliar peer.

Age is also used very early on in a categorical way. Infants aged 6–9 months discriminate in their behaviour between the approach of a child and that of an adult, and infants aged 9–12 months can differentiate between photographs of baby and adult faces. Lewis and Brooks-Gunn (1979) suggest that height, movement, voice and extreme differences in facial and hair characteristics (in baby and adult photographs) are the cues that infants use to categorize by age. Verbal age labels (e.g. baby, mummy, daddy) begin to be used correctly by 18–24 months of age. By the preschool years, age can be used as an explicit criterion for classification. Edwards and Lewis (1979) found that 3.5-year-olds could successfully sort head-and-shoulders photographs of persons into four categories: little children, big children, parents and grandparents.

Differentiation of people by gender also occurs early. Nine- to 12-month-olds respond differentially to photographs of both female and male strangers (Brooks-Gunn & Lewis, 1981) and to direct approach by male and female strangers (Smith & Sloboda, 1986). Verbal gender labels (e.g. mummy, daddy, boy, girl) begin to be used correctly after 18 months of age. The development of gender identity is considered further later in this chapter. The child's sense of self is also closely bound up with the expression and management of emotions.

We saw in Chapter 4 how the intensity and quality of the attachment relationship between child and parent/caregiver have a profound impact on the ways in which the child expresses feelings and on the way in which feelings are managed.

In the next section, we describe a range of studies that have examined the ways in which children produce their emotions, how they recognize emotions in others and how they come to understand the complexity of emotions as experienced by themselves and as observed in others.

EMOTIONAL DEVELOPMENT

Producing Emotions

Historically, emotions were viewed as subjective states that existed separately from cognition and behaviour but more recent research suggests that there are multiple components of emotion. For example, an individual's expression of emotion communicates their intentions to those with whom they interact, and this in turn influences the ways in which the others respond. Recent work tends to consider emotions as part of a dynamic system connected to other psychological processes. The quality and nature of the response of the adults around babies facilitate the process. Meins et al. (2002) emphasize how important it is for parents to treat their infant as a person with a mind rather than as a helpless creature with needs. They call this *mind-mindedness*, where the focus of the parent is on an inferred state of mind rather than only on behaviour.

From birth onwards, babies start signalling their emotional state. Perhaps the earliest distinction one can make for babies is between positive and negative affect—whether they are contented and happy, as indicated by smiling, or discontented and distressed, as indicated by pursing the lips and crying. A study by Ganchrow et al. (1983) showed that at the time of the very first feed, newborns would produce distinct facial expressions to a sweet liquid (slight smile) or bitter liquid (mouth corners down, pursed lips). Observers who watched the babies without knowing which liquid was being given could judge whether the babies liked or disliked the liquid, and also the intensity of response.

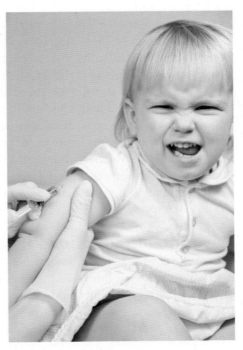

Figure 6.1 After about 7 months of age, it becomes increasingly easy to distinguish pain from anger, as seen in the angry facial expression of this infant being given a routine inoculation (Izard et al., 1987).

Source: Image copyright Dmitry Naumov, used under licence from Shutterstock.com.

Some basic or 'primary' emotions, which may be discernible from the first few weeks onwards, are happiness, interest, surprise, sadness, fear, anger and pain. For example, surprise is indicated by wide-open eyes and mouth, together with a startle response by the trunk and limbs. Fear responses increase considerably after about 7 months of age, when infants become wary and fearful of unfamiliar persons and objects, and sadness can occur in periods of separation from a familiar caregiver. (As we saw in Chapter 4, the balance of different emotional expressions is crucial in scoring the 'Strange Situation' procedure, where intense anger as well as intense happiness can be observed when children are reunited with parents/caregivers after a period of separation.) Anger and pain also become increasingly easily distinguished from each other, especially after about 7 months (Figure 6.1). This was shown in a study by Izard et al. (1987). They looked at babies' facial expressions when they were given routine inoculations. The babies were aged from 2 to 8 months. For younger babies, the reaction was one of generalized distress but for older babies, a distinctly angry expression (brows compressed together, eyelids tensed, mouth compressed or squared) became progressively more frequent.

One of the earliest descriptions of emotional development comes from Charles Darwin (1877), who published an article about the early development of one of his own children. Here is his description of the development of anger.

> It was difficult to decide at how early an age anger was felt; on his eighth day he frowned and wrinkled the skin round his eyes before a crying fit, but this may have been due to pain or distress, and not to anger. When about ten weeks old, he was given some rather cold milk and he kept a slight frown on his forehead all the time that he was sucking, so that he looked like a grown-up person made cross from being compelled to do something which he did not like. When nearly four months old, and perhaps much earlier, there was no doubt, from the manner in which the blood gushed into his whole face and scalp, that he easily got into a violent passion. A small cause sufficed; thus, when a little over seven months old, he screamed with rage because a lemon slipped away and he could not seize it with his hands. When eleven months old, if a wrong plaything was given him, he would push it away and beat it: I presume that the beating was an instinctive sign of anger, like the snapping of the jaws by a young crocodile just out of the egg, and not that he imagined he could hurt the plaything.
>
> *(Darwin, 1877)*

Darwin's account is interesting for several reasons. It brings out clearly both his skill as an observer and the difficulty in interpreting emotions, especially at younger ages. Darwin's account is an example of the diary method (p. 5); though in this case Darwin actually wrote up the article 37 years after keeping the diary on which it was based! Finally, you will see that Darwin suggests that some emotional displays are 'instinctive', in children as well as in animals. The very early development of emotional display in infants does seem to suggest that some of the mechanisms for producing emotion are 'innate' or strongly canalized in development (p. 4). The main alternative view would be that infants learn emotional expression from others, through observation and imitation; this seems less plausible in early infancy but more plausible later, for example in explaining cultural differences in emotional expression.

Recognizing Emotions in Others

The capacity to recognize, discriminate and interpret emotion is fundamental to children's capacity to relate to others and maintain communication with them. It lies at the heart of interpersonal relationships from a very early age (see also Stern's descriptions of mother–baby prelinguistic dialogues in Chapter 12). In order to investigate this process, some studies have looked at dialogues between mother and baby. Usually, mother and baby are interacting happily. What would happen if the mother adopted a sad face or an angry face? Haviland and Lelwica (1987) asked mothers to do this for a short while with their 10-week-old babies, adopting appropriate facial expressions and tone of voice. The babies did react differently. If the mother appeared happy, so did the baby. If the mother appeared angry, so did the baby. If the mother appeared sad, the baby did not particularly look sad, but did engage in chewing, mouthing and sucking. Similarly, Fernyhough (2008, p. 46) noted in his observations of Athena at a few weeks old that: 'She can recognize a few different emotional expressions and reproduce the most basic ones for herself. If I were to change my expression suddenly from happy to angry, for example, she would show surprise. If I suddenly made my face freeze-up altogether, she would stop smiling, look away, and then try to re-engage my attention'.

Infants can imitate the facial expression of an adult but it is only with the emergence of the social smile (at around 6 weeks) that the baby is showing her active emotional resonance with others. Through the dialogical interchanges, as described by Fernyhough with Athena, infants express emotional coregulation with others—a process that leads quite quickly to social expectations and patterns of communication with others.

These studies show that babies can discriminate emotions in others early on. But do babies really understand their parent's emotions? There is some compelling evidence to suggest that they can quite sensibly interpret their parent's emotional expression.

Social referencing: Sometimes, an infant will look carefully at his or her caregiver as if to gauge their emotional expression, before, as it were, deciding how to react to a situation. This is known as *social referencing* (Mumme & Fernald, 2003). Not surprisingly, it is more likely in ambiguous situations where some extra 'advice' is needed by the infant. Two well-studied examples are wary reactions to strangers or to strange toys, and behaviour on the 'visual cliff'.

Wary reactions to strangers: From about 7 months of age, infants do tend to be wary of strangers. Feiring et al. (1984) observed how 15-month-olds would respond to a stranger. They would often turn to the mother when the stranger entered, as if to ascertain her reaction. The experimenters asked the mother to either interact positively with the stranger or ignore the stranger. The reaction of the infants to the stranger was less positive when the mother ignored the stranger. Similar results have been obtained with the reactions of 12-month-old infants to toys, depending on the facial expression of the mother (Klinnert, 1984). Mumme et al. (1996), however, found rather little effect of mothers' facial emotional signals, but stronger effects of negative vocalizations, on the infants' behaviour with a novel toy.

The visual cliff: In the experimental situation called the 'visual cliff' (see Figure 11.8, p. 398), infants generally refuse to move onto a glass surface when it appears that there is a large drop at the boundary. The situation can be made more ambiguous by making the apparent drop smaller. This was done by Sorce et al. (1985) with a sample of 12-month-olds. The mother was opposite the baby, so her face was very visible. Some mothers were asked to adopt a happy face, others a fearful face. Of 19 infants whose mother had a happy face, 14 crossed the visual cliff; of 17 whose mother had a fearful face, none crossed. This suggests that the infants interpreted the mother's expression appropriately, as a commentary on the situation. This is well illustrated by this experiment, as a mother's fearful expression would normally cause an infant to approach the mother for safety but in this experiment, the mother's fearful expression actually prevents approach across the apparent cause of danger, the visual cliff.

Stop and Think

How strong is the evidence that babies can gauge their parent's emotion *before* they respond to a new object or to a stranger?

Some criticisms have been made of these social referencing experiments; while it is clear that the infants are making use of emotional messages in some sense, are they actually using the mother's emotion to refer to the new object, person or situation encountered? Perhaps the mother's emotional signalling simply alters the infant's emotional state, or perhaps the mother is just altering the distance between herself and the baby (Baldwin & Moses, 1996). Such criticisms certainly could apply to the experiments with strangers or novel toys cited above, although less obviously to that with the visual cliff. In any event, a study by Moses et al. (2001) provided rather clear evidence for social referencing in the full sense of the term, in 12–18-month-olds. They found that infants would use vocalizations of an adult (positive, such as 'nice!', 'wow!'; or negative, such as 'iiuu!', 'yeech!') to adapt their behaviour with a strange toy, such as a 'bumble ball'; the infants would often look at the adult when they vocalized. However, they only adapted their behaviour to the toy that the adult was looking at.

UNDERSTANDING OTHERS' EMOTIONS, DESIRES AND BELIEFS

There is considerable evidence that children can understand other people's emotions, desires and beliefs by 3 or 4 years of age, and indeed that the beginnings of this can be seen by 2 years of age. How does this understanding come about? One theory was put forward by Paul Harris in his book *Children and emotion* (1989). Harris proposed that it is a child's awareness of his or her own mental state that allows them to project mental states on to other people using an 'as if' or pretence mechanism; understanding someone else results from imagining yourself in their position. (This is, in fact, similar to the argument by Humphrey, 1984; see p. 4.) On this basis, Harris argues that there are three important precursors, or preconditions, for the child to be able to understand another person's mind: self-awareness; the capacity for pretence; and being able to distinguish reality from pretence.

- *Self-awareness:* as we saw earlier, children are aware of themselves by about 18–20 months of age and can verbally express their own emotional states by 2 years.
- *The capacity for pretence:* in Chapter 7 we see that the ability to pretend that something in the world is something else emerges in pretend play during the second year. Specifically, children start acting out scenes with dolls or stuffed animals, for example feeding teddy 'as if' he were hungry. By 2 and 3 years of age, children are conjuring up animate beings in their pretend play, with emotions and desires of their own.
- *Distinguishing reality from pretence:* when children are in pretend play, they do not usually confuse this with reality. Admittedly, this can happen sometimes. When an adult joins in with a 1- or 2-year-old's play, the child can be confused as to whether the adult is in 'pretend' or 'real' mode; for example, if a child knocks an empty cup over in play and mother says, 'you spilled your tea, better wipe it up', the child may actually pick up a cloth to wipe it. However, more usually, and especially by 3 or 4 years, the pretence–reality distinction is a stable one. Things would be difficult if it was not—suppose a child pretends a wooden block is a cake, for a tea party; if they confused pretence and reality, they would actually try to eat the wooden block! This seldom happens. By 3 years, children often signal the pretend mode in their play; for example, 'Let's pretend to be families. You be daddy …'. Direct interviews with 3-year-olds also confirm that they can distinguish real from imaginary situations, and understand the use of the words 'real' and 'pretend'.

How do all these precursors come together in Harris's theory? He supposes that once a child is aware of his or her own emotional state, he or she can use the ability to pretend in order to project this emotional state onto inanimate beings (in pretend play) or other people, and to realize that the other person's imagined reality may differ from their own reality. Let's take as an example a child who said, 'You sad Mummy. What Daddy do?'. We can suppose that previously this child has experienced sadness herself, and perhaps has experienced sadness because her daddy was nasty to her. Her ability to imagine things in an 'as if' or pretend mode enables her to suppose that mummy may be sad, too, because daddy was also nasty to her. Furthermore, she does not confuse this with her own emotional state; the child does not have to be sad herself in order to imagine that mummy is sad, for a certain reason.

There is one obvious alternative interpretation that would dispense with Harris's 'as if' mechanism. That is that young children learn to link common situations with common emotions. Perhaps they have just learned that mummies are usually sad because daddies have been nasty to them, and it doesn't require any imaginative projection of one's own emotional state.

One way to distinguish this alternative explanation from Harris's theory is to see whether children can understand that someone else's emotion in a given situation depends on what they desire or want. To ascertain this, Harris and his colleagues asked children to listen to stories about animal characters: for example, Ellie the elephant and Mickey the monkey. The children were told that Ellie the elephant is choosy about what she likes to drink. Some were told that she likes milk to drink and nothing else, others that she likes coke to drink and nothing else. Mickey the monkey is mischievous and mixes up the drink containers; for example, he might pour all the coke out of a coke can, fill it with milk and offer it to Ellie. How would she feel when she tastes the drink? Four-year-olds are able to answer correctly that (if she likes milk) she will be pleased or that (if she likes coke) she will be sad, and explain why in terms of Ellie's desires.

This does tend to suggest that, at least by 4 years, children are taking account of someone's desires in predicting their emotional state; they are not just basing their judgement on a stereotyped situation–emotion link (such as: you are pleased if you are given a drink). In a subsequent study, the experimenters also asked children how Ellie would feel before she tasted the drink. How would she feel if she likes coke and is given a coke can (which Mickey has secretly filled with milk)? By 6 years (though in this study, not at 4 years), children correctly judged that Ellie would be happy when given the can, though sad when she tasted the contents. Here, the belief and desire of another are being successfully linked in the prediction of emotion, even when the belief is different from the child's own belief (the child knows the coke can has milk in it, but Ellie has a 'false belief') and the desire may be different from the child's desire—not all children like coke (or milk).

Stop and Think

To what extent do these studies show that children have insights into the ways in which other people feel?

From the above account, we might say that children are developing hypotheses about other persons' emotions, desires and beliefs. This could be described as developing a 'theory of mind' or skills in 'mindreading'. As we saw at the end of Chapter 2, there are similar ideas about the evolutionary origins of intelligence in the higher primates. Further research on development of 'theory of mind' in children is considered in Chapter 15.

By 6 or 7 years, children seem able to understand and manipulate emotions in a more complex way. It would appear that, as well as being able to understand that someone else can feel a different emotion (metarepresentation), they can begin to operate reflectively on such understanding (Harris, 1989). Consider, for example, how children might respond to the following story.

> Diana falls over and hurts herself. She knows that the other children will laugh if she shows how she feels. So she tries to hide how she feels.

What will Diana do, and why? Many 6-year-olds (but not 4-year-olds) are able to say that Diana will look happy, and explain why; for example, 'She didn't want the other children to know that she's sad that she fell over'. This is an embedded sentence with a recursive structure of the form 'I may not want you to know how I feel'. We've seen that 4-year-olds can cope with 'I know how you feel', but only by 6 years does this further recursion seem to become possible (see also discussion of higher-order false belief tasks in Chapter 15).

DEVELOPING EMOTIONAL INTELLIGENCE

Emotional Regulation

Emotions play a regulatory role, for example, when a child's expression of sadness elicits comforting responses on the part of parents. Children must learn to regulate their emotions in order to cope with the range of situations that they encounter in life. Stressful situations are unavoidable, so emotional regulation is a developmental task for children if they are to achieve states of emotional well-being. The capacity to regulate emotions underpins the development of social competence. During infancy and early childhood, children can rely on their parents/carers to help them manage their emotions, but as they grow older their success in forming positive relationships with peers will depend to a large extent on their ability to manage their emotions by themselves. Research with preschoolers indicates a continuing relationship between children's accuracy in recognizing emotions and their acceptance and liking by peers (Denham et al., 1990).

This finding is confirmed by research on vulnerable 'at-risk' children (Izard et al., 2001) and also by research on children who are rejected or bullied by their peers (Mahady Wilton et al., 2000). Children who are victimized are understandably upset by their peers' behaviour. However, if they respond with aggressive reactions and other emotional displays that are perceived by the others as inappropriate or exaggerated (such as excessive crying and distress), these responses appear to perpetuate the bullying by motivating aggressive peers to engage in further attack. Mahady Wilton et al. (2000) found significant differences between the emotional displays of bullies and those of victims during aggressive interactions. The emotional displays of interest, joy, anger, contempt, surprise and sadness accounted for the six most frequent displays of both bullies and victims (Figures 6.2 and 6.3). However bullies showed a significantly greater proportion of joy and anger, while victims showed a significantly

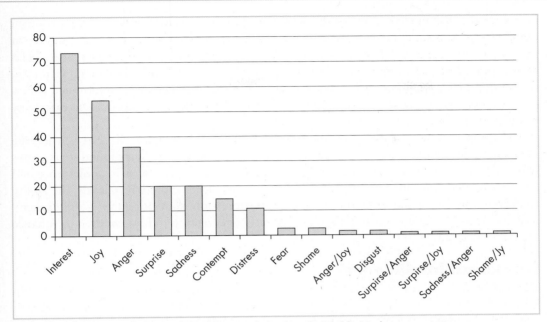

Figure 6.2 Observed frequencies of emotional displays by children who were victims.

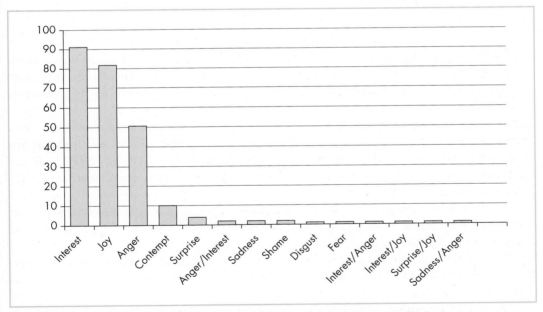

Figure 6.3 Observed frequencies of emotional displays by children who bullied others.

greater proportion of surprise and sadness. There were no significant differences between bullies and victims in displays of interest, or contempt.

The finding that victimized children show high levels of interest and joy during aggressive episodes is at first glance a puzzling result. However, it may indicate that the episode gives them the social interaction (however unpleasant) with peers that at other times they lack. Mahady Wilton et al. (2000, p. 240) conclude that the anger displays of victims confirm that children who are easily aroused and have difficulties in regulating their emotions are 'at higher risk of regulation dysfunction—in effect, their emotional feeling states overwhelm their coping processes'. The fact that there were close parallels between bullies and victims in their emotional displays confirms the view that emotional expression is interpreted differently depending on the social context. What is functional for one child may be extremely dysfunctional for another.

The importance of emotion regulation is confirmed by Moffitt et al. (2011) using the Dunedin Longitudinal Study data from New Zealand (see Table 1.1). They found strong links between failure to regulate one's emotions as a child and later outcomes in adolescence and adulthood, including substance dependency, money problems and crime. Clearly, the ability to delay gratification and to modulate emotional expression is an extremely useful capacity in Western society. These researchers advocate early intervention to help children to enhance the qualities of emotional regulation.

Emotional Intelligence

Research into emotional regulation is one aspect of a much wider concept—emotional intelligence (EI)—the study of which has become increasingly influential in recent years. EI has its origins in Gardner's (1983) concept of two personal intelligences (intrapersonal and interpersonal; see Chapter 17) that he identified as the individual's ability to understand emotions in self and others. Building on this work, Salovey and Mayer (1990) identified five key EI abilities.

1. *Understanding feelings:* understanding the power of your feelings and the feelings of others. The authors highlight a keystone of emotional intelligence—*self-awareness*—which can be heightened by using materials in schools that help children identify their own emotions, build a vocabulary of feelings and recognize links between feelings, thoughts and actions.
2. *Managing feelings:* understanding when and how to use your feelings and helping others to understand when and where to use theirs. Managing feelings so that they are appropriate is regarded as an ability that builds on *self-awareness*. Children can be taught to use strategies such as self-talk, writing down their feelings in a diary, using breathing appropriately, singing, reading or drawing.
3. *Self-motivation:* taking control of your future by making decisions to move towards your goals; developing self-control, like delaying gratification and controlling impulsiveness through self-regulation.
4. *Handling relationships:* relating well to other people; managing emotions in others; understanding how this skill will impinge on abilities that underpin popularity, leadership and interpersonal effectiveness.
5. *Empathy:* caring about the feelings of others but remaining detached enough to be able to give them support. Children can be taught listening and communication skills, problem-solving, stress management and negotiation skills. They can learn to be assertive rather than aggressive or passive. Empathy is viewed as another ability that builds on emotional self-awareness.

However, there is controversy in this field about whether EI is an *ability* or a personality *trait*. As Petrides and Furnham (2001) indicate, it is essential to distinguish between two types of

EI—ability EI and trait EI—each based on the measurement method used. From this perspective, ability EI (or cognitive-emotional ability) concerns the individual's ability to perceive, process and utilize information about emotions, and should be measured by 'maximum performance tests' as you would do in an IQ test. By contrast, trait EI (or emotional self-efficacy) concerns a constellation of emotion-related self-perceptions and dispositions and should be measured by self-report methods.

Salovey and Mayer devised a measure of ability EI called the Mayer Salovey Caruso Emotional Intelligence Test (MSCEIT) (Mayer et al., 2000). On the other hand, Petrides and Furnham (2001) point out that it is very difficult to measure EI as an ability, since by its nature it refers to subjective emotional experience. They measured self-perceptions and dispositions that are compatible with the subjective nature of emotions and EI as a trait. Through content analysis, they identified 15 facets of EI that form the basis of the Trait Emotional Intelligence Questionnaire (TEIQue) (Table 6.2). Studies using the statistical method of factor analysis have shown that the resulting constellation of self-perceptions and dispositions form a distinct construct that predicts depression, life satisfaction, coping styles and truancy (Petrides et al., 2006, 2007) (see Table 6.2 and Box 6.1).

The emotions clearly play a key role in the ways in which adults and children work, interact and learn together. Children who are emotionally competent are significantly more likely to lead productive lives and have satisfying interpersonal relationships. Children with high scores on EI receive more nominations for prosocial than antisocial behaviours from their peers and receive more nominations for kindness, leadership and overall peer competence (Frederickson et al., 2012; Harris, 2000c; Mavroveli et al., 2007; Petrides et al., 2006; and see Box 6.1).

Table 6.2 Common facets in models of emotional intelligence.

Facets	High scorers perceive themselves as . . .
Adaptability	. . . flexible and willing to adapt to new conditions
Assertiveness	. . . forthright, frank and willing to stand up for their rights
Emotion perception (self and others)	. . . clear about their own and other people's feelings
Emotion expression	. . . capable of communicating their feelings to others
Emotion management (others)	. . . capable of influencing other people's feelings
Emotion regulation	. . . capable of controlling their emotions
Impulsiveness (low)	. . . reflective and less likely to give into their urges
Relationships	. . . capable of having fulfilling personal relationships
Self-esteem	. . . successful and self-confident
Self-motivation	. . . driven and unlikely to give up in the face of adversity
Social awareness	. . . accomplished networkers with excellent social skills
Stress management	. . . capable of withstanding pressure and regulating stress
Trait empathy	. . . capable of taking someone else's perspective
Trait happiness	. . . cheerful and satisfied with their lives
Trait optimism	. . . confident and likely to 'look on the bright side of life'

Source: Adapted from Petrides, K.V., Frederickson, N. and Furnham, A. (2004). The role of trait emotional intelligence in academic performance and deviant behaviour at school. *Personality and Individual Differences*, 36(2), 277–293.

Box 6.1 Trait emotional intelligence and children's peer relations at school

This research aimed to examine the role of trait EI in children's peer relations at school, in particular by examining whether individual differences in EI were related to how children are perceived by their peers. Trait EI (or trait emotional efficacy) is a constellation of emotion-related self-perceptions and dispositions. In this study, it was measured by self-report about the subjective nature of emotional experience. The study built on earlier research by two of the authors (see Table 6.2) using factor analysis.

The main hypotheses were as follows.

1. Children with high trait EI scores would receive more nominations for being cooperative.
2. Children with high trait EI scores would receive fewer nominations for being disruptive.

3. Children with high trait EI scores would receive fewer nominations for being aggressive.
4. Children with high trait EI scores would facilitate prosocial behaviour and inhibit antisocial behaviour.

The researchers studied 160 ethnically diverse children (83 girls and 77 boys), mean age 10.8 years. The measures were as follows.

• *Trait Emotional Intelligence Questionnaire Adolescent Short Form (SF)* comprising 30 short statements, two for each of the 15 facets shown in Table 6.2 and designed to measure global trait EI. Some examples include: 'I feel good about myself' and 'I'm good at getting along with my classmates'.

Box Table 6.1.1 'Guess who' behavioural descriptions.

Description	Guess who in your classroom might . . .
1. Cooperative	Be good to have in your group because they are nice and cooperative, they join in, share and give everyone a turn.
2. Disruptive	Have a way of upsetting everything when they get in a group. They don't share and try to get everyone to do things their way.
3. Shy	Be very shy with other children. They always seem to play or work by themselves and it's hard to get to know them.
4. Aggressive	Start fights. They say mean things to other children or push them or hit them.
5. Dependent	Always be looking for help. They ask for help even before they've tried very hard.
6. A leader	Get chosen by the others as the leader. Other classmates like to have them in charge.
7. Intimidating	Be very funny but sometimes in a scary kind of way.

Source: Petrides, K. V., Sangareau, Y., Furnham, A. and Frederickson, N. (2006). Trait Emotional Intelligence and Children's Peer Relations at School. *Social Development*, 15(3), 537–547.

Box Table 6.1.2 Intercorrelation matrix of trait EI scores and nomination proportions for the seven behavioural descriptions.

	Trait EI	Cooperation	Disruption	Shyness	Aggression	Dependence	Leadership
Trait EI							
Cooperation	-.29***	–					
Disruption	.20**	-.61***	–				
Shyness	-.09	.08	-.26***	–			
Aggression	-.15*	-.54***	.81***	-.19**	–		
Dependence	-.35***	-.49***	.37***	.10	.37***	–	
Leadership	-.15*	.37***	-.01	-.23***	.00	-.25***	–
Intimidation	-.03	-.06	.37***	-.25***	.49***	.00	.35***

* $p < .10$
** $p < .05$
*** $p < .01$

Box Table 6.1.3 Means for the nomination proportions as a function of gender and trait EI (high versus low).

Description	Low trait EI			High trait EI		
	Male N=40	Female N=41	Total N=81	Male N=37	Female N=42	Total N=79
Cooperation[a,b]	.28	.37	.32	.37	.42	.40
Disruption[b]	.19	.11	.15	.15	.08	.11
Shyness	.10	.14	.12	.09	.13	.11
Aggression[a,b]	.28	.06	.17	.16	.05	.10
Dependence[a,b]	.18	.12	.15	.10	.07	.08
Leadership	.14	.14	.14	.16	.18	.17
Intimidation[b]	.18	.10	.14	.15	.09	.12

[a]Statistically trait EI difference.
[b]Statistically gender difference.

Source: Petrides, K. V., Sangareau, Y., Furnham, A. and Frederickson, N. (2006). Trait Emotional Intelligence and Children's Peer Relations at School. *Social Development, 15*(3), 537–547.

- 'Guess who' peer assessment technique, an adaptation of a peer assessment method based on unlimited peer nominations (see Chapter 5) and proportion scores (that is, the proportions of classmates nominating each pupil as fitting each description) for each of seven behavioural descriptions as shown in Box Table 6.1.1.

Teachers also completed the assessment form for each child in their class. Testing took place in class with no time constraints. In Box Table 6.1.2 you can see the correlations between trait EI scores and peer nomination proportions for each of the seven behavioural descriptions. The results indicated that high trait EI children received more nominations for cooperation and leadership and fewer for disruption and dependence than low trait EI children. These results supported hypotheses 1, 2 and 3.

On the basis of the analysis of the seven behavioural descriptions as dependent variables, and trait EI scores as independent variables, the researchers found that both gender and trait EI had statistically significant main effects, as shown in Box Table 6.1.3.

- Compared to low trait EI peers, high trait children received more nominations for cooperation and fewer for aggression and dependence
- Girls received more nominations for being cooperative and fewer for being disruptive, aggressive, dependent and intimidating
- In other data not shown here, teachers rated high trait EI pupils as more cooperative and less aggressive.

These results confirmed the four hypotheses. The researchers took these findings to indicate that emotion-related self-perceptions and dispositions influence children's peer relations at school. The children with high trait EI, in comparison with those who have low trait EI scores, were more likely to be perceived by their peers as having leadership qualities and being cooperative; they were less likely to be perceived as disruptive, aggressive and dependent. Their teachers nominated them as higher on prosocial behaviour and lower on antisocial behaviour in comparison with low trait EI children, though the correlations for teachers were low.

Although girls received more nominations than boys for cooperation and fewer nominations for disruption, aggression, dependence and intimidation, the authors suggest that emotional self-efficacy had a direct influence on peer relations over and above gender impact. As they argue, children who perceive themselves as emotionally skilled are more attractive as friends to their peers and so find it easier to form strong social support networks.

This study confirms a body of earlier research that emphasizes the key role of friends and social networks for emotional health and well-being (see Chapter 5). Low trait EI is a key risk factor, the outcome of which may well be feelings of alienation leading to a tendency to engage in antisocial behaviour. The authors recommend testing children for EI early in their school life in order to identify those who are most at risk of developing antisocial behaviour patterns. The results also have implications for training and education to enhance children's EI (as indicated in Chapter 18 in the context of enrichment).

Based on material in Petrides, K.V., Sangareau, Y., Furnham, A. & Frederickson, N. (2006). Trait emotional intelligence and children's peer relations at school. *Social Development*, 15(3), 537–547.

Studies like these support the views of Goleman (1995), in his popular book on EI, where he argued that Western society has overemphasized intelligence and academic achievement at the expense of emotional skills such as empathy, responsibility, persistence, caring for others and the control of anger. He proposed that children should be helped to recognize and understand their emotions and the emotions of others so that they will be more able to control themselves in positive ways. Essentially, Goleman's message was that emotions and reason are equally important in education. From this perspective, adults should be prepared to teach children about self-awareness, life skills, conflict management, self-esteem, empathy and how to work reflectively and cooperatively in groups, since these qualities underpin the strength of each person's emotional competence.

Self-Concept and Self-Esteem

A general term for how people think about themselves is *self-concept* or *identity*. This can refer to all aspects of the self—appearance, personality and ability, as well as gender or ethnic group.

Some aspects of one's self-concept are evaluative; we all compare ourselves with others and think that we are good at some things and not so good at other things. *Self-esteem* refers to the child's subjective evaluation of their own worth as a person and has been linked in many studies, understandably, with happiness and emotional well-being.

It is possible to measure self-esteem by means of questionnaires. For example, in the Harter Self-Perception Profile for Children (Harter, 1985), designed for 8–13-year-olds, children read a series of 36 paired items such as:

Some kids find it hard to make friends BUT some kids find it's pretty easy to make friends.

They decide which statement is true for them, and whether it is 'sort of true' or 'really true'. The answers give scores for the child's own perception of their 'global self-worth', as well as for more specific aspects of self-esteem such as scholastic competence, social acceptance, athletic competence, physical appearance and behavioural conduct.

By the time they enter school, most children will be able to express some form of self-evaluation and over time they can discriminate amongst different domains in their lives, for example, between the social self and the active self. Harter (1999) proposed that the development of a positive sense of self-esteem depended mainly on the child's *perceived competence* in areas that matter to the child and on the child's experience of social support, whether from parents or peers. Good physical appearance and competence at sports, for example, would be more likely to elicit approval from peers while good academic performance would be more likely to win the approval of parents and teachers.

Harter found that there was a change in children's self-concept during the primary school years as their often unrealistic self-perceptions gave way to more accurate perceptions of abilities and competencies. These judgements of self are inevitably linked to self-esteem, though lack of competence in one domain does not necessarily mean that the child has low self-esteem, provided that he himself and those whose opinions he values regularly affirm his competence in the areas that matter to him.

Tatlow-Golden and Guerin (2010) were interested to find out about how children evaluated themselves by inviting 125 Irish 10–13-year-olds to draw and write about their favourite people (the *social self*) and their favourite activities (the *active self*). They found that, with regard to the active self, there were two main categories: physical activities and non-physical activities. Two-thirds of participants represented themselves doing active things like football, ice skating, gymnastics and skipping; just over half drew and wrote about other activities like baking, playing a musical instrument and playing computer games. The children's comments referred mainly to fitness and friendship, enjoyment and fun, relaxation and play. Competitiveness did not feature at all. With regard to the social self, they mentioned family and friends for the most part and commented frequently on the importance of these relationships in terms of emotional and social support. Seven per cent of the participants chose pets as their favourite 'people', mentioning such qualities as the pet's ability to 'understand what I say'. The authors of this study concluded that it is important to consult with children themselves when attempting to understand how they value themselves, the people in their lives and the activities in which they engage. This is especially so when developing interventions to promote self-esteem in the young.

Increasingly, there has been a huge interest amongst policy-makers, parents and educators in developing training for children and young people throughout the preschool, primary school and secondary school years to enhance EI (or *emotional literacy*, as it is sometimes called) and thereby promote social and emotional learning, including self-esteem (Mayer & Salovey, 1997). The programmes have had some very positive outcomes (Cowie & Jennifer, 2008). Evaluations of emotional literacy programmes have been undertaken (Aber et al., 2003; Frey et al., 2005; Greenberg, 2010; Greenberg et al., 1995; Grossman et al., 1997; van Schoiack Edstrom et al., 2002). In Box 6.2 we describe a study that evaluated the impact of one of these interventions, Circle Time (CT), designed to improve the self-esteem and social and emotional competence of primary school children. CT is one of the most widely used interventions in the promotion of social and emotional learning in schools. It provides a safe space where children, often sitting in a circle, can engage in active listening, sharing experiences, expressing worries and concerns, problem solving around issues that have arisen in the class group, learning to respect others; CT gives them space and time to express their views (Mosley, 2009).

Box 6.2 Circle Time for social and emotional learning in primary schools

In this study, the researchers investigated the effectiveness of CT on children's social and emotional learning. They used a semi-randomized control (RCT) design in one Maltese primary school, across Years 1–5. Five classroom teachers volunteered to be trained in CT and to implement it in their classes (the experimental groups) over a period of one year, with another five teachers agreeing to participate with their classes as controls. The experimental class teachers were trained by qualified CT specialists and received a resource pack with detailed lesson

plans on implementation. Topics in the pack included self-awareness; self-esteem; understanding and managing feelings; belonging; friendship and cooperation; challenges and solutions.

All the class teachers completed the Strengths and Difficulties Questionnaire (SDQ) (Goodman, 1997) pre- and post-intervention while the CT teachers additionally completed a questionnaire on their experience of delivering the programme.

Box Figures 6.2.1, 6.2.2 and 6.2.3 show a clear pattern of improvement in the means of the

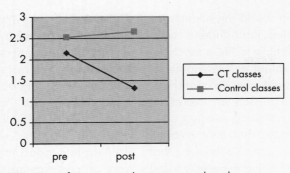

Box Figure 6.2.1 Mean SDQ scores for emotional symptoms subscale.

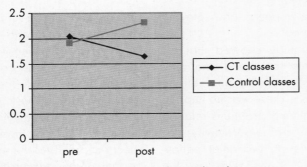

Box Figure 6.2.2 Mean SDQ scores for peer relationships subscale.

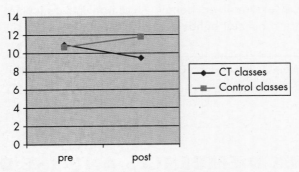

Box Figure 6.2.3 Mean SDQ scores for total difficulties subscale.

experimental classes. Significant effects were found for the emotional symptoms subscale (Box Figure 6.2.1), the peer relationships subscale (Box Figure 6.2.2) and the total difficulties subscale (Box Figure 6.2.3); however, there were no significant differences on conduct difficulties, hyperactivity and prosocial behaviour. In other words, in the CT classes there was an overall decrease of difficulties as well as specifically for those involving peer relationships and emotional symptoms compared with an increase of comparable difficulties in the control group.

All the CT teachers found the experience enjoyable and reported that students were highly engaged. According to these teachers, the students learned valuable listening skills, team work and improved peer relationships. All the CT teachers expressed an interest in using CT again in the following year.

The students reported that they enjoyed CT, would like to do it again and believed that they had learned a lot. They especially liked cooperative games, singing and movement activities and reported that they had improved their social skills, including 'making friends', 'learning how to know peers' and 'playing together without fighting'.

This small-scale study showed that CT contributed to students' social and emotional learning and they showed fewer internalized problems than controls. There was no impact, however, on externalizing problems relating to conduct difficulties and hyperactivity; nor were there differences in prosocial behaviour. One weakness of the study, as the researchers themselves admit, is that a longer period of time was needed in order to have a greater influence on externalized behaviour difficulties and on prosocial behaviour.

The main difficulty experienced by the teachers was lack of time for implementation of CT due to an overloaded curriculum and a general lack of interest in valuing social and emotional learning activities such as CT. This phenomenon has also been noted by Lendrum et al. (2013), who highlighted the need for ongoing staff development and training to support the effective implementation of programmes that aim to enhance children's emotional health and well-being. Cooper and Jacobs (2011, pp. 91–92) have also noted that CT presents challenges to its success due to pressure from other types of curriculum work and teachers' negative views about the empowerment of children. They strongly advocate a whole-school approach in which the values of CT are reflected across the curriculum. They also caution that children who lack theory of mind skills, for example those on the Asperger's spectrum, will find the emphasis on empathy and unconditional positive regard very difficult to manage. The results of the present small-scale study are encouraging but also confirm the difficulties highlighted by other studies in the field.

Based on material in Cefai, C., Ferrario, E., Cavioni, V., Carter, A. & Grech, T. (2014). *Pastoral Care in Education*, 32, 116–130.

EARLY SEX DIFFERENCES AND THE DEVELOPMENT OF GENDER IDENTITY

We will now look at sex differences in behaviour and the development of children's awareness of these differences, and will then compare some hypotheses about why sex differences develop. Rather than using the term 'sex', some authors use the term 'gender' when referring to differences that may have been produced by upbringing or social convention, and reserve the word 'sex' for purely biological differences. In practice, the distinction is not always that easy. Here, we refer to 'sex differences' but to 'gender identity', these being common usages.

Sex Differences among Children in Western Societies

Gender identities and gender roles play a significant part in the structuring of family life. Many studies have been carried out in the UK and the USA on sex differences in infants and young children, most of them involving observations of behaviour in the home or in nursery classes. Individual studies often have rather small samples, say 20 children or so, and measure a large number of behavioural categories, so even by chance, one or two measures may give apparently 'significant' differences. (Remember that a result that is significant at the .05 level occurs by chance 1 in 20 times.) Thus, it is important to look for replication of findings over a number of studies. There are many reviews of this subject area in the literature (e.g. Golombok & Hines, 2002; Maccoby, 1998, 2000).

The results of research in the infancy period (up to 2 years) do not reveal many consistent differences between boys and girls. The similarities certainly outweigh the dissimilarities. However, the replicated findings include: girl infants may be more responsive to people, staying closer to adults, whereas boy infants may be more distressed by stressful situations that they cannot control (such as the 'Strange Situation' separations discussed in Chapter 4, pp. 110–112). Girls also seem to talk earlier.

Among 2-year-olds and in older children, some sex differences in toy choice are apparent. Observations of 2-year-olds at home, and of 3- and 4-year-olds in nursery classes, show that boys tend to prefer transportation toys, blocks and activities involving gross motor activity such as throwing or kicking balls, or rough-and-tumbling; girls tend to prefer dolls, dressing-up or domestic play. Many activities, however, do not show a sex preference at this age.

School-age children tend to select same-sex partners for play, and more so as they get older. Also, boys tend to prefer outdoor play and, later, team games, whereas girls prefer indoor, more sedentary activities, and often play in pairs. Boys more frequently engage both in play-fighting and in actual aggressive behaviour (Maccoby, 1998). Girls tend to be more empathic and remain more orientated towards adults (parents and teacher) longer into childhood.

Girls are more likely to have one best friend with whom they share everything, including the most intimate aspects of their lives. These disclosures play a key role in maintaining the friendship but when such pairings break up (as they often do), there can be intense emotional repercussions with resulting retaliatory behaviour, such as revealing close secrets, spreading nasty rumours or social exclusion of the former best mate. Besag (2006) argues that this instability in relationships can underpin the frequent quarrels and conflicts amongst girls that she observed in her research. Jennifer and Williams (2011, pp. 50–51), on the basis of interviews and focus groups with adolescent girls, concluded that the use of indirect aggression is very influenced by sexualized and gendered discourse. Such behaviours include spreading gossip about another girl's sexual reputation and ridiculing another girl's physical appearance, as well as use of offensive terms like 'slag', 'slapper', 'tart' and 'tramp'. The use of such discourses is the main way in which girls create the gender and sexual norms, identities and hierarchies of their peer groups.

Awareness of Gender Identity and Sex Differences

If you ask a 2-year-old 'Are you a boy or a girl?', quite a few will not know the answer or will be easily confused, although many will answer correctly. The easiest task seems to be to show pictures of a male and female of stereotyped appearance (such as Figure 6.4). In one such study, Thompson (1975) found that 24-month-old children gave 76% correct identification

Figure 6.4 Stereotyped female and male figures.

Source: Image copyright Souped Up Designs. Used under licence from Shutterstock.com.

of sex; this rose to 83% by 30 months and 90% by 36 months. By 3 years, most children can correctly label their own or another person's sex or gender, and are said to have achieved *gender identity*.

The next stage, called *gender stability*, is achieved by around 4 years. This is when a child realizes that gender is normally stable; for example, a girl will say that she will be a mummy when she grows up. A bit later, the child reaches 'gender constancy', a mature awareness that biological sex is unchanging, despite changes in appearance. This is tested by questions such as 'Could you be a girl if you want to be?' (to a boy) or 'Suppose this child [picture of boy] lets their hair grow very long; is it a boy or a girl?'. This is reported to be achieved around 7 years of age, at or soon after the child can conserve physical quantity (see Chapter 13), but may be achieved earlier if children understand the genital difference between the sexes (Bem, 1989).

Sex-role stereotypes also appear to be acquired early; these are beliefs about what is most appropriate for or typical of one sex or the other. In one early study (Kuhn et al., 1978), preschool children were shown a male doll and a female doll and asked which doll would do each of 72 activities, such as cooking, sewing, playing with trains, talking a lot, giving kisses, fighting or climbing trees. Even 2.5-year-olds had some knowledge of sex-role stereotypes. This sex stereotyping increases with age and is well established by the middle school years (Serbin et al., 1993, is an excellent summary).

However, Dunn (2004b) argues that the separation by gender issue is still a focus for debate. The boundaries between the sexes are still much more blurred than some of the earlier research might suggest. For example, Ellis et al. (1981) studied children's interactions in their neighbourhoods and observed that, although 33% of children played in same-gender groups, still 28% were mixed gender. Studies like these indicate that some of the so-called gender segregation may in fact be a function of the nature of school life, where space is in short supply and there is an emphasis on power and evaluation that promotes the separation of boys and girls (Dunn, 2004b, p. 105). Not only that, Dunn argues that there is such a large overlap between boys and girls on most measures of language and behaviour that the emphasis in much of the psychological literature on *differences* actually misrepresents the reality of children's everyday experience.

Furthermore, Frosh et al. (2002), on the basis of in-depth interviews with adolescent boys, argue that many boys suffer from the imposition of conventional constructions of masculinity on their ways of being and relating. The young men in this study reported on how often it was essential to prove their manhood by being contemptuous of vulnerable boys and of people who were perceived to be gay, and by expressing misogynist, sexist views and behaviour. Masculinity was defined by the social situation, with huge pressure from the peer group to behave in stereotypical ways. The boys in their study showed the capacity to be emotionally sensitive and thoughtful, but it was as if they needed permission to express their feelings. Frosh et al. also point out that many intervention projects emphasize conventionally 'male' activities, so perpetuating hegemonic masculinity. They recommend that there should be more attempts on the part of educators to challenge the prevailing myths about what it is to be a boy. It is also important here to reflect on the social constructivist view (see p. 72) that masculinity is constructed differently depending on the social conditions in which the child is growing up, in particular with regard to ethnicity and social class.

Historically, too, attitudes change, as observed by the sociologist Anderson (2013) who 'came out' as gay while a high school sports teacher in 1993 to universal opprobrium. In 2012, he returned to the same high school to run with the teams for 2 weeks and, to his delight, found a radical change:

> Not only was there no homophobia on the team, but young men proudly discussed their other activities that none would have boasted about when I was in high school, or even when I was coaching. One boy talked about wanting to return to ballet lessons, another was establishing his career as a model, and most all of the boys were very soft in their gendered expression. Interestingly, despite the time they took on their appearance, the love they outwardly express for each other on Facebook (and in person) or their feminized physical tactility (long hugs and massaging each other), they ran even faster than the boys did that I coached back in the macho 1980s.
>
> *(Anderson, 2013, p. 130)*

Cross-cultural Studies

The sex differences in behaviour and sex-role stereotypes so far discussed apply to Western urban societies such as the UK and the USA. But how widely do they apply in other societies? Much of what we know here comes from the work of anthropologists. One study made a survey of the anthropological literature on child-rearing in 110, mostly non-literate, societies (Barry et al., 1957). They found that in more than 80% of those societies where accurate ratings could be made, girls more than boys were encouraged to be nurturant, whereas boys more than girls were subject to training for self-reliance and achievement. In many societies, responsibility and obedience were also encouraged in girls more than boys. The degree of pressure for sex-typing does vary with the type of society, and appears to be especially strong in societies where male strength is important for hunting or herding, and less strong in societies with small family groups, where sharing of tasks is inevitable.

A more detailed study of child-rearing was made in the classic 'six cultures study' (Whiting & Edwards, 1973, 1988; Whiting & Whiting, 1975), in which direct observations were made on samples of children in Kenya, Japan, India, the Philippines, Mexico and the USA. In the majority of these societies, girls were more nurturant and made more physical contacts, while boys were more aggressive, more dominant and engaged in more rough-and-tumble play. Differences among the six cultures could often be related to differences in socialization pressures, for example the extent to which older girls were required to do nurturant tasks such as looking after younger siblings.

THEORIES OF SEX-ROLE IDENTIFICATION

Why do boys and girls come to behave in different ways, and to have certain beliefs about sex-appropriate behaviour? There are several theories about this process of acquiring a sex role, or sex-role identification, each giving a different emphasis to the importance of family and societal influences. Here we consider biological factors, social learning theory, social constructionist approaches, the cognitive-developmental approach and gender schemas and social cognitive theory.

Biological Factors

Boys and girls differ in one chromosome pair; girls have two X chromosomes, whereas boys have one X and one Y chromosome. This genetic difference normally leads to differential production of hormones, both in the fetus and later in adolescence. These hormones lead to differentiation of bodily characteristics, such as the genital organs, and may also influence brain growth and hence behaviour patterns.

Much of the evidence linking sex hormones to behaviour comes from animal studies, but there have now been a number of studies on human children who have received unusual amounts of sex hormone early in life, for example while in the uterus. The most common syndrome is called congenital adrenal hyperplasia (CAH), in which, due to a lack of certain enzymes, the adrenal glands produce excessive androgens (a male sex hormone).

A controversial study of this kind was reported by Money and Ehrhardt (1972). They examined girls who had been exposed to unusually high levels of androgen before birth, in this case because of hormone treatment given to some mothers for medical reasons. This treatment sometimes caused physical abnormalities and has consequently been discontinued. In the cases where the hormonal treatment resulted in malformation of the genitals, this was corrected surgically and the children were reared as girls. Compared with a matched group of girls who had not been exposed to excess androgen, these girls were originally perceived as being more tomboyish and less likely to play with other girls or like feminine clothes. Understandably, many of these individuals were deeply affected by their experience and, as adults, reported anger at the surgery inflicted on them and rejected the gender assignment that had been allocated to them. Some requested reassignment of gender and a reversal of surgery. Organizations like the Intersex Society of North America, which celebrate *intersexuality* as a third sex, strongly oppose surgical procedures on the grounds that the benefits are not for the children but for their parents. They propose instead that *intersexed* children should be left as they are until they are old enough to decide for themselves. Similarly, Hird (2003) objects to the idea that both transsex and intersex continue to be framed as individual pathologies.

In a comprehensive review, Collaer and Hines (1995) examined the evidence for the effects of such sex hormone differences on behaviour over a range of outcome variables. They conclude that the effect is strongest for childhood play behaviour. They indicate that in the course of normal fetal development, male sex hormones seem to predispose boys to become more physically active and interested in rough-and-tumble play. They also argued that the evidence is relatively strong in two other areas: aggression (see Chapter 10) and sexual orientation. (For an overview of work on development of sexual orientation, see Patterson, 1995.) Such effects are consistent with evidence that some sex differences appear early in life and in most human societies (such as boys' preference for rough-and-tumble play).

However, while biological factors are probably important in any comprehensive explanation of sex differences, they do not in themselves explain the process of sex-role identification, and they do not explain the variations in sex roles in different societies. The debate continues with arguments on both sides and many social scientists giving consideration to the view that, to an extent, sex, gender and sexuality are sociohistorical constructs.

Social Learning Theory

An early approach to the learning of sex-role identification was that children are moulded into sex roles by the behaviour of adults, especially parents and teachers—the social learning theory approach (Bandura, 1969; Mischel, 1970). In its early version (which Maccoby, 2000, calls 'direct socialization'), this theory postulates that parents and others reward (or 'reinforce') sex-appropriate behaviour in children. Parents might encourage nurturant behaviour in girls and discourage it in boys, for example.

The answer often seems to be that parents do behave differently towards boys and girls. Besides the cross-cultural evidence referred to above, observations have been made in homes and nurseries in Western societies. For example, Fagot (1978) studied children aged 20–24 months in American homes. She found that girls were encouraged by their parents to dance, dress up, follow them around and play with dolls, but were discouraged from jumping and climbing; boys, however, were encouraged to play with blocks and trucks but discouraged from playing with dolls or seeking help. In a similar study of 3–5-year-olds (Langlois & Downs, 1980), mothers, fathers and also same-age peers reinforced sex-appropriate behaviour and discouraged sex-inappropriate behaviour in children.

Nevertheless, many reviews have felt that this evidence has not been very compelling (Golombok & Hines, 2002; Maccoby, 2000). Many differences in parents' behaviour to boys and girls are small in magnitude. Also, it might be that any differential behaviour by parents is simply responding to pre-existing differences in boys' and girls' behaviour.

At times, researchers try hard to find effects. In a study of mothers and fathers playing with a feminine-stereotyped toy (food, plates) and a masculine stereotyped toy (track, cars), Leaper (2000) stated that 'one of the most consistent ways parents treat girls and boys differently is through the encouragement of gender-typed activities and the discouragement of cross-gender-typed activities' (p. 389). However, Leaper's own findings were that 'the hypothesized child gender effects on parent's behaviour were not confirmed' (p. 386).

Does reinforcement actually affect the child's behaviour? Several studies have found that nursery school teachers tend to reward 'feminine' type behaviours (e.g. quiet, sedentary activities near an adult) in both boys and girls equally, yet this does not prevent boys engaging more in noisy, rough-and-tumble play. Fagot (1985) observed 40 children aged 21–25 months in playgroups, looking at what activities were reinforced (e.g. by praise or joining in) and by whom. She found that the teachers reinforced 'feminine' activities in both boys and girls. She also looked at the effectiveness of the reinforcement (in terms of continuation of the activity). This varied with who was reinforcing, and with what was being reinforced. Girls were influenced by teachers and by other girls, but not much by boys. Boys were influenced by other boys, but not much by girls or teachers. Furthermore, boys were not influenced at all by girls or teachers during 'masculine' activities such as rough-and-tumble or playing with transportation toys.

The limited importance of reinforcement by teachers is also brought out in a study by Serbin et al. (1977). They asked teachers in two preschool classes to praise and encourage cooperative play between boys and girls for a 2-week period. This did increase the level of cooperative cross-sex play, but as soon as the special reinforcement was discontinued, cross-sex play declined to just as low a level as before.

In a slightly later version of social learning theory (which Maccoby calls 'indirect socialization'), it is also supposed that children observe the behaviour of same-sex models, and imitate (or 'model') them; for example, boys might observe and imitate the behaviour of male figures in TV films, in their playful and aggressive behaviour. This introduces a more powerful set of influences on behaviour—but at the price of having to acknowledge cognitive factors. Clearly, observation and imitation must be selective. If observation in itself were important, we would expect most young children to acquire a female sex-role identity, as the great majority of caregivers of young children, and of nursery and infant school teachers, are female. If selective modelling is happening, then children must have some sense of gender identity in order to know who to observe and imitate, and perhaps which activities it is appropriate to imitate. In other words, their own cognitions must be playing an important role.

Social Constructionist Approaches

Social constructionist approaches, as we saw in Chapter 2, place far less emphasis on biological factors. They also challenge social learning theory (see previous section), which stresses the influence of parental modelling and reinforcement on the development of the child's gender identity, in the sense that children tend to imitate same-sex models and follow sex-appropriate activities. By contrast, social constructionists focus on the discourses that exist within a particular culture (Kitzinger, 2007). They propose that people who use terms such as 'boy' or 'girl' assume that the person referred to is oriented to gender when, in fact, they are referring to a socially constructed framework of meaning.

Influenced by the social constructionist perspective, Freedman et al. (2002) gathered evidence from studies of the children of transsexual parents. As they point out, clinical audits of case files on families where parents have had sex reassignment treatments provide a unique opportunity to examine whether the children in such families experience particular difficulties in gender identity development. They studied 13 families with 18 children—10 girls and eight boys, age range 3–15 years. Twelve of the transsexual parents were male to female and one was female to male. In only two of the families did the child or children concerned live with their transsexual and non-transsexual parent. In the remaining 11 families, the parents were now divorced or separated and in only two cases was there joint custody; in all other cases, the non-transsexual mother had legal responsibility for the children.

As the authors point out, the revelation to a family of one parent wishing to seek gender realignment is usually a great shock and many non-transsexual parents do not wish the child or children to have access to the transsexual parent. The wider family and community network can also frequently express disapproval and heterosexist prejudice towards the transsexual parent. In the separated or divorced families of the present study, the case records revealed a great deal of conflict and acrimony with regard to parenting. Despite this, 17 of the 18 children showed no signs of any gender identity disorder (GID); one met two of the

 Stop and Think

Do parents behave differently towards boys and girls? If so, why?

criteria for GID (wishing to belong to the other sex and wearing masculine clothes) but neither of these behaviours persisted. In fact, the most frequent reasons for difficulties appeared to arise from marital conflict between the parents, usually focused on highly emotional reactions towards the transsexual parent. The overall conclusion from this study was that the gender identity of the children was not affected by their parent's gender realignment. Rather, the difficulties in relationships between the estranged parents derived from social prejudice towards gender realignment. The authors propose that such families would benefit from clinical intervention to help them to adjust to the changes that are involved when a parent reveals that he or she is transsexual.

Research by Golombok et al. (2003) found that there were no significant differences in emotional and behavioural difficulties as measured by the Strengths and Difficulties Questionnaire (SDQ) (Goodman, 1997) between children of lesbian and heterosexual mothers (see also p. 141). The only difference was greater smacking of children by fathers in the heterosexual couples than by co-mothers in the lesbian couples. Wainright et al. (2004), in a study of 12–18-year-olds, 44 of whom had same-sex parents and 44 of whom had opposite-sex parents, found that, on measures of psychosocial adjustment, there were no differences between the two groups. Analysis of participants' reports of their romantic/sexual relationships also indicated that there was no difference between the two groups in terms of sexual orientation; fewer than 10 of the adolescents in the whole sample reported same-sex attractions and same-sex romantic relationships in the past 18 months. The outcomes in this study were that adolescents with same-sex parents did not differ significantly from those for a representative group of American adolescents.

Similarly, Rivers et al. (2008), in a study of children raised by lesbian and heterosexual couples, also indicate no significant differences in terms of masculine or feminine traits or the ways in which children interact socially with others. These studies confirm that children of same-sex parents do not exhibit difficulties in psychological functioning in comparison with the children of heterosexual parents. However, Rivers and colleagues observed that lesbian parents were less likely to make use of sources of social support at school (for example, from teachers, nurses, counsellors or classroom assistants). This indicated that they might be reluctant to disclose anxieties to school staff for fear of a prejudiced response. Rivers et al. (2008) suggest that families headed by same-sex couples are often unsupported by education systems that regard heterosexual parenting as the only valid reference point for rearing children. One serious outcome may be that the children of lesbian and gay parents may feel marginalized and stigmatized by the educational system.

Like Freedman et al. (2002), Rivers et al. (2008) recommend that there should be an expansion of services for children of same-sex parents and greater acknowledgement of their status as families. Research studies such as those described in this section represent a wider body of literature confirming that individuals and families with minority identity statuses, such as being gay, lesbian or transsexual, face challenges arising from the discourses of their culture, much of it discriminatory.

Cognitive-developmental Theory and Gender Schemas

The cognitive-development approach in this area stems from the writings of Kohlberg (1966, 1969). He argued that the child's growing sense of gender identity is crucial to sex-role identification. Children tend to imitate same-sex models and follow sex-appropriate activities, because they realize that this is what a child of their own sex usually does. This process was termed *self-socialization* by Maccoby and Jacklin (1974), since it does not depend directly on external reinforcement. The difference between the cognitive-developmental and social learning viewpoints is summarized in Figure 6.5.

What evidence is there for this cognitive-developmental view? In a number of studies, the development of gender identity and constancy has been found to correlate with the degree of

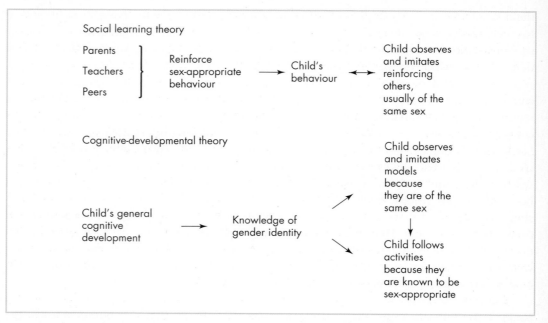

Figure 6.5 Summary of two earlier approaches to sex-role development: social learning theory and cognitive-developmental theory.

sex-typed behaviour. For example, in a study of 2- and 3-year-olds by Weinraub et al. (1984), it was found that the children who had achieved gender identity more securely were also the ones who were observed to make more sex-stereotyped toy preferences. In another study of 4–6-year-olds (Ruble et al., 1981), the level of gender constancy was measured, and each child was shown a film of either same- or opposite-sex children playing with a new toy. Only children high on gender constancy were influenced by the film; if a child high on gender constancy saw opposite-sex children playing with the toy, that child avoided playing with it subsequently.

In the 1980s, ideas of gender schemas were introduced (Bem, 1981; Martin & Halverson, 1981). Gender schemas are cognitive structures that organize gender knowledge into a set of expectations about what it is important to observe, and what it is appropriate to imitate. Schemas also help children to form evaluations of and make assumptions about peers, based on their sex. Martin and Halverson (1981) argued that early gender schemas are formed around a basic in-group/out-group division; the child then focuses on a further understanding of their own gender identity through a grasp of the characteristics of their in-group.

Social Cognitive Theory

Social cognitive theory (Bussey & Bandura, 1999) in effect draws together the ideas of social learning theory and the cognitive-developmental and gender schema insights which, after all, are complementary rather than antagonistic. Social cognitive theorists stress the variety and complexity of mechanisms that are at work—for example:

- *Self-regulatory mechanisms*—children monitor their own behaviour with reference to a self-accepted standard of what is appropriate.

- *Identification with a peer group*—monitoring their behaviour in relation to how they expect same-sex peers might react.
- *Motivational mechanisms*—children are most likely to imitate behaviour that they think they can master and that will enhance their self-efficacy and self-esteem.

Gender schema theorists cite evidence that children not only selectively imitate same-sex models, but also selectively observe and remember information that is relevant to, or consistent with, their own gender schema, or ignore and reject information that is not relevant to or consistent with their gender schema. For example, Martin et al. (1995), in a study of 4–5-year olds, found that if a girl likes a toy, she will assume that girls will like it more than boys (even if it is actually highly attractive to both sexes).

Martin et al. (1999) assessed cognitions or gender schemas held by children aged 3–6 about playing with same- or opposite-sex playmates. As other studies have found, same-sex preference increased over this age period. They also observed the children playing in the day care or after-school care centres they attended. They found that cognitions—assessed by beliefs about what peers would think appropriate, and what partner preferences peers would have—did correlate significantly with the observed same-sex play preference.

We have seen that if reinforcement does have some effects, they are being 'filtered' through other factors. From a number of studies, it seems that the child's own gender identity, and their gender schemas, are important here. In Fagot's (1985) study, however, the children were so young (21–25 months) that gender identity was unlikely to have been achieved. The effects of reinforcement must have been mediated by some early, non-verbal awareness of gender not tapped by the usual tests (see Figure 6.5)—perhaps by a basic in-group/out-group identification, as Martin and Halverson (1981) proposed.

One aspect concerns the influence of the peer group, and cognitions of the peer group. Preference for same-sex peers seems to be a ubiquitous cross-cultural phenomenon, and one that increases through childhood into adolescence. Maccoby (1998, 2000) has documented this thoroughly, and argues that it is a key factor in integrating not only cognitive and social factors, but also the biological factors affecting sex differences (which are often ignored or at least downplayed by social learning theorists). She argues that there are canalized processes of activity preference and behavioural compatibility between the sexes that lead to primarily same-sex peer groups, and that these have an evolutionary basis (as is also believed by evolutionary developmental psychologists, see Chapter 2). Furthermore, boys' and girls' peer groups differ; boys' peer groups tend to be larger, more competitive and risk taking while girls' groups are smaller, more collaborative and based on sharing information. Maccoby argued that the same-sex peer group has a key role in developing sexual identity and sees this pivotal role as requiring biological factors for a full understanding, while not denying the insights that the social learning and cognitive-developmental views have provided. But see also the more recent social cognitive domain approaches proposed by Smetana and by Turiel (as described in Chapter 9) in which the authors emphasize the pivotal role of the social context in specific domains of the child's experience.

Espelage (2013) argues that we need to consider relationships between boys and girls in the context of a gender system that is dominated by normative forms of masculinity. The socialization of men into traditional masculine gender roles emphasizes power and dominance in relationships. Traditional masculinity, she argues, is characterized by antifeminism, homophobia, competitiveness and aggressiveness. As Frosh and colleagues (2002) observed, as boys reach adolescence there is great pressure on them to conform to these traditional male norms.

CHILDREN'S AWARENESS OF AND ATTITUDES TO DIFFERENT ETHNIC AND NATIONAL GROUPS

In this section, we will look at how children become aware of ethnic and national differences and how this affects their behaviour and attitudes towards out-groups. We also explore recent challenges to earlier ways of measuring children's awareness of ethnicity.

Ethnic Awareness and Preference

Ethnic identity can be thought of as awareness of one's own ethnicity, or membership of a particular national or social group. In the past, psychologists such as Aboud (1988) often assessed it by using dolls or photographs, and asking the child to point to one that looked most like them. Aboud (1988) found that children of 4 years and above tended to choose the doll or photograph of someone from their own ethnic group, though there were variations in different studies. Similarly, ethnic awareness of others was assessed by, for example, showing a child photographs of different persons and saying, 'Show me the African-Caribbean person', 'Show me the Chinese person', and so on. By the age of 4 or 5 years, children seemed able to make basic discriminations, for example, between Black and White people, and, during the next few years, between Anglo-American and Hispanic people. A bit later, at around 8 or 9 years, children understood that ethnic identity remains constant despite changes in age or superficial attributes such as clothing. For example, in one study, children were shown a series of photos of an Italian-Canadian boy, labelled as such, putting on Native-American clothes (Figure 6.6). When asked to identify the boy in the final photo, half of the 6-year-olds thought that he was different from the boy in the first photo and that he really was Native American. By 8 years, none made this mistake (Aboud, 1988).

Figure 6.6 By 8 years old, children understand that ethnic identity remains constant despite changes in superficial attributes such as clothing.

Source: Image copyright Hal_P, used under licence from Shutterstock.com.

On the basis of this methodology, Aboud (1988) asserted that dissimilar people were disliked. From her perspective, many children appeared to show racial prejudice from 4 or 5 years of age. For example, they showed such prejudice when asked to put photos of children from different ethnic groups along a scale of liking, or when asked to assign positive descriptions such as 'work hard' and 'truthful', or negative adjectives such as 'stupid' or 'dirty', to all, some, one or none of the photos representing different ethnic groups (Davey, 1983). Aboud (1988, 2008) and Aboud and Doyle (1996) argued that there were definite stages in children's development of prejudice, related to stages in cognitive development. Before about 3 or 4 years of age, ethnic awareness was largely absent and prejudice was not an issue. From 4 to 7 years, Aboud argued, children perceived other ethnic groups as dissimilar to themselves, and because of this tended to have negative evaluations of them. From 8 years onwards, children could think more flexibly about ethnic differences, and in terms of individuals rather than groups.

In recent years, however, such interpretations have been challenged (Quintana, 2011). One challenge concerns the primacy of cognitive development in the origin of racial or ethnic awareness, and its absence in young children until racial categories develop. Hirschfeld (2008) has argued the opposite—that children first acquire racial attitudes, then the ability to sort and classify others into racial categories. As an example, a study by Kelly et al. (2007) showed that preferential attention to own-race rather than different-race faces presented to infants was not present at 3 months, but emerged at 6 months and was clearly present at 9 months.

A strong predictor of racial preference or bias is identification with an ethnic and racial in-group. Two important theories here are Social Identity Theory (SIT) (Tajfel & Turner, 1986) and self-categorization theories (SCT) (Barrett & Davis, 2008). SIT argues that persons maintain self-esteem through identification with an in-group, and SCT that views towards other social groups change once in-group identification occurs. This approach is consistent with young children's ethnocentrism and their apparent bias against out-groups. Measures to assess children's national identifications and attitudes to national groups include the Strength of Identification Scale (SoIS), which can be used to assess children's and adolescents' strength of identification with their own national, state, ethnic, racial or religious groups, and the Perceived Group Status Scale (PGSS), which can be used to assess children's and adolescents' beliefs about how other people view their national, state, ethnic, racial or religious groups (Barrett, 2007).

Graham et al. (2009) found that school students show a preference for same-ethnicity peers in friendship choices and this increases during adolescence. However, much research may have confounded the measurement of positive attitudes towards the in-group with negative attitudes towards the out-group. Brewer (1999) argued that identification with one's own in-group is independent of negative attitudes towards out-groups. However, you can consider the evidence from studies like Ruck and Tenenbaum (2014) as described in Box 9.2 where the authors discovered that secondary school children showed less tolerance of the rights of asylum seekers than did primary school children. They discuss this disturbing result in the light of current media campaigns that emphasize the costs to the host community rather than the potential benefits.

Bennett et al. (2004) studied a sample of 6-year-olds, a group that previous research had identified as being especially prone to racial prejudice (Aboud, 1988). They looked at the attitudes towards out-groups in 594 6-year-olds from five culturally diverse nations—Azerbaijan, UK, Georgia, Russia and Ukraine—proposing that all groups would demonstrate in-group preference, but that specifically negative attitudes towards out-groups would be the exception rather than the rule. They found that, for each national sample, there was indeed in-group favouritism. However, in very few cases were the evaluations of out-groups significantly negative. In fact, in some instances (for example, in the UK about French and Spanish out-groups, and in Georgia and Ukraine about Armenian and Russian out-groups), there was out-group popularity. More typically, however, attitudes towards out-groups were neutral. In other words, these researchers found no evidence that commitment to one's own national identity resulted in widespread judgements against out-groups. The exception was when the out-group belonged to a nation that had posed a threat to the child's own country. For example, Azeri children expressed less positive views towards Russians, though not towards other groups, if they were strongly pro in-group—a finding that was not surprising, since Russia supported the Armenians when they occupied Azeri territory in 1992.

Emphasizing Diversity

In recent years, schools have been a focus for work to reduce racial prejudice in children. This can be assisted by a multiracial curriculum approach that emphasizes the diversity of cultural beliefs and practices and gives them equal evaluation. Procedures such as Cooperative Group Work (Cowie et al., 1994) may help to bring children of different ethnicities and nationalities together in common activities, and thus reduce prejudice in the classroom.

Many studies find some reduction in ethnic prejudice through middle childhood. For example, Takriti et al. (2006), in a study of 5–11-year-old Christian and Muslim children, found a shift away from assigning mainly positive attributes to the in-group and mainly negative attributes to the out-group at 5 years of age, to assigning both positive and negative attributes to both the in-group and the out-group by 11 years of age. While there may be some advantages in same-ethnic friendships in terms of strengthening ethnic identity, as classrooms in Europe and the US become more ethnically diverse, there is a growing literature that investigates the possible benefits of cross-ethnic friendships, including more positive intergroup attitudes (Davies et al., 2011), less tolerance of those who exclude others (Killen et al. 2010), less victimization of peers (Kawabata & Crick, 2011) and feeling safer at school (Munniksma & Juvonen, 2012; and see also pp. 192–193).

CHAPTER SUMMARY

- Research into self-recognition in the mirror indicates that after about 18 months an infant has a reasonable understanding that the reflection in the mirror is a representation of him- or herself.
- The child's sense of self is closely related to the ways in which he or she expresses and manages his or her emotions. The emotions play a key role in the ways in which adults and children work, interact and learn together, and have a strong influence on the quality of children's interpersonal relationships.
- Harris proposed an explanation about how children come to understand other people's emotions, desires and beliefs. He proposed that there are three important preconditions: self-awareness; the capacity for pretence; and being able to distinguish reality from pretence.
- The capacity to recognize, discriminate and interpret emotion in others lies at the heart of interpersonal relationships from a very early age.
- As he or she gets older, the child also needs to develop the skill to regulate emotions; this skill is an important factor in determining the quality of peer relationships.
- Recent work on the development of emotional intelligence has led to some intervention programmes that aim to increase children's prosocial behaviour, reduce aggression and enhance their capacity to relate well to one another.
- Research into sex roles and gender identity is extensive but some controversies continue. There are a number of theoretical explanations for the development of gender identity.
- Children also develop ethnic awareness, and often some degree of ethnic bias; they acquire a sense of national identity and learn to perceive and understand the national identities of others.

DISCUSSION POINTS

1. When does a child develop a sense of self?
2. When can a child understand someone else's emotional state?
3. What causes sex differences in behaviour?
4. How does a sense of ethnic or national identity develop?
5. What is emotional intelligence and how can we measure it?

FURTHER READING

- A good introduction to emotional development in children is Harris, P. (1989). *Children and emotion*, Oxford: Blackwell. Also useful is Dunn, J. (2004). *Children's friendships: The beginnings of intimacy*, Oxford: Blackwell Publications.
- Up-to-date publications in the field of emotional intelligence can be found on the website of the London Psychometric Laboratory (www.psychometriclab.com). For a comprehensive review of evidence-based interventions to promote the well-being of children with emotional and behavioural difficulties, see Cooper, P. & Jacobs, B. (2011). *Evidence of best practice models and outcomes in the education of children with emotional disturbance/behavioural difficulties*. National Council for Special Education Research Report no. 7: www.ncse.ie
- A review of bullying on the grounds of gender and sexual orientation is provided by Rivers, I. & Duncan, N. (Eds.) (2013). *Bullying: Experiences and discourses of sexuality and gender*. London: Routledge.
- For a collection on sex differences see Tenenbaum, H. & Leman, P. (Eds.) (2013). *Gender and development*. Hove: Psychology Press.
- An excellent review of the development of children's perceptions of national identity is Barrett, M. (2007). *Children's knowledge, beliefs and feelings about nations and national groups*. Hove: Psychology Press.

CHAPTER
7
Play

CHAPTER OUTLINE

- Characteristics of Playful Behaviour
- The Development of Play
- Play Theorists
- The Benefits of Play: The Evidence

Play is a very characteristic feature of childhood, but it is quite difficult to define. This chapter first discusses why we consider some behaviour sequences to be playful, what the defining characteristics of play are, and how it differs from the related behaviour of exploration. The next section examines the development of various kinds of play in childhood. The ideas of leading play theorists are then discussed, before the final section examines what empirical studies can tell us about the significance of play in children's development.

CHARACTERISTICS OF PLAYFUL BEHAVIOUR

Three sequences of behaviour are described below. Study them and think what they have in common.

Example 1: A 2-year-old lies in his cot, babbling to himself: 'Big Bob. Big Bob. Big Bob. Big and little. Little Bobby. Little Nancy. Little Nancy. Big Bob and Nancy and Bobby. And Bob. And two three Bobbys. Three Bobbys. Four Bobbys. Six.' (All with giggles and exaggerated pronunciation.)

Example 2: Helen, a 4-year-old, is sitting in a playhouse, by a table with a plastic cup, saucer and teapot. She calls out, 'I'm just getting tea ready! Come on, it's dinner time now!' Charlotte, also 4, answers, 'Wait!'; she wraps up a teddy in a cloth in a pram, comes in and sits opposite Helen, who says, 'I made it on my own! I want a drink.' (She picks up the teapot.) 'There's only one cup—for me!' (pretends to pour tea into only one cup). Charlotte pretends to pour from the teapot into an imaginary cup, which she then pretends to drink from. Darren, a 3-year-old, approaches. Charlotte goes and closes the door, shutting a pretend bolt and turning a pretend key, but Helen says, 'No, he's daddy; you're daddy, aren't you?' (to Darren). Charlotte 'unbolts' and 'unlocks' the door, and Darren comes in.

Example 3: Some 6- and 7-year-olds are in a school playground. One boy runs up to another, laughing, and grabs his shoulders, turns and runs off. The second boy chases the first, catches him by the waist and pulls him round. They tussle and swing around, then fall and roll over on the ground, grappling. They get up and run off, laughing and chasing again.

Most observers would agree in saying that, despite their differences, all three are examples of play, or playful behaviour. Respectively, they could be described as language play, fantasy or pretend play and rough-and-tumble play. However, although there have been numerous attempts to characterize or define play, it has not proved an easy task.

Fagan (1974) made a distinction between two kinds of definition: the functional approach and the structural approach. The functional approach suggests that play does not have an obvious end in itself, or an external goal. Thus, if an external goal is present (such as a need to eat, to seek comfort or to overpower another) then the behaviour is not play. This led to a definition of play as something that has no clear immediate benefits or obvious goal. Symons (1978) advanced this sort of definition for monkey social play, but it can equally apply to human play. If you look at examples 1–3 above, it is not clear when an episode is completed, or obvious what the purpose of the behaviour is. In fact, many theorists *do* believe the child gets benefits from playing, but they are not clear, immediate ones; there is continuing disagreement about exactly what the benefits of play are (see the last section of this chapter).

The structural approach attempts to describe the sorts of behaviour that only occur in play, or the way in which behaviours are performed playfully. The main examples of behaviours that only occur in play are play signals. In mammals, these often take the form of an open-mouth play face (as in monkeys grappling) or a bouncy gambol (as in puppies or kittens initiating a chase). In children, similarly, laughter and the associated 'open-mouth play face' (Figure 7.1) usually signal play. Such play signals are especially use-

Figure 7.1 Play signals: (a) 'open-mouth face' in a chimpanzee; (b) 'play face' in a human child.

Source: (a) Hooff, J. A. R. A. M. Van (1972). A comparative approach to the phylogeny of laughter and smiling. In R.A. Hinde (Ed.), *Non-verbal communication*. Cambridge: Cambridge University Press; (b) Reproduced with permission of Peter K. Smith.

ful in rough-and-tumble play (example 3 above), where they can indicate that no aggressive intention is implied in a chase or wrestle.

Not all play is indexed by play signals, however. Often play is made up entirely of behaviours familiar in other contexts, such as running or manipulating objects. According to the structural approach, we think of these behaviours as being done playfully if they are 'repeated', 'fragmented', 'exaggerated' or 'reordered'. For example, a child just running up a slope may not be playing but if he or she runs up and slides down several times (repetition), runs just halfway up (fragmentation), takes unusually large or small steps or jumps (exaggeration) or crawls up and then runs down (reordering), we would probably agree that it was playful.

This structural approach is not in opposition to the functional one. After all, the child running up and down the slope has no immediate purpose, apart from enjoyment. The two approaches are logically distinct, however.

Another approach, which can encompass both the previous ones, is to say that observers identify play or playfulness by a number of different *play criteria*. No one criterion is sufficient, but the more criteria are present, the more agreement we will have that the behaviour is play. A formal model along these lines, proposed by Krasnor and Pepler (1980), is shown in Figure 7.2. 'Flexibility' sums up the structural characteristics of play—variation in form and content. 'Positive affect' refers to the enjoyment of play, especially indexed by signals such as laughter. 'Non-literality' refers to the 'as if' or pretend element (see example 2 above). 'Intrinsic motivation' refers to the idea that play is not constrained by external rules or social demands, but is done for its own sake.

An empirical test of Krasnor and Pepler's model was made by Smith and Vollstedt (1985). They used the four criteria above, and a fifth—means/ends (i.e. the child is more interested in the performance of the behaviour than in its outcome). They made a video film of nursery school children playing, and designated short, discrete episodes, which they asked 70 adults to view. Some scored each episode as to whether it was playful or not, others as to the applicability of the

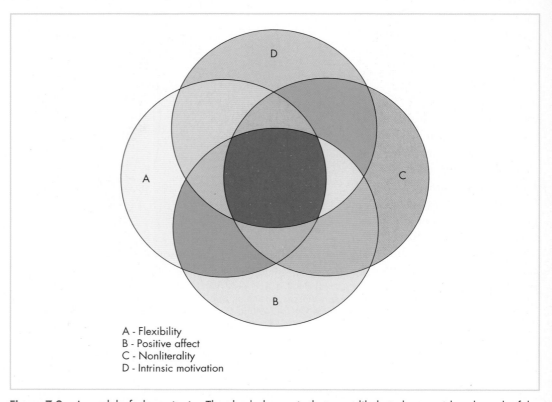

A - Flexibility
B - Positive affect
C - Nonliterality
D - Intrinsic motivation

Figure 7.2   A model of play criteria. The shaded area is that most likely to be considered as playful.
Source: Krasnor, L. R. & Pepler, D. J. (1980) The study of children's play: some suggested future directions, *New Directions for Child and Adolescent Development, 1980*(9), 85–95. Reproduced by permission of John Wiley & Sons Inc.

play criteria. Analyses showed that the episodes seen as playful were often seen as non-literal, flexible and showing positive affect. Furthermore, the more of these that were present, the higher the ratings for playfulness. Means/ends also correlated with play, but did not add anything to the first three criteria. Interestingly, the intrinsic motivation criterion did not correlate with play judgements, despite its common occurrence in definitions of play. Observers often rated non-playful activities (such as watching others or fighting) as intrinsically motivated; equally, some play episodes were externally constrained, for example by the demands of others in social play.

The play criterion approach does not attempt a one-sentence definition of play—a seemingly hopeless task. It does acknowledge the continuum from non-playful to playful behaviour, however, and seeks to identify how observers actually decide to call a behaviour sequence 'play'. The main criteria so far identified for young children, as we have seen, are enjoyment, flexibility and pretence.

Exploration and Play

A behaviour that is sometimes confused with play is exploration. These were often subsumed together in earlier writings, perhaps because of the influence of behaviourism and learning theory. Both exploration and play were awkward for traditional learning theorists, as neither was obviously goal seeking or under the control of reinforcers. It is also true that, with very young children, during sensorimotor development (see Chapter 13) the distinction between

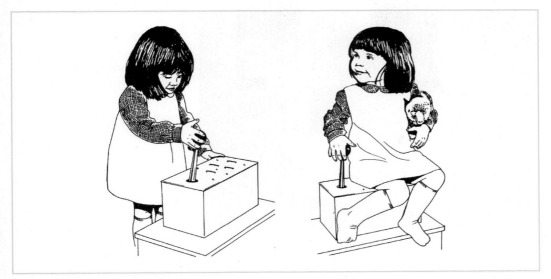

Figure 7.3   A child exploring and later playing with a novel object.
Source: C. Hutt (1966). *Symposia of the Zoological Society of London*, p. 18. © Zoological Society of London, with permission.

exploration and play is difficult to make, as, for young infants, all objects are novel. By the preschool years, however, the distinction is clearer. A classic experiment illustrating this was carried out by Corinne Hutt (1966). She devised a novel toy, a box that children could sit on, with a lever that could sound a bell or a buzzer. Children aged 3–5 years were rather serious when introduced to the toy, feeling it, touching and moving the lever—they were in fact exploring what the novel object could do (see left hand of Figure 7.3). Fairly soon, this changed. Typically a child would relax, and sit on the object making noises with the lever repeatedly or in different ways—seen as more playful activity (see right hand of Figure 7.3). These observations led Hutt to suggest that children typically proceed from specific exploration of the object to more playful behaviour. Exploration was characterized as relatively serious and focused, essentially asking, 'What does this object do?'. Play was characterized as relaxed, and by a diversity of activities essentially asking, 'What can I do with this object?'.

Stop and Think

What do we mean when we talk about children 'playing'?

THE DEVELOPMENT OF PLAY

Play Types and Sequences

Researchers have identified a number of different types of play. These include locomotor or physical activity play (covering exercise play and rough-and-tumble play), play with objects, fantasy and sociodramatic play, and language play. Exercise play is found in most if not all

Figure 7.4 'Practice' or 'functional' play in a 1-year-old infant; simple actions like mouthing, banging or pushing are performed with one or two objects.

Source: Reproduced with permission of Peter K. Smith.

Figure 7.5 This 2-year-old boy is showing constructive play, making a tower from box cubes.

Source: Reproduced with permission of Peter K. Smith.

mammal species (Power, 2000) and over the last decade has been given more attention in human children. Most child developmental research, however, has focused on object and especially pretend play (see the title of Box 7.1 as an example, where 'play' is taken as synonymous with 'pretending').

Piaget (1951) was one of the first to describe a developmental sequence in children's play. This went from practice play, through symbolic play (fantasy/pretend play), to games with rules; Piaget saw these as overlapping stages through the childhood years. By 'practice play', Piaget mainly meant early sensorimotor play in infants, and most animal play. However, if practice play means play that is neither symbolic nor rule governed, then it can occur well beyond the sensorimotor period. Indeed, rough-and-tumble would seem to count as practice play, unless it has symbolic elements (as in monster play) or is rule governed (as in tig).

Smilansky (1968) later postulated a four-fold sequence, from functional play (similar to practice play) to constructive play (making something, e.g. from Lego bricks), then dramatic play (like Piaget's symbolic play) and finally games with rules. She thus suggested that constructive play was intermediate between functional and dramatic play (Figures 7.4, 7.5, 7.6 and 7.7). Some American play researchers have used this scheme as a 'play hierarchy'. Piaget (1951), however, thought that 'constructive games are not a definite stage like the others, but occupy . . . a position halfway between play and intelligent work, or between play and imitation'. The goal-directed nature of much constructive activity, for Piaget, made it more accommodative than purely playful behaviour (see later, and also Chapter 13). Either it was work-like or some symbolic element might be present. The distinct, sequential nature of constructive play in Smilansky's scheme is thus questionable (Takhvar & Smith, 1990).

Physical Activity Play

As anyone watching a yard or school playground can observe, a lot of play involves physical activity, often without objects. In a review of what they argued was a neglected aspect of play, Pellegrini and Smith (1998) suggested there were three developmental phases in physical activity play. First were 'rhythmical stereotypies', bodily movements characteristic of babies, such as kicking legs, waving arms. Then, during the preschool years, there is a lot of 'exercise play'—running around, jumping, climbing—whole-body movements which may be done alone or with others. Overlapping with and succeeding this is rough-and-tumble play, most common in the middle school years.

Figure 7.6 A young child 'feeding' her doll—an example of 'pretend play'.

Source: Image copyright emin kuliyev, used under licence from Shutterstock.com.

Rough-and-tumble Play

The origins of play fighting and chasing may lie in the vigorous physical play that parents often engage in with toddlers—tickling, throwing and crawling after them, for example. Actual play fighting between peers is common from 3 years on through to adolescence.

Figure 7.7 Children engaging in physical activity play.

Source: Reproduced with permission of Tony Pellegrini.

Wrestling generally involves some struggle for superior position, one child trying to get on top of another and pin him or her down, though roles quickly reverse themselves. More fragmentary episodes involve pushing, clasping, leg play and kicking. Chasing play is generally included in rough-and-tumble as well (see example 3, p. 234).

The friendly intent in play of this kind is typically signalled by smiling and laughter. Up to adolescence, play fighting seems distinct from serious fighting, at least in the majority of cases. The former is carried out with friends, who often stay together after the episode. The latter is often not between friends, involves different facial expressions and the participants

Figure 7.8   Children play fighting.
Source: Laurence Mouton/Getty Images.

usually do not stay together after the encounter. Play fights tend to be shorter, they are not watched by others (Figure 7.8) and participants do not hit hard.

Young children themselves are aware of these differences. One study (Costabile et al., 1991) used video films of play fighting and real fighting made in Italy and England. They showed the films to children aged 8 and 11 years, and asked them to say whether each episode was playful or real fighting, and why. Children were very good at this, and gave reasons such as:

'It didn't last long enough to be a [real] fight.'

'It was only a play fight because he didn't hit him hard.'

'It was a real fight because they were both angry.'

'That was a play fight as the other boys didn't watch them.'

Interestingly, children from both countries were just as good at recognizing play fighting in the video film from the other country as their own; the evidence to date suggests that the forms of play fighting are very similar across cultures.

Although play fighting and real fighting are usually distinct, they sometimes get confused. Pellegrini (1988, 1994) has shown that in boys, sociometrically rejected children (see p. 177) are much more likely than other children to be involved in play fights which turn into real fights; whether deliberately or through a lack of social skills, these children may respond inappropriately to the usual play signals. Primary school teachers often say that a lot of play fighting becomes real fighting, and it is possible that they are basing this judgement on the minority of children for whom this is true (Schafer & Smith, 1996). For most children, only around 1% of play fights turn into real fights. However, there is evidence that by adolescence, strength and dominance become more important in the choice of partners in play fighting, and deliberate manipulation of play conventions may then become more common (Boulton, 1992; Pellegrini, 2002; Smith, 1997).

Play with Objects

As will be discussed in Chapter 13, Piaget made detailed descriptions of the ways in which infants manipulate and make use of objects. Initially, this is best described as exploratory: what does this object feel like? Let's suck it and see (literally!). But when we get to the circular reactions, such behaviours are repeated, presumably because the infant finds such actions enjoyable—two criteria for playful behaviour. As the infant moves from primary to secondary and then tertiary circular reactions, such repeated behaviours become more flexible and variable, such that some behaviours would definitely be described as playful—what Piaget calls practice play, such as banging objects together in various ways and laughing.

By 2 and 3 years onwards, toddlers engage in a range of constructive activities; for example, stacking and sorting objects, putting cups of different sizes one inside another, doing simple jigsaw puzzles, starting to sort objects by shape and colour. Also, objects are used in pretend (see below), and war toys are a particular kind of pretend object play (see below).

Much object play is solitary, but much also has a social context, even early on. Mothers and other adults or older siblings can encourage play. Teti et al. (1988) studied mother, father and older sibling play with second-born children, and found bidirectional relationships between mother-created object play and infant's sophistication at solitary object play, from 12 to 18 months.

Social play with objects obviously requires shared attention to the objects concerned. One concept here is the 'referential triangle'. This refers to an adult, a child and a toy that is the focus of shared attention, and the way the child takes account of the adult in this. From 9 to 12 months, the infant starts to follow the adult's gaze to an object, and by 15 months starts to direct the adult's gaze by pointing. According to Tomasello et al. (2005), shared attention and the referential triangle provide a means for the child to be aware of others (the adult) as an intentional agent, and to interact with them, often in cooperative ways. They may point to an object because it is interesting, and not just because they want it for themselves. Tomasello et al. argue that these features distinguish us from the great apes (see also p. 53) and act as a lever up to more advanced human abilities and what they call 'cultural cognition'.

Fantasy and Sociodramatic Play

The beginnings of fantasy play can be seen from about 12–15 months of age. In the course of his extensive observations of his own children, Piaget (1951, p. 69) recorded the following behaviour on the part of his daughter Jacqueline (the numbers refer to Jacqueline's age, in years, months and days):

> . . . every appearance of awareness of 'make-believe' first appeared at 1;3(12) in the following circumstances. She saw a cloth whose fringed edges vaguely recalled those of her pillow; she seized it, held a fold of it in her right hand, sucked the thumb of the same hand and lay down on her side, laughing hard. She kept her eyes open, but blinked from time to time as if she were alluding to closed eyes. Finally, laughing more and more she cried 'Nene' [Nono]. The same cloth started the same game on the following days. At 1;3(13) she treated the collar of her mother's coat in the same way. At 1;3(30) it was the tail of her rubber donkey which represented the pillow! And from 1;5 onwards she made her animals, a bear and a plush dog, also do 'nono'.

The earliest pretend play tends to involve the child directing actions towards herself—in Jacqueline's case, pretending to sleep on a cloth. It is clear from Piaget's records that a month or so later Jacqueline directed the same actions to a toy bear and a stuffed dog. This has been called *decentration*—incorporating other participants into pretend activities. The others may be parents (e.g. the child tries to feed a parent with an empty cup), or stuffed animals or dolls. By around 24 months the child can get the doll itself to act as an agent, rather than have things done to it (see above).

Early pretend play also depends heavily on realistic objects—actual cups, combs, spoons and so on, or very realistic substitutes. *Decontextualization* refers to the ability to use less realistic substitute objects—for example, a wooden block as a 'cake', or a stick as a 'gun'. Experiments have shown that the more different the object from its referent, the more difficulty children have in using it in a pretend way. It has also been shown that adults can help the process by modelling or prompting the pretend use. In one study (Fein, 1975), after modelling by an adult, some 93% of 2-year-olds would imitate making a detailed horse model 'drink' from a plastic cup; however, only 33% would imitate making a horsey shape 'drink' from a clam shell. The less realistic objects made the pretence more difficult, especially as two substitutions were needed (the horsey shape and the clam shell). If the horse alone or the cup alone were realistic, 79% and 61% of the children respectively could imitate successfully.

By 3 years of age, this kind of decontextualized pretence occurs much more spontaneously in children's play. Here we also begin to get quite imaginary objects or actions, without any real or substitute object being present (example 2 on p. 234 has several examples). While possible for 3- and 4-year-olds, this is easier still in middle childhood. When asked to pretend to brush their teeth or comb their hair, one study (Overton & Jackson, 1973) found that 3- and 4-year-olds used a substitute body part, such as a finger, as the brush or comb, whereas most 6–8-year-olds (and indeed, adults) imagined the brush or comb in their hand.

These studies have usually relied on laboratory situations, where infants have been provided with particular toys. A much more naturalistic study was reported by Haight and Miller (1993) in a book, *Pretending at home*. They reported a longitudinal study of nine children (four girls and five boys), each observed in the home environment and video filmed for three or four hours at 12, 16, 20, 24, 30, 36 and 48 months of age. An interesting finding was that three-quarters of pretend play was social—usually with mothers earlier on, though equally often other children by 48 months. Even the earliest pretend play episodes were more likely to be social than solitary. The authors describe one characteristic of this mother–child social, pretend play as being mutual responsiveness, with neither partner initiating or dominating most episodes. Joint episodes were generally longer than episodes of solo pretend play. Another study of this kind, giving detailed descriptions of naturalistic pretend play in small samples (in this case in two cultural contexts), is described in Box 7.1.

Reviewing both laboratory-based and more naturalistic studies, Howes and Matheson (1992) developed a scheme for the development of social pretend play with mothers, older siblings and peers. A slightly simplified version of this is shown in Table 7.1. The work of Howes and others shows the change from predominantly adult-oriented to predominantly peer-oriented social pretend. You could look again at example 2 at the start of this chapter; match the role assignment and negotiation of the action at the end with the 37–48 months stage in Table 7.1.

In Table 7.1, the word 'script' appears from the 25–30-month stage onwards. Pretend play sequences become more integrated with age. Initially, one action is involved; then variations on a single theme, such as stirring the spoon in the cup; then drinking, or feeding two dolls in succession. By 2 years of age, multischeme combinations are in evidence. Mini-stories begin to be acted out, following 'scripts' such as shopping or bedtime. Language plays an increasing role in maintaining the play structure. All these developments come together in *sociodramatic play*, prominent in 3–6-year-olds. Here, two or more children act out definite roles, such as mummy and daddy, spacemen and monsters, doctors and patients (Singer & Singer, 1991).

Table 7.1 Stages in social pretend play with mothers, and with peers

Age period	Play with mother	Play with peers
12–15 months	Mother structures child's actions by commenting, suggesting and demonstrating. Child is corrected when his or her pretend acts violate the real world.	Isolated pretend acts within social play do not elicit a response, but children watch and imitate the partner's pretend.
16–20 months	As above, and child imitates, watches and complies with mother.	Children engage in similar or identical pretend acts, and attempt to recruit partner to joint pretend.
21–24 months	Mother becomes an interested spectator who creates a context and provides support for the child's enactments.	Children engage in similar pretend actions while they simultaneously engage in social exchange: join the pretend of the partner, attempt to recruit the partner to joint play and organize materials for joint pretend.
25–30 months	Child offers storyline or script. Mother requests creation of new elements and prompts child to a more realistic or detailed enactment.	Each partner's pretend reflects the same script but their actions show no within-pair integration. Partners inform each other of the script by comments on their own pretend and telling the other how to act.
31–36 months	Mother praises and encourages independence; may pretend with child.	Joint pretend with enactment of complementary roles. Children discriminate between speech used for enactment and speech about enactment, assign roles, and negotiate pretend themes and plans.
37–48 months	As above.	Children adopt relational roles, are willing to accept identity transformations and generate or accept instruction for appropriate role performance; they negotiate scripts and dominant roles and use metacommunication to establish the play script and clarify role enactment.

Source: Adapted from Howes, C. & Matheson, C.C. (1992). Sequences in the development of competent play with peers: social and pretend play. *Developmental Psychology, 28,* 961–974. American Psychological Association. Adapted with permission.

Box 7.1 Universal, developmental and variable aspects of young children's play: a cross-cultural comparison of pretending at home

This study aimed to provide an in-depth, longitudinal account of pretend play in two different cultural contexts, and thereby suggest not only what were universal trends, but also more culturally specific aspects of this kind of play. All participants were 'relatively well off' intact families with 1–3 children, including a target child aged 2.5 years at the start of the study.

The two cultural contexts were:

- Irish-American families in Chicago, USA: these families lived in spacious, single-family homes, and there were many toys available to play with, including 'extensive and elaborate collections of toy miniatures' (realistic toys such as dolls, cups and trucks). The children had extensive contact with other children and adults in the neighbourhood. Five families participated (three girls, two boys).
- Chinese families in Taipei, Taiwan: these families lived in compact single-family apartments, with a modest number of toys including a few miniatures. Contacts with other children and adults in the neighbourhood were few until children attended formal preschool. Nine families participated (five girls, four boys).

The study proceeded in three phases.

1. Ethnographic fieldwork: researchers familiarized themselves with the community, and collected descriptions of the home and play areas; this period also allowed the children to get acclimatized to the researcher's presence.
2. Naturalistic observations: video records were made of the children's behaviour at home, during the day, with mother present (and sometimes siblings), at 2.5, 3 and 4 years of age; at each age point, two separate 2-hour records were obtained. The video records, including transcriptions of speech in pretend play, were coded.
3. Formal interviews: with parents, to obtain basic information including socialization beliefs and practices.

Altogether, 14 hours of pretend play were recorded: 5 (out of 108 hours) in Taipei and 9 (out of 60 hours) in Chicago. Some features were universal. Firstly, all 14 of the target children showed some spontaneous pretend play. Also, the majority of this play was social, the majority was with the mother and the majority involved objects of some kind. Some developmental changes were also common to both cultures. The proportion of pretend play episodes initiated by the child increased from 30 to 48 months, as did the proportion of responses to others' initiations which elaborated on the play theme. Also, although the mothers started off primarily treating pretend in a purely playful way, their use of pretend in non-play fashion increased over this period; for example, to distract a child from an angry mood, to enliven a tedious task such as clearing up or to teach the child a new social skill.

There were also some pronounced cultural differences. Those shown in Box Table 7.1.1 were all statistically significant on analysis of variance, despite the small sample size. Related to the conditions described in the ethnographic fieldwork, the pretend play of the Taiwanese children was more often with the mother and less often with other children, compared to the US children. Less use was made of toy miniatures

Box Table 7.1.1 Differences in pretend play observed in young children in Chicago, USA, and Taipei, Taiwan

Proportion of pretend play that:	Chicago, USA	Taipei, Taiwan
is social	89	98
is with mother	64	98
is with other children	64	13
uses toy miniatures	57	28
does not use objects	10	36
uses fantasy themes	21	05
involves caretaking roles	29	07
is initiated by the child	.70 (2.5 yrs) to .94 (4 yrs)	.09 (2.5 yrs) to .34 (4 yrs)
involves routine social interactions with non-kin adults	08	70
is used by mother to practise 'proper conduct'	00	38

(they had few of these) but more use of pretence without objects. The US children made more use of fantasy themes (for example, based on TV or comic strips) and more use of caretaking or home-based themes (such as shopping, feeding, cleaning), and more often initiated these themes themselves. The Taiwanese children's play more often involved routine social interactions with non-kin adults (such as with teachers, shopkeepers).

Based on the ethnography and the observations, the researchers also argued that mothers and caregivers generally may use pretend play for somewhat different purposes in these two cultures, based on differing views of socialization. They argue that an important priority for the US parents is developing self-esteem in their children, and they may think that this is fostered by providing many play materials and encouraging the spontaneous initiation of play by the child. On the other hand, an important priority for the Taiwanese parents is to encourage moral development. These parents might

use pretend play to encourage 'proper conduct' in an interpersonal context, such as bowing to the teacher in class.

The strengths of this study are in the high quality of records obtained, by a combination of methods. In particular, the naturalistic observations in the home provide a wealth of detail that is more ecologically valid than laboratory studies on pretend play. The primary limitation, and a severe one, is the small sample size; this was no doubt dictated by the time and expense of obtaining and coding the video records, even for just 14 families. Clearly, the cultural differences cannot be generalized with confidence to families in the USA and in Taiwan in general (especially as all families were relatively prosperous). However, the magnitude of the differences is often substantial and certainly makes the point that, superimposed on a common and probably universal core nature of pretend play, both the physical and social context, and socialization beliefs of parents, can impact on the kinds of pretend play seen in these families.

Based on material in Haight, W.L., Wang, X-L., Fung, H.H-T., Williams K. & Mintz J. (1999). *Child Development*, *70*, 1477–1488.

Imaginary Companions

The ultimate in imagination in childhood play is perhaps the *imaginary companion*, who may follow the child around, or need to be fed at mealtimes or tucked up in bed with the child. Some one-quarter to one-half of children have some form of imaginary companion, especially between 3 and 8 years (they are mostly abandoned by age 10). These children tend to engage in a lot of sophisticated pretend play generally (Taylor et al., 1993). Children are not confused about the imaginary status of these companions and are aware that they are different from real friends.

Majors (2007) carried out a detailed exploration of imaginary companions of children aged 5–10 years, in the UK. Most imaginary companions were human, a few were animal (a duck; a pony). One child, John, had one imaginary companion and created an elaborate imaginary world (sometimes called a 'paracosm') around him. Majors found that the imaginary companions were significant and important for the children, and that they served several functions, including being a pleasurable retreat, dependable companions, wish fulfilment and entertainment. For example, one girl said she needed her imaginary companions 'when I can't get to sleep or when I'm lonely and times when I'm feeling sad or there's no one to play with or talk to'. A boy who created a duck as an imaginary companion explained, 'I was swimming a width [in a swimming pool] and then I thought I would do another with my imaginary friend and I did and I needed it to be a swimming one so I chose a duck'. This boy's swimming had since improved a lot and it is possible the imaginary duck helped him.

Language Play

The most well-known examples of language play come from Weir's book *Language in the crib* (1962). Weir left a tape recorder on under her 2-year-old son's crib at night-time. At this age toddlers often talk to themselves a lot before going to sleep or on waking up. Sample extracts are shown on p. 415 and in Table 12.2. A similar study (Keenan & Klein, 1975) recorded social play, with syllables and words, between twins aged 21 months. Children appear to use these presleep monologues or dialogues to play with and practise linguistic forms they are in the process of acquiring (Kuczaj II, 1986; and p. 415).

The humorous use of language becomes very prominent in the older preschool child. Chukovsky (1963) reports examples of rhyming poems created by 3- and 4-year-old children:

> I'm a whale. This is my tail.
> I'm a flamingo. Look at my wingo.

Preschool children will spontaneously express a whole range of humorous responses, including interactive 'pre-riddles', conventional riddles and joking behaviours. However, what they find amusing changes with age and cognitive development. By about age 2, incongruous language and labelling of objects and events appear humorous.

> J., aged 3 years, while drawing a picture of her mother, put hair all round the circle face and then called it 'Mommy porcupine' with shouts of glee.

By about age 4, conceptual incongruity appears humorous.

C., aged 5, said to her mother 'I can play a piano by ear'. Then she banged her ear on the piano keyboard and laughed.

By about age 6, children begin to understand and enjoy humour with multiple meanings (McGhee, 1979); however, they usually cannot do so when younger, and often laugh inappropriately or make up 'pre-riddles'.

L., aged 3 years, after her older sister told the riddle, 'Why does the turtle cross the road? To get to the Shell station', insisted on telling a 'riddle' also. Her riddle was 'Why does the dog cross the road? To get to the station' (she laughed at the 'riddle').

B., aged 5 years, asked? 'What's red and white? A newspaper' and laughed at his 'riddle'.

S., aged 6, asked his uncle and father this riddle, 'Why was 6 afraid of 7? Because 7, 8, 9!' Everyone laughed at this joke.

(Examples adapted from Bergen, 1990)

Language is often used playfully in sociodramatic play episodes. Several examples have been given by Garvey (1977): 'Hello, my name is Mr Elephant!'; 'Hello, my name is Mr Donkey!'. In school-age children, rhymes and word play are common, and have been documented by Opie and Opie (1959). The repetition of well-known verses, with variations, has more in common with the rule-governed games common by the age of 6 or 7 years (see below and also Chapter 13).

War Toys and War Play

One kind of aggressive play is when children use toy guns or weapons, or combat figures, to engage in pretend fighting or warfare. This kind of play is banned in some nurseries and playgroups. Parents, too, have mixed views about it. Costabile et al. (1992) surveyed parents in Italy and England. Some actively discouraged it:

I do not like it. In fact, children who do war play become less sensible and less obedient.

Some were uncertain, or felt it should be allowed within limits:

Unsure. We don't encourage it, but don't discourage it, either.

Some allowed it unconditionally:

A natural part of a child's development, just as they act out cooking, etc. War/fighting is featured in so many things it would be difficult and unnatural to exclude it from a child's life.

Researchers, too, are divided. Nancy Carlsson-Paige and Diane Levin wrote two books, *The war play dilemma* (1987) and *Who's calling the shots?* (1990), in which they argued that war toys and combat figures encourage stereotyped good-versus-evil aggressive scripts, which impoverish the child's imagination and encourage actual aggressive behaviour. They recognized the difficulties in banning such play entirely (there are plenty of stories of children making toy guns out of Lego, if replica guns are banned in the nursery), but advocated adults intervening to turn such play to more constructive and less aggressive ends (a policy also favoured by most parents, in the survey by Costabile et al., 1992). However, Brian Sutton-Smith (1988) argued that for children, war play is clearly pretend, and just reflects an aspect of real life. As one boy said when his father asked him not to use toy guns:

> But Dad, I don't want to shoot anybody, I just want to play.

The issue bears some similarity to the debate about violent videos and television (see Chapter 8). In England, guidance from the Department for Children, Schools and Families (DCSF, 2007, p. 16) stated:

> Images and ideas gleaned from the media are common starting points in boys' play and may involve characters with special powers or weapons. Adults can find this type of play particularly challenging and have a natural instinct to stop it. This is not necessary as long as practitioners help the boys to understand and respect the rights of other children and to take responsibility for the resources and environment.

This was highlighted in the press (for example, a feature in the *Guardian* newspaper titled 'Let boys play with toy guns, ministers advise nursery staff'; Booth, 2007). In fact, the guidance in the DCSF document was balanced, with its final sentence on rights and responsibility for others and the environment.

We clearly need to consider the interests of children themselves, their parents and families, and the wider society, as well as being aware of the pressures on toy manufacturers to sell their products (Smith, 1994). On the one hand, for most children such activities are natural, separated from real life, and probably do little if any harm. But it is easy to feel uncomfortable when the activity becomes very prominent; although the evidence is uncertain, there is the possibility that for children who are already disturbed or have violent tendencies, sanctioning violent play (or violent videos) can make matters worse. Dunn and Hughes (2001) studied 40 'hard-to-manage' and 40 control children in London, filming them playing alone in a room with a friend when they were 4 years old. They found that the 'hard-to-manage' children showed more violent fantasy; the extent of violent fantasy (across both groups) was related to poorer language and play skills and more antisocial behaviour, and also to less empathic understanding 2 years later at age 6.

 Stop and Think

Should we be concerned about children playing with war toys?

Video and Computer Games

Ever since 'Space Invaders' hit the computer game market in 1979, there has been an increase in the amount of time children spend with computer games or in video arcades (see Table 8.1), at least until the last few years when social networking has become so popular (see Chapters 8 and 19). Playing video games may increase hand–eye coordination and skill at that particular game, but what are the other effects? As with war toys, much of this activity is engaged in by boys, and it is most popular in the 9–15-year age range. Many such games do have aggressive fantasy themes (Singer & Singer, 2005). Some games appear quite addictive, and parents sometimes fear that playing video games leads to social isolation. However, there is generally a lot of social contact with peers in the context of video games, and Singer and Singer (2005) discuss the constructive and prosocial possibilities of computer play. The effects of computer games are considered in more detail in Chapter 8.

Games with Rules

Games with rules ended the developmental sequences of Piaget and Smilansky. The play of preschool children often has some rule structure; for example, if someone is role-playing 'doctor' to a 'patient', there are some constraints on what he or she is expected to do, exerted by the other participants. Nevertheless, any rules or constraints are largely private to that particular play episode, and can be changed at any time ('I'm not the doctor now, I'm a policeman'). By the time children are 6 or 7 years old, rule-governed games like hopscotch, tig or football take up much more playground time. These are games with public rules, sometimes codified, with much less latitude for change. The transition from play to games is nevertheless a gradual one (see also Chapter 9, and Piaget's study of the game of marbles).

Factors Affecting Play

In Western societies, some studies have suggested that children from disadvantaged backgrounds show less frequent and less complex fantasy and sociodramatic play. These studies were criticized by McLoyd (1982) for poor methodology. Some failed adequately to define social class, or confounded it with other variables such as race or school setting. Any effects of social class on play will vary with historical time, cultural group and even location within a country.

If children, for whatever reason, do not engage in much fantasy or sociodramatic play in nursery school, it does seem that nursery staff can encourage it by play tutoring. This technique was pioneered by Smilansky (1968). Such intervention at its least intrusive involves verbal guidance or suggestions; alternatively, more direct involvement in the play may be made by acting as a model for roles and actions, or by giving deliberate training in imaginative activities or fantasy themes. Play tutoring can be made even more effective if appropriate toys are provided (e.g. dressing-up clothes, hospital props) and if children are taken on visits (e.g. to a zoo, hospital or factory).

Several investigators have studied sex differences in children's pretend play (Göncü et al., 2002). Differences in the frequency of pretend play are inconsistent, but there are sex differences in the choice of roles in sociodramatic play. Girls tend to act out domestic scenes—shopping, washing the baby and so on. Boys less often imitate male roles, as they have usually not been able to observe their father at work; rather, they rely on roles familiar from books (e.g. police, fireman), or act out film or television characters.

There does appear to be a reliable sex difference in rough-and-tumble play; this has almost always been found to be preferred by boys. A predisposition for boys to engage more in this activity may be related to the influence of sex hormones during the period of fetal growth, as indicated by Collaer and Hines (1995). However, social factors are likely to be very important too; fathers engage in more rough-and-tumble play with boys, even by 2 years of age, and this kind of play is socially stereotyped as a male activity (Goldstein, 1995; see also Chapter 6).

Play in Different Cultures and the 'Play Ethos'

Both anthropologists and psychologists have studied play in different human societies. Although the main types of play are seen in most if not all societies, there are variations in frequency and in the content of play. Obviously, in many traditional societies, children do not have the great variety of toys available in more affluent societies, but they can play in varied ways with available materials. For example, Baka hunter-gatherer children, living in the African tropical forest, make guns from the stem of a papaya, play hunting animals with stones, shoot plants and inanimate objects with bows and arrows, mimic the forest spirits with songs, and play a flute made of a papaya stem (Kamei, 2005).

Gaskins et al. (2006) describe three types of societies with differing prevailing attitudes to play.

- *Culturally curtailed play* refers to societies where adults will tolerate only minimum amounts of play. The Yucatan Maya people of Mexico are an example; children are busy running errands, accompanying parents, etc. from 3 or 4 years. Parents believe that children need to acquire skills through observation and imitation. Play is seen as 'having little purpose beyond being a distraction for children when they cannot help with the work to be done and as a signal that the children are healthy', and 'extensive pretense in particular is of questionable appropriateness. Adults believe that one should not lie even in jest, and fiction, written or oral, is not a valued genre' (Gaskins et al., 2006, p. 192).
- *Culturally accepted play* refers to societies where parents typically expect children to play and do not disapprove of it, but neither do they invest much time or energy in supporting it. Many traditional societies are of this kind; children, especially by around 6 years, start to be seen as useful in looking after younger siblings and in subsistence tasks, but adults see play as harmless and keeping children busy and out of the way until they are old enough to be useful. When an adult plays with a child, there is no concern with the benefits of play for the development of the child.
- *Culturally cultivated play* refers primarily to urban, middle-class Euro-American families. We have seen how many parents encourage play when it starts to appear in their young children; in these families there are many objects and toys to play with. Parents believe in the importance of play for cognitive development and social skills. MacDonald (1992) argued that this is a form of parental investment in children, which is of recent historical origin.

Smith (1988, 2010) argued that in modern Western industrial societies, the 'cultural cultivation' of play has been supported by a play ethos that developed strongly through the 20th century. This play ethos sees play as vital and essential for development: 'The realization that play is essential for normal development has slowly but surely permeated our cultural heritage' (Department of the Environment, 1973, p. 1). Many play workers and theorists would assume this. Smith (2010) argued that this play ethos has been widely held, but that it may have distorted much previous research. We will review some empirical evidence about this later in the chapter.

PLAY THEORISTS

Theoretical perspectives on the nature of play and on its role in development cover a wide range. Several influential ideas can be traced back to the late 19th and early 20th century. The views of a number of earlier play theorists and educators are summarized here.

Friedrich Froebel. The ideas of Froebel, as expounded in *The education of man* (published posthumously in 1906), were influential in the start of the kindergarten and nursery school movement. 'Kindergarten' translates from German as 'child-garden', and this aptly sums up Froebel's ideas about play and development: 'Play, truly recognized and rightly fostered, unites the germinating life of the child attentively with the ripe life of experiences of the adult and thus fosters the one through the other'. On this view, play exemplifies development from within the child, but can be nurtured by adult guidance and the provision of appropriate materials. Froebel's influence, following that of Pestalozzi (with whom he studied for 2 years), encouraged a positive evaluation of the educational significance of play, as compared with the rote-learning approach which nevertheless became characteristic of many infant schools at the end of the 19th century (Whitbread, 1972).

Herbert Spencer. In his book *The principles of psychology* (1878, final edition 1898), Spencer proposed a less enthusiastic view of play. He believed play is carried out 'for the sake of the immediate gratifications involved, without reference to ulterior benefits'. He suggested that the higher animals are better able to deal with the immediate necessities of life, and that the nervous system, rather than remaining inactive for long periods, stimulates play. 'Thus it happens that in the more evolved creatures, there often recurs an energy somewhat in excess of immediate needs . . . Hence play of all kinds—hence this tendency to superfluous and useless exercise of faculties that have been quiescent' (pp. 629–630). Spencer's approach has been labelled the 'surplus energy' theory.

Karl Groos. At the turn of the 19th century, Groos published two influential works, *The play of animals* (1898) and *The play of man* (1901). Groos criticized Spencer's theory on a number of grounds. He thought that surplus energy might provide 'a particularly favorable condition for play', but was not essential. He also thought play had a much more definite function than in Spencer's theory. Groos argued that a main reason for childhood was so that play could occur: 'perhaps the very existence of youth is largely for the sake of play'. This was because play provided exercise and elaboration of skills needed for survival. This has been called the 'exercise' or 'practice' theory of play, and in its modern form it has many adherents.

G. Stanley Hall. In his book *Adolescence* (1908) and elsewhere, Hall argued that Groos's practice theory was 'very partial, superficial, and perverse'. This was because Groos saw play as practice for contemporary activities. By contrast, Hall thought that play was a means for children to work through primitive atavisms, reflecting our evolutionary past. For example, 'the sports of boys chasing one another, wrestling, making prisoners, obviously gratify in a partial way the predatory instincts' (p. 207). The function of play was thus cathartic in nature, and allowed the 'playing out' of those instincts that characterized earlier human history. This became known as the 'recapitulation theory' of play. In the form proposed by Hall, it has had little or no recent support.

Maria Montessori. The work of Montessori has been another major influence in the education of young children (see Kramer, 1976). Like Froebel, Montessori saw the value of self-initiated activity for young children, under adult guidance. She put more emphasis on the importance of learning about real life, however, and hence on constructive play materials that helped in sensory discrimination and in colour and shape matching. She did not value pretend or sociodramatic play, seeing pretence as primitive and an escape from reality. She preferred to encourage children actually to serve meals, for example, and to clear up around the house themselves, rather than play at mealtimes in a 'play house'. This particular aspect of her philosophy, however, has largely been abandoned by contemporary Montessori schools.

Jean Piaget. The place of play in Piaget's theory of cognitive development has often been misunderstood (see Sutton-Smith, 1966; Piaget, 1966; and Rubin & Pepler, 1982 for reviews). Piaget saw adaptation as depending on the two processes of accommodation and assimilation (see Chapter 13). Play 'manifests the peculiarity of a primacy of assimilation over accommodation'. Children acted out their already established behaviours, or schemata, in play, and adapted reality to fit these. For example, referring to episodes such as his daughter Jacqueline's pretending to sleep (p. 241), Piaget wrote:

> It is clearly impossible to explain this symbolic practice as being pre-exercise; the child certainly does not play like this in order to learn to wash or sleep. All that he is trying to do is to use freely his individual powers, to reproduce his own actions for the pleasure of seeing himself do them and showing them off to others, in a word to express himself, to assimilate without being hampered by the need to accommodate at the same time.

Here is a criticism both of some aspects of Groos's approach (play as pre-exercise) and of play as being important in learning. For Piaget, learning was related more to accommodation to reality. This emphasis may be linked to Montessori's influence, for Piaget carried out his early research at a modified Montessori school, and for many years was president of the Swiss Montessori Society. The functions of play in Piaget's framework are two-fold. Play can consolidate existing skills by repeated execution of known schemas, with minor variations. Also, it can give a child a sense of 'ego continuity', that is, confidence and a sense of mastery. It does this because failure is largely circumvented in fantasy play, where the real properties of the materials are not at issue, and no external goal is aimed for.

Sigmund Freud. Freud himself did not write a great deal about play, but it has come to have an important role within the psychoanalytic movement, and especially in play therapy. Freud thought that play provided children with an avenue for wish fulfilment and mastery of traumatic events. As Peller (1954, p. 180) put it, 'play . . . is an attempt to compensate for anxieties and depression, to obtain pleasure at a minimum risk of danger and/or irreversible consequences'. Thus play provided a safe context for expressing aggressive or sexual impulses which it would be too dangerous to express in reality. In addition, play could, within limits, help achieve mastery of traumatic events: 'Small quantities of anxiety are mastered in play, but anxiety of high intensity inhibits play'. Both aspects are important in play therapy. First, play expresses the child's wishes and anxieties (Peller relates the development of fantasy playthemes to Freud's psychosexual stages). Second, play can help overcome such anxieties, by catharsis or by working through them.

Susan Isaacs. The view of play as essential to both emotional and cognitive growth of young children, strong in the British educational tradition and the 'play ethos', owes much to Susan Isaacs and to her successor at the Institute of Education at London University, Dorothy Gardner. Isaacs combined a belief in the emotional benefits of play (deriving from the psychoanalytic tradition) with a wider view of its benefits for physical, social and cognitive development generally, echoing the evolutionary perspective that animals that learn more also play more: 'Play is indeed the child's work, and the means whereby he grows and develops. Active play can be looked upon as a sign of mental health; and its absence, either of some inborn defect, or of mental illness' (Isaacs, 1929, p. 9).

Lev Vygotsky. Another combination of the affective and cognitive aspects of development occurs in Vygotsky's approach to play (1966; from a lecture given in 1933). Like psychoanalysts,

Vygotsky saw the affective drive behind play as being 'the imaginary, illusory realisation of unrealisable desires'; not with very specific or sexual impulses but in a much more general sense, to do with the child's confidence and mastery (for example, in attitudes to authority in general): 'Play is essentially wish fulfilment, not, however, isolated wishes but generalized affects'. Furthermore, Vygotsky saw play as being 'the leading source of development in the preschool years'. Essentially, this was because the nature of pretend play meant that 'the child is liberated from situational constraints through his activity in an imaginary situation'. The child is getting into the world of ideas (e.g. what an object might become). A very young child cannot separate out an object from its meaning but when he or she starts to engage in pretend play, and uses an object to represent another (for example, a stick for a horse), then meaning begins to be separated from the concrete object. Vygotsky says that the substitute object (e.g. the stick) acts as a pivot, to separate the meaning or concept (e.g. of the horse) from the object itself.

Recent theorists. In recent decades, theorists have tended to argue the benefits of play for cognitive development and creative thinking. Jerome Bruner (1972) suggested that play in the advanced mammals, and especially in human children, serves both as practice for mastery in skills, and as an opportunity for trying out new combinations of behaviour in a safe context. Sara Smilansky (1968; Smilansky & Shefatya, 1990) advanced the value of fantasy and socio-dramatic play in particular, and Dorothy Singer and colleagues (Singer et al., 2006) did so more generally, in their book *Play = Learning*. Brian Sutton-Smith, however, argued against what he saw as the 'idealization' of play (Sutton-Smith, 1986); he later considered different 'rhetorics' of play from varying disciplinary perspectives (Sutton-Smith, 1997). Paul Harris (2000b) has advanced theoretical thinking about children's imaginative thinking and pretend play. Gordon Burghardt (2005) has thoroughly examined the evolutionary origins of play; human play is included, but he mainly concentrates on a great range of animal play.

THE BENEFITS OF PLAY: THE EVIDENCE

Much theorizing about the importance of play was carried out in the absence of any real evidence that play does, or does not, have the effects or benefits postulated. Here we will review the evidence about the importance of play from three different perspectives:

- the forms of play, or 'design characteristics'—does the actual nature of play behaviour reveal something of its value?
- correlational studies—what tends to go with playfulness in children?
- experimental studies—attempts to compare the value of play experiences in controlled conditions.

We will also look at the clinical uses of play, in play therapy.

The Forms of Play

If we look closely at what goes on in playful episodes, we may form hypotheses as to what uses the behaviour has. Indeed, it is this approach that Piaget used, and which led him to his own theory of play (p. 252).

Physical activity play: Byers and Walker (1995) examined the nature of locomotor or physical activity play in mammals generally. Both the form of the play and its peak time of occurrence in development led them to conclude that this kind of play has important functions in affecting brain growth and developing motor skills. Pellegrini and Smith (1998) also argued that it would improve physical strength and endurance. A quite different hypothesis was put forward by Bjorklund and Green (1992). This *cognitive immaturity hypothesis* suggests that in younger children, an impulse to engage in physical activity builds up, and that the resulting physical activity gives them a break from cognitive tasks, relieving memory overload and ultimately enhancing learning.

Rough-and-tumble play: The nature of rough-and-tumble (R&T) play suggests that it could be practice for real fighting or hunting skills. This has been argued for mammals generally, although there is not a great deal of evidence beyond design characteristics. For human children, the rougher nature of R&T in adolescence may be linked to dominance assertion (Pellegrini, 2002). The functional importance of R&T was challenged by Gosso et al. (2005, p. 233) who argued that 'it is our view that play fighting, so important in so many mammals, may have lost nearly all of its relevance for humans …'. This was because some hunter-gatherers show little play fighting, and also because real fighting generally involved weapons (and so was different from play fighting). Nevertheless, Fry (2005, pp. 79–80), reviewing the anthropological literature, found meaningful associations between R&T and fighting skills in different traditional societies, and concluded that 'the manifestation of the R&T theme in children around the world suggests the presence of evolved functions for the behavioural pattern, of which the practice of fighting skills, broadly conceived, and dominance assertion seem likely candidates'.

Play with objects: Play with objects could be important in learning future skills. Bock (2002) studied play pounding in Botswana (Figure 7.9). Here, children pretend to pound grain with sticks, rather as adult women pound real grain to grind it into flour for baking. The age trends in this kind of play suggested that children get more efficient in their actions and that it can help in skill learning, but is only tolerated by parents until actual productive work is possible.

Observations of the flexibility present in play with objects led Bruner (1972) to postulate its role in problem solving and creativity. This argument has since been taken up by a number

Figure 7.9　Children in Botswana (a) playing at pounding and (b) actually pounding grain.
Source: Sara E. Johnson and John Bock. Reproduced by permission of Sara E. Johnson.

of authors, including Bateson and Martin (2013), and Pellegrini and Pellegrini (2013), who argued that object play may be related to children's discovery of novel uses for objects (see also Box 7.2). But how commonly will novel object use actually translate into something useful later on? And could such a function for object play have really been important in human evolution? In a commentary on Pellegrini and Pellegrini (2013), Hewlett and Boyette (2013) stated that:

> Pellegrini and Pellegrini identify three general functions: (1) learning future skills, (2) learning skills for current survival and adaptation, and (3) a source of innovation to adapt to novel environments. The limited hunter-gatherer literature provides strong support for the first, some support for the second, and no support for the third.

Even if hunter-gatherers are not constantly inventing new tools, arguably present-day humans are! Perhaps such functions of object play are more important in modern societies. Pellegrini (2013) also points to another possible function of novel object use in play, which is that it may attract attention from peers and bring related social status benefits.

Fantasy and sociodramatic play: Some theorists have speculated on the importance of pretend play for theory of mind development (see Chapter 15). Leslie (1987) argued that pretend play is an indicator of metarepresentational abilities as early as 18 months, and is important in developing these latter abilities for understanding that someone else may represent things differently (have different knowledge or beliefs) from yourself. Lillard (1993) and Jarrold et al. (1994) reviewed the evidence on pretend play skills and theory of mind, and each concluded that the evidence is not strong. Much early pretend play appears to be largely imitative, as was shown in Table 7.1. On the basis of Howes' model, there is little reason to suppose that social pretend implies metarepresentational abilities on the part of the child until 37–48 months, which is when theory of mind abilities emerge by most criteria; so, it is not necessary to postulate that it has a leading role in theory of mind development. However, quite a lot of talk about mental states does take place in pretend play (see also Chapter 15, pp. 526, 531).

Observations of sociodramatic play suggest there is considerable negotiation about social roles (cf. Table 7.1). Observations of rough-and-tumble show that coordination with a large number as well as partners is often involved, and suggest it may have social functions in terms of making friends, or practising fighting or dominance skills.

Studies on the forms of play are suggestive of functional hypotheses, and may rule some hypotheses out; but are these conclusions supported by other forms of evidence?

Correlational Studies

If playful behaviour has useful developmental consequences, then we would expect that children who practise a lot of a certain type of play should also be more advanced in other areas of development for which play is supposed to be beneficial. A detailed study on the outcomes of various kinds of object and construction play is given in Box 7.2.

One study, by Hutt and Bhavnani (1972), used data from the novel toy experiment mentioned earlier (see p. 237). They traced 48 children who had been observed with the novel toy at around 4 years of age, when they were 4 years older. From the earlier data, they had recorded those children who, after investigating the toy, used it in many imaginative ways (15 of the 48). Four years later, they gave the children some tests designed to measure creativity. The imaginative players scored significantly higher on these tests than did the children who at 4 years had not played much with the novel object.

Box 7.2 Boys' and girls' uses of objects for exploration, play and tools in early childhood

The majority of studies of object play in young children have used rather contrived laboratory settings, with particular sets of play objects; in particular, experimental studies of the effects of object play have been criticized as lacking ecological validity, being of short duration and susceptible to experimenter effects (Smith & Simon, 1984). A more naturalistic approach to look at outcomes of object play was attempted by Pellegrini and Gustafson (2005).

In the first part of the study, they observed the play of 35 children (17 girls, 18 boys) aged 3–5 years, in a US preschool, over an entire school year. Observations were made on three afternoons, every week, using 1-minute focal child sampling (this means a child was watched for 1 minute and his/her behaviour recorded; then the observer watched another child for 1 minute, and so on). These authors distinguished exploration with objects and play with objects (see pp. 237–238), and also distinguished construction with objects (see p. 238) and tool use (in which objects are used for direct functional ends). Thus their 'object play' category primarily refers to pretend play with objects.

Object play was recorded in 26% of the observations, and tool use in 24%; construction play was recorded less frequently, and exploration rather rarely. The most frequent kinds of tool use observed were using an object to transport another, for art work (e.g. painting) or for pouring or emptying. Boys did more object play (often embedded in acting out superhero themes) and girls did more construction play, with few sex differences in tool use. There was considerable individual variation among the children in the proportion of time spent in these different categories, and this made possible the second part of the study.

In this second part, 20 of the children (10 girls, 10 boys) were given two lure retrieval tasks, an associative fluency task and a WPPSI Block design test to measure spatial intelligence (see p. 524). These tests were to look at convergent and divergent problem-solving outcomes, related to different types of object use over the past year.

In the first lure retrieval task, children were given a choice of rake-like objects to help pull in a toy dinosaur that was out of reach; a second, harder task involved the child having to connect together shorter sticks to make a long enough rake. The experimenter measured the time taken to get the dinosaur in each task, the number of hints needed and the number of swipes, or attempts to reach the dinosaur, before succeeding.

In the associative fluency task, each child was asked to generate novel uses for common household objects: a paper cup, a plastic spoon, a marker pen. The number of novel uses (i.e. not conventional ones such as drinking from a paper cup) was scored.

The correlations between the main object use categories and the seven outcome measures from the problem-solving tasks are shown in Box Table 7.2.1. These are partial correlations, controlling for spatial intelligence scores on the WPPSI Block design test; this is to ensure that general spatial ability is not the reason for the correlations, making it more plausible that correlations can be ascribed to the effects of specific object use experiences. For the lure retrieval tasks, negative correlations

Box Table 7.2.1 Partial correlations between observed object use and performance on using objects as tools, controlling for spatial intelligence (N = 20)

		Exploration	Object play	Construction	Tool use
Lure retrieval 1:	Time taken	−.21	.35	−.45*	−.01
choose tool	Hints needed	−.21	.33	−.46*	.12
	Swipes needed	−.24	.33	−.17	−.14
Lure retrieval 2:	Time taken	−.16	.10	−.30	−.32
assemble	Hints needed	−.38	−.15	−.06	−.45(*)
tool from	Swipes needed	−.35	−.11	−.18	−.25
components					
Associative fluency	Novel uses	.04	−.18	.52*	−.34

*$p < .05$ (*)$p < .10$

signify better performance (less time spent, fewer hints, fewer unsuccessful swipes); for the associative fluency task, positive correlations indicate greater success (more unconventional uses).

The three significant correlations are with time children spent in construction activity. Children who had engaged in a lot of construction activities did better on the first lure retrieval task (less time, fewer hints needed) and on the associative fluency task (more novel uses given). They also tended to do better on the second lure retrieval task, as did those children who engaged in a lot of prior tool use. Time spent in exploration also predicted better outcomes, though non-significantly. Interestingly, more time spent in object play did not tend to predict better outcomes; indeed, the opposite was true for the first lure retrieval task, and associative fluency.

The strengths of this study are its delineation of four main different types of object use in early childhood and its combination of detailed observations over a long time period, with a later test design to examine outcomes. In this sense, it differs from a considerable body of experimental work using lure retrieval tasks and associative fluency tasks, which had been strongly criticized. This is essentially a correlational study, but the findings held up even when spatial intelligence was accounted for. A weakness of the study is the small sample, limited to one preschool. Some measures (e.g. some types of tool use) occurred at very low frequencies. In addition, it is not clear that precautions were taken to guard against experimenter effects in the testing.

The findings suggest that practice in construction activities is helpful for new problem-solving tasks. The relevance for play is somewhat uncertain, as the authors defined construction as 'building something that is end oriented (not play)' (p. 121). Their overtly 'play' category, which mainly included pretend use of objects, did not yield positive correlations with problem solving.

Based on material in Pellegrini, A.D. & Gustafson, K. (2005) in A.D. Pellegrini & P.K. Smith (Eds.), *The nature of play: Great apes and humans*, pp. 113–135. New York: Guilford Press.

This is consistent with the idea that imaginative play fosters creativity, but no more than that. An alternative explanation would be that another factor (for example, shyness with adults) was responsible for the poor performance both with the novel object and later in the tests. Or perhaps the playfulness of the imaginative children is just a by-product of their creativity, not a cause of it. As discussed in Chapter 1, correlations may be due to extraneous factors, and we cannot infer causal relations from them.

Many other correlational studies have been reported in the literature. For example, Oostermeijer et al. (2014) obtained parents' ratings of constructive play activities in Dutch 11–12-year-olds. They also assessed their spatial ability (a picture rotation task) and mathematical word problem-solving performance (tasks such as: 'How many picture frames 6 cm long can be made from a piece of framing 200 cm long?'). They found that constructive play activities correlated significantly ($r = 0.55$) with mathematical word problem-solving performance, and that about a third of this relationship was explained by spatial ability. However, they acknowledge (p. 5) that 'the correlational nature of the data . . . made it impossible to draw conclusions about any causal relationships'.

Many correlational studies have been reported on fantasy play. For example, Taylor and Carlson (1997) studied US children aged 3 and 4 years, and correlated various measures of pretend and fantasy play with theory of mind tasks. They found no relationship for 3-year-olds, but a significant relationship for 4-year-olds. The correlation for the whole sample was modest: $r = .16$ for the correlation of a principal fantasy component with theory of mind—significant, but accounting for only 2.6% of the variance. The authors' conclusion that 'The results of this study provide strong evidence that there is a relation between theory of mind and pretend play development in 4-year-old children' (p. 451) seems a very positive gloss on their findings. Smith (2010) reviewed 10 studies that correlated pretend play measures with theory of mind scores. The pattern of results was patchy—many correlations, even if positive, were small or not statistically significant. Smith concluded that pretend play may be helpful for theory of mind, but so also are many other kinds of experience (an equifinality model, see p. 262).

A study by Watson and Peng (1992) was one of the few to look at effects of war toy play. They coded for pretend aggression play and real aggression in 36 preschool children. Parents completed questionnaires saying how much toy gun play the children did at home, and how aggressive were the TV programmes that they watched. There was an association for boys (but not for girls) between a history of toy gun play (based on parents' ratings) and levels of real aggression in the day care centre. However, this finding could simply reflect that temperamentally aggressive children also like playing with toy guns. Pretend aggression in the day care centre did not correlate with real aggression. All these studies are subject to the same caveats about drawing conclusions from correlational evidence.

Experimental Studies

Experimental studies of play take two main forms: deprivation studies and enrichment studies. If participants are randomly allocated to the various conditions, it should be possible to make better causal inferences than is the case in correlational studies.

The effects of depriving children of play opportunities have largely been limited to studies of physical activity play. Pellegrini et al. (1995) examined the effects of keeping children in primary school classrooms for longer (delaying the recess breaks). Greater deprivation led to increased levels of play when opportunities became available. Also, the experience of break time increased children's attention to school tasks when they returned to the classroom, supportive of the *cognitive immaturity hypothesis* proposed by Bjorklund and Green (1992).

The more usual form of experiment on play is in the form of enrichment. The benefits of some form of extra play experience are compared with the benefits of non-play experience. Some experiments have been done on object play, usually using short sessions of about 10 minutes' duration. Children, usually of nursery school age, are given some play experience with objects; others are given an instructional session, or an alternative materials condition (e.g. drawing), or are put in a no-treatment control group. After the session is over, they are then given an assessment, for example, of creativity (e.g. thinking of unusual uses for the objects they have played with), problem solving (e.g. using the objects to make a long tool to retrieve a marble) or conservation (p. 458). A number of such studies claimed some form of superiority for the play experience, but subsequent work has not always borne these claims out.

Smith and Simon (1984) argued that these early studies were methodologically unsound due to the possibility of experimenter effects (see pp. 16–17). When the same experimenter administers the conditions, and tests the participants immediately after, some unconscious bias may come in. Some studies were criticized for inadequate control for familiarity with the experimenter. When these factors are properly taken account of, there is little evidence that the play experience helps, or indeed that such sessions have any real impact. Smith and Simon concluded that either the benefits of play in real life occur over a longer time period, or they are not substantial enough to measure by this sort of experimental procedure.

Experiments on the effects of make-believe and imagery on deductive reasoning in 4–6- year-olds were reported by Dias and Harris (1988, 1990). The results were suggestive of a role of pretence in theory of mind development but unfortunately, full protection against experimenter effects was not taken. Leevers and Harris (1999) have done further studies within this paradigm that led them to reinterpret the earlier work. Harris now argues that it is not the fantasy or pretend component, but simply any instruction that prompts an analytic, logical approach to the premises, which helps at these syllogistic tasks.

A more ecologically valid approach is to look at the effects of play over periods of weeks, or perhaps a school term. This has been done in studies examining the effects of play tutoring (see p. 249) in preschool classes. Several studies on disadvantaged preschool children in the USA found that play tutoring, besides increasing children's fantasy play, also had benefits in a variety of areas on cognitive, language and social development. The problem with these studies was that the play-tutored children were compared with children who received little or no extra adult intervention. Thus, general adult involvement and conversation might have caused the gains, rather than fantasy play *per se*. This alternative idea has become known as the 'verbal stimulation' hypothesis. Some play-tutoring studies since then have embodied controls for 'verbal stimulation' or, more generally, adult involvement (Figure 7.10). These found little superiority for the play-tutoring conditions. This does not mean that play tutoring is not worthwhile, but it does imply that it is of no more value than some other kinds of adult involvement (Smith, 2010).

An experimental study looking at the hypothesis that pretend play assists theory of mind was carried out by Dockett (1998) in an Australian preschool. Four-year-old children were naturally split into two groups and pre- and post-tested on measures of shared pretence and

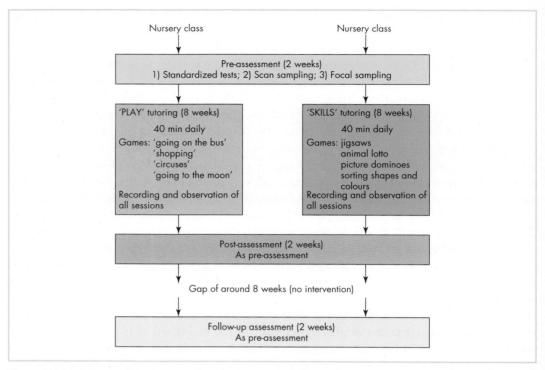

Figure 7.10 Design of experimental study comparing effects of play tutoring and skills tutoring.

on theory of mind ability. One group of children received sociodramatic play training for 3 weeks; the other, control, group experienced the normal curriculum. The play training group significantly increased in frequency and complexity of group pretence, relative to the control group, and improved significantly more on the theory of mind tests, both at post-test and at follow-up 3 weeks later. This study provides the best evidence yet for a causal link from pretend play to theory of mind; however, the groups were small and not well matched, and the testing was not done blind to condition.

Stop and Think

Is it likely that pretend play is important for development of theory of mind skills in childhood?

Play Therapy

A child who is emotionally upset or who has experienced some trauma may express this in their play. Saylor et al. (1992) described preschoolers' play following the experience of Hurricane Hugo; this hurricane struck South Carolina in September 1989, with winds up to 175 mph and a tidal surge of up to 23 feet, causing widespread destruction. Parents described re-enactments of this later, in their children's play. For example (of a 2-year-old boy and 3-year-old girl):

> Our children used to (still do at times) play what they call 'Hurricane'. They pretend the hurricane is coming . . . they have a new version where they are doing repairs—one is the workman, one is the homeowner who cannot live in the house and moves away while the work is being done . . . they also verbalize the noises, trees falling, wind, rain, etc. (p. 145)

It is widely thought that such play can help children work through some of the anxieties by acting out the themes 'at one remove'. Play therapists use play to help understand children's anxieties, and most therapists also believe that it can help the child work towards resolution of them. The role of a play therapist may well be important, as it appears unlikely that children's spontaneous pretend play will function effectively to resolve emotional difficulties. Insecurely attached children and children who have experienced emotional trauma show less pretend play, and it is relatively disorganized and negative in quality. In a review of pretend play and emotion learning in traumatized mothers and children, Haight et al. (2006, p. 211) concluded that ' . . . at the very time when children may benefit most from pretend play, they are less inclined to re-engage in it'. These findings suggest that spontaneous pretend play may be diagnostic of a child's disturbed emotional condition, but they are hardly strong evidence that pretend play functions in itself to help emotional mastery.

Such research challenges any simple cathartic function of fantasy play. It seems that many play therapists, too, are moving away from such a viewpoint—that obsessive repetition of negative play acts is in itself useful—towards using the play therapy setting to help the child think through issues more deeply (Alvarez & Phillips, 1998).

There are a variety of methods of play therapy. The origins of play therapy lie in psychoanalysis, and such approaches emphasize an active interpretation of the child's play by the therapist. The humanistic tradition of Carl Rogers (1951) and the work of Virginia Axline (1947) helped bring about a more child-centred approach in which the therapist is reflective of the child's feelings. Most play therapists now follow a child-centred approach to a considerable extent. In play sessions, the child is presented with a range of play materials and is allowed freedom of expression with these, within certain limits or boundaries. The adult therapist provides a safe, warm and accepting environment, and typically empathizes with the child and reflects their feelings back, helping them to develop self-understanding and gradually come to terms with the issues concerning them. A review of such play therapy procedures is given by Porter et al. (2009).

Evaluations of play therapy generally report positive outcomes, but not necessarily more so than child psychotherapy that does not use play methods. Bratton et al. (2005) carried out a systematic meta-analysis of 93 controlled outcomes studies, published between 1953 and 2000. All had pre- and post-tests and some kind of control group. The average age of children was 7 years, and the mean number of sessions was 16. They reported an overall effect size (p. 116) of .8, which is quite large. Effect sizes were greater for humanistic (child-centred) than non-humanistic treatments. However, many studies had small samples and inadequate control groups: 'because most play therapy research uses the design of play therapy versus absence of intervention, researchers are unable to declare play therapy as the most effective method of treatment', compared to, for example, 'traditional behavioural plans, cognitive techniques, or school guidance curricula' (Bratton et al., 2005, p. 386). Although findings are promising, there is a need for more and rigorous evaluation of different types of play therapy and of what exactly produces beneficial outcomes.

Models of Benefits of Play

The value of play remains a controversial topic. Arguments for its essential function continue to be advanced. For example, Gray (2013) has argued that in hunter-gatherer societies, 'children apparently acquire through play the skills, knowledge, values and character traits essential to hunter-gatherer success' (p. 367). In particular, he viewed social play as requiring sharing and cooperation, important for the kind of egalitarian societies that hunter-gatherers lived in. Gray (2011, p. 443) also argued that in modern societies too, play:

> functions as the major means by which children (1) develop intrinsic interests and competencies; (2) learn how to make decisions, solve problems, exert self-control, and follow rules; (3) learn to regulate their emotions; (4) make friends and learn to get along with others as equals; and (5) experience joy. Through all of these effects, play promotes mental health.

This is a modern restatement of the play ethos referred to earlier (p. 250). Gray goes on to argue that opportunities for free play have declined over the past half century in the USA and other developed nations, and that this is reflected in a decline in indicators of mental health such as depression, feelings of helplessness, and narcissism (see also Chapter 19 for some empirical evidence regarding such historical changes).

This is one end of a spectrum of views. Smith (2010) contrasted three models for the importance of play in development.

1. Play has no particular role in development; it is just a by-product of other abilities (social, cognitive, linguistic) as they develop. It is 'epiphenomenal'
2. Play is one of a number of ways in which a child can learn and acquire skills; it is useful, but not essential. Children also learn through observation, trial and error, work and instruction. This can be called an 'equifinality' model (there are different routes to the same goal)
3. Play is essential, or at least has a very privileged position, for many aspects of development in the preschool years and beyond. In the absence of play, these developmental consequences will not occur or will at least be significantly held back. This 'essential' model is that of the 'play ethos'.

Smith (2010) concluded that so far as pretend play was concerned, the second model, or equifinality, was the most supported in terms of the evidence (see p.258). In a very thorough review of the literature on object and pretend play, Lillard et al. (2013) reviewed three similar models, in relation to a large number of developmental outcomes. Their summary was as follows.

- *Language, narrative, emotion regulation*—there was insufficient evidence.
- *Executive function, social skills*—the evidence was against 'essential', so supporting 'equifinality' or 'epiphenomenal'.
- *Reasoning*—'equifinality' was supported.
- *Problem solving, creativity, intelligence, conservation, theory of mind*—'epiphenomenal' was supported.

They concluded that 'despite over 40 years of research examining how pretend play might help development, there is little evidence that it has a crucial role; equifinality and epiphenomenalism have as much if not more support' (p.27).

The Benefits of Play: An Overview

Considerable empirical investigation has now been made into the benefits of play, but 'the jury is still out'. Most of the investigations have concentrated on the supposed cognitive benefits of play, and have been made in an explicitly educational framework. Yet as we have seen, the evidence for strong cognitive benefits, whether from theory, observation, correlational or experimental studies, is not very convincing. If anything, the evidence is better for the benefits of play for social competence. The 'play ethos', a prevalent view that Sutton-Smith (1986) called 'the idealization of play', has tended to distort research and writing on the topic. In some societies, children seem to play little but develop normally. Thus, the empirical evidence is mixed, and it is arguable that, while play is likely to have benefits, it is unlikely that they are essential. Rather, these benefits could be achieved in a number of ways, of which play would be one. Whatever the final verdict, it will not detract from the enjoyment of play, on the part of both the participant and the observer. This in itself gives an enduring value to play, whatever the extent of its developmental consequences may be.

CHAPTER SUMMARY

- Attempts to define play include functional and structural approaches, and the use of play criteria. Play can be distinguished from exploration.
- Main types of play include physical activity, rough-and-tumble, object, fantasy and sociodramatic, and language play. These show characteristic developmental sequences, with games with rules becoming more important in middle childhood.
- Play behaviours vary by social class, gender and culture, with the attitudes of adults to play being an important factor.
- A number of prominent theorists have written on the nature and possible functions of play.
- The 'play ethos', an uncritical assumption that play is essential, has been a common view that distorted some research findings.
- Empirical studies have used both correlational and experimental methods to try to pin down the functions of various kinds of play; for example, pretend play for theory of mind development.
- There are different views on the conclusions to be drawn so far, and no consensus has been reached. One position would be that play can facilitate many aspects of development, but is not essential, due to alternative ways of acquiring many skills and competencies.
- Play therapy can be helpful for children with emotional disturbances, but further evaluation is needed.

DISCUSSION POINTS

1. How important is it to define play? Does play at different ages require different definitions?
2. Are exploration and play really distinct?
3. How useful is it to distinguish stages in the development of play?
4. Have theorists been too ready to speculate about the value of play, without sufficient evidence?
5. Are experimental studies of play worthwhile?

FURTHER READING

- Both Pellegrini, A.D. (2009). *The role of play in human development*. Oxford: Oxford University Press; and Smith, P.K. (2010). *Children and play*. Oxford: Wiley-Blackwell, are good sources of research and thinking on play. A comprehensive collection is available in Pellegrini, A.D. (Ed.), *The Oxford handbook of the development of play*. Oxford: Oxford University Press. For a detailed overview of play (and exploration!), in non-human species as well as in children, see Power, T. (2000). *Play and exploration in children and animals*. Mahwah, NJ: Lawrence Erlbaum; and Burghardt, G. (2005). *The genesis of animal play: Testing the limits*. Cambridge, MA: MIT Press.

- For those interested in educational relevance, a general text is Johnson, J.E., Christie, J.F. & Yawkey, T.D. (1990), *Play and early childhood development* (2nd ed.). New York: Longman; Roskos, K.A. & Christie, J.F. (Eds.) (2007). *Play and literacy in early childhood*. Lawrence Erlbaum, will also be relevant. Singer, D.G., Golinkoff, R.M. & Hirsh-Pasek, K. (Eds.) (2006). *Play = Learning*. Oxford: Oxford University Press, is a useful collection; many chapters are influenced by the 'play ethos', as the title indicates. Bateson, P. & Martin, P. (2013). *Play, playfulness, creativity and innovation*. Cambridge: Cambridge University Press, makes the case suggested in the title.

- For pretence, see Mitchell, R.W. (Ed.) (2002). *Pretending and imagination in animals and children*. Cambridge: Cambridge University Press; and Harris, P.L. (2000). *The work of the imagination*. Oxford: Blackwell, puts forward his ideas on pretence, role play and imagination. Singer, D.G. & Singer, J.L. (2005). *Imagination and play in the electronic age*. New Haven, CT: Harvard University Press, covers a variety of important topics including war play and computer games. For the nature and benefits of play in school yards, see Pellegrini, A.D. (1995). *School recess and playground behavior*. Albany, NY: State University of New York Press.

- For an anthropological perspective, try Lancy, D.F. (1996). *Playing on the mother-ground*. New York: Guilford Press, an account of play in the life of the Kpelle people of Liberia. Sutton-Smith, B. (1997). *The ambiguity of play*. Cambridge, MA: Harvard University Press, is an idiosyncratic and eclectic account of play in a broad, multidisciplinary perspective.

CHAPTER
8

Children and Media

CHAPTER OUTLINE

- Children's Use of Media
- Children and Television
- Computer Games
- Advertising to Children
- Media Interventions

In this chapter we consider how the media environment in which children live may influence their beliefs and behaviour. Virtually all children in the world now have access to television and most also have access to other media. We describe how media have changed and how traditional media (like television) have influenced children's lives, and we discuss how new technologies may have an impact on children, now and in the future. We look at the controversy around the effects on children's behaviour of exposure to television and video games, and the effects of advertising on children. We also point out the difficulties of media research in an ever-changing media environment, and note that, compared to the extensive research about television, new media have received little attention from developmental researchers.

CHILDREN'S USE OF MEDIA

Virtually all children have access to television, and most have computers, access to the internet, tablets and mobile phones. Children's access to media has generated new questions and new research into the role of media in children's lives. There are three aspects to this research. First, there are studies that have assessed how often and for how long children interact with different types of media. Second, there are studies investigating how children use media. Third, there are studies that consider the effects of media on children's lives. In this chapter we will be mainly concerned with this third aspect of research, as this has the most bearing on issues relating to children's development.

It is typical to begin a chapter on media with data about how much media children consume, but media and children's access to it change very quickly, and any figures will be out of date quickly so we will only give examples of the frequency of media use and how that use has changed in recent years The best way to find out about contemporary children's media use is to check websites that report recent research (e.g. Ofcom in the UK, www.ofcom.org.uk, or the Kaiser Foundation in the US, http://kff.org/). Figures about media use should be treated with caution unless they come with full details of the surveys that generated the figures. Surveys may be carried out by policy groups, by broadcasters, by marketers and by many others. Only rarely are surveys carried out by academic researchers. To assess the importance of survey data, it is essential to know who paid for the survey, exactly what the sample was and exactly what questions were asked. One example of how quickly media use has changed is shown in Table 8.1, from Rideout et al. (2010; see http://kff.org/), for US samples of 8–18-year-olds in 1999, 2004 and 2009. Noticeable is the huge growth in time spent on computers and video games, over a 10-year period. Time spent texting on cell phones (or mobile phones) has also increased; in fact, in 1999 no question was included about phones at all and in 2004 there was only one—and that referred to cell *or* landline phones.

Irrespective of any survey, it is safe to assume that nearly all children in the world already have or very soon will have access to all the major media. It took about 50 years from the time of the very first televisions in the home in the late 1940s (Pecora, 2007) to the time when broadcast programmes could reach even the most isolated children in the world (Charlton et al., 2002). But technological progress is now so rapid that the spread of computers, phones and the internet will take only a fraction of the time it took television to reach all

Table 8.1   Average number of hours spent with each medium, in a typical day, for 8–18-year-olds in the US, in 1999, 2004 and 2009.

Media type	Time spent (hours:minutes)		
	1999	2004	2009
Watching television content	3:47	3:51	4:29
Listening to music	1:48	1:44	2:31
Using a computer	0:27	1:02	1:29
Playing video games	0:26	0:49	1:13
Reading print media	0:43	0:43	0:38
Going to films	0:18	0:25	0:25
Total media exposure	7:29	8:33	10:45
Total time spent in media use, allowing for multitasking	6:19	6:21	7:38
Talking on cell phone	Not asked	Not asked separately	0:33
Texting on cell phone	Not asked	Not asked	1:35

Source: Rideout, V.J., Foehr, U.G. & Roberts, D.F. (2010). *Generation M2. Media in the lives of 8-18 year olds.* Henry J. Kaiser Family Foundation (www.kff.org). Reproduced by permission of The Kaiser Family Foundation.

parts of the globe (Livingstone, 2009). Access to media is free or cheap because media are paid for mainly by broadcasters (and not by consumers). One way that broadcasters make money is by selling part of the time that they broadcast, or by selling part of the space on their web pages to advertisers (see below); this removes most of the costs to the viewer. Because media are cheap, children often have as much access to media as do adults, and children have more time to use them. In the past, using media usually referred to using one source of media at a time. When televisions were large, heavy objects, there was little alternative but to sit in front of one, and there was little opportunity to use other media at the same time. Now children have mobile technology (e.g. phones and tablets), so they have access to media wherever they are, and as technologies have become more sophisticated children can multi-task. As can be seen from Table 8.1, Rideout et al. (2010) estimated that, on average, children and young people aged 8–18 years in the US used media for 7 hours, 38 minutes a day (total media exposure was 10 hours, 45 minutes but this included 3 hours, 7 minutes multitasking, such as downloading music). This total did not count the more than 2 hours 8 minutes a day spent talking and texting on phones.

Children use media in multiple ways. The frequencies for US children are shown in Table 8.1. In the UK, Livingstone (2009) described the internet activities of 9–19-year-olds, in order of frequency, as searching for information; doing school work; playing games; sending or receiving email; instant messaging; downloading music; doing quizzes; searching shops; visiting sites for hobbies; making a website; visiting sports sites; reading the news; seeking personal information; seeking computer information; visiting chat rooms; posting pictures or stories; and visiting porn sites.

In other words, children and young people spend more time with media than they do in school or asleep, and children can already do many things through a screen that would previously have involved travelling to different places or required face-to-face interaction.

Sometimes the media world is an extension of the young person's actual world (Ribak, 2009; Subrahmanyam et al., 2009) and more often it is a virtual world, as in game play (Blumberg, 2014; Durkin, 2006). Either way, the media world offers children immense possibilities and opportunities.

The media world also generates new concerns (Livingstone & Helsper, 2013)—for example, that text messaging will damage children's ability to write English (see Box 8.2) or that unhealthy food advertising will impact on children's diets (see Box 8.1)—and new risks, like cyberbullying (see Chapter 10), pornography (Wright, 2014), sexting (Lippman & Campbell, 2014; and see Chapter 19) and identity theft (Livingstone, 2009). The world that children live in today is very different from the world in which their parents grew up, and as yet, we know little about how living in this new media world affects children's development.

At present, there is still only limited research into new media beyond studies that have logged hours of new media use or listed children's activities. These studies are useful but provide little information about the psychological effects of new media on children. Some aspects of new media have received more attention (e.g. computer games, see below), but consist mainly of studies with adults and adolescents, and we need to know far more about the influence of new media on young children. However, there have been a large number of studies about the effects of traditional media (usually television), and so we will examine these first.

CHILDREN AND TELEVISION

Virtually all children in the world have access to television and most children watch many hours of television a day. Television watching is therefore an important part of viewing. According to Ofcom (2014), children aged 6–15 years in the UK watched nearly 3 hours of television a day. About half this was watching live TV, and the rest was watching on-demand television, recorded television, DVDs and short video clips online (Ofcom, 2014). Older children (11–15-year-olds) were as likely as adults to watch on-demand television (e.g. BBC iPlayer), but were much more likely to watch online video clips, for example on YouTube (Ofcom, 2014).

Children watch television for a variety of reasons (Gunter & McAleer, 1997); when children are asked why they watch television, they may include both positive and negative reasons. Viewing television can be for entertainment, for excitement, for information or just to relax. Children also say that they watch television to avoid doing other activities, out of habit or just to fill in time. Multichannel television provides constant mood-changing opportunities, with programmes ranging in content from serious to funny, from sad to happy, from everyday emotions to fantasy adventures and from romantic stories to horror films (Gunter & McAleer, 1997). Watching television with others is a social activity that leads to shared experiences and conversations with friends, and influences patterns of family activity (Lemish, 2007). The issues or opinions raised in programmes like soap operas or dramas may also provide opportunities to discuss topics that might otherwise be difficult to address.

Young children's attention to television is determined by several factors. Very young children may attend to programmes in response to the superficial features of the programme. Changes of pace, music and sound effects can all attract children's attention (Huston & Wright, 1983). As children get older, their attention is determined less by the programme features and more by their ability to attend effectively to the content of a programme. Lorch et al. (1979) found that by the age of 5 years, children could monitor television effectively, even when they were in a distracting environment. Lorch et al. showed 5-year-olds a 40-minute tape of segments from *Sesame Street* programmes. Half the children watched the programme in an empty room with just a parent present, and the other half watched it with a parent in a room full of toys. An observer noted when the children were looking at the television screen. Immediately after watching it, the children were shown stills from the programme (for example, of a character with a stick in his hand) and asked questions like, 'What does the character want to do with the stick?'. There was a large difference in the proportion of time children spent watching the television. For the group without toys, it was 87% of the time, and for the group with toys it was 44% of the time. But there was no difference in the proportion of questions answered, because both groups answered two-thirds of the questions correctly. Lorch et al. suggested that the children were sophisticated enough to divide their attention between the programme and the toys in such a way that their comprehension of the programme was not affected.

Most television programmes do not present information or a story in a coherent way. In a television drama, characters may appear or disappear depending on scene changes, there may be major changes in time or location between consecutive scenes, and much of the story may be implicit rather than explicitly presented on the screen. Children have to be able to interpret and pull together scenes that may not always portray a consecutive series of events. This ability develops gradually. When Clifford et al. (1995) showed participants police dramas (aimed at adults), they found that even 16-year-olds had a less than complete understanding of the stories, and 9-year-olds only understood about two-thirds of the programme content. Comprehending television depends on at least two factors.

First, children need their own experience of the real world, and Clifford et al. found that children's previous television experience was less important than their general knowledge about police work and crime—though children's comprehension does benefit from having seen similar programmes in the same series or the same programme several times (Crawley et al., 1999).

Second, children need to understand the conventions of television presentation. For example, young children may have difficulty recognizing that replays in sports programmes are repetitions of actions and not new actions each time (Rice et al., 1986). Other features of television, like flashbacks, dream sequences and variations in pacing, all need to be recognized if children are to fully understand what they are watching (van Evra, 2004).

Children also need to distinguish different types of programmes. Programmes can be categorized in different ways, for example by genre (news, drama, comedy), by the intended audience (programmes for children, for boys or girls, or for adults) or by their factual or fictional content. The latter may be particularly difficult to distinguish, because although some types of programmes (like news) are generally 'factual' and other types (like drama) are usually 'fictional', there are many programmes that blur these boundaries (like drama-documentaries or 'reality' shows), and any particular type of programme may include a range of content. For instance, the news may be presented in a dramatic way with music, loud headlines and features that in other contexts are more likely to suggest fictional content. Other programmes, like soap operas, although fictional, may have stories that are 'true' to the real-life situations they are presenting, and deal with personal, social or moral issues in a realistic way.

Distinguishing fact from fantasy in television is therefore difficult. Although very young children can distinguish between broadly different types of programmes (e.g. between cartoons and news broadcasts), it may not be until many years later that children recognize the subtle range of fact and fiction in many programmes (Lemish, 2007). Even when children can label programme content appropriately, they have to recognize that programmes are often broken up by 'idents' (images that identify a channel), previews, trailers for other programmes and advertising, each of which can also embody a range of fact–fictional content.

 Stop and Think

How do young children become successful television viewers?

Learning from Television

Television provides a rich source of information, not only in news and documentaries but also in programmes like quiz shows or travel programmes. Television also provides an opportunity for children to see world-class performances in sport, music, drama or almost any activity. However, in contrast to learning in a school environment, watching television is a passive activity, with little or no interaction from the viewer, and programmes involve a never-ending stimulus of visual images and sound effects. The pace of television is determined by the programme and not by the viewer, and so sometimes content may be too boring to maintain interest; at other times, it may be too complex to be understood (Huston et al., 2007). Unlike a classroom in which a teacher can tailor activities to the needs and abilities of the children, television may therefore be a limited source of effective learning.

For very young children, television may be a poor substitute for direct experience. Several researchers have shown that young children are less likely to learn an activity from seeing it demonstrated on television compared to seeing it demonstrated live (Anderson & Pempek, 2005; Hayne et al., 2003). For example, young children might be shown a novel object and then an experimenter shows the child how to carry out a series of actions with it (e.g. push a lever on a box to release a lid, then move the lid to find out what is inside). Children up to about 2 years of age are better at imitating the actions if they see them carried out live by a person, rather than if they see the same person perform the actions on television.

There is a large market in DVDs aimed specifically at parents of young children, which are sold as educational tools to help children develop basic skills—for example, in learning new vocabulary—but it is not clear whether younger children's vocabulary does benefit from watching television. Robb et al. (2009) compared how well children aged 12–15 months learned new words from watching a DVD. The DVD included 30 words naming objects and rooms that might be found in a house. On the soundtrack, an adult female spoke the name of an object that was illustrated with pictures on the screen. Half the children watched the DVD at home (15 times during a 6-week period). The other half was not given a DVD and their parents were just instructed to keep to their usual family routines. All the children were given a vocabulary test every 2 weeks during the course of the study. Robb et al. did not find any differences between the children who watched the DVD and those who did not. In other words, very young children did not learn new words any faster with the DVD.

In contrast, older children can learn from television. For example, children from about 3 years of age can learn new words from hearing them on television (Rice & Woodsmall, 1988) and there are successful educational programmes that have been designed for preschoolers.

Sesame Street

One of the longest established programmes is *Sesame Street*, originally produced in the 1960s in the US and now broadcast, suitably adapted for local cultures, to more than 100 million children in about 150 countries. *Sesame Street* has wide-ranging aims that go beyond just helping children learn words and language; it includes counting, mathematics, recognizing colours and shapes, and teaching children how to make inferences and solve problems, or deal with social problems (e.g. making friends, getting on with others) and emotional issues (e.g. coping with the death of a pet). *Sesame Street* is designed to reach children from all social classes on the assumption that even children from less advantaged backgrounds will have access to television. Research into the benefits of *Sesame Street* has shown that the programme does help young children, and that it has a positive effect on both girls and boys, and on different social classes (Fisch, 2004; Wright et al., 2001). Not only does the programme have immediate benefits, but Wright et al. also found long-term benefits when they followed up *Sesame Street* viewers until the age of 7 years, because children who had been regular viewers during their preschool years did better at their primary school. Anderson et al. (2001) also found that children who had watched more *Sesame Street* also did better in high school. High school performance is not, of course, dependent on any knowledge learned from a programme designed for preschoolers, but it might be the case that early educational viewing encourages a positive attitude towards learning, and that has a long-term benefit.

A version of *Sesame Street* called *Rechov Sumsum/Shara'a Simsim* was used with 275 Israeli-Jewish, Palestinian-Israeli and Palestinian preschool children (Ciole et al., 2003). This introduced children to the everyday lives of children in the other culture (either Jewish or Palestinian). Exposure to the programme was associated with an increase in the use of prosocial justifications to resolve conflicts, and in the use of positive attributes to describe members of the other group.

Therefore, *Sesame Street* has been a success. However, this is not to say that educational programmes are a panacea. The results from different assessments of *Sesame Street* vary, but some assessments have shown that parents' influence and social class are still factors in how well children learn from the programme (Lemish, 2007). *Sesame Street* demonstrated how, before the widespread use of the internet, media even for very young children had become a shared phenomenon, with programmes developed in one place being watched by millions of children across the globe. Following the success of television programmes like *Sesame Street*, there have been similar educational programmes for young children, such as *Teletubbies* in the UK (Roberts & Howard, 2005) and programmes for older children (Kirkorian & Anderson, 2008). Television can therefore help children to learn, and television may be particularly important when children have limited opportunities for other experiences.

Television in Relation to Other Activities

Whatever the benefits of television, those benefits need to be balanced by the fact that children who are watching a screen are not doing something else. That 'something else' could well be less useful than watching educational media, or it could be activities that promote learning in other ways (e.g. by spending more time interacting with parents, or doing positive activities with other children). Concerns about how much television children watch is one of the reasons why the American Academy of Pediatrics (AAP, 1999) recommended that children under 2 years of age should not watch any screens at all, and that children over the age of 2 years should have no more than 2 hours of high-quality screen time a day. This recommendation would apply to teenagers as well, though as we have noted above, most surveys of older children's media use find that the number of hours that older children are in front of screens is far in excess of these suggested times (Evans Schmidt et al., 2008; Ofcom, 2014; Rideout et al., 2010). The AAP also recommended 'screen-free' zones, so for example there are no televisions or computers switched on in children's bedrooms or while children are having meals. Such zones might be hard to enforce as more children gain greater access to their own phones and tablets.

The AAP stated that young children need to be playing or interacting with their parents to develop their social, emotional and cognitive skills. There is some evidence that the more time young children spend watching television in total (all programmes, including ones aimed at adults), the lower their language and cognitive performance (Linebarger & Walker, 2005), which supports the AAP position. However, as discussed above, some television, like *Sesame Street*, does benefit children, and indeed Linebarger and Walker found that the more time children spent watching educational programmes, the better was their language development. In other words, what television young children watch may be as important as how much they watch, hence the AAP's emphasis on the quality of screen time and the suggestion that parents should watch television with their children This assumes that parents know when their children are watching media.

The AAP recommendation that children's viewing should be limited to 2 hours a day might be feasible for very young children who may not see much more than that in any case, but it would be a major reduction for older children. For older children, there is clear evidence that more time spent with media leads to poorer educational performance. Moessle et al. (2010) carried out a series of studies in Germany after concerns were raised about the poor educational achievement of children from lower socioeconomic or immigrant backgrounds. In Study 1, in 2005, Moessle et al. interviewed over 5,500 German children aged 10–14 years. About 40% of boys had a television or a computer in their bedrooms. The figures were slightly lower for girls. Children without their own television watched 70 minutes of television on a school day, and 101 minutes each day of the weekend. For children with a television, this increased to 124 minutes on schooldays and 185 minutes each day at the weekend. Children who had their own games consoles played computer games for nearly twice as long as children who did not have games consoles. Overall, boys spent more time using media and children from ethnic backgrounds used more than other children. Children with access to their own media were more than twice as likely to watch films or play games rated for 16- or 18-year-olds, and this was particularly the case for boys.

Moessle et al. (2010) considered the educational achievement of children in the context of how often the children used media and what type of media they were using. Children who had their own media had lower marks in German, science and mathematics. For boys, the more time they spent playing games, especially games rated for 18-year-olds, the more likely they were to have poorer school performance. These findings are correlations so we cannot assume that children who spent more time with media did less well at school for that reason. It may have been that children who were already poorer academically were less interested in schoolwork and therefore did less homework and hence had more time to watch media. So Moessle et al. carried out a second, longitudinal, study to investigate possible causal relationships between screen media and academic performance.

In Study 2 (Moessle et al. 2010), the same children in each of four years (in their 2nd grade, about 7–8 years old, in 2005; 3rd grade in 2006; 4th grade in 2007; and 5th grade in 2008) were asked to complete a questionnaire about their activities and how they spent their leisure time. The children's IQ, academic self-image and social behaviour were also assessed. On the same occasions, the children's parents were asked about the family's background and the family's use of media. The children's teachers provided details of each child's school performance. Overall, there were significant negative correlations between the time they spent with media and the children's marks in German, English, science and mathematics. One of the most important effects on later performance was how long children played computer games during the earlier years, and in particular how often children played violent games or watched violent television programmes. From these longitudinal data, Moessle et al. suggested that children who had poor marks in school spent increasingly more time watching games and television and this, in turn, led to even poorer school marks.

Stop and Think

Does television contribute to or detract from children's education?

Influence of Television: Stereotypes

Children not only learn from educational programmes, but are also influenced by the other programmes on television. For example, news and current affairs programmes may help young people form political opinions about national and international events (Lemish, 2007; Matthews, 2009). Even programmes produced mainly for entertainment carry implicit messages influencing attitudes and behaviour.

Through media, children are exposed to ideas about gender, race, families and social class (Gunter & McAleer, 1997). When these are not an accurate reflection of the societies in which children live, television can generate false stereotypes. For instance, Signorielli and Bacue (1999) pointed out that even though there are more women in the US, males appear twice as often as females in television programmes. Male characters also outnumber female characters in video games (Dietz, 1998). Women often have less important roles, or roles that are subservient to the male characters. Women are more likely to be portrayed in traditionally female occupations (e.g. nurse or secretary) and even when women are shown in traditionally male occupations (e.g. as a lawyer or doctor), they are often portrayed as single or separated (Signorielli, 2001).

It is difficult to assess how gender roles on television influence children's thinking about gender, because many factors other than television are involved in the perception of gender (Lemish, 2007). Children who watch more media are more likely to describe male and female roles in traditional terms, identifying women with domestic roles and men with professional roles (Hust & Brown, 2008). But such correlations could mean that children who watch more media are influenced by the way gender is presented on the screen, or could mean that children who accept traditional gender roles, for whatever reason (e.g. the influence of their family, religious or social backgrounds), prefer to watch more media.

Children who watch more educational programmes (which often attempt to avoid gender stereotypes) have less stereotypical attitudes to gender. But again, such findings could mean that such programmes influence children's attitudes or that children who already have non-stereotypical beliefs prefer to watch educational programmes. Nonetheless, when media portray men and women in a variety of ways, children experience a range of role models. In contrast, some aspects of sexuality are ignored. For example, gay and lesbian characters, and homosexual relationships, are rarely included in programmes for young people (Hust & Brown, 2008).

Gender roles are also bound up with attitudes to beauty and attractiveness. Male characters are often portrayed with V-shaped, muscular bodies, and females are portrayed as thin— sometimes thinner than would be recommended for healthy living. Portrayals of males have tended to get heavier (because they have become more muscular) and females have become even thinner (Harrison & Hefner, 2008). Stereotypes of male attractiveness or very thin females are often linked to positive outcomes, like leadership, intelligence and successful lifestyles. In contrast, obese characters are often portrayed as slow, greedy and unpopular (Harrison, 2000). Body size does have an effect on viewers. In typical experiments, girls or young women are shown a scale with stylized pictures of female bodies ranging from very thin to very fat. Girls are first asked to say what they think their own body size is, and what their ideal body size would be. The difference (or lack of difference) between a a girl's perception of what she is and what she would like to be is a measure of her degree of satisfaction with her own body size. Then the girls are exposed to images of thin females in media (for example, in fashion magazines, television programmes or music videos), following which they make further judgements about their own and ideal body sizes. Compared to girls who have seen neutral images, those who have viewed thin models tend to have increased dissatisfaction with their own body size. Such effects have been found in girls as young as 5 or 6 years of age (Dittmar et al., 2006; Hayes & Tantleff-Dunn, 2010).

As with gender, racial portrayals in media may not reflect reality. In the US, the proportion of African-Americans on television watched by children is actually higher than the proportion in the population, but the proportions of other ethnic groups (Latino, Asian Americans and Native Americans) is much lower than their actual proportions in the US population. Similar biases exist in the numbers of minority groups portrayed in films, games and advertisements (Berry, 2007; Greenberg & Mastro, 2008). The almost complete absence of a group, like Native Americans, means that a traditionally important part of the US population is effectively dismissed. Compared to White Americans, other groups may be portrayed negatively in terms of status, behaviour and achievement (Mastro & Greenberg, 2000). Other groups are also more likely to be reported negatively in news broadcasts. As with gender, it is difficult to disentangle the effects of media bias about ethnic groups from all the other influences on children. Early research suggested that White children's television viewing influenced their knowledge about, and attitudes towards, other groups (Zuckerman et al., 1980), and some research showed that positive portrayals of other groups had an effect. For instance, after White children were shown images of White and other race groups playing together, the White children were more likely to say that they would like to have friends from other groups (Gorn et al., 1976).

Research into any aspect of stereotypes is difficult because cultures change rapidly. For example, the contemporary ethnic composition of the US is very different now than one or two generations ago (Berry, 2007). Television changes, too, with some children's programmes attempting to portray gender or ethnic groups more equally (even though, in an age of multichannel, 24-hour broadcasting, the need to fill schedules means that a large number of programmes and films from earlier, more traditional generations are constantly repeated on screen). The most likely difference between the effects of stereotypes in the past and their effects on contemporary children comes from the internet. Whereas children in the past were usually passive viewers of whatever was presented on screen, the unlimited choice provided by the internet means that children can now search out the media that most appeal to them, whether it is for more positive views of their own cultural group or to find information about their own gender or sexual orientation. Such access may reduce the stereotypical effects found in traditional programmes, but there is the danger that the lack of regulation of the internet can result in children viewing far more extreme racial stereotypes or gender stereotypes (e.g. in pornography) than would ever be allowed on television (Ionnotta, 2008).

Influence of Television: Aggression and Violence

Television programmes in general include a large number of violent interactions. Aggressive incidents (physical or verbal) occur in all aspects of television—in films, dramas, comedies, cartoons, news, music videos, trailers and advertisements—so a child may see thousands of examples of aggressive behaviour each year (Wilson et al., 2002). Violence is often glamorized (e.g. when an action hero performs it) or trivialized (e.g. it is shown as entertaining, or the consequences to the victim are ignored).

Several theories—at least five—have been proposed to explain how violence on television might influence children's behaviour. One point of view is that such violence might be 'cathartic'—a word of Greek origin referring to the purging of emotions that was supposed to result from watching classical drama. The implication is that adults or children watching violent media will have their emotions purged or drained in a similar way.

A more prevalent view is that watching television violence may encourage aggression through imitation. The child may copy actions seen on television, especially if they are associated with admired figures or aggression seems to have successful outcomes. Even very young children imitate behaviours they have seen (see Chapters 3 and 13) and will to some extent imitate actions from a screen (see previous section about learning from television; Zack et al., 2009). Older children will also copy behaviours, especially when the behaviours are carried out by an attractive character, or if aggressive behaviours go unpunished (Bandura, 1986; Smith et al., 2002b), or are actually rewarded (e.g. a character achieves a desired outcome by using aggression).

A third theoretical viewpoint focuses on arousal. Any television content may generate pleasure or excitement, and when this occurs in the context of violent scenes, the violence may become associated with the stimulation of positive feelings (Anderson & Bushman, 2002).

Fourth, viewing violent behaviour may desensitize children, who become used to the presence of aggressive actions (Funk et al., 2004). So rather than being upset by aggression in real life, or sympathetic towards the victim, children come to regard aggression as an acceptable behaviour (Drabman & Thomas, 1974).

Fifth, some researchers have suggested that children learn 'scripts' from television (see Chapter 14) so they may come to believe that one way to resolve problems is by using violence (Berkowitz, 1990; Huesmann, 1998).

These theories are not mutually exclusive and it is likely that there are several ways in which aggression experienced on television can lead to increased levels of real-life aggression. The point is that all these theories suggest potential psychological reasons why violent media may have an effect on children. There are also counter-arguments, however. Much television violence involves fantasy contexts, which older children can certainly distinguish from real violence, just as they distinguish play with toy guns from real gun use (see section on war play, Chapter 7). As one researcher has argued, children 'see that television is not to be taken seriously, that the murders are there as stunts, that shooting is a part of entertainment. Thus the violence on television passes them by' (Cullingford, 1984).

In typical past investigations of the effect of media violence, children were shown aggressive or non-aggressive programmes, and then placed in situations where they can hit a punch bag or inflatable doll, or push buttons that supposedly 'help' or 'hurt' another child. Children who watched aggressive films punched the bag or doll, or pushed the 'hurt' button, more. However, such experiments have been criticized as very artificial. Hitting the punch bag might have been playful, not aggressive, and some of the experiments seem so contrived that the main effect being measured may have been obedience to the experimenter (Cullingford, 1984).

We will look in detail at two more naturalistic studies, each with a correlational, longitudinal design.

A Longitudinal, Correlational Study on Adolescents

Lefkowitz et al. (1977) interviewed the parents of 8–9-year-old children (184 boys, 175 girls) to find out their favourite television programmes, and hence measure their exposure to television violence. This score was higher for boys than for girls. The children were also asked to rate the other children in their class for aggressiveness. Lefkowitz et al. found that there was a significant correlation between the two measures for boys, but not for girls. The correlation for boys could mean either that viewing television violence caused aggression or that aggressive boys liked watching violent television programmes. Yet another explanation could be that some other factor—parental discord in the home, for example—led a child both to watch violent television programmes and to be aggressive himself.

The same measures were taken 10 years later when the children were about 19 years old. The correlations between the same two measures at this time, and the correlations between the two time periods, are shown separately for boys and for girls, in Figure 8.1. The results for the boys are the most interesting and the most quoted. They showed that watching a lot of violent television at age 9 was significantly correlated with peer-rated aggression at age 19; however, peer-rated aggression at age 9 was not correlated with watching violent television at age 19. This suggests that watching violent television leads to aggression, rather than vice versa. A similar, though less strong, association was found when aggression was measured by self-ratings or personality questionnaires. Some other factor or factors might still be responsible for the associations, but this technique (known as 'cross-lagged correlation') does give more weight to the findings than a simple correlation would do. Lefkowitz et al. (1977) argued that they had identified a small but statistically reliable influence of television violence on aggressive behaviour in boys. The findings for girls (see Figure 8.1) were much weaker, and tended to go in the opposite direction.

This longitudinal study was continued until the participants were 30 years of age (Eron, 1987). Throughout, there was significant continuity of aggressive tendencies: aggressive youngsters were more likely to have criminal convictions as adults. However, there could be many causal factors producing such continuity, independently of watching violent TV programmes (see Chapter 10).

A Two-site Longitudinal Study

One longitudinal investigation (Anderson et al., 2001) took advantage of two earlier studies of preschool children in the USA, carried out in Topeka, Kansas, and Springfield, Massachusetts. The two studies had been quite independent but had used sufficiently similar methodologies that the findings could later be combined. In particular, in both studies

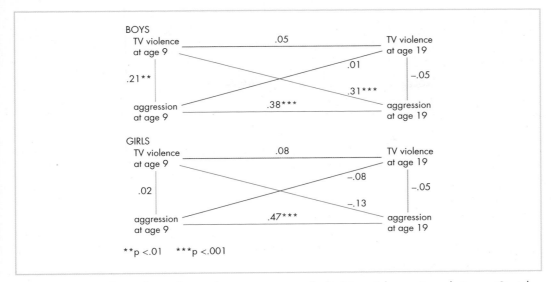

Figure 8.1   Cross-lagged correlations between amount of television violence viewed at ages 9 and 19 and peer-related aggression at ages 9 and 19, for 184 boys and 175 girls.
Source: Adapted from Lefkowitz, M.M., Eron, L.D., Walder, L.O. & Huesmann, L.R. (1977). *Growing up to be violent.* New York and Oxford, Pergamon.

parents had kept diary records of the television viewing of their children, aged 5 years at the time. Mean viewing times were around 15 hours per week in Massachusetts and 19 hours per week in Kansas.

Of 655 children in the original combined samples, the researchers were able to follow up 287 males and 283 females when they were about 16 years (Kansas) or 18 years of age (Massachusetts). According to their own self-reports, the teenagers watched about 12 hours (boys) or 10 hours (girls) of television per week. Of this, about 1–1.5 hours were classified as 'violent' (the researchers included cartoons and action-adventure shows in this category). Some 2.5–3 hours per week were spent watching videos, with a similar amount of time spent on listening to the radio and reading non-school books.

Anderson et al. (2001) were interested in finding out whether the kind of television programmes watched when the children were 5 years were an indicator of their progress around school-leaving age. The researchers also looked at concurrent relationships with their viewing as teenagers. Anderson et al. assessed current academic achievement (from self-report and school marks), aggression (from a self-report scale), and aspects of leisure time use. Some results from their study are shown in Table 8.2. The figures shown are from regression analyses—similar to correlations but taking account of various covariates such as site, parental education and birth order.

The results for school performance (in English, mathematics and science) showed that watching informative programmes as a preschooler correlated positively, significant for boys only, while watching violent programmes as a preschooler had negative relationships, significant for girls only. The relationships were less strong for current viewing as teenagers, although for boys there was a significant negative relationship between school performance and violent television viewing. The results for aggression showed a negative relationship of

Table 8.2 **Some results of regression analyses predicting adolescent characteristics from preschool and current television viewing; two sites combined.**

	Grades		Creativity		Aggression	
	Males	**Females**	**Males**	**Females**	**Males**	**Females**
Preschool TV						
Informative	.21***	.05	.07	.11	−.20**	−.10
Violent	.03	−.19***	.02	.03	.07	.50*
Teen TV						
Informative	.04	.08	−.04	−.004	−.03	.14
Violent	−.12*	.01	.06	−.08	.00	−.24

*p < .05, **p < .01, ***p < .001.
Source: Adapted from Anderson, D.R., Huston, A.C., Schmitt, K.L., Linebarger, D.L. & Wright, J.C. (2001). Early childhood television viewing and adolescent social behaviour. *Monographs of the Society for Research in Child Development, 66*(1), 1–154.

watching informative programmes as a preschooler, for boys only, and a significant positive effect for watching violent programmes as a preschooler, for girls only. These results were mixed in the picture they gave. There is no clear relationship between violent television viewing, either earlier or currently, and aggressive behaviour but for boys only, watching informative programmes as a preschooler had a 'protective' relationship. Concerning school performance, there were different findings for boys and girls, the strongest being the negative effect of early violent programme viewing for girls.

Anderson et al. hypothesized that early television viewing has a greater effect when it counteracts normative developmental trends and predominant sex-typed socialization influences than when it reinforces them. In other words, they argue that early viewing of violent television by boys did not influence boys much, because it is more normative for boys to be aggressive.

There have been other longitudinal studies of a similar kind, and many researchers feel that aggression on television does result in increased levels of real-life aggression (Huesmann & Kirwil, 2007). We also know from case studies of a few abnormal individuals that television violence can on occasion provide a stimulus or model for some violent crime. But it may be that for most children, most of the time, the impact of television is rather small. Although violence on television probably does have an influence on children's behaviour, that influence needs to be considered in the context of other, non-media factors that can also lead to violent behaviour. Actual aggression in the home between parents is not as easily turned off as a television set, and might be a more potent influence than fictitious aggression on television; aggression in the home has consistently been found to predict later conduct disorders (see Chapter 10). Other factors might affect any single child's response to violent television, such as their developmental stage, their social class, how much violent television they watch, what type of violence they view and whether parents discuss the portrayal of violence in the media with them (Lemish, 2007; Wilson, 2008). Television is no longer the only or main source of violent examples, and children can witness aggressive behaviours in other media (like the internet or computer games).

Stop and Think

Do the bad influences of television outweigh the good influences?

COMPUTER GAMES

Computer games have evolved rapidly in a short period of time. Computer games can be used for entertainment and stimulation, for education and training, or for presenting simulations of the real world. A large proportion of people play some form of computer game for entertainment. In the US, recreational games are played by nearly two-thirds of the population (Entertainment Software Association, 2013, cited in Blumberg et al., 2014a). Games are also frequently used for educational purposes—in a survey of US teachers, three-quarters said they used digital games in the classroom (Takeuchi & Vaala, 2014). Simulation games may be an effective way to provide students with experiences that they could not otherwise get easily or safely, or provide simulations of events or places that no longer exist (Hammer & Black, 2009).

Blumberg et al. (2013) summarized why games are such an attractive pursuit. Games are *interactive*, because players respond to the demands of the game and receive *feedback* for their performance. Games allow the player *control* over their actions and their choices in achieving a goal. The player has the opportunity to develop an *identity* by interacting with other characters or becoming a character in the game. Games involve *immersion* which means that players can feel that they are part of the game. Games can become absorbing and provide a strong sense of achievement as players progress to more complex levels and learn more skills to master the game. Games therefore encourage repeated play. All these aspects of games reflect aspects of any learning context, and therefore it is not surprising that game play has been advocated as an effective way to develop new cognitive skills.

Researchers have found a positive relationship between game-playing and cognitive skills in adults, including attention (Bavalier et al., 2012; Boot et al., 2008; Green & Bavelier, 2003, 2006, 2007) and reasoning (Greenfield et al., 1994). Games that feature spatial skills, such as mental rotation (De Lisi & Wolford, 2002), result in improved performance on tests of spatial ability, especially tests that are closely related to the spatial skills involved in the games (Sims & Mayer, 2002). As yet, there is little similar research with children, and the current research with children has inconsistent findings about the effects of games on children's cognitive processes (Best, 2014).

Children can become very involved in games and enjoy the challenge of doing well (Blumberg & Altschuler, 2011; Hamlen, 2013) and therefore games offer new ways to improve children's knowledge. Numerous educational games have been designed to help children with all aspects of school performance, from learning how to spell to understanding sophisticated scientific concepts. As noted above, games are frequently used in the classroom. By using games, teachers are testifying to their advantages but most individual games will not have undergone rigorous psychological testing to find out how much a game improves children's abilities, whether it compares favourably to other forms of learning, or whether skills and knowledge learnt in the context of a game transfer to other contexts (Barnett, 2014; Black et al., 2014). Nonetheless, there is an assumption by educators that games have advantages. These advantages include learners being able to work at their own pace, receiving immediate feedback, working with others online, and the ease with which performance can be recorded and monitored. Most important of all, if games are designed appropriately they should have all the elements described at the beginning of this section and they should be motivating and enjoyable so that children will want to go on playing them. Games can be designed such that the pace of learning is always within a child's zone of proximal development (see Chapter 16) so that the game never becomes so easy that it becomes boring or so hard that a child loses interest.

The process of developing an educational game was described by Evans et al. (2013) who designed a game to help children understand mathematical fractions. Evans et al. described the principles and past research that informed their choice of the elements in the game. Other researchers have used established games to find out if they help young people learn. For example, Black et al. (2014) compared expert players of a history simulation game with other people who were not familiar with the game. The results showed that there was no difference in the historical knowledge of the two groups, so the game did not seem to have benefited the expert players. However, when the two groups were later asked to read a difficult history textbook with similar content to the game, the expert players understood far more from the book than did the other group. Black et al. argued that although playing the game was of no immediate benefit, the play experience prepared the participants for later learning from a different source. Alternatively, it might be the case that learners often benefit from experiencing the same educational material in different formats, and that games provide an additional way to present learning opportunities (Fisch et al., 2014).

Digital game play has generated concerns about the impact of game play on children because some games involve violent actions, and the interactive nature of games means that a player is often directly 'responsible' for aggressive, sometimes excessively aggressive, actions. There have been concerns that violent games may foster aggressive attitudes (Anderson et al., 2007; Gentile, 2009) or desensitize children to real-life violence (Funk et al., 2004), and these are similar to the concerns expressed about violence on television. Anderson et al. (2010) carried out a meta-analysis of 136 studies of violent games. They looked at outcomes in six areas, as shown in Table 8.3, and found significant effect sizes for each of these; that is, violent game exposure was associated with negative outcomes on all these measures. This was true irrespective of research design (experimental, cross-sectional, longitudinal), and gender effects were not significant. Nevertheless, the importance of these findings has been questioned. Ferguson and Kilburn (2010) argued that Anderson et al. (2010) had not included a number of unpublished studies that gave less support to their conclusions, and that the effect sizes were quite small compared to many other factors affecting aggression. They also pointed out that the very rapid increase in the use of violent games had coincided with a reduction in violent crime rates in the USA, UK, Japan and other industrialized countries over the same period.

So, as with the debate on television violence (see above), the conclusion appears to be that there can be harmful effects of game violence but that it is (for most children at least) not a major factor in understanding violent behaviour. As noted above, researchers have

Table 8.3 Effects sizes for effects of violent video game exposure on six outcome measures.

Outcome measure	Number of studies	Effect size
Aggressive behaviour	140	.189
Aggressive cognition	95	.162
Aggressive affect	62	.139
Physiological arousal	29	.135
Empathy/desensitization	32	.177
Prosocial behaviour	23	.101

Source: Anderson et al.,(2010). Violent video game effects on aggression, empathy, and prosocial behavior in Eastern and Western countries: A meta-analytic review. *Psychological Bulletin, 136,* 151–173.

pointed out that action games (even violent ones) can promote learning and reasoning in adults (Bavalier et al., 2012; Green & Bavalier, 2003), and such games can actually promote collaborative work and more positive social attitudes (Dickey, 2011; Ferguson & Garza, 2011).

Another concern is that playing games results in social isolation. This might also apply to children who spend long periods watching television, but games generate more concern because some games offer versions of 'real' worlds, like sports simulations, or virtual worlds (Shapiro et al., 2006), that may be more immersive than anything viewed on television and might result in greater social isolation. Nonetheless, researchers have found that adolescent boys who played more games spent more, rather than less, time visiting friends (Colwell et al., 1995), and although some game play can be a solitary activity, Durkin and Aisbett (1999) found that a third of adolescents who played games did so with friends on the internet. Some multiplayer games may involve hundreds of players at the same time (Williams, 2006).

Like other media activities, playing games is usually a sedentary activity, and therefore games play may be one of the factors in the increase of childhood obesity (Vandewater & Cummings, 2008). Some interactive games, like exergames, involve physical activity, but there has been little research into the effects of exergames on children's physical health (Best, 2013). Maddison et al. (2011) found that 10–14-year olds who played exergames for 6 months gained less weight than children who did not play exergames, but the experience of the exergames did not result in the children taking up more physical activity. As yet, there is little evidence to suggest that exergames encourage greater physical activity by children.

Stop and Think

Are computer games a good or a bad influence on games players?

ADVERTISING TO CHILDREN

Access to media is free or very cheap and this is one reason why children have such easy access to different forms of media. Media content can be provided cheaply because many of the costs of producing and broadcasting media are covered by the income that media companies derive from selling advertising opportunities. Rather than describing a medium like commercial television as programmes separated by advertisements, it is more accurate to consider television as advertisements separated by programmes. If there were no advertisements there would fewer media, and access to those media would become very much more expensive.

Much advertising in media is directed at children because children represent a major market (Blades et al., 2014). In 2000, children under 12 in the US spent nearly $30 billion of their own money and influenced $250 billion of family purchases. The total amounts children spend in other countries is less, but their influence on family spending may be even greater. For example, in China, families have only been permitted to have one child, and therefore this one child is the main focus of his or her parents' and grandparents' spending (Blades & Oates, 2007; Chan & McNeal, 2004). Children in just the main cities of China (one-quarter of all the children in China) spend $6 billion of their own money and influence more than $60 billion of family purchases. Children's direct spending is on a limited range of products, which includes food, entertainment, clothes and toys, and therefore very large amounts of money are spent on advertising such products to children. For example, 44 food and drinks companies in 2006 spent $1.6 billion in the US promoting their products to children and young people (Kovacic et al., 2008).

As marketers have so much money to spend on advertising, they have a major effect on children's lifestyles, and therefore advertising aimed at children raises a number of concerns (Blades et al., 2014). Children's requests for products they have seen advertised is referred to as 'pester power' and can lead to family arguments and conflict. Many parents believe that the children's desire for products makes them more materialistic (Buijzen & Valkenburg, 2003); this may be a particular concern in cultures, like China, that have previously emphasized communal and traditional values over individual possessions (Chan, 2014; Chan & McNeal, 2004).

Unhealthy Food Products

More specific concerns relate to the types of products that are aimed at children. A large proportion of all marketing to children is for unhealthy food and drink products—these are products high in fat, salt and/or sugar content, or 'HFSS' products (Boyland et al., 2014). Hastings et al. (2003) reviewed the literature on children and food advertising and concluded that food advertising to children had a negative impact on their diets. Other researchers have demonstrated this in experiments (an example of such experiments is given in Box 8.1). Halford et al. (2004) asked healthy-weight, overweight and obese children to watch television food advertisements. After the children had watched the advertisements, they were given a variety of high- and low-fat foods to eat (but not the specific foods that they had just seen in the advertisements). The amount of food was unlimited, so children could eat as much as they wanted. On a separate occasion, the same children went through exactly the same procedure but watched non-food advertisements. All three groups of children ate more food, and more high-fat food, after they had watched the food advertisements. Concerns that advertising is a factor in the children's unhealthy eating, and the rise in the number of children with obesity, led the UK government to take action against advertising HFSS products to children (Ofcom, 2006), and in 2008 the UK government prohibited advertisements for HFSS products in or around television programmes aimed at children.

Box 8.1 Food choice and overconsumption: Effect of a premium sports celebrity endorser

Celebrities are often used to advertise products to children, including foods that are generally considered to be unhealthy (for example, ones that contain high proportions of fat, sugar and salt). Boyland et al. (2013) investigated whether celebrities had an effect on children's food choices. To do this, they selected a UK advertising campaign that featured Gary Lineker who had been a famous and popular international football player for England and was, at the time of the study, a frequent sports presenter on national UK television. He was also the voice of a cartoon character on children's TV. In addition, he was the key figure in a national UK campaign to promote Walker's Crisps (potato chips) and had been for over 10 years.

Boyland et al. considered whether exposure to Gary Lineker increased children's consumption of crisps. There were 181 children (with a mean age of 10 years) in the experiment, none of whom had any food allergies. The group was divided, roughly equally, into four conditions. All the children saw a 20-minute video of a cartoon (*The Simpsons*) in which there was a 45-second television clip. The clips varied depending on condition.

- Condition 1: Gary Lineker presenting a television advertisement for Walker's branded crisps.
- Condition 2: an advertisement for a different snack (a brand of salted peanuts called Nobby's Nuts).
- Condition 3: Gary Lineker, presenting a TV football programme (with no references to any food).
- Condition 4: an advertisement for a toy.

The children were shown the video in groups of 5–10 children. Immediately after seeing the video, each child was given two bowls of crisps. Each bowl contained 100 g of Walker's crisps. One bowl had a label with the word 'Walker's' and one bowl had a label with the words 'supermarket brand', and the experimenter told the children that the bowls contained Walker's or a supermarket brand of crisps. Then the children were told they could eat as much as they liked, and that there was more of each type of crisp available if they wanted more. When children had finished eating, the amount that each child had eaten was measured, and the children's weights were measured.

Boyland et al. found that neither the children's age nor weight had any influence on the results. Then they used ANOVA and t tests to compare how much the children had eaten in each condition (see Box Table 8.1.1). Children ate the same amount of the non-branded (supermarket) crisps in all four conditions. The amount of Walker's crisps and the amount of supermarket crisps consumed in condition 4 (with the toy advertisement) was the same. This was an important result because it showed that the children did not prefer Walker's crisps in all circumstances.

In contrast to condition 4, the children did choose more of the Walker's crisps in all the other three conditions. In condition 1, with the Gary Lineker advertisement, the children ate significantly more of the Walker's crisps. This was also the case in condition 3, when children saw Gary Lineker in a sports programme. This suggests that seeing a celebrity associated with a brand will prompt children to eat more of that brand even when the celebrity is not explicitly advertising the brand (as in condition 3). There was no difference in the amount of Walker's crisps that children ate in condition 1 and in condition 3, indicating that

Box Table 8.1.1   Mean weight (in grams) of each type of crisp consumed in each condition. (Means are taken from a graph in Boyland et al., 2013, and are therefore approximate.)

	1 Gary Lineker advertisement for Walker's brand of crisps	2 Advertisement for a brand of peanuts	3 Gary Lineker presenting football programme	4 Advertisement for toy
Walker's brand crisps	36 g	25 g	35 g	20 g
Non-brand crisps	16 g	14 g	17 g	17 g

Source: Based on Boyland, E.J., Harrold, J.A., Dovey, T.M., Allison, M., Dobson, S., Jacobs, M-C. & Halford, J.C.G. (2013). Food choice and overconsumption: Effect of a premium sports celebrity endorser. *Journal of Pediatrics, 163*, 339–343.

the effect of a celebrity alone (condition 3) was as influential as the celebrity actively promoting the product (condition 1).

In condition 2, with the advertisement for a brand of peanuts, children also ate more of the Walker's crisps than the supermarket crisps. This suggests that just seeing an advertisement for a branded snack prompted children to eat more of the branded crisps. However, children ate less of the Walker's crisps in condition 2 than in either condition 1 or condition 3. Therefore, seeing branded peanuts led to greater consumption of the branded crisps, but not to the same amount as when the children saw the celebrity associated with the crisps.

The results showed that seeing a celebrity associated with a brand led to more consumption of that brand (Walker's) than when children saw an advertisement for a different brand (the peanuts) or for a non-food product (the toy). The celebrity had the same effect on children's eating whether or not he was actually advertising Walker's or was just appearing in a television broadcast. As Boyland et al. point out, the effect of a celebrity endorser is such that it can lead to children eating more of a product,

and in this case one that might be considered an unhealthy snack. Boyland et al. discussed the policy implications of their findings, and whether celebrities who are popular with children should be allowed to promote brands. They also advocated further research to investigate the effect of other sports celebrities advertising other products, to find out how people famously associated with sport (considered to be a healthy activity) have an effect on children's snack eating (often an unhealthy activity).

One limitation of this study was the fact that the children were given the crisps to eat very soon after seeing the advertisement. The authors did not say when the advertisement was shown during the cartoon programme, but if it was shown in the middle of the cartoon there was only about 10 minutes between the children seeing the advertisement and being offered the crisps. This does not detract from the importance of the result because children may often have access to snack food during or soon after watching a television programme, but it does mean that the long-term effect of such advertisements was not measured. There may have been less effect on children's choice of food if there had been a longer delay between seeing the advertisement and the presentation of the food. This is a common limitation in the experimental work related to advertising because often only quite short-term effects can be measured. Another limitation that applies to this and similar studies is that children were only shown a single advertisement for the product. The fact that just one viewing of an advertisement (or a celebrity) had a significant effect in Boyland et al.'s study is an important finding, but products are marketed in advertising campaigns that may involve repeated advertisements in different media, advertisements on branded goods (e.g. on clothing bearing the brand logo), and by product placement (e.g. when a brand is shown during a film or programme without being explicitly advertised). Such advertising campaigns may have more effect than a single advertisement.

Based on material in Boyland, E.J., Harrold, J.A., Dovey, T.M., Allison, M., Dobson, S., Jacobs, M-C. & Halford, J.C.G. (2013). Food choice and overconsumption: Effect of a premium sports celebrity endorser. *Journal of Pediatrics, 163*, 339–343.

Children's Understanding of Advertisements

There are two major steps in understanding advertisements: first, being able to recognize an advertisement; and second, realizing that advertisements aim to persuade people to purchase a product. The latter is referred to as understanding 'persuasive intent' (Ali & Blades, 2014).

Levin et al. (1982) found that children could usually distinguish television advertisements from programmes by about 5 years of age. Levin et al. suggested that children might be distinguishing advertisements from their distinctive characteristics, like faster pacing, voiceovers, music and jingles. If children identify advertisements by such criteria, they have some awareness of advertising, but do not necessarily appreciate the persuasive intent of an advertisement.

Children only achieve an awareness of persuasive intent when they can explicitly say that advertisements try to make the viewer go to the shops and spend money (Oates et al., 2002). The American Psychological Association (APA; Kunkel et al., 2004) reviewed the psychological research on children and advertising, and concluded that there was no evidence that children are aware of persuasive intent until about 8 years of age. The APA argued that if younger children are unable to understand the nature of advertising, any advertising aimed at such children should be banned. Although most countries do have limitations on what type of television advertisements can be broadcast when children are watching (e.g. for products like tobacco and alcohol), there are no countries that prohibit all television advertising to children (Gunter et al., 2005). Therefore, the suggestion of the APA, that television advertising to young children should be banned, has never been implemented.

The increasing importance of new media in children's lives has meant that the large sums of money spent targeting children through television marketing have been transferred to marketing in new media like the internet. Although national governments do have control over television broadcasting, the global and rapidly changing nature of the internet means that it is harder to regulate. Ali et al. (2009) investigated when children can identify advertisements on a web page. Children were shown specially designed web pages that incorporated a number of images including advertisements; examples are shown in Figures 8.2a and 8.2b. Children were asked to look at the web pages and point to any advertisements they could see. Two similar studies were carried out, one in England, with 6–10-year-olds, and one in Indonesia, with 6–12-year-olds. The findings were similar in both countries, possibly suggesting common cognitive developmental processes at work. As shown in Table 8.4, 6- and 8-year-olds were poor at identifying the advertisements. The 10- and 12-year-olds were more successful, but even these age groups identified only about three-quarters of the advertisements. Li et al. (2014) replicated Ali et al.'s study in China with similar findings. Children's generally poor ability to identify advertisements on web pages contrasts with their earlier ability to identify advertisements on television (see above). If children cannot distinguish what is and what is not an advertisement on a web page, they may confuse what is factual content and what is a marketing message.

Product Placement and Advergames

On television, a traditional advertisement and a programme cannot occur together but on a web page, advertisements are an integral part of the page; this may be one reason why children find it harder to identify internet advertisements. The integration of advertisements and other content raises particular problems, because children may not even be aware that they are

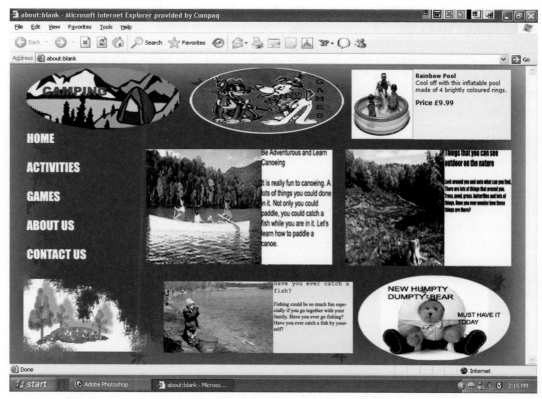

Figure 8.2a   Example of web page with two advertisements (top right and bottom right). Children have difficulty identifying what is and is not an advertisement on web pages like this.

Source: Ali, M., Blades, M., Oates, C. & Blumberg, F. (2009). Young children's ability to recognize advertisements in web page designs. *British Journal of Developmental Psychology, 27,* 71–83.

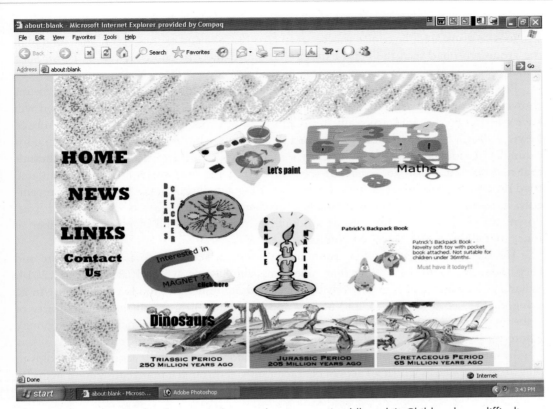

Figure 8.2b Example of web page with one advertisement (middle right). Children have difficulty identifying what is and is not an advertisement on web pages like this.

Source: Ali, M., Blades, M., Oates, C. & Blumberg, F. (2009). Young children's ability to recognize advertisements in web page designs. *British Journal of Developmental Psychology, 27,* 71–83.

Table 8.4 Percentage of web-based advertisements identified correctly as such by children of different ages in England and Indonesia.

Age (years)/percentage correct	6	8	10	12
England	28.3	46.4	73.1	n/a
Indonesia	32.3	53.8	70.4	77.7

Source: Adapted from Ali, M., Blades, M., Oates, C. & Blumberg, F. (2009). Young children's ability to recognize advertisements in web page designs. *British Journal of Developmental Psychology, 27,* 71–83.

watching an advertisement (Owen et al., 2014). Such advertising is sometimes referred to as 'product placement'—this is when marketers arrange or pay for their products to be included in films or television programmes that are aimed at children. Auty and Lewis (2004) investigated the effects of product placement by showing 7- and 12-year-olds extracts from the film *Home Alone*. Half the children were shown a scene in which a family was having a meal. During the meal Pepsi Cola was discussed; there was a bottle of Pepsi on the dinner table and some was spilt. The other half of the children were shown a similar scene from the same film, but without any reference to Pepsi. Up to 4 hours later, the children were given the opportunity to choose a drink, and the choice was between cans of Coke and cans of Pepsi. The children in the group who had seen the Pepsi extract were more likely to choose a can of Pepsi. Such findings show that product placement may have an effect on children's behaviour.

Product placement in traditional media like a television programme usually means showing a product in a positive context with the expectation that such a presentation will have an effect on the child, especially if the child sees the programme more than once (Auty & Lewis, 2004). The opportunities for product placement are more extensive in new media; for example, in video games, players can drive racing cars that have all the logos and brands that might be found on an actual car (Nelson, 2002), and while driving along a simulated road the car passes billboards and posters advertising actual products. Playing games repeatedly, and often being positively rewarded for doing so with higher point scores or 'free' downloads that may include further product information, can all increase the number of times that children experience a product.

The use of 'advergames' is a common way to attract children to a marketing site and keep them involved via a game that repeatedly emphasizes a brand (Rifon et al., 2014; Staiano & Calvert, 2014). Many advergames promote unhealthy foods to children (An & Kang, 2014; Lee et al., 2009), and Moore and Rideout (2007) found that the majority of websites designed by food and drink companies and aimed at children included advergames. About 80 such sites had a total of 50 million visits per year from young children.

To find out the effects of advergames, Pempek and Calvert (2009) asked 10-year-olds to play an advergame in which a Pacman character moved through a maze eating food items. In one version of the game, points were gained if Pacman ate healthy foods (fruit and vegetables) and lost points for eating unhealthy foods. In a second version of the game, the reverse applied and Pacman gained points for unhealthy foods and lost points for healthy foods. After the game, the children were given a choice of food to eat. The children who had played the advergame in which healthy eating led to winning were more likely to choose healthier foods to eat afterwards. Those who played the advergame in which unhealthy eating was rewarded were more likely to choose unhealthy foods afterwards. Pempek and Calvert's study showed the possible negative effect of advergames on children's food choices but also demonstrated that an advergame could be a positive influence if it was used to encourage healthy eating (Calvert et al., 2014).

Effects of Advertising on Children

Advertising has an effect on all children's lives. As discussed in the other chapters of this book, developmental researchers have always considered the effects of other people on children's development. Traditionally, 'other people' has included family, friends, peers, educators and others with whom a child interacts on a frequent or daily basis. But researchers have paid much less attention to the role of advertisers in children's lives. Ever since television was established in children's homes, advertisers have had some influence on children's lives, but with children's increasingly independent use of new media and the expansion of interactive media (like advergames), one of the 'other people' in children's everyday lives is now the marketer. Marketers communicate directly to individual children through websites, and children respond to marketers (e.g. when they type in their personal details to a website). Marketers will also monitor children's web page choices and game playing as part of their company's market research.

Stop and Think

Should we ban some of, all of, or none of the advertisements that are aimed at children?

Box 8.2 Exploring the relationship between children's knowledge of text message abbreviations and school literacy outcomes

The rapid increase in the use of mobile phones and the use of text messages is a widespread phenomenon. The use of text messaging especially by primary school children led to concerns about the effects of texting on children's literacy (Wood et al., 2014). Plester et al. (2009) pointed out that, at the time of their study, half of older primary children (8–11-year-olds) in the UK had mobile phones. This is an age group that is still learning formal ways of writing and communicating in English. If young children are still learning to read and write, will their familiarity with text messaging interfere with their ability to learn conventional words? This was the question that Plester et al. tried to answer in a study with 10–12-year-old British children.

Eighty-eight children (55 boys and 33 girls) with a mean age of 10.6 years took part in the study. Sixty-nine of the children had their own mobile phones and 14 could borrow one when they wanted. Typically, children had first acquired a phone when they were 9 years old. When asked the main use of the phones, one-third of the children said it was for texting, one-third said for talking and the rest said for playing games or taking pictures. When asked with whom they communicated most, more than half said with friends, and one-quarter said with parents. Just over half the children used predictive text sometimes, but the rest never did.

Plester et al. took several measures of the children's abilities. These included measures of their vocabulary, reading, pronunciation and conventional spelling. The children were also given 10 scenarios and asked to write the sort of text message they might use to describe each one. Two of the scenarios are given below.

> Your best friend's birthday is at the weekend, and he or she is having a party. [You decide what kind of party.] You aren't sure what you want to wear to look great, and another friend is always good at helping you decide. You also aren't sure what to get your best friend for a present, and want to see if you might buy something together with this other friend if that's okay with him or her.

> You've just seen your friend riding in his or her dad's brand new car [you decide what kind] and it's brilliant. You'd love to have a ride in it because it's a really sporty, fast one and you love cars. Your friend's dad is pretty good-natured and very proud of his car.

The children's text messages in response to these scenarios were assessed for the number and type of textisms that they used. There were 12 types of textisms.

- Shortenings (bro, sis, tues).
- Contractions (txt, plz, hmwrk).
- G-clippings (swimmin, goin, comin).
- Other clippings (hav, wil, couldn).
- Omitted apostrophes (cant, wont, dads).

- Acronyms (conventional ones like BBC, UK).
- Initialisms (ttfn, lol, tb).
- Symbols (@, &, :-o).
- Letter/number homophones (2moro, l8r, wuu2).
- Misspellings (comming, are [for our], bolinase).
- Non-conventional spelling (fone, rite, skool).
- Accent stylization (wiv, elp [help], anuva).

Overall, one-quarter of the words in the messages were textisms, and the girls used a higher proportion of textisms than did the boys. Box Table 8.2.1 shows the percentage of children who used each type of textism, and the mean number of times each textism was used over the 10 scenarios. The mean numbers are based on the number of children who used a particular textism, so, for example, 84% of the children used contractions, and on average these children used just over nine contractions in producing their 10 text messages.

Factors like the age of the child and how large a conventional vocabulary the child has might contribute to a child's ability to read words, therefore Plester et al. carried out a number of analyses which accounted for these factors. Even when these factors were taken into consideration, Plester et al. found that there was a positive correlation between the number of textisms that a child used and their word reading ability. Some forms of textism (like accent stylization and letter/number homophones) were particularly closely related to children's ability to read words.

Plester et al. pointed out that because children who were better at texting were also better at reading conventional words does not necessarily mean that texting actually contributes to children's reading ability, because other reasons might account for the correlation between better texting and better reading. But the positive correlation between texting and reading suggests that children's use of text messaging is unlikely to interfere

Box Table 8.2.1   Percentage of children using each textism, and mean number of textisms used by those children in the 10 scenarios.

	Percentage of children using textism	Mean number of textisms used by those children who employed them
Contractions	84%	9.01
Non-conventional spellings	84%	6.96
Letter/number homophones	82%	13.81
Accent stylization	81%	13.28
Omitted apostrophes	69%	3.23
Other clippings	67%	3.49
Misspellings	58%	3.04
Shortenings	54%	2.00
G-clippings	46%	2.33
Symbols	38%	4.30
Initialisms	30%	2.88
Acronyms	1%	1.00

Source: Based on Plester, B., Wood, C. & Joshi, P. (2009). Exploring the relationship between children's knowledge of text message abbreviations and school literacy outcomes. *British Journal of Developmental Psychology*, 27, 145–161.

with the development of their reading. Plester et al. carried out other analyses that showed that there was no relationship between texting and children's conventional spelling; in other words, there was no indication that children who texted more had poorer spelling ability.

Plester et al. speculated that textisms often depend on an understanding of conventional letter-sound correspondences. They suggested that using 'nite' instead of 'night', for example, does not break language conventions but reflects a creative way of using sound similarities. Even when children used symbols as a substitute for conventional words, many of the symbols used, like & or @, are already commonly used in informal written English as well as in text messages. Plester et al. also pointed out that the text messages created by the children in the study would have been completely understandable to anyone who was willing to acknowledge that texting is a reflection of spoken words with the addition of some common and recognizable symbols. Plester et al. (p. 158) concluded that there was no evidence 'for the demise of standard English among the young', but rather that 'text literacy is positively associated with standard English literacy'.

This study was one of the first to examine the relationship between texting and literacy. Since then there have been a number of similar studies (see Wood et al., 2014). These have generally confirmed Plester et al.'s original findings. Wood et al. summarize the research by emphasizing that there is no evidence to suggest that texting has a negative impact on children's spelling and writing skills. Indeed, as Plester et al. found, there is often a correlation between knowledge of textisms and knowledge of conventional spellings.

This is a good example of focused psychological research that has been designed to address a new phenomenon and one that initially caused popular concern, with suggestions that text messaging would lead to a decline in the use of 'correct' English, to a general decline of language, even to a revolution by youth against conventional norms and ultimately to the loss of civilization (see Wood et al. for some of the exaggerated claims). As the research has shown, there was no evidence at all for such suggestions.

Based on material in Plester, B., Wood, C. & Joshi, P. (2009). Exploring the relationship between children's knowledge of text message abbreviations and school literacy outcomes. *British Journal of Developmental Psychology, 27*, 145–161.

MEDIA INTERVENTIONS

Given the influence of the media, it is important that children have a good understanding of the nature of the screen media, especially any that might have negative effects. Media interventions can be considered in three categories: those that limit broadcasting to children (restrictive interventions); those that provide guidance about viewing (evaluative restriction, or co-viewing); and those that provide information about media (media literacy).

Restrictive Interventions

Most governments ban the broadcast of some types of television programmes or advertisements. This is an effective way of controlling what is viewed. Many governments also restrict what can be broadcast when children are likely to be watching, and have advisory rating systems for media like films, games and music. Examples of regulations and guidelines for various countries can be found in Calvert and Wilson (2008) and Drotner and Livingstone (2008). If programme content is only restricted, rather than banned, children may still access it.

Sometimes parents will limit what their children are watching, especially on websites. However, Kirwil et al. (2009) found that only about half of parents had rules prohibiting their children going to particular websites (usually violent or sexual ones), and only about half used software to monitor which sites their children went to. Parents will probably only attempt to limit children's viewing if they suspect children are looking at inappropriate media. But not all parents know what their children are watching. Vittrup (2009) asked 7–13-year-olds to list what they had watched on television the day before. Then their parents were asked to list what they thought their children had watched. Only a quarter of the parents correctly listed the programmes seen by their child. There may be occasions when parents are naïve about their children's media use, either because they are less familiar with media technology or because they are unaware of the nature of the sites their children are going to (Newman & Oates, 2014). For example, Cornish (2014) pointed out that parents may not be able to protect children from online advertising because the parents themselves are unaware of the marketing techniques being used or the effects that marketing may have on children.

Greater media use often results in poorer academic performance—see Moessle et al.'s (2010) two studies summarized on pp. 272–273. Therefore Moessle et al. also investigated whether reducing the time children spent with media would benefit their school performance. Moessle et al. examined approximately 1,000 children in 40 German primary schools. Half the children (those in the intervention group) received lessons about media. The other half (those in the control group) did not receive any training about media. Over a period of 3 years (from 3rd to 5th grade), the intervention group received nearly 40 lessons about media use, which included children reading stories about media use, keeping logs of what they watched and agreeing on an appropriate amount to watch. There was particular emphasis on limiting computer games and reducing all electronic media use to no more than an hour a day. As well as the lessons for children, parents were actively involved in the study, and were encouraged to make clear rules about media use and prohibit televisions and games consoles in their children's bedrooms.

During the period of Moessle et al.'s study there was, in fact, an overall increase in the number of children with media in their bedrooms. But the increase in the number of bedroom televisions and games consoles was lower for the children in the intervention group than in the control group, and took place later. The largest increase in bedroom media was in the 3rd grade for the control group, but not until the 4th grade for the intervention group. Therefore, the intervention had a small effect in delaying the bedroom use of media. There were large differences in how much media the two groups watched. Although all the children watched more television in the 5th grade than in the 3rd grade, the increase was four times greater for the children in the control group. Similarly, the length of time spent on computer games increased for all the children, but in each grade the children in the intervention group spent less time playing games than did the children in the control group. The focus of Moessle et al.'s study was on school performance. Compared to expected school performance children's marks for both the intervention and control groups actually declined during the course of the study, but the decline was less for the intervention group.

It would seem that Moessle et al.'s intervention did have positive effects in reducing children's media use and this may have resulted in better school performance. It should be noted that Moessle et al. carried out a well-planned and long-term intervention involving both teachers and parents, which included both restrictive measures *and* media literacy training. It may be the case that for media interventions to be effective, they have to be quite elaborate (e.g. Bickham & Slaby, 2012).

Co-viewing

A second form of intervention is co-viewing, when parents watch the same media as their children (Figure 8.3) and provide comments about what they are watching together (Borzekowski & Robinson, 2007; Fisch et al., 2008). For example, when watching a violent programme, a parent might want to emphasize that violence is rarely rewarded and that victims of violence really do get seriously hurt in real life. Such interventions can reduce children's aggressive behaviour (Nathanson & Cantor, 2000). Parents may also, for instance, want to explain special effects, discuss what is real or fantasy on the screen, counter stereotypes, or warn children about the bias in advertisements. Parents can also explain how different media are produced, who makes media and who profits from media. But as the topics discussed become more general and less specific to the programme being co-viewed, this type of mediation is close to what is usually referred to as media literacy.

Figure 8.3   One form of media intervention is co-viewing, when parents watch the same media as their children and provide comments about what they are watching together.

Source: Image copyright Vinicius Tupinamba. Used under licence from Shutterstock.com.

Media Literacy

Media literacy is more likely to be carried out in formal educational programmes that teach children not only about media content but also about different types of media, media techniques and the role of media in the economy. All this is with the aim of making children more informed, and therefore potentially more critical viewers. Chakroff and Nathanson (2008) reviewed a number of media literacy programmes aimed at children. They concluded that such interventions do increase children's factual knowledge about media, and may change children's attitudes (e.g. about violent content), but there is less clear evidence about the effects of intervention programmes on children's actual behaviour. Most intervention programmes have focused on television and there has been little research into the effectiveness of interventions about the internet and other new media (O'Neill & Hagan, 2009), and very little research into the design of interventions to help children become more aware of specific aspects of media, for example, to help them to better understand how they are targeted by food advertisers (Blumberg et al., 2014b). Teaching children how to be critical and safe users of the internet is still a new challenge for researchers.

CHAPTER SUMMARY

- Media use plays an important but rapidly changing part in the lives of children.
- Over the last decade, the use of new media (mobile phones and the internet) has come to occupy a very important part of children's experience.
- Although research on the effects of new media is growing, there is much more research available on traditional media, especially television.
- There can be many positive aspects of television; the use of programmes like *Sesame Street* provides an example.
- There can also be negative aspects of watching television programmes; for example, they can promote stereotypes. Violent television programmes lead to more violent behaviour, although the strength and generalizability of this link are still debated.
- The use of computer and video games has increased rapidly and such games can have both positive and negative effects.
- The increasing use of advergames and product placement techniques raises important implications about marketing, especially food marketing, to children.
- Interventions to enhance children's experience with media include restrictive interventions, co-viewing and education for media literacy.
- Although this chapter is in sections that largely reflect technological distinctions (e.g. television, computer games, the internet), because researchers have usually worked within a specific domain, these distinctions are disappearing. All children and all age groups, including the very youngest children, will have immediate and continuous access to all media. As yet, we are a long way from having theories that integrate children's media experience with the theories of development described elsewhere in this book, but as children's lives are ever more mediated by their experience through a screen, such theories will become increasingly necessary.

DISCUSSION POINTS

1. Overall, do screen media have a positive or negative effect on the lives of children and young people?
2. Who should control what children see on television and in other media?
3. How can interventions be designed to help children understand more about media?
4. How will the media world that children experience in 5 years' time be different from what it was 5 years ago?

FURTHER READING

- The media world and children's position in that world are always changing rapidly. Any specific data about children's access to media, and how they use media, are likely to be out of date very quickly. To find the most recent information, it is best to look at websites that include reports on children and media use. For example, for the UK see Ofcom (www.ofcom.org.uk/) and for the US see the Kaiser Foundation (http://kff.org/). Most governments maintain websites that include information about media use and media regulation in their own countries.

- A good review of most of the research related to television can be found in van Evra, J. (2004). *Television and child development* (3rd ed.). Mahwah, NJ: Lawrence Erlbaum. The role of the internet in children's lives is described in Livingstone, S. (2009). *Children and the internet*. Cambridge: Polity Press. A book that covers the positive aspects of computer games is Blumberg, F. (2014). *Learning by playing: Video gaming in education*. Oxford: Oxford University Press. For examples of research into violent games, see Anderson, C.A., Gentile, D.A. & Buckley, K.E. (2007). *Violent video game effects on children and adolescents*. Oxford: Oxford University Press.

- A definitive review of some of the television advertising research can be found in Kunkel, D. et al. (2004). *Report of the American Psychological Association task force on advertising and children: Psychological issues in the increasing commercialization of childhood*, at the APA website, www.apa.org/. A more recent publication covering all aspects of advertising to children is Blades, M., Oates, C., Blumberg, F. & Gunter, B. (2014). *Advertising to children: New directions, new media*. Basingstoke: Palgrave Macmillan.

- Calvert, S. & Wilson, B. (2008). *The handbook of children, media and development*. Oxford: Blackwell, is an excellent and comprehensive encyclopaedia that covers most aspects of children and media, particularly in the US.

- Articles and research papers about children and media can be found in a number of different types of journals. For example, a study of computers in the classroom might appear in an educational journal, an applied psychology journal, a developmental psychology journal, a sociology journal or a journal about media and communication. Papers in different types of journals may address the same issues, but often come from different research backgrounds and take different theoretical and methodological approaches. These differences should be kept in mind when comparing the findings from different fields. Some journals are devoted to research about children and media. Two examples of journals that publish brief and readable papers are: *Journal of Children and Media* (Routledge), which has articles on all aspects of media, and *Young Consumers* (Emerald), which includes papers on marketing to children. Other journals may sometimes have special issues dedicated to children and the media—special issues are a good way to keep up with this rapidly changing area of developmental research; for example, for papers on children and computer games, see *Zeitschrift für Psychologie* (2013), vol. 221(2), pp. 65–118. For papers about children and advertising see *International Journal of Advertising* (2014), vol. 33(3), pp. 429–616.

CHAPTER
9

Helping Others and Moral Development

CHAPTER OUTLINE

- The Development of Prosocial Behaviour
- Factors Influencing Prosocial Behaviour
- The Development of Moral Reasoning
- The Age of Moral Responsibility in the Context of Youth Crime
- Can We Teach Moral Values?

In this chapter, we look at the development of prosocial behaviour in children, contrasting experimental studies with observational studies and those carried out in naturalistic conditions. We consider the factors that influence prosocial behaviour in the family and at school. We review studies that document gender and cross-cultural differences in the emergence of prosocial behaviour. Then we move on to consider major explanatory models of the development of moral reasoning in children. We contrast the influential stage theories of Piaget and Kohlberg and review later revisions that have been made, including the social-cognitive domain approach to moral development proposed by Turiel and Smetana. We end by describing some educational interventions that have been designed to teach children moral values, including the PATHS curriculum.

THE DEVELOPMENT OF PROSOCIAL BEHAVIOUR

In a broad sense, prosocial behaviour can be taken to mean helping, comforting and sharing on the part of one person to another. Grusec et al. (2002, p. 2) define prosocial behaviour as:

> Any voluntary, intentional action that produces a positive or beneficial outcome for the recipient regardless of whether that action is costly to the donor, neutral in its impact, or beneficial. In this sense, it is distinguished from 'altruism' which clearly implies that assistance to others came at some cost to the donor.

Although most people believe that it is wrong to harm others, there is considerable ambiguity around the concept of acting prosocially to help others. Individuals in need may respond negatively to being helped; on the other hand, an over-caring approach to others can be damaging to the self-concept of the helper. As above, it is useful to distinguish between *prosocial behaviour*, which can occur for both selfish and unselfish reasons, and *altruistic behaviour*, in which there is no intentional benefit to the helper and where in some cases there may even be disadvantage or danger. Carlo (2006, p. 555) proposes a more detailed classification with six common categories of 'prosocial tendencies'.

1. *Altruistic tendencies* encompass actions intended to benefit others with an explicit cost to the self
2. *Dire* tendencies result from a response to extreme situations
3. *Emotional* tendencies result from a response to affectively laden situations
4. *Public* tendencies are beneficial actions conducted in front of others
5. *Anonymous* tendencies are actions carried out without other people's knowledge
6. *Compliant* tendencies refer to prosocial behaviours that are requested by others.

 Stop and Think

How helpful do you find Carlo's six-fold classification of prosocial behaviour?

Some researchers are greatly concerned about such definitional matters (e.g. Carlo, 2006; Eisenberg & Fabes, 1998), whereas others are happy to label helping and sharing behaviours as prosocial, largely irrespective of context, intent or reward. You may like to compare these definitions of prosocial and altruistic behaviour with ethologists' accounts of altruism in animals given in Chapter 2; they are similar (see also Verbeek, 2006).

Some psychologists have used the concept of costs and benefits in an attempt to explain why it is that apparently self-sacrificing behaviour—where the helper incurs a 'cost'—persists and is not eliminated through natural selection. McGuire (1994), for example, points out that helping often occurs between people who are known to one another, so helping has the benefit of enhancing one's reputation in the social group. Despite the costs, McGuire argues, there are also likely to be benefits to those who act altruistically, such as enhanced self-esteem, the development of empathy and the internalization of socially acceptable norms of cooperation and support.

Other researchers, for example, Trevarthen and Logotheti (1989), have considered the *intrinsic* value of prosocial behaviour from the earliest years of life and argue that, as social beings, we have inborn motivation to form cooperative relationships with one another; strategies for reaching out to others in a spirit of mutual trust and giving are established and developed initially in the context of the family, and children learn how to act towards others by engaging in shared activities and routines with those who are close to them. Eisenberg and Fabes (1998) argue that there is substantial evidence to support the view that children and adolescents often spontaneously express prosocial behaviour intended to help others. From this perspective, proso-cial human qualities are universal, although the ways in which they are expressed will vary from culture to culture, and with age. And, as we have seen in Chapter 4, when attachments within the family are insecure, the capacity to relate in a trusting, empathic way towards others may be impaired where the child has internalized a working model of relationships rooted in the experience of *not* being helped at times of need. It would seem, too, that there is great value in attempting the complex task of classifying different types of prosocial behaviour, just as social scientists have found it helpful to classify different types of aggression (see Chapter 10).

Social practice in Western society has emphasized the role of children as *recipients* of help, when the reality is that there is an enormous, often untapped, potential for harnessing children's capacity to respond prosocially towards peers (Foot et al., 1990). We are only at the threshold of realizing the range of ways in which children could be sources of practical help and emotional support for one another, and so further influence their own and their peers' cognitive and social development. We need to look at prosocial and altruistic behaviour in a wide social context if we are to understand it in all its complexity. One study (Eisenberg, 1983) found that children (aged 7–17 years) clearly differentiated among people whom they might help. When faced with hypothetical moral dilemmas, they indicated that they would be more likely to help family than non-family members, friends rather than non-friends, people they knew rather than people they did not know, people more similar to themselves in race or religion and non-criminals rather than criminals.

Developmental psychologists have known for some time that children are capable of demonstrating prosocial behaviour from a very early age. In all societies, children enter into what Tomasello (2003) calls an *intersubjective world*. From around 18 to 36 months of age, as we will see in Chapter 12, the child becomes increasingly conversational. Through myriad communications with caregivers and peers, the child comes to learn about the perspectives of others and demonstrates a growing capacity for developing a theory of mind(Chapter 15).

Experience of 'internal state' language enables the child to understand their own and others' internal states over time (Meins et al., 2006). Also as we saw in Chapter 6, throughout the preschool period, the child is learning about feelings and what causes them. These experiences are at the heart of mind-mindedness and mark the important transition away from egocentric patterns of thought towards prosocial behaviour.

Carlo et al. (2003), on the basis of their classification of prosocial behaviour into six tendencies, developed a measure of prosocial tendencies (the PTM). They found that young people in mid-adolescence reported more anonymous and altruistic helping than did those in early adolescence. This finding and other studies suggest that, when they adopt anonymous and altruistic forms of helping, adolescents are using a more sophisticated capacity to take the perspective of others. This interpretation is further confirmed by Carlo and colleagues' finding that, in comparison with younger adolescents, altruistically inclined young people in late adolescence were more likely to report that they acted according to moral principles and that they were concerned to understand the perspectives of others. They were less likely to report that they acted selfishly to gratify their own needs, or that they only acted morally to gain the approval of others. Carlo (2006) points out that children and young people may also become aware of the benefits that arise from being prosocial, such as having enhanced feelings of well-being and developing a wider network of friends and associates. This argument is supported by studies of especially altruistic young people, such as peer supporters, who frequently report the emotional satisfaction that they experience in the course of helping others (Cowie et al., 2002). See also Box 9.2 where Ruck and Tenenbaum (2014) demonstrate the multifaceted nature of young people's thinking about moral issues. In this study, adolescents used moral reasoning in some domains but social-conventional thinking in others, so indicating how important it is to take account of the social context within which young people think and behave.

As Grusec et al. (2002) point out, children engage in prosocial behaviours for a variety of reasons. An obvious one relates to *empathy*. Many psychologists distinguish between *cognitive empathy* and *affective empathy*. Cognitive empathy refers to understanding someone else's feelings or emotional state (as discussed in Chapters 6 and 15). Here we are more concerned with affective empathy; if a person sees someone who is sad and then feels sad themselves, they are experiencing affective empathy with the other person. Affective empathy usually leads to *sympathy*. Sympathy, however, is an emotional response that consists of feelings of concern or sorrow *for* the other person (if they are sad). Another reason to engage in prosocial behaviour concerns the urge to adhere to a social or cultural norm. We explore each of these in the sections that follow, where we describe both experimental and naturalistic studies of children's prosocial behaviour, explore the emergence of prosocial action in a range of settings at home and in school, and discuss the effect of social context and culture on its emergence.

Experimental Studies

Early experiments studied the impact on a child who observes an adult demonstrating or 'modelling' a helpful or altruistic act. One study (Grusec et al., 1978) compared the 'modelling' condition with direct exhortation by adults to give to a charitable cause (here called the 'preaching' condition) for its effectiveness as a technique. The participants were 96 boys and girls aged 8–10 years. Children came individually to a research caravan in a school yard to play a marble-bowling game in which they could win marbles (the game was fixed so that all the children won the same number of marbles). Nearby was a poster reading, 'Help poor children: Marbles buy gifts' over a bowl with some marbles already in it. An adult (of the same sex as the child) played the game first; she then either exhorted the child to give half her marbles or said nothing (two preaching conditions), and then either gave or did not give away half her own marbles (two modelling or performance conditions). The child was then left alone to play, but was observed through a one-way mirror to see how many marbles she donated. It was found that most children who saw the adult give marbles did so themselves, irrespective of preaching, whereas few children who saw the adult not giving marbles did so, although preaching did have some effect here. The children were asked to play the game again 3 weeks later and, irrespective of previous conditions, few of them donated any marbles. This and other studies suggest that the behaviour children actually observe in others may be more important than moral exhortations from them, though both do have some effect.

 Stop and Think

To what extent do these studies really measure altruism? If a young person gains a benefit, such as a sense of emotional satisfaction, from helping others, are they still acting altruistically?

The experimental design of these studies enables us to make fairly certain inferences; for example, that modelling (performance) by an adult increases the likelihood of altruism in a child who is watching. However, one could criticize these experiments for being rather artificial. The experimenters are unfamiliar, the situations are contrived and some deception is involved. Is it really helpfulness and altruism that is being measured in these settings, or is it just some kind of conformity to adult demands?

Observational Studies

Many of the problems inherent in such experimental studies of prosocial behaviour can be overcome by observing children in natural settings. Zahn-Waxler and Radke-Yarrow (1982) described a study of 24 children that used a combination of cross-sectional and longitudinal design to span the age range from around 12 to 30 months. These researchers relied on mothers' recordings. Mothers were asked to report on their children's response to events in which negative emotions were expressed. Later, Zahn-Waxler (2001) observed the empathic responses of toddlers aged 14, 20, 24 and 36 months to an adult pretending to be injured. There was an increase with age in the children's expressions of concern, whether facial, vocal or gestural. On the basis of these observations, it is possible to identify progressive levels of empathy on the part of the target child towards another's emotion: *personal distress*, where the child was emotionally affected by the incident; *emotional contagion*, where the child displayed an emotion in sympathy with the other person; and *egocentric empathy*, where the child offered support to the other person in the form of something that they would find comforting themselves, such as a favourite toy or blanket. Two noticeable changes were found between the younger children (aged up to about 20 months) and the older children (20–30 months). The younger children often orientated to someone's distress, and often cried, fretted or whimpered themselves, but only seldom acted prosocially. Such prosocial behaviour as there was usually took the form of simply touching or patting the victim, or presenting objects. Prosocial behaviour was much more likely in the older children, however, and occurred in about one-third of all incidents reported. It took a variety of forms, such as reassurance ('You'll be all right'), combative altruism (hitting an aggressor), giving objects (e.g. bandages, comfort objects) or getting help from a third party. This developmental pattern was similar whether the child was a bystander to the distress or had caused it.

From this study it is clear that children below 3 years of age can show some forms of prosocial behaviour. This is especially so after about 20 months, which is when sensori-motor development is completed (see Chapter 13); that is, when children understand cause–effect relations and the distinction between themselves and other people (see Chapter 6). Before this age, children often seek comfort as much for themselves as for the other person, but after about 20 months they are increasingly aware that the distress is in the other person (and, somewhat later, of whether they have caused it or not), and act more appropriately.

Grusec et al. (2002) noted that the general ability of a child to take the perspective of others affects their capacity to demonstrate emotional responsiveness to the distress of another in a specific context. For example, children who regularly and intensely express negative emotions tend to demonstrate less empathy and more personal upset when faced with the distress of another. By contrast, children who are able to regulate their own emotions effectively show more empathic responsiveness and less personal upset towards another person's distress. (See also the study by Davidov and Grusec (2006) in the next section.)

FACTORS INFLUENCING PROSOCIAL BEHAVIOUR

Parenting

We have seen that parents do not stand idly by when their child does, or does not, show helpful or altruistic behaviour; the evidence is that they often intervene, as do teachers and peers. What effect do such interventions have? We have also seen that interventions may take the form of reinforcement (e.g. praise) or punishment for not being helpful, modelling of altruistic behaviour or moral exhortation. Are some techniques more effective than others? And what does the child contribute to this process?

 Stop and Think

What is the most effective way in which a parent should encourage their child to act prosocially? Does punishment teach children to be 'good'?

There is reasonably consistent evidence to indicate that children's tendency to respond with empathy and sympathy towards another person's distress is learned through the process of socialization (for a detailed review see Eisenberg et al., 2006). Parents who are empathic, who score highly on perspective-taking tasks and who respond sensitively to their children's needs are more likely to have children who are high in empathy towards others (Kochanska et al., 1999; Meins et al., 2006; van der Mark et al., 2002). Davidov and Grusec (2006) investigated the linkages between two different aspects of positive parenting—*responsiveness to distress* and *warmth*—and the social-emotional functioning of children in a sample of 106 6–8-year-olds. For both mothers and fathers, responsiveness to distress was positively and significantly related to more effective regulation of negative emotions on the part of the children. Mothers' responsiveness to distress also predicted children's empathic capacity and their prosocial behaviour towards distressed others. By contrast, warmth did not emerge as a significant predictor of either of these child outcomes but maternal warmth did predict children's adaptive regulation of positive affect as well as boys' (but not girls') peer group acceptance. The authors concluded that warmth and responsiveness to distress are distinguishable aspects of positive parenting and should not (as is often the case) be collapsed into one quality. They recommended a differentiated approach to positive parenting in order to discover more about the pathways through which parents can promote their child's competencies by being sensitive and caring in different ways.

Eisenberg et al. (2006, p. 526) reviewed a number of studies confirming the proposition that there is a strong relationship between empathy-related responsiveness and children's prosocial behaviour. They concluded that children who experience empathy for others' feelings are more likely to understand that person's feelings and respond in a sensitive way towards them. Conversely, children who are negatively aroused when exposed to others' feelings are likely to be self-focused in their social behaviour and less socially competent. This was confirmed by, for example, a study by Gill and Calkins (2003), who found that aggressive toddlers tended to lack concern for others. This extensive line of research provides strong evidence that the ability to maintain an optimal level of arousal in response to the distress of another is conducive to high empathy and relatively low personal distress, whereas becoming over-aroused leads to high personal distress and low empathy.

There are clear links with secure parent–child attachment (see Chapter 4 on attachment theory), with securely attached children demonstrating greater empathy towards their peers. Krevans and Gibbs (1996) also found that, when parents regularly encouraged their children to reflect on the consequences of their behaviour and how it might affect other people, there was a greater likelihood that their children would show empathy for others and demonstrate more prosocial behaviour. Grusec and Goodnow (1994) suggested that this process occurs in two stages through the internalization of parental values.

1. The child's accurate perception of the parent's message through frequent and consistent expression of that value in a form that is appropriate for the child's cognitive level
2. Acceptance of that value by experiencing it as reasonable and appropriate, by being willing to listen to the message and by having some sense of self-generated action.

From this perspective, punishment for failing to act prosocially would not be effective, since it would be perceived by the child as unfair. However, where parents regularly demonstrated empathy for that child, and where the child was happy to respond to parental reasoning and experienced little threat to their own autonomy by helping another, then the internalization of prosocial values was more likely to occur. Similarly, Dunn (2006), on the basis of her extensive in-depth observations of children in naturalistic settings, maintained that positive experiences within the parent–child relationship have a profound impact on children's moral development. She argued that it is the affective dynamics of intimate family relationships that provide strong motivation for children to understand moral issues and conventional rules.

So, what can we learn from situations in real-life settings where children are regularly punished for misdemeanours? An extreme example is demonstrated in the study by Luthar and Suchman (2000), who investigated the social and emotional development of children up to 16 years who were being raised by heroin-addicted mothers. Children in these types of household we are significantly more likely to display behavioural and mental health difficulties than children being reared by parents who are not addicted to drugs. Luthar and Suchman found that many of the mothers reported having been exposed as children to inadequate parenting, including excessively lax or excessively punitive disciplinary styles, as well as physical, emotional and sexual abuse. Such adversities (see Chapter 18) deeply affected their capacity to function as effective parents, and they in turn demonstrated tendencies to use harsh, authoritarian discipline and to maltreat their children.

 Stop and Think

What is the most effective way in which a parent can encourage their child to act prosocially? Praise? Modelling? Moral exhortation? Punishment?

At the same time, and in line with the findings of Werner and Smith (1982) (whose longitudinal study is discussed in Chapter 18), Luthar and Suchman (2000) were prepared to work with the potential resilience and coping strategies of this challenging group. They had already found that addicted mothers, despite their ineffective parenting styles, were nevertheless (and contrary to expectation) highly concerned about the emotional well-being of their children. The researchers devised a developmentally informed programme of psychotherapy, the Relational Psychotherapy Mothers' Group (RPMG), which focused on the following four aspects.

1. *Supportive therapists' stance:* this encompassed a client-centred approach (Rogers, 1951) based on constructs of acceptance, empathy and genuineness and designed to meet the developmental needs of the mothers themselves.
2. *Interpersonal, relational focus:* this aspect had its roots in gender-sensitive perspectives on women and addressed the interpersonal isolation and stress that featured in these addicted women's lives.
3. *Group treatment:* these sessions were led by a clinical psychologist assisted by a drugs counsellor from the methadone clinic, so bringing expertise across diverse domains, including child development, women's psychology and addiction-related issues. To accommodate to the chaotic schedules of the mothers, these sessions were offered in a flexible way and made allowances for the fact that the parents were often unable to attend regularly.
4. *Insight-oriented parenting skill facilitation:* instead of 'instructing' the mothers about appropriate parenting, the therapists encouraged them to explore their own strengths, as well as the limitations of their current practices, and guided them towards using more effective approaches. The goals were reached through discussions, role-play and brainstorming exercises. This discovery-based learning approach empowered the mothers, acknowledged their wish to become better parents and fostered the positive development of their families.

Stop and Think

How similar are these therapeutic methods to the mind-mindedness approach proposed by Meins and her colleagues (see Chapter 6) to foster prosocial behaviour?

The results were very encouraging. In comparison with similar mothers receiving standard drugs counselling intervention, the RPMG mothers fared much more positively in most of the parenting domains measured in the study. At the end of treatment, RPMG mothers displayed significantly lower maltreatment scores based on reports by both mothers and their children; they felt more satisfied with their roles as parents and showed marginally lower levels of depression; they also viewed their children's psychosocial difficulties as less severe. The children's self-reports reflected these positive changes. Most of these improvements were maintained at the time of a follow-up study 6 months later, with the exception, however, of children's reports of mothers' maltreatment risk. This study indicated the value of working with the mothers' psychological and parenting concerns in order to address the needs of extremely vulnerable children over the long term (see also the discussion of Sure Start outcomes in Chapter 18).

Siblings

Experiences with siblings are also important in promoting prosocial behaviour because of the age differences between them. This has implications for the emergence of sensitivity and empathy towards others. There were some quite striking age consistencies reported in a longitudinal study on siblings (Dunn & Kendrick, 1982; see also Chapter 5); for example, Dunn and Kendrick found that children (aged 1–3 years) who showed friendly interest and concern for a new baby in the first 3 weeks after birth were also likely to respond with concern if their younger sibling was hurt or distressed at a follow-up 6 years later (the correlation was .42, significant at the .05 level). They also noticed interplay between helping and rivalry. The help that children offered their siblings was not necessarily appreciated by the recipients! The giving of help by an older child could, for example, elicit anger from a younger sibling.

When Dunn et al. (1991) followed up the siblings who had been observed as preschoolers, they found that there were links between the quality of the relationships between the siblings in the preschool period and the children's behaviour at a later stage. Those who had grown up with a sibling who was unfriendly or aggressive were more likely as adolescents to have emotional difficulties in their relationships with others than were those whose siblings had been warm and affectionate towards them. Children who perceived that their sibling was receiving more attention and affection from the mother were more likely to show aggressive or difficult behaviour in childhood and adolescence. It appeared that relative differences in how loved a young person feels have an influence on how socially adjusted they are. Dunn and her colleagues suggested that the growth of social understanding develops out of the child's experience of balancing his or her preoccupation with self against responsiveness to the feelings and emotions of others. Dunn (1995) argued that participation in the moral discourse of the family begins very early on in the child's life and that prosocial behaviour can only be fully understood if we consider it in the context of the dynamic web of family relationships.

Dunn is convinced that the growth of understanding involves more than 'an unfolding of cognitive abilities' and that 'self-concern and affective experience play central roles in the interactions in which moral and social rules are articulated and fostered, and the development of the child's theory of mind' (see Chapter 15) (Dunn, 1995, p. 341). In other words, the complexity of a young child's social understanding and awareness of others' mental states is closely linked to the nature of their family interactions and interpersonal relationships. Dunn (2004b, p. 42) proposed that children's views on the needs and rights of their friends may be different from their views on what is the right way to behave towards members of the family. She quotes an extract from an interview with 4-year-old Kevin to illustrate.

Interviewer: What about if you took a toy from your sister? Would that be OK or not OK?

Kevin: (cheerfully) OK . . . because she's my sister and I hate her guts . . . well I don't actually hate her, but . . .

Interviewer: How about if you took a toy from Jeff?

Kevin: (solemnly) I would never do it. Because he's my best friend. My best, best, best friend!

Dunn's research suggested that psychologists should place more emphasis on social understanding as a phenomenon that *emerges from* relationships rather than as an *individual* characteristic of a particular child. The study of siblings in the family context has highlighted the importance of differences in family discourse about the social world in influencing the nature of a child's social development. For example, children who grow up in families where there is a great deal of discussion about feelings and causality perform better than other children on assessments of social understanding 14 months later. Dunn (1992) suggested that the foundations for such qualities as caring, consideration and kindness are well established by the age of 3 years.

> For a young child whose own goals and interests are often at odds with—and frustrated by—others in the family, it is clearly adaptive to begin to understand those other family members and the social rules of the shared family world. The study of siblings has highlighted why it is important that social understanding should be high on the developmental agenda.

School and the Peer Group

Boulton et al. (1999) found that young people who have a reciprocated best friend are much more likely to be protected from aggressive acts of social exclusion on the part of the peer group. The implications of this finding are that, in the context of a reciprocated friendship, young people are motivated to help one another against peer relationship difficulties (see Chapter 5). This confirms the view that vulnerable young people can be protected by appropriate befriending interventions, but that in the absence of such support they cannot rely on their peers to act prosocially. The influence of peer group values on young people is very important (Craig & Pepler, 1995; Ruck & Tenenbaum, 2014 in Box 9.2; see also Chapter 10 on bullying and social exclusion). A study by Bosacki et al. (2006) illustrated how adolescents may passively condone antisocial behaviour and fail to act prosocially in defence of vulnerable members of the peer group. The researchers were interested to find out from children what their moral views were on how bullies justify their actions, as well as how they portrayed the emotions experienced by bullies, victims and (if they included them) bystanders. They asked 82 children aged between 8 and 12 years to draw a bullying episode. Once the drawing was complete, they asked the children the following questions.

- In your picture, how do you think the bully feels?
- What is the bully thinking?
- Why would he or she want to bully?
- How do you think the one being picked on in your drawing feels?
- What is he or she thinking?
- Why is he or she being picked on?
- What would he or she do so that he or she is not picked on?

Although the majority of the drawings depicted a pair, the number of characters in the bullying scenarios increased amongst the older children, indicating that, as they get older, children develop a view of bullying as a more complex, social process involving bystanders in different roles. Most of the drawings showed the bully as bigger than the victim (40%) or the same size (57%). Most of the bullies were portrayed as smiling (78%) whereas victims tended to be crying or upset (48%). In the older children's drawings, the victims were given voice bubbles much less frequently than in the younger children's drawings, dropping from 53% among the 8-year-olds to 40% for 10-year-olds and 23% for 12-year-olds. The authors noted that this 'silencing' of the victims is also expressed in the passive acceptance of the situation, which appeared more frequently among the older children. When interviewed about their drawings, 70% of children indicated that bullies had psychological motives for behaving the way they did (for example, wanting to make someone sad), often in a sadistic manner for the fun of it, confirmed by the fact that so many of the bullies were smiling in the drawings. The children also commented that 'being different' was a feature common to many bullied children rather than the possession of a skills deficit.

 Stop and Think

Do you agree with Bosacki et al. that the 'silencing' of the cartoon victims indicates that older children accept bullying as a fact of life?

These are not surprising findings, but they do put helping behaviour in a social context. Rogers and Tisak (1996) found that 6-, 8- and 10-year-olds, when asked to explain peers' responses to aggression, reasoned out of a concern for the well-being of all peers involved in a conflict and showed awareness of the relationship between victim and perpetrator. Yet, despite their awareness of the injustice of bullying behaviour, many young people bow to group pressure and remain inactive. It may well be that the most effective ways of promoting prosocial behaviour are those that strengthen children's altruistic tendencies and also appeal to the child's developing sense of reasoning or justice.

The school is one arena in which these ideas about training young people to act prosocially can be put to the test. There is a great deal of evidence supporting the idea that, in order to foster prosocial behaviour in educational settings, teachers must incorporate values of trust and cooperation into the whole school community, and not simply 'teach' prosocial behaviour as a series of separate lessons, such as a once-a-week discussion of social and moral issues (Cowie & Jennifer, 2007; Foot et al., 1990; Hertz-Lazarowitz & Miller, 1992; Howe, 2010).

Peer Support Systems in Schools

In order to create a structure in which prosocial behaviour can be enhanced, many schools are developing systems of peer support to supplement the work of pastoral care staff (Boulton, 2014; Cowie et al., 2002, 2008; Cowie & Wallace, 2000). Peer support systems take many forms, but there are three broad approaches.

1. *Befriending/mentoring:* schemes in which specially trained pupils support peers who are, for example, new to a school or have particular learning difficulties. In some cases (as in buddying or peer tutoring), pupils are paired with another pupil. In others, befrienders look out for pupils who may be socially excluded or bullied during break times, and offer companionship and try to integrate them into appropriate friendship groups.
2. *Mediation/conflict resolution:* these schemes offer a structured method for empowering young people to defuse interpersonal disagreements among their peers, including bullying, racist name-calling, fighting and quarrelling. These methods are reported to result in a substantial reduction in the incidence of aggressive behaviour. During the mediation, the peer supporters are responsible for facilitating a resolution of the conflict and for working out a joint solution. For a more detailed description see Box 9.2.
3. *Counselling:* these schemes extend befriending and mediation approaches into interventions based more overtly on counselling models. Training is often carried out by a qualified counsellor or psychotherapist, who will offer supporters a wider range of counselling skills. Supervision is modelled on professional counselling supervision, usually facilitated by a person with knowledge of experiential work. These approaches are usually implemented through a system of formal referral soon after the request for help has been received and can include telephone helplines, individual meetings or small group sessions.

Given the appropriate training and supervision, peer helpers demonstrate that they are able to offer themselves as a resource to peers troubled by experiences of victimization, rejection, isolation, relationship difficulties and other problems common during childhood and adolescence. Other studies have confirmed that this prosocial behaviour has benefits for the helpers, as well as for those who seek help and for the school as a whole (Boulton, 2014; Cowie & Wallace, 2000).

Sex Differences in Prosocial Behaviour

Researchers have not documented particular gender differences in the emergence of prosocial behaviour during the preschool stage. At the same time, it is widely believed that girls are more prosocial than boys, and any studies in the school years seem to confirm this view. Cowie et al. (2002), in their longitudinal study of peer support in 35 secondary schools, found that girls (80%) regularly outnumbered boys (20%) in the ranks of peer supporters. In interviews, 80 peer supporters described threats to boys' sense of masculinity if they participated in caring activities such as peer support.

It is seen as wimpy . . . Yeah, they (boys) dropped out—peer pressure.

(13-year-old girl peer supporter)

We used to get called 'queer supporters'.

(15-year-old boy peer supporter)

Only a minority of boys felt strong enough to challenge the stereotype.

When I became a peer supporter, we all thought it unmanly, but now all my friends think it brilliant. There are none of my mates that call me names because they know that you are there and you can help them, and I have helped a lot of my friends.

(15-year-old boy peer supporter)

There was no evidence to suggest that boys were incapable of acting in the role of peer supporters. In fact, in an earlier study in single-sex boys' schools (Cowie, 2000), teachers who organized peer support schemes were inundated with offers of help. But in the context of coeducational schools, boys appeared to find it difficult to withstand the pressure from peers to maintain a distance from caring activities. Eisenberg and Fabes (1998) found that there was a large discrepancy between observations of gender differences in real-life prosocial behaviour and experimental findings. They suggested that, to some extent, gender differences found in empirical studies may be due to children's conformity to gender stereotypes rather than their actual behaviour and emotions.

Similarly, Frosh et al. (2002) found that it was very difficult for boys to stray outside the strict rules provided by their peer group culture on what it is to be 'masculine'. The boys in this study reported in one-to-one interviews (but much less frequently in group interviews with other boys present) that they had to find strategies for dealing with the sanctions of bullying, ostracism and name-calling meted out mercilessly to those who did not fit. The most common terms of abuse concerned being 'gay', but boys who were studious, sensitive or in some way emotionally vulnerable did not fare any better at the hands of the peer group. Even boys who were willing to defend ostracized peers had to be careful in case the group turned on them. Yet most of the boys in the study had a clear awareness of moral codes and understood the need for close supportive relationships. Possibly the culture has changed since these studies were done. With regard to their willingness to make use of a peer support service in schools, Boulton (2014) found no gender differences, in contrast to previous studies where it was found that girls were more likely to confide in a peer supporter than boys.

Björkqvist et al. (2000) argued that girls are better at peaceful conflict resolution, just as they are more skilled than boys at indirect aggression (see Chapter 10). One explanation is that both types of conflict behaviour require a relatively high level of social intelligence, so girls can use their skills either to escalate conflict or to resolve it. At the same time, they found that empathy correlates strongly with peaceful conflict resolution. They argued that indirect aggression requires more social intelligence than direct verbal aggression, which, in turn, requires more social intelligence than physical aggression. Since empathy mitigates interpersonal aggression, empathy training has a key role to play in reducing aggression in young people. Similarly, Cunningham et al. (1998) (Box 9.1) found gender differences in involvement in conflict resolution interventions in junior schools. They concluded that, since boys are less likely to experience or employ indirect or verbal aggression, they may be less likely to detect this type of aggressive interaction, especially when it involves girls. In addition, if boys are less disturbed by relational aggression, they may assume that it is not worth intervening to prevent it.

Box 9.1 The effects of primary division, student-mediated conflict resolution programs on playground aggression

In this Canadian study, the researchers sought to discover the effects of a student-mediated conflict resolution programme on levels of playground aggression in primary schools. Mediation teams of Grade 5 students (approximately age 10 years) participated in 15 hours of training in mediation skills.

The study employed a multiple baseline design with weekly observations of aggressive behaviour in three schools serving as baselines. The researchers used observational methods at three time-points—before the intervention, during the intervention and at a follow-up—to evaluate the effect of introducing the mediation service into three primary schools on a staggered basis. Following seven weekly baseline observations, mediators began intervening in conflicts on the playground of School 1. Mediators began intervening in conflicts in School 2 following 11 weekly baseline observations. Mediation was introduced onto the playground of School 3 following 14 weekly baseline observations. Weekly observations were continued throughout the school year, with follow-up observations the following year.

A team of three coders conducted the observations once weekly during two 20-minute break times, with one observer assigned to each of the three schools. In general, observations were conducted at the same time, from the same location, by the same observer. The coders did not attend the mediation training programme, were not told the identity of the mediators, and were not told when the programme began in each of the schools. Before the study began, the coders engaged in 2 months of coder training. The coders' ratings were carried out independently and then compared, a method known as interrater reliability. The interrater reliability in this study was high since it averaged .90 for coder 1, .72 for coder 2 and .90 for coder 3.

The following behaviours were recorded at regular intervals.

- *Physical aggression:* this category included instances of physical aggression, such as taking equipment from peers, pushing another pupil, or hitting.
- *Adult intervention:* instances in which adults intervened to prevent or resolve conflicts.

The multiple baseline design of this study was selected as a controlled design and provided immediate and continuous feedback about the impact of the programme on children's behaviour in the playground in three different contexts, variability across time and longer term stability.

Peer mediators carried a clipboard with a prompt sheet (called a mediator monitoring form) for examples of behaviours that warranted or did not require intervention. For each conflict in which they intervened, mediators noted the gender and grade of the disputants, the nature of the conflict (*physical* versus *verbal/relational*) and whether the conflict was resolved successfully. Mediators coded *physical conflict* when disputants engaged in aggressive behaviour with physical contact, for example pushing, kicking or hitting. *Verbal/relational conflict* referred to aggressive behaviours such as nasty teasing of another person or social exclusion.

Mediation was judged to be successful if:

- both disputants agreed to mediate in the conflict
- a solution was agreed on, and
- the mediator felt that the solution solved the problem.

Checks on the interrater reliability were conducted for 51 mediators from the three schools. Overall agreement on the outcome of mediation was .86. Agreement on the grade of disputants, the gender of disputants and the type of dispute (physical versus verbal/relational) was 1.00.

The results were analysed in terms of both the mediator monitoring forms and the direct observations. The mediator monitoring forms showed that the three mediation teams recorded 1,010 mediations during year 1. Box Table 9.1.1 shows the number of disputes between boys, between girls, and boys versus girls at grades 1–5 in which mediators intervened. (Data

for kindergarten pupils are not included here.) Mediations involving conflicts between boys, and between boys and girls, declined from grade 1 to grade 5. The number of mediations involving only girls, by contrast, remained relatively stable from grade 1 to grade 5.

There were significant gender differences in the types of conflict that required mediation. Conflict involving boys was more likely to be physical, whether it was boys versus boys (61.5% of disputes) or boys versus girls (56.7%); for girls versus girls, only a minority of disputes were physically aggressive (29.1%).

Box Table 9.1.2 shows that for both verbal/relational and physical aggression, mediators

Box Table 9.1.1   Number of mediations at grades 1–5.

	Grade 1	Grade 2	Grade 3	Grade 4	Grade 5
Two boys	117	95	76	58	49
Two girls	59	47	45	28	48
Boy vs girl	67	71	46	38	26
Total	243	213	167	124	123

Source: Cunningham, C.E., Cunningham, L.J., Martorelli, V., Tran, A., Young, J. & Zacharias, R. (1998): The Effects of Primary Division, Student-mediated Conflict Resolution Programs on Playground Aggression. *Journal of Child Psychology & Psychiatry*, 39(5), 653–668.

Box Table 9.1.2   Percentage of the disputes, mediated by boys and girls, that involved disputants who were both boys, both girls, or boys and girls.

	Gender of disputants				
	Boys vs boys	Boys vs girls	Girls vs girls	X^2	p
	Verbal/relational conflicts				
Boy mediator	55.1	22.5	22.5	33.74	<.001
Girl mediator	26.5	26.9	46.5		
	Physical conflicts				
Boy mediator	63.1	27.3	9.6	17.16	<.001
Girl mediator	45.1	22.3	32.6		

The figure of 32.6 on the bottom row is a correction for what appears to be a mistake in the original article.

Source: Cunningham, C.E., Cunningham, L.J., Martorelli, V., Tran, A., Young, J. & Zacharias, R. (1998): The Effects of Primary Division, Student-mediated Conflict Resolution Programs on Playground Aggression. *Journal of Child Psychology & Psychiatry*, 39(5), 653–668.

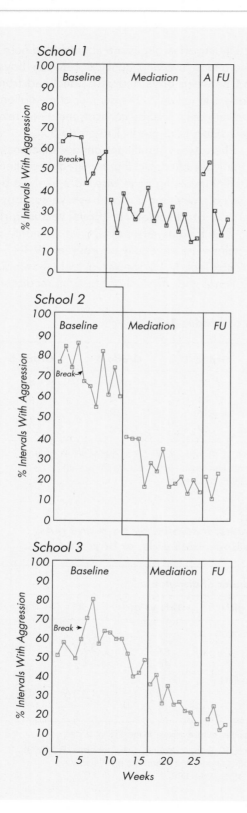

Box Figure 9.1.1 Percentage of 120 intervals in which physically aggressive behaviour was observed each week during baseline, mediation and follow-up (FU) conditions at three primary division schools. 'A' indicates a reversal when the mediation team was reduced from eight to two members.

Source: Cunningham, C.E., Cunningham, L.J., Martorelli, V., Tran, A., Young, J. & Zacharias, R. (1998): The Effects of Primary Division, Student-mediated Conflict Resolution Programs on Playground Aggression. *Journal of Child Psychology & Psychiatry, 39*(5), 653–668.

showed a significant gender preference. The percentage of disputes mediated by boys and girls did not differ significantly from the proportions predicted on the basis of their membership in the team. However, boys were more likely to intervene in disputes involving boys: 77.6% of the verbal/relational and 90.4% of the physical conflicts that boys mediated involved either boys or boys versus girls. Girls showed a similar (though less pronounced) preference to mediate in disputes involving girls: 73.4% of the verbal/relational and 54.9% of the physical disputes mediated by girls involved girls or girls versus boys.

The results from the direct observations of aggressive playground behaviour in School 1 are shown in Box Figure 9.1.1 (playground observation during baseline, mediation and follow-up). Aggressive behaviour remained stable for 5 weeks; rates dropped after the winter break, then increased over the next 4 weeks. After the introduction of mediation, rates dropped abruptly from an average of 57% during baseline observations to an average of 28% during mediation. These effects were still evident during the follow-up period. Similar results were found for Schools 2 and 3.

On the basis of the observations, the authors concluded that the introduction of the mediation scheme resulted in a sustained drop in aggressive behaviour in the playground in each of the three schools. The multiple baseline design of the study suggested that the decline in physically aggressive behaviour was not due to the passage of time, but specifically to the introduction of the mediation programme. The authors found that mediators successfully resolved 90% of the playground conflicts in which they intervened. The mediator monitoring records confirmed that pupils cooperated with the mediation team. Staff were unanimous in recommending that the programme should be maintained in each of the schools after the experiment was over. In fact, all of the schools in the study selected and trained a second generation of mediators in the following year. The mediators detected conflict early and were able to intervene quickly before it escalated. Although boys and girls contributed equally to the mediation teams' efforts, they displayed distinct preferences: boys intervened more in disputes involving boys and girls intervened more in disputes involving girls. The authors conclude that, as a relatively low-cost intervention, it merits wider use and further study as part of an antiviolence school programme.

Based on material in Cunningham, C.E., Cunningham, L.J., Martorelli, V., Tran, A., Young, J. & Zacharias, R. (1998). The effects of primary division, student-mediated conflict resolution programs on playground aggression. *Journal of Child Psychology & Psychiatry*, 39(5), 653–668.

However, Grusec and Hastings (2008) overview studies that indicate the need to view such results critically. Girls, they suggest, are more likely than boys to be kind or considerate but not more inclined to share, comfort or help. They are more likely to act prosocially when the person in need is an adult rather than another child. They are also more likely to be judged as prosocial when the measure is one of self-report, but less so when it is a direct observation or where physiological measures of empathy are used. Grusec and Hastings consider that these results may be due to differential socialization practices on the part of parents towards their sons and daughters. For example, girls may be praised for altruistic actions while boys are criticized for them. Researchers in this domain currently focus much more than they did in the past on studying the socialization of gender as a phenomenon that is embedded in a wider social structure (Leaper & Friedman, 2008). It is useful to consider this issue with reference to Rogoff's studies of boys' and girls' development in particular cultural contexts (see Chapters 16 and 18).

Cross-cultural Differences in Prosocial Behaviour

Research into cross-cultural differences in prosocial behaviour provides us with further insights into the process through which individuals acquire views on the nature of the social world, develop sets of values and understand the meaning of events within their community. Cross-cultural studies add a new perspective, since there are quite wide variations in the values that different cultural groups place on prosocial behaviour and altruism (see Howe (2010) in relation to her work on cooperation in the classroom).

In a classic study, Whiting and Whiting (1975) observed children between 3 and 11 years in six different cultures. They found that children from Kenya, Mexico and the Philippines acted more prosocially than those from Okinawa, India or the USA. One especially important difference among the cultures lay in the assignment of household chores, especially in the case of younger children (Figure 9.1). The more prosocial cultures were those in which women's contribution to the family economy was highest. As a result, these women delegated more responsibility to their children, so giving them opportunities to develop their prosocial behaviour.

By contrast, cultures that place high value on individual success are more likely to foster competitiveness than cooperation in their children in order to enhance their chances of personal success in the future.

Robarchek and Robarchek (1992) studied two cultures' different sets of values and consequent behaviour towards one another. The Waorani people of the Amazon are extremely warlike, fight constantly with their neighbours and have a strong philosophy of individualism. If there is a raid from a neighbouring tribe, each person will save themselves regardless of the fate of friends or members of their family. By contrast, the Semai of the Malaysian rain-

Figure 9.1   Research into cross-cultural differences in prosocial behaviour suggests that one important difference lies in the assignment of household chores, with more prosocial cultures being those in which women's contribution to the family economy is highest. As a result, more responsibility is given to their children, so giving them opportunities to develop their prosocial behaviour (Wainryb, 2006).

Source: Image copyright Hurst Photo, used under licence from Shutterstock.com.

forest are an extremely cooperative society, and place great emphasis on mutual support among family members and the community. The children in these two contrasting societies are exposed to different value systems and, not surprisingly, develop differently with regard to prosocial behaviour. Yet it would be mistaken to assume that these people differ in the extent to which they love their children. In everyday life, both the Waorani and the Semai adults are affectionate and non-punitive towards their children, so there is evidence of the caring, supportive patterns of behaviour that we expect to find in families and communities.

 Stop and Think

How can we explain the contrasting ways in which prosocial behaviour is expressed in different social settings?

Some psychologists (for a review see Wainryb, 2006) argue that there is a collective dimension, as opposed to individual functioning, in social processes and that shared discourses about conflict resolution and social responsibility are socially constructed within a particular context. As Wainryb (2006, p. 211) wrote, 'Persons, including children, are capable of reflecting on social interactions embedded in the practices and traditions of their culture; disagreements about what is right or valuable are common'. In fact, on the basis of her review of studies of moral development in a range of traditional societies, she concluded that children seem to form a mixture of judgements that vary with the particular features of the context and do not conform blindly to the concerns of the collective society. Although there is still controversy over the existence of a direct relationship between cultural values and specific manifestations of prosocial behaviour in children, in a broad sense we can justifiably conclude that there are cultural variations in what constitutes desirable prosocial behaviour within any society.

One broad distinction has been made between societies that have *individualistic* values and those that have *collective* values. For example, as we have seen, qualities of reciprocity and responsiveness to others' needs are judged more positively in a culture that values interdependence and compliance with social roles than in one that values autonomy and feelings of self-generation. This has led a number of researchers in the field to ask whether current Western emphases on autonomy and self-generation may need to be replaced: 'The growing heterogeneity of Western culture challenges researchers to rethink some very basic theoretical issues in the study of socialization' (Grusec et al., 2002).

 Stop and Think

In the context of prosocial behaviour and moral development, what are the relative advantages of individualistic and collective values?

THE DEVELOPMENT OF MORAL REASONING

So far, we have examined the development of prosocial behaviour. In this section we examine how children and adolescents develop the capacity to act and reason morally. Moral reasoning refers to how we reason, or judge, whether an action is right or wrong. Often, of course, we do follow our moral reasoning when we decide on a course of behaviour. For example, we might reason that it is right to give some money for overseas aid, and then do so. It is equally clear that we do not always follow our moral reasoning. For example, if we are incorrectly given extra change in a supermarket, we might reason that it is wrong to keep it, but still do so.

We are concerned here with the way in which moral reasoning (often referred to as moral judgement) develops. One important strand in the study of moral reasoning by psychologists is closely linked to cognitive development, and is often referred to as the *cognitive developmental approach*. Work in this area was pioneered by Piaget, and this tradition has been carried on in the USA by Kohlberg and others. The models developed by Piaget and by Kohlberg have also been described as *global stage theories*, since they propose that the child learns to act and think morally through a gradual process that culminates in learning to differentiate between acting through conformity to convention and acting according to some moral principle.

Piaget's Theory

Piaget turned his attention to moral reasoning in children early in his career. He spent time in the suburbs of Geneva watching children at play and also posing them moral dilemmas. The results of his investigations were reported in *The moral judgement of the child* (first English publication in 1932). Piaget described how he studied the boys' game of marbles. He was interested in how children acquired the rules of the game, where they thought the rules came from and whether the rules could be altered. Here, the 'rules of the game' are taken as corresponding to the 'rules of society' for adults—you should follow the rules; you can break them, but there are sanctions if you do so. Piaget used four methods here.

1. He asked the children directly ('Teach me the rules')
2. He played with a child, pretending to be ignorant so that the child had to explain the rules—though not too ignorant in case the child gave up in frustration!
3. He watched the child play with others
4. He interviewed children about where rules came from and whether they could be changed.

From his results, Piaget distinguished three stages in children's awareness of rules. In the first (up to 4–5 years), rules were not understood. In the second stage (from 4–5 to 9–10 years) the rules were seen as coming from a higher authority (e.g. adults, God, the town council) and could not be changed. In the third (from 9–10 years onwards) rules were seen as mutually agreed by the players, and thus open to change if all the players agreed. (Piaget also distinguished corresponding stages in how the child's awareness of rules was put into practice. He also examined a girls' game, a version of hide-and-seek, in much less detail and described similar stages occurring somewhat earlier, perhaps as the game was simpler.)

Over time, the child's conception of rules changes, from their being absolutely fixed (Piaget called this 'heteronomous' morality) to their being mutually agreed (Piaget called this 'autonomous' morality). In other words, a unilateral respect for adult or higher authority changes towards a sense of equality with peers. These are cognitive changes, which in Piaget's later theory can be linked to the decline in egocentrism and the growth of operational thought (see Chapter 12). Important other factors are the growing independence from parents and especially increased interaction with same-aged peers. Different children may have acquired slightly different versions of the rules, and through playing together these discrepancies will come to light and have to be resolved. This contact with divergent viewpoints, Piaget thought, was a crucial element in evolving the autonomous morality that involved respect for others and a sense of reciprocity or sharing through equal relationships with others in the peer group.

Piaget also reported the results of another study in his 1932 book. In this, he presented children with several pairs of short episodes or stories that posed a problem of moral judgement. An example is given below.

> A little boy who is called John is in his room. He is called to dinner. He goes into the dining room. But behind the door there was a chair, and on the chair there was a tray with 15 cups on it. John couldn't have known that there was all this behind the door. He goes in, the door knocks against the tray, bang go the 15 cups and they all get broken!

> Once there was a little boy whose name was Henry. One day when his mother was out he tried to get some jam out of the cupboard. He climbed up on the chair and stretched out his arm. But the jam was too high up and he couldn't reach it and have any. But while he was trying to get it he knocked over a cup. The cup fell down and broke.

Piaget would tell children this pair of stories, and get them to repeat each to make sure that they remembered them. Then he would ask them to make a judgement as to which child in the two stories was the naughtiest. He found that before 9 or 10 years, children often judged on the basis of the amount of damage, whereas after this age the child judged by motive or intention.

In the first of these stages, children judge by the objective amount of damage, and also tend to see punishment as inevitable and retributive. Piaget called this stage 'moral realism', as compared with the 'moral subjectivism' of the following stage, in which subjective intent is taken account of, and punishment is seen more as a lesson suited to the offence. Piaget related these stages to his idea of heteronomous and autonomous morality from the marbles study. A summary of his stages is given in Table 9.1.

 Stop and Think

Can you spot any methodological difficulties about Piaget's method of eliciting children's views on morality?

There are problems with Piaget's dilemma method; many were pointed out in a critique by Turiel (1998). Characteristically, Piaget makes it difficult for the child by having unequal consequences in the two stories (15 cups versus one cup broken), thus in effect tempting the child to ignore intention. The stories are badly designed: for example, it is not clear that Henry was being naughty in going to get the jam, and he probably didn't intend to break the cup, he was just careless. So the 'bad intention' in this story has to be inferred. There are also considerable memory demands made on young children (Kail, 1990). Several studies have shown that when methodological improvements are made (e.g. contrasting intent and accident when there is equal damage), children as young as 5 years will judge on the basis of intent.

Also, as pointed out by Turiel and Wainryb (2000) (and as we have seen in the earlier part of this chapter), children's moral reasoning develops in a complex social context in which there is not one dominant view on right and wrong, but a diverse, sometimes conflict-ridden set of experiences.

Further research has shown that young children do not have a monolithic conception of rules as constraints. For a useful summary, see Turiel (2006). Children can distinguish between

Table 9.1 Summary of Piaget's stages of moral judgement.

Up to 4 or 5 years	From 4–5 years to 9–10 years	After 9–10 years
Premoral judgement	Moral realism (Heteronomous morality of constraint)	Moral subjectivism (Autonomous morality of cooperation)
Rules not understood	Rules come from higher authority and cannot be changed	Rules are created by people and can be changed by mutual consent
	Evaluate actions by outcomes	Evaluate actions by intentions
	Punishment as inevitable retribution	Punishment as chosen to fit crime

Source: Based on Piaget (1932).

behaviours that violate purely social conventions (e.g. not putting your belongings in the right place), and those that violate moral conventions (e.g. not sharing a toy, hitting a child). A study by Smetana (1981) of children aged 2–5 in two American nursery schools found that children distinguished between these two kinds of behaviour in terms of whether it was dependent on context (home or school) and on the amount of punishment it deserved. Children are able to distinguish between different kinds of social rules and acts, and they are able to demonstrate conceptions of autonomy, rights and democracy. Even young children have moral concepts that are independent of authority or existing social rules, and their moral judgements are sensitive both to the context of these rules and the context of their application (Helwig & Turiel, 2002).

Despite limitations, the approach of presenting children and young people verbally with moral dilemmas has been pursued by a number of psychologists in the USA. It was used especially by Kohlberg, over a longer age span than Piaget and on a more ambitious scale.

Kohlberg's Theory

Kohlberg researched the development of moral reasoning for some 30 years, and his theory proved influential in education and criminology, as well as psychology. The work started with, and extended from, research for his doctoral thesis, in which he commenced in 1955 a longitudinal study of 50 American males initially aged 10–26 years. These participants were reinterviewed every 3 years. Kohlberg asked them questions, such as, 'Why shouldn't you steal from a store?', and also posed them story dilemmas. Of a number of dilemmas, the most famous is that of Heinz and the druggist (Kohlberg, 1969, p. 379).

> In Europe, a woman was near death from a special kind of cancer. There was one drug that the doctor thought might save her. It was a form of radium that a druggist in the same town had recently discovered. The drug was expensive to make, but the druggist was charging 10 times what the drug cost him to make. He paid $200 for the radium and charged $2,000 for a small dose of the drug. The sick woman's husband, Heinz, went to everyone he knew to borrow the money, but he could only get together about $1,000, which is half of what it cost. He told the druggist that his wife was dying, and asked him to sell it cheaper or let him pay later. But the druggist said 'No, I discovered the drug and I'm going to make money from it.' So Heinz got desperate and broke into the man's store to steal the drug for his wife.
> Should Heinz have done that? Why or why not?

This might seem an artificial dilemma, but in fact something very similar can occur in real life! (see Table 9.2). On the basis of these questions and dilemmas, Kohlberg postulated three levels of moral reasoning, each subdivided to make six stages in all. These levels and stages are defined in Table 9.3. We look briefly at each level in turn.

Level One: Preconventional Morality This is similar to Piaget's morality of constraint. Kohlberg (1976, p. 33) thinks of it as 'the level of most children under 9, some adolescents and many adolescent and adult criminal offenders'. On this level, the individual reasons in relation to himself and has not yet come fully to understand and uphold conventional or societal rules and expectations. Here is a level-one response from Joe, aged 10 years, one of Kohlberg's original longitudinal sample.

Kohlberg: Why shouldn't you steal from a store?
Joe: It's not good to steal from a store. It's against the law. Someone could see you and call the police.

(Kohlberg, 1976, p. 36)

> **Table 9.2   'Man Tells Police that he Robbed Bank to Pay for Wife's Cancer Treatment'.**
>
> A man told police he robbed a bank so he could afford cancer treatment for his terminally ill wife. Larry A., 22, was arrested at a police roadblock after a chase on Tuesday following a holdup at the Mid-South Bank.
>
> Detective Rick E. said that Larry A.'s account of his wife's illness was true. A woman who answered the telephone at Larry A.'s home and identified herself as his mother said his wife has ovarian cancer.
>
> Larry A. told police he decided to rob the bank after several banks turned him down for a loan. In the hold-up, a man handed a teller a note demanding $10,000 and threatened to 'blow you up', Detective E. said. The robber had no weapons.
>
> Larry A. was given $4,000, police said. He was jailed on charges of robbery. Bail was set at $200,000.
>
> *Source: Japan Times*, 25 November 1994.

Level Two: Conventional Morality This is 'the level of most adolescents and adults in our society and in other societies' (Kohlberg, 1976, p. 33). At this level, the individual thinks of what is right as conforming to and upholding the rules, expectations and conventions of society. Here is a level-two response from Joe, now aged 17 years.

Kohlberg:	Why shouldn't you steal from a store?
Joe:	It's a matter of law. It's one of our rules that we're trying to help protect everyone, protect property, not just to protect a store. It's something that's needed in our society. If we didn't have these laws, people would steal, they wouldn't have to work for a living, and our whole society would get out of kilter.

(Kohlberg, 1976, p. 36)

Level Three: Postconventional Morality This level 'is reached by a minority of adults and is usually reached after the age of 20' (Kohlberg, 1976, p. 33). Someone at this level broadly understands and accepts the rules of society, but only because they accept some general moral principles underlying these rules. If such a principle comes into conflict with society's rules, then the individual judges by principle rather than by convention. Here is a level-three response from Joe, now aged 24 years:

Kohlberg:	Why shouldn't you steal from a store?
Joe:	It's violating another person's rights, in this case to property.
Kohlberg:	Does the law enter in?
Joe:	Well, the law in most cases is based on what is morally right so it's not a separate subject, it's a consideration.
Kohlberg:	What does 'morality' or 'morally right' mean to you?
Joe:	Recognizing the rights of other individuals, first to life and then to do as he pleases as long as it doesn't interfere with somebody else's rights.

(Kohlberg, 1976, pp. 36–37)

Table 9.3   Kohlberg's stages of moral judgement.

Level	Stage	What is right
Preconventional	Stage 1 Heteronomous morality	To avoid breaking rules backed by punishment, obedience for its own sake, avoiding physical damage to persons and property.
	Stage 2 Individualism, instrumental purpose, and exchange	Following rules only when it is in someone's immediate interest; acting to meet one's own interests and needs, and letting others do the same. Right is what's fair, an equal exchange, a deal, an agreement.
Conventional	Stage 3 Mutual interpersonal expectations, relationships and interpersonal conformity	Living up to what is expected by people close to you or what people generally expect of people in your role. 'Being good' is important and means having good motives, showing concern about others and keeping mutual relationships, such as trust, loyalty, respect, and gratitude.
	Stage 4 Social system and conscience	Fulfilling the actual duties to which you have agreed. Laws are to be upheld except in extreme cases where they conflict with other fixed social duties. Right is contributing to society, the group, or institution.
Postconventional or principled	Stage 5 Social contract or utility and individual rights	Being aware that people hold a variety of values and opinions, that most values and rules are relative to your group but should usually be upheld in the interest of impartiality and because they are the social contract. Some non-relative values and rights like life and liberty, however, must be upheld in any society and regardless of majority opinion.
	Stage 6 (hypothetical) Universal ethical principles	Following self-chosen ethical principles. Particular laws or social agreements are usually valid because they rest on such principles. When laws violate these principles, one acts in accordance with the principle. Principles are universal principles of justice: the equality of human rights and respect for the dignity of human beings as individual persons.

As a cognitive-developmental theorist, Kohlberg supposed that the level of moral reasoning was dependent on having achieved a level of cognitive development, and also of social perspective or role-taking (see Chapter 13 on Piaget). He thought that someone still at the concrete operational stage would be limited to preconventional moral judgement (stages 1 and 2). Someone at early formal operations would be limited to conventional morality (stages 3 and 4). Postconventional morality would be dependent on late formal operations being achieved.

Kohlberg hypothesized that in all societies, individuals would progress upwards through these stages, in sequence (stages would not be skipped, and subjects would not regress). He also hypothesized that an individual would be attracted by reasoning just above their own on the scale, but would not understand reasoning more than one stage above; if true, this would have obvious implications for moral education.

Early Criticisms of Kohlberg's Theory

Kurtines and Greif (1974) made a substantial number of criticisms of Kohlberg's methodology. They pointed out that the moral judgement score of an individual was assessed from his or her scores on a number of dilemmas, yet the different dilemmas were designed intuitively by the researchers and there was no indication that they were measuring similar things. The scale was criticized as being unreliable, and the 'clinical method' of interview (similar to Piaget's) as being subjective. The validity of the scale was also called into question, since the proposition that children progressed through certain stages in fixed order could not be properly proved from Kohlberg's sample if that was the sample from which he derived the sequence in the first place.

 Stop and Think

Try out the Heinz dilemma on another student who is unfamiliar with Kohlberg's research. Interpret this person's response according to Kohlberg's stages. How accurately do you think this measures the person's level of moral reasoning?

Damon (1977) elaborated the criticism that the original dilemmas were intuitive, and in many ways unrealistic. How does the 'Heinz' problem appear to a 10- or 17-year-old? Damon listened to actual moral debates among children, and made up a number of interview items, such as:

> All of these boys and girls are in the same class together. One day their teacher lets them spend the whole afternoon making paintings and crayon drawings. The teacher thought that these pictures were so good that the class could sell them at the fair. They sold the pictures to their parents, and together the whole class made a lot of money.
> Now all the children gathered the next day and tried to decide how to split up the money. What do you think they should do with it? Why?
> Kathy said that the kids in the class who made the most pictures should get most of the money. What do you think? [More probe questions follow.]

From using these more realistic items, Damon derived a six-step 'positive-justice sequence', which describes children's reasoning about sharing, fairness and distributive justice. Other scales and sequences have also been published.

Another criticism has been that Kohlberg's original participants were all male, and that the consequent sequence of stages reflects the development of male morality and is male biased. This viewpoint was put strongly by Carol Gilligan in her book *In a different voice: Psychological theory and women's development* (1982). In fact, Gilligan argues quite widely for a 'female psychology' to complement the predominantly 'male psychology' so far developed. So far as moral reasoning is concerned, Gilligan described a short-term longitudinal study in which she interviewed 29 women, aged 15–33, who were attending abortion and pregnancy counselling services. These women were faced with a very real moral dilemma—whether to have an abortion or go through with the pregnancy. Gilligan found that these women considered their dilemma in somewhat different terms from what she calls the 'justice' orientation of Kohlberg; rather, they focused more on 'responsibility'. Instead of abstract, principled judgements that are universally applicable, as in Kohlberg's stages 5 and 6, these women made rational, context-dependent judgements that were more concerned about the impact of behaviour on people's actual feelings. Put simply, it is a question of whether you put principles before people (a 'male' characteristic) or people before principles (a 'female' characteristic). On this basis, Gilligan suggested an alternative ethic of care and responsibility as being more representative of women's moral reasoning development.

Later Revisions of Kohlberg's Theory

Kohlberg and his co-workers, especially Anne Colby, revised some aspects of the theory. This, and independent replications, went some way to answering earlier criticisms. A new scoring system, called Standard Issue Scoring, was published in 1978 (Colby et al., 1987). This scores, separately and with clear criteria, the responses to the issue chosen by the respondent for each dilemma; in the Heinz dilemma, for example, this would be the law issue if the respondent says Heinz should not steal, the life issue if they say Heinz should save his wife. High reliabilities are reported for this scoring method. A rescoring of the original American longitudinal sample produced the results shown in Figure 9.2. The stage sequence model is well supported for the first four stages. The low incidence of stage 5 is noticeable. Stage 6 is absent. Kohlberg therefore considered this to be a hypothetical stage, which has not been established empirically (Colby et al., 1983).

This sequence of stages has now been broadly confirmed in many other societies. A review by Snarey (1985) listed studies in 27 different cultural areas; most are cross-sectional, but there have been longitudinal studies in the Bahamas, Canada, India, Indonesia, Israel, Turkey and the USA. Naturally the dilemmas are adapted slightly for different cultures; the Turkish version of the Heinz dilemma, for example, involves a man and his wife who have migrated from the mountains and are running out of food so that the wife becomes sick; there is only one food store in the village, and the storekeeper charges so much that the man cannot pay. Here is an example of a level one (stage 2) response from Turkey (Snarey, 1985, p. 221).

Should the husband have stolen the food?
Yes. Because his wife was hungry . . . otherwise she will die.
Suppose it wasn't his wife who was starving but his best friend; should he steal for his friend?
Yes, because one day when he is hungry his friend would help.
What if he doesn't love his friend?
No, [then he should not steal] because when he doesn't love him it means that his friend will not help him later.

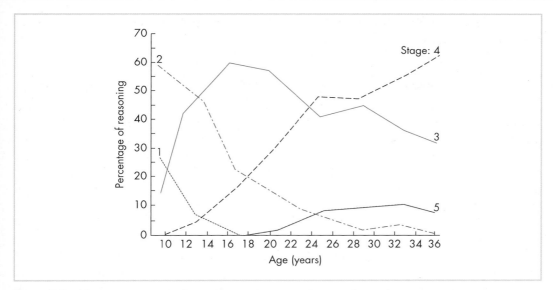

Figure 9.2 Mean percentage of moral reasoning at each stage for each age group.
Source: Colby, A., Kohlberg, L., Gibbs, J. & Liebermann, M. (1983). A longitudinal study of moral judgment. *Monographs of the Society for Research in Child Development, 48*(1-2), 1–124.

In his review, Snarey found that almost all the studies in different societies agreed in finding a progression from stages 1 through to 4, at reasonably appropriate ages. There was some discordance about stage 5, however. Very few studies found true stage 5 reasoning, and even transitional stage 5 reasoning was only found in urban societies. It was not found at all in rural or village societies (e.g. Alaskan Eskimos, Guatemala, rural Kenya, New Guinea, rural Turkey). Rather than argue that individuals in these societies are in some sense inferior in moral reasoning, Snarey and other psychologists argue that Kohlberg's level three (stage 5) is significantly culturally biased. It reflects the individualistic, capitalistic orientation of middle-class, Western, urban society. Other religions, such as Hinduism, may put less value on individual human life than does the Christian religion. Other societies, socialist or rural, may put more emphasis on collectivist values based on reciprocity and on conflict resolution by inter-personal means. This is illustrated by an extract from an interview with an Israeli kibbutz male (Snarey, 1985, p. 222).

> Should Moshe steal the drug? Why or why not?
> Yes . . . I think that the community should be responsible for controlling this kind of situation. The medicine should be made available to all in need: the druggist should not have the right to decide on his own . . . the whole community or society should have the control of the drug.

In this example, the person interviewed is somewhat at cross-purposes with the assumptions of the interviewer. Such responses may be difficult to score on Kohlberg's scheme, but (Snarey and others argue) should not therefore be devalued. Oser (1996) criticizes Kohlberg for orienting his theory of moral development too far towards cognitive development and ignoring social contextual influences.

The Social-Cognitive Domain Approach to Moral Development

Social-cognitive domain theory takes account of the diversity of values within cultures. This perspective proposes that moral concepts are universal but that social conventions will differ (Smetana, 2006; Turiel, 2002). Thus, children's moral knowledge is constructed out of myriad reciprocal relationships amongst the individual children, their social environment and the important people in their lives. Turiel (2006, p. 31) argues that it is misleading to categorize people's morality as either absolute or relative.

> . . . morality appears absolute because issues of welfare, justice and rights, as we have seen, are not judged as arbitrary but as obligatory across settings. Morality appears relative because issues of welfare, justice and rights, as we have seen, are not applied uniformly in all situations.

Social-cognitive domain theorists propose that children's moral development grows from specific personal experiences. Over time, children become increasingly more capable at applying moral criteria to abstract and unfamiliar situations. Turiel, in contrast to Piaget and Kohlberg, proposes that children's thinking is organized from an early age into the domains of *morality* and *social convention*. The moral domain refers to issues of fairness, harm and rights, while the social-conventional domain consists of behavioural uniformities that serve to coordinate social interactions in social systems, for example, through dress codes, rules of classrooms, etiquette at meals and so on. Smetana (2006) added a third category—the *psychological* domain—pertaining to personal choice.

Turiel assessed children's moral development in two ways. The first concerns *criterion judgements*. For example, judgements about hitting and stealing are found to be generalizable, that is, wrong across contexts; and non-rule contingent, that is, wrong even if there were no rule against them. Rules that pertain to moral acts are viewed as unalterable. By contrast, social-conventional transgressions, such as calling a teacher by his or her first name or eating with your fingers, are seen as relative to the social context, or contingent on a specific rule. Such rules that are to do with social conventions are seen to be alterable by authority.

Secondly, Turiel (1998) measured the judgements that children use to *justify* their own opinions or actions. He found that children can distinguish between the two domains (morality and social convention) and reason about them in different ways. For example, children judge it acceptable to call a teacher by his or her first name in a school where there is no rule to prohibit it. By contrast, hitting is judged to be wrong, even if a teacher permitted it, and children do not consider that rules about hitting can be altered by the commands of those in authority. Children's judgements of acts are independent of social-conventional aspects of the social system, and many studies have shown that they distinguish between morality and social convention from quite an early age. Turiel criticized Kohlberg's theory for failing to acknowledge the different ways in which children learn to distinguish between social rules and conventions on the one hand (for example, 'You shall not undress in public' is a social convention) and, on the other, moral rules that apply to principles of justice, truth and right (for example, 'It is wrong to kill' is a moral rule). Social conventions can be negotiated and changed, but moral rules have an intrinsic quality.

This is nicely illustrated in the study by Ruck and Tenenbaum (2014) in which they investigated the views of 60 adolescents (half in early to middle adolescence and half in late adolescence) about the rights of asylum-seeking youth. Reasoning about rights, the authors argue, may involve either negative attitudes (e.g. when the rights of asylum seekers are rejected) or positive attitudes (e.g. when tolerance and empathy are shown). This study used vignettes, each involving a 12-year-old refugee, matched to the gender of the participant. Two of the vignettes described a situation where the refugee wished to exercise a self-determination right (e.g. choosing where to live or refusing to carry ID) and two described a situation where the refugee child wanted to have a nurturance right upheld (e.g. being provided with food or clothing). The results indicated that, in each of the age groups, the participants favoured the refugee child's nurturance rights over their self-determination rights. When considering refugee children's nurturance rights, participants were more likely to invoke moral concepts like fairness and justice; when considering self-determination and decision-making rights, they were more likely to invoke social-conventional arguments, such as the necessity to adhere to authority. In other words, nurturance rights evoked *moral* reasoning while self-determination rights evoked *social-conventional* reasoning. A follow-up study, also grounded in social-cognitive domain theory (Ruck & Tenenbaum, 2014), is described in Box 9.2.

Box 9.2 Does moral and social-conventional reasoning predict British young people's judgements about the rights of asylum seeker youth?

The objective of this study was to measure young people's moral and conventional reasoning when discussing the religious and secular self-determination and nurturance rights of young asylum seekers in the UK. Specifically, the study investigated young people's reasoning about asylum seeker youth's religious and secular *self-determination* and *nurturance* rights. The researchers predicted that:

1. adolescents' endorsement of rights and reasoning would be based on the particular situation involved
2. young people would endorse fewer secular self-determination rights than other types.

Social-cognitive domain theory provided the theoretical perspective for this study in which moral and social-conventional reasoning were related to young people's decisions about the justification of the wishes of asylum seekers

to assert their rights. While there is quite a large literature on how young people view their own rights, there is very little on how they view the rights of out-group members. In this study, 260 British young people were asked for their opinions on the rights of young asylum seekers, in particular, their views on their religious and secular rights to *self-determination* and *nurturance*. The sample of youth was divided into naturally occurring groups based on school year groups: 11–12 years; 13–14 years; 15–16 years; 17–18 years; and final 2 years of university: 19–24 years.

Eight hypothetical vignettes were presented to each participant. Half of the vignettes depicted situations involving an asylum-seeking child's nurturance rights while the remaining four concerned self-determination rights. Two of the nurturance vignettes described situations where the child asylum seeker desired to have a religious right fulfilled while the other two depicted secular rights. Similarly, for the self-determination rights, two involved religious and the other two involved secular rights. All the vignettes depicted situations where a child asylum seeker wanted to have a child's right fulfilled that was in conflict with authority or government practices. Half of the situations took place in a detention centre while the others took place in a school context. For each vignette, the age and gender of the character in the story were matched to the participant.

A researcher read each vignette to the participants. For each vignette, the participant was presented with a single-item endorsement rating scale to assess whether the story character should be allowed to exercise the right in question using a five-point scale ranging from *not at all* (–2) to *very much* (+2). In addition, the participants were asked to provide a justification for their response. The researchers developed a justification coding system based on four categories: *moral*, *social-conventional*, *outcomes* and *practicality*. Box Table 9.2.1 gives definitions of the coding categories.

ANOVA analyses showed that, with regard to *Endorsement of rights*, as predicted, there was a main effect of situation.

1. Participants showed the greatest level of support for the asylum seeker child's nurturance right to parental support and the right to practise his or her religion.
2. Participants were most likely to support the religious self-determination right of wearing a headscarf.
3. Participants were less likely to support the nurturance right of the school paying for the asylum seeker child's school uniform, the religious nurturance right of food preparation according to religious beliefs and the asylum seeker's right to privacy.
4. Participants did not support the child asylum seeker's self-determination right to choose where to live.

The ANOVA also showed a main effect of age. In general, the young people extended fewer rights as they grew older, with 11–12-year-olds endorsing all vignettes more than did the 15–16-year-olds or the 17–18-year-olds. Their justifications depended on the context or situation where the right was embedded. For example, with regard to the nurturance right about having food prepared according to religious beliefs, 11–12-year-olds were more likely to

---

Box Table 9.2.1 Justification categories.

1. **Moral**: Includes references to fairness, rights and equality; appeals to the importance of respecting the asylum seeker's customs or religious beliefs (e.g. 'Everyone should have the right to live where they want').
2. **Social-conventional**: Includes reference to group norms, such as parents being responsible for looking after children; adhering to authority and rules; reference to asylum seekers being grateful for being allowed into the host country (e.g. 'Those people should be grateful for being here').
3. **Outcomes**: Includes reference to positive or negative outcomes of the situation (e.g. 'He will get into trouble with his religion if he does that').
4. **Practicality**: Includes reference to practical issues or alternatives to solve the situation (e.g. 'The school should lend him a uniform and when he has money he can buy his own').

Source: Ruck, M. D. and Tenenbaum, H. R. (2014). Does Moral and Social Conventional Reasoning Predict British Young People's Judgments About the Rights of Asylum-Seeker Youth? *Journal of Social Issues, 70*(1), 47-62.

support this right than were 15–16-year-olds. There was also a significant age effect regarding the non-religious self-determination vignette on whether the child should be able to choose where to live, with 11–12-year-olds more likely to endorse this vignette than 15–16-year-olds or 19–20-year-olds. For freedom of religious expression involving gender differentiation, the youngest participants were more likely than the older ones to endorse this form of religious freedom. The same applied to freedom of religious expression involving food preparation. Thus younger British youth were more likely to support religious self-determination for asylum seekers than older British youth. Similarly, the younger participants were more likely than the older ones to favour the asylum seeker's right to choose where to live.

As regards *Justifications*, Box Table 9.2.2 shows the main effects for the two categories of moral reasoning and social-conventional reasoning. With regard to the correlation between young people's endorsement of a right and their reasoning, the results were complex and multifaceted, indicating confirmation of social-cognitive domain theory. In particular, results for justification in religious nurturance and self-determination scenarios were as follows.

1. Here participants' justifications generally focused on moral reasoning the most, second on outcomes, third on social-conventional reasoning and last on practical considerations.
2. With regard to religious expression involving gender differentiation, they were most likely to mention outcomes and practicality, next moral reasoning and rarely social-conventional reasoning.
3. With regard to freedom of religious expression, they were more likely to use moral reasoning and least likely to use social-conventional reasoning.

Box Table 9.2.2 Correlations between young people's endorsement and reasoning.

Type of vignette	Moral reasoning	Social-conventional reasoning
Freedom of religious expression involving food preparation	.54***	−.07
Freedom of religious expression involving gender differentiation	.23***	−.02
Freedom of religious expression (unspecified)	.47***	−.09
Freedom of religious expression involving wearing a headscarf	.02	−.64***
Access to parental support	.15**	−.26***
School provision of school uniform	.26***	−.21***
Right to choose where to live	.67***	−.57***
Right to personal privacy	.64***	−.53***

Note:
*$p < .05$ **$p < .01$ ***$p < .001$.

Source: Ruck, M. D. and Tenenbaum, H. R. (2014). Does Moral and Social Conventional Reasoning Predict British Young People's Judgments About the Rights of Asylum-Seeker Youth? *Journal of Social Issues, 70*(1), 47-62.

For freedom of religious expression involving the wearing of a headscarf, participants were least likely to use social-conventional reasoning. As regards Justification in *non-religious nurturance and self-determination scenarios*, the participants made reference to outcome, social-conventional and moral justifications. For rights to privacy, they were most likely to use moral reasoning.

In summary, the participants showed the greatest level of support for asylum seeker rights to parental emotional support and the right of freedom of religious expression but the lowest level of support of the asylum-seeking child's choosing where to live. In general, the younger participants extended more rights than did the older participants.

A strength of this study is that it demonstrated the multifaceted nature of young people's thinking. Participants clearly took account of the particular aspects of each situation in the different vignettes. Overall, they invoked moral justification with regard to freedom of religious expression, but social conventional justification when considering access to parental emotional support and choosing where to live. They invoked moral reasoning where they endorsed the asylum seeker's rights but social-conventional reasoning when they condoned social exclusion. One weakness is that the study authors did not examine whether the ethnic and religious backgrounds of the participants influenced their thinking. Given that the students were reasoning about Muslim asylum seekers, these factors probably influence participants' reasoning.

There are implications from these findings for the management of prejudice towards out-groups. Educators need to develop interventions that encourage open discussion about the issues and that increase knowledge about different cultural practices and beliefs. This can be challenging in the light of current campaigns against immigration and confusion over the contribution that incomers give to their host country.

Based on material in Ruck, M.D. & Tenenbaum, H.R. (2014). Does moral and social conventional reasoning predict British young people's judgments about the rights of asylum-seeker youth? *Journal of Social Issues*, 70(1), 47–62.

Turiel observed that children as young as 4 years could understand the difference between the two domains of moral and social-conventional reasoning in that they saw moral rules as more binding than conventions.

From an early age, children are aware of the consequences of moral actions, and understand the emotions felt by other children when they experience pain or injury. Most observational studies have shown that young children do not respond as frequently to conventional violations as to moral transgressions. By contrast, adults more frequently focus on children's violations of social conventions, such as untidiness, rule keeping and obedience. In the view of Helwig and Turiel (2002), these findings confirm the view that children's domain distinctions are based on early social experiences. Their findings are certainly consistent with Dunn's research on siblings in the family and the much greater social understanding that young children demonstrated in naturalistic surroundings than they did in the laboratory (p. 166). Turiel's research similarly challenges Kohlberg's view that the principles only outweigh the conventions at a later stage of development—that is, during adolescence.

However, we need to consider carefully the implications of such research for establishing in law the age at which a young person may be deemed to be morally culpable for their actions.

 Stop and Think

Think back to Dunn's interview with 4-year-old Kevin earlier in this chapter (p. 306). How moral was Kevin's judgement about how he should behave towards his friend in comparison to how he should behave towards his sister?

THE AGE OF MORAL RESPONSIBILITY IN THE CONTEXT OF YOUTH CRIME

The issues that we have been discussing are not only of theoretical interest. They have important applications in real life. A key question concerns the age at which a child may be considered to be morally responsible. This issue has been especially salient in recent years, with public moral debate (often highly emotional) over the culpability of children who commit violent crimes, including high-profile cases where children have been killed by other children, for example, the killings in the UK of the toddler James Bulger by two 10-year-old boys; and the more recent case of two brothers, aged 10 and 11, who were sentenced in 2014 for an extremely sadistic attack on two other boys of a similar age who were lucky to escape with their lives.

The age of criminal responsibility in the UK is 10 years—currently one of the lowest in Europe. However, any system of justice for children must be viewed in the wider context of the social, political and economic climate in which it takes place. In the judgement of the European Court of Human Rights, child offenders should be treated differently from adults, since such children are still going through the process of development and there is some chance that they can change. Account should be taken not only of their maturity of reasoning and grasp of moral issues and their capacity for impulse control, but also of the extremely difficult circumstances of their experiences within their families. Hickey et al. (2003), in a study of 280 children, mean age 13.9 years, referred to Child and Adolescent Mental Health Services (CAMHS) for their sexually abusive behaviour, found that the majority had been physically, sexually or emotionally abused themselves, and many had experienced traumatic loss, for example the death of a parent. These children were characterized by extreme cruelty to animals and a strong association with inappropriate sexual behaviour towards other children (59%) or towards animals (9%). Typically they lacked empathy for others' feelings, had difficulty in controlling their own anger and had a grandiose sense of self-worth.

Questions about differences in moral development—for example, with regard to gender, ethnicity and social class—are central to current debates about youth justice. From a social-cultural perspective (see Chapter 16), moral development does not occur in the same way for each individual in a social group. Rather, it is specific to the social-cultural context within which that individual exists. The child perpetrators of violent crimes represent extreme examples of children whose families and society have failed to provide a nurturing environment within which they could develop empathy and prosocial attitudes towards others, as other children typically do (see also Chapter 18 on the debates around difference and deficit).

Stop and Think

To what extent should society blame children who engage in violent crimes? At what age is it reasonable to expect that they are capable of moral reasoning about the nature and consequences of their violent acts? Should they be punished or given therapeutic treatment?

These arguments are extremely important in the particular context of youth offending. Some facts and figures help to contextualize the issue. According to the Prison Reform Trust (2013) report, in England there were 1,320 children under the age of 18 in custody—a decrease of 553 from the same report in the previous year. Also, 85,000 children were under the supervision of youth justice services—20% fewer than the previous year. Around 25% of children who offend have special educational needs; 29% have literacy and numeracy difficulties. Children who are, or who have been, in care are overrepresented among the offender population since; although fewer than 1% of all children in England are in care, looked-after children make up 30% of boys and 44% of girls in custody.

The social experiences of young offenders reveal that almost all of them have endured various kinds of abuse and deprivation during their childhood and adolescence (Carlile, 2006; Cowie et al., 2007; Hickey et al., 2003; Utting et al., 1993). Neglect and family conflict, poor domestic care and the absence of a good relationship with either parent have all been shown to increase the risk of behaviour problems and subsequent juvenile offending (Farrington, 1995)

Stop and Think

Do you think that the criminal justice system should take more account than it does of the social and family circumstances of young people who break the law?

Young offenders have significant risk factors for mental health difficulties. The Prison Reform Trust (2013) found that the rates of all mental disorders (psychosis, depression, posttraumatic stress disorder, substance misuse) are substantially higher in young offenders than in young people in the community. This is unsurprising, given that so many of them have experienced events in their lives that are known to increase the risk of mental disorder. These risk factors include inconsistent and erratic parenting, over-harsh discipline, hyperactivity as a child and additional family stressors. The levels of previous physical, sexual and emotional abuse, school exclusion, low educational achievement and unemployment are all high, and many are teenage parents. They are more likely than adult prisoners to suffer from mental health problems, and are more likely to commit or attempt suicide. Various aspects of risky behaviour such as offending may in themselves cause mental health problems (Mental Health Foundation, 2002). Being incarcerated causes extreme stress and anxiety, sometimes due to fear of bullying and violence within prison itself (Ireland & Monaghan, 2006). Furthermore, research has suggested that the detection of mental health problems in the young offender population is imprecise, and tends towards underestimation (Carlile, 2006; Mental Health Foundation, 2002).

Despite the extent of mental health difficulties being experienced by young people in custody, Carlile (2006) expressed grave concern that their access to treatment and protection, during and after detention, was less than that offered to children in society at large. The mental health services provided to young people in custody are generally inadequate in comparison to the adolescent population as a whole, despite their increased risk (Prison Reform Trust, 2013). There is growing concern about this lack of provision for a particularly vulnerable group of young people (Newman et al., 2013). This contravenes their rights according to the Children Act 2004 and the United Nations Convention on the Rights of the Child (United Nations, 1989) (see also Chapter 1). Together, these pieces of legislation dictate that children should be consulted in matters that affect them, yet rarely are young offenders given a voice on their own mental health issues and the provision of services that they feel they need.

As Wolff and McCall Smith (2000, p. 136) urged, 'the only purpose of detaining juveniles should be the protection of society and rehabilitation, the second of course promoting the first'. The moral development of children must also be viewed in the context of the family and the community. The harsh treatment of children and young people who commit crimes (for example, the use of tasers to control children in detention) is inappropriate, particularly if these are individuals who have been raised in homes that are poverty-stricken and by parents who are themselves inadequate or under severe stress. In this instance, the reason for the child's offending behaviour may clearly lie in the adverse circumstances in which he or she was brought up (see also Chapter 18). This leads to another critical question: can we teach children to act and judge morally?

CAN WE TEACH MORAL VALUES?

Kohlberg's research has encouraged psychologists and some educators to consider the cognitive-developmental principles at the heart of moral reasoning. For example, Osler (2011) proposes education for global citizenship to encompass local, national and global affinities as an important way of broadening students' perspectives beyond narrower ethno-nationalistic attitudes that can foster prejudice and intolerance. Although Piaget emphasized the role of peer interaction in the formation of moral judgements, he did not sufficiently explore the ways in which these kinds of social interaction promote further changes in the child's thinking.

The social-cognitive domain approach to moral reasoning has been very influential, with definite implications for moral education. In becoming self-aware, children and young people are engaging in a process of learning about significant relationships and social roles. By cooperating with others in a social group that is significant to them, they can gain direct experience of learning about what is morally right for that group, as well as the opportunity to learn that reciprocity is of greater value than the maximization of individual benefits.

Schools are in a position to create this kind of context by actively promoting participative involvement in responsible action (being elected to the school council, being a class representative and taking part in a peer support service would all be examples of this in practice). In addition, schools can teach democratic procedures and social responsibility through such curriculum initiatives as citizenship education (Cowie & Jennifer, 2007).

At the same time, the citizenship curriculum by its nature is likely to be controversial in its implementation, and requires teachers to reflect deeply on their own values, with particular reference to social and cultural practices in the home and the community. Parents, too, will make their voices heard and may not always be in accord with the values being promoted in school. Valsiner (2000) made the point that adolescents may often develop an antiestablishment stance despite efforts on the part of the state to inculcate in them dominant social values. In fact, by their participation in a number of social groups, not all of which are likely to be mainstream, adolescents may reject the political system by, for example, becoming apathetic or by embracing antiestablishment ideologies. Compare, too, the perspectives of impoverished Brazilian youth from the *favelas* of Rio de Janeiro (see Chapter 18) on the need to join gangs for safety, protection and self-affirmation with the dominant view that such behaviour is dysfunctional.

Oser (1996) argued that the ethos of a community depends as much on its moral heart or emotional conviction, and frequently the 'heart' and the 'head' are not in agreement. In many everyday situations, teachers may find themselves mediating among conflicting parties. This situation is likely to involve discussing the moral values at stake and considering the options that meet criteria of truth, justice and care. Oser suggests that, from an educational point of view, no dilemma discussion leading to a higher developmental stage should occur without relation to action and context. For example, in the case of the Heinz dilemma, there should be discussion around, 'What would I really do in this situation?'. A more concrete form would exist in real-life dilemmas where, for example, helping behaviour would be the required outcome of the discussion (for example, through peer support). Most concrete of all would be the decision of a community that was voted upon and enforced by this whole community, and where the outcomes of the decision-making processes were evaluated collectively. From this perspective, educators would not only need to be familiar with cognitive stimulation techniques, but also be embedded in what Oser call 'participatory pedagogy' (see also collective argumentation, Chapter 16).

Emotional Literacy

Research on emotional intelligence (Mayer et al., 2000; Petrides et al., 2007) (see Chapter 6) gives further useful insights into the teaching of moral values. The emotional literacy movement, popularized by Goleman (1995), recognizes the need for schools to educate young people in the management of emotions, in settling disputes peacefully and in learning to live cooperatively with one another. Emotional literacy programmes such as the Promoting Alternative Thinking Strategies (PATHS) curriculum (Greenberg, 2010; Greenberg et al., 2005) are designed to educate school-aged children about issues involved in the expression, understanding and regulation of emotions. The components of an emotional literacy curriculum include the following.

- *Self-awareness*: self-monitoring and recognition of feelings; building a vocabulary of feelings and making links between thoughts, feelings and behaviour.

- *Personal decision making*: self-monitoring of actions and recognition of their consequences; distinguishing between thought-led and feeling-led decisions.
- *Managing feelings*: self-monitoring of 'self-talk'; challenging negative self-messages; recognizing triggers for strong feelings; finding ways of handling fears, anxieties, anger and sadness.
- *Handling stress*: self-monitoring for signs of stress; recognition of sources of stress; learning to use relaxation methods.
- *Empathy*: understanding others' feelings and concerns; recognizing that different people have different perspectives.
- *Personal responsibility*: taking responsibility for self-management; recognizing consequences of actions and decisions; accepting feelings and moods; persisting to achieve goals and commitments.
- *Conflict resolution*: understanding the difference between need and want; using a 'win-win' model for negotiating solutions.

The PATHS Intervention

Here we describe one attempt to teach children about their own and others' emotions and about the ways in which emotions can be managed and regulated in social settings. We have selected this particular intervention because it has been evaluated by a research team (Greenberg, 2010; Greenberg et al., 2005), and has been used in the Fast Track project (also described in Chapter 10).

PATHS is a preventive intervention that places importance on the developmental integration of affect (emotion), behaviour and cognitive understanding as they relate to social and emotional competence. By the end of the preschool years, most children are able to interpret the emotional states of themselves and others (see Chapter 6), but the development of more complex social cognitions about the emotions has a major impact on children's moral behaviour, for example in thinking through the implications of acting prosocially or antisocially. They need to cope with unpleasant emotions, and learn to regulate emotions with positive outcomes for self-awareness, self-esteem, self-control, awareness of others' emotions and the capacity to act prosocially. Cognitive processes that are devoid of emotion, defined as 'cold' cognitive processes (see Chapter 15 on theory of mind), are most effective if the child has also developed the capacity to feel empathy for the emotion of others involved in a particular situation. The peer group plays a key role in developing this empathic awareness, and the school curriculum provides an influential arena for the facilitation of change.

PATHS is a 60-lesson intervention composed of units on self-control, emotions and problem solving. Lessons involve didactic instruction, role-play, class discussions, modelling by teachers and peers, social and self-reinforcement, and worksheets. A critical aspect of PATHS focuses on the relationship between cognitive-affective understanding and real-life situations. The evaluation by Greenberg and his colleagues involved 286 children attending 1st and 2nd grade at pretest, and 2nd and 3rd grade at posttest. Ages ranged from 6 years 5 months to 10 years 6 months at pretest (mean age 8 years) and from 7 years to 11 years 2 months (mean 8 years 10 months) at posttest. One hundred and thirty received the intervention (83 in mainstream education, 47 in special education) and 156 were in control classrooms (109 in mainstream education and 47 in special education). Special education children received a modified version that placed more emphasis on self-control and less emphasis on the more advanced steps of problem solving.

Children were individually interviewed in the autumn or spring prior to the intervention year; during the following spring, around 1 month after the end of the intervention, they were interviewed again using the same measure, the Kusche Affective Interview Revised (KAI-R), to assess their emotional understanding and to probe a wide range of affective situations and emotional states. Five domains of emotional understanding were assessed: ability to discuss one's own emotional experiences; cues used to recognize emotions; issues regarding the simultaneity of emotions; display rules for emotions; and whether and how emotions can change. A list of the summary variables is given in Table 9.4.

Results of the PATHS intervention

Overall, the evaluation indicated the effectiveness of the 1-year PATHS curriculum in improving children's range of feelings vocabulary, their ability to provide appropriate personal examples of the experience of basic feelings, their beliefs that they can hide, manage and change their feelings, and their understanding of cues for recognizing emotions in others.

Table 9.4   Affective interview summary variables using the Kusche Affective Interview Revised (KAI-R).

1. Ability to discuss one's own emotional experience
   a) Feelings vocabulary
      Total number of positive feeling words
      Total number of negative feeling words
      Total definitions score: proud, guilty, jealous, nervous, lonely
   b) General questions about feelings
      'Are all feelings okay to have?' ('How do you know that?')
   c) Discussion of own emotional experiences
      Proportion of appropriate responses for self:
      Happy, sad, mad, scared, love
      Proud, guilty, jealous, nervous, lonely
2. Cues used to recognize emotions
      Self: happy, mad, jealous
      Other: happy, mad, jealous
3. Understanding simultaneous feelings
      Sad/mad; sad/happy; love/anger
4. Display rule for emotions
      'Can you hide your feelings?' 'How can you do that?'
      'Can other people hide their feelings from you?' 'How can they do that?'
5. Changing emotions; 'Can feelings change?'
      'If you felt upset, could your feelings change?' 'Tell me what would happen.'
      Sum of developmental level for pictures: happy/sad, jealous/happy

Source: Adapted from Greenberg, M.T., Kusche, C.A., Cooke, E.T. & Quamma, J.P. (1995). Promoting emotional competence in school aged children: The effects of the PATH curriculum. *Development and Psychopathology, 7,* 7–16, with permission.

In special education classes, the intervention also significantly improved their understanding of how others manage and hide their feelings, and how feelings can be changed. In some instances, there was greater improvement in children whose teachers had rated them as having behavioural difficulties. Among mainstream education children only, the intervention improved their comprehension of complex feeling states. On the other hand, there were no effects on children's self-awareness about their own feelings, or in understanding that feelings can happen simultaneously. PATHS' most influential impact was on the children's fluency in discussing basic feelings, as well as their beliefs in their own efficacy about managing and changing feelings.

However, not all evaluations in other countries have been so positive. For example, an evaluation of PATHS in the Netherlands, with intervention and control schools, failed to find effects on internalizing and externalizing behaviours, including victimization (Goossens et al., 2012). A similar design failed to find any long-term effects of PATHS in Swiss schools (Malti, Ribeaud & Eisner, 2012).

This research gives some support to the idea that cognitive knowledge about emotion may affect how we respond to others and how we reflect about ourselves. Thinking ahead about one's actions and their effects on others may therefore lead to greater empathy towards others and a more reflective, responsible stance. More advanced knowledge of emotions may also lead to more advanced strategies for regulating emotions, so to less impulsivity in action. Greenberg and his colleagues acknowledge that there was a wide variation among the teachers in the extent to which they modelled emotional awareness, shared their own emotions and created an ethos of respect for others in the classroom. This may explain some of the cultural variations in the success or otherwise of this intervention. In this sense, progress is likely to be slow in the early stages, as educators become used to working more directly with emotions in schools. It could be argued, therefore, that the potential for interventions such as PATHS is much greater than the present results indicate, especially in the context of preventing difficulties before they escalate (Greenberg, 2010).

It is also interesting to note that this type of intervention is part of a wider movement on the promotion of emotional literacy in children and young people (Bywater & Sharples, 2012). The evaluations of PATHS illustrate that it is possible to teach aspects of emotional fluency and understanding in school settings, in both mainstream and special education, with positive outcomes. But we must also remember that there are many ways of teaching emotional literacy, with set programmes such as PATHS being only one. For example, moral values can be explored through classroom discussions of drama and literature, or through games, or in current affairs lessons, or through direct experience of community action. Administrators and educators need to take account of cultural factors in the wider society in which any particular programme is being taught (see Chapter 18). For a useful metaanalysis of a number of Social and Emotional Learning (SEL) programmes see Durlak et al. (2011) and for a comprehensive overview of approaches to SEL that have been evaluated scientifically see Cefai and Cavioni (2014).

CHAPTER SUMMARY

- Constructs such as prosocial behaviour, altruism and empathy are defined. Examples of experimental and observational studies are given.
- Various factors in the family and the school encourage prosocial behaviour in young people. According to Grusec and colleagues, there are key aspects to the parent–child relationship that are conducive to the internalization of prosocial values: being warm and nurturing; offering unconditional approval of their children's actions; fostering secure attachment through sensitive, empathic relationships; responding positively to the child's reasonable demands.
- Research supports the idea that reasoning is a better strategy than punishment or authoritarian interventions to control the child; reasoning helps children to consider the outcomes of their actions and is conducive to the emergence of empathy to others' feelings. It is also important for adults to model good practice in the course of everyday interactions with children.
- The reciprocal nature of peer and sibling relationships also plays a crucial part in the development of prosocial behaviour, both through direct experience of others' responses and through witnessing the distress of others. Interactions among peers and siblings provide many opportunities to help and comfort others and so offer a rich source of influence on prosocial development.
- The peer group provides the social setting in which children and adolescents discover how to deal with their own emotions, how to interact with others in distress, how to deal with relationship difficulties and how to maintain their status within the peer group. In school settings, peer support systems have been found to be effective methods for training young people to act prosocially when faced with conflicts or social problems among their peer group.
- The development of prosocial behaviour takes place in a social and cultural framework of moral values. The chapter considers gender and cultural differences in the emergence of prosocial behaviour, as well as antisocial and criminal behaviour.
- This links to the discussion of how the child develops the capacity for moral reasoning. The two influential stage theories of Piaget and Kohlberg are compared and contrasted. New ideas are being researched and discussed in the context of social-cognitive domain theory as proposed by Turiel and Smetana.
- Curriculum materials have been developed to enhance the moral and prosocial development of children. These are reviewed in the final section.

DISCUSSION POINTS

1. How should we define prosocial behaviour? How important is it to take account of cultural differences when doing so?
2. Contrast the use of naturalistic and experimental designs for studying what influences prosocial behaviour and altruism.
3. Compare Piaget's two methods of studying moral reasoning. Do they give children full opportunity to describe their processes of making a moral judgement?
4. Is Kohlberg's way of obtaining levels of moral reasoning biased towards male, upper/middle-class, urban, Western-educated respondents?
5. Does social-cognitive domain theory offer a more convincing alternative explanation? How does this approach illuminate our understanding of youth attitudes towards asylum seekers?
6. Is it possible to teach children moral values? How can schools and families collaborate to do this?
7. Should young offenders be punished more severely than they are at present within the criminal justice system?

FURTHER READING

- For a clear account of the domain approach to moral development, see Killen, M. & Smetana, J. (2006). *Handbook of moral development*. Mahwah, NJ: Lawrence Erlbaum; and Helwig, C.C. & Turiel, E. (2011). Children's social and moral reasoning, in P.K. Smith & C.H. Hart (Eds.), *Wiley-Blackwell handbook of childhood social development* (2nd ed.), pp. 567–583. Chichester: Wiley.
- Piaget, J. (1977, 1932). *The moral judgement of the child*. Harmondsworth: Penguin, is worth reading for an insight into Piaget's style and methods; the theoretical excerpts are, however, rather dated and heavy going. Unfortunately, there is not a good, simple primer on Piaget's and Kohlberg's theories. For a useful critique of Kohlberg's ideas in practice, read Oser, F.K. (1996). Kohlberg's dormant ghosts: The case of education. *Journal of Moral Education, 25*, 253–275.
- A useful overview of emotional literacy theory and practice in action is Cefai, C. & Cavioni, V. (2014). *Social and emotional education: Integrating theory and research into practice*. New York: Springer. Howe, C. (2010). *Peer groups and children's development*. Oxford: Wiley-Blackwell considers the value of cooperative learning in schools from a sociocultural perspective. For up-to-date information on SEL, see the website of the European Network for Social and Emotional Competence (ENSEC): www.enseceurope.org.

CHAPTER

10

Social Dominance, Aggression and Bullying

CHAPTER OUTLINE

- Dominance in Children
- Aggression in Children
- Bullying in School

In Chapter 9 we examined how children often show prosocial behaviours. In this chapter, we examine how they may take advantage of or hurt others. We look first at the phenomenon of social dominance: how some children get their own way and dominate others in social encounters. Aggression is usually defined as behaviour that intentionally hurts another; we examine the nature and development of aggression between children. Research on aggression in older children often overlaps with research on antisocial behaviour more generally, and delinquency; these are usually defined in terms of the impact of the behaviour on society (antisocial behaviour) and whether the behaviour is illegal (delinquency). Finally, we examine the rapidly expanding area of work on bullying. Bullying refers to repeated aggression where there is an imbalance of power; at an interpersonal level, much of this happens in school settings and there are well-developed intervention procedures.

DOMINANCE IN CHILDREN

Dominance refers to being able to get one's own way or take precedence over others, for example when there is some potential conflict over resources. Winning fights is one criterion of dominance, but more generally it is taken as getting one's own way or influencing others, which may or may not involve actual conflict. Thus, the concept is close to that of 'leadership', or social status. The 'dominance hierarchy' concept has been helpful in understanding social structure in animal social groups. It also appears useful for understanding human social groups, and a number of psychologists have used it in the context of children's peer groups. The concept is often referred to as 'social dominance', as it is in a social context.

Social Dominance in Younger Children

Some of the relevant research has involved direct observation of which children win conflicts. Strayer and Strayer (1976) observed children in a Canadian preschool. They separated out three kinds of conflict behaviours: 'threat-gesture', 'physical attack' and 'objection/position struggles'. They then examined the usefulness of a dominance hierarchy for each of these three kinds of behaviour, separately, whenever there was a clear winner or loser. They did this by calculating the linearity of the hierarchies. A linear hierarchy means that you can order individuals in a vertical hierarchy, such that (for example) if A dominates B, and B dominates C, then you can predict that A will dominate C. If instead C dominated A, this would be a 'reversal' of order, and the hierarchy would be less linear. Strayer and Strayer found that the linearity values were very high, though slightly lower for 'object/position struggles' than for the other two behaviours.

Besides observations, a common procedure is to get ratings or rankings from children, using questions such as 'Who is the toughest?' or 'Who is the strongest?' in their class. Several psychologists have confirmed that this can be done reliably from about 4 or 5 years of age onwards. Children generally agree, especially regarding the top and bottom positions (Edelman & Omark, 1973). Also, the consensus of ratings or rankings from classmates usually shows good agreement with observational measures.

An interesting exception to this reliable estimation is that an individual child will often overestimate his or her open dominance position in the class. One of the authors (P.K.S.) noticed this with one of his own children; when his son was 5 years old, on the way to his primary school one morning, he was asked, 'Who is the strongest in your class?' and without hesitation he replied, 'I am!'. In fact, he was probably around the middle of his class, as far as strength and dominance were concerned. But this overestimation is common, as Edelman and Omark found, and generalizes to overestimating one's friends' position as well (Boulton & Smith, 1990). From an evolutionary developmental psychology perspective (see Chapter 2), Bjorklund (2007) argues that these and other examples of overestimating performance in young children may be adaptive (if not carried too far!) by encouraging attempts and stretching their abilities.

Social Dominance in Older Children

Sluckin (1981) carried out an intensive study of playground behaviour in a first school and a middle school in Oxford, England, that illustrates how social dominance can operate in middle childhood. In the first school, he describes how a boy called Neill was known by his peers as the 'boss' of the playground. Neill was often observed in conflicts, although usually these were not overt fights (Neill was not particularly strong physically), but verbal conflicts by which Neill sought to enhance his prestige and manipulate social situations. Neill disliked losing, and would try to redefine or reinterpret situations so that it appeared he had won. For example, in a race with Ginny, where they finished at the same time, Neill cried out, 'Yes, yes' (I'm the winner). Ginny called out 'Draw', to which Neill replied, 'No, it wasn't, you're just trying to make trouble'. In another example, playing football, Neill said, 'I'm in goal, bagsee'. Nick replied, 'No, I'm in goal'. Neill retorted, 'No, John's in goal' and John went in goal. Here (perhaps avoiding a fight), Neill kept the initiative and gave the impression of being 'in charge' even though he did not get his own way entirely. Neill was clearly a leader of sorts, but he does not seem to have been especially popular. His leadership was often disruptive, since he always insisted on winning games. However, he had a high dominance status in the playground, and would seem to qualify as 'controversial' in sociometric status terms (see p. 173).

Dominance hierarchies need to be established, and this will normally be in the early stages of a new group or class being formed. Savin-Williams made studies of dominance formation in groups of American teenagers (aged 10–16 years), mostly previously unacquainted, who came together in 5-week summer camps. In one report (Savin-Williams, 1976), he studied intensively one cabin group of six boys aged 12 and 13. It took about 3 days for a stable, ordered hierarchy to emerge; it then remained very consistent throughout the duration of the camp. Observational measures of dominance correlated highly ($r < .90$) with a sociometric measure from the children themselves. The most frequently observed dominance behaviours were verbal ridicule (seen 235 times), giving a verbal command that was obeyed (seen 190 times) and ignoring or refusing to comply with another's command (seen 158 times). The most dominant boy also was usually the leader in hiking and athletics, and was well liked. However, the least dominant boy, quiet, serious but friendly, was also popular.

Another study (Savin-Williams, 1980) was of four groups of five girls (aged 12–14) at summer camp. Again dominance hierarchies formed, although they did not seem as clear-cut as in boys' groups, perhaps because girls more often formed smaller groups (pairs or threesomes).

Verbal ridicule was again the most frequently observed indicator of dominance. The position in the dominance hierarchy correlated significantly with ratings of leadership. However, Savin-Williams distinguished between 'maternal leaders' who were perceived by peers as a source of security and support, and 'antagonists' who imposed themselves on others.

Although dominance, when acknowledged, can reduce aggression (the person lower in dominance gives way), if dominance is challenged or uncertain then aggression may be used to sort out the hierarchy. Pellegrini and Bartini (2001) studied boys in US schools as they made the transition from primary to middle school (11 to 12 years). These boys moved from being the oldest and most dominant to the youngest and least dominant in their school settings. Aggression increased at the start of the new school, and aggressive behaviour was related positively to dominance status. It seems that aggressive behaviour was being used to assert social dominance. This changed by the end of the year, as the hierarchy was established; aggressive behaviour decreased and the more dominant boys were not more aggressive. The 'payoff' to dominant boys was that they were more attractive to girls, at an age when heterosexual relationships were just beginning to be of interest (see Chapter 19).

AGGRESSION IN CHILDREN

Aggression is usually defined as intentional behaviour that hurts another person. The 'intentional' qualifier is to distinguish it from behaviour that might accidentally hurt someone. If I am rushing for a bus and by mistake knock someone over, while that deserves an apology, it would not normally be taken as 'aggressive behaviour'.

Given that sort of definition, how do we describe some hitting and pushing behaviours seen in 12–18-month-old infants? Early peer interactions (see Chapter 5) not infrequently involve such physical acts. Indeed, Richard Tremblay (2003) has documented how what might be physically aggressive behaviours are actually most frequent around 2 years of age! Up to 2 years, however, this is sometimes referred to as 'exploratory aggression', since it is not clear that one infant intends to hurt the other when they hit or push them—they are still finding out about the effects of their actions. Tremblay argues that from around 2 years, toddlers are usually increasingly 'socialized' into realizing this is not acceptable behaviour.

As with Parten's study of social participation (p. 171), some of the early studies on aggressive behaviour in young children were based on observational studies in nurseries and child-care centres. For example, Jersild and Markey (1935) observed conflicts in 54 children at three US nursery schools. Many kinds of conflict behaviour were defined; for example, *snatches* as 'takes or grabs toys or objects held, used, or occupied by another child; uses, tugs at, or pushes material away with hands or feet; all contacts with material which, if completed, would deprive the other child of the use and possession of material'; and *unfavourable remarks about persons* as comments like 'You're no good at it'; 'You don't do it right'; 'I don't like you'. Jersild and Markey recorded who was the aggressor and who was the victim, what the outcome of the struggle was and the role of the teacher. They found some decline in conflicts with age, and overall boys took part in more conflicts than girls. A follow-up was made of 24 children after about 9 months. Conflicts had become more verbal, but individual differences between children in types and frequencies of conflict tended to be maintained. Very similar results were found in an observational study over 50 years later by Cummings et al. (1989); they reported that the overall level of physical aggression declined between 2 and 5 years of age. Nevertheless, the more aggressive boys tended to stay relatively more aggressive over this period.

In another early study, Appel (1942) made observations in 14 different nursery schools. She delineated 15 kinds of adult responses to children's aggression. Five were 'ending techniques': diverting; separating or removing; restraining; arbitrary decision making; enforcing a rule. Ten were 'teaching techniques': explaining property rights; urging self-defence; suggesting a solution; suggesting the child find a solution; interpreting; encouraging friendly acts; making light of troubles or hurts; requiring good manners; disapproval; retaliation. An evaluation of the effectiveness of these different techniques was made, by deciding whether the conflict continued or ended after the adult intervention. Some techniques were much more effective than others at ending the immediate conflict. Least effective was suggesting to the children that they find a solution themselves. Appel concluded that 'teachers should not intervene too readily in children's conflicts. Children will teach each other a great deal. Too much interference prevents self-reliance'.

Through the 1950s and early 1960s, direct observation was neglected, and more constrained investigations in laboratories, often experimental in nature, were seen as the preferred method (see p. 5). Aggression was assessed by means of observing children punching inflatable dolls and pressing buttons to supposedly deliver punishment to another child. These studies have subsequently been criticized as lacking ecological validity (p. 16). By the late 1960s, direct observation had started to make a comeback. For example, Blurton Jones (1967) observed the social behaviour of children in an English nursery school. Most aggressive behaviour occurred in the context of property fights. Blurton Jones drew a clear distinction between aggressive behaviour, evidenced by beating or hitting at another with a frown or angry face, and rough-and-tumble play, where children chased and tackled each other, often smiling or laughing. These two kinds of behaviour can be confused because of their superficial similarity (see pp. 239–240).

Types and Typologies of Aggressive Behaviour

As observations and studies of aggressive behaviour accumulated, researchers started distinguishing the main categories.

One set of distinctions focuses on the intent or motivation for the aggressive act. Some researchers distinguish *instrumental* and *hostile* aggression. This is based on whether the distress or harm is inferred to be the primary intent of the act; instrumental aggression is supposed to be carried out to achieve some external aim, to which hurting the other is incidental—for example, a child pushes or hits another in order to get a toy that the other child has. Hostile aggression is when a child deliberately attacks another in order to hurt them.

A related distinction is between *reactive* and *proactive* aggression. This distinction focuses more on the precursors of the aggression. Reactive aggression is in response to some provocation (real or perceived); a child feels insulted by what another child has said or done, perhaps, and hits out at them in angry retaliation. Proactive aggression is dominant behaviour employed to achieve a specific goal (so similar to instrumental aggression, though without the presumption that any hurt is incidental).

The distinction between reactive and proactive aggression has been used by proponents of the Social Information Processing model (see p. 176). Crick and Dodge (1996) showed that reactively aggressive children tended to differ from others in the stage of attributing intent to another's actions—they showed a *hostile attribution bias*, very readily assuming aggressive intent in a peer. By contrast, proactively aggressive children differed in the stage of evaluation of consequences—they evaluated aggressive acts more positively, in terms of their outcomes.

Another set of distinctions refers more descriptively to the type and context of actions. It is possible to distinguish individual and group aggression (depending on whether more than one child attacks another), and a long-standing distinction was between physical and verbal aggression. For example, in the Jersild and Markey (1935) study above, both kinds of aggressive acts were clearly observed.

However, more recent work has extended this physical/verbal typology. The kind of physical and verbal attacks usually described are 'direct' or face-to-face—hitting or insulting someone. Björkqvist et al. (1992) added a third category, of *indirect* aggression. This is aggression not aimed directly at someone but via a third party; for example, spreading nasty rumours about someone. In a study in Finland, they obtained nominations and ratings of peers, for behaviours such as:

- *Physical aggression*: hits, kicks, pushes.
- *Direct verbal aggression*: insults, calls the other names.
- *Indirect aggression*: tells bad or false stories, becomes friends with another as revenge.

As is clear from Table 10.1, girls were less nominated for physical aggression at all ages, but there is not much difference in verbal aggression, and girls were consistently nominated more for indirect aggression. This sex difference has been generally confirmed by subsequent studies, including Crick and Grotpeter (1995) in the USA, who used the term 'relational aggression'. Galen and Underwood (1997) used the similar term 'social aggression', as aggression intended to damage another's self-esteem or social status.

For example, in the Crick and Grotpeter (1995) study, peer nominations were obtained from 8–11-year-old US children for overt aggression (e.g. starts fights) and relational aggression (e.g. when mad at a person, ignores them or stops talking to them). The researchers also obtained data on sociometric status, loneliness and depression. They found that overt and

---

Table 10.1   Peer-estimated aggression of different types, at different ages, for boys (B) and girls (G).

		8 years	11 years	15 years	18 years
Physical aggression (e.g. kicking)	B	.61	.82	.50	.15
	G	.15	.22	.07	.07
Verbal aggression (e.g. verbal abuse)	B	.44	.96	.95	.75
	G	.15	1.09	.98	.90
Indirect aggression (e.g. gossip)	B	.32	.83	.81	.60
	G	.40	1.30	1.14	1.06

Source: Adapted from Björkqvist, K., Lagerspetz, K. M.J. & Kaukainen, A. (1992). Do girls manipulate and boys fight? Developmental trends in regard to direct and indirect aggression. *Aggressive Behaviour, 18*, 117–127.

relational aggression tended to be related—children who did more of one did more of the other; the correlation was r = .54, so moderate in size. Nevertheless, the two concepts are clearly partly distinct, and this was especially noticeable when gender differences were examined. The researchers looked at which children were especially high on each type of aggression. For overt aggression, this included 15.6% of the boys but only .4% of the girls. For relational aggression, it included only 2.9% of the boys but 17.4% of the girls. They also found that children high in relational aggression tended to be 'controversial' and also to be high on depression and loneliness (see pp. 178–180).

The utility of these different typologies will depend on the focus of the study, but it has generally been accepted that aggression should now embrace the 'indirect' and 'relational' as well as the more straightforward hits and insults studied in earlier decades. This has been revealing about gender differences, and there are important age changes.

Stop and Think

Is it important to discriminate between different types of aggression?

Developmental Changes in Aggression

Physical aggression is the earliest kind of aggressive behaviour, but for most children this declines through childhood. Based on mother's reports of hitting, biting or kicking by children from 2 through to 11 years, Tremblay and colleagues (2004) have shown that this starts around 1 year of age and actually is actually highest at around 2–3 years. Toddlers are the most physically aggressive age group. Most children gradually learn to inhibit physical aggression, as adults (mostly) tell them that this is not acceptable; but although generally children become socialized out of physical aggression, rates of indirect aggression increase with age. This is shown in Table 10.2, which gives rates of mother-rated physical and indirect aggression from 2 to 8 years, from a longitudinal study of 1,183 Canadian children. For both sexes, there is a steady decrease in physical aggression and a steady increase in indirect aggression,

Table 10.2 Mother-estimated physical and indirect aggression, at different ages, for boys (B) and girls (G).

		2 years	4 years	6 years	8 years
Physical aggression	B	1.31	1.30	1.05	.92
	G	1.15	1.03	.80	.75
Indirect aggression	B	n/a	.58	.73	.76
	G	n/a	.64	.96	1.13

Source: Adapted from Cote, S.M. et al. (2007) The joint development of physical and indirect aggression: Predictors of continuity and change during childhood, *Development and Psychopathology, 19*: 37–55, with permission.

Table 10.3   Self-reports of bullying, sexual harassment, and dating aggression in children and adolescents aged 11 to 17 years, for boys (B) and girls (G).

		11 years	12 years	13 years	14 years	15 years	16 years	17 years
Bullying	B	1.25	1.43	1.57	1.63	1.48	1.61	1.33
	G	1.16	1.17	1.26	1.39	1.13	1.15	1.11
Same-sex sexual harassment	B	1.11	1.16	1.21	1.41	1.44	1.38	1.35
	G	1.16	1.02	1.04	1.18	1.16	1.09	1.04
Opposite-sex sexual harassment	B	1.05	1.15	1.25	1.40	1.36	1.36	1.32
	G	1.15	1.06	1.10	1.31	1.21	1.17	1.18
Social dating aggression	B	1.02	1.10	1.09	1.21	1.20	1.20	1.36
	G	1.10	1.02	1.09	1.38	1.21	1.30	1.20
Physical dating aggression	B	1.03	1.06	1.07	1.02	1.07	1.05	1.06
	G	1.06	1.01	1.03	1.08	1.03	1.05	1.03

Source: Adapted from Pepler, D. J. Et al (2006) A developmental perspective on bullying, *Aggressive Behavior, 32*: 376–384.

although both trends are more marked for girls (Côté et al., 2007). As can be seen in Table 10.1, physical aggression continues to decrease from 8 or at least 11 to 18 years, while verbal and indirect aggression increase, although starting to decline by 18 years.

Data from a different Canadian sample are shown in Table 10.3, which gives more detail on forms of aggression common in adolescence (Pepler et al., 2006). This includes bullying (see p. 358), sexual harassment (such as making sexual comments, spreading sexual rumours) and dating aggression to a current or recent romantic partner. Bullying increases up to around 13–14 years (or 16 for boys), then declines; sexual harassment peaks at around 14–15 years; while dating aggression is naturally low in the early adolescent years (and stays low for physical dating aggression), with social dating aggression increasing in later adolescence.

These studies generally find substantial overlap amongst the different types of aggression, with children high on one also tending to be high on another. For example, children who bullied also tended to be high on sexual harassment and dating aggression (Pepler et al., 2006). From longitudinal data it is also possible to look at individual trajectories over time. For example, in the Côté et al. (2007) study, most children (63%) showed decreasing physical aggression and low levels of indirect aggression, from 2 to 8 years; some 14% showed moderately decreasing physical aggression and rising indirect aggression; and another 14% showed high-level trajectories for both kinds of aggression.

Is Aggression Maladaptive?

For some decades, there has been a prevalent view in much North American and some European developmental psychology that aggressive behaviour in children was unskilled and maladaptive. This view was often associated with the Social Information Processing (SIP) model (see p. 176). Here, Crick and Dodge (1996, p. 994) wrote that, 'Skilful processing at each step is hypothesized to lead to competent performance within a situation, whereas biased or deficient processing is hypothesized to lead to deviant social behaviour (e.g. aggression)', and 'Social maladjustment is related to the formulation of social goals that are likely to be relationship-damaging'. This view is often found in textbooks from that period; for example, in *Child psychology: A contemporary viewpoint*, Hetherington and Parke (1993, p. 603) stated that, 'Aggressive children may behave in a hostile and inappropriate fashion because they are not very skilled at solving interpersonal problems'. In *Child development*, Berk (2000, p. 515) stated that, 'Social-cognitive deficits and distortions add to the maintenance of aggressive behavior'.

This view has been challenged (see Hawley et al., 2007). Proponents of an alternative view argue that aggression is seen throughout animal species as one part of the normal behavioural repertoire, and this can be argued to be true of humans, including children. Also, there is considerable evidence that some degree of aggressive behaviour, especially when used strategically by children, is associated with social competence, not social incompetence. Box 10.1 gives an example of an empirical study illustrating this kind of finding in young children. In another study at this age range, of 471 US 3-year-olds in Head Start programmes, Vaughn et al. (2003) summarized that, 'for the most part, aggression and negative behaviour measures were positive predictors of social competence', and 'we are inclined to see these negative episodes as opportunities for learning and for social-cognitive development'.

It is important to distinguish 'socially incompetent' from 'socially undesirable'. A lot of aggressive behaviour in a child may be socially undesirable, but it does not necessarily mean that child is socially incompetent. For most children, a certain amount of aggressive behaviour is normal. It is usually kept within reasonable bounds such that they are not overly disruptive of peer group activities and hence rejected by peers. However, some children show high levels of aggression, often of a hostile or harassing nature, which can be quite stable over time and for which some adult intervention seems justified. If not dealt with at the time, such children who show persistent high aggressiveness through the school years are at greatly increased risk for later delinquency antisocial and violent behaviour (Farrington, 1995; Lahey et al., 1999). We will look next at the origins of individual differences in aggressive behaviour, and why some children may be highly aggressive.

Box 10.1 Strategies of control, aggression and morality in preschoolers: an evolutionary perspective

This study is one of a number challenging the consensus view (at the time) that aggression in children is maladaptive. It takes as a starting point what the author refers to as *resource control theory*. This postulates that socially dominant individuals get preferred access to resources in a social group, and that various strategies may be used to achieve social dominance. In particular, there are coercive strategies and prosocial strategies. Coercive strategies involve threats and aggression. Prosocial strategies involve reciprocity, help and alliances.

The conventional view would be that coercive strategies would be associated with reduced social competence and popularity, compared to prosocial strategies. However, Hawley proposed that the picture is more complicated. She argued that some children were 'bistrategic controllers'—successful at using both coercive and prosocial strategies, perhaps depending on the situation—and that these children would be the most competent and would not be unpopular.

In this study, she obtained data from 14 classrooms in six preschools, with, altogether, 163 children (mostly 3–5 years) and their teachers participating. The teachers provided the following ratings for each child.

- Use of prosocial strategies (six items: e.g. 'He/she is someone who influences others by doing something in return').
- Use of coercive strategies (six items: e.g. 'He/she bullies or pushes others to do what He/she wants').
- Resource control (six items: e.g. 'He/she gets what she wants even if others don't').
- Overt aggression (three items).
- Relational aggression (three items).

In addition, interviews with each child produced the following data.

- Language ability (Peabody Picture Vocabulary Test).
- Moral cognition (three vignettes to assess knowing what is right and wrong, and reasons for this).
- Moral affect (three vignettes to assess whether guilt is felt at transgressions, and reasons for this).

- Use of prosocial strategies (six items; e.g. 'He/she is someone who influences others by doing something in return').
- Social problem-solving strategies (six vignettes).
- Social preference (nominations of children they liked to play with, or did not play with).

As well as reporting correlational data, Hawley divided her children into different types of resource controllers. Children rated high (top third) on both coercive and prosocial strategies were labelled bistrategic (19 girls, 6 boys). Those only high on coercive strategies were coercive controllers (13 girls, 14 boys). Those only high on prosocial strategies were prosocial controllers (25 girls, 17 boys). Non- controllers scored low (bottom third) on both dimensions (12 girls, 17 boys) and the remaining children were labelled typical (20 girls, 20 boys). These groups were then compared on the range of measures obtained. Some of the findings are shown in Box Table 10.1.1.

The means in the table show standardized scores, so the average score would be zero. Three results are very highly significant, statistically. First, bistrategic controllers score highest for success in resource control; not surprisingly, non-controllers score the lowest. Second, both bistragetic and coercive controllers are high on both overt and relational aggression—again, not unexpected, as this enters into the definitions of these categories. The findings on moral cognition and moral affect are a bit more complex and for some measures not significant, but those that are statistically significant (shown in the table) indicate that the bistrategic controllers come out as morally mature; they are high or highest on recognizing that transgressions (such as taking a candy from another child) are wrong, giving reasons for this related to the victim's feelings, and giving rule-based reasons to explain their feelings. Finally, and importantly for the hypotheses

Box Table 10.1.1   Mean standardized scores on various measures, comparing five different types of children based on resource control strategies; significance levels from MANOVA.

Variable	Bistrategic	Coercive	Prosocial	Typical	Non-controller	Significance
Resource control	.74	.49	.06	−.40	−.67	$p < .0001$
Overt aggression	.80	1.11	−.44	−.54	−.36	$p < .0001$
Relational aggression	1.07	.44	−.20	−.39	−.55	$p < .0001$
Cognition: wrong to take	.38	.26	.07	.01	−.57	$p < .05$
Cognition: emotion reasons	.42	.08	−.32	.41	.22	$p < .04$
Moral affect: rule reasons	.48	−.03	−.39	−.16	.48	$p < .02$
Peer social preference	.52	−.57	.45	−.18	−.30	$p < .01$

Source: Adapted from Hawley, P. H. (2003). Strategies of control, aggression and morality in preschoolers: An evolutionary perspective. *Journal of Experimental Child Psychology*, 85, 213–235.

of the study, the bistrategic controllers, together with prosocial controllers, come out highest on social preference. The coercive controllers come out lowest on social preference.

Two important strengths of this study are: taking a theoretical approach (resource control theory) to test out specific and possibly counterintuitive hypotheses; and going beyond a simple notion of 'aggressive children', splitting up the aggression construct depending on how aggression is used with other strategies such as prosocial behaviour. The findings of this study show very clearly that, in this sample at least, the strategic use of aggression is quite compatible with success in gaining resources, being liked rather than disliked, and moral maturity. However, this is only so for children who can combine, probably in flexible and situation-dependent ways, the use of prosocial and coercive strategies. Those children who only (or primarily) use coercive strategies are indeed not liked, even though they often get their own way.

One limitation of the study is that the measures of moral cognition and moral affect did not assess actual behaviour; moral reasoning is interesting in its own right, but measures of actual behaviour would give further insight. Also, the measures of aggression and resource control were based on teacher's ratings. Teacher's ratings are considered relatively accurate for preschool children, but nevertheless direct observations would ultimately give more valid indicators of these.

Based on material in Hawley, P. H. (2003). Strategies of control, aggression, and morality in preschoolers: An evolutionary perspective. *Journal of Experimental Child Psychology*, 85, 213–235.

Origins of Aggression: Genetic Factors and Temperament

There is some clear evidence for the role of genetic factors in individual differences in aggressiveness, and more generally for antisocial behaviour. Much of this evidence comes from both twin and adoption studies (see Chapter 2). Rhee and Waldman (2002) carried out a meta-analysis of 51 twin and three adoption studies that included measures of antisocial behaviour. They found that genetic influences accounted for 41% of the variance, shared environment 16% and non-shared environment 43%, with no differences between males and females. Tuvblad et al. (2006) reported findings from a Swedish twin study, with 1,133 twin pairs, on antisocial behaviour in adolescence (16–17 years). They found that the proportions of variance (genetic, shared and non-shared environment) showed some variation by gender and by socioeconomic circumstances. Genetic influences were stronger for adolescents from higher socioeconomic backgrounds, whereas shared environment was more important in lower socioeconomic backgrounds. This makes sense; environmental factors may have more relative impact in impoverished than in advantaged backgrounds. Genetic influence was (contrary to the Rhee and Waldman findings) higher in girls than boys.

Of course, it is not the case that a propensity for specific aggressive or criminal acts is inherited. So how do genetic effects operate? One approach is to consider aspects of brain development. We know (see Chapter 1) that different parts of the brain—frontal, temporal and parietal cortex, and limbic system structures—have effects on aspects such as emotional control, behavioural inhibition and moral judgement. Both genetic and social-environmental factors can affect aspects of brain functioning, and hence psychological outcomes such as these (Raine, 2008). One example of a relevant and partly heritable aspect of behaviour is temperament. For example, poor anger and behavioural control (related to frontal cortex functioning) may be picked up as difficult temperament (see Chapter 3, p. 101). In the Dunedin longitudinal study in New Zealand (see Table 1.1), Caspi et al. (1995) assessed temperament on a sample of 800 children at ages 3, 5, 7 and 9 years and behaviour problems at 9, 11, 13 and 15 years. They found that early 'lack of control' (emotional lability, restlessness, short attention span and negativism) correlated with later externalizing problems (such as aggressiveness). In a similar kind of study in the USA, Guerin et al. (1997) assessed 100 children over 10 years; children with difficult temperament at 1.5 years showed more attention problems and aggressive behaviour at 4–12 years.

How parents respond to children of different temperament may set up a transactional pathway leading to different outcomes (see Chapter 3). If some genetic factors work through temperamental characteristics, we would then expect that the extent of aggressive behaviour would also depend on aspects of parenting. This is an example of a gene–environment interaction, and early evidence for this was reported by Caspi and colleagues (2002) from the Dunedin longitudinal data. Of 442 males followed from birth to age 26, boys who were severely maltreated in childhood were more likely to show antisocial/criminal behaviour as adults. However, this depended on genotype, specifically the high- or low-activity variants of a gene encoding for the enzyme MAOA (which metabolizes neurotransmitters such as dopamine). Maltreated boys with the low-activity genotype were at high risk (85% of them showed violent behaviour, and 50% had criminal convictions); maltreated boys with the high-activity genotype were not. Figure 10.1 shows this interaction between genotype and environment in the expression of antisocial behaviour. Since then several other studies have

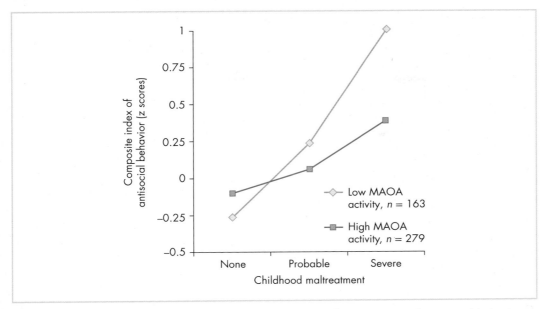

Figure 10.1   An example of gene–environment interaction in the expression of antisocial behaviour.
Source: Caspi et al. (2002). Role of Genotype in the Cycle of Violence in Maltreated Children, Science.,
297: 851–854. Reprinted with permission from AAAS.

broadly replicated this finding. As noted in Chapter 2, this effect has been interpreted within the diathesis-stress model, but may actually be an example of differential susceptibility if the boys with the low-activity genotype do better in favourable situations.

The Caspi et al. study focuses on a particular gene variant and on environments that included severe maltreatment—so not a typical situation. Another study has suggested that within the normal range of children's behaviour, temperament is important and often outweighs family factors. Russell et al. (2003) carried out a study of preschool children in two countries, the USA and Australia. Irrespective of country, they found that the best predictor of teacher-rated aggression was parent-rated temperament. They also obtained measures of parenting, but found that they contributed little, with one important exception: father's authoritarian parenting was a significant predictor of physical aggression in the child.

Temperament is not the only likely mediator from genes to aggressive behaviour. Another is empathy and regard for others' feelings (also influenced by the frontal cortex). In fact, some researchers have argued that this is a very important factor for a subset of children who have what they call 'callous-unemotional' traits.

Callous-unemotional Traits

Callous-unemotional (CU) traits refer to lack of guilt, lack of empathy and callous use of others for one's own gain (Frick & White, 2008). These, in fact, are diagnostic of psychopathy in adults, together with deceitful and manipulative behavioural style and impulsive, poorly planned behaviour.

Research suggests that CU traits are a particularly important diagnostic criterion for disruptive and antisocial behaviour, and aggression, from childhood through adolescence (Frick et al., 2014). As such, CU traits have recently been included as a specifier for Conduct Disorder in DSM-V (APA, 2013). They are also an important predictor of future antisocial behaviour and poor outcome (Fontaine et al., 2011; Kahn, Byrd & Pardini, 2013).

Callous-unemotional traits appear to be relatively stable from later childhood to early adolescence and appear to have high heritability. Two twin-based studies (Viding et al., 2005, 2008) have assessed the level of conduct problems in over 3,000 twin pairs, at 7 and at 9 years. It was found that for those with conduct problems who were high on CU traits, heritability was very high whereas for those with conduct problems who were low on CU traits, heritability was much lower and there was substantial shared environmental influence— perhaps pointing to parenting factors as influential.

This differentiation of high-CU and low-CU groups has been further substantiated through brain imaging work (Jones et al., 2009; Marsh et al., 2013), demonstrating a decreased brain response to fear and pain in others. Differentiating the different developmental pathways involved in CU traits is important as it is likely to have implications for intervention strategies (Hawes, Price & Dadds, 2014).

 Stop and Think

Are aggressive children born that way, or made that way by their environment?

Origins of Aggression: Parenting

There is considerable evidence that home circumstances can be important influences leading to aggressive and later antisocial behaviour (see also Chapter 4). Insecure and disturbed attachment relationships may be one factor (Van IJzendoorn, 1997). Another consideration is early day care arrangements. As we saw in Chapter 4, there are mixed findings on the developmental impact of day care. Specifically looking at outcomes for aggression, Borge et al. (2004) found that for high-risk families, children in day care were significantly *less* physically aggressive, suggesting that here day care was a protective factor (see Table 4.5). More usually, the concern has been that early day care might make children *more* aggressive, as indicated by the NICHD longitudinal studies (see Chapter 4).

However, the dominant approach in this area of home background factors relates to parenting skills. Patterson et al. (1989) suggested that certain key aspects of parenting are involved in producing highly aggressive or antisocial children. They argued that children who experience irritable and ineffective discipline at home, and poor parental monitoring of their activities, together with a lack of parental warmth, are particularly likely to become aggressive in peer groups and at school. Such children are experiencing aggressive means of solving disputes at home, and are not being given clear and effective guidance to do otherwise. According to this view, antisocial behaviour at middle school is likely to be linked to academic failure and peer rejection; in adolescence, especially if parental monitoring is lax, these young people are likely to be involved in deviant and delinquent peer groups. This hypothesis is

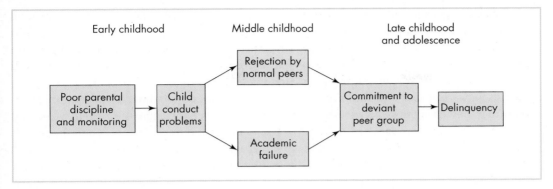

Figure 10.2   A developmental progression for antisocial behaviour.

Source: Patterson, G.R., DeBaryshe, B.D. & Ramsey, E. (1989). A developmental perspective on antisocial behavior. *American Psychologist, 44,* 329–335.

shown in Figure 10.2. (You may find it interesting to compare Figure 10.2 with Figures 4.2 and 5.4; all relate to different linked aspects of parenting and peer relations. Do you feel they can be linked together, or are some aspects in disagreement?)

A number of studies have provided some support for this kind of theorizing. For example, Florsheim et al. (1998) studied boys aged 10–15 years, in the USA. They found that externalizing behaviour problems (which would include aggression) was more common in boys in single-parent than dual-parent families. However, looking beyond this to what aspects of parenting were involved, the difference appeared to be explained by lower cohesion, less effective parental monitoring and absence of a positive male family member.

Smith and Farrington (2004) examined continuities in antisocial behaviour and parenting across three generations, using longitudinal data from 411 inner-London males (born in 1953; labelled G2 generation), their parents (G1 generation) and their children (G3 generation). They found a complex pattern of intergeneration effects, but some intergenerational continuity; for example, antisocial G1 mothers and fathers predicted conduct problems in G2 children and G3 children. This is supportive of Patterson's model (see Figure 10.2), but such continuities could be explained by genetic factors (see above) as well as by parenting factors. Also, the authors found that spouses tended to share similar values regarding antisocial behaviour ('assortative mating'); in both G1 and G2 generations, an antisocial adult was likely to have an antisocial spouse.

Patterson's approach suggests that the social skills of parenting are very important in early prevention of antisocial behaviour, and his interventions focus on helping parents improve their child management skills, for example via manuals and videotaped materials. However, another component of this model is the importance of the deviant peer group in adolescence. In early and middle childhood, aggressive behaviour often leads to peer rejection, but the picture becomes more complex in adolescence.

Origins of Aggression: Peer Group Factors

Patterson's model suggests that by early adolescence there are peer networks of antisocial children who may reinforce each other's behaviour. There is considerable evidence for this. Studies by Cairns on social networks of US adolescents confirm that aggressive pupils tend to associate with other aggressive pupils (Cairns et al., 1988). Dishion et al. (1995) also found that in 13–14-year-olds, highly antisocial boys had more antisocial friends; these friendships were more coercive and of shorter duration than those between less antisocial pupils, but were still seen as satisfying by those involved. It seems that at this age, an aggressive child may not necessarily be rejected, but may congregate with others of a similar antisocial tendency in ways that they can find rewarding. In one longitudinal study, Adams et al. (2005) found that having aggressive friends maintained high levels of aggression in 12-year-olds. Another longitudinal study, of 13–14-year-olds, by Berndt and Keefe (1995) found that pupils with disruptive friends tended to become more disruptive themselves over a half-year period. Although pupils with high-quality friendships (intimate, reciprocal) were generally less likely to be disruptive, those whose friends were both of high quality *and* disruptive were particularly at risk of becoming more disruptive themselves.

Again as predicted in this model, antisocial peer group affiliations may be linked to family factors and to a developmental progression of antisocial behaviour. Ferguson and Horwood (1999) examined prospective childhood predictors of deviant peer affiliations in adolescence in a longitudinal study of 900 children in Christchurch, New Zealand, up to age 15 years. Predictors of deviant peer group affiliation (antisocial behaviour, substance abuse) were low family socioeconomic status, poor family functioning (parental conflict, low emotional responsiveness, childhood sexual abuse), poor parental functioning (alcoholism, criminality, drugs) and earlier child problems at 10 years.

Reputation enhancement theory suggests that 'deviant' adolescents and adolescent peer groups have different values concerning antisocial behaviour; for non-deviant groups, antisocial behaviour might be a reason for exclusion, but for deviant groups it is a reason for inclusion (Carroll et al., 1999; Emler et al., 1987). This can explain an important finding, that peer-based interventions can have iatrogenic (negative) effects (Dishion et al., 1999). If antisocial children are selected out to take part in some group-based intervention (such as social skills training or empathy training), then their sharing and reinforcement of each other's values, and enhancing of in-group reputation by performing antisocial acts, may outweigh any possible positive effects of the intervention programme itself.

Low self-esteem (and underlying insecurity) is often thought to be an explanation of aggressive behaviour, but this is not well supported by research. Baumeister et al. (1996) argued that often aggression is associated with *threatened egotism*—that is, highly favourable views of oneself (not necessarily realistic) that are disputed or threatened by someone; aggression serves to buttress the favourable view of oneself, by belittling the other person.

Origins of Aggression: Neighbourhood Factors

Another important aspect in the even wider ecological context (see p. 11) is the neighbourhood the young person is growing up in. Linares et al. (2001) studied 160 children growing up in high-crime neighbourhoods in the USA. Exposure to community violence (including witnessing violent acts) predicted child behaviour problems in 3–5-year-olds, although how mothers coped with community violence was also an important mediating factor. At 10–12 years, Brody et al. (2001) found that community disadvantage predicted deviant peer affiliations, especially when combined with a lack of nurturant or involved parenting. Pettit et al. (1999) found that at 12–13 years, lack of neighbourhood safety, especially combined with low parental monitoring and unsupervised peer contacts, predicted teacher ratings of externalizing behaviour problems.

It is clear that a range of factors needs to be considered together to get a balanced picture of the more important predictors of aggressive and antisocial behaviour. Large samples are also needed. For example, Romano et al. (2005) examined multilevel correlates of childhood physical aggression and prosocial behaviour, in a Canadian study of 2,745 11-year-olds. At the individual level, significant predictors of physical aggression were male sex and experience of maternal hostility. At the family level, significant predictors were depressed mood of mother and punitive parenting style. At the neighbourhood level, the effects sizes were smaller, but growing up in a problem and impoverished neighbourhood remained a significant predictor even when the other factors were taken into account.

Disruptive Behaviour and Oppositional Defiant Disorder

Externalizing symptoms in children include both aggressive and defiant behaviours. The latter include being disobedient, disruptive, argumentative, antagonizing and vindictive. Oppositional defiant disorder (ODD) is a clinical diagnosis of this kind of antisocial behaviour syndrome. It overlaps to some extent with conduct disorder (CD).

Davies and Cicchetti (2014) looked at both genetic factors and maternal unresponsiveness in relation to disruptive and externalizing behaviour, in a predominantly Black US sample of 2-year-olds from disadvantaged backgrounds. They were interested in the 5-HTTLPR gene, which is involved in the neurotransmitter serotonin. In a longitudinal study over 2 years, they found that maternal unresponsiveness did predict later externalizing problems (see also p.37, and p.133). However this was moderated by genotype (assessed from cheek swabs for DNA analysis). Those with the long-long (l/l) version of the HTTLPR gene were more susceptible to the extent of maternal unresponsiveness; they did better (fewer externalizing symptoms) when mothers were more responsive, and less well when mothers were more unresponsive. This is a classic crossover interaction, similar to that shown in Figure 2.16(b), and described as *differential susceptibility*. As mentioned in Chapter 2, ethnicity seems to be important here, as in predominantly Caucasian samples it is those children with a short (s) allele of this gene who are more susceptible.

Why might 5-HTTLPR have such effects? The researchers also measured emotional reactivity to mother's behaviour. In particular, what they called angry reactivity appeared to play a key role—an aspect of emotional regulation that might plausibly be affected by this genotype. Such a reaction to maternal unresponsiveness might set up a vicious cycle of maternal irritation and hostility and further child externalizing reactions—or conversely, an emotionally responsive child may benefit more, when mothers are responsive to the child's needs.

With slightly older children, how they think and reason about others will become more important. A study in Canada by Dinolfo and Malti (2013) obtained ratings of ODD in 4- and 8-year-olds by their parents/caregivers. These correlated negatively with feelings of sympathy for others, and some aspects of reasoning about moral issues. However, interpretive understanding (a theory of mind task about understanding others' emotions) played an important role; for example, those children who showed feelings of sympathy in combination with high interpretive understanding showed lowest levels of ODD.

Delinquency

Delinquency is the legal definition of antisocial behaviour. As such, it overlaps greatly with violent and aggressive behaviour, although it also includes crimes such as vandalism and shoplifting, which do not cause harm to people directly.

Patterson et al. (1989, 1991) described 'early starters' and 'late starters' for delinquency. 'Early starters' are those who are aggressive and disruptive in primary and middle school, and often peer rejected at that time (see Figure 10.2), but who associate with others like them in secondary school and form the core of antisocial peer groups. They commit offences from around 10–12 years, and are more likely to reoffend. 'Late starters' are those who follow a more normal developmental path but show some aggressive and antisocial behaviours for a period, as they get drawn into the risk-taking behaviours of antisocial peer groups during adolescence. They only commit offences from around 15 years, and desist after a few years of involvement with a deviant peer group.

Farrington (1995) described findings from his longitudinal study of 411 working-class boys in London (see p. 353) that support this distinction. Of those convicted of an offence between 10 and 15 years, 23 boys (about one-third of offenders) were chronic offenders, having at least six offences by 18 years. These boys were responsible for half of all the convictions from the 411 boys in total. By contrast, none of those first convicted after 15 were classified as chronic offenders. (For a long-term follow-up of this sample to age 48, see Farrington et al., 2006.) Farrington's work also delineated risk factors for delinquency, quite similar to those often found for aggression; in this sample, the seven most powerful predictors from middle childhood to chronic delinquency in adolescence were: troublesomeness in school (from both teacher and peer ratings); hyperactivity/poor concentration; low intelligence and poor attainment; family criminality; family poverty (low income, large family size, poor housing); and poor parental child rearing. Moving out of London was a protective factor!

As with high aggression, family factors have been implicated in studies of delinquency. For example, Pagani et al. (1998, 1999) reported findings from a longitudinal study in Montreal of more than 400 French-Canadian boys. Their first study (1998) examined the impact of family transition on the development of delinquency in these boys between 12 and 15 years, and especially the effects of divorce and of remarriage while the boy was 6–11, or 12–15 years, on self-reported delinquency. They did not find main effects of divorce, but a specific finding was that those boys in families with a remarriage while they were aged 12–15 were more delinquent; these boys saw their parents as less expressive, and monitoring their behaviour less. Their second study (1999) examined the effects of poverty on academic failure and delinquency in these boys, and whether parenting practices would mediate any such effects. They found that delinquency at age 16 was predicted by poverty, independent of family configuration, and that lack of parental supervision and academic failure predicted delinquency, independently of poverty.

As reputation enhancement theory would predict, peer group factors are very important in understanding delinquent behaviour. Again using longitudinal data from boys aged 14–16 years growing up in Montreal, Gatti et al. (2005) studied youth gangs, delinquency and drug use. They found that delinquent behaviour was much higher in gang members, as might be expected. They then tried to ascertain whether this was an influence of selection (delinquent youth choose to join a gang), and/or an influence of facilitation (youth become delinquent through the influence of other gang members). In fact, their results supported the conclusion that both of these influences were at work.

Stop and Think

What would reputation enhancement theory predict about gang behaviour and ways of changing it?

Interventions

There are a great many programmes designed to reduce aggression, antisocial behaviour and conduct disorders in school, including social skills interventions (similar to those used for peer rejection, described earlier), and anti-bullying programmes (see next section). Generally, effects have been rather limited; as a result, more comprehensive programmes have started early (well before adolescence, so as to tackle the 'early starters'), and have attempted to incorporate parent/family components as well as the child in the school setting (Sutton et al., 2006).

An ambitious intervention programme in the USA has been the Fast Track project (Conduct Problems Prevention Research Group, 1999). This was based at four sites: Durham, North Carolina; Nashville, Tennessee; Seattle, Washington; and central Pennsylvania, a rural area. A multistage screening procedure was used to identify behaviourally disruptive kindergarten children, who would be at high risk of later problems in school. Entire schools in the sample areas were then assigned either to intervention (445 children in 191 classrooms) or to control (446 children in 210 classrooms) conditions. The intervention included a school-based social skills curriculum (an adaptation of the PATHS model, described in Chapter 9), and various interventions directed at the target parents and children, including emotional understanding and communication, social problem solving and home-based tutoring.

A variety of assessment measures was used. Table 10.4 shows a few of a large number of outcomes, for which there were pretest measures before or at the start of grade 1 (6 years) and posttest at the end of grade 1. The first three are child measures, based on responses to vignettes; the intervention group did not change on hostile attribution scores, but did improve more than controls on aggressive retaliation scores and on social problem-solving skills. The non-significant findings for parent-rated social competence of the child, and teacher-rated externalizing behaviours, indicate the difficulty in having substantial effects, even with such an ambitious programme; however, there were some other significant trends on some measures.

The project has continued through to grade 12. Slough et al. (2008) reported that by grade 10, the strongest effects were seen in grade 1, but that improvements have continued in many areas, though often with modest effect sizes. For example, at the end of grades 4 and 5 there were significant intervention effects for involvement with deviant peers, and for home and community problems such as delinquency. The Conduct Problems Prevention Research Group (2011) reported some findings by grade 12, on conduct disorder, oppositional defiant disorder, attention deficit hyperactivity disorder (ADHD) and externalizing disorders generally. No significant main effects of the intervention were found. However, dividing the sample into highest risk (16% of the total) and moderate risk (the remaining 84%), significant

Table 10.4   Some pre- and posttest measures for intervention and control group children in the Fast Track project, at grade 1.

| | Intervention | | Control | | |
	Pretest	Posttest	Pretest	Posttest	Significance
Social problem solving	.61	.70	.63	.67	$p < .002$
Hostile attribution	.67	.66	.67	.67	n.s.
Aggressive retaliation	.43	.31	.42	.35	$p < .04$
Parent-rated social competence	2.45	2.41	2.45	2.44	n.s.
Teacher-rated externalizing behaviour	61.64	62.68	61.31	62.76	n.s.

Source: Conduct Problems Prevention Research Group (1999). Initial impact of the Fast Track Prevention trial for conduct problems, II: Classroom effects. *Journal of Consulting and Clinical Psychology, 67,* 648–657.

differences were found on all these outcome measures—the highest risk intervention children were doing noticeably better. In the control groups only 18% were free of any externalizing diagnosis, but the intervention condition raised this to 32%. The converse finding was that for the moderate-risk children, the intervention condition resulted in slightly worse outcomes on all outcome measures, though only significant for one of these. The researchers argue that the substantial success with the highest risk group is important, as these individuals would normally often become a substantial burden to society.

BULLYING IN SCHOOL

Bullying is usually taken to be a subset of aggressive behaviour, characterized by an imbalance of power, and often by repetition (e.g. Olweus, 1999). The victim cannot defend him/herself easily for one or more reasons: he or she may be outnumbered, or smaller, less physically strong or less psychologically resilient than the person(s) doing the bullying. Also, the behaviour is repetitive; that is, a victim is targeted a number of times. The definition 'a systematic abuse of power' (Smith & Sharp, 1994) also captures these two features.

These two criteria (power imbalance and repetition) are now widely used, although debated as regards their relevance to cyberbullying (see below). In an empirical study using two data sets of US adolescents, Ybarra, Espelage and Mitchell (2014) showed that episodes of bullying where these two criteria were present had the most detrimental effects on daily functioning. Bullying, by its nature, is likely to have particular characteristics (such as fear of telling by the victim) and particular outcomes (such as development of low self-esteem and depression in the victim). The relative defencelessness of the victim implies an especial obligation on others to intervene, if we take the democratic rights of the victim seriously. Nevertheless, as Ybarra et al. (2014) point out, some victims of peer aggression may not meet the criteria for being bullied, but may also have problems which should not be ignored.

Over the last two decades, research on school bullying has expanded greatly worldwide, and especially in Europe, North America, Japan and Australasia (Jimerson et al., 2010; Smith, 2014). This growth in knowledge, combined with media interest that has at times been intense, has led to action to reduce school bullying and its effects. This started in the early 1980s in Norway, with the first national campaign against bullying. The reported success of this inspired many other projects. In recent years there has been widespread circulation of antibullying materials, plus, in some countries, legal requirements for schools to have an antibullying policy or to tackle bullying effectively.

Bullying can happen in many contexts—the workplace, the home, the armed forces, prisons and so on (Monks et al., 2009). Indeed, topics such as workplace bullying are growing research areas. In school, too, we can think of teacher–teacher, teacher–pupil and pupil–teacher bullying, as well as pupil–pupil bullying. However, it is pupil–pupil bullying that has been the main focus of research up to now.

The roles considered in early bullying research were *bully*, *victim* and *non-involved* (neither a bully nor a victim). In addition, victims were often divided into *passive victims*, who did nothing to provoke any attacks, and *aggressive* or *provocative victims*, who can be seen to be behaving in annoying ways. This latter category overlaps somewhat with so-called *bully-victims* (pupils who are both a bully and a victim). Salmivalli et al. (1996) refined the bully and non-involved categories further, by describing six participant roles in bullying: *ringleader bullies* (who take the initiative), *follower bullies* (who then join in), *reinforcers* (who encourage the bully or laugh at the victim), *defenders* (who help the victim) and *bystanders* (who stay out of things), as well as the victims themselves.

Finding Out about Bullying

There are obvious difficulties in getting data on school bullying. Nevertheless, a number of methods can be used.

- *Teacher and parent reports*: these are of limited value as regards pupil–pupil bullying, as teachers and parents are usually unaware of a lot of the pupil–pupil bullying that is occurring. Teacher reports may be most valid for younger children whose behaviour is more easily observed.
- *Self-reports by pupils* as to whether they have been bullied or taken part in bullying others (usually, over a definite time period); these are widely used in anonymous questionnaires, such as the Olweus questionnaire (Olweus, 1999), and are the usual method for large surveys.
- *Peer nominations*, in which classmates are asked who is a bully or a victim: this is often considered the most reliable method for class-based work, as information is collated from multiple informants. Two common instruments are those of Rigby and Slee (1995) and the Salmivalli Participant Role Scale (Salmivalli et al., 1996).
- *Direct observations of behaviour*, for example in the playground: Pepler and Craig (1995) used radio microphones plus a telephoto camera. Observations have high validity but are expensive and time-consuming to carry out and analyse.
- Interviews with individuals, focus groups with, say, 4–8 pupils and incident reports kept by a school are other ways of getting information.

As can be seen, a lot of information is normally obtained from the pupils or young people themselves. One point to bear in mind here is that not all pupils (or indeed adults) necessarily share the same understanding of the term 'bullying' as researchers do (i.e. that it is aggression with repetition and imbalance of power). The understanding that pupils and adults have of 'bullying', at different ages and also in different societies, has been studied using a 'cartoon test' (Smith et al., 2002a). Here, various stick figure cartoons, with a caption, are shown to children, as in Figure 10.3. They are asked whether this shows 'bullying' or not. It is also possible to ask if they correspond to other terms, such as 'teasing' or 'harassment' in English, or to similar terms such as 'prepotenza' in Italian or 'ijime' in Japanese.

Some data, using these cartoons with English children and adults, show that there are age variations in using the term 'bullying' (Monks & Smith, 2006). Some of these data are shown in Table 10.5, which gives percentage 'yes' responses (to 'Is this bullying?') to three of the cartoons. (Many more were used in the actual study; the three cartoons in Table 10.5 are included in Figure 10.3.) For the cartoon 'Mary starts a fight with Linda, who is smaller', where there is obviously an imbalance of power, almost all respondents say it is bullying, irrespective of age. For the cartoon 'Helen and Jo don't like each other and start to fight', however, there is no obvious imbalance of power—it is just a fight. Neither adults nor 14-year-olds think of this as bullying, but most 4–6- and 8-year-olds do. This illustrates a well-replicated finding, that younger children have a broader definition of bullying; they think of it as 'nasty things happening to you'. This is obviously important to know when gathering information from younger children. Also interesting is the response to the cartoon

Figure 10.3   Cartoon stick figures used to assess understanding of bullying at different ages and in different cultures.

Source: Images provided by Peter K. Smith.

Table 10.5 Percentage 'yes' responses as to whether particular stick cartoon figures/captions are 'bullying', from pupils of different ages and adults.

Cartoon	4–6 years	8 years	14 years	Adult	X^2
Helen and Jo don't like each other and start to fight	82	90	15	8	111.76*
Mary starts a fight with Linda, who is smaller	73	93	98	93	19.52*
Fran spreads nasty stories about Melanie	77	90	85	53	18.34*

*$p < .01$.
Source: Adapted from Monks, C. P. & Smith, P. K. (2006). Definitions of bullying: Age differences in understanding of the term, and the role of experience. *British Journal of Developmental Psychology, 24,* 801–821.

'Fran spreads nasty stories about Melanie'. Here, the lowest figure comes from the adults. Although not directly shown as such in this study, this is very likely a historical effect rather than an age effect (cf. pp. 6, 8). For a long time, physical and verbal abuse has been seen as bullying, but indirect/relational aggression only came to be recognized as such in the 1990s (p. 344). Many middle-aged or older adults may not see this as bullying, even though almost all younger people do.

Although many studies of bullying are carried out in English-speaking countries, many others are carried out in different languages. Do the terms used in these different languages truly correspond to bullying? This, again, is an important question, especially when comparisons are made of bullying rates in different countries (Elgar et al., 2009). This was also studied using the cartoon task (with appropriate captions that only stated the behaviours rather than using terms such as 'bullying'), as there is no indication in the stick figure cartoons of clothes or skin colour and they can be used cross-nationally. In reporting the findings (Smith et al., 2002a), the 25 cartoons used were grouped into five similar clusters, as shown in Table 10.6: non-aggressive; physical aggression (an even-handed dispute or a provoked retaliation); physical bullying (with power difference between the disputing parties in terms of size, strength, number and consistency); verbal bullying (direct and indirect); and social exclusion.

An analysis of 67 terms used in 14 different countries found a variety of meaning profiles; a few examples are shown in Table 10.6. The English terms *bullying* and *harassment* have similar profiles; both are high on physical and verbal bullying, moderately high on social exclusion and less high on physical aggression. By contrast, *teasing* is high on verbal bullying but not on physical bullying; it has a more restricted meaning. The German term *schikanieren* corresponds reasonably well to English *bullying*, although it does not capture physical bullying so strongly. By contrast, the French term *violence* does not correspond so closely to *bullying*: it is high on physical bullying but low on social exclusion and rather high on physical aggression (thus, physical aggression and physical bullying are not well distinguished using this term). The Italian terms *violenza* and *prepotenza* are higher on social exclusion but, even more than French *violence*, they fail to distinguish physical aggression and physical bullying. These two Italian terms have broad meaning profiles. Indeed, early

Table 10.6   The mean percentage of 14-year-olds who included the cartoons in each cluster as part of their 'definition' of terms similar to bullying, in different countries.

	Non-aggressive	Physical aggression	Physical bullying	Verbal bullying	Social exclusion
England					
Bullying	4	34	94	91	62
Harassment	10	42	88	84	49
Teasing	15	43	35	83	51
Germany					
Schikanieren	6	20	58	80	55
France					
Violence	3	56	83	60	26
Italy					
Prepotenza	10	71	92	86	90
Violenza	10	93	96	63	59

Source: Adapted from Smith, P. K., Cowie, H., Olafsson, R. F. & Liefooghe, A. P. D. (2002). Definitions of bullying: A comparison of terms used, and age and gender differences, in a fourteen-country international comparison. *Child Development, 73,* 1119–1133.

findings of high levels of 'bullying' in Italian schools may have been because these terms were used in the Italian questionnaires (Fonzi et al., 1999).

Clearly, when one tries to translate the term *bullying* into other languages, it is difficult or sometimes impossible to get an equivalent word that covers fully the meaning of bullying. In Latin languages (e.g. French, Italian, Spanish, Portuguese) several terms exist, but none is a very good match. As the research area on bullying has expanded and public concern has grown, the English word *bullying* has been adopted or adapted in some countries. In Germany, the term *bully* is now used as well as *täter*. In Spain, *bullying* is an increasingly recognized term. And in Italy, the term *Il bullismo* has been introduced, as in *Il Bullismo in Italia* (Fonzi, 1997), *Bullismo: Che fare?* (Menesini, 2000) and *Il Bullismo Elettronico* (cyberbullying) (Genta et al., 2009).

 Stop and Think

How important is language, and the linguistic terms used, when we make comparisons across cultures?

Types of Bullying

What might be called the 'traditional' (or offline) forms of bullying include physical, verbal and indirect/relational, as found in typologies of aggression generally. Physical bullying includes hitting, kicking, punching and taking or damaging someone's belongings. Verbal bullying includes teasing, taunting and threats. Indirect/relational includes spreading nasty rumours (done indirectly rather than face to face) and systematic social exclusion ('You can't play with us'); these damage a person's relations or social network, rather than being a direct physical or verbal attack.

Some bullying is based on the victim being a member of a particular group, often a marginalized or disadvantaged one, rather than on individual characteristics. This has been referred to as identity-based bullying, or 'bias bullying'.

Gender-based bullying: This is specifically targeted at an individual's gender, generally based on sexist attitudes or stereotypes. A common form is of boys to girls, for example harassment using sexually abusive and aggressive language such as 'bitch', 'slag', etc. (Duncan, 1999). Less commonly, girls can bully boys, and girls may also engage in sexual bullying of other girls, for example spreading nasty gossip about a girl's sexual reputation. Williams (2013) found that girls may now use social networking sites as a forum for this.

Racist bullying: This is related to a child's race or ethnicity. A number of studies have been made of racist bullying, but while it clearly exists, findings do not consistently suggest that minority groups are more at risk. As an example, a UK study by Tippett, Wolke and Platt (2013) examined ethnicity and bullying involvement in a sample of 10–15-year-olds. They found that White children were not more involved than other ethnic groups, even when controlling for age, gender, parental qualifications and economic situation. African children were the least likely to be victims, and Caribbean and Pakistani children were most often involved in bullying others—these differences being significant for girls but not for boys.

Bullying related to disability: This is typically bullying directed to someone with physical or sensory or learning difficulties. A survey in Northern Ireland by RSM McClure Watters (2011) found that the prevalence of being bullied for children with a disability was significantly higher, compared to those without; the prevalence of bullying others was also higher for those with a disability. Similarly, a study in Sweden by Holmberg and Hjern (2008) compared children diagnosed with varying degrees of ADHD with controls. Rates of being bullied were around eight times higher in children with ADHD, and rates of bullying others were around three times higher. In a review of the topic, Mishna (2003) suggested three reasons for this greater involvement: first, having fewer friends and less social acceptance; second, in some cases a lack of social skills in coping; and third, some characteristics of a disability, such as clumsiness or a stammer or poor hearing, may make someone an easy target for those who enjoy bullying others.

Homophobic bullying: This is bullying directed to lesbian, gay or bisexual (LGB) people, or those perceived to be LGB, because of their real or perceived sexual orientation. Some studies include transgendered individuals (T), with prevalence reported for LGBT individuals combined. A number of studies have consistently shown that LGBT young people are considerably more at risk of victimization. A meta-analysis by Toomey and Russell (2013) found 18 studies where a direct comparison of school-based victimization between sexual minority (LGBT) and heterosexual pupils was possible. They found the risk of victimization was significantly higher for LGBT pupils, and especially for boys.

This gender difference was also found in a longitudinal study in England, by Robinson, Espelage and Rivers (2013). They followed up over 4,000 young people from 13–14 to their leaving secondary school aged 17–18. Over the 6 years of the study, there was a fairly steady decrease in victimization in the total sample (this is an age trend found rather generally for victimization). But the 4.5% of their sample who identified themselves as LGB experienced nearly twice as much victimization as their heterosexual peers. For males, their relative risk increased over the 6 years, from 1.78 to 3.95; for females, their relative risk decreased from 1.95 to 1.18. Thus although victimization experiences were higher for LGB young people generally, they declined with age, but the relative risk compared to heterosexual peers got worse for males but better for females.

Cyberbullying

What is now commonly called 'cyberbullying' (or online bullying) has become an important issue in this century. Cyberbullying describes forms of bullying using mobile phones and the internet, that have become prevalent in the last decade as the use of these devices has spread rapidly among young people (see Chapter 8). There are many types of cyberaggression, including attacks and threats, denigration (put-downs), flaming (online verbal fights), cyberstalking (persistent online intimidation), exclusion (from an online group), masquerade (pretending to be someone else to send/post material to damage someone), outing (sharing embarrassing information or images of someone) and putting up false profiles and distributing personal material against someone's wishes (Livingstone & Smith, 2014).

There are some distinctive features of cyberbullying, one of which is 'no place to hide'. Unlike traditional forms of bullying—where, once the victim gets home, they are away from the bullying until the next day—cyberbullying is more difficult to escape from; the victim may continue to receive text messages or emails, or view nasty postings on a website, wherever they are. Another is the breadth of audience: cyberbullying can reach particularly large audiences in a peer group compared with the small groups that normally witness traditional bullying. For example, when nasty comments are posted on a website, the audience that may see these comments is potentially very large. In addition, those doing the bullying often have more anonymity than in traditional physical or verbal bullying, and may use online pseudonyms on the internet.

The characteristics of cyberbullying do raise definitional issues. Where is the imbalance of power, in cyberbullying? And how important is the 'repetition' criterion, when one act (sending a nasty text or posting a demeaning comment on the internet) can be seen or duplicated many times? These issues are being debated as the study of cyberbullying gathers momentum; some researchers prefer to use terms such as cyberaggression rather than cyberbullying (see Bauman, Walker & Cross, 2013). Nevertheless, a six-country cross-national study by Menesini et al. (2012) gave 11–17-year-olds scenarios and asked them to judge whether they were cyberbullying or not. Imbalance of power was the most important criterion used, followed by intentionality, and anonymity of the perpetrator as a substitute for imbalance of power. This study found repetition to be a less important criterion for cyberbullying. However, the Ybarra et al. (2014) study, based on young people's experiences, found both power imbalance and repetition to be important criteria for outcomes.

In contrast to other forms of bullying, prevalence rates of cyberbullying have been found to be greater outside school than inside (see Table 10.7). Schools do often place restrictions on or supervise mobile phone and internet use. As some pupils wrote on the questionnaires, 'Inside, teachers can track them down'; outside school, 'No one is checking you'. However, those involved often know each other through school. Another feature of cyberbullying is how the media used are changing quite rapidly as technology develops. Initially mainly text messaging and emails, much cyberbullying now takes place on social networking sites (Livingstone & Smith, 2014).

Stop and Think

How is modern technology changing the forms of bullying behaviour?

Incidence and Structural Features of Bullying

Incidence figures for bullying vary greatly depending on measurement criteria (for example, what frequency and time span are asked about; whether the information comes from self, peer, teacher or parent report). The figures in Table 10.7 are high, because pupils were asked if they had *ever* been bullied. More usually, questions are asked about being bullied, or taking part in bullying others, in the previous school term.

Table 10.7 Reports from pupils as to whether they have ever been bullied in a traditional way, or cyberbullied, in school, out of school or both.

	In	Out	Both
Traditional bullied	37%	5%	12%
Cyberbullied	3%	11%	3%

Source: Based on Smith, P. K. et al. 2008. Cyberbullying: its nature and impact in secondary school pupils, *Journal of Child Psychology and Psychiatry, 49*: 376–385.

A source of international data is provided by the Health Behaviour in School-aged Children (HBSC) surveys (www.hbsc.org), carried out every 4 years on 11-, 13- and 15-year olds. The 2009–2010 survey provided data from 38 countries, mostly European, but also including the United States, Canada, Russian Federation, Armenia and Ukraine. Questions on bullying used a standard definition (mentioning repetition and imbalance of power), and as reported by Currie et al. (2012), victim or bully rates were calculated from 'at least two or three times in the past couple of months' or more (so, ignoring 'it only happened once or twice'). The rates for bullying others averaged at 10.3%, and for being bullied (victims) at 11.3%.

Another cross-national data set comes from the EU Kids Online survey carried out in spring/summer 2010 (Livingstone, Haddon, Görzig & Ólafsson, 2011). This reported findings on traditional bullying and cyberbullying from 25 European countries, for children aged 9–16 years. Self-report questionnaires were given face to face, in children's homes. Taking a similar frequency cutoff of more than once or twice a month, bully prevalence was 5% and victim prevalence was 9%. The main discrepancy with the HBSC findings is the lower prevalence of bullying others. This is unexplained, but might be due to a greater unwillingness to admit to bullying others in a face-to-face interview compared to an anonymous class-based questionnaire.

In sum, there are appreciable minorities of children and young people involved in bullying, which is a matter of concern because of the suffering caused by bullying and the long-term effects. Incidence information is important both for raising awareness about the issue and for monitoring effects of intervention.

A great deal has been found out about the nature of bullying, mainly from large-scale surveys using anonymous self-report questionnaires. Many findings replicate across studies and across cultures. It is a fairly common finding that boys report, and are reported as, bullying more than girls whereas boys and girls report being bullied about equally. Girls' bullying more usually takes the form of behaviours such as social exclusion or spreading nasty rumours, rather than the physical behaviours used more by boys.

One finding, very important for intervention work, is that a substantial proportion of self-reported victims say that they have not told a teacher or someone at home about the bullying. The proportion that has not told anyone increases with age, and boy victims are less likely to tell anyone than girl victims. Another finding relates to attitudes about bullying in the peer group as a whole. Although most pupils say they do not like bullying, a significant minority do say they could join in bullying. Perhaps surprisingly, these 'probullying' or 'anti-victim' attitudes increase with age up to 14–15 years (after which they start to decline) (Rigby, 2002). Such antivictim attitudes are more marked in boys than girls—and especially for boys as regards boy victims (Olweus & Endresen, 1998).

Causes of Bullying

Many levels of causation are typically invoked in understanding bullying and victimization. At the broadest level are society factors, such as tolerance of violence, bullying and abuse of power in society, and portrayals in the mass media. At the community level, relevant factors are neighbourhood levels of violence and safety, and socioeconomic conditions (Bowes et al., 2009; Elgar et al., 2009). At the school level, the school climate and quality of teacher and pupil relationships can have powerful effects (Anderson et al., 2001; Utting et al., 2007). It is through the school and the peer group that most antibullying interventions have tried to operate, although work with parents and families is clearly also relevant. For example, involvement in bullying others is associated with family predictors such as insecure attachment and harsh physical discipline; and being a victim with overprotective parenting (Lereya, Samara & Wolke, 2013). Parental maltreatment and abuse is a likely risk factor in the bully/victim or aggressive victim group (Schwartz, Dodge, Pettit & Bates, 1997).

Regarding young people who bully others, aggressive behaviour and inequalities of power are commonplace in human groups, including peer groups in school, so bullying can be a temptation; there are potential rewards for bullying behaviour, such as getting money or other resources from the victim, or displaying one's power to the peer group. Caravita et al. (2009) found that children who bullied others were high on perceived popularity (see Chapter 5), though not particularly high on social preference scores; in other words, bullies were perceived as popular or at least having high status, even though not so many pupils actually liked them a lot. Salmivalli (2010) argued that some children who bully are driven by a desire for dominant status in the peer group. This is supported by evidence that the likelihood of a child taking part in bullying another is influenced by peer group norms and expectations about bullying and defending, as well as what support the victim might have. Correspondingly, children with high popularity or peer group status can be the most effective defenders (Caravita et al., 2009).

A traditional view from the Social Information Processing (SIP) model is that bullies, being aggressive children, lack social skills; Camodeca and Goossens (2005) describe bullies as showing proactive aggression, and both bullies and victims as showing reactive aggression and interpreting scenarios in aggressive ways. But there is considerable controversy regarding the social skills of bullies; Sutton et al. (1999, and commentaries) suggested that many bullies, especially the ringleaders, may be skilled manipulators, possessing good theory of mind abilities that enable them to organize a gang effectively and hurt a victim while avoiding detection by teachers. Peeters, Cillessen and Scholte (2010), in a Dutch sample of 13-year-olds, found from cluster analysis that three kinds of pupils were peer nominated as bullies. One group was popular and socially intelligent; a second group was relatively popular and with average social intelligence scores; a third group, the smallest numerically, was unpopular and had lower than average scores on social intelligence.

Bullies may be low on affective empathy (sharing others' feelings) but not necessarily low on cognitive empathy (understanding others' feelings)—a combination that has been labelled 'cold cognition'. Related to the concept of empathy is that of moral disengagement—a process by which someone can bypass the normal kinds of reasoning which would hold us back from severely hurting or even killing another person. In a meta-analysis, Gini, Pozzoli and Hymel (2013) found that perpetrators of both traditional bullying and cyberbullying showed greater scores on moral disengagement—such as cognitive restructuring (seeing the attack as justified—'he deserved it'), minimizing one's agentive role ('I didn't start it'), disregarding or distorting the consequences ('it was just for fun'), or blaming the victim ('he started it'). These associations were similar for boys and girls, but were significantly stronger for adolescents compared to younger children.

Victims do seem to lack some social skills, for example in coping assertively, and may be temperamentally timid or shy (Cook et al., 2010). Fox and Boulton (2003) found that a social skills training programme could be helpful for victims of bullying. At an interpersonal level, the attitudes of the main peer groups in the school, as well as the nature and quality of friendships that a child has, are amongst the most important risk factors for victimization. Victims are more likely to report being alone at break time, and to feel less well liked at school; having some good friends can be a strong protective factor against being bullied. Hodges et al. (1997) found that having few friends, or friends who cannot be trusted or who are of low status, and sociometric rejection (dislike by peers) were risk factors for being a victim. Hodges et al. (1999), in a longitudinal study of 10-year-old US children, found that internalizing behaviour (being tearful or anxious) was a risk factor in victimization, but that this risk was lessened if the child had a good friend.

Family and peer influences may interact for aggressive victims. Schwartz et al. (2000) found similar results in two US-based studies on 8–9-year-olds: earlier harsh home environment (harsh discipline, marital conflict, abuse) predicted both victimization and aggression scores at school, but only for children with few friends (defined in terms of reciprocated high liking). This suggests a protective effect of friends for children strongly at risk from their home environment.

Consequences of being Victimized

For children being bullied, their lives are made miserable, often for some considerable period of time. Kochenderfer and Ladd (1996) found that in 5–6-year-olds, continued victimization led to loneliness and school avoidance. Already probably lacking close friends at school, victims of bullying are likely to lose confidence and self-esteem even further. Victims of bullying often experience anxiety and depression, low self-esteem, physical and psychosomatic complaints (Cook et al., 2010). The more serious forms of bullying, at least, can have very serious consequences. In extreme cases, victims may commit suicide (Kim & Leventhal, 2008).

Longer-term effects: although involvement in school bullying has immediate consequences, research using retrospective data suggests that children and young people who are persistently victimized are at increased risk for relationship difficulties later in life. Such long-term effects can be brought out by in-depth case study interviews. The following extract, from an interview with a woman aged 28 who experienced being bullied throughout much of her school career and is now engaged to be married, illustrates this.

> Do you feel that it's left a residue with you . . . what do you feel the effects are?
>   I'm quite insecure, even now . . . I won't believe that people like me . . . and also I'm frightened of children . . . and this is a problem. He [fiancé] would like a family. I would not and I don't want a family because I'm frightened of children and suppose they don't like me? . . . those are things that have stayed with me. It's a very unreasonable fear but it is there and it's very real.

A number of longitudinal survey studies have demonstrated long-term effects. These have typically followed young people up from secondary school into early adulthood an average of 6 or 7 years later. Meta-analyses of such studies by Ttofi, Farrington and Lösel (2012) and Farrington, Lösel, Ttofi and Theodorakis (2012) show that being a victim at school significantly predicts depression in later life. By contrast, bullying behaviour at school significantly predicts later violent behaviour and offending. These findings held up even when adjusting for other factors including child impulsivity, parent criminality, parent–child conflict, income and neighbourhood crime.

There can also be long-term effects on educational achievement and earnings. Using data from the National Child Development Study in the UK (see Table 1.1), Brown and Taylor (2008) found that both victims and perpetrators of school bullying had lower educational attainment later in life, even after controlling for some school and family characteristics; victims (but not bullies) also had lower earnings.

In a longitudinal study using US data, Wolke, Copeland, Angold and Costello (2013) obtained bully and victim measures at ages 9, 11 and 13 years, and a range of outcome measures between 19 and 26 years. Analyses controlled for childhood hardships and childhood psychiatric problems. The longitudinal associations showed that in early adulthood, being a victim (only) was related to poorer health, wealth and social relationships. Being a bully (only) was related to greater risky/illegal behaviour, and poorer wealth and social relationships. Being a bully/victim was associated with poorer outcomes in all domains.

All these findings provide strong arguments for developing school-based interventions to tackle bullying.

Interventions against Bullying

Bullying in school is a systemic problem. The whole-school approach, as described in detail in Cowie and Jennifer (2007), takes account of different aspects of the system: the whole-school and classroom level, including the school ethos; the environment of the school; the peer group; the role of parents and carers; and individual pupils, including not only bullies and victims but also those involved as bystanders or outsiders to the bullying.

The whole-school and classroom level: within the UK, a whole-school policy against bullying is taken as a basic first step, and since 1999 it has been a legal requirement in England and Wales for all schools to have some form of antibullying policy. This is a written document that should define the issue comprehensively, and state the responsibilities of all concerned in the school and what actions will be taken to reduce bullying and deal with incidents when they occur. School policies provide a framework for the school's response involving the whole school community.

Classroom activities can be used to tackle issues associated with bullying, progressively and in an age, gender and culturally appropriate way. These can include literature, audiovisual materials, videos, drama/role-play, music, debates, workshops, puppets and dolls (in early years) and group work. Such curricular approaches can raise awareness of bullying and the school's antibullying policy, and develop skills, empathy and assertiveness in confronting bullying. One curriculum approach that can enhance interpersonal relationships and may reduce victimization is cooperative group work, in which small groups of pupils cooperate in a common task—for example, designing the front page of a class newspaper (see pp 574–575). Such methods appear to be positive for academic achievement (Jacobs et al., 2002), but can also involve/integrate vulnerable children (victims) and children from ethnic minorities—although, unless handled carefully, it can be disrupted by bullying children (Cowie & Berdondini, 2001).

The school environment: pupil–pupil bullying predominantly takes place outside the classroom in corridors, school grounds and outside the school gates (Blatchford, 1998). An effective playground policy and well-designed play area can help to reduce bullying. Work on the physical environment of the playground—structuring or redesigning it to provide more creative opportunities for pupils during break and lunch times, and reduce boredom and bullying—can be a participatory and inclusive process for pupils.

The peer group: peer support uses the knowledge, skills and experience of children and young people themselves in a planned and structured way to tackle and reduce bullying. There is a wide variety of forms, most of which involve some training of the peer supporters; they include befriending, which involves the assignment of a pupil or pupils to 'be with' or 'befriend' a peer; conflict resolution/mediation, a structured process in which a neutral third party assists voluntary participants to resolve their dispute, using a step-by-step process that helps pupils agree to a mutually acceptable solution; and active listening/counselling-based approaches, which extend the befriending and mediation approaches into interventions that are based more overtly on a counselling model, with pupil helpers trained and supervised to use active listening skills to support peers in distress (Cowie & Wallace, 2000). Users report that peer supporters offer helpful interventions, and most pupils and teachers believe that such approaches have an impact on the school as a whole.

Parents and carers: parents have an important role, since family and parenting characteristics do have an influence on the risks of being in bully or victim roles. Communication between parents and the school will be important in terms of recognizing symptoms of bullying and taking early steps to deal with it. The role of parents was particularly emphasized in an intervention project in Ireland (O'Moore, 2013). Through parents' evenings, parents were introduced to a discussion covering what is bullying; misconceptions of bullying; types of bullying; signs and symptoms; effects of bullying on the victims and aggressors; and risk factors associated with victims and bullies. In addition, aspects of parenting were discussed, such as love and care, cruelty, inconsistent discipline, management of aggressive behaviour, excessive physical punishment and violence between adults.

Individual pupils: in a preventive sense, assertiveness training has been recommended as one way to help victims (or potential victims) of bullying to cope in non-passive but non-aggressive ways. These techniques can be taught to pupils, and appear to be helpful at least to some. It is not reasonable to use this as the only strategy, but it can be one part of a more comprehensive package. Working with individual pupils is also an important part of the reactive strategies used to deal with bullying episodes when they happen.

Reactive strategies: these deal with bullying situations when they have arisen. They range from direct sanctions-based approaches, through restorative practices, to more indirect and non-punitive approaches. Direct sanctions vary in severity and can be used on a graded scale if bullying persists. They can range from reprimands/serious talks to involving parents or carers, temporary removal from class, withdrawal of privileges and rewards, disciplinary measures such as detentions and punishment (litter picking or school clean-ups), through to temporary or permanent exclusion. Direct sanctions are expected to impress on the perpetrator that what he or she has done is unacceptable, and promote understanding of the limits of acceptable behaviour, as well as giving an opportunity for pupils who bully to face up to the harm they have caused and learn from it, deter them from repeating that behaviour, signal to other pupils that the behaviour is unacceptable and deter them from doing it, and demonstrate publicly that school rules and policies are to be taken seriously.

Direct sanctions are seen as a form of retributive justice; this contrasts with the idea of restorative justice (Braithwaite, 2002). Restorative justice refers to a range of practices that focus on the offender or bullying child being made aware of the victim's feelings and the harm they have caused, and making some agreed reparation. Although originally developed in the area of youth justice and criminal behaviour, restorative approaches are increasingly being used in schools for bullying, vandalism, theft, assault and conflicts between teachers and pupils. Restorative justice is based around three main principles.

1. *Responsibility*: the offender, along with their parents, learns to accept responsibility for the offence caused through their actions.
2. *Reparation*: the victim is involved through consultation, mediation and participation, and reparative activities are devised to help the offender alleviate some of the damage and distress they have caused.
3. *Resolution*: successfully ending a dispute so that pupils and their families are free to interact without threat of further conflict.

The actual restorative practices used will depend on the nature and severity of the bullying incident, ranging from simple, pupil-based discussions through to a full restorative conference. Effective use of restorative justice depends on pupils being able to talk about feelings and relationship issues.

At the opposite pole to direct sanctions are approaches in which the bullying child(ren) do not have to directly acknowledge their responsibility, although there is encouragement to recognize the plight or suffering of the victim, and pressure on them to do something helpful to ease this. In the UK, the *support group approach*, developed by Robinson and Maines (2007), follows this philosophy. It is a non-punitive approach that aims to change problem behaviours through a mixture of peer pressure, to elicit a prosocial response, and self-realization of the harm and suffering caused to the victim. There are seven steps: the facilitator talks individually to the bullied pupil; a group meeting of 6–8 students is then set up, some of whom are suggested by the victim but without his or her presence; the facilitator explains to the group that the victim has a problem, but does not discuss the incidents that have taken place; the facilitator assures the group that no punishment will given, but instead that all participants must take joint responsibility to make the victim feel happy and safe; each group member gives their own ideas on how the victim can be helped; the facilitator ends the meeting, with the group given responsibility for improving the victim's safety and well-being; individual meetings are held with group members 1 week after the meeting to establish how successful the intervention has been.

Not everyone agrees that bullying children should not be blamed; the alternative view is that bullying children must acknowledge their own responsibility in the bullying, and accept any negative sanctions that follow when this is discovered. This is an issue that needs to be handled carefully, bearing in mind the age of the pupils, the duration of the bullying and the ethos of the school.

For an overview of antibullying procedures and the evidence base for them see Thompson and Smith (2012) and in the UK the Anti-Bullying Alliance website (www.antibullyingalliance.org.uk).

Large-scale School-based Intervention Programmes

There have been quite a number of large-scale school-based antibullying interventions, which have been carefully evaluated. Reviews of such studies (Farrington & Ttofi, 2009) suggest that they are often effective, although the degree of effectiveness does vary markedly. In the most successful programmes, reductions in bullying of about 50% can be achieved.

The first large-scale school-based intervention campaign was launched at a nationwide level in Norway in 1983; this is described in Box 10.2. Since then, Olweus (Olweus & Limber, 2010) has further developed his Olweus Bullying Prevention Programme (OBPP). This has continued to have considerable success in Norway. Altogether, six evaluations in Norway have produced reductions in victim rates from 24% to 64%, and reductions in bully rates of from 21% to 53% (see Smith, 2014). However, its use in other countries such as the USA has not so far been so consistently successful (Bauer, Lozano & Rivara, 2007).

In Finland, the KiVa Koulu programme started in 2006, funded by the Finnish Ministry of Education and led by Christina Salmivalli and Elisa Poskiparta. This has universal interventions (lessons and an antibullying virtual learning environment) and targeted interventions (individual discussions with victim and bullying children; using prosocial, high-status peers to help), together with teacher training. An innovative element in this project is the use of virtual learning via the KiVa computer game. This embodies 'I KNOW' (learning facts about bullying, testing what has been learned during the lessons), 'I CAN' (learning skills and strategies to support the victim/counteract bullying), and 'I DO' (applying the skills learned to everyday life at school). A first evaluation of the programme utilized a randomized control trial (RCT) (Kärnä et al., 2011, 2012) and reported reductions in victim rates of round 30%. Further (non-RCT) evaluations in Finland have continued to be promising, and KiVa is now being introduced in several other countries.

Internationally, schools and teachers now have many more resources to help them tackle bullying, and awareness and recognition of the problem are much greater than one or two decades ago. Overall, there does appear to be some reduction in rates of bullying in many countries, as evidenced by the regular HBSC surveys and other longitudinal studies (Rigby & Smith, 2011), perhaps as a result of all these efforts.

Box 10.2 Bully/victim problems among schoolchildren: basic facts and effects of a school-based intervention programme

Norway has been very active in researching and intervening in problems of school bullying. Local and then nationwide surveys of the extent of the problem revealed that some 9% of the school population were fairly regular victims of bullying, and some 7–8% engaged in bullying others. Often, these children and young people did not tell teachers or parents about their involvement in bullying. In 1982, three young people in Norway took their own lives because of bullying at school. This and the associated media interest and public concern, combined with the previous research findings, led to the Ministry of Education supporting a nationwide Norwegian Campaign Against Bullying. This commenced on 1 October 1983.

The intervention programme, aimed at students, teachers and parents, had a number of components.

- A 32-page booklet for school personnel, giving detailed suggestions about what teachers and school can do to counteract bullying.
- A four-page folder with information and advice for parents.
- A 25-minute video cassette showing episodes from the everyday lives of two bullied children, a 10-year-old boy and a 14-year-old girl. Child actors were used in making this video, which could be used as a basis for class discussion.
- A short inventory or survey given to pupils, to ascertain the level and nature of bully/victim problems in each school.

In an evaluation carried out by Dan Olweus in the Bergen area of Norway, the effects of an advanced version of this intervention programme were assessed in 42 primary and junior high schools, with some 2,500 students. Children only started school at 7 years in Norway; these students were aged around 11 and 14 years. A cohort-sequential design was used (cf. pp. 9–10 and Figure 1.2), and is illustrated in Box Figure 10.2.1. The four grade (age) cohorts started at grades 4, 5, 6 and 7 (ages 11, 12, 13 and 14) in May 1983, shortly before the intervention campaign was started. Measurements were taken at this point (time 1), and again in May 1984 (time 2) and May 1985 (time 3).

This cohort-sequential design was important for interpreting any results. Suppose that there was some improvement in bullying problems with time. This could be due to the intervention programme or it could be due to age or historical changes. Usually in a study of this kind we would control for these by comparing the results for other children who did not experience the intervention, or 'treatment'. However, as the intervention campaign was on a national basis, there could not be any 'no-treatment' control groups. What could be done was to make 'time-lagged contrasts between age-equivalent groups'. For example, the children who were grade 6 at time 2, and had experienced 1 year of intervention, could be compared with those who were grade 6 at time 1, before the intervention started. Later, the same comparison could be made with children who were grade 6 at time 3, after 2 years of intervention. Altogether, five such time-lagged comparisons can be made (see broken lines in Box Figure 10.2.1).

These comparisons are matched for age, obviously an important factor. The children are different, but in the same schools, and given

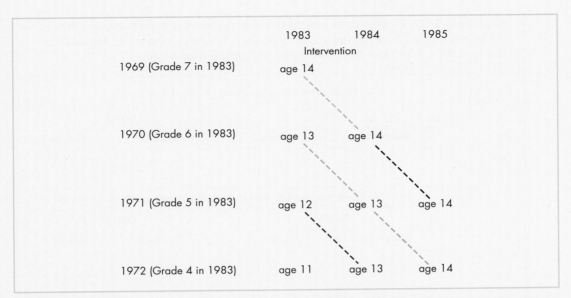

Box Figure 10.2.1   Design of cohort-sequential study of effects of an intervention programme against school bullying. Year of assessment is shown horizontally, and cohort (year of birth/initial grade level) vertically. The approximate ages of each sample of children from each cohort and at each year of study are shown in years.

the large sample size this should not matter. Also, you will be able to see from the design that the same children, starting in grades 5 and 6, serve as both baseline groups and treatment groups in different comparisons.

The measurements made at the three time points were based on anonymously filled-in questionnaires from the students. These indicated the frequency of being bullied and bullying others, and of spending playtime alone; self-ratings of antisocial behaviour; ratings of satisfaction with school life; and ratings of the number of peers in the class being bullied or bullying others.

The results were encouraging. There were substantial reductions in the levels of both being bullied and bullying others, reported by both boys and girls. Box Table 10.2.1 shows the changes for the two time 1–time 3 comparisons (shown in Box Figure 10.2.1), on the questionnaire scores for 'How often

have you been bullied in school?' and 'How often have you taken part in bullying other students in school?'. Similar reductions were found for ratings of peers involved in being bullied or bullying. The bullying was not just displaced elsewhere; there were no changes in reports of bullying on the way to and from school. There were some decreases in the self-reports of antisocial behaviour, and some increases in student satisfaction with school life, such as liking playground time.

This research programme provides a convincing account of the application of psychological research to diagnosing a social problem, helping devise an intervention programme, and then assessing the results of such an intervention. The independent variable is time of assessment, while the dependent variables are the questionnaire measures. The data do depend largely on self-reports, which could be open to distortion or to effects of

Box Table 10.2.1 Effects of intervention programme: questionnaire scores for (a) being bullied and (b) for bullying others, for boys and girls, for each of the two time 1 to time 3 comparisons (at grade 6 and grade 7).

| | How often have you been bullied in school? | | | |
| | BOYS | | GIRLS | |
(a)	Grade 6	Grade 7	Grade 6	Grade 7
Time 1	.36	.47	.46	.19
Time 3	.19	.18	.11	.07

| | How often have you taken part in bullying other students in school? | | | |
| | BOYS | | GIRLS | |
(b)	Grade 6	Grade 7	Grade 6	Grade 7
Time 1	.49	.47	.26	.23
Time 3	.33	.31	.10	.04

repeated testing, but are supported by ratings of peers.

The cohort-sequential design overcomes the absence of conventional no-treatment control groups. However, the comparisons do not control for historical effects. For example, suppose some other events had happened in 1984, such as severe economic depression or increased racial tension; these might influence the comparisons. The comparisons are measuring the effects of the intervention programme itself an historical effect!) and any other large-scale effects felt in 1983–85. Nevertheless, there were no other such obviously important effects in Norway in the period concerned.

Based on material in Olweus, D. (1991). In K. Rubin and D. Pepler (Eds.), *The development and treatment of childhood aggression*. Hove, Sussex: Psychology Press.

CHAPTER SUMMARY

- Dominance behaviour is important in children's peer groups, but it is conceptually distinct from aggression.
- Aggression can take various forms. Indirect aggression was a term introduced in the 1990s.
- Although much aggression is seen as antisocial, it is not necessarily maladaptive for the individual or indicative of a lack of social skills.
- There are many roots to aggressive behaviour in childhood and adolescence, including genetic factors and temperament, parenting, the peer group and neighbourhood factors.
- Delinquency is the legal definition of antisocial behaviour, and overlaps with aggression, but includes damage not directly to persons; intervention programmes such as Fast Track attempt to intervene at several levels to reduce delinquent behaviours.
- Bullying is aggressive behaviour characterized by repetition and imbalance of power. It is widely studied using anonymous self-report questionnaires. Cyberbullying is a new form of bullying. A range of interventions is available to reduce school-based bullying.

DISCUSSION POINTS

1. Discuss the definitions of dominance, aggression, antisocial behaviour, delinquency and bullying.
2. Is aggression always socially undesirable? And is it always socially maladaptive?
3. What might explain family influences on aggression?
4. How important is the peer group in understanding aggression and bullying in school?
5. What would be the best ways of tackling bullying in schools?

FURTHER READING

- Flannery, D.J., Vazsonyi, A.T. & Waldman, I.W. (Eds.) (2007). *The Cambridge handbook of violent behaviour and aggression*. New York: Cambridge University Press, provides a very detailed and comprehensive coverage of violence, and especially the more physical aspects of aggression. Hawley, P.H., Little, T.D. & Rodkin, P.C. (Eds.) (2007). *Aggression and adaptation: The bright side to bad behaviour*. London: Lawrence Erlbaum, counters the traditional view that all aggression is maladaptive.

- For an overview of research on school bullying see Smith, P.K. (2014). *Understanding school bullying: Its nature and prevention strategies*. London: Sage. McGrath, H. & Noble, T. (Eds.) (2006). *Bullying solutions*. Frenchs Forest, NSW: Pearson Education, is a readable collection from Australia with a lot of general material on school bullying. For a comprehensive selection, see Jimerson, S.R., Swearer, S.M. & Espelage, D.L. (Eds.) (2010). *Handbook of bullying in schools: An international perspective*. New York: Routledge. For cyberbullying, see Mora-Merchan, J. & Jager, T. (Eds.) (2010). *Cyberbullying: A cross-national comparison*. Landau, Germany: Verlag Empirische Padagogik; and Bauman, S.D. (2011). *Cyberbullying: What counsellors need to know*. Alexandria, VA: ACA.

PART IV

CHILDREN'S DEVELOPING MINDS

Chapter 11 Perception

Chapter 12 Language

Chapter 13 Cognition: Piaget's Theory

Chapter 14 Cognition: The Information Processing Approach

Chapter 15 Children's Understanding of Mind

Chapter 16 Learning in a Social Context

Chapter 17 Intelligence and Attainment

Chapter 18 Deprivation and Enrichment: Risk and Resilience

CHAPTER
11
Perception

CHAPTER OUTLINE

- Methods for Studying Infants' Perception
- Visual Perception
- Auditory Perception
- Intermodal Perception

In this chapter we focus on one aspect of young children's development—their perceptual abilities. To begin with, we discuss the difficulties of working with infants and young children. The main difficulty is that infants are too young to give meaningful verbal responses, and therefore numerous and often ingenious ways have been invented to elicit responses from infants. These ways can be more or less appropriate depending on the ability being investigated and the age of the child. We then summarize some of the results from research into young children's visual and auditory perception. Research into these perceptual abilities often touches on issues of great importance. One important question, and one that has stimulated much of the research, is: what are infants' perceptual abilities when they are born? And if infants' early abilities are limited, how quickly do they develop the abilities typically found in older children and adults? The latter leads on to a further question: what types of stimuli and experience do infants need for their perceptual abilities to develop? We give examples from the work of researchers who have investigated the answers to these questions.

Psychologists make a distinction between sensation and perception. 'Sensation' refers to the way that information about the environment is picked up by sensory receptors and transmitted to the brain. It is known that infants have certain sensory abilities at birth because they respond to light, sound, smell, touch and taste. 'Perception' refers to the interpretation by the brain of this sensory input. It is through perception that we gain an understanding about the events, objects and people that surround us.

As adults, we can discriminate speech from birdsong or a distant tree from a nearby flower. But can infants, with their limited experience, understand the variety of stimuli that their sensory receptors detect? Are they born with certain perceptual capacities or must these be acquired through learning and experience?

The debate about the relative influence of heredity and environment in perception has a long history. Empiricists, following the tradition of the philosopher John Locke (1690/1939), argued that the newborn infant is a *tabula rasa* (blank slate), on which experiences are imprinted. For example, the psychologist William James (1890) asserted that, to the infant, sensory inputs become fused into 'one blooming, buzzing confusion' and that it is only later, through experience, that children can discriminate among them. In other words, children's ability to perceive develops as the result of a long learning process.

A contrasting view was proposed by nativists, who claimed that many perceptual abilities are present at birth. Philosophers such as Descartes (1638/1965) and Kant (1781/1958) argued that infants' capacity to perceive space, for example, is innate. Later, psychologists of the Gestalt school (in the early 20th century) lent support to the idea that certain perceptual abilities were present at birth because of the structural characteristics of the nervous system. Furthermore, they argued that the infant, far from being a *tabula rasa*, actively tries to create order and organization in his or her perceptual world.

In recent years, experimental psychologists have been able to make an important contribution to our knowledge of perceptual development in the infant. Researchers have found that infants are born with a wider range of perceptual abilities than empiricists suggest, and that infants' capacity to learn rapidly from experience is greater than the nativists propose. The newborn infant possesses many abilities for exploring events and objects in his or her world, and this is enough to form the basis for rapid learning and development. In this chapter we will give some examples of infants' perceptual abilities, and we will concentrate on the research that has been carried out with newborn and very young infants.

METHODS FOR STUDYING INFANTS' PERCEPTION

It is not easy to work with young infants, because they cannot tell you what they are thinking, and therefore what they know has to be inferred from their behaviour. But infants' repertoire of behaviours is limited, and researchers have had to invent ingenious techniques for measuring their perceptual abilities.

Preference Technique

In this procedure, a researcher presents two stimuli to an infant at the same time; for example, these might be two pictures (A and B). The researcher can then measure how long the infant looks at each picture. If, over a period of time, the infant looks at each picture equally it may be because he or she does not differentiate between them. If the infant looks at A more than B it can be inferred that he or she 'prefers' A, and two conclusions follow from this: first, that the infant can in fact distinguish between the two pictures (having a preference is indicative of discriminating between the two stimuli); second, that for some reason, the infant finds A to be the more stimulating picture to look at, and whatever infants find particularly stimulating may give us clues about which aspects of the environment are contributing to their development.

The preference technique is comparatively easy to employ if accurate measures of the infants' looking can be made. The early research was based on an observer watching the infant's face and measuring how long he or she looked at a stimulus. But contemporary research is carried out by filming an infant's face, and then the film can be scored objectively to measure accurately what the child looked at. Infants' eye fixations can also be recorded, so that researchers can measure not only how long an infant looks at a stimulus, but also on which parts of the stimulus the infant focuses. An example of research based on a preference technique is given in Box 11.1.

Habituation

Another method involves habituation and dishabituation to a stimulus. If an infant is shown an interesting stimulus (A), he or she may look at it for some time, but eventually he or she will lose interest in it. If A is presented again and again, it is likely that each time it is presented the infant will spend less and less time looking at it (i.e. habituates to it). Then, if A is changed for a different stimulus (B), the infant is likely to show a renewed interest in the novel stimulus and start looking at it for some time (i.e. dishabituates to it).

A researcher can exploit this pattern of habituation and dishabituation. For example, suppose the researcher wanted to know whether an infant can distinguish between two very

Box 11.1 Is face processing species-specific during the first year of life?

Pascalis et al. (2002) tested very young children's ability to distinguish between monkey faces. To do this, they used a visual paired comparison (VPC) task. In this task, a child is shown an image (say 'A') long enough to become familiar with it. Then the participant is shown image A and a new image ('B') at the same time. The child will, of course, look at both A and B. However, if the child looks longer at B than A, an experimenter can infer that the child 'prefers' B and that the child can distinguish between the two images. As the VPC task depends on nothing more than the child looking at a pair of pictures, it is a suitable way to test very young children's perception.

Pascalis et al. used a VPC procedure to find out if 6-month-olds, 9-month-olds and adults could distinguish between pairs of faces. Sometimes the faces were human ones and sometimes they were the faces of monkeys. If the 6-month-olds discriminated between the human faces, it could have been because they had some very early ability to do so (see this chapter), or because even 6-month-olds have had a great deal of experience of human faces and have learned how to differentiate between them. However, the infants that Pascalis et al. included in their study would have had little if any experience of monkeys, and if they could distinguish between two monkey faces, it might imply that they did have a general ability to discriminate between all types of faces. However, previous researchers (e.g. Pascalis & Bechevalier, 1998) had shown that adults are poorer at recognizing monkey faces than human faces, and this might imply that humans' face recognition

skills are tuned specifically to human faces, and not to faces in general.

Adult Participants and Procedure

Eleven adults (mean age 28.5 years) took part in the experiment. All the adults were Caucasian and there were five males and six females. The adults were tested sitting 60 cm away from a screen, and they were instructed to 'look at the screen as if you were watching TV'.

There were several parts to each trial. First, in the familiarization stage, the colour image of a face was projected on the screen so that it was 15 cm high and 10 cm wide. This image was projected in the centre of the screen for 5 seconds. The faces were presented against a uniform background, looking towards the viewer and with as neutral an expression as possible (see Box Figure 11.1.1). Then there was a blank screen for 5 seconds.

Then two images were presented side by side, separated by 12 cm, for 5 seconds. One image was a 'familiar' face, i.e. the image that the adults had just seen. The other was a 'novel' face, which the adults had not seen before. The faces in each pair were chosen so that they were similar, but they were not so similar that it would be difficult for adults to distinguish between them. The adults were filmed while looking at the screen, so that the experimenters could later analyse the film and assess how long the adults looked at each face in the pair.

Each adult carried out a trial with monkey faces and then, after a delay of 30 seconds, they carried out a second trial with human faces. The position of the familiar and the novel face was counterbalanced across trials and

Box Figure 11.1.1 Examples of the face stimuli used by Pascalis et al. (2002).

Source: Pascalis, O., De Haan, M. & Nelson, C.A. (2002). Is face processing species-specific during the first year of life? *Science*, *296*, 1321–1322. Reproduced with permission.

across participants, so that each face could appear on the left or the right.

Infant Participants

There were 30 infants (16 males and 14 females) aged 6 months, and 30 infants (13 males and 17 females) aged 9 months. Another seven infants were included but did not complete the experiment because of fussiness.

The infants sat on their parents' laps, 60 cm in front of the screen. Each infant went through a procedure that was similar to the one used for the adults, but for the infants the familiarization period was equivalent to 20 seconds and they saw pairs of faces for a total of 10 seconds. The infants had a single trial. Half the infants were shown pictures of monkey faces and the other half of the infants were shown human faces. The infants

had only one trial for a couple of reasons: to avoid interference effects between trials with human faces and monkey faces, and because very young children do not always complete more than one trial without getting distracted.

Results

The results of this study were that, for the adults, the mean time spent looking at the novel face in the pair of human faces was 2.79 seconds (during the 5-second exposure). This was significantly longer than they spent looking at the familiar face (1.63 seconds). The adults' preference for the novel face demonstrated that they could distinguish the two faces. However, when they were looking at the pair of monkey faces, the adults looked for as long at the novel face (2.42 seconds) as they did at the familiar face (2.31 seconds), and this implied that the adults did not distinguish the two monkey faces.

The 9-month-olds showed the same pattern of responses as the adults did. The 9-month-olds who were shown the human faces looked significantly longer at the novel face in the pair (4.5 seconds out of 10 seconds) than at the familiar face (3.63 seconds). The 9-month-olds who saw the monkey faces looked as long at the novel face (3.86 seconds) as the familiar one (3.74 seconds). Therefore, like the adults, the 9-month-olds were poor at distinguishing monkey faces.

In marked contrast to the other participants, the 6-month-olds preferred to look at the novel human face *and* the novel monkey face. For the pair of human faces, the 6-month-olds looked at the novel one for 4.55 (out of 10) seconds. That was significantly longer than the time they looked at the familiar face

(3.57 seconds). For the pair of monkey faces, the 6-month-olds looked at the novel monkey face for 4.04 seconds, and this was significantly longer than the time they spent looking at the familiar monkey face (2.31 seconds).

Pascalis et al. argued in conclusion that the 'perceptual window' for face processing narrows during the first year. Whereas very young children can distinguish faces of another species (in this case monkeys), older children and adults no longer have this ability. Instead, the successful performance of the older participants was limited to the human faces. In other words, the face perception skills of the older children have become specialized for just faces of their own species. This loss of ability in face recognition may parallel the loss of ability that young children experience in speech perception (see this chapter).

Based on material in Pascalis, O., de Haan, M. & Nelson, C.A. (2002). Is face processing species-specific during the first year of life? *Science, 296,* 1321–1323.

similar pictures. The researcher could show the infant picture A until he or she has habituated to it. Then the researcher shows picture B. If the infant does not start looking at B, it is as if he or she treats it as A (which he or she's already lost interest in). It can then be inferred that the infant cannot distinguish B from A. If, however, the infant does start looking at B, it can be assumed, from this dishabituation, that the infant can discriminate between A and B. This technique is effective for finding out just how large or small a difference there needs to be between two stimuli for an infant to detect the difference between them.

Conditioning

Infants will learn to carry out behaviours if those behaviours are reinforced, and this is called conditioning. For example, an experimenter might condition infants to turn their head to one side by 'rewarding' the infant every time he or she turned her head. The reward could be an adult popping up into the infant's line of sight and playing 'peek-a-boo' (something that infants like). At the start of such an experiment, the adult has to wait until the infant naturally moves his or her head to one side, and then gives a peek-a-boo response. If the adult does this every time the infant turns his or her head, the infant will learn to make the head movement each time he or she wants to get the same response.

Some experimenters have used infants' responses in a manner similar to the habituation and dishabituation paradigm described above. For example, suppose an infant is sucking on a teat; if the infant increases his or her sucking rate above the usual rate, this can be rewarded by presenting a stimulus (e.g. sound A). The infant will learn that every time he or she increases her sucking rate he or she is rewarded by hearing the sound. For as long as the sound remains an interesting stimulus, the infant is likely to go on sucking to hear it. However, there will come a point when the infant's interest in the sound declines and he or she no longer sucks so frequently (i.e. has habituated to it). At that point, the experimenter can alter the sound (e.g. to sound B). If the infant does not increase sucking, the experimenter can assume that the infant does not differentiate between A and B, but if he or she does increase sucking (i.e. dishabituates) when first hearing B, it can be inferred that the infant treats B as a different sound from A. In this way, researchers can find out how well infants distinguish between different stimuli.

As well as behaviours that can be observed (like looking, sucking or head turning), other less obvious responses can also be measured. In particular, researchers have measured changes in infants' heart rate. If infants are surprised or upset, their heart rate increases, and if they are focusing or attending to a stimulus, their heart rate tends to slow down. To use the example of differentiating sounds again, an infant hearing sound A for the first time may show a decline in heart rate (assuming that A is not such a frightening noise that the infant's heart rate increases rapidly). After having heard sound A several times, he or she will habituate to it and then the researcher can present sound B. If the infant's heart rate slows down at the sound of B, it indicates dishabituation, which can be taken as evidence that the infant distinguishes between sounds A and B.

Summary of Methods

Infants' preferences, habituation and conditioning are all important in their own right. Preferences indicate those aspects of the environment that an infant finds most stimulating at the time. Habituation is important because it means that an infant will not just concentrate on one object, but after a time will lose interest in that object and therefore seek out new stimuli. Habituation is, in effect, a constant encouragement to explore new things. Conditioning allows an infant to have some control over his or her environment (e.g. by turning his or her head an infant can make an adult appear to play peek-a-boo, or by sucking harder on a teat the infant can hear an attractive sound). These responses reflect infants' understanding of patterns and relationships within the world and are the first signs of learning.

It should be added that none of the above methods can be used without difficulty. Very young children are hard to work with; they may be easily distracted, they may become upset, or they may even fall asleep during an experiment. Apart from these problems, researchers may sometimes find it difficult to measure or interpret the sort of infant behaviours (like head turning or heart rate change) that are fundamental to the investigation of perceptual abilities. Nonetheless, the application of different experimental techniques permits researchers to approach each question about perceptual development in several ways, and if researchers using different techniques all find similar results, it gives confidence in the reliability of those results.

Stop and Think

Why is there no single best way to test very young children's abilities?

VISUAL PERCEPTION

Investigating Infants' Visual Perception

The visual abilities of a newborn infant are different from those of an adult (Hainline, 1998; Kellman & Arterberry, 2006; Slater, 2001). For example, a newborn infant has much poorer visual acuity. Visual acuity is a measure of how well an individual can detect visual detail. People can be asked to look at a visual display made up of vertical black and white lines (of equal width) while the lines are made progressively narrower. There will be a point at which people can no longer distinguish the lines as separate, and the display will appear to be a gray image. Newborn infants can only detect the separation of the lines if they are about 30 times wider than the minimum width that adults can detect (Atkinson & Braddick, 1981). Children's acuity does improve rapidly (Atkinson, 2000) but their limited acuity during the first few months means that young children view a world that is more fuzzy and blurred than an adult's.

The vision of a newborn infant is also limited in other ways. For example, infants younger than 2 months cannot track a moving object very smoothly; instead, they tend to follow a moving object by making a series of jerky eye movements (Aslin, 1981). To take in the whole of an object, it is usually necessary to scan across the object, but infants may have less effective scanning abilities. Salapatek (1975) investigated the eye movements of young infants as they scanned geometric shapes such as triangles, circles and squares. Salapatek found that at 1 month of age, infants tended to focus on a single or limited number of features in the shape (for example, just part of the boundary of the shape—see Figure 11.1). By 2 months of age, infants have adopted more comprehensive scanning strategies and prefer to scan internal features more than the boundaries of a shape.

Figure 11.1 Visual scanning of a geometrical figure by 1- and 2-month-old children. The older infants scanned more of the figure.

Source: From Schaffer (1985).

Newborn infants have only a limited ability to detect colours. Adams et al. (1994) found that newborn infants could distinguish between red and white, but not between white and other colours. By the age of 2 months, infants can discriminate several other colours from white, including orange, blue, some greens and some purples (Teller et al., 1978) and by about 4 months, infants' colour vision approaches adults' ability to discriminate colours (Kellman & Arterberry, 2006).

In summary, young infants have a functional and effective visual system, but the quality of their vision, at least in the first few weeks and months of life, is poorer than adults' vision.

Nonetheless, as Hainline (1998) has emphasized, what might be classed as 'limitations' when compared to adults' vision may not be detrimental for very young infants. Although infants' limitations may reduce the range of stimuli they experience, this may actually help them to focus on the most important aspects of their environment during the first few months of life.

Pattern Perception

Infants may have very early preferences for particular patterns. Fantz (1961) found that very young infants could discriminate between patterned and unpatterned shapes. For example, they preferred to look at striped, bulls-eye or checkerboard patterns rather than at plain discs or squares (see Figure 11.2). Fantz therefore concluded that infants prefer to look at more complex patterns. In another experiment, Fantz and Fagan (1975) showed 1- and 2-month-old children two stimuli

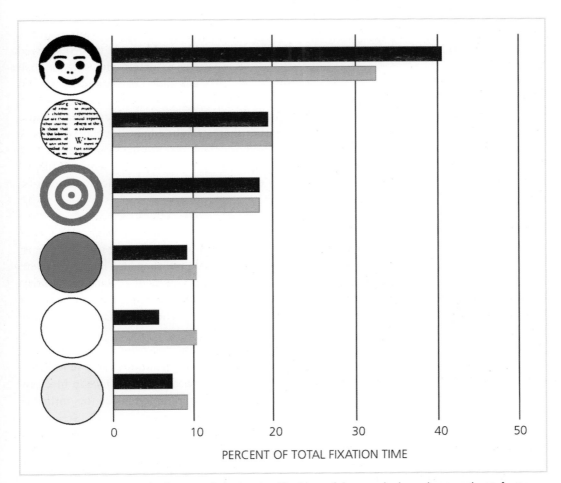

PERCENT OF TOTAL FIXATION TIME

Figure 11.2 Time spent looking at each pattern. The bars of the graph show the time that infants looked at each pattern as a percentage of the total time they looked at all the patterns. Blue bars represent the results from infants who were 2–3 months of age, and orange bars represent the results from infants who were more than 3 months of age.

Source: Adapted from Fantz, R.L. (1961). The origin of form perception. *Scientific American, 204* (May), 66–72.

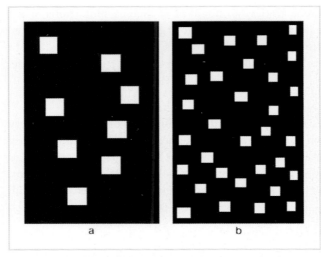

Figure 11.3   Stimuli similar to those used by Fantz and Fagan (1975).

that each had identical amounts of light and dark areas on them, but differed in the complexity of their patterns (see Figure 11.3). The 1-month-old infants preferred the less complex stimuli (with eight 1-inch squares), and the 2-month-old infants preferred the more complex pattern (with 32 smaller squares). It may be that as infants' acuity improves and they can see more detail, the more complex patterns become more interesting and stimulating.

Infants may also prefer patterns with particular shapes. For example, Fantz and Miranda (1975) showed patterns to infants who were less than 1 week old. These patterns, shown in Figure 11.4, were presented in pairs (e.g. the curved and straight contoured versions of the type 1 pattern would be presented together). Fantz and Miranda found that infants had a preference for patterns that had curved edges rather than straight edges. But this preference disappeared if the patterns were placed in a surround (see the lower two rows of Figure 11.4). This may be because, as mentioned above, infants often prefer to look at the edges of figures or shapes. In other words, if there are curves within a pattern they will attract less attention than if the shape itself is curved.

Face Perception

Faces are an important aspect of infants' environments (see Chapter 3). Not only do infants have frequent experience of faces from immediately after birth, but they also have to learn to interpret the faces they see. Researchers investigating the development of face recognition have considered many issues. For example, when do infants first recognize faces? Do infants have a specialized ability to process information about faces? When do infants distinguish between different faces?

In one of the earliest studies of face recognition, Fantz (1961) showed infants aged 1 week to 15 weeks three stimuli based on a face. Fantz showed the infants three flat objects the size and shape of a head (Figure 11.5). One was painted with a stylized face in black on a pink background, one had the same features but these were scrambled inside the outline of the face, and one was painted with a solid area of black that was equivalent to the area of the features on the first two stimuli. Fantz observed which stimuli the infants preferred to look at, and found that they had a very slight preference for the 'real' face compared to the scrambled face, and a strong preference for both the real and scrambled faces over the solid pattern. But it was not clear from Fantz's experiment why the infants preferred the face and the scrambled face. Fantz himself found that infants prefer to look at more complex patterns. Both the face and the scrambled face were more complex than the non-face, and the infants may have simply preferred to look more at the two complex patterns.

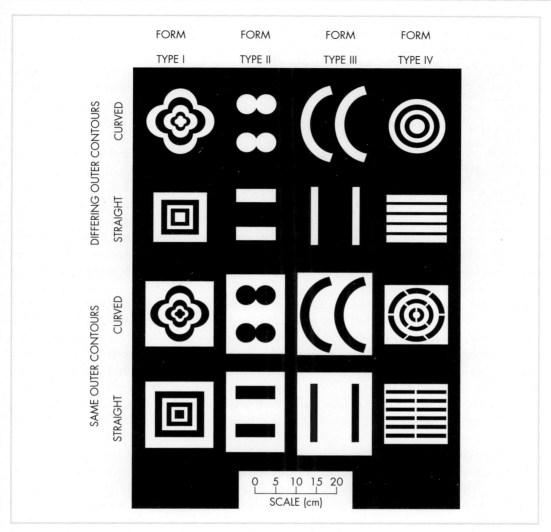

Figure 11.4   Patterns with straight and curved edges used by Fantz and Miranda (1975).

Source: Fantz, R.L. & Miranda, S.B. (1975). Newborn infant attention to form of contour. *Child Development, 46,* 224–228.

Figure 11.5   Face stimuli used by Fantz (1961).

Source: Adapted from Fantz, R.L. (1961). The origin of form perception. *Scientific American, 204* (May), 66–72.

Maurer and Barrera (1981) overcame the issue of complexity by using the three stimuli illustrated in Figure 11.6 with 1- and 2-month-old infants. One stimulus was a 'natural' face, the second was a symmetrical scrambled face, and the third was an asymmetrical scrambled face. All the stimuli had the same facial features, and thus the same complexity. There was no difference in how

Figure 11.6   Face stimuli used by Maurer and Barrera (1981).

Source: Maurer, D. & Barrera, M. (1981). Infants' perceptions of natural and distorted arrangements of a schematic face. *Child Development, 52*, 196–202.

long the 1-month-old infants looked at any of the stimuli, but the 2-month-olds looked longer at the natural face than either of the other two stimuli. This suggested that any preference for natural faces at 2 months of age was more than just a preference for more complex stimuli.

However, other researchers have found, using different techniques, that newborn infants can recognize faces. Goren et al. (1975) showed newborn infants a schematic face, a schematic symmetrical scrambled face, or a blank outline. While an infant lay on her back, Goren et al. moved the stimuli in an arc from one side of the infant to the other. The infant's eye and head movements were measured to assess how long she tracked each stimulus. The infants tracked the schematic face more than the other two stimuli; this suggests that infants have some ability to detect face-like stimuli from birth.

Johnson et al. (1991) confirmed Goren et al.'s findings with newborn infants, but also found that by the age of about 3 months infants no longer spent more time tracking the schematic face than the other stimuli. Johnson and Morton (1991) pointed out this contrast in the findings. If children are shown moving faces, they show a face preference at birth but not after about 3 months. If children are shown a static face (as in Maurer & Barrera, 1981), they do not show a face preference until about 2 months. To explain these results, Johnson and Morton proposed that early face recognition may be based on two different processing systems. They proposed a very early system that operates during the first few weeks of life to draw infants' attention to moving faces. As faces are one of the most important stimuli in an infant's environment, such processing would be advantageous in helping infants select what is relevant in the world around them. By attending to moving faces, infants can begin to learn about different faces, and then after about 2 months a second processing system takes over and contributes to infants' ability to distinguish between human faces and other stimuli (including the faces of other species). At this time, infants can also begin to distinguish static faces.

Over recent years, much evidence has accumulated to show that very young infants have good face recognition skills and can learn faces very rapidly. For example, Walton et al. (1992) demonstrated that newborn infants can distinguish their mother's face. Walton et al. showed 1–4-day-old infants a video showing their mother and a similar-looking but unfamiliar female. All the adults maintained a neutral expression, and the use of video meant that there were no olfactory cues. Infants were first shown one face, and if they sucked on a teat that face remained on the screen. If they did not suck, the second face appeared, and remained on the screen as long as the infants sucked; otherwise, the first face reappeared. In this way, the infant could control the picture at which they were looking. Walton et al. measured the number of times that infants sucked while keeping their mother's face visible and how often they sucked to keep the stranger's face in view. All but one of the infants in the study sucked more to see their mother's face. This result showed that infants can distinguish a specific familiar face, like their mother's face, at a very early age.

How do newborn infants distinguish their mother's face from another person's? Pascalis et al. (1995) found that 4-day-old infants could discriminate between their mother and an unfamiliar female, which confirmed Walton et al.'s findings. But Pascalis et al. then carried out a further study in which the mother and the unfamiliar female both wore headscarves, so that only their internal facial features were visible. The infants in this experiment did not distinguish between their mother and another female, and Pascalis et al. concluded that early recognition of familiar faces may be based on the external contours of the face.

Pascalis et al.'s finding suggests that very young infants do not process the internal features of a face, and if that is the case we would not expect them to recognize facial expressions (De Haan & Nelson, 1998). Nonetheless, newborn infants do respond to internal features when those features move. For example, newborn infants will imitate an adult's facial expression, like tongue protrusions or mouth opening (Meltzoff & Moore, 1983) (see p. 98 and p. 453). Newborns can also recognize eye-gaze in pictures of faces. Farroni et al. (2002) tested infants who were 1–5 days old with pairs of pictures of the same adult female face. In one picture the female was shown with her eyes averted (i.e. looking towards the left or right side of the picture), and in the other the female was shown looking directly out of the picture, as if towards the viewer. The infants spent more time looking at the latter face than at the one with the eyes averted. Some researchers have argued that very young infants can recognize expressions. For example, Field et al. (1982) showed newborn infants happy, sad and surprised expressions that were posed by an adult. The adult maintained one expression until the infants stopped looking at her (i.e. until they had habituated to the expression) and then the adult changed to one of the other expressions. When the expression changed, the infants started to look again (i.e. dishabituated). Field et al. argued from this result that the infants could discriminate between different facial expressions.

Some researchers have found that infants a few days old have a preference for attractive faces. Slater et al. (2000) tested infants between 1 day and 1 week old with a number of female faces. Prior to the infants being tested, a group of adults rated the faces; half were rated attractive and half were rated unattractive. The infants were then shown pairs of faces, one attractive and one unattractive, and the infants looked longer at the attractive face; in other words, they discriminated between the faces in ways that corresponded to the adults' categorization of the faces. Quinn et al. (2008) also found that 3–4-month-olds preferred attractive faces when they were looking at faces from another species (cats and tigers), and this suggests that infants may have a very early and general ability to recognize attractive faces.

All these results suggest that even very young infants have a number of face-processing skills, and these will be the basis for the rapid development of more sophisticated face perception during the first few months of life. We discuss other aspects of early face recognition in the section on the effects of the environment on perceptual development (see below and Box 11.1).

Stop and Think

Why do very young children look at some faces more than others?

Perceptual Constancies

As a person or object moves relative to the viewer, the visual size, shape and colour information it projects on the eye will change. Yet we perceive a given object as the same, even though its apparent size, shape and colour change in this way. This effect is referred to as a 'perceptual constancy'. Size constancy can be illustrated with the following example. If we observe a car driving away from us along a road, the image of the car on the retina becomes smaller, but we do not perceive the car as getting smaller. We perceive that the car remains the same size, but is actually getting further away. To perceive this way is to display 'size constancy'; in other words, we understand that the size of an object remains constant even though the object may be at a different distance. This is an observation that seems obvious to the adult, but does the infant have the same knowledge at birth, or must he or she learn to respond to the appropriate cues?

Bower (1965) carried out one of the first investigations into size constancy with infants who were 6–8-weeks-old. The infants were rewarded for turning their heads to the left. An adult, who was hiding out of sight, knew when the child had turned her head, because the infant's action operated a sensitive pressure switch on a pad behind the infant's head. The adult then stood up and gave a 'peek-a-boo' response, then disappeared again. As described in Chapter 3, infants enjoy contingent responses like an adult playing peek-a-boo and therefore they learn to make head turns to get the adult's response.

Once the head-turning response was firmly established, Bower changed the procedure slightly. Sometimes a 30 cm cube was placed at a 1-metre distance from the infant. The infant only received the reward (the peek-a-boo response) if she turned her head when the cube was present. In this way, infants learned (or were 'conditioned') to make a head turn only when they saw the cube at that distance.

In a later test phase, Bower (1965) presented various stimuli. For example, the original 30 cm cube to which the infant had been conditioned was placed 3 metres away from the infant. At the greater distance this cube projected a smaller retinal image than at the original distance of 1 metre. Bower also used a 90 cm cube that was placed 3 metres away. This larger cube at a greater distance produced the same size retinal image as the original stimulus.

Bower (1965) argued that if infants did have size constancy, they would continue to display head turning when they saw the 30 cm cube, even though it was placed further away. If the infants did not have size constancy and were responding on the basis of the size of an object's retinal image, then they would not respond to the 30 cm cube further away, but they would respond to the 90 cm cube at 3 metres, because this projected the same retinal image to which the infants had been conditioned. Bower found that the infants responded three times more often to the 30 cm cube than the 90 cm cube. In other words, the infants responded on the basis of the size of the object rather than the size of its retinal image, so Bower concluded that young infants do have size constancy.

The infants in Bower's experiment were a few weeks old, but other researchers have suggested that even younger children may also have size constancy. Slater et al. (1990a) showed newborn infants the same cube six times, and each time the cube was shown at different distances from the infant. In this way the infant was familiarized with the cube. Slater et al. then showed the infant two cubes at the same time. One cube was the original cube that the child had seen six times (but shown at a distance that had not been used previously) and the other cube was a new one of a different size. The two cubes were positioned so that they both formed the same size image on the infant's retina. Slater et al. found that all the infants looked longer at the new cube (presumably because they had habituated to the original, which they had already seen six times) and this demonstrated that the children could distinguish between the two cubes even though they both produced the same retinal image. Slater et al. argued that if newborn infants could distinguish between the cubes, they must have been doing so on the basis of the actual size of the cubes. In other words, size constancy is present from bith.

Shape constancy refers to the fact that we see the shape of an object as the same even when its orientation changes. Several researchers have shown that young infants have shape constancy. For example, Caron et al. (1979) showed 3-month-olds a shape (e.g. a rectangle) several times, and each time the rectangle was tilted at a different angle. Then on a test trial Caron et al. showed infants the rectangle (tilted to a new angle) paired with a new shape and measured the infants' preference. Although the infants had never seen the rectangle tilted at the angle used in the test trial, they still preferred to look at the new shape. The infants' preference for the new shape suggested that they had habituated to the rectangle, and this habituation applied even when the rectangle was presented at a new angle. If the angle of presentation did not make any difference to the children, this implies that the infants had achieved shape constancy for the rectangle, i.e. the infants treated the rectangle as the same shape in whatever position they saw it. Slater and Morison (1985) used a similar procedure to Caron et al. (1979) to test newborn infants, and found that newborn infants also had shape constancy.

The research into perceptual constancies shows the same pattern of discoveries. As described above, researchers first found that infants have, for example, size and shape constancy, and progressively more experimentation demonstrated the same constancies in newborn infants. In areas like this, the increase in studies with newborn infants has supported the idea of the competent infant—one that is born with many abilities (Slater, 2001).

If newborn infants have size and shape constancy, it is unlikely that the infant's experience will have much effect on the ability to detect such constancies. However, other perceptual abilities may be only partially developed, or not developed at all, at birth and these are ones that will be dependent on learning and experience. In the following sections we give examples of how children's experience contributes to the development of visual abilities.

Object Separation

Most studies of infants' object perception involve infants looking at one or two separate objects, but the real world is made up of many objects, with some objects touching or occluding others (Johnson, 1998). Given the complexity of most real-world environments, when can infants perceive distinct objects in the world around them?

Kellman and Spelke (1983) investigated this by showing 3–4-month-old infants a rod moving from side to side behind a box. The rod was never fully visible but both ends of the rod could be seen above and below the box (Figure 11.7a). Even though it would be possible to imagine the two parts of the rods as separate, when adults see this display they assume that the two parts of the rod are part of a common object. Presumably adults see the rod as a single object because the two parts are aligned with each other, and the fact that they move in unison strengthens the impression of a single object. Do infants also perceive the scene as a single rod behind a box?

After Kellman and Spelke (1983) had shown infants the rod and box display, the infants were presented with two stimuli. One was a complete rod and one was a broken rod (see

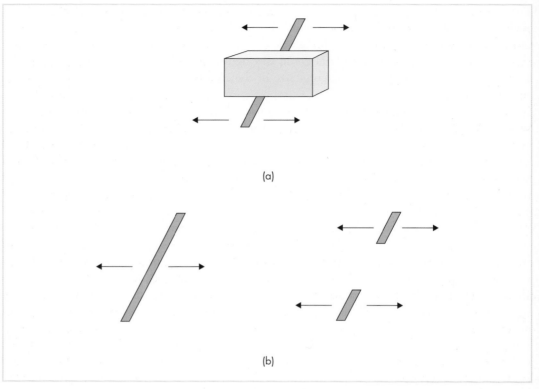

(a)

(b)

Figure 11.7 (a) Rod and box display and (b) test stimuli, used by Kellman and Spelke (1983). The arrows on either side of the rods indicate that the rods moved from side to side during the display.

Source: Kellman, P.J. & Spelke, E.S. (1983). Perception of partly occluded objects in infancy. *Cognitive Psychology, 15*, 483–524.

Figure 11.7b). Kellman and Spelke argued that if the infants had interpreted the rod behind the box as a complete object, they would have habituated to it and would therefore prefer to look at the broken rod. Alternatively, if the infants had treated the rod behind the box as two separate objects, they would have habituated to those and preferred to look at the complete rod. In fact, the infants looked more at the broken rod, and this implied that they had seen the rod behind the box as a complete object.

The infants tested by Kellman and Spelke (1983) were 3 months of age, and other researchers have also found the same result for 2-month-old infants (e.g. Johnson & Aslin, 1995). But do newborn children also perceive occluded objects as complete ones? Slater et al. (1990b) used the same procedure as Kellman and Spelke to test newborn infants and found that they preferred to look at the complete rod rather than the broken one. This implied that the infants had habituated to the broken rod; that is, they had treated the rod behind the box as two separate parts, and if so newborn infants do not perceive occluded objects as ones that are made up of seen and unseen parts. However, Condry et al. (2000) found that young children had difficulty interpreting movement in visual displays, so infants' performance in tasks like the one used by Kellman and Spelke may have been less to do with children's ability to interpret partially hidden objects and more to do with their ability to understand the movement of objects.

In contrast to previous researchers who had used smoothly moving displays, Valenza et al. (2006) showed newborn infants a partially hidden rod that 'jumped' back and forth behind another object. Infants who experienced such a display later showed a preference for looking at a broken rod, rather than a complete rod. This preference suggested that the newborn infants had interpreted the partially hidden 'jumping' rod as a whole object. Therefore, Valenza et al. demonstrated that in some contexts newborn children interpret two parts of the same object as a whole object even when they cannot see the complete object. The study by Valenza et al. is another example of how different techniques can lead to new interpretations of very young children's abilities, and that in some cases, these new interpretations suggest that infants are born with more advanced visual abilities than previously supposed. But this is not to say that infants have very sophisticated visual processing abilities because they are still very dependent on experience in the world to develop their perceptual skills, and below we give examples of the importance of experience in shaping children's perceptual abilities.

Many researchers have demonstrated the importance of experience in perceptual development. For example, Needham and Baillargeon (1998) showed 4-month-olds a scene that included two objects touching each other. While the infant watched, the objects were sometimes moved individually and sometimes moved together. The infants spent as long looking at the objects moving separately as they did looking at the objects moving together. In other words, they did not show surprise when the objects moved together, and Needham and Baillargeon suggested that infants of this age were not sure when objects in a visual scene were separate or not. In a second experiment, Needham and Baillargeon showed infants one of the objects on its own before showing them the objects moving separately or together. In this experiment the infants looked longer (i.e. showed surprise) when the two objects moved together. These results suggested that when the infants had first experienced an object on its own they could later distinguish it when they saw it as part of a complex scene, and demonstrated the importance of experience in the development of perceptual abilities. Needham and Baillargeon's studies are summarized in Box 11.2.

Depth Perception

Other perceptual abilities may develop more directly as a result of experience. For example, Gibson and Walk (1960) used the 'visual cliff' to investigate infants' depth perception. The visual cliff was a glass table with a checkerboard pattern underneath the glass. There was a central platform and on the shallow side of this platform the pattern was immediately below the glass. At the other, deep, side the pattern was several feet below the glass (Figure 11.8). Gibson and Walk argued that if infants had no depth perception they would be willing to crawl over the 'deep' side of the table. But if infants did have depth perception, they might be unwilling to go over the edge. The children were 6–14 months old— that is, they were old enough to crawl—so Gibson and Walk placed infants on the central platform and observed which way they moved. The infants were willing to crawl on the shallow side of the table, but would not crawl over the 'cliff' even when encouraged to do so by their mothers.

Although Gibson and Walk's (1960) result demonstrated depth perception in infants after 6 months of age, their experiment depended on the infants crawling (or not crawling) over different sides of the visual cliff. As younger infants are not able to crawl, later researchers have used other measures to find out if they have depth perception. Schwartz et al. (1973)

Box 11.2 Effects of prior experience on 4.5-month-old infants' object segregation

When adults look at a scene, they do not see a confused mixtures of lines, shapes and surfaces. Instead, adults see distinct objects in the scene. We know, for example, that a cup standing on a saucer is a separate object and not fixed to the saucer. Do young infants also understand that features that may touch or occlude each other are still distinct objects? Several researchers have shown that infants have difficulty distinguishing separate objects in a three-dimensional scene, and Needham and Baillargeon (1998) confirmed these findings in their first experiment.

Needham and Baillargeon tested 32 infants aged 4.5 months. The infants could see through the front wall of a wooden cubicle (1.8 m high, 1 m wide and .45 m deep). The floor of the cubicle was coloured blue and the walls were white. The cubicle contained a blue-and-white rectangular box and a yellow zigzag-edged cylinder (see Box Figure 11.2.1). In other words, the two objects had different sizes, shapes, textures and colours. The two objects were placed in the cubicle so that they were touching each other. The right end of the cylinder was covered with a metallic end and inside the box (but not visible to the infants) there was a magnet, so that the box and the cylinder could be moved together. When the box and cylinder were moved separately, the magnet was covered and a weight placed in the box.

Half the infants took part in one of two conditions. In the move-apart condition, infants saw a gloved hand reach into the apparatus through

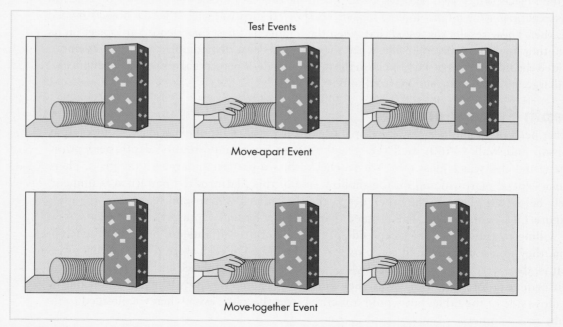

Test Events

Move-apart Event

Move-together Event

Box Figure 11.2.1   Apparatus similar to that used by Needham and Baillargeon (1998).

Source: Adapted from Needham, A. & Baillargeon, R. (1998). Effects of prior experience on 4.5-month-old infants' object segregation. *Infant Behaviour and Development*, 21, 1–24.

a curtained opening on the left. The hand slowly pulled the cylinder to the left so that it was separate from the box. After a pause, the hand pushed the cylinder back to its starting position. This procedure was repeated several times, and at the end of these movements a curtain was lowered across the front of the apparatus. Exactly the same procedure was used for the move-together condition, except that the hand pulled the cylinder and the box together.

Infants sat on their parent's lap about .65 m from the apparatus. Two observers viewed the infant through peepholes in the apparatus. Each observer had a button box connected to a computer and pressed the button each time the infant attended to the events. There was high agreement between the two observers' recording of the infants' gaze. Each trial was finished when infants had looked away from the event for at least 2 seconds, or when they had looked at the event for 60 continuous seconds. Each infant had six trials.

Needham and Baillargeon argued that infants would look more at events that were surprising. On the one hand, if infants saw the items as two separate objects, they would be surprised if the objects moved together and should spend more time looking at such an event. On the other hand, if infants saw the two items as a unit, they would be surprised if they saw the objects moving individually and should attend more to this event. Needham and Baillargeon used analysis of variance to compare infants' performance in the two conditions (move-apart and move-together). There was no difference in how long the infants looked at either of the events. Needham and Baillargeon (1998, p. 7) concluded that the infants 'were uncertain whether the cylinder and box constituted one or two units and thus tended to look equally at the move-together and move-apart test events'.

Having shown that 4.5-month-old infants were unsure whether objects that touched each other were a single item or two individual objects, Needham and Baillargeon went on to investigate whether infants could learn from the experience of seeing the objects as separate items. If infants have had experience of an object as a single entity, will they then distinguish this object when they see it as part of a scene? Needham and Baillargeon tested 16 infants aged 3.5 months in a second experiment with nearly the same procedure as their first study. The only difference was that before the trials, when the infants saw the cylinder and the box together, they were given experience of one object on its own. Prior to the test trials, the infants saw just the box in the apparatus and saw the hand lift and tilt the box for a period of 5 seconds. Then they had the test trials as in the first study. Half the infants took part in the move-apart condition and half took part in the move-together condition.

In the second experiment, Needham and Baillargeon found that infants looked significantly longer at the objects in the move-together condition; they interpreted this result to mean that the infants were more surprised when the objects moved together than when they moved separately. This implies that as infants gain experience of individual objects, they become better at separating them in complex scenes. In other words, infants may need experience of individual objects so that they can segregate information from scenes that include those objects, and Needham and Baillargeon's experiments demonstrated the importance of such experience in contributing to perceptual understanding.

Based on material in Needham, A. & Baillargeon, R. (1998). Effects of prior experience on 4.5-month-old infants' object segregation. *Infant Behaviour and Development*, 21, 1–24.

Figure 11.8 Baby girl reaches out to her mum but fears crossing the visual cliff.
Source: Mark Richards/PhotoEdit, Inc.

placed 5- and 9-month-olds on the shallow and deep sides of the visual cliff and measured their heart rate. As we pointed out earlier, infants' heart rate tends to increase if they are surprised or frightened and slows down during periods of increased attention. Shwartz et al. found that the 9-month-olds' heart rate increased when they were over the deep side of the cliff, but the 5-month-olds' heart rate decreased over the deep side. The fact that the younger infants' heart rate changed showed that they noticed a difference between the sides, but as their heart rate did not increase (which would have reflected fear or surprise) there was no evidence that they recognized they were over a drop.

Some researchers have argued that, rather than age, experience is an important factor in developing the depth perception needed to recognize the drop on the deep side of the visual cliff. Campos et al. (1992) found that the heart rate of infants who could crawl increased when they were placed over the deep side of the cliff, but the heart rate of similarly aged infants who could not crawl decreased on the deep side. In a similar study, infants who did not crawl on their own were given several hours of experience of moving in a wheeled walker and were then placed on the visual cliff. The heart rate of these infants increased when they were over the deep side. These findings suggest that learning not to move onto the deep side of the cliff is the result of experience that infants have gained from crawling.

 Stop and Think

In what ways do young children become better at interpreting the world they see?

AUDITORY PERCEPTION

For adults, vision is the most important of the senses. For young infants, this may not be so. Relative to adults, the auditory acuity of newborn infants is much better than their visual acuity (Burnham & Mattock, 2014); for example, newborns will turn their heads towards a sound, which suggests they can locate sounds very soon after birth. In this section we will give examples of young infants' responses to voices and speech sounds, as these are important auditory stimuli for both the early development of attachment relationships (Chapter 4) and the development of language (Chapter 12).

Auditory perception develops before birth (Lecanuet, 1998). Recordings within the uterus have demonstrated that sounds like voices, and in particular the mother's voice (because it is transmitted both externally and internally through bones and body tissue), can, to some extent, be heard in the uterus. Several researchers have shown fetal reactions to sound, and some of these studies are described in Chapter 3. Typically an external sound is played and the fetal reaction (called a startle response) is measured by asking the mother if she is aware of any fetal movement, by observing that movement by ultrasound scanning, or by measuring changes in fetal heart rate. Reactions to some sounds can be identified from about 20 weeks (Shahidullah & Hepper, 1993a). The discrimination of sounds becomes better over time and, near term, fetuses can distinguish between male and female voices (Lecanuet et al., 1993).

In studies with newborn infants, researchers have tested their auditory perception by, for example, giving them the opportunity to suck on a teat to hear sounds. Infant preferences are measured by how much they suck on the teat. DeCasper and Fifer (1980) found that when 3-day-old infants could suck to hear their mother's voice or the voice of a stranger, the infants sucked more to hear their mother's voice. By this age the infants had only had about 12 hours' contact with their mothers and their preference would imply either very rapid learning after birth or some learning before birth. When DeCasper and Prescott (1984) tested 2-day-old infants' preference for their father's voice or the voice of another male, the infants showed no preference, even though they had had several hours' contact with their father. The preference for mother's voice and the lack of preference for father's voice in the first few days after birth suggests that the preference is less to do with postnatal learning and more to do with prior experience. Fifer and Moon (1989) and Moon and Fifer (1990) showed that infants may recognize their mother's voice from before birth. They gave infants the choice between listening to their mother's voice in a way that simulated the way they would have heard it in the uterine environment and listening to their mother's voice as they heard it after birth. Moon and Fifer found that the infants preferred the former version of their mother's voice. Taken together, these findings suggest that infants have learned to recognize their mother's voice before they are born.

There is evidence that other learning is also possible before birth. Moon et al. (1993) gave 2-day-old infants the opportunity of hearing an unfamiliar adult speaking the native language of the infant's mother or hearing an adult speaking an unfamiliar language. The infants preferred to listen to the mother's language, suggesting that they had become familiar with some aspects of that language before birth. In another study, DeCasper and Spence (1986) showed that young infants could even distinguish different passages in the same language. They asked mothers to read a story out loud twice a day for 6 weeks before they gave birth. At 2 days old, their infants were tested with that story and a new story, and the infants sucked more to hear the story they had been exposed to before birth, even when the story was read by a stranger. The fact that the infants could recognize the same story in a different voice suggests some aspects of the rhythm or pacing of the story itself were recognized by the infants. All these findings indicate prenatal learning.

Newborn infants can distinguish between different syllables (Moon et al., 1992) and there is evidence that young infants can distinguish speech sounds in the same way as adults

(Jusczyk et al., 1998). Speech sounds like 'ba' and 'pa' are part of a continuum in the sense that by a series of gradual changes 'ba' can be changed into 'pa'. On such a continuum there will be a range in the middle of the continuum where it is difficult to distinguish between the two sounds. However, adults do not hear a range of sounds; rather there is a point on the continuum and before that point adults perceive a sound as a 'ba' and after that point they perceive it as a 'pa'. For this reason, the perception of such sounds is referred to as 'categorical perception' to reflect the fact that we only hear those sounds in either one or other category.

Several researchers have shown that, like adults, infants also have categorical perception. Eimas et al. (1971) tested 1–4-month-old infants' ability to distinguish sounds that were between category (i.e. 'ba' compared to 'pa') and sounds that were within a category (e.g. different 'ba' sounds). The infants distinguished between the former, but not the latter. Other researchers have shown that by about 6 months of age, infants can distinguish between consonants that sound similar but differ in the way they are articulated (e.g. 'b', 'd' and 'g'), and also distinguish between different vowel sounds. For example, Kuhl (1979) trained 6-month-old infants to turn their heads towards a loudspeaker whenever contrasting vowel sounds interrupted background noise. The infants were able to identify the vowel 'i' (as in 'peep') against a background noise of 'o' (as in 'pop'). These vowels were heard in a variety of voices and intonations, nonetheless the infants were very successful and Kuhl concluded that infants are sensitive to the acoustic dimensions of speech long before they understand language.

Identifying sounds is not enough for speech perception, because to understand spoken language infants have to identify individual words. Mandel et al. (1995) found that 5-month-olds can distinguish their own name from other names; that is, infants can recognize very familiar words by this age. Older children, about the age of 8 months, can also distinguish typical words (i.e. ones that are not highly familiar) even when those words are heard in the middle of sentences (Jusczyk & Aslin, 1995). Once infants can distinguish individual words, they can attach meanings to those words and then progress to an understanding of the speech they hear as meaningful utterances.

Effects of the Environment on Perceptual Development

As we pointed out in the previous section, young infants can distinguish between many sound contrasts before they understand language. Infants in different cultures (who therefore have exposure to different languages) can make the same sound discriminations. However, some sound contrasts may not actually be used in the infant's native language, and adults speaking that language may have difficulty distinguishing those sound contrasts (Werker & Lalonde, 1988). There is a paradox here, because within a particular culture adults may not be able to make some sound discriminations, but infants can. For example, Japanese adults find it difficult to distinguish 'r' and 'l' even though Japanese infants are sensitive to differences between these consonants.

When do infants lose the ability to discriminate sounds that are not part of their own language? Werker and Tees (1985) found that 6–8-month-old infants from an English-speaking community could distinguish consonantal contrasts in Hindi but, by 12 months of age, the same infants could no longer detect the differences. By comparison, Hindi infants retained their ability to perceive the consonantal contrasts in Hindi (Figure 11.9). These findings suggest that infants are born with the underpinnings of language but, without the reinforcing experience of hearing particular sound contrasts, the ability to distinguish certain sounds is lost during the first year of life.

Pascalis et al. (2002) suggested that the pattern for language development described above might also apply to the development of face recognition. They compared 6-month-old and 9-month-old infants' ability to discriminate between human faces, and between the faces of monkeys. Both age groups were able to distinguish similar but different human faces; however, only the 6-month-olds could discriminate similar monkey faces. By 9 months of age, the children

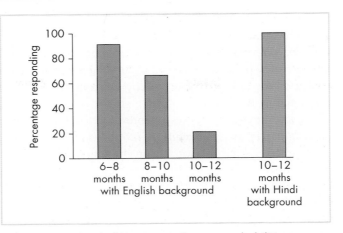

Figure 11.9 The decline in unused perceptual abilities among infants from English backgrounds compared to those from Hindi backgrounds. Between 6 and 12 months the infants from English backgrounds became less able to make sound discriminations that were not used in their environment.

Source: Adapted from Kuhl, P.K. (1979). Speech perception in early infancy: Perceptual constancy for spectrally dissimilar vowel categories. *Journal of the Acoustical Society of America, 66,* 1168–1179.

treated the different monkey faces as the same (see Box 11.1). Pascalis et al. argued that infants' face-processing abilities are tuned by their experience of human faces, and therefore their initial, more general, ability that allowed them to distinguish other species is lost. Pascalis et al. (2005) considered whether infants older than 6 months could distinguish monkey faces if they were given experience of such faces. Parents were asked to show 6-month-olds a set of photographs of monkey faces for 1–2 minutes each day for 2 weeks, and then less frequently for the next 3 months. Then, the infants' ability to distinguish monkey faces was tested again (i.e. when the infants were 9 months old). At 9 months these children were able to discriminate between similar but different monkey faces. Presumably the experience of looking at monkey faces had provided these infants with the opportunity to adapt their face-processing system to monkey faces.

The research into auditory and face-processing abilities demonstrates the effect of the environment on perceptual abilities. Infants will tune their perceptual systems depending on their experience, and so their abilities become more specialized with age. Infants living in different language environments will therefore develop different abilities to recognize speech sounds, and infants who experience different types of faces will develop different face-processing abilities.

INTERMODAL PERCEPTION

So far, we have examined visual and auditory perception separately. In everyday life, however, it is unusual to receive perceptual information from one source only. Normally we coordinate information from a number of senses—vision, audition, touch, taste and smell. For example, we see, taste and smell our food as we eat. We see a bus approaching and hear the sound of its engine getting louder. This coordination of information from different sensory modalities is called *intermodal perception*. Adults use their knowledge of intermodal perception in a number of ways. It can be used to direct a person's attention, so, for example, the increasing sound of the engine round the corner from the bus stop results in a visual search for the approaching bus.

There are several types of intermodal relationships (Bahrick, 2000) and these include *amodal perception* and *arbitrary intermodal perception*. Some events result in two (or more) senses receiving information from the same event. For example, a hammer will be seen and heard hitting an object at the same time; this is called amodal perception because the sight and sound of a hammer being used always occur together. Other sensory combinations may be specific to a particular event. For example, the sound that a hammer makes when hitting a nail will be different from the sound it makes when hitting glass, and could not be specified in advance of hearing those sounds. This is referred to as arbitrary intermodal perception. In the same way, a speaker's voice is always synchronized with the movements of the speaker's mouth, and these aspects of perception are therefore amodal. But Jill's voice and Jo's voice are different and associating Jill's voice with Jill and Jo's voice with Jo means learning arbitrary relationships.

Amodal perception may be an early achievement. For example, Muir and Field (1979) found that when newborn infants heard a sound, they would usually turn their head towards the source of the sound. Bahrick (1992) showed 4-week-old infants films of various objects hitting a surface and making a noise as they did so. The infants were shown these events until they habituated to them (i.e. showed little interest in them). Then Bahrick presented the same events again, but this time the soundtrack of the film was not in synchrony with the event. The infants dishabituated to this change and began looking again. From this result, Bahrick argued that very young infants are sensitive to the synchrony involved in events like an object making a sound as it hits a surface, and this implies early amodal perception.

Slater et al. (1997) also claimed that very young infants can learn arbitrary intermodal relationships. They tested newborn infants with two arbitrary combinations of auditory and visual stimuli. At the same time as hearing the word 'teat' the infants saw a green line, and at the same time as hearing the word 'mum' the infants saw a red line. After the infants had experienced both auditory-visual pairs several times they were tested with two pairs of stimuli. One pair was a familiar one (for example, the word 'mum' and the red line) and one was a novel pair (for example, the word 'mum' and the green line). During the test the infants preferred the novel combination. Their preference for the novel pair implied that the infants had learned (and habituated to) the original combination. If so, this showed that newborn infants can learn associations between two concurrent stimuli; in other words, they have the ability to learn arbitrary intermodal relationships.

Stop and Think

In what ways can very young children be called 'competent'?

CHAPTER SUMMARY

- Research with very young children can address fascinating questions about early abilities and there has been a rapid increase in research with infants during the past few years. This is not just because of the importance of this period in development, but also because of the advent of resources like video filming and computer-controlled stimuli that result in much greater objectivity in the design and scoring of empirical studies with infants.
- As experimental techniques have improved, so has our understanding of early perceptual abilities. The increased focus on infants has shown that they demonstrate some abilities at earlier ages than previously thought.

DISCUSSION POINTS

1. Discuss some of the difficulties of working with very young children and explain how researchers have attempted to overcome those difficulties.
2. Why do psychologists refer to the 'competent infant'?
3. How does face recognition develop?
4. Explain how an infant's own experience contributes to his or her perceptual development.

FURTHER READING

- A very good introduction to infant perception is Bremner, G. & Wachs, T.W. (Eds.) (2014). *The Wiley-Blackwell handbook of infant development*, 2nd edition. Chichester: Wiley-Blackwell, which includes chapters on visual perception, auditory perception and early cognitive development as well as several related topics.
- A collection of papers on infant perception can be found in Slater, A. (Ed.) (1998). *Perceptual development: Visual, auditory and speech perception in infancy*. London: Psychology Press. For encyclopaedic coverage of infancy research, see Damon, W. & Lerner, M. (Eds.) and Kuhn, D. & Siegler, R.S. (Volume Eds.) (2006). *Handbook of child psychology. Volume 2, Cognition, perception and language*, 6th edition. Chichester: Wiley. This handbook has critical reviews of the research into infants' visual and auditory perception, and other reviews about most aspects of infant development.

CHAPTER
12

Language

CHAPTER OUTLINE

- Main Areas of Language Development
- Sequences in Language Development
- The Transition to Literacy
- Learning to Read
- Dyslexia
- Theories of Language Development

In this chapter we look at the main areas of language competence that the child must master—*phonology*, *semantics*, *syntax* and *pragmatics*—and the sequences of language development that children usually go through. We consider the role of narrative skills in enabling children to engage in extended discourses with adults and other children in their social worlds and in preparing them to read and write. We also describe major theories of language development and some of the controversies that continue in this field. As you will see, despite the wealth of empirical research, there remain quite radical differences of opinion amongst theorists about how children's language develops. These and other issues will be explored in the following sections as we examine the sequences of language development through which children progress and the contexts in which this happens. We will look at some research findings in the field and major theoretical explanations of the processes involved in learning language. Throughout the chapter, we present empirical studies in a range of contexts, both experimental and naturalistic, which attempt to illuminate the complex processes of children's language development.

MAIN AREAS OF LANGUAGE DEVELOPMENT

Barrett (1999, p. 1) defines spoken language as 'a code in which spoken sound is used in order to encode meaning'. The way in which children acquire the complex system of language in the early years of life is not yet fully understood. It is likely that children are in some way programmed to learn language (canalized development, see Chapter 2) but psychologists also emphasize the role of dialogue between child and significant others in the achievement of meaning.

> To become a competent speaker of a natural language it is necessary to be conventional: to use language the way that other people use it. To become a competent speaker of a natural language it is also necessary to be creative: to formulate novel utterances tailored to the exigencies of particular communicative circumstances.
>
> *(Tomasello, 2000, p. 209)*

There are four main areas of language competence that the child must acquire. These are the rules of sounds (phonology), meaning (semantics), grammar (syntax) and knowledge of social context (pragmatics).

Phonology is the study of the system that governs the particular sounds (or phonemes) used in the language of a child's community in order to convey meaning. For example, an English speaker treats the sounds 'l' and 'r' as two separate phonemes; to a Japanese speaker they are one. Scottish people use the speech sound 'ch' (as in 'loch'), which many English people cannot pronounce properly. Phonology investigates the ways in which these phonemes can be combined into syllables, morphemes (the smallest meaningful linguistic unit) and words.

Semantics refers to the meanings encoded in language. Phonemes, which are by themselves meaningless, are combined to form morphemes, the smallest meaningful units of language. These may be whole words ('dog' in English, 'chien' in French) or grammatical markers, such as '-ed' at the end of a verb to make the past tense. The child learns that morphemes, words and longer utterances refer to events, people, objects, relationships—in short, that they convey meaning.

Syntax refers to the form in which words are combined to make grammatical sentences. The child progresses, for example, from saying, 'Anna cup' to saying, 'Anna, please pass me that cup over there'. The words themselves are not the only things that convey meaning, as we see in the following sentences:

> Yasmin hit Jane.
> Jane hit Yasmin.

Each phrase has the same words but the sentences express different meanings. The difference comes from the sequencing of the words. The rules that govern such sequences are known as *syntax*. The word *grammar* refers to the study of all the rules that determine sequences of morphemes and words in any language. These grammatical rules determine how words and morphemes in a language can be combined and sequenced to produce meaningful sentences.

Pragmatics is knowledge about how language is used in different contexts. The young child must learn to adapt his or her language to the situation in which he or she finds him- or herself. A toddler may shout out loudly in the restaurant, 'That man's greedy!'. The sentence shows understanding of phonology, syntax and semantics, but lacks sensitivity to others.

SEQUENCES IN LANGUAGE DEVELOPMENT

There seem to be great similarities in all human societies in the sequence of language development, as children progressively master the rules of sounds (phonology), of meaning (semantics) and of grammar (syntax), and learn to combine words in ways that are acceptable and understandable (pragmatics) within their linguistic community. For example, whether the child speaks pidgin, dialect, patois, Japanese, French or English, he or she constructs a grammar with rules and strategies.

 Stop and Think

Do children go through identical stages as they learn to talk?

Let us start with the newborn baby to see how this complex process of acquiring language begins (see also pp. 399-400 for phoneme perception).

Shared Rhythms

In Chapter 3, we saw how babies can pass on vital information about their needs to their parents through different patterns of crying. From around 1 month, babies produce the vowel 'ooo', a sound that seems to grow out of pleasurable social interactions, especially out of the dialogues that occur spontaneously during normal caregiving activities like nappy changing and bathing. This is the period of 'shared rhythms and regulations'.

Stern (1995, 1998) proposed that when a mother becomes pregnant and gives birth, she forms a new mental organization that Stern called 'the motherhood constellation', which remains prominent during the child's very early years. The strands of this constellation consist of concern for the child's safety and well-being (see Chapter 4 on attachment theory) as well as the need to form a 'maternal matrix' or network of close family and friends (ideally including a close relative like the maternal grandmother). The function of the constellation is to create an emotional environment within which mother and baby interact with one another in mutually satisfying dialogue.

Stop and Think

Is there any connection between the non-verbal sounds and gestures that a baby produces and later speech? What part do adults play in creating a context in which a child's language will flourish?

Stern (1990) collected detailed observational data on the interactions between caregiver and baby in the early months of the baby's life. These observations indicate that the interaction is distinctively different from typical adult–adult interaction. When adults interact with infants there is close proximity, an emphasis on exaggerated facial expressions, much repetition and more eye contact—the sort of interaction that might sometimes occur between adults when acting playfully towards one another or at points in the course of a very intimate relationship. Stern plots 'phrases of interaction' organized into 'runs'—sequences that have a common characteristic. Stern explains the rationale for this characteristic form of interaction as being one that ensures optimal attention on the part of the infant. The adult tries to make sure that the baby is neither bored nor overaroused by engaging in a sort of 'dance' with the infant in which each trades similar responses back and forth. These exchanges are rhythmic and both partners contribute to the rhythm. Stern's key point is that exchanges between the parent and Joey involve a communication of affect (Table 12.1). During the prelinguistic stage, mother and child show a very sensitive attunement to each other's emotional state. The 'gaze coupling', in which caregiver and baby appear to take different roles in their 'dialogue', may anticipate later turn taking, or alternative speaker–listener roles, that are at the heart of conversation.

Babbling and Echolalia

From 6 to 9 months the baby produces more vowels and some consonants. He or she no longer confines him- or herself to cries and cooing sounds. Echolalia is the frequent repetition of sounds—like 'dadadadad' or 'mummummummum'. The baby can also shout for attention or scream with rage; he or she spends time making noises when alone. During this stage, infants begin to develop a whole range of behaviours, some of which are directed only at familiar people. For example, certain gestures, facial expressions and sounds seem to be reserved only for the mother or primary caregiver (see Chapter 4 and Figure 12.1).

There is still disagreement among researchers about the extent to which babbling and later speech are related to one another. It would seem, however, that babies' vocalizations at

Table 12.1   Joey at 4.5 months: a face duet.

Adult perspective	Joey's perspective
Joey is sitting in his mother's lap, facing her. She looks at him intently but with no expression on her face, as if she were preoccupied and absorbed in thought elsewhere. At first, he glances at the different parts of her face but finally looks into her eyes.	I enter the world of her face. Her face and its features are the sky, the clouds and the water. Her vitality and spirit are the air and the light. It is usually a riot of light and air at play. But this time when I enter, the world is still and dull. Neither the curving lines of her face nor its rounded volumes are moving. Where is she? Where has she gone? I am scared. I feel that dullness creeping into me. I search around for a point of life to escape to.
He and she remain locked in silent mutual gaze for a long moment. She finally breaks it by easing into a slight smile. Joey quickly leans forward and returns her smile. They smile together, or rather, they trade smiles back and forth several times.	I find it. All her life is concentrated into the softest and hardest points in the world—her eyes. They draw me in deep and deeper. They draw me into a distant world. Adrift in this world, I am rocked from side to side by the passing thoughts that ripple the surface of her eyes. I stare down into their depths. And there I feel running strong the invisible currents of her excitement. They churn up from those depths and tug at me. I call after them. I want to see her face again, alive. Gradually life flows back into her face. The sea and sky are transformed. The surface now shimmers with light. New spaces open out. Arcs rise and float. Volumes and planes begin their slower dance. Her face becomes a light breeze that reaches across to touch me. It caresses me. I quicken. My sails fill with her. The dance within me is set free.

Source: Adapted from Stern (1990), pp. 57–59.

this stage have some of the phonetic characteristics of speech and that there is a process of continuity in the ways in which vocal abilities develop. In any event, parents tend to believe that their babies' babbling is an attempt to communicate meaningfully and seem to spend a lot of time guessing at the intentions that underlie the baby's actions and sounds.

Fernyhough (2008, p. 75), in observations of his baby daughter, Athena, emphasizes the fact that Athena appeared to be finely attuned to the rhythmic properties of her parents' speech, and they in turn were eager to hear her vocalizations as meaningful. For example, when Athena, at 6 months, suddenly said, 'Laggy loo!', as she played with a plastic toy, her parents interpreted this profound utterance as 'an expression of wishful optimism'. These

Figure 12.1   A mother and her 9-month-old baby engage in 'turn-taking' during their 'conversation'; although he cannot talk, he responds to her with speech-like rhythms, gestures and facial expressions (Fogel & Garvey, 2007).

Source: Image copyright Mika Heittola, used under licence from Shutterstock.com.

'conversations' with Athena are similar to the images, metaphors, space and movement described in Table 12.1.

The fact that doting parents often go beyond the actual meaning of the baby's actions (as far as we can determine) plays a crucial part in their integration of the young child into their social system, and provides an early example of scaffolding (that is, offering guided support to the novice learner; see Chapters 4 and 16). Tomasello et al. (2005) indicate the early capacity to engage in collaborative activity. This means that the very young child can interpret the mother's meaning when she points at an object. Similarly, the child can point to something to show that he/she wants it. By 18 months, most infants can draw the attention of an adult to an object of mutual interest and offer some form of commentary. In all cultures, children in this way enter what Tomasello calls an *intersubjective world* of shared knowledge and mutually satisfying communication.

Typically, parents speak to babies in a very special way known as Infant-Directed Speech (IDS) characterized by exaggerated intonation, rising and falling curves of sound and higher pitch than usual (Saxton, 2010). Mithen (2005) notes how satisfying IDS is to babies through its musical rhythms and tones. It is certainly clear that, long before the first words appear, the baby shows signs of understanding some of what is said to him or her.

Stern's observational work is consistent with the research findings of Fogel (1993) and his colleagues (e.g. Fogel & Garvey, 2007) in their detailed analysis of the dynamic nature of communication between mother and baby. Fogel and Garvey (2007) propose the concept of 'alive communication' in which each expression and gesture is new and meaningful. Take, for example, a tickling game between mother and baby. Each moves in close relationship to the other and each movement is adjusted to the next on a second-by-second basis. Mutual enjoyment emerges out of this dynamic process.

Fogel (1993) identifies complex microinteractions or 'coregulation of intentions' during the communication process between adult and child. This process of coregulation, he claims, is a form of ongoing elaboration of actions and intentions in response to the other's actions. Fogel uses the metaphor of the jazz band to demonstrate how the communication between adult and child is a shared achievement, not an individual one. Just as members of a jazz group respond to one another's rhythms and sounds to create their music, so parents and babies engage in a process of improvisation as they communicate with each other in mutually enjoyable ways (see also p. 99).

First Words and Sentences

It is easy to miss the first words a baby utters, since they are often sounds not found in the dictionary! However, they can be considered as words if the child uses them consistently in the presence of a particular object or situation. One 12-month-old baby, for example, said 'da' every time he pointed at something that he wanted, and 'oof' whenever he saw animals.

These first words have the function of naming or labelling the people and objects in the child's environment. But they also condense meaning. 'Milk' can mean 'I want milk' or 'My milk is spilt'. Even though the child can only say one word at a time, variations in context, intonation and gesture can convey a richer meaning. Single words used in this way are known as *holophrases*, since the one word can be interpreted as expressing a whole idea. Gestures play a part here in enhancing meanings and intentions, and it seems likely that hand gestures and spoken language are linked in evolutionary terms.

Research into 'baby signing' (BS) provides evidence that babies can be taught to sign their intentions to their parents or to make combinations of first words and gestures to form two-item strings (e.g. *give* + point to a cup = 'give cup'). Where babies are taught specific gestures, there appears to be an extension of the 'gesture + word' combination into 'gesture + gesture' combinations before the occurrence of two-word utterances (Doherty-Sneddon, 2008.) It can take 3 or 4 months after the emergence of the first words before vocabulary increases very much, but after that the acquisition of new words is extraordinarily rapid. Vocabulary typically grows from around 20 words at 18 months to around 200 words at 21 months. New words are mainly object names ('daddy', 'car', 'cat') but also include action names ('look', 'gone'), state names ('red', 'lovely', 'sore') and some 'function' words referring to types of events ('there', 'more', 'bye-bye'). The vast majority of object names refer to objects that the child is able to manipulate (e.g. shoes, toys, foodstuffs) or that are spontaneously dynamic (e.g. people, animals, vehicles) (Dromi, 1999; Nelson, 1981).

At around 18 months the child starts to combine single words into two-word sentences. Of course, single-word utterances continue to be used for some time, but they gradually give way to more complex word combinations. The child becomes more 'conversational' and this capacity is closely linked to the child's *theory of mind* (see Chapter 15). Frequent communication with adults and other children is crucial for facilitating the child's growing understanding of her world and the people in it (Hoff, 2010). The child's first sentences are often described as 'telegraphic' speech, i.e. speech in which the highly condensed meaning is transmitted from the child to another person. 'Ben shoe' means 'That is Ben's shoe' or 'Put on my shoe'. The child may also have a characteristic way of asking for more information—'Who dat?' or of making observations—'Mummy gone', 'Sammy here', often repeated. However, as Fogel's research indicates, fluid musical metaphors seem to provide more accurate representations of the process than the more static (and dated) metaphor of the telegraph. Typically, when the child produces a holophrase the adult will expand it to clarify meaning.

Child: More.
Adult: You want more milk?

Early studies, such as the classic one by Nelson et al. (1973), investigated the impact of different kinds of adult feedback on children's grammatical constructions by comparing the effects of expanding children's incomplete sentences (that is, putting them in their complete form) and recasting them (that is, keeping the topic the same but giving the child a new way of talking about it). For example:

Child's incomplete sentence:	Doggy eat.
Adult expansion:	Doggy is eating.
Adult recasting:	What is the doggy eating?

Children whose sentences were recast performed better in a sentence imitation task than children whose sentences were only expanded. Furthermore, the children whose utterances were recast used more complex grammatical forms in their spontaneous speech than those whose sentences were simply expanded. An even more specific effect was found when an experimenter recast children's utterances into questions or into complex verb constructions: each treatment group showed growth in the use of negative 'wh-' questions or complex verb constructions depending on the type of adult intervention. Box 12.1 gives the details of this study.

As Tomasello (2000) points out, most of children's early language is 'grammatical' from the adult point of view. However, there are different ways of explaining this. Some psychologists (e.g. Ingram, 1999) propose that children begin to use properties of phonological organization that are part of those that underlie the adult language, though in a less complex form. On the basis of his detailed phonological case study of the developing syllables, vowels and consonants of one child, Alice, from the age of 16 months, Ingram claimed that children's phonological systems develop in ways that are parallel to adult languages. By contrast, Tomasello (2000, p. 210) suggests that children are learning to use specific linguistic items and structures (or, in other words, specific words and phrases) in the ways that adults use them 'with the proviso that they can substitute nominals (or nouns) for one another relatively freely'.

There are different ways of testing these proposals, such as focusing on language that goes beyond what the child could possibly have heard from adults. One method examines spontaneous speech, looking at the ways in which the child uses particular items or structures. For example, if a child said 'sheeps', you could infer that he or she was applying the principle that plural nouns end in 's'. Another method is to teach the child novel linguistic items and see what they do with them. For example, introduce a new noun, like 'gop' or 'tam' and see if the child uses it grammatically.

By 24–27 months, the child is regularly producing three- and four-word utterances. There are many sentences that are in a strict sense 'ungrammatical' but that reveal that the child is in fact using grammatical rules of syntax. These errors are 'logical errors'. The child will produce sentences like 'Mouses gone away' in which the normal rule for plurals is extended to exceptions like 'mouse'. These 'errors' are made because the child is applying a basic set of rules (in this case, adding 's' to make a noun plural). Idiosyncratic words are also common. For example, one child called a chocolate biscuit a 'choskit', a word that he had invented himself. Grammatical rules are applied to such words; for example, the plural is formed by adding 's'—choskits.

After the three-and four-word linking stage, there is a rapid increase in use of grammatical rules. Prepositions (such as 'in', 'on', 'beneath' or 'against') and irregular verb endings appear (such as 'written' or 'fought'). Now the child can begin to reorder the words of a sentence, for example to make questions or negative statements. Thus, 'John is swimming?' becomes 'Is John swimming?'. 'Wh-' questions are formed, though often at first in an unorthodox form—'Where my glove?' or 'Why John is eating?' in which the 'wh-' form is just tacked on to the beginning of the sentence. The negative is used more, though also in unusual forms, such as 'Not my

Box 12.1 Facilitating children's syntax development

Nelson had already shown (Nelson et al., 1973) that the recasting of children's incomplete sentences by adults had a positive effect on both performance on a sentence imitation task and complexity of grammar use in spontaneous speech. In this experiment she aimed to discover whether these effects were specific. Would children whose utterances were recast into complex questions show improvement in the use of question forms? Would children whose utterances were recast into sentences that contained complex verbs show greater use of verbs? To answer these questions, Nelson devised an experimental intervention study.

Her sample was 12 children (six boys and six girls) aged 28–29 months who all lacked two categories of syntactic structures in their spontaneous speech. These were complex questions and complex verbs of the type shown below.

Complex questions

1. Tag questions: for example, 'I changed them round, didn't I?', where 'didn't I?' is tagged on to the end of a statement.
2. 'Wh-' negative questions: negative questions beginning with 'what', 'why', 'where' 'who' and so on (e.g. 'Why can't I go?').
3. Other negative questions: for example, 'Doesn't it hurt?' or 'It won't fit?'.

Complex verbs

1. Single verbs in future or conditional tense: for example, 'He will help me' or 'He would help me'.
2. Sentences in which two verbs were used: for example, 'He will run and jump' or 'The bear ate the girls who visited'.

Two 1-hour sessions with each child were taped to determine initial language levels. Assignment of children to groups was based on mean length of utterance (MLU) in words. Three boys and three girls were assigned to an intervention schedule focused on complex questions; the remaining six children were assigned to receive an intervention designed to facilitate the use of complex verbs. Each group had an average MLU of 3.69 words per utterance (range 3.09–4.29). Both groups were closely comparable in terms of the presence or absence of complex verbs and complex questions in their spontaneous speech during these two sessions.

Five 1-hour sessions of intervention were scheduled for each child. Three women were the experimenters, each one working with four children (two assigned to question intervention and two to verb intervention).

In question intervention sessions, the experimenter frequently recast the child's sentences in the form of tag or negative questions. For example, when one child said, 'You can't get in', the researcher replied, 'No, I can't get in, can I?'. If recastings did not come readily, the experimenter constructed new examples. When one child said, 'And you're a girl', the experimenter replied, 'Right! And aren't you a little girl?'.

Similarly, in verb intervention sessions both recastings and new constructions were used. If the child said, 'Where it go?', the adult replied, 'It will go there'. When one child said, 'I got it, I reached it', the adult said, 'You got under the bed and reached it'.

The children's utterances during the fourth and fifth sessions (the last two intervention sessions) were recorded. Each child's transcript was scored for presence or absence of sentences containing complex questions or complex verbs, using the measures shown in

Box Table 12.1.1   Type of sentence structure used by each participant (numbered) after intervention but not prior to intervention.

Sentence type	Question intervention						Verb intervention					
	1	2	3	4	5	6	1	2	3	4	5	6
Tag questions	+		+	+	+							+
'Wh-' negative questions			+									
Other negative questions		+										
Future tense (one verb)							+			+		
Conditional tense (one verb)							+	+	+			+
Future tense (two verbs)								+	+			+
Conditional tense (two verbs)							+					
Past tense (two verbs)							+		+	+		+

Note: Sign tests show the results to be significant ($p<.01$) for both question and verb intervention. MLU for both groups was not affected. Examples of sentences with complex questions or verb structures that appeared after intervention are given in the text.
Source: Nelson, K. (1977). Facilitating children's syntax development. *Developmental Psychology, 13,* 101–107.

Box Table 12.1.1. Analysis of the data revealed clear-cut effects of the interventions. Complex questions, which had been lacking before intervention, were used by all six children in the question intervention group; only one of the children in this group (subject 6) also showed use of complex verbs. The opposite pattern held for the acquisition of new verb forms. All the children in the verb intervention group used complex verbs that they had not expressed before intervention; only one (subject 6) also used new complex questions. Sign tests showed the results to be significant for both question and verb intervention. MLU was not affected for either group.

Nelson concluded that this experiment increases our understanding of how children get information from adults about syntax. In comparing the experimenters' recasting with normal parental responses, she noted that in real life adults do use negative and tag questions and complex verbs when they talk to their children, but they do not use them frequently. So why did recastings of children's sentences have the effect shown by this experiment?

Nelson suggested that the experimental recasting probably drew the child's attention to the new forms. The experience of hearing complex questions and verbs was not a wholly new one to the child, but the researchers, by reworking the child's own sentences, pointed attention to a more complex form that was close to the child's existing language use and that made immediate sense to the child. The experimenter's response to 'Donkey ran' of 'The donkey did run, didn't he?' was more complex but also entirely appropriate in a playful, conversational content. The child was thus able to make a direct comparison between his or her own utterances and the sentence structure of the adult's reply. The introduction of new grammatical forms that are still closely tied to the child's language use thus seems to be one way of extending language development.

Based on material in Nelson, K. (1977). Facilitating children's syntax development. *Developmental Psychology, 13,* 101–107.

daddy work'; 'I no want it'; 'Not shut door, no!'. In these sentences, 'no' or 'not' is put in to express negation. Later, the child will reorder the sentence in a more 'adult' way, e.g. 'My daddy not working'.

Children at this age show a great interest in rhymes and will sing songs they have learned, though sometimes in a distorted form. Imaginative play reflects developing language (see Chapter 7). Conversations acted out in play or commentaries that accompany actions contribute greatly to the expression of ideas and experience. Presleep monologues (Table 12.2)

Table 12.2 Presleep monologues.

Weir (1962) studied her child Anthony as he talked himself to sleep each night between the ages of 28 and 30 months (see also Chapter 7). The monologues she recorded took the form of social exchanges, even though Anthony was alone. Anthony asked questions, responded to an imaginary companion, invented words and created rhythmical songs. It seems that his language served three purposes. First, he seemed to be practising new words and grammar forms that he had recently learned. Second, he was playing with sounds for their own sake and creating poetic rhythms. Third, he seemed to be trying to make sense of his world by ordering events in a systematic way. Here is an example of one of Anthony's monologues.

> That's for he
> Mamamama with Daddy
> Milk for Daddy
> OK
> Daddy dance
> Daddy dance
> Hi Daddy
> Only Anthony
> Daddy dance
> Daddy dance
> Daddy give it
> Daddy not for Anthony
> (Weir, 1962, pp. 138–139)

Weir argues that Anthony is practising language as well as trying to make sense of the non-linguistic world of which he is a part—the sharing of his attachment between Mama and Daddy is one theme, his offer of milk 'for Daddy' another. The second example shows sound play with no clear meaning at all.

> Bink
> Let Bobo bink
> Bink ben bink
> Blue kink

You will notice the use of rhyming and alliteration, a skill that will have implications for the future process of learning to read.

Source: Weir (1962), p. 105.

may also be important for the processing of interpersonal experiences and their subsequent organization in memory. Schank (1982) and Nelson (1989) argued that autobiographical memories are processed, reprocessed and cross-indexed into a system of interlinked schema categories that retain aspects of the structure of the experienced event in terms of time, space, movement and causality. These become 'scripts' (for example, the script of putting a doll to bed or the script of a mealtime routine). A study by Bruner and Lucariello (1989) of the monologues of Emmy as she talked herself to sleep between the ages of 21 months and 3 years gives insight into the process of organizing information into such meaningful units. Emmy would often repeat the stories and add her own predictions and inferences. As the analysis of the tapes suggests, Emmy was actively constructing experience, not simply reflecting it.

Research into bilingualism provides useful insights. Bilingual first language (BFL) acquisition is very similar to monolingual acquisition but has some important differences. Bilingual children reach a number of milestones within the same age range as monolinguals, for example, in babbling, first words and rate of vocabulary growth. However, bilingual children can also show differences in vocabulary size, depending on the extent of the exposure to the language (for example, if they hear more of the mother's language than that of the father). This can also depend on the extent of the overlap between the two languages. But from a very early age, most BFL learners are able to manage their two languages very well for communication purposes. In general, as Genesee and Nicoladis (2007, pp. 336–337) indicate, the acquisition of BFL is 'an active, creative process that draws on the linguistic, communicative and cognitive resources of the developing child'.

As we have seen, the role of adult discourse is important throughout this period in facilitating the child's learning about how to highlight events in a particular scene in order to communicate intentions and meaning effectively. However, there is considerable disagreement among theorists about the extent to which children's early meanings and the words they use to express them arise directly from the input of adults. Intrinsic factors related to the child's cognitive functioning have also been shown to play a significant part. Findings in the literature are actually quite diverse about the initial mapping of new words, the child's growing ability to use words out of context and the refinement of meaning relationships among the different words in the child's *lexicon* (or vocabulary). Here we present two models of word acquisition that present contrasting interpretations: the *syntactic bootstrapping hypothesis* (Gleitman, 1990) and the *multi-route model* (Barrett, 1986).

Gleitman's Syntactic Bootstrapping Hypothesis

Gleitman (1990) called children's ability to infer the meanings of words from cues *syntactic bootstrapping*. By this she means that young children use grammatical information from the *structure* of sentences to infer meanings of unfamiliar target words—as if they are 'pulling themselves up by their own bootstraps' or, in other words, improving their own performance by their own strenuous efforts. In this sense, syntax helps the young child to learn, for example, when the sentence structure around a new verb provides clues about its meaning. Gleitman and her colleagues (Fisher & Gleitman, 2002; Hirsh-Pasek & Golinkoff, 1996) argue that from an early age children are sensitive to syntactic and semantic correspondences that exist in the language. They designed ingenious experiments using invented words to prove that young children can extract the meanings of verbs from syntactic cues.

For example, in one study, 27-month-old children were shown two different videos. In one, Big Bird and Cookie Monster rotated next to each other; in the other, Big Bird rotated Cookie Monster. As the children watched the videos they heard sentences, each using a novel verb. The first sentence was: 'Big Bird is gorping with Cookie Monster'; the second was 'Big Bird is gorping Cookie Monster'. Note that the first verb is intransitive (that is, it has a subject but no object), while the second verb is transitive (Big Bird is the subject while Cookie Monster is the object of the verb). When hearing the intransitive verb form, the children were more likely to look at the video in which the two puppets performed the same action. When hearing the transitive verb form, they tended to look at the video that showed Big Bird performing an action on Cookie Monster. Gleitman's conclusion is that young children bring the verb's meaning into alignment with the syntax and not the other way round. Gleitman's model is grounded in linguistic theory.

Barrett's Multi-Route Model

By contrast, Barrett's multi-route model of early lexical development takes account of the interactions he observed among the timing of acquisition, the child's linguistic experience and the cognitive representational abilities. Barrett (1986), Harris et al. (1988) and Barrett et al. (1991) distinguished two classes of early words.

1. *Context-bound* words that are only used in a specific behavioural context. For example, Emmy says 'duck' when she hits a toy duck off the edge of the bath; duck is only used in this context.
2. *Referential* words that are used in a variety of different behavioural contexts. As examples, James initially uses 'teddy' to refer to one large teddy bear; later, 'teddy' is extended to apply to a little teddy. James also initially uses 'more' to request or comment on recurrence of an object; later, he uses 'more' to request repetition of a set of actions.

Barrett proposed that these two classes of words follow different routes in order to reach adult conventional meaning. Context-bound words are mapped on to what he calls 'holistic *event* representations' (that is, the child's global construction of an event), while referential words are mapped on to *mental* representations of either specific *objects* (object names) or *actions* (action names). Barrett's approach was strongly influenced by Nelson's argument (see Box 12.1) that during late infancy children build up holistic mental representations of the events that occur in everyday life. These representations of events underlying context-bound words are gradually analysed into their constituent components—people, objects, actions and relations—and so the child eventually learns to sort them into logical categories. Barrett agrees that maternal input has a critical role in helping the child establish the initial uses for words, but argues that children also rely on their own cognitive processing to establish subsequent use of words. In other words, while the initial focus is on external stimuli, later children focus more on their own inner representations in order to form theories about the linguistic system.

From 3 to 5 Years

The 3-year-old's speech is largely understandable to adults, even outside the family. His or her vocabulary is now around 1,000 words, the length and complexity of utterances have increased, and he or she can carry on reasonable conversations, though these still tend to be rooted in the immediate present. Despite these skills, however, the child is still perfecting various linguistic systems, such as pronouns (for example, 'I' and 'we'), auxiliary verbs (for example, the word 'am' in 'I am dancing'), passive verbs (for example, 'the door *was* opened') and irregular verbs ('he *thought*' or 'I *knew*').

By 3 years, children begin to use complex sentences containing relative clauses. Sentences like 'See the car that I got' appear before 'The car that I got is a red one'. The second sentence is more difficult for children, since the relative clause 'that I got' is embedded.

By the time a child enters school at around 5 years, she can understand and express complex sentences and her use of language is very similar to that of an adult. She can also adjust her speech in a number of ways to suit listeners of different ages with whom she is communicating. She may still produce logical errors like 'That one's the bestest'. Some specific aspects of syntax continue to pose difficulties. In general, however, by the time children enter school their language use is correct, and their basic sentence types are similar to those used by adults.

THE TRANSITION TO LITERACY

When children enter formal schooling at around the age of 5 years, they are expected to make the important transition to literacy. Literacy is an essential part of the child's development, opening up access to education, future employment prospects and complex forms of communication in society that go beyond face-to-face talk and gesture. Ritchie and Bates (2013), using longitudinal NCDS data (see Table 1.2), found that early reading ability is significantly associated with academic motivation and duration of education, and later socioeconomic status (SES), independently of other variables such as SES at birth. They speculate that early reading ability helps to boost cognitive activity, resulting in greater academic motivation and longer experience of education which, in turn, leads to enhanced access to higher-status occupations.

Reading and writing are social constructs which need specific instruction and which build on previous linguistic competence (Snow, 2009) and in order to make the transition smoothly children are at a distinct advantage if they come to school with an existing repertoire of *prereading and prewriting skills*. It also helps if they have developed some understanding of narrative through their capacity to take account of *their own and others' perspectives* on a situation. We consider these aspects in the next two sections.

Prereading and Prewriting Skills

By 6 or 7 years of age, most children have begun the process of learning to read and write. Obviously some perceptual skills are needed, but other aspects of language development in the preschool years may also be necessary if a child is to become a proficient reader and writer a few years later. These are called 'prereading skills' and 'prewriting skills'. As well as the usual skills of perception and discrimination, these include the understanding of reading conventions and the concept of story, and the awareness of rhyming ('roses' and 'posies') and alliteration (the recurrence of the letter 'r' in 'ring a ring o' roses' and 'p' in 'a pocket full of posies', or the repetition of 'p' in 'Peter Piper picked a peck of pickled peppers'). From an early age, the child can be helped to develop these skills.

When a child begins to read and write he needs to consider visual information as well as the sound and sense of words (for an example, see 5-year-old Javier's writing in Figure 12.2). During the preschool years, the child's perceptual skills can be sharpened by encouraging him to observe specific aspects of his environment. Training in visual discrimination can be done in an enjoyable way through games; for example, jigsaws, picture-matching games or exercises in grading shapes and objects by size or colour, or the experience of noticing differences and similarities between objects can give the child useful preparation for discriminating among words and letters. It is also useful if the child understands concepts of 'up', 'down', 'forwards' and 'backwards'.

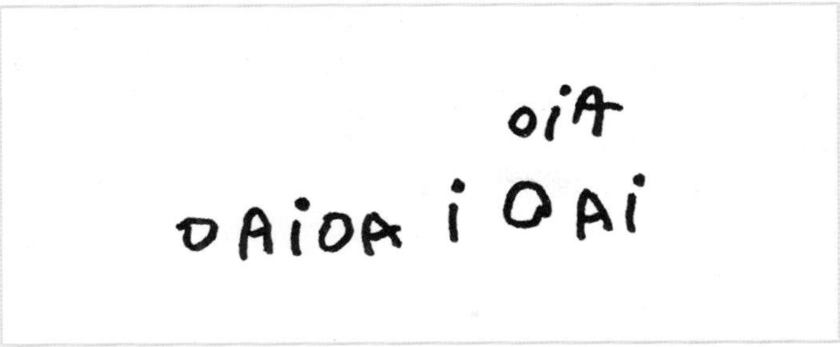

Figure 12.2 Writing by Javier, aged 5 years 5 months. Top row, 'Gatito' (little cat); bottom row, 'Gatitos' (three little cats in the picture). He explains as he is writing: 'One little cat' (the first three letters); 'the little cats here' (six letters); 'another cat' (the three remaining letters). You can see that the plural is obtained by repeating the original word as many times as there are cats to be represented.

Source: Ferreiro, E. (1985). Literacy development: a psychogenic perspective. In D. Olson, N. Torrance & A. Hildyard (Eds.), *Literacy, language and learning*. Cambridge: Cambridge University Press. Reproduced by permission.

Bryant and Bradley (1985) and Bryant et al. (1990) argue that young children's awareness of rhyming and alliteration indicates a skill in analysing the constituent sounds of words, which is essential for learning to read. Young children usually respond with delight to nursery rhymes such as 'Ring a ring o' roses' that contain rhyming and alliteration, and will often create their own rhymes, as we see in the rhyming couplets created by 3-year-olds (Chukovsky, 1963) and the alliteration in some of the presleep monologues produced by 2-year-old Anthony (Weir, 1962; see p. 415).

Bryant and Bradley (1985, pp. 47–48) quote (from Chukovsky) jingles by 3-year-olds that also demonstrate the children's ability to change words to suit the rules of rhyme.

The red house
Made of strouss
The duckling and the big goose
Sat on the broken sail-oose.

Bryant and Bradley argue that 'all these children know a great deal about how to spot the common sounds in different words. Children show this every time that they produce rhyme'. In the process of becoming familiar with rhymes and alliteration, they are also developing an awareness of speech sounds (*phonological awareness*) that will have an influence on their later ability to read and spell. Bryant and Bradley hypothesize a direct link between sensitivity to sounds (as shown in responses to rhyming and alliteration games) and competence in learning to read. The delayed reader is likely to be a child who has not developed this skill in detecting speech sounds during the preschool years. In a longitudinal study of 65 3- and

4-year-olds, Bryant et al. (1990) provided further evidence for the strong link between children's sensitivity to rhyme and alliteration and their success in reading. The awareness of rhyme, argue these authors, helps children to form spelling categories. For example, if the child knows how to read 'beak', it gives him a strategy to read and pronounce the new word 'peak'. Some support for these ideas is found in the study reported in Box 12.2.

Box 12.2 Categorizing sounds and learning to read: a causal connection

The investigators in this study wished to test the hypothesis that the child's experience of categorizing sounds, as in rhyming and alliteration, has a considerable effect on later success in learning to read and spell. To do this, they used two methods: a large-scale correlational study and a small-scale experimental study.

The correlational study started with 118 4-year-olds and 285 5-year-olds. None could yet read. The children were tested on their ability to categorize sounds by detecting the odd word out (i.e. the one that did not share a common sound) in a series of words. This common sound could be at the end of the word (bun, hut, gun, sun), the middle (hug, pig, dig, wig) or the beginning (bud, bun, bus, rug). Where it came at the end or the middle of the word, the task was to spot words that rhymed. Where it came at the beginning of the word, the children's awareness of alliteration was tested.

In addition, each child was given a test of verbal intelligence (the English Picture Vocabulary Test, or EPVT) and a memory test. Four years later, when the children were 8 or 9 years old, Bradley and Bryant gave them standardized tests of reading and spelling. They also tested their IQ, using the WISC-R, and their mathematical ability on a standardized test. (By this time, 368 of the original 403 children remained in the project sample.)

There were high correlations between the initial sound categorization scores (at ages 4–5 years) and the children's reading and spelling scores 4 years later (Box Table 12.2.1). This in itself does not prove the hypothesis that the ability to categorize sounds has a

Box Table 12.2.1 Correlations between initial sound categorization, EPVT and memory scores, and final reading and spelling levels.

| | | Initial scores | | | | | |
| | | Sound categorization | | EPVT | | Memory | |
	Age (yr)	4	5	4	5	4	5
Final reading score (Schonell test)		.57	.44	.52	.39	.40	.22
Final spelling score (Schonell test)		.48	.44	.33	.31	.33	.22

Source: Adapted by permission from Macmillan Publishers Ltd: NATURE Bradley, L. & Bryant, P.E. (1983) Categorizing sounds and learning to read - a causal connection, *Nature*, *301*: 419-421, copyright 1983.

causal connection with reading success. Some third factor might lie behind both abilities. For example, general intelligence, or perhaps memory for words, might help in both. However, as can be seen in Box Table 12.2.1, the correlations of reading and spelling scores with sound categorization are a bit higher than with the EPVT or memory scores. This means that while intelligence and memory may explain some of the association between sound categorization and reading and spelling, it is unlikely that they can explain all of it.

To provide more definite evidence for the causal relationship that this suggested, the investigators carried out a training study with an experimental design (a field experiment, see Chapter 1), using 65 children from the larger sample. They were selected from those whose original scores on sound categorization were at least two standard deviations below the mean.

Two experimental groups received training in sound categorization skills for 40 individual sessions over two years. In Group 1 (N=13), coloured pictures of familiar objects were used to teach the children that the same word could share common beginning (hen, hat), common middle (hen, pet) and common end (hen, man) sounds with other words. This training experience was purely concerned with increasing awareness of rhyming and alliteration. For Group 2 (N=13), in addition to the rhyming and alliteration training, the children were shown plastic letters and taught how to identify the sounds that the names of the pictures had in common with particular letters ('c' for 'cat' and 'cup'). The relationship between common sounds and letters of the alphabet that represented them was made clear (Box Figure 12.2.1).

Two control groups were also used. Group 3 (N=26) was taught over the same period of time to categorize the same pictures in a

Box Figure 12.2.1 Children receiving training in sound categorization skills: (a) selecting pictures with names which have common sounds (e.g. bat, mat, hat); (b) identifying sounds with the aid of plastic letters.

conceptual way (e.g. hen and bat are animals; hen and pig are farm animals) but received no tuition in sound categorization. Group 4 (N=13) received no training at all. All four groups were matched for age, initial EPVT scores and initial scores on sound categorization. The results are shown in Box Table 12.2.2. Group 1, the experimental group that had been trained on sound categorization only, was ahead of Group 3 (the group trained to categorize conceptually) by 3–4 months in reading and spelling levels. The second experimental group, Group 2, which had been trained on sound categorization and alphabetic letters as

Box Table 12.2.2 Mean final reading, spelling and mathematics levels, and intelligence test scores, in groups from the training study.

	Experimental groups		Control groups		Significance of group differences
	1	2	3	4	
Reading age in months (Schonell test)	92.2	97.0	88.5	84.5	$p < .01$
Spelling age in months (Schonell test)	86.0	98.8	81.8	75.2	$p < .001$
Mathematics score	91.3	91.1	88.0	84.1	n.s.
Final IQ (WISC-R)	97.2	101.2	103.0	100.2	n.s

Source: Adapted by permission from Macmillan Publishers Ltd: NATURE Bradley, L. & Bryant, P.E. (1983) Categorizing sounds and learning to read - a causal connection, *Nature, 301*: 419-421, copyright 1983.

well, performed best of all in reading and spelling. The authors conclude that not only does training in sound categorization have an influence on reading and spelling but that, if it is combined with alphabetic teaching, it will be even more effective. They also argue that the effect is specific to reading and spelling, since the differences among the four groups in scores in the mathematics test were considerably smaller and not statistically significant.

The drawbacks of this training study are that the numbers in the experimental groups are small, and some differences are not statistically significant (for example, the scores for Group 1 in themselves do not differ significantly from those in Group 3). Also, as the investigators point out, we do not know how well such experimental results would generalize to a wider spectrum of children in real-life teaching conditions.

This is where the strength of combining two methods comes in. The original correlational study strongly suggests that the relationship between sound categorization skills and later reading and spelling abilities is an ecologically valid one. Taken together, these results provide strong evidence for a moderate degree of causal influence along the lines the investigators hypothesized. The educational implications are considered further in Bryant and Bradley (1985) and in Bryant et al. (1990). In view of the large number of children who do experience reading difficulties, this study offers practical guidelines for identifying specific problem areas and intervening to overcome them.

Based on material in Bradley, L. & Bryant, P.E. (1983). Categorizing sounds and learning to read: A causal connection. *Nature, 301*, 419–421.

While acknowledging the great value of phonological awareness in forming a strong foundation for reading, Snowling and her colleagues argue that semantic skills are also extremely important (for detailed reviews, see Snowling, 2002, 2009). Snowling recommends reading methods—such as the widely acclaimed New Zealand Reading Recovery method

(Clay, 1985)—that integrate a structured phonological programme with meaningful use of context and content to help children develop effective reading strategies. This is where extensive experience of narrative is an important preparation for literacy.

Taking Account of One's Own and Others' Perspective Through Narrative Experiences

Children extend their literacy skills by engaging in accounts of everyday events where they have the chance to express their own stance through appropriate repetition, emphasis, exclamations and other indicators of the capacity to make the shift between their own and others' perspectives. This ability usually emerges by the age of 4–5 years when children describe personal experiences. But this is an evolving process. In retelling events from a book or a drama, it is not until much later—usually around 9 years—that children begin to move clearly among the perspectives of the author of the storyline, the characters, the events and their own views on the narrative.

Children need to learn to make appropriate use of linguistic indicators to show that they are aware of the listener's perspective, for example, by manipulating words like 'this' and 'that' or 'I' and 'you' to differentiate the speaker's from the listener's stance. They also need to be able to distinguish between what they know as speakers and what the listener may not know, for example by contextualizing information or putting the listener into the picture ('Isabel—she's a girl in my class' or 'That programme I saw yesterday on TV'). More subtly, children need to adjust their language to different contexts, for example saying 'please' and 'thank you' when in the company of older relatives, or adjusting their language to the social conventions of the community outside the family.

Oppenheim et al. (1997) found that there were clear associations between children's co-constructed narratives with their mothers and two aspects of their development: their ability to construct emotionally well-organized and regulated narratives independently and their behavioural and emotional regulation in everyday life. Children who were rated higher on their capacity to express emotions appropriately during co-constructed narrative making had higher ratings on their independently created stories in terms of emotional coherence, the presence of prosocial themes and the absence of aggressive themes. They were rated by their mothers as having fewer behavioural and emotional problems at the time of the study and also when retested 1 year later.

By encouraging children to tell and write stories, parents and teachers can give them the opportunity to encompass both subjective and objective ways of knowing the inner world of experience as well as external reality. In order to explore preschoolers' understanding of their own and others' internal emotional states, Meins et al. (2006) asked children to describe what they saw in a wordless picture book about a pet frog which escapes from his owner, a little boy. The pictures illustrate a range of emotional reactions, including mistaken identity and deception. The researchers recorded the preschoolers' use of such words as 'see', 'want', 'look', 'taste', 'think', 'know', and 'remember'. Responses like 'The lady was shocked' indicated that the child could infer a feeling from the picture. One child spoke on behalf of the frog in a croaky voice, saying, 'Mmm! That looks tasty!', indicating his capacity to take the frog's perspective. Meins and her colleagues linked the children's knowledge and understanding of inner states with the extended use of vocabulary describing their own and others' feelings and perspectives. This process is, of course, best developed in a playful way and in the context of enjoyable shared experiences, such as bedtime stories or the shared recall of important family events.

There are wide individual differences in children's capacity to create and respond to stories, and research studies of adult–child interaction indicate that these processes may be nurtured or inhibited by the responses of other people, especially those who are significant to the child. The literature about children's personal narratives indicates that narratives are central for several developmental processes, including:

- Autobiographical memory.
- Integration into a particular social-cultural context.
- The capacity for self-awareness and emotional organization.
- The capacity to view interpersonal situations from multiple perspectives.
- The capacity to see the self as having multiple sides or 'narrative voices'.

By 3 years, children are developing in their skills as narrators of fictitious stories, using beginnings ('Once upon a time') and endings ('They all lived happily ever after'). These stories are based on real-life experiences or on stories that they have heard from books and the media. Bruner (1990) suggests that we learn about the physical world by devising paradigms or models that are logical and rule bound, whereas we come to understand the cultural world in a more personal, dynamic way—by, for example, telling stories. He argues that not only do children devise narratives as a way of understanding their own experiences, but they also use narrative as a medium for communicating to others what these experiences mean.

With particular regard to emergent literacy, the telling and retelling of stories can also enable children to become familiar with the convention of written stories, thus providing motivation and a framework for help with reading. Parents have a crucial part to play in the period before the child begins to read by making stories an enjoyable, shared experience through turn-taking, sharing and empathizing. The discourse processes that began in the preschool years can be fostered by sensitive parents and teachers and harnessed to the emerging skills of reading and writing.

 Stop and Think

Why is it important for parents to tell their children stories or recall shared family experiences? How does this help children to develop useful prereading and prewriting skills?

LEARNING TO READ

There are different methods for teaching children to read with a continuing debate about which one is the most effective. One major approach places emphasis on the teaching of *phonics* in the context of meaningful use of text. This approach adopts a logical progression from recognizing individual letters and letter sounds, to sounding out consonant-vowel-consonant words (like c-a-t), to recognizing blends of letters to make new sounds (like 'ch-ip' and 'sh-ip'), to recognizing more complex sounds (like 'igh' or 'ou') and split diagraphs (like 'kite' and 'tape'), to alternative sounds (like 'show' and 'frown'), to phonically regular sounds (like 'cat', 'mat' and 'sat') before combining these words into sentences (like 'the cat sat on the mat'). Bryant and Bradley (1985) (as we have seen) and Goswami (1995) argue that phonological awareness underpins success in learning to read. But other theorists, such as Snowling (2002, 2009), place much more emphasis on reading as a search for meaning and argue that individual letter sounds and words are best learned in the context of reading longer texts that are interesting to the child. This approach draws strongly on the value of semantic skills.

Most children learn to read with enjoyment, whatever the method they experience, but some find it an overwhelmingly difficult task and require remedial support. The early years are critical for identifying children at risk of failing to learn to read and write. Some remedial programmes offer highly structured phonics. For example, one successful approach is the Literacy Programme (Hornsby & Shear, 1993) which uses phonics in a structured sequence starting with letter sounds before moving on to blending, word reading and spelling, then sentences and finally longer texts. Others focus on using meaningful texts. One widely used reading scheme is the research-based New Zealand Reading Recovery programme (Clay, 1985) which integrates knowledge of phonics with meaningful use of content. In this programme, the children are given many opportunities for speaking and listening as an integral part of learning to read and write. Its main aim is to *accelerate* literacy and to *reduce* reading and writing difficulties by specifically targeting children in the lowest 20% of literacy competence at an early stage. Evaluation studies (e.g. Timperely et al., 2006) indicate immediate and long-term gains for children who follow the Reading Recovery programme and success in preventing a cycle of failure and discouragement.

In the next section we look in some detail at the particular challenges faced by children with *dyslexia*. Children who experience difficulties in reading and writing are more prone to have later learning problems as well as emotional and behavioural difficulties. Expert teaching and support are essential if children with literacy difficulties are to catch up with their peers. The section on dyslexia indicates how important it is for educators and parents to adopt a range of strategies that not only encompass reading and writing skills but also address the child's self-concept and social confidence.

DYSLEXIA

Developmental dyslexia is the most common of the developmental disorders. There are a number of different definitions. The World Health Organization (2010) defines dyslexia as 'a disorder manifested by difficulty in learning to read, despite conventional instruction, adequate intelligence and sociocultural opportunity. It is dependent upon fundamental cognitive disabilities which are frequently of constitutional origin'. The British Dyslexia Association (BDA) (2014) adopts the following definition:

> Dyslexia is a specific learning difficulty that mainly affects the development of literacy and language related skills. It is likely to be present at birth and to be life-long in its effects. It is characterized by difficulties with phonological processing, rapid naming, working memory, processing speed and the automatic development of skills that may not match up to an individual's other cognitive abilities. It tends to be resistant to conventional teaching methods but its effect can be mitigated by appropriately specific intervention, including the application of information technology and supportive counselling.

Children with dyslexia are likely to have problems with writing, spelling, word recognition, reading comprehension and speaking. Since reading and writing skills are central to education systems, children with dyslexia are at risk of reading failure, a consequent lack of motivation to engage in school work, low self-esteem and even school dropout. Children in the UK are protected under the Special Educational Needs and Disability Act and the Equality Act (2010), so schools are required by law to ensure that children with dyslexia are treated fairly and given appropriate support.

Although the criteria for measuring dyslexia vary, it is thought to affect between 5% and 10% of the population. This means that in the average classroom, there will be at least one child with dyslexia who needs specific specialist teaching. Early research (Badian, 1984) suggested that dyslexia was four times more common in males than females but later studies (e.g. Zabell & Everatt, 2002) indicate a more even balance.

The analysis of the development of a child with dyslexia typically shows a range of differences in their language development. Many, for example, will have had some form of speech therapy in the preschool period. Others may show subtle impairments in their speech, ranging from mislabelling to mispronunciation to word-finding difficulties. The most consistently reported phonological difficulties are limitations of verbal short-term memory and problems with phonological awareness. Children with dyslexia have difficulties with long-term verbal learning, for example in memorizing the days of the week or the months of the year, and with learning a foreign language. They also find it hard to retrieve phonological information from long-term memory (Shaywitz et al., 2008; Snowling, 2002, 2009). Miles (1982, 1993) describes problems in repetition of polysyllabic words, in acquiring familiar sequences, such as the months of the year, in correctly labelling left and right, and learning tables, as well as the characteristic problems in reading and spelling. The problems of dyslexia interest a wide range of researchers, because it seems that whichever area of research you are interested in, people with dyslexia show intriguing deficits in just that area.

Explanations of Dyslexia

There are a number of explanatory models in the study of dyslexia but the 'core phonological deficit' model is the one that is most commonly used today (Bradley & Bryant, 1983; Snowling, 2002); in other words, dyslexia is a language-based learning disability in which individuals have difficulty with phonological coding (Washburn et al., 2014). Children with dyslexia have particular difficulty with the sounds of words, so that when they try to link the phoneme (the sound 'sss') to the grapheme (the letter squiggle 's') they make mistakes. Children who are going to have difficulties of this type can be identified in preschool by their problems in rhyming and alliteration (see Box 12.2). These children appear to have missed the stage of playing with words, which seems to come naturally to most children. Later on, they may have problems in segmenting a word (i.e. breaking it down into sounds).

By the late 1980s, the phonological deficit hypothesis had become the dominant explanation for the difficulties children with dyslexia suffer in reading and spelling, largely based on the work of researchers such as Bradley and Bryant (1985). On the basis of their research in the Jyvaskyla Longitudinal Study of Dyslexia (JLD), Lyytinen et al. (2007) argued that, despite a teaching system that is highly effective for most children within the first 3–4 months of schooling, the acquisition of reading may fail to happen for some children. The reason is that the majority of children have already learned most of the letter-sound correspondences before they go to school. This means that their only remaining task is to assemble these learned letter-sounds in the same order that they are written/heard in order to produce the words that they represent. In the JLD, the researchers found that infants' ability to process aspects of speech predicted their early reading skills. Additionally, the single most accurate predictor of early reading skill was the development of letter knowledge in the years before formal schooling began.

Nicolson and Fawcett (1990, 1996) suggested that the key to the dyslexic deficit seems to be early problems in articulation, which has been found to be significantly slower and more error-prone in dyslexia (Snowling et al., 1986). Snowling (2002, 2009) suggests that children with dyslexia may be able to compensate for their difficulties by relying on contextual cues to support decoding processes.

It may be that in the early stages of speech, children with dyslexia are simply less efficient at repeating words correctly. These articulation difficulties lead to problems in basic phonological skills such as segmentation, which impacts on the development of grapheme–phoneme conversion skills, leading to reading difficulties. Reading and spelling are the most severely impaired skills in dyslexia, because not only does a child with dyslexia have problems in acquiring the basic building blocks, such as the grapheme–phoneme correspondence, they also have problems in becoming expert in these skills. This leads to problems in identifying whole words, or noting the sequences of letters that traditionally occur together (these are known as orthographic regularities). The result is that at each stage, children with dyslexia are investing too many resources in just coping with the basics, which leaves them less spare capacity for acquiring new information.

Nicolson and Fawcett's research has been seen as controversial, particularly in linking dyslexia with problems in motor skills and learning, as has Stein's work on dyslexia and visual symptoms. Interestingly, however, because it is known that dyslexia is hereditary, with around a 50% chance of being dyslexic if you have a parent with dyslexia, family studies have helped to unravel some of these controversies. Studies of families with dyslexia have shown that it is not just the phonological skills that are important in whether or not a child shows problems in learning to read. In a series of important studies, Snowling and her colleagues have shown that, contrary to predictions, many of the children in this at-risk group who have phonological problems do not go on to show dyslexic problems in reading. Reading deficits are also not linked to the severity of their phonological problems, but depend on the number of associated or comorbid problems in visual and language skills. Moreover, Lyytinen's group (Lyytinen et al., 2007) has shown that children with delayed motor milestones showed problems at age 7–8 in word, nonsense word and text reading.

It has to be said, however, that some psychologists challenge the very concept of dyslexia itself on the grounds that the term is unscientific and has a poor evidence base. They argue, controversially, that it may be socially desirable to have a child who is labelled as dyslexic rather than cognitively weak since this reduces the parents' feelings of shame and guilt around having a child who struggles with literacy. Elliott and Grigorenko (2014) propose that, rather than a global diagnosis of dyslexia, it would be far more helpful to focus on specific reading deficits with regard to reading comprehension, reading fluency, spelling and writing. In practice, whether or not you agree with the label *dyslexia*, there is still a great need for specialist intervention to help children with literacy problems. Research from all groups is now converging on the need to consider comorbid problems in order to understand and support children with dyslexia. Early screening tests (Fawcett & Nicolson, 1996), which cover a broad range of skills, and appropriate specialist intervention (Shaywitz et al., 2008) allow many children with dyslexia and those with more generalized difficulties to receive the help they need before they fail.

Helping Children with Dyslexia to Cope

Early identification and appropriate support should allow children with dyslexia to progress through the education system at a normal rate, thus limiting the impact of dyslexia on children's development. It should then be possible for children with dyslexia to express their strengths without being hampered by their weaknesses.

A study focusing on coping strategies of children with dyslexia has shown encouraging results. Firth et al. (2013) implemented a dyslexia coping programme, Success and Dyslexia, in two Australian primary schools. One hundred and two Year 6 children aged 10–11 years, 23 of whom had dyslexia, completed questionnaires pretest, posttest and at 1-year follow-up. A 10-session universal coping programme was given to all Year 6 students, including those who had dyslexia. The programme was based on cognitive behaviour therapy principles and involved awareness of current coping strategies, use of positive thinking, assertiveness, goal setting and problem solving. Students were encouraged to think positively rather than blaming themselves, opting out or ignoring the problem. They were then trained in cognitive restructuring strategies including recognition of links between thought and feeling, avoidance of overgeneralizing difficulties and replacing *negative* self-talk with *empowering* self-talk. Finally, the students were given role-play activities that fostered verbal assertiveness and assertive body language. The whole programme was designed to enhance the children's capacity to take control of their own lives, whether through drawing, drama or discussion; written material was kept to a minimum. The children with dyslexia received an additional coping programme specifically focused on dyslexia. This included talks by successful adults with dyslexia, coaching in how to cope with one's own dyslexia, discussions about dyslexia and opportunities to do projects on dyslexia.

By the end of the programme, students with dyslexia had similar profiles with regard to school connectedness and well-being to students who did not have dyslexia. Furthermore, students with dyslexia achieved a greater reduction in non-productive coping strategies and more internal locus of control. One explanation is that the students with dyslexia had developed a greater sense of control over their situation and less tendency to rely on maladaptive coping responses, such as giving up or worrying. These positive outcomes were enduring as indicated by follow-up tests a year later when the children had made the transition to secondary school.

Studies like these indicate the importance of complementing literacy training with activities that boost self-esteem and foster a sense of control of thoughts and feelings in everyday life.

THEORIES OF LANGUAGE DEVELOPMENT

Our review of sequences in language development has outlined the remarkable achievements that can be made during the preschool years. The child masters the phonology of her language. She has acquired grammatical morphemes (e.g. pluralizing nouns or adding modifiers such as '-ed' to verbs to indicate past tense) and learned how to produce declarative statements (e.g. 'I have a cup'), 'wh-' questions (e.g. 'Where is my cup?' or 'Why is my cup on the floor?') and the negative ('I do not have a cup'). Sentences have become more complex and relative clauses appear ('The cup, which is on the table, is red'). Semantic development has progressed in that children can express quite subtle meanings in their language. Their skill as tellers of stories, jokes and riddles is increasing as they realize the layers of meaning embedded in language. The pragmatics of communication have improved and there is growing awareness that they need to adapt language to particular contexts and adjust speech to suit the requirements of different people.

How does the child achieve this? In the next sections, we review a number of theories of language development. We begin with Chomsky's influential theory, the emphasis of which is on the universal properties of all languages.

The Innate Basis of Language: Chomsky's Views

Some theorists focus on the universal properties of language, pointing out that the sequences of language acquisition are broadly similar in all societies; language occurs in all human cultures, and all languages have certain features in common (Chomsky, 1965; McNeill, 1970).

The essence of Chomsky's argument is that the relationship between speech sounds and meaning is not a simple one of association. Instead, we need to distinguish between the surface structure of the language and its deep structure; that is, between the arrangement of words in the utterance and the logical, grammatical relationships among the elements in that utterance. The connection between the two is specified by the transformational procedures or rules of grammar. Different languages use different transformational rules, but the universal features are to be found in deep structure.

Chomsky proposed that humans have an innate 'language acquisition device' (LAD), without which language could not develop. The LAD is so constructed that it can 'perceive' regularities in the utterances that the child hears. The LAD generates hypotheses about these regularities (for example, that the plural is formed by adding -s to the noun). These are then tested against new utterances and so come to be rejected or accepted as appropriate. The LAD can acquire any language and, faced with the utterances of a particular language, it develops a grammar. Brown and Bellugi (1964) analysed the early speech of two children, Adam and Eve, and noted the overgeneralization of inflections described earlier. For example, the use of -s to form plurals was observed as 'deers', 'sheeps', 'knifes', 'tooths'. The use of -ed to form the past tense was observed as 'comed', 'doed', 'growed', 'hurted', 'swimmed', 'caughted', 'drinked'. The child's innate propensity to use rules, argued Brown and Bellugi, leads to 'errors' from which the linguist can infer the grammar being used. The incorrect grammatical constructions made by Adam and Eve did not come from adult models; it seemed that the children had produced them themselves on the basis of simple grammatical 'hypotheses'. This would be consistent with the LAD theory.

What are these universal characteristics of language? First, they refer to phonological aspects of language, since every language has consonants, vowels and a syllabic structure. They also apply to syntax. All languages have sentences, noun phrases, verb phrases and a grammatical structure underlying them. Chomsky (1965) argued that there are deep structures and surface structures in all languages, as well as rules of transformation that connect the two. The surface structure (that is, the ordering of words in a sentence) can vary but still reflect the same deep structure (that is, the underlying meaning). For example:

The dog bit the man.
The man was bitten by the dog.

These two sentences have the same deep structure in the sense that they are about the same occurrence, but the surface ordering of words is different. The relationship between deep and surface structures is achieved through the rules of transformation. These rules make the connection between sound and meaning in a language. Table 12.3 shows sentences that, by contrast, show differences in deep structure but a similar surface structure.

We understand that, although the three sentences in Table 12.3 have the same surface structures, different relationships among the words are implied and thus different meanings. Finally, some sentences can have two meanings, for example, 'The peasants are revolting'. It is the rules of transformation that enable us to understand whether the peasants 'are in revolt' or 'revolt us'. As McNeill (1970) writes: 'Every sentence, however simple, has some kind of underlying structure related to some kind of surface structure by means of certain transformations'.

Chomsky stresses the intuitive knowledge that we all have of the structure of language, even though we may not be able to describe the structures using the language of linguistics experts. Even young children have a tacit knowledge. By 5 years, most children, whatever their background or culture, have a good grasp of the basic rules of their language. So who teaches them? Not the parents—most are not professional linguists. Chomsky proposes that it must be because of innate knowledge. This theory, then, encompasses not just specific languages, but the general form of human language, and proposes that 'the theory of grammar and its universal constraints describes the internal structure of LAD, and, thus, of children' (McNeill, 1970, p. 151). The ability to infer such transformational rules from surface structure utterances was, Chomsky and McNeill both thought, embodied in the LAD.

Chomsky's theory of transformational, generative grammar provided the impetus for a great deal of research into child language. He called it 'generative grammar' because the application of rules generates actual sentences. His own work investigated grammars in which deep structure or 'meaning' had transformational rules applied to it in order to change it to a surface or spoken utterance. Chomsky argued that the child was involved in the creative process of generating language, as utterances like 'Two sheeps' or 'All done milk' seemed to show.

Brown and Fraser (1963), studying telegraphic speech in children, concluded that the utterances could all be classified as grammatical sentences from which certain words had been omitted. For example, 'Mummy hair' only omitted the possessive inflection ('Mummy's hair'); 'chair broken' was an acceptable sentence if 'is' was added. Similarly, McNeill (1966)

Table 12.3 Examples of sentences with similar surface structure but a different deep structure.

Sentence	Paraphrase	Non-paraphrase
They are buying glasses.	–	–
They are drinking glasses.	They are glasses to use for drinking.	They are glasses that drink.
They are drinking companions.	They are companions that drink.	They are companions to use for drinking.

Source: McNeill, D. (1970). *The Acquisition of Language*. New York: Harper & Row. Reproduced by permission of Professor David McNeill.

noted other grammatical relationships in the telegraphic speech of young children. Ordering was important in the structure of children's speech even though it was not in direct imitation of the order of adult language. The child might say 'Me want that coat', but phrases like 'Want that coat me' did not appear.

Linguistic research has also investigated transformational rules in child language. We will look at one kind of transformation—the question. Table 12.4 gives examples of a child using telegraphic speech and shows the gradual development of the correct form of question. This is one type of transformation; there are many others (e.g. use of the past tense, the negative, the use of plurals) that also seem to demonstrate that the child, from an early age, acts as though she expects language to be governed by a set of rules.

The analysis of children's utterances in terms of deep structure, surface structure and the transformational rules that relate the two (Brown, 1973; McNeill, 1970; Slobin, 1973) greatly enriched our understanding of early language development. Children's language does seem to be governed by rules and does seem to develop in a systematic way. Children do seem to progress through similar stages in the acquisition of language. However, many contemporary psychologists question the notion of an inborn LAD. As we will see in the following sections, many psycholinguists (for example, Tomasello & Brooks, 1999) challenge the whole concept of underlying structure.

Chomsky himself revised his views on transformational grammar. In a later version of his theory (Chomsky, 1986) he proposed the principles and parameters theory (PPT), in which he adds to his concept of deep and surface structures the idea of processes through which the

Table 12.4   Stages in the development of question forms.

Ages for Adam	Questions	Commentary
28 months	Sit chair? Ball go? What that? Where mummy go? What mummy doing?	Expressed by intonation only. The child has developed a routine form of the question.
38 months	Will you help me? Does the kitty stand up? What I did yesterday? Why the Christmas tree going? How he can be a doctor?	The child has developed the use of *auxiliary verbs*. For questions expecting the answer yes or no, there is inversion of the verb, but not for 'what' and 'why' questions.
42 months	Are you thirsty? Why can't we find it? I have two turn, huh? We're playing, huh? That's funny, isn't it? Why can't they put on their swimming suits?	Inversion of the verb in 'why' questions. Development of 'tag' questions (e.g. tags on 'huh?' at the end of a sentence). Later, inversion of auxiliary verbs appears too.

Source: Cazden, C. B., *Child Language and Education*. Holt, Rinehart & Winston Inc, New York, copyright © 1972 Dr Courtney B. Cazden.

child must pass in order to achieve grammatical utterances. He still holds to the assumption that humans have an innate capacity for language, but in the recent formulation of his theory puts more emphasis on the psychological processes of learning different kinds of grammatical structure. As with the earlier version, it is difficult to test PPT theory formally.

Pinker and the Evidence from Pidgin and Creoles

Pinker (1994), in *The language instinct*, provides evidence for the innate basis of language. He argues (p. 32) that 'complex language is universal because *children actually reinvent it*, generation after generation—not because they are taught, not because they are generally smart, not because it is useful to them, but because they just can't help it'. As one source of evidence for this view, he investigated *pidgin* languages, for example the language developed by labourers who were imported into the sugar plantations in Hawaii around the turn of the 20th century (Bickerton, 1990). These people came from China, Japan, Korea, Portugal, the Philippines and Puerto Rico, and developed a pidgin language in order to communicate with one another. Typically, this pidgin did not have the usual grammatical structures; it had 'no consistent word order, no prefixes or suffixes, no tense or other temporal and logical markers, no structure more complex than a simple clause, and no consistent way to indicate who did what to whom' (Pinker, 1994, p. 34). Pinker quotes examples from two speakers (p. 33).

Speaker 1: Me cape buy, me check make.
Speaker 2: Good dis one. Kaukau any-kin' dis one. Pilipine islan' no good. No mo money.

The meaning intended by these pidgin speakers is as follows.

Speaker 1: He bought my coffee; he made me out a check.
Speaker 2: It's better here than in the Philippines; here you can get all kinds of food, but over there there isn't any money to buy food with.

Pinker points out that, in each case, the meaning has to be filled in by the listener since pidgin does not have the grammatical resources to convey complex messages. But for the children who grew up in Hawaii, it was a totally different matter. Pinker indicates how pidgin languages were transformed—by children learning and changing them—into full languages. Linguists call these languages *creoles*, that is, stable languages that originated from a combination of other languages. Their language (which is now called Hawaiian Creole) became grammatical, since it contained standardized word orders, markers for present, future and past tenses, and subordinate clauses, despite the fact that they had been exposed only to the pidgin of their parents. Here are some examples (Pinker, 1994, p. 34), each followed by a 'translation'.

Speaker 3: One time when we go home inna night dis ting stay fly up.
Speaker 4: One day had pleny of dis mountain fish come down.

The meaning of Speaker 3's sentence is: 'Once when we went home at night this thing was flying about'. Note that the event is contextualized by the use of 'one time'; there is a subordinate clause, 'when we go home' and the verb tense is indicated through the use of 'stay fly up'.

The meaning of Speaker 4's sentence is: 'One day there were a lot of these fish from the mountains that came down (the river)'. Note the contextualization ('One day') and the use of the past tense ('had').

Bickerton proposes that sentences like these are not haphazard, but indicate a consistent use of the rules of Hawaiian Creole grammar. He concluded that creole languages that have been formed from unrelated language mixtures have strong similarities that support the concept of a basic common grammar.

Similar insights come from research into sign language (Kegl et al., 1999; Morford & Kegl, 2000; Senghas & Coppola, 2001). In Nicaragua, deaf children were not introduced to any form of sign language other than the basic signs that their families had separately devised to communicate with one another. After 1979, special schools for the deaf were founded in which the teachers tried to teach the children to lip-read, with small success. At the same time, and spontaneously, the children were devising their own sign language based on the signs that they had each individually developed within the family—a form of pidgin that linguists have named Lenguaje de Signos Nicaraguense (LSN). (However, unlike pidgin speakers who had a native language, these deaf children could *only* rely on visual and motor cues to convey meaning.) Over time, this developed into a creole created by the younger children who had been exposed to the pidgin of the older children in the school. In other words, the children had formed a community in which their gestural communication system developed into a full-blown language. This is now known as Idioma de Signos Nicaraguense (ISN) and has become a standardized language with grammatical devices absent in LSN.

The new language is so sophisticated that a dictionary of its signs has been published. The children use ISN to tell one another stories, make jokes and plays on words, and share experiences in their linguistic community. The children who were introduced to LSN before the age of 6 years showed the strongest tendency to produce grammatical innovation, suggesting that they were within the optimal period for language development. These researchers suggest that this is clear evidence of the claim that language has universal rules. Kegl and colleagues point out that the older students, who had entered school in their teens, failed to achieve the level of fluency that was obtained by the younger children, who had gained exposure to one another and had signed to one another at an earlier age. Reflecting on this research, Clay et al. (2014) conclude that young children spontaneously bring properties of language into their gestural communication systems. (This supports the idea of a sensitive period in language development; see also the case study of Genie in Chapter 18.)

Language and Cognition: A Piagetian Perspective

Chomsky and his colleagues suggested that the child has an innate knowledge of the basic rules and constraints of language, and of her community. But some psychologists have suggested that the rule-bound nature of children's speech arises not so much from an innate LAD as from the child's prelinguistic knowledge, since the child, it is argued, already has some ability to categorize her world even before she can communicate with others in language.

From this perspective, the investigator focuses on the *precursors* of early language, for example, gestures, facial expression, actions. This approach moves the emphasis away from grammatical competence to the study of understanding and communication. As we will see in Chapter 13, Piaget claims that during the first 2 years of life, the child's intellectual skills do not rely on symbols, such as words and images, but are rooted in sensorimotor experiences, such as seeing, hearing and touching. Symbolic actions do not appear until the end of the sensorimotor period. Although interactionists would accept that children develop a system of rules, they would not accept that the rules grow out of an innate LAD, but rather that they come from a much wider cognitive system. Children talk alike because they share many similar experiences and their language is facilitated by the sensorimotor schemas of early infancy. This hypothesis, called the 'cognition hypothesis' (Cromer, 1974), states that:

1. we understand and use particular linguistic structures only when our cognitive abilities enable us to do so (for example, the child can gesture that he wants an apple before he uses the holophrase 'Apple')
2. even once our cognitive abilities allow us to grasp an idea, we may say it in a less complex way because we have not yet acquired the grammatical rule for expressing it freely. Thus the child may not be able to say 'Have you looked?' but he can express the same meaning in the less complex sentence 'Did you look yet?'.

What Piagetians suggested was that children form schemas to explain events in their lives and only then talk about them. Language development reflects the stages of cognitive development through which the child is progressing. This is a reciprocal relationship, in which the child plays an active part. However, the child is not applying an innate LAD to the talk that he hears. Instead, his understanding arises out of his existing knowledge of the world.

Many observations support this interactionist approach. In Chapter 13, we examine Piaget's work on the object concept, which shows that by the end of the first year the child understands that objects exist independently of herself, whether in her sight or not. In Piaget's view, the child needs to have this sense of object permanence before she can begin to understand that words can represent things. Observations of first words show that children usually focus on familiar actions or objects. In this way, they are using words to express aspects of their environment that they already understand non-verbally, and there seem to be regularities in the ways in which children combine their early one- and two-word utterances with gestures or with knowledge of the context in which the word occurs.

This cognitive approach to children's language development was very influential in the 1970s, until some psychologists began to suggest that it gave a rather narrow view of the child. It ignored, for example, the child's social skills and the effect of the social environment on a child's capacity to learn. It is this shift of emphasis towards the child as communicator in a social world that we will consider next.

Cognitive-Functional Linguistics

 Stop and Think

What is the function of language? How important is it to examine the child's growing competence in a socially meaningful context?

Recent developments in linguistics, broadly categorized as cognitive-functional linguistics, also challenge Chomskian theory. They suggest that a child's competence in language consists of her mastery of its various linguistic symbols and constructions, each of which has one or more linguistic forms (signifier) each with a communicative function (signified). Recent empirical findings appear to contradict the Chomskian position. For example, Chomskian theory would interpret such phrases as 'allgone sticky' as evidence that the child had an abstract category of the nominal (naming word or 'noun', 'sticky' being defined as a noun). Instead, the cognitive-functional interpretation would be that young children's capacity to generate novel utterances is still quite limited. As we will see, Tomasello's verb island hypothesis suggests that children's early language is structured around individual verbs—in other words, it is specific to each particular verb rather than an abstract construct. Tomasello proposed that children of around 2 years develop their repertoire of verbs to apply to specific scenes in their everyday life, and only after they have heard them in specific adult discourse.

Influenced by cognitive-functional linguistics, Tomasello argues that children acquire language gradually, beginning with concrete linguistic structures based on words and morphemes, and building up to more abstract structures based on linguistic schemes and constructions. As we have seen, by the time children begin to produce holophrases, they have already become quite skilled at communicating through gestures and vocalizations. Children's early one-word utterances have both semantic and pragmatic dimensions (e.g. 'Da!' meaning 'That is a dog!' and 'Milk!' meaning 'Give me that cup of milk because I am thirsty!') but at this stage they are only able to communicate in a condensed, 'telegraphic' way without detailing the scene or marking the various participant roles of the other people involved in the conversation. By 18 months, children begin to combine words, initially to talk in more detail about the same kinds of scenes as they did through their holophrases. On the basis of extensive studies (both naturalistic and experimental), Tomasello (2000) concludes that before the age of 3 years children do not possess the abstract structures that would enable them to generate verb combinations that they have not actually heard.

Tomasello's model is grounded in children's cognitive understanding of the various 'scenes' that make up their lives, for example, pushing and pulling, eating, seeing objects move up and down, people going in and out of rooms, objects being broken and mended. In his view, children move through specific steps in their language development: *holophrases, word combinations, verb island combinations* and *adult-like constructions*. At each step the child produces creative new utterances, suggesting, Tomasello argues, that they have constructed some kind of schema or category based on the specific utterances that they have heard from adult speakers (Tomasello & Olguin, 1993). But children are creative with their language in different ways at different developmental points. When given novel object labels ('Look! A wug!'), 18-month-old children were able to use the new label in combination with words they already knew (for example, 'Wug gone!' or 'More wug'). But at the same age, they had difficulty in being creative in their use of verbs. Tomasello (2000) argues that children's creativity with language has been overestimated. Instead, he claims, the child produces novel utterances in a very limited way. For example, if the child hears 'The window broke' and no other uses of this verb, she is not able to produce 'He broke it' or 'It got broken'.

Tomasello et al. (1997) tested children's capacity to make word combinations with new nouns and verbs. The researchers did this by teaching the children novel words, e.g. 'gop' and 'tam', that they could never have encountered before. Ten children, aged between 18 and 23 months, were taught four new words—two nouns and two verbs—over many sessions. All four words were modelled by the experimenters without providing any contextual clues as to what these novel words meant. For example, the researcher would simply say, 'That's a gop' in the noun condition and 'It is gopping' in the verb condition. The researchers then gave the children frequent opportunities to reproduce the words and to create morphological endings, such as plurals for nouns and past tense endings for verbs. What they found was that the children combined the novel nouns with already known words 10 times more often than they did with the novel verbs. For example, several children produced plurals ('some gops') but none formed a past tense with the verb ('it gopped').

Tomasello and colleagues concluded that children of this age have some form of category of noun or noun phrase; they called it a *pivot grammar* on which the children can 'hang' new nouns as they are learned. They appeared to have learned that a noun could be a subject ('the wug is kissing') and an object ('kissing the wug'). They had a construct of the order patterns characteristic of subject (the wug as kisser) going before object (the wug as one being kissed). They could also form plurals ('wugs'). But they could not do the same on the basis of the category of verb. In other words, Tomasello concluded, children between 18 and 24 months do not have a general schema of subject-verb-object.

For the child, after the age of around 24 months, the pattern changes. Tomasello developed the *verb island hypothesis* to describe early sentences produced by his own daughter in the second year of her life: 'Each verb seemed like an island of organization in an otherwise unorganized language system' (Tomasello & Brooks, 1999, p. 170). His daughter did not appear to know how to describe events in a general way, but rather appeared to develop her language in a 'verb-specific' way. Some verbs were only used in one type of simple sentence frame (e.g. 'Cut paper') whereas others were used in more complex frames of several types (e.g. 'Draw teddy', 'Draw teddy on table', 'Draw picture for Mummy' or 'Me draw on floor').

Tomasello concluded that she did not have a general category of verb as instrument, but rather something that was more verb specific, for example 'thing to draw with' or 'thing to cut with'. His explanation is that the child is exposed to rich discourse involving multiple participants and a range of pragmatic functions for some activities (in his daughter's case, for the verb 'draw') while in others the child is not exposed to complex talk involving multiple participants and functions (in his daughter's case with regard to the verb 'cut'). Clearly, these experiences would vary from child to child. As a result, each verb is developed on a verb-by-verb basis to apply to specific scenes in the child's everyday life. That is, the child of around 2 years produces new verbs only after she has heard them in specific adult discourse—for example 'a thing to draw with' or 'a person to kiss'.

> Early in their linguistic development, young children are not primarily creating a lexical category of verb for purposes of syntax, but rather they are creating different types of schemas or constructions, with particular verbs as their central organizing elements.
> *(Tomasello et al., 1997, pp. 385–386)*

As Tomasello and colleagues have shown, once children have acquired an inventory of verb islands, they use them in increasingly differentiated ways. During the preschool years, they move beyond verb island construction and show their ability to make more abstract linguistic constructions. They use transitives ('Imtiaz broke the vase'), locatives ('Jason picked it up' or 'Put that down!'), datives ('Give it to me' or 'I sent it to Flora') and passives ('He was hurt').

Tomasello proposes that syntax develops *out of* the child's experience of learning specific verbs and nouns before they are able to partition events in a general way. In his view, children

Table 12.5 Tomasello's construction grammar: children's early syntactic development and the characteristics in which they are defined.

	Lexical partitioning of scenes	Syntactic marking of participant roles	Categorization of specific scenes
Holophrases (12 months)			
Word combinations (18 months)	+	+	
Verb island construction (24 months)	+	+	
Adult-like constructions (36+ months)	+	+	+

Source: Adapted from Barrett, M. D. (ed.) 1999: *The Development of Language*, London: Psychology Press with permission.

do not generalize across scenes to make syntactically similar participant roles in similar ways without first having heard them in adult discourse. From this perspective, it is adult discourse that plays a critical role in the child's production of syntax.

The cognitive-functional approach can explain a whole range of linguistic abilities, from core competencies (e.g. using regular verbs) to idiosyncratic phrases, such as ritualized greetings (e.g. 'Hiya, dude!'), proverbs (e.g. 'It's an ill wind . . .'), to metaphors and similes (e.g. 'We are poised on the edge of an abyss . . .'). Such competence represents general cognitive abilities that are expressed in many domains, not only in language. From this linguistics perspective, there is no need for the concept of a universal grammar. Furthermore, it does not make sense to begin with formal grammars as used by adults and then use them uncritically with children.

Syntactic development depends on the child's ability to divide scenes into events, states and people and then to work out the common features in the construction of language, using the same cognitive processes that they use to interpret other aspects of their worlds. Table 12.5 summarizes Tomasello's types of early syntactic development and their characteristics from holophrases through to adult-like speech. According to Tomasello (2000), there is no empirical evidence in support of the Chomskian position; language development need not be characterized in terms of a universal grammar. Rather, the child's language develops through social interaction with key people in their culture (Rogoff, 2003) and the gradual building up of grammatical structures. Also, there are new explanatory models, such as functional and cognitive linguistics, which offer sophisticated accounts of children's learning processes.

Adult–Child Speech

Research into adult–child (A–C) speech (sometimes called infant-directed speech, or IDS) also challenges the Chomskian position. In the 1960s, it was believed that A–C speech was similar to that between adults. Chomsky (1965) took this position, indicating that language acquisition was very difficult—too difficult for the young child to do unless some innate capacity was present. But empirical research since that time has indicated that A–C speech is distinctively different from adult–adult (A–A) speech.

As we have seen, parents typically speak to babies with exaggerated intonation and use distinctively musical rhythms and tones (Mithen, 2005). Adults also adjust their speech to the cognitive ability of the child, whether it is first or later born, and whether siblings are present. Messer (1994) argues that adults do in fact modify their speech when talking to young children, as is evidenced in the work of Snow (1977) and Snow et al. (1996). The most commonly used measure of grammatical complexity has been the mean length of utterance (MLU). Messer shows that when you compare A–C speech with A–A speech, there are very clear differences. A–C speech has a higher pitch, a greater range of pitch and is simpler in meaning. The mean length of utterance is shorter; A–C speech is also simpler, for example, through number of verbs or conjunctions per utterance. It is also more likely to be in the present tense. It is easier to process; it is slower; it has more repetitions and an exaggerated form. It is more likely to concern events that are happening in the here and now, contains more concrete nouns, uses proper names rather than pronouns. It will also use special words like 'tummy', 'poo', 'dummy', 'doggy'.

Babies indicate soon after birth that they prefer A–C speech to the adult–adult speech they hear (see also Chapters 3 and 11). Why is this? Before infants are able to speak or even to respond to words, they seem to be able to respond to the sound patterns—or 'prosodic' characteristics—of speech. This refers to the general pattern of sound, which is not related to individual words. Stern et al. (1983) identified a number of distinctive prosodic patterns in speech to infants. For example, when infants were inattentive, parents would typically raise the pitch of their voice, so a form of bell-shaped pitch contours—a pattern of rising and falling pitch—took place as a means of capturing and then maintaining the infant's attention.

Papousek et al. (1987) found that A–C speech has the following kinds of melodic units: level, rising, falling, U-shaped, bell-shaped or complex sinusoidal. These were found across three languages—English, Mandarin and German. They are used in consistent ways in a culture and, in addition, are attuned to the perceptual preferences and abilities of infants (see Chapter 11). Papousek et al. (1991) found that Chinese mothers use similar melodic contours, suggesting that there are universal patterns across languages and cultures which parents use to communicate with their infants. They are also present in non-Western cultures, for example the Kaluli of New Guinea (Schieffelin & Ochs, 1983).

As Saxton (2010) argues, child-directed speech is not only confined to well-educated, middle-class parents but appears in all cultures in some form or another. Current research emphasises the learning mechanisms and knowledge that the child brings to the task of language acquisition and the focus now is more on the processes of interaction between child and adult—in other words, the social and emotional contexts within which the child's language develops. In Saxton's words, the only way to engage a young child in conversation is to follow their lead. "Try talking to a two-year-old about your council's recycling policy and see how far you get. Now try talking about the book that the child is holding in their hands. Note the difference?" (Saxton, 2010, p. 105). In this view, child-directed speech evolves naturally from everyday communication with the child. By following the child's lead, the adult can most easily maintain a conversation and mirror back what the child has said with appropriate modifications where, for example, the child's grammatical forms are 'incorrect'. This is communication rather than teaching.

Stop and Think

What is it about the nature of adult–child talk that makes it meaningful to infants?

It would appear that the prosodic contours enable infants to understand the intent of speech before they can identify the meaning of individual words. In addition, they must identify individual words in the speech that they hear before they can produce words themselves. But how do they reach the point where, like adults, they can distinguish individual words in the speech that they hear? Gleitman (1990) suggested that infants are predisposed to attend to smaller segments of speech (such as stressed syllables) and that this is how they eventually identify words. First of all, they identify whole utterances by silences before and after them, the melody of the utterance and its rhythm. At the same time as the infants begin to segment or split an utterance into smaller units, the parents also stress words in their speech in ways that help the infants to locate them in speech—for example, by stressing the ones which are especially important or by speaking loudly at particular points in the 'conversation'. Gleitman calls this process 'syntactic bootstrapping', as we saw earlier in this chapter.

Some support for this idea came from a study by Messer (1981) of the amplitude (or emphasis) of words in mothers' speech to 14-month-old infants. He found that labels for objects were more likely than any other word class to be the loudest in an utterance. This emphasis, on the part of the mothers, clearly helps infants to identify the words for everyday objects in the child's world. These labels also occurred more frequently in the last position in an utterance and therefore were more likely to be remembered.

Such findings were confirmed by Fernald and Mazzie (1991). They found that mothers consistently gave new words prominence when reading a story to an infant of 14 months. Again these new words were more likely to be positioned at the end of the utterance and be spoken with more emphasis. This suggests that there are a number of strategies that infants use to identify certain words, but also that the mother provides useful cues that help the infant to identify important words.

A Continuing Debate

Research into children's developing language (see Box 12.1) indicates that adults' and peers' feedback plays an important role in children's language learning, but that the principles of reinforcement and imitation are not in themselves sufficient to explain how the process occurs. The value and nature of the role of adult discourse in child language development remain controversial. Some researchers argue that the sentences which parents use to children are 'finely tuned' to the child's needs as a learner (e.g. Fernyhough, 2008; Furrow et al., 1979); others disagree (e.g. Gleitman, 1990). A number of questions remain unanswered. How short should the parent's MLU ideally be, for example? No one has suggested that parents should speak in one-word utterances! One theory might be that optimal MLU should be longer, but only a bit longer, than child MLU, through a process of scaffolding (as discussed in Chapters 2 and 16).

Researchers have also explored the ways in which social interaction between adults and children reflect cultural attitudes and beliefs about children. Schieffelin (1990) reports on the Kaluli of Papua New Guinea, who develop language despite the fact that mothers and babies do not appear to engage in mutual eye contact, as is customary in Western society. In this society, conversation is given a high status. However, the Kaluli do not talk at any length about their feelings. Kaluli mothers usually put babies in such a position as to be seen by others and to see others, but they do not engage in mutual gaze. Although Kaluli mothers are very attentive to their infants, they do not seem to view them as conversational partners, so they are rarely addressed except to call them by name or in the use of expressive vocalizations. When the babies are 6–12 months old, adults begin to speak to them using short utterances. Teaching is done by giving the child a model utterance and then instructing the child to repeat it. When an adult talks to an infant, the mothers reply on the part of their infants in a high-pitched, child-like voice and these exchanges seem to be designed to foster certain social relationships. Clearly, some aspects of child-directed speech are present in Kaluli communities, and the children still become fluent speakers of their own language.

Work with blind children, who also learn to speak without mutual eye-gaze and peek-a-boo games, indicates that parents are able to engage in their child's joint attention in non-visual ways. Babies who are blind obviously do not 'look', but they learn how to direct their parents' attention and may even use the word 'look'. Transcripts of Kaluli children and parents talking indicate that they also develop mutual points of focus. It is highly likely that interactions between adults and babies adapt their methods of communication in different ways depending on a range of circumstances rather than according to one particular biologically designed choreography (Schieffelin & Ochs, 1983, p. 127). Ethnographic studies by linguistic anthropologists have shown a range of ideologies about language, which may well differ from middle-class, Western views.

As we have seen, explanations, as opposed to description, of the course of language development vary in emphasis. Some theorists have suggested that there is a biological basis for language acquisition, with innate mechanisms underlying it. Piagetians emphasize the importance of cognitive development. Still others take the interactionist approach and argue that the development of linguistic competence needs to be studied within its social context. The cognitive-functional approach focuses more on linguistic competencies in the context of the general study of cognitive development across a range of domains, not only in language.

We have considered major approaches to language development in this chapter and described a range of empirical studies of children's language as it evolves. To date, there is no one theory that successfully encompasses all aspects of language development, and the debate continues.

CHAPTER SUMMARY

- Children typically become competent across four main areas: phonology, semantics, syntax and pragmatics.
- Children benefit if they come to school with a repertoire of prereading and prewriting skills, including the concept of story and some knowledge of rhyming and alliteration.
- Themes in the study of child language development focused initially on the wider debate in developmental psychology between nativists and developmentalists (see Chapter 2).
- More recent positions, influenced by cognitive-functional linguistics and by sociocultural theories, place much more emphasis on the social context in which children grow, and on the child's construction of language through discourse with others (see also Chapter 16).
- The child also seems to be equipped with cognitive resources to enable her to learn quickly from those around her, as indicated by the phenomena of gaze following, pointing, social referencing and the myriad meaningful interactions that emerge before speech.
- Further debate concentrates on whether the child's language is domain general (that is, reflects the child's changing representations of concepts, categories, events and scripts across cognitive domains) or domain specific (that is, the child's linguistic processes are specialized and arise out of domain-specific information processing systems).
- As the painstaking analysis of real-life conversations between parents and their children and of children's usage of grammar has shown, children do not directly imitate adult language and adults do not normally use reinforcement techniques to teach their children to speak. The presence of involved adults and other children who use a form of discourse closely adapted to the child's level, and who recast sentences in a form to which the child has access, seems to provide an environment in which language will flourish.
- To date, however, there is still no agreement among theorists about the precise ways in which the child's phonological, syntactic, semantic and pragmatic language development takes place.

DISCUSSION POINTS

1. What is the developmental importance of prelinguistic communication between adult and baby?
2. Discuss how research findings on A–C speech can help parents to talk more effectively with their young children.
3. How important is it to take semantic (or meaning) aspects into account when examining the language of young children?
4. Does the study of pidgin languages and creoles help us to understand the process of speaking grammatically?
5. How convincing is Tomasello's verb island hypothesis?

FURTHER READING

- Fernyhough, C. (2008). *The baby in the mirror*. London: Granta, uses scientific observation to provide a detailed and imaginative account of his daughter's voyage of discovery during her first 3 years.
- Hoff, E. & Shatz, M. (2007). *Blackwell handbook of language development*. Oxford: Blackwell, gives a comprehensive overview of the major issues in current thinking about language development. Barrett, M. (Ed.) (1999). *The development of language*. London: Psychology Press, gives a thoughtful and wide-ranging overview of the main strands in language development. Messer, D. (1994). *The development of communication from social interaction to language*. Chichester: Wiley, describes the development of communication and language from birth to 3 years. He discusses a number of research traditions in the field, notably those that emphasize language as an innate process and those that stress language as the outcome of learning. A review of recent developments in research into dyslexia can be found in Nicolson, R.I. & Fawcett, A.J. (2008). *Dyslexia, learning and the brain*. Massachusetts: MIT Press.
- A clear introduction to Chomsky's ideas is provided by Lyons, J. (1985). *Chomsky*. London: Fontana. See also the website: www.chomsky.info
- For a readable account of child language acquisition, see Saxton, M. (2010). *Child language: Acquisition and development*. London: Sage. If you are interested in the links between music and language development, do read Mithen, S. (2005). *The singing Neanderthals*. London: Phoenix.
- Pinker, S. (1994). *The language instinct*. London: Penguin, argues persuasively that language has a biological, modular basis. The book is scholarly but also immensely readable and draws on research from a wide range of sources.
- For a challenging review of research and practice in dyslexia, see Elliott, J.G. & Grigorenko, E.L. (2014). *The dyslexia debate*. New York: Cambridge University Press.

CHAPTER
13

Cognition: Piaget's Theory

CHAPTER OUTLINE

- Underlying Assumptions: Structure and Organization
- The Stages of Cognitive Development
- The Sensorimotor Stage
- Reinterpretations of Piaget: The Sensorimotor Stage
- The Preoperational Stage
- Reinterpretations of Piaget: The Preoperational Stage
- The Concrete Operational Stage
- Reinterpretations of Piaget: The Concrete Operational Stage
- The Formal Operational Stage
- Reinterpretations of Piaget: The Formal Operational Stage
- Piaget's Theory: An Overview
- Educational Implications

In this chapter we outline Piaget's theory of cognitive development. Piaget proposed that children, from birth, progress through a number of identifiable stages, and that within those stages particular aspects of development can be observed. For this reason, Piaget's description of child development is usually referred to as a stage theory. Using examples taken from Piaget's own writing, we describe the main features of each of these stages. For each stage, we have also included a section that refers to work by more recent researchers. Although the *findings* from Piaget's original studies are rarely disputed, the *interpretation* of those findings has been a matter of debate. Many researchers believe that Piaget thought that children had more limited cognitive abilities than is the case. For this reason, many of the more recent studies have been designed to demonstrate that children have more sophisticated ways of thinking and reasoning (in particular stages) than Piaget supposed. Nonetheless, Piaget's theory was, for many years, the dominant framework for thinking about children's cognitive development. As we will explain, Piaget's pioneering empirical work provided many new insights into children's development and set the agenda for much of the research that followed. For the latter reason, it is important to be aware of Piaget's research and theory, and of the terminology that he introduced for describing the way that children's thinking changes as they develop.

Jean Piaget (1896–1980) was born in Neuchâtel, Switzerland. At an early age, he showed a keen interest in observing animals in their natural environment. At the age of 10 he published his first article, a description of an albino sparrow that he had observed in the park, and before he was 18 years old journals had accepted several of his papers about molluscs. During his adolescent years he developed an interest in philosophy, in particular the branch of philosophy concerned with knowledge—'epistemology'. His undergraduate studies, however, were in the field of biology and his doctoral dissertation was on molluscs.

Piaget then worked for a period at Bleuler's psychiatric clinic in Zurich, where he became interested in psychoanalysis. As a result, he went to the Sorbonne University in Paris in 1919 to study clinical psychology. There he pursued his interest in philosophy. While in Paris, he worked at the Binet Laboratory with Theodore Simon on the standardization of intelligence tests (see Chapter 17). Piaget's role was to examine children's correct responses to test items, but he became much more interested in the mistakes the children made, and came to believe that a study of children's errors could provide an insight into their cognitive processes.

Piaget saw that, through the discipline of psychology, he had an opportunity to forge links between epistemology and biology. By integrating the disciplines of psychology, biology and epistemology, Piaget aimed to develop a scientific approach to the understanding of knowledge—the nature of knowledge and the ways in which an individual acquires knowledge. Although the quantitative methods of the French intelligence testers did not appeal to Piaget, he was strongly influenced by the developmental work of Binet. Binet was a French psychologist who had pioneered studies of children's thinking, and his method of observing children in their natural settings was one that Piaget followed himself when he left the Binet Laboratory.

Piaget integrated his experiences of psychiatric work in Bleuler's clinic with the questioning and observational strategies that he had learned from Binet. Out of this fusion emerged the 'clinical interview'—an open-ended, conversational technique for eliciting children's thinking processes. His interest was in the child's own judgements and explanations. He was not testing a particular hypothesis, but rather looking for an explanation of how the child comes to understand his or her world. The method is not easy, and Piaget's researchers were trained for a year before they actually collected data. They learned the art of asking the right questions and testing the truth of what the children said.

Piaget's life was devoted to the search for the mechanisms of biological adaptation on the one hand, and the analysis of logical thought on the other (Boden, 1979; Miller, 2011). He wrote more than 50 books and hundreds of articles, revising many of his early ideas in later life. In essence, Piaget's theory is concerned with the human need to discover and to acquire deeper knowledge and understanding. Piaget's prolific output of ideas suggests that he was constantly constructing and reconstructing his theoretical system, but this, as we shall see, was quite consistent with his philosophy of knowledge.

In this chapter we will describe the model of cognitive structure developed by Piaget. We will also take notice of modifications and reinterpretations that subsequent researchers have made to Piaget's ideas. Although many aspects of Piaget's theory are now questioned, no one denies the valuable contribution he made to our understanding of the thinking processes of both children and adults.

Piaget argued that to understand how children think, we have to look at the qualitative development of their ability to solve problems. Let us look at two examples of children's thinking. These examples show how children develop more sophisticated ways to solve problems.

The first example is taken from one of Piaget's dialogues with a 7-year-old.

Adult:	Does the moon move or not?
Child:	When we go, it goes.
Adult:	What makes it move?
Child:	We do.
Adult:	How?
Child:	When we walk. It goes by itself.

(Piaget, 1929, pp. 146–147)

From this, and other similar observations, Piaget described a period during childhood that was characterized by egocentrism. Because the moon appears to move with the child, the child concludes that it does indeed do so. But later, with the growth of logic, the child makes a shift from their own egocentric perspective and learns to distinguish what they see from what they know. Gruber and Vonèche (1977) give a good example of how an older child used logic to consider the movement of the moon. This child sent his little brother to walk down the garden while he himself stood still. The younger child reported that the moon moved with him, but the older boy could disprove this from his own observation that the moon did not move with his brother.

The second example is adapted from Piaget's research into children's understanding of quantity. Suppose John, aged 4 years, and Mary, aged 7 years, are given a problem. Two glasses, A and B, are of equal capacity but glass A is short and wide and glass B is tall and

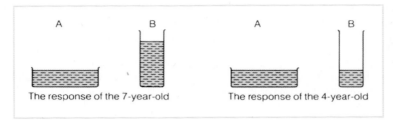

Figure 13.1   Estimating a quantity of liquid.

narrow (see Figure 13.1). Glass A is filled to a certain height and the children are each asked, separately, to pour liquid into glass B so that it contains the same amount as glass A. In spite of the striking difference in the proportions of the two containers, John cannot grasp that the smaller diameter of glass B requires a higher level of liquid. To Mary, John's response is incredibly silly: of course you have to add more to glass B. From Piaget's perspective both responses are revealing. John cannot 'see' that the liquid in A and the liquid in B are not equal, since he is using a qualitatively different kind of reasoning, not yet having the mental operations that will enable him to solve the problem. Mary finds it difficult to understand why John cannot see his mistake. We will discuss this aspect of children's problem solving in more detail later.

Piaget proposed that the essence of knowledge is activity. This may refer to the infant directly manipulating objects and so learning about their properties. It may refer to a child pouring liquid from one glass to another to find out which has more in it. Or it may refer to the adolescent forming hypotheses to solve a scientific problem. In all these examples, the child is learning through action, whether physical (e.g. exploring a wooden brick) or mental (e.g. thinking of different outcomes and what they mean). Piaget's emphasis on activity was important in stimulating the child-centred approach to education because he believed that, to learn, children not only need to manipulate objects; they also need to manipulate ideas (Halpenny & Pettersen, 2014). We discuss the educational implications of Piaget's theory later in this chapter.

UNDERLYING ASSUMPTIONS: STRUCTURE AND ORGANIZATION

Using observations, dialogues and small-scale experiments, Piaget suggested that children progress through a series of stages in their thinking, each of which corresponds to broad changes in the structure or logic of their intelligence (see Table 13.1). Piaget called the main stages of development the sensorimotor, preoperational, concrete operational and formal operational stages, and emphasized that they occur in that order.

Piaget's structures are sets of mental operations, which can be applied to objects, beliefs, ideas or anything in the child's world. Such a mental operation is called a *schema*. The schemas are seen as evolving structures; in other words, structures that grow and change from one stage to the next. We will look at each stage in detail in the next section, but first we need to look at Piaget's concepts of the unchanging (or 'invariant', to use his term) aspects of thought; that is, the broad characteristics of intelligent activity that remain the same at all ages. These are the *organization* of schemas and their *adaptation* through *assimilation* and *accommodation*.

Piaget used the term *organization* to refer to the inborn capacity to coordinate existing cognitive structures, or schemas, and combine them into more complex systems. For example,

Table 13.1 The stages of intellectual development according to Piaget.

Stage	Approximate age (years)	Characteristics
Sensori-motor	0–2	The infant knows about the world through actions and sensory information. Infants learn to differentiate themselves from the environment, begin to understand causality in time and space, and develop the capacity to form internal mental representations.
Preoperational	2–7	Through the symbolic use of language and intuitive problem solving, the child begins to understand about the classification of objects. But thinking is characterized by egocentrism, children focus on just one aspect of a task and lack operations like compensation and reversibility. By the end of this stage, children can take another's perspective and can understand the conservation of number.
Concrete operational	7–12	Children understand conservation of mass, length, weight and volume, and can more easily take the perspective of others; can classify and order, as well as organize objects into series. The child is still tied to the immediate experience, but within these limitations can perform logical mental operations.
Formal operational	12	Abstract reasoning begins. Children can now manipulate ideas; can speculate about the possible; can reason deductively, and formulate and test hypotheses.

a baby of 3 months has learned to combine looking and grasping with the earlier reflex of sucking. She can do all three together when feeding, an ability which the newborn baby did not have. Or, to give another example, at the age of 2 Ben has learned to climb downstairs, to carry objects without dropping them and to open doors. He can combine all three operations to deliver a newspaper to his grandmother in the basement flat. In other words, each separate operation combines into a new action that is more complex than the sum of the parts.

Organization also grows in complexity as the schemas become more elaborate. Piaget described the development of a particular action schema in his son Laurent as he attempted to strike a hanging object. At first Laurent only made random movements towards the object, but by the age of 6 months the movements had become deliberate and well directed. As Piaget described it, by 6 months Laurent possessed the mental structure that guided the action involved in hitting a toy. He had also learned to accommodate his actions to the weight, size and shape of the toy, and its distance from him.

This leads us to the other invariant function identified by Piaget—*adaptation*. By adaptation, he meant the striving of the organism for balance (or equilibrium) with the environment, which is achieved through the complementary processes of *assimilation* and *accommodation*. Through assimilation, the child 'takes in' a new experience and fits it into an existing schema. For example, a child may have learned the words 'dog' and 'car'. For a while, all animals are called 'dogs' (i.e. different animals taken into a schema related to the child's understanding of 'dog'), or all four-wheeled vehicles might be considered 'cars'. This process is balanced by accommodation, in which the child adjusts an existing schema to fit in with the nature of the environment. From experience, the child begins to perceive that cats can be distinguished from dogs (and may develop different schema for these two types of animals) and that cars can be discriminated from other vehicles.

Through the twin processes of assimilation and accommodation, the child achieves a new state of equilibrium. This equilibrium, however, is not permanent. The balance will soon be upset as the child assimilates further new experiences or accommodates their existing schemas to another new idea. In a sense, equilibrium only prepares the child for disequilibrium, that is, further learning and adaptation; the two cannot be thought of separately. Assimilation helps the child to consolidate mental structures; accommodation results in growth and change. All adaptation contains components of both processes, and striving for balance between assimilation and accommodation results in the child's intrinsic motivation to learn. When new experiences are close to a child's capacity to respond, then conditions are at their best for change and development to occur.

THE STAGES OF COGNITIVE DEVELOPMENT

Piaget considered intellectual development to be a continuous process of assimilation and accommodation. Although we go on here to describe the four stages he identified, there is no sharp dividing line between each. The order of stages is the same for all children, but the ages at which they are achieved may vary from one child to another.

THE SENSORIMOTOR STAGE

During the sensorimotor stage, the child changes from a newborn, who focuses almost entirely on immediate sensory and motor experiences, to a toddler who possesses a rudimentary capacity for thinking. Piaget described in detail the process by which this occurs by carefully documenting his own children's behaviour. On this basis of such observations carried out over the first 2 years of life, Piaget divided the sensorimotor period into six substages (see Table 13.2).

The first stage, *reflex activity*, included the reflexive behaviours and spontaneous rhythmic activity with which the infant was born. Piaget called the second substage *primary circular reactions*. His use of the term 'circular' was to emphasize the way that children will repeat an activity, especially one that is pleasing or satisfying (e.g. thumb sucking). The term 'primary' refers to simple behaviours that are derived from the reflexes of the first period (e.g. thumb sucking develops as the thumb is assimilated into a schema based on the innate suckling reflex).

Secondary circular reactions refer to the child's willingness to repeat actions, but the word 'secondary' points to behaviours that are the child's own. In other words, she is not

Table 13.2 Substages of the sensori-motor period according to Piaget.

Substage	Age (months)	Characteristics
Reflex activity	0–1	Infants practise innate reflexes (e.g. sucking, looking). Behaviour is largely, but not entirely, assimilative.
Primary circular reactions	1–4	Behaviour is primary in the sense that it is basically made up of reflexes or motor responses; it is circular in the sense that the child repeats it. Primary circular reactions centre on the infant's own body. There appears to be no differentiation between self and outside world.
Secondary circular reactions	4–10	Infants now focus on objects rather than on their own body. They begin to make interesting things happen (e.g. moving a hanging toy by hitting it). They have begun to change their surroundings intentionally.
Coordination of secondary circular reactions	10–12	Infants begin to combine schemas to achieve goals, and to solve problems in new situations (e.g. they will use the hitting schema to knock down a barrier between themselves and a toy).
Tertiary circular reactions	12–18	Infants actively use trial-and-error methods to learn about objects. Increased mobility enables them to experiment and explore. They learn new ways of solving problems and discover more about the properties of the environment.
Internal representation	18–24	The beginning of mental action and insightful solutions to problems. Objects and people can be represented symbolically; behaviour can be imitated from previous observations.

limited to just repeating actions based on early reflexes, but, having initiated new actions, can repeat these if they are satisfying. At the same time, such actions tend to be directed outside the child (unlike simple actions like thumb sucking) and are aimed at influencing the environment around her.

This is Piaget's description of his daughter Jacqueline, at 5 months of age, kicking her legs (in itself a primary circular reaction) in what becomes a secondary circular reaction as the leg movement is repeated not just for itself, but is initiated in the presence of a doll.

> Jacqueline looks at a doll attached to a string which is stretched from the hood to the handle of the cradle. The doll is at approximately the same level as the child's feet. Jacqueline moves her feet and finally strikes the doll, whose movement she immediately notices . . . The activity of the feet grows increasingly regular whereas Jacqueline's eyes are fixed on the doll. Moreover, when I remove the doll Jacqueline occupies herself quite differently; when I replace it, after a moment, she immediately starts to move her legs again.
>
> *(Piaget, 1936/1952, p. 182)*

In behaving as she did, Jacqueline seemed to have established a general relation between her movement and the doll's, and was engaging in a secondary circular reaction.

Coordination of secondary circular reactions. As the word coordination implies, it is in this substage that children start to combine different behavioural schema. In the following extract, Piaget described how his daughter (aged 8 months) combined several schemas, such as 'sucking an object' and 'grasping an object' in a series of coordinated actions when playing with a new object.

> Jacqueline grasps an unfamiliar cigarette case which I present to her. At first she examines it very attentively, turns it over, then holds it in both hands while making the sound apff (a kind of hiss which she usually makes in the presence of people). After that she rubs it against the wicker of her cradle then draws herself up while looking at it, then swings it above her and finally puts it into her mouth.
>
> *(Piaget, 1936/1952, p. 284)*

Jacqueline's behaviour illustrates how a new object is assimilated to various existing schema in the fourth substage. In the following stage, that of *tertiary circular reactions*, children's behaviours become more flexible, and when they repeat actions they may do so with variations, which can lead to new results. By repeating actions with variations children are, in effect, accommodating established schema to new contexts and needs.

The last substage of the sensorimotor period is called the substage of *internal representation*. Internal representation refers to the child's achievement of mental representation. In previous substages the child has interacted with the world via her physical motor schema; in other words, she has acted directly on the world. But by the final substage she can act indirectly on the world because she has a mental representation of the world. This means that instead of just manipulating the world around her directly, she can also manipulate her mental representation of the world—that is, she can think and plan.

What evidence did Piaget put forward to demonstrate that children have achieved mental representations by the end of the sensorimotor period? He pointed out that by this substage children have a full concept of *object permanence*. Piaget noticed that very young infants ignored even attractive objects once they were out of sight. For example, if an infant was reaching for a toy but then the toy was covered with a cloth, the infant would immediately lose interest in it, she would not attempt to search for it and might just look away. According to Piaget, it was only in the later substages that children demonstrated an awareness (by searching for and trying to retrieve the object) that the object was permanently present even if it was temporarily out of sight. Searching for an object that cannot be seen directly implies that the child has a memory of the object (i.e. a mental representation of it).

Piaget suggested that it was only towards the end of the sensorimotor period that children demonstrated novel patterns of behaviour in response to a problem. For example, if children want to reach for a toy but there is another object between them and the toy, younger children might just try to reach the toy directly. It may be that in the course of trying to reach the toy they happen to knock the object out of the way and succeed in reaching the toy itself, but this is best described as 'trial-and-error' performance. A child in the later substages of the sensorimotor period might solve the problem by not reaching for the toy immediately, but first removing the object and then getting the toy easily. If a child carries out such structured behaviour it implies that she was able to plan ahead and to plan ahead indicates that she had a mental representation of what she was going to do.

Piaget gave an example of planned behaviour by Jacqueline at 20 months. She was trying to solve the problem of opening a door while carrying two blades of grass at the same time.

> She stretches out her right hand towards the knob but sees that she cannot turn it without letting go of the grass. She puts the grass on the floor, opens the door, picks up the grass again and enters. But when she wants to leave the room things become complicated. She put the grass on the floor and grasps the door knob. But then she perceives that in pulling the door towards her she will simultaneously chase away the grass which she placed between the door and the threshold. She therefore picks it up in order to put it outside the door's zone of movement.
>
> *(Piaget, 1936/1952, pp. 376–377)*

Jacqueline solved the problem of the grass and the door before she opened the door. In other words, she must have had a mental representation of the problem, which permitted her to work out the solution before she acted.

A third line of evidence for mental representations comes from Piaget's observations of *deferred imitation*. This is when children carry out a behaviour that is copying other behaviour that they have seen some time before. Piaget provided a good example of this.

> At 16 months Jacqueline had a visit from a little boy of 18 months who she used to see from time to time, and who, in the course of the afternoon got into a terrible temper. He screamed as he tried to get out of a playpen and pushed it backward, stamping his feet. Jacqueline stood watching him in amazement, never having witnessed such a scene before. The next day, she herself screamed in her playpen and tried to move it, stamping her foot lightly several times in succession.
>
> *(Piaget, 1951, p. 63)*

If Jacqueline was able to imitate the little boy's behaviour a day later, she must have retained an image of his behaviour; in other words, she had a mental representation of what she had seen from the day before, and that representation provided the basis for her own copy of the temper tantrum.

In summary, during the sensorimotor period the child progresses from very simple and limited reflex behaviours at birth to complex behaviours at the end of the period. The more complex behaviours depend on the progressive combination and elaboration of schema, but are, at first, limited to direct interaction with the world—hence the name Piaget gave to this whole period, because he thought of the child developing through her sensorimotor interaction with the environment. It is only towards the end of the period that the child is freed from immediate interaction by developing the ability to mentally represent her world. With this ability, the child can then manipulate her mental images (or symbols) of her world—in other words, she can act on her thoughts about the world as well as on the world itself.

REINTERPRETATIONS OF PIAGET: THE SENSORIMOTOR STAGE

Piaget's observations of babies during this first stage have been largely confirmed by subsequent researchers, but he may have underestimated children's capacity to organize the sensory and motor information they take in. Several researchers have shown that children have abilities and concepts at an earlier age than Piaget thought.

Bower (1982) examined Piaget's hypothesis that young children did not have an appreciation of objects if they were out of sight. Children a few months old were shown an object, then a screen was moved across in front of the object, and finally, the screen was moved back to its original position. There were two conditions in the experiment: in one condition, when the screen was moved back the object was still in place but in the second condition the object had been removed and there was only an empty space. The children's heart rate was monitored to measure changes, which reflected surprise. According to Piaget, young children do not retain information about objects that are no longer present, and if this is the case there would be no reason for them to expect an object behind the screen when it was moved back. In other words, children should not show any reaction in the second condition. However, Bower found that children showed more surprise in the second condition than in the first condition. Bower inferred that the children's reaction was because they *had* expected the object to reappear. If so, this would be evidence that young children retained an image or representation of the object in their head, and this could be interpreted as children having a concept of object permanence at an earlier age than Piaget suggested.

In another experiment, Baillargeon and DeVos (1991) showed 3-month-old children objects that moved behind a screen and then reappeared from the other side of the screen. The upper half of the screen had a window in it. In one condition children saw a short object move behind the screen. The object was below the level of the window in the screen and therefore it was not visible again until it had passed all the way behind the screen. In a second condition a tall object was moved behind the screen. This object was large enough to be seen through the window as it passed behind the screen. However, Baillargeon and DeVos created an 'impossible event' by passing the tall object all the way behind the screen but without it appearing through the window. Infants showed more interest by looking longer at the event when it included the tall object than when it included the short object. Baillargeon and DeVos argued that this was because the children had expected the tall object to appear in the window. This is further evidence that young children are aware of the continued existence of objects even when they have been out of view. Studies like this one by Baillargeon and DeVos have led to new research into children's interpretation of the appearance and disappearance of objects, and have resulted in the development of more elaborate theories about children's reasoning about the physical world (Baillargeon et al., 2011).

Other researchers have considered Piaget's conclusion that it is only towards the end of the sensorimotor period that children demonstrate planned actions that reflect their ability to form a mental representation of the event. Willatts (1989) placed an attractive toy out of reach of 9-month-old children. The toy was placed on a cloth (and therefore children could pull the cloth to move the toy closer). But the children could not reach the cloth directly because Willatts placed a light barrier between the child and the cloth (and therefore they had to move the barrier to reach the cloth). Willatts found that children were able to get the toy by carrying out the appropriate series of actions—first moving the barrier and then pulling the cloth to bring the toy within reach. Most importantly, many of the children carried out these actions on the first occasion they were faced with the problem, and did not need to go through a period of 'trial-and-error' learning to work out how to get the toy. As children at this age can demonstrate novel, planned actions, it can be inferred from such behaviour that the children are operating on a mental representation of the world which they can use to organize their behaviour before carrying it out. This is earlier than Piaget had suggested.

Piaget pointed out that deferred imitation was evidence that children must have a memory representation of what they had seen at an earlier time. From soon after birth, babies can imitate an adult's facial expression or head movement (Meltzoff & Moore, 1983, 1989), but this type of imitation is performed while the stimulus being imitated is present (in other words, there is no need to store a memory of the stimulus). According to Piaget, imitation based on stored representations only develops towards the end of the sensorimotor period. However, Meltzoff and Moore (1994) showed that 6-week-old infants could imitate a behaviour a day after they had seen the original behaviour. In Meltzoff and Moore's study, some children saw an adult make a facial gesture (for example, stick out her tongue) and others just saw the adult's face while she maintained a neutral expression (see p. 98). The following day all the children saw the same adult again, but on this occasion she maintained a passive face. Compared to children who had not seen any gesture, the children who had seen the tongue protrusion gesture the day before were more likely to make tongue protrusions to the adult the second time they saw her. To do this, the infants must have had a memory representation of the gesture they had seen a day before, and this is evidence of mental representations at a much earlier age than Piaget proposed.

As infants get older, they are able to imitate more than just a single action like a facial gesture. For example, Barr et al. (1996) showed 6-month-olds a hand puppet and then demonstrated a series of actions (taking off a glove that was on the puppet's hand, shaking the glove so that the infant could hear a bell which was inside the glove and then putting the glove back on the puppet). The infants were able to repeat this sequence of actions themselves when they were given the puppet again a day later, indicating successful recall of what they had seen the first day. In other words, as infants get older they are able to retain representations of more complex actions, and they are also able to recall actions for longer periods (Barr & Hayne, 2000). That such development is taking place during the period that Piaget referred to as the sensorimotor period weakens Piaget's contention that infants in this period have little or no ability for deferred imitation (Meltzoff & Moore, 1999).

 Stop and Think

Why might Piaget have underestimated children's cognitive abilities during their early years?

THE PREOPERATIONAL STAGE

Piaget divided this stage into the preconceptual period (2–4 years) and the intuitive period (4–7 years).

The Preconceptual Period

The preconceptual period builds on the capacity for internal, or symbolic, thought that has developed in the sensorimotor period. In the preconceptual period there is a rapid increase in children's language which, in Piaget's view, results from the development of symbolic thought.

Piaget differs from other theorists who argue that thought grows out of linguistic competence. Instead, Piaget maintained that thought arises out of action and (as we saw in

Chapter 12) this idea is supported by research into the cognitive abilities of deaf children who, despite limitations in language, are able to reason and solve problems. Piaget argued that thought shapes language far more than language shapes thought, at least during the preconceptual period. Symbolic thought is also expressed in imaginative play (see Chapter 7). Despite the rapid development of children's thinking and language in the preconceptual period, Piaget identified limitations in the child's abilities in this stage. For example, Piaget pointed out that the preoperational child is still centred in her own perspective and finds it difficult to understand that other people can look at things differently. Piaget called this 'self-centred' view of the world *egocentrism*.

Egocentric thinking occurs because of the child's view that the universe is centred on herself. She finds it hard to 'decentre', that is, to take the perspective of another person. The following dialogue illustrates a 3-year-old's difficulty in taking the perspective of another person.

Adult:	Have you any brothers or sisters?
John:	Yes, a brother.
Adult:	What is his name?
John:	Sammy.
Adult:	Does Sammy have a brother?
John:	No.

John's inability to decentre makes it hard for him to realize that from Sammy's perspective, he himself is a brother.

Children's egocentrism is also apparent in their performance in perspective-taking tasks. One of Piaget's most famous studies was the three mountains experiment (see Figure 13.2).

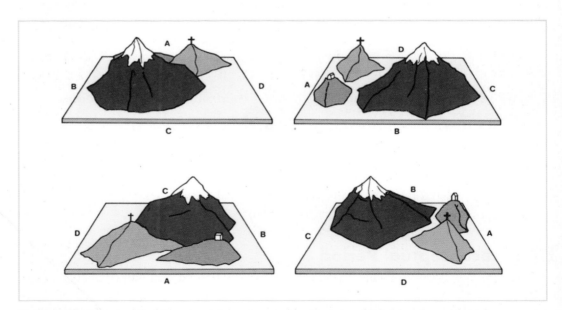

Figure 13.2 The model of the mountain range used by Piaget and Inhelder viewed from four different sides.

Piaget and Inhelder (1956) asked children between the ages of 4 and 12 years to say how a doll, placed in various positions, would view an array of three mountains from different perspectives. For example, in Figure 13.2, a child might be asked to sit at position A, and a doll would be placed at one of the other positions (B, C or D). Then the child would be asked to choose, from a set of different views of the model, the view that the doll could see. When 4- and 5-year-old children were asked to do this task, they often chose the view that they themselves could see (rather than the doll's view) and it was not until 8 or 9 years of age that children could confidently work out the doll's view. Piaget interpreted this result as an example of young children's egocentricity—that they could not decentre from their own view to work out the doll's view.

Several criticisms have been made of the three mountains task (Newcombe, 1989). Some researchers (e.g. Donaldson, 1978) have pointed out that it is a particularly unusual task to use with young children who might not have much familiarity with model mountains or be used to working out other people's views of landscapes. Borke (1975) carried out a similar task to Piaget's, but rather than model mountains, she used layouts of toys that young children typically play with themselves. She also altered the way that children were asked to respond to the question about what another person looking at the layout might see. Borke found that children as young as 3 or 4 years of age had some understanding of how another person would view the layouts from a different position. This was much earlier than suggested by Piaget, and shows that the type of procedures and materials that are used in a task can have a marked effect on how well children perform the tasks. By using a model of mountains, Piaget may have selected a particularly difficult context for children to demonstrate their perspective-taking skills. Borke's experiment is described in Box 13.1.

Piaget used the three mountains task to investigate visual perspective taking, and it was on the basis of this task that he concluded that young children were egocentric. There are also other kinds of perspective taking, and these include the ability to empathize with other people's emotions and the ability to know what other people are thinking. Researchers have found that by 4 or 5 years of age children do understand that different people can interpret the world in different ways (Wimmer & Perner, 1983). In other words, young children are less egocentric than Piaget assumed. The research concerned with children's insights into other people's minds is discussed in Chapter 15.

The Intuitive Period

Piaget suggested that there was a further shift in thinking about the age of 4 years, and that it is about this time that a child begins to develop the mental operations of ordering, classifying and quantifying in a more systematic way. Piaget applied the term *intuitive* to this period, because even though a child can carry out such operations, she is largely unaware of the principles that underlie the operations and cannot explain why she has done them, nor can she carry them out in a fully satisfactory way.

If a preoperational child is asked to arrange sticks in a certain order, this poses difficulties. Piaget gave children 10 sticks of different sizes from A (the shortest) to J (the longest), arranged randomly on a table. The child was asked to seriate them, that is, to put them in order of length. Some preoperational children could not do the task at all. Some children arranged a few sticks correctly, but could not sustain the complete ordering. And some put all

Box 13.1 Piaget's mountains revisited: changes in the egocentric landscape

Borke questioned the appropriateness for young children of Piaget's three mountains task (described on p. 454). Borke thought it possible that aspects of the task not related to perspective taking might have adversely affected the children's performance. These aspects included the following possibilities. First, viewing a mountain scene from different angles may not have been an interesting or motivating problem for young children. Second, Piaget had asked children to select pictures of the doll's views and young children might have had difficulty with such a response. Third, because the task was so unusual, children may have performed poorly because they were unfamiliar with the nature of the task. Borke considered whether some initial practice and familiarity with the task might improve performance. With those points in mind, Borke repeated the basic design

of Piaget and Inhelder's experiment, but changed the content of the task, avoided the use of pictures and gave children some initial practice. She used four three-dimensional displays: these were a practice display and three experimental displays (Box Figure 13.1.1).

Borke's participants were eight 3-year-old children and 14 4-year-old children attending a day nursery. Grover, a character from the popular children's television programme *Sesame Street*, was used instead of Piaget's doll. There were two identical versions of each display (A and B). Display A was for Grover and the child to look at, and display B was on a turntable next to the child.

The children were tested individually and were first shown a practice display. The practice display was a large toy fire engine. Borke placed Grover at one of the sides of practice

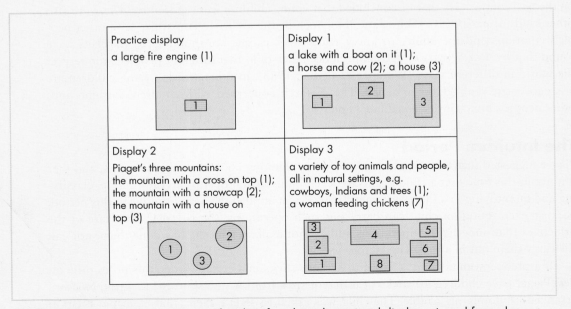

Box Figure 13.1.1 A schematic view of Borke's four three-dimensional displays viewed from above.
Source: Borke, H. 1975: Piaget's mountains revisited: changes in the egocentric landscape. *Developmental Psychology, 11*, 240–243.

display A so that Grover was looking at the fire engine from a point of view that was different from the child's own view of this display.

An exact duplicate of the fire engine (practice display B) appeared on the revolving turntable, and Borke explained that the table could be turned so that the child could look at the fire engine from any side. Children were asked to turn the table until they were looking at display B in the same way that Grover was looking at display A. If necessary, Borke helped the children to move the turntable to the correct position or walked the children round display A to show them how Grover saw it.

After this practice period the child was ready to move on to the experiment itself. Here the procedure was the same, except that the experimenter provided no help. Each child was shown three experimental displays, one at a time (see Box Figure 13.1.1). Display 1 included a toy house, lake and animals. Display 2 was based on Piaget's model of three mountains. Display 3 included several scenes with figures and animals. There were two identical copies of each display. Grover was placed at different places round one copy of each display, and children then rotated the other copy on the turntables to demonstrate Grover's point of view.

Most of the children were able to work out Grover's perspective for display 1 (3- and 4-year-olds were correct in 80% of trials) and for display 3 (3-year-olds were correct in 79% of trials and 4-year-olds in 93% of trials). For display 2, however, the 3-year-olds were correct in only 42% of trials and 4-year-olds in 67% of trials. Borke used analysis of variance, and found that the difference between the displays 1 and 3 and display 2 was significant at $p < .001$. As for errors, there were no significant differences in the children's responses for any of the three positions—31% of errors were egocentric (i.e. the child rotated display B to show their own view of display A, rather than Grover's view).

Borke demonstrated clearly that the task itself had a crucial influence on the perspective-taking performance of young children. When the display included recognizable toys and the response involved moving a turntable, the children could work out Grover's perspective even when the display was a comparatively complex one like display 3. This demonstrated that the poor performance of young children in Piaget's original three mountains task was due in part to the unfamiliar nature of the materials that the children were shown.

Borke's conclusion was that the potential for understanding another's viewpoint is already present in children as young as 3 and 4 years of age—a strong challenge to Piaget's assertions that children of this age are egocentric and incapable of taking the viewpoint of others. It would seem that young children make egocentric responses when they misunderstand the task, but given the right conditions they are capable of working out another's viewpoint.

Based on material in Borke, H. (1975). Piaget's mountains revisited: changes in the egocentric landscape. *Developmental Psychology, 11*, 240–243.

the small ones in a group and all the larger ones in another. A more advanced response was to arrange the sticks so that the tops of the sticks were in the correct order even though the bottoms were not (see Figure 13.3). In short, the child at this stage is not capable of ordering more than a very few objects.

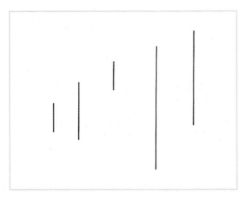

Figure 13.3   The preoperational child's ordering of different-sized sticks. An arrangement in which the child has solved the problem of seriation by ignoring the length of the sticks.

Piaget found that preoperational children also have difficulty with class inclusion tasks. These are tasks that involve part–whole relations. Suppose a child is given a box that contains 18 brown beads and two white beads; all the beads are wooden. When asked, 'Are there more brown beads than wooden beads?', the preoperational child will typically reply that there are more brown beads. According to Piaget, the child finds it hard to consider the class of 'all beads' at the same time as considering the subset of beads, the class of 'brown beads'.

Such findings tend to be true of all children in the preoperational stage, irrespective of their cultural background. Investigators found that Thai and Malaysian children gave responses very similar to Swiss children and in the same sequence of development. In the following example, a Thai boy, shown a bunch of seven roses and two lotus, states that there are more roses than flowers when prompted by the standard Piagetian questions.

Child:	More roses.
Experimenter:	More than what?
Child:	More than flowers.
Experimenter:	What are the flowers?
Child:	Roses.
Experimenter:	Are there any others?
Child:	There are.
Experimenter:	What?
Child:	Lotus.
Experimenter:	So in this bunch which is more, roses or flowers?
Child:	More roses.

(Ginsburg & Opper, 1979, pp. 130–131)

One aspect of the preoperational child's thinking processes that has been extensively investigated is what Piaget called *conservation*. Conservation refers to a person's understanding that superficial changes in the appearance of a quantity do not mean that there has been any fundamental change in that quantity. For example, if you have 10 dolls standing in a line, and then you rearrange them so that they are standing in a circle, this does not mean that there has been any alteration in the number of dolls. If nothing is added or subtracted from a quantity then it remains the same (i.e. it is conserved).

Piaget discovered that a preoperational child finds it hard to understand that if an object is changed in shape or appearance, its qualities remain the same. There is a series of conservation tests; examples are given in Figures 13.4 and 13.5. If a child is given two identical balls of clay and asked if they each have the same amount of clay in them, the child will agree that they do. But if one of the two balls is rolled into a sausage shape (see Figure 13.4b) and the

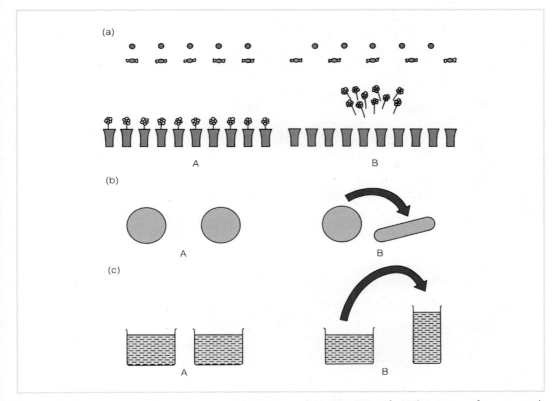

Figure 13.4   Some tests of conservation: (a) two tests of conservation of number (rows of sweets and coins; flowers and vases); (b) conservation of mass (two balls of clay); (c) conservation of quantity (liquid in glasses). In each case illustration A shows the material when the child is first asked if the two items or sets of items are the same, and illustration B shows the way that one item or set of items is transformed before the child is asked a second time if they are still the same.

child is asked again whether they have the same amount of clay, she is likely to say that one is larger than the other. When asked why, she will not be able to give an explanation, but will just say something like 'because it is larger'.

Piaget suggested that a child has difficulty in a task like this because she can only focus on one attribute at a time. For example, if she focuses on length she may think that the sausage shape, being longer, has more clay in it. According to Piaget, for a child to appreciate that the sausage of clay has the same amount of clay as the ball means understanding that the greater length of the sausage is *compensated* for by the smaller cross-section of the sausage. Piaget said that preoperational children cannot apply principles like compensation.

In another example of a conservation task, a child is shown two rows of sweets with the same number of sweets in each row, and presented in a one-to-one layout (as in Figure 13.4a). She is asked if there is the same number of sweets in each row and will usually agree that there is. Then one row of sweets is made longer by spreading them out, and the child is asked again whether there is the same number of sweets in each row. The preoperational child often says that there are now more sweets in one of the rows. She may, for example, think that a longer row means that there are more objects in that row. She does not realize that the greater length of the row of sweets is compensated for by the greater distance between the sweets.

Figure 13.5 A 4-year-old puzzles over Piaget's conservation of number experiments; he says that the rows are equal in number in arrangement (a), but not in arrangement (b) 'because they're all bunched together here'.

Source: Photographs courtesy of H. Cowie.

According to Piaget, compensation is only one of several processes that can help children overcome changes in appearance. Another process is *reversibility*. This means that children could think of 'reversing' the change they have seen. For example, if children imagine the sausage of clay being rolled back into a ball, or the row of sweets being pushed back together, they may realize that once the change has been reversed the quantity of an object or the number of items in the row is the same as it was before. According to Piaget, preoperational children lack the thought processes needed to apply principles like compensation and reversibility, and therefore they have difficulty in conservation tasks.

In the next stage of development, the concrete operational stage, children have achieved the necessary logical thought processes that give them the ability to use appropriate principles and deal with conservation and other problem-solving tasks easily.

REINTERPRETATIONS OF PIAGET: THE PREOPERATIONAL STAGE

As explained above, Piaget claimed that the preoperational child cannot cope with tasks like part–whole relations or conservation, because they lack the logical thought processes to apply principles like compensation. However, other researchers have pointed out that children's lack of success in some tasks may be due to factors other than ones associated with logical processes.

The preoperational child seems unable to understand the relationship between the whole and the part in class inclusion tasks, and will happily state that there are more brown beads than wooden beads in a box of brown and white wooden beads 'because there are only two white ones'. However, some researchers have pointed out that the questions that children are asked in such studies are unusual; for example, it is not often in everyday conversation that we ask questions like: 'Are there more brown beads or more wooden beads?'.

Even slight variations in the wording of the questions that help to clarify the meaning of the question can have positive effects on the child's performance. McGarrigle (quoted in Donaldson, 1978) showed children four toy cows, three black and one white, all lying asleep on their sides. If the children were asked, 'Are there more black cows or more cows?' (as in a standard Piagetian experiment) they tended not to answer correctly. If the question was rephrased, 'Are there more black cows or more sleeping cows?', preoperational children were more likely to respond correctly. McGarrigle found that in a group of children aged 6 years, 25% answered the standard Piagetian question correctly. When it was rephrased, 48% of the children were correct, a significant increase. In other words, some of the difficulty was in the wording of the question rather than just an inability to understand part–whole relations.

Donaldson (1978) put forward a different reason from Piaget for why young children performed poorly in conservation tasks. Donaldson argued that children build up a model of the world by formulating hypotheses that help them anticipate future events on the basis of past experience. The child, therefore, has expectations about any situation, and the child's interpretation of the words she hears will be influenced by the expectations she brings to the situation. In a conservation experiment, for example, an experimenter asks a child if there are the same numbers of sweets in two rows (see Figure 13.4a). Then the experimenter changes one of the rows while emphasizing that it is being altered. Donaldson suggested that it is quite reasonable for a child to think that there must be a link between that action (changing the display) and the following question (about the number of sweets in each row). Why should an adult ask the child such a question if there hasn't really been a change? If the child thinks that adults don't usually carry out actions unless they want to alter something, then the child may assume that there really has been a change in the material.

McGarrigle and Donaldson (1974) explored this idea in an experiment that included a character called 'Naughty Teddy'. It was Naughty Teddy, rather than the experimenter, who muddled up the display and the change was explained to the children as an 'accident'. In this context the child might have less expectation that a deliberate action had been applied to the material, and that there was no reason to believe that a real change had taken place. This was the case, because McGarrigle and Donaldson found that children were more likely to give the correct answer (that the material remained the same after being messed up by Naughty Teddy) in this context than in the classic Piagetian context (see Box 13.2).

Piaget was right to point out difficulties that preoperational children have with conservation and other reasoning tasks. But researchers since Piaget have found that, given appropriate wording and context, young children seem capable of demonstrating at least some of the abilities that Piaget thought only developed later. In the right social context, the child emerges as more competent than Piaget's work would suggest (Siegal, 1997).

Piaget also found that preoperational children had difficulty with *transitive inferences*. He showed children two rods, A and B. Rod A was longer than rod B. Then he put rod A away and showed the children rods B and C. Rod B was longer than rod C. Then he asked children which rod was longer, A or C. Young children find such questions difficult and Piaget

Box 13.2 Conservation accidents

McGarrigle and Donaldson set out to discover whether young children could succeed at conservation tasks if a different procedure from Piaget's was used. McGarrigle and Donaldson tested 80 children, aged between 4 years 2 months and 6 years 3 months, in two situations involving conservation of number (with equal or unequal numbers) and two situations involving conservation of length (with equal or unequal lengths of string). Each child performed each conservation task under two conditions.

1. An 'accidental' transformation when the materials were disarranged 'accidentally' by a mischievous teddy bear.
2. An 'intentional' transformation when the transformation of materials was clearly intended by the experimenter. This corresponded to the traditional Piagetian procedure.

The children were divided into two groups of 40, each balanced for age and gender. Group 1 had the accidental condition before the intentional condition. Group 2 had the intentional condition before the accidental one. Within each of the two groups, half of the children were given the number conservation task first and half were given the length conservation first (thus counterbalancing for the order of the tasks).

In the number equal situation, four red and four white counters were arranged in a one-to-one correspondence in two rows of equal length (see Box Figure 13.2.1). Transformation occurred when the counters of one row were moved until they touched one another. In the intentional condition, the experimenter did this deliberately. In the accidental condition, a 'Naughty Teddy' appeared and swooped over the counters and pushed them together. The child, who had already been warned that Teddy might 'mess up the toys', helped to put Teddy back in its place. Before and after the transformation the child was asked, 'Is there more here or more here, or are they both the same number?'.

In the number unequal situation, rows of four and five counters were used and the child was asked, 'Which is the one with more—this one, or this one?' (Box Figure 13.2.2). A similar procedure was carried out for the conservation of length, using lengths of black and red string. As can be seen in Box Table 13.2.1, the largest effect was between the accidental and the intentional conditions. Correct responses were more frequent when the transformation was accidental: 72% of the responses were correct when the display was moved accidentally, but only 34% were correct in the intentional transformation condition (i.e. the usual Piagetian procedure). There was little difference between the equal and unequal conditions.

Before transformation   After transformation

Box Figure 13.2.1 Transformation of counters in the number equal situation, either accidentally or intentionally.

Before transformation   After transformation

Box Figure 13.2.2 Transformation of counters in the number unequal situation, either accidentally or intentionally.

Source: McGarrigle, J. & Donaldson, M. 1974: Conservation accidents. *Cognition*, 3: 341-50.

Box Table 13.2.1   Number of correct responses given by Groups 1 and 2 under accidental (A) and intentional (I) conditions.

	A	then	I	I	then	A
Number equal	32		19	14		22
Number unequal	36		18	13		22
Length equal	34		15	8		24
Length unequal	37		12	9		23
Total	139		64	44		91

Group 1 N=40
Group 2 N=40

Source: McGarrigle, J. & Donaldson, M. 1974: Conservation accidents. *Cognition*, 3: 341–50.

However, the order in which the displays were presented did affect children's responses.

When McGarrigle and Donaldson compared performance by Group 1 and 2, the difference was significant ($p < .05$), because children who were given the accidental condition before the intentional condition performed better than those who did the tasks in the reverse order (see Box Table 13.2.1). This might mean that experiencing Naughty Teddy first could have helped the children realize in the later intentional condition that the change to the materials was superficial rather than a real alteration.

McGarrigle and Donaldson concluded that the experimenter's behaviour towards the task materials can influence the interpretation a child makes of the situation because the child will be trying to make sense of the situation and understand what the experimenter wants. Unless the setting is considered, the child's ability to conserve may be underestimated. The original experiments in number conservation might have made the child think that a real change in the materials had taken place—why else would an adult alter something? However, if the change was of no obvious importance (because something was simply messed up by a 'Naughty Teddy' who was only playing about), the child's ability to conserve improved markedly. This result indicated that how children interpret the social context of the conservation experiments may be a factor in whether or not they demonstrate the ability to conserve.

Based on material in McGarrigle, J. & Donaldson, M. (1974). Conservation accidents. *Cognition*, 3, 341–350.

suggested that they cannot make logical inferences such as: if A is longer than B and B is longer than C, then A must be longer than C.

Bryant and Trabasso (1971) also considered transitive inference tasks. They wondered if children's difficulties were less to do with making an inference and more to do with remembering all the information in the task. For children to make a correct response, they not only have to make the inference but they also have to remember the lengths of all the rods they have seen. Bryant and Trabasso thought it was possible that young children, who have limited working memory capacity (see Chapter 14), were unable to retain in memory all the information they needed for the task. They investigated transitive inferences using a task similar to Piaget's original task, but before asking the children to carry out the task itself, they trained them to remember the lengths of the rods. Of course they did not train them using rods A and C together, but the children were trained on the other comparisons they needed to remember (i.e. that A was longer than B and that B was longer than C). Only when Bryant and Trabasso were satisfied that the children could remember all the relevant information were they asked the test question. Bryant and Trabasso found that the children could now answer correctly. In other words, the difficulty that Piaget noted in such tasks was to do more with forgetting some of the information needed to make the necessary comparisons, rather than a failure in making logical inferences.

 Stop and Think

How did the way that Piaget designed his studies affect the results of those studies?

THE CONCRETE OPERATIONAL STAGE

From about the age of 7 years, children's thinking processes change again as they develop a new set of strategies that Piaget calls *concrete operations*. These strategies are called 'concrete' because children can only apply them to immediately present objects. Nonetheless, thinking becomes much more flexible in the concrete operational period because children no longer have a tendency just to focus on one aspect of problem; rather, they are able to consider different aspects of a task at the same time. They have processes like compensation and reversibility. For these reasons, children succeed on conservation tasks. For example, when a round ball of clay is transformed into a sausage shape, children in the concrete operational stage will say, 'It's longer but it's thinner' or 'If you change it back, it will be the same'. Conservation of number is achieved first (about 5 or 6 years), then conservation of weight (around 7 or 8 years), and conservation of volume is fully understood about 10 or 11 years. Operations like addition and subtraction, multiplication and division become easier. Another major shift comes with the concrete operational child's ability to classify and order, and to understand the principle of class inclusion. The ability to consider different aspects of a situation at the same time enables a child to perform successfully in perspective-taking tasks. For example, in the three mountains task, a child can consider that she has one view of the model and that someone else may have a different view.

There are still some limitations on thinking, because children are reliant on the immediate environment and have difficulty with abstract ideas. Take the following question: 'Edith is fairer than Susan. Edith is darker than Lily. Who is the darkest?'. This is a difficult problem for concrete operational children, who may not be able to answer it correctly. However, if children are given a set of dolls representing Susan, Edith and Lily, they are able to answer the question quickly. In other words, when the task is made a 'concrete' one, in this case with physical representations, children can deal with the problem but when it is presented verbally, as an abstract task, children have difficulty. According to Piaget, abstract reasoning is not found until the child has reached the stage of formal operations.

REINTERPRETATIONS OF PIAGET: THE CONCRETE OPERATIONAL STAGE

Many of Piaget's observations about the concrete operational stage have been broadly confirmed by subsequent research. For example, Tomlinson-Keasey (1978) found that conservation of number, weight and volume are acquired in the order stated by Piaget.

As in the previous stage, children's performance in the concrete operational period may be influenced by the context of the task. In some contexts, children in the concrete operational stage may demonstrate more advanced reasoning than would typically be expected of children in that stage. Jahoda (1983) showed that 9-year-olds in Harare, Zimbabwe, had more advanced understanding of economic principles than British 9-year-olds. The Harare children, who were involved in their parents' small businesses, had a strong motivation to understand the principles of profit and loss. Jahoda set up a mock shop and played a shopping game with the children. The British 9-year-olds could not explain about the functioning of a shop, did not understand that a shopkeeper buys for less than he sells, and did not know that some of the profit has to be set aside for purchase of new goods. The Harare children, by contrast, had mastered the concept of profit and understood about trading strategies. These principles had been grasped by the children as a direct outcome of their own active participation in running a business. Jahoda's experiment, like Donaldson's studies (1978), indicated the important function of context in the cognitive development of children, and we discuss this issue more in Chapter 16.

THE FORMAL OPERATIONAL STAGE

We have seen that during the period of concrete operations the child is able to reason in terms of objects (e.g. classes of objects, relations between objects) when the objects are present. Piaget argued that it is only during the period of formal operations that young people are able to reason hypothetically. Young people no longer depend on the 'concrete' existence of things in the real world. Instead, they can reason in terms of verbally stated hypotheses to consider the logical relations among several possibilities or to deduce conclusions from abstract statements. For example, consider the syllogism, 'All green birds have two heads'; 'I have a green bird at home called Charlie'; 'How many heads does Charlie have?'. The young person who has reached formal operational thinking will give the answer that is correct by abstract logic: 'two heads'. Children in the previous, concrete operational stage will usually not get beyond protesting about the absurdity of the premise.

Young people are also better at solving problems by considering all possible answers in a systematic manner. If asked to make up all the possible words from the letters A, S, E, T, M, a person at the formal operational level can do this in a logically ordered way. She can first consider all combinations of two letters AS, AE, AT, etc., checking whether such combinations are words, and then going on to consider all three-letter combinations, and so on. In earlier stages children attempt tasks like this in an unsystematic and disorganized way.

Inhelder and Piaget (1958) described the process of logical reasoning used by young people when presented with a number of natural science experiments. An example of one of their tasks was called the pendulum task. In this task a person is given a string (that can be shortened or lengthened) with a weight on it. The person is also given a set of weights and is asked to find out what determines the speed of swing of the pendulum. Possible factors are the length of the string, the weight at the end of the string, the height of the release point and the force of the push. In this problem the materials are concretely in front of the person, but the reasoning, to be successful, involves formal operations. These operations would include a systematic consideration of the various possibilities, the formulation of hypotheses (e.g. 'What would happen if I tried a heavier weight?') and logical deductions from the results of trials with different combinations of materials.

Other tasks considered by Inhelder and Piaget (1958) included determining the flexibility of metal rods, balancing different weights around a fulcrum and predicting chemical reactions. These tasks mimic the processes of scientific inquiry, and Piaget argued that formal scientific reasoning is one of the most important characteristics of formal operational thinking. From his original work, carried out in schools in Geneva, Piaget claimed that formal operational thinking was a characteristic stage that children or young people reached between the ages of 11 and 15 years, having previously gone through the earlier stages of development.

REINTERPRETATIONS OF PIAGET: THE FORMAL OPERATIONAL STAGE

Piaget's claim has been modified by more recent research. More recent researchers have found that the achievement of formal operational thinking is more gradual and haphazard than Piaget assumed. It may be dependent on the nature of the task and is often limited to certain domains.

Shayer et al., (1976; Shayer & Wylam, 1978) gave problems such as the pendulum task to schoolchildren in the UK. Their results (see Figure 13.6) showed that by 16 years of age, only about 30% of young people had achieved 'early formal operations'. Martorano (1977) gave 10 of Piaget's formal operational tasks to girls and young women aged 12–18 years in the USA. At 18 years of age, success on the different tasks varied from 15% to 95%, but only two children out of 20 succeeded on all 10 tasks. Young people's success on one or two tasks might indicate some formal operational reasoning, but their failure on other tasks demonstrated that such reasoning might be limited to certain tasks or contexts. It may only be much later that young people can apply formal reasoning across a range of problem tasks.

Some researchers have shown that formal thinking can be trained. Figure 13.7 shows the results of a study by Danner and Day (1977). They coached students aged 10 years, 13 years and 17 years in three formal operational tasks. As would be expected, training only had a limited effect at 10 years, but it had marked effects at 17 years.

In summary, it seems that the period from 11 to 15 years signals the start of the potential for formal operational thought, rather than its achievement. Formal operational thought may only be used some of the time, in certain domains we are familiar with, are trained in, or which are important to us. Often formal thinking is not used. After all, most adults know of areas of life where they should have thought things out logically, but in retrospect realize they failed to do so!

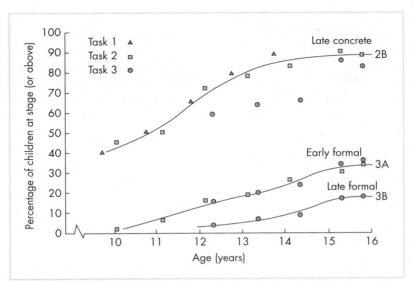

Figure 13.6 Proportion of boys at different Piagetian stages as assessed by three tasks.

Source: Shayer, M. & Wylam, H. (1978). The distribution of Piagetian stages of thinking in British middle and secondary school schildren: II. *British Journal of Educational Psychology, 48,* 62–70.

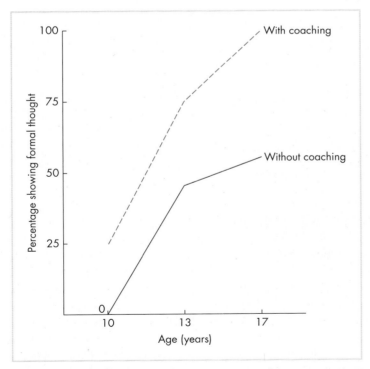

Figure 13.7 Levels of availability of formal thought. Percentage of adolescents showing formal thought, with and without coaching.

Source: Danner, F.W. & Day, M.C. (1977). Eliciting formal operations. *Child Development, 48,* 1600–1606.

Stop and Think

How have more recent researchers modified Piaget's conclusions about children's thinking in the concrete operational and formal operational stages of development?

PIAGET'S THEORY: AN OVERVIEW

No one denies the stature of Piaget's achievement, beginning his work as he did in the 1920s, when scientific psychology was in its infancy. However, several objections have been raised as to his methods. He seldom reported quantitative information on the number of children tested, or the percentage who passed a certain test (although researchers who replicated his findings in the 1950s and 1960s did support their findings with statistical analyses). He used a flexible method of interviewing children, the 'clinical method', which meant that he adapted his procedure to suit the child rather than following a standardized approach. This has advantages, but it puts a heavy premium on the interviewer's skill and makes replication of his experiments difficult. Piaget has also been criticized for putting too much emphasis on the child's failures rather than successes.

Piaget's emphasis on distinct cognitive stages, although very influential in the past, no longer provides a framework for developmental research. This is not to say that Piaget's research is no longer of any importance, because his individual studies are still highly cited, but contemporary developmental researchers would put much less emphasis on Piaget's theory of stages. Nonetheless, Piaget's research cannot be underestimated, because he set the agenda for so much later research. The reason why developmental psychologists still investigate and debate issues like 'deferred imitation' or 'egocentrism' and many others (albeit using different terms and using different methodologies from Piaget) is because Piaget was the first to point out the importance of such issues, and the first to find ways to investigate them. In so doing, he provided insights into children's minds that inspired the wealth of developmental research that succeeded his original work.

EDUCATIONAL IMPLICATIONS

Whatever its shortcomings, Piaget's approach provided the most comprehensive account of cognitive growth ever put forward. It has had considerable implications for education, most notably for child-centred learning methods, especially in nursery and infant schools (Davis, 2003). Piaget argued that young children think quite differently from adults and view the world from a qualitatively different perspective. It follows that a teacher must make a strong effort to adapt to the child and not assume that what is appropriate for adult learning is necessarily right for the child. At the heart of this child-centred approach to education lies the idea of active learning.

From the Piagetian standpoint, children learn from actions rather than from passive observations; for example, telling a child about the properties of materials is less effective than creating an environment in which the child is free to explore, touch, manipulate and experiment with different materials. First, a teacher must recognize that each child needs to construct knowledge for him- or herself, and that active learning results in deeper understanding. A teacher's role is therefore to create the conditions in which learning may best take place, since the aim of education is to encourage the child to ask questions, try out experiments and speculate, rather than accept information unthinkingly. Second, a teacher should also be concerned with process rather than end-product. From this it follows that a teacher should be interested in the reasoning behind the answer that a child gives to a question rather than just in the correct answer. Conversely, mistakes should not be penalized, but treated as responses that can give a teacher insights into the child's thinking processes at that time.

A teacher's role is not to impart information, because in Piaget's view knowledge is not something to be transmitted from an expert teacher to an inexpert pupil. It is the child, according to Piaget, who sets the pace. A teacher's part in the educational process is to create situations that challenge the child to ask questions, to form hypotheses and to discover new concepts. A teacher is the guide in the child's process of discovery, and, whenever possible, the curriculum should be adapted to each child's individual needs and intellectual level so that tasks are appropriate to individual children's level of understanding.

However, Piaget did not ignore the importance of social interaction in the learning process. He recognized the social value of interaction and viewed it as an important factor in cognitive growth (Davis, 2003). Piaget pointed out that through interaction with peers a child can develop through cooperation with others and by arguments and discussions. By listening to other children's opinions, by having one's own view challenged and by experiencing through others' reactions the illogicality of one's own concepts, a child can learn about perspectives other than her own. The need to agree or disagree with the views of others means that a child has to communicate her own beliefs in the most effective way, and in so doing will refine her own thinking in a continual process that improves her own understanding of the world.

CHAPTER SUMMARY

- Piaget described children's cognitive development in a theory that he applied from birth to adulthood. Piaget was the first psychologist to put forward such a comprehensive theory, and his theory formed the basis for much of the succeeding research into children's cognitive development.
- Piaget described cognitive development in four main stages (and several substages) and believed that all children progress through each stage in turn.
- Piaget's theory no longer has the influence that it once did. This is because more recent researchers have found children to be more competent than Piaget suggested, and have argued that children in particular stages are not as limited as Piaget believed.
- Other researchers have also put forward theories of cognitive development, some of which have been derived from Piaget's original description of cognitive development (see Chapter 14).

DISCUSSION POINTS

1. Piaget said that by the end of the sensori-motor stage, children have achieved 'internal representations'. What evidence led him to this conclusion?
2. What did Piaget mean by egocentrism? How have his ideas on egocentrism been challenged?
3. Did Piaget underestimate children's abilities in the preoperational stage of development?
4. Discuss ways in which Piaget seems to have misjudged the age when formal operations are acquired. Illustrate with examples from your own experience.
5. What are the implications of Piaget's theory for education? Discuss in relation to your own educational experiences.

FURTHER READING

- Wood, D. (1998). *How children think and learn* (2nd ed.). Oxford: Blackwell, includes a brief introduction to Piaget's work in the context of other developmental theories. A longer introduction that focuses on the educational implications of Piaget's theory is Halpenny, A.M. & Pettersen, J. (2014). *Introducing Piaget: A guide for practioners and students in early years education*. Abingdon: Routledge. This book explains the jargon of Piaget's theory in a clear and understandable way, and integrates numerous examples of Piaget's original studies with well-selected examples from recent research. A good starting point to understanding Piaget's theory in more depth.
- An extensive description and critique of Piaget's theory can be found in Miller, P.H. (2011). *Theories of developmental psychology* (5th ed.). New York: Worth. A briefer critique of Piaget's work is in Meadows, S. (2006). *The child as thinker: The development and acquisition of cognition in childhood* (2nd ed.). Hove, East Sussex: Routledge.
- For a good summary of Piaget's sensorimotor period, see Bremner, J.G. (1994). *Infancy* (2nd ed.). Oxford: Blackwell.

CHAPTER

14

Cognition: The Information Processing Approach

CHAPTER OUTLINE

- Information Processing Limitations
- Stage-Like Performance in Information Processing
- Memory Development
- Metacognition
- Knowledge and Memory Development
- Constructive Memory and Knowledge
- Summary of the Information Processing Approach
- Children's Eyewitness Research
- Children's Suggestibility
- Interviewing Procedures
- Stress and Recall
- Summary of Eyewitness Research

In the previous chapter we described the theory put forward by Piaget to describe the development of children's thinking. In this chapter we discuss several theories that developed from Piaget's original theory. For example, some researchers have suggested that limitations in memory processing may have been an underlying constraint on children's ability to reason in some cognitive tasks. We also discuss how researchers have analysed Piagetian and similar tasks in great detail to establish how children approach those tasks and what types of difficulties children have when attempting them. The detailed analysis of tasks has demonstrated the complexity of the processes involved in any problem-solving context, and has resulted in experimenters noting that children may attempt a single task in a number of different ways, often alternating between several different ways at the same time, rather than in stages. Such focused approaches have moved the study of cognitive development away from the wide and all-embracing theories put forward by researchers like Piaget. In the later part of the chapter we consider some of the applied implications of the research into cognitive development, especially how that research has contributed to a better understanding of children's memory and information processing in real-life contexts. We use the example of eyewitness research to do this. Children who have witnessed crimes or been the victims of crime are sometimes interviewed about what they have experienced, and (based on the studies of children's cognitive development) researchers have developed guidelines to help interviewers elicit the most accurate and complete testimony from a child.

Some of Piaget's work was reevaluated by researchers like Donaldson (1978), who argued that Piaget's tasks may have measured not only children's developing cognition, but also their understanding of other factors associated with the task, including the language used in the instructions, the context of the information which is used in the experiment, and the familiarity of the materials (see Chapter 13).

The discovery that apparently minor changes in experimental materials and procedures could affect children's performance is important for several reasons. First, it made researchers aware that what might be thought of as quite superficial changes (e.g. in the way that a question is phrased) could have an impact on the way that children interpret a task. Second, knowing that factors associated with the presentation of a task may influence children's success led to the identification of important aspects of cognitive development—for example, compared to older children, young children may be more dependent on the context of the task, or more dependent on the clarity of the instructions if they are to succeed in solving a problem. Third, if children can succeed on some tasks earlier than Piaget predicted, it influences how we interpret his theory.

However, as Piaget himself emphasized, describing development means more than just describing task factors; it means understanding the *cognitive* factors that influence the way that children approach problem-solving tasks. As pointed out in Chapter 13, Piaget described children's intellectual development in terms of their ability to apply processes (like 'compensation' and 'reversibility') in progressively more effective ways. Other researchers have also investigated the cognitive processes associated with cognitive development, but rather than following Piaget's description of mental operations, they used the *information processing approach* to describe the development of cognitive abilities.

One of the first models of information processing was put forward by Atkinson and Shiffrin (1968), who described cognitive processing in terms of three memory stores and the control processes that operate on those stores (see Figure 14.1). This model emphasized the flow of information through or between the different components. Any information in the environment that is attended to will be encoded via the *sensory register*. This will encode what is seen, heard or otherwise sensed, in full, but only for a very brief period of time before the information decays or is overwritten by new information coming into the sensory register. Some of the information from the sensory store may be selected for processing in *short-term memory*.

Atkinson and Shiffrin's (1968) model of short-term memory was of a store that could only retain a limited number of 'units' of information. More recent theorists have placed less emphasis on the 'capacity' of short-term memory and more emphasis on short-term memory as the conscious part of information processing, which is constrained by the number and the processes being carried out at the same time (Baddeley et al., 2014). Processes will vary, depending on how well practised they are. For example, a novice car driver may need all her attention just to drive the car, but for an experienced driver many aspects of driving are automatic and require little active thought—this will leave the experienced driver with available cognitive resources (perhaps to listen to the car radio and carry out a conversation at the same time as driving). Some processes (if they are relatively unpractised) may require a lot of capacity, but others (which are well learned and automatic) may make little demand on capacity. This emphasis on processing capacity has led to the original term *short-term memory* being replaced by the term *working memory* (Andrade & May, 2004; Cowan & Alloway, 2009; Henry, 2012; Schneider, 2015).

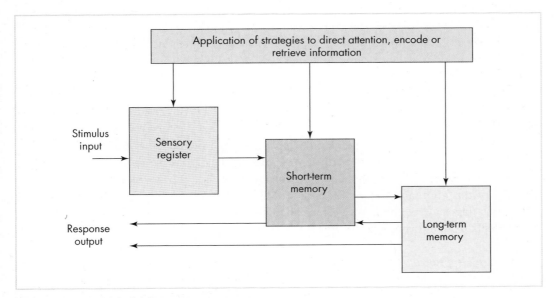

Figure 14.1 Model of information processing.

Source: Atkinson, R.C. & Shiffrin, R.M. (1968). Human memory: A proposed system and its control processes. In K.W. Spence and J.T. Spence (Eds.), *Advances in the psychology of learning and motivation, vol. 2*. New York: Academic Press.

How information is processed in working memory will determine whether it is transferred into long-term memory. Long-term memory is unlimited and retains information indefinitely, and information from that store can be retrieved and reentered into working memory. Information can be processed by various control mechanisms as it flows through the system, and such mechanisms include strategies for retaining information in working memory—these are called *encoding strategies*. We will discuss how children develop effective encoding strategies later in this chapter.

To provide an example of the flow of information through the different components, think about glancing at the front page of a newspaper for a moment and then closing your eyes. You might, very briefly in the sensory register, retain an image of the whole page, but only that part of the page that is specifically attended to (e.g. the headline) will be transferred to working memory. The headline will only be kept in working memory if it is actively processed—for instance, you may need to keep repeating the headline to retain it in working memory, or you may link the words in the headline with some information you already know in long-term memory. Such strategies increase the likelihood that the headline will be transferred to long-term memory. If some time later you want to recall the headline, you may be able to retrieve the words directly from long-term memory, or you may find that you cannot immediately remember them and you need to find some way of recalling them. You might, for example, try to think what the headline was about, or what you associated it with when you first encoded it. The latter processes are referred to as *retrieval strategies* and we will describe some of these later in the chapter.

INFORMATION PROCESSING LIMITATIONS

The flow of information is subject to many limitations. As well as attentional limitations, there are also processing limitations. For example, few adults could calculate a mathematical problem like $(123 \times 456)/78$ in their working memory. That is not because adults do not know the appropriate rules for multiplication and division, it is simply because the complexity of the calculation will exceed the processing space available in working memory. However, most adults can solve $(12 \times 34)/5$ without using a calculator, because the figures in the problem and the calculation itself can be held in working memory. But children have more limited processing abilities than adults and therefore, even if they understand multiplication and division, they may not find it possible to solve $(12 \times 34)/5$ by mental arithmetic.

Models such as Atkinson and Shiffrin's provided the basis for describing cognitive development with reference to the components described in information processing models. One early example of this approach was by Brainerd (1983), who considered how different processing limitations might affect children's performance. Brainerd's approach illustrated how some of the concepts from information processing theories might be applied to a problem-solving task.

1. *Encoding limitations*: children may not encode the appropriate information about a problem. In a problem like $(12 \times 34)/5$, a child might not encode the multiplication symbol correctly, and add the figures in the bracket rather than multiply them. Brainerd pointed out that failure in some Piagetian problem-solving tasks (e.g. those that involve part–whole relationships—see Chapter 13) may be because when children listen to the question in that task, they fail to encode the crucial information about the required comparison.

2. *Computational limitations*: children may encode all the relevant information about a problem and retain it in working memory, but they may not have appropriate strategies in long-term memory that they can apply to the encoded information. For example, they may not be able to solve the mathematical problem because they do not know a procedure for multiplying two digit numbers.

3. *Retrieval limitations*: children may have the necessary strategies in long-term memory, but when they try to retrieve the strategy from their long-term store, they retrieve an inappropriate strategy. For example, instead of retrieving the procedures for multiplication, they retrieve, in error, the procedures for division.

4. *Storage limitations*: children may have encoded all the information, and have retrieved the appropriate strategies from long-term memory, but they may not be able to retain all the relevant information in working memory while they carry out the calculation. For example, while children are calculating (12×34) they may forget the information relating to the rest of the original equation (the need to divide by 5) and be unable to complete the problem.

5. *Workspace limitations*: as working memory is limited, children will only be able to retain a few items of information at the same time. For example, if a mathematical problem only involves two digits and one calculation ($4 + 5$), this may all be held in working memory (as the two digits, the addition and the sum of the two digits). But if the problem is ($4 + 5$)/($6 + 7$), the need to retain information about several digits, addition and division might mean there is no storage space left to hold information about the subtotals that are needed to achieve the final answer.

After a consideration of these limitations, Brainerd (1983) investigated Piaget and Inhelder's (1951) 'probability judgement' task. In one version of this problem, 4- and 5-year-old children were shown 10 tokens. Seven of the tokens had a picture of a rabbit on them and three had a picture of a horse. All the tokens were placed in an opaque bag, which was shaken, and then the experimenter pulled out one of the tokens and held it in his hand so that the child could not see it. Children were asked to predict the picture on the token in the experimenter's hand. After one trial the token was replaced in the bag (without the child seeing it) and then the procedure was repeated for another four trials.

The best way to be correct in this task is always to predict that the token that will be pulled out is the one that occurs most frequently in the bag (i.e. rabbit). But Piaget and Inhelder (1951) found that young children were poor at this task—children did not consistently predict the picture with the higher frequency. Brainerd carried out a series of studies to find out why children had difficulty. He found that on the first trial, the majority of children predicted that the token taken out of the bag would have a rabbit on it. This meant that most of the children realized the need to choose the more frequent picture (and if they knew this they did not have an encoding problem). However, on the remaining four trials, the children did not go on predicting the rabbit tokens (e.g. after the first trial they might just predict the horse and rabbit tokens alternately).

Brainerd's first hypothesis was that the children had *storage limitations* so that by the second and later trials, the children had forgotten the frequency of the pictures in the bag and were simply guessing. Therefore, in a further experiment Brainerd placed a second set of seven tokens with rabbits and three tokens with horses on the table in front of the child throughout the experiment, to help children retain the relative frequency of the tokens.

However, children's performance did not change (they still did poorly after the first trial). As there was no need to store information about the frequency of the tokens (because that information was always in front of them), Brainerd assumed that something other than storage limitations was the cause of the children's difficulty.

Brainerd therefore considered what was different between the first (often successful) trial and the later (unsuccessful trials). He thought that after the first trial, the most recent information in children's working memory was their own response to the previous trial, and that this might have been influencing their predictions—for example, on the second trial children remembered that they had said rabbit (or horse) on the first trial and in recalling that response some children went on to repeat that response, and some decided to say the alternate response. In other words, they based their later predictions on the recall of their previous response, and this strategy was not related to the crucial information about the relative frequency of the tokens. Brainerd called this a retrieval problem because the children were retrieving the wrong information (their own previous response) as the basis for their predictions and ignoring the frequency information. When Brainerd changed the experimental procedure so that the most recent item in working memory (before the children made a prediction) was information about token frequency, the children were successful on all the trials.

We have described Brainerd's (1983) research in some detail because it illustrates how a model of information processing can provide the stimulus for a series of studies that identify not just whether children succeed or fail a task at a certain age, but can explain why children have difficulty with a task. In the case of the probability task, Brainerd's first studies supported Piaget and Inhelder's (1951) conclusion that young children were poor at the task, but by generating a series of hypotheses based on a theoretical model, Brainerd was able to go beyond the initial findings, identify children's retrieval difficulties and then demonstrate that when these difficulties were overcome children could perform successfully. This latter finding leads to a very different conclusion about children's ability and illustrates the need to have a specific model of the processes that may be involved in a task.

STAGE-LIKE PERFORMANCE IN INFORMATION PROCESSING

Case (1978, 1985), like Piaget, thought that cognitive development could be interpreted as a series of stages. But unlike Piaget (who described stages in the development of children's logical thinking and reasoning—see Chapter 13), Case described children's stage-like performance on particular problem-solving tasks in information processing terms. This can be exemplified by Case's analysis of Noelting's (1980) orange juice problem (see Figure 14.2).

In Noelting's problem, children were shown two sets of glasses. In each set, some of the glasses contained orange juice and some contained water. Children were also shown two empty jugs and told that the contents of one of the sets of glasses would be poured into one jug, and the other set would be poured into the second jug. The children were then asked which of the two jugs would taste more strongly of juice. For example, in Figure 14.2 one set of glasses includes a glass of orange juice and a glass of water, and the second set includes two glasses of orange juice and three of water. Children have to compare the proportion of orange juice in each set and (if they do this correctly) say that the first jug will taste more strongly of orange. Noelting described children's performance in terms of four age-related strategies.

Figure 14.2 An example of the juice problem. Children are shown each set of glasses and told that each set will be poured into a different jug. The children are asked which jug will taste more strongly of juice.

Source: Based on Noelting, G. (1980). The development of proportional reasoning and the ratio concept. *Educational Studies in Mathematics*, *11*, 217–253.

- 3–4-year-olds only considered whether orange was present or absent in each set. They could only succeed if one set of glasses had some orange in it and the other did not. If both sets included glasses of orange, they would say that both jugs would taste more strongly of orange juice.
- 5–6-year-olds chose the set that had more glasses of orange (so, in the example in Figure 14.2, they would make an incorrect prediction).
- 7–8-year-olds compared the number of glasses of water and orange in each set, and if one set had more glasses of orange than glasses of water, they said that the jug receiving that set would taste more strongly of juice. If both or neither sets had more glasses of orange, the children just guessed.
- 9–10-year-olds were able to use more appropriate strategies to select the correct set of glasses (e.g. by subtracting the number of glasses with water from the number with orange and choosing the set with the larger remainder—this works for many but not all problems).

Each of the strategies described above takes into account an additional aspect of the task, and therefore the later strategies can be applied successfully to a larger number of different problems. Case (1978) suggested that information processing limitations restricted younger children to the less effective strategies. For example, the strategy used by the 3- and 4-year-olds can be described in the following terms:

> Look for orange juice in one set of glasses. If there is orange juice say that set will taste more strongly of juice. If there is no orange juice say that it won't taste of juice.

This strategy only requires a minimum of information in working memory (the colour of the glasses in the set). Then children can turn to the other set of glasses and repeat the strategy:

> Look for orange juice in the other set of glasses. If there is orange juice say that set will taste more strongly of juice. If there is no orange juice say that it won't taste of juice.

Again, this only requires one item of information (the colour of the glasses) in working memory. Of course, this is not a very effective strategy because, as we have pointed out, it sometimes leads children to make apparently contradictory responses, such as both jugs will taste more strongly of orange juice.

The strategy used by 5- and 6-year-olds requires the children to count the number of glasses of juice in one set (and retain this number in working memory); then count the number of glasses of orange in the other set (and retain this number in working memory); then compare the two numbers and predict that the set with the greater number will taste more strongly of orange. Thus, to complete this strategy, children need to hold two items (the numbers) in working memory, as well as having the processing space to carry out the comparison of these items. The other two strategies, used by older children, each require increasing amounts of working memory capacity for completion.

Case (1985) analysed the strategies required for a number of Piagetian and other problem-solving tasks and concluded that one of the main constraints on children's performance was their information processing capacity. Other factors will also influence children's cognitive development, which we will discuss later, but if a particular problem-solving strategy requires more processing capacity than a child has available, it will be difficult for the child to apply that strategy.

Stop and Think

What different cognitive limitations might affect children's performance on problem-solving tasks?

Problem-solving Strategies

Noelting's (1980) analysis of the orange juice problem focused on the strategies that children used in attempting to solve the problem. Many such analyses are carried out after an experimenter has collected data, because then the experimenter can look for patterns in the children's performance (when they were correct, when they were incorrect, the type of errors they made and so on). Having analysed the performance, an experimenter can often suggest the likely strategies that children brought to the problem.

An alternative way of investigating children's strategies was used by Siegler (1976, 1978). He examined the way in which children of different ages attempted a balance scale task. In this task the children were shown a balance scale that already had several weights placed on either side of the fulcrum. The scale was fixed by a wedge and the children were asked which way the scale would tip if the wedge was removed. In contrast to most researchers who specify the possible task strategies that children use after testing them, Siegler considered the possible strategies prior to testing the children. He outlined four progressively more sophisticated strategies that could be used and then predicted how a child using one of those strategies would perform across a set of different balance scale problems (see Box 14.1). This meant that if a child's pattern of performance matched one that he had predicted, he could infer that the child was using a specific strategy. Older children used progressively more effective strategies to solve the balance scale problems and Siegler described children's development on this problem as a series of steps (or stages) as the children adopted more successful strategies to solve the problems.

Although Siegler described development on tasks like the balance scale in terms of steps or stages, he also suggested that this approach has limitations (Siegler, 1996). First, he pointed out that although children's performance on tasks like the balance scale can be described in

Box 14.1 Strategies of scientific reasoning

Siegler (1976) investigated the strategies that children used in Inhelder and Piaget's balance scale problem. In this task, children were shown a balance scale with four equally spaced pegs on either side of the fulcrum (see Box Figure 14.1.1). A number of weights (each of the same value) were placed on some of the pegs. While the weights were placed, the balance was held in place by a wedge. Then the child was asked to predict which side of the balance would go down, or whether it would remain in balance if the wedge was removed.

Rather than test children with the balance scale and then interpret their performance in terms of the strategies that they might have used, Siegler first considered what strategies were possible, and only then did he test children. Siegler's (1976) methodology involved four steps. First, he considered the dimensions of the balance scale problem and the potential strategies that could be used to solve it. Second, he designed a set of tasks. Third, he predicted how a child who used a specific strategy would perform on the set of tasks. Fourth, he used the set of tasks to test a large number of children at different ages to establish developmental differences in the way they approached the task.

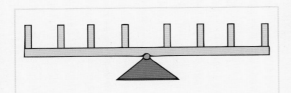

Box Figure 14.1.1 Balance scale.

Source: Adapted from Siegler, R.S. (1976). Three aspects of cognitive development. *Cognitive Psychology, 8*, 481–520.

Strategies

According to Siegler, there were four strategies that children might use (and there was also the possibility that they would have no strategy at all and just guess the answer).

- No strategy (i.e. just a guess).
- Strategy I: if there are a different number of weights, then say the side with more weights will go down. If the number of weights is the same on both sides, then say the scale will balance. (This strategy considers only the number of weights on either side of the fulcrum and ignores the distance of the weights.)
- Strategy II: if there are a different number of weights, then say the side with more weights will go down. If the number of weights is the same on both sides, then say the side with the weights furthest from the fulcrum will go down.
- Strategy III: if the number of weights and the distance of the weights from the fulcrum on both sides are equal, then predict that the scale will balance. If both sides have the same number of weights then consider the distance of the weights and say that the side with weights furthest from the fulcrum will go down. If both sides have weights at equal distance from the fulcrum, then say the side with the greater number of weights will go down. If one side has more weights and the other side has weights at greater distance from the fulcrum, then guess.
- Strategy IV: follow Strategy III, unless one side has more weights and one has weights at greater distance. In this case, calculate torques by multiplying weights times distance. Then predict that the side with the greater torque will go down.

These strategies are shown diagrammatically in Box Figure 14.1.2. As can be seen particularly well from these diagrams, each strategy incorporates the preceding strategy. In other words, each strategy is like the preceding one, but with additional components which contribute to progressively more accurate solutions to the balance problem.

Designing the tasks

Having described the possible strategies, Siegler then generated a set of different balance weight problems (these problems are shown in Box Figure 14.1.3).

1. Balance problems: have the same configuration of weights on either side of the fulcrum.
2. Weight problems: have unequal number of weights, but at the same distance on either side of the fulcrum.
3. Distance problems: have equal number of weights on both sides, but at different distances.

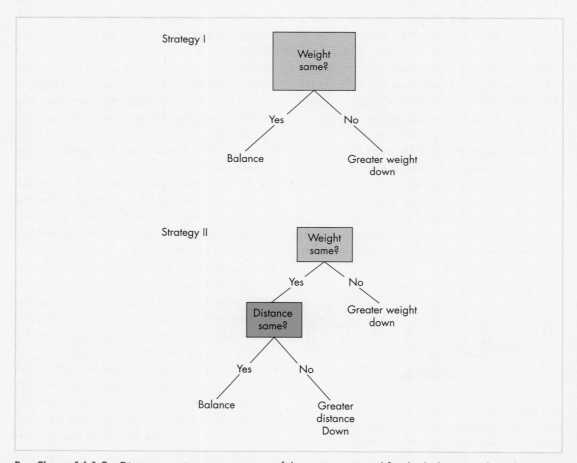

Box Figure 14.1.2 Diagrammatic representation of the strategies used for the balance scale task.

Source: Adapted from Siegler, R.S. (1976). Three aspects of cognitive development. *Cognitive Psychology, 8,* 481–520.

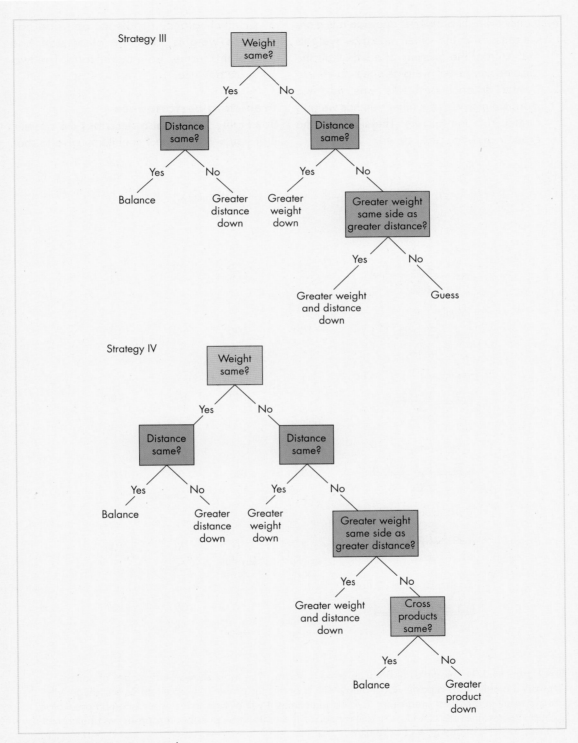

Box Figure 14.1.2 *Continued*

4. Conflict-weight problems: one side has more weights, and the other side has weights further from the fulcrum. The side with the greater number of weights goes down.

5. Conflict-distance problems: one side has more weights, and the other side has weights further from the fulcrum. The side with the greater distance goes down.

6. Conflict-balance problems: one side has more weights, and the other side has weights further from the fulcrum. The two sides balance.

Predicting performance

Box Figure 14.1.3 also describes the answer that you would expect a child to give to that

| | | Strategy | | |
	I	II	III	IV
Balance				
	100	100	100	100
Weight				
	100	100	100	100
Distance				
	0 say balance	100	100	100
Conflict (weight)				
	100	100	33 Chance	100
Conflict (distance)				
	0 say right down	0 say right down	33 Chance	100
Conflict (balance)				
	0 say right down	0 say right down	33 Chance	100

Box Figure 14.1.3 Examples of balance scale problems. The table shows percentages of correct answers if a child uses a particular strategy with a particular problem. In some cases a strategy will always result in a correct prediction (100%), sometimes it will always leads to an incorrect prediction (0%) and sometimes the child has to guess and (as there are three possible responses) will be correct, by chance, on 33% of that type of problem.

Source: Adapted from Siegler, R.S. (1976). Three aspects of cognitive development. *Cognitive Psychology*, 8, 481–520.

problem if she was using one of the four strategies. For example, if a child is applying Strategy I to the balance, weight and conflict-weight problems she will give correct answers each time. However, if she uses Strategy I with distance problems, conflict-distance and conflict-balance problems, not only will she be wrong but it is possible to predict her incorrect answer. With the set of tasks designed by Siegler, the use of each strategy will generate a different pattern of responses. In other words, if children are given a set of tasks, it is then possible to identify the strategy that they are using from the pattern of their answers.

An intriguing aspect of Box Figure 14.1.3 is that on conflict-weight problems, children who use Strategy III will perform worse than children who use the less sophisticated Strategy I. It is not often in developmental psychology that children using a less advanced problem-solving strategy are predicted to perform better than children using a more complete strategy.

Testing children

Siegler asked 5–17-year-olds to carry out balance scale problems (like the ones described above) and he found that most of them consistently used one of the expected strategies. Five-year-olds usually used Strategy I; 9-year-olds used Strategy II or III, and older children used Strategy III. Very few children used Strategy IV. Siegler also found that 5-year-olds (who nearly always used Strategy I) were correct on 89% of the conflict-weight problems, but the 17-year-olds (who generally used Strategy III) were correct on only 51% of these problems. These findings support Siegler's predictions about the use of the strategies.

Siegler's approach provides a good example of how cognitive development can be investigated by generating hypothetical models (in this case, the description of possible strategies prior to the data collection) and making specific predictions (in this example, the expected performance of children), which can then be empirically tested.

Based on material in Siegler, R.S. (1976). Three aspects of cognitive development. *Cognitive Psychology, 8*, 481–520.

---

terms of distinct and progressively more complex cognitive strategies, other tasks cannot be analysed in the same way. Second, he argued that the most important aspect of development is how children progress from one stage to another, but most researchers have focused on describing the stages and few have investigated the way in which children progress from one stage to the next. We will discuss these two points in turn.

Many researchers have used tasks that have well-defined dimensions. For example, in the juice problem (see above), children need to consider the number of glasses of juice and water in each jug, and in the balance scale task (see Box 14.1) children need to work out the weight and distance of the weight from the fulcrum. The tasks are also ones with which children are unfamiliar. Young children are unlikely to have been asked to work out the strength of a jug of juice or estimate which way a balance scale will tip. Siegler (1996) suggested that the salience of particular dimensions in these sorts of tasks might lead children to attempt just one or two particular strategies. He also pointed out that when children have had little experience of a task, they will not have had time to develop diverse strategies. On other, less novel tasks, children might not show such clearly defined strategies, and Siegler and Robinson (1982) showed that this was the case when they analysed children's strategies for adding numbers.

Siegler and Robinson (1982) gave 4- and 5-year-olds addition problems like 'How much is 1+2?'. Each child was given several problems and took part in six sessions. Some of the problems were repeated in different sessions. Siegler and Robinson found that children used four strategies. These were: (a) counting fingers (for instance, to work out 1 + 2 children would put up one finger and then two fingers and count them out loud); (b) the same strategy but without counting out loud; (c) counting out loud without using fingers; (d) when children showed no audible or visible behaviour, Siegler and Robinson classed this as 'retrieval' and assumed that children were retrieving the answers from memory. They found that only 20% of the children used one of the four strategies for all the addition problems. Rather, 23% used two strategies, 30% used three strategies and 27% used four strategies. Siegler and Robinson also found that when children were given the same problem in different sessions, a third of them used different strategies each time. This was not necessarily because children used a less sophisticated strategy the first time (e.g. counting fingers) and a more sophisticated strategy the second time (e.g. retrieval), because many children actually used a less advanced strategy the second time.

Siegler and Robinson's (1982) results demonstrated that children used different rules at the same time and even for the same problems. This stands in contrast to the more distinct and age-related strategies that can be identified on tasks like the balance scale, and led Siegler (1996) to suggest that the use of multiple strategies is most likely when children have a moderate amount of experience at a task. When tasks (like the balance scale) are unfamiliar, children may attempt to solve them using just one strategy for all examples of the task. When tasks are very familiar (e.g. adults solving addition problems), people will have established the best strategy they can, and will use that strategy consistently for all similar problems. However, when children are still learning (as in Siegler and Robinson's addition problems), they may use a range of different strategies and be willing to use several different ones at the same time. This is in contrast to the neat stage-like progression described for very unfamiliar or very familiar tasks, and led Siegler to describe the use of multiple strategies as 'overlapping waves'. He used this metaphor to capture the idea that children's progression on tasks they are still learning might involve the increase and decrease in the use of several strategies at the same time, and this metaphor is best expressed graphically—see Figure 14.3. This metaphor is in contrast to the traditional view of strategy development as a series of distinct steps or stages (see Figure 14.4).

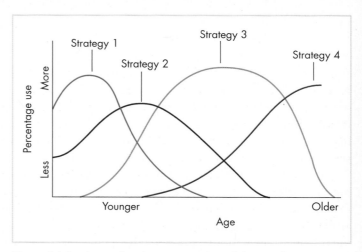

Figure 14.3 A graphical representation of the overlapping waves metaphor used by Siegler to describe children's strategy use over time. At any specific age children might be using two or more strategies.

Source: Siegler, R.S. (1996). *Emerging Minds: The Process of Change in Children's Thinking*. New York, Oxford University Press. By permission of Oxford University Press, USA.

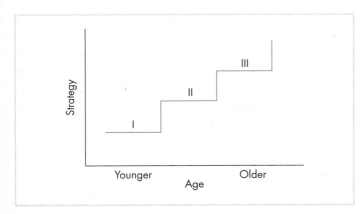

Figure 14.4 A graphical representation of children's strategy development as distinct steps or stages. This example represents the distinct stages implied in the development of better strategies in tasks like the balance scale task.

Source: Adapted from Siegler, R.S. (1996). *Emerging Minds: The Process of Change in Children's Thinking.* New York, Oxford University Press.

Siegler (1996, 2006) argued that the period when children are learning a new task is a period of rapid change as children identify and experiment with different problem-solving strategies. However, traditional methodologies for studying children's development tend to ignore these periods. The most commonly used methodologies for developmental research are cross-sectional (when several different age groups are tested) and longitudinal (when the same children are tested at intervals over a period of time). Most longitudinal studies test children at intervals of weeks or months. Such methods will identify major differences in performance, but they may not be appropriate for examining periods of rapid learning. Siegler suggested that changes in children's strategy use are best investigated by taking a *microgenetic* approach. This means studying change in children's performance as it is occurring, and this implies intensive and repeated testing of the same children over very short periods of time.

Siegler and Jenkins (1989) used the microgenetic approach to investigate the development of one particular addition strategy, called the 'min' strategy, which can be illustrated with an addition problem like 'What is 3 + 4?'. A child using the min strategy will identify the larger number and then count up by the value of the smaller number (in this case, counting '5, 6, 7' to achieve the answer). Siegler and Jenkins identified eight children aged 4–5 years who could do addition problems but did not use the min strategy. The children were given problems (that required the addition of two numbers) three times a week for 11 weeks, and their performance was assessed from videotape records and by interviewing the children about their strategies. Siegler and Jenkins found (like Siegler & Robinson, 1982) that children's strategies varied both within and between sessions. During the course of the study, all but one of the children discovered the min strategy and Siegler and Jenkins then examined the context in which it occurred for each child.

Previous researchers had suggested that the min strategy developed from children realizing that they could count from either of the numbers in the problem. For instance, in the example above (3 + 4), children might realize that they could count from 3 to 4, 5, 6, 7. Earlier researchers had assumed that children would first notice that counting from either number would be successful before realizing that counting from the larger number (the min strategy) was the most effective way to solve the problem. However, Siegler and Jenkins found that only one child in the study went from counting from either number before adopting the min strategy, and this finding contradicted earlier assumptions. Nearly all the children who discovered the min strategy did so after using a strategy that researchers had not noted before. Given a problem like 3 + 4, the children started counting at 1 to 2, 3, 4, 5, 6, 7. Soon after using this strategy, children would move to the min strategy and count from the higher number.

This was a new finding and provided some insight into the way that children progress to the min strategy.

Siegler and Jenkins's study demonstrated how the detailed investigation and analysis of children's performance over a short period of time can elicit information about strategy change. Those studies that have used the cross-sectional methodology to examine children in different age groups have been important for finding out what children can do at different ages, but say little about how children progress from one strategy to another, because changes may be subtle and short-lived. Siegler and Jenkins found that most children used the 'counting from 1' strategy only once or twice before adopting the min strategy.

However, discovering exactly how children progress to more effective strategies does not explain *why* children realize the importance of a new strategy. Siegler and Jenkins found that even after children had started to use the min strategy, they used it for only 12% of the addition problems. But halfway through the testing sessions, Siegler and Jenkins moved from just giving children sums like 3 + 4 and included ones with larger numbers like 3 + 20. For the latter additions, the min strategy is by far the most effective way to solve the problem. When faced with these additions, children used the min strategy for two-thirds of such problems, and then quickly went on to use the min strategy for all addition problems irrespective of the size of the numbers. This pattern of development suggested that children may discover new strategies and use those strategies alongside other older strategies, as implied by Siegler's (1996) wave metaphor. But as the context changes (in the above example the context changed as the difficulty of the addition problem increased), children will focus on the most effective of the several strategies they use. Once children have used their most effective strategy more frequently, that strategy is then applied to all problems. As children get older, they will develop other new strategies alongside the min strategy, and eventually will drop the min strategy and adopt further and more effective addition strategies.

The above provides a neat example of how strategy change might apply to many tasks (Siegler & Svetina, 2002). First, children may use a variety of strategies, some of which will be more or less effective, and then as the context alters, children realize the importance of using one particular strategy. This process indicates the dual role of children's increasing cognitive sophistication (developing new strategies) and the environment that creates a context in which children realize the usefulness of one particular strategy. The interaction between the child's developing cognition and the environment is a key factor in learning. We can also see the implications for education. Vygotsky stressed the importance of helping children progress with their 'zone of proximal development' (see Chapter 16) and Siegler's idea of overlapping waves is complementary to the zone of proximal development. If a child is already on the point of using a new strategy (or using a new strategy but only rarely) then just a little support from a teacher can encourage the child to focus more on that strategy and help to channel the child's learning. Piaget emphasized the importance of giving children the opportunity to explore and experiment for themselves (see Chapter 13), and as exemplified by Siegler and Jenkins's (1989) addition study, when children attempt more difficult problems they come to select the most effective strategy they have. In other words, the more children explore new problems and new contexts, the more likely they are to identify and refine their problem-solving strategies.

Eventually children will learn that for simple sums like 3 + 4 the answer is always 7, and that knowledge will become part of long-term memory. Once this information is encoded in long-term memory, there is no longer any need to calculate the answer in working memory, which reduces processing time in working memory and leaves working memory free to process other information. As children become familiar with more arithmetic problems and the answers to those problems, they can draw on ever increasing amounts of knowledge stored in long-term memory and this makes them more efficient at carrying out such tasks. The same applies in any problem-solving context, because once the solution to a problem is known from past experience, children can retrieve an appropriate response from their long-term memory. In this way, the solution to a problem becomes an automatic response, rather than one that needs processing effort to solve. Increasing age usually brings increasing knowledge, and this is one of the reasons why older children are better at most problem-solving tasks than younger children.

Stop and Think

How has the analysis of problem-solving tasks contributed to an understanding of how children's thinking develops?

Attention

It is a truism that for any information to be processed at all, it must be attended to in the first instance. One difference between young children and older children is in the ability to identify the most crucial aspects of a task and pay attention to those aspects. Vurpillot (1968) demonstrated differences in the attentional strategies of children between 3 and 9 years of age. Vurpillot showed the children drawings of two houses, each of which had six windows (see Figure 14.5). Some pairs of houses were identical, but other pairs of houses had different windows (e.g. in one house a specific window might have a blind, but the corresponding window in the other house might have curtains). Children were asked to look at the drawings and say whether the two houses were the same or different.

An appropriate strategy in this task is to look at a window in one house and then check that the corresponding window in the other house is the same, and to continue this until either a difference is found or all six windows in each house have been examined. Then you can conclude that there are no differences. While the children were looking at the houses, Vurpillot recorded their eye movements and found that all the children aged 5 years or below only examined a few windows, and made few comparisons between corresponding windows. As a result, the younger children often concluded incorrectly that the houses were

Figure 14.5 Pairs of houses used by Vurpillot (1968). Children were asked whether the houses were the same or different.

Source: Vurpillot, E. (1968). The development of scanning strategies and their relation to visual differentiation. *Journal of Experimental Child Psychology*, 6, 632–650.

the same because they had not detected differences in unchecked windows. Children from the age of 6 years were more likely to examine pairs of windows, and between 6 and 9 years of age the children used this strategy more effectively, by considering all the windows exhaustively.

If the houses were the same in Vurpillot's task, children needed to check all the pairs of windows, something that young children had difficulty doing. Young children may also have difficulty in tasks that require attention to just a selection of, rather than all, the material they are shown. Miller and Seier (1994) described a task in which children were shown 12 boxes. Six of the boxes contained a picture of an animal and six contained household objects. The boxes were not placed in any particular order, but the ones with animals had a label on the outside with a picture of a cage, and the ones with the household objects had a label with a picture of a house. Children aged 3–10 years were given half a minute to learn the positions of all the animals, and Miller and Seier made a note of which boxes the children opened during this time. The most effective strategy in this task is to attend selectively to just the six boxes that contain an animal (i.e. the boxes with a label showing a cage), and ignore the other boxes altogether because they are not relevant to the task. But 3- and 4-year-olds often opened all the boxes irrespective of their label. Older children tended to open more boxes labelled with cages, but still opened some with the house picture, and it was not until about 9 or 10 years of age that children focused exclusively on the boxes labelled with a cage.

MEMORY DEVELOPMENT

The word 'strategy' is used in two ways, either to refer to the strategies used in specific problem-solving tasks (like Noelting's juice problem or Siegler's balance scale problem) or to refer to general strategies that can be applied across a range of different tasks. Such general strategies include memory strategies like *encoding* and *retrieval* strategies (Bjorklund, 2011; Pressley & Hilden, 2006; Schneider, 2015).

Encoding Strategies

Rehearsal: This refers to the mental repetition of information. For example, if you want to remember a telephone number you can repeat it to yourself until you have a chance to write it down. To investigate children's use of rehearsal, Flavell et al. (1966) showed groups of 20 5-, 7- and 10-year-olds a set of seven pictures. The experimenters pointed to some of the pictures and told the children that they should try to remember those specific pictures. Then 15 seconds later, the children were asked to say, aloud, all the pictures they could recall. During the 15-second interval, the children were observed by a lip reader to assess what they might be saying to themselves while waiting to recall the pictures. Only two of the 5-year-olds repeated the pictures to themselves, but more than half the 7-year-olds and nearly all the 10-year-olds could be seen repeating the pictures. Flavell et al. found that children who rehearsed recalled more pictures than children who did not use rehearsal, and therefore they concluded that some age-related differences in memory might be the result of developmental differences in the use of strategies like rehearsal.

Flavell et al. were among the first researchers to investigate rehearsal and this experiment stimulated many other studies into the development of memory. However, Flavell et al.'s methodology was limited, because some children might have been rehearsing without making any observable behaviours like lip movements. McGilly and Siegler (1990) carried out an experiment like Flavell et al.'s study with similar age groups, but as well as assessing children's observable behaviour they also asked the children, after the test, to report how they had tried to remember the material. On the basis of observable behaviour, McGilly and Siegler found that children appeared to use rehearsal on 39% of the trials, but when the evidence from children's self-reports was included they found that rehearsal was used on 74% of the trials.

If children do use rehearsal (McGilly & Siegler, 1990) then why are age differences in recall found in the studies of rehearsal (Flavell et al., 1966; Kunzinger, 1985)? One reason might be that younger children do not use rehearsal as effectively as older children. Ornstein et al. (1975) asked 7-year-olds and adults to remember a list of words, which were presented at the rate of one every 5 seconds. During this task, participants were asked to say what they were thinking while they tried to remember the words. Ornstein et al. found a difference in the way that the children and adults rehearsed the words. The children's rehearsal was sometimes limited to repeating a word when it was presented, and then repeating the next word and so on. The adults grouped a number of words and rehearsed these as a group. For example, imagine a list made up of the words 'cat . . . dog . . . house . . . car . . .'. Children might try to remember this list by saying 'cat, cat, cat' and then 'dog, dog, dog' as each word is presented. In contrast, adults might begin by saying 'cat, cat, cat' and then after the presentation of the second word say 'cat, dog, cat, dog' and then 'cat, dog, house' and so on. The latter procedure is a more effective way of encoding the list, but it depends not only on the use of rehearsal but also on realizing the benefits of organizing (or 'chunking') information together to increase the likelihood of remembering it (see below).

The results from studies like Ornstein et al. (1975) suggest that developmental changes are less to do with using or not using rehearsal, and more to do with how effectively children apply the strategy. As children get older they use rehearsal in more sophisticated ways (Lehmann & Hasselhorn, 2007). The importance of using rehearsal effectively was demonstrated by Naus et al. (1977), who trained 8-year-olds to rehearse by grouping items in sets of three. In a later memory test, the 8-year-olds recalled as much information as 12-year-olds. But Naus et al.'s results beg a further question—if young children can learn and use an effective rehearsal strategy, why do they not use that strategy spontaneously? We will discuss this below, in the section on the development of memory strategies.

Organization: Grouping information together is another aspect of encoding. If information is linked together it may be encoded more effectively than unlinked information, and this effect will be greater when the information can be linked in a meaningful way. Moely et al. (1969) showed children a set of pictures that were laid out in front of them in no particular order. Within the set of pictures there were several showing animals, several showing pieces of furniture, and other categories of items. The children were asked to learn the names of all the pictures and were told that they could rearrange the pictures if they thought that would help them to remember the pictures. Moely et al. found that it was only after the age of 10 years that children realized the usefulness of rearranging the pictures into categories so that they could learn all the animals as a group, then all the furniture as a group, and so on.

Children younger than 10 years do show evidence of organizing material, but often they do so in only a partially effective way. Organizing a set of items is achieved best if the items are grouped into a small number of categories containing several items each, but young children may use a large number of categories with only a couple of items in each

(Frankel & Rollins, 1982). Like the development of rehearsal, the development of organization as a strategy may depend on children learning more sophisticated ways to use it.

Elaboration: Elaboration means making associations between items to help recall them better. For example, to remember that two words like 'fish' and 'hat' occur together in a list of items, they could be linked together in several ways. One way would be to include them in a sentence like 'the fish put her hat on', and another way would be to form a mental image of a fish wearing a hat. In general, the more unusual the image that is generated, the more likely it is that the information will be remembered. Foley et al. (1993) suggested images to 6- and 9-year-olds to help them remember pairs of words like 'ant' and 'comb'. At both ages, the children recalled the words better if they thought of images like 'the large black ant was using a comb to fix its hair' than if they thought of images like 'the black ant crawled in and out of the teeth of the comb'.

Pressley and Levin (1980) found that 7-year-olds did not use elaboration spontaneously to learn pairs of English and Spanish words, but could use elaboration if they were provided with an effective mnemonic at the time of learning the pairs. For example, if children had to learn that the word 'carta' in Spanish means 'letter' in English, they were shown a picture of a giant envelope in a cart. Given this support, the 6-year-olds learned the pairs of words nearly as well as 11-year-olds.

If children do have the potential to use elaboration with support, then developmental differences may be because, like other encoding strategies, children's use of elaboration becomes progressively more sophisticated. For example, Buckhalt et al. (1976) found that when children started to use elaboration spontaneously, they tended to use less effective elaborations than older children. Buckhalt et al. asked children to think of ways to remember pairs of words like 'broom' and 'lady'. They found that younger children used what might be called 'static' elaborations like 'the lady had a broom', but older children were more likely to use 'active' elaborations like 'the lady flew on the broom on Hallowe'en'. The latter are often more effective because they generate a more memorable and distinctive image.

Retrieval Strategies

Adults are familiar with the feeling of knowing something but not being able to recall it immediately, and most adults have learned ways to retrieve information from long-term memory. For instance, when trying to recall the name of a person, it is useful to go through the letters of the alphabet and sometimes the initial letter of the name will trigger the rest of the person's name. As with encoding strategies, the use of retrieval strategies is an ability that develops gradually. In one study of retrieval strategies, Kreutzer et al. (1975) told 5- and 10-year-old children a story about a boy who wanted to remember which Christmas he was given a puppy, and then they were asked what the boy could do to remember the correct Christmas. Possible ways to do this include working out the age of the dog, thinking about other presents received at the same time as the puppy, or going back from the most recent Christmas to each previous Christmas in turn until the one when the puppy was received. All the 10-year-olds were able to suggest at least one appropriate retrieval strategy, but only about half the 5-year-olds were able to do so.

In another study of retrieval strategies, Kobasigawa (1974) showed 6-, 8- and 11-year-olds a set of 24 pictures. The pictures showed items from eight different categories (for example, toys, musical instruments, vehicles or playground equipment). Children were shown all 24 pictures and asked to learn them, and at the same time they were shown eight cue cards that reflected the categories (for example, the cue cards showed a playpen, music book, street and park). Later the children were shown (just) the cue cards and asked to recall as many of the original pictures as they could. Only one-third of the 6-year-olds spontaneously used the cue cards as an aid, but the majority of the older groups did so, and what was of particular interest was how the children used the cues. The 6- and 8-year-olds who used the cues did so by looking at a cue card and recalling one of its associated small pictures, and then they moved on to the next cue card. In contrast, 11-year-olds looked at a cue card and tried to recall as many associated pictures as possible before moving on to the next cue. In this way, the oldest children were able to recall the majority of the small pictures effectively.

How Do Memory Strategies Develop?

Most researchers suggest that there is a gradual progression in how effectively children apply memory strategies (e.g. Buckhalt et al., 1976; Frankel & Rollins, 1982; Ornstein et al., 1975). Nonetheless, there are several studies showing that young children can be taught more effective strategies for specific memory tasks (e.g. Naus et al., 1977; Pressley & Levin, 1980; Sodian et al., 1986). Although such experiments show that children are capable of more effective strategies, a typical finding is that young children do not always apply the strategy they have learned in one task to other similar tasks. For example, Keeney et al. (1967) identified 6-year-olds who did not use rehearsal and then prompted them to use this strategy— the children were told to keep whispering the names of several items to themselves until they needed to recall them. After this instruction, the majority of the children were able to use rehearsal effectively. But they only used rehearsal in tasks when they were explicitly prompted to do so by the experimenters; they did not spontaneously apply the new strategy to other tasks.

Some researchers have suggested that young children might not use a strategy that they have been taught because they find that the strategy requires cognitive effort to use (Bjorklund & Harnishfeger, 1987). If the strategy itself takes up young children's limited processing capacity then they may not have enough capacity left to encode the material that they are trying to remember. Bjorklund and Harnishfeger examined 8- and 12-year-olds' ability to use organization. Children were given a list of items that could be recalled in categories. Children were trained in the use of an organizational strategy that emphasized the usefulness of considering which items could be grouped together at encoding. When Bjorklund and Harnishfeger tested the children's recall, they found that when the older children used the strategy their recall improved significantly, but using the strategy did not improve the younger children's recall. Bjorklund and Harnishfeger suggested that the lack of improvement in the younger children's recall was because the cognitive processing they needed to apply the strategy left the children too little processing capacity in working memory to encode additional items. Such an interpretation would explain why young children are capable of learning a strategy in experimental contexts (e.g. Keeney et al., 1967) but do not use the same strategy outside those contexts. If children attempt to use a strategy that does not result in improved recall they will have little incentive to use it. As children's processing capacity improves with age, they will have the capacity to use strategies without detriment to the material they are encoding.

As well as increased processing capacity, older children also have other abilities that contribute to strategy use and successful recall. For example, to employ a strategy like elaboration, children need to make memorable connections between diverse words or items.

Compared to younger children, older children have more general knowledge and may therefore be better at inventing useful mnemonics for elaboration. Similarly, older children may use their greater knowledge to group items in better and more effective ways when using strategies like organization. The importance of knowledge will be discussed below.

As children get older they use an increasing number of memory strategies (rather than just one) in a single task, and the more strategies children use, the more information they encode successfully (Coyle & Bjorklund, 1997). In addition, older children usually know more about their own abilities and are therefore better able to assess when a strategy will be effective. Knowing about one's own abilities is called *metacognition*.

Stop and Think

Consider all the memory strategies you use to remember information—could all your memory strategies be categorized under the types of strategies described in this chapter?

METACOGNITION

Metacognition refers to a person's awareness of his or her own cognitive abilities and limitations. For example, most adults know that they can only hold six or seven items in working memory at one time. Adults know that to retain information for more than a short time, it is necessary to process that information in such a way that it is retained in long-term memory. Adults also know that encoding information can be affected by the learning context. An awareness of one's own memory capacity, processes and limitations is an understanding that develops gradually (Joyner & Kurtz-Costes, 1997).

Awareness of learning context: Young children may know that learning and remembering can be affected by various factors. Wellman (1977) showed 3–5-year-olds pairs of pictures of variables that might influence learning and recall. For example, one pair (about number of items) showed a boy who had three objects to remember and a second picture with a boy who had to remember 18 objects. Another pair (about distraction) showed a boy in a quiet room and another boy in a room with a noisy radio and noisy pets; and another pair (about age) showed a drawing of a baby and a drawing of an adult. By 5 years of age children understood most of these factors—they were able to choose the picture that indicated when recall was likely to be better.

Awareness of capacity: Flavell et al. (1970) showed children cards with up to 10 pictures on them and asked them how many pictures they thought they could remember. The children were later given a test to find out how many pictures they could actually remember. Young children were unrealistic in the number they said that they would remember. Four- and 5-year-olds actually recalled only three or four pictures, but thought they would be able to recall at least eight pictures. It was only after about the age of 9 years that the majority of children made accurate predictions about the number of items they were likely to remember.

How do children develop a better understanding of their own memory capacity? They may learn from experience. Kail (1990) cited a study by Markman, who showed 5-year-olds a set of items, asked the children how many they thought they could remember, and then tested their actual recall. Markman repeated this procedure several times with the same children and found that with repeated testing, they became more realistic about how many items they could remember. Children may also learn about memory by considering how well other people can recall information. For example, Yussen and Levy (1975) asked 4- and 8-year-olds to estimate how many items they could remember (from a large number of items that they were shown). The children were also told what an average child of their own age would be able to recall, and this information helped the 8-year-olds to make realistic estimates about their own ability. The information had little effect on the 4-year-olds, who may not have realized that knowing how other 4-year-olds performed had implications for their own performance.

Awareness of strategies: Children must also become aware of the usefulness of memory strategies and which ones are the most appropriate for a particular task. Kreutzer et al. (1975) asked 5-, 6-, 8- and 10-year-olds how they would remember to take their skates to school. The strategies suggested by the children could be divided into several categories: using the skates as a direct reminder (e.g. putting them with other things to be taken to school); using an external aid (e.g. writing a note and putting it where it would be seen); relying on someone else's memory (e.g. asking parents to remind them); or just relying on their own memories. The older children could suggest more different types of strategy, and were more likely to suggest the most effective ones.

Just as children need to monitor their own performance to develop a better awareness of their capacity (see above), so children need to consider their performance if they are to work out whether using memory strategies is useful or not. Ringel and Springer (1980) taught 8–9-year-olds how to use an organizational strategy in a picture learning task. The children were told how to put the pictures in particular groups that would help them remember the pictures. The children learned this strategy and their recall increased. Ringel and Springer gave some (but not all) of the children feedback on how their performance had improved. Then all the children were given a new memory task, one in which the grouping strategy would also be effective. The children who had received the feedback did apply the grouping strategy to the new task. In other words, when children became aware that the memory strategy led to better recall, they realized its appropriateness for other, similar tasks. In contrast, many of the children who had not received the feedback failed to use the grouping strategy in the new task. Ringel and Springer's results indicated the importance of feedback from carrying out tasks, and the importance of children realizing the relationship between applying a strategy and performing better as a result.

KNOWLEDGE AND MEMORY DEVELOPMENT

An important aspect of memory development is the knowledge that children can bring to bear on a memory task—knowledge here does not just mean a knowledge of memory strategies, but children's general knowledge and experience. As children learn more, they can build up a rich information base and newly learned information can be linked to the known information in a more meaningful and effective way. As children know more, they become better at processing and encoding novel information that can be related to preexisting knowledge.

The importance of knowledge was demonstrated by Chi (1978), who compared the memory of children who were experienced chess players with the memory of adults who knew how to play chess but were not particularly proficient. Both groups were asked to carry out two memory tasks; in one they were asked to learn lists of 10 digits, and in the other they were asked to memorize chessboard positions with an average of 22 pieces. The adults were better at remembering the digits, but the children were much better at learning the chess positions. It is unusual for children to perform better than adults in a memory task, and Chi argued that the children's greater knowledge of chess contributed to their performance. As they were familiar with chess positions, it may have been easier for them to 'chunk' groups of pieces into meaningful patterns and encode them more effectively than the less experienced adult chess players. This advantage only applied to learning chess positions, and indicated the importance of having an established knowledge base that was directly relevant to the task.

Other researchers have also demonstrated that if children have established information in a particular domain of knowledge, it is easier for them to encode new information related to that domain (Schneider et al., 1989). For example, Schneider and Bjorklund (1992) divided a number of 7–9-year-olds into a group who knew a lot about soccer and a group who only knew a little. The children were asked to learn two sets of drawings. One set included drawings of unrelated items and the other set included drawings that were related to soccer. There was no difference between the two groups in their recall of unrelated items, but the group who knew more about soccer was better at remembering the related items. Such studies have demonstrated how relevant knowledge can increase the likelihood of information being learned successfully.

Bjorklund et al. (1990) suggested that having good knowledge of a subject allows a child to recognize and understand information about that subject more readily, and therefore more processing capacity remains in working memory. Having more capacity leads to more effective or more extensive encoding. In other words, as children get older they have more information and they can make more links and connections between that information. Over time these connections will become automatic and require little explicit processing. Therefore strategies like grouping and elaboration become easier to apply, and as they become easier more information can be encoded successfully.

CONSTRUCTIVE MEMORY AND KNOWLEDGE

Constructive memory refers to a person's ability to infer, extrapolate or invent information that might never have been directly experienced. Suppose a person hears sentences like 'The box is to the right of the tree' and 'the chair is on top of the box'. If that person is later given several similar sentences and asked to say which ones they heard previously, they may be convinced that a sentence like 'The chair is to the right of the tree' is one they heard before. From the original information, people may infer the scene being described and then come to believe that a sentence that includes information corresponding to the inferred scene must be one that they had heard previously. In this example, constructive memory leads to an incorrect inference.

Brown et al. (1978) showed that children can make false inferences. They told 7- and 12-year-olds a story about an invented group of people called the Targa. All the children heard the same story, but half were told that the Targa were Eskimos and half were told that the Targa lived in the desert. Later, the children were asked to retell the story from memory. Brown et al. examined the recalled stories for any intrusions that were related to assumptions about where the Targa lived. For example, the original story included a reference to bad weather, and some of the children who had been told that the Targa were Eskimos recalled this reference as a mention of cold conditions. But the children who thought that the Targa lived in the desert recalled it as a reference to hot weather. The older children made many more of this type of error than the younger children. Brown et al. suggested that the intrusions were due to the children introducing information from knowledge they already had about Eskimos or desert people, and the larger number of intrusions by the older children reflected their greater knowledge of such cultures.

Constructive memory is related to 'scripts' and 'schema'. The term 'script' was used by Schank and Abelson (1977) to describe a sequence of actions that are appropriate in a particular context and which lead to a specific goal. For example, you might have a script for going to a restaurant, and this would include an expected sequence of actions involving specific aspects of the restaurant. The script would include sequences for entering (locating a table, sitting down, etc.); ordering (reading menu, speaking to the waiter, etc.); eating (being served, eating courses in expected sequence, etc.); and leaving (paying bill, leaving a tip, etc.). Each part of the script can be thought of as a 'slot' that needs to be filled, with both obligatory and optional actions. For example, it would be obligatory to order before eating, but leaving a tip might depend on how much you liked the service. Adults may have any number of scripts relating to different events. They are important because without generalized script knowledge, it would be difficult to function in new contexts. When we go into almost any new restaurant, most of what happens can be predicted from a script derived from previous visits to other restaurants.

Do children structure their knowledge of the world as scripts? Nelson and Gruendel (1981) investigated eight preschool children's scripts by asking them what happened in different eating contexts (at lunch in their day care centre, eating dinner at home and going to McDonald's). Most of the children mentioned the same actions for each event, and focused on main actions. For example, children typically said they ate food, but did not usually specify what they ate—in other words, they reported the events as if they had an 'open slot' that could be filled with more specific information if that was required. All the children reported, without error, the sequence of actions involved in eating a meal, with the significant exception that children reported paying for food at McDonald's after eating it. This error suggests that children were referring to script-based knowledge about what it means to go out for food, because at nearly all restaurants, payment is made at the end of a meal but the procedure at McDonald's is an exception. On the one hand, children's ability to develop scripts is important in structuring their experience in such a way that they can use and adapt their knowledge of previous events to make sense of similar, but novel events. On the other hand, a dependence on script-based knowledge can lead to inaccurate assumptions when recalling information, if specific events do not correspond to the script (as in the McDonald's example). With age and experience, children's scripts become more elaborate, and they become better at distinguishing specific events from generalized script knowledge (Fivush, 1997).

A schema is similar to a script because it refers to an organized grouping of knowledge, but unlike a script, the term 'schema' denotes what is known (for example) about a scene, a place or an object. A schema can generate expectations about what a scene should include. For instance, a schema for a kitchen might include 'slots' for sink, cooker, refrigerator, table and so on. Even young children can have established schema for objects or places that are well known. Blades and Banham (1990) asked children to learn a realistic model of a kitchen.

The model included 10 items of typical kitchen furniture, but it did not include a cooker. When the children had learned the model layout, all the items were removed and placed in a box with an additional 10 items of toy furniture (for example, a bed, an armchair, bookshelves). These additional items included a cooker. The children were asked to use the box of toy furniture to reconstruct the model kitchen from memory as accurately as possible. The reconstruction was generally accurate, and very few of the children included non-kitchen items in their models. However, nearly two-thirds of the children included the cooker in their reconstructions. Blades and Banham suggested that the inclusion of the cooker indicated that children's reconstructions were based not only on recall of the model they had learned, but also on their knowledge, or schema, about kitchens in general.

Generating schemas and scripts is an important way to represent knowledge and to use that knowledge effectively to make inferences and predictions about the world. However, in using schema-based knowledge, it is also important to retain flexibility, because there may sometimes be exceptions to the schema (e.g. paying for food before eating it at McDonald's, or kitchens without cookers) and this flexibility may only develop with age and experience (Nelson, 1986). As Kail (1990, p. 95) said:

> Knowledge is a double-edged sword. On the one hand, knowledge allows us to understand novel versions of familiar experiences (e.g. going to a restaurant) that would be completely uninterpretable if knowledge consisted only of specific previous experiences. On the other hand, knowledge does so at the cost of introducing some distortions into our perception of experiences and our later recall of those experiences.

 Stop and Think

Think of ways in which memory strategies, metamemory and knowledge might interact to help or hinder children's accurate recall of information.

SUMMARY OF THE INFORMATION PROCESSING APPROACH

In the previous sections we described some examples of the information processing approach to the study of children's cognitive development. The emphasis of this approach is on the mechanisms that children bring to bear in any task, coupled with an appreciation of the limitations that might affect children's performance. The research related to the information processing approach includes detailed studies of children's performance in specific tasks (see Box 14.1) as well as investigating the more general processes (such as memory strategies) that might be applied across a range of different tasks. Researchers in the information processing tradition attempt to explain developmental change with reference to a number of interrelated factors. These include, for example, changes in children's ability to focus attention; changes in children's processing capacity as they mature; the development of memory strategies; the ability to apply progressively more sophisticated strategies in a particular task; the growth of children's knowledge base (i.e. the development of long-term memory); and children's increasing awareness of their own abilities (i.e. their metacognitive abilities).

CHILDREN'S EYEWITNESS RESEARCH

Much of the research into children's memory has focused on the development of memory capacity and strategies. Such research can be carried out successfully using well-established and appropriate paradigms—for example, asking children to learn lists of words, remember the names of pictures or recall stories they have heard. However, the focus of memory research has since moved away from studies about children's strategies to investigations of how children recall real life events (Schneider, 2015). In particular, researchers have investigated memory development in the context of children's ability to give accurate testimony about events that they have witnessed. These investigations were driven by the realization that more, and younger, children were taking part in court proceedings. One of the reasons for children's greater involvement in courts was a growing awareness about the frequency of child abuse and the need to bring abusers to court. The nature of child abuse often means that the child himself or herself may be the only witness that the prosecution can call on for evidence (Lamb et al., 2008).

In the past, children were rarely called as witnesses, because there was a general belief that children would be unreliable when giving testimony, and it is only comparatively recently that researchers have investigated how well children recall real-life events (Ceci & Bruck, 1995; Odegard & Toglia, 2013). In one of the first studies of its kind, Marin et al. (1979) tested the recall of 6-, 9- and 13-year-olds and adults for a brief staged incident (an argument between two people). A few minutes after seeing the event, participants were given an unexpected recall test. They were asked to recall as much as they could about the incident, answer 20 objective questions about it, and then pick out a photograph (from a set of six) of one of the people who took part in the argument.

In free recall, the youngest children gave little information about the event (only one or two items), but there was an age-related increase in the number of items of information recalled (the adults mentioned seven or eight items). However, the youngest participants made virtually no errors in free recall, but on average the adults gave approximately one incorrect item of information in free recall. In other words, the children said very little but what they did say was nearly always accurate, and this finding has been replicated in many studies of children's memory for events, because in free recall young children say very little but their reports are generally accurate if they have not been given deliberately misleading information by an interviewer (see below).

The most surprising result from Marin et al. (1979) was that there was no difference between the age groups for the objective questions—all groups answered three-quarters of the questions correctly. Nor were there any age differences for the photograph recognition task. The results from Marin et al. demonstrated that children could be as accurate as adults in reporting information about an event, at least when answering specific objective questions about it. This finding contradicted the earlier assumptions that children would be poor eyewitnesses.

However, Marin et al.'s experiment was limited in two ways. First, the participants were only exposed to a brief incident lasting a few seconds, and the task may have been so difficult that all age groups did poorly and this could have masked developmental differences. Second, Marin et al. only asked a single misleading question (and found that about half of each age group answered it correctly). Nonetheless, their study was an important stimulus for later experiments, most of which did confirm Marin et al.'s original findings.

One such experiment was by Goodman and Reed (1986), who used a more elaborate event and then asked 6-year-olds and adults objective and leading questions about it. The participants were told that they were taking part in an experiment about motor skills (i.e. physical movement) and were introduced to a confederate of the experimenters who asked them to copy a series of arm movements. Four days later, the participants were given a surprise recall test. They were asked for free recall and to say everything they could about the event, and they were shown five pictures and asked to pick out the confederate. They were also asked 17 objective questions (e.g. 'What colour was the man's hair?' or 'Did the man have a ring on?') and four leading questions (e.g. 'The man was wearing a sweater, wasn't he?' or 'Was the man wearing a watch on his right or left hand?').

Goodman and Read found that in free recall, the adults reported three times more information than the 6-year-olds. But, as Marin et al. (1979) found, although the adults said more in free recall, they also reported more inaccurate information than the children. On the identification task, 95% of the 6-year-olds picked out the confederate's picture correctly, which was better than the adults (74%). There was no difference in the accuracy of 6-year-olds and adults on the objective questions. This replicated Marin et al.'s (1979) finding for 6-year-olds and confirmed that children of this age could answer questions accurately. In summary, when children were asked objective questions that required brief one-word answers or yes/no responses, they could report information as well as adults could. (Later we will say more about the effects that the type of questioning can have on children's responses.) However, Goodman and Reed found that the children were more likely than the adults to give incorrect answers to the misleading questions.

This pattern of findings is a common one in most of the more recent research. Young children generally recall less about an event than adults do, but if children are asked clear and unbiased questions they can be quite accurate. Children become much less accurate if they are given deliberately misleading questions, something that did happen in the past (Ceci & Bruck, 1995), or accidentally misleading questions. Unfortunately, there are many circumstances when a question can be accidently misleading, even when an interviewer is trying to be objective (Eisen et al., 2002; Lamb et al. 2008; Poole & Lamb, 1998), and this is the most serious problem in interviewing children. Even though an adult might not recognize any ambiguity in a phrase, a child might interpret that phrase in a different way from the way the interviewer intended. Much of the psychological research into children's testimony has investigated when and how seriously children can be misled.

CHILDREN'S SUGGESTIBILITY

Children are easily misled. Leichtman and Ceci (1995) demonstrated this in an elaborate study in which they interviewed 3–6-year-olds repetitively about an event. The event was a visit by 'Sam Stone' to their classroom. This visit involved no more than Sam Stone walking round the classroom and saying a few words. When children were later interviewed in a neutral and objective way about what had happened during the visit, they were nearly always correct in reporting details. But if the children were given misleading questions that implied that Sam Stone had damaged a book and a toy, they began to report that such events had actually happened. Leichtman and Ceci also introduced a condition in which children were told (in advance of the event) that Sam Stone was a careless and clumsy man. Some of the children who had been given this 'stereotypical' information also came to believe, incorrectly, that they had seen Sam Stone damage the items. In other words, even though Sam Stone had done nothing but walk around the classroom, interviewers who used suggestive questions and suggestive information led the children into saying that they had seen things happen that had never been part of the event. This study is summarized in Box 14.2.

Box 14.2 The effects of stereotypes and suggestions on preschoolers' reports

Leichtman and Ceci (1995) were interested in the suggestibility of young children. They pointed out that many researchers had found that, compared to older children and adults, young children are much more susceptible to misleading and suggestive questions. However, Leichtman and Ceci noted that these findings were derived mainly from small laboratory-based experiments in which children were interviewed just once. They argued that it was difficult to extrapolate from these studies to the sort of interviews that children experience in forensic and other contexts when they may undergo many repeated interviews over a period of weeks or months. At the time of this study it was common for children to experience many interviews about the same event. Partly as a result of research like this study, the procedures for interviewing children in many countries have been changed; for example, children in the UK are now interviewed as few times as possible (e.g. Ministry of Justice, 2011)—see below.

Leichtman and Ceci also discussed court cases in which children's testimony had been influenced because adults had earlier told the children that the accused was a 'bad man'. For these reasons, Leichtman and Ceci investigated the effects of multiple interviews and stereotypical information on children's recall and suggestibility.

Ninety 'early preschoolers' (3- and 4-year-olds) and 86 'older preschoolers' (5- and 6-year-olds) took part in the study. Roughly equal numbers of each age group took part in four conditions.

All the children experienced the same event. A stranger visited their classroom during a story-telling session and was introduced as Sam Stone. He said hello to the teacher and commented on a story that was being read by saying, 'I know that story; it's one of my favourites!'. He walked round the sides of the classroom and then left the room, waving goodbye. Sam Stone's visit lasted for 2 minutes.

There were four conditions in the experiment.

1. *Control condition*: children were not given any information about Sam Stone prior to his visit. These children were interviewed once a week for 4 weeks after the visit. They were asked what Sam Stone had done during the visit, but they were not given any suggestions about Sam Stone or his visit.
2. *Stereotype condition*: each week for 4 weeks *before* Sam Stone visited the classroom, the children were given information about him.

He was described as a well-meaning but clumsy person. For example, the children were told: 'You'll never guess who visited me last night. That's right, Sam Stone! And guess what he did this time? He asked to borrow my Barbie [doll] and when he was carrying her down the stairs, he accidentally tripped and fell and broke her arm. That Sam Stone is always getting into accidents and breaking things! But it's okay, because Sam Stone is very nice and he is getting my Barbie doll fixed for me.' After Sam Stone's visit, the children in the stereotype condition were treated in exactly the same way as children in the control condition (i.e. they received the four neutral interviews each week following the visit).

3. *Suggestion condition*: children in this condition did not receive any information about Sam Stone before his visit, but during the four interviews *after* his visit they were given erroneous suggestions. In the first of the four interviews, they were shown a book with a torn page and asked who they thought might have ripped it. Then they were shown a dirty teddy bear and asked who they thought had made it dirty. In the second interview they were shown the torn book again and given leading questions like, 'Remember when Sam Stone ripped the book? Did he rip it on purpose or by accident?'. Then they were shown the dirty teddy bear again and asked questions like, 'When Sam Stone got the bear dirty was he in the classroom, the hallway, or the bathroom?'. Children heard three leading questions about the book and three about the teddy bear. In the third and fourth interview, the children were also asked similar questions.

4. *Stereotype plus suggestion condition*: this group received both the stereotype information before Sam Stone's visit (like condition 2)

and the suggestive questions in the four interviews after the visit (like condition 3).

All the children were give a further interview 10 weeks after Sam Stone's visit. This interview was carried out by a new interviewer. The children were asked what had happened when Sam Stone had visited the classroom; whether they had 'heard something' about the book or the teddy bear, and whether they had seen Sam Stone do anything to those items. If children did say they had seen Sam do something to the book or the bear, they were asked a further question to find out how sure they were: 'You didn't really see him do this, did you?'. The percentage of children in each condition who gave incorrect answers is shown in Box Table 14.2.1. The children in the control condition (especially the older ones) rarely gave incorrect answers. They described what happened when Sam Stone visited their classroom without inventing events that did not happen. In all the other conditions children gave more incorrect answers than in the control condition.

Leichtman and Ceci used 2 (age) × 4 (group) multivariate analyses of variance (MANOVA) to analyse any differences in the children's answers about what happened during Sam Stone's visit (the row labelled 'made errors' in Box Table 14.2.1). There were effects for age and for group. Taking all the conditions together, the 5–6-year-olds were less likely than the 3–4-year-olds to say that events had happened when they had not. Those in the control group were less likely to invent events than those in the stereotype group, who were less likely to invent events than those in the suggestion group, who in turn were less likely to invent events than those in the stereotype plus suggestion group. In other words, the more strongly that children had been given suggestions about Sam Stone's behaviour, the more likely they were to

Box Table 14.2.1 Percentage of responses from each condition and age group.

| | (a) Control | | (b) Stereotype | | (c) Suggestions | | (d) Stereotype plus suggestions | |
	3–4 yrs (%)	5–6 yrs (%)	3–4 yrs (%)	5–6 yrs (%)	3–4 yrs (%)	5–6 yrs (%)	3–4 yrs (%)	5–6 yrs (%)
Made errors	10	4	37	18	50	38	72	37
Said seen	5	0	18	10	38	11	44	12
Maintained	2.5	0	10	2.5	12	9	21	6

Note: The row labelled 'Made errors' shows the percentage of incorrect responses children made to the questions about what Sam Stone did (rip the book or dirty the teddy bear). The row labelled 'Said seen' shows the percentage of incorrect responses when children were asked if they had actually seen Sam Stone do either of the actions. The row labelled 'Maintained' shows the percentage of responses in which children continued to say that they had seen something even after being asked, 'You didn't really see him do this, did you?'. (NB: Leichtman and Ceci did not provide a data table and therefore some of the percentages are taken from the graphs they included in their paper. For this reason, some figures are approximate.)
Source: Leichtman, S.D. & Ceci, M.J. (1995). The effects of stereotypes and suggestions on preschoolers' reports. *Developmental Psychology, 31,* 568–578.

believe that they had seen him do damage to the book or the teddy bear. Leichtman and Ceci concluded that repeated suggestions and stereotypical information could result in young children inventing events that had not actually occurred. In particular, a combination of both suggestion and stereotypical information had the greatest effect, especially on the younger age group.

As Leichtman and Ceci showed, some of the children said that they had actually seen the invented events, and a few maintained that an invented event had taken place even after being asked a question like, 'You didn't really see him do this, did you?'. Some of the children did not just answer 'yes' or 'no' to a suggestive question about what Sam Stone had done, but elaborated details. For example, one claimed that Sam Stone had taken the teddy bear into a bathroom and soaked it in hot water before marking it with crayon. Such invented detail might lead an interviewer to believe that the child really had witnessed the event.

Leichtman and Ceci also investigated whether adults could discriminate between children who were reporting events correctly or incorrectly. They showed videotapes of three interviews to 119 researchers and clinicians. The videotapes showed three children during their final interview in the stereotype plus suggestion condition. Child 1 was shown saying that Sam Stone had tossed things in the air, ripped a book and made the teddy bear dirty, and had visited the classroom with 'another Sam Stone'. Child 2 said only that Sam Stone had visited the classroom, said hello, and walked round the classroom (all of which was accurate). Child 3 initially said only that Sam Stone had walked around the classroom, but when asked the suggestive questions the child agreed that Sam Stone had ripped the book and put ice cream on the teddy with a paintbrush while in the school yard.

The adults were told that all the children had witnessed the same visit by Sam Stone, and were then asked to decide what had happened during the visit from the children's reports. The adults were asked to rate (on a seven-point scale) the events described by the children as ones that had definitely occurred or ones that had definitely not. The adults rated Child 1 as the most credible, Child 3 as the next most credible and Child 2 as the least credible. In other words, the two children who included inaccurate details were rated as more credible than the child who gave the perfectly accurate account. The adults were unable to identify which of the specific events reported by children were accurate or not. The adults usually believed the reports of items being tossed in the air and the book being ripped. They could not decide about the teddy bear, but were unlikely to think that there had been two visitors both named Sam Stone.

Leichtman and Ceci suggested that Child 1 and Child 3 were seen as more credible because they provided more detail about the event. As Leichtman and Ceci (1995, p. 575) conclude, 'the accuracy of children's reports is extremely difficult to discern when children have been subjected to repeated erroneous suggestions over long retention intervals, especially when coupled with the induction of stereotypes'.

This study has implications for the way in which children are interviewed. In the past, children who had witnessed a crime, or had been the victims of a crime, might have been interviewed many times about the events that had happened (e.g. by parents, teachers, social workers, police officers, lawyers and so on), but now children are interviewed as little as possible. Teachers and other professionals should know not to engage in a lengthy discussion with any child who seems to be reporting a genuine case of abuse. Rather than talk much to the child, they should contact specialist police officers as soon as possible to avoid a child experiencing multiple interviews. The specialist officers should make sure that a child can be interviewed in one session that is appropriately videotaped and recorded (Ministry of Justice, 2011) (see this chapter).

One positive aspect of Leichtman and Ceci's findings was the performance of the children in the control group. The children in this group received no suggestions about Sam Stone nor about the event and this group was, in general, quite accurate in reporting what happened. This reinforces the findings from several studies referred to in this chapter—children can be good witnesses if they are questioned appropriately.

Based on material in Leichtman, M.D. & Ceci, S.J. (1995). The effects of stereotypes and suggestions on preschoolers' reports. *Developmental Psychology, 31*, 568–578.

In another study, Ceci et al. (1994) gave preschool children repeated interviews for several weeks. The researchers asked the children's parents for details of distinctive events that had actually happened to the child (e.g. a particular accident or injury). Ceci et al. also included events that had never happened (e.g. getting a finger caught in a mousetrap and having to go to hospital for treatment). During each interview, the interviewer read out brief details of actual or invented events, asked the children to think hard about the events and prompted them to think about any details associated with it (e.g. who else might have been around at the time). The children were asked to consider the same events in interviews each week for

10 weeks. Then, in the 11th week, each child was questioned by a new interviewer. The new interviewer went through each event and asked the children if the event had really happened. Ceci et al. found that more than half the children claimed that at least one of the invented events had actually taken place. Some children even provided elaborate 'details' of the fictitious events; for example, they explained how they got their fingers caught in the mousetrap, or who took them to the hospital or what sort of treatment they had had. Ceci et al. (1994) demonstrated that just getting young children to think about invented events during repeated interviews led some of them to believe that the invented event had really happened.

The examples above, with young children, included extensive repeated interviewing and suggestions about brief events that did not happen but might have done (a toy being damaged or an accident at home). Other researchers have demonstrated that quite complex events can also be suggested, even to much older children. Loftus and Ketcham (1994) gave an example of two brothers, Jim and his younger brother Chris (aged 14). Unknown to Chris, Jim invented an event that supposedly happened in the past about Chris being lost in a shopping mall when he was 5 years old. The invented description included information about the mall and Chris's emotional state, and included a description of the man who was supposed to have found Chris and brought him back to his parents. Each day, for a few days after the event was first described to him, Chris was asked to write down how he had felt about being lost. Then 2 weeks later Chris was interviewed about the event. Chris then provided a lengthy description, including some of the details he had been told and many others that he had invented, including, for example, 'facts' about man who had found him, such as the man's hair colour and the colour of the shirt the man had been wearing. Chris also described emotions and thoughts about how scared he had been and how he remembered thinking he would never see his family again. Chris was asked how he rated his memory of being lost and he rated the memory as very clear. Both children and adults 'recalling' childhood events can be susceptible to suggestions and suggestive questioning (Ceci & Bruck, 1995; Davies & Dalgleish, 2001).

Quite unlikely events have been suggested by some experimenters. For example, Otgaar et al. (2009) interviewed 8-year-olds about their first day at school, when they had been 4 years of age. The interview included accurate information about that day (obtained from the children's parents) and a false suggestion that the children had been abducted by a UFO. Children were also shown an invented 4-year-old newspaper article about UFOs being seen in the children's town at the time. Even during a first interview, some of the children agreed with the false suggestion that they had been abducted, and a few maintained this belief in a later interview.

Why are Children Misled?

There are several reasons why children might be suggestible (Ceci & Bruck, 1995). They may encode less information about an event than adults, for example, if they have less effective strategies for attention (Miller & Seier, 1994; see above). Or children may attend to information but, because of working memory constraints, encode that information less completely than adults. Such limitations may mean that children have more 'gaps' in memory that can be filled with information implied by suggestive questioning. Even if children encode information, it may be encoded only weakly, for example, because they have fewer schema and less existing knowledge to which they can link new information (see above). Some researchers have found that if some aspects of an event are only weakly encoded, it is those aspects that are most open to suggestive questioning (Warren et al., 1991).

Children may also have more difficulty than adults at distinguishing information that they have actually experienced and different information that was mentioned during a later interview. For example, suppose a child saw a man with a brown shirt during an event. Perhaps during a first interview about the event the child is asked, 'Did the man have a red shirt?'. The child may well reply accurately that the man had a brown shirt. However, at a second interview the child might be asked again, 'What colour was the man's shirt?'. At this point, the child has to realize that she actually saw a brown shirt, but only heard that the man might have had a red shirt during the first interview. The ability to recall the origin of memories is called *source monitoring* (Roberts, 2000). Young children sometimes have difficulty recalling the sources of their memories and this means that they may confuse something that actually happened with something that they had only thought about. For example, Foley and Johnson (1985) compared the source monitoring of 6-year-olds and adults. The participants were asked to either carry out several brief actions (e.g. wave goodbye) or just to imagine performing such actions. A few minutes later the participants were given a surprise memory test and asked which actions they had really carried out. Foley and Johnson found that the adults were more accurate than the children at recalling which actions they had actually performed. Sometimes the 6-year-olds thought that they had actually done something that they had only imagined doing (and vice versa). Source confusions may be one of the reasons why some children in Ceci et al. (1994) believed that events that they had only thought about during the course of the interviews had actually happened.

As well as cognitive factors (like encoding and source monitoring), there are other factors associated with the conduct of an interview that may influence children's suggestibility. These include questions that are deliberately suggestive, for example, when an interviewer asks a misleading question to obtain a particular answer ('The man had a red shirt on, didn't he?'). There may be other questions that, because of their structure, may result in children giving inappropriate answers. When children are asked questions with a limited choice of answers (e.g. ones that seem to require a yes or no response: 'Was the man wearing a red shirt?'), they may be tempted to guess an answer. If children do not appreciate that they should say 'don't know' to questions they do not understand or cannot answer, they may also be vulnerable to suggestive questioning.

Children may think that if an adult asks a question there should be an answer, and they will try to give a response. Hughes and Grieve (1980) asked 5- and 7-year-olds questions like 'Is red heavier than yellow?' and found that most of the children answered yes or no. None of the children said that the question was impossible to answer. Questions asked by police officers and lawyers may be hard for children to understand because they include difficult vocabulary or phrasing (Carter et al., 1996). Hughes and Grieve's finding implies that, even if children do not understand a question, they are more likely to give an answer than say they don't know, and in doing so they may give a misleading response.

Hughes and Grieve (1980) asked only nonsensical questions that could be answered with yes or no. In another study, Waterman et al. (2000) asked 5–8-year-olds nonsensical yes/no questions, and also asked 'open' nonsensical questions that required an answer, for example, questions like 'What do bricks eat?'. Waterman et al. found, like Hughes and Grieve, that children answered most of the yes/no questions but, in contrast, children hardly ever tried to invent an answer for the nonsensical open questions. Even though all the questions in

Waterman et al.'s study were nonsensical ones, questions with different formats prompted different patterns of responses from the children. This has implications for interviewing children, because variations in the style of questions can result in different answers.

In a similar study, Waterman et al. (2001) read 5–9-year-olds a brief story about Mary and her family having a picnic at the seaside, and then asked the children questions about what had happened in the story. Some of the questions were impossible to answer, not because they were nonsensical but because the relevant information had not been included in the story. If the unanswerable questions required an answer (e.g. 'What flavour ice cream did Mary have?'), children usually said they didn't know. But if the unanswerable questions implied a yes/no response (e.g. 'Did they drink lemonade?'), children often gave an answer. These studies demonstrated the importance of the exact form of questioning in eliciting correct answers from children. Some types of questions (like ones that require a yes/no response) may tempt children to give inappropriate answers to questions that they do not understand, or to speculate about information that they do not know. For these reasons, interviewers are recommended to use yes/no questions only after other types of questions have been exhausted (see below).

Suggestibility can also occur when an interviewer repeats a question several times, if this results in a child thinking that a previous answer was incorrect, or thinking that an answer has to be given before the interview can continue, even though the child does not have anything more to say. Krähenbühl et al. (2010) considered the types of questions used by police interviewers in interviews with 4–11-year-old children who had alleged abuse. About 100 police interviews were analysed and, on average, each interview included nearly 200 questions. Krähenbühl et al. pointed out that a large number of questions were repeated, sometimes several times each. Such repetition frequently led to children changing their answers. Often the changes were because children gave new answers with additional information (which might be seen as a positive outcome for repeating a question), but on other occasions children gave a different answer from their first response. If a child changes his or her answer to a question when it is repeated, it may be difficult for an interviewer to know whether the child's first or second (or third or fourth) answer is the correct one. Experimental research has shown that children often change their answers in response to a repeated question (Krähenbühl & Blades, 2006; Poole & White, 1991). For example, Moston (1987) asked 6-year-olds the same question twice. The first time the children were asked the question about an event, two-thirds of the children's answers were correct but when the question was repeated, only about one-third of the responses were correct. Children may have assumed that being asked a question more than once implied that their first answer was wrong. After all, teachers and parents do not usually ask a question a second time if they receive an adequate answer the first time. Hence, repeating a question can mislead a child witness and result in less accurate testimony.

Stop and Think

Why do children have problems answering questions when they are interviewed by an adult?

INTERVIEWING PROCEDURES

The Cognitive Interview

Most researchers have found that children are unlikely to offer much information in free recall, even when they know a lot about an event (Goodman & Reed, 1986; Marin et al., 1979) and for this reason researchers have considered ways to maximize the amount of information given by a witness. One technique is called the *cognitive interview* (Fisher & Geiselman, 1992).

The cognitive interview relies on established cognitive principles to maximize what witnesses recall. These include four specific techniques.

- *Context reinstatement*: a witness is asked to reconstruct the original context of the event by describing the scene (e.g. by closing their eyes and trying to visualize the scene) and how they felt at the time.
- *Report everything*: a witness is encouraged to report as much as possible, even if some details are only partially remembered or not considered important.
- *Variety of perspectives*: the witness is asked to report the events from different perspectives (e.g. by describing what someone else who was involved would have seen and heard).
- *Temporal order*: the witness retells the event in different orders (e.g. from the last thing that happened to the first).

A cognitive interview begins with open-ended questions about neutral topics and then the context reinstatement. Following this, the witness is asked for free recall of an event and encouraged to report everything (but without guessing). Then the interviewer asks more specific questions, asking the witness to imagine details of the event (e.g. to form a mental image of where it happened or imagine the face of someone in the event).

Compared to an interview in which witnesses are just asked to recall as much as they can, the cognitive interview can elicit twice as much information from adults without increasing the amount of inaccurate information reported (Fisher et al., 1987). The cognitive interview can also be effective with children, though the improvement in children's recall is usually less than the improvement found in studies with adults. For example, McCauley and Fisher (1995) asked 7-year-olds to play a game with an unfamiliar adult, and a few hours later the children were interviewed about the game using either a typical interview or a cognitive interview. The children who were given the cognitive interview reported about 50% more information than the children who received the other interview. However, McCauley and Fisher found that the amount of inaccurate information the children gave also increased in the cognitive interview. A small increase in inaccurate information from children is a common finding and therefore interviewers may have to emphasize to children that they should avoid guessing (Memon et al., 2010). Nonetheless, the large gain in correct information makes the cognitive interview an effective way to interview children.

Different parts of the cognitive interview, such as context reinstatement, may be particularly useful with children (Memon & Bull, 1991), and some parts may be less appropriate for children; for example, Holliday (2003) omitted the perspective-taking aspect and found that the revised version of the interview was still effective. The cognitive interview may be difficult to use with young children (Memon et al., 1996) because it requires a certain amount of concentration and some self-awareness of memory processes (see the section above on metacognition) so some researchers have investigated whether alternative measures might also help children's recall. For example, Natali et al. (2012) showed children a film of a bank robbery and then asked the children questions about what they had seen. Half the children answered the questions as in a typical interview and half answered the same questions with their eyes closed. The children with their eyes closed answered more questions correctly. This may have been because the children were less likely to be distracted with their eyes closed. Although this effect has not been found consistently in children (Kyriakidou et al., 2014), the investigation of such measures may result in new ways to improve children's performance in interviews.

Achieving Best Evidence

In the UK, police officers and social workers interviewing children should follow the interview protocol described in *Achieving best evidence in criminal proceedings* (ABE) (Ministry of Justice, 2011). The ABE is an extensive document that describes how interviews with children (and other vulnerable witnesses, such as adults with learning difficulties) should be conducted and filmed. The ABE also includes the procedures that should be used when questioning children, and describes the stages that interviewers must follow. These include a 'rapport' stage during which the interviewer discusses neutral topics to relax the child and emphasizes that the child should say when she does not understand a question, or say 'don't know' when she does not know an answer. The interviewer should also check that a child knows the difference between telling the truth and telling a lie. The following stage is 'free narrative' when the interviewer asks a child to report as much as she can remember, and only prompts the child with neutral comments, like 'Tell me more'. After the free narrative there is a stage of questioning, beginning with open-ended questions (which do not suggest the answer, such as 'Tell me about him hitting you with the bat'), then more specific questions (i.e. ones with a limited range of possible responses, often 'who', 'what' 'when' or 'where' type of questions), and then closed questions (which are ones with two or three possible responses, such as 'yes', 'no' or 'don't know'). At the end of this stage, when other question types are exhausted, the interviewer may use leading questions. The last stage of the interview is 'closure' when the interviewer should summarize the evidence, ask the child if she has any questions, thank the child, give her advice about getting help if she needs it after the interview, and then return to neutral topics.

The ABE guidelines are closely based on developmental studies of children's performance as eyewitnesses, and embody many principles (e.g. about the order in which questions should be asked) that are derived from psychological research. For these reasons, the ABE provides an appropriate way to interview children, and evidence gained from ABE interviews will often be the basis for a court case. Similar interviewing guidelines have been developed in other countries (see Lamb et al., 2008).

STRESS AND RECALL

As witnesses, children may often have to report events that were stressful, and stress may influence memory in different ways (Marche & Salmon, 2013; Quas & Fivush, 2009). Some researchers have found that stress has little effect on recall. For example, Goodman et al.

(1986) compared two groups of children, aged between 3 and 7 years. Both groups visited a clinic; the 'high stress' group were taken to the clinic to have a blood sample taken, and the 'low stress' group went through the same procedure, but instead of a blood sample they had a washable transfer placed on their arm. A few days later, the children were questioned about the visit. Both groups had good recall of the events that had happened at the clinic and there was no difference between the groups—the children in the high stress group recalled as much as the other children. Some researchers have found that in conditions of high stress, for example when children undergo medical operations, they are less likely to recall information about the experience (Merritt et al., 1994). But other researchers have argued that highly stressful events may be remembered better than more mundane ones (Baker-Ward et al., 2009; Howe et al., 2004).

The different conclusions may reflect the variety of stressful events that have been studied by researchers. These have included events like visits to clinics for examinations that may be embarrassing or cause distress (Goodman et al., 1986; Saywitz et al., 1992), events such as painful injury or medical operations (Baker-Ward et al., 2009), and natural disasters (Fivush et al., 2004). The level of discomfort, pain and personal involvement is likely to vary from study to study.

A further issue is that individual children may have different reactions to stress. In most of the studies investigating the effects of stressful events on children's recall, one group has experienced a stressful event and a second, separate group has experienced a non-stressful event. In studies involving real-life events, it is not always possible to allocate children randomly to the stressful and non-stressful groups. Therefore most studies have compared not only different events, but also different groups of children. It is possible that children who experience stressful real-life events are different from children who do not. For example, some children who have been involved in a real-life stressful event might have experienced similar events before, and this could make them more (or less) susceptible to the stress of the particular event they are asked to recall. One way to avoid this issue is to assess the recall of both stressful and non-stressful events in the same group of children. Fivush et al. (2003) did this by questioning 5–12-year-old children about both positive and negative events. The children's parents provided examples of each type of event (e.g. positive events included parties and family outings, and negative ones included injuries or witnessing violence). The children also provided their own examples of positive and negative events. The children were asked to recall the events in as much detail as possible using mainly open-ended questions, and the researchers coded the recall for details about actions, people, places, references to time, and emotions. On nearly all the measures, there was no difference in the amount recalled for the stressful event and for the non-stressful event, though children recalled more emotions associated with negative events. Therefore, stress did not affect the number of details recalled.

One added complication in any research about stressful and non-stressful real-life events is whether children have discussed the events since. It might be the case that children are asked more about a stressful event and therefore this event becomes more salient in their memory. Fivush et al. (2003) tried to take this into account by asking the parents and children if they had discussed the events included in the study, and found no difference in how frequently the positive and the negative events were talked about. Overall, therefore, Fivush et al. showed that there was little difference in the way that positive and negative events were treated in the family, and little difference in how well children recalled those events.

Children may not only experience stress at the time of witnessing an event, but also at the time of reporting it, for example, if they have to give testimony in open court. There is little research into the effects of stress at recall. For obvious ethical reasons, there are limitations on how much stress children can be subjected to for the sake of an experiment. In one of the few relevant studies, Saywitz and Nathanson (1993) showed 8–10-year-old children a staged event. Then half the children were interviewed on their own by an interviewer in a classroom at their school, and the other half were interviewed in a full mock courtroom (in a university law school) with actors representing all the key court figures as well as jurors and spectators. The children in the court condition found the experience more stressful than the ones interviewed in the classroom. Most importantly, the children in school recalled more correct information about the event than did the children in court, and the children in school were less likely to make errors in response to misleading questions. In this study it was clear that stress at the time of recall had a negative effect on children's performance as witnesses.

 Stop and Think

How can interviewers help children to recall information fully and accurately?

SUMMARY OF EYEWITNESS RESEARCH

Research into children's ability as witnesses is important for what it can reveal about memory in everyday contexts. Such research has implications for interviewing children who have been involved in events that might become the focus of legal proceedings, and the results from the research have made a significant contribution to the treatment of children in courts. For example, in the UK there are now carefully constructed guidelines about the initial interviewing of children who may later have to appear in court (Ministry of Justice, 2011). The frequent publication of psychological research in legal and other journals has meant that all those involved in the interviewing of children are now more aware of the issues relating to the development of children's memory abilities.

CHAPTER SUMMARY

- Children's performance in reasoning tasks is dependent on their information processing. Younger children may have more limited processing capacity than older children and this may be reflected in younger children's less sophisticated ways of attempting problem-solving tasks.
- Researchers have analysed individual problem-solving tasks, or groups of similar tasks, to assess how children of different ages approach those tasks. Sometimes children's ability to solve tasks can be seen as a stage-like progression that is related to their underlying information processing abilities.
- But on other tasks children may apply a variety of strategies at the same time, only gradually focusing on the most efficient one.
- One factor in children's cognitive development is attention, and how well children attend to all aspects of a task may affect their performance.
- Some strategies, like memory strategies, can be applied across a range of contexts, and children need to recognize what is the most effective strategy for a particular context. Children's insight into their own memory and information processing abilities is called metacognition.
- There is an interaction between task-specific strategies, non-specific strategies (like memory strategies) and children's increasing knowledge about the world. These aspects of thinking interact to contribute to ever more powerful ways to deal with problem-solving tasks.
- Understanding more about children's reasoning and memory has many applied implications. For example, research into cognitive development has contributed to better ways of interviewing child eyewitnesses.

DISCUSSION POINTS

1. Contrast Piaget's approach to studying cognitive development with the information processing approach.
2. Does children's problem-solving and strategy use develop gradually or in distinct stages?
3. What factors contribute to children's memory development?
4. What advice would you give to someone who needed to interview young children about events that they had witnessed?
5. In what ways is the ABE interviewing protocol based on psychological research with children?

FURTHER READING

Memory and Information Processing

- Bjorklund, D.F. (2011). *Children's thinking: Cognitive development and individual differences* (5th ed.). Belmont, CA: Wadsworth, is a very good introduction to all aspects of children's memory, thinking and reasoning.
- The most comprehensive survey of the literature on memory development is Schneider, W. (2015). *Memory development from early childhood through emerging adulthood*. New York: Springer.
- Cowan, N. & Alloway, T. (2009). Development of memory in childhood. In M.L. Courage and N. Cowan (Eds.), *The development of memory in infancy and childhood*. Hove, East Sussex: Psychology Press, has a collection of chapters about different aspects of memory development.
- Definitive reviews of most aspects of children's cognitive development can be found in Damon, W. & Lerner, R.M. (Eds.) and Kuhn, D. & Siegler, R.S. (Vol Eds.) (2006). *Handbook of child psychology, Volume 2, Cognition, perception and language*. Hoboken, NJ: Wiley.

Children's Eyewitness Memory

- Lamb, M., La Rooy, D.J., Malloy, C. & Katz, C. (Eds.) (2011). *Children's testimony: A handbook of psychological research and forensic practice*. Chichester: Wiley-Blackwell, has a good selection of chapters on different topics related to children as eyewitnesses. This book is a more recent version of Westcott, H.L., Davies, G.M. & Bull, R.H.C. (Eds.) (2002). *Children's testimony. A handbook of psychological research and forensic practice*. Chichester: Wiley, which has a number of chapters that are still relevant.
- Holliday, R.E. & Marche, T.A. (2013). *Child forensic psychology*. Basingstoke: Palgrave Macmillan, contains a good set of chapters about child witnesses, including ones about court testimony.
- Lamb, M.E., Hershkowitz, I., Orbach, Y. & Esplin, P.W. (2008). *Tell me what happened: Structured investigative interviews of child victims*. Chichester: Wiley-Blackwell, describes the research behind the development of interview protocols designed to help interviewers who have to question children. This book focuses on US and international interviewing practice.
- The best source of information about UK interviewing practice is the guidelines that interviewers in the UK are expected to use when questioning children; see Ministry of Justice (2011). *Achieving best evidence in criminal proceedings: Guidance on interviewing victims and witnesses, and guidance on using special measures*. This document (usually called the ABE) applies to all interviews with vulnerable people, including children, and there are some sections that in addition specifically apply to children (see the ABE contents page).

'....see Ministry of Justice website at www.justice.gov.uk.'

CHAPTER
15

Children's Understanding of Mind

CHAPTER OUTLINE

- The False-Belief Task

- Children's Knowledge of Mind Before About 4 Years of Age

- When is Theory of Mind Achieved?

- Theory of Mind After 4 Years of Age

- Theories About the Development of Understanding the Mind

- Do Children with Autism or ASD Lack an Understanding of Others' Minds?

- How Far Can a Deficit in Understanding Mental Representations Contribute to an Explanation of ASD?

In this chapter we will consider how a child comes to realize that other people have knowledge and beliefs, and that other people's beliefs may be different from the child's own. Appreciating that other people have a set of beliefs and that everyone may have a differing set of beliefs is an important aspect of human cognition and is referred to as having 'theory of mind'. Without an awareness of theory of mind, communication and conversation between individuals would be difficult. In particular, understanding theory of mind means that children can predict another person's behaviour from knowing that person's beliefs and intentions. We describe the ways in which theory of mind is measured in children and how it develops during the early years. We also discuss children with autism who, usually, lack theory of mind.

In Chapter 2 we discussed the possible evolution of 'mind reading' in primates. As Byrne and Whiten (1987) argued, there are some observations of chimpanzees that are most easily interpreted as examples of deliberately deceptive behaviour. The presence of deceptive behaviour in other primates is the best evidence we have that some animals may be able to take into account the beliefs of others. Deception means altering the beliefs of others. In the example given in Chapter 2, p. 50, one chimpanzee did not immediately go to some food that was available, but rather acted as if the food was not there at all. This was because a second chimpanzee was nearby and would have made an attempt to grab the food for himself. The first chimpanzee was, in effect, generating a false belief in the mind of the second chimpanzee, and this implies that the first chimpanzee had some understanding that the beliefs of the other chimpanzee could be manipulated. Put simply, the first chimpanzee understood that the other chimpanzee had a mind.

This chapter will concentrate on children's understanding of the mind. With a few exceptions (discussed later in the chapter), we assume that all adults have an awareness that other people have minds. It is basic to our everyday human understanding that both we and others have beliefs. We know this in many ways: we know that we ourselves have beliefs about the world, that our beliefs change, that they might be wrong, and that what we say and what we do are based on our beliefs. We also assume that other people have beliefs; they can tell us those beliefs directly, or we can work out their beliefs indirectly from the way they behave.

Understanding that most individual behaviour is based on individuals' beliefs about the world is not just a useful facet of human knowledge; it is vital if we are to make sense of what others say and how they act. For example, if we know that there is some chocolate in the kitchen cupboard but there is none anywhere else in the house, and a friend goes to look for the chocolate on the dining room table, our friend's behaviour would make no sense to us at all if we could not interpret it in terms of what our friend believed about the world. We would assume she thought the chocolate was on the table, because we know that she has a mind, which includes beliefs that, as in this case, are incorrect. If we did not take into account her beliefs it would be very difficult to explain why she went to the dining room (except as some form of random behaviour).

Having an understanding of other people as people who have desires, beliefs and their own interpretations of the world is often referred to as having a 'theory of mind'. Calling it a 'theory' stresses two aspects of understanding about the mental world. First, we cannot directly see or touch the mind, and therefore we have to infer (or theorize) about others' mental states from what they say or the way they behave. Second, a theory is usually a complex interconnected set of ideas, and an adult's understanding of the mental world, taking into account emotions, desires, pretence, deception, beliefs and different perspectives of the world, is certainly a rich and complementary set of concepts, which it might be appropriate to call a 'theory'. However, the phrase 'theory of mind' is also troublesome, because it cannot be defined with precision (how much knowledge about the mind do you have to have for a theory of mind?). Some researchers have argued explicitly that the development of understanding the mind is similar to the development of theories in science (see below), but others are against drawing too close an analogy between the development of understanding minds and the development of scientific theories (Russell, 1992).

What does it mean to have an understanding of the mind? The mind can be considered in different ways. We understand that we have emotions and feelings (e.g. we can feel happy or sad) and that we have desires (I want some chocolate) and that desires and feelings are related (I will be happy if I find some chocolate). We realize that the mind includes knowledge (I know what chocolate is, I know where it is); that we can think about information (I am thinking about chocolate); that there is a difference between thoughts and real things (I can only touch or eat real chocolate); and that we have beliefs about the state of the world (I believe that the chocolate is in the cupboard). Adults also have an appreciation of some aspects of how the mind can be used, for example, in learning new information or using mnemonics (see discussion of metacognition in Chapter 14); and we know that knowledge is derived from particular sources, for example, if I see the chocolate in the cupboard, then I know where it is and that my knowledge is derived from looking.

One of the most important aspects of understanding the mind is the realization that, just as I have a mind, so do other people. They, too, have feelings, desires and beliefs and, just as I behave on the basis of my beliefs about the world, so do they. One of the most crucial points about understanding other people's minds is the realization that they may have beliefs that differ from our own. To put this another way, a person's set of beliefs about the world can be referred to as their (mental) representation of the world. Different people may represent the world in different ways; I believe the chocolate is in the cupboard, but my friend believes it is on the table. It is possible that we are both wrong about these beliefs (perhaps unknown to either of us someone has come along and eaten all the chocolate), but we cannot both be right about the same block of chocolate. If I'm right and the chocolate is still in the cupboard, then my friend's belief is incorrect and she has a false belief about the world.

THE FALSE-BELIEF TASK

Do children, like adults, appreciate that other people can have false beliefs? In an influential experiment, Wimmer and Perner (1983) investigated this question (see Box 15.1). They used models to act out a story about a little boy called Maxi who put some chocolate in a blue cupboard. Then Maxi left the room, and while he was out of the room the children saw Maxi's mother transfer the chocolate to a green cupboard. The children were asked to predict where Maxi would look for the chocolate when he came back into the room. Four-year-olds usually said that he would look in the green cupboard. From an adult point of view, this is a very surprising response because, of course, Maxi could not possibly know that the chocolate had been moved. We can infer from such a result that young children do not understand that Maxi's beliefs about the world are different from how the world really is, and they do not understand that he will act on the basis of his beliefs and not on the actual state of the world.

Box 15.1 Beliefs about beliefs: representations and constraining function of wrong beliefs in young children's understanding of deception

Wimmer and Perner carried out the first investigation of children's understanding of false belief. In their study, children heard a story about a boy (Maxi) who was looking for some chocolate. The children knew where the chocolate actually was, but they were told that Maxi thought the chocolate was in another place. The children were asked to predict where Maxi would look for the chocolate, and the key aspect of the experiment was whether children would predict that Maxi would look for the chocolate where they knew it was or where he thought it was. Of course, this is not a difficult task for most adults, who reason that Maxi can only look for the chocolate in the place where he believes it to be (i.e. people's behaviour is based on what they believe about the world rather than how the world really is). Wimmer and Perner wanted to find out if children would also reason in the same way. They tested three groups of 12 children, aged 4, 6 and 8 years, in Austria.

The children were told a story that was also acted out in front of them with three differently coloured matchboxes that were glued high up on a model wall, and paper cut-outs for the characters. The story was given in two versions. One was called the cooperative story (because one character offers to help Maxi find the chocolate) and one was called the competitive version (because another character may take the chocolate from Maxi).

The story was as follows (taken from Wimmer and Perner, 1983, in which it was translated into English).

Mother returns from her shopping trip. She brought chocolate for a cake. Maxi may help her put away the things. He asks her: 'Where should I put the chocolate?'. 'In the blue cupboard', says the mother.

'Wait, I'll lift you up there, because you are too small.'

Mother lifts him up. Maxi puts the chocolate into the blue cupboard. [A toy chocolate is put into the blue matchbox.] Maxi remembers exactly where he put the chocolate so that he could come back and get some later. He loves chocolate. Then he leaves for the playground. [The boy doll is removed.] Mother starts to prepare the cake and takes the chocolate out of the blue cupboard. She grates a bit into the dough and then she does not put it back into the blue but into the green cupboard. [Toy chocolate is thereby transferred from the blue to the green matchbox.] Now she realizes that she forgot to buy eggs. So she goes to her neighbour for some eggs. There comes Maxi back from the playground, hungry, and he wants to get some chocolate. [Boy doll reappears.] He still remembers where he had put the chocolate.

Children were then asked the 'belief' question: 'Where will Maxi look for the chocolate?' and had to indicate one of the three matchboxes.

Then in the cooperative story, children were told: 'OK, there he'll look, but he is too small to reach up there. There comes Grandpa and Maxi says: "Dear Grandpa, please could you help me get the chocolate from the cupboard?" Grandpa asks, "Which cupboard?".'

The children were then asked the 'utterance' question: 'Where will Maxi say the chocolate is?' and had to indicate one of the matchboxes.

In the competitive story, children were told: 'However, before Maxi gets a chance to get at the chocolate his big brother comes into the kitchen. He, too, is looking for the chocolate. He asks Maxi where the chocolate is. "Good grief", thinks Maxi, "now big brother wants to eat up all the chocolate. I will tell him something completely wrong so that he won't find it, for sure"'.

As with the cooperative story, the children were then asked an 'utterance' question: 'Where will Maxi say the chocolate is?' and had to indicate one of the matchboxes.

Then, to make sure that the children had paid attention to the story, the children were asked two questions. First, to check that they had not forgotten where the chocolate actually was, they were asked the 'reality' question: 'Where is the chocolate really?'. Second, to check that they also remembered where the chocolate had been put, they were asked the

'memory' question: 'Do you remember where Maxi put the chocolate in the beginning?.'

There was also a second story, with the same structure as this one, but it was set in a nursery school room where a little girl hid her favourite book. While she was out of the room the caretaker moved it to a different place. In the cooperative version, when the girl came back into the room, she offered to show the book to her friend. In the other version, another child was competing for the book and the girl tried to mislead him. The questions paralleled the ones in the Maxi story.

Each child heard both stories. Box Table 15.1.1 shows the number of children giving correct answers to the belief question 'Where will Maxi look for the chocolate?' (or 'Where will the little girl look for the book?'). The children could have been correct for both stories, for one, or for neither.

As shown in the table, the two older age groups were successful, but the 4-year-olds did comparatively poorly. It was important to be sure that the younger children's poor performance was not just due to them forgetting information from the story. When Wimmer and Perner examined the children who gave incorrect answers to the belief question, they found that 100% gave correct responses to the reality question and 80% gave correct responses

Box Table 15.1.1 Number of children giving correct answers to the belief questions in Wimmer and Perner's first experiment.

Age	Number of correct answers		
	2	1	0
4 years	4	2	6
6 years	11	0	1
8 years	11	1	0

Source: Wimmer, H. & Perner, J. (1983). Beliefs about beliefs: Representations and constraining function of wrong beliefs in young children's understanding of deception. *Cognition, 13*, 103–128.

to the memory question. In other words, all the children had paid attention to the stories and remembered the details. Therefore, the 4-year-olds' poor performance was not likely to be due to task factors, it was more likely that they only had a limited understanding that Maxi might hold an incorrect belief about the location of the chocolate.

Of the children who were correct on the belief question (predicting where Maxi would look for the chocolate, or where the girl would look for the book) in the cooperative versions, 85% gave appropriate answers to the utterance question (e.g. they said that Maxi would tell Grandpa that the chocolate was in the blue cupboard). Similarly, of the children who were correct on the belief question in the competitive versions, 82% gave an appropriate answer to the utterance question (e.g. they said that Maxi would tell his brother that the chocolate was not in the blue cupboard, but in one of the others).

Children who were incorrect on the belief question (and said that Maxi would look for the chocolate in the green cupboard) tended to indicate the green cupboard in response to the utterance questions. For example, in the cooperative version they said that Maxi would tell Grandpa that the chocolate was where it actually was, and in the competitive version they also said that Maxi would tell his brother where the chocolate really was. These responses were inappropriate given Maxi's false belief, and even if these children thought that Maxi would know that the chocolate was in the green cupboard, it was rather ineffective for him to tell his brother where he thought the chocolate was if he wanted to stop his brother getting it. In other words, these children did not seem to understand how to deceive the brother.

Wimmer and Perner went on to rule out some of the possible reasons why the youngest children gave inappropriate replies to the belief question. They thought that because the children had seen the toy chocolate put in

the green box and it was still there when they were asked the questions, the knowledge of where the chocolate was may have encouraged inappropriate responses from the 4-year-olds. One possibility was that the 4-year-olds were responding without much reflection and simply pointing to where they knew the chocolate was. Wimmer and Perner also suggested another possibility—that Maxi's belief, 'the chocolate is in the blue cupboard', might have been overridden by the child's own, similar knowledge that 'the chocolate is in the green cupboard', and that this effect was less likely to apply to the older children. (For similar arguments about the dominance of knowledge in false-belief tasks, see Hughes and Russell (1993).)

Therefore, in a second experiment, Wimmer and Perner introduced two new conditions (as well as the one they had used in the first experiment). Hence there were three conditions.

1. *Displaced condition*: this was the same as in the first experiment—children saw the chocolate moved from the blue to the green cupboard.
2. *Stop and think displaced condition*: to reduce the possibility of unconsidered responses, the children were told, before the belief question, to pause and think carefully before they answered.
3. *Disappear condition*: the children were told that the chocolate was all used up in the baking (in other words, it no longer existed in any cupboard).

Both the chocolate story and the book story were modified as necessary. Wimmer and Perner tested 20 3-year-olds, 42 4-year-olds and 30 5-year-olds. Box Table 15.1.2 shows the number of children in each condition answering the belief question correctly. (As there were two stories, children could have been right on both, one or neither.) Wimmer and Perner did not

Box Table 15.1.2 **Number of children in each condition answering the belief questions correctly in Wimmer and Perner's second experiment.**

Age	Condition	No. of children	Number correct		
			2	1	0
3 years	2. Stop and think displaced	10	0	0	10
	3. Disappear	10	0	3	7
4 years	1. Displaced	14	6	1	7
	2. Stop and think displaced	14	4	2	8
	3. Disappear	14	11	0	3
5 years	1. Displaced	10	5	0	5
	2. Stop and think displaced	10	10	0	0
	3. Disappear	10	10	0	0

Source: Wimmer, H. & Perner, J. (1983). Beliefs about beliefs: Representations and constraining function of wrong beliefs in young children's understanding of deception. *Cognition, 13*, 103–128.

report any results for 3-year-olds in the displaced condition, and presumably they did not test such young children in this condition on the assumption that they were unlikely to succeed if most of the 4-year-olds in the first experiment had failed in this condition.

As can be seen in the table, 5-year-olds were always correct in conditions 2 and 3, though they were poorer in the original task. Four-year-olds also did well in condition 3. In other words, the older children in this experiment performed best in the disappear condition, and this was support for Wimmer and Perner's suggestion that some of the 4-year-olds in the first experiment may have had difficulty because of the continuing presence of the chocolate. However, the 3-year-olds performed poorly irrespective of condition and there was no evidence that this age group could appreciate Maxi's false belief. Most of these children gave no response at all to the belief question (or, because they had seen the experimenter remove the toy chocolate in the course of telling the story, they suggested that Maxi would look behind the model for it).

Taken together, these experiments demonstrated that young children had difficulty ascribing a false belief to another person. In particular, 3-year-olds were unable to appreciate Maxi's false belief even in the 'disappear' condition of the second experiment, when there was little direct conflict between Maxi's belief (chocolate in cupboard) and their own knowledge (chocolate disappeared).

Wimmer and Perner's experiment has been criticized because of the length of the story, and the amount of information children had to remember to understand it. Although 4-year-olds performed poorly in Wimmer and Perner's first experiment, other researchers have shown that when the task is presented in the context of a briefer story (as in the Sally–Anne task described in this chapter), 4-year-olds can give appropriate answers to belief questions.

Based on material in Wimmer, H. & Perner, J. (1983). Beliefs about beliefs: Representations and constraining function of wrong beliefs in young children's understanding of deception. *Cognition, 13*, 103–128.

This was a very important result, because it indicated that young children's reasoning about other people's behaviour may be quite different from the assumptions that adults make about other people's behaviour. The discovery of such a major developmental difference has generated a wealth of research into how children think about the mind and the relationship between mind and behaviour.

Wimmer and Perner's (1983) task is referred to as a 'false-belief' task because Maxi's belief that the chocolate is in the blue cupboard is an incorrect belief after the chocolate is moved. Some researchers questioned the length of Wimmer and Perner's (1983) story, and suggested that children may have had difficulty with the amount of information they needed to consider to fully understand the story. Therefore, other researchers (Baron-Cohen et al., 1985) reduced the complexity of the story, with a version called the Sally–Anne task (see Figure 15.1). In this version, children are shown two dolls: Sally (who has a basket) and Anne (who has a box). Sally puts a marble in her basket and then leaves. While she is absent Anne takes the marble from the basket and puts it in the box. Sally returns and children are asked, 'Where will Sally look for her marble?'. The typical result from this task is that 4-year-olds realize that Sally will look in the basket and 3-year-olds say that she will look in the box. In other words, with this briefer version of the false-belief task, children perform correctly at a slightly earlier age, but 3-year-olds seem unable to understand how Sally will act. Indeed, Wimmer and Perner (1983) found that by altering the story about Maxi and the chocolate so that some features of the story were more salient, the 4-year-olds succeeded but the 3-year-olds remained unable to work out what Maxi would do (see Box 15.1).

Other false-belief tasks, such as the 'Smarties task', have produced the same result (Perner et al., 1987). In the Smarties task, children are shown a closed box of Smarties (chocolate sweets popular with children) and asked to say what is in the box. Children nearly always say 'sweets'. Then the lid is taken off and the children are shown that the box actually contains pencils. After this the lid is replaced and children are asked what one of their friends will think is in the box: 'When X [friend's name] comes in I'm going to show her this box. What will X think is in the box?'. The correct answer is 'sweets', and although this is the most common answer given by 4-year-olds, younger children answer that their friend will say there are pencils in the box. Children can also be asked what they thought was in the box before it was opened. Four-year-olds give the correct answer ('sweets'), but 3-year-olds say (incorrectly) that they thought there were pencils in it. In other words, 3-year-olds seem to lack insight into their own mind—they do not acknowledge that at an earlier time they believed there were sweets in the box.

It is clear from experiments like these that children before the age of about 4 years have difficulty understanding that another person can have a false belief about the world. They respond as if Sally (in the Sally–Anne task) or their friend (in the Smarties task) will know what the actual state of the world is, even though they could not possibly know this.

However, even if 3-year-olds fail the false-belief task, it does not mean that they understand nothing at all about the mind. In the next section we will give examples of the research into very young children's understanding of the mind.

 Stop and Think

Why is testing children's awareness of *false* beliefs an essential way to assess theory of mind?

Figure 15.1 The Sally–Anne task.

Source: Frith, U. (2003). *Autism: Explaining the enigma* (2nd ed.). Oxford: Wiley-Blackwell.

CHILDREN'S KNOWLEDGE OF MIND BEFORE ABOUT 4 YEARS OF AGE

Distinguishing Mental States in Language

From about 2 years of age, children start to use words that refer to internal states of perception or emotion—words like 'want', 'see', 'look', 'taste' (see Chapter 6)—and by the age of 3 years children also use cognitive terms like 'know', 'think' and 'remember'. When children use such words spontaneously, it may be difficult to work out whether they use them to refer to mental states or whether they are being used in a more casual manner (for example, adults say 'you know' or 'know what' without any implication that the word 'know' refers to a mental state).

Shatz et al. (1983) examined 3-year-old children's spontaneous use of mental terms; to avoid instances of casual use, they focused on utterances that included a contrasting use of terms. The statements collected by Shatz et al. included ones like:

> 'I thought it was an alligator. Now I know it's a crocodile.'
> 'I was teasing you. I was pretending 'cept you didn't know that.'
> 'I thought there wasn't any socks [in the drawer], 'cept when I looked I saw them. I didn't know you got them.'

In these examples, children spontaneously contrasted reality and a belief—for instance, in the first example, the belief was that an animal was an alligator, the reality was that it was a crocodile. Shatz et al. inferred from such examples that these 3-year-olds could distinguish between mental states and external reality.

In another study, Wellman and Estes (1986) showed 3-year-olds two story characters and the children were told that character A had a biscuit and that character B was, for example, thinking about a biscuit. The children were then asked which of the two biscuits (the physical one or the mental one) could be touched, be seen by the character, or be seen by another character. Different stories were used so that several contrasts could be made between the physical object (with character A) and the same object that character B was thinking about, dreaming about, remembering or pretending about. Wellman and Estes found that three-quarters of the children's judgements accurately reflected the distinction between physical and mental entities.

Understanding the Relationship between Seeing and Knowing

Children from the age of 2 years have some understanding of the relationship between seeing and knowing. Lempers et al. (1977) asked 2-year-olds to show another person a picture that was glued to the inside bottom of a box. The children realized the need to angle the box so that the other person could see into it. Children of the same age also appreciated that if a person had their hands over their eyes it was necessary to move their hands if they were to see a picture. By the age of 3 years, children understood that if they hid something from another person, that person would not be able to see it. In other words, by 3 years of age children realize something of the relationship between seeing an object and knowing about that object.

Three-year-olds also understand that different people may have a different view of the same object. For example, Masangkay et al. (1974) used a card with a cat drawn on one side and a dog drawn on the other. The card was placed with one side facing the child and the other facing the experimenter, and children were asked what each person could see. Three-year-olds realized that the experimenter saw a different picture from the one they were looking at. More than this, children of this age are aware that if people see something they will know about it, but if they do not see something they will be unaware of it. For example, if an object is hidden in a box, 3-year-olds understand that if person A has looked into the box she will know what is in it and if person B has not looked in the box she will not know its contents (Hogrefe et al., 1986). The results of these experiments show that young children appreciate that different people can have different knowledge about the world, and that some people may have less complete knowledge than others.

However, it is not until about 4 years of age that children realize that people may have different views of an object that is equally and completely visible to both. Masangkay et al. (1974) had a child (aged 3–5 years) sit opposite an experimenter, and between the two of them was a picture showing the side view of a turtle. The experimenter explained that when the turtle appeared as if it was standing on its feet, it was the right way up and when it appeared as if it was on its back it was 'upside down'. The picture was placed flat on the table and children were asked which of the two views they saw and which the experimenter saw. All the children were correct in describing their own view of the turtle, but only a third of the 3-year-olds could describe the experimenter's view, and it was not until 4 years of age that children understood that their view and the experimenter's were different. This is an important realization, because it means that, at least in perspective-taking tasks, children by the age of 4 can recognize that the same object can be thought about in different ways.

Understanding the Appearance–Reality Distinction

Most adults know that a realistic-looking apple that is made of wax is not a real apple, and they can distinguish what it looks like—an apple (its appearance)—from what it is—wax (the reality). In other words, they realize that the *same* person can think about an object in different ways—it can represent the same object as fruit and as wax. However, young children have difficulty in tasks that involve distinguishing appearance and reality. For example, Flavell et al. (1986) showed children a sponge, which looked like a rock. The children were shown it from a distance (when it could be interpreted as a rock) and then they had an opportunity to feel it, and discovered that it was a sponge. After this they were asked two questions: 'What does it look like?' (the correct answer was, of course, a rock) and 'What is it really and truly?' (a sponge). Three-year-olds had difficulty in this task; once they had found out that it was a sponge they tended to answer 'sponge' to both questions.

The 3-year-olds had difficulty considering two (contradictory) representations of the object at the same time. As Flavell (1988, p. 246) said: '. . . they do not clearly understand that even though something may be only one way out there in the world, it can be more than one way up here in our heads, in our mental representations of it'. At the age of 3 years children do not realize that the appearance of an object is only a representation (that can be changed); instead, they only consider one interpretation of the object—what they know it to be. It is only after about the age of 4 years that children begin to appreciate that an object can be represented as both what it looks like and what it is. Such an appreciation includes an awareness that at least one of the representations is false (as when the sponge is represented as a rock). Children may also realize that it is possible for one person to have a true belief about an object (in this case, know that the object is a sponge), but another person might have a false belief about the same object (and think it is a rock).

Predicting Behaviour

Two-year-olds understand that people have desires, and that these can influence the way they behave. Wellman (1990) told children a story about a character called Sam who wanted to find his rabbit so he could take it to school. The children were told that the rabbit could be hiding in one of two locations, and they saw Sam going to one of the two locations. At that location Sam either found his rabbit (the desired object) or he found a dog. After Sam had looked in one location, the children were asked, 'Will he look in the other location, or will he go to school?'. Two-year-olds answered correctly (if Sam found the rabbit) that he would then go to school, and (if he found the dog) that he would go on searching. In other words, they predicted what Sam would do from what they knew about his desires.

By the age of 3 years, children understand that people not only have desires, they also have beliefs about the world. Wellman (1990) showed 3-year-olds two locations (for example, a shelf and a toy box), and the children were shown that there were books on the shelf and in the box. Then a character was introduced: 'This is Amy. Amy thinks there are books only on the shelf; she doesn't think there are books in the toy box. Amy wants some books. Where will Amy look for books?'. (The children could have answered 'shelf' or 'toy box' or 'both places'). Two-thirds of the responses made by the children were correct—they realized that Amy's beliefs would lead to her looking for the books on the shelf.

In this last experiment, Amy had a true belief about the world: she thought that there were books on the shelf, and there were books in that place; and 3-year-olds appreciated the relationship between a true belief and behaviour. However, as noted in the previous section, 3-year-olds cannot predict someone else's behaviour when that person has a false belief (as in the Sally–Anne or Smarties tasks). In other words, 3-year-olds realize that other people's behaviour is based on their beliefs about the world, and that those beliefs may be incomplete (as in the case of Amy). But 3-year-olds do not yet realize that people can act on the basis of a belief that is inaccurate (as in the case of Sally).

WHEN IS THEORY OF MIND ACHIEVED?

Wellman et al. (2001) reviewed nearly 180 studies involving false-belief tasks (like the Sally–Anne and the Smarties tasks) and found that the results from these studies were generally consistent. Only a very few 2-year-olds and a minority of 3-year-olds were ever successful in tasks that required an understanding of false belief, but children above 4 years of age usually passed false-belief tasks. Different researchers have used different types of false-belief tasks and have used different ways to phrase the questions given to children during the tasks, but variations in the task and style of question made little difference to the age when children achieve an understanding of false belief (Wellman et al., 2001).

In summary, children usually have an understanding of false belief from about 4 years of age, and it is then that they appreciate that other people's behaviour may be based on incorrect assumptions about the world. This is an important achievement, because 4-year-olds realize that when a person behaves in a certain way, that person does so on the basis of her own representation of the world rather than on the basis of what the world is really like. Realizing that other people have representations of the world in their minds (and that different people may have different representations of the world) is a very significant developmental achievement. From the age of 4 years, children can interpret and predict the behaviour of the people around them with a fair degree of accuracy, and during the next couple of years they develop even more profound insights into social behaviour (see the following section).

Even though children do not achieve an understanding of false belief until 4 years of age, slightly younger children may already have an implicit understanding of belief. 'Implicit' means that children have some understanding but are unaware, or unconscious, of their own understanding. Clements and Perner (1994) gave false-belief tasks to 2- and 3-year-olds. These were typical tasks in which a character put an item in box A, then left the scene and a second character moved the item to box B. Clements and Perner asked the children where the first character would search for the item when he returned. They found, as expected, that most of the 3-year-olds said, incorrectly, that the character would search in box B. But Clements and Perner also observed where the children looked when they were asked the question, and found that the majority of them actually looked at box A—the correct place. Why the 3-year-olds looked at box A but said box B is not easy to explain, but may indicate an implicit awareness of false belief somewhat earlier than children can express their understanding verbally in a false-belief task (Leslie, German & Polizzi, 2005). Clements and Perner found that the 2-year-olds said that the character would search in box B and also looked at box B, which indicated that they had no understanding of false belief at all. However, other researchers using similar procedures have found that 2-year-olds did look at box A (Southgate et al., 2007), and Onishi and Baillargeon (2005) found that children who were just 1 year of age showed appropriate patterns of looking in a false-belief task. The age when children develop an implicit awareness of false belief is important because it has consequences for theories about how theory of mind develops. If there is unambiguous evidence that very young children have some recognition of theory of mind, this would support a view that understanding others' minds is a very early achievement (Hughes, 2011).

There are several factors that might contribute to children achieving an explicit understanding of belief at about the age of 4 years. Milligan et al. (2007) reviewed over 100 studies of theory and mind and found that the development of theory of mind was related to language development. Children who performed well in belief tasks had better language abilities than those who performed poorly. The relationship between theory of mind and language has also been demonstrated in studies with children who have delayed language abilities. For example, children with hearing impairments often have difficulty on false-belief tasks, and may not succeed on them until well after the age of 4 years (Schick et al., 2007; Woolfe et al., 2002).

A child's interaction with other members of their family will also have an effect on theory of mind development. Taumoepeau and Ruffman (2006, 2008) found that the way mothers used mental state terms (about desire, belief and knowledge) to children at 15 months and 24 months of age correlated with how much their children used and understood such terms up to a year later. Meins et al. (2002) found that mothers who referred to mental states when interacting with their children at the age of 6 months had children who performed better on false-belief tasks at the age of 4 years.

Children do, of course, interact with other people as well as their mothers. Brown et al. (1996) investigated the way that 4-year-olds talked to mothers, siblings and friends, and found that children were more likely to talk about thoughts and beliefs when interacting with their siblings and friends than when talking with their mothers. Brown et al. also found a correlation between children's talk of thoughts and beliefs with their siblings and friends and their performance on false-belief tasks. Dunn (1999) pointed out that there is a rapid increase in the amount of child–child interaction between 2 and 4 years of age, and suggested that during this period children may learn more from interacting with other children than with adults. Other children may be more likely than adults to take part in shared make-believe and pretend activities, and planning, discussing and acting out such activities necessitate children discussing their thoughts and ideas with each other. In particular, children may benefit from interacting with children of a slightly different age; for example, Ruffman et al. (1998) found that children with older siblings had a better understanding of false belief (see also p. 167). The presence of older siblings may provide more opportunities for social interaction, as well as more opportunities for young children to hear the use of language involving mental state terms, either from their siblings or from their parents, as their parents interact with older siblings. As well as siblings, children may benefit from interacting with other children of different ages. For instance, Wang and Su (2009) found that 4-year-olds who were taught in classes with mixed ages had a better understanding of false belief.

Family size is also likely to be important (Carpendale & Lewis, 2006). For example, Lewis et al. (1996) carried out a study with children who lived in extended families in the Greek communities on Crete and Cyprus. Lewis et al. gave the children several false-belief tasks and gathered details about the number of people with whom the children interacted on a daily basis. They found that children who were the most successful on false-belief tasks were those who interacted most with adults and had more older siblings and older friends. Lewis et al. suggested that those young children who have a greater opportunity to talk to and interact with older children and adults will have a better chance of developing their theory of mind skills at an earlier age.

Although there are several factors (like family size, siblings and language ability) that all influence exactly when children succeed on false-belief tasks, none of these factors has a major effect on when children achieve an understanding of false belief. Most typically, developing children achieve this understanding between 4 and 5 years of age.

 Stop and Think

What factors contribute to the development of theory of mind?

THEORY OF MIND AFTER 4 YEARS OF AGE

After children understand that people's behaviour is based on their representations of the world, they come to realize that emotional responses are also based on a person's representation. For example, in Chapter 6 we referred to a study by Harris (1989). In one condition of Harris's study, children were told about Ellie the elephant, who only liked to drink Coke. Ellie was given a can of Coke that, unknown to her, had been filled with milk (which she did not like). Children were asked how Ellie would feel when she received the can (and before she had drunk from it). Four-year-olds realized that Ellie would not know what was in the can, but when the children were asked how she would feel, most of them said that she would feel sad. However, by the age of 5 years, children realized that Ellie would feel happy when she was given the can of Coke. In other words, by the age of 5 children appreciated that Ellie's incorrect representation of the world (i.e. her false assumption that the can contained Coke) would actually make her happy when she saw the can.

Adults would assume that when Ellie tasted the liquid in the can she would be surprised that it was milk, because the contents were contrary to her representation of the situation. In other words, being able to predict someone else's surprise depends on knowing that their view of the world is about to be disconfirmed. Children only understand surprise reactions some time after they have achieved an understanding of false belief. Hadwin and Perner (1991, experiment 4) told 4- and 5-year-olds a story about a boy called Tommy. Tommy's mother buys him a box of chocolate sweets (Smarties) but while Tommy is out of the room and before he has opened the box, the experimenter changes the Smarties for jelly-babies. Nearly all the children were old enough to realize that Tommy would look at the box and (wrongly) think there were Smarties in it, but Hadwin and Perner also asked the children to pick one of two pictures to show how Tommy would feel when he opened the box. One picture showed a face with a surprised expression and one showed a face with a neutral expression. The 5-year-olds tended to pick the surprised face, but the 4-year-olds just guessed which face was correct. So, even though the 4-year-olds recognized that Tommy had a false belief about the content of the Smarties box, they did not use this knowledge to predict that Tommy would be surprised when he opened the box.

Once children realize that people can have false beliefs, they also become aware of the possibility of deceptive behaviour. Deception involves planting a false belief in another person's mind, and this is only possible if you realize that other people can have false beliefs. Peskin (1992) investigated young children's ability to deceive another person: 3-, 4- and 5-year-olds were shown four stickers and each child was told that she could have the one she liked best. But the children were also told that two puppet characters would each be allowed to choose a sticker before the child could take the one she wanted. Children were told that one puppet was friendly, and would never take a sticker that the child wanted, but the other puppet was mean and always wanted the same sticker that the child wanted.

After the child had said what sticker she wanted, the friendly puppet came and, before choosing its own sticker, the friendly puppet asked the child which sticker she wanted. Nearly all the children, truthfully, pointed out the one they preferred and the friendly puppet chose a different one. Then the mean puppet arrived and also asked the child which she wanted. Nearly all the 3- and 4-year-olds pointed out the one they wanted and the mean puppet took it. Most of the 5-year-olds pointed to a sticker they did not want. This result could be taken as evidence that the younger children did not have any understanding of how to deceive the mean puppet. They did not seem to realize that by telling the puppet a lie, they could instill a false belief in the puppet so that he would not take the sticker they wanted.

What is particularly interesting about Peskin's experiment is that after the first trial (that we have just described), Peskin gave the children a further four trials using the same procedure. Not surprisingly, the 5-year-olds were as good in the later trials as they were in the first trial. The 4-year-olds showed a rapid improvement in performance and by their second trial half of them realized the need, when the mean puppet was around, to point to a sticker that was not their preferred one. Presumably these children's rapid learning was based on an awareness that others can have a false belief. However, the 3-year-olds did not improve; even by the fifth trial nearly all of them continued to point to the sticker they wanted and every time the mean puppet took it from them. Despite the children's disappointment and frustration, and despite the repeated trials, it appeared that the 3-year-olds had no way of deceiving the mean puppet—they did not realize that they could generate a false belief in the mean puppet by pointing to a sticker they did not want.

As children get older, they can interpret more complex social situations that involve theory of mind. A false-belief task like the Sally–Anne task involves a 'first-order' belief (i.e. I think that Sally thinks that the marble is in the basket). A 'second-order belief' is one that involves understanding that someone else can have beliefs about a third person (for example, I think that Jack thinks that Jill thinks that the marble is in the basket). Working out second-order false beliefs is a slightly later achievement (Miller, 2012). For example, Sullivan et al. (1994) gave 4–8-year-olds the following story:

> Tonight it's Peter's birthday and Mom is surprising him with a puppy. She has hidden the puppy in the basement. Peter says, 'Mom, I really hope you get me a puppy for my birthday'. Remember, Mom wants to surprise Peter with a puppy. So, instead of telling Peter that she got him a puppy, Mom says, 'Sorry Peter, I did not get you a puppy for your birthday. I got you a really great toy instead.' Now, Peter says to Mom, 'I'm going outside to play'. On his way outside, Peter goes down into the basement to fetch his roller skates. In the basement Peter finds the birthday puppy! Peter says to himself, 'Wow, Mom didn't get me a toy, she really got me a puppy for my birthday'. Mom does *not* see Peter go down to the basement and find the birthday puppy. Now the telephone rings, ding-a-ling! Peter's grandmother calls to find out what time the birthday party is. Then Grandma says to Mom, 'What does Peter think you got him for his birthday?'.

The last question in the story is a second-order belief question, because the answer depends on what Mom thinks Peter thinks. At this point the children were asked what Mom's answer to the last question would be. Sullivan et al. (1994) found that some 4-year-olds and most of the 5-year-olds gave a correct response, indicating that these children had worked out that Mom would have a false belief about what Peter thought.

From the above examples it can be seen that children develop a rapid understanding of false belief from about the age of 4 years. Within a year or so, they can begin to apply their awareness that other people can have false beliefs in a variety of contexts, including ones that involve working out second-order beliefs, judging how people might react or feel on the basis of false beliefs, and manipulating false beliefs in others. These are all major achievements. However, this is not to say that all aspects of reasoning about others' minds has been fully achieved by the age of 5 years, and some researchers have emphasized that the development of more sophisticated theory of mind abilities may take longer (Chandler & Sokol, 1999). To demonstrate this, Carpendale and Chandler (1996) gave 5–8-year-olds a false-belief task based on Wimmer and Perner's (1983) Maxi task (see above). The children were then given a second task involving an ambiguous drawing that could be interpreted as either a duck or a rabbit (see Figure 15.2).

Figure 15.2   An ambiguous drawing that can be interpreted as a duck or a rabbit.
Source: Jastrow, J. (1900). *Fact and fable in psychology*. Boston, MA: Houghton Mifflin.

Carpendale and Chandler checked that children could recognize both interpretations and then introduced a puppet called Ann. The children were asked, 'Now we will show this picture to Ann; do you think Ann will think it's a duck or a rabbit, or wouldn't you know what she would say?'. If children said that Ann would say it was (for example) a rabbit, they were asked, 'How can you tell what she will think?'. If children said they did not know what Ann would think, they were asked, 'Why is it hard to tell what Ann will think?'. All the children succeeded on the false-belief task, but most of the 5-year-olds were unable to answer the questions about Ann appropriately. They either made a clear and specific prediction about how Ann would interpret the picture, or if they said they did not know what Ann would say, they could not explain why it is impossible to predict another person's response to the picture. In other words, 5-year-olds did not appreciate that another person has to interpret the picture and that such an interpretation cannot be predicted. Children's ability to answer the questions appropriately improved with age, but even some of the 8-year-olds had difficulty answering them. From these results, Carpendale and Chandler argued that even after children have achieved success on a false-belief task, it may be some years before they are fully aware that, in all contexts, the mind is always an interpreter of reality.

 Stop and Think

Why is theory of mind an essential part of human understanding?

THEORIES ABOUT THE DEVELOPMENT OF UNDERSTANDING THE MIND

Several theories have been put forward to explain how children develop an understanding of their own and other people's minds. We will only mention these very briefly to give an indication of the different approaches that researchers have taken. We described a couple of Wellman's (1990) experiments earlier, and on the basis of such studies Wellman suggested that children's understanding develops in three phases. Two-year-olds have a 'theory' based on 'desire psychology'—they assume that people's desires influence their behaviour. For example, in the experiment with Sam looking for his rabbit, Sam's behaviour (searching) is determined by his desire (to take the rabbit to school).

By the age of 3, children have a 'theory' based on 'belief-desire psychology'—they take into account not only a person's desires but also their beliefs about the world. For example, in the experiment with Amy looking for some books, 3-year-olds realize that, although there are books in two places, if Amy only knows that they are in one place she will go there. This means that 3-year-olds are able to take Amy's beliefs into account—they can predict her behaviour on the basis of Amy's representation of the world. However, Amy had a true (if incomplete) belief about the world—her representation reflected the actual state of the world. Wellman (1990) originally suggested that 3-year-olds may think of beliefs as a 'copy' of the world and they do not realize that a belief is not a copy but an interpretation of the world. As Bartsch and Wellman (1995, p. 203) said, 'three-year-olds can conceive that people either have a belief about the world or they don't; if they have one, however, it reflects the world veridically, like a good photograph would'. Such a view of 3-year-olds excludes the possibility that children of this age can understand false belief. However, Bartsch and Wellman examined the conversation of 10 children as they developed from infants into young children and found that at the age of 3 years, children occasionally showed a realization that a person's beliefs and reality could be different. For these reasons, Bartsch and Wellman concluded that 3-year-olds have some awareness that other people can have false representations of the world, but for the most part their theory of mind is still very much based on desire psychology (as in the case of younger children). It is only after about 4 years of age that children consistently adopt a theory that includes the crucial realization that beliefs are interpretations, and like all interpretations they may be inaccurate (like Sally's belief in the Sally–Anne task).

Wellman (1990) referred to children's understanding as progressively more sophisticated 'theories' about the mind. Put another way, they are developing a 'theory of mind'. By describing development in this way, Wellman made an explicit comparison between children's developing understanding and the way that scientific theories develop. A scientist tries to understand a large number of facts or events by proposing a theory that explains the relationships between those facts, and then on the basis of that theory the scientist can predict the existence of other facts or relationships. Wellman suggested that in the same way that a scientist uses a theory to explain the world around her, so a child (who sees and experiences a constant stream of information about others' actions and behaviours) also tries to make sense of all this information by establishing a 'theory'. At first, this may be quite a simple theory (e.g. one based on 'desire psychology'). Such a theory may explain some behaviours, but as the child comes across examples of behaviour that cannot be explained simply from knowing a person's desires, she will be forced to consider a more elaborate theory (e.g. one based on belief-desire psychology). This shift in theories is rather like a scientist considering new facts that do not fit into an already established scientific theory—at a point when the old theory no longer helps understand the new facts, the scientist has to develop a new theory.

Wellman (1990) suggested that children's understanding of the mind progresses through several theory changes between the ages of 2 and 4 years. Support for the theory view of children's development comes from research that has shown that children achieve success on several different tasks at roughly the same age (Astington, 1994). For example, children's perspective-taking ability (that two people can have different, and contrary, views of the same picture); children's appreciation of the distinction between appearance and reality (that the same person can have different, contradictory representations of an object); and children's awareness of false belief (that different people can have contrary representations of the world) are all achieved about the same time. That children start to succeed on a variety of tasks at the same age can be taken as evidence that there has been a significant underlying change in their thought, which is influencing their understanding of a number of related mental concepts. Such a change might well be described as a shift in their 'theory' about the mind.

Rather than postulating several phases, Perner (1991) put great emphasis on the major change that occurs at about 4 years when children can understand false belief. He argued that the most important aspect of understanding the mind occurs when a child has acquired the concept of 'metarepresentation'. This means an understanding of the distinction between what is being referred to (the referent) and what it is represented as. For example, consider a photograph (i.e. a representation) of a pyramid. If the photograph is taken from the ground, the pyramid will be represented by a triangular shape; if taken from a plane flying directly above the pyramid, it will be represented as a square shape; if taken from a satellite, it will be represented as a dot. These are all representations of the pyramid, but they are not copies of the pyramid. To think of representations simply as copies of reality is to misunderstand the nature of representations. It is only when you understand that representations are not copies of reality that you have the concept of metarepresentation, so that when a 4-year-old succeeds on a false-belief task like the Maxi task, she can make the distinction between *what* is represented (chocolate in location A) and *how* it is represented (by Maxi, as chocolate in location B).

As Perner (1991) pointed out, having the concept of metarepresentation, at about the age of 4 years of age, is an important achievement. Perner said that younger children can, of course, understand a lot about minds (see the examples we gave in the previous section) but he argued that they can do so without an understanding of the nature of mental representations (Perner, 1991). In other words, Perner put most emphasis on a major change in children's representational thinking at the age of 4 years.

Leslie (1987) also used the word 'metarepresentation' but in a different way from Perner (1991). Leslie used the word in relation to young children's pretend play. He pointed out that children start to demonstrate pretend play from about 18 months of age (see Chapter 7) and he also noted that pretend play should actually be very confusing for a child who is still learning to categorize objects. For example, suppose a child has learned that yellow curved fruits are called bananas and that mechanical instruments you put to your ear are called telephones. Children do not usually mistake bananas for telephones or vice versa. However, in pretend play the child herself or someone else (e.g. her mother) might pick up a banana, put it against her ear and pretend to be using it as a telephone. It might be expected that relabelling the banana as a telephone has every potential to disrupt a child's categorization of objects. But this does not happen; young children are quite happy to pretend that a banana is a telephone, or a block of wood with wheels is a car, and they do not then get so confused that they start calling all bananas 'telephones' or all blocks of wood 'cars'.

In considering why children can indulge in pretend play without getting confused, Leslie (1987) suggested that children must have two types of representations when they indulge in pretend play. One is a primary representation (thinking about the banana as a banana) and the other is a secondary representation. The latter is the child's re-representation of the primary representation (so that the banana is also thought of as a telephone). Leslie called these secondary representations 'metarepresentations'. He also pointed out that in pretend play with others, young children interact with what other children are pretending (and not what they are actually doing). Children's ability to coordinate pretend play implies that they understand what is in the minds of the children they are playing with.

If young children can represent representations, and have some insight into other's minds, this might be thought of as a good basis for developing a fuller understanding of other minds. But it is at least 2 years between the beginning of pretend play and succeeding on a false-belief task. This is a surprisingly long time if the representational abilities proposed by Leslie (1987) really are the foundation for later understanding of minds. For this reason, several researchers have argued that pretend play is not dependent on representational abilities at all, and suggested that children can pretend by acting out behaviours. They can act out picking up a banana and talking into it, because that is what they would do with a telephone. In other words, the pretence is based on applying well-known actions to an object, and to do this children do not necessarily need to have a representation of the banana as a telephone, all they need to do is think about all the actions they would use with a telephone and then apply those to the banana (Lillard, 1993; Perner, 1991).

Wellman (1990), Perner (1991) and Leslie (1987) all suggested that children's understanding of mind is based on the development of their representational abilities. In contrast, Harris (1989) suggested that children can understand others' minds without necessarily understanding that others have mental representations; instead, children could use a process that Harris called 'simulation'. In Chapter 6 we discussed how children might develop an understanding of emotions. Harris pointed out that young children know about their own emotions and that they have the ability to pretend. With this knowledge and ability they can project emotions onto others (e.g. if they have felt upset when they have fallen down, then in doll play they can pretend that the doll feels upset when it has fallen down). In the same way, children can project emotions and explanations for those emotions onto other people.

Harris (1991, 1992) argued that by simulation, children can work out not only other people's emotions but also their desires and beliefs. It is worth noting that adults probably use simulation all the time to imagine other people's feelings and behaviour. For example, if you hear that a friend has just passed an important examination, you may be able to imagine your friend's emotions and how she felt immediately before and after she received the result. You could also imagine her behaviour—what she will do and what plans she can make now that she knows that she has passed. This simulation can be achieved by considering how you felt and behaved in a similar situation and applying that information to your friend. In the same way, a child faced with the Sally–Anne task could imagine what she herself would think and do if she were Sally, and then work out what actions and consequences would follow.

Harris suggested that children at the age of 3 years can work out what someone else is thinking even if the other person is focusing on an aim or object different from the child's own. For example, if child A wants chocolate and her friend B wants ice cream, child A can still work out B's thoughts and beliefs. She can predict B's behaviour from simulating how she herself might feel and act towards the chocolate, and applying that simulation to work out B's likely responses with regard to the ice cream. By the age of 4 years, children realize that different people may have different attitudes towards the same object, and can take into account alternative views of the same situation. This involves reasoning about situations that are counter to reality; so, in the Sally–Anne task, the child knows that the marble is in the box, but to work out how Sally construes the same situation the child has to imagine a hypothetical situation in which the marble is in the basket (and can then simulate Sally's likely behaviour).

Simulating another's behaviour may help a child work out what is in someone else's mind, and this may well be how children interpret another's beliefs and behaviours in many situations, but as Doherty (2009) has emphasized, there are several contexts in which it is impossible to simulate another person's beliefs successfully. Doherty gives the example of simulating another person's knowledge when that person is looking into a box. If you have previously looked in the box and know what is inside it (e.g. an apple), then you can imagine the other person looking into the box and seeing the apple. From that simulation you can work out that the other person will then have a belief about the content of the box. However, if you do not know what is inside the box, then no amount of imagining will help you know what is inside it. All you will be able to conclude is that you have no belief about the contents, but if from this you reason that the other person has no belief about the contents, you will be incorrect.

Simulation can work sometimes and may be one way to interpret another's mind, but on other occasions children may need to fall back on other forms of reasoning. In the case of the box, a child will know from many past experiences that if a person has looked in a box they will know what is in it, and hence the child will be able to predict that once someone has seen inside a box, that person will have a belief about the contents. The latter form of reasoning is akin to having a theory about the relationship between seeing and knowing (see p. 522). In other words, there may be several ways to interpret another person's mind, and some will be more appropriate and successful depending on the context and on the knowledge of the child. Simulation may work sometimes; working things out from past experience (i.e. from theories about the patterns in the world) may work at other times.

DO CHILDREN WITH AUTISM OR ASD LACK AN UNDERSTANDING OF OTHERS' MINDS?

Autism was described by Kanner (1943) and by Asperger (1944) who both (independently) used the term 'autism' to label a disorder that they described in children who usually, but not always, had a low IQ. Kanner described two main features in the children he saw. One was 'autistic aloneness', which referred to children's inability to relate to others—for example, they made little physical contact with parents, made little eye contact, preferred to be alone, and preferred playing with objects to playing with people. The second feature was a 'desire for sameness', because children often became very upset by changes in their surroundings or routine (for example, insisting on always having the same furniture arrangement in a room, or wanting the same food at every meal).

Kanner also discussed several secondary features in the children he examined. These included difficulties with language; children with autism might have a good vocabulary, but may use language without meaning, may use correct language but in inappropriate contexts, and may demonstrate 'echolalia' (repeating what another speaker has just said). Children with autism also lack spontaneous activities, they have repetitive behaviours, restricted interests, and sometimes have an obsessive interest in what most people might think are obscure activities. They may also be oversensitive to particular stimuli, reacting excessively to noises or to particular objects.

The criteria for defining autism have varied at different times, and have been subject to much debate. The most commonly used criteria have been ones that emphasize three major impairments. These are impairments in social interaction (e.g. impairment of non-verbal behaviours such as a lack of eye-to-eye contact or a failure to develop peer relations); impairments in communication (e.g. delay in the development of language, or a lack of varied, spontaneous make-believe play); and evidence of restricted and repetitive patterns of behaviour and activities (e.g. maintaining inflexible routines, including ones that have no practical function).

One other feature of autism is that people often show 'islets of ability' (Frith, 2003). This means that in contrast with their generally poor performance in most areas, they may be as good if not better than typically developing people on specific tasks. For example, people with autism often have good rote memory and good performance on some spatial tasks (like finding a hidden shape in a complex pattern).

The way that autism is defined is crucial for several reasons. One of the most important reasons is that, in practice, being labelled 'autistic' may give recognition to a group of children with similar problems (Evans, 2014), and that in turn may give those children access to treatment and resources they would otherwise not receive.

A second consequence is that the definition of autism will affect the number of people who are labelled as autistic, and this number may increase or decrease. In the past, different definitions have led to very different estimates about the frequency of autism. For many years, typical estimates of the prevalence of autism were about four or five people in 10,000, but over the last couple of decades far more people have been diagnosed with autism, and different researchers have suggested that autism may have a prevalence of anything from eight people in 10,000 to as many as 60 in 10,000 (Wing & Potter, 2002). This is not to say that there has been an increase in the number of cases of autism, only that clinicians are more likely to use the label than they were in the past.

The increase in the number of people diagnosed with autism means that there is a range of individuals who may show quite different degrees of autism, from mild to severe forms, and for this reason the term 'autistic spectrum disorder' (or ASD) rather than the word 'autism' is more often used. Using the term ASD is a way of acknowledging that within the group of people called autistic, there will be individuals with a wide range of different abilities and disabilities. At one end of the spectrum there are individuals with severe learning difficulties and at the other end, there are individuals with average or even higher than average levels of intelligence (Frith, 2003).

Autistic spectrum disorder is formally defined in the *Diagnostic and statistical manual of mental disorders*, fifth edition (DSM-5) of the American Psychiatric Association (2013). This definition focuses on two criteria. First, people with ASD will have problems in social communication (including more limited or less appropriate non-verbal behaviour during social interaction, being less likely to empathize with others during interactions, and having difficulty forming and maintaining social relationships). Second, people with ASD will also have restricted patterns of behaviour (e.g. repetitive speech, dependence on fixed routines, and very focused interests) and they may also be unusually sensitive to external stimuli (e.g. have an extreme reaction to a particular sound), or be insensitive to stimuli (e.g. less aware of extreme temperatures). People with ASD will have had such symptoms (in some form or other) from early childhood, and the symptoms will be severe enough to limit the person's everyday life and interactions.

A third consequence of the changing definitions of ASD is that participants with ASD in psychological studies may vary, depending on the prevailing definition of ASD at the time of the study. Matson et al. (2012) have pointed out that the contemporary definition of ASD (like DSM-5) means that someone must have more symptoms (and usually more severe symptoms) to be labelled as a person with ASD than was the case in the past. This means that not all the participants in older studies of ASD would necessarily be included in contemporary studies. Matson et al. considered the diagnoses of 2,493 children, some of whom had ASD. Each child's diagnosis was compared to criteria derived from DSM-5 and criteria based on earlier editions of DSM (DSM-IV, American Psychiatric Association, 1994). Matson et al. found that using the criteria from DSM-IV, the number of children classified as having ASD was 773. When the criteria from DSM-5 were used, the number of children was 404. This was a decrease of nearly half. Such a major change in the number diagnosed with ASD has all the consequences mentioned above, i.e. for monitoring the proportion of people with ASD in the population, for comparing between past and present studies of ASD, and for allocating treatment and resources to individuals.

The challenge for any researcher investigating ASD is to explain how one syndrome can lead to all the criteria that typify a person with ASD (DSM-5, American Psychiatric Association, 2013), as well as explaining many of the other phenomena associated with ASD (e.g. those people who have 'islets of ability').

Several theories were put forward to explain ASD (see Frith, 2003; Happé, 1994) but most of these only explained a small part of the pattern of impairments seen in people with ASD. Then researchers began to consider whether people with ASD had an understanding of minds, using the same types of experiment that had been used to investigate typically developing children's understanding. Baron-Cohen et al. (1985) were the first to do this, using the Sally–Anne false-belief task. They tested children with ASD who had a mental age of over 4 years, because it is about this age that typically developing children succeed on false-belief tasks. Baron-Cohen et al.

also tested a group of typically developing children aged 4 years and a group of children with Down syndrome (see pp. 38–39) with a mental age of 4 years or more. (For an explanation of the need for matched groups in experiments that include children with ASD, see Box 15.2.)

Baron-Cohen et al. (1985) found that more than 80% of the typically developing children and the children with Down syndrome succeeded on the Sally–Anne task, but only 20% of the children with ASD were successful. Failure on the task was unlikely to be due to learning difficulties in general (otherwise the children with Down syndrome would have failed as well), but it seemed to be specific to the group with ASD. Perner et al. (1989) also tested children with ASD using the Smarties false-belief task and found similar results—most of the children with ASD failed the task.

Children with ASD also have difficulty in other tasks that require an appreciation of another's false belief. Baron-Cohen et al. (1986) showed children with ASD sets of four pictures, each of which made a story (see Figure 15.3). One type of story was called a 'mechanical' story because the action in the story did not involve any people.

- Picture 1: shows a balloon leaving a person's hand.
- Picture 2: the balloon in the air.

A mechanical story

A behavioural story

A mentalistic story

Figure 15.3 Examples of pictures from the Baron-Cohen et al. (1986) experiment.

Source: Baron-Cohen, S., Leslie, A.M. & Frith, U. (1986) Mechanical, behavioural and intentional understanding of picture stories in autistic children. *British Journal of Developmental Psychology 4,* 113–125.

- Picture 3: the balloon near a tree.
- Picture 4: the balloon bursts on the tree.

Another type was called a 'behavioural' story because it included people but did not require any understanding of what the people were thinking.

- Picture 1: shows a girl walking in a street.
- Picture 2: the girl goes into a sweet shop.
- Picture 3: the girl buys sweets at the counter.
- Picture 4: the girl leaves the shop with the bag of sweets.

The third, 'mentalistic' type of story required an understanding of the beliefs about the characters in the pictures.

- Picture 1: shows a boy putting a sweet into a box.
- Picture 2: the boy leaves the room, to play soccer outside.
- Picture 3: mother takes the sweet out of the box and eats it.
- Picture 4: the boy comes back to the box and looks surprised.

The children were given the pictures in a mixed-up order and were asked to put them in an appropriate sequence, and they were asked to explain what was happening in the story. The children with ASD could order and describe the events in both the mechanical and the behavioural stories, but they were poor at understanding the mentalistic stories—they put the pictures in a jumbled order and only reported what they could see in them. They did not refer to the 'mentalistic' aspect of the story (for example, in the story about the boy and the chocolate, they could not explain why the boy was surprised when he found that the box was empty).

We said earlier that having an understanding of another person's mind is essential if you want to deceive them by giving them a false belief. If children with ASD have difficulty understanding other people's minds, how well can they deceive others? This question was examined by Sodian and Frith (1992), who showed children a closed box that contained a sweet. The children were then told about a robber puppet (who would take the sweet). They were also told that the robber was lazy and would not try to open the box if it was locked. In the 'sabotage' condition of the experiment, children had a key and could decide whether to leave the box unlocked or to lock it when they were told that the robber was coming. In the 'deception' condition, children did not have a key and therefore could not lock the box, but before the robber reached the box he asked the child whether the box was open or locked (and therefore the children could deceive him by saying that the box was locked).

In the sabotage condition the children were, in effect, manipulating the robber's *behaviour* (by locking the box so that he could not look in it). In the deception condition they were manipulating the robber's *beliefs* (by telling him that the box was locked). Children with ASD were successful in the sabotage condition, but failed to think of ways to deceive the robber in the other condition. Even though they understood the task and were motivated to stop the robber getting the sweet (as demonstrated by their success in the sabotage condition), they were unable to manipulate the robber's belief in the deception condition. This again demonstrated the difficulty children with ASD have in a task that depends on understanding the mind of someone else.

These studies have shown that children with ASD have difficulty in tasks that involve mental representations. But is this difficulty specific to understanding mental representations, or do children with ASD have difficulty understanding all types of representations? There are several 'non-mental' representations of the world: maps represent the landscape; drawings and photographs represent scenes in the world. As we pointed out before, all these represent the world in a (single) specific way, and they may often no longer portray the world in its current state. If children with ASD have a general difficulty with representations, they might also have difficulty understanding the nature of pictures, photographs and other such representations, because they often portray a 'false' view of the world. Leslie and Thaiss (1992) investigated this issue. They tested typically developing children and children with ASD using a false-belief task (a test of understanding a mental representation) and a 'false' photograph task (a test of understanding a non-mental representation). Leslie and Thaiss's procedure and findings are described in Box 15.2. It was clear that, although the children with ASD performed poorly in the false-belief task, they performed very well in the 'false' photograph task, suggesting that children with ASD have a specific deficit in understanding *mental* representations, rather than in understanding all representations. If so, the research into photographs and maps leads to a similar conclusion as the other research, described above, demonstrating that children with ASD have particular problems in tasks involving understanding other people's thoughts and beliefs.

Box 15.2 Domain specificity in conceptual development: neuropsychological evidence from autism

Several experiments had shown that people with ASD often have difficulty appreciating that other people behave on the basis of their beliefs about the world (Baron-Cohen et al., 1985; Perner et al., 1989). A belief about the world is usually referred to as a representation, and we all have a mental representation of the world derived from our knowledge and experience of the world. Most adults also realize that other people may have different representations from our own, and that both we and other people may have a representation of the world that is inaccurate, but this realization often seems to be lacking in people with ASD.

Leslie and Thaiss pointed out that, as well as mental representations, there are other types of representations (pictures, photographs, maps and so on). If children with ASD are impaired in their understanding of mental representations, are they also impaired in understanding other forms of representation?

In any experiment with people with learning difficulties, it is very important to find an appropriate control group. If, for example, children with ASD aged 12 years were compared with typically developing children aged 12 years, it is likely that on almost any cognitive measure, the typically developing children would perform better than the children with ASD, because the typically developing children would have a mental age that was approximately the same as their chronological age, but the children with ASD would have a much lower mental age. Discovering that a group of children with a typically developing mental age performed better than a group of children with a comparatively low mental age would not be very surprising or informative.

Therefore, to measure the abilities of children with ASD, it is usual to compare them to other children who have the same mental age (but who do not have the diagnosis of autism). For example, if a group of children with ASD who have a mental age of 6 years are compared to a group of typically developing children who also have a mental age of 6 years, and the children with ASD perform less well than the typically developing children on a task, it can be assumed that their poorer performance is due to their autism.

However, in such an experiment it would be likely that the chronological age of the typically developing children would be about 6 years, but the children with ASD might (say) have a chronological age of 12 years. In other words, there might be a large difference in the actual age, and therefore the experience of the two groups. To overcome this, some researchers have compared children with ASD with children with other learning difficulties. For example, researchers might find a group of children with ASD with an average chronological age of 12 years and an average mental age of 6 years, and a group of children with learning difficulties who also have an average chronological age of 12 years and an average mental age of 6 years. If both groups carried out the same test, and the children with ASD performed less well than the

children with learning difficulties, it can be inferred that the deficit in the performance of the children with ASD was due to some factor associated with autism, because other factors like chronological and mental age were the same for both groups.

Leslie and Thaiss compared 15 children with ASD with 20 typically developing children who had a similar average mental age. The details of the children are given in Box Table 15.2.1.

All the children were given two tasks. In one task, the children's understanding of mental representations was tested by asking them about a false belief. In the other task the children's understanding of a non-mental representation (a photograph) was tested by asking them about the content of the photograph.

The false-belief task was based on the Smarties task (see p. 520). The children were shown a chocolate sweets (Smarties) box and asked what it contained. All the children said 'sweets'. The top was then removed and the child was shown that the box actually contained a pencil. The pencil was then replaced in the box and the top put back. The child was then asked, 'Now [name of child's friend] has not seen this box before. When I show this box to [name of friend] before I take the top off—what will [name of friend] say is in here?'.

Box Table 15.2.1 Mean ages and age ranges of children in Leslie and Thaiss's (1992) experiment.

	Chronological age	Mental age
Children with ASD	Mean 12:0 Range 7:10–18:7	Mean 6:3 Range 4:4–14:5
Typically developing children	Mean 4:0 Range 3:8–4:5	Mean 4:5 Range 2:6–7:3

Source: Leslie, A.M. & Thaiss, L. (1992). Domain specificity in conceptual development: Neuropsychological evidence from autism. *Cognition, 43,* 225–251.

The children were also asked a 'reality' question ('What is really in here?') to check that they remembered what was actually in the box.

The photograph task involved a story about three puppets and a toy box. A cat puppet took a photograph of Polly the horse puppet while Polly was sitting on the toy box. After the photograph was taken it was placed face down (without the child seeing it). Then Polly was moved from the toy box and a mouse puppet was put in Polly's place. The child was then asked the photograph question: 'In the photograph, who is sitting on the toy box?.'

The child was also asked a 'memory' question ('Who was sitting on the toy box when the cat took the photograph?') and a 'reality' question ('Who is sitting on the toy box now?') to check that they had remembered all the story details.

Four of the children with ASD and three of the typically developing children failed one or both of the memory and reality questions and were excluded from the analysis.

Box Table 15.2.2 shows the percentage of children in each group who gave a correct answer to the belief question in the Smarties task, and the percentage who gave a correct answer to the photograph question.

There was a significant interaction in the performance of the children ($p < .001$). As can be seen in the table, the typically developing children performed similarly on both the false-belief and the photograph task. In contrast, the children with ASD performed poorly in the false-belief task and were all correct in the photograph task. Their poor performance in the false-belief task (a task that required an appreciation of someone else's mental representation) is typical of the findings from other researchers (see this chapter).

The children with ASD had no difficulty in the photograph task, so Leslie and Thaiss suggested that any impairment that children with ASD have in understanding representations does not extend to non-mental representations like photographs.

In a second experiment, Leslie and Thaiss carried out a similar study, but instead of showing children a photograph they showed them a map of a model room (and a sticker on the map marked the position of a puppet character, who later moved). The children were then asked where the character was sitting 'in the map' to test whether they realized that the map did not change even though the character had moved. As in the photograph task, the children with ASD were much better in the map task than in a false-belief task.

This experiment by Leslie and Thaiss (and similar studies with photographs by Leekam and Perner, 1991, and with drawings by Charman and Baron-Cohen, 1992) demonstrated that although children with ASD have an impaired understanding of mental representations, they are not impaired in understanding non-mental representations such as photographs and maps.

Box Table 15.2.2 Percentage of children in each age group who were correct in the false-belief and photograph tasks.

	False belief task (%)	Photograph task (%)
Children with ASD	33	100
Typically developing children	75	66

Source: Leslie, A.M. & Thaiss, L. (1992). Domain specificity in conceptual development: Neuropsychological evidence from autism. *Cognition, 43*, 225–251.

However, other researchers have argued that understanding false photographs (or drawings) is not the same as understanding false beliefs, because a photograph does not show a false representation of the current situation (Leekam et al., 2008). In the case of a typical false-belief task like the Sally–Anne task, Sally has a false belief about the current position of a marble. Therefore in the Sally–Anne task a child has to differentiate between two representations: the child's current representation of the position of the marble and Sally's current representation about the marble. In contrast, in the photograph task a child has to distinguish the current position of a toy from the past position of the toy. Leekam et al. argued that the photograph task and the false-belief task were therefore not equivalent, and require different aspects of understanding about representations. This interpretation emphasizes that it is differences in the way that children with ASD and typically developing children reason about representations that account for the pattern of performance in false-belief and photograph tasks (Apperly, 2011; Bowler et al., 2005), rather than differences in performance being due to the mental or non-mental aspects of the task (Leslie & Thaiss, 1992).

Based on material in Leslie, A.M. & Thaiss, L. (1992). Domain specificity in conceptual development: Neuropsychological evidence from autism. *Cognition, 43*, 225–251.

HOW FAR CAN A DEFICIT IN UNDERSTANDING MENTAL REPRESENTATIONS CONTRIBUTE TO AN EXPLANATION OF ASD?

One problem for any explanation of ASD based on children's lack of understanding of mental representations is the fact that in most studies, a proportion of children with autism succeed on false-belief tasks (e.g. in Baron-Cohen et al., 1985; in Leslie and Thaiss, 1992—see Box 15.2). As Charman (2000) has emphasized, if a failure to understand minds is not a universal deficit in ASD, any explanation based on understanding minds is very much weakened.

However, even though some people with ASD can pass a first-order false-belief task like the Sally–Anne task, when the same people are given a second-order false-belief task they rarely succeed (Baron-Cohen, 1989). It seems that some people with ASD may be able to pass first-order tasks, but the fact that they fail second-order tasks suggests that they do not have a secure understanding of other people's minds. It could be that people with ASD may succeed on first-order tasks using strategies that do not necessarily include an understanding of mental representation (Happé, 1994).

If people with ASD do not have an understanding of minds, does this explain the impairments seen in people with ASD? Major social impairments might be expected in anyone who does not realize that other people have thoughts and beliefs about the world, and that their behaviour is based on those beliefs. A failure to understand that people have independent beliefs, and a failure to appreciate that people's beliefs may not coincide with reality, must make it very difficult to interpret why other people act as they do, and this will limit effective social understanding. It will also make it difficult to communicate, because people with ASD will not realize that what a speaker says is a statement based on the speaker's thoughts, and requires interpretation. Being unable to interpret what people do and what they say may lead to a world in which many things appear to be, at best, puzzling and confusing and, at worst, arbitrary and disturbing. In such a world, it would not be surprising if people with ASD insist on sameness and routine, because at least in this way some sense of consistency and predictability might be maintained.

The finding that people with ASD have a deficit in understanding of minds was a major discovery. It led to the recognition of many previously unrecognized aspects of the autistic syndrome, it has stimulated much new and original research into ASD, and it goes part of the way to explaining some of the impairments, especially social ones, that typify ASD. However, a deficit in understanding minds does not help us to understand all the impairments associated with ASD. For example, it is not obvious how specific language problems (e.g. echolalia), obsessive behaviours or 'islets of ability' could be linked to a lack of understanding minds.

Some researchers accept that the poor performance of children with ASD on false-belief tasks does reflect a deficit in their understanding of mind, but do not accept that this is a core impairment in ASD. For instance, Baron-Cohen (1995) suggested a more fundamental deficit. He described a 'shared attention mechanism', which combines information about your own direction of gaze and another person's direction of gaze. This includes information like: I see that X sees the object; X sees that I see the object. For example: I see that Mummy sees a toy; Mummy sees that I see the toy. Baron-Cohen suggested that the shared attention mechanism allows a child to work out whether she and someone else are both looking at the same thing. Such a mechanism would also mean that a child could understand the perceptual mental state of another person (i.e. that Mummy sees the toy). More than this, a child may also be able to interpret another's look in terms of desire—for example, young typically developing children know that, if someone is looking at one of four blocks of chocolate, she wants that particular block (Baron-Cohen et al., 1995). Baron-Cohen argued that from an early understanding about gaze, a young typically developing child can gain insights into another's mental state, and that these insights are the foundation for children's later understanding of mind. Baron-Cohen et al. (1995) found that, in contrast to typically developing children, when children with ASD saw someone looking at one of four blocks of chocolate, they did not realize that it was that block that the person wanted.

In an extensive study, Baron-Cohen et al. (1996) screened 16,000 infants at the age of 18 months using five tests, including a test of shared attention. Only 12 children failed all five tests. When these children were followed up at 42 months of age, nearly all of them had been diagnosed with ASD. This implies that lack of shared attention is one of the early deficits in ASD, and Baron-Cohen (1995) argued that the lack of a shared attention mechanism in children with ASD could explain the later deficit in their understanding of mind.

We have mentioned only one or two examples of the theories that have been put forward to explain ASD, and a deficit in theory of mind is only one suggested explanation for ASD. Nonetheless, the realization that children with ASD may lack theory of mind has generated a great deal of research and provided new insights into both ASD and typical development.

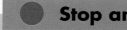 **Stop and Think**

What are the implications of not having a theory of mind?

CHAPTER SUMMARY

- Research into how children develop an understanding of another person's mind has become a large and very important area of developmental study.
- The discovery that typically developing 3-year-olds have difficulty understanding the concept of mind has stimulated many new studies, and has led to the generation of new theories about early cognitive development.
- Researchers now recognize that the development of theory of mind abilities in young children is crucial because theory of mind is linked to so many other aspects of development.
- Once children make the discovery that other people have minds and that all people are interpreters (rather than just receivers) of information about the world, they have made the first step to the sophisticated reasoning they will employ in later life. They can begin to develop all the skills they need for successful interaction, and for understanding others' emotions and behaviour, as well as those other necessary social skills like deception that all, crucially, depend on an awareness of theory of mind.
- The importance of all these achievements is highlighted by the difficulties experienced by a few children, those with ASD, who lack full insight into others' minds. Realizing that children with ASD lack insight into others' minds has stimulated new directions of research into ASD, and a better understanding of the difficulties faced by children and adults with this diagnosis.

DISCUSSION POINTS

1. What does 'false belief' mean, and why are false-belief tasks important?
2. When do children succeed on false-belief tasks?
3. Is children's achievement of theory of mind a major cognitive change which occurs during a brief period of time, or is it a gradual development over several years?
4. How much has the research into children's theory of mind contributed to an understanding of ASD?

FURTHER READING

- The best introduction to research into theory of mind is Doherty, M.J. (2009). *Theory of mind. How children understand others' thoughts and feelings*. Hove: Psychology Press. This book is the best source of references to the literature, and Doherty provides a well-balanced view of the competing theories that have been put forward to explain the development of theory of mind.
- A very clear review is provided by Miller, S.A. (2012). *Theory of mind: Beyond the pre-school years*. Hove: Psychology Press. This reviews studies of second- and higher order theory of mind (from primary school to adults) but there are also chapters summarizing research with younger children.
- A very good and readable book is Hughes, C. (2011). *Social understanding and social lives: From toddlerhood through to the transition to school*. Hove: Psychology Press. This book covers all aspects of theory of mind, but focuses on young children and their development in a social context.
- Carpendale, J. & Lewis, C. (2006). *How children develop social understanding*. Oxford: Blackwell, covers all aspects of the research into theory of mind, and includes several chapters on the interaction between cognitive and social development in relation to theory of mind development. A specialist book is Apperly, I. (2011). *Mindreaders: The cognitive basis of 'theory of mind'*. Hove: Psychology Press.
- An advanced collection of essays on theory of mind can be found in Baron-Cohen, S., Tager-Flusberg, H. & Lombardo, M.V. (2013). *Understanding other minds: Perspectives from developmental social neuroscience*. Oxford: Oxford University Press.
- Frith, U. (2003). *Autism: Explaining the enigma* (2nd ed.). Oxford: Blackwell, is still a good readable introduction to ASD, which includes a history of the concept of autism, as well as vivid examples of the impairment. The National Autistic Society of the UK (www.autism.org.uk) has extensive web pages that cover every aspect of ASD, including references to the academic literature, much practical guidance about ASD and advice about supporting people with ASD.

CHAPTER
16

Learning in a Social Context

CHAPTER OUTLINE

- The Challenge of Vygotsky
- Individual Mental Functioning: Its Sociocultural Origins
- Language and Thought
- The Impact of Bruner
- Collective Argumentation
- Implications for Education
- Is Synthesis Possible?

We saw in Chapter 13 Piaget's account of how children develop as thinkers and learners. Essentially, the Piagetian model shows us children as individual 'scientists' who formulate and test increasingly complex hypotheses about their world and about their own experiences and interactions. By and large, it is the inanimate world of objects to which Piagetian psychologists have paid most attention. Donaldson and her colleagues, however, demonstrated young children's competence at taking the perspective of another person in tasks that are socially meaningful to them. In this chapter, we explore the idea of the child as someone who negotiates meaning and understanding in a *social* context and the critical role that language plays in enabling children to enter into their culture.

First we describe the influential work of Vygotsky, who proposed that learning must be viewed in the context of the person's culture and the tools and aids that exist in that culture. Here we explore the role of language as a tool for learning through complex processes of social interaction in children's communities. The child develops repertoires of shared meanings even before the emergence of language, starting with such phenomena as 'joint attention'. But, with language, the child gains a much more powerful entry point into the images, metaphors and ways of interpreting events that are distinctive in his or her own culture. These social representations give the child a framework for constructing knowledge.

Second, we discuss the ethnographic research carried out by Cole and his colleagues in non-Western cultures to investigate the role of the individual's social world as an arena within which thinking develops.

Third, we examine Bruner's contribution to this approach, in particular its application to educational contexts. Bruner developed the concept of 'scaffolding', that is, the wide range of activities through which the adult, or the more expert peer, assists learners to achieve goals that would otherwise be beyond them.

Finally, we view the proposal by Rogoff and her colleagues in the neo-Vygotskian tradition that significant learning occurs in communities of learners through a process of guided participation. We provide a number of examples that illustrate these learning processes in action.

THE CHALLENGE OF VYGOTSKY

A major challenge to Piaget's theory comes from the more recent emphasis, within the field of developmental psychology, on the intricate and reciprocal relationship between the individual person and the social context. One influential strand in this shift of perspective comes from Russian psychologists, in particular from the writings of Vygotsky (1896–1934). By the end of the 20th century, he was increasingly cited in the literature; there were several new translations of his work and biographies were written of his life. In the 21st century, his ideas continue to influence a growing number of empirical and theoretical studies, and are currently viewed as highly relevant to applied fields such as education.

Vygotsky created an ambitious model of cognition with a sociohistoric approach at its centre. Vygotsky was a brilliant student of law, literature and cultural studies at the University of Moscow. He also studied at Shaniavskii People's University, an unofficial university that appeared in Moscow when the authorities expelled staff and students from Moscow University on suspicion of being involved in anti-tsarist activities. Like Piaget, he saw the child as an active constructor of knowledge and understanding. But he differed from Piaget in his emphasis on the role of direct intervention by more knowledgeable others in this learning process. It is as a result of the social interactions between the growing child and other members of that child's community, he argued, that the child acquires the 'tools' of thinking and learning. In fact, it is out of this cooperative process of engaging in mutual activities with more expert others that the child becomes more knowledgeable. Instruction, according to Vygotsky, is at the heart of learning.

During his short life, despite poor health, Vygotsky worked intensely and productively. Yet much of his work was censored or simply hidden by his colleagues out of fear. *The psychology of art* (Vygotsky, 1971), which led to the award of his PhD in 1925, was not published even in Russian until 1965; *Thought and language*, his best-known work, was first published in 1934, but was suppressed by the Stalinist authorities in 1936 and did not reappear until 1956. During this period, a distorted interpretation of Pavlov's work predominated in Russia, as in the USA. This reductionist model of mind (which Pavlov himself never endorsed) said that higher mental processes, such as reasoning, and even consciousness itself, could be accounted for within the conditioned reflex approach. Vygotsky distanced himself from this dominant view.

> A human being is not at all a skin sack filled with reflexes, and the brain is not a hotel for a series of conditioned reflexes accidentally stopping in.
>
> *(Vygotsky, quoted in Joravsky, 1989, p. 260)*

By contrast, he argued that consciousness is central to the science of mind and that human beings are subject to ongoing interplay between biological and cultural factors.

Vygotsky's psychology was consistent with Marxism, but it was far more sophisticated than the psychology favoured by Stalinist party ideologists. He had to tread a minefield and, for the most part, managed to avoid head-on conflict with the authorities while stating his own views with integrity. It says a great deal for him that he was able to separate himself from the Stalinist pressure to reject 'bourgeois' aspects of science and to address himself to the study of the self-directed, conscious mind.

INDIVIDUAL MENTAL FUNCTIONING: ITS SOCIOCULTURAL ORIGINS

According to Vygotsky, children use the knowledge from their culture to solve problems in everyday life. They interpret this knowledge in terms of their own understanding and then use that information in new ways to fit the immediate task. They use that interpretation for action, which, in turn, they introduce back into their culture. As we saw in Chapter 9 in the discussion of social cognitive domain theory, children's constructions of knowledge— for example, their development of moral understanding—are not direct copies of their parents' views. Psychological mediational tools, such as problem-solving skills and language, shape children's thinking processes within the social, cultural and historical context that they inhabit. From Vygotsky's perspective, we can only understand mental functioning in the individual if we take account of the social processes on which it is based.

> Children solve practical tasks with the help of their speech, as well as with their eyes and hands. This unity of perception, speech and action . . . constitutes the central subject matter for any analysis of the origins of uniquely human forms of behaviour.
>
> *(Vygotsky, 1978, p. 26)*

Although Vygotsky placed a greater emphasis on language than Piaget did, he stressed that this process must also be seen in the context of the person's culture, and the tools and aids that exist in that culture. The interactions between the individual child, the significant people in her immediate environment and her culture can be represented diagrammatically (Figure 16.1). From this diagram, we can see that Vygotsky saw mental functioning as action, and he argued that before this conscious, self-directed control develops, action is the way in which the child responds to the world. Furthermore, it is the action of turning round and, using language, reflecting on one's own thoughts that enables one to see things in a new way. Learning is achieved, first, through cooperation with others in a whole variety of social settings, with peers, teachers, parents and other people who are significant to the child, and, second, through the 'symbolic representatives' of the child's culture, through her art and language, through play and songs, through metaphors and models. In this two-way process, the child's development as a learner reflects her cultural experience; in turn, significant cultural experiences become internalized into the structure of the child's intellect. Vygotsky's theory stresses the

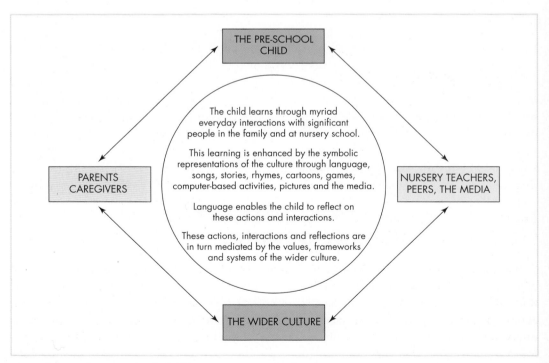

Figure 16.1   The pre-school child learns in a social-cultural context.
Source: Image provided by Helen Cowie. Used with permission from Helen Cowie.

role of interpersonal processes and the role of society in providing a framework within which the child's construction of meaning develops.

Vygotsky (1981, p. 163) stated that 'social relations or relations among people genetically underlie all higher functions and their relationships'. In contemporary Western psychology, the terms 'cognition', 'memory' and 'attention' are automatically assumed to be individual characteristics. We only place them in the social plane by adding markers such as 'socially shared' or 'socially distributed'. Vygotsky was especially interested in the cognitive processes that are directly influenced by the specific culture in which the person happens to exist. Out of this evolved the concept of *intersubjectivity of social meanings*, by which we mean the shared understandings that occur when people communicate with one another. These social meanings develop out of the negotiations that occur within social groups. As we saw in Chapter 2, Rogoff (2003) proposed that children learn in cultural communities, where they participate in and observe adult behaviour and so create their own interpretations of the world.

The kinds of changes in activity that could have an impact on higher cognitive processes were documented in an early study by Vygotsky's colleague, A.R. Luria, who investigated the effect of Marxist reforms and the introduction of schooling on the cognitive processes of the peasants of Uzbekistan (Luria, 1979). Luria compared traditional, non-literate peasants with similar villagers who had experienced a literacy course and training in new farming methods. One of his experiments was to test his participants' capacity for reasoning by presenting them with problems in logic. He found differences between those who had experienced formal schooling and those who had not. For example, uneducated peasants would respond on the basis of their everyday knowledge and not in terms of the logical nature of the problem. When presented with the following syllogism: 'In Siberia all the bears are white; my friend Ivan was in Siberia and saw a bear; what colour was it?', an uneducated peasant would typically reply: 'I have never been to Siberia, so I can't say what colour the bear was; Ivan is your friend, ask him.'

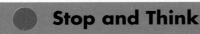
Stop and Think

Why did the uneducated peasant find this problem hard to solve?

Luria concluded that the extensive changes brought about by economic reconstruction of traditional peasant farming methods and formal schooling were paralleled by changes in the ways in which the peasants formed concepts and drew logical conclusions. The implication appeared to be that schooling develops a particular kind of abstract thinking.

Cole's Work with the Kpelle

Influenced by this work, Cole and his colleagues (Cole et al., 1971; Scribner & Cole, 1978) carried out a similar intensive study of the Kpelle of Liberia, a tribal group whose culture is very different from that of Western societies, at a point in their history where economic and educational changes were taking place. However, these researchers came to a more complicated conclusion than Luria. They found that in some domains the adult Kpelle performed less well than Americans, but that in others they were greatly superior. For example, the Kpelle were very good at estimating various amounts of rice; by contrast, they performed less well than Westerners when asked to estimate length. This difference could be explained by the fact that, for the Kpelle, rice farming is central to their culture and so involves a whole network of related activities. They have an elaborate system for measuring rice in its harvested and processed form. As Cole et al. (1971, pp. 36–37) wrote:

> The rice . . . is measured by the cup, bucket, tin and bag. Rice is normally sold for ten cents a cup, which is the size of two English measuring cups or one pint dry measure. However, the price varies according to the season and the availability of rice. The largest measure for harvested rice is the bag. There are nearly 100 cups of rice in the typical bag in which rice is imported or sold from one part of Liberia to another. This fact is known to the Kpelle, who value a bag of rice at 100 times the going rate per cup.

Consequently, their ability to estimate quantity is very highly developed. When it comes to measuring length, however, this activity is specific to the task and depends on the object being measured. The Kpelle are not nearly as accurate in doing length measurement as Westerners are.

Cole gives another example of cultural differences in cognitive ability. The Kpelle had quite complex reasons for preferring to plant their rice on the upland hillsides rather than on more convenient, low-lying swampland, including the taste of the rice, the social cohesion that arises from communal planting activity, the lesser yield from swamps, and their custom of growing other crops (not suited to swamps) within the rice plantations. But when Western agriculturalists, for reasons of apparent efficiency, tried to persuade them to plant instead in swamplands, the Kpelle did not articulate their objections and often gave the casual observer the impression of being stupid and irrationally recalcitrant.

 ## Stop and Think

Why did the Kpelle farmers appear 'stupid' to some Westerners?

On the basis of extensive ethnographic observations such as these, Cole and his colleagues concluded that, in order to understand a people, the researcher must consider their social life as a central arena within which much thinking is manifested. Cole drew comparisons with the underperformance of minority groups on standard psychological tests, which, he argued, was the result of situational factors and not the result of deficits. He also suggested that the observations made among the Kpelle could be applied to the problem of subcultural differences in Western societies, in that cultural differences in cognition resided more in the situation to which cognitive processes are applied than in the existence of a process in one cultural group and its absence in another. But he recognized that members of minority cultures were not always able to make appropriate connections between the knowledge of their own culture and the knowledge that is required in a Western classroom. In other words, Cole and his colleagues concluded that cultural variations in logical thinking are the result of differences in the cognitive content brought to the task, rather than differences in generalized thinking skills.

Cole's research in the Vygotskian tradition pioneered psychological research into the relationship between culture and learning, and it challenged the widespread view at the time that non-literate peoples in developing countries were less intelligent than Western people, or that some cultures did not push young people far enough (as, for example, schooling does) so that their cognitive structures operated at a lower level. In particular, this research undermined the view that a psychologist could administer cognitive tests that had been developed in one culture in order to measure the abilities of people in another culture. Rogoff and Waddell (1982) confirmed this perspective in a study of Mayan children's performance on a memory task. The researchers constructed a miniature model of a Mayan village and then added 20 small objects, including animals, people and furniture that were familiar to the children, out of an array of 80 and placed them in the model. The objects were then removed and placed back with the other 60 objects. Then the researchers asked the children to reconstruct the scene that they had been shown. The Mayan children performed slightly better than Western children, so indicating how crucial it is to take account of the child's sociocultural context when inviting him or her to take part in a test.

Within Western societies, this principle has frequently been applied to 'culturally disadvantaged children' to explain their relative underachievement in comparison with more privileged groups (see also Chapter 18 for a discussion of the *deficit* and *difference* models). Kirshner (2014) worked with ethnically diverse youth activist groups from deprived areas to empower them to organize grassroots campaigns, for example, winning the right to subsidized bus passes for young people on low incomes or persuading the community of the need for a playground and then raising the money to build it. As we saw in Chapter 2, Rogoff (2003), building on Vygotsky's theory, proposed that children learn in cultural communities, where they participate in and observe adult behaviour and so create their own interpretations of the world. Kirshner applied similar principles when he helped the low-income young people to acquire the *cultural tools* that would facilitate and strengthen their campaigning. Such endeavours build bridges between school and community and can play a significant part in preventing school dropout and consequent marginalization from mainstream society.

The Zone of Proximal Development (ZPD)

A central concept of Vygotsky's is the zone of proximal development, or ZPD, which provides an explanation for how the child learns with the help of others. The ZPD is the distance between the child's actual developmental level and his or her potential level of development under the guidance of more expert adults or in collaboration with more competent peers. To Vygotsky, the child is initiated into the intellectual life of the community and learns by jointly constructing his or her understanding of issues and events in the world. Unlike Piaget, Vygotsky did not wait for the child to be 'ready'. Instead, he argued, children learn from other people who are more knowledgeable (Figure 16.2).

How does this 'expert intervention' enable the child to learn? It should be at a level beyond the child's existing developmental level so that it provides some challenge, but not too far ahead, so that it is still comprehensible. This is then within the ZPD, and the child can accomplish something he or she could not do alone and learn from the experience. When the child's level of understanding is deliberately challenged (but not challenged too much), then he or she is more likely to learn new things effectively without experiencing failure. Instruction itself should be geared to the ZPD of the person receiving the instruction (Wertsch, 2008). The intervention is at its most effective when it is contingent upon the child's existing repertoire of skills and knowledge—that is, when it is within the ZPD.

Gunawardena et al. (2009) applied the Vygotskian model to the domain of social networking as a foundation for building online communities of practice. Social networking makes it possible for people with shared interests to communicate with one another from any place and at any time. Web technology provides the online tools for learning that mediate

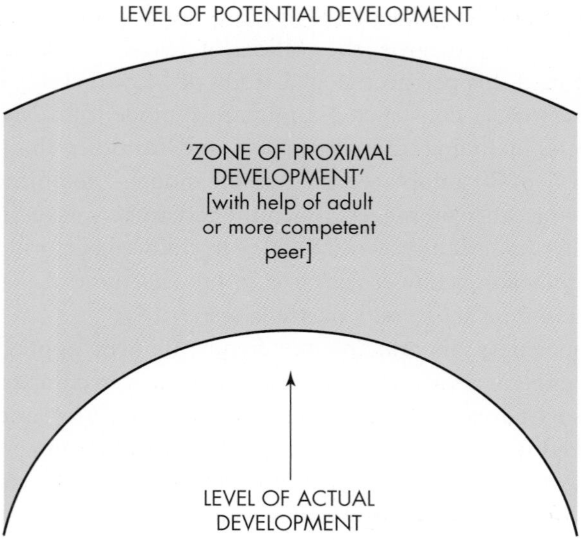

LEVEL OF POTENTIAL DEVELOPMENT

'ZONE OF PROXIMAL
DEVELOPMENT'
[with help of adult
or more competent
peer]

LEVEL OF ACTUAL
DEVELOPMENT

Figure 16.2   Vygotsky's concept of the zone of proximal development (ZPD) (Vygotsky, 1978).

between the knowledge of the individual and their contribution to knowledge building within the community. As Gunawardena et al. (2009, p. 9) put it, 'Learning to navigate on online social networking sites challenges the novice and creates a ZPD . . . In an online environment, the ZPD is often scaffolded by tutorials and a help option that guides the user in correct navigation and procedures'. By using technologies like wiki and social bookmarking, members of an online community exchange knowledge and the space enhances engagement in learning because of the shared common discourse amongst members of the community—a form of *socially shared cognition.*

However, as we see in the section 'Implications for education' later in this chapter, some social contexts are not conducive to learning and may even inhibit it; for example, where the teacher asks too many closed questions, or where the child is in a group of domineering or intimidating peers. In the next section, we see an example of Vygotskian principles as they were applied in one Danish classroom to enhance the quality of children's thinking.

 Stop and Think

Think of an example from your own learning in which you have been guided through the ZPD by a tutor or another student.

Hedegaard's Teaching Experiment

Hedegaard (1996) described a teaching experiment based on the methodology developed by Leontiev (1981) and other followers of Vygotsky. From this perspective, the children's understanding grows out of the process of making the shift from *actions*, through *symbolization*, to *formulation.* Action involves direct exploration of the subject through research based on, for example, observation in the field, at the museum or through film. Symbolization is achieved once the children are able to find ways of representing relationships among things that they have observed; this may be done by means of charts, drawings or models of their research findings. Formulation of broader principles comes when the children can clearly state principles that go beyond the specific subjects of their research. At each stage, the concept of the ZPD provides an essential framework for evaluating children's development as thinkers.

Hedegaard's longitudinal study involved teaching a class of 8–10-year-old Danish elementary school children, using a method for integrating three distinct but related areas of the curriculum: evolution of species, origin of humans and historical change in societies. In order to achieve this aim, she and the teachers in the project designed carefully structured learning experiences to give the children the 'tools' to tackle questions like: 'How can an animal population adapt to changes in its habitat while many individual animals do not succeed in managing this adaptation and so die?'. As an abstract question, this would be difficult for elementary school children to answer. But, claimed Hedegaard, if the problem is presented through the direct study of, say, the polar bear and how it adapts to its Arctic surroundings, children can use this information first to symbolize adaptations of the polar bear and later, on the basis of other similarly concrete studies, to formulate broader laws about survival and change in a whole species. Hedegaard proposed that theoretical knowledge has a 'tool character'; the initial models proposed by the children may become the tools that guide the next stage of the inquiry. By the direct experience of finding contradictions in their active modelling of the problem area under study, pupils' concepts become richer and clearer.

Stop and Think

Why was the process of dialogue influential in developing these children's understanding of the evolution of species?

The teachers' method of deliberately working within the ZPD built on shared, concrete activities using whole-class dialogue, cooperative group work and collective problem-solving tasks. At the heart of the method was the tool of research activity, which in turn led to a critical appraisal on the part of the children of the models that they themselves had constructed. These intellectual tools were then applied to other learning situations that the children encountered.

Hedegaard's results demonstrated that teachers could successfully work with the ZPD in a whole-class context. The children developed a qualitative change in their interest in the subject matter and in the methods used to discover new things. They showed loss of interest in specific animals when they became too familiar and shifted instead to an interest in general formulation of models applicable in a more general way to the issue of animals' adaptation to living conditions. They also developed a critical interest in the teaching methods as they related to problem identification and solution. Overall, the children demonstrated a shift in interest from the concrete to general principles that might, in turn, be applied to new concrete situations. Significantly, Hedegaard found that fast learners were stimulated by the approach but that the less able children, too, maintained interest and motivation.

LANGUAGE AND THOUGHT

Vygotsky demonstrated how higher-order psychological functioning (e.g. problem solving, emotional regulation, thinking and learning) is socially acquired, first existing in the external world and later internalized as dialogue. Behaviour is mediated by use of cultural tools that can be externally oriented, leading to changes in the world (for example, the young activists changing their community by creating a playground), or internally oriented, leading to changes in language and self-mastery (for example, the children learning about evolution). You can see another example of the use of cultural tools such as drama in Box 18.1 in which Veale and her colleagues describe the processes through which girls traumatized by war were reintegrated back into their home communities.

This view has strong implications for education and differs quite sharply both from the child-centred model of education, which sprang from Piaget's theory, and from traditional, didactic models of education. From the Vygotskian standpoint, children do not operate in isolation, but make knowledge their own in a community of others who share a common culture. Language plays a key part in this process. Vygotsky suggested that it was through speech—which had been formed through the processes of social interaction as outlined above—that the child developed as a thinker and learner.

Vygotsky argued that language reflects our culture and its forms, whether in academic texts, professional practice, the arts, folklore or customs. The person as a conscious thoughtful being could accomplish very little without the aids and tools that are provided by his or her history and culture. Piaget had not stressed the importance of language as the principal source of cognitive development. As discussed in Chapter 13, he maintained that language was strongly influenced by the underlying cognitive structures in the child. We have already examined one of his major theoretical constructs, egocentrism. Piaget made extensive observations of children at the Rousseau Institute in Geneva and, on that basis, concluded that up to half of the utterances made by children under the age of 7 years are examples of egocentric speech; in other words, they show no sign that the children have attempted to communicate with another person or adapted their speech so that another might understand it. Piaget observed further that young children often did not seem to care whether anyone else could understand them or not. He noticed that young children would often talk at length to themselves while engaged in solitary activity; these monologues were like commentaries on the children's own actions rather than forms of communication. They might also carry out collective monologues where children were close to one another and spoke in pairs or a group, but where the utterances were not made in response to other children's speech.

Piaget interpreted this behaviour as a sign of the child's inability to take account of the perspective of another, and argued that, with maturity, the child comes to decentre and also becomes more logical. He or she is then able to take the perspective of others and engage in socially meaningful verbal exchanges. This process of decentration, according to Piaget, unfolds between the ages of 4 and 7 (see also Chapter 13). By the age of 7, the child's speech would become more fully socialized.

Vygotsky's view was quite different. He did not accept that the young child's language is largely egocentric and that monologues have no part to play in cognitive development. To Vygotsky, the monologues of younger children were highly social and represented the transition from language as a tool for regulating action and communicating needs, to language as a tool for thought (see also Chapter 12). In fact, he argued that the monologues show children's development in their capacity, already socially formed, to regulate their own activities.

Table 16.1 The contrasting views of Piaget and Vygotsky on preschoolers' private speech.

Piaget's model	Vygotsky's model
Repetition: the child merely repeats sounds.	Social dialogue between adult and child: children and adults engage in joint activities (e.g. peek-a-boo play).
Monologue: the child alone speaks to herself as if she were thinking aloud.	Monologues or overt inner speech: these are internalized to regulate a child's activity, and originate from social dialogues.
Collective monologue: the child uses monologue in social settings but does not take the listeners' viewpoint into consideration. True dialogue does not emerge until around age 7.	Inner speech: utterances internalized in private speech to guide behaviour. Inner speech is internalized by the end of the preschool period.

The monologues, as a form of communication with the self, help children to plan and organize their behaviour. Three-year-old Ben, for example, talks to himself as he cuts out a paper figure: 'Now I'm going to make a man. Cut round here. This is his magic wand. He's a wizard now. Oops! Too far. Oh! Start again'.

Vygotsky suggested that monologues become internalized at around 7 years to become inner speech—the dialogue with ourselves in which we all engage—which becomes thought. You may even still experience a tendency to revert to *externalized* monologues when tasks are too challenging, for example, talking yourself through a difficult problem ('Now, how do I open this door now that the high-tech new lock has been installed?') or commenting on your lack of expertise ('Stupid! Try turning the key the other way!' or 'I'd better ring the locksmith')! Vygotsky's and Piaget's contrasting views are summarized in Table 16.1.

In Vygotsky's words, language reflects 'the organizing consciousness of the whole culture' (see Figure 16.1). He argued that the child's development as a thinker arises both from the dialogue with parents and other adult carers, and in relation to the wider society of which the parents are a part. His perspective encompasses the use of language as a framework for thought and the use of language as a representation of the culture. The two are inextricably intertwined. This is a fundamental point of disagreement between Vygotskian and Piagetian thinking and many developmental psychologists have become increasingly critical of the lack of emphasis on social and cultural context in Piaget's model, with its concentration on the child as an individual progressing through developmental stages. The debate continues in the field of academic developmental psychology but it is of more than academic significance. There are important practical implications for the ways in which we educate and socialize our children.

THE IMPACT OF BRUNER

Vygotsky's ideas were extensively developed and applied in educational settings by the American psychologist Jerome Bruner. Vygotsky's *Thought and language* was not translated into English until 1962. Bruner (1986, p. 72) describes how he welcomed the invitation to write an introduction to the book and how he read the ongoing translation with 'astonishment'. Vygotsky's ideas on thought and speech as instruments for planning out action were in tune with Bruner's views. Bruner was intrigued by Vygotsky's suggestion that society provides the tools that enable the child to become more advanced as a thinker. Bruner was especially interested in the concept of the ZPD and the role that other people play in helping the child to learn and reflect on things. Bruner called this help 'the loan of consciousness'. However, Vygotsky had not actually spelled out in any detail how the more expert adult might 'lend' consciousness to the child who did not already have it. Bruner and his colleagues proposed the concept of 'scaffolding' (Wood et al., 1976) to refer to the wide range of activities through which the adult, or the more expert peer, assists the learner to achieve goals that would otherwise be beyond them, for example by modelling an action, by suggesting a strategy for solving a problem or by structuring the learning into manageable parts. The metaphor of scaffolding is illuminative. Imagine the tutor has erected scaffolding that could help the child to climb to a higher level of understanding. To be more effective, scaffolding has to be constructed so that the child is not asked to climb too much at once. It has to take account not only of the child's existing level, but of how far he or she can progress with help; essentially the idea of Vygotsky's ZPD.

Scaffolding in Practice

Stop and Think

How useful do you find the metaphor of 'scaffolding' in explaining how adults can help children to learn new concepts?

Scaffolding does not imply a rigid structure or a didactic teaching method, but rather a flexible and child-centred strategy which supports the child in learning new things and enables the child to have a sounding board for action. As the child becomes more independent in the mastery of a new skill, the adult is able gradually to remove the scaffolding until the child no longer needs it. The idea of scaffolding is, of course, a metaphor, since the more expert adult or peer does not literally build a structure of scaffolding to support the child! However, the concept of scaffolding has been extremely useful to educators in giving a theoretical justification for methods that structure learning without being unnecessarily didactic, and in exploring the area that covers the distance between learning with adult support and performing without help (that is, the ZPD).

Figure 16.3 A child shows her knowledge of the sun as a sphere, but she still thinks that the earth is a flat disc beneath it (Vosniadou et al., 2001).

Source: Vosniadou, S. (1994). Capturing and modelling the process of conceptual change. *Learning and Instruction, 4*, 45–69.

Vosniadou et al. (2001) provide a good illustration of scaffolding in their study of how children come to understand the physical world. As they indicate, teachers very rarely initiate a discussion of gravity as it relates to children's understanding of the shape of the earth (Figure 16.3). One key problem for children is to understand why people do not fall off the earth. Instruction based only on the presentation of scientific facts cannot by itself lead to conceptual change if it does not give children all the information they need to counteract their naive theories. If this is not acknowledged, children will retain inconsistencies in their thinking. Vosniadou et al. (2001) suggest that instead of focusing on misconceptions, educators might be better advised to focus on naive presuppositions through finely tuned scaffolding (see Box 16.1).

Box 16.1 Capturing and modelling the process of conceptual change

This is a study of the ways in which young children acquire knowledge about the physical world. Stella Vosniadou argued that children have a naive framework theory of physics from early on in infancy. The presuppositions of this framework theory act as constraints on the ways in which children interpret both their own observations and the information they receive from their culture. As we saw in Chapter 11, there are basic principles that seem to guide the infant's process of learning about the properties of the physical world. Children generate specific theories derived from observations of the objects in their physical world and from information that is presented to them by their culture.

The theories that children form through this process are continuously *enriched* and *revised*. Some kinds of conceptual change require the simple addition of new information to an existing conceptual construct (enrichment). For example, primary school children find it easy to add to their existing concept of the moon the information that the moon has craters.

Other theories are accomplished only when existing beliefs and presuppositions are modified (revision). Such conceptual change is difficult to achieve, argued Vosniadou. In an earlier study of 8-year-olds' understanding of the day–night cycle, she found that they could learn in class that the sun does not move, as stated in their textbook, but that later, when asked to describe the day–night cycle, many continued to explain that 'the sun goes down behind the mountains'. Clearly the children were more confused after reading the text than they had been before, since their framework theory had been challenged.

Vosniadou was particularly interested to investigate the nature of children's misconceptions when they were asked to assimilate new information into existing conceptual structures that contain information that is contradictory to the scientific view. Learning failures can happen at any time during the knowledge acquisition process, but especially when the process requires the revision of deeply entrenched presuppositions that belong to the framework theory. Inconsistencies are produced when children attempt to reconcile conflicting pieces of information.

Vosniadou developed a methodology that consisted of a series of questions about the concept in question. Some required a verbal response, some elicited drawings and others required the construction of physical models. There are two aspects of this method: the *types of question* used and the *test of internal consistency*. Here we focus on her study of children's developing mental models of the earth. Young children find it difficult to believe that the earth is a sphere, because this information contradicts their naive framework theory that space is organized in terms of 'up' and 'down' and that the earth appears to be flat.

Types of question

If children are asked factual questions like 'What is the shape of the earth?' or 'Does the earth move?', they can often repeat information that they have been exposed to during instruction. The fact that their answers are scientifically correct does not necessarily mean that they fully understand the concept. Generative questions, by contrast, are those that confront children with phenomena about which they have not yet received any instruction. For example, when asked 'Does the earth have an edge?' or 'Would you ever reach the end of the earth?', children retrieve the answers from their own mental model of the earth and use this model to answer the question. Generative questions, argued Vosniadou, have greater potential than factual questions to unravel the underlying mental models of the earth that children use.

Test of internal consistency

This aspect of the method is concerned to determine for each child whether the pattern of his or her responses can be explained by a single, underlying mental model. A first example comes from Kirsti, aged 6 years.

E: What is the shape of the earth?

Kirsti: Round.

E: Can you make a drawing which shows the real shape of the earth?

Kirsti: (Child draws a circle.)

E: If you walked and walked for many days in a straight line, where would you end up?

Kirsti: You would end up in a different town.

E: Well, what if you kept on walking and walking?

Kirsti: In a bunch of different towns, states, and then, if you were here and you kept on walking here (child points with her finger to the 'edge' of the circle which she had drawn to depict the earth) you walk right out of the earth.

E: You'd walk right out of the earth?

Kirsti: Yes, because you just go that way and you reach the edge and you gotta be kinda careful.

E: Could you fall off the edge of the earth?

Kirsti: Yes, if you were playing on the edge of it.

E: Where would you fall?

Kirsti: You'd fall on this edge if you were playing here. And you fall down on other planets.

Here Kirsti demonstrated that she can answer a factual question about the shape of the earth correctly but that her overall responses are not consistent with the model of a spherical earth. Rather, Kirsti's model appears to be that the earth is a suspended disc or a truncated sphere. A second example comes from Venica, aged 8 years, who, in answer to previous questions, has inconsistently stated that 'the earth is round' but that 'it has an edge'.

E: Can people fall off the end or edge of the earth?

Venica: No.

E: Why wouldn't they fall off?

Venica: Because they are inside the earth.

E: What do you mean inside?

Venica: They don't fall, they have sidewalks, things down like on the bottom.

E: Is the earth round like a ball or round like a pancake?

Venica: Round like a ball.

E: When you say that they live inside the earth do you mean they live inside the ball?

Venica: Inside the ball. In the middle of it.

Venica appears to have constructed a mental model of the earth as a hollow sphere with people living on flat ground inside it.

On the basis of their responses to all the questions designed to investigate a given concept, Vosniadou placed children in a 'mental model' category. Her study of the concept of the earth showed that 80% of children used one out of a small number of well-defined mental models of the earth in a consistent fashion (see Box Figure 16.1.1 for a graphical representation of these mental models). Younger children view the earth as a rectangle or a disc supported by ground underneath and surrounded by sky and solar objects above its flat top. Vosniadou called these *initial* models, since they are based on everyday experience and show no

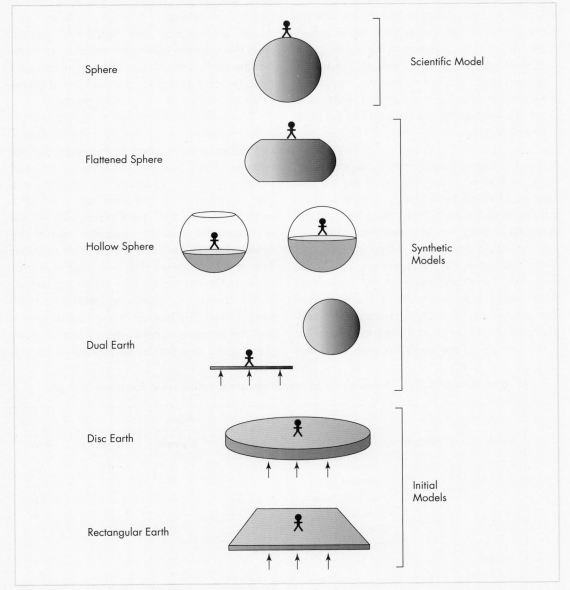

Box Figure 16.1.1 Children's mental models of the earth.

Source: Adapted from Vosniadou, S. (1994). Capturing and modelling the process of conceptual change. *Learning and Instruction*, *4*, 45–69.

influence from the scientific model of the earth. Older children tend to form models that combine aspects of the *initial* model with aspects of the culturally accepted spherical model. Vosniadou called these *synthetic* models, which included the following.

- *Dual earth*: consisting of two earths, one flat on which people live and the other spherical, which is a planet up in the sky.
- *Hollow sphere*: in which people live on flat ground deep inside the sphere.
- *Flattened sphere*: in which the earth is a sphere flattened at the top and bottom parts where people live.

The distribution of these models by age is shown in Box Table 16.1.1. Only 23 of the 60 children had formed the culturally accepted spherical model of the earth. The others had either a synthetic or initial model or were mixed up.

Having identified the mental models children used to answer her questions, Vosniadou was able to unravel some of the underlying theoretical structures and begin to understand the process of conceptual change. She concluded that children find it hard to construct a mental model of the earth because it violates certain entrenched presuppositions of the naive framework theory of physics within which their concept of the earth is embedded.

Children seem to begin by categorizing the earth as a physical object rather than as an astronomical object and applying it to fit the properties of other physical objects in their environment, that is, with reference to solidity, stability, 'up/ down' organization and 'up/down' gravity. From this presupposition, the children conclude that the earth is flat, supported and stable, and that solar objects and the sky are located above it. Vosniadou calls this their initial model.

Later, the children have to reconcile their initial model with the culturally accepted model of a spherical earth, which Vosniadou called the synthetic model, and they do so by a number of modifications. For example, by adopting the misconception of the dual earth, they resolve the conflict between their initial concept of the flat earth and the culturally accepted view of the spherical earth, and so they are able to retain their initial framework theory through a modification but do not change their underlying beliefs. Partial changes in underlying beliefs are achieved through the models of the hollow sphere and the flattened sphere. These children have given up the idea that the earth needs to be sup-

Box Table 16.1.1 Frequency of earth shape models as a function of age.

Earth shape models		Age			
		6 years	8 years	10 years	Total
Culturally accepted	Sphere	3	8	12	23
Synthetic	Flattened sphere	1	3	0	4
	Hollow sphere	2	4	6	12
	Dual earth	6	2	0	8
Initial	Disc earth	0	1	0	1
	Rectangular earth	1	0	0	1
Mixed		7	2	2	11
Total		20	20	20	60

Source: Vosniadou, S. (1994). Capturing and modelling the process of conceptual change. *Learning and Instruction*, 4, 45–69.

ported and have abandoned the 'up/down' gravity presupposition so far as it applies to the earth itself. This is the first step that children take in the differentiation of the concept of the earth from the concept of the physical object to which it initially seemed to belong. These children accept the notion that the earth is a sphere surrounded by space, but continue to operate under the constraints of the 'up/down' gravity presupposition when they consider the physical objects located on the earth. So they cannot understand how it is possible for people and objects on earth to stand outside it without falling down. In order to resolve this conflict, they create a model in which the spherical earth is hollow and people live on flat ground inside it. In the model of the flattened sphere, children have revised their 'up/down' gravity presupposition but still believe that the ground on which people walk is flat.

Vosniadou concluded that the process of conceptual change is slow and it proceeds through the gradual suspension and revision of the presuppositions of the naive framework theory and their replacement with a different explanatory framework. By the end of the primary school years, most children seem to have constructed the concept of a spherical earth, as an astronomical object, suspended in the sky and surrounded by space and solar objects. There are implications for education at school. It is important for teachers to take account of children's deeply held naive presuppositions and beliefs when they design science lessons. For example, telling a child who believes that people live on flat ground inside a hollow sphere that the earth is not hollow will not resolve this child's misconception. A lesson on gravity and a lesson on how round things can sometimes appear flat might allay some of this child's confusion.

Vosniadou et al. (2001) argued, on the basis of this study and others in the domain of children's understanding of scientific concepts, that knowledge is acquired in specific domains and that learning is a process that requires the substantial *reorganization* of existing knowledge structures and not just their *enrichment*. Vosniadou's conceptual change approach to learning proposes that, for children to learn about science, they must create new, qualitatively different representations of the physical world. Children need to be helped to become aware of their existing beliefs and presuppositions in ways that are more consistent with scientifically accepted views.

However, we still need to be cautious in interpreting these findings. Panagiotaki, Nobes and Potton (2009), for example, found that when the questions are asked differently, children (and adults) give very different types of answers. Nobes et al. (2005), using different methods from those used by Vosniadou, reported that even young children had some understanding of the fact that the earth is spherical. They showed children picture cards representing the flat disc earth, the hollow sphere and the spherical (scientific) earth. Like adults, the children showed a marked preference for the scientific earth pictures. Nobes and his colleagues conclude that, rather than having naive mental models of the earth, children build up their understanding through the acquisition of 'fragments' of knowledge that are communicated to them piecemeal by their culture. From this perspective, mental models, like the one described by Vosniadou, may still be methodological artefacts. We need to consider whether early beliefs are a theory or simply fragmented and isolated pieces of scientific information. The search to understand the basis of children's early understanding of scientific concepts continues through ingenious experiments such as the one described in this box.

Based on material in Vosniadou, S. (1994). Capturing and modelling the process of conceptual change. *Learning and Instruction*, 4, 45–69.

Guided Participation in Sociocultural Activity

A useful concept that has grown out of the metaphor of scaffolding is that of *guided participation*, a form of apprenticeship in which children actively engage in cultural practices where adults model, guide and regulate performance while creating temporary scaffolds that offer a form of bridge between old patterns and new. Guided participation allows novices to increase their familiarity and control over the diverse activities involved in a particular culture. As they become more accomplished, these novices reconstruct the knowledge and appropriate it for themselves. Progress towards competence arises through a complex interplay among social factors. Despite the diversity of the contexts studied, a common feature in the research is the role of scaffolding within guided participation.

Paradise and Rogoff (2009) examined the cultural practices that underpin everyday informal learning as children 'pitch in' with family and community activities. A key feature of this kind of learning is that it is embedded in the child's sense of *belonging* with all the personal and emotional commitment that is involved. As Paradise and Rogoff (2009, p. 110) point out, learning in family and community life is often based on a process of observing with intense concentration on the part of the young child. They provide the example of Tz'utujil Mayan toddlers eagerly observing their mothers engage with novel objects.

> For example, one toddler stood watching his mother intently, bending forward to observe her demonstration of an object, with his arms held straight behind him, taut fingers revealing his effort to suppress the impulse to touch, so that he could gain information by observing.

This motivation appears to be based on the child's intuitive understanding of the importance to themselves as well as to their community of what is being learned. Paradise and Rogoff note that this type of observation takes place without any coercion on the part of the adults. The skills that they need to acquire in their community are evident so no pressure is necessary. Contrast this with formal schooling where children will often be reluctant to learn. See also Box 16.2 where you can contrast the competent mathematical knowledge of child street traders with their incompetence at formal maths in the classroom.

Some observation involves active demonstration by an adult. Spoken language is an essential part of this learning but it depends on the child's keen observation and active participation in the life of the community. Paradise and Rogoff (2009, p. 138) also point out that narrative—e.g. gossip, stories, conversations—contextualize the knowledge that the child is acquiring and often carry a message or moral, in their words, 'human age-old sociocultural practice that has evolved culturally over millennia'. The process also illustrates the *collective memory* through which 'members of a group share a similar set of cultural tools, especially narrative forms, when understanding the past' (Wertsch & Roediger, 2008, p. 324).

 Stop and Think

How useful is Rogoff's concept of 'guided participation'? Can you think of an example from your own learning or from your observations of other people in the process of learning?

From this perspective, individual cognitive development is inseparable from interpersonal and community processes. Another study (Rogoff et al., 1995) used the concept of guided participation to study a particular social practice, not, in this instance, the study of a remote culture but a reflective investigation into cultural practices in their own community—Girl Scout cookie sales. Rogoff analysed a number of interlocking practices at different levels, including active contributions from individuals involved (the Girl Scouts), their social partners (mothers and other mentors) and the historical traditions of their community (the cultural history of the Girl Scout movement). This example, drawn from community life, shows the collaborative nature of the learning process and suggests that language, foremost among the social representations, provides a framework within which the growing child comes to interpret and understand experience.

Rogoff developed a research method for investigating guided participation at three levels of analysis: community, interpersonal and individual, each integrated one with the other. She defined the different planes of analysis as follows.

- *Community plane of analysis*: focuses on people participating with others in a culturally organized activity that is guided by cultural values and goals. This could refer to formal systems, such as education, or informal ones, such as voluntary activities.
- *Interpersonal plane of analysis*: focuses on how people communicate and coordinate efforts in face-to-face interaction. This also refers to choices about who may be involved and who should be excluded from the activity. Parents and more experienced peers played a key role here.
- *Individual plane of analysis*: focuses on how individuals change through their involvement in the activity, a process that prepares them for further, related activities in the future. For example, we can study the process of children's growing responsibility through participation in an activity under the guidance of adults or more experienced peers. This includes their increased confidence in the role of door-to-door salesperson, their accomplishment in managing accounts and the efficiency in arranging deliveries of cookies. All of these social and conceptual skills could also be built on for future activity.

A detailed account of the study with Girl Scouts is given in Box 2.2, where you can see in practice how Rogoff provides empirical evidence for her assertion that development (whether in the personal, interpersonal or community plane) is a process of transformation through people's participation in shared activities.

Rojas-Drummond (2000) has also evaluated the impact of guided participation in classroom settings. She compared Mexican preschool children following a specially designed guided participation curriculum, known as 'High Scope' (see p. 632), with matched preschoolers who followed the official state curriculum. By the end of 1 year, the High Scope children's performance in problem solving was significantly higher. Further qualitative analysis of the children's performance indicated that by the end of the year the High Scope children could solve virtually all the problems unaided, while the control children still required help and prompting from the experimenter.

Rojas-Drummond argues that, given the homogeneity of the two populations, the nature of the guided participation and daily discourse between pupil and teacher facilitated this change in the problem-solving competence of the children. Table 16.2 indicates the actions, categorized here under five dimensions, that expressed the guided participation offered to the children. High Scope teachers engaged in these actions significantly more frequently than control teachers.

Table 16.2 Dimensions for describing how teachers and students enact the process of teaching and learning.

I. Learning is a social-communicative process
For example, pupils are used as a resource for the social-cognitive support of fellow pupils; group work is organized so that there are interchanges of viewpoints between pupils and sharing of responsibility in solving problems.

II. Knowledge can be jointly constructed
For example, there is frequent use of reformulations, elaborations and recaps; teachers regularly ask questions that explore pupils' levels of understanding; they also negotiate meanings with pupils.

III. Becoming educated includes learning ways to solve problems
For example, teachers make frequent use of 'why?' questions to get pupils to justify answers; they elicit problem-solving strategies from the pupils; they create opportunities for constructing knowledge jointly with pupils.

IV. Emphasis placed on the process of learning
For example, teachers take time to recap or review learning with pupils; they emphasize the meaning or purpose of tasks.

V. Learning can be nurtured by a teacher
For example, teachers encourage the active participation of pupils; they provide elaborated feedback on a pupil's response to a problem; they gradually withdraw expert support when pupil demonstrates competence.

Source: Adapted from Rojas-Drummond, S. (2000). Guided participation, discourse and the construction of knowledge in Mexican classrooms. In H. Cowie and G. van der Aalsvoort (Eds.), *Social interaction in learning and instruction*, pp. 193–213. Amsterdam: Pergamon, Elsevier Science.

Collective Argumentation

A related pedagogical strategy that has also been systematically researched is *collective argumentation*, another sociocultural approach to classroom learning. Central to this approach is the emphasis on the process whereby cultural tools, such as language, are transformed into internal tools of thinking. This process from the social to the internal plane of functioning requires active engagement on the part of children as they interact with adults and peers to share perspectives and construct new ideas through a collective rather than an individual process. Key aspects of collective argumentation are:

- Individual representations of the issue.
- Comparisons of these representations with those of others in the class.
- Explanations and justifications of a position.
- Co-construction of a perspective by the group.
- Presentation of the group co-construction to the whole class, leading to.
- Validation or testing for acceptance in the wider community of the class.

The teacher's role in the groups is highly proactive as he or she observes, challenges and listens critically to the quality of argumentation at each stage of the process. The final validation stage is especially important, as the teacher rephrases and re-represents the views from the various groups. The teacher also makes connections back to previous argumentations in order to maintain a sense of continuity in the process of inquiry.

Schwarz and Linchevski (2007) investigated the role of argumentation in enhancing children's mathematical understanding. They compared the capacity of 60 high school students to understand a concept known as 'proportional reasoning' in two different conditions: as individual learners and in pairs. They found that in a situation where the young people were testing out a hypothesis in a pair, under the guidance of the experimenter who mediated when opinions differed, there were greater cognitive gains than when the students worked alone. The researchers were testing out the idea that dialogue is needed when there are contradictions that challenge a person's prior knowledge. The ingenious experiment, using various configurations of bricks arranged in blocks (A, B, C and D) of different sizes and weights, is described in detail by Schwarz and Linchevski (2007, p. 513). Essentially, the students are told the relative weight of blocks A and B and they are then asked to infer the relative weights of C and D from the information given. The task is deliberately designed in such a way that there is likely to be disagreement between the students as they try to solve the problem.

Here is an example of the argumentation that took place between two boys, Av and Ita.

Av: C weighs more than D. Here (B) I see one more box than in A, and there (D) there is one more box (than in C). She (the experimenter) said that A weighs more than B. It's more or less the same. They simply added one box. You got it?

Ita: The same. My answer is the same as Av's. This (C) is bigger than that (D).

Av: [to the experimenter] You said that A weighs more than B. Then C here weighs more than D, because there is one more box in B (than in A) and in D there is one more box (than in C) too.

Ita: It's impossible to tell.

The two different conclusions led naturally to further discussion.

Av: Why is it impossible to tell? But this and this (an A-box and a C-box) weigh the same. And this and this (B and D) weigh the same. They simply added boxes.

Ita: What's the link with the structures?

Av: Why one more box? Here (in B) there are four boxes and here (in A) three and here (in C) also three. It's the same, only more boxes.

The researchers indicate that this type of dialogue shows two-sided argumentation. Because Ita and Av have arrived at different conclusions, they had to become more explicit in their arguments. Av had consistently adopted a strategy of adding the number of boxes. It was a less clear about the logic leading to his conclusion. The experimenter intervened to stimulate further argumentation.

Experimenter: *Convince each other!*

Here Av continues the argument.

Av: Again, here A weighs more than B.

Ita: I understand you! Here (B) there is one more cube and here (D) there is one more cube . . . I understand.

Av: They simply added . . .

Finally, Ita was faced with Av's well-argued conclusion that conflicted with his own and conceded. Ita was able to recognize that he did understand Av and throughout he was open to Av's logic. Several processes appear to be at work in such argumentation.

- Confrontation between differing opinions.
- The adult's elicitation of argumentation.
- The readiness of participants to listen to each other and to admit that they are wrong.
- Argumentative moves that lead to the integration of different claims into a new argument.

The outcome is growth in understanding. Argumentation is a form of social exchange that leads to an advance in the participants' knowledge. In other words, we have an example of argumentation as a tool for shared thinking.

Frijters et al. (2008) evaluated the impact of learning through dialogue and discussion on critical thinking in a sample of 297 Dutch pupils during biology lessons. Like Schwarz and Linchevski (2007), they were interested to investigate how interaction between students enhanced learning. However, instead of focusing on internal logical consistencies (as in the study of proportional reasoning described above), they explored the political nature of arguments in the context of discussing an issue that involves emotions and moral reasoning, for example the relationship between people and the environment. In this experiment, the stimulus is a simulated dialogue between two young people about recycling computers in developing countries. The students then, in pairs, analyse the simulated dialogue and then formulate their own joint opinion. Here is an extract from the simulated dialogue (Frijters et al., 2008, p. 80).

Soeraya and Glenn are watching TV. They see how old computers from Europe are dismantled in India. The different materials are sorted—plastic with plastic, etc. The company employs children too.

Glenn:	That's a good example of recycling! Our old computers are then reused.
Soeraya:	Why do they first take those computers all the way to India? Surely, that must cost lots of money?
Glenn:	No that's good. Here a worker costs 40 euros a day, in India only 1 euro. That saves a lot of money . . . It's a really good way of recycling, otherwise we have to burn the things or something. Recycling in the Netherlands costs far too much money.
Soeraya:	But you can see that they're children doing the work in India.
Glenn:	But these people are really poor, now the children are earning a bit extra too. And the computers are recycled for us. So we're helping India a bit.
Soeraya:	But children, Glenn! It's terrible to pay children a pittance to take our computers apart. It's just not fair to recoup our recycling costs on those poor children . . .

The simulated dialogue ends with a commentary.

Glenn hadn't thought about it like this before. He was just so pleased that the computers were being recycled. Things are sometimes more complicated than we think. Soeraya explained to Glenn why she thinks it's not fair to recycle our computers in India.

Then, the students are given the joint assignment: 'Recycling computers costs money. What are Glenn's and Soeraya's opinions and arguments and what are yours?'.

In the non-dialogic condition, the same information was presented in a coherent text rather than in a dialogue. Here is an extract (Frijters et al., 2008, p. 81).

> Every year lots of computers are thrown away. Some are broken, sometimes the model is out-of-date. What happens to these thousands of old computers? They're collected and dismantled. The different materials are sorted—metal with metal, plastic with plastic, etc. These materials are made really small and melted down, ready to use again . . . But did you know that this recycling of computers is done in India? Our computers are taken apart in India. In Europe a worker costs 40 euros a day and in India only 1 euro. That saves a lot of money . . . Children recycle our computers . . . We call this child labour . . .

The students analyse the arguments individually and then formulate their own opinions. Their assignment is structured in the following way.

1. What is the best solution for all our old computers in your opinion?
   I think the best solution for our old computers is . . . because . . .
2. What do you think about recycling our old computers in India?
   I think recycling our old computers . . . because . . .
3. What do you think about child labour?
   I think child labour is . . . because . . .

Students were tested for their subject-matter knowledge, their attitudes towards dialogic learning and the quality and fluency of their reasoning. As predicted, students in the two learning conditions reached very similar levels of subject-matter knowledge. However, students in the dialogic condition scored much more highly on fluency of reasoning than did students in the non-dialogic classes, including more points of view and more arguments to support their position. Students in the dialogic condition also produced more value orientations around the social issues involved in the lessons.

Stop and Think

Why did the students in the dialogic condition become more fluent and critical in their capacity to reason?

This indicated that the higher scores on critical thinking were not gained at the expense of subject-matter knowledge. At the same time, with regard to subject-matter knowledge, there was an interaction effect between student characteristics and learning. The better the students' general reasoning skills in the first place, the more they profited from the dialogic condition. The authors conclude that educators should place more emphasis on training students in the competences that they need to play an active part in a democratic society.

Similarly, Brown and Renshaw's (2000) research with Australian 10–11-year-olds provides another example of sociocultural theory in practice. Students in classes that practised collective argumentation produced significantly higher levels of verbal interaction than students in control classes that engaged in unstructured open discussion of the same topics. Collective argumentation groups produced more requests for clarification, justification and elaboration of ideas. In these classes there was a substantially higher percentage of student talk than in control classes. The larger number of restatements, rephrasings, evaluations and explanations by students indicated that they were working more with one another's ideas rather than with those of the teacher only.

An interesting outcome in one class was that the students developed their own charter of values, which incorporated such qualities as sharing, persistence, patience in waiting turns, respect for others, peer support, honesty and humility. As a result, in this particular school, aspects of collective argumentation were incorporated into school policy documents for both English and mathematics, indicating that the method had in turn become recognized as an important part of the school culture by senior management and administrators. The researchers consider that studies of this form of social construction of knowledge show how exploratory discourse can be used in ordinary classrooms to enhance children's learning. In their words (Brown & Renshaw, 2000, p. 66): 'Collective Argumentation is only one of many possible ways—one of many different types of social scaffolds—that promote the occurrence of such discourse'.

The Community of Inquiry

Just as Cole and his co-researchers carried out intensive observations of the Kpelle in order to make deductions about their thinking processes, so some current researchers treat classrooms as miniature cultures from the observation of which it is possible to make wider generalizations about how young people reflect on their own learning processes (Rogoff, 2003). As Rogoff et al. (2001) argue, truly democratic education empowers everyone involved to create a learning community. The metaphor of the community of inquiry has been devised by Elbers and Streefland (2000) as a guideline for structuring lessons as a communal rather than individual activity. In a community of inquiry, children are given the opportunity to take responsibility for their own learning and that of others, and to become aware of a relationship with their teachers that is different from that normally allowed in a formal classroom. The idea of the community of inquiry is strongly influenced by Rogoff's (1994, 2003) research into communities of learners where pupils play a far more active role in guiding their own learning than they do in traditional, teacher-centred classrooms.

The study by Elbers and Streefland (2000) of 11–13-year-olds in the Netherlands took place at a point where a new mathematics curriculum was being introduced into state schools. The teacher began by announcing to the class that both he and the students would work under new, discursive rules as the experimental curriculum was introduced. Specifically, the children were given a new role, that of 'researcher', with their teachers (the usual class teacher and a researcher) as 'senior researchers'. This announcement immediately created a 'zone of uncertainty' as teachers and children redefined their roles and negotiated new patterns of interaction in the classroom. The teacher began each of the weekly 90-minute lessons with the reminder: 'We are researchers. Let us do research'. The children were then given a mathematical problem as the subject for their research. They worked in small groups or as a whole class, but never individually.

 Stop and Think

How easily might this experimental study be incorporated into everyday teaching in schools?

The children responded very positively to their new roles as researchers, and even when the 'senior researchers' occasionally slipped back into traditional roles, they had to remind them that 'we are all researchers now'. The children quickly adapted to the active inquiry that was expected of them and worked productively in collaborative groups to solve real mathematical problems. The teachers, too, had to reflect carefully on their roles as senior researchers and to keep a balance between imposing their knowledge (for example, of correct solutions to a maths problem) on the children and facilitating inquiry even when, at times, the pupils were making inadequate deductions. The teachers addressed this issue by paraphrasing what the children said and recasting it in a more acceptable form, by eliminating incorrect terminology and errors, and by reminding the young researchers of earlier deductions. This approach follows very closely the idea of apprenticeship as developed by Rogoff and her colleagues.

The metaphor of the 'community of inquirers' was an effective framework within which to guide activities and identify new social roles within that community. Critically, the concept of learning changed from one of reproducing knowledge to one of learning to listen, learning to use evidence constructively and learning to critique another person's statement. Their identities as researchers gave the children a critical stance so that the teachers in turn had to give good arguments and justifications for what they said. Elbers and Streefland gave insight into how young people view themselves as learners and how they learn and work together.

IMPLICATIONS FOR EDUCATION

The teacher in the Piagetian tradition is a facilitator who provides the right materials for the child's level of development and helps the child to 'discover' by herself, through the conflict between her existing schemas and the evidence facing her. The teacher does not confront the child with these discrepancies, but stands back and allows the child to find out for herself. The view of Vygotsky and of Bruner is that the adult and child can work together to construct new schemas, and that intervention by the more expert adult is positively helpful in moving the child's thinking on. The adult's expertise should be actively harnessed to the child's level of competence and to the ZPD. Concepts are jointly constructed through interaction with those who already embody them, together with the ways of doing and thinking that are cultural practices, recreated with children through processes of formal and informal teaching (Wood, 1998). It is important, from this standpoint, to give help to the child that is contingent on her failure to give a correct response. If the child succeeds, it is important to give less help. The more the teacher's behaviour is contingent on the child's behaviour in these sorts of ways, the more able the child becomes to work independently.

Bruner argued forcefully that educators need to be concerned with the role of structure in learning. Teachers must address the issue of enabling students to grasp the structure of a discipline rather than simply mastering facts. By structure, he means the principles and concepts of a discipline, relative to the needs of the learner. The mastery of structure gives the learner purpose and direction; it is a process that enables the child to go beyond the information given in order to generate ideas of her own. Bruner also stressed the need to encourage students to make links and to understand relationships between and across subjects. Curriculum planning should be concerned to enhance learning as an active and problem-solving process.

Even if children do not properly understand something, they may know enough for the adult to be able to direct them to a relevant activity. If this activity is within the ZPD, then, as we have seen, the scaffolding function supports the young learners: 'Contingent control helps to ensure that the demands placed on the child are likely neither to be too complex, producing defeat, nor too simple, generating boredom or distraction'. In fact, the commentary from more expert people helps the child integrate existing knowledge into a wider framework. Thus it supports existing understanding while giving the opportunity to branch out into new regions.

Children may also need help in having their attention directed towards significant features of a task or a situation, when, left alone, they might not make the right connections. The interventions by the knowledgeable adult give the child a structure within which to formulate meaning. By helping the young learner to use language as an instrument of thought, the adult frees the child from the world of immediate perceptions and enables him or her to 'go beyond the information given'.

Bruner pointed out that the invention of 'schooling' itself has had a great impact on the nature of thinking, since schooling creates particular ways of looking at problems and of acting on the world. Teachers are not, he argues, simply handing on knowledge, but actively recreating distinctive ways of thinking. This can be enabling or inhibiting. Donaldson's research has shown how children's will to learn may be unwittingly crushed by the educational experience. Competence, where not recognized or fostered, can wither. Failure to scaffold on the part of teachers, failure to build on the knowledge that the child brings to the classroom, may well lead the child to learn to fail in school settings. In Box 16.2, for example, we see that Brazilian street children are more expert at mathematical calculation in the marketplace than in the classroom.

There are some similarities here with Piaget's theory (Chapter 13). Both Bruner and Piaget view action as important in cognitive development. There are also similarities in the ways in which the two psychologists consider that abstract thinking grows out of action and perception. Both would agree that competence in any area of knowledge must be rooted in active experience and concrete mental operations. Where the two theorists differ, and where Bruner has been greatly influenced by the work of Vygotsky, is: first, in how language and interpersonal communication play a role in the process; and second, in the need for active intervention by expert adults (or more knowledgeable peers) at a suitable level, so enabling the child to develop as a thinker and problem-solver. Like Vygotsky, Bruner argues that instruction is an essential part of learning.

Box 16.2 **Mathematics in the streets and in schools**

Mathematical problem solving in the street market is significantly superior to that carried out with paper and pencil. This was the conclusion of Nunes Carraher and her colleagues, using a research method combining participant observation and the Piagetian clinical method in their study, which demonstrated that youngsters who work on the streets have developed computational strategies that are different from those taught in schools. These young people performed better in problems that were embedded in real-life contexts than they did when asked to solve context-free problems involving the same numbers and mathematical operations.

Nunes Carraher and her colleagues carried out this research in Recife, Brazil, among the children of street vendors who often helped out their parents from the age of 8 years onwards. Young people may also develop their own small businesses selling peanuts, popcorn or coconut milk. As part of this work, the children have to be able to carry out mathematical problem solving, usually mentally, involving addition (4 coconuts and 12 lemons cost x + y), multiplication (one coconut costs x; 4 coconuts cost 4x), subtraction (500 cruzeiros minus the purchase price = the amount of change to be given) and, less frequently, division (where a customer wants a fraction of a unit, such as .5 kilo of oranges).

In the study there were four boys and one girl, age range 9–15, with a mean age of 11.2. All were from poor backgrounds. They were recruited to the study from street-corner stalls where they were working with their parents or alone. The researchers acting as customers in the course of a normal transaction posed test items. The children were asked to take part in a formal test a week later administered by the same researcher. There were 99 questions in the formal test and 63 questions in the informal test. The order of testing was the same for all participants.

The informal test

This was carried out in Portuguese in the naturalistic setting of the street-corner market. A researcher, posing as a customer, asked the children successive questions about potential purchases. Another researcher wrote down the responses. After receiving the answer, the researcher asked the child how they had solved the problem. Here is an example of an informal test taken by M., a 12-year-old vendor.

Researcher: How much is one coconut?
M.: 35.

Researcher: I'd like 10. How much is that?
M.: [Pause] Three will be 105; with three more, that will be 210. [Pause] I need four more. That is . . . [pause] . . . 315 . . . I think it is 350.

M. has solved the problem in the following way.

a) 35 × 10
b) 35 × 3 (a sum which he probably already knew)
c) 105 + 105
d) 210 + 105
e) 315 + 35
f) 3 + 3 + 3 + 1

Even though he had been taught in school that to multiply any number by 10 you simply add a zero to the right of that number, M. used a different problem-solving routine.

The formal test

After the test in a naturalistic setting, participants were invited to take part in the second part of the study. This took place on the street corner or at the child's home. The items for the formal test were devised on the basis of the problems that the child had successfully solved in the naturalistic context. These test items were presented as 38 mathematical problems dictated to the child (e.g. 105 + 105) and 61 word problems (e.g. Mary bought x bananas; each banana cost y; how much did she pay altogether?). In either case, the child solved problems involving the same numbers as those that were used in the informal test. The children were given paper and pencil and were encouraged to use them if they wished. When the problems were solved mentally, the child was still asked to write down the answer. Only one of the children refused to do this, on the grounds that he did not know how to write.

As you can see in Box Table 16.2.1, problems that were embedded in the context of the street market were much more easily solved

Box Table 16.2.1 Test results in three conditions: each participant's score is the percentage of correct items divided by 10.

Child	Informal test score	Formal test score
M	10	2.5
P	8.9	3.7
Pi	10	5.0
MD	10	1.0
S	10	8.3

Source: Adapted from Nunes Carraher, T., Carraher, D.W. & Schliemann, A.D. (1985). Mathematics in the streets and in schools. *British Journal of Developmental Psychology*, 3, 21–29.

than those that were context free. In the informal test, 98.2% of the 63 problems presented were correctly solved. By contrast, in the formal test, word problems (which provided some context) were correctly answered in 73.7% of cases; mathematical problems with no context were solved in only 36.8% of cases. The frequency of correct answers for each child was converted into scores from 1 to 10, reflecting the percentage of correct answers. A two-way analysis of variance of score ranks compared the scores of each participant in the three types of testing situation. The scores differ significantly across conditions ($X^2 = 6.4$, $p < .039$). Mann-Whitney Us were calculated. The children performed better on the informal test than on the formal test ($U = 0$, $p < .05$).

How can we interpret these results? One possible explanation is that errors in the formal test were related to the transformations that had been performed on the informal test problems in order to construct the formal test. But when the researchers tested this hypothesis by separating items that had been changed— by inverting the operation or changing the decimal point from those which remained identical to their informal test equivalents—they found no significant difference between the rates of correct response in each of these conditions.

A second explanation is that the children were still 'concrete' thinkers. This meant that in their natural setting they could solve problems about coconuts and lemons because these items were physically present in front of them. But the researchers rejected this interpretation on the grounds that the presence of the food items in itself does not make a mathematical calculation any easier. In any case, the children can carry out the calculations mentally, without external memory aids in the form of coconuts!

A third interpretation was confirmed by a qualitative analysis of the interview protocols. This analysis suggested that the children were using different routines in each of the two situations. In the context of the street market, they were using familiar groups of objects; in the formal context, they were using school-based routines. Let's look again at how 12-year-old M. solved the same problem in informal and formal contexts.

Informal test

Researcher: I'm going to take four coconuts. How much is that?

M.:   Three will be 105, plus 30, that's 135 . . . one coconut is 35 . . . that is . . .140.

Formal test

M.:
[Asked to solve 35×4] 4 times 5 is 20, carry the 2; 2 plus 3 is 5, times 4 is 20.
[Written answer] 200.

Here are two examples from M.D., aged 9 years.

Informal test

Researcher:
OK, I'll take three coconuts (at the price of Cr$40.00 each). How much is that?

M.D.:
[Without gestures calculates out loud]: 40, 80, 120.

Formal test

M.D. solves the problem 40×3 and obtains 70. She says: 'Lower the zero; 4 and 3 is 7'.

Informal test

Researcher:
I'll take 12 lemons (1 lemon is Cr$5.00).

M.D.:
10, 20, 30, 40, 50, 60 [while separating out two lemons at a time].

Formal test

In solving 12×5, she proceeds by lowering first the 2, then the 5 and the 1, obtaining 152. She explains this to the researcher when she is finished.

When solving the informal test items, the children relied on mental calculations closely linked to the quantities that they were dealing with. The strategy for dealing with multiplication was a form of successive addition. When the addition became too difficult, the child would 'decompose' a quantity into 10s and units. But in the formal tests, the children would try, unsuccessfully, to use school-based routines in which mistakes were frequent. They did not show any sign of checking the final answer in order to assess whether it was reasonable.

The researchers conclude that thinking that is sustained by daily 'common sense' can be at a higher level than thinking out of context. They are, therefore, critical of teaching mathematical operations in a disembedded form before they are applied to real-world problems. In many of the cases that they observed, the school-based routines actually seemed to interfere with the successful solution of the problem. Even when the answers were absurd, children would not notice. Further support comes from Saxe (1988) who found that children engaged in selling actually outperformed non-vendors on a variety of mathematical tasks. He concludes that children construct novel understandings as they address problems that emerge in their everyday cultural practices.

The researchers do not conclude that teachers should allow children to develop their own strategies independently of conventional systems devised in our culture! However, they point out that the mathematics taught in school has the potential to serve 'as an "amplifier" of thought processes' (Bruner, 1971). They recommend that schools should develop methods in which mathematical systems are introduced to children in ways that allow them to be sustained by common sense, rooted in everyday contexts. This study has demonstrated that children have the potential for devising their own efficient routines that have little to do with the formal procedures of school. The study also suggests that teachers need to recognize children's existing *funds of knowledge* (Moll & Greenberg, 1990).

Based on material in Nunes Carraher, T., Carraher, D.W. & Schliemann, A.D. (1985). Mathematics in the streets and in schools. *British Journal of Developmental Psychology*, 3, 21–29.

The Role of Peers as Tutors

We have seen how teachers can use Vygotskian principles in whole-class settings.

Stop and Think

Are there ways in which pupils might also play a part in scaffolding one another's learning?

Slavin, a proponent of cooperative learning, asserts that children can work within the ZPD to challenge existing beliefs and so move peers on in their thinking (Slavin, 1987, p. 1166). Group learning environments, if properly structured, encourage questioning, evaluating and constructive criticism, leading to restructuring of knowledge. For example, in these learning settings a child may need to explain something to another, defend his or her own viewpoint, engage in debate or analyse a disagreement. This can result in learning with understanding, and, many proponents claim, in fundamental cognitive restructuring.

Peer tutoring provides a good example of interaction as a necessary condition for cognitive growth, since it is through the processes involved in this interaction between tutor and tutee—for example, using language to make explicit diverging points of view—that the less expert child masters a new skill (Shamir, 2000; Topping & Ehly, 1998). Here the expert tutor is a fellow pupil. Foot et al. (1990) stress the appropriateness of Vygotsky's model in explaining how peer tutoring works. One child (the tutor) is more knowledgeable than the other (the tutee) and each is aware of the distinctiveness of their roles as expert and novice; it is clear to each child that the aim is for the expert to impart his or her knowledge to the novice. However, the 'expert' is not likely to be that much ahead of the 'novice', and so more readily appreciates the latter's difficulties and thus can scaffold effectively within the latter's ZPD.

Note that it is not simply the encounter between child and child that brings about the change, but the impact of communication and instruction from the more capable peer. As Shamir (2000) found, the enhancement of mediation skills was demonstrated not only by the trained peer tutors who participated in a peer mediation intervention, but was also transferred to the children who were taught by their qualified peers. In other words, the tutees benefited from the mediating style used by peer tutors and were more likely to adopt this style of interaction themselves in other contexts. Studies like these demonstrate how such joint intellectual activity becomes internalized. The instruction is effective when it is slightly ahead of the tutee's actual level and when the assistance from the peer tutor lies within the ZPD.

Cooperative group work (CGW) in the classroom (Cowie & Berdondini, 2001; Howe, 2010) can offer one effective method for enabling children in the role of experts to act contingently upon one another, so guiding their peers through the ZPD. For example, the Jigsaw method (Aronson, 1978) is designed in such a way that children work interdependently by splitting a task into four or five sections. Each pupil has access to only part of the material to be mastered and must work with others to fit together all the pieces of the 'jigsaw'. The pupils work in groups where they become expert in one section; the expert pupils then return to their home groups where they tutor other members of their team in the material that they have mastered.

Bennett and Dunne (1992) investigated the effect of three types of grouping arrangement (one of which was Jigsaw) on primary school children's talk. They noted an increase in the quality of children's language and thinking when they were given the opportunity to work in small, interactive cooperative groups. The children who participated in cooperative group work showed less concern for status, less competitiveness and were significantly more likely to express evidence of logical thinking. This was particularly so when the children were encouraged to engage in an exchange of views, often conflicting, and to explore a range of possible perspectives. Even the most stilted discussions were characterized by talk in abstract modes rarely found in individualized work.

IS SYNTHESIS POSSIBLE?

There are a number of ways in which Piaget's and Vygotsky's theories differ. They have contrasting views on language and thought. Piaget argues that thinking develops out of action rather than out of language. Language does not create thought but enables it to emerge. Before the age of around 7, that is, before the onset of concrete operations, the child, in Piaget's view, is unable to think or discuss things rationally. Preschoolers' language and thought are primarily egocentric since the child is unable to enter into the perspective of another person. Children do not enter into discussions with one another since there is no real reciprocity or attempt at mutual understanding.

Vygotsky, by contrast, did not view children's speech as egocentric, but as highly social. Vygotsky saw the collective monologues in which preschoolers typically engage as representing a transition between the communicative function of language and its function as a tool of thought—that is, between the social and the intellectual. The child who talks to herself, then, is involved in a process of regulating and planning ongoing activity. This overt commentary will later be internalized as inner speech or thought. Vygotsky proposed that language arises out of social interaction.

With regard to learning and thinking, Piaget claimed that children pass through a series of stages of intellectual development before they are able to reason and think logically. Teaching, from this standpoint, is only effective if the child is 'ready' to assimilate the new idea or experience. Conflicting viewpoints can lead to cognitive change through the twin processes of assimilation and accommodation. Piaget emphasized the key part of action for the child's learning. Vygotsky agreed that action underlined thinking and learning, but placed much more emphasis on the role of language, and of direct intervention and help by others more skilled in a task. However, it is sometimes overlooked that Piaget, too, valued peer interactions as playing a significant part in facilitating children's intellectual development.

Contemporary psychologists have begun to examine ways in which the insights from both Piaget's and Vygotsky's perspectives might be synthesized (Smith et al., 2000). Piagetian researchers such as Doise and Mugny (1984) have documented the types of cooperative context in which children progress in their understanding. Conflict of views and perspectives can encourage children to rethink. Doise and Mugny have shown that children working in pairs or small groups come to solve problems more effectively than when they work alone. The reason seems to be that it is through social interaction that they come to see the solution. When the child encounters conflicting views, this stimulates cognitive imbalance that the child is motivated to resolve. The social process of negotiating with peers erects a 'scaffold' that helps each child to reconstruct his or her ideas. This interpretation by Doise and Mugny starts from a Piagetian standpoint but takes account of the social context of peer interaction within which the child operates.

Studies in both the Piagetian and the Vygotskian traditions have given us great insights into cognitive development, but there is still a great deal to be discovered about the interface between social perceptions, personal emotions and cultural constructions on the one hand and the nature of the learning context on the other. We have much to learn about the most productive ways to engage in collaborative work and about working with conflicts as well as cooperation. These issues challenge both Piagetians and Vygotskians, indicating a case for a much fuller integration of developmental and social theories.

Grossen (2000) identifies two critical problems. The first, she argues, is to think that social organizations are homogeneous and to forget that an activity may be situated in various, sometimes oppositional, institutions. The second is to consider that institutions are static and that the rules, routines and habits are unchanging. Grossen's research indicates that participants and institutions are actively engaged in the process of framing both the adult's and the child's representations of the body of knowledge that is to be taught in school. In this way, they influence both the construction of knowledge and the negotiation of social identities. Grossen's critical perspective is useful when we consider ways in which Western-style educational systems have been imposed on developing cultures by powerful political forces without due respect for the traditions that have worked well for these cultures in the past. Cole (1998) warns about social disruption, human misery and other negative outcomes that occur in the name of 'progress' when too little thought is given to local values.

Nearly one hundred years on, the issues are still being fiercely debated in contemporary psychology precisely because they continue to be of such importance for our personal and social development as individuals in society, and for our understanding of wider social processes.

CHAPTER SUMMARY

- Vygotsky's sociocultural proposal is that learning must be viewed in the context of the person's culture and the tools that exist in that culture.
- Vygotsky's concept of the zone of proximal development (ZPD) explains how the child learns with the help of others in a social learning community.
- From the Vygotskian position, language is a very important tool for learning, since it facilitates complex processes of social interaction in children's communities and so enables children to enter into the shared meanings of their culture. This gives the child a framework for constructing and reconstructing the knowledge that is of value in his or her particular society.
- Ethnographic research by Cole and his colleagues in non-Western cultures gives additional insights into this proposal that the child's social world is an arena within which thinking develops.
- Bruner applied Vygotksy's ideas to the educational curriculum and provided alternative ways of structuring learning in social contexts, in contrast to Piaget's child-centred but still individualistic approach. His concept of scaffolding has been particularly influential in educational settings, since it proposes more structure than traditional Piagetian child-centred methods.
- These ideas have been taken further by such researchers as Rogoff, who propose the concept of guided participation as a powerful method for learning in communities. We gave examples of children in the process of negotiating meanings and understanding in a range of interactional contexts.
- Finally, we discussed the possibility of a synthesis between the two major approaches proposed initially by Piaget and Vygotsky. Nearly one hundred years on, the issues are still being debated by practitioners and researchers in contemporary educational and developmental psychology, but there appears to be some scope for common ground.

DISCUSSION POINTS

1. Vygotsky argued that instruction is at the heart of developing and internalizing new ideas. How can the adult most effectively help children to do this?
2. Think of the strategies that teachers might use to scaffold children's learning in the classroom. Can you think of examples from your own experience as a student?
3. Bruner claimed that 'any subject can be taught in some intellectually honest form to any child at any stage of development' (Bruner, 1963, p. 33). Do you agree? For example, how could you teach a 10-year-old about developmental psychology?
4. How do the views of Piaget and Vygotsky differ? In what ways might they be reconciled?
5. Does language structure our thinking, or thinking structure our language?

FURTHER READING

- Rieber, R.W. & Robinson, D. (Eds.) (2004). *The essential Vygotsky*. New York: Springer, gives a very useful overview of Vygotsky's ideas and how they apply to educational contexts. See also Bodrova, E. & Leong, D.J. (2006). *Tools of the mind: The Vygotskian approach to early childhood education*. Harlow: Pearson Education, for deep insights into how teachers can influence their students' development by working through the ZPD.

- Piaget, J. (1959). *The language and thought of the child*. London: Routledge & Kegan Paul, was originally written in 1923. It contains his ideas on children's egocentric speech, which Vygotsky disagreed with in Vygotsky, L. (1962). *Thought and language*. Cambridge, MA: MIT Press. This actually dates from 1934, and was the first of Vygotsky's writings to be widely available in English (though in truncated form).

- Rogoff, B. (2003). *The cultural nature of human development*. New York: Oxford University Press, presents an account of human development that looks at both the differences and the similarities between cultures, including the influence of culture on cognition. See also Rogoff, B., Turkanis, C.G. & Bartlett, L. (2001). *Learning together: Children and adults in a school community*. New York: Oxford University Press, which describes how children learn best in a cooperative community where adults share their interests.

CHAPTER
17

Intelligence and Attainment

CHAPTER OUTLINE

- The Development of Intelligence Tests
- Reliability and Validity
- The Early Uses of Intelligence Tests
- Concepts of Intelligence
- Savants
- Intelligence in a Social-Cultural Context
- The Use of Intelligence Tests
- Attainment Tests

In this chapter we discuss the ways in which 'intelligence' has been measured in children. Intelligence testing has a long history, and finding ways to measure children's abilities predates some of the research into children's development. The first intelligence tests were designed at the end of the 19th century, and several contemporary tests are still modelled on those original scales. We have therefore included a brief history of intelligence testing, because without knowing how the tests were developed it is hard to appreciate the reasons for the form and content of present-day intelligence tests. We also give examples of the tests that are most commonly used with children. All tests should meet certain criteria of reliability and validity and we summarize what those terms mean. Despite the well-established use of intelligence tests, there has been controversy about what 'intelligence' means. Indeed, there are many different definitions and concepts of intelligence. We summarize some of these different concepts in the chapter. We also consider special groups of children, like gifted children who may perform exceptionally well on measures of intelligence.

THE DEVELOPMENT OF INTELLIGENCE TESTS

As we have seen in previous chapters, psychologists studying cognitive development have been interested in the processes of intellectual growth, but the 'psychometric' approach is a rather different way of looking at intelligence. In the psychometric tradition, psychologists have devised tests to measure a person's ability with an emphasis on comparing individuals' performance in a way that can be quantified; usually, people are given a score to indicate their performance on a test. The best known tests of ability are 'intelligence' tests.

The First Tests

Galton, in England in the 1880s, was the first to attempt the scientific measurement of intelligence with a series of tests (Mackintosh, 1998; Sternberg, 2002). These tests included both physical measures, like the strength of hand squeeze or the capacity of the lungs, and behavioural measures, like reaction time tests (e.g. how quickly a person could make a response after they heard a sound). Galton believed that intelligence was an underlying trait that would influence a person's performance on all tasks. In other words, if one person had more intelligence than someone else, they would generally be better on all tests, whatever the type of test. Galton also believed that there would be a relationship between a person's status (i.e. their rank in society) and their performance on his tests. But he failed to find such a relationship, and when other researchers compared how well college students performed on Galton's tests and how well they performed academically, they too found little relationship between the tests and academic achievement (e.g. Wissler, 1901).

Early in the 20th century, two French psychologists, Binet and Simon (1905), published tests that, they claimed, could identify children who were failing to make progress within the normal school system. Their aim was to identify such children so that they could be removed from the overcrowded French schools and be given special education. The battery of tests that Binet and Simon devised represented the kinds of abilities that, in their view, children typically used during the school years. The tests included word definitions, comprehension tests, tests of reasoning and knowledge of numbers. Binet and Simon spent a long time in schools using different tests with students who had a range of ability to find out which tests distinguished between younger and older children and between good and poor learners. The latter were defined by teachers; in other words, Binet and Simon selected tests on which children who were rated as bright by their teachers did well, and on which children who were considered less able did poorly. Therefore, the selection of the original tests by Binet and Simon was based on purely practical considerations—the tests that most effectively differentiated between good and poor students.

Once Binet and Simon (1905) had identified the 30 most effective tests, they listed them in order of difficulty (see Table 17.1). For example, a younger child might be able to repeat three numbers; an older child would not only be able to do this but could also repeat a sentence with 15 words in it. Any particular child would then attempt test items of increasing difficulty until he or she consistently failed them, at which point the tester could calculate the

Table 17.1 Items used in the 1905 Binet–Simon scale.

1. Follows a moving object with the eyes.
2. Grasps a small object that is touched.
3. Grasps a small object that is seen.
4. Recognizes the difference between a square of chocolate and a square of wood.
5. Finds and eats a square of chocolate wrapped in paper.
6. Executes simple commands and imitates simple gestures.
7. Points to familiar objects (e.g. 'show me the cup').
8. Points to objects represented in pictures (e.g. 'put your finger on the window').
9. Names objects in pictures.
10. Compares two lines of markedly unequal length.
11. Repeats three spoken digits.
12. Compares two weights.
13. Shows susceptibility to suggestion.
14. Defines common words by function.
15. Repeats a sentence of 15 words.
16. Tells how two common objects are different (e.g. paper and cardboard).
17. Names from memory as many as possible of 13 objects displayed on a board.
18. Reproduces from memory two designs shown for 10 seconds.
19. Repeats a series of more than three digits.
20. Tells how two common objects are alike (e.g. butterfly and flea).
21. Compares two lines of slightly unequal length.
22. Compares five blocks to put them in order of weight.
23. Indicates which of the previous five weights the examiner has removed.
24. Produces rhymes for given words.
25. Word completion test.
26. Puts three nouns in a sentence (e.g. Paris, river, fortune).
27. Given set of 25 comprehension questions.
28. Reverses the hands of a clock.
29. After paper folding and cutting, draws the form of the resulting holes.
30. Distinguishes abstract words (e.g. boredom and weariness).

child's mental level. The average 5-year-old, for example, would complete test items at the 5-year-old level; a less able 5-year-old might fail to solve test problems beyond the 4-year-old level, and would be said to have a mental level of 4.

The use of Binet and Simon's ordered series of tests (or 'scale') was an effective way of measuring children's abilities: it was simple to administer, it could be used by teachers, it made it easy to compare different children and it was successful. Not surprisingly, given the reasons behind the choice of tests, if a child did well on the Binet–Simon scale, she was likely to be successful academically; if a child did poorly on the scale, she was likely to have difficulties in school. In other words, the test was an effective way of identifying those children who might be in need of extra help.

Revisions of the Binet–Simon Scale

After Binet and Simon had produced their scale of items for measuring mental age, it was adapted by Terman at Stanford University in California for use in the USA. Terman increased the number of tests to 90, and the new version, called the Stanford–Binet Intelligence Scale, was introduced in 1916. In this new scale were two main types of test item, verbal and non-verbal. Verbal tests relied on language abilities (e.g. general knowledge, comprehension, vocabulary and understanding similarities between concepts). Non-verbal or performance tests measured perceptual skills and non-verbal reasoning, such as the ability to arrange pictures in a logical sequence to make a coherent story, to copy designs using a set of coloured blocks or to assemble pieces of a jigsaw-type puzzle into the right arrangement as quickly as possible.

One of the limitations of the original Binet–Simon scale was the way it led to a comparison between a child's mental level, as tested on the scale, and her chronological age. For example, if a child aged 7 years performed at the level of a 4-year-old it could be said that the 7-year-old had a developmental delay of 3 years. However, if a child aged 12 years performed at the level of a 9-year-old then she also would be classified as delayed by 3 years. However, a 3-year delay at the age of 7 years might have different implications from the same length of delay at 12 years. A better measure of the ability of a child can be calculated by taking a ratio of mental level to chronological age. This gives the child's mental age as a fraction (MA/CA), and Terman suggested multiplying the fraction by 100 and describing the result as the 'intelligence quotient' (or IQ).

This change was introduced with the first Stanford–Binet scale. The average child's IQ by this calculation is 100 and the IQs of children above or below the average can be calculated accordingly. The numerical scores of the IQ were less cumbersome than the original age scores and made it possible to make direct comparisons between the intellectual capability of individuals, even at different ages. The IQ assessment also made it easier to calculate correlations between intelligence and other variables. Nonetheless, the idea of labelling people with an 'IQ' has always been controversial. Binet had died before the use of IQ was introduced, but Simon described the concept of IQ as a betrayal of his and Binet's original objectives in assessing children (Gregory, 1992). From something that had been intended to identify children who needed special education, the scale had become a way to make comparisons between all people and rank them according to 'IQ'. The Stanford–Binet scale has undergone many revisions, and its most recent form, the fifth edition (SB5), is still used today.

Every scale has to be 'standardized'. This means that when a scale has been designed, it should be tested on a large sample of children who are representative of those for whom it is intended. For example, if the test was for use in the UK, it would be important that the sample included girls and boys in the same ratio as girls and boys are found in the UK population; that the sample included children from different ethnic backgrounds in the same proportions as in the population as a whole; and that there were children from differently sized communities and from different geographical regions. Each time a scale is revised, this process has to be repeated. If a scale that has been standardized in one country is used in another country, then it has to be standardized again with an appropriate sample of children from the new country.

It is important that intelligence scales are tested on large samples, because IQ is no longer calculated by the MA/CA formula. Instead, a person's performance on an intelligence scale is compared to the distribution of the performance of everyone else of the same age on the same scale. Intelligence scales are designed so that at each age, the average performance of all people of that age will be a score of 100. For example, if several thousand 10-year-olds were assessed using an intelligence scale, their average score would be 100, and the scores of all the children would be normally distributed. This means that there will be a large number scoring 100, and only a slightly smaller number scoring 99 (or 101) with slightly fewer scoring 98 (or 102), slightly fewer again with a score of 97 (or 103) and so on, with only very small numbers of children having particularly low or high scores.

Intelligence scales are also designed so that the distribution of scores at each age follows the same pattern. If the mean score is 100 then 34% of scores will fall between 85 and 100 and 34% will be between 100 and 115. Fourteen per cent will fall between 70 and 85, and 14% between 115 and 130. Two per cent will fall between 55 and 70, and 2% between 130 and 145. In this way, a child's score can be compared easily with the expected scores for the whole of his or her age group.

Other Intelligence Scales

One of the tests most commonly used nowadays was designed by Wechsler in the US. His first test, for adults in 1939, was based on other tests that existed at the time (including the Stanford–Binet). Since then, the Wechsler scale has been revised many times and a version for children was first produced in 1949. The most recent children's version is the Wechsler Intelligence Scale for Children Fifth Edition (WISC-V) (Wechsler, 2014). The scales have been adapted for use in different countries and the most recent UK versions of the scales are:

- *For adults (16–90 years):* Wechsler Adult Intelligence Scale Fourth UK Edition (WAIS-IV UK) (Wechsler, 2010).
- *For children (6–16 years):* Wechsler Intelligence Scale for Children Fourth UK Edition (WISC-IV UK) (Wechsler, 2014).
- *For young children (2–7 years):* Wechsler Preschool and Primary Scale of Intelligence Fourth UK Edition (WPPSI-IV UK) (Wechsler, 2013).

Examples of the type of items in the WISC are given in Table 17.2.

As well as the Stanford–Binet and Wechsler scales, there are other tests that include similar batteries of tests. For example, the British Ability Scales Third Edition (BAS-3) (Elliot et al., 2011) is a battery of 20 tests including ones to assess verbal and non-verbal ability, spatial ability and information processing speed.

Table 17.2   The Wechsler Intelligence Scale for Children.

The WISC-IV UK includes 15 subtests that are administered in the order given below. Where we include examples below, these are similar to, but not the same as, the ones actually used in a subtest.

1. Block design	A child is given a set of four cubes. Each cube has some sides that are painted all white, some sides that are all red and some that are half white and half red. The child is shown a pattern (on a card) and asked to rearrange the cubes so that the top surface of the four cubes, placed together, shows the target pattern. The child then has further trials with other four cube patterns, and then with nine cube patterns. All the trials have a time limit.
2. Similarities	A child is asked how two items are alike (e.g. 'In what ways are a pear and a plum alike?' or 'In what ways are secrets and lies alike?').
3. Digit span	A list of numbers (e.g. '8–2–5' or '9–1–4–5–8–2–6–3–7') is read out and the child is asked to repeat the numbers in the same order. On other trials, the child is asked to repeat the numbers in reverse order.
4. Picture concepts	The child is shown two or three rows of pictures with three pictures in each row (e.g. top row: bottle, golf ball and clock; middle row: step ladder, golf club, envelope; bottom row: wristwatch, box, pencil). The child is asked to pick three pictures, one from each row, that go together.
5. Coding	The child is asked to match symbols with numbers according to a key that is provided. For example, on the key, the number 1 could be symbolized by a triangle, number 2 by an X, number 3 by a circle, and so on. The child is given a list of numbers, in random order, and against each number has to write down its corresponding symbol. This test is scored by how quickly and accurately the child completes the task.
6. Vocabulary	The examiner asks the child to explain the meaning of words, for example, 'What is a horse?' or 'What does "inconsequent" mean?'.
7. Letter-number sequencing	The examiner reads out a combination of numbers and letters (e.g. 'K–5–A–4' or '7–T–1–M–9–D–4–Q') and the child then has to say the numbers, in order, followed by the letters, in alphabetical order. A correct response for the first example would therefore be 4–5–A–K.
8. Matrix reasoning	A child is shown matrices with up to nine components. One component is missing and the child is asked to choose the missing component from a choice of five alternatives.
9. Comprehension	The examiner asks a child to explain why certain courses of action are appropriate or explain the purpose behind social policies. For example, 'What should you do if you break a friend's toy by mistake?' or 'Tell me some of the reasons why there are surveillance cameras in public places'.

Table 17.2 (Continued)

10. Symbol search	The child is shown rows containing several abstract shapes. For each row, the child is given a target shape and has to indicate whether or not the target is present in the row. Scoring depends on how accurately and how quickly this is done.
11. Picture completion	The examiner shows the child a picture and asks what is missing from the picture (for example, a car without a wheel or a telephone keypad with a button missing).
12. Cancellation	The child is given a large sheet of paper on which are printed several hundred small pictures of animals, cars, fruit, trees, clothes, musical instruments, tools and other objects, randomly spread across the page. The child is asked to circle all the animal pictures as quickly as possible. The task is scored for speed and accuracy.
13. Information	The examiner asks general knowledge questions, for example, 'What month comes right after September?' or 'How far is it from London to Paris?'.
14. Arithmetic	The child is asked questions like: 'John had six sweets. He ate three and gave one to Jill. How many does he have left?' or 'Amy is visiting her friend Beth. Amy has a 3-hour train journey to reach the station nearest to Beth's home. Beth lives 10 miles from the station. Beth drives at 30 miles per hour. If Amy's train leaves at 11am, what time does Beth need to start driving from home to get to the station 10 minutes before Amy arrives?'.
15. Word reasoning	The examiner says, 'Tell me what I'm thinking of' and then gives a clue like 'It's something you wear on your feet' or 'It's made by people, and it's not real, and it can be heard'. The child is scored correct for any appropriate answer.

Intelligence scales like the Wechsler scales are to some extent dependent on verbal abilities. Not only are there specific items that test children's performance in various verbal tests (like 'vocabulary' or 'similarities'), but the instructions and many of the children's responses also depend on verbal abilities. Tests with a verbal component may underestimate the intellectual capacity of children who speak a different dialect or for whom the language of the test is not their mother tongue. In other words, children who have language difficulties or who come from another cultural background may be at a disadvantage when taking the test.

Tests like the Stanford–Binet and the Wechsler scales have to be administered individually (see Figure 17.1), usually in clinical or educational settings, to help in the diagnosis of learning difficulties. Psychologists have also devised tests that can be given to groups of people, and these are often used for personnel selection. Correlations between performance on individually administered tests and on group tests are fairly high and therefore it is assumed that they are each measuring the same abilities. However, group testing has some disadvantages. For example, the tester may not notice signs of anxiety in those being tested, which would be more obvious in a one-to-one context, and people with language difficulties may be at a disadvantage if they find it hard to read the instructions for each item.

Figure 17.1   A preschool child is tested on one of the subscales of the WPPSI.
Source: Reproduced with permission of Peter K. Smith.

One example of a test that can be administered to a group is Raven's Progressive Matrices. This test also has the advantage that it requires little specific verbal ability—the way that a person completes the test can, if necessary, be demonstrated with examples that avoid verbal instructions, and the tests do not depend on people giving verbal responses. Raven's Progressive Matrices are available in different versions for different levels of ability, but the principle behind each test is the same. A person is shown a set of patterns (called a 'matrix') with one of the patterns missing. Below the matrix there is a selection of different patterns and the person is asked to choose the one that they think best fits the missing piece in the matrix. The test is called 'progressive' because a person completes a number of different matrices, which are presented one at a time, in a booklet, in order of increasing difficulty. The Coloured Progressive Matrices (Raven, 2008) is designed for children aged 5–11 years, and the Standard Progressive Matrices is for use with older children and adults (Raven, 2008). A person's performance on Raven's Progressive Matrices correlates with their performance on other intelligence tests. Other non-verbal tests include picture analogies (see Figure 17.2).

RELIABILITY AND VALIDITY

All tests of intelligence should meet several criteria if they are to be effective ways of measuring a person's ability (Domino & Domino, 2006).

Reliability

A test must be 'reliable'. This means that each time a person takes a test, they should achieve the same result. For example, if someone is given an intelligence scale one day and then the same scale on the next day, it is essential the person's level of performance is the same both times. Of course, there is a difficulty in checking reliability in this way, because if someone has done a test once it is likely that practice and familiarity will lead to better performance the second time. One way round this problem is to give a person half the test (perhaps alternate questions from it) on one occasion and the other half of the test on a second occasion. The person should have the same level of performance on both halves of the test. The most frequently used intelligence scales, like the Stanford–Binet and Wechsler scales, have very high levels of reliability.

Validity

Concurrent validity means assessing a scale against either another scale or an independent measure of performance. For example, if a child performed well on the Stanford–Binet scale it would be expected that the same child would also perform well on the WISC. Similarly, if a teacher thought that a child was at the top of the class, it would be expected that the child would have one of the highest levels of performance in the class when tested with an intelligence scale.

Predictive validity means that performance on a test should predict future performance. For example, if a child scores highly on an intelligence test, it would be expected that the child will do well academically. Similarly, the level a student achieves in a college entrance exam should predict the grade they achieve at the end of college.

Content validity (which is also called 'face validity') refers to how appropriate a test is. For example, if you wanted to test a person's driving ability, it would be appropriate to test how well she actually drove a car on the road and how well she answered questions about driving. It would not be appropriate to test that person's short-term memory or vocabulary. This example makes content validity appear rather obvious, and for many practical abilities (like driving) it is not difficult to see the relationship between the test and what it is measuring. However, as we will explain later, intelligence is not easy to define, and the content validity of a test depends on what the test designers believe intelligence to be. If you believe that intelligence is mainly about how accurately people process and remember information, you might include several measures of short-term memory, comprehension and general knowledge. If you think that intelligence is about how well a person adapts to the world around her, you might want to include tests of social and practical skills.

Content validity is difficult to define if there is no common agreement about what the word 'intelligence' means. Although many researchers have considered that tests of memory, reasoning and knowledge are appropriate ways to measure intelligence, other researchers have developed concepts of intelligence that include skills and abilities that are not directly tested by the more established intelligence scales. We will discuss the different concepts of intelligence in a later section.

THE EARLY USES OF INTELLIGENCE TESTS

The Binet–Simon scale was initially used simply to differentiate between average children and children with learning difficulties who might be in need of special education. However, during World War I (1914–1918) when large numbers of people were being categorized to meet the requirements of different work roles, there was a proliferation of intelligence testing (Mackintosh, 1998). After the war, large industrial companies also demanded batteries of tests, which could measure specific aptitudes in skills such as engineering, typing or dressmaking. This type of selection procedure, it was claimed, provided an effective means of assigning individuals to occupations appropriate to their abilities. In the UK, Cyril Burt was one of the first psychologists in the National Institute of Industrial Psychology. Burt was committed to the idea that intelligence was innate, static throughout a person's lifetime and measurable using intelligence tests.

Burt proposed that intelligence tests also be used in schools with the aim of providing all children with an education appropriate to their level of mental ability. He argued that in any group of children, the variations in mental ability would be large and he therefore recommended that the organization of school classes should be on the basis of mental ability rather than chronological age. It was this view, that the individual should be assigned a place in society according to his or her intellectual ability, which was to have far-reaching effects on the educational system in Britain (Broadfoot, 1996). In his day Burt was highly respected as an educational psychologist, although he is now largely discredited because of his fraudulent research into the heritability of intelligence (Hearnshaw, 1979).

In the early days of intelligence testing, it was believed that intelligence tests were objective and accurate means of assessing mental ability. The tests appeared to offer a fairer measure of the potential ability of children from differing backgrounds than did conventional examinations and school reports, and they were thought to be less susceptible to social biases that might affect teachers' evaluations. If, as Burt believed, intelligence is an innate, stable factor, it would follow logically that once suitable measures had been devised, children could be grouped according to ability levels for educational purposes. This belief had a strong influence on educational policy in the UK in the years following World War I, and the Hadow Report (1926) recommended several types of school for children after the age of 11 years. These were 'modern' schools, 'technical' schools and traditional grammar schools. To assign children to appropriate schools, some form of assessment had to take place, and by the late 1930s it was standard practice to select children on the basis of an 11-plus examination which assessed children's English and mathematical abilities, and their performance on an intelligence test.

It was only after World War II (1939–1945) that attitudes changed, and there was a growing awareness that a selective system discriminated against children from underprivileged backgrounds. The 1944 Education Act aimed to provide equality of opportunity for all children 'according to age, aptitude and ability'. But the selective system was so firmly entrenched that the change to a comprehensive system of secondary education in the UK was achieved only many years later.

The original intelligence scales were designed primarily to meet educational needs (e.g. to distinguish children who had learning difficulties) and therefore they focused on tasks that related to knowledge, reasoning and memory. Other researchers have argued that such tasks may only reflect a rather narrow concept of intelligence, and that many other aspects of a person's abilities should be taken into account when assessing intelligence. We will discuss different concepts of intelligence in the following section.

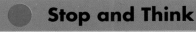

Stop and Think

Do we need intelligence tests?

CONCEPTS OF INTELLIGENCE

As we pointed out earlier, Galton, who was the first to invent intelligence tests, believed that intelligence was a general ability that would be reflected in any test or task undertaken by an individual. The implication of Galton's view is that any test that produces differences in individual performance could be used as an intelligence test. Some tests (e.g. stating your name) are unlikely to produce many individual differences but many others (like vocabulary tests) result in a range of performance and might therefore be used to compare people. Other researchers also came to the conclusion that intelligence was an underlying trait that affected performance across all the tasks used in typical intelligence scales. For example, Spearman (1904) found that there were correlations between children's performance on different academic tests. Spearman (1927) found the same when he gave adults a range of different mental tests (i.e. those who did better than others on one test also tended to do better on other tests). From this, Spearman concluded that there was a single factor, which he labelled 'g' (for 'general' intelligence), which influenced a person's performance on all tests.

Galton and Spearman can be seen as part of the tradition of researchers who put most emphasis on a single general intelligence permeating an individual's performance. In contrast, other psychologists have emphasized the independence of the different factors that might make up a person's intelligence. Thurstone (1931) suggested that there were seven factors that accounted for performance on the type of tests found in traditional intelligence scales. Thurstone called these 'primary mental abilities' and labelled them 'verbal meaning' (e.g. vocabulary and comprehension), 'word fluency' (e.g. speed of naming all the words in a category, like all the animal names beginning with C), 'numerical reasoning' (e.g. mental arithmetic), 'spatial' (e.g. imagining what objects look like after they are rotated), 'perceptual speed' (e.g. being able to quickly check through lists of items for a specific target item), 'memory' (e.g. recall of words or sentences) and 'inductive reasoning' (e.g. completing number series). This 'group factor' approach has the implication that a child might perform differently on different sets of items; for example, a child might have very good memory and good verbal meaning, but average numerical reasoning and poor spatial ability. This means that children cannot easily be assessed in terms of general intelligence; rather, they may perform differently across a number of tasks.

Although Spearman argued for a single underlying factor that affected performance across all measures of intelligence and Thurstone argued for a set of separate abilities, the difference between these two viewpoints is somewhat artificial. Many researchers have pointed out that Thurstone's factors are not independent, but some of them may be closely related (Carroll, 1993). For example, a child who does well on a test involving inductive reasoning will often do well on a test of memory, and a child who does well on tests of verbal ability will tend to do well on tests of numerical ability. Therefore reasoning and memory can be combined into a higher order factor, and verbal and numerical ability can also be combined into a higher order factor. These higher order factors can also be combined together to produce a single factor (in Spearman's term's, the 'g' factor).

In summary, some researchers have preferred to emphasize the differences between the abilities that make up intelligence (Thurstone) and others have preferred to focus on the close relationships between those abilities (Spearman). But most contemporary researchers would agree that intelligence is best thought of as a hierarchy of interrelated factors (Cooper, 1999).

In the 1980s Gardner (1983, 1999, 2011) proposed a more radical view of intelligence. He proposed a theory of 'multiple intelligences' and suggested that there were six distinct kinds of intelligence: linguistic, logical-mathematical, spatial, musical, body-kinaesthetic and personal. The first three are already familiar from our discussion of intelligence scales, but the last three constitute a marked departure in thinking about intelligence. Musical intelligence refers to the abilities to comprehend and play or compose music. Bodily-kinaesthetic intelligence refers to bodily control and grace of movement, as shown, for example, in athletics, dance or skating. Personal intelligence refers to an awareness of one's own behaviour and that of others, and this is related to social and interpersonal skills and to role-taking ability. By putting forward the theory of multiple intelligences, Gardner was effectively criticizing the use of conventional intelligence scales that do not measure abilities like musical, athletic or social skill. Gardner's theory was also the stimulus for other researchers to define further kinds of intelligences (for example, emotional intelligence, which we discussed in Chapter 6).

Sternberg's Theory of Intelligence

Other researchers have also pointed out that conceptions of intelligence based only on academic abilities are too narrow and that other aspects of human performance must be taken into account to provide a full picture of intelligent behaviour. Sternberg et al. (1981) asked a number of people to give examples of what they thought of as intelligent or unintelligent behaviour (see Box 17.1). Sternberg et al. collected 250 different types of intelligent behaviour and classified these under different headings. What was notable about the behaviours that they collected is that people included many aspects of practical and social behaviour in their examples of intel-

Box 17.1 People's conceptions of intelligence

Sternberg et al. asked 186 people to list behaviours that they thought were characteristic of 'intelligence', 'academic intelligence', 'everyday intelligence' and 'unintelligence'. The people included 61 studying in a Yale college library, 63 waiting for trains and 62 shoppers at a supermarket. In total, Sternberg et al. collected 250 different behaviours, which included 170 examples of intelligent behaviour and 80 examples of unintelligent behaviour.

Sternberg et al. then found two further groups of people. One group were 'laypersons' recruited through newspaper advertisements and the other group were 'experts', all of whom had higher degrees in psychology and were carrying out research in universities. These groups were given questionnaires that included the list of 250 behaviours and they were asked to rate each behaviour, on a 1 (low) to 9 (high) scale, according to how important they thought that behaviour was in defining the concept of (a) an intelligent person, (b) an academically intelligent person, and (c) an everyday intelligent person.

The experts' view of an ideally intelligent person could be divided into three factors that Sternberg et al. labelled as 'verbal intelligence', 'problem-solving ability' and 'practical intelligence'. The first factor included behaviours like: 'displays a good vocabulary', 'reads with high comprehension', 'displays curiosity' and 'is intellectually curious'. The second factor included behaviours such as 'able to apply knowledge to problems at hand', 'makes good decisions', 'poses problems in an optimal way' and 'displays common sense'. The third factor included behaviours like 'sizes up situations well', 'determines how to achieve goals', 'displays awareness of world around him or herself' and 'displays interest in the world at large'.

Laypersons' views of an ideally intelligent person could also be divided into three main factors that were labelled 'practical problem-solving ability', 'verbal ability' and 'social competence'. Although there was an overlap with the experts' views, there was also an important difference, because laypersons put more emphasis on social competence, a category that included behaviours such as 'accepts others for what they are', 'admits mistakes' and 'is on time for appointments'.

Experts' views of academic intelligence were divided into three factors: problem-solving ability, verbal ability and motivation. Clearly there was an overlap between their views of ideal intelligence and ideal academic intelligence, but with the difference that experts also stressed motivation in the context of academic intelligence. This was a factor that included behaviours like 'displays dedication and motivation in chosen pursuits', 'gets involved in what he or she is doing', 'studies hard' and 'is persistent'. The layperson's view of academic intelligence was slightly different because they included behaviours linked to verbal ability, problem-solving ability and social competence, rather than motivation.

For everyday intelligence, the experts' views could be divided into three factors: practical problem-solving ability, practical adaptive behaviour and social competence. The layperson's description of everyday intelligence included four factors. The first two were the same as the first two factors proposed by the experts, but laypersons also thought that character and an interest in learning and culture were important factors.

As all the participants were asked to describe types of intelligence, it is not surprising that there were many similarities in the patterns that Sternberg et al. identified. Nonetheless, there were also differences, both in the way that the same groups described different types of intelligence and between the groups. These differences reflect the difficulty of describing intelligence with any brief or single definition of the term. What is most noticeable about Sternberg et al.'s data is the very large number of behaviours that people were willing to include as examples of intelligent behaviour. As Sternberg et al. say in summing up their results, no one theory of intelligence is likely 'to do justice to the full scope of intelligence' (1981, p. 55).

Based on material in Sternberg, R.J., Conway, B.E., Ketron, J.L. & Bernstein, M. (1981). People's conceptions of intelligence. *Journal of Personality and Social Psychology*, 41, 37–55.

ligent behaviours. Although researchers like Gardner (1983) pointed out the importance of social intelligence, other theorists had not included such behaviours under the heading of intelligence. Sternberg (1985) proposed a triarchic theory of intelligence, which recognized the importance of social and practical skills as well as purely academic ones.

Sternberg's (1985) triarchic theory was so called because it consisted of three subtheories. One was called the 'experiential subtheory', which emphasized how effectively a person learns new skills. For instance, many skills (e.g. driving a car) become automatic; that is, they do not require much conscious attention and an experienced driver can not only drive, but also hold a conversation at the same time. Sternberg pointed out that how quickly someone achieves task automaticity could be a reflection of their intelligence. For instance, a person might be able to achieve automaticity in a task after so many hours of experience. Another person might also achieve automaticity on the same task, but only after twice as much experience. Such differences are not examined by conventional intelligence scales, but may be important. Vygotsky (see Chapter 16) made a similar point when he criticized testing children's intelligence. He argued that finding out that one child scored the same as another on an intelligence scale might not mean very much unless there were also other measures of the children's potential to learn—one child might progress faster than another if she was able to gain more from her environment and the support she received from others. However, assessing how quickly and how well a person achieves automaticity on a task, or assessing a child's potential to learn, are both very difficult to measure. In practice, it is unlikely that a convenient and realistic test of such abilities could be devised. As it is, most intelligence scales include novel tasks and measure a child's reasoning and knowledge at one point in time—they do not measure a child's ability to learn from practice or experience.

Sternberg (1985) called another subtheory the 'contextual subtheory', which referred to the way that people interact with their environment (e.g. in school, at home, with their families, with friends and so on). Sternberg pointed out that people can adapt themselves to the environment they find themselves in at the time, or they can try to change their environment, or they can select an alternative environment. Much of what Sternberg said applied more to adults than children; nonetheless, the idea of adapting to an environment is important at all ages (for example, children who adapt most successfully to school may do better academically).

The contextual subtheory has important implications for measuring intelligence, because Sternberg (1985) suggested that this aspect of intelligence is best measured with tests of practical and social skills. Practical measures might include sets of tests that, for example, include filling in forms, reading street maps, understanding bus and railway timetables, following technical instructions and so on. Measures of social skills might include tests of how well a person interprets non-verbal information. For example, Sternberg took photographs, in the street, of couples standing together. Sometimes the couples were genuine couples, but at other times they were two strangers who had been asked to stand together just for the purpose of the photograph. Sternberg then used the photographs as a test to find out if people could work out, from just looking at the photographs, which couples were 'genuine' and which couples were 'fake'. Such tests of practical and social intelligence have been designed primarily for adults, but they are mentioned here because they highlight how the concept of intelligence has been broadened and extended by researchers like Sternberg. As yet, little emphasis is placed on the measurement of children's abilities in social and practical contexts.

The other subtheory was called the 'componential subtheory' and was concerned with the information processing aspects of tasks typically used in tests of intelligence. For example, Sternberg and Rifkin (1979) analysed the components required for the picture analogy task shown in Figure 17.2. They suggested that one way to solve the task involved six components.

1. *Encoding* (e.g. considering the type of hat, footwear, clothing, etc. of all five figures)
2. *Inference* (this involves working out the changes needed to make A into B, e.g. changing A's hat to match B's hat)
3. *Mapping* (means comparing A and C, e.g. in this example noting that they have the same hat but all their other features are different)

Figure 17.2 Picture analogy task (as A is to B, so C is to . . . ?)

Source: Sternberg, R. J. & Rifkin, B. 1979: The development of analogical reasoning processes. *Journal of Experimental Child Psychology*, 27: 195–232.

4. *Application* (means applying the changes worked out by the inference component to C, e.g. changing C's hat, to produce an 'ideal' answer for the analogy, and then the ideal answer can be compared to the two alternatives and the appropriate figure selected)
5. *Justification* (if neither of the given figures matches, choosing the better one and justifying this choice)
6. *Respond* (giving the answer).

The analysis we have described is not the only way to solve the problem in Figure 17.2—in this example, one of the given figures is the correct match and therefore, there is no need for the justification component. Sternberg (1985) made the point that if such a task was included in an intelligence scale, a person's answer would be scored as correct or incorrect without any reference to how they reached their answer. But Sternberg and Rifkin (1979) found that adults and children approached the picture analogy in different ways. At the encoding stage, adults attended to all the information in the picture (i.e. all the features of the figures) before applying the other components, and at this stage they were actually slower than 10-year-olds. The children, probably because of limited working memory capacity (see Chapter 14), may only have encoded one or two features before moving on to the other components. The latter would either result in more errors or mean that sometimes the children had to return to the encoding process again to consider other features. Analysing such tasks provides a greater insight into children's approach to the problem than simply scoring them as right or wrong on the basis of their final response.

Sternberg's (1985) triarchic theory is an ambitious theory of intelligence. However, the three subtheories are not very well integrated into the whole, and this weakens the attempt to bring all the different aspects of intelligence together. Nonetheless, Sternberg demonstrated how extensive a description of intelligence needs to be if it is to include all the contemporary ideas about intelligence. The triarchic theory focused on adults, but Sternberg has also discussed how contemporary approaches to intelligence can be applied to children's developing intelligence (Sternberg, 2010).

SAVANTS

Savants are individuals who usually have a low intelligence score as measured on traditional scales, but may have one (or sometimes more than one) exceptional ability. For this reason, such people used to be referred to as 'idiot savants'. Howe and Smith (1988) described the case of

'Dave' who, despite having a low IQ, had an exceptional ability to calculate calendar dates. When Dave was asked what day of the week a certain date would be he was able to answer almost perfectly for any date between 1900 and 2060. Howe and Smith tried to work out how Dave was able to calculate such dates so accurately (for a summary of their study, see Box 17.2).

Savants with other outstanding skills are also known, including those with exceptional memories, mathematical abilities, musical abilities or drawing skills (Hermelin et al., 1999; Howe, 1989). For instance, Smith and Tsimpli (1995) described Christopher, an English boy who had a much lower than average IQ but despite this, had an outstanding linguistic ability. Smith and Tsimpli found that Christopher knew elements of at least 16 foreign languages and was fluent in some. In addition, he could read and write several different scripts; for example, he was fluent in reading and writing modern Greek. Most of these languages he had learned himself from textbooks and grammars. Christopher's remarkable language abilities stand in contrast to his lack of other abilities; for example, he was unable to play noughts and crosses (tic-tac-toe) or even draw the simple grid needed for this game. It is difficult to explain how the same person can learn fluent Greek, among many other languages, but remain unable to play a simple game of noughts and crosses.

The performance of savants like Dave or Christopher has implications for the different theories of intelligence that we discussed earlier. Savants are people with generally low intelligence but one exceptional skill, and this pattern of performance may be easiest to consider in the context of theories that emphasize that 'intelligence' is made of a number of different

Box 17.2 Calendar calculating by 'idiot savants'. How do they do it?

Howe and Smith carried out a case study with a 14-year-old boy called 'Dave' (not his real name), who had a low IQ but a remarkable ability to work out dates. Dave attended a non-residential school for children who were developmentally delayed. Howe and Smith used a series of tests to establish Dave's IQ and found that he scored 50 on the Stanford–Binet test and 54 on the Wechsler Intelligence Scale for Children. As typically developing children have an average score of 100 on such intelligence scales, Dave's scores were very low. Howe and Smith also used a reading test to establish Dave's reading age and found it was about 6 years (i.e. 8 years behind his chronological age).

Dave was withdrawn and said very little, and when he did speak, what he said was often irrelevant to the situation. He showed lit-

tle interest in other people and resented interference from others. Dave's solitariness meant that it was difficult for Howe and Smith to ask him questions because he often chose not to answer. Nonetheless, Howe and Smith were able to get Dave to answer a number of questions that involved calculating dates. They asked him questions like, 'What day of the week was it/will it be on the . . . th of . . ., in the year of . . .?'. The range of dates included ones between 1900 and 2060 and Dave gave the correct day of the week for 94% of the questions. It goes without saying that this was a remarkable achievement from a child who was otherwise so developmentally delayed.

Earlier researchers who have investigated other individuals with calendar calculating skills have suggested several ways in which savants might be able to work out dates. First, the day of the week for a particular date can be calculated using published mathematical formulae, and these can be learned and practised (see Howe, 1989, for examples of these formulae). Second, some calendar calculators have memorized a large number of specific dates (e.g. the days and dates of the birthdays of everyone they have ever met) and they might use these as reference points for other dates by working forwards or backwards from the ones they have already memorized. Third, some may use a form of visual imagery to imagine a calendar. For example, Roberts (1945) reported one savant who could recall dates and the colour of those dates as they appeared on a printed calendar. Of course, none of the approaches are mutually exclusive and a calendar calculator could use a combination of them. Nonetheless, Howe and Smith tried to find out if they could exclude any of these methods in the case of Dave.

It did not seem likely that Dave was using any published formula, because his reading ability was poor and there was no reason to believe he had access to such formulae. Howe and Smith asked Dave to answer questions like, 'In what years will the 9th October be on a Wednesday?' because this type of question cannot be answered by using any available formula. Dave was able to answer all the questions in this form quickly and without difficulty. This showed that Dave was quite capable of calendar calculating in contexts where no formula was possible.

Howe and Smith had asked Dave to name the day of the week for particular dates between 1900 and 2060. Dave was thought to know the days and dates of the birthdays of all the pupils and staff at his school, and he might have been able to use these as reference points for dates in the past. But it would not have been possible to use this technique for working out dates that would occur in the future. When

Howe and Smith asked Dave to give the day of the week for future periods they found that he remained very accurate. This suggested that Dave had some way of calculating dates without relying on reference dates.

Howe and Smith came to the conclusion that Dave was probably using some form of visual imagery. He often drew calendars, and included in his drawings the additional details sometimes included on printed calendars (e.g. representations of the moon). When recalling dates, he sometimes made comments like 'Thursdays are always black' or 'It's on the top line' as if he was recalling an image of a page of a calendar. Howe and Smith asked Dave to say which month of each year began with a Friday. They reasoned that this would be a very difficult task if Dave had to calculate the day of the week for the first of every month for every year, but would be possible if Dave had an image of a calendar that he could work through. In fact, Dave was able to name correctly and quickly all the months beginning with a Friday between 1970 and 1990. Howe and Smith suggested that Dave's speed and accuracy indicated that he was able to access some image of each month as a whole.

Given the difficulty of eliciting information from anyone who, like Dave, has limited language abilities and is generally withdrawn, any findings from this study must be speculative. Nonetheless, Howe and Smith showed that it was possible to hypothesize several ways that dates could be calculated, and then, by carefully designing the questions they asked, to eliminate some of these ways in the case of Dave. By using this method, they concluded that Dave's calendar calculating was based on a mental image, perhaps derived from printed calendars he had seen. This does not necessarily mean that all savants with calendar calculating skills use the same method, because there is evidence that other savants do have some appreciation of calendar regularities (O'Connor & Hermelin, 1992) or may have memorized so many individual dates they can recall them easily (Kahr & Neisser, 1982, cited by Howe & Smith, 1988).

As yet, we know little about how savant skills develop, but studies of savants like Dave will undoubtedly continue. They will continue partly because of the fascination of observing such exceptional skills, and partly because the fact that some people with generally low IQ can have one or more outstanding abilities has many implications for theories of intelligence.

Based on material in Howe, M.J.A. & Smith, J. (1988). Calendar calculating in 'idiot savants': how do they do it? *British Journal of Developmental Psychology*, *79*, 371–386.

---

abilities. As discussed above, Gardner (1983) suggested that different 'intelligences' may be independent abilities. A person can be poor in one area of skill but excellent in another domain, and if this is the case it would not be surprising to find a person with a low IQ who does have an outstanding ability.

An alternative explanation for the skills shown by savants has been put forward by Howe (1999), who emphasized the role of extensive practice in the development of many of the skills shown by savants. As Howe argued, many savants are solitary and withdrawn individuals who show little interest in the world around them, but may spend many hours practising one particular skill, whether it is calculating dates or learning a language. Anyone, irrespective of their IQ, who focuses their attention and effort on one particular task is likely to become an expert at that task. For example, Ericsson and Charness (1994) estimated that a 20-year-old first-class violinist will have already spent over 10,000 hours practising the instrument, and will know many long and complex pieces of music. Howe would argue that we are not surprised when we learn that an expert musician has devoted many thousands of hours to rehearsing music. We should therefore not be surprised when savants, who may well have spent very long periods of time practising a skill like calendar calculating, also demonstrate remarkable abilities (Howe et al., 1999).

INTELLIGENCE IN A SOCIAL-CULTURAL CONTEXT

Several early researchers have pointed to the importance of considering intelligence in the context of the real world. Binet and Simon (1916) described intelligence in the following terms:

> It seems to us that in intelligence there is a fundamental faculty, the impairment or the lack of which is of the utmost importance for practical life. This faculty is judgement, otherwise called good sense, practical sense, initiative, the faculty of adapting oneself to circumstances. To judge well, to reason well, these are the essential activities of intelligence.

And Wechsler (1944) said:

> Intelligence is the aggregate or global capacity of the individual to act purposefully, to think rationally, and to deal effectively with his environment.

However, despite these early descriptions of intelligence, it is only more recently, in the work of psychologists like Sternberg (1985) described above, that specific emphasis has been placed on the context of intelligent behaviour. Children's performance can differ markedly depending on context. Nunes Carraher et al. (1985) asked children to solve mathematical problems in the context of their everyday activities (helping their parents at a street market) by asking them, for example, to calculate the cost of several items of fruit that the experimenters purchased at the market. At a different time, the children were given the same problems as a paper and pencil test in their own homes. Even though the problems were the same, the children performed much better in the market context than in the more 'formal' test at home (see Chapter 16). Nunes Carraher et al.'s results showed how children's performance cannot be divorced from the context of that performance.

Contextualists take the view that intelligence should be defined within a particular cultural context, and that comparisons across cultures can only be made with caution (Miller, 1997; Sternberg, 1999). For example, Berry (1984) argued that it is important to define intelligence in terms of the 'cognitive competence' that is needed in a particular culture, and that psychologists should take local conceptions of intelligence into account when they design tests. For example, the ability to construct and use a bow and arrow is irrelevant for most people in our society, but such skills may well be of prime importance among hunter-gatherers. Intelligence scales that have been validated in a technologically advanced society would not assess skills like using a bow and arrow, but it cannot be concluded that the hunter-gatherers are less intelligent.

The constructs of intelligence vary across cultures (Sternberg, 2007a). Some cultures (e.g. Western industrial societies) place most emphasis on the intelligence 'within' an individual, but other cultures have conceptualized intelligence more in terms of the relationship between the individual and society. An individual's relationship with society can refer to personal relationships with friends and family, to a wider understanding of what is acceptable social behaviour within a society, and to an even wider appreciation of the history and religious beliefs of a society and how those inform behaviour (Demetriou & Papadopoulous, 2004). An intelligent child will therefore be one who can understand and adapt appropriately to the requirements of his or her society. These aspects of intelligent behaviour may be recognized more explicitly in some non-Western cultures.

Many cultures relate intelligence to good behaviour and good interpersonal skills. Serpell (1977) asked adults in Zambia to explain why particular children could be labelled intelligent. The adults not only referred to the children being clever (i.e. having good mental abilities) but also said that intelligent children were ones who were obedient, who could be trusted to follow instructions, and who had respect for their elders. Similarly, Harkness and Super (1992) found that in Kenya the concept of children's intelligence included reference to the children's competence in carrying out family duties effectively and obediently (Figure 17.3). In another study in rural Kenya, Grigorenko et al. (2001) found that people had four distinct ways to describe intelligence: having knowledge; having real-world problem-solving skills; having the ability to take initiatives; and understanding how to show respect. Showing respect may be a reflection of a child's increasing awareness of their role in a community, and the development of interpersonal skills like politeness, modesty and consideration for others, as Baral and Das (2004) found in descriptions of intelligence collected in India.

Concepts of intelligence that go beyond interpersonal skills to emphasize a child's relationship with the whole of society are found in many cultures. Wober (1974), in Uganda, found that intelligence referred to shared knowledge and wisdom, and in particular the way

Figure 17.3   In Kenya, the concept of children's intelligence includes reference to the children's competence in carrying out family duties effectively and obediently.

Source: Adam Hart-Davis/Science Photo Library.

an individual acted to the benefit of their community. Shared knowledge and wisdom may be seen in religious or philosophical contexts. For example, Yang and Sternberg (1997) asked people in Taiwan to describe intelligence; the descriptions included responses about cognitive skills and about interpersonal skills, like behaving generously and compassionately, but also referred to self-control, self-awareness and recognizing one's role in life. Yang and Sternberg suggested that the development of such a personal philosophy was a reflection of Confucian teaching in Eastern societies, because that teaching emphasized an individual's duties and obligations to their society. These beliefs about intelligence are quite different from the beliefs about intelligence most often expressed by people in Western cultures (see Box 17.1).

Sternberg (1985) argued that it is much more useful to see intelligence as being embedded in a particular context than as a static quality possessed by an individual; what is important is the relative emphasis that different cultures place upon certain skills at different historical times. For example, skills needed for reading are present in individuals from preliterate societies but are not developed, and are thus not important until literacy becomes widespread. As a second example, consider the children in contemporary Western society, who have gained familiarity with computers for both academic work and for recreation. Interacting with a computer may depend more on visual, auditory and manual aspects of intelligence that are skills that are not so readily measured by traditional intelligence tests. In other words, the contextualist view emphasizes a malleable concept of intelligence that can accommodate different ideas about intelligence in different places and at different times. The cultural context of intelligence will also have implications for teaching and assessing children. For example, if a child is brought up in a culture that emphasizes social and practical skills, it may be appropriate for the child's curriculum to reflect those skills more than just traditional academic abilities, and there is evidence that when this is the case, children's performance in school improves (Sternberg, 2007b).

   Stop and Think

Why are there so many different concepts of intelligence?

THE USE OF INTELLIGENCE TESTS

Despite concerns about the content validity of traditional intelligence scales, they are still used frequently, because they are one way to find out about a child's strengths and weaknesses. Over and above just measuring a child's performance, many educational psychologists treat intelligence tests like a clinical interview in which they can gain insights into the child's personality, self-image, attention span and motivation as well as level of intelligence. Thus, in the hands of an experienced clinician, a test can be of important diagnostic value. From this point of view, intelligence scales can be useful. They can identify children with particularly low levels of ability who may need special help and schooling (which was Binet's original intention in designing tests); they can identify gifted children who may also need special educational provision; and they can also identify distinctive patterns of performance. For example, adults with dyslexia (see Chapter 12) may have a pattern of performance on the WAIS that is called the 'ACID' profile; this means that they have below average scores on four tests on this scale (i.e. arithmetic, coding, information and digit span tests; these are similar to but more advanced versions of the tests described in Table 17.2), but they may have average or above average scores on the other tests. This particular profile is typical of adults who have dyslexia.

Children with Learning Difficulties

In assessing children who perform poorly in school, educational psychologists may rely only partly on the results from an intelligence test. They would also try to assess children in the context of their home background, medical history of life events and in relation to the problems that the children might be experiencing. For example, if a child has had prolonged periods of illness or a traumatic event such as the loss of a parent, then these circumstances would need to be taken into account when assessing the child's level of attainment.

Some learning difficulties have been ascribed to general intellectual impairment. Others, however, may be due to an unstimulating or stressful home background, to emotional disturbance, to a physical condition, to poor diet or to a combination of factors, and therefore psychologists may use methods of assessment that best identify such potential problems. In addition to intelligence scales, many other measures can be used; for example, naturalistic observation of the child's behaviour as recorded by parents and teachers can lead to a greater understanding of the child's difficulties. Social assessment can also be helpful to indicate a child's communicative abilities, social skills and emotional adjustment. Psychologists can also use attainment tests to measure performance in specific areas, such as mathematics and reading, and diagnostic tests can help to unravel the reasons for a child's poor performance. We will say more about attainment tests later in this chapter.

Gifted Children

A child may be described as 'gifted' who is outstanding in either a general domain, such as exceptional performance on an intelligence test, or a more specific area of ability, like music or sport (Howe, 1999; Radford, 1990). The borderline between gifted children and others is not clearly defined, and different researchers have used different levels of performance on intelligence scales to define a gifted child as one with an IQ of more than 120, more than 130 or more than 140. Children with such high scores are rare: only 1 in 10 children has scores over 120; 1 in 40 has scores over 130; 1 in 200 has scores over 140; and 1 in 1000 has scores over 150. Fewer than 1 in a million has an IQ score over 180.

The most famous investigation of giftedness is Terman's (1925) longitudinal study in California that began in 1921 with children aged about 10 years. Terman used 'gifted' to refer to children with IQ scores about or above 140 (on the Stanford–Binet scale) and all the children in his sample had scores of between 130 and 190. Terman published regular reports about their achievements for nearly 35 years (Terman & Oden, 1959) and other researchers have reported on the same group in old age (Holahan and Sears, 1996).

Terman found that his sample of gifted children had superior physical health and growth from birth on; they walked and talked early and excelled in reading, language and general knowledge. A follow-up in 1947 when the average age was 35 indicated that the initial level of intelligence had been maintained (Terman & Oden, 1947). Sixty-eight per cent had graduated from college, and many had been outstanding in their professions; for example, they had produced a large number of publications and patents. In 1959, another follow-up found that they had continued to maintain their high achievements in their occupations. Seventy-one per cent were in professional, semi-professional or managerial positions (compared with 14% of the Californian population as a whole) and their average income was higher than that of the average college graduate (Terman & Oden, 1959).

Terman's study showed that gifted children are, perhaps not surprisingly, very likely to become successful adults. However, one limitation of his study should be noted. The children in Terman's sample were selected partly on the basis of teachers' ratings and, in this way, home background factors may have been confounded with his criterion of high intelligence; for instance, working-class and ethnic minority children may have been underrepresented from the start of the study. In other words, the children in the sample may have come from advantageous social environments, and some of their success may have been due as much to this factor as to their high IQ.

Most of the participants in Terman's sample appeared to be well-integrated, healthy and well-adjusted individuals. However, some researchers have pointed out the problems and difficulties that some gifted children can face, especially amongst those with the highest ability levels (Winner, 1996). For example, Gross (2004) described the case of Ian who, at the age of 5 years, hated school, was uncontrollable in class, was aggressive towards other children, and was to be referred to a special school for children with behavioural problems. As part of the referral process, Ian was assessed by an educational psychologist. Ian had an IQ over 170 and the reading age of a 12-year-old, and the psychologist suggested that any behavioural problems were most likely to be the result of frustration. When measured at the age of 9, Ian's IQ was about 200, and therefore he was performing as well as a typical 18-year-old, but his school insisted that he undertook a curriculum designed for 9-year-olds. Clearly, this was insufficient to be challenging or stimulating for Ian, but it was not until later that he was allowed to study at a level more appropriate to his abilities. During his school years, Ian began attending university courses, and then enrolled for a degree at the age of 16.

Ian was one of several highly gifted children described by Gross (2004), all of whom were exceptional as young children and who nearly all went on to be both academically and professionally successful. Nonetheless, some of the children had difficult experiences at school, finding (like Ian) that the school work they were expected to do was unrewarding, or that they had problems relating to other children of their age because their knowledge, abilities and interests were so different. Some children were bullied for being different and some deliberately underachieved in attempts to make themselves more acceptable to their peers.

Gross suggested several reasons why gifted children may not thrive: teachers who do not recognize exceptional children; school policies that are not flexible enough to provide them with stimulating environments; and governments that do not provide special support for such children. Other researchers have pointed out additional reasons, suggesting that some gifted children have to cope with unreasonable parental expectations and with the pressure always to excel (Freeman, 2000, 2001).

Being gifted can therefore be both an advantage, because of the greater opportunities and success that often accompany high academic achievement, and a disadvantage, when young children find it difficult to adjust socially and emotionally to a peer group who may be many years behind them intellectually. Interventions like special teaching or special classes can help gifted children overcome the disadvantages (Gross, 2004), but such interventions are not always straightforward, because they may have wider social implications about the use of additional educational resources to benefit a particular group of able children, rather than using those resources to raise the standard of all children (Winner, 1996).

 ## Stop and Think

How might intelligence testing benefit gifted children and children with learning difficulties?

ATTAINMENT TESTS

Measures of intelligence usually include tests that are unfamiliar to the person taking the test—in other words, the test designers are attempting to measure the performance of a person on tests that are novel and that have not been practised. In contrast, tests of attainment measure what a person has achieved after specific training (Black, 1998). Examples of attainment tests include school examinations, driving tests, examinations for music, tests of sporting achievement and so on. Such measures have a variety of purposes, and we will give examples of the different ways in which attainment tests can be used.

Certification and selection: Passing an examination is an indication that a person has achieved a specified level of competence. Examinations were first introduced in the UK in 1815 for doctors, and were later also used by other professions (e.g. solicitors and accountants) to determine entry into the profession. They were also used from the mid-19th century to assess candidates for the Civil Service, and for university entrance. These examinations were meant to be a way of giving more (middle-class) people access to the professions or university, because previously such opportunities had been based on family background or payment. The early professional examinations were all written ones and established the tradition of written examinations throughout school and university. The use of tests for selection at all ages and levels is one of the main perceived uses of examinations, and earlier we mentioned the use of the 11-plus examination for selection to secondary school. In the present educational system in England and Wales performance in GCSE examinations at 16 years of age determines the opportunity to study for AS-level and A-level examinations, and they in turn determine access to higher education.

Motivation: Assessment is a way to motivate children to be successful. At a minimum, examinations focus attention on hard work and channel behaviour into what is educationally and socially desirable. But more than this, assessment may be seen as both intrinsically rewarding (because children learn as they prepare for tests) and externally rewarding (if success in an examination gives access to the next step on the educational ladder). At all stages, children can be given feedback, which should contribute to both their learning and their motivation to improve.

Record keeping: All assessment (e.g. examinations or teachers' judgements) can contribute to a record of a child's performance. This can be used to check on a child's progress, and is particularly important if a child is having difficulties, as the course and extent of those difficulties can be identified.

Screening and diagnostic assessment: Screening means that all the children at a certain age or level are given the same test, or set of tests, to identify any who might be in need of special help. Once a child who needs special help has been identified, he or she can be given diagnostic tests to find out about their particular weaknesses. For example, if a child is poor at reading, diagnostic tests can be used to discover the specific reading disabilities that he or she may have. Measures used for screening are usually standardized tests.

Standardized tests: There is a wide range of tests designed to measure attainment in reading, verbal reasoning, English, numeracy, comprehension and so on. Standardized tests (like intelligence scales) have been pretested on large numbers of children to eliminate badly worded questions or items that fail to discriminate between different children. The instructions for administering the tests are also standard so that all children take the test under the same conditions. Such tests have been used on large numbers of children, so that the test designers can state how an average child at any given age should perform on the test. This allows a teacher to make a meaningful assessment of an individual child's abilities by comparing his or her performance to other children of the same age. Performance on many attainment tests may correlate quite highly with IQ, but the primary function of an attainment test is to measure achievement within a particular subject area rather than general intelligence.

Criterion-referenced tests: These are tests that measure whether a child can achieve a specified level of performance on a task. For example, a teacher might want to know whether a child understands how to do long division, and might set the criterion of understanding as successfully solving 20 long division problems. A criterion-referenced test is different from a standardized test (which is based on comparisons between children of the same age) because set criteria are given. For example, a driving test is a criterion-referenced test, because a person either meets the requirements of the test and passes, or does not meet them and fails. In other words, you either pass or fail; the test is the same whatever your age. If all driving test candidates met the required criteria then 100% could pass the test. In contrast, on a standardized test, 50% of children at any age will be below the average score and 50% will be above that score.

Curriculum control and school evaluation: One use of assessment is to determine what is taught in schools. If children are to take a particular examination, the school syllabus must include the appropriate teaching needed for that examination. The National Curriculum in England and Wales includes specific attainment targets. Pupils are assessed at several ages between 7 and 14 years of age, either by teachers or using tests that are the same nationally. These are criterion-referenced assessments because, ideally, all children, at each age, should have achieved the knowledge and ability to succeed on them. The use of common tests for all pupils can provide important information about the progress of individual children, and at the same time both teachers and schools can be assessed in terms of their pupils' performance.

Stop and Think

Which are more important, intelligence tests or attainment tests?

CHAPTER SUMMARY

- Intelligence and attainment tests are useful for assessing an individual child. They can often be of great importance for identifying children who are exceptional (in terms of either learning difficulties or giftedness) or in identifying a particular child's strengths and weaknesses.
- The most frequently used intelligence measures (e.g. the Wechsler scales, the British Ability Scales and Raven's matrices) are based on conceptions of intelligence that focus on cognitive and academic skills such as memory, reasoning and problem solving, and these measures are, to some extent, independent of context and culture.
- In contrast, some researchers have emphasized the importance of other abilities in human performance (including, for example, emotional, social, practical and musical intelligences) and these may be related to contextual and cultural factors.
- The inclusion of a wider range of abilities in the concept of intelligence can provide us with much richer insights into human performance. However, if the concept is extended to take into account more abilities, one implication is that children's intelligence should be measured using not a single IQ scale, but many different tests that capture a range of children's abilities. But it is not clear how this could be achieved, because we would need age-appropriate, culturally appropriate, standardized measures for each of the possible abilities that can be linked to intelligence, and as yet such measures hardly exist.

DISCUSSION POINTS

1. What does 'intelligence' mean?
2. Is an individual's 'intelligence' a single trait or is it made up of many different abilities?
3. Do different concepts of intelligence have different implications for the way we measure people's intelligence?
4. Do school and college examinations measure intelligence?
5. Should children with very high IQs be educated any differently from children with average IQs?

FURTHER READING

- A good and very readable introduction to intelligence research is Cooper, C. (1999). *Intelligence and abilities*. London: Routledge. A very good and detailed summary of all the issues related to intelligence and intelligence testing can be found in Maltby, J., Day, L. & Macaskill, A. (2013). *Personality, individual differences and intelligence* (3rd ed.). Harlow: Pearson. These two books (like most books about intelligence and intelligence testing) focus on adults rather than children; however, a chapter by Sternberg places some of the theories and issues about intelligence in a developmental context: see Sternberg, R.J. (2010). Individual differences in cognitive development. In U. Goswami (Ed.), *Blackwell handbook of childhood cognitive development* (2nd ed.). Oxford: Blackwell.
- Robert J. Sternberg is probably the most prolific writer on intelligence research, including the educational implications of that research, and his websites include a large number of relevant references.
- Gardner's theory of intelligence is described in Gardner, H. (2011). *Frames of mind. The theory of multiple intelligences* (2nd ed.). New York: Basic Books. This edition has an introduction by Gardner describing the impact of his theory since it was first published in the 1980s.

A note about intelligence and attainment tests. Many intelligence and attainment tests can be purchased. However, the publishers of tests only sell them to registered users. Before registering a user, the publishers require evidence of the user's qualifications and, in addition, for specific tests they may require evidence that a user has been on an appropriate course for training in the use of that test. These procedures are followed to ensure that tests are used responsibly and correctly, and that both test material and test results are always kept confidential. For these reasons, you cannot borrow tests from libraries or other sources. Nonetheless, most publishers maintain extensive websites and you can find information about specific tests by searching these.

CHAPTER
18

Deprivation and Enrichment: Risk and Resilience

CHAPTER OUTLINE

- Deprivation
- Extreme Deprivation and Neglect
- The Effects of Institutional Rearing on Children's Development
- Socially Disadvantaged Children
- Explanatory Models
- Interventions: The Role of Families
- Nurture Groups
- Compensatory Education Programmes in the USA
- Compensatory Education Programmes in the UK
- A Continuing Debate

In this chapter we look at deprivation and enrichment and the part played by families, by schools and by society itself in the cognitive and emotional development of children, with particular emphasis on those from less advantaged environments. We will consider the role of risk and protective factors in the psychological development of the child. There are ethical considerations to take into account when undertaking the study of deprivation since children cannot, of course, be deliberately deprived of essential experiences. So, as you will see, many of the research studies tend to be carried out in naturalistic settings in circumstances that were occurring anyway. This makes for particular problems in research design (see Chapter 1). By contrast, it is ethically permissible to provide enrichment for children in conditions of adversity, and we will review studies, both experimental and in naturalistic settings, that attempt to evaluate the effect on children of improving the conditions of their lives.

DEPRIVATION

> Deprivation takes many different forms in every known society. People can be said to be deprived if they lack the types of diet, clothing, housing, household facilities and fuel and environmental, educational, working and social conditions, activities and facilities which are customary, or at least widely encouraged and approved, in the societies to which they belong.
>
> *(Townsend, 1987, p. 126)*

From this perspective, the concept of deprivation encompasses four critical aspects (Morgan & Baker, 2006, pp. 31–32).

- It is *multidimensional*, as people can be deprived in different ways, because of their lack of the basic necessities of diet or clothing or the poor environment or social conditions in which they live.
- It concerns *material* as well as *social* aspects. The *material* dimension of deprivation concerns access to goods and resources, whereas the *social* dimension concerns the ability of individuals and families to participate as active members of their society, for example through attendance at family and social events, entertaining friends or engaging in community activities.
- Deprivation is *relative*, since it refers to minimum standards of living based on socially accepted norms that differ from one society to another and from one historical point in time to another. Measures of deprivation need to be updated regularly in order to remain in line with social perceptions of acceptable standards.
- Deprivation concerns *individuals* just as much as regions or areas. A person does not become deprived simply with regard to the area in which they live. Morgan and Baker (2006), discussing the relationship between relative deprivation and health, indicate the need to take account of both environmental factors (for example, living in a poor inner-city area, Figure 18.1) and individual factors (for example, socioeconomic factors like family composition, low income and poor housing).

Figure 18.1 Children make the most of a dismal inner-city environment, using available materials for play (Morgan & Baker, 2006).
Source: Peter Ginter/Getty Images.

Stop and Think

Why are some children at a disadvantage in society? Can interventions and policies compensate for deprivation? How does the wider culture shape the direction of a child's aspirations and achievements?

None of the answers is simple, because these questions concern the complex interaction of many factors, from the parent–child relationship to the social context within which the child develops. It may help to consider Baltes' emphasis on historical factors and Bronfenbrenner's ecological model of human development, summarized in Chapter 1. Both Baltes and Bronfenbrenner warn of the dangers of focusing on the individual without taking into account the context within which he or she exists or the processes of interaction through which the behaviour of individuals in a particular system or historical period develops. It is useful to bear their ideas in mind as you consider the issues raised in this chapter.

EXTREME DEPRIVATION AND NEGLECT

Feral Children

We look first at studies of the effects of extreme deprivation and neglect on young children. There have, for example, been anecdotal accounts of 'feral' children; that is, children discovered in the wild with apparently no form of human contact. When rescued, these children have tended to display behaviour more characteristic of animals, such as running on all fours, and this led some to believe that the children had survived through being reared by and among animals. Such cases are often inadequately documented. Whatever the circumstances of their rearing, the prognosis for feral children has been poor. Their linguistic and cognitive attainment has tended to remain at a low level, and their social behaviour is usually strange. However, we cannot be sure that such children were developing 'normally' when their parents abandoned them, and some investigators have suggested that feral children may have been psychotic or developmentally delayed in the first instance. We do have a few more reliable case studies of children who have been reared in conditions of extreme deprivation in their own homes and who have subsequently been rescued. These accounts can help answer the question of how far an enriched environment can compensate for the effects of very severe neglect in the early years.

The Koluchova Twins

Koluchova's (1972, 1991) case study of Czechoslovakian twins, Andrei and Vanya, born in 1960, gives evidence to support the argument that the effects of severe neglect need not be irreversible. The twins' mother died when they were born and they spent the next 11 months in an institution where they were said to be making normal progress. The father then took them back into his home but, on his remarriage, they were again put into care until the new household was formed. From around the age of 18 months until 7 years, the twins lived with their father and his new wife. However, the stepmother kept them in conditions of extreme deprivation. She forbade her own children to talk to the twins and denied them any affection herself. They spent their time either in a bare, unheated room apart from the rest of the family or, as a punishment, were locked in the cellar. They never went out, and lacked proper food, exercise and any kind of intellectual or social stimulation apart from what they could provide for themselves. Neighbours did not know of their existence but from time to time heard strange, animal-like sounds coming from the cellar. By the age of 7, when the authorities became aware of the twins' existence, they had the appearance of 3-year-olds; they could hardly walk because of rickets, they could not play, their speech was very poor and they relied mainly on gestures to communicate. On their discovery, they were removed from the family and placed in a home for preschool children.

They had experienced such severe emotional, intellectual and social deprivation that the prognosis seemed very poor, but once placed in a supportive environment they began to make remarkable gains. After a year, they were ready to be placed in a school for children with special educational needs. There they made such progress that they were transferred the next year to the second class of a mainstream infant school. At the same time, they were placed in the care of an unmarried middle-aged woman with a long experience of rearing children in her extended family. At the time, she lived with her sister, who had already adopted an 11-year-old girl. The two sisters gave the twins the emotional security and intellectual stimulation that had been so lacking in their own family environment.

As a result, in the next 15 months, the twins' mental age increased by 3 years, showing clearly how the environmental change had compensated for early neglect. Prior to that, Koluchova had estimated their intelligence to be around an IQ of 40, although no formal assessment was possible because of their unfamiliarity with any of the tasks that appear in intelligence tests. A follow-up at the age of 14 found complete 'catch-up' in the twins' language development; school performance was good and motivation high. They were now functioning at an average academic level in a class of children who were only 18 months younger than they.

They were socially adjusted and had realistic aspirations to go on to take vocational training. They finished schooling at the age of 17, when their educational standard corresponded broadly to that of their peers. After leaving school, they went to college to train as typewriter mechanics, where they were among the best in their class. They lived in a students' residence while maintaining strong relationships with their adoptive family. Figure 18.2 indicates the intellectual progress made by the twins from 3 months after intervention began.

Following military service, one twin worked as an instructor in technical vocational training and the other as a technician specializing in computers. Andrei and Vanya are now in their 50s with a wide circle of friends and family. Both have married and each has three children.

Koluchova's study indicates how removal from an extremely impoverished environment can reverse the effects of deprivation. It could be argued, of course, that the success of the intervention was only possible because the twins had experienced some normal nurturing in the first few months of their lives; second, they were not totally isolated, since they had the support of one another; third, the twins were discovered when they were still relatively young. But their case illustrates how the straightforward improvement of life circumstances can lead to children's rehabilitation despite being exposed to extreme emotional and physical

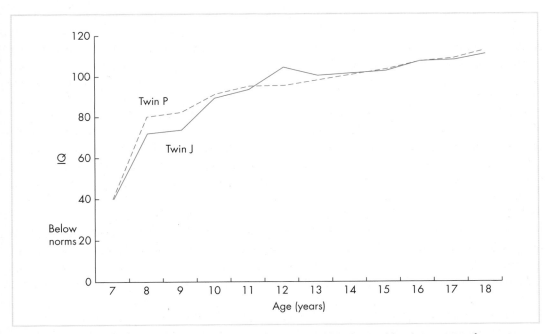

Figure 18.2   Changes in the IQ score of the Koluchova twins, measured by the WISC, after intervention began (Koluchova, 1972).
Age 7: placed in institutional care
Age 8–9: attend school for children with special needs
Age 10: attend second class of mainstream infant school
Age 11–13: progress through mainstream primary school
Age 14–16: progress to secondary school class of pupils 18 months younger than twins
Age 17: complete schooling; attain school leaving certificate
Age 18: attend college for vocational training

Source: Koluchova, J. (1972). Severe derivation in twins: A case study. *Journal of Child Psychology and Psychiatry* 13(2): 107–114.

deprivation in early life. Masten (2014) comments that this resilience results from what she calls 'ordinary magic'—the quality that exists in the minds and bodies of children, their carers and communities.

 Stop and Think

Think of your own examples of 'ordinary magic'. What can families and communities do to create the magic and live in a more positive way?

In other words, by ending the deprivation and replacing it with ordinary life experiences, it is possible to shift individuals back onto a positive developmental path. A less favourable outcome, however, was found in the case study of a girl called 'Genie', where crucial ameliorative factors were absent (Curtiss, 1977).

Genie

Genie's isolation was even more extreme than that of the Czechoslovakian twins and lasted for a longer period of time. From the age of 20 months until she was 13 years old, she was imprisoned alone in a darkened room. By day, she was tied to an infant potty chair in such a way that she could only move her hands and feet; at night, she was put in a sleeping bag and further restrained by a wire straitjacket. Her father beat her if she made any sound and he forbade other members of the family to speak to her. She lived in an almost silent world, deprived of warmth, proper nourishment and normal human contact. She was kept in these conditions until her mother, who was partially blind and dominated by Genie's father, finally escaped with her. At this point, Genie could not walk; she was emaciated, weighing around 27 kilos, she spent much of her time spitting and salivating, and was virtually silent apart from the occasional whimper. When tested soon after admission to hospital, she was functioning at the level of a 1-year-old.

Curtiss (1977), a graduate student of linguistics at the time, has given a detailed account of Genie's development for the 7 years and 2 months during which she was studied by psychologists and linguists for research purposes. Despite the terrible conditions she had endured, Genie responded to treatment. She soon learned to walk. Her level of intellectual functioning (measured by a non-verbal intelligence test developed for use with deaf children) increased (see Figure 18.3) and in some perceptual tasks, such as the Mooney Faces Test, which required subjects to distinguish between real and distorted faces, she performed well above average. She also became able to form relationships with other people.

In the area of language, however, Genie's development proved puzzling. During the first 7 months in care she learned to recognize a number of words, and then began to speak. At first she produced one-word utterances like 'pillow'; later, like any normal toddler, she produced two-word utterances, first nouns and adjectives (e.g. 'big teeth') and later verbs ('want milk') (as you read in Chapter 12 on language development). She was even able to use words to describe her experience of isolation and neglect (Curtiss records Genie as saying, 'Father hit arm. Big wood. Genie cry'). However, there were unusual aspects to her language development. She never asked questions, she never learned to use pronouns and the telegraphic speech did not develop into more complex sentences. In fact, she was more inclined to use gestures in order to convey meaning.

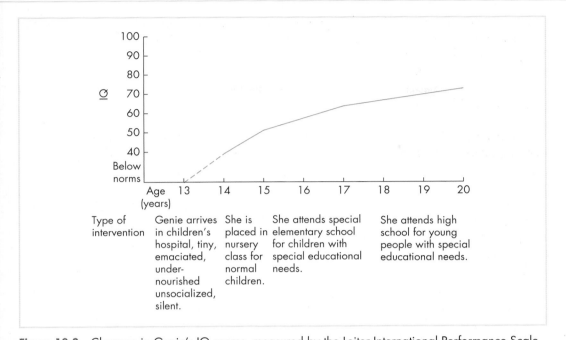

Figure 18.3 Changes in Genie's IQ scores, measured by the Leiter International Performance Scale (a non-verbal test), after intervention began (Curtiss, 1977).

Source: Curtiss, S. (1977). *Genie: A psycholinguistic study of a modern-day 'wild child'.* New York: Academic Press.

Thus, although Genie showed great interest in language and developed some competence, she did not catch up with other children of her own age.

Stop and Think

Why did Genie not catch up in the way that the Koluchova twins did?

Curtiss speculated that Genie was using the right hemisphere of the brain for language, not the left as is usual. Since the right hemisphere is not predisposed to language, this could explain some of the strange aspects of Genie's speech. Such an interpretation is confirmed by Genie's competence at discriminating faces, which is a right hemisphere task. Curtiss's explanation of Genie's unusual language development is that when language is not acquired at the right time, the cortical tissue normally committed for language and related abilities may cease to function. If Curtiss is right, Genie provides support for the idea that there is indeed a critical or sensitive period for the development of some left hemisphere functioning.

Some of the questions remain unanswered, since all research into Genie's development stopped in 1975 when guardianship was transferred to her mother. She was initially cared for by her mother but soon after was placed in a series of foster homes. Genie's reaction to this dramatic change in her life was to regress, 'shedding by degrees the skills in comportment and communication that she had developed over the previous several years' (Rymer, 1993, p. 155).

Skuse (1984, p. 567), in a review of studies of extreme deprivation (including the Koluchova twins and Genie), concluded that 'in the absence of genetic or congenital anomalies or a history of gross malnourishment, victims of such deprivation have an excellent prognosis. Some subtle deficits in social adjustment may persist'. Having a secure attachment to a good caregiver is a key factor in recovery. Skuse argued that, with regard to Genie, it is possible that the help came after a critical or sensitive period for normal language development; further, he did not rule out the possibility of organic dysfunction (that is, a brain disorder) in the left hemisphere in her case. Jones (1995), however, disagrees with this view and argues convincingly that the disruption, separation and loss that were happening in Genie's life provide a sufficient explanation of her failure to develop linguistically after 1975. On the basis of his analysis of Genie's language development in three time periods, he argues that Genie *was* able to acquire the morphology and syntax of English and was still in the process of acquiring it when the research stopped. He concludes that a definitive judgement on the extent of Genie's language development cannot be given. Intervention did have a considerable impact on Genie's development, but clearly without such dramatic success as was obtained with the twins in Koluchova's study.

THE EFFECTS OF INSTITUTIONAL REARING ON CHILDREN'S DEVELOPMENT

Early Studies

Another area of research that provides information about the impacts of deprivation on children's development focuses on the experience of children reared in orphanages or children's homes. Pioneering studies in this field began in the years before and soon after World War II. Spitz (1946) noted that infants in institutions fared very badly in comparison with infants reared at home. They were underweight, reached developmental milestones later and were more vulnerable to illness. Two early studies showed the effects that could be achieved by enriching the environment for institutionally reared children. Skeels and Dye (1939) chanced to notice the effect of environmental change on two developmentally delayed children who had been transferred at 18 months from an orphanage to the women's ward in an institution for adults with severe learning difficulties, which had an associated school. Their new environment was in fact an enriched one in comparison with the orphanage. Both staff and patients lavished attention and affection on them, played with them and took them on outings, and the children were given a much more stimulating experience than they had had previously. The gains were dramatic, and after 15 months of this experience the children were considered to be within the normal range of intelligence. By contrast, children who had remained in the stultifying environment of the orphanage did not make progress in the same way.

Skodak and Skeels (1945) then carried out a more systematic longitudinal study in which 13 developmentally delayed infants from the orphanage were transferred in the same way as the earlier two. The infants were aged 11–21 months, and had a mean IQ of 64. Again the children made dramatic gains; after an average of 19 months' stay their mean IQ was 92. By the age of 3 or 4, most were adopted by families and went on to attend mainstream schools.

Stop and Think

Was it the intervention in the women's ward that had the effect, or was it the continuing long-term stimulation and care from the adopted families?

Although these studies have been criticized for their small number of participants, possible lack of random assignment to experimental and control groups, and the diversity of the sample, the striking results provide a strong indication that environmental stimulation can undo at least some of the negative effects of deprivation. Later studies in different cultures tell a very similar story. Dennis (1973) carried out a series of studies in The Crèche, a Lebanese orphanage run by French nuns. The children were fed and kept clean, but were given very little intellectual stimulation; the ratio of caregivers to children was 1–10; the babies were kept in cribs with white sheets round them; if they cried, no one came; the caregivers rarely talked to them. Dennis also investigated the intellectual development of those children from The Crèche who were adopted, following a change in legislation in the Lebanon in the 1950s. He found that children who were adopted by the age of 2 regained normal IQs, even though their average IQ at the time of adoption was 50. However, Crèche children who were adopted at a later age were less likely to 'catch up' intellectually. Dennis concluded that deprivation up to the first 2 years of life can be overcome if the later environment is normal, and that if there was a critical period (see Chapter 2) for intellectual development it would be later—between 2 and 8 years. Alternatively, the difficulties older children experience might be because they suffer more deficits. For example, a 4-year-old with an IQ of 50 has a mental age of 2 years; an 8-year-old with an IQ of 50 has a mental age of 4 years. By 12 years of age, the 4-year-old had 8 years of normal growth, but the 8-year-old had only 4 additional years of normal growth.

Romanian Adoptees: The English and Romanian Adoptees (ERA) Study

Ongoing rigorous longitudinal, multimethod research by Rutter and his colleagues (Beckett et al., 2006; O'Connor et al., 2000; Rutter et al., 1998, 2009a, 2009) has investigated the deficit and developmental 'catch-up' following adoption to the UK of Romanian children who had spent the first years of their lives in orphanages where they suffered neglect and deprivation. This was at a time when Romania was going through a period of acute political upheaval; the previous regime, under communist President Nicolae Ceauşescu, had encouraged policies that resulted in many children being placed in orphanages in conditions ranging from poor to appalling. The Romanian children in the ERA study, who were severely developmentally delayed on their entry to the UK, were compared with a sample of UK children placed for adoption before the age of 6 months. Both groups of children have been assessed at 4, 6, 11 and 15 years of age.

Initial measurements at 4 years (Rutter et al., 1998) indicated considerable resilience with regard to cognitive and physical development on the part of the Romanian adoptees. The strongest predictor was the children's age on entry to the UK. For those who were adopted before 6 months, there appeared to be almost complete cognitive and physical catch-up by 4 years; for those adopted after 6 months, the mean was one standard deviation below that of adopted UK children. Rutter and his colleagues also considered the impact of emotional deprivation on these children, since there had been malnutrition and possibly abuse in some cases. However, despite this, there appeared to be a high degree of emotional resilience.

A later study of the same children in comparison with UK-born adoptees included the separate analysis of the scores of a subsample of 48 Romanian children who were adopted after more than 2 years of severe global deprivation (that is, deprivation in every physical, social, emotional and cognitive aspect of their development) (O'Connor et al., 2000). The first finding was that the Romanian children demonstrated virtually complete cognitive catch-up, provided adoption occurred before 6 months (as in the earlier study). A second finding was that those who had been adopted between 6 and 24 months scored significantly higher on cognitive tests than those who had been adopted between 24 and 42 months. A third finding, focused on the late-placed adoptees, was that in comparison with earlier-placed groups there was general developmental impairment.

Figure 18.4 illustrates cognitive differences at age 6 according to age of adoption. The analysis of the cognitive scores indicated that the UK and Romanian 0–6-month-old adoptee groups did not differ from one another. In other words, in comparison with UK adoptees, the early-placed Romanian children had achieved and maintained the cognitive catch-up that was indicated at age 4. Both groups (UK and Romanian early-placed adoptees) scored significantly

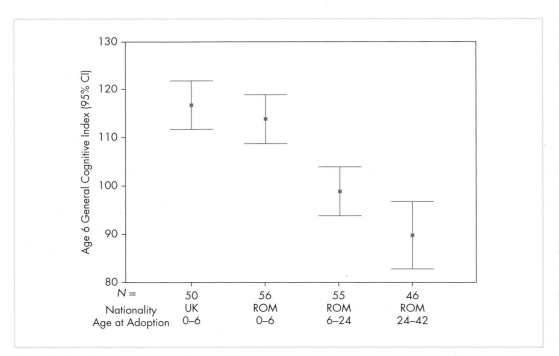

Figure 18.4   Cognitive scores of UK and Romanian adoptees at 6 years of age as a function of age at adoption in months.

Source: O'Connor, T. G. et al, 2000: The effects of global severe privation on cognitive competence: extension and longitudinal cover-up, *Child Development, 71*(2), 376–90.

higher, on average, than the 6–24-month-old and the 24–42-month-old groups. In turn, the 6–24-month and 24–42-month groups were significantly different from one another ($p < .001$).

The latest-placed adoptees (in the 24–42-month group) exhibited low to average cognitive scores as a group. These children had long-term difficulties. As a group they showed lower cognitive scores and a general developmental impairment in comparison with those children who had been adopted earlier. Despite the fact that they had been adopted by supportive and caring families, the early deprivation continued to have a negative influence on their emotional adjustment at 6 years. While there was some improvement, unfortunately there was no differential catch-up for these later-placed adoptees between the ages of 4 and 6, even though the length of time with their adoptive families was by now longer than the period of time spent in the Romanian orphanages. These findings suggest that early deprivation rather than the time spent in the adoptive home beyond a period of 2 years seemed to be the key factor in explaining the extent of their cognitive and physical developmental catch-up.

Beckett et al. (2006) explored these issues further by examining the links between duration and timing of deprivation and IQ scores when the children were 11 years of age, and compared their findings with cognitive results gathered from 128 of the adoptees at the age of 6 years. There was substantial heterogeneity among individual children in terms of cognitive outcomes at both age 6 and age 11. There was also high continuity in terms of impairment category at both 6 years and 11 years. The most significant changes at age 11 were for the most impaired group of children, given that marked cognitive catch-up occurred for most of the children in this category. Despite this, many of these children remained within the most impaired group. Most strikingly, Beckett et al. (2006) found that there was no measurable effect of institutional deprivation that did not extend beyond 6 months of age, but there was a substantial decrement in IQ associated with institutional deprivation above that age.

Certain emotional and behavioural difficulties emerged, especially where the institutional deprivation had lasted beyond 6 months. For example, as younger children they were more likely to display a lack of wariness of strangers and a willingness to wander away from caregivers. They had some difficulties in social interaction with adults outside the family and with the peer group, for example being the victims of bullying and social exclusion at school. Often these children might find it hard to 'read' social situations and pick up social cues. In other words, for some, there was impaired theory of mind. Some showed unusual preoccupations and intense interest in one particular topic. They were also more likely to display inattention and overactivity similar to attention deficit hyperactivity disorder (ADHD).

Some of these emotional and behavioural difficulties persisted beyond the age of 11, especially amongst those who had experienced more than 6 months of deprivation (Kumsta et al., 2010). The follow-ups, at 15 years of age and into young adulthood, indicate the continuation of a number of emotional, conduct and peer relationship problems and some difficulties in finding employment (Rutter et al., 2010).

 Stop and Think

What do these findings add to our understanding of resilience and catch-up? What is the impact of the ongoing care from supportive families and schools?

On the other hand, for most of the young people in this sample of adoptees, there were substantial improvements over time. Many of the children who had been intensely preoccupied with particular topics broadened out their range of interests, in harmony with the usual pursuits of young people in their age group. In some instances, they developed enhanced skill in music and sport. There were many examples of outstanding resilience and adaptation—processes that continued through adolescence and beyond. As adolescents, most of the adoptees were extremely positive about the experiences within the families. By the age of 15, around a quarter of the young people had visited Romania and valued this opportunity to discover more about their country of origin.

Rutter and his colleagues on the ERA study conclude that if children are rescued from extreme deprivation before 6 months of age, there is evidence that they will demonstrate considerable resilience and catch-up (Rutter et al., 2008, 2010). Additionally, provided that the adoptive family is caring and supportive, the catch-up of the immediate adoption period is maintained and not 'washed out'. At the same time, deprivation is associated with impairment and there are long-term difficulties for those children who experience severe deprivation for more than the first 6 months of their lives (in partial confirmation of the earlier research by Skodak and Skeels and by Dennis). There is also the possibility that there may be genetically influenced variations in the susceptibility of individual children to environmental hazards such as those experienced in the harsh conditions of the Romanian orphanages (Kumsta et al., 2010). Beckett et al. (2006) speculate that the influence of education could have been a factor in the catch-up of the children with the lowest scores at age 4, since extra individual help was provided by the schools for those children with lowest academic attainment. A second factor, they suggest, could have been the additional time in the adoptive homes. Whatever the reason, they argue that, even though cognitive impairment persists in this group of children, continuing improvement may go on for much longer than previous research might have predicted. In their words (Beckett et al., 2006, p. 706), 'the window of opportunity for intellectual gains post adoption between 6 and 11 years seems wider than appeared likely at 6, but there are clear limits, as shown by the relative persistence in cognitive impairment'.

This 'natural experiment' arose out of a humanitarian response to a social problem. The study enabled researchers to examine basic questions about risk and resilience in development and the causal role of early experience on later outcomes. As we saw, there was strong evidence of resilience, but also long-term difficulties for some children, depending on their age at adoption.

SOCIALLY DISADVANTAGED CHILDREN

Another key line of research examines the impact of severe social disadvantage, continuing through childhood and adolescence, on young people's development.

Social Disadvantage in the UK

Historically, concern about the impact of social disadvantage on children coincides with the philosophy of 'equality of opportunity' that emerged in most Western societies, including Britain and the USA, in the years following World War II. As the Newsom Report (1963) put it, 'all children should have an equal opportunity of acquiring intelligence, and developing their talents and abilities to the full'. It was assumed by many that this would also result in an equality of achievement among different social class and racial groups. Yet, despite decades of research, policy making and intervention, huge inequalities in UK society remain to this day. Surveys consistently show that children from working-class groups and ethnic minorities, and those experiencing adverse social conditions, have, on average, achieved poorly in the school system.

A large body of international research indicates strong links between poverty and negative outcomes for children at all ages (Belsky et al., 2007a). Adverse outcomes include behaviour problems and difficulties with peer relationships; adjustment difficulties and delinquency; lesser likelihood of going on to further or higher education; and a greater likelihood of becoming unemployed as an adult. It is not simply poverty itself but the stresses associated with poverty that make it hard for parents and children to function as well as they might.

The Impact of Racial Prejudice and Discrimination

A series of reports in the 1980s (Commission for Racial Equality, 1988; Eggleston et al., 1986; Rampton Report, 1981; Swann Report, 1985) provided large-scale statistical evidence about the educational underachievement of ethnic minority groups in the UK. The reports looked at the examination results and destinations of school leavers from schools with high concentrations of ethnic minority children. All the reports recommended that it is the responsibility of schools to give their pupils, regardless of gender, class or ethnic background, the confidence and the ability to have an equal opportunity in society. Later studies, for example Wright et al. (2005), proposed that since the 1990s there had indeed been a change in the extent to which youth stayed on for a longer period in education. However, they found that, although minority young people continued for longer in full-time education, their participation in degree study was still lower than for White youth and they were more likely to achieve a lower class of degree. Recent research indicates that these issues continue to be of concern but that it is essential to consider the dimension of social class. For example, Stroud (2014) found that, at age 16, the achievement gap associated with *social class* was twice as high as that for *ethnicity* and he argued that there are complex interactions between social class and ethnicity with key influences coming from the extent of parental involvement, the academic self-concept of the student as well as the incidence of truancy and exclusion from school. White working-class boys are particularly at risk of dropping out of school and higher education. The complexity of the pathways towards social mobility of ethnic minority students is confirmed by Collins et al. (2013), who found that the postcodes (in Birmingham, UK) with the highest proportion of Black and Minority Ethnic (BME) students were those with the highest vulnerability in terms of examination grades in the General Certificate of Secondary Education (GCSE) achieved. For example, 46.7% of students in the bottom 30% were BME boys; some areas with very high BME populations had rates of 90% and 100%. Additionally, the poorer areas of the city also recorded the highest rates of low-achieving students, indicating a strong link between deprivation and academic underperformance. Studies like these indicate that there is no room for complacency with regard to the promotion of equality of opportunity for all children and young people, regardless of social class and ethnicity. Collins et al. (2013) conclude that schools should do far more to close the performance gap between students from different socioeconomic and cultural backgrounds through the involvement of positive role models, modification to the curriculum and promotion of relevant extracurricular activities designed to raise aspirations.

One area of particular concern is the excessively high rate of school exclusions for some groups of young people (Hayden, 2007; Osler et al., 2002), including travellers of Irish heritage, African-Caribbean pupils and pupils of mixed ethnic origin. In addition, pupils perceived as 'different' may be symbolically excluded through the marginalization of their histories, beliefs and cultures, so leading to disaffection and underachievement (Gillborn & Gipps, 1996). There is evidence that racist bullying of traveller children results in self-exclusion and poor attendance (Derrington, 2005; Lloyd & Stead, 2001). As Hayden (2007) and Wright et al. (2005) demonstrate, school exclusions have extremely negative consequences for young people's sense of identity, ambition and potential for successful transfer to adulthood. Permanent exclusion from school is often linked to long periods without education, consequent underachievement, reduced employment opportunities and involvement in crime. Wright et al. (2005) found that, although some minority excluded pupils were sent to a pupil referral unit (PRU), most were left without any educational provision and expressed a strong sense of injustice and discrimination. As a result, these young people missed out on taking important examinations and so found it even harder to reintegrate into mainstream school. However, Wright et al. (2005) also documented the positive role played by community-based voluntary groups in advising these young people, assisting them with appeals and in helping them access further education and training.

To address such concerns, the Council of Europe produced a report (Barrett et al., 2014) arguing that now, more than ever, there is a need to tackle racial prejudice in the light of the frequency of discrimination and hate speech in contemporary society and the consequent resurgence of political parties that advocate extreme attitudes towards ethnic minorities. The report discusses the development of intercultural competence through education and recommends a range of pedagogical approaches for the promotion of the fundamental values of the Council of Europe—namely, *human rights*, *democracy* and the *rule of law*. The authors argue that it is possible to promote *intercultural competence* through action which enables the person to:

- Understand and respect people who are perceived to have different cultural affiliations from oneself.
- Respond appropriately, effectively and respectfully when interacting and communicating with such people.
- Establish positive and constructive relationships with such people.
- Understand oneself and one's own multiple cultural affiliations through encounters with cultural 'difference'.

The promotion of intercultural competence involves the following components—attitudes, knowledge and understanding, skills and actions—all of which can be promoted and developed in educational contexts, both formal (as in schools) and informal (as in the community). For children and young people, a whole variety of approaches can encourage learners to experience and discover multiple perspectives, challenge existing attitudes, analyse opinions, compare ideas, reflect on their own and others' views and engage in cooperative activities, through, for example, participation in sport or involvement in role plays or musical groups. As we saw, Wright et al. (2005) had already documented the valuable role of community projects in overcoming some of the effects of racial prejudice. Similarly, Barrett et al. (2014) advocate the need to provide opportunities for young people from diverse backgrounds to cooperate in shared projects, to enact situations and explore emotions through drama and role play and to gather information about their own cultural identity through ethnographic approaches such as oral history. Barrett et al. also highlight the importance of social media and other online tools in developing intercultural competence, provided that they are carefully moderated.

Street Children

In some countries, considerable numbers of children live on the streets, apparently without family or social support. Researchers in Brazil (Huggins, 2000; Huggins et al., 1996) studied street children through their work in shelters and on street programmes for impoverished youth in São Paulo, Rio de Janeiro and Recife. Their statistical data were gathered from morgue and police records, newspaper archives and work with children's rights groups.

They discovered that the official statistics greatly underestimated (in fact, by nearly 50%) the actual number of youth homicides in Brazil. Between 1988 and 1991 alone, more than 7,000 poor children and adolescents were murdered in Brazil, mostly by strangers who were on- and off-duty police, citizen 'justice-makers', death-squad exterminators and private security police; most of the murderers received a fee for their services and the vast majority were never identified or prosecuted. In July 1991, the going rate for killing a street youth was half 1 month's adult minimum wage. The authors estimated that, in 1993 in Brazil's four biggest cities, up to five youths were murdered each day; 80% of these victims were aged between 15 and 17.

Ethnicity determines the probability of being among Brazil's poorest and of having to live on the streets, and influences who among poor youth bear multiple social stigmas (since they are both poor and Black). Where goods, services and justice are allocated and awarded according to a group's relative class and colour, poor Black youth are in a highly disadvantaged position—excluded economically and socially, and also in terms of their political representation in their local communities as well as nationally (Huggins et al., 1996; Rodrigues, 2006). At this age, the more privileged young people are usually given opportunities to engage in studies and to prepare for life in their society. By contrast, hard-core street youths devote most of their time trying to survive harsh conditions by day and by night, with a constant requirement to maintain vigilance against danger. This study identifies particular conditions that transform certain types of Brazilian young people into 'social problems' or even 'non-persons'. These young people are often labelled by society as seriously delinquent or deviant. However, qualitative studies of their lives reveal a complex picture in which, from the young person's perspective, the gang is experienced as a protective place in a dangerous world. Moignard (2007) describes the harsh reality of everyday living amongst Brazilian gang members in Rio de Janeiro and the stoical acceptance amongst these young people of the brevity of their lives. The gang becomes a resource and a refuge, as well as adding meaning to life. As one young gang member commented, 'It is necessary to feel yourself alive. It is necessary to live well, even if life is short'.

 Stop and Think

What are the particular challenges to society presented by the existence of violent gangs? How can the needs of these marginalized young people be met?

The Social Reintegration of Children Associated with Armed Forces

The Brazilian street children are marginalized even in their own society. Some children grow up in societies experiencing chronic political instability and often violence. These children see violence, death and destruction as part of their daily lives and respond in a variety of ways. In Box 18.1 we explore the impact on girls abducted by armed forces and document the complexity of the factors involved when they returned to their home communities. Veale, McKay,

Box 18.1 Participation as principle and tool in social integration: young mothers formerly associated with armed groups in Sierra Leone, Liberia and Northern Uganda

Children associated with armed forces or armed groups (CAAFAG) face huge challenges when they return to their home communities. The present study focuses particularly on girls, who have suffered the same stressors as abducted boys but have also experienced gender-specific stressors, such as rape, enforced marriage and sexual abuse, and who, by the time of their return, in many cases are mothers. Consequently, they have reduced opportunities for employment; they have low status; they have limited chances of marriage; there is often a cultural stigma associated with their children's absent (or unknown) father. These young survivors tend to have lower levels of confidence and self-esteem, and higher levels of depression, anxiety and hostility compared to boys.

The participants were 658 young mothers with more than 1,200 children from rural and urban communities across 20 study sites in Sierra Leone, Liberia and northern Uganda. All participants had conceived or given birth while under the age of 18. At the start of the study, 22% had one child, 44% had two children, 25% had three children and 9% had four or more children. Sixty-six per cent were formerly associated with armed forces or groups and 33% were other vulnerable young mothers.

The young mothers were formed into groups of around 30 participants who met weekly or bimonthly to share stories about their daily lives, solve problems and identify their priorities. They also conducted family visits to each other's houses to gain the support of families for their activities. The groups planned social actions to address their priorities. Many of the groups initiated community dramas, dance and poetry performances that gave insight into their experiences and that challenged misconceptions about their lives. Many started small savings schemes and implemented social action projects, including group gardens, petty trading, bakery and restaurant businesses, goat rearing, community cleaning, help at funerals, home visits and visits to other vulnerable young mothers. Skill-building initiatives were introduced, such as managing group dynamics, business skills, health and hygiene, gathering and analysing data. The detailed informed consent process assured confidentiality. Participants owned the data for the research project and liaised with staff to identify a secure locked storage space for their meeting minutes. The participants decided whether they wanted to share ideas from their group meeting with the researchers or not. Academics trained the young mothers to organize and present their data. Individual responses were anonymized and were confidential.

The research team carried out a thematic analysis of the data that emerged from the monthly reports, team meetings and ethnographic field work. Their analysis was guided by a form of participatory understanding (see Chapter 1) since the researchers were experientially involved in the project. There were two major themes that emerged from this analysis: (1) *From other-regulation to self-regulation* and (2) *Shifts in identity, role and community membership.*

From other regulation to self-regulation

Community members noted changes that took place in the young mothers during the development of the project. They observed that the discomfort felt by the young mothers was expressed either as aggression or as withdrawal and non-participation. As one young mother from northern Uganda said (p. 837):

> In the beginning you would really know the difference. Those who were formerly abducted would not participate, they would look down, say nothing, and other girls dominated the meeting. Now, you would not know the difference. The stigma is almost over. No one points at them, the participation in the group is equal, those formerly abducted speak their minds out.

Over time, the anger and aggression often expressed by some of the young mothers began to calm down and, by contrast, where the young mothers were depressed and withdrawn they become more lively and outgoing. The dynamics of the groups changed as all participants shared their stories and recognized commonalities of their experiences of stigmatization. In the course of the group sessions, the participants began to find a voice of support, affirmation and action and to reject the negative identities that had been forced upon them. The external dialogue (as expressed in the supportive groups) became internalized as self-dialogue and so changed the young mothers' constructions of self. In many contexts, there was evidence of change in self-concept and self-efficacy as the group members began to undertake a variety of social actions, such as literacy classes, hairbraiding, trading and group businesses. Here one young mother from Liberia describes the process (p. 839):

> The benefit of being in the group is firstly, to learn how to take care of myself and my child and how to stay in the group and build friendships. Because of this group—at first we were traumatized and isolated—but as a group we share our experiences and we appreciate each other's struggles.

An important social action tool that the young mothers chose to engage with was community dramas. Typical dramas that the group members devised were:

- A baby boy whose grandfather rejects him as his mother was formerly abducted; group members visit him, he changes his attitudes, the family is reconciled.
- A girl who was abducted comes back; her parents, friends and community do not talk to her; she becomes part of the young mothers' group where she is welcomed 'though shy and not easily talked to'; she becomes confident, able to participate in many activities, and is accepted by her parents.
- The story of a girl who is captured by rebels, taken to the bush, taken as a wife where she has a child, is redeemed from the bush and is befriended by a pastor's wife who helps her and her children.
- A school girl who was 'fooled' by a boy, becomes pregnant and drops out of school.

The young mothers enjoyed performing their dramas and children and adults would gather round to watch the performances which tended to be long and with several acts. They evoked laughter as well as deep reflection on unpleasant topics like abduction, alcoholism and child abuse. The community advisors came to recognize these dramas as a key cultural tool that mediated participation and transformed relationships within the group. As one adviser in Uganda observed (p. 840):

> In the beginning we could see the two groups (never abducted and formerly abducted young mothers) separating. Through the songs and dramas, this really made a difference. As roles in the drama would be given to someone, it was a way to get people to participate. So through this, the singing and the drama they became all the same.

Shifts in identity, role and community membership

In a similar way, the principle of participation itself began to act as a symbolic tool. All sites were in war-affected areas. The research methods included study reports and ethnographic fieldwork. The research indicates how the young mothers transformed their identity and membership within communities of return through drama, songs and poetry, as well as through social engagement in meaningful action. The authors argue forcefully that meaningful participation offers a culturally grounded intervention in which the impacts of traumatic stressors on individual functioning and the social relational world are directly targeted, resulting in a positive modification of developmental trajectories for young women and their children. The model adopted by the researchers is a sociocultural account of participation as embedded in social activity (see Chapter 16). Over time, the principle of participation embedded in participatory

action research (PAR) acted as a symbolic tool mediating how psychosocial workers engaged with the young mothers on planning, problem solving and decision making. This was demonstrated in transcripts of workshop meetings (p. 842):

> The role was not to impose what we wanted on the girls but to help them to work through the process themselves. (PAR team, Liberia)
>   Imparting a sense of personal responsibility in solving their problems has helped a lot. (PAR team member, northern Uganda)

Key priorities in the three countries were health, education and income generation. A core decision that the young mothers had to make was how to use the limited funds available in order to engage in activities that would meet these priority needs. For the agency workers, there was a dilemma involved in acting on participatory principles since if they handed over all decision making to the young mothers, there was a risk of failure. It would have been tempting to intervene and offer strategic advice based on their professional experience but the agency workers decided that the learning experience would be much more productive if the girls were at the heart of the participatory process in line with the principles that underpinned PAR.

Here is an example of how the experience of failure was turned into success, so affirming the value of PAR principles. One decision made by the young mothers was to run a restaurant. However, after a while, it became clear that the restaurant was making no profits. There were problems: rent was high, the money was perceived by the young mothers as belonging to the NGO, the girls were giving free food to friends and boyfriends, a few members were stealing funds. The young mothers themselves decided to hold a series of meetings to address the problems and at the same time agency staff arranged classes in book-keeping. The young mothers decided to approach a local leader for support. Here is an extract from his account of the meeting (p. 844):

> What I saw, immediately, is these girls began mobilizing themselves. It was no longer a hard thing for (the organization) to do. They totally sacrificed their time, not demanding any payment. They maintained their spirit. Some hope was coming somewhere. Then when it came to identifying their priorities they said, 'We want a restaurant' because that's what we can do ourselves . . . I went there—there was an issue with accountability— one girl was taking money. They handled it and put someone else in charge of money. When I saw that spirit, they are now embracing ownership.
>
> (Commuity leader, northern Uganda)

The strength of this study lies in the fact that the researchers were able to build up trust with their young participants and to provide opportunities for these young women to share traumatic experiences from their time in captivity. Thus they were able to chart the ups and downs of the whole process of reintegration back into their home communities. One weakness of the study might lie in the fact that the research material had to be gathered when and where the young women were willing to share their past and present experiences. Since some of the material was extremely distressing to them and in some cases could only be expressed indirectly through drama and story-telling, there is the danger that the observations and interviews were not as systematically collected as they would be in a more traditional research design. However, the strengths greatly outweigh the weaknesses since, with a more conventional research design, there would simply have been no material to analyse!

Veale et al. overview the main issues that emerged from this research.

1. At a local level, the young mothers' social reintegration occurred in a relational context, mediated by material, social and symbolic tools and involving the young mothers' families, community advisors, psychosocial workers, PAR team members and academics.
2. There were clear shifts from other-regulation to self-regulation on the part of the young mothers in many directions: from young mothers to other young mothers; from agency staff to young mothers; from young mothers to agency staff. This complex web of relationships was central to the reintegration process and led to greater collective efficacy and social connectedness.
3. The majority of the young mothers took the opportunity to address their priority survival needs which they themselves identified as health, education, making a living and reduced stigma.
4. The CAAFAG young mothers learned to modify their communication style and behaviour in ways that better adjusted them to their civilian home communities. The non-CAAFAG young mothers also gained confidence in how to survive. Group members gained confidence in speaking their minds and some developed leadership ability in the process.

Based on material in Veale, A., McKay, S., Worthen, M. & Wessels, M.G. (2013). Participation as principle and tool in social integration: Young mothers formerly associated with armed groups in Sierra Leone, Liberia and Northern Uganda. *Journal of Aggression, Maltreatment & Trauma, 22*, 829–848.

Worthen and Wessells (2013) describe a community-based participatory action research (PAR) project in three sub-Saharan African communities. The theoretical model was that of participation embedded in social activity as a means of understanding how the young mothers engaged with the *social* (people in the community), *material* (money) and *symbolic* (dialogue and drama) resources within their groups and communities. The core principle was (p. 831) 'If it doesn't come from the girls, it's not PAR'.

The aim of the study was to explore how the young mothers engaged with the negative impact of the stressors that they had experienced (marginalization, disempowerment, damaged social relationships) and took greater control of their lives and their children. This process over time enabled the girls to bring about change in their psychological and social worlds. Drama was used as a tool to engage shy members of the group as well as those whose voice had been silenced by the community. This created a structure for participation that enabled those on the periphery of the group to move to positions of fuller participation. It also gave group members the opportunity to take the perspective of another person (a grandfather, a baby boy, a community member, a young mother) and experience their position.

EXPLANATORY MODELS

The 'Deficit' and 'Difference' Models

During the 1960s and early 1970s, many psychologists and educational researchers thought that the reasons for the relative failure in school of children from working-class and ethnic minority groups must lie in psychological factors such as the quality of parent–child language in the home or parental attitudes to school. It was felt that parents of these children did not provide the intellectual stimulation that children needed. In the UK, the Newsom Report (1963) identified linguistic disadvantage in some home backgrounds; the abilities of boys and girls, it stated, were often unrealized because of their 'inadequate powers of speech'. These ideas came to be known as the 'deficit' model, which places blame on the home for failing to give an adequate socialization experience for the children; as a result, children have poor language skills and/or inadequate intellectual skills to cope at school.

Advocates of an alternative approach, known as the 'difference' model, argued that schools are essentially White, middle-class institutions in terms of their values, the language used by teachers and the content of courses. Hence, children from different backgrounds achieve less well. Difference theorists advocated greater tolerance of the values, attitudes and behaviour that children bring to school from their home background, or even separate kinds of schooling for ethnic minorities. For example, Labov (1969) demonstrated the verbal skills that American ghetto children can display in the right context, but also argued that educators seldom valued or encouraged the non-standard English of inner-city children. Both the deficit and the difference positions indicate the 'social disadvantage' of some social class and ethnic minority groups, for example through lower income, poor housing and more difficult family circumstances. However, difference theorists argued more strongly that so-called 'deficits' produced by the culture were exacerbated by actual discrimination against working-class or ethnic minority children in schools.

Since the 1950s, there have been great improvements in the living conditions of most people in the economically developed countries. However, while physical health is considerably better in these countries, social and psychological health may actually have deteriorated, for example with regard to the incidence of depression and the effects of drug and alcohol abuse (Cowie et al., 2004). Services for children in need have grown in volume and extent of provision, but there is still no firm agreement among professionals about when and how to respond to the needs of children and their families (Little & Mount, 1999). While prevention in the field of physical health has been effective (for example, in the near elimination of some illnesses, including tuberculosis and childbed fever, that were widespread in previous centuries), it has been far more difficult to reduce social and psychological problems.

It has been found useful to identify different types of intervention, as follows (Little & Mount, 1999, p. 49).

- *Prevention*: this implies activity to stop a social or psychological problem happening in the first place.
- *Early intervention*: this aims to stop those at highest risk of developing social or psychological problems, or those who show the first signs of difficulty (see the section on Sure Start later in this chapter).
- *Intervention or treatment*: this seeks to stabilize or achieve realistic outcomes among those who develop the most serious manifestation of a social or psychological problem.
- *Social prevention*: this seeks to reduce the damage that those who have developed a disorder can inflict on others in a community and on themselves.

The potential impact of these kinds of intervention can be better assessed by consideration of *risk* factors and *protective* factors.

Risk and Protective Factors

Rutter and Smith (1995) and Rutter (2000) have identified the more general social context within which young people develop, and they have taken account of the changes over time associated with changed risks of individual vulnerability to disorders. Since the beginning of the 21st century, there have been huge changes in the social, economic, educational and family structures within which children and young people develop. These changes have led to increased risk factors on the one hand and the potential for resilience on the other. It is also important to be aware of the tensions between care and control, and between welfare and justice, when considering children who are at risk of offending or engaging in antisocial behaviour (Hayden, 2007).

There is growing recognition of individual differences in children's responses to stress and adversity (Masten, 2014). Even family-wide experiences impact differently on each child in the family. There are also protective mechanisms both in the child and in the interplay between the child and the environment. Masten (2014) argues forcefully that families, schools and community have a crucial role to play in promoting resilience among children and young people, even where there are adverse circumstances, such as poverty and severe family difficulties. Changes for the better can occur even in adult life, provided that the right 'turning point' experiences occur (Werner & Smith, 2001). Research evidence shows the importance of influences outside the parent–child relationship, including peers, siblings, the community and school.

Risk factors are those factors that render an individual more likely to develop problems, such as delinquency or poor mental health, in the face of adversity; they do not in themselves necessarily *cause* these problems. Risk factors (many considered in earlier chapters) can include:

- Family factors: violence, abuse, neglect, discordant family relationships, being a young person who is looked after outside the family.
- Psychosocial factors: poverty, economic crises, deprivation.

- Individual factors: low intelligence, brain damage, chronic physical illness.
- Rejection by parents or peers.
- Being a member of a deviant peer group.

Protective factors are those factors that act to protect an individual from developing a problem even in the face of adversity and risk factors such as those described above. Although the presence of risk factors, such as a poor environment or unsupportive relationships with primary caregivers, or being looked after outside the family, increases the likelihood of a negative outcome for the individual, studies of competence and resilience have shown that, regardless of background, children are generally resourceful (Frydenberg, 1997, 2004). Competence has been shown to be a mediating variable that predicts positive or negative outcomes; so, too, is the belief that others are available to offer support when it is needed. Protective factors include:

- Supportive relationships with adults.
- Access to good educational facilities.
- A sense of competence.
- Participation in activities, sports and outside interests.
- Being a member of a non-deviant peer group.
- Small family size.
- Personal attributes, such as good health, even temperament, positive self-esteem, intelligence or good social skills.
- Material resources, such as adequate family income.
- Religious affiliation.

Resilience in the face of adversity: the Kauai study

Emmy Werner (1989, 2004) reported on a 40-year longitudinal study on the Hawaiian island of Kauai that demonstrates how some individuals can triumph over physical disadvantages and deprived childhood. Werner and her colleagues aimed to assess the long-term consequences of prenatal and perinatal stress, and to document the effects of adverse early rearing conditions on children's physical, cognitive and psychosocial development. The women of Kauai reported 2,203 pregnancies in 1954, 1955 and 1956; there were 1,963 live births and 240 fetal deaths. The researchers chose to focus on the cohort of 698 infants born in 1955 and followed the development of these individuals at 1, 2, 10, 18, 31 and 40 years of age. The majority (422) were born without complications and grew up in supportive environments. Some, however, grew up in families where they experienced disadvantage and neglect. But the researchers observed a subset of these 'high-risk' children who, despite exposure to reproductive stress, discordant and impoverished homes and uneducated, alcoholic or mentally disturbed parents, grew into competent young adults who worked well and related positively to others. Take the examples of Michael and Mary.

> Michael was born prematurely to teenage parents, weighing four pound five ounces. He spent the first three weeks of life in hospital, separated from his mother. Immediately after his birth, his father was sent with the US army to Southeast Asia where he remained for two years. By the time Michael was 8 years old he had three siblings and his parents were divorced. His mother had deserted the family and had no further contact with her children. His father raised Michael and his siblings with the help of their grandparents.

Mary's mother experienced several miscarriages before that pregnancy and the birth was difficult. Her father was an unskilled laborer with four years of formal education. Between Mary's 5th and 10th birthdays her mother became severely mentally ill and was hospitalized several times. She had also subjected Mary to frequent physical and emotional abuse.

Despite having been exposed to these risk factors in their childhood, by the age of 18 both Mary and Michael were individuals with high self-esteem and sound values who cared about others and were well-liked by their peers. They were successful at school and looked forward to their future careers and relationships.

(Werner, 1989, p. 108)

Stop and Think

What contributed to the resilience of these children?

The researchers identified a number of protective factors in the families, outside the family circle and within the children themselves. Children such as Mary and Michael tended to have temperamental characteristics that included being active and sociable and having a low degree of excitability and distress. They were often described as 'easygoing', 'even-tempered' and 'affectionate'. Their teachers noted that they concentrated well in class and were alert and responsive; they were physically active and excelled at sports like fishing, swimming, riding and hula dancing. These children also tended to have formed a close bond with at least one caregiver from whom they received positive attention during their early years. The nurturing came from grandparents, older siblings, aunts and uncles, or from regular babysitters. As these resilient children grew older, they seemed to be adept at seeking out surrogate parents when a biological parent was unavailable or incapacitated. Resilient girls seemed to gain a sense of responsibility from looking after younger siblings; resilient boys, by contrast, tended to be firstborns who did not have to share attention with younger siblings, but they, like girls, had a structured routine of household chores and duties; they usually had a male in the family who served as a role model. Resilient children also seemed to find a great deal of support outside the family from classmates, neighbours and elders in the community. School became a refuge from a disordered home and many retrospectively recalled a favourite teacher who had supported them in times of crisis. With the help of the support networks, these resilient children developed a sense of meaning in their lives and a belief that they had control over their future.

Clearly, not all of the deprived children in this community fared so well. Those with the poorest outcomes at age 40 tended to be people with prolonged exposure during childhood to parental alcoholism and/or mental illness. (Boys were particularly affected.) Men and women who had encountered stressful events in childhood, such as loss of a close family member or frequent disruption in the family, reported more health problems at age 40 than those who had not. Resilient children's competence and hopefulness contrasted starkly with feelings of futility and helplessness expressed by troubled peers within the same cohort. Resilience does not happen in a vacuum. A key feature was that each of the resilient children had at least one person in their lives who accepted them unconditionally. They also had temperamental characteristics that enabled them to take advantage of the support networks available to them in the community, even when their biological parents were unable to look after them well. As a result of this study, several community action and educational programmes were established on Kauai to provide opportunities and caring people that could compensate for the difficulties being experienced by high-risk children and offer them an escape from adversity.

 Stop and Think

How could this risk-focused intervention model be applied to violent gangs?

In the next sections, we examine evaluations of the role that families themselves play in responding with resilience to adversity. We also look at large-scale government initiatives to combat inequalities in opportunities provided for certain groups of children in society.

INTERVENTIONS: THE ROLE OF FAMILIES

One American study gives evidence of the vital part that can be played by families themselves in ensuring that their children achieve well in the educational system. Caplan et al. (1992) reviewed key factors that, in their view, contributed to the outstanding academic achievement of refugee children in their study. During the 1970s and 1980s, many Vietnamese and Lao people sought a new life in the USA. The children of these families had lost months or years of formal schooling, they lived in relocation camps and had suffered trauma and disruption as they escaped from South-East Asia. They had little knowledge of English and had experienced extreme poverty and material hardship. The researchers surveyed 6,750 members of refugee families and, from this larger group, selected a random sample of 200 nuclear families and their 536 children of school age; 27% of the families had four or more children, a factor not usually associated with high academic achievement. At the time of the study, the children had been in the USA for an average of 3.5 years. All attended schools not known for their scholastic success in low-income, inner-city areas.

The children did outstandingly well in their academic grades, with their mean grade point average at B (27% had an A, 52% had a B, 17% had a C and only 4% were below C). As expected, their grades in English and liberal arts were unexceptional. But in mathematics and science almost half had A scores; another third earned Bs. These grades were matched by test scores on the California Achievement Test, which indicated that they outperformed 54% of all students taking the test, placing them just above the national average. These achievements held for the majority of the children, not just a few gifted individuals.

The researchers explored aspects of the family context that might be encouraging the high academic achievement of these children. They found through interviews conducted in the language of the families that in the evenings the whole family would typically collaborate on the children's homework. The children spent an average of 3 hours and 10 minutes each evening on their homework. (American students spend, on average, only 1 hour and 30 minutes on their homework each day.) The parents were usually unable to engage in the content of the homework, but they set standards and goals for each evening and took responsibility for the household chores so that the children could get on with their studies. In addition, the parents read regularly to their children, either in English or in their own language, and it seemed to be the experience of reading that strengthened emotional ties between parent and child, strengthened cultural understanding of traditions, and transmitted the wisdom of the culture through stories. Not only that, the experience was enjoyable and shared by all members of the family.

Caplan et al. concluded that the parents had carried their cultural heritage with them to the USA and handed it on to their children. This meant that the families were securely linked to their own past as well as to the realities of the present and the possibilities of a future in their new environment. This study explored the role of the family in the academic performance of Indochinese children from refugee families, and the results confirm the need for close integration between home and school, the importance of familial commitment to education, and the need for the creation of an environment that is conducive to learning.

Barn et al. (2006) found a very similar situation in their study of 385 parents from diverse ethnic backgrounds in the UK. The parents in this study tried to compensate for their own lack of formal education by ensuring that their children were aware of the crucial role to be played by education in leading them out of poverty and exclusion from mainstream society. As Barn et al. (2006, p. 4) quote:

> I'm always asking . . . making sure their homework is done, are they studying, are they reading, have they done their reading? I find . . . because I work full-time and I'm single that I always have to be nagging them more than spending any pleasure time with them.
> *(Lone Asian mother)*

> Obey the teacher, listen to the teacher, respect the teacher as they respect the parents . . . I tell them that the teachers in school must be obeyed, you must not misbehave.
> *(Bangladeshi father)*

> Young people need education in school. Without education you get nowhere in life. That's the main point.
> *(Caribbean mother)*

The researchers also found that Asian parents with poor education themselves were most likely to make arrangements for their children to go to a private tutor. The families in this study believed in the crucial importance of giving their children a strong sense of their own ethnic identity, including their language of origin, but reported that they would benefit from support in raising bilingual children.

 Stop and Think

How can families in disadvantaged circumstances be helped to realize their ambitions for their children?

It is unfair to expect poor families to overcome adversity all by themselves; nor do the authors of these papers suggest this. Families need acknowledgement of what they are doing and some sense that their own experiences are valued within the school system. Studies like these can help us identify some of the cultural components that contribute to the academic success or failure of children in order to provide practitioners and policy makers in the fields of education, health and social care with the insights and knowledge to help children in need.

NURTURE GROUPS

For over 30 years, nurture groups (NGs) have demonstrated that, with the right type of emotional support, children who are having emotional and behavioural difficulties at home and school can be successfully included in mainstream schools. NGs create a school-based environment specifically designed for pupils whose behaviour indicates unmet early emotional needs; the theoretical underpinning is attachment theory (Bennathan & Boxall, 2014). Many of the children who are placed in nurture groups have experienced disruptive or dysfunctional parenting in their early years and their social and language skills tend to be poorly developed. In order to address this, some NGs begin the day with 'breakfast', which usually occurs mid-morning. Pupils and teachers share a simple meal (usually toast and jam) and interact socially as they eat it. As relationships in the NG grow and develop, the breakfast experience may be phased out. The essential point is that the relationship with the nurture group teachers is supportive and these teachers provide a role model that the children observe and, over time, begin to incorporate into their own relationships. While NGs have many of the features of family life, such as soft furnishings, kitchen and dining facilities, they are not designed to replace family life but rather to complement it. The trained NG staff work collaboratively with the parents and, in fact, the experience of the NG appears to have a positive influence on the ways in which parents interact with their children. Scott Loinaz (2015) identifies five distinctive features of the NG in comparison with other psychosocial interventions.

- *Length of provision*: NG provision is available long term (1–4 school terms);
- *Frequency of provision*: NG provision is made available nearly every school day (whether full time or part time) while still allowing children to be part of the mainstream class.
- *Modelling*: NGs always have two adults present in the room (usually a teacher and a classroom assistant) to model cooperation and positive social skills.
- *Breakfast*: NGs typically start the day with breakfast, providing a valuable link between home and school. This group occasion helps the pupils relate to one another and improves both cognitive function and academic performance as well as social skills, though over time as the relationships develop the breakfast may be phased out.
- *Attachment*: NGs focus primarily on internalizing models of effective relationships and forming attachments to loving and caring adults, so allowing the children to achieve a sense of security and safety at school.

Scott Loinaz (2015) compared NGs with 122 other effective evidence-based psychosocial interventions for children with emotional and behavioural difficulties, including FRIENDS, a form of cognitive behavioural group therapy for children and adolescents (Barrett, 2005). She concluded that NG provision shares most of its therapeutic procedures with other effective interventions, such as consensual goal setting, modelling, cognitive restructuring, role playing, relaxation techniques and affective education; similarly, NG provision can help children and adolescents address both externalizing and internalizing behavioural difficulties. What makes the NG distinctive is that the length of time involved helps the young people to form strong, trusting relationships with adults who show them affection, give them attention and reassure them of their self-worth and personal value. This greatly helps the process of reintegrating back into their mainstream class. Other evaluations of the impact of NGs (e.g. Bennathan & Boxall, 2014; Cooper & Whitebread, 2007; Seth-Smith et al., 2010) reveal statistically substantial improvements in terms of children's social and emotional development, social engagement and behaviours showing secure attachment. NG pupils make significant gains in self-esteem, self-image, emotional maturity and attainment in literacy compared with those without NGs, and the social-emotional developments are, on the whole, maintained by children after they leave the NG (OFSTED, 2011).

COMPENSATORY EDUCATION PROGRAMMES IN THE USA

As we have seen, in the later 1960s a deficit or cultural deprivation model became the most accepted hypothesis to explain the educational disadvantage and underachievement of working-class and ethnic minority children. This led to a large number of programmes of compensatory education for preschool children in the USA (and also in the UK). Following the apparent success of these kinds of programmes, a massive policy of intervention occurred in the USA with 'Project Head Start'. This began in the summer of 1965 and built up over subsequent years until millions of preschool children across the USA had participated in some form of Head Start programme. The general goal was to give 'deprived' children a head start in schools by some form of early intervention to stimulate cognitive and linguistic development. Up to the 1960s, nursery schools had tended to be more orientated towards the needs of the middle-class child. Much of the emphasis was on social and emotional development through free play and unstructured imaginative activities. Preschool programmes of compensatory education, in contrast, aimed directly to prepare children for entry into infant school and to give them skills that, it was felt, their homes had failed to provide. Programmes were often based on the assumption that the children's language was deficient, that they lacked cognitive strategies appropriate for school learning, and that their parents used ineffective modes of control. However, no detailed syllabus was laid down and the exact nature and length of programmes varied widely.

USA Compensatory Programmes Evaluated

Some of the early evaluation studies showed disappointing results for the compensatory programmes. The Westinghouse Learning Corporation carried out the first national evaluation of Project Head Start in Ohio University in 1969. This research study showed that the intervention programmes had very little, if any, effect on the children who had taken part. Also, any benefits seemed to be very transient, disappearing after a year or so at school. Some psychologists, such as Arthur Jensen (1969), took this to confirm the view that children from poor families had *inherited* low academic ability, which no amount of compensatory education could change. Others thought there should be greater intervention. This might mean more intensive intervention, involving parent as well as child education; or starting intervention earlier; or following intervention through into the early school years. At an extreme, this might virtually involve removing a young child from a 'deficient' home environment. Yet others—the difference theorists—argued that the whole premise of intervention was biased or racist. As Baratz and Baratz (1970, p. 43) put it, 'Head Start has failed because its goal is to correct a deficit that simply does not exist'. By now, the ignorance and insensitivity that many White researchers had shown to Black culture and to the thoughts and feelings of Black mothers and children had become more obvious. Baratz and Baratz claimed that the 'Head Start programmes may inadvertently advocate the annihilation of a cultural system which is barely considered or understood by most social scientists'.

However, the Ohio-Westinghouse study took place only 5 years after Project Head Start began. By 1976, researchers who were following the long-term effects of intervention programmes began to report more encouraging results. One major research project (Lazar & Darlington, 1982) was a collaborative study in which 11 preschool research teams came together to pool their results for a group named the Consortium for Longitudinal Studies. Each researcher had independently designed and carried out preschool programmes in the 1960s; the children who had participated, mainly Black children from low-income families, were followed up in 1976 when their ages ranged from 9 to 19.

For example, the High Scope Perry Preschool Project, organized by Weikart et al. (1970) in Ypsilanti, Michigan, involved 123 children from low-waged Black families. Half of them, selected at random, experienced an intervention programme; the other half, the control group, had no preschool educational provision. The programme children spent 12.5 hours per week for 2 years in a special preschool intervention programme that stressed active learning and a great deal of communication between child and adult and between child and child. There were also home visits by the teachers.

The results for IQ scores from the project and later follow-ups are shown in Table 18.1. The programme group children showed an initial increase (more than the control group) in the year or so immediately following the intervention, but through the middle school years this showed a familiar falling-off or wash-out effect. However, some long-term effects of the intervention were found in other areas. By the age of 15, the programme group scored on average 8% higher on reading, arithmetic and language tests than the control group. By the end of high school only 19% of the programme children had been placed in remedial classes, compared with 39% in the control group. There were social effects too. The programme youngsters were less likely to be delinquent (36% as compared with 42% of the control group). Ten per cent of the programme group went on to college but none of the control group did. These findings were fairly typical of the other 10 projects in the survey.

A follow-up of the children at the point when they were in their late 20s showed some dramatic results (Weikart, 1996). The researchers managed to interview 95% of the original

Table 18.1 Changes in IQ with age, for programme and control group children, in Weikart's preschool programme.

	Pretest	3	4	5	6	7	8	9	10	14
Programme group	79.6	79.9	92.7	94.1	91.3	91.7	88.1	87.7	85.0	81.0
Control group	78.5	79.6	81.7	83.2	86.3	87.1	86.9	86.8	84.6	80.7

Source: Adapted from Lazar, I. & Darlington, R. (1982) Lasting effects of early education, *Monographs of the Society for Research in Child Development*, 47, nos 2–3, 1–151. Reproduced by permission of John Wiley & Sons Inc.

study participants when they were 27, and additional data were gathered from their school, social services and arrest records. There were significant differences between programme and control groups. One-third more programme than control members had graduated from high school; they were also significantly more likely to be literate and to score more highly on achievement tests. By the age of 27, only one-fifth as many programme members as control members had been arrested five or more times (7% versus 35%) and only one-third as many were arrested for drug dealing. Those who had experienced the programme were four times as likely to earn $2,000 per month as controls; they were three times as likely to own their own homes and to own a second car.

Weikart (1996, p. 120) concluded that the evidence gave very strong support for the effectiveness of preschool interventions and argued that the benefits are long term because they empower:

- Children by enabling them to initiate and carry out their own learning activities and to make independent decisions.
- Parents by involving them in ongoing relationships as full partners with teachers in supporting their children's development.
- Teachers by providing them with systematic in-service training, supportive curriculum supervision and observational tools to assess children's development.

The Consortium for Longitudinal Studies concluded that early intervention programmes could have significant, long-term effects (Lazar & Darlington, 1982). The interpretation of achievement test scores was difficult because of variability in the tests themselves. However, the authors reported some evidence that children who had experienced early intervention performed better on school attainment tests than controls. But perhaps more important were the non-cognitive differences—the changes in attitudes towards themselves as learners and in their aspirations and beliefs in their own competence. Research into this controversial area continues, as you see in Box 18.2.

Box 18.2 What makes a difference: Early Head Start evaluation findings in a developmental context

Love, Chazan-Cohen, Raikes and Brooks-Gunn (2013) were part of a large US team that evaluated the impact on 3,001 children in 17 sites from poor families, half of whom received Early Head Start (EHS) interventions in the first 3 years of life and half of whom did not. This was one of the largest, multisite, multistate longitudinal experiments in the US. The children and families were randomly assigned to experimental and control groups. The intervention began before birth in 25% of cases and under 1 year of age for the rest and lasted until the children were 3 years old. The children were assessed at 2 years, 3 years and 5 years in order to capture the impact of the programme on their lives. The research addressed issues that are relevant to practitioners, policy makers, developmental psychologists and evaluators of interventions for low-income families in the early years.

The aims of the study were to:

- Examine the impact of EHS on children and their parents.
- Examine the role of programme features in modifying the impact.
- Explore the extent to which families with a range of demographics (e.g. urban, rural, ethnicity, family risk) were differentially affected by the intervention experience.

The researchers also aimed to investigate the impact on the children's cognitive and language skills and health as follows:

- The extent to which aggressive behaviours were reduced.
- The impact on higher engagement with the parent during play episodes.

The main findings were that many of the impacts that were noted at ages 2 and 3 years were still present when the children were assessed at age 5. Significantly, the intervention reduced behaviour problems and enhanced social skills and approaches to learning in comparison with the control group. Specifically, EHS enhanced vocabulary among the Spanish-speaking children though not among the English speakers. By contrast, there was no impact on school-related achievement outcomes, such as letter-word identification and applied problems or on parent–child play interactions.

The children and their families who experienced EHS followed by services in the 3–5-year-old age period fared the best overall. Benefits in social, emotional and parenting outcomes came primarily from EHS whereas benefits in achievement-oriented outcomes appeared to come from formal programme participation between ages 3 and 5 years. Early intervention seemed to have the strongest effects when followed by preschool education. The children from high-risk families seemed to benefit from comprehensive services from birth through to 5 years.

The researchers concluded that EHS children continued to do better than peers in the control group 2 years after programme participation. The most consistent effects were on aggressive behaviour (significantly reduced in the experimental group) and attention to learning (which was enhanced in the experimental group). Additionally, parents in the experimental group were significantly more likely to read to their children than were parents in the control group. But gains in cognitive and language skills were not sustained except with Spanish-speaking children. One explanation for this is that control group children were able to 'catch up' when they enrolled in preschool programmes between the ages of 3 and 5 years.

A strength of this longitudinal study is that great care was taken in assigning the children and their families randomly to the experimental and control groups. The sample is very large and the children came from a wide range of environments and communities. A weakness is that it was impossible to anticipate the extent to which the control group children would experience equally enriching education between the ages of 3 and 5 years. In the end, we learn very little that is new if we compare these findings with earlier evaluations such as Lazar and Darlington (1982). Furthermore, we lack qualitative data on the actual experiences of the children and their families, to include their reflections on the whole process of participating in EHS. It would have been useful, for example, to have deeper insights into why the Spanish-speaking children in particular sustained the gains in cognitive and language skills. To understand this, we would have benefited from more information on the lifestyles and child-rearing practices of Spanish-speaking communities.

The researchers argue that there are cumulative effects in that children who experience EHS and formal preschool programmes fare best at age 5. They also argue that their findings indicate the value of a positive relationship of educators with primary caregivers in the first years of life coupled with programmes that enhance the children's cognitive abilities. They conclude that the period from birth to 3 years is crucial for intervening to support families and to promote positive changes in parenting practices. This points to the value of involving parents in all programmes and of targeting particular parenting behaviours (such as play and story-telling) that are important for children's development. The researchers also indicate the importance of continuity between interventions such as EHS whose emphasis is on the child–parent relationship (0–5 years) and more formal preschool programmes (3–5 years). Children from high-risk families especially benefit from this type of continuity.

Based on material in Love, J.M., Chazan-Cohen, R., Raikes, H. & Brooks-Gunn, J. (2013). What makes a difference: Early Head Start evaluation findings in a developmental context. *Monographs of the Society for Research in Child Development, 78*, 1–172.

COMPENSATORY EDUCATION PROGRAMMES IN THE UK

The Plowden Report of 1967 (HMSO, 1967) advocated a policy of positive discrimination in favour of children from poor areas throughout Britain, through the provision of more resources, more teachers and better school buildings. These areas were to be designated 'Educational Priority Areas' (EPAs). In response to the recommendations of the Plowden Report, Halsey (1972) mounted a large project, the Educational Priority Area Project, to initiate and evaluate compensatory education programmes in exceptionally deprived communities in London, Birmingham, Liverpool, Yorkshire and Dundee. Each area formulated its own programme within the wider framework of the project in order to take account of the particular needs of the region. Halsey's overall conclusion was a positive one. He argued that the concept of EPAs was a useful one that enabled positive discrimination to be made in favour of underprivileged children. He advocated the use of structured programmes that were flexible enough to accommodate to local needs and he recommended the development of community schools as one means of bridging the gap between home and school. Although he did not claim that programmes like this could fully compensate for deprived social conditions, he argued that education could play an important role in extending young children's cognitive and linguistic abilities.

Sure Start

In the late 1990s, a number of government initiatives were implemented to help parents and children deal with issues before they become acute, and to promote effective interventions for children and young people most at risk. Interventions for preschool children included free nursery education for 3- and 4-year-olds, an official early childhood curriculum, the Neighbourhood Nurseries programme for the most deprived communities and a national network of children's centres. The Sure Start programme, launched in 1998, was a major strategic initiative by New Labour to end child poverty by changing the ways in which services were delivered to preschool children and their families, including hard-to-reach groups such as homeless families, and by specifically targeting highly deprived geographical areas in the UK. A funding package of over £450 million was provided to set up 250 Sure Start Local Programmes (SSLPs) in areas with high concentrations of 4-year-olds living in poverty. The programme aimed to enhance the life chances of children living in areas of greatest need by improving their learning, health, social and emotional development, and by strengthening families and communities. To avoid stigma, the initiatives targeted areas rather than individual families, and there was a strong emphasis on involving the local communities in making decisions about what their needs were and how they might be met. SSLP services aimed to address the health and social, emotional and economic development of the children, the health and social, emotional and social development of the parents, and the general wellbeing of the wider community. Provision included, for example, postnatal support for mothers, sessions on nutrition and dental health, playgroups and toy libraries. Parents were given opportunities to attend vocational and non-vocational adult education courses, as Sure Start also provided childcare.

Two large research projects—the NESS and the Effective Provision of Preschool Education (EPPE) (Sylva et al., 2003, 2004)—had a large influence on the implementation of policy through their identification of the successes and failures of Sure Start.

The research teams reported a number of key difficulties in implementing Sure Start (Tunstill et al., 2005). Policy recommendations were constrained by tensions between local and national provision, including potential conflict between meeting the needs and rights of children and addressing the needs and rights of parents. For example, some parents with problems related to drugs or alcohol abuse, domestic violence, criminality or mental health (that is, the parents of children who were particularly at risk) were reluctant to access the Sure Start services because they distrusted professionals and did not wish to allow professionals or volunteers into their homes. This meant that many families in greatest need of support were not reached. In addition, in areas where there was no critical mass of one particular ethnic minority group, such parents might also feel reluctant to take advantage of SSLP provision. It made sense to undertake outreach work with other areas with a similar ethnic group population rather than be constricted by the local Sure Start provision.

After 5 years of systematic research examining the effectiveness and impact of SSLPs, Belsky et al. (2007a) produced a comprehensive evaluation addressing the following aspects of the programme:

- The nature of the communities that were targeted and how they changed over time
- The early effects of SSLPs on children and families
- Specific features of SSLPs that contributed to the success or failure of the intervention.

The evaluation addressed the key question, 'What was the effect of SSLPs, all other things being equal?' and answered it under the four headings shown in Table 18.2 (Belsky & Melhuish, 2007).

Stop and Think

What was the major impact of the Sure Start Local Programmes (SSLPs)? Why did some initiatives not succeed?

Table 18.2   The effects of SSLPs.

Did children/families in SSLPs receive more services or experience their communities differently from children/families in comparison communities?

Unfortunately, the effects, both negative and positive, were very small. Mothers of neither 9- nor 36-month-olds in SSLP areas reported greater use or usefulness of services than mothers in the comparison communities. In terms of reporting the favourability of the community as a place to live and bring up children, there were no effects of SSLPs among the families of 9-month-olds. Indeed, the families with 36-month-olds in the SSLPs actually rated their communities less favourably than the comparison groups.

Did families function differently in SSLP areas than in comparison communities?

Here the results were more positive. The households of mothers of 9-month-olds in SSLP communities were rated as less chaotic (less noise and more regular childcare routines) than comparison groups, and the mothers of 36-month-olds were more accepting of their children's behaviour (less smacking, scolding and physical restraint). Non-teenage mothers of 36-month-olds also demonstrated less negative parenting practices than mothers in comparison communities. Though many other outcomes showed no significant differences, these results indicated important impacts of the programme.

Did effects of SSLPs extend to children themselves?

There were both positive and negative outcomes for some of the child outcomes but many were non-significant. However, the significant outcomes were considered by the researchers to be important ones; 36-month-olds living in SSLPs showed fewer behaviour problems and demonstrated greater social competence than those in comparison communities. The adverse effects were amongst the children of teenage mothers (14% of the sample) who scored lower on verbal ability and social competence and higher on behaviour problems. Children from workless households (40% of the sample) and from lone-parent families (33% of the sample) also showed evidence of adverse effects, such as lower scores on verbal ability. In general, then, the children from *relatively less* disadvantaged families (non-teenage mothers) benefited from the SSLPs, while those who were *relatively more* deprived (that is, teenage mothers, workless households and lone parents) appeared to be adversely affected by living in an SSLP community.

How did effects on children come about?

The researchers were interested to find out whether the effects on the children were mediated by the impact of SSLPs on the parents themselves. In the case of the non-teenage parents, the results supported this view, since the positive impact on behaviour and social competence appeared to be mediated by SSLP interventions to reduce negative parenting practices. Mediation effects were not, however, evident in other subgroups in the sample.

Source: Adapted from Belsky, J. & Melhuish, E. (2007). Impact of Sure Start Local Programmes on children and families. In J. Belsky, J. Barnes and E. Melhuish (Eds.), *The national evaluation of Sure Start* (pp. 133–153). Bristol: The Policy Press, with permission from The Policy Press, Bristol.

The general conclusions to be drawn from the data in Table 18.2 are that the families/parents in deprived areas who have some personal, social and economic resources available to them are more able to take advantage of interventions such as Sure Start. By contrast, those without such resources, including lone parents, families in workless households and teenage mothers, continue to be deprived of resources, even when they are literally provided within walking distance. Belsky et al. (2007a) recognized the need to engage with the whole community in order to mobilize its resources to the full and to ensure that participation from 'at-risk' families actually took place. The researchers speculate that these parents may have felt intimidated or alienated at the offers of help, and recommend that additional training and sensitivity may be required in order to gain access to children in these hard-to-reach families. The families who were adversely affected by SSLPs were, fortunately, in the minority.

A CONTINUING DEBATE

The apparent failure of Project Head Start around 1970 led many educationalists to reject the idea of compensatory education and to replace the deficit model with the difference model. The deficit theorists had certainly been naive in their assumptions. Nevertheless, the difference model, too, may be naive if taken to the extreme of supposing that all kinds of rearing conditions are equally valid. Poor material conditions, inadequate housing and poverty will affect the quality of a child's development. Working-class groups, and many ethnic minorities, tend to suffer from these material and social disadvantages, as well as possible prejudice or bias within and outside the educational system.

The best schemes of compensatory education appear to be those that involve the families, since those that focus on the child alone tend to have only short-term effects (Little & Mount, 1999). If parents are involved throughout, they can sustain the effects after the programme is over. Bronfenbrenner recommends childcare education for young people before they become parents, and support for them once the children are born, as well as a network of community support services among parents and other members of the community (Bronfenbrenner, 1989). However, he concluded that programmes of compensatory education are not effective for the most deprived groups if they concentrate only on the parent–child relationship. He calls also for intervention at other levels (see Figure 1.3) to alleviate the desperate conditions in which some families are forced to live. Removal of educational disadvantage requires that the families themselves have adequate healthcare, reasonable housing, enough food and a sufficient income. Programmes of compensatory education cannot by themselves undo the inequalities that continue to exist in our society, and should not replace efforts to tackle poverty and racial prejudice.

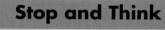 **Stop and Think**

Is there any reason to hope that as a society we can create better conditions for the children of the future?

More recent research shows that material disadvantage and discrimination in the educational system remain convincing explanations of much educational underachievement. There is plenty of evidence to show that poor children perform less well at school than children from better-off families, are less healthy and have a narrower range of opportunities in later life.

The evidence from large-scale interventions such as High Scope and Sure Start is clear in its demonstration of the positive effects of high-quality preschool provision on the cognitive and social development of children. Good preschool provision can play a crucial role in enhancing the experiences of children from deprived areas by providing them with a better preparation for primary school. There is also strong evidence that the quality of the home environment can be changed through government policies and appropriate intervention by well-trained practitioners. Clearly this is a topic in which the values of society and the political possibilities of the times must be considered together with our psychological knowledge of the processes of children's development. Deprivation and disadvantage arise out of a complex interaction among biological, ecological, cultural, historical, demographic and psychological risk factors. Given that there are so many varied factors and given the different theories and explanations offered for disadvantage, it may be thought to be unrealistic to expect an easy solution to such a complex problem. Rutter (2000) argued that the main benefits come from circumstances in which it is possible to bring about a long-lasting change in the environment. Much less is achieved by inputs—however effective at the time—when overall deprivation and disadvantage continue. He proposes the need for rigorous research that puts environmental mediation mechanisms under scrutiny, so that we understand more clearly what the specific risk and protective factors are. We need multimethod, cross-disciplinary research methods that integrate perspectives on the individual children in their social contexts, such as that provided by the EPPE project (Sylva et al., 2004).

As we saw in the study by Veale et al. (2013; and Box 18.1), participatory principles facilitate resilience. Empowerment plays an important part in healing of young people traumatized by political violence and war through individual and group self-regulatory processes as well as action to lead them back into full membership of their communities. Ongoing research into the impact of political violence on children's emotional health reveals a complex pattern, with some children demonstrating incredible resilience (Cummings et al., 2014). Of course, many studies document the huge risk to well-being that living with political violence incurs, including internalizing disorders, such as depression and posttraumatic stress disorder, and externalizing disorders, such as aggressive behaviour. But much depends on the context in which the conflict takes place. For example, strength of identity with in-group members can support processes that buffer the negative effects of violence through positive social support from other in-group members. However, this higher in-group identity is associated with greater likelihood of aggression towards the out-group. So strength of identity can have positive outcomes in one domain but very negative ones in another.

Stop and Think

**Divide a sheet of paper into four columns headed as follows:
1. Individuals; 2. Families; 3. Communities; 4. Wider society.**

Next, under each heading, list ways in which people and groups have shown that they can work together to enhance the social and cognitive development of children from disadvantaged backgrounds. Draw on the research reported in this chapter and on your wider reading around the subject.

Now, drawing on your reading of this chapter, make a second list of the barriers that prevent these initiatives from being fully realized.

Finally, list ways in which individuals, families, communities and the wider society have demonstrated that they can overcome the barriers.

CHAPTER SUMMARY

- Studies of severe institutional deprivation, for example among children reared in orphanages, or children (like the Koluchova twins or Genie) severely neglected by their parents, provide key insights into the impact of later interventions on cognitive and emotional development and into the processes of resilience in the face of adversity.
- We know from the research that children who have experienced bad parenting do not necessarily mature into adults who lack parenting skills. Street children do not necessarily stay on the street. Asylum seekers can integrate into their new communities. Children born into poor families can make good. History does not need to repeat itself.
- As we have seen, children and their parents are capable of incredible resilience in the face of adversity. However, children who live in impoverished conditions are strongly affected by them, even if they have the qualities of resilience and the opportunities to rise above them. Rescuing them individually is not enough. The environmental conditions need to be changed in order to offer to all children the opportunity to realize their potential. This surely is a fundamental human right. We should not wait until their presence on the streets and in the inner-city slums occurs in such numbers that they are a threat or a disgrace to society.
- In his commentary on Sure Start, Rutter (2007) argues that there is sufficient evidence that early intervention does make a difference to preschool children living in deprived circumstances but, at the same time, it is also essential to continue to give support throughout childhood and into adolescence.
- We know enough from the child development literature to understand that there are many ways in which society must continue to give respect, initiative, autonomy and opportunity to disadvantaged children and their families. This requires strong intervention and strategic planning at government level.

DISCUSSION POINTS

1. Discuss the meaning of the terms 'disadvantage', 'deficit' and 'difference' in explaining educational underachievement.
2. How useful are the concepts of 'risk' and 'protective' factors?
3. Consider the problems involved in evaluating the effects of a programme of compensatory education such as Sure Start. How would you attempt to do this?
4. Discuss the advantages and disadvantages of targeting deprived areas in order to intervene to help children and their families.
5. Identify some ways, for example nurture groups, in which policies and practices might be developed in order to reach the most 'at-risk' children.
6. Discuss ways in which participatory methods might be used to address the outcomes of political violence on the emotional well-being of children.

FURTHER READING

- For an overview of the English Romanian Adoptees (ERA) see Rutter, M., Beckett, C., Castle, J., Kreppner, J., Stevens, S. & Sonuga-Barke, E. (2009). *Policy and practice implications from the ERA Study: Forty-five key questions*. London: BAAF. A comprehensive and readable review of the policies, interventions and evaluation of Sure Start is given in Belsky, J., Barnes, J. & Melhuish, E. (2007). *The national evaluation of Sure Start*. Bristol: The Policy Press; there is also an insightful commentary by Professor Sir Michael Rutter.
- An earlier collection of useful articles can be found in Clarke, A.M. & Clarke, A.D.B. (1976). *Early experience: Myth and evidence*. London: Open Books. The authors challenged the belief that the early years have an irreversible effect on later development. The book included chapters on the effects of parent–child separation, the effects of institutionalization on children's cognitive development, and the case study of severe deprivation of the Czech twins. A later book, Clarke, A.M. & Clarke, A.D.B. (2000). *Early experience and the life path*. London: Jessica Kingsley, also challenged the assumption that early experience has a 'disproportionate' effect on later development. Here they presented recent evidence in support of the idea of children's resilience in the face of adversity. Of interest too is the book by Masten on the 'ordinary magic' of resilience: Masten, A.S. (2014). *Ordinary magic*. New York: Guilford Press.
- For a detailed account of the Genie case, see Pines, M. (1981). The civilizing of Genie. *Psychology Today*, 15(Sep), 28–34. This describes the effects that an intensive programme of intervention had on the social, intellectual and linguistic development of Genie. A number of important theoretical and practical issues are raised about deprivation and the extent to which its effects can be reversed. See also Rymer, R. (1994). *Genie: A scientific tragedy*. Harmondsworth: Penguin, where you can read about the professional rivalries among the scientists who studied Genie's progress.

PART V

ADOLESCENCE

Chapter 19 Adolescence

CHAPTER
19
Adolescence

CHAPTER OUTLINE

- The Biological and Physical Changes of Puberty
- Psychological Effects of Puberty
- Effects of Early and Late Maturation
- Relations with Peers
- Romantic Development
- Adolescent Sexuality
- Adolescence as a Period of Turmoil, or 'Storm and Stress'
- Risk-Taking Behaviours
- Adolescence in Different Cultures
- Historical Changes in Adolescent Behaviour

Adolescence is the period of transition between childhood and life as an adult, covering basically the teenage years. Biologically, it is marked by the onset of puberty, and by some aspects of brain reorganization. After puberty, a person is sexually mature and could potentially become a mother or father of a child. Socially, adolescence is marked by an increasing independence from parents, and importance of the peer group, as the young person prepares to leave home, to complete his or her education, to form sexual partnerships and to seek some vocation or employment. These are universal features of adolescence, but there are also important cultural and historical variations.

The historian Philippe Aries (1962) actually argued that adolescence was a modern invention, and that in the Middle Ages 'children were mixed with adults as soon as they were considered capable of doing without their mothers or nannies' (p. 411). However, historians since then have criticized Aries' views as 'simplistic and inaccurate' (Hanawalt, 1992, p. 343); in medieval literature, adolescence was characterized in not unfamiliar ways, and potential conflict with the adult world was recognized.

In a review of the anthropological literature in different traditional (non-urban) societies, Schlegel and Barry (1991) agree that many of the phenomena of adolescence appear universal—a theme we return to at the end of the chapter. Although only about one-third of societies have a particular linguistic marker such as 'adolescent', these authors point to 'social adolescence' as being the disjuncture between sexual maturity, reached at puberty, and full social maturity, which comes later. This delay 'appears to be universal for boys; for girls, in the majority of societies, at least a short period of adolescence intervenes between puberty and the full assumption of adult roles, usually at marriage' (Schlegel & Barry, 1991, p. 19).

Adolescence is characteristically thought of as a difficult period, as indeed times of transition often are. This conflict was rather overemphasized by some writers in the earlier 20th century; phrases such as 'the identity crisis of adolescence' and the turmoil or 'storm and stress' of the adolescent period became familiar. Around the 1970s and 1980s, more normal features of adolescence were reasserted. In this century, insights from evolutionary psychology and neuroscience have again suggested that adolescence has distinctive features that can often involve impulsive and risk-taking activities.

In this chapter we will look at the nature of adolescence and examine how well the evidence supports these various views. In doing so, we shall note again the importance of the social and historical context in considering development. We need to keep a balance between the real cultural and historical variations and the relatively invariant features that characterize adolescence. The most obvious universal feature is the onset of puberty, and we will start with an overview of the biological and physical changes that this involves.

THE BIOLOGICAL AND PHYSICAL CHANGES OF PUBERTY

The precise timing of puberty depends on the measure used, but in girls the onset of menstruation (menarche) provides a fairly definite marker, and in boys the time of first ejaculation (spermache). Puberty comes later for boys. The typical age sequence of physical changes is shown in Table 19.1.

Table 19.1 Approximate age and sequence of appearance of sexual characteristics during puberty.

Age (years)	Boys	Girls
9–10		Growth of bony pelvis Budding of nipples
10–11	First growth of testes and penis	Budding of breasts Pubic hair

11–12	Activity of prostate gland
	  producing semen
		Changes in lining of vagina
		Growth of external and internal
		  genitalia

12–13	Pubic hair	Pigmentation of nipples Breasts fill out

13–14	Rapid growth of testes and penis	Axillary hair (under armpits)
		Menarche (average: 13.5 years;
		  range 9–17 years). Menstruation
		  may be anovulatory for first
		  few years

14–15	Axillary hair (under armpits) Down on upper lip Voice change	Earliest normal pregnancies
15–16	Mature spermatozoa (average: 15 years; range: 11.25–17 years)	Acne Deepening of voice
16–17	Facial and body hair Acne	Skeletal growth stops
21	Skeletal growth stops	

Source: Adapted from Katchadourian, H. (1977). *The Biology of adolescence.* San Francisco: W.H. Freeman.

The physical differences between boys and girls become much more obvious at puberty, due to hormonal changes. The reproductive organs become fully functional. In girls both the external genitalia (the vulva, including the clitoris) and the internal genitalia (the ovaries, fallopian tubes, uterus and vagina) become enlarged. The clitoris becomes more sensitive to stimulation, and the lining of the uterus and the vagina are strengthened. Menarche follows these changes. In boys, the testes and penis become larger, and so does the prostate gland, which is important for the production of semen. This is followed by the first ejaculation. Other changes are linked to these, but are not directly part of the reproductive system. In both sexes there is a growth of body hair, especially under the armpits and in the pubic areas. In boys there is more coarse body and facial hair, and the beginnings of beard growth. There are skin changes and the sweat glands become more active, often leading to acne. The voice deepens, especially in boys. In girls, breast development occurs.

Another feature of the pubertal period is the adolescent growth spurt. Throughout the school years, growth in height is fairly steady, averaging about 5 or 6 cm per year. This increases early on in puberty, reaching about 9 cm per year in girls and 10 cm per year in boys, before falling off sharply at adulthood (Figure 19.1 shows these changes in growth

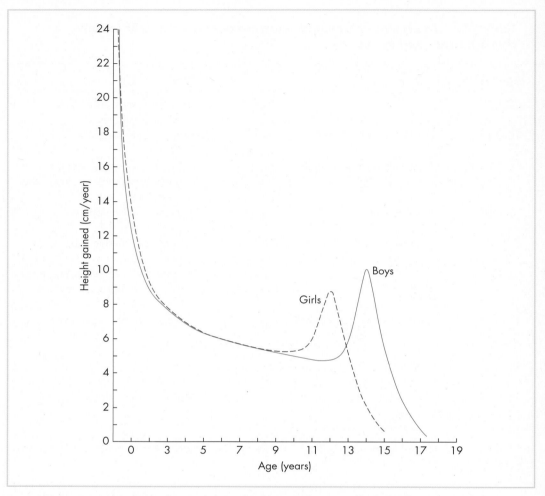

Figure 19.1 Typical individual curves showing velocity of growth in height for boys and girls.
Source: From Katchadourian, H. (1977). *The Biology of adolescence*. San Francisco: W.H. Freeman.

velocity for an average boy and girl). The extent of this growth spurt is largely independent of the child's previous height and some 35% of the variation in adult height is due to these rapid changes in adolescence.

All of the physical changes at puberty are linked to biological changes in the body. These are summarized in Figure 19.2. The key role is played by the hypothalamus, as it controls the action of the pituitary gland that produces the necessary hormones. The action of the hypothalamus resembles that of a thermostat regulating temperature—it 'shuts down' when high enough levels of sex hormones are circulating in the body. These sex hormones (especially androgen, testosterone, oestrogen and progesterone) are produced by the adrenal cortex, and by the gonads (the testes and ovaries). The growth of the latter is in turn stimulated by hormones released by the pituitary gland. At puberty, there is a change in the 'setting' or sensitivity of the hypothalamus. As a result, the pituitary gland works harder and sex hormone levels are raised.

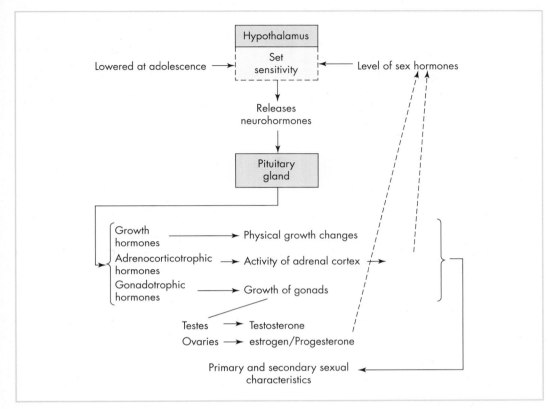

Figure 19.2 Summary of hormonal changes at puberty.

Variations in Physical Maturation Rates

The age of pubertal development can vary a great deal between individuals. This is dramatically illustrated in Figure 19.3, which shows the growth and sexual development of three boys, each aged 14 years and 9 months, and of three girls, each aged 12 years and 9 months.

To a considerable extent this variation appears to be genetic. For example, two randomly chosen girls will differ in age of menarche by, on average, 19 months; for two sisters, however, the average difference is only 13 months, and for identical twins, less than 3 months (Tanner, 1962). Behaviour genetic studies (see Chapter 2) indicate that 50% or more of the variability is genetic in origin (Ellis, 2006).

Environmental factors can also have pronounced effects on the timing of pubertal maturation. Undernourishment or malnutrition can slow down growth and retard the onset of puberty. This is not surprising, as caloric requirements increase with puberty. Although it is difficult to prove, it is highly likely that nutritional differences are largely responsible for social class and cultural differences in the timing of puberty. In less wealthy countries especially, social classes may differ by about a year in the age of menarche; the difference is less marked or absent in richer countries, where most young people get adequate nourishment (Katchadourian, 1977).

More recently, attention has been drawn to the possible effects of endocrine-disrupting compounds (EDCs). EDCs interfere with endocrine action and hormone production. They may be synthetic (for example, insecticides) or natural (for example, lead or other heavy metal compounds). The presence of EDCs in the diet or in the environment has raised concerns about decreased sperm counts in recent years. They may also affect the onset and process of puberty, although the nature of this (acceleration, delay or disruption) does vary between studies (Zawatski & Lee, 2013).

The Secular Trend in Age of Puberty

A fascinating phenomenon in western Europe and North America has been the secular trend in the age of menarche, illustrated in Figure 19.4. This is based on records from the Scandinavian countries, going back to the mid-19th century, and more recent records, including those in the UK and the USA. Figure 19.4 indicates that the age of menarche in girls declined over a 100-year period from an average of around 16 or 17 in the 1860s to around 13 in the 1960s. The change averaged about 0.3 years per decade. There have been similar secular trends in height. Over the same period, the average height of 12-year-olds increased by about 1.5 cm per decade; the trend for adult height was less—about 0.4 cm per decade—

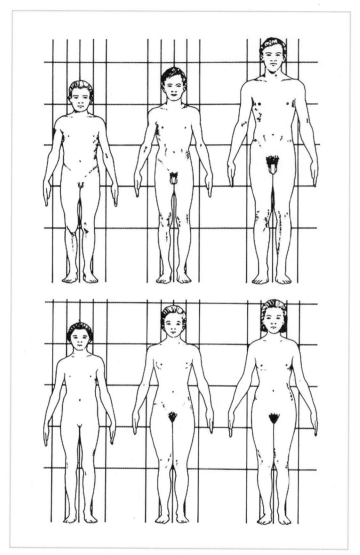

Figure 19.3 Individual variation in pubertal development: each of the three boys is $14\frac{3}{4}$ years old, and each of the three girls is $12\frac{3}{4}$ years old.

Source: From Tanner, J.M. (1973). Reproduced by permission of Tom Prentiss.

since some 'catching up' occurs in later maturers in early adulthood. Since the 1960s these changes in height and in age of menarche have slowed down (Roche, 1979). Nevertheless, a study in West Germany reported a continuing decrease in menarcheal age, from 13.3 years in 1979–1980 to 13.0 years in 1989 (Ostersehlt & Danker-Hopfe, 1991). Another study in North America found only a very small decline, from 12.9 years in 1948 to 12.8 years in 1992, but possibly with other aspects of puberty such as breast development coming earlier (Hermann-Giddens et al., 1997).

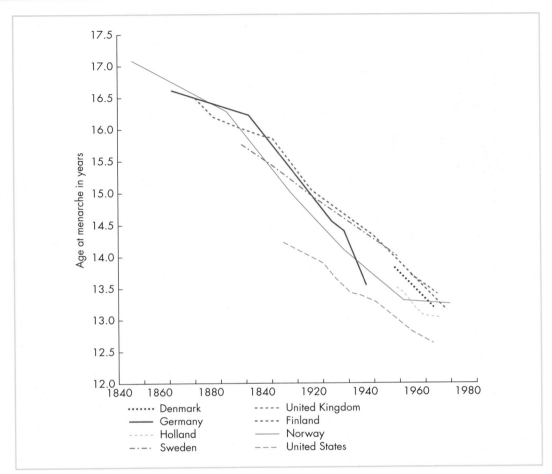

Figure 19.4 Changes in age of menarche over the past 120 years.

Source: Tanner, J. M. 1973: Growing Up, *Scientific American*, *229* (Sept), 35-43. Reproduced with permission. Copyright © 1973 Scientific American, Inc. All rights reserved.

Figure 19.4 has been extensively reproduced in textbooks, but in fact it seems that some of the earlier data are incorrect. Bullough (1981) reexamined available data from the 19th century, which suggest that menarche occurred between 14 and 16 years of age. The data for the 19th century in Figure 19.4 suggesting an age of 17 years are based on very small samples from Scandinavia that are not representative. Nevertheless, no one denies that there has been a secular trend. The historian Herbert Møller (1985, 1987) has looked at available evidence for still earlier periods, and for males. One source of evidence was records of Bach's choir-boys in Leipzig for 1727–1747. Their voices broke distinctly later, at around 17 years, than would be the case nowadays (14–15 years; see Table 19.1). An analysis of beard growth in males, from writings and portraits, suggests that before the 19th century many young men did not grow a beard until their 20s; for example, the series of Rembrandt self-portraits only show him with a beard by age 24. Nowadays beard growth happens at around 17 years (see Table 19.1).

The secular trend is believed to have been due to improving nutritional and health stand-ards. Decreases in mean family size may have been a contributing factor (see Malina, 1979, and Frisch, 1988, for a discussion). Research by Hinobayashi (2007) in Japan has shown that among Japanese females, the age of menarche was around 14–15 years, but slowly declining from 1900 to the 1940s. However, it increased by nearly a year in the late 1950s, a likely consequence of the devastation suffered by Japan at the end of World War II (ending in 1945). Japan made a rapid economic recovery from the 1950s onwards, and the age of puberty there has steadily decreased again, reaching 12.2 years by 1999.

 Stop and Think

Why might there be variations in the timing of puberty? Would we expect the secular trend to continue?

Theories Concerning Pubertal Timing

While acknowledging the importance of genetic factors, there has been considerable study and theorizing about environmental determinants of pubertal timing. Some theories come from the perspective of evolutionary developmental psychology (Chapter 2); that is, these theories focus on why it may be adaptive to enter puberty early or late.

Frisch (1988) argued a *relative fatness* theory, which suggested that girls especially needed to have adequate fat reserves to enter into the energy-demanding process of puberty; she suggested that a threshold of relative fatness (i.e. fat reserves and body weight relative to height) was required. This is consistent with evidence of the effects of nutrition on pubertal timing, and also with observations that some women athletes in very rigorous training, who lose fat reserves, may become amenorrhoeic (temporarily stop having periods). Data from the NICHD longitudinal study in the USA (see Table 1.1) found that body mass index (BMI) scores as early as 36 months, and rate of increase over the next few years, predicted earlier onset of puberty (Lee et al., 2007). Data from the ALSPAC study in the UK (see Table 1.1) found similar findings, although both studies found that early age of menarche in the mother is also predictive of daughters' age of menarche, pointing to a possibly complex interaction between genetic and environmental factors (Ong et al., 2007).

In a review, Ellis (2006) contrasts two main approaches, which superficially at least make some opposite predictions. The *energetics theory* supposes that a poor nutritional environment will lead to slower growth and to delayed puberty. There is considerable evidence for this, dating from Frisch's work and supported by the secular trend in puberty noted above. A generalization of this approach to include psychosocial as well as nutritional stressors is the *stress suppression theory*, which supposes that it would be advantageous to delay reproduction for less stressful times in the future. However, Ellis (2006) found rather little support for this latter theory.

An opposite kind of prediction comes from the *psychosocial acceleration theory*, stem-ming from Belsky et al. (1991). These authors proposed that some kinds of psychosocial stress, and especially low parental investment and/or stressful early family circumstances such as parental conflict and divorce, bring forward the onset of puberty. They argued that such stressors may 'signal' a difficult and unpredictable prevailing environment and thus the advantage of reproducing early rather than waiting for an uncertain future—a faster 'life history strategy'.

There is quite a lot of supportive evidence for this theory. For example, a longitudinal study of 87 adolescent girls in the USA found that both stressful relationships with their mothers and the presence of a stepfather contributed independently to earlier pubertal maturation (Ellis & Garber, 2000). A study by Belsky et al. (2010), using the NICHD longitudinal cohort (see Table 1.1) at age 15, found that greater maternal harshness at 54 months predicted earlier age of menarche, and in turn this predicted greater risk taking, an aspect of adolescence we discuss later.

A more recent longitudinal study by Simpson et al. (2012) separated out harshness (based on socioeconomic status—SES) and unpredictability (based on changes in parental employment, residence and partners). These were assessed at both 0–5 years and 6–16 years, and related to outcomes at age 23 such as number of sexual partners, engagement in aggressive and delinquent behaviours, and being associated with criminal activities. These authors found that unpredictability of the child's environment in the 0–5 period significantly predicted all of these; unpredictability at 6–16, and harshness at either time period, did not do so. The authors suggest that children respond to cues such as maternal depression and insensitivity in unpredictable early environments, develop corresponding internal working models of relationships, and become more likely to adopt a faster life history strategy. This study did not measure age of puberty, however.

PSYCHOLOGICAL EFFECTS OF PUBERTY

Through this chapter we will discuss a number of psychological changes associated with puberty, including a decrease in parent–child closeness and an increase in risk-taking behaviours (Arnett, 1999). But how does puberty actually bring about such changes? The relevant factors include direct and indirect effects of the physical changes themselves, the increased level of sex hormones, changes in the brain and the cognitive and self-definitional changes characteristic of this period.

Effects of Physical Changes

We have seen how the onset of puberty produces marked physical changes. These in their turn have psychological effects on the young person. The adolescent is becoming aware of his or her sexual development, and of associated changes in body size and shape, depth of voice, skin texture and facial and body hair. Many writers on adolescence have ascribed the awkwardness or self-consciousness that is often thought to characterize this period to awareness of these changes.

A number of studies have examined the psychological impact of menarche on girls (Greif & Ulman, 1982). Retrospective studies, in which women are asked to recall their menarcheal experience, suggest that it remains a clear and vivid event in the memory; it is recalled in rather negative terms, as an unpleasant experience for which social support was lacking. These conclusions are limited by the samples (mainly middle-class American) and historical period studied (mainly of menarche several decades ago). Box 19.1 gives details of a more recent study with Turkish adolescents.

A few studies have looked at attitudes in pre- and postmenarcheal girls. After menarche, girls tend to report more negative emotions or experiences than they had expected, despite

Box 19.1 The associations among perceived pubertal timing, parental relations and self-perception in Turkish adolescents

This study aimed to examine perceptions of early, on-time and late pubertal timing in Turkish adolescents, and how these related to feelings about maturation, relationships with parents and self-perception.

A total of 697 participants (360 girls, 337 boys) came from four urban schools, with a mean age of 16 years (range 14–18 years). They were given a package of questionnaire-based assessments.

Perceived pubertal timing: this was based on retrospective reports on six items (growth spurt, body hair, skin changes; and for males, voice change, erection/ejaculation, facial hair; for girls, breast development, menarche, widened hips). For each item, they were asked whether this had happened much or somewhat earlier than most other boys/girls their age, about the same, or somewhat or much later. In addition, they were asked to recall age of spermache or menarche.

Feelings about pubertal maturation: for each of the six developmental items above, they were asked if they reacted in a negative, neutral or positive way.

Parent–adolescent relationship: three subscales of the Parent–Adolescent Relationship Questionnaire (PARQ), translated into Turkish: global distress (15 items on conflict and dissatisfaction); communication with mother (13 items on manner of communication, defensive comments); and communication with father (13 items corresponding to the mother scale).

Self-perception: four subscales of Harter's Self-Perception Profile for Adolescents (SPPA) (this is a variant of the SPPC, see Chapter 6, p. 215), translated into Turkish: romantic appeal; physical appearance; close friendship; and global self-worth.

The authors first looked at the distribution of responses on perceived pubertal timing. Overall, they classified 61% as on-time maturers (66% boys, 57% girls), 23% as early maturers (25% boys, 21% girls) and 16% as late maturers (9% boys, 22% girls).

They then examined feelings about maturation. The average feelings for each of the six items (with 3.0 representing the neutral point) are shown for boys and girls in Box Table 19.1.1. Overall, boys were somewhat more positive than girls. However, for both sexes feelings were generally positive, especially as regards the growth spurt, but slightly negative as regards skin changes.

Perhaps the most interesting results concern the differences between early, on-time and late maturers. As regards overall feelings about pubertal maturation (summing over the six items in the table), the findings are shown in Box Figure 19.1.1. For boys, those who matured early felt good about it, as good or slightly (though non-significantly) better than on-time maturers, whereas boys who matured late did not feel so good about it. For girls the picture was different, as it was those who matured early who felt least good about it. On-time maturers felt best, although the difference between them and late-maturing girls was not statistically significant.

Examining the relationship between pubertal timing and parent–adolescent relationships, it was found that early maturers reported more conflict with parents than did on-time maturers.

Box Table 19.1.1 Mean scores (1 = very negative to 5 = very positive) on feelings about six aspects of pubertal development, for boys and girls.

Girls		Boys	
Growth spurt	3.45	Erection/ejaculation	3.70
Breast development	3.35	Growth spurt	3.57
Body hair	3.26	Voice change	3.54
Menarche	3.24	Body hair	3.49
Widening of hips	3.17	Facial hair	3.39
Skin change	2.93	Skin change	2.99

Source: Adapted from Gure, A., Ucanok, Z. & Sayil, M. (2006). The Associations Among Perceived Pubertal Timing, Parental Relations and Self-Perception in Turkish Adolescents, *Journal of Youth and Adolescence*, *35*, 538–548.

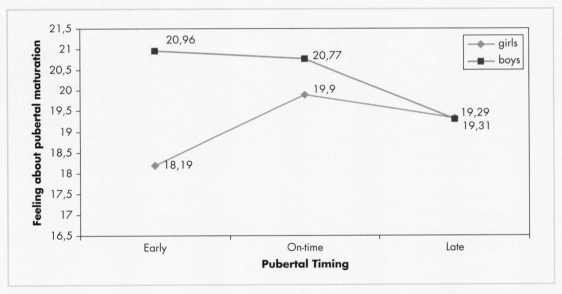

Box Figure 19.1.1 Early, on-time and late-maturing boys and girls on the measures of feelings about pubertal maturation.

Source: Reproduced from Gure, A., Ucanok, Z. & Sayil, M. (2006). The Associations Among Perceived Pubertal Timing, Parental Relations and Self-Perception in Turkish Adolescents, *Journal of Youth and Adolescence*, *35*, 538–548. With kind permission from Springer Science and Business Media.

They also communicated with fathers more negatively, although differences for communication with mothers were not significant. These analyses controlled for mother's educational level (because this was found to correlate with some of the variables). The authors do not report whether boys and girls differed in terms of these relationships but from personal communication with the authors, it appears that there were no significant main effects or interaction effects of sex in terms of the three measures of adolescents' family relations.

Finally, there were no significant differences between early, on-time and late maturers on the four measures of self-perception from the Harter scales when these were analysed on their own. However, subsequent regression analyses, also taking account of sex and of parent–adolescent relationships, found that physical appearance and global self-worth showed significant effects, with lower scores on these related to more negative feelings about pubertal maturation.

This study is interesting in showing clearly how feelings about puberty are affected by sex and by timing, as in Box Figure 19.1.1. Early-maturing boys generally feel good about this, but not early-maturing girls, for reasons discussed later (pp. 666–667). The least-liked aspect of puberty for both sexes is skin changes; issues such as acne affect appearance in negative ways, to which adolescents may be very sensitive.

The study also confirms, in a Turkish sample, how early maturation may well have negative effects on conflict and communication with parents, in effect accelerating and perhaps heightening what is a normative trend in the adolescent period. The lack of difference for communication with mothers (compared to that found for fathers) may, the authors suggest, reflect cultural aspects of Turkish society, with mothers being more supportive and acting as a buffer between fathers and adolescents.

The strengths of this study are having data from a relatively understudied population (in Turkey) and presenting a range of measures of adolescent adjustment. One drawback is the reliance on self-reports for all measures. This may not be considered an issue when the interest is on adolescents' own perceptions and feelings, but nevertheless measures beyond self-report, such as parent ratings, would increase validity as regards, for example, relationships with parents. Another limitation is the use of retrospective reports of pubertal development and feelings. However, the authors cite other work showing that adolescents' perceptions of pubertal timing do correlate highly with actual timing. Finally, they acknowledge that longitudinal study is needed to go beyond associations to a more developed model of the causal processes involved.

Based on material from Gure, A., Ucanok, Z. & Sayil, M. (2006). The Associations Among Perceived Pubertal Timing, Parental Relations and Self-Perception in Turkish Adolescents, *Journal of Youth and Adolescence*, 35, 538–548..

some educational preparation and support, usually from mothers. In a longitudinal study of 120 girls through menarche, Ruble and Brooks-Gunn (1982) found that menarche did initially create some inconvenience, ambivalence and confusion, but that typically it did not seem to be a traumatic experience. The negative feelings were greater for early maturers, and also for girls who thought themselves poorly prepared for the experience. There can be positive features to menarche as well. Some studies have found that menarche can serve as a focal reference point, bringing a girl closer to her mother and heightening an awareness of and interest in her femininity. Menarche, or at least general changes associated with menarche, may be correlated with greater maturity on some personality characteristics (Greif & Ulman, 1982).

Some authors believe that the experience of menarche was better handled in traditional cultures, in which there were or are well-defined rituals surrounding menstruation that give it a symbolic meaning and importance (Greif & Ulman, 1982; Mead, 1949). In the village of Lesu in Melanesia, for example, the focus of a classic anthropological study by Powdermaker

(1933), the onset of menstruation was an important ritual event for the women in the community. The girl was washed in the sea before sunrise by an old woman, who dipped the leaves of a branch in the water and over the girl, saying: 'Leaf, leaf I wash her; Soon her breasts will develop; I take away sickness of blood'. The leaves were then mixed with white lime and rubbed over the girl's body. This ritual was thought necessary if the girl's breasts were to develop and full womanhood achieved. A feast was held later the same day.

In many traditional societies, boys also go through initiation ceremonies, often grouped together into an 'age set' spanning some 5 years. For example, among the Karimojong, a cattle-herding people of Uganda, boys who are to be initiated first have to spear an ox. Semi-digested food from the stomach sack of the slaughtered animal is smeared over the initiate's body, while the elders call out: 'Be well. Become wealthy in stock. Grow old. Become an elder'. After further rituals, the boy has become a man and is allowed to grow his hair long in the fashion of men in the tribe (Dyson-Hudson, 1963).

These rituals are important in signalling the transition point from child to adult. Some anthropologists believe that they also reinforce the authority of the elders of the tribe, who perform the ceremonies. Another idea is that male initiation rites serve to break the close link children have with the mother; elaborate initiation rites were especially likely in societies where mothers nursed infants and shared the same bed with their child for a long period (Whiting et al., 1958). However, other explanations are possible for this finding. It may simply be that in male-dominated societies, men may have several wives (so prolonged nursing and postpartum sex taboos are tolerated) and, independently, male initiation rites are important in forging male solidarity (Young, 1965).

Effects of Hormones

Puberty is brought about by hormonal changes and, as well as any indirect effect through response to physical changes, some researchers have argued that hormones have a fairly direct effect or *activational* effect on psychological functioning in adolescence. Steinberg (1987) reported that pubertal maturation was associated with increased emotional distance from parents, in a US sample. This could just reflect an effect of chronological age (older adolescents being less close to parents), but utilizing individual variations in age of puberty, Steinberg showed that the effect of pubertal maturation was independent of chronological age. This was a cross-sectional study; further evidence that it is the pubertal maturation that causes the changes in parent–child relationships (rather than vice versa) came from a similar, longitudinal study (Steinberg, 1988); in fact, Steinberg found influences in both directions. Puberty was associated with adolescent autonomy and parent–child conflict, and decreased closeness. Some subsequent studies, for example Steinberg et al. (2008) and Burnett et al. (2011), have linked puberty status (rather than age) to aspects such as sensation seeking and understanding of social emotions.

However, besides any activational effects, Peper and Dahl (2013) argue that sex hormones also have *organizational* effects on the brain—for example, affecting the myelination and branching of neurons. The study of how the brain is reorganized at puberty has now become a major area of research.

Brain Development at Puberty

Recent work in developmental cognitive neuroscience (see Chapter 1, and Romer & Walker, 2007) has had implications for our understanding of both cognitive and social development in adolescence (Burnett, Sebastian, Kadosh & Blakemore, 2011; and see special issue of *Current Directions in Psychological Science* on 'The Teenage Brain', Vol 22(2), 2013). These new insights into the adolescent brain, according to Steinberg (2010, pp. 160–162), have 'the potential to structure a new, overarching model of normative and atypical adolescent development', and the phenomena are 'among the most dramatic and important to occur during the human lifespan'.

Some main features of these changes are shown in Table 19.2. A lot of remodelling of the brain is going on in adolescence, in areas that affect emotional regulation, response inhibition and planning. But they do not all take place at the same time. The earlier changes will impact on emotional experience and reward, while those mediating cognitive regulation are more gradual. The phased combination of these neural changes may contribute to aspects such as greater self-focus in adolescence and greater risk taking.

Steinberg and colleagues have proposed a *dual systems model* of risk taking and decision making in adolescence (Strang, Chein & Steinberg, 2013). The two systems are: (1) the socioemotional or reward system, stimulated by the increase in dopaminergic activity around

Table 19.2　Changes in the adolescent brain and their implications.

Timing	Changes in the adolescent brain	What these changes may mean
Preadolescence and early adolescence	A decrease in grey matter (mainly cell bodies and dendrites) in prefrontal areas of the brain, probably a kind of synaptic pruning.	The initial synaptic pruning can be seen as a stepping stone to the growth and reorganization that are to come.
Early adolescence, around puberty	Dopamine receptors in the paralimbic and prefrontal cortex are remodelled (proliferation, then reduction and redistribution of receptors).	Steinberg (2008) argues that the remodelling of dopaminergic systems at puberty leads to increased sensation seeking and reward seeking, since dopamine receptors are critical in the reward circuitry of the brain.
During adolescence and into early adulthood	An increase in white matter (mainly axons transmitting information) in prefrontal areas of the brain.	The increase in white matter is thought to reflect myelination, the sheathing of nerve fibres or possibly changes in axonal diameter, which improves their efficiency. As the prefrontal areas are implicated in thinking ahead, planning, executive function and response inhibition, this would improve such functions.
Through adolescence	An increase in connections between cortical and subcortical areas.	The increased connectivity with subcortical areas such as the limbic system could improve cognitive control over emotional response.

puberty (Table 19.2, row 2); and (2) the cognitive control system, which increases its connections through adolescence and early adulthood (Table 19.2, rows 3 and 4). The socioemotional system follows a curvilinear pattern, peaking at around puberty before declining; the cognitive control system shows a steady upward trend. Thus in puberty there is a temporary imbalance, with relatively less cognitive control of the socioemotional reward system, compared to before in childhood and later in adulthood.

In empirical work with nearly 1,000 US participants aged 10–30 years, Steinberg et al. (2008) found that sensation seeking was linked to pubertal maturation, and increased from 10 to 15 years before declining; on the other hand, impulsivity was unrelated to puberty and decreased steadily from 10 years onwards. Thus, Steinberg argues (2009, p. 744) that 'heightened risk taking in adolescence is the product of an easily aroused reward system and an immature self-regulatory system'. He also argues (Steinberg, 2008) that adolescents are not deficient in their cognitive understanding of the risks involved (for example, in drunk driving, sex without contraception, etc.), but rather in the balance of emotional impulse and cognitive control, plus other factors such as enhanced peer influence (see pp. 663–664). If so, then intervention programmes that focus on impulsiveness or awareness of risks might be expected to be less effective than strategies to make risk-taking behaviours more difficult (such as regulating alcohol sales, raising driving age, improving access to contraceptives).

Blakemore and Mills (2014) point to areas of the prefrontal cortex related to mentalizing, especially perspective taking and impulse control. These include the dorsal medial prefrontal cortex, temporoparietal junction, posterior superior temporal sulcus and anterior temporal cortex—a set of regions they call the *social brain* (p. 663). Neuroimaging studies have shown that these areas are particularly activated during social cognitive tasks, with changes in patterns of activation through adolescence.

This area of neuroscience research on the adolescent brain is developing rapidly and leading to exciting insights. The findings integrate well with the more traditional foci on cognitive and behavioural changes, but do open up new possibilities for understanding and intervention.

Effects of Cognitive Changes

Entering the period of formal operational thought, adolescents are increasingly able to think about abstract issues and hypothetical situations (Chapter 13). Thus, they may well reflect on how they are perceived by hypothetical others, and have problems adjusting to their changing physical appearance. A study in the USA found that girls (but not boys) experienced increased dissatisfaction with their bodies over the period 13–18 years; furthermore, this dissatisfaction was only weakly related to how other adolescents rated their physical attractiveness (Rosenblum & Lewis, 1999).

Elkind (1967) suggested that adolescents often imagine how their appearance or behaviour would seem to an 'imaginary audience' of others, hence their own self-consciousness. Elkind also argued that adolescents often thought that their own actions were very important in the eyes of others, and that they became bound up or obsessed with their own feelings, constructing a 'personal fable', an imaginary story of their own life, perhaps containing fantasies of omnipotence or immortality. These concepts of the 'imaginary audience' and the 'personal fable' led Elkind to postulate that a new kind of egocentrism appeared in adolescence (cf. Chapter 13). In this 'adolescent egocentrism', young people are unable to differentiate their own feelings about themselves from what others might be feeling.

Elkind was writing at a time when the 'storm and stress' view of adolescence was popular and empirical work on his concepts has yielded rather mixed results (Buis & Thompson, 1989). However, subsequent research has suggested that, similar to the imaginary audience, adolescents become increasingly aware of others' perspectives, as well as developing their own identity, leading to greater self-consciousness and awareness of how others may evaluate them (Sebastian, Burnett & Blakemore, 2008).

 Stop and Think

Are the hormonal, brain development and cognitive explanations of the changes in adolescence compatible?

EFFECTS OF EARLY AND LATE MATURATION

At 11 years, a girl would be early in experiencing menarche; at 14 she would be late. Similarly a 12-year-old boy would be early, a 16-year-old late in reaching puberty. Do these differences have important psychological consequences?

Early-maturing boys tend to be at an advantage socially, as their growth spurt favours strength and sporting achievement, usually highly valued in boys' groups (Chapter 5). A boy who is late in reaching puberty may feel less confident socially and be rated as less mature, attractive or popular (Mussen & Jones, 1957). The data in Box 19.1 indicate how early-maturing Turkish boys (as compared to early-maturing girls) feel positive about their pubertal development.

Research in Sweden found a more complex picture for early-maturing girls (Magnusson et al., 1985). Data on 466 girls were obtained before puberty, after puberty at 14 years and in a follow-up at 25 years. At 14 years it was clear that girls who had reached puberty early (before 11 years) were much more likely to be involved in drinking alcohol, smoking hashish, playing truant and generally breaking social norms than girls who matured on time or late. However, this was found to be the case because these girls were more likely to mix with an older peer group who were more likely to engage in these activities. In other words, early maturation often led to associating with older peers and, if and when this happened, the norm breaking followed. This was a temporary effect; by age 25 the differences between early and late maturers in terms of drinking alcohol had vanished. Nevertheless, there was a more permanent effect of early maturation on education. Early-maturing girls tended to engage in sexual activity earlier, and get married and have children earlier, and were less likely to be in tertiary education than late maturers.

A study by Caspi et al. (1993) drew on data from the Dunedin longitudinal study (see Table 1.1) to examine whether early maturation in girls was related to delinquency, and also whether such a link was related to dispositional factors (childhood history of externalizing problems) and contextual factors (single- or mixed-sex secondary school; single-sex schools are still common in New Zealand). The authors assessed 165 girls who entered all-girl second-ary schools at age 13 and 132 who entered mixed-sex schools. At 13, girls filled in an early delinquency scale (activities such as breaking windows, getting drunk, making prank telephone calls, stealing from pupils at school), and a familiarity with delinquent peers scale (whether their friends, or other kids they knew, did these behaviours). At 15, they filled in a delinquency scale (whether they had engaged in activities such as shoplifting, car theft, smoking marijuana, using weapons). To examine effects of maturational timing, the researchers used self-reports of menarche to divide their sample into early maturers, on-time and late maturers.

Some findings are shown in Table 19.3. Early-maturing girls are more at risk but the effect is a complex one, interacting with type of school. There is more familiarity with other girls' delinquency in the mixed-sex schools than in the same-sex schools, and this effect is largest for early-maturing girls. Early-maturing girls are more at risk of being delinquent themselves, but only in mixed-sex schools. However, by age 15, both early and on-time maturers are scoring higher than late maturers on delinquency. The authors argue that early-maturing girls are likely to associate with older peers, who are more into norm-breaking activities. Also, such peer pressures may be particularly strong in mixed-sex schools, with higher delinquency rates among boys, and possibly greater opportunities for observing or engaging in delinquent activities. These effects of peers were particularly strong for early-maturing girls with no earlier history of externalizing problems. Probably, those who did have an earlier history of externalizing problems were already familiar with delinquent acts by age 13 and did not need peer familiarity to get into such activities.

Partly on the basis of these sorts of findings, Moffitt (1993) proposed a 'maturity gap' theory. This starts with the assumption that there is a gap between biological and social maturity at adolescence—certainly true in modern societies but also, in fact, found through the anthropological literature (Schlegel & Barry, 1991), and also consistent with the recent evidence from brain development in puberty reviewed above (Steinberg, 2008). Moffitt argued that this maturity gap can lead to adolescence-limited delinquent behaviour (see also Chapter 10) in certain circumstances: if the adolescent is motivated to overcome the maturity gap; if he or she has access to role models for delinquent behaviour; and if there is reinforcement for such behaviour. Since earlier biological maturity might make the maturity gap more obvious, this would predict more delinquent and problem behaviour, especially when associating with older peers, or for girls in mixed-sex schools (since boys generally show higher rates of delinquency).

Table 19.3 Rates for early delinquency, familiarity with delinquent peers, and delinquency, at ages 13 and 15, by onset of physical maturation.

		Early maturers	On-time maturers	Late maturers
Age 13: early delinquency	All girl	2.0	2.5	1.3
	Mixed sex	4.3	2.4	1.2
Age 13: delinquent peers	All girl	14.1	13.7	12.1
	Mixed sex	19.3	17.0	13.6
Age 15: delinquency	All girl	1.8	2.5	1.5
	Mixed sex	3.2	3.5	1.3

Source: Adapted from Caspi, A., Lynam, D., Moffitt, T.E. & Silva, P.A. (1993). Unravelling girls' delinquency: Biological, dispositional and contextual contributions to adolescent misbehaviour. *Developmental Psychology, 29,* 19–30.

Some further studies clearly support this kind of explanation. A longitudinal study of 200 adolescent girls in the USA (Ge et al., 1996) found that early-maturing girls were more vulnerable to deviant peer pressure, and Lynne et al. (2007), in a longitudinal study of 1,366 US participants at 6th, 7th and 8th grades (11–14 years), found that, irrespective of gender or ethnicity (African-American, Latino), early maturers were higher on aggression and delinquency; this link was fully mediated by association with delinquent peers in 6th grade.

But for boys, not all studies give quite such a straightforward result. Williams and Dunlop (1999) carried out a study in the UK of 99 boys aged 14 years, and found delinquency to be higher in boys with 'off-time' puberty, whether this was early *or* late. And Graber et al. (2004), in a survey of over 1,500 US participants followed up to age 24, found a clear sex difference; early-maturing females were more at risk of antisocial behaviours but it was late-maturing males who were at more risk of deviant behaviours and substance abuse. So, while there is a rather consistent pattern for early-maturing girls, it is not so consistent for early-maturing boys.

Maturational timing may also impact on academic achievement. A longitudinal study in the UK by Douglas and Ross (1964) was based on the National Survey of Health and Development, which followed children born in one week in March, 1946 (see Table 1.1). At secondary school, it emerged that both boys and girls who were early maturers scored higher than late maturers on tests of mental ability and performance while at school. Some other studies have reported similar results. However, the superior performance of early maturers might not be due to the physical changes of puberty and greater physical maturity. First, the effect seems to interact with social class, being larger in lower social class groups. Also, family size may explain much of the effect. Puberty tends to be later in large families, and being a member of a large family also tends to depress intelligence and school achievement in a slight but consistent fashion (p. 169). When children of similar family size are compared, the differences between early and late maturers are small (Douglas & Ross, 1964).

A similar study in Sweden used a sample of 740 children followed from 9 to 14 years (Westin-Lindgren, 1982). In relation to achievement in Swedish, English and mathematics, the effects of social class were generally much greater than effects of early or late maturation. Thirteen- to 14-year-old early maturers did score better in Swedish and English if they came from families of manual workers, but there was little effect for children from families of salaried workers or employers. There were no effects of early or late maturation on mathematics scores. The possibly confounding effects of family size were not looked at in this study.

Effects of early or late maturation are clearly complex. Skoog and Stattin (2014) summarize psychological theories, and suggest applying a diathesis-stress model (see Chapter 2); early puberty is a diathesis or risk factor, and when combined with an adverse environment, problem behaviours can develop. Association with older and/or more deviant peers might be the adverse environment, or dual risk. However, is it correct to think of early (or late) puberty as a risk? Belsky (2012) summarizes an evolutionary-biological perspective which rather than viewing early puberty as a risk and some consequences as problem behaviours, instead sees different optimal pathways of development for the individual, dependent on actual or predicted environmental circumstances. From this life-history viewpoint, early puberty can be seen as a strategy that is the best one in certain conditions, as in the *psychosocial acceleration theory* discussed earlier. Of course, what is optimal for the individual may not always be what is best for society—as discussed in the context of aggression in Chapter 10.

RELATIONS WITH PEERS

As adolescents become independent from their parents, they may spend more time with peers and turn to peers more for social support and identity. Lam, McHale and Crouter (2014) used a combination of questionnaires and regular telephone interviews to get information on how time with peers changed from middle childhood (8 years) into late adolescence (18 years), and also adjustment correlates—problem behaviours (drinking alcohol, smoking, skipping school), depressive symptoms, social competence (Harter Self-Esteem Scale, see p. 215) and school performance. Time spent with same-sex peers increased from age 8 to age 14 and then started to decline. Time spent with opposite-sex peers increased steadily, but especially after around 13 years, overtaking time spent with same-sex peers later in adolescence (earlier for girls than boys). So far as adjustment was concerned, the researchers differentiated between what they called supervised time with peers (when an adult or older person was present) and unsupervised (when this was not the case). Longitudinally, more supervised time with peers correlated with improved academic performance. However, more unsupervised time with peers predicted greater problem behaviours and depressive symptoms (perhaps because of the influence of older peers, cf p. 660).

The nature of an adolescent's social relationships with peers is substantially different from those with his or her parents or caregivers. Through childhood, the parental relationship is often characterized as one of 'unilateral authority', in which parents strive to impart an already constructed set of knowledge and attitudes to their children. Friendship, however, is a form of mutually reciprocal relationship in which divergent opinions may be expressed and new ideas discussed. We have come across these conceptions previously, in discussing the development of friendship (Chapter 5) and Piaget's views of the development of moral reasoning (Chapter 9). While parent–child relations may become more mutual during adolescence, it is thought that they do not become as truly mutual or reciprocal as peer relationships (Youniss, 1980).

The social brain

Blakemore and Mills (2014), reviewing a range of studies, argue that adolescence is a sensitive period for adapting to one's social environment. Several main areas around mentalizing and social cognitive abilities show distinctive changes in adolescence.

Face processing: this is important for understanding the emotions and mental states of others. Monk and colleagues (2003) looked at the kinds of attention paid by adolescents and adults to aspects of fearful and neutral faces, and (using functional magnetic resonance imaging [fMRI] techniques) the brain areas activated. Sometimes participants were asked to look at the emotional expressions but at other times they were asked to focus on a non-emotional aspect, such as nose width. They found that the adults activated frontal cortex areas more for the non-emotional task, whereas the adolescents showed more brain activation in response to the emotional aspects of the stimuli, even when asked to focus on nose width. The authors suggest that 'maturation between adolescence and adulthood may involve increased ability to engage relevant brain regions for goal-directed attention when emotionally evocative, attention-grabbing events occur' (Monk et al., 2003, p. 427).

In another study, Kadosh, Heathcote and Lau (2014) compared 11- and 17-year-olds on a task involving attention to face stimuli with fearful, neutral or happy emotions. The 11-year-olds were less good than the 17-year-olds generally, but showed particularly poor attentional control over the fearful faces, suggesting that the emotion of fear was particularly salient to them.

Processing social emotions: fear is a basic emotion, like anger and happiness—they can be evoked by non-social as well as social situations. But social emotions, such as guilt, embarrassment, shame and pride, are more complex and depend upon an understanding of how others think about your actions. Understanding of these seems to develop rapidly during adolescence. For example, Burnett et al. (2011) compared responses to social scenarios in 11-, 13- and 15-year-olds. Basic emotions (anger and fear) showed little change with age or pubertal status but social emotions (embarrassment, guilt) increased—as a function of pubertal status rather than age.

Peer evaluation and fear of rejection: early research by Coleman (1980) showed that anxieties about friendships with peers peak in mid-adolescence. He asked adolescents to complete unfinished sentences about friendships in a small group, and analysed the results for their emotional content. Themes of anxiety and fear of rejection by friends increased from 11 to 13 and then to 15 years, but declined by 17 years.

A more recent laboratory paradigm called *Cyberball* has been used to examine feelings about social rejection or ostracism by peers. Cyberball is an internet ball-passing game which the young person thinks they are playing with two other players (in fact, the other players are controlled by computer algorithms, so as to include or exclude the participant). Mood and anxiety following exclusion are assessed. A study by Sebastian et al. (2010) compared young adolescents (11–13 years), mid-adolescents (14–15 years) and adults (22–47 years) in this game. The adolescents showed greater distress at this kind of social exclusion, with anxiety being raised most noticeably in the young adolescent group. In a related paradigm, adolescent girls showed greater social anxiety to peer evaluation, related to activation of brain areas concerned with processing emotions.

Peer influence: some evidence has suggested that conformity with peers, especially in antisocial situations, increases up to around 14 years before declining again (Berndt, 1979). Steinberg and Monahan (2007) argued that this was probably limited to antisocial behaviours, and that part of the cognitive and social development of adolescence should be an increase in autonomy and maturity such that peer influence could be resisted if it went against one's own values. They constructed a measure of Resistance to Peer Influence (RPI), which included items such as 'Some people go along with their friends just to keep their friends happy, BUT other people refuse to go along with their friends just to keep their friends happy', with the respondent asked how true this is of them (a format similar to Harter's Self-Esteem Scale, described in Chapter 6). They found a general increase in RPI with age from 9 to mid-20s, especially from 14 to 18 years (although there does appear to be a small dip at 14 years). Girls scored higher on RPI than boys. It seems likely that through adolescence there is an increasing potential for autonomy and resistance to peer influence, but that nevertheless the influence of the peer group is very considerable, and especially so for risky or antisocial behaviours in the mid-adolescent period; this is considered further in the section on risk taking.

Concern for self versus ideas of trust and sharing: a number of studies have used *behavioural economic games* to examine trust and sharing between two peers (Crone, 2013). For example, in the *Ultimatum Game*, two players are given a sum of money: player 1 has to decide on how to split this, and player 2 has the option of accepting this or declining (in which case neither gets any money). Fairness in this increases through childhood and adolescence, and has been related to mentalizing abilities. In the *Trust Game*, again two players have a sum of money to share. Here, player 1 can either decide on a split or they can trust player 2 to decide the split, in which case the amount is tripled. This is a one-off game, so although letting player 2 decide could be very advantageous, it does mean player 1 trusting player 2 to give a fair share. In early adolescence, players tended to make more self-oriented choices; in later adolescence they considered the consequences for others more. These changes have been related to shifts in activity in the social brain areas.

ROMANTIC DEVELOPMENT

Puberty is usually associated with increased interest in relationships with the opposite sex. Although children may have close 'best friends' in childhood, usually of the same sex, it is typically in adolescence that intimate partnerships start to be formed, usually with someone of the opposite sex, and with romantic and possibly sexual elements to the relationship. Indeed, 'identity' followed by 'intimacy' are seen as normative aspects of development in adolescence and early adulthood, in Erikson's model (described shortly); although he saw intimacy as a challenge of early adulthood, the origins are found in adolescence.

Brown (1999) developed a four-phase model of the development of romantic partner relationships, based on US adolescents.

1. *Initiation phase*: an awakening of interest in the opposite sex (usually) but focus on the self and one's own confidence and ability. Dating occurs in the context of and with the assistance of same-sex peers.
2. *Status phase*: romantic relationships are primarily seen in the context of status with same-sex peers, the emphasis being on having a desired or high-status partner ('You're going out with who?').
3. *Affection phase*: here there is a shift of focus onto the romantic relationship itself. The peer group has less influence and there is a greater sense of commitment to the relationship, often with increased sexual activity.
4. *Bonding phase*: the relationship is seen as a long-term commitment.

A longitudinal study of German adolescents by Seiffge-Krenke (2003) has provided some empirical support for this kind of model. Semi-structured interviews were carried out with 103 young people, at ages 13, 15, 17 and 21 years. The qualitative data obtained were broadly supportive of Brown's model. In addition, as shown in Table 19.4, the proportion of young people with a romantic partner, and the duration of the current intimate relationship, increased steadily with age.

Table 19.4 **Romantic partners in adolescence in a German sample.**

Age in years	13	15	17	21
Percentage with romantic partner	40	43	47	65
Duration of relationship in months	3.9	5.1	11.8	21.3

Source: Seiffge-Krenke, I. (2003). Testing theories of romantic development from adolescence to young adulthood: Evidence of a developmental sequence. *International Journal of Behavioral Development, 27,* 519–531.

Connolly et al. (2004) found some support for a four-stage model, with some similarity to Brown's model. Their first stage is primarily being in same-sex groups. The second phase involves hanging around with both boys and girls and going to clubs and sports activities in mixed-sex groups. The third phase refers to dating activities, but in a group. The fourth phase involved dyadic dating and having a romantic partner. The researchers found good supportive evidence for these as sequential phases, in a sample of Canadian 12–15-year-olds, although they point out that this progression is not inevitable and some reversals or changes of sequence can occur. In their sample, 21% said they had a boyfriend or girlfriend.

While some younger adolescents claim to have an intimate, romantic relationship, it is only later in adolescence that these become more normative and the duration of such relationships becomes substantial. There are also cultural differences: Connolly et al. (2004) in Canada and Collins (2003) in the USA both reported that young people of Asian origin were later in dating and forming romantic relationships, perhaps because of cultural and familial expectations.

Collins (2003) suggested five important aspects to assess in adolescent romantic relationships: (1) involvement—the timing and duration of such relationships; (2) partner selection—characteristics of preferred partners such as age, personality; (3) content—what kind of shared activities were engaged in; (4) quality—aspects such as intimacy, affection and nurturance; and (5) cognitive and emotional processes—attachment style, and the internal representation of the relationship (similar to internal working models as discussed in Chapter 4).

An example of a study looking at content and also quality of adolescent romantic relationships is provided by Carlson and Rose (2012). They studied 12-, 15- and 18-year-olds in the midwestern USA. Those who had a heterosexual romantic relationship checked which of 32 activities they engaged in together. The most frequent were talking on the telephone (88%), talking about non-personal things (77%), talking about personal things (70%), listening to music (68%), talking in school (66%), and going to each other's houses after school/weekends (66%). Communication by emails/instant messages was only mentioned by 51% and social networking sites were not on the list so it would be relevant to know the year in which data were collected for this study, but—as is too often the case—this is not stated. Many of the activities mentioned increased with age, and many showed a positive relationship with a measure of romantic relationship satisfaction—a quality measure.

This last finding suggests the positive nature of most early romantic experiences. However, as with all relationships there can be a 'dark side'. Barter (2009) reviewed the topic of partner abuse and violence in teenage relationships, discussing physical violence, sexual violence and coercion, and emotional abuse. While such activities may end a relationship, unfortunately for those who stay in an abusive relationship there is a high probability of the violence or abuse continuing. A number of studies have linked childhood sexual abuse (see Chapter 4) to the likelihood of later partner violence, including in the teenage years as romantic partnerships develop.

In a comprehensive review, Stonard et al. (2014) examined the incidence of these different kinds of dating violence and abuse (physical, sexual and emotional). The incidence figures vary greatly between studies, due to many factors, especially around definition and measurement procedures; however, their tables suggest a ballpark figure of at least 20% of adolescent dating relationships involving some kind of violence or abuse. Stonard et al. also review how technology is playing an increasing role in dating violence.

Sexting

Sexting has been defined as 'the sending, receiving and forwarding of sexually explicit messages, images or photos to others through electronic means, primarily between cellular phones' (Klettke, Hallford & Mellor, 2014). A boy may ask a girlfriend for such photos of herself and the majority of sexual images and texts pass between consenting adolescents without harm. In Europe, the EU Kids Online project found that 15% of 11–16-year-olds had received peer-to-peer sexual messages or images (Livingstone, Haddon, Görzig & Ólafsson, 2011). Of those, 3% said they had sent or posted such images.

But if the relationship becomes abusive, such photos may be shared very widely without the girl's consent—a shattering and very demeaning experience. Young women are particularly at risk, as they often feel pressurized or coerced to send sexual images or 'sexts' (Mitchell, Finkelhor, Jones & Wolak , 2012). Drouin and Tobin (2013) found that in females, anxious attachment in close relationships was associated with consenting to unwanted involvement in sexting, often to avoid an argument. In the UK, the Child Exploitation and Online Protection Centre (CEOP) has produced films, resources and guidelines for schools about sexting. A short film called *Exposed* portrays the effects of an unwanted sexting experience. A 'ClickCEOP' button is linked to 1,700 different websites for children to report abuse. The button links to a team of specialist NSPCC child protection advisors.

ADOLESCENT SEXUALITY

Human societies vary in attitudes to adolescent sexuality. The review by Schlegel and Barry (1991) found that the majority of traditional societies were relatively tolerant, but it did depend on factors such as the usual age of marriage and the type of property transferral. Although early teenage fertility is generally lower than it is a few years later, obviously pregnancies can result from intercourse, and this usually results in marriage. When property exchange is an important part of a marriage, parents and relatives will be more concerned about adolescent sexual behaviour and choice of partners. As Schlegel and Barry comment (p. 132), 'given the absence of property exchanges at marriage, along with alternatives to abstinence for preventing pregnancy, it is understandable that Europeans and Americans have become tolerant toward premarital sexuality'.

A study in the UK, based on the ALSPAC longitudinal study (see Table 1.1), documented the beginnings of intimate and sexual behaviour in 11–12 and 12–13-year-olds (Waylen, Ness, McGovern, Wolke & Low, 2009). A first step was holding hands (25% and 41% respectively at these two age levels), and kissing on the mouth (17% and 33%). Only the 12–13-year-olds were asked about more intimate behaviours. By this age, 12% had 'lain down together', 5% had been touched under their clothes, but fewer than 1% had had oral sex or sexual intercourse.

As shown later in Table 19.9, other surveys have shown that the percentages of adolescents who have had sexual intercourse increases rapidly through the teen years, and in many samples reaches a majority by 17 years. However, there are great variations by sample characteristics and also by historical period; more data on this are given in the final Historical Changes section of the chapter.

Just as the extent of sexual experience in young people varies considerably, so do aspects such as the number of sexual partners and the use of condoms. A study by Boislard and colleagues (2009) examined risky sexual behaviours (not using condoms and having many sexual partners) in young Canadian and Italian adolescents over a 2-year period. Association with similar peers was strongly predictive of such risky behaviours, although parenting practices had some influence, probably through influencing or approving choices of friends and of sexual partners.

Lesbian and Gay Adolescents

In their review of traditional societies, Schlegel and Barry (1991) found that, in many, there are relatively tolerant attitudes towards casual homosexual acts during adolescence. These are usually seen as a substitute for heterosexual intercourse, and do not necessarily lead to homosexuality in adults.

In Western societies, tolerance of homosexuality has increased greatly in recent decades. Recently, actuarial estimates suggest that between 5% and 7% of young people in the UK grow up to be lesbian or gay (Department of Business, Enterprise and Regulatory Reform, 2004). In the US, demographic data collected from the Youth Risk Behavior Surveys between 2001 and 2009 suggest that between 1.0% and 2.6% of youth in junior high school and high school identify as lesbian or gay, between 2.9% and 5.2% identify as bisexual, and between 1.3% and 4.7% are unsure of their sexual orientation (Centers for Disease Control and Prevention, 2011). Awareness of same-sex attraction and self-labelling are sensitive to historical and cultural contexts (Floyd & Bakeman, 2006). Studies on lesbian and gay adolescent development in Western societies suggest that, today, some young women and men first start to become aware of their attraction to members of the same sex between the ages of 10 and 15 years. D'Augelli et al. (1998) surveyed 260 lesbian and gay youth in the US, and found that initial awareness of same-sex orientation often started at around 10 years, but that self-labelling as lesbian or gay tended to occur around 15 years (a bit earlier for boys than girls), with first disclosure at around 16.5 years for both sexes. Retrospective data collected by Floyd and Bakeman (2006) from 767 lesbians and gay men in the US indicated that boys become aware of their same-sex orientation at an average of 11.4 years of age and girls again somewhat later at 15.3 years.

D'Augelli (1994) suggested that lesbian and gay identity formation occurs after the individual has considered the implications of disclosure—popularly known as 'coming out'. The process is complex, as it often requires young people to review and, in some cases, renew their relationships with others as they take on an outwardly different identity to that perceived by their family, friends, school and local community. Young lesbians and gay men have to consider questions such as: 'What does it mean to be lesbian or gay?'; 'How do I behave and how should I behave?'; 'How will my parents react?'; 'How will my family react?'; 'How will my peers/friends react?'; 'Can I be openly lesbian or gay?'; 'What does the law, religion, family or social custom say about homosexuality?' (Rivers & Gordon, 2010).

Reactions to 'coming out' are varied. Mothers sometimes show the strongest reactions—sometimes they are the most rejecting compared to fathers, brothers or sisters, sometimes the most accepting of their lesbian or gay child. D'Augelli et al. (1998) found that gay men tend to tell their mothers first rather than their fathers, while lesbians tend to tell both parents at the same time. Floyd and Bakeman (2006) found that although young people tend to tell their mothers first rather than their fathers, the gap between telling one parent and then telling another is relatively small. Parental reactions are often intensified by the reactions of other adults and family members to a young person's disclosure, and the way in which a young person is received by their own peers (Willoughby et al., 2006). Family rejection was found to be the primary cause of homelessness (46%) among lesbian, gay, bisexual and transgender youth surveyed by Durso and Gates (2012).

ADOLESCENCE AS A PERIOD OF TURMOIL, OR 'STORM AND STRESS'

In the earlier half of the 20th century, many theorists thought of adolescence as a time of acute identity crisis and turmoil. One influence here was that of psychoanalysis. Sigmund Freud's view of human psychosexual development was that much of an individual's psychic energy was taken up with trying to cope with unacceptable sexual impulses early in childhood. In the 'oral', 'anal' and 'Oedipal' stages, the very young child experiences frustration and anxiety at his or her developing sexual impulses, resulting in psychological defences and repression of these impulses during a 'latency period' from about 5 years of age to puberty. However, at puberty there is a renewed upsurge of sexual 'instincts' that reawakens old conflicts.

The psychoanalytic approach was developed by Peter Blos (1962) in his book *On Adolescence*. Blos likened the adolescent transition to independence to the earlier transition that the infant went through to become a self-reliant toddler; in both, ambivalence and regression were likely. Blos called adolescence a 'second individuation process' because of this parallel. Freud's and Blos's theories received much criticism later in the 20th century. The 'instinct' model is outdated (Chapter 2), and the emphasis on sexual concerns is generally felt to be exaggerated. However, a revision of the psychoanalytic approach made by Erik Erikson (1902–1994) attracted a lot of support. Erikson realized that Freud emphasized innate impulses too strongly; he gave a much larger role to cultural influences in personality formation. He accepted Freud's insight into the importance of sexual desires, but regarded other concerns as equally, or more, strong at various stages of the life cycle. He therefore described 'psychosocial' rather than 'sexual' stages of development. Finally, he thought that adolescence (rather than early childhood) was the most decisive period in the formation of adult personality. A summary of Erikson's eight stages in the life cycle is shown in Table 19.5. In each stage there is a 'normative crisis'—the area in which Erikson considered conflict to be most characteristic.

The idea of adolescence as a turbulent, rebellious period was popular in the 1960s and 1970s, a period of considerable social and attitudinal change (for example, in sexual permissiveness, see pp. 684–685), increased use of drugs and social protest (for example, against the Vietnam War in the USA). In the later 1970s and 1980s, however, more researchers stressed the view that the conflicts in adolescence were by no means universal, and were often about mundane matters such as mode of dress or getting home times. These may have overstressed the 'normality' of the adolescent period; later reviews tend to point out that there are indeed stresses particular to the adolescent period. Arnett (1999), in a review of the 'storm-and-stress' view, contended that it is 'a real part of life for many adolescents and their parents' (p. 324). He reviewed three main areas: conflict with parents; mood disruption; and risk behaviour.

Table 19.5 The eight developmental stages proposed by Erikson (1968).

Normative crisis	Age (year)	Major characteristics
Trust versus mistrust	0–1	Primary social interaction with mothering caretaker; oral concerns; trust in life-sustaining care, including feeding
Autonomy versus shame and doubt	1–2	Primary social interaction with parents; toilet training; 'holding on' and 'letting go' and the beginnings of autonomous will
Initiative versus guilt	3–5	Primary social interaction with nuclear family; beginnings of 'Oedipal' feelings; development of language and locomotion; development of conscience as governor of initiative
Industry versus inferiority	6–puberty	Primary social interaction outside home among peers and teachers; school age assessment of task ability
Identity versus role confusion	Adolescence	Primary social interaction with peers, culminating in heterosexual friendship; psychological moratorium from adult commitments; identity crisis; consolidation of resolutions of previous four stages into coherent sense of self
Intimacy versus isolation	Early adulthood	Primary social interaction in intimate relationship with member of opposite sex; adult role commitments accepted, including commitment to another person
Generativity versus stagnation	Middle age	Primary social concern in establishing and guiding future generation; productivity and creativity
Integrity versus despair	Old age	Primary social concern is a reflective one: coming to terms with one's place in the (now nearly complete) life cycle, and with one's relationship with others; 'I am what survives of me'

Source: Adapted from Erikson, E. (1968). *Identity: Youth and crisis*. London: Faber.

He also remarked on cultural variations in these. We will look at some evidence regarding all these areas, following a description of Erikson's work on identity, and the 'identity crisis'.

Identity Development and the 'Identity Crisis'

Erikson elaborated his ideas about role confusion and identity in adolescence in an influential book, *Identity: Youth and crisis* (1968). He argued that while identity was important throughout the life cycle, it was in adolescence that the most turmoil in this area could normally be expected. He thought that adolescents typically went through a psychological or psychosocial 'moratorium', in which they could try out different aspects of identity without finally committing themselves. For example, a young person might temporarily adopt different religious beliefs or change views about their vocation, without adults expecting this necessarily to be a final choice. After this period of crisis, a more stable, consolidated sense of identity would be achieved.

There are good reasons why one's sense of identity might change considerably through adolescence. We have seen how marked physical changes occur, which will affect one's body image or sense of physical self. At this time also, a pattern of sexual relationships needs to be decided upon. Society expects a young person to make some choice of vocation by around 18 years, and in many countries they also get the vote at this age and have to decide on their political preferences. Nevertheless, Erikson's ideas were not obtained from any large-scale survey; they were based on his own observations and on his clinical practice. They certainly needed to be tested against empirical findings.

An interesting longitudinal case study that tested Erikson's ideas was reported by Espin et al. (1990). They carried out a content analysis of 71 letters written by a Latin-American girl to her former teacher, over a 9-year period, between the ages of 13 and 22. Besides her adolescence, this was a traumatic period for her, since she and her parents were imprisoned for political reasons. According to the content analysis, themes to do with identity predominated in the earlier letters. These increased from 13 to 18 years, then declined. Themes to do with intimacy increased steadily through the period and became predominant after age 19. Themes to do with generativity were very low at first, but did start to increase after age 19. This single case study does support the notion of three successive overlapping stages from Erikson's model (Table 19.5), but clearly more normative studies are needed.

A more thorough attempt to do this was made by James Marcia (1966, 1980). Marcia developed an interview technique to assess 'identity status' in certain areas, notably those of occupation, religion, political belief and attitudes to sexual behaviour. He would ask questions such as, 'Have you ever had any doubts about your religious beliefs?'. Depending on the answer to these and other questions, a person would be characterized as in 'diffusion' (D) (or 'confusion'), 'foreclosure' (F), 'moratorium' (M) or 'achievement of identity' (A) (Marcia, 1966).

Someone in diffusion status has not really started thinking about the issues seriously, let alone made any commitment. Thus in answer to the above question, they might answer, 'Oh, I don't know. I guess so. Everyone goes through some sort of stage like that. But it really doesn't bother me much. I figure one's about as good as the other!'. By contrast, someone in foreclosure status has formed a commitment but without ever having gone through a crisis or seriously considered alternatives. They probably accept parental or conventional beliefs unquestioningly. They might answer, 'No, not really, our family is pretty much in agreement on these things' to the question about religious doubts.

Someone in moratorium status is going through the crisis predicted by Erikson. They are going to form a commitment, but at present are still considering various alternatives. They might answer, 'Yes, I guess I'm going through that now. I just don't see how there can be a god and yet so much evil in the world, or ...'. Finally, someone in achievement status has been through the crisis and has reached a resolution. They have consolidated their identity in this respect. Thus, they might answer, 'Yeah, I even started wondering whether or not there was a god. I've pretty much resolved that now, though. The way it seems to me is ...'.

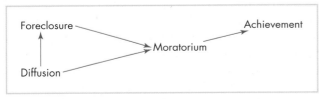

Figure 19.5 Most likely predicted changes in identity status.

In this scheme, diffusion is seen as the least mature status and achievement as the most mature. The most likely transitions in identity status are shown in Figure 19.5. There is some support for such a sequence (Al-Owidha et al., 2009). The results of a cross-sectional

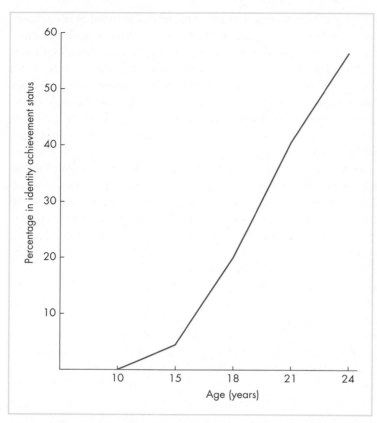

Figure 19.6 Percentage of males who were in identity achievement status at five age levels.

Source: Meilman, P.W. (1979). Cross-sectional age changes in ego identity status during adolescence. *Developmental Psychology, 15,* 230–231.

study (Meilman, 1979) on 12–24-year-old males are shown in Figure 19.6. It can be seen that only just over half those interviewed had reached identity achievement at 24 years. Thus, identity achievement may go on well into adulthood. This is borne out by a study by O'Connell (1976), who carried out retrospective interviews with married women who had school-aged children. Most of the women said that they had experienced an increasingly strong sense of identity as they moved from adolescence through to when they married, then had their first child, then had their children going to school. Such findings suggest that identity development is not so strongly focused in adolescence as Erikson suggested.

We can have more confidence in identity status measures if they correlate with, or predict, other variables. Persons in moratorium for vocation are indeed more likely to change their academic plans. Students in identity achievement have a wider range of cultural interests and express more interest in expressive writing and poetry (Waterman, 1982). Sex differences in identity status are not very marked (Archer, 1982), except in the area of sexual attitudes (discussed on p. 684). Identity status has been related to family background. Those in foreclosure report close relationships to parents, those in moratorium and achievement more distant or critical ones.

Later research has differentiated Marcia's two concepts of exploration and commitment. Exploration has been described as being either in breadth or in depth. Exploration in breadth refers to comparing a variety of possibilities before making a choice (for example, looking carefully at all the political party manifestos before deciding how to vote); exploration in depth means reflecting on one's current commitments (perhaps wondering if you were right to vote for the party that you chose). A cohort-sequential study in the Netherlands by Klimstra et al. (2010) suggested that early adolescence is more characterized by exploration in breadth and moving to some choice or commitment whereas later adolescence is more characterized by exploration in depth, with a possible reevaluation of an earlier choice. This suggests some movement to-and-fro between moratorium (M) and achievement (A)—a process called a MAMA cycle.

Studying these processes needs detailed longitudinal research, and some studies have examined how identity changes over periods of months or even on a day-to-day basis. One study of Dutch students in later adolescence, by Kunnen et al. (2008), looked at changes over 6 months in six domains—philosophy of life, parents, friends, studies, self, and intimate relationships. The patterns of change over 6 months varied considerably by domain, but many students were either stable or showed an M to A trajectory. Students with stable commitment (in A, but also in F) had the highest levels of well-being.

Conflicts with Parents

Adolescence is often seen as a period when relations with parents become less close and more conflictual. This perception has some basis in fact. Figure 19.7 shows data drawn from a large-scale study by Rossi and Rossi (1991) in the USA. The figure shows ratings for closeness to parents, at ages 10, 16 and 25, for different parent–child dyads and for two birth cohorts (those born in 1925–1939 who were adolescents in the 1940s–1950s, and those born during 1950–1959 who were adolescents in the 1960s–1970s). What is apparent is that in every

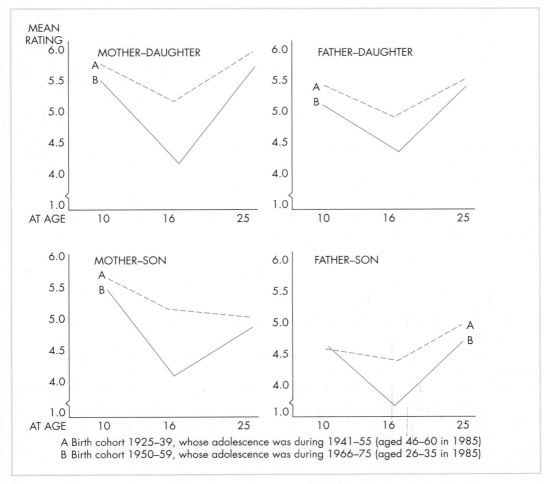

A Birth cohort 1925–39, whose adolescence was during 1941–55 (aged 46–60 in 1985)
B Birth cohort 1950–59, whose adolescence was during 1966–75 (aged 26–35 in 1985)

Figure 19.7 Affective closeness of children and their parents: cohorts whose adolescence was in 1941–1955 (dotted lines) versus 1966–1975 (full lines). (Mean rating on 1–7 closeness scale.)

case, rated closeness is lower at 16 than at 10 years, though it recovers by 25. This dip in closeness is more pronounced (and rates of closeness generally are lower) in the later cohort, probably reflecting the turbulence and social protest of the 1960s (see p. 669).

The dip in closeness seems to be related to a rise in conflicts. What are such conflicts about? A study of 11–14-year-old African-American adolescents in the USA (Smetana & Gaines, 1999) found the most frequent conflicts were about choice of activities (24%), doing chores (21%), or issues of interpersonal relationships such as choice of friends (17%). The researchers found that parents seemed to see the conflicts primarily as being matters of 'social convention' (see also Chapter 9); for example, one African-American mother stated:

> I want her to share the load in the household. This is a team effort, and she knows she has two working parents.
>
> *(Smetana & Gaines, 1999, p. 1459)*

However, the adolescents themselves seemed to view these conflicts as being about issues of personal autonomy. They were seeking to develop their own rights in decision making, rather than automatically give way to parents' wishes. Thus, even though many conflicts are about mundane matters, they may contribute to a decrease in parent–child closeness if parents resist this bid for autonomy.

A similar study of parent–adolescent conflicts in families in Hong Kong and in Shenzhen, China, was reported by Yau and Smetana (2003). Hong Kong is a very densely populated urban community, while Shenzhen is a mainland Chinese city bordering Hong Kong. In both, the Chinese population presents a somewhat different picture of socialization to Western norms, with more emphasis on family obligations and responsibility to elders. Nevertheless, Yau and Smetana found that a range of typical conflicts with parents were reported by young people, aged 11–18. The percentages who reported various kinds of conflicts are shown in Table 19.6. Many were about choice or regulation of activities (using the phone, watching TV, bedtimes) and doing household chores. In Shenzhen especially, there were more conflicts over achievement (studying, homework), consistent with a greater emphasis there on good school grades as a route to advancement, but there were fewer interpersonal conflicts (over relationships with parents, siblings and friends), perhaps because most were in one-child families and thus had no siblings to quarrel with. Some conflicts were also about money and looks/health.

Table 19.6 **Types of parent–adolescent conflict reported by young people in Hong Kong and Shenzhen.**

Type of conflict	Activities	Chores	Achievement	Interpersonal	Money	Looks/ health	Other
Hong Kong	40	17	9	15	9	5	4
Shenzhen	31	10	34	6	5	10	2

Source: Yau, J. & Smetana, J. (2003). Adolescent–Parent conflict in Hong Kong and Shenzhen: A comparison of youth in two cultural contexts. *International Journal of Behavioral Development, 27,* 201–211.

Lichtwarck-Aschoff, Kunnen and van Geert (2009) carried out an intensive diary-based study of 17 adolescent girls in the Netherlands. The girls were aged 15 years at the start of the study, and every 6 weeks they kept a 2-week diary (either in a booklet or online) of any conflicts with their mothers. The girls received a small reward of 5 euros for each completed diary week, with altogether six batches of 2 weeks over a 1-year period. A total of 147 conflicts were recorded. These were classified by the researchers as *autonomy* (e.g. when to go to bed, when to do homework), the most frequent category at 51%; *not like me* (a discrepancy between how the girl saw herself and how she was seen and reacted to by her mother), 20%; *dependency* (the daughter wanting help or advice from the mother), 13%; unfairness (the daughter feels she is treated unfairly), 9%; and a remaining 7% coded as *minor-scope* conflicts (e.g. brushing hair painfully, losing a sandwich box).

The researchers were interested in what emotions the girls felt during these conflicts, and how much variation there was in the types of conflicts and the emotions experienced. Generally, having more conflicts meant experiencing a greater range of emotional states, but the researchers actually found a curvilinear relationship here; for a small number of girls who reported the most conflicts, the range of emotional variability was less. These girls and their mothers seemed caught in a rigid pattern of re-enacting similar conflicts, through the year.

Autonomy comes out of many studies as a key area for conflict. A study of Asian-American adolescents in the USA (Juang et al., 1999) found that in families where parents allowed an earlier timetable of autonomy, adolescents reported greater closeness to parents and higher self-esteem. This might suggest that parents should 'give in' to adolescent demands, but clearly there are arguments both ways, and a lot may depend on how autonomy is defined.

Wang, Pomerantz and Chen (2009) distinguished three relevant aspects, which they labelled as *psychological control* (including guilt induction, love withdrawal and authority assertion), *psychological autonomy support* (facilitating choices, opinion exchange), and *behavioural control* (talking about free time activities, having rules about time out). Early adolescents aged 12–13 years took part in a 6-month longitudinal study, in Chicago, USA, and Beijing, China. They reported on their parent's behaviour to them, and their own psychological functioning; and their academic grades were the same. On the whole, the findings were similar in the two countries. First, psychological control predicted negative effects over time on emotional well-being. Second, psychological autonomy support predicted positive effects over time for both emotional well-being and academic achievement—these effects being stronger in the USA than China. Third, behavioural control predicted gains in academic achievement. This suggests that parents of adolescents have a fine line to tread—some rules are important, but discussion and flexibility that acknowledge the young person's own feelings and desires are also necessary.

Adolescent bedtimes

One area where some parent–adolescent conflict may be difficult to avoid concerns adolescent bedtimes. Wolfson and Carskadon (1998) documented how, in a US sample of over 3,000 young people aged 13–19 years in Rhode Island schools, sleep patterns changed through the adolescent period. Late bedtimes became more frequent, together with much later rising at weekends (a pattern called *delayed phase preference*). Despite the late weekend rising, these students got less sleep overall than they wanted or needed, and those getting less sleep reported greater negative or depressed moods, and also did less well at school.

Kelley et al. (2015) have reviewed evidence that the delayed phase preference is a natural consequence of the biological changes in adolescence. Adolescents typically have what they call a *wake maintenance zone*, in which a pacemaker in the hypothalamus maintains a state of alertness later into the evening than was the case in childhood; this appears to be linked to the onset of puberty, and occurs earlier in girls. It only starts to reverse from around 20 years.

Sleep duration also decreases with age, from infancy onwards, but adolescents still need more sleep than adults. The consequence, Kelley et al. argue, is that normal adult wake times mean that adolescents are typically sleep deprived, with adverse consequences for learning and well-being (as well as associated conflicts with teachers and grumpiness at school in the morning). They suggest that normal biological wake time for adolescents is about 8 am at 16 years and 9 am at 18 years and thus that optimal times to start school for them would be at 10 am or even 11 am.

Dr Paul Kelley, the first author of this review, was previously Head Teacher at Monkseaton High School in North Tyneside, England, and he carried out a pilot study at this school in 2010, starting school at 10 am, over a 2-year period. He reported that:

> There were very positive outcomes, both academic and in terms of health. Academic results went up, illness down and the atmosphere in the school changed. The students were not only much nicer to each other, they were much nicer to teachers. It was bliss . . . Nothing I had ever done in my teaching made such a difference.

A follow-up project, funded by the Wellcome Trust and the Educational Endowment Foundation, will involve 106 schools starting lessons at 10 am; it will also include lessons about sleep as part of the personal, social and health education curriculum (www.theguardian.com/lifeandstyle/2014/oct/09/study-teenage-sleep-patterns-assess-impact-learning).

Mood Disruption

Mood disruption—feeling depressed or having fluctuating moods—was identified by Arnett (1999) as another factor contributing to adolescent difficulties. Larson and Ham (1993) carried out an ingenious study with 483 10–14-year-olds in the USA. Students carried an electronic pager for 1 week, and recorded their emotional affect in response to randomized signals. They also filled in a life-events questionnaire. The 12–14-year-olds experienced significantly more negative affect than the 10–11-year-olds, and this was related to negative life events connected with family, as well as school and peers.

The 'Isle of Wight' study carried out by Michael Rutter and colleagues made an important contribution to examining mood disruption and the 'storm and stress' hypothesis of adolescence. The Isle of Wight, in the English Channel off the coast of Hampshire, provided a bounded area of population living in small towns and villages. Behavioural questionnaires were completed by parents and teachers for all the 14–15-year-olds on the island, numbering 2,303. The most detailed results, however, were obtained from two subsamples. One, of 200 teenagers, was a random sample of the total population; the other, of 304 teenagers, was of those with extreme scores from the parent and teacher questionnaires, which pointed to 'deviant' behaviour. The adolescents in both these subgroups were given further questionnaires and tests, and were interviewed individually by psychiatrists. Their parents and teachers were also interviewed. Two main areas are explored in the report (Rutter et al., 1976): one is the extent of conflict between adolescents and their parents (the 'generation gap'); the other, the extent of inner turmoil and of observed behavioural or psychiatric disorder (mood disruption or 'storm and stress'). A selection of the results are shown in Tables 19.7 and 19.8, based on

Table 19.7 Percentages of parents and 14-year-old children in the Isle of Wight study reporting conflicts and feelings of inner turmoil.

	Boys	Girls
Parental interview		
any altercation with parents	18	19
physical withdrawal	12	7
communication difficulties	24	9
Adolescent interview		
any altercation with parents	42	30
any criticism of mother	27	37
any criticism of father	32	31
any rejection of mother	3	2
any rejection of father	5	9
Often feel miserable or depressed (questionnaire)	21	23
Reported misery (psychiatric interview)	42	48
Observed sadness (psychiatric interview)	12	15

Source: Adapted from Rutter, M., Graham, P., Chadwick, O. & Yule, W. (1976). Adolescent turmoil: Fact or fiction? *Journal of Child Psychology and Psychiatry, 17,* 35–56.

Table 19.8 Percentages of those interviewed in the Isle of Wight study having any psychiatric disorder, at different ages.

	10 years	14–15 years	Adult (parent)
Males	12.7	13.2	7.6
Females	10.9	12.5	11.9

Source: Adapted from Rutter, M., Graham, P., Chadwick, O. & Yule, W. (1976). Adolescent turmoil: Fact or fiction? *Journal of Child Psychology and Psychiatry, 17,* 35–56.

the random sample of 200. Regarding the extent of conflicts, only about one parent in six reported any altercations or arguments with their children about when and where they went out, or about their choice of activities (Table 19.7). About one parent in three, however, said they disapproved of their youngster's clothing or hairstyles. The great majority of parents approved of their children's friends, and nearly all had discussed with them their plans after leaving school. Rather more of the teenagers themselves reported having altercations with parents. However, only about one-third made any criticism of their mother or father during the interview, and only a small percentage expressed outright rejection of either parent.

By and large, these results confirmed that the average adolescent was not in a state of crisis and severe conflict with parents. Nevertheless, such conflict did characterize a minority (for example, 9% of girls expressed outright rejection of their father; see Table 19.7). These difficulties were much greater in the children with some behavioural or psychiatric disorder (the second subgroup). Altercations with parents, physical withdrawal of children from the rest of the family and communication difficulties or problems parents had in 'getting through' to adolescents were all some three times more common in this sample.

What about mood disruption? Only about one-fifth of the adolescents reported on the questionnaire that they often felt miserable or depressed; from the psychiatric interview, nearly half were diagnosed as reporting miserable feelings, though a much smaller proportion actually looked sad in the interview (see Table 19.7). It would seem from this study that severe clinical depression is rare, but that some degree of inner turmoil may well characterize many adolescents.

In making judgements about adolescence as a stage, it is obviously necessary to compare with other ages and stages of development. In the Isle of Wight study, such comparisons were made for the prevalence of psychiatric disorder, as based on parental interview. Table 19.8 shows the rates of disorder for the teenagers at 14–15 years, for the same children at the age of 10 from a previous survey of psychiatric disorder, and for adults (the parents of the teenage sample). There was a rather modest peak in adolescence (though the adolescent interview data gave a slightly higher figure for disorder of 16.3% at this age). Again, this suggested that adolescent turmoil is not a myth, but that it should not be overexaggerated. As Rutter et al. (1976) concluded at the time, 'adolescent turmoil is a fact, not a fiction, but its psychiatric importance has probably been over-estimated in the past'.

Stop and Think

The Isle of Wight study was carried out several decades ago. Does Rutter's conclusion still seem valid?

RISK-TAKING BEHAVIOURS

Some degree of deviant or risk-taking behaviour, such as substance abuse, and minor delinquencies such as shoplifting are quite common in adolescence. Some more serious risk-taking behaviours, such as reckless driving, can have serious consequences. A study of various kinds of risk taking in Danish adolescents is described in Box 19.2. We saw earlier how Steinberg (2009) has seen increased risk taking as in part a consequence of brain changes in adolescence. These can affect both the balance of sensation seeking as opposed to self-regulation, and the sensitivity to rejection by peers.

In adolescence, peer groups may reinforce risk-taking behaviour. In an experimental study, Gardner and Steinberg (2005) simulated risky car-driving activities in a computer game. They compared adolescents and younger/older adults, either playing the game alone or with two peers. They also assessed risk preference and risk decision making in response to scenarios. On all three risk measures, there was a decrease with age but greater risk was taken when peers were present; however, there was a significant interaction between age and the peer condition. The presence of peers increased risk taking in adolescents (more than doubling the number of risks), much more than in younger or older adults. In another study using the risky car-driving game and fMRI measures of brain activity, Chein et al. (2011) showed that the peer condition increased activity in reward areas of the brain.

Box 19.2 Cultural bases of risk behaviour: Danish adolescents

In this study, risk behaviour (similar to, but wider than, reckless behaviour or delinquency) was assessed in 1,053 Danish adolescents. The authors wished to assess absolute levels of types of risk behaviour, and also see how these varied by community size and family type. In addition, they made comparisons with similar behaviours in the USA.

Like most Western societies, Denmark tends to what Arnett calls 'broad socialization', with few restrictions on adolescent behaviour; however, car driving is not permitted until 18 (and per capita, car ownership is about one-half of US levels). There is much better provision for cyclists than in many countries such as the USA or even the UK. Sex education, including knowledge of contraception, is provided in schools before adolescence.

Denmark had a rather homogeneous population of about 5 million at the time. One million lived in Copenhagen; there were three cities of 100,000–150,000, including Odense; and about four-fifths of the population lived in small cities (population less than 50,000). The researchers chose three schools/colleges each, in Copenhagen, Odense and Varde, a small town. Risk behaviours were measured by a short self-report questionnaire on the frequency of engaging in a variety of risk activities over the past year; participation rates were 99%. Family measures were taken using a family relationships questionnaire.

A sample of the results, broken down by age and sex, is given in Box Table 19.2.1. There are low rates of driving a car while drunk, but much higher rates of riding a bicycle while drunk. Rates of sex without contraception are quite considerable in older adolescence, although less than rates with contraception

(included not as a risk behaviour, but for comparison); in fact, those who engaged in sex with contraception were also more likely to do so without contraception. Marijuana use and cigarette dependency were fairly frequent, but use of cocaine or other drugs was very rare. All these risk behaviours increased with age, but shoplifting and vandalism peaked in the 16–17- year period. Generally, risk-taking behaviours were less frequent in girls, with the exception of sexual behaviours and cigarette dependence.

Family influences did not appear to be very strong in this study. There were few differences between intact and divorced or lone-parent families, for example, and no effects of parental strictness. However, lower parental monitoring did predict increased drink/ cycling, marijuana use and cigarette dependency, and poorer family relationships generally did predict greater risk of shoplifting and vandalism.

Many types of risk behaviour were greatest in Copenhagen (large city) compared with the smaller communities; for example, sex without contraception, cigarette dependency and marijuana use, and shoplifting; however, vandalism was more frequent in Odense (mid-size city).

Drawing comparison with US studies, the authors concluded that rates of sex without contraception are somewhat similar but since teenage pregnancy rates are much lower in Denmark, this may reflect occasional lapses in the Danish adolescents rather than a consistent pattern. The low rates of drink/driving (but high rates of drink/cycling) can be related to legal restrictions and cultural opportunities. Surprisingly, the authors do not comment on

Box Table 19.2.1   Prevalence (at least once during last year) of risk behaviours, in male (M) and female (F) Danish adolescents.

		12–13 years	14–15 years	16–17 years	18–20 years
Drink/cycling	M	18	56	77	76
	F	13	52	61	63
Drink/car driving	M	0	0	7	15
	F	0	0	2	8
Sex without contraception	M	4	4	25	42
	F	2	12	20	34
Sex with contraception	M	2	14	53	65
	F	3	15	43	75
Marijuana use	M	12	22	33	32
	F	10	13	22	24
Cigarette dependency (20 days in last month)	M	6	18	23	19
	F	5	18	18	33
Cocaine use	M	2	0	0	1
	F	0	0	1	2
Shoplifting	M	14	21	25	17
	F	5	16	14	11
Vandalism	M	18	38	33	34
	F	5	12	14	10

Source: Adapted from Arnett, J. & Balle-Jensen, L. (1993). Cultural bases of risk behaviour: Danish adolescents. *Child Development, 64*, 1842–1859.

the very low rates of hard drug use; they do comment that cigarette dependency is higher than in US studies, perhaps because of more intensive media anti-smoking campaigns in the US.

This study, cross-sectional in design, does potentially confound historical factors with what are apparently age changes (in Box Table 19.2.1, for example) but it could be argued that historical changes might not be very large over the 8-year period that represents the total age range in the study, at least compared with the size of age changes obtained. The data on risk behaviour and on family factors are all obtained from adolescent self-report, as is quite common in research of this kind, but other sources of data could help validate the conclusions. A strength of the study is the way it takes account of the social and legal context of the country of study, Denmark, and contrasts it with much more widely studied populations in the USA.

Based on material in Arnett, J. & Balle-Jensen, L. (1993). Cultural bases of risk behaviour: Danish adolescents. *Child Development, 64*, 1842–1859.

The reward could be showing off to gain status with peers; we also saw in Chapter 10 how the values of some (antisocial) peer groups may diverge greatly from those of teachers and parents in adolescence, and association with deviant peers may encourage delinquent behaviour, and earlier in this chapter, how early-maturing girls may be influenced in this way by an older peer group.

Monahan et al. (2009) used data from a longitudinal study of 1,354 juvenile offenders in the US (mainly male) to try to disentangle the effects of selection (choosing antisocial peers to affiliate with) and socialization (the effects of delinquent peers on the individual) (cf. discussion of gangs in Chapter 10). In middle adolescence they found evidence that both processes were at work but from ages 16 to 20, socialization appeared more of a factor than selection. After age 20, the impact of peers declined, a finding that the authors ascribe to greater autonomy with increased maturation.

Risk taking is usually considered in the psychological literature as a kind of problem behaviour. However, Ellis et al. (2012) suggested some reconceptualization of this, taking an evolutionary life-history perspective, rather similar to that of Belsky (2012) and colleagues on early puberty. They argue that risk taking can have adaptive functions for the individual adolescent; it may be a strategy to impress others in the peer group, and especially for boys to impress girls as romantic interests and dating become more important. Risk taking may be especially adaptive for adolescents growing up in harsh and unpredictable environmental situations—they have 'less to lose' by taking risks. This perspective is aimed not at condoning risk taking, but at understanding its causes. From a societal viewpoint, delinquency and risky driving (for example) have important negative consequences. But Ellis et al. argue that their perspective has important implications for which kind of interventions will or will not be effective. They suggest that exhortations and programmes to raise awareness of risks may even be counterproductive, as they could increase the status of the risk-taking activities. Rather, interventions should tackle the adverse environmental conditions that lead to an increase in risk taking; give clear incentives for reducing risk taking; and provide alternative status-enhancing routes for adolescents, which are not so risky for them or potentially harmful to others.

ADOLESCENCE IN DIFFERENT CULTURES

So far, we have looked mainly at adolescents in Western societies. We have seen that the view of adolescence as a difficult period does have some validity, even if it has probably been exaggerated by some writers (perhaps especially by psychoanalytic or clinical authors, such as Blos or Erikson, who would have come into most contact with the minority of adolescents who are particularly disturbed). But are such difficulties an inevitable part of puberty, sexual maturity and gaining independence from parents, or merely a product of our particular kind of society and the way we treat adolescents? Different cultures vary widely in the treatment of adolescents, as we have noted earlier in connection with puberty rites. However, although the extent of parent–child conflict may be less in some traditional societies, it has been argued to be a common feature (Schlegel & Barry, 1991).

Margaret Mead and Samoa

One study has often been quoted to support the view that adolescence can be a tranquil and conflict-free period. This is Margaret Mead's book *Coming of age in Samoa* (1928). In this, Mead described adolescence as 'the age of maximum ease', with 'an absence of psychological maladjustment'. Indeed, Samoan society as a whole was described as 'replete with easy solutions for all conflicts'. This picture of an island paradise was supported by drawing attention to two important differences between Samoan and American society at the time. The first related to the context of child-rearing. Compared with what, at its extreme at least, can be the oppressive and confining atmosphere of the Western nuclear family, the Samoans had a more open and extended family-rearing system, in which 'the child is given no sense of belonging to a small intimate biological family'. As a result, an adolescent who might be in disagreement with parents could easily go and stay with another relative. Human relationships were thus warm but diffuse.

The second point related to methods of child-rearing. There was little physical punishment of children by parents, and little repression or sense of guilt. Therefore, there was little for teenagers to rebel against. According to Mead, Samoan society 'never exerts sufficient repression to call forth a significant rebellion from the individual'. There was 'no room for guilt'. In particular, there was no guilt about sexual behaviour and experimentation before marriage. According to Mead, adolescents had 'the sunniest and easiest attitudes towards sex', and promiscuity and free love were the norm in the adolescent period.

Samoan society would thus seem to be about as different from the 'storm and stress' model of adolescence as one could imagine. Mead's work, and that of other anthropologists such as Ruth Benedict, suggested that the adolescent experience was entirely a matter of social structure and cultural pressures. The biological impact of puberty was of little consequence. As Franz Boas, the eminent anthropologist who supervised Mead's work in Samoa, put it: 'much of what we ascribe to human nature is no more than a reaction to the restraints put upon us by our civilization' (Boas, 1928).

Mead's work was influential for a long time, but not all writers on Samoa agreed with her interpretations. These disagreements were publicized by Australian anthropologist Derek Freeman (1983, 1999); he argued that Mead's methodology was poor and that she had simply found what she was looking for. The study was Mead's first (in a long and distinguished career) and at the age of 23 she did not 'really know much about fieldwork' (as Mead herself said). Although Mead reported that she had spent 9 months in Samoa, 'speaking the language and living in the conditions in which they lived', she only spent 6 weeks learning Samoan, and only 3 months on her study of adolescence. She did not live in the native way, but stayed with the only white family on Ta'u, the island where her interviews were carried out. Thus, it is not clear how much trust or rapport she had with the adolescents whom she interviewed (often about very personal matters such as sexual experience). Mead interviewed 50 girls and young women, but only half of these (aged 14–20) were past puberty. In fact, only 11 of these reported having heterosexual experience. Thus, Freeman suggested that Mead was selective in the way she interpreted her results, and was also misled by some female adolescents who, taking advantage of her naivety and poor understanding of the language, fooled her about the extent of their sexual adventures. One elderly Samoan lady, Fa'apua'a Fa'amu, who had known Mead well, testified to Freeman of just such hoaxing in a 1987 interview (Freeman, 1999, 2000). Freeman stated that both earlier and later studies of Samoa give a different overall picture from Mead's. Recent studies (and reports by older Samoans of their society in the 1920s) suggest that family bonds are strong, that physical punishment is used, that brides are expected to be virgins (in one survey, Freeman (1999) found that about three-quarters are virgins), and that strong emotions including sexual jealousy and competitiveness are common.

Not all researchers agree with all Freeman's conclusions. He based many of his contentions on his own work in Samoa in the 1940s and 1960s yet, due to the influence of Christian missionaries and American military bases, Samoan society might have already changed greatly since the 1920s. But further analysis of Mead's writings and of how she obtained her evidence (Freeman, 2000, plus commentaries) does strongly suggest that the picture of an adolescent paradise may have been more of a wish-fulfilment dream than a reality. An interesting archive of material on Mead's work in Samoa, including photographs, letters and field notes, is available at www.loc.gov/exhibits/mead/field-samoa.html.

Stop and Think

Have Mead's conclusions about adolescence in Samoa in the 1920s been effectively challenged?

Broad and Narrow Socialization

Arnett (1992) has drawn attention to the trend in Western societies for adolescents to be overrepresented in categories of what he calls 'reckless behaviour', primary components of which are: having sex without contraception; delinquency and crime; illegal drug use; and driving at high speeds and while drunk. While reviewing evidence that these may be influenced by hormonal changes, cognitive factors such as adolescent egocentrism and peer influences, he also draws attention to marked cultural differences. He summarizes this in terms of a distinction between narrow and broad socialization patterns.

Arnett argues that narrow socialization is characterized by firm expectations of, and restrictions on, personal (including adolescent) behaviour. He argues that this will be typical of smaller societies, usually preindustrial, in which neighbours know each other. Family, peers and community (and the mass media, if present) will all tend to act to reduce reckless behaviour, though at the expense of producing conformity and reducing independence and creativity. By contrast, broad socialization is characterized by few personal restrictions. There are more expectations of self-expression and autonomy. Arnett argues that this will be typical of modern Western societies, with large diverse communities. There is less conformity and more creativity, but also more reckless behaviour. An example of a study in this framework, carried out in Denmark, was given in Box 19.2.

Arnett does not make judgements about which system is better. Each has costs and benefits. Some societies have been in transition; Russia, the Eastern European countries and to some extent China, for example, have relaxed personal restrictions, but with consequent increases in delinquency and sexual experimentation, often in adolescents.

HISTORICAL CHANGES IN ADOLESCENT BEHAVIOUR

We have already seen how, even within a culture, there can be important historical changes in adolescent behaviour. Earlier, we noted the considerable historical changes in the age of puberty through the later 19th and 20th centuries, and Figure 19.7 showed differences in affective closeness to parents, in cohorts only 20–25 years apart. We will end the chapter with a look at historical changes in three other areas: sexual attitudes and behaviour; leisure interests and ICT; and adolescent mental health.

Sexual Attitudes and Behaviour

Attitudes to sexual matters generally changed markedly during the latter half of the 20th century (Herold & Marshall, 1998; Wellings, 2009). For example, masturbation was seen as a vice in parents' manuals 100 years ago, but it became much more socially acceptable by the 1970s, and current medical opinion is that masturbation is normally harmless and is the usual way in which young males first reach orgasm following puberty.

Attitudes to premarital sexual intercourse also changed. Over the 1960s and 1970s, surveys showed that older generations had much less permissive attitudes on such matters than younger people. A historical trend has been working through Western populations and, although premarital sexual intercourse is far from universally accepted, in many societies a majority regard it as permissible (indeed, rates of marriage have also fallen in recent decades, as discussed in Chapter 4). However, there is still a lot of cultural variation in such matters. Ma (1989) reported a comparison of attitudes to premarital sex in university students in the USA and in Taiwan. In the USA, this was widely seen as permissible within an affectionate relationship, but amongst the Chinese students in Taiwan no sexual intercourse before marriage was most common.

These general changes in attitudes are reflected in changes in behaviour, noticeably an earlier age of first intercourse. A lot of this work was done in the 1960s and 1970s; the interest shown by social scientists at this time probably reflects the considerable changes happening in sexual attitudes and behaviour. There was then a drop in interest until the spread of the AIDS virus in the 1980s (Cowan & Johnson, 1993).

In the UK, the Schofield Report of 1965 was based on a sample of 2,000 adolescents aged 15–19. They reported going through successive stages of sexual experience. Dating was usually the first form of independent contact with a member of the opposite sex, often leading to kissing. Further forms of petting included breast stimulation under clothes and direct touching or stimulation of the partner's genitals. These heavier forms of 'petting' usually preceded full sexual intercourse, which only a minority of the sample reported having had (Table 19.9). A similar survey in the UK was reported by Farrell in 1978. This showed that the increased permissiveness in sexual attitudes had been reflected by an increased incidence of sexual behaviour in young people. Table 19.9 shows how the proportion of teenagers reporting having had sexual intercourse at 17 and 19 years of age approximately doubled in males and tripled in females over the period between the two studies.

Breakwell and Fife-Schaw (1992) surveyed sexual behaviour in over 2,000 16–20-year-olds. The pattern of results for sexual intercourse (see Table 19.9) suggests a continuing trend to earlier sexual activity, and a disappearance of any 'double standard' of greater permissiveness for males than females.

Table 19.9   Percentage of participants reporting having had sexual intercourse in three UK studies of adolescents.

	At 17 years		At 19 years	
	Males	**Females**	**Males**	**Females**
Schofield, 1965	25	11	37	23
Farrell, 1978	50	39	74	67
Breakwell & Fife-Schaw, 1992	60	60	77	80

Note: Figures from Breakwell and Fife-Schaw (1992) are an average of their 16–17/17–18 and 18–19/19–20 percentages.

A similar change over historical time has been found in American studies, and in Norway and Sweden (Sundet et al., 1992), but the same trend has not been found in many non-Western societies (Wellings, 2009). No doubt many factors contributed to these changes in attitudes and behaviour, including increased affluence and a greater availability of effective contraceptives.

Leisure Pursuits

Adolescents spend a great deal of time in leisure pursuits, often with media products: watching TV and videos, playing computer games, surfing the internet and using social networking sites, playing music; these can take up a half or more of a young person's waking hours (see Table 8.1). They also spend a lot of time 'hanging out' with friends.

Some of these leisure activities, such as watching TV, may be rather passive activities. However, Larson (2000) pointed to the positive aspects of leisure activities such as sports, arts, hobbies and clubs. He argued that modern Western societies lack such clear roles and responsibilities for adolescents as are found in most traditional societies, and that as a result many adolescents lack activities suitable for developing initiative in a context that can build identity and self-esteem. He thinks that such activities require both *intrinsic motivation*—the young person must want to take part—and *concerted engagement*, a concentration in order to meet some challenge in the activity. In work on high-school adolescents (aged about 15 years) in the USA, he assessed these in four major contexts (Table 19.10). School and classwork experiences

Table 19.10   High-school adolescents' ratings of their psychological state, in four contexts.

	Intrinsic motivation	Concentration
In class	−.46	+.20
With friends	+.34	−.12
During sports	+.48	+.37
Arts and hobbies	+.53	+.60

From high (+1) to low (1).
Source: Adapted from Larson, R.W. (2000). Towards a psychology of positive youth development. *American Psychologist*, 55, 170–183.

are moderately challenging, but are not self-chosen and score low on intrinsic motivation (for most pupils); time with friends is enjoyable, but does not usually evoke much concentration. However, both sports activities and arts and hobbies score high on both counts. The activities of Girl Scouts selling cookies, described in Box 2.2, would be just such an activity.

Larson argued that such activities provide a context for 'positive youth development' and that outcome studies show benefits for higher aspirations and self-esteem and lower rates of delinquency. A difficulty with many such outcome studies is that they are prone to self-selection: adolescents who are already better adjusted may preferentially choose such activities. The context is very important. A study in Sweden of youth recreation centres (Mahoney et al., 2001) found that these were often attended by youths with problem behaviour, and that attendance at the youth centres actually correlated with increased criminal offending! This finding may relate to the influence of deviant peer groups in adolescence, discussed earlier (p. 660) and in Chapter 10.

However, the nature of leisure pursuits in adolescence has changed rapidly over the last decade with the increased use of information and communication technologies (ICT), discussed also in Chapter 8.

Mobile Phones and the Internet

The 21st century has seen a tremendous increase in penetration and use of mobile phones and the internet. Their proliferation has been a remarkable history-related change (see Figure 8.1 and pp. 87–9), which in its effects may exceed those of the advent of television in the 1950s. Much use of the internet is for surfing, emailing, chatrooms, blogging and getting information generally, but an increasing use among young people has been *social networking*. Social networking sites such as Facebook, MySpace and Bebo are open to all ages but are heavily used by adolescents.

A European research project, EU Kids Online, has examined online activities amongst children and adolescents across 25 European countries (Livingstone, Haddon, Görzig & Ólafsson, 2011). A major part of this was a quantitative survey of about 1,000 children aged 9–16 years, in each country. The survey, carried out in 2010, encompassed questions about internet use, digital literacy, coping responses, perceptions and safety practices. The survey found that 93% of 9–16-year-olds went online at least weekly, and 60% daily; for 15–16-year-olds, 80% went on the internet daily. The main activities online for the 13–16-year-olds were school work (89% over the past month), watching video clips (86%), visiting a social networking profile (81%), playing games (80%), instant messaging (77%) and sending/receiving emails (75%). A majority—73% of 13–14-year-olds and 82% of 15–16-year-olds—had a social networking profile.

This survey found that the majority of online activity is sociable and useful or enjoyable, but there are risks as well as opportunities. A focus of this survey was on risks and safety on the internet. Risks could include sexting (see earlier section), exposure to inappropriate content such as pornographic materials or content of a violent or racist nature, and receiving unwelcome contact, perhaps sexual (e.g. grooming, sexual harassment) or being cyberbullied (discussed in Chapter 10). Meeting an online contact offline without adequate precautions, which can be particularly dangerous, was much less frequent.

There were gender differences in risk, with boys more likely to be involved in conduct risks and with girls more affected by content and contact risks. Exposure to risks increased with age—49% of 13–14-year-olds and 63% of 15–16-year-olds said they had encountered one or more. However, not all risks are perceived by them as harmful—for example, sexting is only perceived as harmful in certain circumstances. A minority, 12% of 13–14-year-olds and 15% of 15–16-year-olds, said that they had been bothered or upset by something on the internet.

In the UK, Ofcom provides yearly surveys of media use, and these have documented a steady increase in ICT usage since they started in 2003. Detailed patterns of usage change rapidly; for example, the use of tablet computers has increased in the last few years. An Ofcom (2014b) report gives information on children's media use and attitudes from data gathered in 2012–2014. Some relevant findings for adolescents aged 12–15 years are shown in Table 19.11.

Social networking site profiles are now an important aspect of affirming identity for most adolescents in Western societies (Boyd, 2014). Just as teenagers decorate their bedrooms with images and posters, they also design and adorn their personal web pages and their profiles. Livingstone and Brake (2009) quote Danielle, aged 13, as saying, 'You can just change it all the time [and so] you can show different sides of yourself' (p. 76).

The evidence suggests that adolescents move flexibly between many forms of media use and communication (obviously facilitated by the development of mobile phones that can access the internet). Often, they are sustaining friendships that are also present in the offline world. However, the internet probably helps maintain a very wide circle of friends. There has been debate about how the internet has impacted on adolescent friendships. Valkenburg and Peter (2011) discuss two competing hypotheses. The *displacement hypothesis* supposes that online friendships are more superficial than face-to-face contacts, whereas the *stimulation hypothesis* claims that the quantity and quality of online communication can enhance close-ness and intimacy. While the latter seems more supported by the evidence so far, this is a fast-developing area. Amichai-Hamburger, Kingsbury and Schneider (2013) have considered

Table 19.11 Some main findings on media use in UK adolescents aged 12–15 years, from Ofcom (2014b).

Almost 80% own a mobile phone; 59% go online using a mobile phone.

Ownership of a smart phone rises from 41% of 12-year-olds to 67% of 13-year-olds.

Of those using a smart phone, popular activities are arranging to meet friends (71%), messaging friends (53%), looking at photos posted online (47%) and sharing photos they have taken (45%).

Although the TV set remains the most used media device for younger children, 12–15-year-olds spend more time going online (17.2 hours/week) than watching television (15.7 hours/week); and 37% say they would miss their mobile phone, whereas only 18% say they would miss TV.

Three-quarters (76%) have watched YouTube channels.

Of those going online, 70% have a social media profile, Facebook being the most popular. Also popular are YouTube (especially boys), and Instagram and SnapChat (especially girls).

Concerns or dislikes about social media sites are more common in girls (73%) than boys (52%); and parents of girls are more likely than parents of boys to mediate their media use by checking and supervising.

Source: Ofcom (2014b). *Children and parents: Media use and attitudes report.* London: Office of Communications.

internet friendships in the light of the functions and characteristics of friendships (as reviewed in Chapter 5).

In a discussion of teenagers' use of social networking sites, Boyd (2014) uses the phrase *networked publics* to describe how adolescents can congregate on virtual communities online, just as they might previously have congregated in public spaces such as shopping malls. She also argues that networked publics create new opportunities or affordances: *persistence* (the durability of online expressions and content); *visibility* (the potential audience); *spreadability* (the ease with which content can be shared); and *searchability* (the ability to find content). In the US context at least, she argues that there are reduced offline opportunities, with parents increasingly concerned about safety, and that 'social media . . . is a release valve, allowing youth to reclaim meaningful sociality as a tool for managing the pressures and limitations around them' (p. 95).

There have been some concerns about the effects of adolescents spending so much time on ICT activities. The EU Kids Online project (Livingstone et al., 2011) found that about 29% of 13–14-year-olds and 36% of 15–16-year-olds said that they had spent less time than they should with friends, family or doing schoolwork because of time spent online. Excessive or problematic internet use, often referred to as *internet addiction* or *problematic internet use* (Caplan, 2010; Leung & Lee, 2012), can be associated with a range of risks, including cyber-bullying and harassment, invasion of privacy, and exposure to pornographic and violent content. However, while acknowledging possible dangers, Boyd (2014) argues that generally the concerns of parents and others are misplaced, and that in most cases any addiction of teenagers is to social networking rather than to the technology itself.

One study in Finland, by Punamaki et al. (2009), surveyed 10- and 13-year-olds from seven urban schools; they were asked about four types of ICT use, three measures of peer relations and four measures of parent–child communication (Table 19.12). The first thing to notice is that all the correlations are fairly low; it does not appear that ICT usage is having a major impact on, or relationship to, the peer and parents variables measured. However, a lot of playing digital games did relate negatively to quality of friendships (Bukowski's scale; see Chapter 5) and to open and positive communication with mothers. On the other hand, a lot of emailing and internet chatting correlated with being less lonely with peers (as measured by Asher's loneliness scale; see Chapter 5), although there was less easy and positive communication with both mothers and fathers. A lot of internet surfing also related to negative parent communication, whereas using the internet for information seeking did not.

Adolescent Mental Health

It is a common complaint that adolescent behaviour, and problems such as delinquency, are getting worse. As we saw in Chapter 1 (p. 212), these worries can date back a long time, even centuries. But is there any truth in recent concerns? A couple of studies in the UK suggested there were grounds for concern, up to the beginning of the 21st century, with recent follow-ups producing conflicting trends.

A report from Scotland by West and Sweeting (2003) compared Scottish 15-year-olds living in or around Glasgow on mental health (the General Health Questionnaire or GHQ, a well-established measure) in 1987 and 1999. Scores had got worse with time, not significantly for boys but significantly for girls. A further report by Sweeting et al. (2008) also used similar data obtained in 2006. There was a continued worsening of scores, now significant for both sexes but more marked for girls.

Table 19.12 Correlations of ICT use with peer and parent relationships in early adolescence.

Type of ICT use	Playing digital games	Learning and information seeking	Communication by email and chatting	Internet surfing
Peer popularity	−.07	.05	.02	.00
Loneliness	.05	−.04	−.09*	.02
Friendship quality	−.17***	.03	.08	−.04
Open communication with mother	−.12**	−.02	−.15***	−.15**
Open communication with father	−.06	−.00	−.18***	−.16**
Conflicting communication with mother	.04	.05	.08	.08
Conflicting communication with father	.02	−.01	.09	.07*

*p < .05 **p < .01 ***p < .001.
Source: Punamaki, R. L. et al. (2009). The associations between information and communication technology (ICT) and peer and parent relations in early adolescence. *International Journal of Behavioral Development, 33,* 556–564.

Another report, by Collishaw et al. (2004), was based on representative sampling across the UK, using Child Benefit records. It obtained Strengths and Difficulties Questionnaire (SDQ) ratings from parents of 15-year-olds in 1974, 1986 and 1999. The authors reported that conduct problems had consistently increased over the three time periods, for both sexes; there was also some increase in emotional problems, but no consistent trend for hyperactivity. This work, funded by the Nuffield Foundation, led to a booklet, *Time trends in adolescent well-being* (Nuffield Foundation, 2004). Maughan et al. (2008) produced a further analysis with data obtained in 2004 (see also Nuffield Foundation, 2009). On most measures there were small improvements from 1999 to 2004, plus a small increase in prosocial behaviour. This was true for the parental reports (used in the previous surveys) but also for teacher reports, and young-people's self-ratings on the same dimensions. This research, contrary to the Scottish study, suggests that any increase in problems has levelled off and perhaps declined modestly, although as the authors state, 'rates of emotional and behavioural problems remain considerably higher than in the 1970s and 1980s' (Maughan et al., 2008, p. 310).

As the Nuffield report also makes clear, there have been some increases in adolescent problems reported in the USA, but which levelled off in the 1990s, and no notable increase in the Netherlands in the same period. We know there are considerable cross-national differences in child and adolescent well-being (see Chapter 1 and Table 1.2), with the Netherlands doing well on such indices and the UK and USA doing poorly—at least using data from around the 2001–2003 period. These indices may give some clues to understanding the reasons for the increases in problems in the UK. Maughan et al. (2008) did examine a range of demographic factors (education, family type, income, housing) in relation to the changes, but only family size interacted significantly in the 1999–2004 comparison, with improvements more noticeable for larger families. Overall, they comment, 'As yet, the factors underlying time trends in child emotional and behavioural difficulties are largely unknown' (Maughan et al., 2008, p. 310).

Nevertheless, these trends are likely to have major societal ramifications. A report from the Sainsbury Centre for Mental Health (2009), *Childhood mental health and life chances in post-war Britain* , uses data from three national birth cohort studies (see Table 1.1) to document that 'Mental health problems in childhood and adolescence are common and they cast a long shadow over our lives. They affect not only our mental health as adults but also our chances of doing well at school and in work, of forming strong families and of becoming good citizens' (p. 2).

CHAPTER SUMMARY

- Adolescence is signalled by the onset of puberty. Timing of puberty varies between individuals and also shows changes over historical time. Puberty is accompanied by physical changes, hormonal changes and changes in brain organization. It brings about increased interest in romantic and sexual behaviours, usually but not always with the opposite sex.
- Early or late maturation can have psychological consequences; for example, in girls, some greater risk of delinquent behaviour.
- Adolescence is often seen as a time of 'storm and stress', as young people gain independence from parents and seek out their identity in various domains. This period can be marked by increased conflict with parents, mood disruption and risk-taking behaviours.
- There are cultural variations in the nature of adolescence but an early attempt to portray Samoa as a culture where adolescence was 'the age of maximum ease' has been largely discredited.
- There are notable historical effects in the nature of adolescence, including changes in sexual attitudes and behaviours; increased use of new communication technologies and social networking sites; and some indications in the UK that mental health problems have increased in the last few decades.

DISCUSSION POINTS

1. Does the biological phenomenon of puberty have any direct psychological effects?
2. How have recent advances in studying the adolescent brain thrown light on behavioural changes?
3. Is there an 'identity crisis' at adolescence?
4. Why might parent–child closeness change during adolescence?
5. Is adolescence inevitably a period of 'storm and stress'?

FURTHER READING

- A good general overview remains Coleman, J.C. (2010). *The nature of adolescence* (4th ed.). London: Routledge, while Steinberg, L. (2010). *Adolescence* (10th ed.). New York: McGraw-Hill, is another very successful textbook. Smetana, J.G. (2011). *Adolescents, families, and social development*. Chichester, Wiley-Blackwell, focuses most on parent–adolescent relations. A useful edited collection is Lerner, R.M. & Steinberg, L. (Eds.) (2009). *Handbook of adolescent psychology*. Hoboken, NJ: John Wiley & Sons. Arnett, J. (2010). *Adolescence and emerging adulthood: A cultural approach*. Englewood Cliffs, NJ: Prentice Hall, and Kerig, P.K., Schulz, M.S. & Hauser, S.T. (Eds.) (2012). *Adolescence and beyond*. Oxford: Oxford University Press, take work on adolescence through to the early adult years.
- Tanner, M. (1973). Growing up. *Scientific American, 229*, 35–43 gives a succinct overview of the now classical work on physical aspects of adolescence. More detail is available in Tanner's books (e.g. (1978). *Fetus into man* (2nd ed., 1990), Cambridge, MA: Harvard University Press; and (1981). *A history of the study of human growth*, Cambridge: Cambridge University Press). For work on identity, see Kroger, J. (2004). *Identity in adolescence* (3rd ed.). London: Psychology Press.
- For adolescent mental health see Hagell, A. (2012). *Changing adolescence: Social trends and mental health*. Bristol: Policy Press.
- For updates on the EU Kids Online research, visit www.lse.ac.uk/media@lse/research/EUKidsOnline/Home.aspx

INDEX

Note: Abbreviations used: ASD for autism spectrum disorder; ToM for theory of mind; vs. for *versus*

11-plus examination 588
5-HTTLPR gene 37, 133, 355

ABE (achieving best evidence)
    guidelines, eyewitness
    testimony 507
ability EI (emotional
    intelligence) 211
absent fathers 137–8, 141
abstract reasoning, formal
    operational stage 465–6
abuse
    effects on mental health 329,
      330–1
    leading to offending
      behaviour 330
    and maltreatment 149–54
academic achievement/
    performance
    family interventions 628–9
    link to media use 272–3,
      277–8, 292–3
    and timing of maturation
      662
accommodation, Piaget 448
acculturation 192
active engagement
    collective argumentation
      564–8
    in cultural practices 562–3
    important educational tool
      569–70
active vs. social self 215–16
adaptability and intelligence
    592
adaptation, Piaget 447–8
adolescence
    anonymous & altruistic
      helping 300
    antiestablishment stance 332
    biological and physical
      changes 646–53
    boys' aggression linked to
      TV violence 276
    characteristics of perceived
      popularity 179
    'cliques'/'crowds'/'gangs'
      171–2

conflicts with parents 673–5
conventional morality
    320
cultural variations 681–3
friendships, instability of
    185–7
historical changes in
    behaviour 684–90
identity development 670–3
maturation, effects of early
    and late 660–2
mood disruption 676–8
passive acceptance of
    bullying 306–7
peer relations 663–5
as period of turmoil 669–78
psychological effects of
    puberty 653–60
risk-taking behaviours
    678–81
romantic development 665–7
sexuality 667–9
sleep patterns 675–8
social-cognitive map of peer
    group structure 173
views on rights of asylum-
    seekers 324–8
and youth crime 329–31
adoption studies 34–5
Adult Attachment Interview
    (AAI) 119–20
    AAI scores linked to infant's
      SS coding 122–3
adult-child (A-C) speech 437–9
advergames 288
advertising 282–8
    advergames 288
    children's understanding of
      285–6
    effects on children 288
    product placement 286–8
    unhealthy foods 282–5
age of moral responsibility
    329–31
aggression 342–3
    callous-unemotional (CU)
      traits 351–2
    and delinquency 356–7

developmental changes
    345–6
and dominance status 342
evolutionary perspective
    347–9
genetic factors 350–1
interventions to reduce
    357–8
linked to video game play
    280–1
as maladaptive behaviour or
    social competence
    346–9
mediation reducing 310–13
neighbourhood factors
    354–5
oppositional defiant disorder
    (ODD) 355
and parental social skills
    352–3
peer group factors 353–4
and popularity 178
on television, influence of
    275–8
and temperament 350–1
and toy guns/war play
    247–8, 258
types of 343–5
Ainsworth, Mary 109, 110,
    116
alliteration 418–20
    training study 420–2
altruistic behaviour 298
    charitable giving experiment
      300–1
ambiguous drawing, interpreta-
    tion of 528–9
ambivalent (C type) attachment
    110, 115, 118, 122, 123,
    129
American Academy of
    Pediatrics (AAP), screen
    viewing times 271–2
animal communication 47–8
anthropological studies
    58–61
antipathetic relationships
    190–1

antisocial behaviour
    callous-unemotional (CU)
        traits predicting 352
    delinquency 356
    developmental progression
        352–3
    gene-environment interaction
        350–1
    intergenerational effects 353
    low trait EI as risk factor
        214
    reinforced by peer group
        353–4
    risk factors 625–6
Apgar scoring technique 88
appearance-reality distinction
    523
apprenticeship learning,
    guided participation
    562–4
argumentation, role in learning
    565–6
Arnett, J., risk behaviour
    679–80
articulation problems 427
assertiveness training, victims
    of bullying 369–70
assessment of IQ see intel-
    ligence tests
assimilation, Piaget 448
asylum seeking youth, rights of
    325–8
attachment relationships
    108–9
    Adult Attachment Interview
        119–20
    beyond infancy 117–19
    criticism of attachment
        theory 124
    and day care quality 132
    disorganized attachment
        116–17
    in Dogon people, Mali
        113–15
    environmental vs. genetic
        influences 112, 116
    security of attachment
        110–12
    stability over generations
        122–4
    stability over time 120–1
attainment tests 601–3
attention
    shared 241, 541
    tasks for strategy
        development 487–8

attractiveness
    early recognition of attractive
        faces 391
    facial proportions 55, 56
    and social status 174, 178,
        179
    and TV stereotypes 274, 275
auditory perception 398–401
authoritarian parents 142, 143
authoritative parents 142, 143
autism spectrum disorder
    (ASD) 533–41
Autonomous adults, attach-
    ment 120, 122, 123
autonomous morality, Piaget
    316, 317
avoidant (A type) infants 110,
    111, 115, 118, 122, 123

babbling 408–10
baby signing (BS) 411
Baillargeon, R., object
    separation 395, 396–7
balance scale problem,
    children's strategies
    478–83
Balle-Jensen, L., risk behaviour
    679–80
Baltes, Paul, life-span
    development 8
Baron-Cohen, S., theory of
    mind 534–5, 540–1
Bavarian Longitudinal Study,
    very preterm babies 92–4
befriending, peer support 308
behavioural genetics 32–6
beliefs see understanding of
    mind
Belsky, J
    day care studies 131, 133–4
    parenting model 154–6
bias 19–20
bilingualism 416
Binet, A. 444–5, 580–2, 596
Binet-Simon scale 581–2, 587–8
    revisions of 582–3
bipedalism 86
birth canal, restrictive width 86
birth order 169–70
birth process (parturition) 86–8
blind children, language
    development 440
body-kinaesthetic intelligence
    590
body mass index (BMI) and
    pubertal timing 652

body size satisfaction in
    girls, media
    influence 274
Bofi foragers and farmers,
    weaning 59–61
bonding of mother with
    newborn 100
Bowlby, John
    maternal deprivation
        hypothesis 125–9
    phases in development of
        attachment 108–9, 118
Boyland, E.J., celebrity
    endorsement and food
    choice 283–5
Bradley, L., learning to read
    420–2
brain development 40–1
    at puberty 657–9
brain size 55, 85, 86
Brazilian street vendors,
    mathematical
    competence of 570–3
breastfeeding 89–90, 103
Bronfenbrenner, Urie 5, 15, 21,
    22, 607, 638
    ecological model of human
        development 10–12
Brooks-Gunn, J., Early Head
    Start evaluation 633–5
Bruner, Jerome 555–6, 569–70
Bryant, P.E., learning to read
    420–2
bullying (in school) 358–9
    acceptance of by older
        children 306–7
    attitudes towards 366
    causes of 366–7
    consequences of victimiza-
        tion 367–8
    cyberbullying 364–5
    disclosure 366
    gathering data on 359–62
    gender differences in 366
    incidence figures 365–6
    interventions against
        368–74
    types of 362–4
Burt, Cyril 21, 588

calendar calculating, savant
    ability 594–6
callous-unemotional (CU)
    traits 351–2
'canalization' of behaviour
    42–4, 63

Cappotelli, H., sociometric status 173, 174–5

Carraher, D.W., maths of street vendors 570–3

cartoon test, bullying 360–1

categorical perception, sounds 400

categorization of others, infants 202–3

Ceci, S.J., preschoolers' reports, effect of stereotypes 499–502

Cefai, C., Circle Time for social & emotional learning 216–18

celebrity endorsement and children's choice of food 283–5

certification, attainment tests 601

Chan, A., adolescent friendship instability 185–7

Chazan-Cohen, R., Early Head Start evaluation 633–5

child abuse and maltreatment 149–54

child-directed speech 438

child-rearing
cross-cultural studies 221
Samoan society in the 1920s 682

childcare patterns, UK 156–7

childminding 130–1

children with learning difficulties 599

Children Act (2004) 23–4, 25, 331

Children's Rights Alliance for England (CRAE) 24

children's knowledge about the physical world, Vosniadou 556–61

Chinese parenting styles 143

Chomsky, innate basis of language 429–32

chromosomal abnormalities 38

chromosomes 32, 33

Circle Time (CT) 216–18

circular reactions, sensorimotor stage 448–50

citizenship curriculum 332

class inclusion tasks 458, 460–1

co-viewing, media intervention 293

coaching in formal thinking 467

code switching, Harris 195

cognition hypothesis of language development 434

cognition, Piaget's theory 444–6
assumptions 446–8
educational implications 468–9
overview of theory 468
stages 447, 448
concrete operational 464–5
formal operational 465–8
preoperational 453–64
sensorimotor 448–53

cognitive behaviour therapy (CBT), dyslexia programme 428

cognitive deficits, children born very prematurely 92–4

cognitive development
and breastfeeding 89–90
genes linked to 37–8
see also information processing approach

cognitive developmental approach 28, 225–6, 315

cognitive-functional linguistics, Tomasello 434–7

cognitive immaturity hypothesis 254, 259

cognitive interview (CI) 506–7

cognitive neuroscience 39–40, 657–9

cognitive skills from computer game playing 279

cohort and cohort-sequential designs 9–10

Coie, J.D., sociometric status 173, 174–5

Cole, ethnographic research 549–50

collective argumentation 564–8

collectivist vs. individualistic values 314–15, 323

colostrum, first milk after birth 89

communal child-rearing, Israeli kibbutzim 109, 129

communication systems in mammals 47–8

community of inquiry 568–9

community-based participatory action research (PAR) 620–4

compensation ability, Piaget 459

compensatory education programmes
continuing debate 638–40
in the UK 635–8
in the USA 631–5

competent infant 393

componential subtheory of intelligence 592–3

computational limitations 475

computational strategies, street children 570–3

computer games 248–9, 279–81

concrete operational stage, cognitive development 464–5
Piaget's views 464–5
reinterpretations of Piaget 465

conditioning 45–6
of infants' behaviour 384–5

confidentiality, research ethics 20–1

conflict and rivalry between siblings 165–6

conflict behaviours, dominance hierarchies 340

conflict resolution
girls better at 309
student-mediated 308, 310–13

conflict resolution between friends 182, 184–5

conservation, Piaget 458–60, 464
reinterpretations 461, 462–3

constancies, perceptual 392–3

constructive memory 494–6

constructive play 238, 256–7, 258

content validity 587

context of task and cognitive ability 465

contextual subtheory of intelligence 592

contextual view of intelligence 596–8

contingent responding, infants 96–8

controlled experiments 14

controlling parents 143
'controversial' children 173, 175, 178
conventional morality 319, 320
cookie sales study, sociocultural model of development 68, 69–71
cooperative group work (CGW) 574–5
cooperative learning 574–5
corporal punishment (CP) 147–9
correlational analyses 12–13
counselling, peer support in schools 308
creativity and play 255, 258
creole languages 432–3
criminal responsibility, age of 329–31
criterion-referenced tests 602
critical/sensitive period 44, 100, 611–12
cross-country differences, terms used for bullying 361–2
cross-sectional design 6, 9
crying, neonates 96
cultural context model of development, Cole 66–7
cultural differences
  adolescence 681–3
  attitudes to play 250
  in behaviour 63
  cognitive abilities 549–51
  in concept of intelligence 596–8
  early attachments 109–10
  language development 440
  parenting styles 143
  pretend play at home 244–5
  prosocial behaviour 313–15
  sex-role stereotypes 221
  Strange Situation 112, 114
cultural-ecological models 66–8
cultural experience and learning 548–9
cultural tools 551, 554, 562, 564
culturally disadvantaged groups, empowering 551
culture in animals 47, 49
culture and development 65–6
Cunningham, C.E., conflict-resolution study 310–13

curricular approaches to bullying 369
curriculum control 602
custody issues, divorced parents 145–6
cyberbullying 364–5

Danish adolescents, study of risk behaviour 679–80
Darwin, Charles 5, 55, 56, 204
data analysis 12–13
data recording 15–16
data types 19
dating violence 666
day care
  home-based, childminding 130–1
  NICHD study, USA 132–4
  nursery or centre-based 131–2
  overview of 134
deception
  evolution of 50–1
  failure in children with ASD 536
  false belief task 515–21
  in non-human primates 514
  young children's understanding of 516–19, 527
'deconstruction' of developmental psychology 73–4
decontextualization, pretend play 241–2
deferred imitation, Piaget 451, 453, 468
'deficit' model of deprivation 624–5
delayed phase preference 675–6
delinquency 660–2, 681
  Bowlby's link to separation 126
  concerns 21–2
  link to child abuse 153
  risk factors for 356
  sons, inverse link to father involvement 137
democratic education, learning communities 568–9
depression
  in children from divorced families 145, 146
  children high in relational aggression 345

and instability of early adolescent friendships 185–7
maternal, and insecurely attached infants 116
mood disruption in adolescents 676–8
victims of bullying 368
deprivation 606–7
  and academic underperformance 617–18
  explanatory models 624–5
  extreme cases of 607–12
  institutional rearing 612–16
depth perception 395, 398
development, defined 6
developmental changes in aggression 345–6
developmental cognitive neuroscience 40–1
developmental niche 68
diagnostic assessment 602
dialogical learning 564–8
diasthesis-stress model 64–5
'difference' model of deprivation 624–5
differential susceptibility 65
direct sanctions, bullying 370
disability-related bullying 363
disadvantaged children see socially disadvantaged children
discipline
  effect of harsh physical 148
  parenting styles 141–2
  smacking 148–9
discrimination 617–19
  positive 635
dishabituation 381, 384, 385
Dismissive adult, attachment 120, 122, 123
disorganized (D type) attachment 110, 111, 115, 116–17, 122, 123
disruptive behaviour 355
distress of others, responsiveness to 301–3
divorce 144–6
  grandparent involvement with children 139–40
dizygotic (DZ) twins 34
DNA sequencing 36–7
Dodge, K.A., sociometric status 173, 174–5

Dogon people, Mali, infant-mother attachment 113–15
domestic violence 143–4
dominance behaviour 340–2
Down syndrome (DS) 38–9
DRD4 7-repeat allele, interaction with quality of childcare 133–4
drug-addicted parents 304–5
dual-risk model 64–5
dyslexia 425–8, 599

E-S model of sex differences 81–2
early adversity, resilience 626–8
early intervention 625
    Project Head Start, US 631–5
    Sure Start, UK 635–8
early social behaviour/interactions 95–100
the earth, children's understanding of 556–61
echolalia 408
ecological model of development, Bronfenbrenner 10–12
ecological validity 15, 16
education
    imposition of Western style on developing cultures 576
    policy in the UK 588
    Vygotsky's and Bruner's views 569–70
    see also schooling; teaching methods
Education Act (1944) 588
educational games 279–80
educational underachievement
    compensatory education programmes 631–8
    'deficit' and 'difference' models 624–5
    discrimination & racial prejudice 617–18
    and poverty 638–9
egocentric speech, Piaget's observations 554, 555
egocentrism, Piaget 445, 454–5
    Borke's challenge 456–7
elaboration, encoding strategy 490
emotion in others, recognition of 204–6

emotion regulation 208–10
emotional abuse 150, 151
emotional development 203–6
    production of emotions 203–4
    recognition of emotion in others 204–6
    understanding of others' emotions, desires and beliefs 206–8
emotional intelligence 210–11
    and children's peer relations at school 212–14
    regulation of emotion 208–10
emotional literacy curriculum 332–3
    PATHS programme 333–5
emotional literacy programmes 216
empathy 300, 333
    and conflict resolution 309
    and emotion regulation 302, 333
    lack of, effect of abuse 329
    link to fetal testosterone levels 81–2
    and positive parenting 302–3
    progressive levels of 301
    and prosocial behaviour 300, 303
    sibling relationships 305
empowerment
    from preschool interventions 633
    young people traumatized by war 639
encoding strategies 474, 488–90
enemies 190–1
energetics of gestation and growth (EGG) hypothesis 86
energetics theory, pubertal timing 652
English and Romanian Adoptees (ERA) study 613–16
Enmeshed adults, attachment 120, 121, 122, 123
environment
    effects on perceptual development 400–1
    shared and non-shared 35–6, 194

epigenesis 41–2
'epigenetic landscape' 43–4
'epiphenomenal' model of play 262–3
'equifinality' model of play 262–3
Erikson, Erik
    eight developmental stages 669, 670
    'identity crisis' in adolescence 670–1
'essential' model of play 262
ethical issues in research 20–1
ethnicity
    and academic excellence 629
    and academic underachievement 617–18
    asylum seekers' family values 628–9
    and bullying 363
    cross-ethnic friendships 192–3
    differential susceptibility 355
    ethnic awareness/identity 228–9
    'social disadvantage' 624
    street children 619
    unbalanced media portrayal 274
ethnographic research 549–51
EU Kids Online survey, bullying 365
European Forum on the Rights of the Child 22
evolutionary approaches
    aggression 347–9
    criticisms of 63
    risk-taking behaviour 681
evolutionary developmental psychology 62–3
evolutionary psychology 62–3
evolutionary theory 55–8
    and human behaviour 58–62
examinations, selection purposes 601
exclusion from school 618
exercise play 237–8, 239, 251
exergames 281
experiential subtheory of intelligence 591–2
experimental techniques 16
experimenter effects, early studies of play 259

experts
  children as 574–5
  helping children learn,
    ZPD concept 551–2,
    569–70
  views of intelligence 590–1
exploration vs. play 236–7,
    256–7
externalizing problems
  antipathetic relationships
    191
  boys in single-parent families
    353
  and childcare quality 133
  and family status 157
  harsh maternal physical
    discipline 148
  interventions 357–8
  link to peer rejection 180
  maternal unresponsiveness 355
  and parental conflict 144
extreme deprivation 607–12
eye contact, mother-baby,
    language development
    408, 409, 440
eye-gaze, recognition by
    newborns 391
eyewitness research 497–8
  children's suggestibility
    498–505
  interview procedures 506–7
  stress and recall 507–9
  summary 509

face processing/recognition
    388–91, 663–4
  facial expression, infants'
    recognition of 391
  monkey faces, before 6
    months 382–4, 401
  mother's face 390–1
  neonates' interest in faces 96
  preference technique 381
false belief tasks
  Maxi task 515–20
  Sally-Anne task 520–1, 528,
    532, 534–5, 540
  Smarties task 520, 527, 535,
    538
false belief understanding 167,
    168
false inferences 494–5
falsification 27, 28
family
  and aggression in children
    354

and bullying 366, 367
composition and child
    outcomes 157
and delinquency 356
in development of prosocial
    behaviour 302–6
and peer relationships 193
role in children's academic
    performance 628–30
size, impact on development
    169–70
support, role of grandparents
    138–40
types 140–1
fantasy play see pretend play
Fantz, R.L., pattern perception
    387–9
Fast Track project, USA
    357–8
fathers
  fathering and child outcomes
    136–7
  involvement in child care
    134–6
  non-resident/absent 137–8
feelings, understanding of,
    PATHS curriculum
    332–5
female genital mutilation
    (FGM) 22–3
femininity 73–4
feral children 607–8
fetal learning 82
fetal reaction to mother's voice
    399
field experiments 14–15
first-borns
  jealousy and ambivalence
    towards new baby 164
  social competence of 168
  Sulloway's theory of birth
    order 170
'first-order' belief 528, 540
flexibility of behaviour 42–3
focus groups 16
food choice, effect of celebrity
    endorsement 283–5
formal operational stage of
    cognitive development
    465–8
  Piaget's work 465–6
  reinterpretations of Piaget
    466–8
fostering 130
Fouts, H.N., parent-offspring
    conflicts 59–61

free recall 497, 498, 506
Freud, Sigmund, views on play
    252
friendship 181–2
  adolescent, instability of
    185–7
  children's ideas about 183,
    184
  impact of internet on
    687–8
  importance of 188–90
  in multicultural settings
    192–3
  origins of 182–3
  quality of 183–5
  and sociometric status 190
Friendship Qualities Scale
    184–5
Froebel, Friedrich, ideas about
    play 251
functional play 234, 238

'g' factor, intelligence 589
games
  rule-based 249
  video and computer 248–9
games, infant-mother
    interaction 98
gangs
  in adolescence 171–2
  and delinquency 15–16,
    356–7
  street children, Brazil 619
Gardner, H., 'multiple
    intelligences' 590, 591,
    596
gay adolescents 668–9
gay parents 141
gender-based bullying 363
gender differences see sex
    differences
gender-identity
  awareness of 219–21
  cognitive-development
    approach, Kohlberg
    225–6
gender role portrayal on
    television 273–4
gender schemas 226, 227
gene-environment interaction
    36, 350–1
general intelligence 589
genetics 32–3
  adoption studies 34–5
  aggression in children 350–1
  and childcare quality 133–4

chromosomal abnormalities 38
Down syndrome (DS) 38–9
Human Genome Project 36–8
shared and non-shared environment 35–6
twin studies 33–4
Genie case study, extreme deprivation 610–12
genome 32
gestation periods 85–6
Gibson, E.J., visual cliff 395
gifted children 599–601
Girl Scout cookie sales study 68, 69–71
girls abducted by armed forces, social integration of 620–4
Gould, Steven 19–20
grammar 407
    Chomsky's views 429, 430, 431
    early sentences 411–12
    pidgin language 432–3
    pivot grammar 436
grandparents 138–40
Groos, Karl, play theory 251
Gross, M., gifted children 600–1
group effects, day care 133
group learning
    collective argumentation 564–8
    community of inquiry 568–9
    peer tutoring 574–5
group socialization theory 194–5
group tests, intelligence 585–6
guided participation in sociocultural activity 562–4
Gure, A., perceived pubertal timing 654–6
Gustafson, K., object play 256–7

habituation to a stimulus 381, 384
Haight, W.L., pretend play 244–5
Hall, G. Stanley, play theory 252
harm prevention, research ethics 20
Harris, Judith, group socialization theory 194–5

Hawley, P., strategies of control in preschoolers 347–9
Head Start, USA 631–5
Health Behaviour in School-age Children (HBSC) survey 25–6, 365
Hedegaard, teaching experiment 552–3
Heinz dilemma, moral reasoning 318, 322
helping others see prosocial behaviour
Hepper, P. G., fetal & newborn response to human voice 83–4
heritability 34, 35, 36
heteronomous morality, Piaget 316, 317, 320
HFSS (high in fat, salt and/or sugar content) products 282
high intelligence, evolution of 50–1
High Scope Perry Preschool Project 632–3
historical changes, adolescent behaviour 684–90
Holocaust, generational effects 123–4
holophrases 411, 435
homophobic bullying 363
homosexuality 668
hormonal changes in puberty 648–9
hostile aggression 343, 344, 347
Howe, M.J.A., calendar calculating by savants 594–6
Human Genome Project 36–8
human plasticity, models of 63–5
human voice, newborn and fetal response to 83–4
humour, language play 246–7
Humphrey, Nicholas, homo psychologicus 4
hypotheses, role of 27

ICT use by adolescents 688, 689
identity 215–16
    development in adolescence 670–3
    ethnic/national 228–30
    gender 219–20, 224–7

'imaginary audience', adolescent egocentrism 659–60
imaginary companions 246
imaginative play
    novel toy experiment 255, 258
    see also pretend play
imitation 46
    and infant learning 98
    of television violence 275
imitative learning 54
immigrant children
    acculturation 192
    friendships 192
    strong influence of peer group 195
immigrant paradox phenomenon 192
implicit awareness of false belief 525
imprinting 44–5
'in-group/out-group' identification 226, 227, 229, 639
incarceration, effect on mental health 331
indirect aggression 219, 309, 344, 345, 346
indirect/relational bullying 363
individualistic vs. collective values 314–15, 323
infant-directed speech (IDS) 410, 437–8
infant facial features eliciting caring/parental behaviour 55, 56
information processing approach 472–4
    constructive memory and knowledge 494–6
    knowledge and memory development 493–4
    memory development 488–92
    metacognition 492–3
    processing limitations 474–5
    stage-like performance 476–88
    summary 496–7
informed consent, research ethics 20, 21
insecure attachment 111–12, 115, 116, 117, 119
    change over time 120–1

and day care controversy 131
link to abusing parents 153
low maternal sensitivity/
responsiveness 121,
122, 132
and maternal upbringing 123
instinct 42
institutional care/rearing
behavioural & emotional
problems 127–8
Bowlby's maternal deprivation
hypothesis 124–6
early studies 612–13
and failure to form strong
attachments 127, 129
Israeli kibbutzim 109, 129
Romanian adoptees 613–16
instrumental aggression 343
intellectual development *see*
cognitive development
intelligence 589–90
social-cultural context
596–8
people's conceptions of
590–1
savants 593–6
Sternberg's theory of
590–3
intelligence tests 580–8
attainment tests 601–2
early uses of 587–8
reliability and validity 586–7
use of 599–601
intensive neonatal care, ethical
issues 95
interactions
and growth of social
understanding 305–6
mother-baby 408–10
interactive specialization, brain
areas 41
intercultural competence
618–19
intergenerational continuity
in abuse 154
antisocial behaviour 353
attachment 122, 123–4
intermodal perception 401–2
internal representation, Piaget
449, 450
see also mental
representation
internal working models 118,
154
internalizing behaviours
antipathetic relationships
191

and attachment security 111
and conflict between parents
144
and family status 157
rejected children 177, 180
risk factor in victimization 367
internet
advertisements 285–6
multiplayer games 281
and stereotypes 274–5
time spent on 267
internet addiction 688
internet use 686–8, 689
intersubjective world,
Tomasello 299–300,
410
intersubjectivity of infants,
Trevarthen 99
intersubjectivity of social
meanings, Vygotsky 549
interventions
aggression reduction 354,
357–8
antibullying 368–74
breastfeeding promotion
89–90
compensatory preschool
eduction 631–8
different types of 625
drugs counselling for
addicted mothers
304–5
extreme deprivation/neglect
607–12
for gifted children 601
to improve parental
sensitivity & attachment
security 155–6
media 291–3
nurture groups 630–1
PATHS, emotion regulation
333–5
peer support in schools 308,
310–13
play therapy 260–2
role of families 628–30
social or psychological
problems 625
social & emotional training,
Circle Time 216–18
social skills training 191
syntax development 413–14
interview method 16
interviewing children
achieving best evidence
(ABE) 507
cognitive interview 506–7

intimate partner violence,
effects on children 143–4
intonation, exaggerated, when
speaking to babies 410,
438
intuitive period, Piaget 455,
458–60
Isaacs, Susan, play theory 252
Israeli kibbutzim, effects of
communal child-rearing
109, 129

jealousy towards new baby
164
Jigsaw method 574–5
Joshi, P., textisms 289–91
juvenile offenders, history of
abuse and deprivation
330
Jyvaskyla Longitudinal
Study of Dyslexia
(JLD) 426–7

Kaluli of Papua New Guinea,
language development
440
Kauai study, resilience 626–8
Kellman, P.J., object separation
393–4
kin selection theory 57–8
knowledge and memory 486–7,
493–6
knowledge of mind *see* theory
of mind (ToM)
knowledge transfer 54
Kohlberg's theory of moral
development 318–21
early criticisms 321–2
later revisions 322–3
stages of moral judgement
320
Koluchova twins, case study
608–10
Kpelle tribe, Liberia, cognitive
abilities 549–50
Kuhn, Thomas, paradigms 28
Kusche Affective Interview
Revised (KAI-R) 334

language
bullying terms in different
countries 361–2
learning from DVDs/TV 270
mental state-reality
distinction 522
and ToM development 525
Vygotsky vs. Piaget 554–5

language acquisition device (LAD), Chomsky 429, 430, 431
language deficits, children born very prematurely 92–4
language development
  decline in unused sounds during first year 400–1
  dyslexia 425–8
  main areas of 406–7
  and quality of childcare 132
  reading 424–5
  sequences in 407–18
  theories of 428–40
  transition to literacy 418–24
language play 246–7
large-scale school-based bullying prevention programmes 371–4
laypersons' views of intelligence 590–1, 598
learned symbolic communication 49
learning 42
  from computer games 279–80
  cultural 54
  and culture 67
  fetal 82
  by imitation 46, 54, 98
  imprinting 44–5
  individual 45–6
  of mother's voice before birth 399
  neonates 96
  social 46, 47
  social context 546–76
  social & emotional 216–18
  from television 270, 271
  'trial-and-error' 46, 450–1, 452
legislation against smacking 148, 149
Leichtman, M.D., preschoolers reports, effect of stereotypes 499–502
leisure pursuits of adolescents, changes in 685–6
lesbian adolescents 668–9
lesbian parents 141, 225
Leslie, A.M., mental respreseration in ASD 537–40
lexical development 417
life-span development, Baltes notion of 8–9

Lineker, Gary, influence on children's food choice 283–5
literacy, effects of texting 289–91
logical deductions, formal operational stage 465–6
logical thinking 549, 550, 575
lone/single-parent families 137, 140, 141, 157
loneliness 179–80
long-term memory 474, 475, 486–7
longitudinal design 6–8, 9–10
Love, J.M., Early Head Start evaluation 633–5
low birthweight babies 90–5
low peer acceptance, effects of 189–90
Lurin, A. R., schooling introduction 549
lying see deception

Machiavellian intelligence 50
maladaptiveness of aggression 346–7
male–female differences and early levels of sex hormones 81–2
maltreatment 149–50
  assessment and extent of 150–2
  causes of 153–4
  and drug-addicted parents 304–5
  effects of 153
marijuana use 679, 680
masculinity 220–1, 227
maternal deprivation hypothesis, Bowlby 124–9
maternal face recognition by infants 390–1
Maternal Sensitivity Hypothesis 114, 115, 116, 117
maternal unresolved state of mind, link to disorganized attachment in child 117, 122, 123
maternal unresponsiveness predicting later externalizing problems 355
mathematical problem-solving
  children as researchers 568–9
  role of argumentation 565–6
  street vendors, informal vs. formal methods 570–3
maturation 42

and changes in parent–child relationships 657
effects of early and late 660–2
Turkish adolescents 654–6
variations in physical development 649–50
Maxi task, false beliefs 515–20
Mead, Margaret 65–7
  work in Samoa 682–3
mean length of utterance (MLU) 438, 439
media interventions 291–3
  co-viewing 293
  media literacy 293
  restrictive measures 291–3
media literacy 293
media use
  by adolescents 687–8
  by children 266–8
mediation, conflict resolution 308, 310–13
memory development 488–92
  constructive memory 494–6
  and knowledge 486–7, 493–4
  see also eyewitness research
menarche
  age of 647, 649, 650–2
  psychological impact 653, 656–7
mental functioning, Vygotsky's views 547–9
mental health problems
  and abuse/maltreatment 153, 329
  in adolescence 688–90
  and decline of play ethos 262
  and low peer acceptance 188
  and punishment 304
  young offenders 24–5, 330–1
mental models of the earth 558–9, 560
mental representation
  achieved by end of sensorimotor period 450–3
  age of development of 523
  ASD children's deficit in 537–41
  sensorimotor substage, Piaget 449, 450
  use of language for 522
mental state–reality distinction 522

mentoring schemes, peer support in schools 308
metacognition 492–3
metapelet, caregiver in Israeli kibbutzim 109, 129
metarepresentation 530–1
    evolution of 51–2
microgenetic approach, problem-solving strategies 485–6
milk, composition of 89
Millennium Cohort Study (MCS) 156–7
    infant care at 9 months 103
'min' strategy, addition problems 485–6
'mindreading' see theory of mind (ToM)
mnemonics for memory tasks 490, 492
mobile phone use 686, 687
mobile phones, texting and literacy 289–91
modelling of altruistic behaviour 300–1
monkey faces
    ability to distinguish 382–4, 401
    discrimination between, before 6 months 382–4, 401
monologues, child and adult 554–5
monozygotic (MZ) twins 33–4
Montessori, Maria, views on play 251
mood disruption in adolescence 676–8
moral disengagement, bullies 367
moral reasoning
    age of moral responsibility 329–31
    Kohlberg's theory 318–23
    Piaget's theory 315–18
    and prosocial behaviour 300
    social-cognitive domain theory 324–9
    teaching of moral values 331–5
mother-baby communication 409–10
motherhood constellation 408
mother's voice
    neonates' preference for 399
    newborn and fetal response to 83–4

motivation
    assessment tests 601–2
    intrinsic 235, 236, 685–6
    and prosocial behaviour 300
moving faces, infants' attention to 390
moving objects
    newborns' visual scanning of 386
    separate objects perception 395, 396–7
multi-route model of lexical development, Barrett 417
multicultural settings, friendships in 192–3
'multiple intelligences', Gardner 590, 591, 596
murders of street children, Brazil 619
musical intelligence 590

naive framework theory of physics 557, 560, 561
narration of stories 423–4
national identity, development of 228–9
National Institute of Child Health and Development (NICHD) Longitudinal Study 132–4
nature and nurture, interaction of 41–2
Needham, A., object separation 395, 396–7
negative emotion regulation, link to parental responsiveness to distress 303
neglect 150–2
    extreme deprivation 607–12
neglected peer status 173, 175
    behavioural profiles 175
    loneliness and social withdrawal 179–80
neighbourhood factors, aggression 354–5
Nelson, K., syntax development 413–14
networked publics 688
neuroimaging techniques 39–40
neuroscience 39–41, 657–9
non-resident fathers 137–8
non-shared environment 36, 194
nonsensical questions 504–5

novel objects, exploration & play 237
novel toy experiment 255, 258
number conservation 459, 460, 461, 462–3
Nunes Carraher, T., maths of street vendors 570–3
nurture groups (NGs) 630–1

obesity concerns
    food advertising 282
    sedentary computer games 281
object permanence 450, 452
object play 240–1
    benefits of 254–5
    experiments on 259
    exploration preceding 237
    study on outcomes of 256–7
    Vygotsky on 253
object realism, early pretend play 241–2
object separation 393–4
    effects of prior experience on 395, 396–7
objective vs. subjective measures of child well-being 25–6
objectivity of investigations 19–20
observational methods 5, 15–16, 27
observer effects 17
obstetric dilemma (OD) hypothesis 86
offending behaviour 329–31
Olweus, D., bullying prevention 371–4
online activities, adolescents 686–8
online communities of learning 551–2
only children 168–9
oppositional defiant disorder (ODD) 355
organization
    encoding strategy 489–90, 491, 493
    Piaget's use of term 446–7
others, children's understanding of
    categorization of others 202–3
    emotions, desires and beliefs 206–8
    national identity 228–30
'overlapping waves' metaphor, Siegler 484

paradigms 28
Paradise, R., guided
        participation 562
parent-offspring conflict,
        Trivers 57–8
    weaning study 59–61
parental conflict 143–4
parental responsiveness to
        distress, link to empathy
        in child 303
parental role in bullying
        prevention 369
parental sexual orientation,
        effects on children 224–5
parental values, internalization
        of 303
parenting
    inadequate/ineffective 304
    models 154–6
    positive 302–3
    skill facilitation 304–5
    skills and aggression in
        children 352–3
    styles 141–3
participant characteristics 17
participatory principles 620–4
Pascalis, O., face processing
        382–4, 391, 401
PATHS intervention 333–5
pattern perception by infants
        387–8, 389
pedagogy 54
peer group factors
    and aggression 353–4
    and delinquency 356–7
    and passive acceptance of
        bullying 306–7
    peer evaluation and fear of
        rejection 664
    peer group identification 227
    peer influence during
        adolescence 664
    peer relations, during
        adolescence 663–5
    social-cognitive map 173
    support for victims of
        bullying 369
peer rejection 175, 177–8, 180,
        191, 193
peer relationships
    controversial children 178
    and family 193
    importance of 188–90
    infants and toddlers 162–3
    loneliness 179–80
    low peer acceptance 189–90

measurement of 172–3
neglected children 179–80
perceived popularity 178–9
popular children 178
in preschool and school 170–2
and psychopathology 188–9
rejected children 177–8, 180
SIP model 176
social withdrawal 179–80
sociometric status 173–6
peer support systems in schools
        308
    gender differences 308–9
peer tutoring 574–5
Pellegrini, A.D., object play
        256–7
pendulum task, Piaget 466
perception 380–1
    auditory perception 398–401
    of infants, methods for
        studying 381–5
    intermodal perception 401–2
    visual perception 386–98
perinatal risk factors 90–5
permissive parents 142, 143
Perner, J., deception under-
        standing 516–19
'person permanence' 200
    familiarity, age and gender 202
personal distress, responsive-
        ness to 301–3
personal intelligence 590
perspective taking 299–300, 454–5
    effect of task difficulty 456–7
    and emotional responsiveness
        302
    and prosocial behaviour 300
'persuasive intent', advertising
        285
Petrides, K.V., trait emotional
        intelligence 212–14
phonological awareness 419,
        424, 426
phonological deficit hypothesis
        426
phonology 406
physical abuse 150, 153
physical activity play 239, 254
    effects of deprivation 258–9
physical aggression of children
        131–2
physical assault 151, 152
physical attractiveness and
        sociometric status 178
physical neglect 150–1, 152
physical punishment 147–9

physical world, children's
        understanding of
        556–61
Piaget, Jean
    background 444–5
    cognitive processes in
        problem-solving 472–3
    language and cognition
        433–4
    language theories 554–5
    moral reasoning theory
        315–18
    play theories 238, 240, 241,
        249, 252
    synthesis with Vygotsky's
        views 575–6
    see also cognition, Piaget's
        theory
picture analogy task 592–3
pidgin languages 432, 433
Pinker, S., pidgin & creole
        languages 432–3
placenta 81
planned actions/behaviour
        450–1, 452
plasticity of human behaviour,
        models of 63–5
play 234–63
    benefits of 253–63
    characteristics of 234–7
    development of 237–50
    factors affecting 249
    theorists 250–3
play criteria, Krasnor &
        Pepler's model 235–6
'play ethos' 250, 252, 262, 263
play fighting 239–40, 247, 254
play signals 235
play theories 250–3
    benefits of play 262–3
    Freud, Sigmund 252
    Froebel, Friedrich 251
    Groos, Karl 251
    Hall, G. Stanley 252
    Isaacs, Susan 252
    Montessori, Maria 251
    Piaget, Jean 252
    recent theorists 253
    Spencer, Herbert 251
    Vygotsky, Lev 252–3
play therapy 252, 260–2
play tutoring 249, 259–60
play types 237–8
    fantasy/pretend play 241–5
    language play 246–7
    object play 240–1

physical activity play 239
rough-and-tumble play 239–40
Plester, B., textisms 289–91
pointing by infants 53
political violence, risk to children's well-being 639
Popper, Karl, falsification 27
popular peer status 175, 178
perceived popularity 178–9
positive parenting, and empathy in children 302–3
postconventional morality 319, 320, 321
Poulin, F., adolescent friendship instability 185–7
poverty
compensatory education 631–8
and deprivation 606–7
families overcoming disadvantage of 628–30
and low academic achievement 617
and negative outcomes 617, 625
street children, Brazil 619
practice/functional play 238
practice theory of play, Groos 251
pragmatics 407
preconceptual period, Piaget 453–5
preconventional morality 318–19, 320
prediction of behaviour 524
predictive validity 587
preference technique, infant perception 381, 382–4
pregnancy sickness 85
premature/preterm babies 90–5
prenatal development and birth
breastfeeding 89–90
from conception to birth 80–5
interaction after birth 88–9
nature of birth 85–8
premature & low birth-weight babies 90–5
prenatal growth stages 80–1
prenatal risk factors 82, 85
preoperational stage, cognitive development 453–64

intuitive period 455–60
preconceptual period 453–5
reinterpretation of Piaget 460–4
prereading skills 418–23
deficits in children born very prematurely 92–4
preschool education pro-grammes 631–8
pretence, chimpanzees 49–50
pretend play 206, 241–2
between siblings 165, 166
correlational studies 258
cross-cultural comparison 244–5
encouragement of 249
'equifinality' model of play 262
examples of 234, 239
experiments on effects of 259
and friendship development 181, 182–3
metarepresentation 531
and play therapy 261
pretence-reality distinction 206–7
role in ToM development 255, 259, 260
sex difference in 249
stages in 243
war toys and war play 247–8
prewriting skills 418–23
primary intersubjectivity 99
primates, advanced abilities 49–50
private speech of preschoolers, Piaget vs. Vygotsky 554–5
proactive aggression 343–4
'probability judgement' task, retrieval problem 475–6
problem-solving 478–87
group work more effective 553, 576
guided participation improv-ing 563–4
mathematical 565–6, 568–9, 570–3
microgenetic approach 485–6
Piaget's findings 445–6, 450–1, 458, 465–6
product placement 286–8
Project Head Start, US 631–5
Promoting Alternative Thinking Strategies (PATHS) 333–5

prosocial behaviour 298–315
cross-cultural differences 313–15
definitions 298–9
development of 299–302
family factors 302–6
intrinsic value of 299
modelling of 300–1
observational studies 301–2
peer support systems in schools 308
sex differences 308–9, 313
teaching in school 306–8
prosodic sound patterns, infants' response to 438
protective factors 626
proximal processes 12
psychopathology and peer rejection 188–9
psychosocial acceleration theory 652–3
psychosocial risk factors, premature babies 90–5
psychotherapy, drug-addicted mothers 304–5
puberty
brain development 657–9
growth spurt 647–8
hormonal changes 648–9
psychological effects of 653–60
secular trend in age of menarche 650–2
theories of pubertal timing 652–3
timing of 646–7
variations in maturation rates 649–50

qualitative methods 19
quality of day care 131–4
quality of friendships 183–5
quantitative methods 19
quantity, understanding of 445–6, 458, 459, 460
quasi-experiments 13–14
questioning children
achieving best evidence 507
cognitive interview 506–7
suggestibility problems 503–5
questionnaires 16

racial portrayals in media 274
racial prejudice 617–19
reduction of 230
racist bullying 363

Raikes, H., Early Head Start evaluation 633–5
Raven's Progressive Matrices 586
reactive aggression 343–4
reactive strategies, bullying 370
reactive vs. proactive aggression 343–4, 367
reading 424–5
  and dyslexia 425–8
  prereading skills 418–23
real-world context, intelligence 596–8
reality-pretence distinction 206–7
reality vs. representation 522, 523, 530, 539
reasoning tasks
  balance scale task, Siegler 478–83
  counting tasks 484, 485
  proportionality 476–8
recall
  effect of stress on 507–9
  see also memory development
'reciprocal altruism' 58
reciprocated friendship, protection against bullying 306
reckless behaviour, adolescents 678–81, 683
recognition of self, infant 201–2
Rees, J., institutional rearing 127–8
referential triangle 241
reflex activity, sensorimotor stage 448, 449
reflexive behaviours, neonates 96
regulation of emotion 208–10
  PATHS intervention 333–5
rehearsal, encoding strategy 488–9
rejected peer status 173
  behavioural profile 175
  home background factors 193
  loneliness of 180
  long-term study 190
  and psychopathology 190
  social skills training 191
  subtypes of 177–8
rejection, fear of 664
Relational Psychotherapy Mothers' Group (RPMG) 304–5

see also relationships
  see also attachment relationships
relative fatness theory, puberty 652
reliability 16–17
  IQ tests 586–7
reputation enhancement theory 354, 356–7
research
  correlational evidence 12–13
  data recording methods 15–16
  design issues 6–10
  ecological 10–12
  ethical issues in 20–1
  experimental methods 13–15
  objectivity & bias 19–20
  participants 17–18
  quantitative and qualitative methods 19
  reliability and validity 16–17
research activity involving children
  community of inquiry 568–9
  Hedegaard's teaching experiment 552–3
resilience in the face of adversity 626–8
restorative justice, bullying 370
retrieval limitations 475, 476
retrieval strategies 490–1
reversibility, Piaget 460
rhyming awareness 419–20
  training study 420–2
rights
  of asylum seeker youth 325–8
  of child offenders 329, 331
  of children 22–5
  individual, Kohlberg 319, 320
rigidity of behaviour 42–3
risk factors 625–6
  perinatal and psychosocial 90–1, 95
risk-taking behaviours 667–8, 678–81
Rogoff, Barbara 67–8
  community of inquiry 568
  guided participation 69–71, 562–3
romantic development 665–7
rough-and-tumble play 239–40, 249, 254

routine(s)
  ASD children's insistence on 533, 534, 541
  expectations in infant-mother games 98
Ruck, M.D., moral & social-conventional reasoning 325–8
rules
  acquisition of, Piaget 315–16, 317
  boys' peer group 309
  and Kohlberg's levels of morality 318–20
  social, family relationships teaching 306
  social vs. moral domains 324
Rutter, Michael 126, 129, 195, 625, 639
  Isle of Wight study 676–8
  Romanian adoptees (ERA) study 613–16

Sally-Anne task, false beliefs 520–1, 528, 532, 534–5, 540
same-sex parents 224–5
Samoan society, adolescence 682–3
sanctions-based approaches, bullying 370
savants 593–6
'scaffolding' concept 99, 546, 556
  in guided participation 562
  peer tutoring 574, 575–6
  in practice 556–61
schemas
  constructive memory 495–6
  gender 225–6
  Piaget 446–8, 450
Schliemann, A.D., maths of street vendors 570–3
school exclusions, effects of 618
schooling
  and abstract thinking 549
  impact on nature of thinking 570
schools
  evaluation of, attainment tests 602
  later starting times 676
  moral education 331–2
  prosocial behaviour in 306–8

scientific concepts, understanding of 557–61
scientific status of psychology 27–8
Scott, D., newborn & fetal response to maternal voice 83–4
screening
    attainment tests 602
    for dyslexia 427
scripts
    constructive memory 495
    language development 416
    infants' pre-sleep monologues 415
'second-order' belief 528
    deficit in ASD 540
secondary altriciality 86
secondary intersubjectivity 99
secure (B type) attachment 110, 111, 112
security of attachment 110–12
    and empathy 303
    interventions to improve 155
    stability over generations 122–4
    stability over time 120–1
seeing and knowing, understanding link between 522–3
self and others, understanding of 200–3
    children's categorization of others 202–3
    others' emotions, desires and beliefs 206–8
self-awareness 200, 206, 210, 332
self-concept 215
    and friendships 188
self-consciousness in adolescence 659–60
self-esteem 215–16
self-monitoring 332–3
self-recognition
    infants 201–2
    non-human primates 49
semantics 406–7
sensitive/critical period 44
    attachment 100, 124, 125
    language development 611–12
sensorimotor stage, cognitive development 448–53
    Piaget's theory 448–51
    reinterpretation of Piaget 451–3
sentences
    3 to 5 years 417–18

early language development 411–16
separation
    and maternal deprivation, Bowlby 125–6
    of parents 137, 140, 143–6
    Strange Situation 110, 114, 117
Separation Anxiety Test (SAT) 118–19
'separation protest', babies 108–9
Sesame Street 271
sex differences 62
    aggression 344–6
    awareness of 219–21
    biological factors 222
    bullying perpetrators & victims 366
    children in Western societies 219
    cross-cultural studies 221
    and fetal testosterone levels 81–2
    homophobic bullying 363–4
    in play types 249
    prosocial behaviour 308–13
sex-role identification theories 221–2
    biological factors 222
    cognitive-development approach 225–6
    gender schemas 226, 227
    social cognitive theory 226–7
    social constructionist approaches 224–5
    social learning theory 223–4
sexting 667
sexual abuse 150, 151, 152, 153
sexual attitudes, changes in 684–5
sexuality, adolescent 667–9
Shahidullah, S., newborn & fetal response to maternal voice 83–4
shape constancy 393
'shared attention mechanism', lack of in ASD 541
shared attention, social play with objects 241
shared environment 35–6, 194
shared rhythms, language development 407–8
sharing concept, adolescence 664–5

short-term memory see working memory
siblings 163–4
    birth order 169–70
    conflict and rivalry 165–6
    and family size 169–70
    in home environment 164–5
    only children 168–9
    pretend play 165
    relationships in preschool years, and emotional outcomes in later life 305
    social comparison 166
    teaching 165
    and ToM development 167
    twins and multiplets 167–8
Siegler, R.S., origins of scientific reasoning 479–83
sign language 47, 433
Simon, Theodore 444, 596
    Binet-Simon scale 580–3
simulation of another's behaviour 531–3
simulation games 279
single/lone-parent families 137, 140, 141, 157
Six Cultures Study 67, 221
size constancy 392–3
skill learning, brain areas 41
sleep patterns, adolescents 675–8
smacking debate 147–9
Smarties task, false beliefs 520, 527, 535, 538
Smetana, J. 317–18, 324, 674
smiling, neonates 96
Smith, J., savants' calendar abilities 594–6
social brain 663–5
social class and underachievement 617
social-cognitive domain theory 324–8
social-cognitive maps, peer group structure 173
social cognitive theory 226–7
social comparison, siblings 166
social competence
    and aggression 347, 348
    layperson's view of intelligence 590–1
    only children 168–9
social constructionist approaches 71–4
    gender identity 224–5

social context of learning 546–76
  Bruner's impact 555–6, 559–70
  collective argumentation 564–8
  educational implications 569–75
  Hedegaard's experiment 552–3
  Piaget & Vygotsky on language 554–5
  scaffolding teaching methods 556–62
  sociocultural origins of individual cognition 547–52
  Vygotsky 546–7
social conventions, reasoning about 324–8
social-cultural context of intelligence 596–8
social development and day care quality 133
social dominance
  in older children 341–2
  and perceived popularity 179
  strategies used to achieve 347–8
  in younger children 340–1
social emotions, processing of 664
social impairments, ASD children 540–1
Social Information Processing (SIP) model 176
  maladaptive nature of aggression 346–7
  reactive vs. proactive aggression 343–4, 366–7
social interactions
  infants 95–100
  and ToM development 525–6
social isolation concerns, computer game playing 281
social learning 45–6
  precondition of culture 47
social learning theory, gender identity 223–4
social meanings, shared 549
social networking 686–8
  use by adolescents 688
  and ZPD concept 551–2
social re-integration, abducted girls 620–4

social referencing 205–6
social skills
  of parents, link to child's aggression 352–3
  peer interaction, SIP model 176
  training in 191
  victims of bullying 367
social understanding, link to interpersonal interactions 305–6
social vs. active self 215–16
social withdrawal 179–80
socialization
  broad and narrow 683
  of gender differences 313
  prosocial behaviour 302–3
socially disadvantaged children
  racial prejudice/discrimination 617–19
  reintegration of girls abducted by armed forces 620–3
  street children 619
  in the UK 616–17
sociobiological theory 57–8
sociocultural model, Rogoff 67–8
  cookie sales study 69–71
sociodramatic play 242, 247, 249, 255, 260
sociograms 172–3
sociometric status 173–5, 177–80
  long-term study linking friendship to 190
sociometry 172–3
sounds
  auditory perception 398–401
  categorizing, training in 420–2
  conditioning infants to respond to 385
  discrimination of different syllables 399–400
  and language learning 400–1
  of speech, neonates' orientation towards 95–6
source monitoring, recalling origins of memories 504
spanking methods 148–9
spatial ability, link to constructive play 258
Spearman, Charles, general factor of intelligence 589

speech
  adult-child 437–9
  telegraphic 411–12, 430–1
  perception, early infancy 399–400, 401
Spelke, E.S., object separation 393–4
spelling 420–2
  dyslexic children 426, 427
Spencer, Herbert, play 251
SSLPs (Sure Start Local Programmes) 636–7
stage-like performance on problem-solving tasks 476–84
  vs. 'overlapping waves' idea 484–5
stage model of children's strategy development 485
standardized tests 602
Stanford-Binet scale 582, 585, 587
stepfamilies/step-parenting 146–7
  and child abuse 153
  and child's emotional well-being 157
stereotypes
  effect on suggestibility of eyewitness reports 499–502
  television generating false 273–5
Sternberg, R.J., intelligence theories 590–3, 597, 598
stillbirth experience, predicting disorganized attachment 117
storage limitations, memory tasks 475–6
stories, creation of and response to 423–4
Strange Situation (SS) 110–11
  coding linked to parent AAI scores 122–3
  continuity over time 120–1
  cross-cultural studies 112
  Dogon people, Mali 114, 115
strangers, wary reactions to 205
street children, Brazil 619
  mathematical abilities 570–3
stress
  influence on recall 507–9
  and pubertal timing 652–3

structural approach to play 235
subcultural differences, cognitive processes 550
subjective vs. objective measures of child well-being 25–6
suggestibility of children 498–505
Sulloway, Frank J., birth order theory 170
supervision neglect 151, 152
support group approach, bullying 370–1
Sure Start, UK 635–8
surrogate parents, grandparents as 139–40
symbolic communication 49, 52
symbolic play 238
symbolic thought, Piaget 453–4
sympathy, motivating prosocial behaviour 300
syntax 407
    Chomsky's views 429–30
    development of 412–15, 417–18
    syntactic bootstrapping hypothesis, Gleitman 416–17
    Tomasello's views 436–7
systematizing, link to fetal testosterone levels 81–2

tactical deception 50, 51
teaching
    animal examples 48, 53
    of moral values 331–5
    pedagogy 54
    sibling influence 165
teaching methods
    dialogical learning 564–8
    guided participation 562–4
    learning communities 568–9
    research activity, Hedegaard 552–3
    see also 'scaffolding' concept
telegraphic speech 411–12, 430–1
television 268–78
    aggression & violence 275–6
    attentiveness to 268–9
    comprehension of programmes 269
    fact-fiction distinction 269–70
    limited learning from 270
    longitudinal studies 276–8
    reasons for watching 268

    in relation to other activities 271–3
    Sesame Street 271
    and stereotypes 273–5
temperament 100–3
    and aggression 350–1
    interaction effect, low-quality childcare 133
    and parental response 36, 156, 195, 350
    and resilience 627–8
Tenenbaum, H.R., moral and social-conventional reasoning 325–8
Terman, Lewis
    adaptation of Binet-Simon scale 582
    giftedness study 600
testosterone levels in utero and subsequent systematizing 81–2
tests *see* intelligence tests
text messaging, effects on school literacy 289–91
Thaiss, L., mental respresentation in ASD 537–40
theories, role of 27
theory of mind (ToM) 514–15
    after 4 years of age 526–9
    age at which achieved 524–6
    children with ASD 533–41
    development of 524–6
    early communications 299–300
    early knowledge of mind 522–4
    evolution of 51–3
    explanations/theories 529–33
    false-belief task 514–21
    precursors of 206–7
    and pretend play 255, 258, 259–60
    sibling influences 167
therapy, play 260–2
thinking/thought
    language as tool for 554–5
    in non-human primates 49–50
three mountains task, Piaget 454–5
    Borke's version of 456–7
Thurstone, L.L., primary mental abilities 589
Tizard, B., institutional rearing 127–8
tool making and use

chimpanzees 46, 49, 50, 52
    in early childhood 256–7
toy guns and weapons 247–8, 258
traditions, in animals 47, 49
training
    assertiveness 369–70
    in emotional literacy 216–18
    in formal thinking 467
    and learning new skills 41
    in mediation skills 310
    peer tutoring 574–5
    play tutoring 249, 259–60
    in social skills 191, 367
    sound categorization skills 421–2
    in visual discrimination 419
trait EI (emotional intelligence) 211, 212–14
transitive inference tasks 461, 463–4
transsexual parents 224
trial-and-error vs. planned behaviour 450–1, 452
triarchic theory of intelligence, Sternberg 591–2, 593
true (controlled) experiments 14
True, M.M., infant-mother attachment, Mali 113–15
trust of peers, in adolescence 664–5
Turiel, E. 317, 324, 328–9
Turkish adolescents, puberty study 654–6
turmoil of adolescence 669–78
tutoring *see* training
twin studies 33–4, 35
    attachment type 36, 112
    callous-unemotional traits 352
    case study of severe neglect 608–10
    closeness of twins 167–8
    delinquency in adolescence 36, 350
    intelligence, Cyril Burt's data 21
    language development 167–8
    premature infants 91
    temperament and aggression origins 350

ultrasound scanning 16, 83, 399
UN Convention on the Rights of the Child (UNCRC) 22, 24, 25, 331
understanding of emotions, PATHS 333–5
understanding of mind *see* theory of mind (ToM)
unhealthy food products, advertising of 282–5, 288
UNICEF, well-being report cards 25
Unresolved adults, attachment 120, 122, 123–4
unresolved maternal state of mind 117, 122

validity 15, 16–17
  IQ tests 587
vantage sensitivity 65
Veale, A., young mothers' social reintegration 620–3
verb island hypothesis 435, 436
verbal aggression 309, 344
'verbal stimulation' hypothesis 259
very preterm infant (VPI) 90–5
victimization
  consequences of 367–8
  risk factors for 367
video games 248–9
violence
  between parents 143–4
  child maltreatment 149–54

in teenage relationships 666
on television, influence of 275–8
in video games 281
virtual communities 688
visual cliff experiments 205, 395, 398
visual perception 386–98
VLBW (very low birthweight) infants 90, 91, 95
vocabulary learning from DVDs 270
Vosniadou, S., scaffolding in practice 556–61
VPI (very preterm infant) 90–5
Vygotsky, Lev 546–7
  language and thought 554–5
  play theory 252–3
  social context of cognition 547–9
  synthesis with Piaget's views 575–6
  zone of proximal development (ZPD) 551–2

Walk, R. D., visual cliff 395
Walton, G.E., maternal face recognition 390
war toys and war play 247–8
weaning, conflict associated with 59–61
web-based advertisements 286–7
Wechsler intelligence scales for children (WISC) 583–6

well-being of children 25–6
  and family status 157
Westermarck effect 58, 62
whole-school approach, bullying prevention 368–9
Wimmer, H., deception understanding 516–19
Wolke, D., cognitive development of very preterm children 92–4
Wood, C., textisms 289–91
word learning 411–17
word recognition at very early age 400
working memory 473–4
  basing recall on 476
  improved by knowledge in long-term memory 486–7
  limited in younger children 474, 475, 478
young mothers' social integration, Africa 620–4
young offenders' rights 24–5
young people
  as researchers 17–18
  rights of 23–4
youth crime
  alarmist writings 21
  and moral development 329–31

zone of proximal development (ZPD) 551–2
zygote 80